A-Z MANCHESTER

CONTENTS

Key to Map Pages	2-3
Manchester Large Scale City Centre	4-11
Map Pages	12-173
Other Selected Large Scale Town Centres	174-179
Postcode Map	180-181

D0331094

-381
-384
Cover

REFERENCE

Motorway	**M60**	Airport		✈
A Road	**A6**	Car Park (Selected)		P
Proposed		Church or Chapel		†
B Road	**B5085**	Cycleway (Selected)		...🚲...
Dual Carriageway		Fire Station		■
One Way Street		Hospital		Ⓗ
Traffic flow on A Roads is also indicated by a heavy line on the driver's left.		House Numbers (A and B Roads only)	20	40
Restricted Access		Information Centre		🛈
Pedestrianized Road		National Grid Reference		³70
Track / Footpath		Police Station		▲
Residential Walkway		Post Office		★

Railway — Station, East Lancashire Railway, Level Crossing, Tunnel

Metrolink (LRT)
The boarding of Metrolink trams at stops may be limited to a single direction, indicated by the arrow.

Toilet:
without facilities for the Disabled ▽
with facilities for the Disabled ▽
for exclusive use by the Disabled ▽

Built Up Area	BRIDGE ST.	Viewpoint	☀
Local Authority Boundary	— ∙ — ∙ —	Educational Establishment	▀
National Park Boundary		Hospital or Hospice	▀
Posttown Boundary		Industrial Building	▀
Postcode Boundary (within Posttown)	— — —	Leisure or Recreational Facility	▀
		Place of Interest	▀
Map Continuation **34**	Large Scale City Centre **4**	Public Building	▀
		Shopping Centre or Market	▀
		Other Selected Buildings	▀

SCALE

Map Pages 12-173
1:18103 3½ inches (8.89cm) to 1 mile
5.52cm to 1 km

0 — ¼ — ½ Mile
0 — 250 — 500 — 750 Metres

Map Pages 4-11 & 174-179
1:9051 7 inches (17.78cm) to 1 mile
11.05cm to 1 km

0 — ⅛ — ¼ Mile
0 — 100 — 200 — 300 Metres

Copyright of Geographers' A-Z Map Company Ltd.

Fairfield Road, Borough Green, Sevenoaks, Kent TN15 8PP
Telephone: 01732 781000 (Enquiries & Trade Sales)
01732 783422 (Retail Sales)
www.a-zmaps.com

Copyright © Geographers' A-Z Map Co. Ltd.

O S Ordnance Survey® This product includes mapping data licensed from Ordnance Survey® with the permission of the Controller of Her Majesty's Stationery Office.

© Crown Copyright 2007. All rights reserved. Licence number 100017302

EDITION 11 2008

Every possible care has been taken to ensure that, to the best of our knowledge, the information contained in this atlas is accurate at the date of publication. However, we cannot warrant that our work is entirely error free and whilst we would be grateful to learn of any inaccuracies, we do not accept any responsibility for loss or damage resulting from reliance on information contained within this publication.

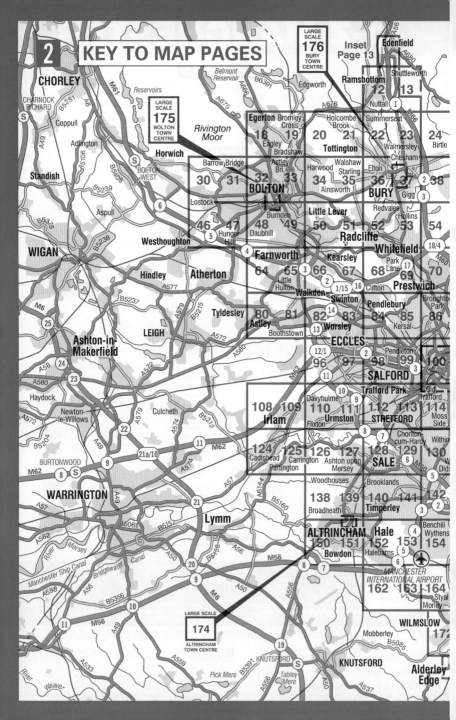

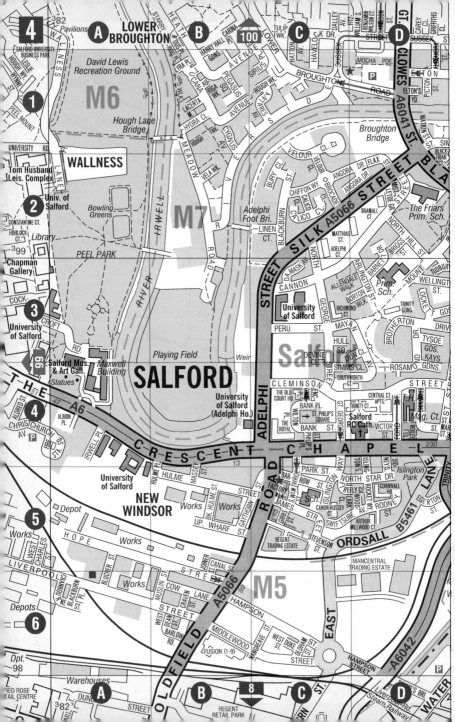

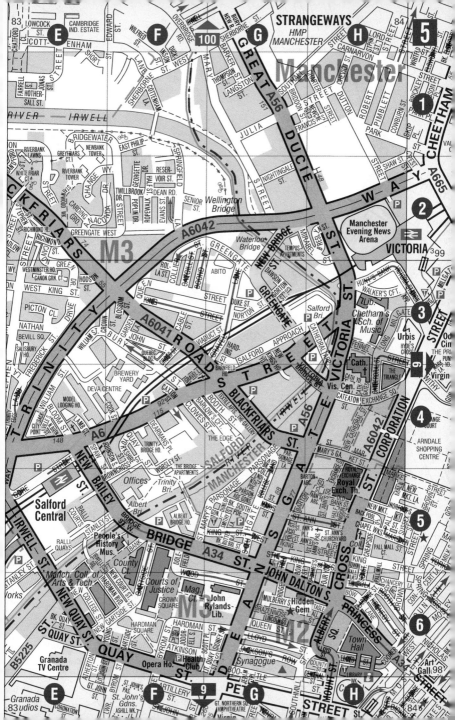

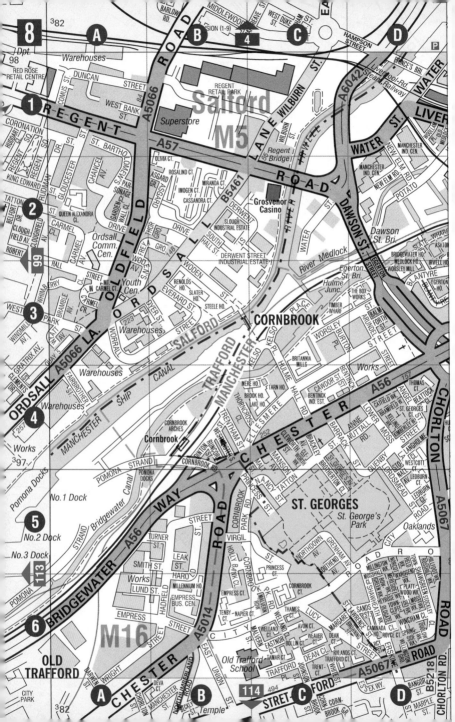

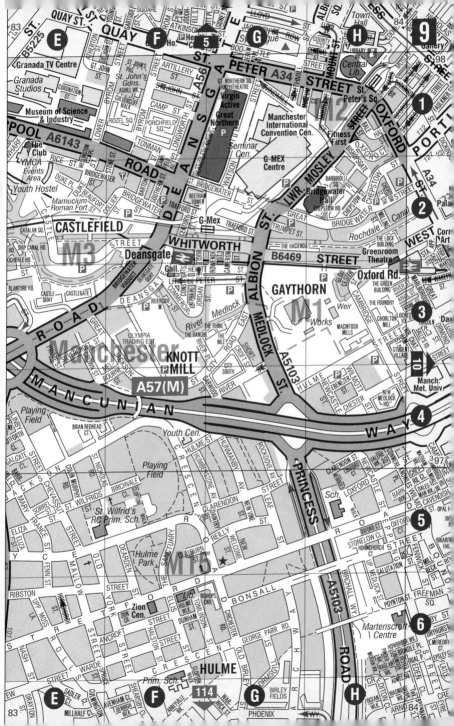

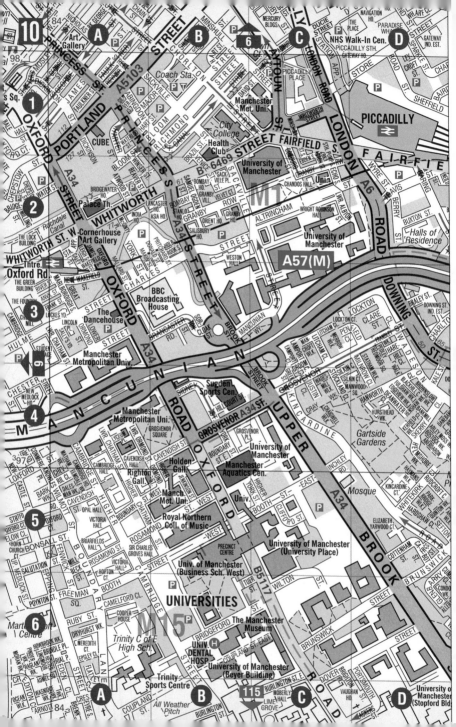

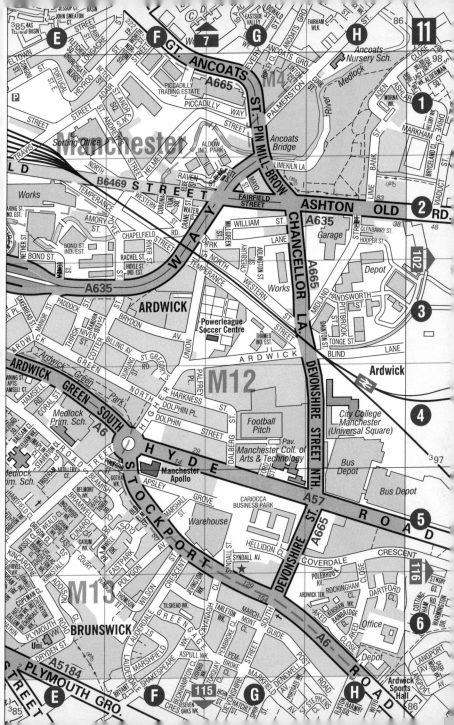

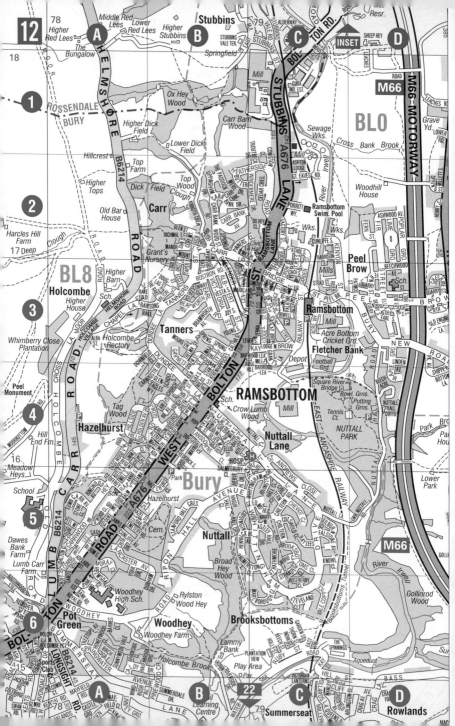

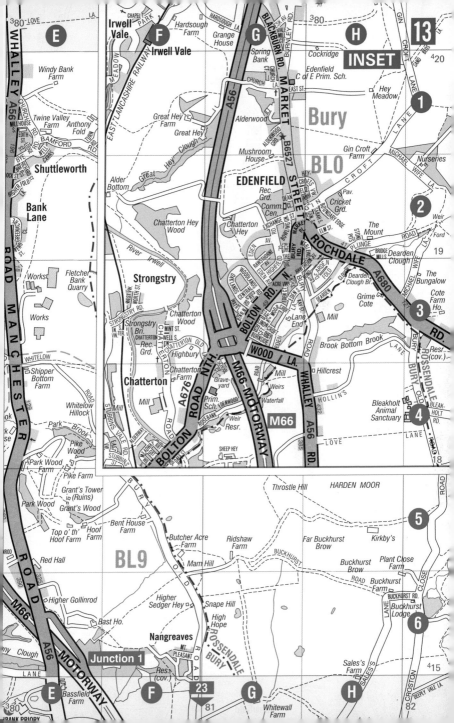

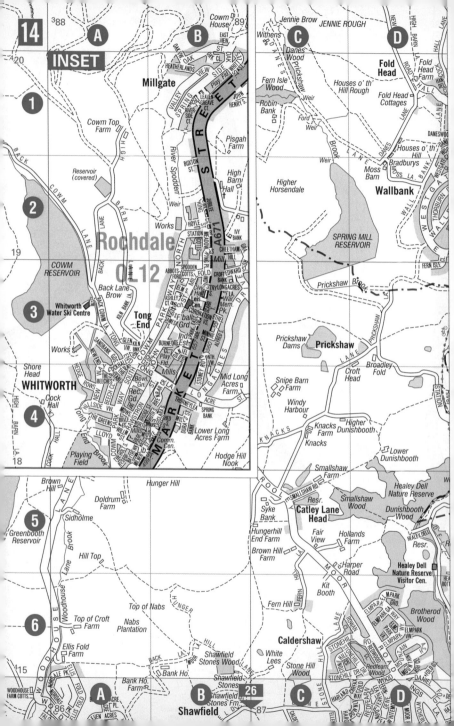

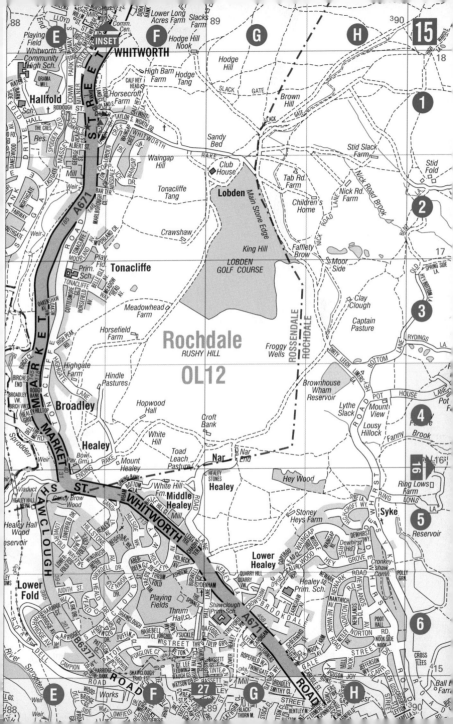

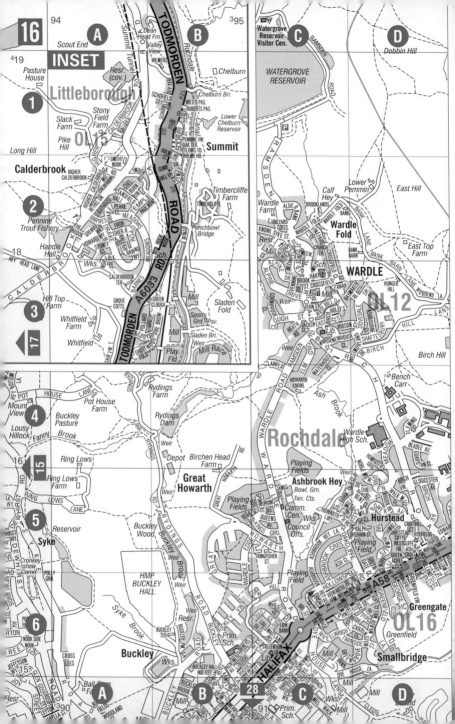

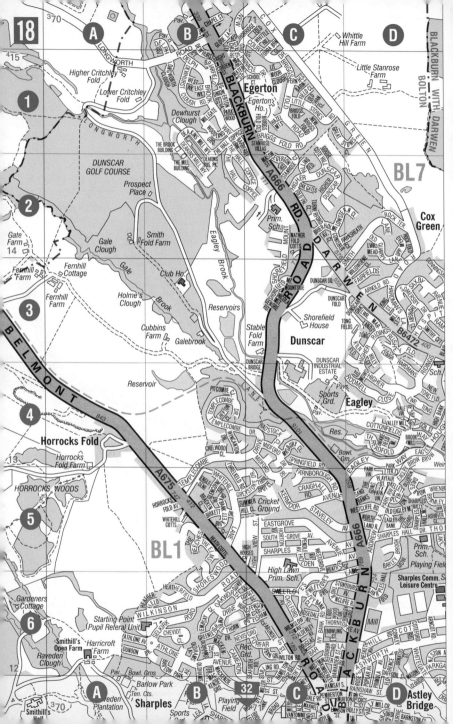

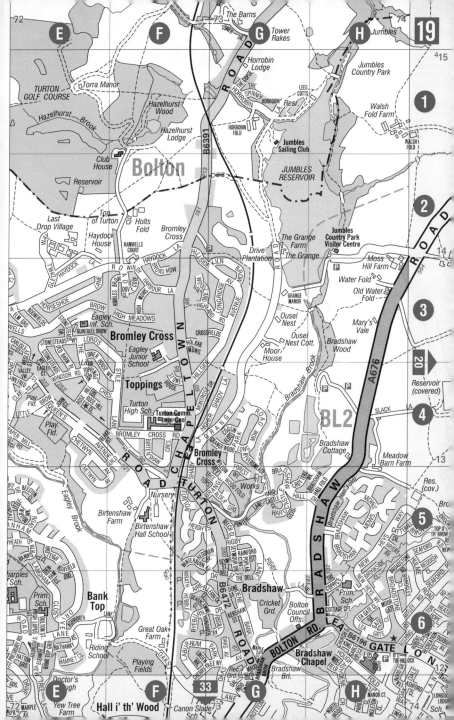

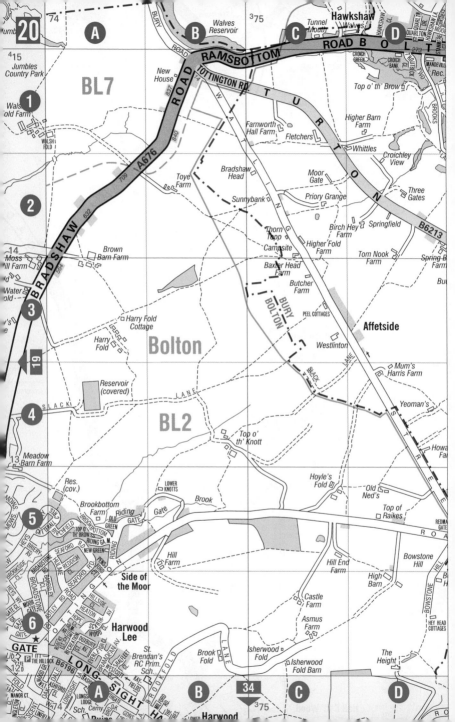

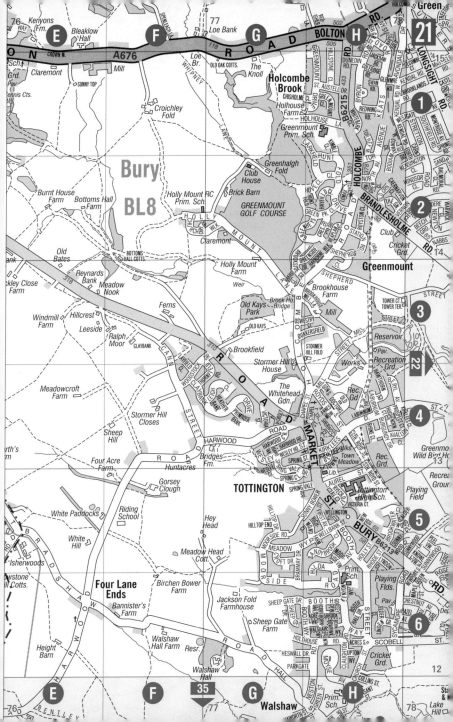

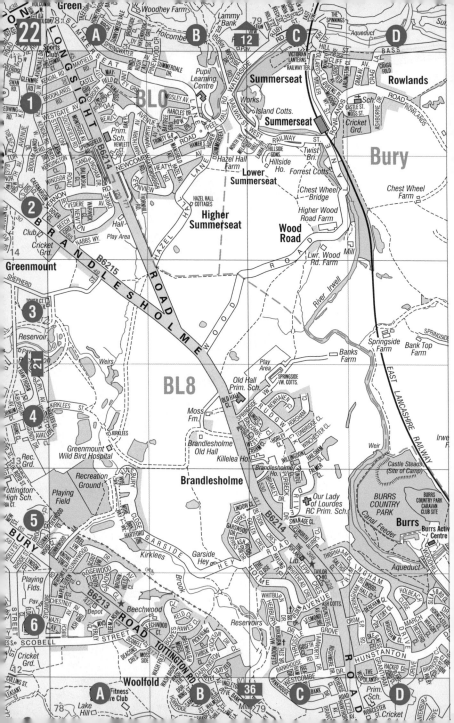

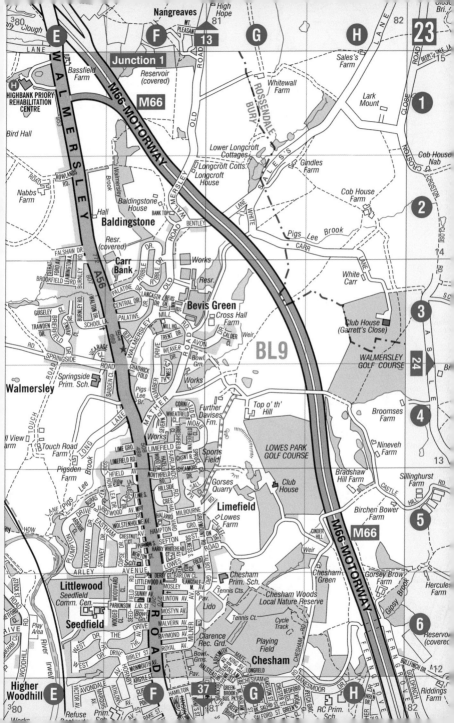

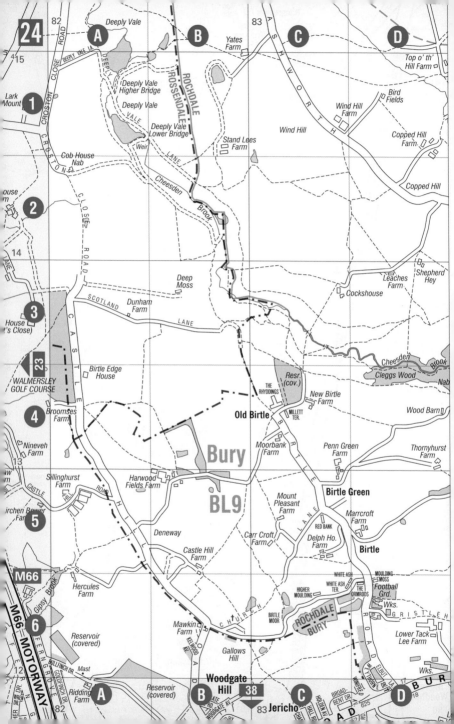

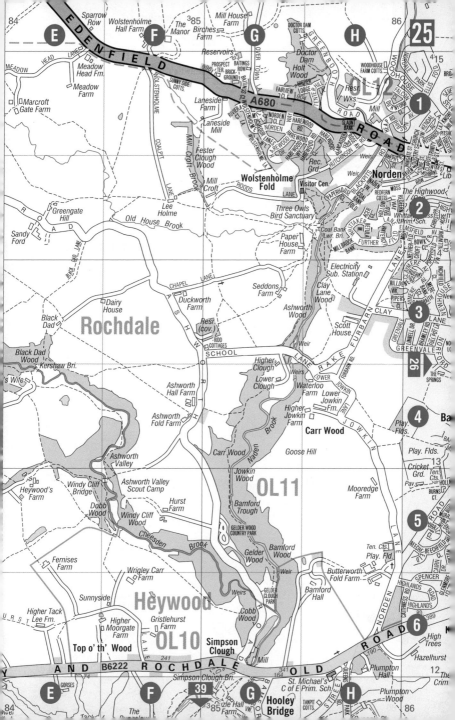

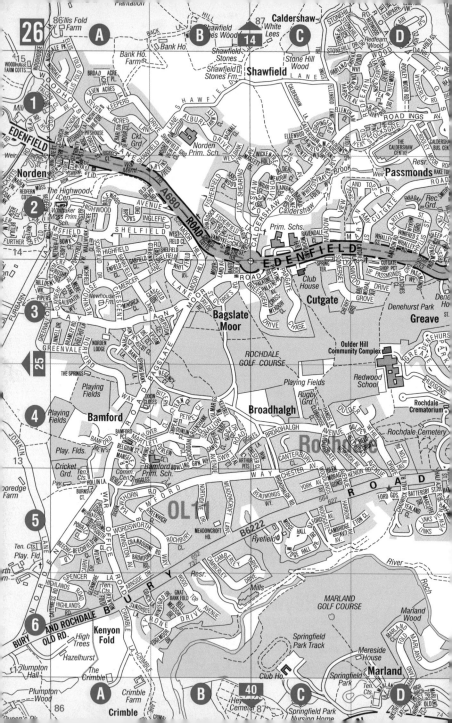

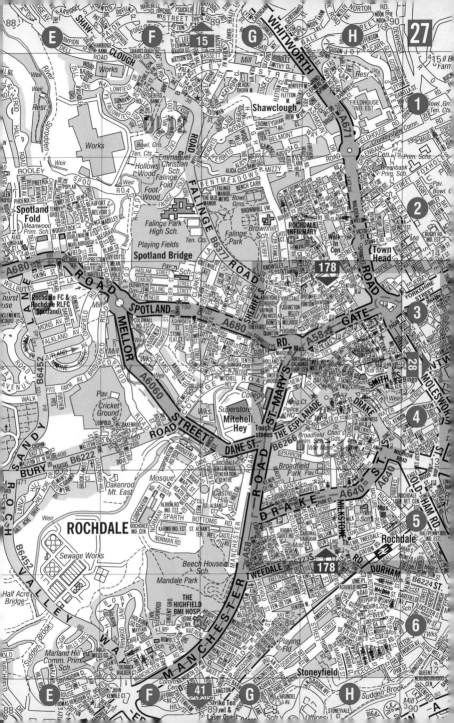

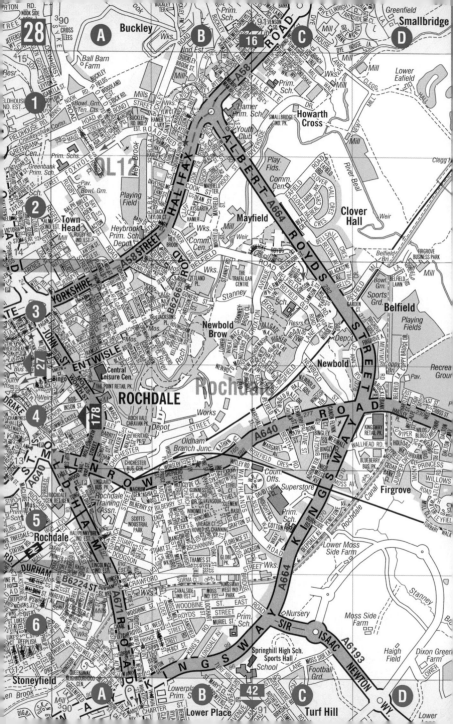

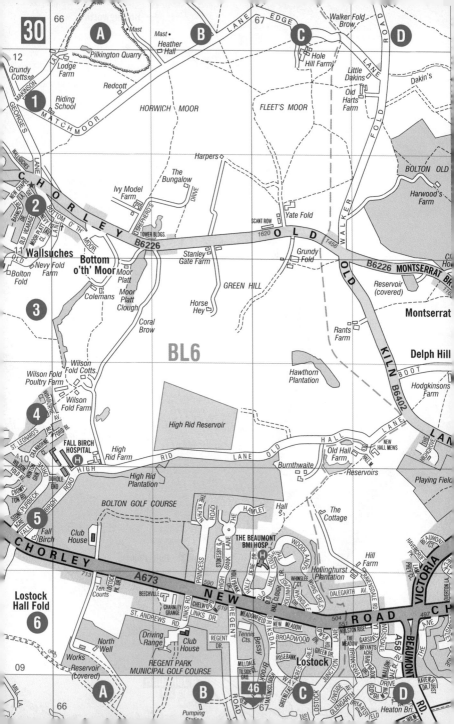

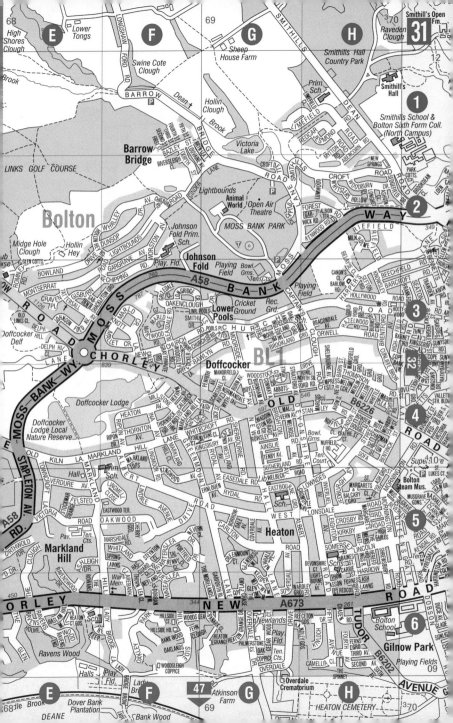

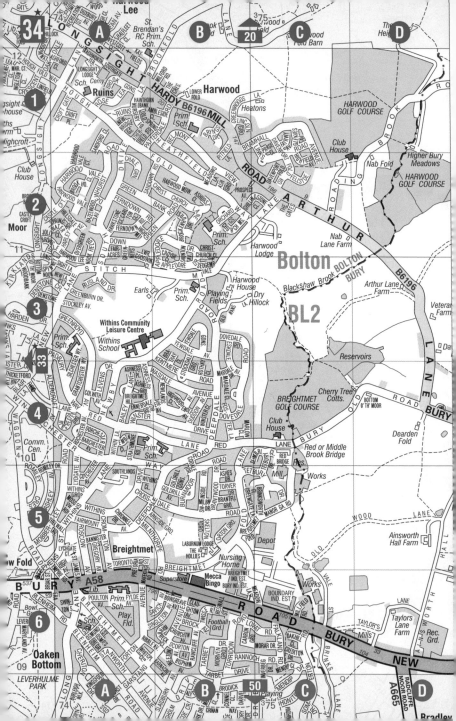

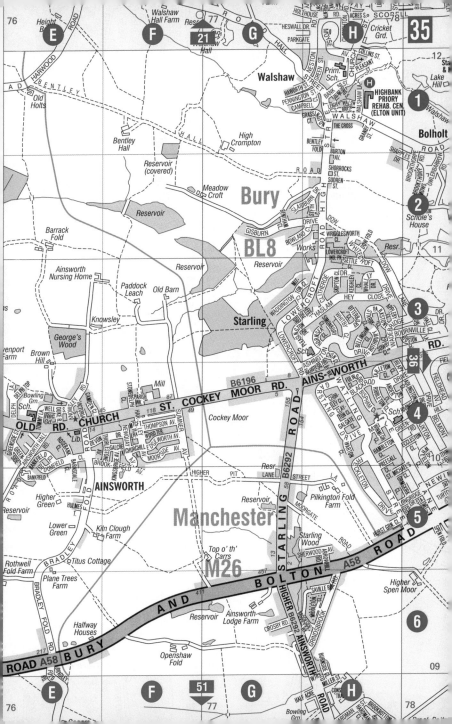

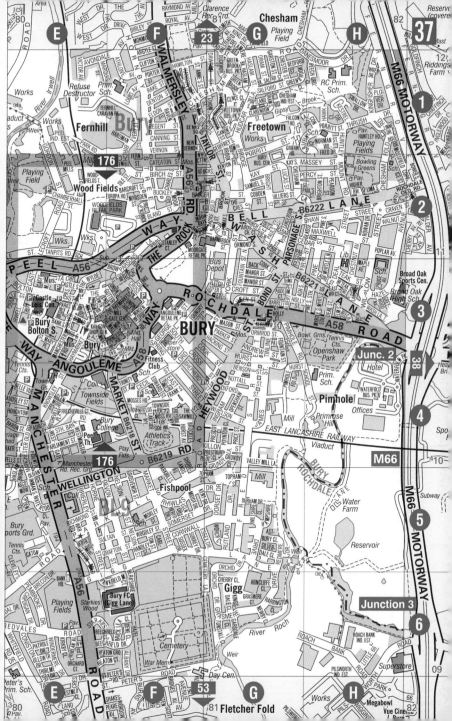

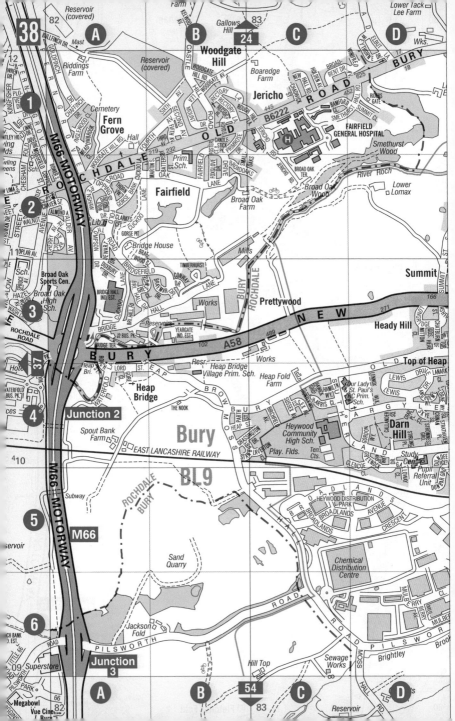

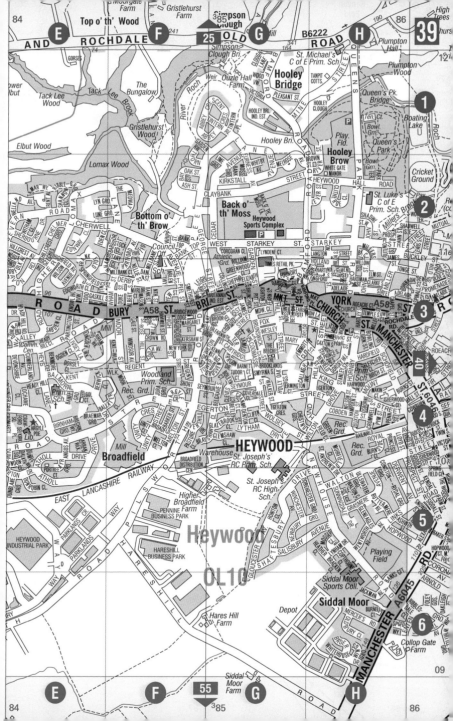

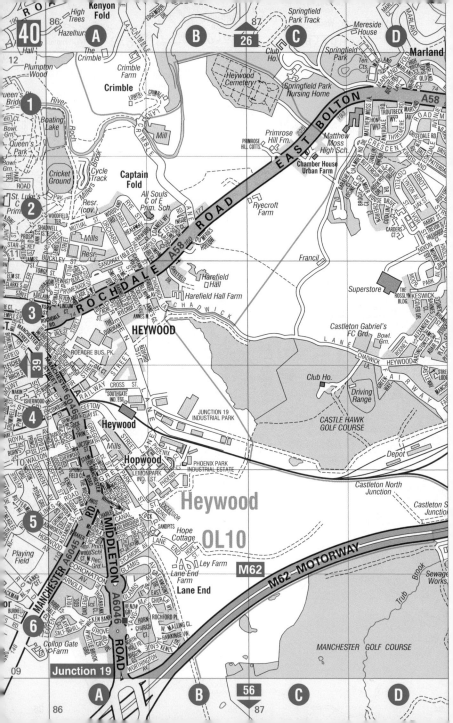

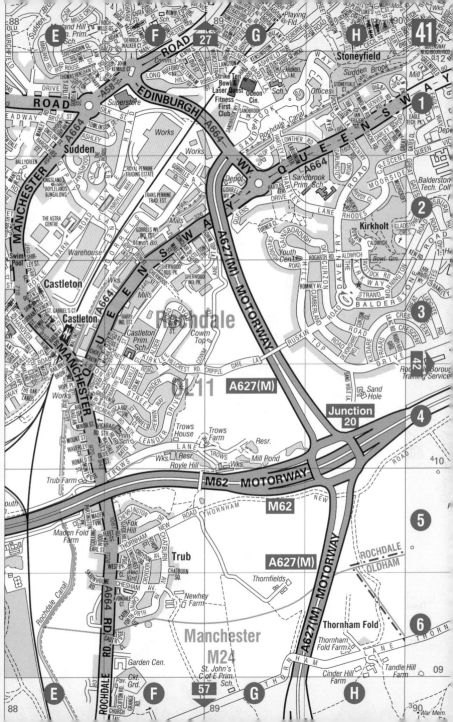

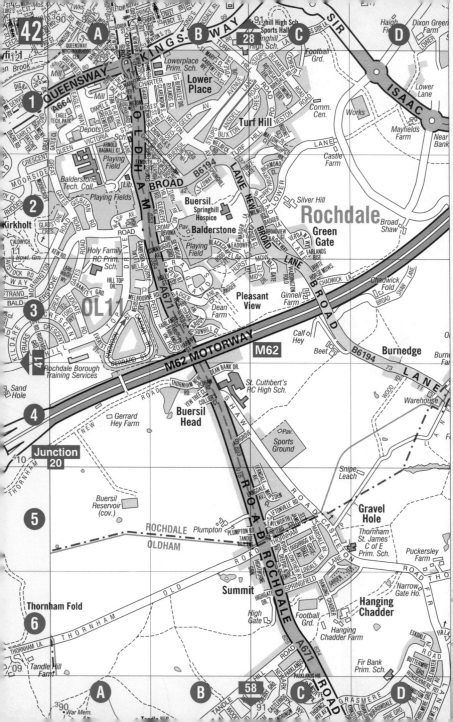

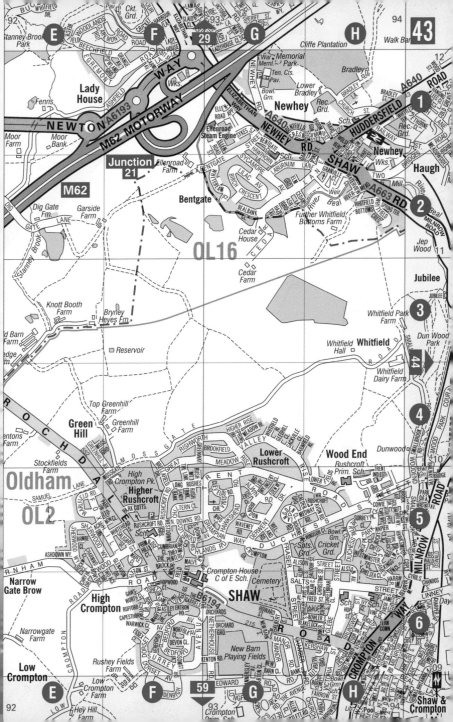

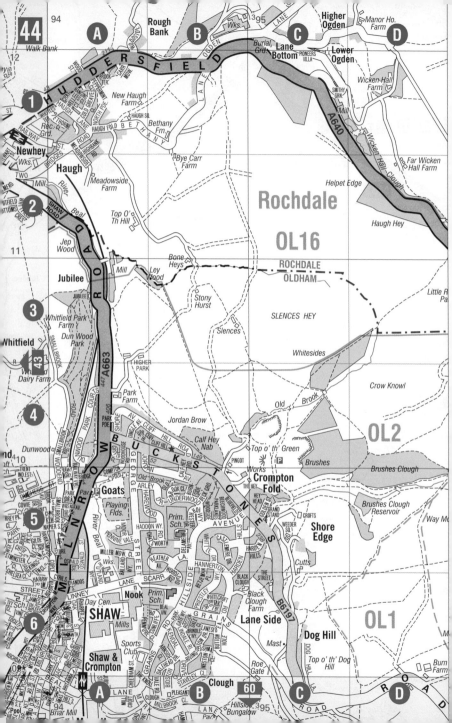

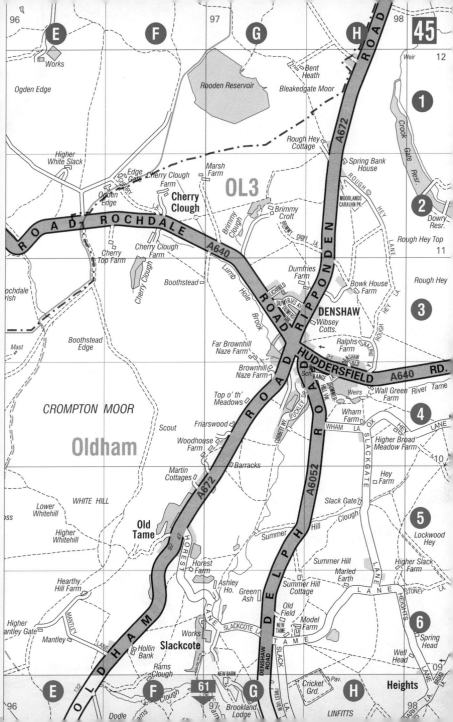

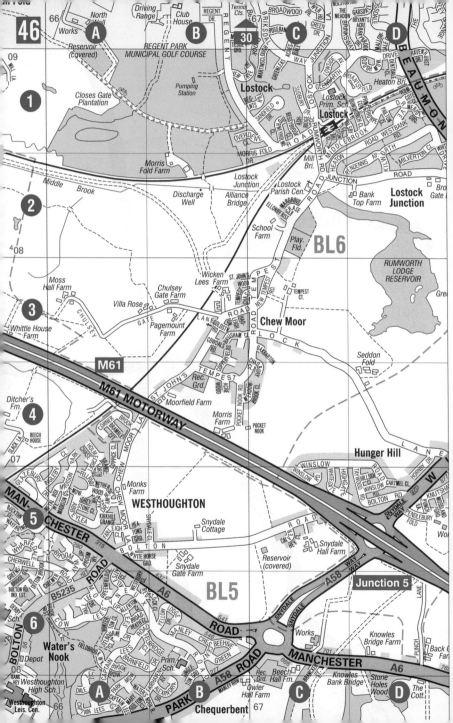

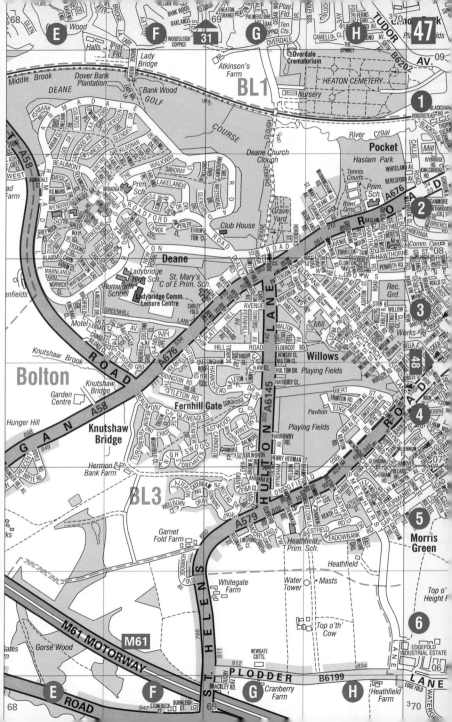

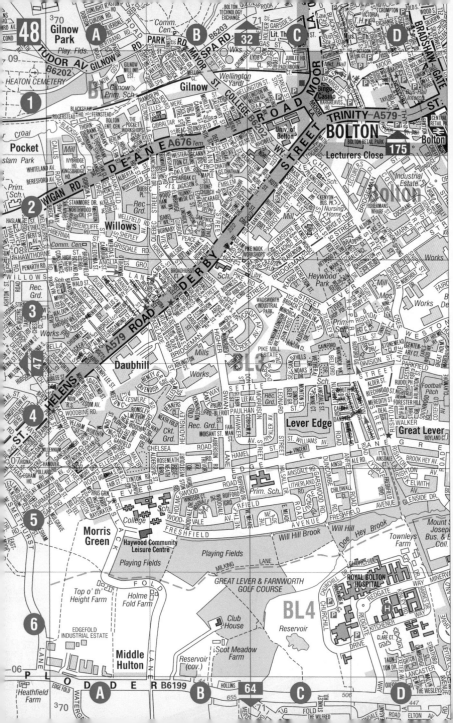

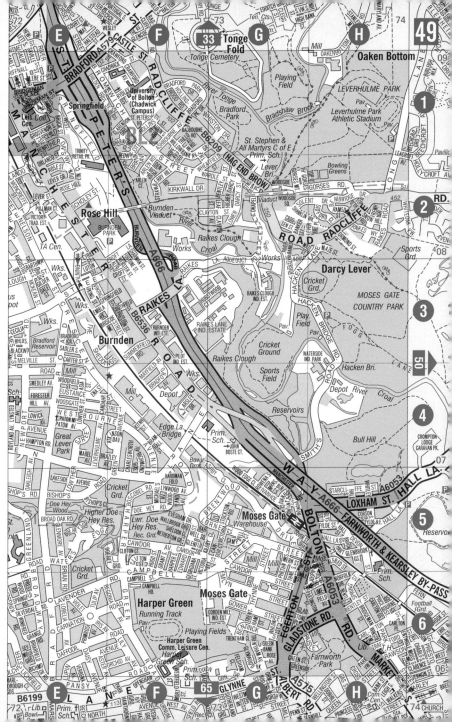

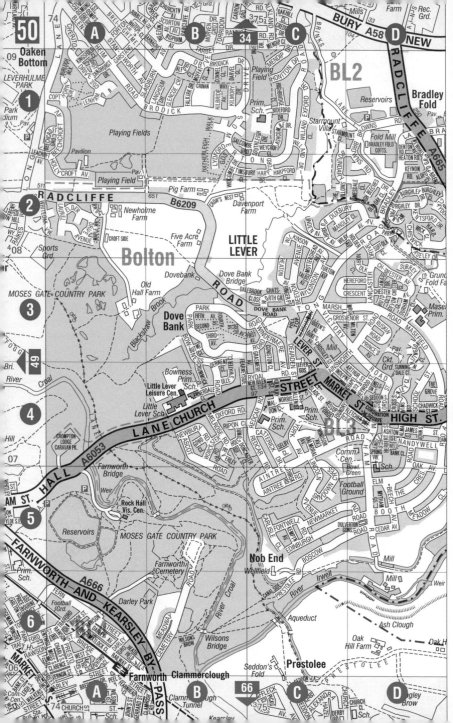

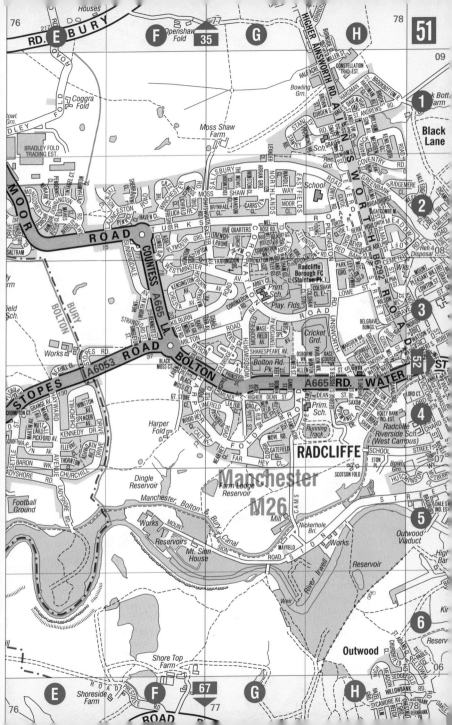

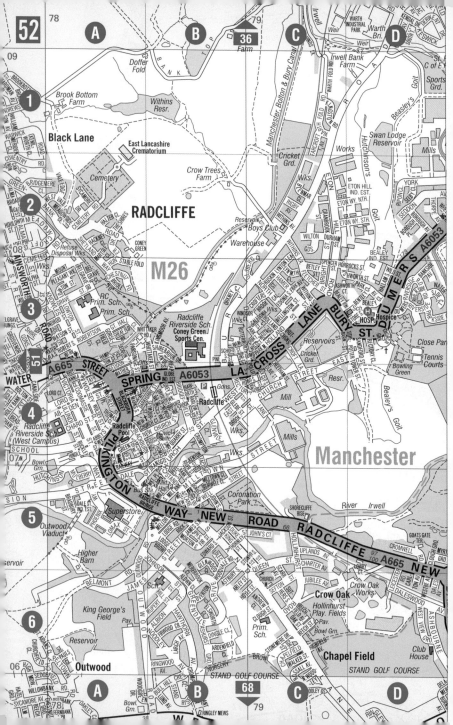

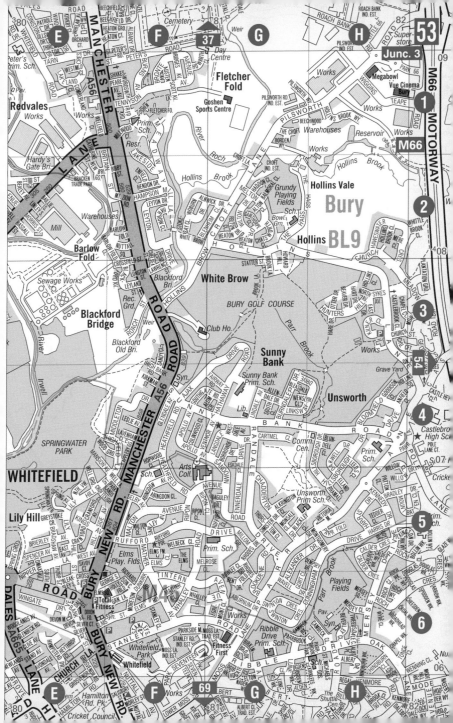

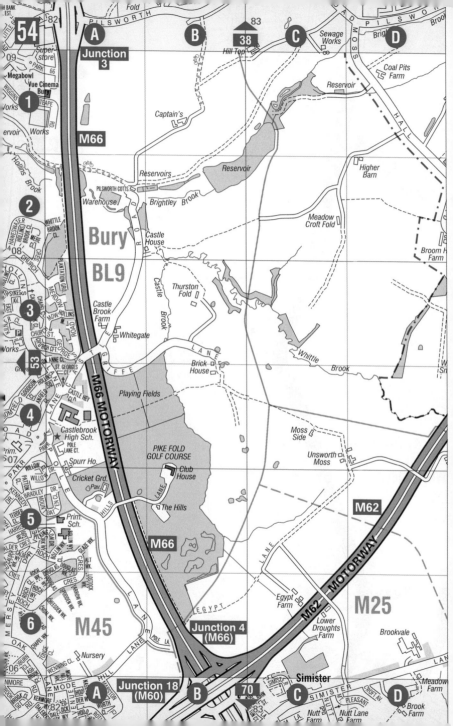

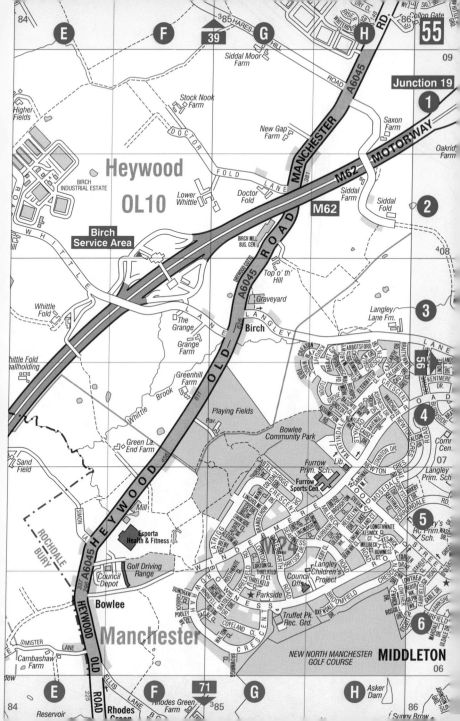

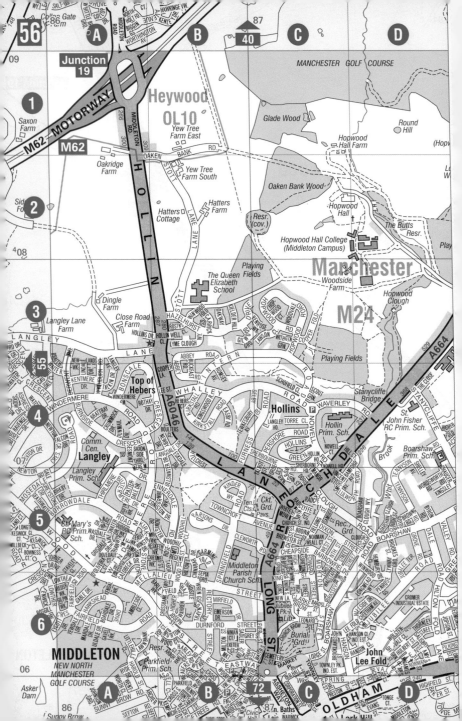

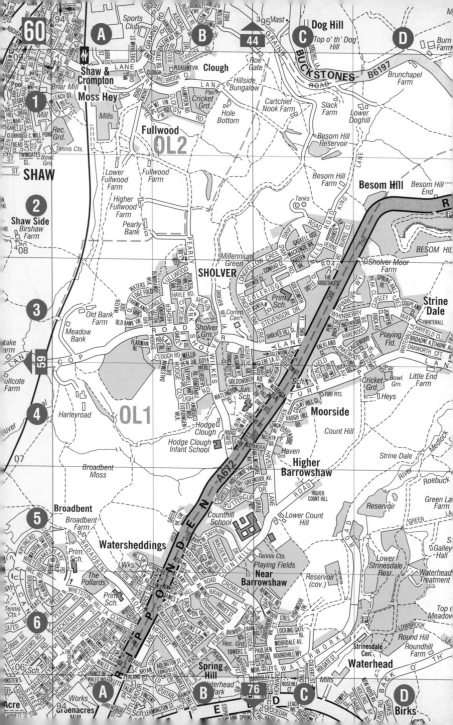

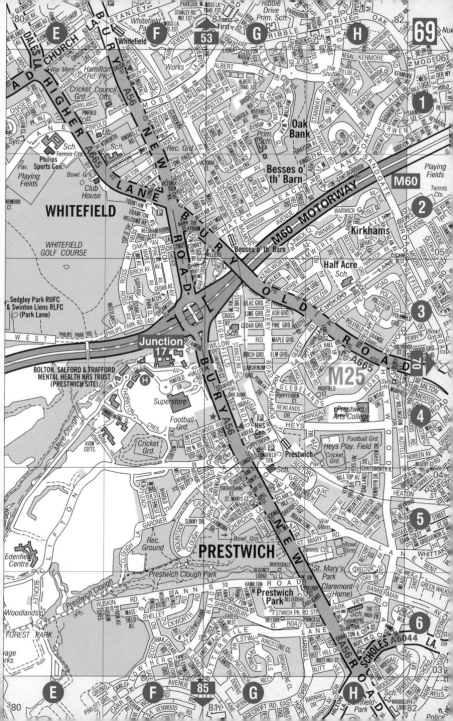

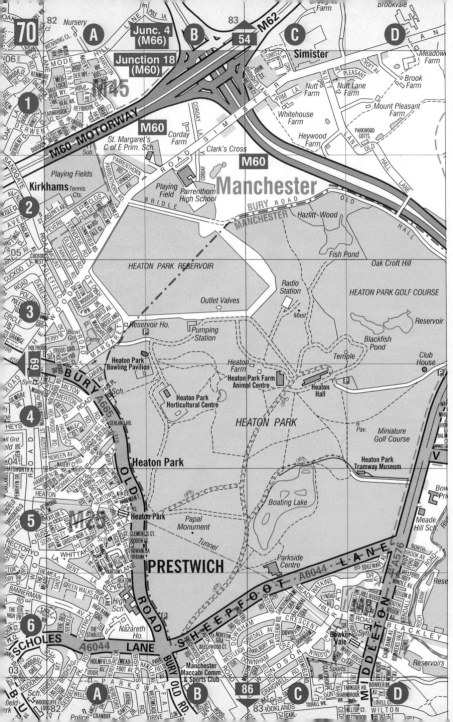

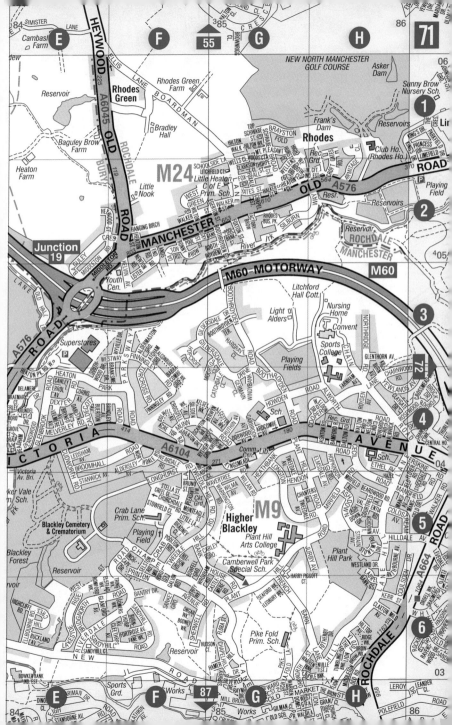

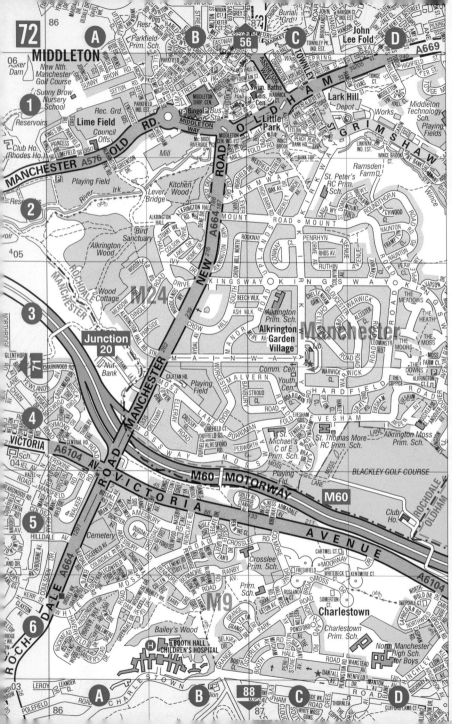

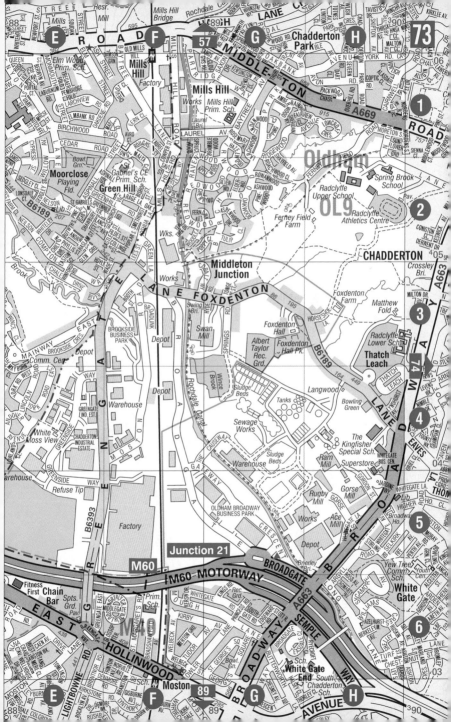

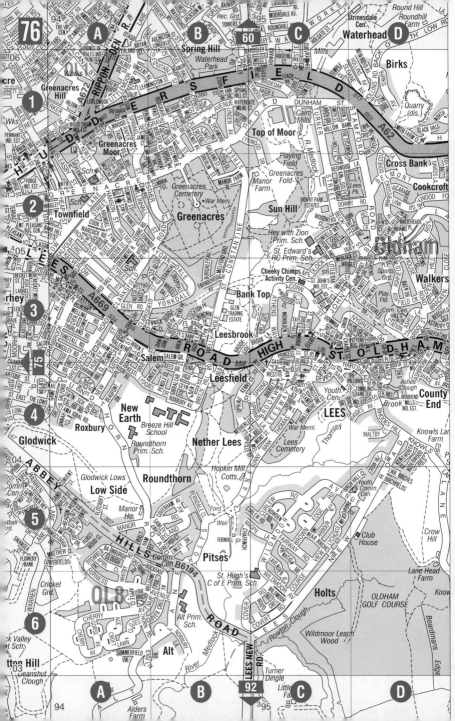

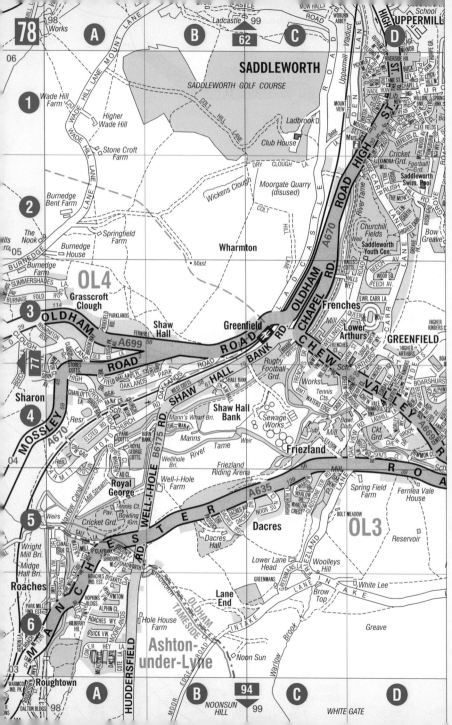

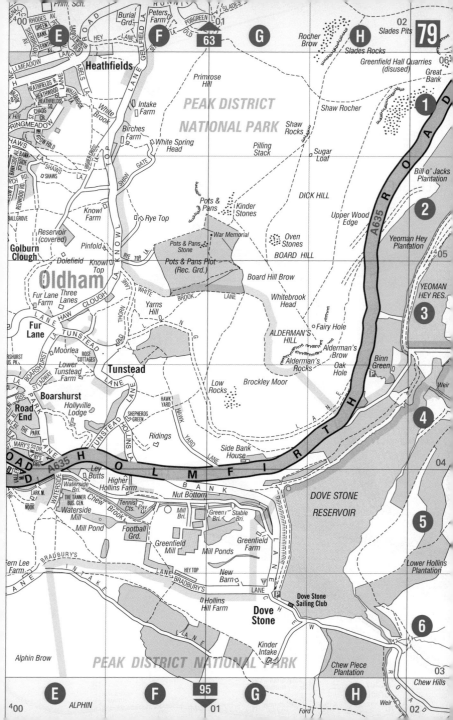

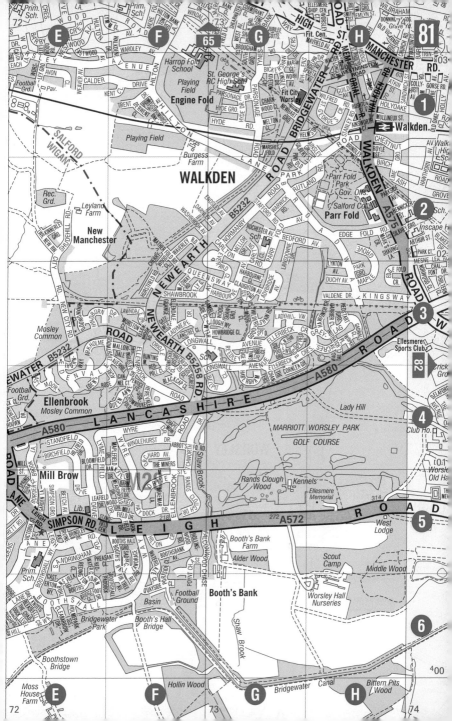

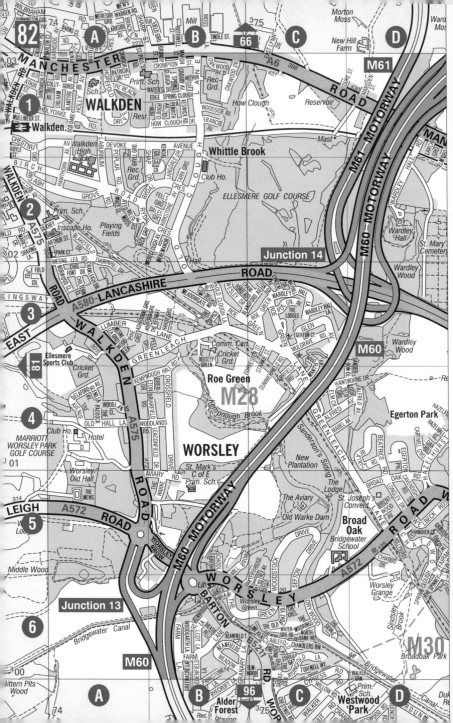

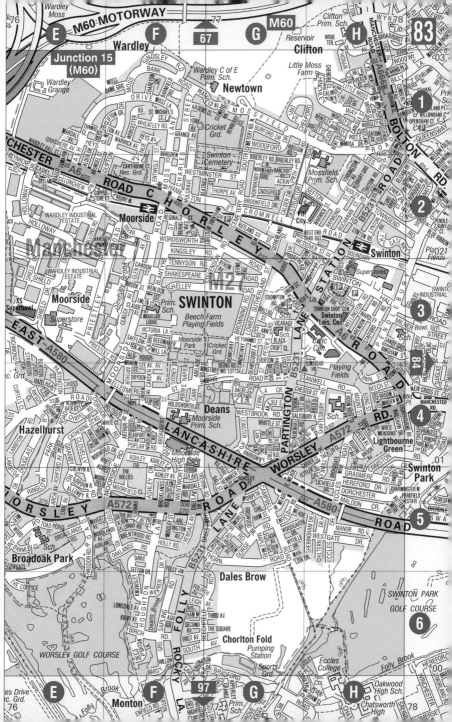

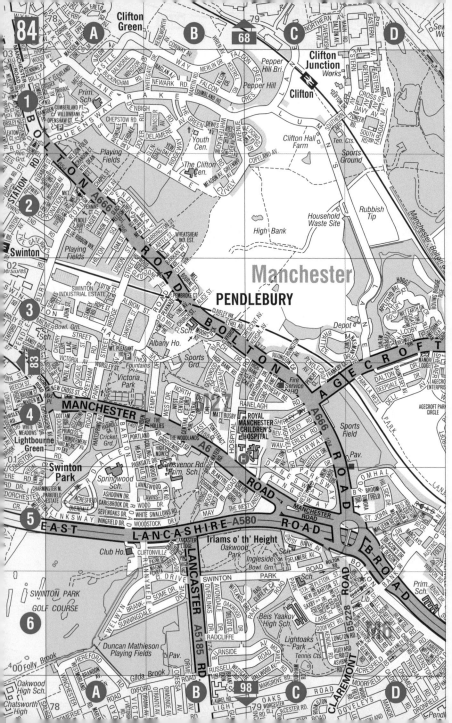

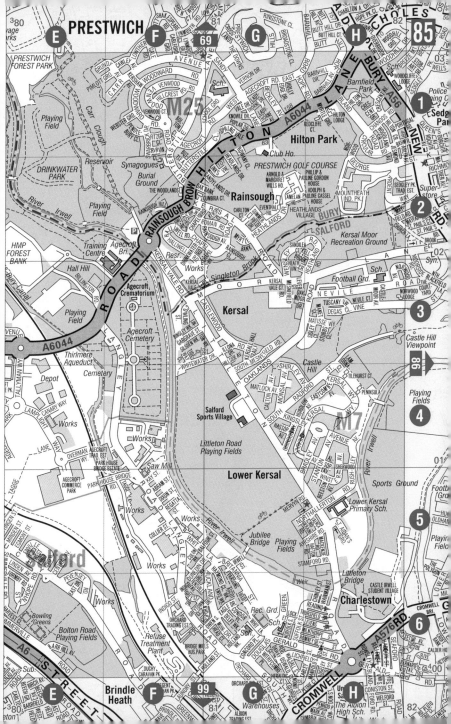

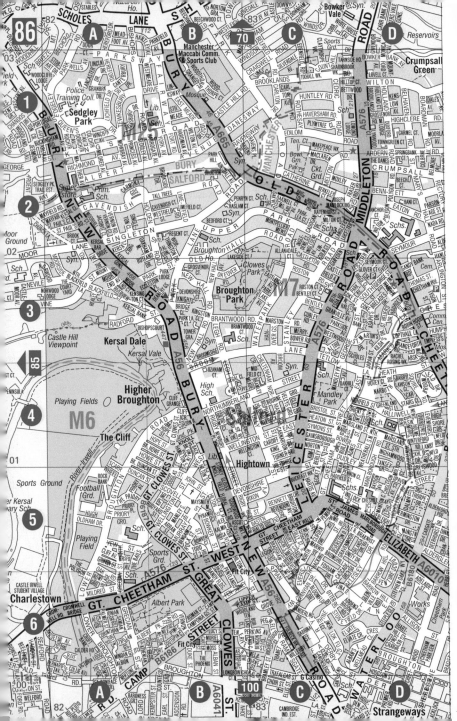

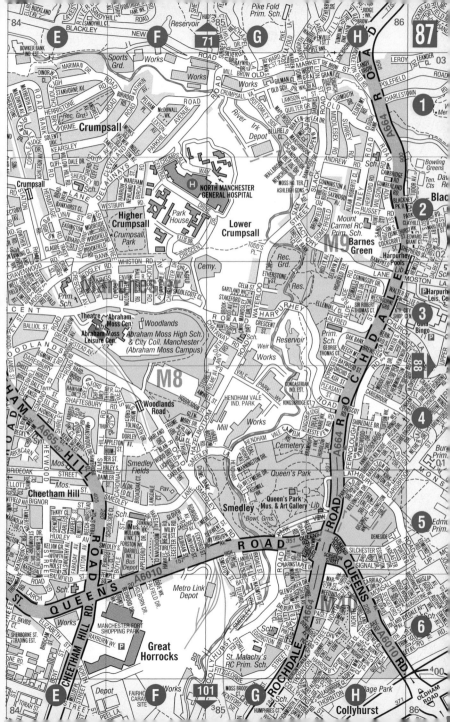

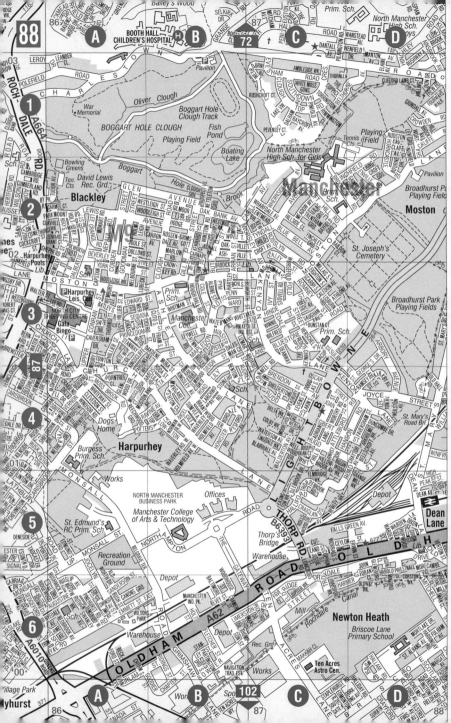

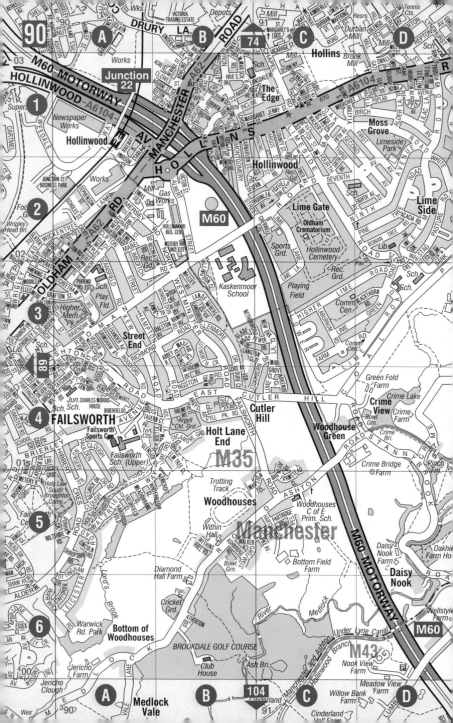

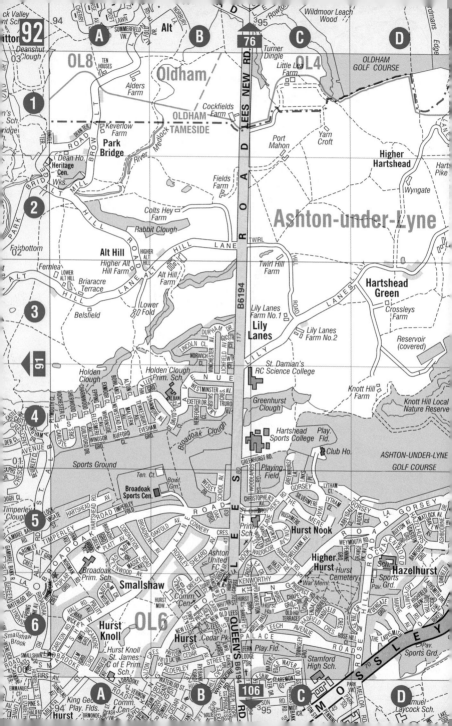

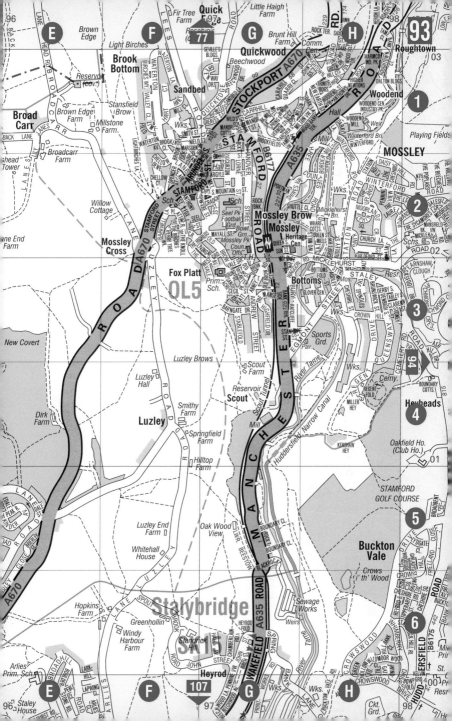

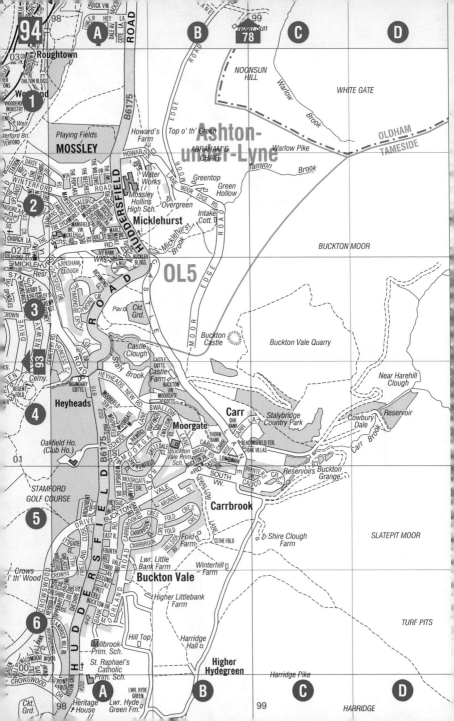

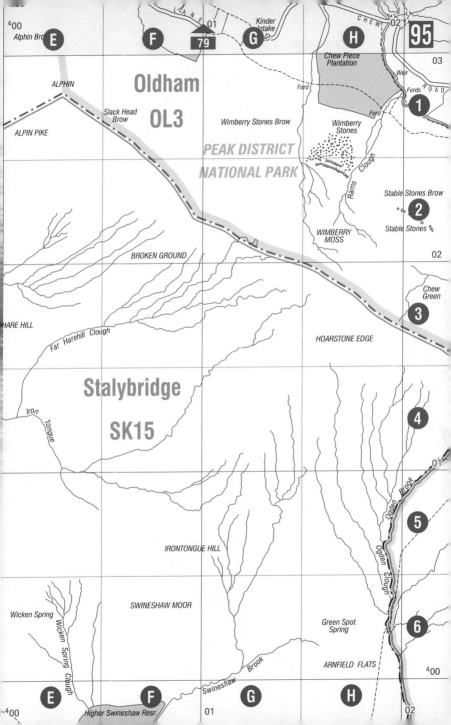

LANE

01

79

Kinder
Intake

G

CHEW

02

03

H

ROAD

400
Alphin Brow

E

Oldham

OL3

Chew Piece
Plantation

Weir

Fords

1

ALPHIN

Slack Head
Brow

Wimberry Stones Brow

Ford

Ford

Wimberry
Stones

ALPIN PIKE

PEAK DISTRICT

NATIONAL PARK

Rams Clough

Stable Stones Brow

2

Stable Stones

BROKEN GROUND

Wimberry
Moss

02

HARE HILL

Far Harehill Clough

HOARSTONE EDGE

Chew
Green

3

Stalybridge

SK15

Iron Tongue

4

01

5

IRONTONGUE HILL

Ogden Brook

Ogden Clough

Wicken Spring

SWINESHAW MOOR

Green Spot
Spring

6

Wicken Spring Clough

ARNFIELD FLATS

400

Swineshaw Brook

E

F

G

H

400

Higher Swineshaw Resr.

01

02

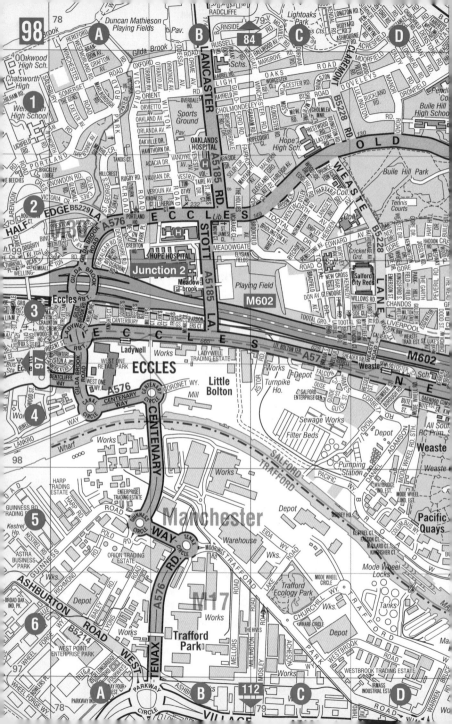

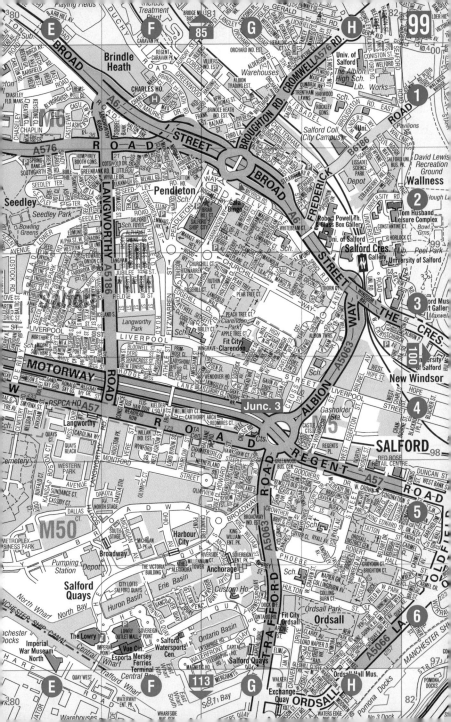

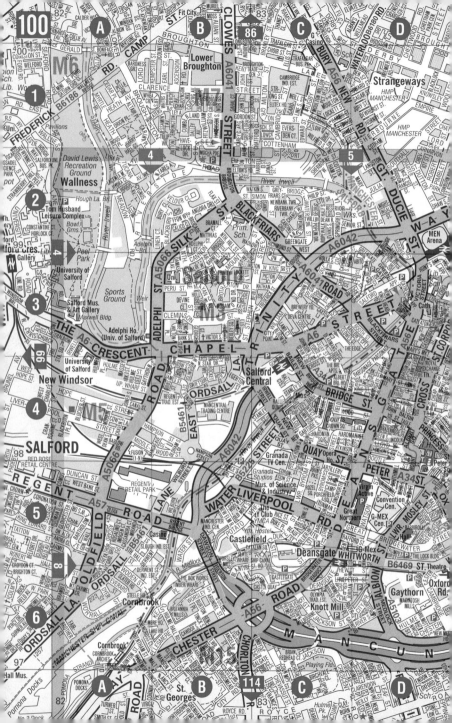

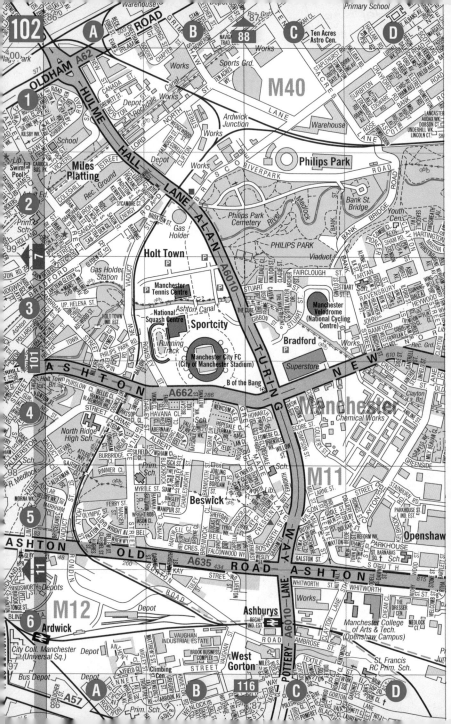

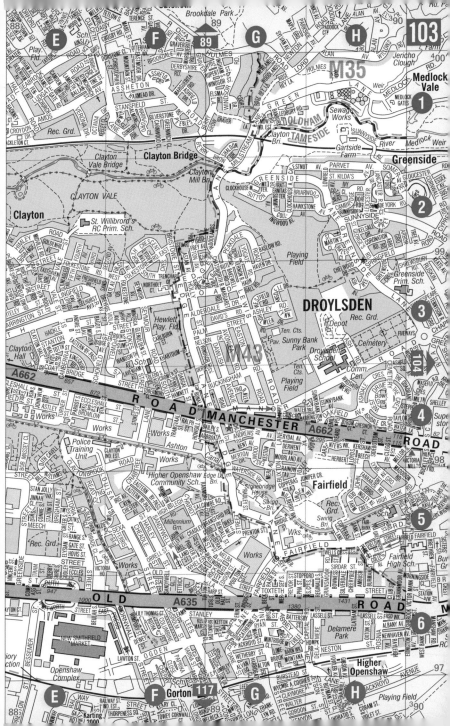

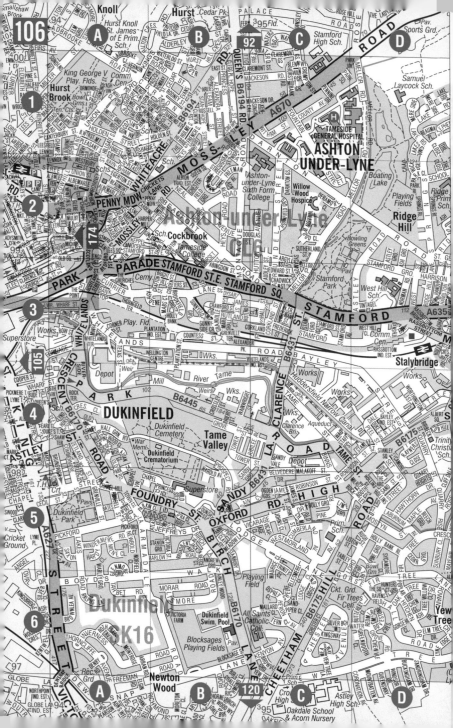

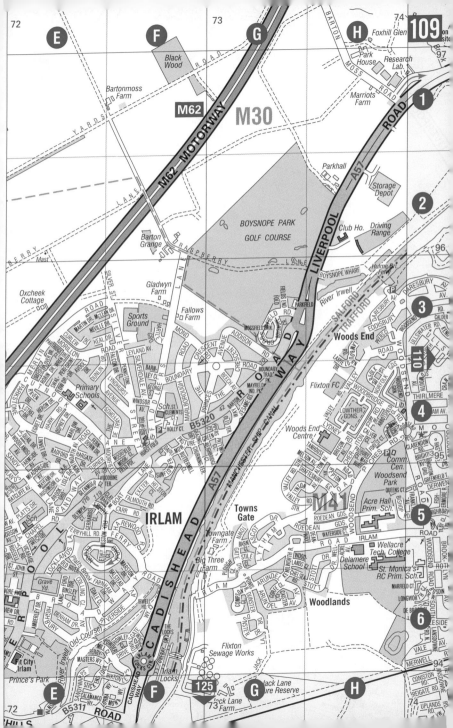

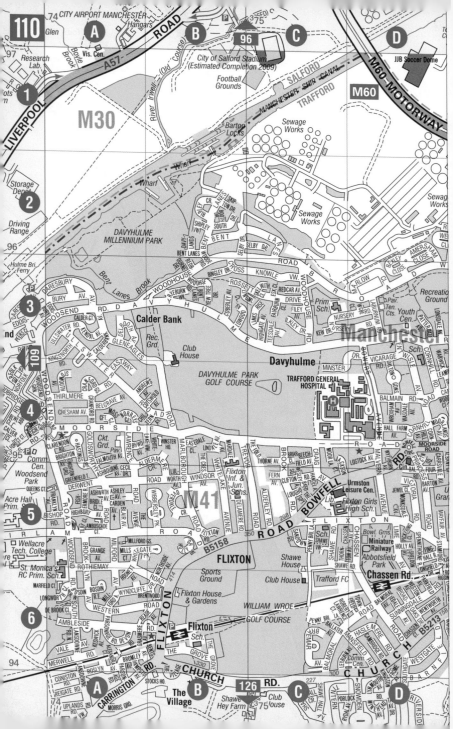

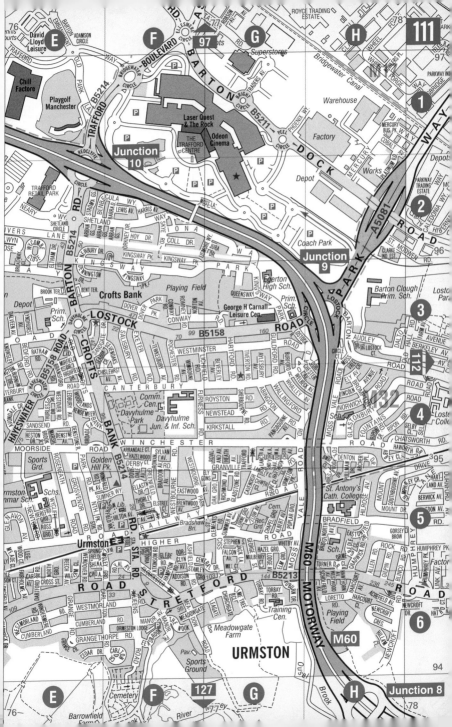

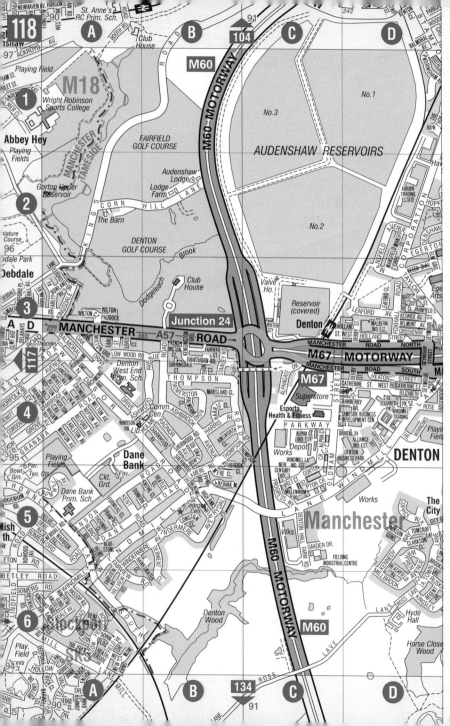

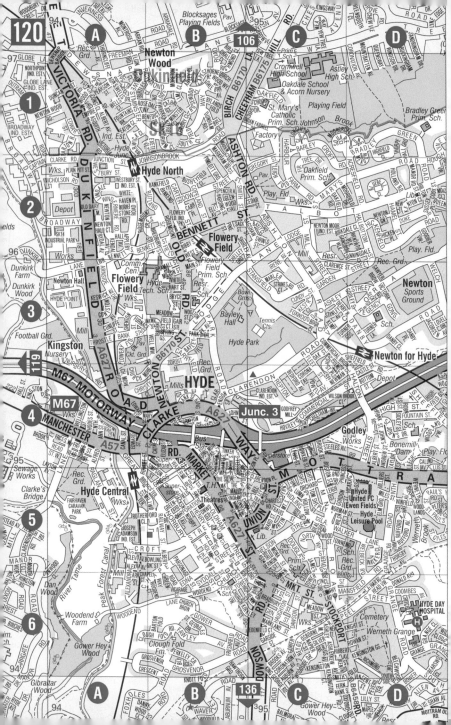

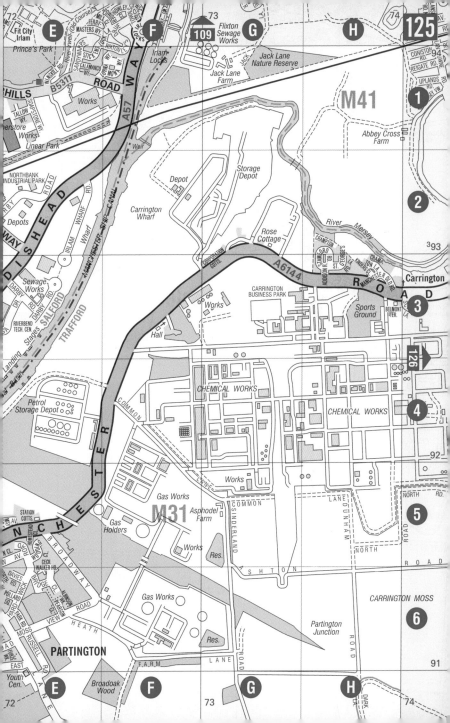

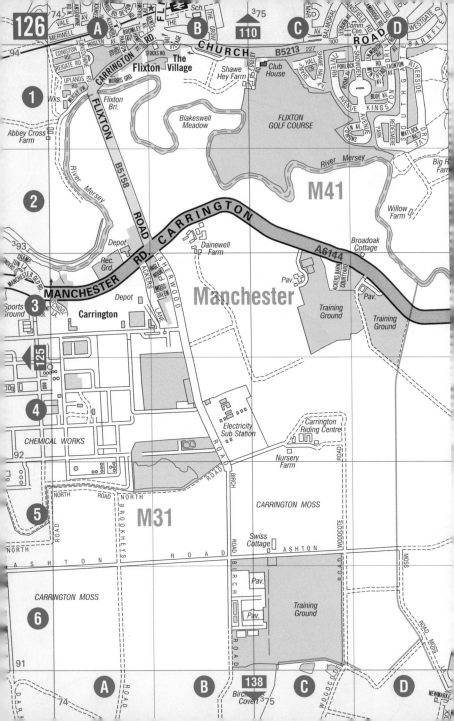

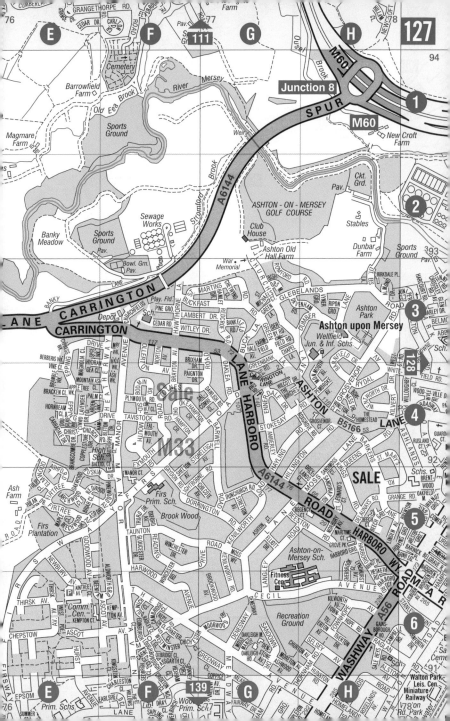

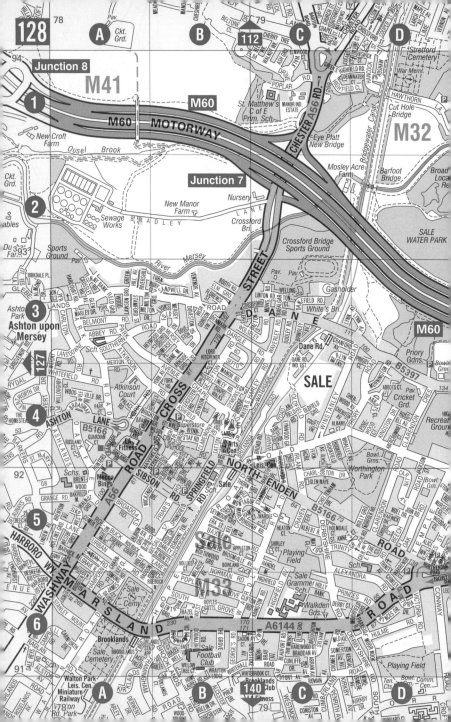

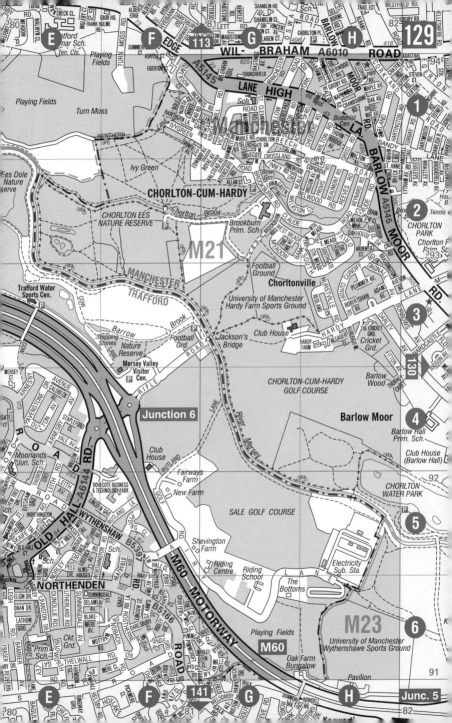

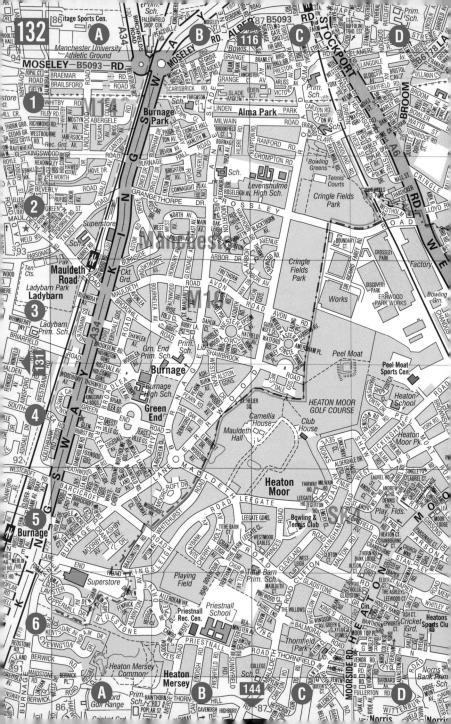

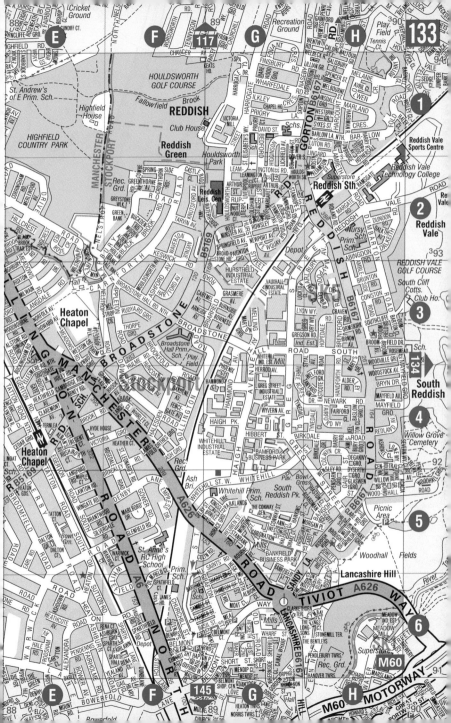

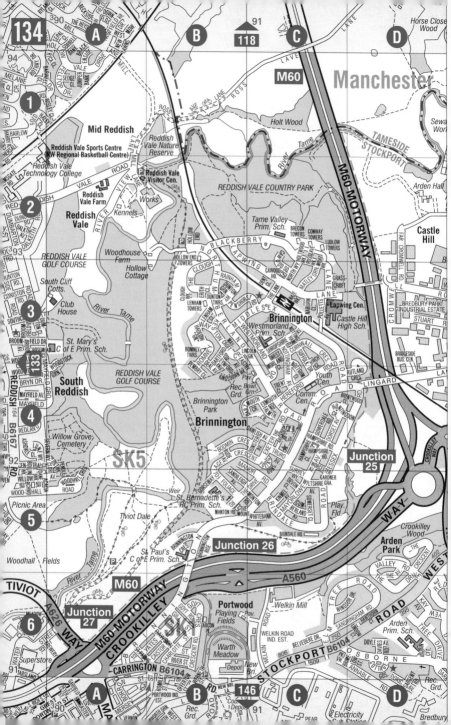

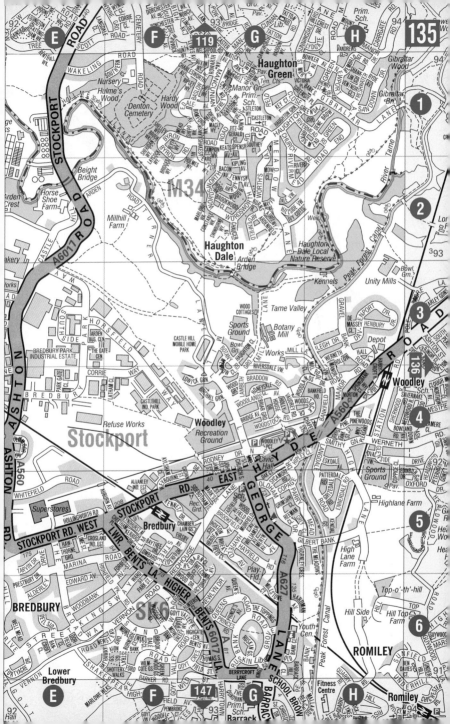

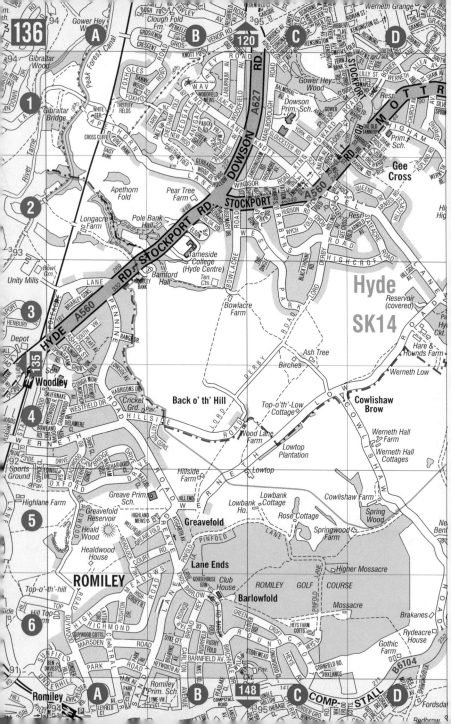

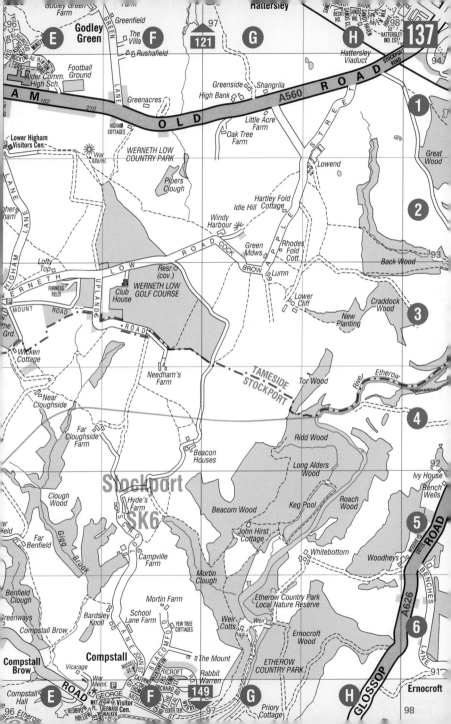

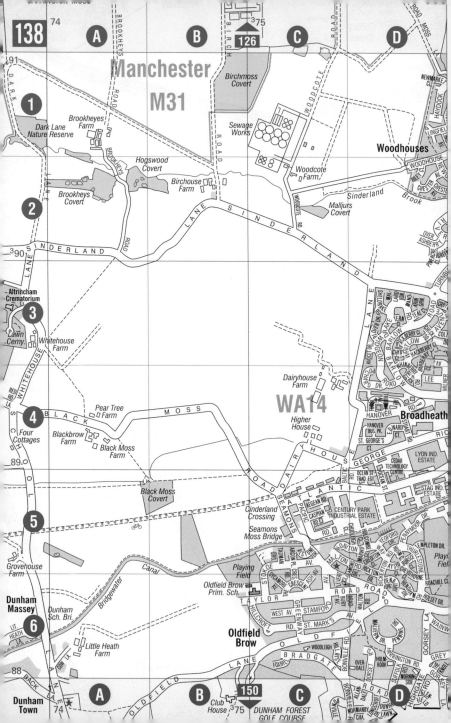

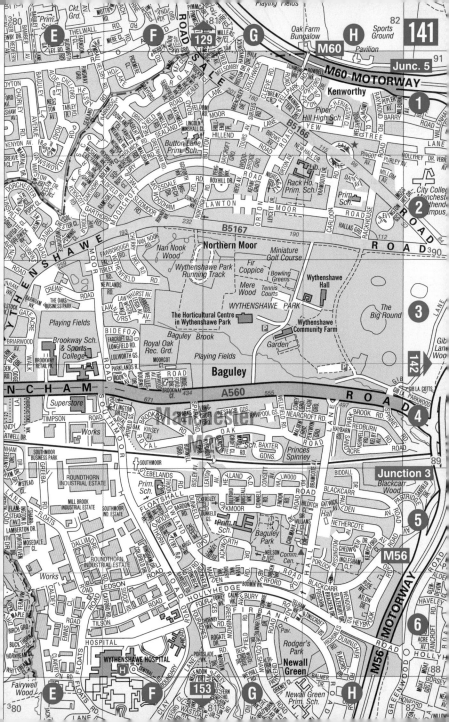

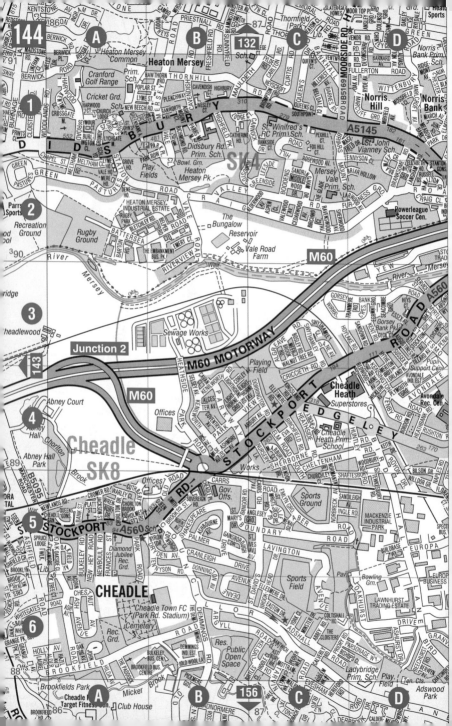

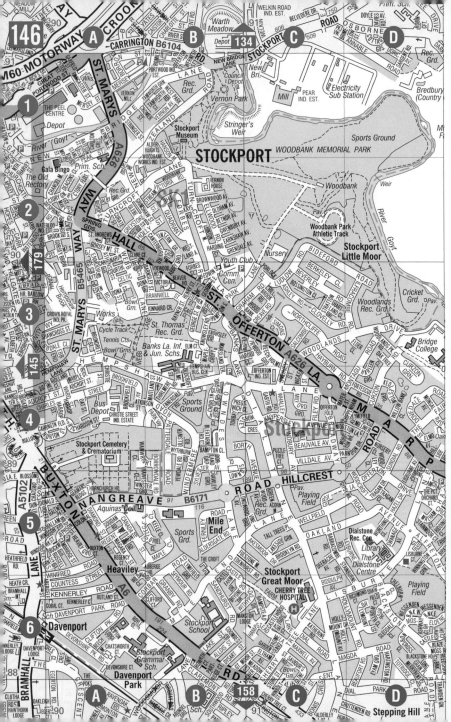

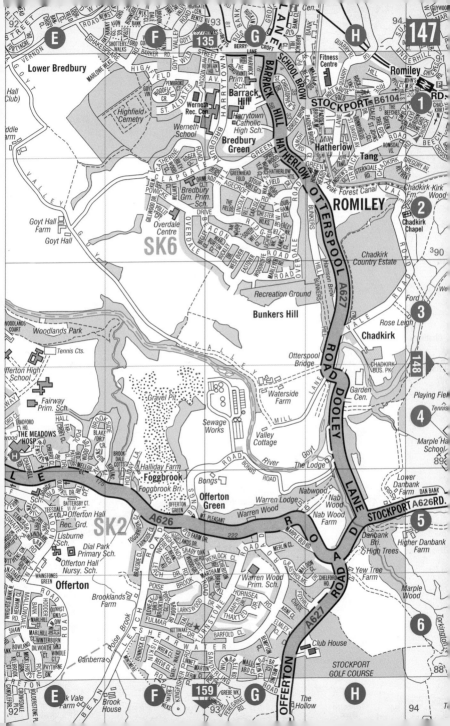

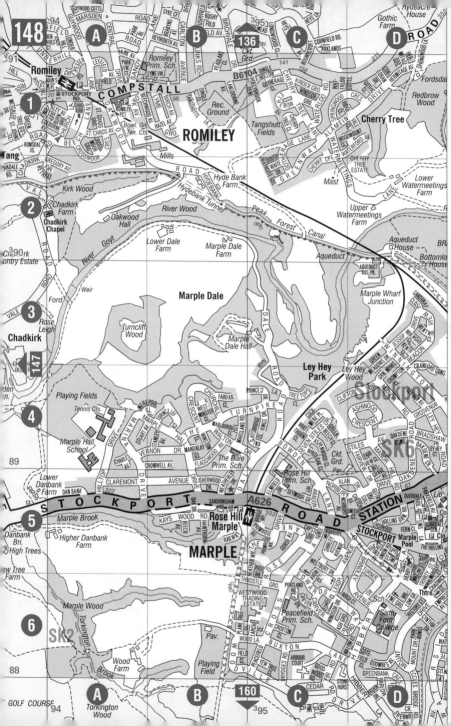

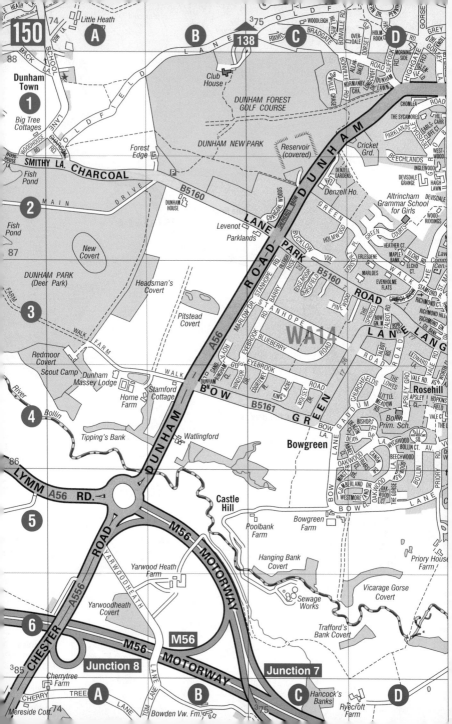

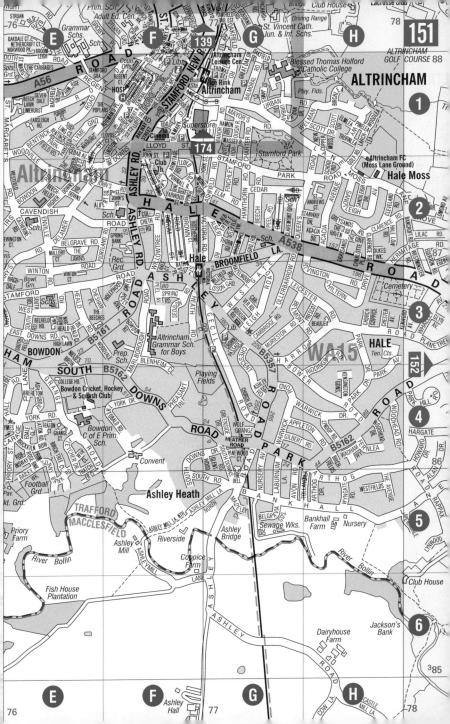

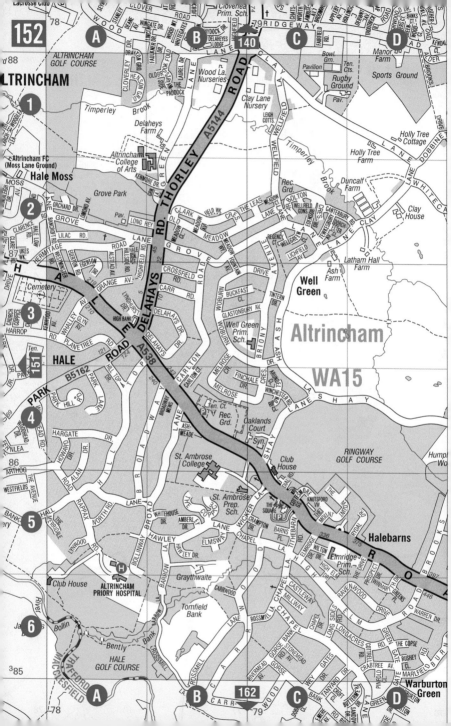

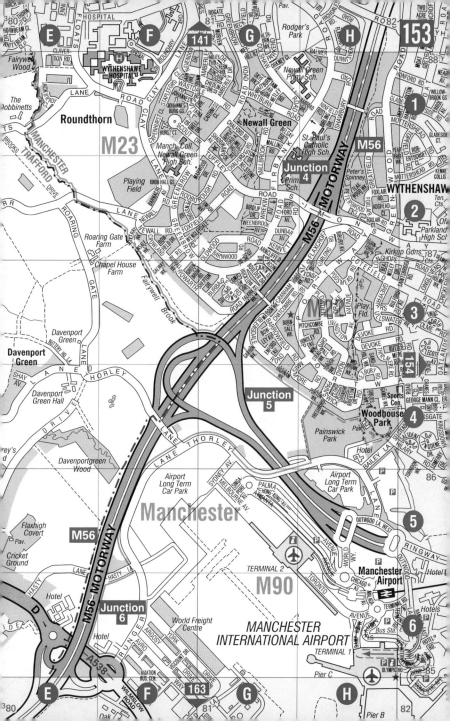

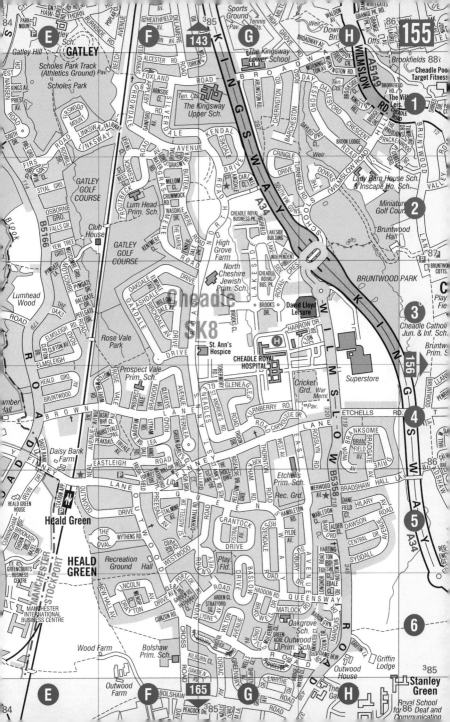

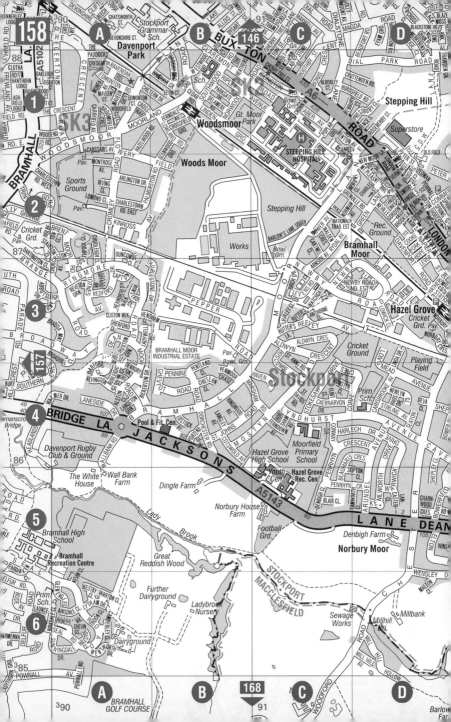

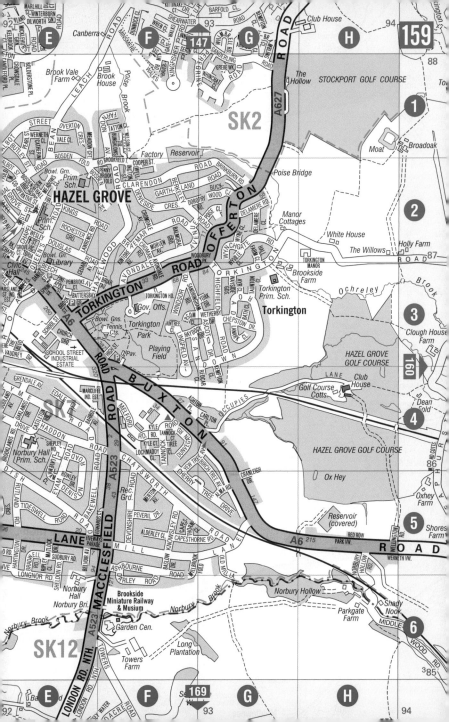

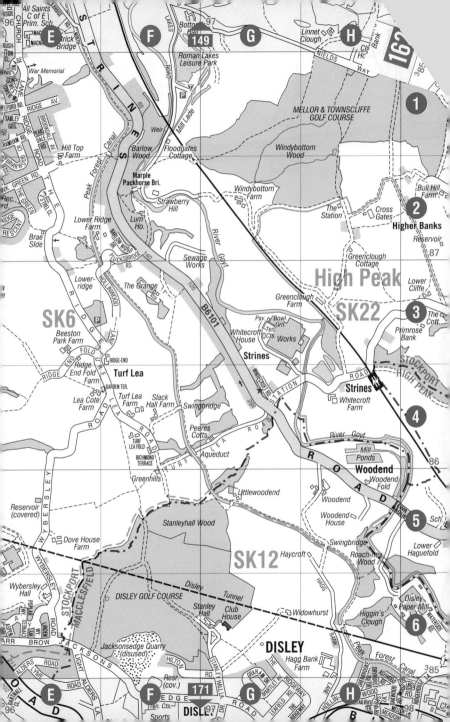

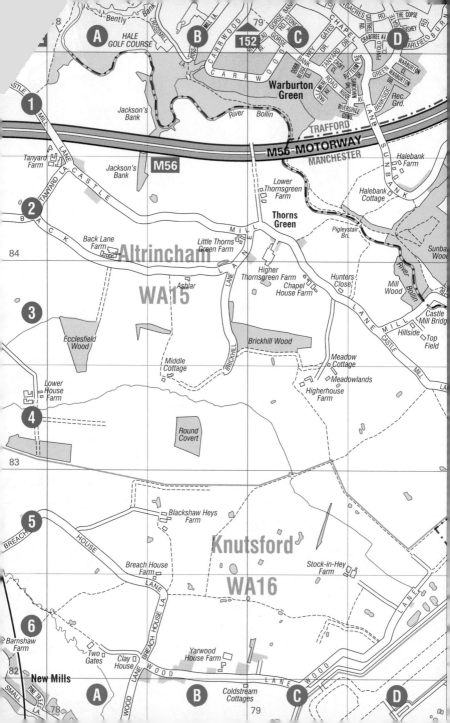

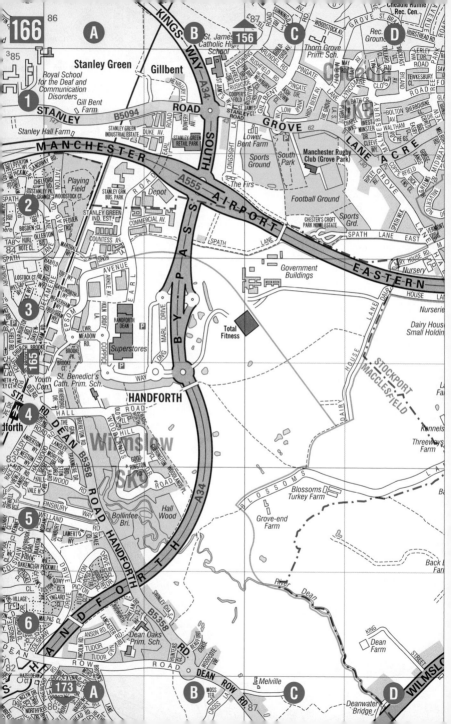

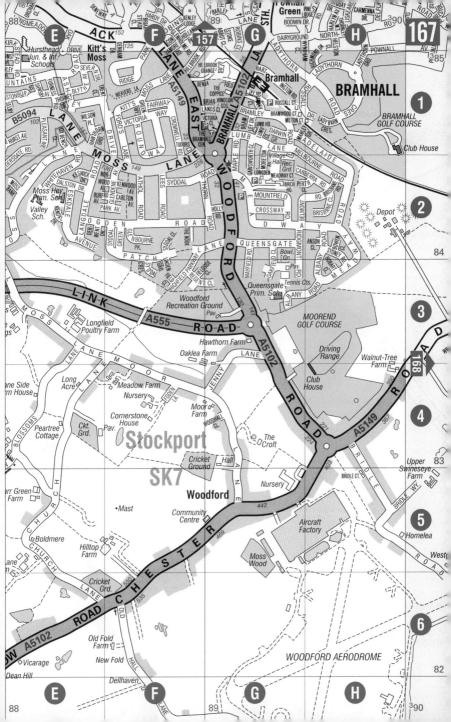

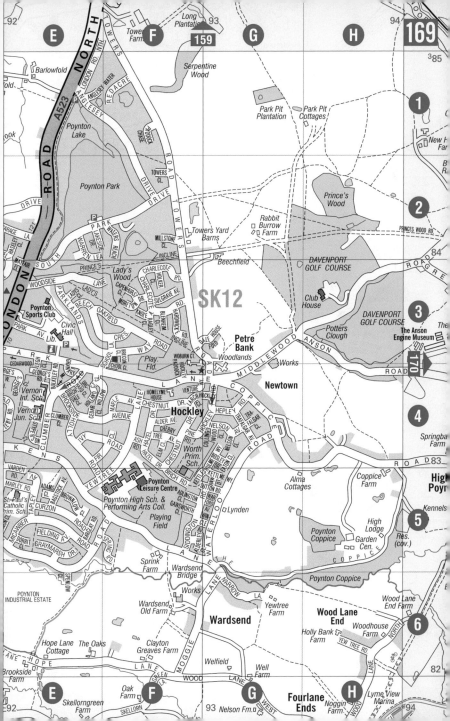

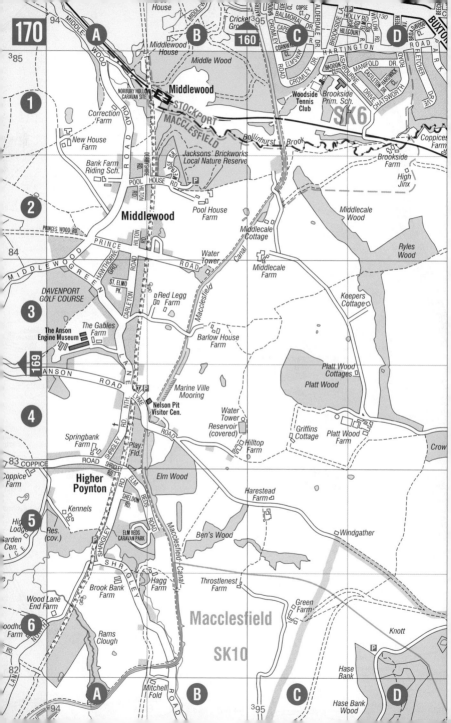

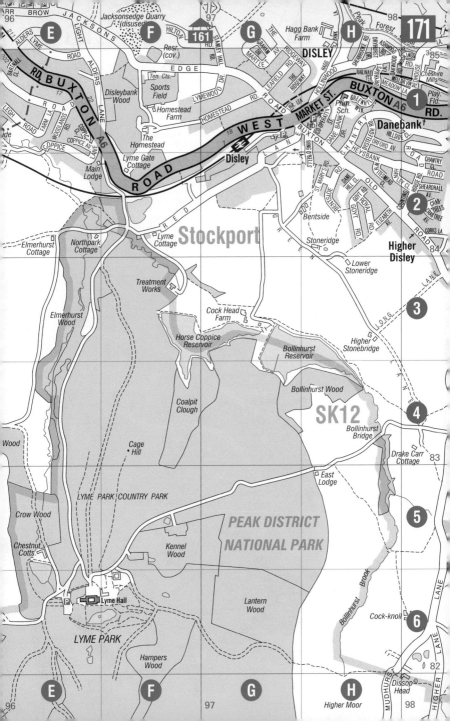

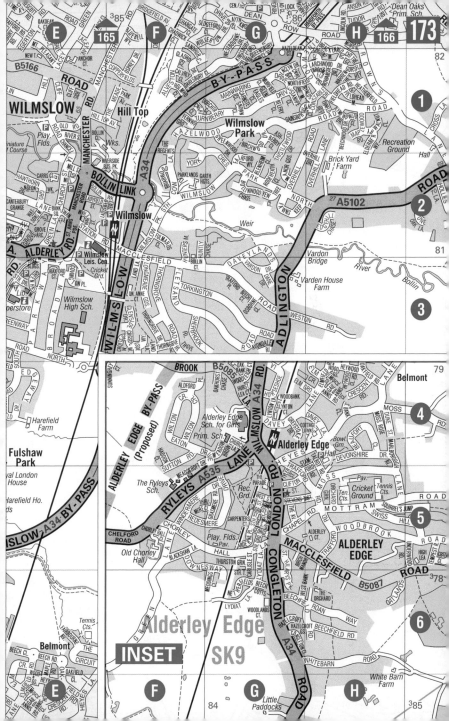

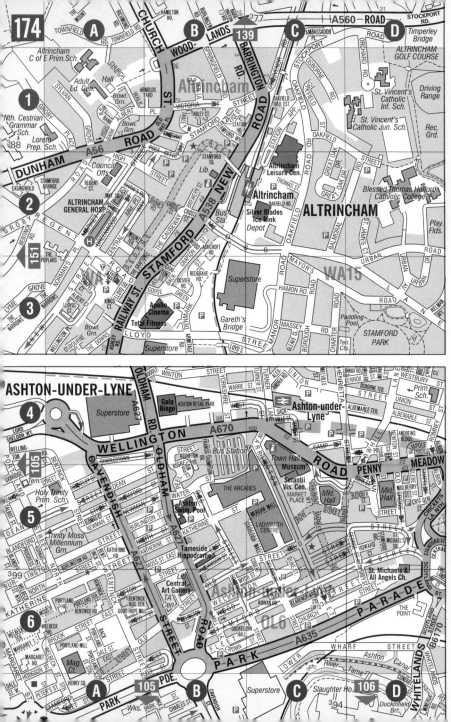

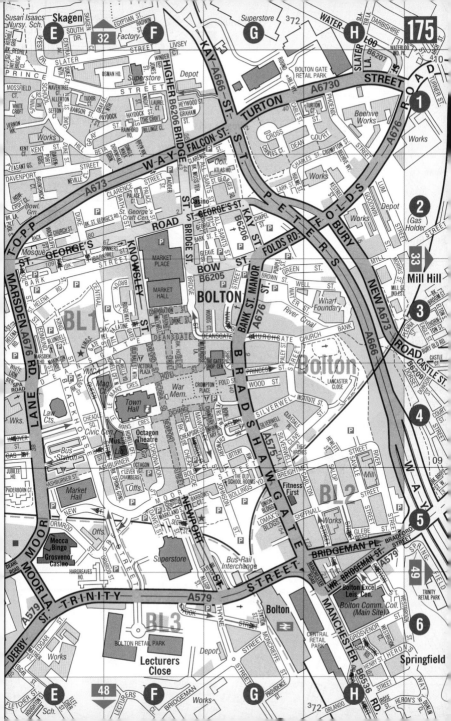

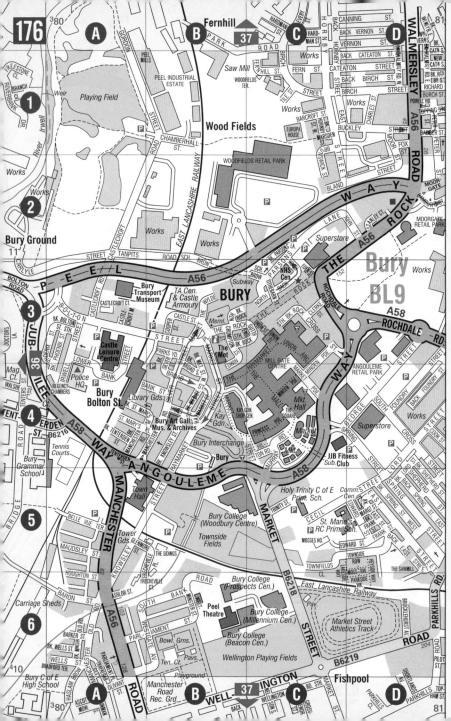

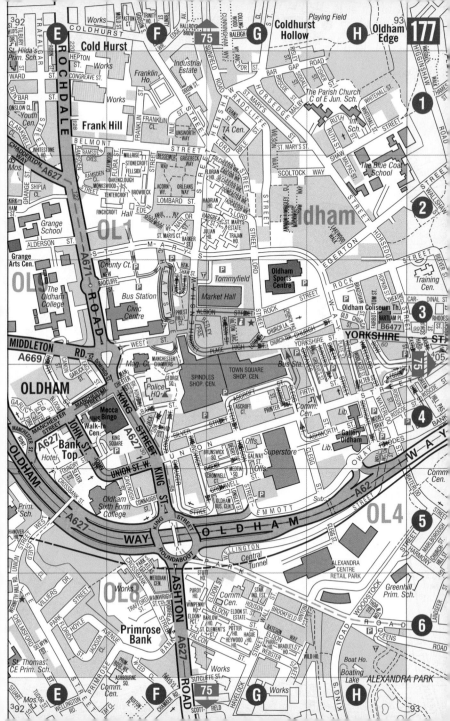

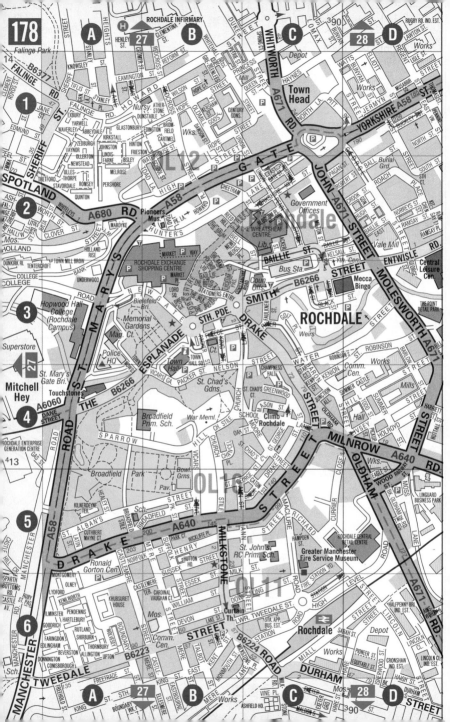

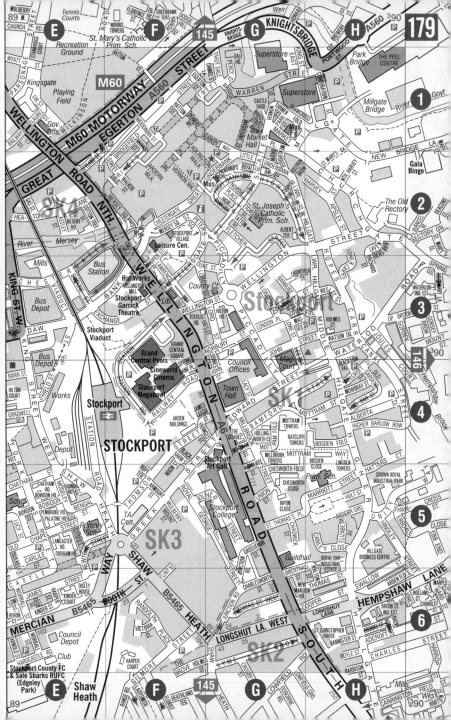

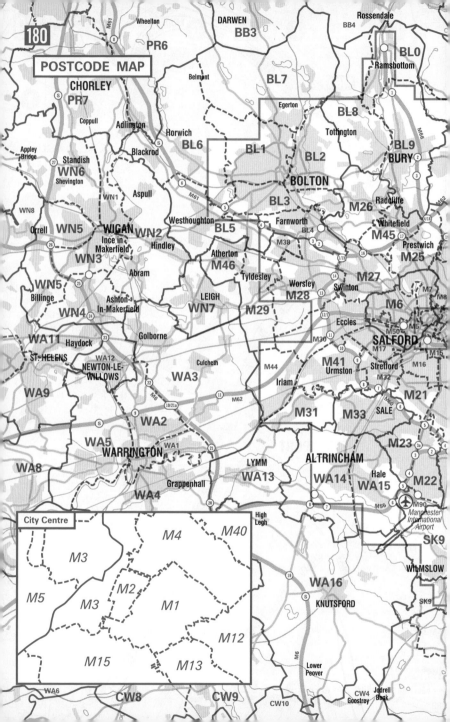

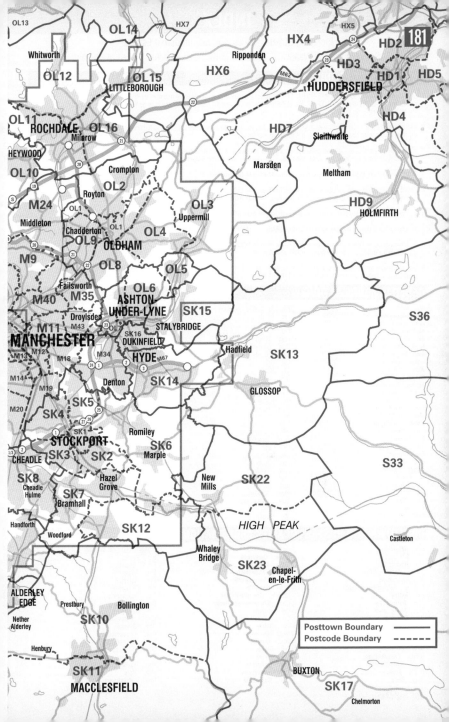

INDEX

Including Streets, Places & Areas, Industrial Estates,
Selected Flats & Walkways, Junction Names and Selected Places of Interest.

HOW TO USE THIS INDEX

1. Each street name is followed by its Postcode District, then by its Locality abbreviation(s) and then by its map reference;
   e.g. **Abbey Dr.** BL8: Bury . . . .4A **36** is in the BL8 Postcode District and the Bury Locality and is to be found in square 4A on page **36**.
   The page number is shown in bold type.

2. A strict alphabetical order is followed in which Av., Rd., St., etc. (though abbreviated) are read in full and as part of the street name;
   e.g. **Ash La.** appears after **Ashlands Rd.** but before **Ashlar Dr.**

3. Streets and a selection of flats and walkways too small to be shown on the maps, appear in the index with the thoroughfare to which it is
   connected shown in brackets; e.g. **Abbeyfield Ho.** M28: Walk . . . .5G **65** (off Mountain St.)

4. Addresses that are in more than one part are referred to as not continuous.

5. Places and areas are shown in the index in **BLUE TYPE** and the map reference is to the actual map square in which the town centre or area is
   located and not to the place name shown on the map; e.g. **ADSWOOD** 5F **145**

6. An example of a selected place of interest is **Anson Engine Mus., The** 3A **170**

7. An example of a station is **Alderley Edge Station (Rail)** . . . .4G **173**. Included are Rail **(Rail)** and Metro **(Metro)**

8. Junction names and Service Areas are shown in the index in **BOLD CAPITAL TYPE;**
   e.g. **CROWN POINT** . . . .4F **119** (junc. of A57 with A6017)

9. Map references for entries that appear on large scale pages **4-11** and **174-179** are shown first, with small scale map references shown in
   brackets; e.g. **Abbeydale** OL12: Roch 1A **178** (3G **27**)

GENERAL ABBREVIATIONS

All. : Alley	**Ent.** : Enterprise	**Mus.** : Museum
App. : Approach	**Est.** : Estate	**Nth.** : North
Arc. : Arcade	**Ests.** : Estates	**No.** : Number
Av. : Avenue	**Fld.** : Field	**Pde.** : Parade
Bk. : Back	**Flds.** : Fields	**Pk.** : Park
Blvd. : Boulevard	**Gdn.** : Garden	**Pas.** : Passage
Bri. : Bridge	**Gdns.** : Gardens	**Pl.** : Place
B'way. : Broadway	**Ga.** : Gate	**Pct.** : Precinct
Bldg. : Building	**Gt.** : Great	**Ri.** : Rise
Bldgs. : Buildings	**Grn.** : Green	**Rd.** : Road
Bungs. : Bungalows	**Gro.** : Grove	**Rdbt.** : Roundabout
Bus. : Business	**Hgts.** : Heights	**Shop.** : Shopping
Cvn. : Caravan	**Ho.** : House	**Sth.** : South
Cen. : Centre	**Ho's.** : Houses	**Sq.** : Square
Chu. : Church	**Ind.** : Industrial	**Sta.** : Station
Chyd. : Churchyard	**Info.** : Information	**St.** : Street
Circ. : Circle	**Intl.** : International	**Ter.** : Terrace
Cl. : Close	**Junc.** : Junction	**Twr.** : Tower
Comn. : Common	**La.** : Lane	**Trad.** : Trading
Cnr. : Corner	**Lit.** : Little	**Up.** : Upper
Cott. : Cottage	**Lwr.** : Lower	**Va.** : Vale
Cotts. : Cottages	**Mnr.** : Manor	**Vw.** : View
Ct. : Court	**Mans.** : Mansions	**Vs.** : Villas
Cres. : Crescent	**Mkt.** : Market	**Vis.** : Visitors
Cft. : Croft	**Mdw.** : Meadow	**Wlk.** : Walk
Dr. : Drive	**Mdws.** : Meadows	**W.** : West
E. : East	**M.** : Mews	**Yd.** : Yard
Emb. : Embankment	**Mt.** : Mount	

POSTTOWN AND POSTAL LOCALITY ABBREVIATIONS

Adl : **Adlington**	Cad : **Cadishead**	D Mas : **Dunham Massey**
Aff : **Affetside**	C'ook : **Carrbrook**	Ecc : **Eccles**
Ain : **Ainsworth**	C'ton : **Carrington**	Eden : **Edenfield**
A Edg : **Alderley Edge**	Chad : **Chadderton**	Edg : **Edgworth**
Alt : **Altrincham**	Char : **Charlesworth**	Eger : **Egerton**
A Lyme : **Ashton-under-Lyme**	Chea : **Cheadle**	Fail : **Failsworth**
Ast : **Astley**	Chea H : **Cheadle Hulme**	Farn : **Farnworth**
Aud : **Audenshaw**	Chor : **Chorlton-cum-Hardy**	Gam : **Gamesley**
Aus : **Austerlands**	Clif : **Clifton**	Gat : **Gatley**
Bel : **Belmont**	Comp : **Compstall**	G'ook : **Glazebrook**
Bolt : **Bolton**	Del : **Delph**	Glos : **Glossop**
Bow : **Bowdon**	Dens : **Denshaw**	Gras : **Grasscroft**
Bram : **Bramhall**	Dent : **Denton**	G'fld : **Greenfield**
Bred : **Bredbury**	Dig : **Diggle**	G'mount : **Greenmount**
B'tom : **Broadbottom**	Dis : **Disley**	Grot : **Grotton**
B'ath : **Broadheath**	Dob : **Dobcross**	Had : **Hadfield**
Bro X : **Bromley Cross**	Droy : **Droylsden**	Hale : **Hale**
Bury : **Bury**	Duk : **Dukinfield**	Haleb : **Halebarns**

Hand : **Handforth**
Hat : **Hattersley**
Haw : **Hawkshaw**
H Gro : **Hazel Grove**
H Grn : **Heald Green**
H'rod : **Heyrod**
H'ood : **Heywood**
H Lan : **High Lane**
Holc : **Holcombe**
Holl : **Hollingworth**
Hor : **Horwich**
Hyde : **Hyde**
Irl : **Irlam**
Kea : **Kearsley**
Lees : **Lees**
Lit B : **Little Bollington**
L'ough : **Littleborough**
Lit H : **Little Hulton**
Lit L : **Little Lever**
Los : **Lostock**
Lyd : **Lydgate**
Man : **Manchester**
Man A : **Manchester Airport**
Mar : **Marple**
Mar B : **Marple Bridge**
Mat : **Matley**
Mel : **Mellor**
Mid : **Middleton**
Mill : **Millbrook**
Miln : **Milnrow**

Mob : **Mobberley**
Mos : **Mossley**
Mot : **Mottram**
N Ald : **Nether Alderley**
N Mil : **New Mills**
Nor : **Northenden**
O'ham : **Oldham**
Old T : **Old Trafford**
O Hul : **Over Hulton**
Part : **Partington**
Pen : **Pendlebury**
P Shr : **Pott Shrigley**
Poy : **Poynton**
Pres : **Prestwich**
Rad : **Radcliffe**
Ram : **Ramsbottom**
Ring : **Ringway**
Rix : **Rixton**
Roch : **Rochdale**
Rom : **Romiley**
Rost : **Rostherne**
Sale : **Sale**
Sal : **Salford**
Scout : **Scouthead**
Shar : **Sharston**
Shaw : **Shaw**
Spri : **Springhead**
Stal : **Stalybridge**
Stoc : **Stockport**
Stre : **Stretford**

Stri : **Strines**
Sty : **Styal**
Sum : **Summerseat**
Swin : **Swinton**
Tim : **Timperley**
Tin : **Tintwistle**
Tot : **Tottington**
T Pk : **Trafford Park**
Tur : **Turton**
Tyld : **Tyldesley**
Upp : **Upperhill**
Urm : **Urmston**
Walk : **Walkden**
Warb : **Warburton**
W'le : **Wardle**
Ward : **Wardley**
Wat : **Waterhead**
W Tim : **West Timperley**
W'ton : **Westhoughton**
W Ran : **Whalley Range**
White : **Whitefield**
Whitw : **Whitworth**
Wilm : **Wilmslow**
W'ford : **Woodford**
Wood : **Woodley**
Wors : **Worsley**
Wyth : **Wythenshawe**

A

Abberley Dr. M40: Man 1F **89**
Abberton Rd. M20: Man 3E **131**
Abbey Cl. M26: Rad 2G **51**
M32: Stre 4H **111**
SK14: Mot 4B **122**
WA14: Bow 4C **150**
Abbey Ct. M18: Man 1G **117**
M26: Rad 3G **51**
M30: Ecc 3G 97
(off Abbey Gro.)
SK1: Stoc 3B 146
(off Abbey Gro.)
SK12: Poy 4D **168**
Abbey Cres. OL10: H'ood 1F **39**
Abbeycroft Cl. M29: Ast 5A **80**
Abbeydale Cl. OL12: Roch . . .1A **178** (3G **27**)
Abbeydale Cl. OL6: A Lyme 5C **92**
SK8: Chea H 6A **156**
Abbeydale Gdns. M28: Walk 6G **65**
Abbeydale Rd. M40: Man 3E **89**
Abbey Dr. BL8: Bury 4A **36**
M27: Swin 3G **83**
OL15: L'ough 6F **17**
Abbeyfield Cl. SK3: Stoc 5G **145**
Abbeyfield Ho. *M28: Walk 5G 65*
(off Mountain St.)
Abbeyfield Sq. *M11: Man 5D 102*
(off Herne St.)
Abbey Gdns. SK14: Mot 4B **122**
Abbey Gro. M30: Ecc 3G **97**
OL9: Chad 5A **74**
SK1: Stoc 3B **146**
SK14: Mot 4B **122**
ABBEY HEY .1H **117**
Abbey Hey La. M11: Man 6G **103**
M18: Man 2G **117**
Abbey Hills Rd. OL4: O'ham 4H **75**
OL8: O'ham 4H **75**
Abbey Lawn M16: Old T 4H **113**
Abbeylea Cres. BL5: W'ton 5A **46**
Abbeylea Dr. BL5: W'ton 5A **46**
Abbey Rd. M24: Mid 3B **56**
M29: Ast 4A **80**
M33: Sale 3A **128**
M35: Fail 3B **90**
M43: Droy 2H **103**
OL3: Del 2A **62**
SK8: Chea 6C **144**

Abbeystead Av. M21: Chor 1B **130**
Abbeyville Wlk. M15: Man 6F **9**
Abbey Way M26: Rad 4A **52**
Abbeywood Av. M18: Man 3G **117**
Abbotsbury Cl. M12: Man 1C **116**
SK12: Poy 2D **168**
Abbots Cl. M33: Sale 4D **128**
Abbots Ct. M33: Sale 4D **128**
Abbotsfield Cl. M41: Urm 4H **109**
Abbotsfield Ct. M8: Man 4E **87**
Abbot's Fold Rd. M28: Wors 4F **81**
Abbotsford OL12: Whitw 3B **14**
Abbotsford Dr. M24: Mid 3H **55**
Abbotsford Rd. WA14: Tim 3G **139**
Abbotsford Pk. Miniature Railway
. . . . .5D **110**
Abbotsford Rd. BL1: Bolt 4G **31**
M21: Chor 5H **113**
OL1: O'ham 6H **59**
OL9: Chad 1G **73**
Abbotside Cl. M16: W Ran 4B **114**
Abbotsleigh Av. M23: Wyth 3F **141**
Abbotsleigh Dr. SK7: Bram 3H **157**
Abbott St. BL3: Bolt 2C **48**
OL11: Roch 2D **40**
Abden St. M26: Rad 4A **52**
Abels La. OL3: Upp 1E **79**
Aber Av. SK2: Stoc 1C **158**
Abercarn Cl. M8: Man 4E **87**
Abercorn Rd. BL1: Bolt 2H **31**
Abercorn St. OL4: O'ham 3B **76**
Abercrombie Ct. M33: Sale 4D **128**
Aberdare Wlk. *M9: Man 4A 72*
(off Crossmead Dr.)
Aberdeen *M30: Ecc 3G 97*
(off Monton La.)
Aberdeen Cres. SK3: Stoc 3F **145**
Aberdeen Gdns. OL12: Roch 5F **15**
Aberdeen Gro. SK3: Stoc 3F **145**
Aberdeen Ho. M15: Man 2F **115**
Aberdeen St. M15: Man 2F **115**
Aberford Rd. M23: Wyth 6G **141**
Abergele Rd. M14: Man 1A **132**
Abergele St. SK2: Stoc 6A **146**
Aberley Fold
OL15: L'ough 2F **17**
Abernant Cl. M11: Man 4B **102**
Aber Rd. SK8: Chea 5C **144**
Abersoch Av. M14: Man 1A **132**
Abingdon Av. M45: White 5F **53**

Abingdon Cl. M45: White 5F **53**
OL9: Chad 5B **74**
OL11: Roch 6G **27**
Abingdon Rd. BL2: Bolt 5G **33**
M41: Urm 4G **111**
SK5: Stoc 2H **133**
SK7: Bram 3G **157**
Abingdon St. M1: Man 1A **10** (5E **101**)
OL6: A Lyme 3B **106**
Abinger Wlk. *M40: Man 1F 103*
(off Eastmoor Dr.)
Abington Rd. M33: Sale 6C **128**
Abito M3: Sal 3G **5** (3D **100**)
Abney Grange OL5: Mos 3A **94**
Abney Rd. OL5: Mos 3G **93**
SK4: Stoc 4E **133**
Abney Steps *OL5: Mos 3G 93*
(off Manchester Rd.)
Aboukir St. OL16: Roch 3B **28**
Abraham Moss Cen. 3F **87**
Abraham Moss Leisure Cen. 3E **87**
Abraham Moss Theatre 3E **87**
Abram Cl. M14: Man 6E **115**
Abram St. M6: Sal 5F **85**
Absalom Dr. M8: Man 3D **86**
Abson St. OL1: Chad 6C **58**
Acacia Av. M27: Swin 5G **83**
M34: Dent 4G **119**
SK8: Chea H 3C **156**
SK9: Wilm 4C **172**
WA15: Hale 2H **151**
Acacia Dr. M6: Sal 2B **98**
WA15: Hale 2H **151**
Acacia Gro. SK5: Stoc 5H **133**
Acacia Rd. OL8: O'ham 2D **90**
Acacias *M41: Urm 4G 111*
(off Granville Rd.)
Academy Wlk. *M15: Man 2C 114*
(off Wilberforce Cl.)
Acer Cl. OL11: Roch 2H **25**
SK14: Hyde 5E **121**
Acer Gro. *M7: Sal 4B 86*
(off Wellington St. W.)
Acheson St. M18: Man 2F **117**
Acheson Way M17: T Pk 6C **98**
Ackers Barn Courtyard M31: C'ton . . .3C **126**
Ackers La. M31: C'ton 3A **126**
Ackersley Ct. SK8: Chea H 5E **157**
Ackers St. M13: Man 6D **10** (2F **115**)
Acker St. OL16: Roch 2C **178** (3H **27**)
Ack La. E. SK7: Bram 6E **157**

Ack La. W. SK8: Chea H 5D 156
Ackroyd Av. M18: Man 1H 117
Ackroyd St. M11: Man 6G 103
Ackworth Dr. M23: Wyth 5G 141
Ackworth Rd. M27: Swin 2G 83
Acme Dr. M27: Pen 3B 84
Acomb Ho. M15: Man 2F 115
    (off Dilworth St.)
Acomb St. M14: Man 4F 115
   M15: Man 2F 115
Acorn Av. SK8: Chea 6A 144
   SK14: Hyde 1C 136
    (not continuous)
Acorn Bus. Pk. SK4: Stoc 2F 145
Acorn Cen., The OL1: O'ham 1H 75
Acorn Cl. M19: Man 1B 132
   M45: White 3F 69
Acorn Ho. M22: Shar 5C 142
    (off Altrincham Rd.)
Acorn Ho., The SK15: Mill 1H 107
    (off Bramble Ct.)
Acorn M. SK2: Stoc 5C 146
Acorn St. OL4: Lees 3C 76
Acorn Way OL1: O'ham 2F 177 (2E 75)
ACRE 1H 75
Acre Barn OL2: Shaw 5E 43
Acre Cl. BL0: Eden 2G 13
Acre Fld. BL2: Bolt 1H 33
Acrefield M33: Sale 6A 128
Acrefield Av. M34: Aud 4C 104
Acrefield Cl. M27: Swin 5A 84
Acrefield Rd. M6: Sal 6D 84
   M24: Mid 4D 56
   M38: Lit H 5F 65
   SK14: Hyde 2D 120
   WA15: Tim 3A 140
Acres Fold Av. M22: Wyth 2C 154
Acres La. SK15: Stal 4F 107
Acres Pass M21: Chor 1G 129
Acres Rd. M21: Chor 1G 129
   SK8: Gat 6E 143
Acres St. BL8: Tot 6H 21
Acre St. M26: Rad 4G 51
   M34: Dent 4E 119
   OL9: Chad 1B 90
   OL12: Whitw 4B 14
Acre Top Rd. M9: Man 4F 71
Acre Vw. BL0: Ram 3G 13
Acre Wood BL6: Los 4B 46
Acton Av. M40: Man 1D 102
Acton Sq. M5: Sal 3H 99
Acton St. OL1: O'ham 1G 75
   OL12: Roch 2A 28
Actonville Av. M22: Wyth 2B 154
Adair St. M1: Man 1E 11 (5G 101)
   OL11: Roch 3D 40
Adam Cl. SK8: Chea H 1D 156
Adams Av. M21: Chor 3H 129
Adams Cl. SK12: Poy 5E 169
Adamson Circ. M30: Urm 6E 97
Adamson Gdns. M20: Man 6D 130
Adamson Ho. M5: Sal 1G 113
    (off Elmira Way)
   M16: Old T 1H 113
Adamson Rd. M30: Ecc 5E 97
Adamson St. SK16: Duk 1A 120
Adamson Wlk. M14: Man 4F 115
    (off Walmer St.)
Adam St. BL3: Bolt 2D 48
   OL6: A Lyme 2A 106
   OL8: O'ham 1F 91

Adastral Ho. M21: Chor 1A 130
Ada St. BL0: Ram 4B 12
   M9: Man 2H 87
   OL12: Roch 1A 28
Adbaston Rd. M32: Stre 2A 112
Adcroft St. SK1: Stoc 6H 179 (4H 145)
Addenbrook Rd. M8: Man 6C 86
Adderley Pl. SK13: Glos 6H 123
Adderley Rd. SK13: Glos 6H 123
Addingham Cl. M9: Man 5F 71
Addington Rd. BL3: Bolt 4F 47
Addington St. M4: Man 3C 6 (3F 101)
Addison Av. OL6: A Lyme 2B 106
Addison Cl. M13: Man 6E 11 (1G 115)
Addison Cres. M16: Old T 3H 113
Addison Dr. M24: Mid 5E 57
Addison Grange M33: Sale 6C 128
    (off Princes Rd.)
Addison Rd. M31: C'ton 3H 125
   M32: Stre 5B 112
   M41: Urm 6F 111
   WA15: Hale 3G 151
Adelaide Rd. SK3: Stoc 3E 145
   SK7: Bram 1H 167
Adelaide St. BL0: Ram 5A 12
   BL3: Bolt 3B 48
   M8: Man 6D 86
   M24: Mid 1C 72
   M27: Swin 4F 83
   M30: Ecc 4F 97
   OL10: H'ood 3H 39
Adelaide St. E. OL10: H'ood 3A 40
Adelphi Ct. M3: Sal 2C 4 (2B 100)
Adelphi Dr. M38: Lit H 4F 65
Adelphi Gro. M38: Lit H 4F 65
Adelphi St. M3: Sal 4C 4 (3B 100)
   M26: Rad 2H 51
Aden Cl. M12: Man 1H 11 (5H 101)
Aden St. OL4: O'ham 4B 76
   OL12: Roch 2A 28
Adisham Dr. BL1: Bolt 4D 32
Adlington Cl. BL8: Bury 4A 36
   SK12: Poy 5F 169
   WA15: Tim 5D 140
Adlington Dr. M32: Stre 3F 113
Adlington Ind. Est. SK10: Adl 6C 168
Adlington Pk. SK10: Adl 6C 168
Adlington Rd. SK9: Wilm 3G 173
Adlington St. BL3: Bolt 3B 48
   M12: Man 2G 11 (5H 101)
   OL4: O'ham 6B 60
Adlington Wlk.
   SK1: Stoc 1F 179 (2G 145)
Adlington Way M34: Dent 6G 119
    (off Two Trees La.)
Admel Sq. M15: Man 6H 9
Adolph & Pauline Cassel Ho.
   M25: Pres 2H 85
Adrian Rd. BL1: Bolt 3A 32
Adrian St. M40: Man 4C 88
Adrian Ter. OL16: Roch 5C 28
Adria Rd. M20: Man 6G 131
Adscombe St. M16: W Ran 3C 114
Adshall Rd. SK8: Chea 6C 144
Adshead Cl. M22: Wyth 2H 153
Adstock Wlk. M40: Man 2F 7
Adstone Cl. M4: Man 5H 7 (4H 101)
ADSWOOD .5F 145
Adswood Cl. OL4: O'ham 6B 60
Adswood Gro. SK3: Stoc 5F 145
Adswood Ind. Est. SK3: Stoc 5F 145
Adswood La. E. SK2: Stoc 5H 145
Adswood La. W. SK3: Stoc 5H 145
Adswood Old Hall Rd.
   SK8: Chea H 1F 157
Adswood Old Rd. SK3: Stoc 5G 145
Adswood Rd. SK3: Stoc 5G 145
   SK8: Chea H 1E 157
Adswood St. M40: Man 3A 102
Adswood Ter. SK3: Stoc 5G 145
Advent Ho. M4: Man 6G 7
Aegean Gdns. M7: Sal 6A 86

Aegean Rd. WA14: B'ath 5C 138
AFFETSIDE .3D 20
Affetside Dr. BL8: Bury 3H 35
Affleck Av. M26: Rad 1C 66
Afghan St. OL1: O'ham 1H 75
Age Cft. OL8: O'ham 6A 76
Agecroft Commerce Pk. M27: Pen 5E 85
Agecroft Crematorium M27: Pen 3F 85
Agecroft Ent. Pk. M27: Pen 4D 84
Agecroft Pk. Circ. M27: Pen 4D 84
Agecroft Rd. M27: Pen 4C 84
   SK6: Rom 2G 147
Agecroft Rd. E. M25: Pres 1G 85
Agecroft Rd. W. M25: Pres 1F 85
Agecroft Trad. Est. M6: Sal 4E 85
Agincourt St. OL10: H'ood 3F 39
Agnes Cl. OL9: O'ham 5C 74
Agnes Ct. M14: Man 2G 131
Agnes St. M7: Sal 4D 86
   M19: Man 5C 116
   OL9: Chad 4B 74
Agnew Pl. M6: Sal 1G 99
Agnew Rd. M18: Man 2E 117
Aigburth Gro. SK5: Stoc 5G 117
Ailsa Cl. M40: Man 6H 87
Ailsa Ho. M6: Sal 4F 99
    (off Langworthy Rd.)
Aimson Pl. WA15: Tim 5C 140
Aimson Rd. E. WA15: Tim 5C 140
Aimson Rd. W. WA15: Tim 4C 140
Aines St. M12: Man 6C 102
Ainley Rd. M22: Wyth 2B 154
Ainley Wood OL3: Del 2A 62
   SK16: Duk 6B 106
Ainsbrook Av. M9: Man 6D 72
   OL3: Del 3B 62
Ainsbrook Ter. OL3: Dig 2F 63
    (off Harrop Ct. Rd.)
Ainsdale Av. BL8: Bury 3B 36
   M7: Sal 2B 86
Ainsdale Cl. OL8: O'ham 5D 74
   SK7: Bram 6A 158
Ainsdale Cl. BL3: Bolt 4D 48
Ainsdale Cres. OL2: O'ham 5E 59
Ainsdale Dr. M33: Sale 1G 139
   OL12: Whitw 2F 15
   SK8: H Grn 4F 155
Ainsdale Gro. SK5: Stoc 1H 133
Ainsdale Rd. BL3: Bolt 5C 48
    (not continuous)
Ainsdale St. M12: Man 1B 116
Ainsford Rd. M20: Man 4H 131
Ainsley Gro. M28: Walk 1H 81
Ainsley St. M40: Man 6E 89
Ainslie Rd. BL1: Bolt 4G 31
Ainsty Rd. M14: Man 3E 115
AINSWORTH 4E 35
Ainsworth Cl. M34: Dent 4B 118
Ainsworth Ct. BL2: Bolt 6G 33
   M28: Walk 1H 81
Ainsworth Hall Rd. BL2: Ain, Bolt 6D 34
Ainsworth La. BL2: Bolt 4F 33
Ainsworth Rd. BL3: Lit L 4C 50
   BL8: Bury 4H 35
   M26: Rad 1H 51
Ainsworth Sq. BL1: Bolt 3A 32
    (off Ainsworth St.)
Ainsworth St. BL1: Bolt 3A 32
   OL16: Roch 6D 178 (5A 28)
Ainthorpe Wlk. M40: Man 6F 89
    (off Droyden Rd.)
Aintree Av. M33: Sale 6E 127
Aintree Cl. SK7: H Gro 3F 159
Aintree Dr. OL11: Roch 3A 26
Aintree Gro. SK3: Stoc 5G 145
Aintree Rd. BL3: Lit L 5C 50
Aintree St. M11: Man 4D 102
Aintree Wlk. OL9: Chad 2C 74
    (off Bentley St.)
Airedale Cl. SK8: Chea 5G 143
Airedale Cl. WA14: Alt 6G 139
    (off Mill St.)
Aire Dr. BL2: Bolt 6F 19

Air Hill Ter.—Aldermary Rd.

Air Hill Ter. OL12: Roch 2E **27**
Airton Cl. M40: Man 1F **7** (2G **101**)
Aitken Cl. BL0: Ram 4B **12**
Aitken St. M19: Man 6E **117**
Ajax Dr. BL9: Bury 4F **53**
Ajax St. BL0: Ram 4B **12**
OL11: Roch 2D **40**
Aked Cl. M12: Man 6H **11** (1H **115**)
Akesmoor Dr. SK2: Stoc 5C **146**
Alamein Dr. SK6: Rom 1C **148**
Alan Av. M35: Fail 6H **89**
Alanbrooke Wlk. *M15: Man 2C* ***114***
(off Rankin Cl.)
Alandale Av. M34: Aud 6E **105**
Alandale Dr. OL2: O'ham 2C **58**
Alandale Rd. SK3: Stoc 4E **145**
Alan Dr. SK6: Mar 5C **148**
WA15: Hale 5A **152**
Alan Rd. M20: Man 3G **131**
SK4: Stoc 6C **132**
Alan St. *BL1: Bolt 2B* ***32***
(off Newry St.)
Alan Turing Way M11: Man 2B **102**
Alasdair Cl. OL9: Chad 1H **73**
Alba Cl. M30: Ecc 4E **97**
Alban Ct. OL6: A Lyme 4B **92**
Alban St. M7: Sal 6B **86**
Albany Av. M11: Man 6H **103**
Albany Cl. M38: Lit H 3F **65**
Albany Ct. *M20: Man 3F* ***131***
(off Redcar Av.)
M33: Sale 4C **128**
M41: Urm 4D **110**
Albany Dr. BL9: Bury 6F **37**
Albany Gro. M29: Ast 3B **80**
Albany Rd. M21: Chor 6H **113**
M30: Ecc .2D **96**
SK7: Bram 3G **167**
SK9: Wilm 4C **172**
Albany St. M24: Mid 2D **72**
OL4: O'ham 6B **60**
OL11: Roch 6A **28**
Albany Trad. Est. M21: Chor 6H **113**
Albany Way *M6: Sal 2G* ***99***
(off Salford Shop. City)
SK14: Hat 5A **122**
Alba St. BL8: Holc 3A **12**
Alba Way M32: Stre 2A **112**
Albemarle Av. M20: Man 3E **131**
Albemarle Rd. M21: Chor 1G **129**
M27: Swin 4G **83**
Albemarle St. M14: Man 3E **115**
Albemarle Ter.
OL6: A Lyme 4D **174** (2A **106**)
Alberbury Av. WA15: Tim 4D **140**
Albermarle St.
OL6: A Lyme 4D **174** (2A **106**)
(not continuous)
Alberta St. BL3: Bolt 2A **48**
SK1: Stoc 4H **179** (3H **145**)
Albert Av. M18: Man 3H **117**
M25: Pres .2A **86**
M28: Walk 4G **65**
M41: Urm 5G **111**
OL2: Shaw 2G **59**
SK16: Duk 1A **120**
Albert Bri. Ho. M3: Sal 5F **5** (4C **100**)
Albert Cl. M45: White 1G **69**
SK8: Chea H 3C **156**
Albert Cl. Trad. Est.
M45: White 1G **69**
Albert Ct. WA14: Alt 3A **174** (1F **151**)
Albert Dr. M45: White 6H **53**
Albert Fildes Wlk. *M8: Man 4D* ***86***
(off Greenland St.)
Albert Gdns. M40: Man 6F **89**
Albert Gro. BL4: Farn 1H **65**
M12: Man 3C **116**
(not continuous)
Albert Hill St. M20: Man 6F **131**
Albert Mt. OL1: O'ham 6H **59**
ALBERT PARK 4E **131**
Albert Pk. Rd. M7: Sal 6A **86**
Albert Pl. M13: Man 4B **116**
M45: White 6H **53**
OL4: Lees .4C **76**
WA14: Alt 1A **174** (6F **139**)
Albert Rd. BL1: Bolt 5G **31**
BL4: Farn .1G **65**
M19: Man 6B **116**
M30: Ecc 3H **97**
M33: Sale 5C **128**
M45: White 1G **69**
SK4: Stoc 6C **132**
SK8: Chea H 3C **156**
SK9: Wilm 3D **172**
SK14: Hyde 5B **120**
WA14: Alt 3A **174** (1F **151**)
WA15: Hale 2G **151**
Albert Rd. E. WA15: Hale 2G **151**
Albert Rd. W. BL1: Bolt 4F **31**
Albert Royds St. OL16: Roch 1B **28**
Albert Sq. M2: Man 6H **5** (4D **100**)
SK15: Stal 4D **106**
WA14: Bow 2E **151**
Albert St. BL0: Ram 3B **12**
BL3: Lit L .4D **50**
BL4: Farn .2H **65**
BL4: Kea 1A **66**
BL9: Bury .3G **37**
M11: Man 4B **102**
M24: Mid .1C **72**
M25: Pres .5A **70**
M30: Ecc 3H **97**
M34: Dent 4F **119**
M43: Droy 4B **104**
M44: Cad 3C **124**
OL2: O'ham 3D **58**
OL2: Shaw 6G **43**
OL4: Lees .4C **76**
OL8: O'ham 2B **90**
OL9: Chad 6B **74**
OL10: H'ood 3F **39**
OL12: Whitw 1E **15**
OL15: L'ough 4H **17**
OL16: Miln 6G **29**
SK3: Stoc 2F **145**
SK7: H Gro 2D **158**
SK13: Had 2H **123**
SK14: Hyde 4D **120**
Albert St. W. M35: Fail 5F **89**
Albert St. Works M43: Droy 4B **104**
Albert Ter. SK1: Stoc 2G **179**
Albert Wlk. OL7: A Lyme 4G **105**
Albine St. M40: Man 3B **88**
Albinson Wlk. M31: Part 6E **125**
Albion Cl. SK4: Stoc 6G **133**
Albion Ct. BL8: Bury 3D **36**
Albion Dr. M43: Droy 3A **104**
Albion Fold M43: Droy 3A **104**
Albion Gdns. SK15: Stal 3F **107**
Albion Gdns. Cl. OL2: O'ham 3F **59**
Albion Gro. M33: Sale 5A **128**
Albion Ho. SK15: Stal 3F **107**
Albion Pl. M5: Sal 4A **4** (3A **100**)
M7: Sal 6A **86**
M25: Pres .5G **69**
SK7: H Gro 2D **158**
Albion Rd. M14: Man 6G **115**
OL11: Roch 5F **27**
Albion Rd. Ind. Est. OL11: Roch 5F **27**
Albion St. BL3: Bolt 2D **48**
BL4: Kea 2C **66**
BL8: Bury 3D **36**
M1: Man 3G **9** (6D **100**)
M16: Old T 3B **114**
M26: Rad 6B **52**
M27: Pen 3A **84**
M33: Sale 5B **128**
M35: Fail 4G **89**
OL1: O'ham 3F **177** (2F **75**)
(not continuous)
OL6: A Lyme 4D **174** (2A **106**)
(not continuous)
OL9: Chad 2A **74**
OL11: Roch 4E **41**
Albion St. OL15: L'ough 4G **17**
SK15: Stal 3F **107**
Albion Ter. BL1: Bolt 2H **31**
Albion Towers M5: Sal 3H **99**
Albion Trad. Est. M6: Sal 1G **99**
OL6: A Lyme 2B **106**
Albion Way M5: Sal 4H **99**
Albury Dr. M19: Man 1H **143**
OL12: Roch 1B **26**
Albyns Av. M8: Man 4E **87**
Alcester Av. SK3: Stoc 4B **144**
Alcester Cl. BL8: Bury 2B **36**
M24: Mid .3D **72**
Alcester Rd. M33: Sale 1B **140**
SK8: Gat 1F **155**
Alcester St. OL9: Chad 6A **74**
Alcester Wlk. M9: Man 4G **71**
Alconbury Ct. *M43: Droy 5B* ***104***
(off Florence St.)
Alconbury Wlk. M9: Man 3F **71**
Aldborough Cl. M20: Man 3F **131**
Aldbourne Cl. M40: Man 1H **101**
Aldbury Ter. *BL1: Bolt 4B* ***32***
(off Eskrick St.)
Aldcroft St. M18: Man 1H **117**
Alden Cl. M45: White 1G **69**
Alden Wlk. SK4: Stoc 2F **133**
Alder Av. BL9: Bury 2A **38**
SK12: Poy 4F **169**
Alderbank OL12: W'le 5C **16**
Alderbank Cl. BL4: Kea 3B **66**
Alderbrook Rd. M38: Lit H 6D **64**
Alder Cl. BL8: Bury 3C **36**
OL6: A Lyme 4H **91**
SK8: H Grn 5H **155**
SK13: Had 3H **123**
SK16: Duk 5E **107**
Alder Ct. M8: Man 2D **86**
Aldercroft Av. BL2: Bolt 4H **33**
M22: Wyth 3A **154**
Alderdale Cl. SK4: Stoc 5C **132**
Alderdale Dr. M43: Droy 3F **103**
SK4: Stoc 4C **132**
SK6: H Lan 6C **160**
Alderdale Gro. SK9: Wilm 4B **172**
Alderdale Rd. SK8: Chea H 1E **157**
Alder Dr. M27: Ward 2E **83**
SK15: Stal 2G **107**
WA15: Tim 1D **152**
Alder Edge M21: Chor 6F **113**
Alderfield Ho. M21: Chor 6F **113**
Alderfield Rd. M21: Chor 6F **113**
Alderford Pde. M8: Man 5D **86**
ALDER FOREST 1C **96**
Alder Forest Av. M30: Ecc 1C **96**
Aldergate Ct. M27: Swin 4E **83**
Aldergate Gro. OL6: A Lyme 6D **92**
Alderglen Rd. M8: Man 5D **86**
Alder Gro. BL7: Bro X 5G **19**
M32: Stre 5E **113**
M34: Dent 4G **119**
SK3: Stoc 3E **145**
Alder Hgts. SK1: Stoc 1B **146**
Alder La. OL8: O'ham 1D **90**
Alderley Av. BL1: Bolt 6C **18**
Alderley Cl. SK7: H Gro 5F **159**
SK12: Poy 5F **169**
Alderley Ct. SK2: Stoc 1C **158**
SK9: A Edg 5H **173**
Alderley Dr. SK6: Bred 6E **135**
ALDERLEY EDGE 5G **173**
Alderley Edge Station (Rail) 4G **173**
Alderley Lodge SK9: Wilm 4D **172**
Alderley Rd. M33: Sale 1E **141**
M41: Urm 5C **110**
SK5: Stoc 4H **133**
SK9: Wilm 4D **172**
Alderley St. OL6: A Lyme 6B **92**
Alderley Ter. SK16: Duk 4H **105**
Alderley Way SK3: Stoc 1G **157**
Alderman Foley Dr. OL12: Roch 1C **26**
Alderman Sq. M12: Man 1H **11** (5A **102**)
Aldermary Rd. M21: Chor 4B **130**

Aldermaston Gro. M9: Man 3F 71
Aldermere Cres. M41: Urm 4B 110
Alderminster Av. M38: Lit H 4E 65
Aldermoor Cl. M11: Man 5E 103
Alder Rd. M24: Mid 5E 57
　M35: Fail 6H 89
　OL11: Roch 3F 41
　SK8: Chea 6A 144
ALDER ROOT 3B 74
Alders Ct. OL8: O'ham 3G 91
Aldersgate Rd. SK2: Stoc 5B 146
　SK8: Chea H 2E 167
Alders Grn. Av. SK6: H Lan 6D 160
Aldershot Wlk. M11: Man 4B 102
　　(off Newcombe Cl.)
Alderside Rd. M9: Man 3H 87
Aldersley Av. M9: Man 4F 71
Alderson St. M6: Sal 1G 99
　OL9: O'ham 2E 177 (2E 75)
Alders Rd. M22: Wyth 6A 142
　SK12: Dis 6E 161
Alder St. BL3: Bolt 4D 48
　M6: Sal 3F 99
　M30: Ecc 1C 96
Aldersyde St. BL3: Bolt 4B 48
Alderue Av. M22: Wyth 5B 142
Alderway BL0: Ram 4F 13
Alderwood Av. SK4: Stoc 2C 144
Alderwood Fold OL4: O'ham 4D 76
Alderwood Gro. BL0: Eden 1G 13
Alderwood Wlk. M8: Man 5D 86
　　(off Ermington Dr.)
Aldfield Rd. M23: Wyth 2F 141
Aldford Cl. M20: Man 6G 131
Aldford Gro. BL2: Bolt 2D 50
Aldford Pl. SK9: A Edg 4F 173
Aldham Av. M40: Man 1E 103
Aldow Ind. Pk. M12: Man . . .1G 11 (5G 101)
Aldred Cl. M8: Man 5F 87
Aldred St. BL3: Bolt 4H 47
　M5: Sal 4A 4 (3H 99)
　M30: Ecc 4E 97
　M35: Fail 4G 89
Aldridge Wlk. M11: Man 5B 102
　　(off Bell Cres.)
Aldsworth Dr. BL3: Bolt 3C 48
Aldwick Av. M20: Man 6G 131
Aldwinians Cl. M34: Aud 2E 119
Aldworth Dr. M40: Man 5A 88
Aldworth Gro. M33: Sale 6F 127
Aldwych OL11: Roch 2H 41
　　(not continuous)
Aldwych Av. M14: Man 4F 115
Aldwyn Cl. M26: Rad 6B 52
　M34: Aud 2E 119
Aldwyn Cres. SK7: H Gro 3C 158
Aldwyn Pk. Rd. M34: Aud 5C 104
Alexander Av. M35: Fail 3A 90
Alexander Briant Ct. BL4: Farn 2G 65
Alexander Ct. M5: Sal 5G 99
　　(off Rowland St.)
Alexander Dr. BL9: Bury 6G 53
　OL16: Miln 5E 29
　WA15: Tim 5A 140
Alexander Gdns. M7: Sal 1B 100
Alexander Ho. M16: Old T 3G 113
Alexander Pk. OL6: A Lyme 3B 106
Alexander Rd. BL2: Bolt 4G 33
Alexander St. M6: Sal 3E 99
　OL11: Roch 3D 40
Alexandra, The M14: Man 1H 131
　M50: Sal 6F 99
Alexandra Av. M14: Man 5D 114
　M45: White 1G 69
　SK14: Hyde 5A 120
Alexandra Cen. Retail Pk.
　OL4: O'ham 5H 177 (3F 75)
Alexandra Cl. SK3: Stoc 5E 145
Alexandra Ct. M31: Part 6D 124
　　(off Bailey La.)
　M41: Urm 6A 110
Alexandra Cres. OL1: O'ham 1H 75
Alexandra Dr. M19: Man 2B 132

Alexandra Gro. M44: Irl 1D 124
Alexandra Ho. M30: Ecc 4E 97
　　(off Liverpool Rd.)
　OL1: O'ham 1H 75
Alexandra M. OL8: O'ham 4G 75
Alexandra Mill OL3: Upp 2D 78
ALEXANDRA PARK 5C 114
Alexandra Pk.
　Alexandra Rd. Sth. 5C 114
　Queens Rd. 6H 177 (4G 75)
Alexandra Rd. BL4: Kea 3C 66
　M16: W Ran 4C 114
　M26: Rad 1C 66
　M28: Walk 4G 65
　M30: Ecc 4D 96
　M33: Sale 6C 128
　M34: Dent 3G 119
　OL6: A Lyme 4C 174 (7H 105)
　OL8: O'ham 5G 75
　SK4: Stoc 6E 133
Alexandra Rd. Sth.
　M16: W Ran 4C 114
　M21: Chor 4C 114
Alexandra St. BL3: Bolt 3B 48
　BL4: Farn 2H 65
　M7: Sal 1D 4 (2B 100)
　OL6: A Lyme 1B 106
　OL8: O'ham 4G 75
　OL10: H'ood 5A 40
　SK14: Hyde 6A 120
Alexandra Ter. M19: Man 6C 116
　OL4: O'ham 4B 60
Alexandria Dr. BL5: W'ton 6B 46
　OL7: A Lyme 3E 105
Alford Av. M20: Man 1E 131
Alford Cl. BL2: Bolt 1B 50
Alford Rd. SK4: Stoc 3D 132
Alford St. OL9: O'ham 1B 90
Alfred Av. M28: Wors 4C 82
Alfred James Cl. M40: Man 2G 7 (2G 101)
Alfred Morris Ct. M23: Wyth 1G 141
　　(off Fellpark Rd.)
Alfred St. BL0: Ram 4B 12
　BL3: Bolt 3F 49
　BL4: Farn 5H 49
　BL4: Kea 1B 66
　BL7: Eger 1B 18
　BL9: Bury 5G 37
　M9: Man 6H 65
　M28: Walk 6H 65
　M30: Ecc 2F 97
　M35: Fail 3H 89
　M44: Cad 3C 124
　　(off Dean Rd.)
　OL2: Shaw 6G 43
　OL6: A Lyme 1B 106
　OL9: O'ham 3C 74
　　(not continuous)
　OL12: Whitw 3B 14
　OL15: L'ough 3G 17
　SK14: Hyde 4A 120
Alfreton Av. M34: Dent 1G 135
Alfreton Rd. SK2: Stoc 5D 146
Alfreton Wlk. M40: Man 5C 88
　　(off Halliford Rd.)
Alfriston Dr. M23: Wyth 1G 141
Alger M. OL6: A Lyme 1B 106
Algernon Rd. M28: Walk 5G 65
Algernon St. M27: Swin 3F 83
　M30: Ecc 2F 97
Alger St. OL6: A Lyme 1B 106
Algreave Rd. SK3: Stoc 3C 144
Alice Ingham Ct. OL12: Roch 2E 27
Alice St. BL3: Bolt 2A 48
　M27: Pen 3B 84
　M33: Sale 5D 128
　OL12: Roch 2B 28
　SK14: Hyde 2C 136
Alicia Ct. OL12: Roch 2G 27
Alicia Dr. OL12: Roch 2G 27
Alison Ct. SK4: Stoc 5D 132
Alison Kelly Cl. M9: Man 3B 88

Alison St. M14: Man 4D 114
　OL2: Shaw 5G 43
Alker Rd. M40: Man 2H 7 (2H 101)
Alkrington Cl. BL9: Bury 5G 53
Alkrington Ct. M24: Mid 4D 72
ALKRINGTON GARDEN VILLAGE 4C 72
Alkrington Grn. M24: Mid 3B 72
Alkrington Hall M24: Mid 2B 72
Alkrington Hall Rd. Nth.
　M24: Mid 2B 72
Alkrington Hall Rd. Sth. M24: Mid . . .3A 72
Alkrington Pk. Rd. M24: Mid 1A 72
Allama Iqbal Rd. OL4: O'ham 4A 76
Allanadale Ct. M7: Sal 2C 86
Allan Ct. M21: Chor 2G 129
Allandale WA14: Alt 1D 150
Allandale Rd. M19: Man 6B 116
Allan Roberts Cl. M9: Man 2H 87
Allanson Rd. M22: Nor 2C 142
Alldis Cl. M12: Man 2A 116
Alldis St. SK2: Stoc 6B 146
Allen Av. SK14: Hyde 1D 136
Allenby Rd. M27: Swin 5E 83
　M44: Cad 5B 124
Allenby St. OL2: Shaw 6G 43
Allenby Wlk. M40: Man 6G 87
　　(off Dalbury Dr.)
Allen Cl. OL2: Shaw 1G 59
Allendale Dr. BL9: Bury 4G 53
Allendale Gdns. BL1: Bolt 3C 32
　　(off Jennaby Wlk.)
Allendale Wlk. M3: Sal . . .3C 4 (3B 100)
Allen Hall M14: Man 5H 115
Allen Rd. M41: Urm 5H 111
Allen St. BL3: Lit L 4C 50
　BL8: Bury 2C 36
　M26: Rad 4G 51
　　(not continuous)
　OL8: O'ham 4D 74
　OL16: Roch 5A 28
Allerdean Wlk. SK4: Stoc 6B 132
Allerford St. M16: W Ran 3C 114
Allerton Cl. BL5: W'ton 6A 46
Allerton Ct. BL1: Bolt 1E 175
Allerton Ho. OL2: O'ham 3E 59
　　(off Royton Hall Pk.)
Allerton Wlk. M13: Man 6D 10
Allesley Cl. BL5: W'ton 6A 46
Allesley Dr. M7: Sal 6C 86
Allgreave Cl. M33: Sale 2E 141
Alliance Ind. Est. M34: Dent 4D 118
Alligin Cl. OL9: Chad 1A 74
Allingham St. M13: Man 3A 116
Allington OL11: Roch 6A 178
Allington Dr. M30: Ecc 1G 97
Alliott Wlk. M15: Man 2C 114
　　(off Elverdon Cl.)
Allison Gro. M30: Ecc 4D 96
Allison St. M8: Man 6D 86
Alonby Wlk. M24: Mid 5G 55
Allotment Rd. M44: Cad 3B 124
Alloway Wlk. M40: Man 5C 88
　　(off Halliford Rd.)
All Saints BL8: Bury 2C 36
All Saints Cl. OL2: O'ham 2D 58
All Saints Ct. M32: Stre 5B 112
　　(off Manor Rd.)
All Saints Pl. BL8: Bury 2C 36
All Saints' Rd. SK4: Stoc 5F 133
All Saints St. BL1: Bolt 2F 175 (5D 32)
　M40: Man 6E 89
All Saints Ter.
　OL12: Roch 1B 28
Allsopp St. BL3: Bolt 6G 175 (1D 48)
Alma Ct. M15: Man 3C 114
　　(off Moss La. W.)
Alma Ind. Est. OL12: Roch 2H 27
Alma La. SK9: Wilm 3D 172
ALMA PARK 1D 132
Alma Rd. M19: Man 1C 132
　M33: Sale 1G 139
　SK4: Stoc 4D 132
　SK7: H Gro 5G 159

Alma St. BL3: Bolt 3A **48**
  BL3: Lit L 4D **50**
  BL4: Kea 4D **66**
  M26: Rad 2H **51**
  M30: Ecc 4H **97**
  OL12: Roch 2H **27**
  SK15: Stal 3F **107**
Alma Works SK16: Duk 4H **105**
Alminstone Cl. M40: Man 1F **103**
Almond Av. BL9: Bury 2A **38**
Almond Cl. M6: Sal 3G **99**
  M35: Fail 5H **89**
  OL15: L'ough 3F **17**
  SK3: Stoc 3E **145**
Almond Ct. SK16: Duk 4A **106**
  (off Combermere St.)
Almond Dr. M33: Sale 3H **127**
Almond Gro. BL1: Bolt 2D **32**
Almond Rd. OL4: O'ham 6B **60**
Almond St. BL1: Bolt 1D **32**
  BL4: Farn 1G **65**
  M40: Man 1F **101**
Almond Tree Rd. SK8: Chea H 4C **156**
Almond Wlk. M31: Part 6B **124**
  (off Wood La.)
Almond Way SK14: Hyde 5E **121**
Alms Hill Rd. M8: Man 4E **87**
Almshouses M33: Sale 5E **129**
Alness Rd. M16: W Ran 4C **114**
Alnwick Dr. BL9: Bury 2F **53**
Alnwick Rd. M9: Man 4H **71**
Alperton Wlk. M40: Man 1F **103**
  (off Thaxmead Dr.)
Alphabet Zoo Adventure Play Cen.
  . . . . .4H **105**
Alpha Ct. M34: Dent 4C **118**
Alpha Ct. Ind. Est. M34: Dent 4C **118**
Alphagate Dr. M34: Dent 4C **118**
Alpha Pl. M15: Man 3F **9**
Alpha Rd. M32: Stre 5C **112**
Alpha St. M6: Sal 2F **99**
  M11: Man 6G **103**
  M26: Rad 3H **51**
Alpha St. W. M6: Sal 2E **99**
Alphin Cl. OL3: G'fld 4D **78**
  OL5: Mos 6A **78**
Alphingate Cl. SK15: C'ook 1H **107**
Alphin Sq. OL5: Mos 2H **93**
Alphonsus St. M16: Old T 3A **114**
Alpine Dr. OL2: O'ham 4C **58**
  OL12: W'le 6C **16**
  OL16: Miln 4G **29**
Alpine Rd. SK1: Stoc 1A **146**
  (not continuous)
Alpine St. M11: Man 2D **102**
Alpington Wlk. M40: Man 1E **89**
  (off Ogmore Wlk.)
Alport Av. M16: W Ran 5A **114**
Alport Gro. SK13: Gam 5G **123**
  (off Melandra Castle Rd.)
Alport Lea SK13: Gam 5G **123**
  (off Hathersage Cres.)
Alport Way SK13: Gam 5G **123**
  (off Melandra Castle Rd.)
Alresford Rd. M6: Sal 6D **84**
  M24: Mid 4B **72**
Alric Wlk. M22: Wyth 5C **154**
Alsager Cl. M21: Chor 3H **129**
Alsham Wlk. M8: Man 5E **87**
  (off Heatherdale Dr.)
Alsop Av. M7: Sal 4H **85**
Alstead Av. WA15: Hale 2A **152**
Alston Av. M32: Stre 4B **112**
  M33: Sale 6H **127**
  OL2: Shaw 5H **43**
Alston Cl. SK7: H Gro 4A **158**
Alstone Dr. WA14: Alt 5C **138**
Alstone Rd. SK4: Stoc 3E **133**
Alston Gdns. M19: Man 4B **132**
Alston Rd. BL3: Bolt 4C **48**
  M18: Man 2G **117**
Alston St. BL8: Bury 2C **36**
Alston Wlk. M24: Mid 5G **55**

ALT 6B **76**
Altair Av. M22: Wyth 4B **154**
Altair Pl. M7: Sal 1A **100**
Altcar Gro. SK5: Stoc 5G **117**
Altcar Wlk. M22: Wyth 3A **154**
Alt Gro. OL6: A Lyme 5H **91**
Altham Cl. BL9: Bury 6D **36**
Altham Wlk. M40: Man 5C **88**
  (off Craiglands Av.)
ALT HILL 2A **92**
Alt Hill La. OL6: A Lyme 3H **91**
Alt Hill Rd. OL6: A Lyme 2A **92**
Althorn Wlk. M23: Wyth 6G **141**
Althorpe Wlk. M40: Man 1F **103**
  (off Eastmoor Dr.)
Alt La. OL6: O'ham 1A **92**
  OL8: O'ham 1A **92**
Alton Av. M41: Urm 5H **109**
Alton Cl. BL9: Bury 2G **53**
  OL6: A Lyme 4A **92**
Alton Rd. SK9: Wilm 1C **172**
Alton Sq. M11: Man 6G **103**
Alton St. OL8: O'ham 6F **75**
Alton Towers M16: W Ran 6B **114**
ALTRINCHAM 2B **174** (1F **151**)
Altrincham Crematorium
  WA14: D Mas 3A **138**
Altrincham FC 2H **151**
Altrincham Garrick Playhouse 5F **139**
Altrincham Leisure Cen.
  . . . . .2C **174** (1G **151**)
Altrincham Retail Pk.
  WA14: B'ath 4E **139**
Altrincham Rd. M22: Shar 4A **142**
  (not continuous)
  M23: Wyth 4D **140**
  SK8: Gat 5B **142**
  SK9: Sty 3C **164**
  SK9: Sty, Wilm 4G **163**
Altrincham Station (Rail)
  . . . . .2C **174** (1G **151**)
Altrincham St. M1: Man 2C **10** (5F **101**)
Alt Rd. OL6: A Lyme 5H **91**
Alt Wlk. M45: White 5A **54**
Alum Cres. BL9: Bury 4G **53**
Alvanley Cl. M33: Sale 2B **140**
Alvanley Cres. SK3: Stoc 5E **145**
Alvanley Ind. Est. SK6: Bred 5F **135**
Alvanley Sq. M11: Man 6G **103**
Alva Rd. OL4: O'ham 5B **60**
Alvaston Av. SK4: Stoc 6D **132**
Alvaston Rd. M18: Man 3G **117**
Aveley Av. M20: Man 4G **131**
Alverstone Rd. M20: Man 3G **131**
Alveston Dr. SK9: Wilm 1F **173**
Alvington Gro. SK7: H Gro 4A **158**
Alvon Ct. SK14: Hyde 5E **121**
Alwin Rd. OL2: Shaw 5G **43**
Alwinton Av. SK4: Stoc 6A **132**
Alworth Rd. M9: Man 4H **71**
Alwyn Dr. M13: Man 3A **116**
Ambassador Pl.
  WA15: Alt 1C **174** (6G **139**)
Amber Gdns. SK16: Duk 5H **105**
  (off Railway St.)
Amberhill Way M28: Wors 6D **80**
Amber St. BL3: Bolt 2F **47**
Amberley Dr. M23: Wyth 1G **153**
  M44: Irl 6E **109**
  WA15: Haleb 5B **152**
Amberley Rd. M33: Sale 4G **127**
Amberley Wlk. OL9: Chad 2C **74**
Amberwood OL9: Chad 1G **73**
Amberwood Dr. M23: Wyth 5D **140**
Amblecote Dr. E. M38: Lit H 3E **65**
Amblecote Dr. W.
  M38: Lit H 3E **65**
Ambleside SK15: Stal 2E **107**
Ambleside Av. OL7: A Lyme 1F **105**
  WA15: Tim 6C **140**
Ambleside Cl. BL2: Bolt 1B **34**
  M24: Mid 6A **56**

Ambleside Ct. SK8: Chea 6G **143**
  SK15: Stal 2E **107**
Ambleside Rd. M41: Urm 6A **110**
  SK5: Stoc 3H **133**
Ambleside Wlk. M9: Man 1C **88**
Amblethorn Dr. BL1: Bolt 6B **18**
Ambrose Ct. M22: Nor 2B **142**
  (off Kenworthy La.)
Ambrose Cres. OL3: Dig 4D **62**
Ambrose Dr. M20: Man 5C **130**
Ambrose Gdns. M20: Man 5B **130**
Ambrose St. M12: Man 6C **102**
  OL11: Roch 6H **27**
  SK14: Hyde 2C **136**
Ambuscade Cl. M41: Urm 5A **110**
Ambush St. M11: Man 6H **103**
Amelan Ho. M25: Pres 2G **85**
Amelia St. SK14: Hyde 5C **120**
  (off Lumn Hollow)
Amelia St. W. M34: Dent 3F **119**
Amersham Cl. M41: Urm 2D **110**
Amersham Pl. M19: Man 3C **132**
Amersham St. M5: Sal 4F **99**
Amesbury Gro. SK5: Stoc 4H **133**
Amesbury Rd. M9: Man 5A **72**
Amherst Rd. M14: Man 2G **131**
  M20: Man 2G **131**
Amlwch Av. SK2: Stoc 5D **146**
Ammons Way OL3: Del 2B **62**
Ammon Wrigley Cl.
  OL1: O'ham 2G **177** (2F **75**)
Amory St. M12: Man 2E **11** (5G **101**)
Amos Av. M40: Man 1E **103**
Amos St. M6: Sal 3E **99**
  M9: Man 4B **88**
Ampleforth Gdns. M26: Rad 2G **51**
Ampney Cl. M30: Ecc 4D **96**
Amport Wlk. M40: Man 1E **89**
Amwell St. M8: Man 4F **87**
Amy St. M24: Mid 6D **56**
  OL12: Roch 2D **26**
Anaconda Dr. M3: Sal 2E **5** (2C **100**)
Ancaster Wlk. M40: Man 1E **89**
Anchorage Quay M50: Sal 5G **99**
Anchorage Rd. M41: Urm 6A **112**
Anchorage Station (Metro) 5G **99**
Anchorage Wlk. M18: Man 1E **117**
  (off Briercliffe Cl.)
Anchor Cl. M19: Man 6E **117**
Anchor Ct. M8: Man 2D **86**
  SK9: Wilm 1E **173**
Anchor La. BL4: Farn, Walk 1D **64**
Anchorside Cl. M21: Chor 2H **129**
Anchor St. OL1: O'ham 1G **177** (1F **75**)
ANCOATS 5C **6** (4F **101**)
Ancoats Gro. M4: Man 6G **7** (5H **101**)
Ancoats Gro. Nth.
  M4: Man 6G **7** (4H **101**)
Ancoats St. OL4: Lees 3C **76**
Ancroft Gdns. BL3: Bolt 5A **48**
  (off Maltby Dr.)
Ancroft St. M15: Man 6F **9** (1C **114**)
Anderton Cl. BL8: Bury 4H **35**
Anderton Gro. OL6: A Lyme 6C **92**
Anderton Way SK9: Hand 4H **165**
Andoc Av. M30: Ecc 4A **98**
Andover Av. M24: Mid 4D **72**
Andover St. M30: Ecc 4E **97**
Andover Wlk. M8: Man 3E **87**
Andre St. M11: Man 3E **103**
Andrew Cl. BL8: G'mount 2H **21**
  M26: Rad 6C **52**
Andrew Ct. M20: Man 3F **131**
  (off Aldborough Cl.)
Andrew Gro. SK16: Duk 5B **106**
Andrew Ho. SK4: Stoc 5D **132**
Andrew La. BL1: Bolt 5D **18**
  SK6: H Lan 4C **160**
Andrew Rd. M9: Man 2H **87**
Andrews Av. M41: Urm 4A **110**
Andrews Bldgs. OL5: Mos 2A **94**
  (off Bk. Micklehurst Rd.)
  OL6: A Lyme 4D **174**

Andrews Cl. M34: Dent 6H **119**
Andrew St. BL9: Bury 3G **37**
  M24: Mid 2E **73**
  M35: Fail 3G **89**
  M43: Droy 1C **104**
  OL5: Mos 3G **93**
  OL6: A Lyme 6B **92**
  OL9: Chad 1B **74**
  SK4: Stoc 1F **145**
  SK6: Comp 1E **149**
  SK14: Hyde 4D **120**
Andy Nicholson Wlk.
  M9: Man 3B **88**
  (off Amos St.)
Anerley Rd. M20: Man 5F **131**
Anfield Cl. BL9: Bury 4H **53**
Anfield Rd. BL3: Bolt 4C **48**
  M33: Sale 4C **128**
  M40: Man 2F **89**
  SK8: Chea H 3B **156**
Angela Av. OL2: O'ham 5E **59**
Angela St. M15: Man 4D **8** (6B **100**)
Angel Cl. SK16: Duk 5H **105**
Angelico Ri. OL1: O'ham 4B **60**
Angelo St. BL1: Bolt 2B **32**
Angel St. M4: Man 2B **6** (2E **101**)
  M34: Dent 3G **119**
  SK7: H Gro 2D **158**
Angel Trad. Est. M4: Man 2B **6**
Angier Gro. M34: Dent 4F **119**
Anglers Rest M44: Cad 4C **124**
Anglesea Av. SK2: Stoc 5H **145**
Anglesey Cl. OL7: A Lyme 5G **91**
Anglesey Dr. SK12: Poy 1E **169**
Anglesey Gro. SK8: Chea 5C **144**
Anglesey Rd. OL7: A Lyme 5F **91**
Anglesey Water SK12: Poy 1E **169**
Angleside Av. M19: Man 5A **132**
Angle St. BL2: Bolt 4F **33**
Anglia Gro. BL3: Bolt 3A **48**
Angora Dr. M3: Sal 2C **4** (2B **100**)
Angouleme Retail Pk.
  BL9: Bury 4D **176** (3F **37**)
Angouleme Way
  BL9: Bury 5B **176** (4E **37**)
Angus Av. OL10: H'ood 4E **39**
Aniline St. M11: Man 4D **102**
Animal World 2G **31**
Anita St. M4: Man 3D **6** (3F **101**)
Annable Rd. M18: Man 1G **117**
  M43: Droy 4B **104**
  M44: Irl 1D **124**
  SK6: Bred 6D **134**
Annald Sq. M43: Droy 5A **104**
Annan St. M34: Dent 3F **119**
Anne Cl. OL7: A Lyme 5G **91**
Annecy Cl. BL8: Bury 1B **36**
Anne Line Cl. *OL11: Roch* 6A **28**
  (off Wellfield St.)
Annersley Av. OL2: Shaw 1G **59**
Annesley Cl. M30: Ecc 3G **97**
Annesley Gdns. *M18: Man* 1F **117**
  (off Keary Cl.)
Annesley Rd. M40: Man 2G **89**
Anne St. SK16: Duk 5B **106**
Annie Darby Ct. M9: Man 4H **87**
Annie St. BL0: Ram 5A **12**
  M6: Sal 3E **99**
Annis Cl. SK9: A Edg 4H **173**
Annisdale Cl. M30: Ecc 3D **96**
Annisfield Av. OL3: G'fld 4D **78**
Annis Rd. BL3: Bolt 3H **47**
  SK9: A Edg 4H **173**
Annis St. M9: Man 4A **88**
Ann La. M29: Ast 6A **80**
Ann Sq. OL4: O'ham 1B **76**
Ann St. BL4: Kea 2A **66**
  M34: Dent 4E **119**
  OL7: A Lyme 5F **105**
  OL10: H'ood 2H **39**
  OL11: Roch 5B **178** (5H **27**)

Ann St. *OL12: Roch* 6D **16**
  (off Oakcliffe Rd.)
  OL16: Roch 5B **178** (5H **27**)
  SK5: Stoc 5G **133**
  SK14: Hyde 4A **120**
Anscombe Cl. M40: Man . . .2H **7** (2H **101**)
Ansdell Av. M21: Chor 1A **130**
Ansdell Dr. M43: Droy 3G **103**
Ansdell Rd. OL16: Roch 1B **42**
  SK5: Stoc 6A **118**
Ansdell St. M8: Man 4E **87**
Ansell Cl. M18: Man 1F **117**
Ansford Wlk. *M9: Man* 5G **87**
  (off Hendham Va.)
Ansleigh Av. M8: Man 2E **87**
Ansley Gro. SK4: Stoc 6D **132**
Anslow Cl. M40: Man 6H **87**
Anson Av. M27: Swin 5G **83**
Anson Cl. SK7: Bram 2H **167**
Anson Engine Mus., The 3A **170**
Anson Rd. M14: Man 3H **115**
  M27: Swin 5G **83**
  M34: Dent 5A **118**
  SK9: Wilm 6A **166**
  SK12: Poy 3H **169**
Anson St. BL1: Bolt 2D **32**
  M30: Ecc 2D **96**
Answell Av. M8: Man 1E **87**
Antares Av. M7: Sal 1C **4** (2B **100**)
Anthistle Ct. *M5: Sal* 3D **98**
  (off Sheader Dr.)
Anthony Cl. M12: Man 6A **102**
Anthony St. OL5: Mos 2F **93**
Antilles Cl. M12: Man 3C **116**
Anton Wlk. *M9: Man* 4H **87**
  (off Shiredale Dr.)
Antrim Cl. M19: Man 1H **143**
Anvil St. M1: Man 3H **9**
Anvil Way OL1: O'ham 2F **177** (2E **75**)
Apethorn La. SK14: Hyde 1A **136**
Apfel La. OL9: Chad 2B **74**
Apollo Av. BL9: Bury 4F **53**
Apollo Cinema
  Altrincham 3B **174** (1F **151**)
Apollo Wlk. *M12: Man* 1C **116**
  (off Bridgend Cl.)
Apperley Grange M30: Ecc 1G **97**
Appian Way M7: Sal 5C **86**
Appleblossom Gro.
  M44: Cad 5B **124**
Appleby Av. M12: Man 4C **116**
  SK14: Hyde 2A **120**
  WA15: Tim 6C **140**
Appleby Cl. BL8: Bury 3H **35**
  SK3: Stoc 6F **145**
Appleby Gdns. BL2: Bolt 4E **33**
  BL9: Bury 4F **53**
Appleby Lodge M14: Man 5H **115**
Appleby Rd. SK8: Gat 1F **155**
Appleby Wlk. *OL2: O'ham* 3E **59**
  (off Shaw St.)
Apple Cl. OL8: O'ham 6A **76**
Applecross Wlk. *M11: Man* 5E **103**
  (off Bill Williams Cl.)
Appledore Dr. BL2: Bolt 3B **34**
  M23: Wyth 4D **140**
Appledore Wlk. OL9: Chad 3B **74**
Appleford Av. M23: Wyth 1G **153**
Appleford Dr. M8: Man 5F **87**
Apple St. SK14: Hyde 2G **137**
Appleton Av. M8: Man 4F **87**
Appleton Ct. M33: Sale 5B **128**
Appleton Gro. M33: Sale 1G **139**
Appleton Rd. SK4: Stoc 3F **133**
  WA15: Hale 4G **151**
Appleton Wlk. *SK9: Wilm* 4G **167**
  (off Colshaw Dr.)
Apple Tree Ct. M5: Sal 3G **99**
Apple Tree Wlk. M33: Sale 4E **127**
Apple Way M24: Mid 3D **72**
Applewood OL9: Chad 2F **73**
Appleyard Cl. M27: Pen 3D **84**

Apprentice Ct. *M9: Man* 3A **88**
  (off Caversham Dr.)
Apprentice La. SK9: Sty 4D **164**
April Cl. *M13: Man* 2H **115**
  (off Markfield Av.)
  OL8: O'ham 5A **76**
Apsley Cl. WA14: Bow 4D **150**
Apsley Gro. M12: Man 5F **11** (1G **115**)
  WA14: Bow 4D **150**
Apsley Pl. OL6: A Lyme 3G **105**
Apsley Rd. M34: Dent 3F **119**
Apsley Side *OL5: Mos* 3G **93**
  (off Abney Rd.)
Apsley St. SK1: Stoc 2H **179** (2H **145**)
Aquarius La. *M6: Sal* 1A **100**
  (off Gemini Rd.)
Aquarius St. M15: Man 2E **115**
Aqueduct Bus. Pk. SK6: Mar 3D **148**
Aqueduct Rd. BL3: Bolt 3G **49**
Aragon Dr. OL10: H'ood 3G **39**
Aragon Way SK6: Mar 5C **148**
Arbor Av. M19: Man 2B **132**
Arbor Dr. M19: Man 2B **132**
Arbor Gro. M38: Lit H 5C **64**
  M43: Droy 2H **103**
Arbory Av. M40: Man 3D **88**
Arbour Cl. BL3: Bolt 5E **23**
  M6: Sal 2F **99**
Arbour Ct. SK6: Mar 6C **148**
Arbour Rd. OL4: O'ham 5C **76**
Arbroath St. M11: Man 4G **103**
Arbury Av. OL11: Roch 6G **27**
Arcade, The SK5: Stoc 4C **134**
  SK15: Stal 5D **106**
Arcades, The
  OL6: A Lyme 5B **174** (2H **105**)
Arcadia Av. M33: Sale 2A **140**
Arcadia Sports Cen. 6C **116**
Archer Av. BL2: Bolt 5G **33**
Archer Gro. BL2: Bolt 5G **33**
Archer Pk. M24: Mid 1A **72**
Archer Pl. M32: Stre 4H **111**
Archer St. M11: Man 3C **102**
  M28: Wors 4C **80**
  OL5: Mos 1G **93**
  SK2: Stoc 6C **146**
Arches, The BL1: Bolt 4G **175**
Archie St. M5: Sal 6G **99**
Arch St. BL1: Bolt 1H **175** (4E **33**)
Archway M15: Man 6G **9** (2D **114**)
Arclid Cl. SK9: Wilm 5A **166**
Arcon Cl. OL16: Roch 5E **29**
Arcon Dr. M16: W Ran 4C **114**
Arcon Pl. SK1: Stoc 6B **134**
  WA14: Alt 5C **138**
Ardale Av. M40: Man 1E **89**
Ardcombe Av. M9: Man 4G **71**
Ardeen Wlk. M13: Man 5E **11**
Arden Av. M24: Mid 4D **72**
Arden Bldgs. SK3: Stoc 4F **179**
Arden Bus. Cen. SK6: Bred 3E **135**
Arden Cl. BL9: Bury 5E **37**
  OL6: A Lyme 5D **92**
  SK8: H Grn 6G **155**
Arden Ct. M21: Chor 2H **129**
  SK7: Bram 4F **157**
Ardenfield M34: Dent 2G **135**
Ardenfield Cl. M26: Rad 6B **52**
Ardenfield Dr. M22: Wyth 2C **154**
Arden Gro. M40: Man 2E **89**
Arden Ho. OL2: O'ham 3E **59**
Arden Lodge Rd. M23: Wyth 4E **141**
ARDEN PARK 6D **134**
Arden Rd. SK6: Bred 2E **135**
Ardens Cl. M27: Swin 1F **83**
Arden St. OL9: Chad 6A **74**
Ardent Way M25: Pres 2H **85**
Arden Wlk. M33: Sale 4E **127**
Arderne Pl. SK9: A Edg 5G **173**
Arderne Rd. WA15: Tim 3A **140**
Ardern Fld. St.
  SK1: Stoc 6H **179** (4H **145**)

Ardern Gro. SK1: Stoc 5H **179** (3H **145**)
Ardern Rd. M8: Man 1D **86**
Ardern Wlk. SK1: Stoc 2F **179**
Ardingley Wlk. M23: Wyth 3D **140**
Ardmore Wlk. M22: Wyth 3C **154**
ARDWICK 4E **11** (6G **101**)
Ardwick Grn. Nth.
　　M12: Man 3E **11** (6G **101**)
Ardwick Grn. Sth.
　　M13: Man 3E **11** (6G **101**)
Ardwick Sports Hall 6H **11** (2A **116**)
Ardwick Station (Rail) 4H **11** (6A **102**)
Ardwick Ter. M12: Man 6H **11**
Argo St. BL3: Bolt 3B **48**
Argosy Dr. M30: Ecc 6B **96**
　　M90: Man A 6F **153**
Argus St. OL8: O'ham 1C **90**
Argyle Av. M14: Man 3A **116**
　　M28: Walk 4G **65**
　　M45: White 1G **69**
Argyle Cres. OL10: H'ood 4F **39**
Argyle Pde. OL10: H'ood 4E **39**
Argyle St. BL9: Bury 1F **37**
　　M18: Man 2F **117**
　　M27: Swin 4G **83**
　　M43: Droy 4A **104**
　　OL1: O'ham 1H **75**
　　OL5: Mos 2G **93**
　　OL10: H'ood 4D **38**
　　OL16: Roch 1A **42**
　　SK7: H Gro 3E **159**
Argyll Av. M32: Stre 5B **112**
Argyll Cl. M35: Fail 4B **90**
Argyll Pk. Rd. M35: Fail 4B **90**
Argyll Rd. OL9: Chad 6H **73**
　　SK8: Chea 6B **144**
Argyll St. OL6: A Lyme 2C **106**
Arkendale Cl. M35: Fail 4C **90**
Arkholme M28: Wors 3E **81**
Arkholme Wlk. M40: Man 4D **88**
Arkle Av. SK9: Hand 3A **166**
Arkle Dr. OL9: Chad 1H **73**
Arkley Wlk. M13: Man 5D **10**
Ark St. M19: Man 5C **116**
Arkwright Cl. BL1: Bolt 4A **32**
Arkwright Dr. SK6: Mar 5E **149**
Arkwright Rd. SK6: Mar 4E **149**
Arkwright St. OL9: O'ham 3C **74**
Arkwright Way OL11: Roch 3A **42**
Arlen Ct. BL2: Bolt 2F **49**
Arlen Rd. BL2: Bolt 2F **49**
Arlen Way OL10: H'ood 3F **39**
Arley Av. BL9: Bury 5E **23**
　　M20: Man 4D **130**
Arley Cl. SK16: Duk 1B **120**
　　WA14: W Tim 3F **139**
Arley Dr. M33: Sale 1A **140**
　　OL2: Shaw 5A **44**
Arley Gro. SK3: Stoc 1F **157**
Arley Ho. M23: Wyth 1G **153**
Arleymere Cl. SK8: Chea H 2B **156**
Arley St. M26: Rad 6B **52**
Arley Way M34: Dent 6G **119**
　　　　　　　　　(off Two Trees La.)
Arlies Cl. SK15: Stal 1E **107**
Arlies La. SK15: Stal 1F **107**
Arlies St. OL6: A Lyme 1B **106**
Arlington Av. M25: Pres 1H **85**
　　M27: Swin 5F **83**
　　M34: Dent 5G **119**
Arlington Cl. BL9: Sum 1C **22**
　　OL2: O'ham 5E **59**
Arlington Cres. SK9: Wilm 4B **172**
Arlington Dr. SK2: Stoc 2A **158**
　　SK12: Poy 4D **168**
Arlington Rd. M32: Stre 5B **112**
　　SK8: Chea 1G **155**
Arlington St. BL3: Bolt 4D **48**
　　M3: Sal 3D **4** (3B **100**)
　　M8: Man 3D **86**
　　OL6: A Lyme 2A **106**
Arlington Way SK9: Wilm 4B **172**

Arliss Av. M19: Man 1C **132**
Armadale Av. M9: Man 5C **72**
Armadale Cl. SK3: Stoc 6G **145**
Armadale Ct. BL3: Bolt 2E **47**
Armadale Rd. BL3: Bolt 1E **47**
　　SK16: Duk 5A **106**
Armdale Ri. OL4: O'ham 6C **60**
Armentieres Sq. SK15: Stal 4E **107**
Armentieres Way SK15: Stal 4E **107**
　　　　　　　　　(off Melbourne St.)
Armitage Av. M38: Lit H 5D **64**
Armitage Cl. M24: Mid 2H **71**
　　OL8: O'ham 6C **74**
　　SK14: Hyde 1C **136**
Armitage Gro. M38: Lit H 5D **64**
Armitage Ho. M6: Sal 2C **98**
　　　　　　　　　(off Edgehill Rd.)
Armitage Owen Wlk. M40: Man 4C **88**
　　　　　　　　　(off Brendon Av.)
Armitage Rd. WA14: Alt 3B **174** (2F **151**)
Armitage Sports Cen. 6A **116**
Armitage St. M30: Ecc 4E **97**
Armit Rd. OL3: G'fld 5A **78**
Armour Pl. M9: Man 1G **87**
　　　　　　　　　(off Oakworth St.)
Armoury St. SK3: Stoc 5F **179** (3G **145**)
Arm Rd. OL15: L'ough 4E **17**
Armstrong Hurst Cl. OL12: Roch 6B **16**
Arncliffe Cl. BL4: Farn 6H **49**
　　　　　　　　　(off Spring St.)
　　BL9: Bury 6G **37**
Arncliffe Dr. M23: Wyth 2G **153**
Arncliffe Ri. OL4: O'ham 3E **61**
Arncot Rd. BL1: Bolt 6D **18**
Arncott Cl. OL2: O'ham 3G **59**
Arndale Shop. Cen.
　　M4: Man 4A **6** (3E **101**)
　　M32: Stre 6C **112**
Arne Cl. SK2: Stoc 6G **147**
Arnesby Av. M33: Sale 4E **129**
Arnesby Gro. BL2: Bolt 5F **33**
Arne St. OL9: Chad 4A **74**
Arnfield Dr. M28: Wors 5F **81**
Arnfield Rd. M20: Man 3F **131**
　　SK3: Stoc 6F **145**
Arnold & Margaret Wills Ho.
　　M25: Pres 2G **85**
Arnold Av. OL10: H'ood 6A **40**
　　SK14: Hyde 2D **136**
Arnold Bagnall Ct. OL11: Roch 1A **42**
Arnold Cl. SK16: Duk 6E **107**
Arnold Ct. M16: W Ran 6C **114**
　　　　　　　　　(off Wilbraham Rd.)
Arnold Dr. M24: Mid 4E **57**
　　M43: Droy 4A **104**
Arnold Rd. BL7: Eger 3D **18**
　　M16: W Ran 6C **114**
　　SK14: Hyde 2D **136**
Arnold St. BL1: Bolt 3A **32**
　　OL1: O'ham 1G **75**
　　OL6: A Lyme 1A **106**
　　SK3: Stoc 6E **179** (4G **145**)
Arnolds Yd. WA14: Alt 1B **174** (6F **139**)
Arnold Wlk. M34: Dent 2G **135**
　　　　　　　　　(off Wordsworth Rd.)
Arnott Cres. M15: Man 6H **9** (2D **114**)
Arnside Av. OL9: Chad 4A **74**
　　SK4: Stoc 3F **133**
　　SK7: H Gro 3C **158**
Arnside Cl. OL2: Shaw 6B **44**
　　SK6: H Lan 5C **160**
　　SK8: Gat 1F **155**
Arnside Dr. M6: Sal 2B **98**
　　OL11: Roch 6A **26**
　　SK14: Hyde 3A **120**
Arnside Gro. BL2: Bolt 5B **34**
　　M33: Sale 3B **128**
Arnside St. M14: Man 5F **115**
Arosa Ct. M20: Man 2G **131**
Arran Av. M32: Stre 5A **112**
　　M33: Sale 6C **128**
　　OL8: O'ham 6F **75**
Arran Cl. BL3: Bolt 1E **47**

Arran Ct. SK8: Chea H 3C **156**
　　　　　　　　　(off Vaudrey Dr.)
Arrandale Ct. M41: Urm 4F **111**
Arran Gdns. M41: Urm 2E **111**
　　　　　　　　　(not continuous)
Arran Gro. M26: Rad 2G **51**
Arran Rd. SK16: Duk 6A **106**
Arran St. M7: Sal 5B **86**
　　M40: Man 3B **88**
Arran Wlk. OL10: H'ood 4E **39**
Arras Gro. M34: Dent 4H **117**
Arreton Sq. M14: Man 4H **115**
　　　　　　　　　(off Rusholme Gro.)
Arrivals Way M90: Man A 6H **153**
Arrowfield Rd. M21: Chor 3B **130**
Arrowhill Rd. M26: Rad 5H **35**
Arrowscroft Way SK14: Holl 2F **123**
Arrowsmith Wlk. M11: Man 4B **102**
　　　　　　　　　(off Redfield Cl.)
Arrow St. BL1: Bolt 5C **32**
　　M7: Sal .6B **86**
Arrow Trad. Est. M34: Aud 2D **118**
Arthington St. OL16: Roch 3B **28**
Arthog Dr. WA15: Hale 5H **151**
Arthog Rd. M20: Man 6G **131**
　　WA15: Hale 5H **151**
Arthur Av. M28: Walk 4G **65**
Arthur La. BL2: Ain, Bolt 2C **34**
Arthur Millwood Ct. M3: Sal 5D **4**
Arthur Rd. M16: Old T 4A **114**
Arthurs La. OL3: G'fld 3D **78**
Arthur St. BL3: Lit L 4D **50**
　　BL4: Farn 1H **65**
　　　　　　　　　(off Ellesmere St.)
　　BL8: Bury 3C **36**
　　M25: Pres 5F **69**
　　M27: Swin 4F **83**
　　　　　　　　　(not continuous)
　　M28: Walk 1B **82**
　　　　　　　　　(Old Clough La.)
　　M28: Walk 2A **82**
　　　　　　　　　(Walkden Rd.)
　　M30: Ecc 4E **97**
　　OL2: Shaw 6H **43**
　　OL10: H'ood 3H **39**
　　OL12: Roch 3F **27**
　　SK5: Stoc 2G **133**
　　　　　　　　　(not continuous)
　　SK14: Hyde 6A **120**
Arthur Ter. SK5: Stoc 2G **133**
　　　　　　　　　(off Arthur St.)
Artillery Ct. M13: Man 4E **11**
Artillery Pl. M22: Wyth 1D **154**
Artillery St. BL3: Bolt 2D **48**
　　M3: Man 1F **9** (5C **100**)
ArTzu Gallery 4C **6**
Arundale Av. M16: W Ran 6C **114**
Arundale Cl. SK14: Mot 4B **122**
Arundale Ct. M16: W Ran 6C **114**
　　　　　　　　　(off Arundale Av.)
Arundale Gro. SK14: Mot 4B **122**
Arundel Av. M41: Urm 6G **109**
　　M45: White 2H **69**
　　OL11: Roch 1G **41**
　　SK7: H Gro 5D **158**
Arundel Cl. BL8: Bury 5C **22**
　　SK15: C'ook 5B **94**
　　WA15: Hale 4C **152**
Arundel Ct. M9: Man 4E **71**
Arundel Gro. SK2: Stoc 1B **158**
Arundel Rd. SK8: Chea H 1C **166**
Arundel St. BL1: Bolt 6C **18**
　　M15: Man 3D **8** (6B **100**)
　　M27: Ward 2E **83**
　　OL4: O'ham 2A **76**
　　OL5: Mos 2F **93**
　　OL6: A Lyme 3C **106**
　　OL11: Roch 1G **41**
Arundel Wlk. OL9: Chad 3A **74**
Asbury Ct. M30: Ecc 2E **97**
Asby Cl. M24: Mid 5H **55**
Ascension Rd. M7: Sal 1B **100**

Ascot Av. M32: Stre 4F 113
M33: Sale .6E 127
Ascot Cl. OL9: Chad 2C 74
OL11: Roch 3A 26
Ascot Ct. M7: Sal 5B 86
SK7: H Gro 3G 159
Ascot Dr. M41: Urm 5G 109
Ascot Mdw. BL9: Bury 6A 176 (5E 37)
Ascot Pde. M19: Man 3B 132
Ascot Rd. BL3: Lit L 4B 50
M40: Man 1D 102
Ascot Wlk. M6: Sal 6G 85
Ascroft Ct. OL1: O'ham 4G 177
Ascroft St. OL1: O'ham 4G 177 (3F 75)
OL9: Chad 4A 74
Asgard Dr. M5: Sal 2B 8 (5A 100)
Asgard Gro. M5: Sal 2B 8
Ash Av. M44: Cad 4B 124
SK8: Chea 6A 144
WA14: Alt 6C 138
Ashawe Cl. M38: Lit H 6C 64
Ashawe Gro. M38: Lit H 6C 64
Ashawe Ter. M38: Lit H 6C 64
Ashbank Av. BL3: Bolt 1E 47
Ashbee St. BL1: Bolt 2C 32
Ashberry Cl. SK9: Wilm 1G 173
Ashborne Dr. BL9: Bury 1D 22
Ashbourne Av. BL2: Bolt 1F 49
M24: Mid .3A 56
M41: Urm 5A 110
SK8: Chea 5B 144
Ashbourne Cl. OL12: W'le 6D 16
Ashbourne Dr.
OL6: A Lyme 5D 92
SK6: H Lan 1C 170
Ashbourne Gro. M7: Sal 4C 86
M28: Wors 3A 82
M45: White 6D 52
Ashbourne Rd. M6: Sal 6C 84
M30: Ecc .4G 97
M32: Stre 3A 112
M34: Dent 5E 119
SK7: H Gro 5F 159
Ashbourne Sq.
OL8: O'ham 6F 177 (4E 75)
Ashbourne St. OL11: Roch 2A 26
Ashbridge M17: T Pk 1B 112
(not continuous)
Ashbridge Rd. M35: Fail 5B 90
Ashbrook Av. M34: Dent 4B 118
Ashbrook Cl. M34: Dent 4B 118
M45: White 6H 53
SK8: H Grn 4F 155
Ashbrook Cres. OL12: Roch 5C 16
Ashbrook Farm Cl. SK5: Stoc 5H 117
ASHBROOK HEY 5C 16
Ashbrook Hey La.
OL12: Roch 5C 16
Ashbrook La. SK5: Stoc 5H 117
Ashbrook Rd. OL4: Spri 4D 76
Ashbrook St. M11: Man 6A 104
Ashburn Av. M19: Man 4B 132
Ashburne Hall M14: Man 6H 115
Ashburne Ho. M14: Man 3H 115
(off Conyngham Rd.)
Ashburner St. BL1: Bolt 5E 175 (1C 48)
(not continuous)
Ashburn Flats OL10: H'ood 3G 39
(off School St.)
Ashburn Gro. SK4: Stoc 6F 133
Ashburn Rd. SK4: Stoc 6E 133
Ashburton Cl. SK14: Hat 5A 122
Ashburton Rd. SK3: Stoc 1G 157
Ashburton Rd. W.
M17: T Pk 6F 97
M41: Urm 6F 97
Ashbury Cl. BL3: Bolt 2C 48
Ashbury Pl. M40: Man 1A 102
Ashburys Station (Rail) 6C 102
Ashby Av. M19: Man 5A 132
Ashby Cl. BL4: Farn 5G 49
Ashby Gro. M45: White 2H 69

Ash Cl. OL6: A Lyme 6B 92
OL12: Roch 5C 16
SK2: Stoc 6C 146
SK4: Mot 3C 122
Ashcombe Dr. BL2: Bolt 1C 50
M26: Rad .2F 51
Ashcombe Wlk. M11: Man 4B 102
(off Newcombe Cl.)
Ash Cotts. BL8: Bury 6C 22
Ashcott Av. M22: Wyth 1B 154
Ashcott Cl. BL6: Los 2E 47
Ash Ct. M16: W Ran 5C 114
SK4: Stoc 6D 132
SK6: Wood 4G 135
Ashcroft OL12: Roch 5D 16
Ashcroft Av. M6: Sal 1E 99
Ashcroft Ho. WA14: Alt 2B 174
Ashdale Av. BL3: Bolt 2E 47
Ashdale Cl. SK5: Stoc 4H 133
Ashdale Cres. M43: Droy 4H 103
Ashdale Dr. M20: Man 4H 131
SK8: H Grn 3F 155
Ashdene OL6: A Lyme 3B 106
OL12: Roch 6F 15
Ashdene Cl. OL1: Chad 6C 58
OL4: Spri 2D 76
Ashdene Cres. BL2: Bolt 6H 19
Ashdene Ri. OL1: O'ham 3B 60
Ashdene Rd. M20: Man 3H 131
SK4: Stoc 1H 143
SK9: Wilm 4C 172
Ashdown Av. M9: Man 5H 71
SK6: Wood 4A 136
Ashdown Cl. SK8: Chea H 1C 166
Ashdown Dr. BL2: Bolt 2G 33
M27: Swin 5A 84
M28: Wors 4E 81
Ashdowne Lawns
SK15: Stal 2H 107
Ashdown Rd. SK4: Stoc 6E 133
Ashdown Ter. M9: Man 5H 71
Ashdown Way OL2: Shaw 5E 43
Ash Dr. M27: Ward 1E 83
Asher St. BL3: Bolt 5A 48
Ashes Cl. SK15: Stal 5G 107
Ashes St. BL2: Bolt 5B 34
Ashes La. OL4: Spri 3D 76
OL16: Miln 4E 29
SK15: Stal 5G 107
Ashfell Ct. M21: Chor 1F 129
Ashfield M34: Dent 2G 119
Ashfield Cl. M6: Sal 2E 99
Ashfield Cres. OL4: Spri 3D 76
SK8: Chea 5H 143
Ashfield Dr. M40: Man 1F 103
M18: Man 3H 117
M44: Irl 3C 124
SK3: Stoc 1H 157
Ashfield Gro. BL1: Bolt 5E 19
SK6: Mar B 2F 149
Ashfield Ho. OL11: Roch 6C 178 (6H 27)
Ashfield La. OL16: Miln 1F 43
Ashfield Lodge M20: Man 1D 142
SK3: Stoc 1H 157
Ashfield Rd. M13: Man 4A 116
M33: Sale 4B 128
M41: Urm 5F 111
OL11: Roch 1G 41
SK3: Stoc 1H 157
SK8: Chea 5H 143
SK13: Had 4H 123
WA15: Alt 2G 151
Ashfield Sq. M43: Droy 3H 103
Ashfield St. OL8: O'ham 6C 74
Ashford M33: Sale 5E 127
Ashford Av. M27: Swin 5E 83
M28: Wors 5D 80
M30: Ecc .5E 97
SK5: Stoc 5H 117
Ashford Cl. BL2: Bolt 1A 34
BL8: Bury 4B 36
SK9: Hand 3G 165

Ashford Ct. OL4: O'ham 6B 60
SK5: Stoc 5H 117
(off Ashford Av.)
Ashford Grn. SK13: Gam 6G 123
(off Youlgreave Cres.)
Ashford Gro. M28: Wors 3B 82
Ashford M. SK13: Gam 6F 123
Ashford Rd. M20: Man 2E 131
SK4: Stoc 3F 133
SK9: Wilm 5D 172
Ashford St. OL10: H'ood 3D 38
Ashford Wlk. BL1: Bolt 4C 32
OL9: Chad 3B 74
Ashgate Av. M22: Wyth 1C 154
Ashgill Wlk. M9: Man 4A 88
(off Osborne Rd.)
Ash Gro. BL0: Ram 1H 21
BL1: Bolt .5H 31
BL2: Bolt .2B 34
BL8: Tot 6A 22
M14: Man 3A 116
M25: Pres 3G 69
M27: Swin 6F 83
M28: Walk 2H 81
M32: Stre 1C 128
M43: Droy 5A 104
OL2: O'ham 1D 58
OL4: Spri 2E 77
(not continuous)
OL15: L'ough 4F 17
OL16: Miln 2G 43
OL16: Roch 4B 42
SK4: Stoc 4F 133
SK6: Mar .6C 148
SK8: H Grn 5F 155
SK9: Hand 4G 165
(off Sagars Rd.)
SK14: Holl 2F 123
SK15: Stal 2D 106
WA14: Bow 4E 151
WA15: Tim 4H 139
Ash Hill OL5: Mos 4A 94
(off Staley Rd.)
Ash Hill Dr. OL5: Mos 3A 94
Ashia Cl. OL16: Roch 5A 28
Ashill Wlk. M3: Man 1F 9
Ashington Cl. BL1: Bolt 2H 31
Ashington Dr. BL8: Bury 4H 35
Ashkirk St. M18: Man 2F 117
Ashlands M33: Sale 4A 128
Ashlands Av. M27: Swin 5E 83
M28: Wors 4E 81
M40: Man 2E 89
Ashlands Cl. BL0: Ram 3G 13
(off Bolton Rd. Nth.)
Ashlands Dr. M34: Aud 1E 119
Ashlands Rd. WA15: Tim 2A 140
Ash La. WA15: Hale 3C 152
Ashlar Dr. M12: Man 1H 11 (5H 101)
Ash Lawns BL1: Bolt 6H 31
Ash Lea SK15: Stal 2D 106
Ash-Lea Ct. M25: Pres 5G 69
(off Greengate La.)
Ash Lea Grange M30: Ecc 2H 97
Ashlea Gro. OL4: Grot 3F 77
Ashleigh Cl. OL2: O'ham 5E 59
Ashleigh Dr. BL1: Bolt 5E 31
Ashleigh Gdns. M9: Man 2G 87
Ashleigh Rd. WA15: Tim 3B 140
Ashley Av. BL2: Bolt 5H 33
M16: Old T 3B 114
M27: Swin 5F 83
M41: Urm 5A 110
Ashley Cl. OL11: Roch 1E 41
Ashley Ct. M27: Pen 1H 83
(off Hall St.)
M40: Man 1H 89
M44: Cad .4B 124
OL12: Whitw 3B 14
SK4: Stoc 5D 132
(off Heaton Moor Rd.)
WA15: Hale 4G 151
Ashley Ct. Dr. M40: Man 2H 89

Ashley Cres. M27: Swin 4F 83
Ashley Dr. M27: Swin 4F 83
  M33: Sale 1G 139
  SK7: Bram 1E 167
Ashley Gdns. SK6: H Lan 5B 160
  SK14: Hyde 6C 120
Ashley Gro. BL4: Farn 1G 65
  (off Westminster St.)
ASHLEY HEATH 4F 151
Ashley La. M9: Man 3B 88
Ashley M. M45: White 2H 69
  SK14: Hyde 6C 120
Ashleymill La. WA14: Alt 5F 151
Ashley Mill La. Nth. WA14: Hale . . .5F 151
Ashley Rd. M43: Droy 3G 103
  SK2: Stoc 3C 146
  SK9: Wilm 6F 165
  WA14: Alt 3A 174 (2F 151)
  WA15: Alt 6G 151
  WA15: Hale 3F 151
Ashleys, The SK4: Stoc 6D 132
Ashley St. M4: Man 2C 6 (2F 101)
  M6: Sal 3E 99
  OL9: O'ham 1C 74
  SK14: Hyde 3C 120
Ashling Ct. M29: Tyld 2A 80
Ash Lodge SK12: Poy 3D 168
Ashlor St. BL9: Bury 6A 176 (4E 37)
Ashlyn Gro. M14: Man 1H 131
Ashlynne OL6: A Lyme 2A 106
Ashmeade WA15: Hale 4B 152
Ashmill Wlk. M9: Man 5G 87
Ashmond OL4: Spri 3D 76
Ashmond Rd. OL4: Spri 3D 76
Ashmoor Rd. M22: Wyth 4C 154
Ashmoor Wlk. M22: Wyth 4C 154
Ashmore Av. SK3: Stoc 4B 144
Ashmore St. M29: Tyld 3B 80
Ashmount Ct. SK4: Stoc 1B 144
Ashmount Dr. OL12: Roch 1H 27
Ashness Dr. BL2: Bolt 4A 34
  M24: Mid 4H 55
  SK7: Bram 5G 157
Ashness Gro. BL2: Bolt 4A 34
Ashness Pl. BL2: Bolt 4A 34
Ashover Av. M12: Man 1B 116
Ashover Cl. BL1: Bolt 5D 18
Ashover St. M32: Stre 4E 113
Ashridge Cl. BL6: Los 1C 46
Ashridge Dr. M30: Ecc 5E 97
  SK16: Duk 6H 105
Ash Rd. BL4: Kea 4B 66
  M31: Part 6B 124
  M34: Dent 4H 117
  M43: Droy 3H 103
  SK12: Poy 4F 169
Ash Sq. OL4: O'ham 1B 76
Ashstead Rd. M33: Sale 2C 140
Ash St. BL2: Bolt 5H 175 (1E 49)
  BL9: Bury 3G 37
  M6: Sal 3F 99
  M9: Man 4H 87
  M24: Mid 6E 57
  M34: Aud 6D 104
  M35: Fail 3G 89
  OL4: O'ham 3H 75
  OL10: H'ood 2F 39
  OL11: Roch 3E 41
  SK3: Stoc 3D 144
  SK7: H Gro 2D 158
Ashton Av. WA14: Alt 5G 139
Ashton Ct. M33: Sale 5G 127
  M34: Aud 1F 119
Ashton Cres. OL9: Chad 6A 74
Ashton Fld. Dr. M28: Walk 5G 65
Ashton Gdns. OL11: Roch 6G 27
Ashton Gro. M9: Man 5H 71
Ashton Hill La. M43: Droy 5A 104
Ashton Ho. M4: Man 2A 6 (2E 101)
  (off Aspin La.)
  M15: Man 2D 8
Ashton La. M24: Mid 1C 72
  M33: Sale 4H 127

Ashton Lodge BL0: Ram 2C 12
Ashton New Rd.
  M11: Man 5H 7 (4A 102)
  M12: Man 4A 102
Ashton Old Rd. M11: Man 5H 101
  M12: Man 2H 11 (5H 101)
Ashton on Mersey Health & Fitness Cen.
  . . . . .6G 127
Ashton Pl. SK7: H Gro 4F 159
Ashton Retail Pk.
  OL6: A Lyme 4B 174 (2H 105)
Ashton Rd. M9: Man 4H 71
  M31: C'ton 6G 125
  M34: Dent 2E 119
  M35: Fail 5C 90
  M43: Droy 5C 90
  OL8: O'ham 6F 177 (4E 75)
  SK6: Bred 4E 135
  SK14: Hyde 1B 120
Ashton Rd. E. M35: Fail 3H 89
Ashton Rd. W. M35: Fail 4G 89
Ashton St. BL3: Bolt 3H 47
  BL3: Lit L 4D 50
  OL9: Chad 6A 74
  OL10: H'ood 3G 39
  OL11: Roch 6G 27
  SK6: Wood 3A 136
  SK16: Duk 6F 105
Ashton Swimming Pool . . .5B 174 (2H 105)
ASHTON-UNDER-LYNE 4C 174 (2H 105)
Ashton-under-Lyne Station (Rail)
  . . . . .4C 174 (2H 105)
ASHTON UPON MERSEY 4F 127
Ash Tree Av. M43: Droy 3H 103
Ash Tree Dr. SK16: Duk 6D 106
Ash Tree Rd. M8: Man 2E 87
Ashurst Av. M11: Man 3D 102
Ashurst Cl. BL2: Bolt 2B 34
  SK14: Hyde 6E 121
Ashurst Dr. SK3: Stoc 6D 144
Ashurst Gdns. OL6: A Lyme 6H 91
Ashurst Gro. BL2: Rad 6B 52
Ashurst Rd. M22: Wyth 1D 154
Ash Vw. OL6: A Lyme 1A 106
Ashville Ter. M40: Man 2B 88
Ash Wlk. M24: Mid 3B 72
  M33: Sale 4F 127
  OL9: Chad 1B 74
Ashway OL6: A Lyme 5A 174 (2G 105)
Ashway Clough SK2: Stoc 6D 146
  (not continuous)
Ashwell M. BL2: Bolt 2G 33
Ashwell Rd. M23: Wyth 4H 141
Ashwell St. BL2: Bolt 2G 33
Ashwin Wlk. M8: Man 5D 86
  (off Ermington Dr.)
Ashwood M26: Rad 2D 66
  OL9: Chad 5B 74
  WA14: Bow 5D 150
Ashwood Av. BL0: Ram 2D 12
  M20: Man 5C 130
  M28: Walk 4G 65
  M33: Sale 6G 127
  M34: Dent 4A 118
Ashwood Cres. SK6: Mar 4D 148
Ashwood Dr. BL8: Bury 5B 22
  OL2: O'ham 2C 58
  OL15: L'ough 4F 17
Ashwood Rd. SK12: Dis 1H 171
Ashworth Av. BL3: Lit L 4E 51
  M34: Aud 6F 105
  M41: Urm 5A 110
Ashworth Cl. OL2: O'ham 3F 59
  OL9: Chad 5B 74
  OL15: L'ough 2G 17
  WA14: Bow 4D 150
Ashworth Ct. M26: Rad 3C 52
  OL2: Shaw 1H 59
  (off Ashworth St.)
Ashworth Gdns. OL3: G'fld 4D 78
Ashworth La. BL1: Bolt 6D 18
  SK14: Mot 5B 122

Ashworth Rd.
  OL10: H'ood 3F 25
  OL11: Roch 1C 24
Ashworth St. BL4: Farn 1G 65
  BL8: Bury 2C 36
  (not continuous)
  M26: Rad 3D 52
  M34: Dent 3E 119
  M35: Fail 5F 89
  OL1: O'ham 4H 177 (3F 75)
  (not continuous)
  OL2: Shaw 1H 59
  OL10: H'ood 5H 39
  OL12: Roch 2A 178 (3F 27)
Ashworth Ter. BL2: Bolt 1A 34
Ashworth Way SK14: Mot 4B 122
Asia Ho. M1: Man 2B 10 (5E 101)
Asia St. BL3: Bolt 4E 49
Askern Av. M22: Wyth 2B 154
Askett Cl. M40: Man 5F 89
Askrigg Wlk. M13: Man 3B 116
  (off Bates St.)
Aspell Cl. M24: Mid 1B 72
Aspen Cl. SK4: Stoc 2C 144
  WA15: Tim 6E 141
Aspen Gdns. OL12: Roch 2C 26
Aspen Grn. M34: Dent 5G 119
Aspens, The SK8: Gat 5E 143
Aspen Way SK6: H Lan 6E 161
Aspen Wood SK14: Hyde 4D 120
Aspenwood Cl. SK6: Mar 4C 148
Aspenwood Dr. M9: Man 1H 87
  M33: Sale 5E 127
  OL9: Chad 2G 73
Aspinall Cl. M28: Walk 6D 64
Aspinall Cres. M28: Walk 6D 64
Aspinall Gdns. M24: Mid 2F 73
Aspinall Gro. M28: Walk 6D 64
Aspinall St. M24: Mid 2E 73
  M30: Man 4G 115
  OL10: H'ood 3A 40
Aspin La. M4: Man 2A 6 (2E 101)
Aspland Rd. SK14: Hyde 2D 136
Aspull St. OL4: O'ham 4A 76
Aspull Wlk. M13: Man 6F 11 (1G 115)
Asquith Av. SK16: Duk 1A 120
Asquith Rd. M19: Man 3B 132
Asquith St. SK5: Stoc 6H 117
Assheton Av. M34: Aud 4C 104
Assheton Cl.
  OL6: A Lyme 4B 174 (2H 105)
Assheton Cres. M40: Man 1F 103
Assheton Ho. OL6: A Lyme 4B 174
Assheton Rd. M40: Man 1F 103
  OL2: Shaw 6F 43
Assheton St. M24: Mid 5C 56
Assheton Way M24: Mid 1C 72
Assisi Gdns. M12: Man 1D 116
Assumption Rd. M24: Mid 4H 55
Astan Av. M43: Droy 2F 103
Astbury Av. M21: Chor 5A 130
  M34: Aud 4D 104
Astbury Cl. BL9: Bury 5G 37
  OL4: Spri 3D 76
  WA15: Alt 5G 139
Astbury Cres. SK3: Stoc 5F 145
Astbury St. M26: Rad 6B 52
Astbury Wlk. SK8: Chea 6C 144
Aster Av. BL4: Farn 6E 49
Aster Ho. OL1: O'ham 6E 59
Aster St. OL1: O'ham 6E 59
Aster Wlk. M31: Part 6D 124
  (off Cross La. W.)
ASTLEY 4A 80
ASTLEY BRIDGE 1D 32
Astley Cheetham Art Gallery 3E 107
  (off Trinity St.)
Astley Cl. OL2: Shaw 6F 43
Astley Ct. M44: Irl 1C 124
Astley Gdns. SK16: Duk 5H 105
ASTLEY GREEN 6A 80
Astley Green Colliery Mus. 6B 80
Astley Gro. SK15: Stal 2D 106

Astley Hall Dr.—Avro Cl.

Astley Hall Dr. BL0: Ram 5C **12**
M29: Ast 5A **80**
Astley La. BL1: Bolt 2C **32**
Astley Rd. BL2: Bolt 6A **20**
M44: Irl 2A **108**
SK15: Stal 3D **106**
Astley St. BL1: Bolt 3C **32**
M11: Man 4E **103**
SK4: Stoc 2E **179** (2G **145**)
SK15: Stal 5E **107**
SK16: Duk 6G **105**
Astley Ter. *SK16: Duk 4A **106***
(off Peel St.)
Aston Av. M14: Man 5D **114**
Aston Cl. SK3: Stoc 5E **145**
Aston Ct. OL1: O'ham 1F **177**
Aston Gdns. *BL4: Farn 6H **49***
(off Spring St.)
Aston Gro. M29: Tyld 2A **80**
Aston Ho. BL1: Bolt 6A **32**
Aston Way *SK9: Hand 2H **165***
(off Spath La.)
Astor Rd. M19: Man 2A **132**
M50: Sal 4C **98**
Astra Bus. Pk. M17: T Pk 5H **97**
Astra Cen., The OL11: Roch 2E **41**
Astral M. M14: Man 5H **115**
Atcham Gro. M9: Man 3F **71**
Athenian Gdns. M7: Sal 6A **86**
Athens Dr. M28: Walk 1G **81**
Athens St. SK1: Stoc 2A **146**
Athens Way OL4: Lees 3C **76**
Atherfield BL2: Bolt 1A **34**
Atherfield Cl. M18: Man 1H **117**
Atherley Gro. M40: Man 1H **89**
OL9: Chad 1H **89**
Atherstone OL12: Roch 1B **178**
Atherstone Av. M8: Man 1E **87**
Atherstone Cl. BL8: Bury 1C **36**
Atherton Av. SK14: Mot 3C **122**
Atherton Cl. M35: Fail 6B **90**
Atherton Gro. SK14: Mot 3C **122**
Atherton La. M44: Cad 4C **124**
Atherton St. M3: Man 6E **5** (4C **100**)
M30: Ecc 4D **96**
OL4: Lees 4C **76**
OL4: Spri 3D **76**
(not continuous)
SK3: Stoc 3F **145**
Atherton Way M30: Ecc 4D **96**
Athlone Av. BL1: Bolt 6A **18**
BL9: Bury 1F **37**
M40: Man 3C **88**
SK8: Chea H 6E **145**
Athole St. M5: Sal 4F **99**
Atholl Av. M32: Stre 5A **112**
Atholl Cl. BL3: Bolt 1F **47**
Atholl Dr. OL10: H'ood 4E **39**
Athol Rd. M16: W Ran 6C **114**
SK7: Bram 2F **167**
Athol St. BL0: Ram 2C **12**
M18: Man 4G **117**
M30: Ecc 4D **96**
OL6: A Lyme 2A **106**
OL12: Roch 2B **28**
(not continuous)
SK4: Stoc 6F **133**
Athos Wlk. M40: Man 1E **89**
Atkinson Av. BL3: Bolt 4F **49**
Atkinson Ho. *M33: Sale 4B **128***
(off Atkinson Rd.)
Atkinson Rd. M33: Sale 3A **128**
M41: Urm 5F **111**
Atkinson St. M3: Man 6F **5** (4C **100**)
OL9: O'ham 1D **74**
OL11: Roch 3E **41**
SK1: Stoc 4A **146**
Atkin St. M28: Walk 1H **81**
Atlanta Av. M90: Man A 5G **153**
Atlantic Bus. Cen. WA14: B'ath 4E **139**
Atlantic St. WA14: B'ath 5C **138**
Atlantic Wlk. *M11: Man 4B **102***
(off Yeoman Wlk.)
Atlas Bus. Pk. M22: Wyth 4D **154**
Atlas Fold BL8: Bury 2C **36**
Atlas Ho. BL1: Bolt 2G **175**
Atlas St. OL7: A Lyme 6G **91**
OL8: O'ham 5F **177**
SK16: Duk 5B **106**
Atlow Dr. M23: Wyth 6H **141**
Atrium, The M45: White 2F **69**
Attenburys La. WA14: Tim 3G **139**
Attenbury's Pk. Est.
WA14: Tim 3G **139**
Attercliffe Rd. M21: Chor 2G **129**
Attewell St. M11: Man 5C **102**
Attingham Wlk. M34: Dent 6E **119**
Attleboro Rd. M40: Man 4C **88**
(not continuous)
Attlee Way M12: Man 4A **102**
Attock Cl. OL9: Chad 4B **74**
Attwood Rd. WA15: Tim 6B **140**
Attwood St. M12: Man 4C **116**
Atwood Rd. M20: Man 6G **131**
Atwood St. M1: Man 2A **10** (5E **101**)
Auberge Ho. SK2: Stoc 5B **146**
Auberson Rd. BL3: Bolt 4B **48**
Aubrey Rd. M14: Man 2A **132**
Aubrey St. M50: Sal 5G **99**
OL11: Roch 6H **27**
Auburn Av. SK6: Bred 5F **135**
SK14: Hyde 6C **120**
Auburn Dr. M41: Urm 6G **111**
Auburn Rd. M16: Old T 3H **113**
M34: Dent 5E **119**
Auburn St. BL3: Bolt 3B **48**
M1: Man 1C **10** (4F **101**)
Auckland Dr. M6: Sal 6G **85**
Auckland Rd. M19: Man 1B **132**
Audax Wlk. M40: Man 1D **102**
Auden Cl. M11: Man 4F **103**
Auden Ct. *M11: Man 4F **103***
(off Auden Cl.)
AUDENSHAW 1F **119**
Audenshaw Ct. M34: Aud 1E **119**
Audenshaw Hall Gro.
M34: Aud 6B **104**
Audenshaw Rd. M34: Aud 6B **104**
(not continuous)
Audlem Cl. M40: Man 3H **7** (3H **101**)
Audlem Wlk. SK8: Chea 6C **144**
Audley Av. M32: Stre 3H **111**
Audley Rd. M19: Man 5D **116**
Audley St. OL5: Mos 2H **93**
(not continuous)
OL6: A Lyme 3C **106**
Audlum Ct. BL9: Bury 3G **37**
Audrey Av. M18: Man 2G **117**
Audrey St. M9: Man 4B **88**
Augusta Cl. OL12: Roch 1G **27**
Augusta St. OL12: Roch 2G **27**
Augustine Webster Cl. M9: Man 3A **88**
Augustus St. BL3: Bolt 3E **49**
M3: Man 1A **6** (1E **101**)
Augustus Way M15: Man 3C **114**
Auriga Wlk. M7: Sal 1B **4**
Austell Rd. M22: Wyth 5B **154**
Austen Av. BL9: Bury 1F **53**
Austen Rd. M30: Ecc 4F **97**
Austen Wlk. OL1: O'ham 3C **60**
Auster Cl. *M14: Man 1E **131***
(off Bethnall Dr.)
AUSTERLANDS 1E **77**
Austin Ct. *M20: Man 5G **131***
(off Milden Cl.)
Austin Dr. M20: Man 5G **131**
Austin Gro. M19: Man 1B **132**
Austins Fold M6: Sal 5D **84**
Autunm St. M13: Man 3G **115**
Avallon Cl. BL8: Tot 4H **21**
Avalon Dr. M20: Man 3G **143**
Avebury Cl. M7: Sal 5D **86**
Avebury Rd. M23: Wyth 6G **141**
Avenham Cl. M15: Man 6F **9** (2C **114**)
Avening Wlk. M22: Wyth 3A **154**
Avens Rd. M31: Part 6D **124**
Avenue, The BL2: Bolt 6F **33**
BL9: Bury 6F **23**
M7: Sal 6A **86**
M20: Man 4C **130**
M28: Wors 4A **82**
(Delaford Av.)
M28: Wors 1A **96**
(Rock Rd.)
M30: Ecc 4F **97**
M33: Sale 6F **127**
M41: Urm 5A **110**
OL2: Shaw 1G **59**
SK6: Bred 6D **134**
SK8: H Grn 4E **155**
SK9: A Edg 5G **173**
SK13: Had 3H **123**
WA15: Hale 5H **151**
Avenue St. BL1: Bolt 5B **32**
SK1: Stoc 1H **145**
Averhill M28: Wors 3F **81**
Averill St. M40: Man 6F **89**
Averon Ri. OL1: O'ham 3B **60**
Aveson Av. M21: Chor 3H **129**
Avian Cl. M30: Ecc 6B **96**
Avian Dr. M14: Man 1F **131**
Aviary Rd. M28: Wors 5B **82**
Aviator Way M22: Wyth 5A **154**
Aviemore Cl. BL0: Ram 1A **22**
Avis St. OL2: Shaw 6H **43**
Avocet Dr. M44: Irl 4E **109**
WA14: B'ath 3D **138**
Avon Bank SK6: Bred 6F **135**
Avonbrook Dr. M40: Man 1H **89**
Avoncliff Cl. BL1: Bolt 2B **32**
Avon Cl. M28: Walk 1E **81**
OL16: Miln 5G **29**
SK6: Mar 6C **148**
Avon Cotts. M25: Pres 4E **69**
Avon Ct. M15: Man 6C **8**
Avoncourt Dr. M20: Man 5E **131**
Avondale M27: Clif 1A **84**
Avondale Av. BL9: Bury 1E **37**
SK7: H Gro 3F **159**
Avondale Ct. OL11: Roch 6F **41**
Avondale Cres. M41: Urm 4E **111**
Avondale Dr. BL0: Ram 1H **21**
M6: Sal 6B **84**
M29: Ast 5A **80**
Avondale Ind. Est. SK3: Stoc 4D **144**
Avondale Lodge *M33: Sale 6B **128***
(off Whitehill Rd.)
Avondale Recreation Cen. 4D **144**
Avondale Ri. SK9: Wilm 3G **173**
Avondale Rd. BL4: Farn 1D **64**
M32: Stre 3E **113**
M45: White 6E **53**
SK3: Stoc 4D **144**
SK7: H Gro 3F **159**
Avondale St. BL1: Bolt 4A **32**
M8: Man 4E **87**
OL8: O'ham 5E **75**
Avon Dr. BL9: Bury 3F **23**
Avon Flats *OL10: H'ood 3G **39***
(off Kay St.)
Avon Gdns. M19: Man 3C **132**
Avonlea Dr. M19: Man 3A **132**
Avonlea Rd. M33: Sale 2F **139**
M43: Droy 3G **103**
Avonleigh Gdns. *OL1: O'ham 6A **60***
(off Clyde St.)
Avon Rd. BL4: Kea 4D **66**
M19: Man 3B **132**
M29: Ast 4A **80**
OL2: Shaw 5H **43**
OL9: Chad 1H **73**
OL10: H'ood 3E **39**
SK8: H Grn 6F **155**
WA15: Hale 5G **151**
Avon St. BL1: Bolt 4H **31**
OL8: O'ham 5F **75**
SK3: Stoc 4G **145**
Avril Cl. SK5: Stoc 1H **133**
Avro Cl. M14: Man 6F **115**

Avro Ct. M24: Mid 1F **73**
Avroe Rd. M30: Ecc 6B **96**
Avro Way M90: Man A 6F **153**
Awburn Rd. SK14: Hat 6A **122**
Axbridge Wlk. M40: Man 3H **7**
Axford Cl. M7: Sal 5D **86**
Axminster Wlk. SK7: Bram 6G **157**
Axon Sq. M16: W Ran 3D **114**
Aycliffe Av. M21: Chor 4B **130**
Aycliffe Gro. M13: Man 4A **116**
Aylesbury Av. M34: Dent 6F **119**
   M41: Urm 3G **111**
Aylesbury Cl. M5: Sal 4G **99**
Aylesbury Gro. M24: Mid 5E **57**
Aylesby Av. M18: Man 3D **116**
Aylesby Ct. M21: Chor 6A **114**
Aylesford Rd. M14: Man 4H **115**
Aylesford Wlk. BL1: Bolt 4C **32**
           (off Blackburn Rd.)
Aylestone Wlk. M40: Man 4C **88**
              (off Hugo St.)
Aylsham Cl. SK6: Bred 4F **135**
Aylsham M. M27: Swin 6F **83**
Aylwin Dr. M33: Sale 6C **128**
Ayr Av. OL8: O'ham 6F **75**
Ayr Cl. SK7: H Gro 3G **159**
Ayres Rd. M16: Old T 3G **113**
Ayr Gro. OL10: H'ood 4E **39**
Ayrshire Rd. M7: Sal 5H **85**
Ayr St. BL2: Bolt 1G **33**
Ayrton Gro. M38: Lit H 4E **65**
Aysgarth OL16: Roch 2B **28**
Aysgarth Av. M18: Man 1G **117**
   SK6: Rom 5B **136**
   SK8: Chea 5G **143**
Aysgarth Cl. M33: Sale 6F **127**
Ayshford Cl. WA14: Alt 5D **138**
Ayton Ct. M16: Old T 3B **114**
             (off Ayres Rd.)
Ayton Gro. M14: Man 3A **116**
Aytoun St. M1: Man 6B **6** (4E **101**)
Azalea Av. M18: Man 1F **117**

B

Babbacombe Gro. M9: Man 4F **71**
Babbacombe Rd. SK2: Stoc 5C **146**
Baber Wlk. BL1: Bolt 1C **32**
            (off Warwick St.)
Bk. Acton St. M1: Man 1C **10**
Bk. Adcroft St. SK1: Stoc 6H **179**
Bk. Ainscow St. BL1: Bolt 5C **32**
            (off Vernon St.)
Bk. Albion Pl. BL9: Bury 1F **37**
            (off Hanson St.)
Bk. Alfred St. BL0: Ram 4B **12**
            (off Mary St.)
Bk. Andrew St. BL9: Bury 3G **37**
           (off Andrew St.)
   OL5: Mos 3G **93**
           (off Fox Platt Ter.)
Bk. Andrew St. Nth. BL9: Bury 3G **37**
           (off Andrew St.)
Bk. Apple Ter. BL1: Bolt 3B **32**
Bk. Ashford Wlk. BL1: Bolt 4C **32**
            (off Vernon St.)
Bk. Ashley St. M4: Man 2C **6**
Bk. Bark St. BL1: Bolt 3E **175**
Bk. Bell La. BL9: Bury 2G **37**
            (off Church St.)
Bk. Benson St. BL9: Bury 4G **37**
           (off Benson St.)
Bk. Birch St. BL9: Bury 1D **176**
          (not continuous)
Bk. Blackburn Rd. BL1: Bolt 4D **32**
   BL7: Eger 1B **18**
           (off Blackburn Rd.)
Bk. Blackburn Rd. E. BL7: Eger 1B **18**
            (off Albert St.)
Bk. Bolton St. Sth. BL9: Bury 3A **176**
Bk. Bond St. W. BL9: Bury 3G **37**
            (off Croft St.)

BACKBOWER 6C **120**
Bk. Bower Fold SK15: Stal 5G **107**
            (off Bower Fold)
Bk. Bower La. SK14: Hyde 1D **136**
Bk. Bradford St. W. BL2: Bolt 5H **175**
          (not continuous)
Bk. Bradshaw Brow BL2: Bolt 1G **33**
         (off Bradshaw Brow)
Bk. Bradshaw Brow E. BL2: Bolt 1G **33**
         (off Bradshaw Brow)
Bk. Bradshaw Rd. BL2: Bolt 6H **19**
         (off Bradshaw Rd.)
Bk. Bradshaw St. OL16: Roch 3A **28**
Bk. Bridge St. M3: Man 5G **5**
Bk. Broad St. BL9: Bury 3B **176**
Bk. Broom St. BL2: Bolt 3H **175** (6E **33**)
   OL16: Miln 1H **43**
          (off Broomfield St.)
Bk. Caley St. BL1: Bolt 3F **31**
            (off Caley St.)
Bk. Cambridge St. OL7: A Lyme 4F **105**
           (off Bennett St.)
Bk. Camp St. M7: Sal 6B **86**
Bk. Canning St. BL9: Bury 1F **37**
           (off Hornby St.)
Bk. Cateaton St. BL9: Bury 1D **176**
          (not continuous)
Bk. Cecil St. OL5: Mos 3G **93**
           (off Park Ter.)
Bk. Chapel St. BL8: Tot 4H **21**
   M19: Man 6C **116**
           (off Bankley St.)
   M30: Ecc 3H **97**
           (off Church St.)
   OL12: W'le 6C **16**
   SK7: H Gro 2E **159**
Back Cheapside BL1: Bolt 4F **175**
Bk. China La. M1: Man 6C **6** (4F **101**)
Bk. Church St. BL1: Bolt 2E **175**
          (not continuous)
Bk. Cobden St. BL9: Bury 2G **37**
           (off Cobden St.)
Bk. College Land M3: Man 4G **5**
Bk. Cowm La. OL12: Whitw 2A **14**
Bk. Cres. Av. BL1: Bolt 5B **32**
           (off Crescent Av.)
Bk. Crostons Rd. BL8: Bury 2D **36**
Bk. Dale St. OL16: Miln 6F **29**
            (off Dale St.)
Bk. Darwen Rd. BL7: Bro X 4E **19**
           (off Darwen Rd.)
Bk. Darwin St. BL1: Bolt 3B **32**
            (off Darwin St.)
Bk. Deacon's Dr. M6: Sal 5D **84**
Bk. Deane Church La. BL3: Bolt 3H **47**
        (off Deane Church La.)
Bk. Deyne Av. M25: Pres 5H **69**
Bk. Drake St.
   OL16: Roch 5C **178** (5H **27**)
Bk. Duncan St. M7: Sal 4A **86**
Bk. Durham St.
   OL11: Roch 6D **178** (6A **28**)
Bk. East St. BL9: Bury 5D **176**
          (not continuous)
Bk. Elsworth St. M8: Man 1A **6**
Bk. Eskrick St. BL1: Bolt 3B **32**
            (off Carl St.)
Bk. Ewart St. BL1: Bolt 3C **32**
           (off Ewart St.)
Bk. Fletcher St. BL9: Bury 3G **37**
            (off York St.)
   M26: Rad 2D **66**
Backford Wlk. M20: Man 2E **131**
Bk. Foundary St. BL9: Bury 4D **176**
Bk. Frank St. BL9: Bury 5D **176**
Bk. George St. M1: Man 1A **10** (5E **101**)
          (not continuous)
Bk. Gladstone St. OL4: O'ham 3H **75**
Bk. Grafton St. WA14: Alt 3B **174**
Bk. Greaves St. OL1: O'ham 3H **177**
Bk. Grosvenor St. SK15: Stal 4E **107**
Bk. Hadwin St. BL1: Bolt 1F **175**
         (off Higher Bri. St.)

Bk. Halliwell Rd. Sth. BL1: Bolt 3B **32**
Bk. Hamel St. SK14: Hyde 2D **120**
            (off Hamel St.)
Bk. Hamilton St. M7: Sal 4B **86**
Bk. Hampson St. M40: Man 1H **101**
           (off Hampson St.)
Bk. Haslam St. BL9: Bury 1G **37**
Bk. Heywood St. E. BL9: Bury 3G **37**
          (off Heywood St.)
Bk. Heywood St. W. BL9: Bury 4G **37**
          (off Heywood St.)
Bk. High St. BL3: Bolt 3B **48**
            (off High St.)
Bk. Hilton St. M7: Sal 4B **86**
Bk. Hope St. M7: Sal 4B **86**
Bk. Horbury St. BL8: Bury 3C **36**
           (off Horbury Dr.)
Bk. Hornby St. E. BL9: Bury 1C **176**
Bk. Hornby St. W. BL9: Bury 1C **176**
Bk. Howe St. M7: Sal 4A **86**
Bk. Hulme St. M5: Sal 5B **4** (4A **100**)
Bk. Hurst St. BL9: Bury 4G **37**
            (off Hurst St.)
Bk. Ingham St. BL9: Bury 4G **37**
           (off Ingham St.)
Bk. Ingham St. E. BL9: Bury 4G **37**
           (off Ingham St.)
Bk. James St. OL15: L'ough 4F **17**
           (off James St.)
Bk. Kershaw St. BL9: Bury 3G **37**
          (off Kershaw St.)
Bk. King St. OL1: O'ham 4F **177** (3E **75**)
Bk. Knowl St. SK15: Stal 3F **107**
Bk. Knowsley St. BL9: Bury 4B **176**
Back La. BL1: Bolt 2E **175** (5C **32**)
   BL5: O Hul 3A **64**
   OL4: O'ham 6E **77**
   OL4: Scout 6G **61**
   OL6: A Lyme 1E **93**
   OL7: A Lyme 6E **91**
          (not continuous)
   OL12: Roch 6B **14**
   OL12: Whitw 3A **14**
   SK14: Mot 4C **122**
   WA14: D Mas 1A **150**
   WA15: Alt 2A **162**
Bk. Lee St. OL3: Upp 1D **78**
Bk. Lord St. BL9: Bury 5D **176**
Bk. Louise St. OL12: Roch 6C **16**
            (off Louise St.)
Bk. Manchester Old Rd.
   BL9: Bury 6A **176**
Bk. Manchester Rd. BL9: Bury 4A **176**
Bk. Manor St. BL9: Bury 3G **37**
Bk. Market St. BL9: Bury 4B **176**
Bk. Market St. W. BL9: Bury 3B **176**
Bk. Mason St. BL9: Bury 3G **37**
           (off Mason St.)
Bk. Massie St. SK8: Chea 5H **143**
Bk. Mawdsley St. BL1: Bolt 4F **175**
Bk. Melbourne St. SK15: Stal 3E **107**
Bk. Merton St. BL8: Bury 2D **36**
           (off Merton St.)
Bk. Micklehurst Rd. OL5: Mos 2A **94**
Bk. Millett St. BL9: Bury 3D **36**
           (off Millett St.)
Bk. Mill La. OL5: Mos 1G **93**
Back Moor SK14: Mot 3C **122**
Bk. Moorgate W. BL9: Bury 2G **37**
            (off Bold St.)
Bk. Moss Ter. BL1: Bolt 2F **175**
Bk. Oldham Rd.
   OL16: Roch 5D **178** (5A **28**)
Bk. Olga St. BL1: Bolt 3B **32**
          (off Wordsworth St.)
Bk. Olive Bank BL8: Bury 1B **36**
            (off Elson St.)
Bk. Ormrod St. BL9: Bury 3G **37**
           (off Ormrod St.)
BACK'O'THE' BANK 4D **32**
BACK O' TH' HILL 4B **136**
Bk. o' th' Low Rd. OL4: Wat 1D **76**

BACK O' TH' MOSS 2G 39
Back o' th' Moss La. OL10: H'ood 2G 39
Bk. Oxford St. BL9: Bury 4G 37
   (off Oxford St.)
Bk. Parkhills Rd. Sth. BL9: Bury 5E 37
Bk. Parsons La. BL9: Bury 2C 176
Bk. Patience St. OL12: Roch 2E 27
   (off Patience St.)
Bk. Peter St. BL9: Bury 2G 37
   (off Peter St.)
Bk. Phoenix St. BL9: Bury 4A 176
Back Piccadilly M1: Man 5B 6 (4E 101)
Bk. Pine St. OL16: Miln 2H 43
   (off Pine St.)
Bk. Pool Fold M2: Man 5H 5 (4D 100)
Bk. Portland St.
   OL6: A Lyme 6A 174 (3G 105)
Bk. Quay St. M3: Man 6E 5
Bk. Queen St. BL1: Bolt 4E 175
Bk. Red Bank M4: Man 1B 6 (2E 101)
Bk. Redhill Gro. BL1: Bolt 1E 175
Bk. Richard Burch St. BL9: Bury 1D 176
Bk. Rochdale Rd. BL9: Bury 3G 37
   (off Rochdale Rd., not continuous)
Bk. Rochdale Rd. Sth. BL9: Bury 3G 37
   (off Foundary St.)
Bk. Roman Rd. M7: Sal 5C 86
   (off Appian Way)
Bk. St George's Rd. BL1: Bolt 2E 175
   M4: Man 2D 6 (2F 101)
Bk. St George's Rd. Nth. BL1: Bolt 5C 32
   (off Ruth St.)
Bk. St Helens Rd. BL3: Bolt 5G 47
   (off Moorlands Vw.)
Bk. St James St. OL1: O'ham 2H 75
Bk. St Marks' La. M8: Man 3D 86
   (off Cheetham Hill Rd.)
Bk. St Mary's Pl. BL9: Bury 4A 176
Bk. Salford St. BL9: Bury 1G 37
Bk. Sankey St. BL9: Bury 3D 36
   (off Sankey St.)
Bk. Scott St. OL8: O'ham 4F 75
   (off Scott St.)
Bk. Shepherd St. BL9: Bury 4D 176
Bk. Silver St. BL9: Bury 3B 176
Bk. South Cross St. E. BL9: Bury 4G 37
   (off Sth. Cross St.)
Bk. South Pde. M3: Man 5G 5
Bk. Spear St. M1: Man 4C 6
Bk. Spring Gdns. BL1: Bolt . . .5F 175 (1D 48)
Bk. Spring St. E. BL9: Bury 5D 176
Bk. Spring St. W. BL9: Bury 5D 176
Bk. Square St. BL0: Ram 3C 12
Bk. Teak St. BL9: Bury 3H 37
Bk. Tenterden St. BL9: Bury 3D 36
   (off Tenterden St., not continuous)
Bk. Thomas St. M4: Man 4B 6
Bk. Tinline St. BL9: Bury 3G 37
   (off Tinline St.)
Bk. Tonge Moor Rd. BL2: Bolt 2F 33
   (off Tonge Moor Rd.)
Backton Pl. M40: Man 1H 101
   (off Sawley Rd.)
Bk. Tootal Rd. M5: Sal 3D 98
   (off Tootal Rd.)
Bk. Turner St. M4: Man 4B 6 (3E 101)
Bk. Vernon St. BL1: Bolt 5C 32
   (off Merehall Dr.)
   BL9: Bury 1D 176
   SK14: Hyde 5C 120
   (off Vernon St.)
Bk. Viola St. BL1: Bolt 2C 32
Bk. Walmersley Rd. E. BL9: Bury 1D 176
Bk. Walmersley Rd. W. BL9: Bury 1D 176
Bk. Water St. BL7: Eger 1B 18
   (off Water St.)
   OL6: A Lyme 1A 106
   SK1: Stoc 1H 145
   (off Gt. Portwood St.)
Bk. Wellington Rd. Sth. BL9: Bury . .6B 176
Bk. Wells St. BL9: Bury 6A 176
Back Whitegate OL15: L'ough 5E 17
   (off Whitegate)

Bk. Willows La. BL3: Bolt 3A 48
Bk. Young St. BL4: Farn 2A 66
Bacon Av. M34: Dent 2G 135
Bacup St. M40: Man 3C 88
Badby Cl. M4: Man 5H 7 (4H 101)
Baddeley Cl. SK3: Stoc 6F 145
Badder St. BL1: Bolt 2F 175 (5D 32)
Bader Dr. OL10: H'ood 6H 39
Badger Cl. OL16: Roch 2C 42
   SK6: Mar 2D 160
   SK14: Hyde 3C 120
Badger Edge La. OL4: O'ham 4G 61
Badger La. OL16: Roch 3B 42
   (not continuous)
Badger Rd. WA14: W Tim 3E 139
Badgers Wlk. M22: Wyth 4C 154
Badminton Rd. M21: Chor 6A 114
Bagnall Cl. OL3: Upp 6E 63
   OL12: Roch 1B 26
Bagnall Ct. M22: Nor 3C 142
Bagnall Wlk. M22: Nor 3C 142
Bagot St. M11: Man 3E 103
   M27: Ward 2E 83
Bagshaw St. SK14: Hyde 2C 120
BAGSLATE MOOR 3B 26
Bagslate Moor La. OL11: Roch 3B 26
Bagslate Moor Rd. OL11: Roch 4B 26
Bagstock Av. SK12: Poy 5E 169
BAGULEY 4F 141
Baguley Cres. M24: Mid 2E 71
   SK3: Stoc 5A 145
Baguley Dr. BL9: Bury 5G 53
Baguley La. M33: Sale 6E 129
   (not continuous)
Baguley Rd. M33: Sale 5E 129
Baguley St. M43: Droy 4B 104
Baildon Rd. OL12: Roch 2D 88
Baildon St. M40: Man 2C 88
Bailey La. BL2: Bolt 4A 34
   M31: Part 6D 124
   M90: Man A 4H 153
Bailey Rd. M17: T Pk 6A 98
Bailey St. M11: Man 4G 103
   M25: Pres 5A 70
   OL1: O'ham 3H 177 (2G 75)
Bailey Wlk. WA14: Bow 5E 151
Baillie St. M26: Rad 2E 53
   OL16: Roch 3H 27
   (Milton St.)
   OL16: Roch 3B 178 (4H 27)
   (Yorkshire St.)
Baillie St. E. OL16: Roch . . .2D 178 (3A 28)
Bails, The M7: Sal 5A 86
   M28: Walk 6H 65
Bainbridge Cl.
   M12: Man 6H 11 (1H 115)
Bainbridge Rd. OL4: O'ham 6B 60
Bainburgh Clough OL8: O'ham 5A 76
Baines Av. M44: Irl 1D 124
Baines St. BL1: Bolt 5H 31
Bain St. M27: Swin 4H 83
Bainton Wlk. M9: Man 4G 71
   (off Munn Rd.)
Baird St. M1: Man 1D 10 (5F 101)
Baitings Cl. OL12: Roch 1G 25
Baitings Row OL12: Roch 1G 25
Baker Ho. OL2: O'ham 3E 59
   (off Royton Hall Pk.)
Bakersfield Pl. M33: Sale 5C 128
Baker's La. OL3: Upp 5G 63
Baker St. BL0: Ram 4B 12
   BL4: Kea 3D 66
   M24: Mid 1D 72
   OL10: H'ood 5A 40
   SK4: Stoc 6G 133
   SK15: Stal 4F 107
   WA15: Tim 4C 140
Bakery Cl. OL6: A Lyme 6B 92
Bakewell Bank SK13: Gam 6F 123
   (off Melandra Castle Rd.)

Bakewell Cl. SK13: Gam 6F 123
   (off Youlgreave Cres.)
Bakewell Fold SK13: Gam 6F 123
   (off Youlgreave Cres.)
Bakewell Gdns. SK13: Gam 6F 123
   (off Youlgreave Cres.)
Bakewell Grn. SK13: Gam 6F 123
   (off Bakewell M.)
Bakewell Gro. SK13: Gam 6F 123
   (off Youlgreave Cres.)
Bakewell Lea SK13: Gam 6F 123
   (off Youlgreave Cres.)
Bakewell M. SK13: Gam 6F 123
Bakewell Rd. M30: Ecc 5E 97
   M32: Stre 4A 112
   M43: Droy 3G 103
   SK7: H Gro 5E 159
Bakewell St. M18: Man 3E 117
   SK3: Stoc 3F 145
Bakewell Wlk. SK13: Gam 6F 123
   (off Totley M.)
Bala Cl. M5: Sal 3G 99
Balcary Gro. BL1: Bolt 5H 31
Balcombe Cl. BL8: Bury 4B 22
BALDERSTONE 2B 42
Balderstone Rd. OL11: Roch 3H 41
BALDINGSTONE 2F 23
Baldock Rd. M20: Man 6H 131
Baldwin Rd. M19: Man 3B 132
Baldwin St. BL3: Bolt 2C 48
Bale St. M2: Man 1H 9 (5D 100)
Balfour Gro. SK5: Stoc 1H 133
Balfour Rd. M41: Urm 5D 110
   OL12: Roch 2E 27
   WA14: B'ath 4F 139
Balfour St. BL3: Bolt 1B 48
   M6: Sal 5G 85
   M8: Man 3E 87
   OL2: Shaw 6H 43
   OL4: O'ham 2A 76
Balham Wlk. M12: Man 1B 116
   (off Pollitt Cl.)
Ballantine St. M40: Man 1E 103
Ballard Cl. OL15: L'ough 2H 17
Ballard Way OL2: Shaw 5A 44
Ballater Av. M41: Urm 6C 110
Ballater Cl. OL10: H'ood 4E 39
Ballater Wlk. M8: Man 4D 86
   (off Heath St.)
Ballbrook Av. M20: Man 4E 131
Ballbrook Ct. M20: Man 5F 131
Balleratt St. M19: Man 6C 116
Ball Grn. M32: Stre 2B 112
Ballgrove OL3: Upp 2E 79
Balliol Cl. SK6: Wood 5A 136
Balliol Ct. M33: Sale 4F 127
   M27: Swin 3G 83
Balloon La. M4: Man 3A 6
Balloon St. M4: Man 3A 6 (3E 101)
Ball St. OL16: Roch 2D 178 (3A 28)
Ball Wlk. SK14: Hat 6B 122
Ballycreen OL11: Roch 2E 41
Balmain Av. M18: Man 4E 117
Balmain Rd. M41: Urm 4D 110
Balmer St. M23: Wyth 1H 153
Balmfield St. M8: Man 6E 87
Balmforth St. M15: Man 3D 8
Balmoral Av. BL3: Lit L 4C 50
   M32: Stre 4D 112
   M34: Aud 6D 104
   M41: Urm 6D 110
   M45: White 2G 69
   OL2: O'ham 3F 59
   OL11: Roch 3D 26
   SK8: Chea H 3C 156
   SK14: Hyde 1C 136
Balmoral Cl. BL8: G'mount 2A 22
   BL9: Bury 2G 53
   OL16: Miln 5G 29
Balmoral Ct. M9: Man 4E 71
   OL7: A Lyme 4G 105
   (off Victoria St.)

Balmoral Dr. M34: Dent 3A **118**
  OL10: H'ood 4E **39**
  SK6: H Lan 6C **160**
  SK12: Poy 4D **168**
  SK15: Stal 2E **107**
  WA14: Tim 3H **139**
Balmoral Grange M25: Pres 6C **70**
Balmoral Gro. SK7: H Gro 2F **159**
Balmoral Ho. *M30: Ecc* *3E 97*
  (off Queen Victoria St.)
Balmoral Rd. BL4: Farn 2G **65**
  M14: Man 1H **131**
  M27: Clif 1A **84**
  M41: Urm 6C **110**
  SK4: Stoc 6C **132**
  WA15: Alt 2C **174** (1G **151**)
Balmoral St. M18: Man 3E **117**
Balmoral Way SK9: Wilm 3D **172**
Balmore Cl. BL3: Bolt 4G **47**
Balm St. BL0: Ram 5A **12**
Balsam Cl. M13: Man 4E **11** (6G **101**)
Balshaw Av. M44: Irl 5D **108**
Balshaw Cl. BL3: Bolt 2A **48**
Balshaw St. M44: Irl 5E **109**
Baltic Rd. WA14: B'ath 5C **138**
Baltic St. M5: Sal 3E **99**
Baltimore St. M40: Man 6B **88**
Bamber Av. M33: Sale 6E **129**
Bamber Wlk. *BL3: Bolt* *2B 48*
  (off Weber Dr.)
Bamburgh Cl. M26: Rad 2E **51**
Bamburgh Dr. OL17: A Lyme 6E **91**
Bambury St. BL9: Bury 2D **176** (2F **37**)
BAMFORD .5A **26**
Bamford Av. M24: Mid 5C **56**
  M34: Dent 1F **135**
Bamford Bus. Pk. SK4: Stoc 4G **133**
Bamford Cl. BL9: Bury 1C **38**
  SK8: H Grn 5H **155**
Bamford Ct. OL11: Roch 5D **26**
Bamford Fold *SK13: Gam* *6G 123*
  (off Castleton Cres.)
Bamford Gdns. WA15: Tim 5D **140**
Bamford Grn. *SK13: Gam* *6G 123*
  (off Castleton Cres.)
Bamford Gro. M20: Man 6E **131**
  OL6: A Lyme 5D **92**
Bamford La. SK13: Gam 6G **123**
Bamford M. OL11: Roch 4A **26**
  SK13: Gam 6G **123**
Bamford Pl. OL12: Roch 2G **27**
Bamford Pct. OL11: Roch 4A **26**
Bamford Rd. BL0: Ram 1E **13**
  M9: Man 4H **71**
  M20: Man 6E **131**
  OL10: H'ood 1G **39**
Bamfords Pas. OL15: L'ough 3H **17**
Bamford St. M11: Man 3D **102**
  OL2: O'ham 4E **59**
  OL9: Chad 1C **74**
  OL15: L'ough 3F **17**
  (Cote La.)
  OL15: L'ough 4F **17**
  (Featherstall Rd.)
  SK1: Stoc 4G **179** (3H **145**)
Bamford Way OL11: Roch 5A **26**
Bampton Cl. SK2: Stoc 4B **146**
Bampton Rd. M22: Wyth 4B **154**
Bampton Wlk. M24: Mid 5A **56**
Banbury Dr. WA14: Tim 3G **139**
Banbury M. M27: Ward 2F **83**
Banbury Rd. M23: Wyth 6F **141**
  M24: Mid 4B **72**
  M35: Fail 1G **103**
Banbury St. BL2: Bolt 4G **33**
  SK1: Stoc 3G **179** (3H **145**)
Bancroft Av. SK8: Chea H 4C **156**
Bancroft Cl. SK6: Bred 6E **135**
Bancroft Ct. *WA15: Hale* *2A 152*
  (off Bancroft Rd.)
Bancroft Fold SK14: Hyde 2F **121**
Bancroft Rd. M27: Swin 2G **83**
  WA15: Hale 2A **152**

Bandy Flds. Pl. M7: Sal 6B **86**
Banff Gro. OL10: H'ood 4E **39**
Banff Rd. M14: Man 3G **115**
Bangor Rd. SK8: Chea 5B **144**
Bangor St. BL1: Bolt 1E **175** (5C **32**)
  M15: Man 6D **8** (2B **114**)
  OL6: A Lyme 3C **106**
  OL16: Roch 5B **28**
  SK5: Stoc 5H **133**
Bank OL12: W'le 5C **16**
Bank, The OL16: Roch 2B **178** (3H **27**)
Bank Barn OL12: W'le 5D **16**
Bank Barn La. OL12: W'le 5D **16**
Bankbottom SK13: Had 2H **123**
Bank Bri. Rd. M11: Man 2D **102**
Bank Cl. OL15: L'ough 6G **17**
Banker St. BL3: Bolt 2G **49**
Bankfield BL2: Ain 5E **35**
  SK14: Hyde 2B **120**
Bankfield Av. M13: Man 4A **116**
  M43: Droy 3A **104**
  M44: Cad 4B **124**
  SK4: Stoc 1E **145**
Bankfield Bus. Pk. SK5: Stoc 5G **133**
Bankfield Cl. BL2: Ain 4E **35**
Bankfield Cotts. OL3: Dob 5B **62**
  SK6: Wood *4H 135*
  (off Woodlands Dr.)
Bankfield Dr. M28: Wors 4F **81**
  OL8: O'ham 1H **91**
Bankfield Ho. SK6: Wood 4H **135**
Bankfield La. OL11: Roch 3A **26**
Bankfield M. BL9: Bury 6F **37**
Bankfield Rd. BL4: Farn 3H **65**
  M29: Tyld 5C **80**
  M33: Sale 3G **127**
  SK6: Wood 4H **135**
  SK8: Chea H 4B **156**
Bankfield St. BL3: Bolt 2A **48**
  (Anglia Gro.)
  BL3: Bolt 2A **48**
  (Deane Rd.)
  M9: Man 3H **87**
  M26: Rad 2F **67**
  SK5: Stoc 5G **133**
Bankfoot Wlk. *M8: Man* *6E 87*
  (off Barnsdale Dr.)
Bankgate SK14: B'tom 6C **122**
Bank Gro. M38: Lit H 4D **64**
Bankhall Cl. BL8: Bury 3A **36**
Bankhall La. WA15: Hale 5G **151**
Bankhall Rd. SK4: Stoc 6C **132**
Bankhall Wlk. *M9: Man* *4A 88*
  (off Craigend Dr.)
Bank Hey BL5: W'ton 6A **46**
Bank Hill St. OL4: O'ham 2A **76**
Bankhirst Cl. M8: Man 2E **87**
Bank Ho. BL9: Bury 6F **37**
Bank Ho. Cl. M29: Tyld 2C **80**
Bank Ho. Rd. M9: Man 5F **71**
Bankhouse Rd. BL8: Bury 6C **22**
Banklands Cl. M44: Cad 4B **124**
BANK LANE 2D **12**
Bank La. M6: Sal 6D **84**
  M27: Pen 6D **84**
  M38: Lit H 3D **64**
  OL3: G'fld 5F **79**
  OL12: W'le 5D **16**
  SK13: Tin 1H **123**
Bankley St. M19: Man 6C **116**
Bankmill Cl. M13: Man 4D **10**
Bank Pl. BL8: Bury 2C **36**
  M3: Sal 4C **4**
Bank Pl. Apartments *SK9: Wilm* . . .*2E 173*
  (off Green La.)
Bankquay Ct. M44: Irl 6F **109**
Bank Rd. BL1: Bolt 6C **18**
  M8: Man 1E **87**
  SK6: Bred 6G **135**
  SK15: C'ook 6A **94**
Banks Ct. WA15: Tim 6D **140**
Banks Cft. OL10: H'ood 6H **39**
Bank Side OL5: Mos 3G **93**

Bankside SK14: Hat 6H **121**
  WA15: Haleb 1D **162**
Bankside Av. M26: Rad 3D **52**
  OL3: Upp 2E **79**
Bankside Cl. OL3: Upp 2E **79**
  OL9: O'ham 3D **74**
  SK6: Mar B 2G **149**
  SK9: Wilm 5H **165**
Bankside Ct. M12: Man 3C **116**
  SK4: Stoc 1C **144**
Bankside Rd. M20: Man 4F **143**
Bankside Wlk. SK14: Hat 5H **121**
Banks La. SK1: Stoc 3B **146**
Banksman Way M27: Pen 3D **84**
Bank Sq. SK9: Wilm 2E **173**
Bank St. BL0: Ram 2E **13**
  BL1: Bolt 3G **175** (6D **32**)
  BL4: Farn 1H **65**
  BL8: Bury 1H **35**
  BL9: Bury 4B **176** (3E **37**)
  M3: Sal 4C **4** (3B **100**)
  M7: Sal 3D **86**
  M11: Man 2C **102**
  M26: Rad 5B **52**
  M33: Sale 4C **128**
  M34: Aud 1F **119**
  M34: Dent 1H **135**
  M43: Droy 5H **103**
  M45: White 6E **53**
  OL2: Shaw 6G **43**
  OL4: O'ham 3B **76**
  OL7: A Lyme 3H **105**
  OL10: H'ood 3F **39**
  (not continuous)
  OL11: Roch 1A **42**
  SK6: Wood 4H **135**
  SK8: Chea 5A **144**
  SK13: Had 2H **123**
  SK14: B'tom 6C **122**
  SK14: Hyde 4B **120**
  WA3: G'ook 4A **124**
Bankswood Cl. SK13: Had 3H **123**
Bank Ter. OL12: Whitw 1E **15**
  SK13: Had 2H **123**
BANK TOP . . . .
  BL2 . . . . .6E **19**
  OL4 . . . . .3B **76**
  OL8 . . . . .4E **177** (3E **75**)
Bank Top BL9: Bury 2F **23**
  M24: Mid 2C **72**
  M26: Bury, Rad 1B **52**
  OL6: A Lyme 3A **106**
  OL10: H'ood 2F **39**
Bank Top Gro. BL1: Bolt 6E **19**
Bank Top Pk. OL4: O'ham 3B **76**
Bank Top St. OL10: H'ood 2F **39**
Bank Top Vw. BL4: Kea 2C **66**
Bankwell St. M15: Man 2C **114**
BANKWOOD 6E **123**
Bank Wood BL1: Bolt 6F **31**
Bankwood Ct. M9: Man 2H **87**
Banky La. M33: Sale 3E **127**
Bannach Dr. OL9: Chad 6A **58**
Bannatyne Ct. M40: Man 2G **89**
Bannatyne's Health Club
  Manchester, Quay St. 6F **5**
  Manchester, Whitworth St. 1B **10**
Banner Dale Cl. *M13: Man* *4B 116*
  (off Bowscale Cl.)
Bannerman Av. M25: Pres 6H **69**
Bannerman Rd. M43: Droy 4B **104**
Banner Wlk. *M11: Man* *4B 102*
  (off Pilgrim Dr.)
Bannister Dr. SK8: Chea H 3B **156**
Bannister St. BL2: Bolt 5A **34**
  SK1: Stoc 6H **179** (4H **145**)
  Bank St. SK3: Stoc 4E **179** (3G **145**)
Banstead Av. M22: Nor 4B **142**
Bantry Dr. M9: Man 6F **71**
Bantry St. BL3: Bolt 2C **48**
  OL12: Roch 1A **28**
Baptist St. M4: Man 2C **6** (2F **101**)
Barathea Cl. OL11: Roch 2C **40**

Barbara Rd. BL3: Bolt 5G 47
Barbara St. BL3: Bolt 3B 48
Barbeck Cl. M40: Man 2H 7 (2A 102)
Barberry Bank BL7: Eger 1B 18
Barberry Cl. WA14: B'ath 4D 138
Barberry Wlk. M31: Part 6D 124
(off Wychelm Rd.)
Barber St. M11: Man 6G 103
Barbican St. M20: Man 2F 131
(not continuous)
Barbirolli Sq. M2: Man 2H 9
Barbury Ct. BL4: Farn 2A 66
Barchester Av. BL2: Bolt 4A 34
Barcheston Rd. SK8: Chea 1G 155
Barcicroft Rd. M19: Man 5A 132
Barcicroft Wlk. M19: Man 5A 132
Barclay Dr. M30: Ecc 2G 97
Barclay Rd. SK12: Poy 5E 169
Barclays Av. M6: Sal 5D 84
Barcliffe Av. M40: Man 1E 89
Barclyde St. OL11: Roch 6G 27
Barcombe Cl. M32: Stre 4H 111
OL4: O'ham 5B 60
Barcombe Wlk. M9: Man 4H 87
(off Fernclough Rd., not continuous)
Barcroft Rd. BL1: Bolt 3H 31
Barcroft St. BL3: Bury 1C 176 (2F 37)
Bardell Cres. SK12: Poy 5D 168
Bardon Cl. BL1: Bolt 4B 32
(off Kirkhope Dr.)
Bardon Rd. M23: Wyth 5F 141
Bardsea Av. M22: Wyth 4B 154
BARDSLEY 3G 91
Bardsley Av. M35: Fail 4H 89
Bardsley Cl. BL2: Bolt 6H 19
SK14: Hat 5A 122
BARDSLEY GATE 1A 122
Bardsley Ga. SK15: Stal 1A 122
Bardsley St. M24: Mid 6C 56
M40: Man 6F 89
OL4: Lees 4C 76
OL4: O'ham 1C 76
OL9: Chad 6H 73
SK4: Stoc 6F 133
Bardsley Va. Av. OL8: O'ham 3G 91
Barehill St. OL15: L'ough 3H 17
Bare St. BL1: Bolt 6E 33
Barff Rd. M5: Sal 3C 98
Barfold Cl. SK2: Stoc 6G 147
Barford Dr. SK9: Wilm 6G 165
Barford Wlk. M23: Wyth 1H 153
Bar Gap Rd. OL1: O'ham 1G 177 (1F 75)
Baric Cl. M30: Ecc 3F 97
(off Lane End)
Baring St. M1: Man 2D 10 (5F 101)
Baring St. Ind. Est.
M1: Man 2E 11 (5G 101)
Barkan Way M27: Pen 3B 84
Barker Rd. SK6: Bred 1F 147
Barkers La. M33: Sale 4H 127
Barker St. BL9: Bury 6A 176 (4E 37)
M3: Man 1G 5 (2D 100)
OL1: O'ham 2F 177 (2E 75)
OL10: H'ood 4F 39
Barke St. OL15: L'ough 6F 17
Barking St. M40: Man 2A 102
Bark St. BL1: Bolt 6C 32
BL4: Kea 4D 66
Bark St. E. BL1: Bolt 2F 175 (5D 32)
Bark Wlk. M15: Man 5H 9
Barkway M32: Stre 5A 112
Barkwell La. OL5: Mos 2F 93
Barkworth Wlk. M40: Man 5D 88
(off Harold Priestnall Cl.)
Bar La. BL1: Bolt 6C 18
Barlby Wlk. M40: Man 5D 88
(off Harold Priestnall Cl.)
Barlea Av. M40: Man 2F 89
Barley Brook Mdw. BL1: Bolt 5D 18
Barleycorn Cl. M33: Sale 6G 129
Borley Cft. SK8: Chea H 4B 156

Barleycroft SK13: Had 3H 123
Barley Cft. Rd. SK14: Hyde 1C 120
Barleycroft St. M16: W Ran 3D 114
Barley Dr. SK7: Bram 6G 157
Barleyfield Wlk. M24: Mid 6B 56
Barley Hall St. OL10: H'ood 2A 40
Barleywood Wlk. SK15: Stal 5H 107
Barlow Cl. BL9: Bury 6F 23
Barlow Ct. M28: Walk 6A 66
Barlow Cres. SK6: Mar 1D 160
BARLOW FOLD 2E 53
BARLOWFOLD 6C 136
Barlow Fold BL9: Bury 2F 53
SK6: Rom 6B 136
Barlow Fold Cl. BL9: Bury 2E 53
Barlow Fold Rd. SK5: Stoc 1H 133
SK6: Rom 6B 136
Barlow Hall Rd. M21: Chor 4A 130
Barlow Ho. BL1: Bolt 3H 31
OL8: O'ham 6G 177 (4E 75)
Barlow La. M30: Ecc 3E 97
Barlow La. Nth. SK5: Stoc 1H 133
BARLOW MOOR 4A 130
Barlow Moor Cl. OL12: Roch 1A 26
Barlow Moor Ct. M20: Man 5D 130
Barlow Moor Rd. M21: Chor 6H 113
Barlow Pk. Av. BL1: Bolt 6B 18
Barlow Rd. M5: Sal 6B 4 (4A 100)
M19: Man 6C 116
M32: Stre 3F 113
SK9: Wilm 6F 165
SK16: Duk 5B 106
WA14: B'ath 3D 138
Barlow St. M35: Fail 4F 5 (3C 100)
Barlow's La. Sth. SK7: H Gro 2C 158
Barlow St. M26: Rad 4B 52
M28: Walk 5H 65
M30: Ecc 4F 97
OL4: O'ham 3G 75
OL10: H'ood 5A 40
OL16: Roch 3D 178
Barlow Ter. M21: Chor 3A 130
Barlow Wlk. SK5: Stoc 1H 133
(off Barlow La. Nth.)
Barlow Wood Dr. SK6: Mar 2F 161
Barmeadow SK13: Dob 5B 62
Barmhouse Cl. SK14: Hyde 4E 121
Barmhouse La. SK14: Hyde 4E 121
(Rowanswood Dr.)
SK14: Hyde 4E 121
(Sheffield Rd., not continuous)
Barmhouse M. SK14: Hyde 4E 121
Barmouth St. M11: Man 5B 102
Barmouth Wlk. OL8: O'ham 1B 90
Barnaby Rd. SK12: Poy 5D 168
Barnacre Av. BL2: Bolt 6B 34
M23: Wyth 2F 153
Barnard Av. M45: White 2H 69
SK4: Stoc 1D 144
Barnard Cl. OL7: A Lyme 6F 91
Barnard Rd. M18: Man 4D 116
Barnard St. BL2: Bolt 5G 33
Barnbrook St. BL9: Bury 2G 37
Barnby St. M12: Man 4C 116
Barn Cl. M41: Urm 5G 109
Barnclose Rd. M22: Wyth 4B 154
Barn Ct. BL2: Bolt 3G 33
Barncroft Dr. BL6: Hor 2A 30
Barncroft Gdns. M22: Wyth 6A 142
Barncroft Rd. BL4: Farn 1H 65
Barnes Av. SK4: Stoc 1C 144
Barnes Cl. BL0: Ram 6A 12
BL4: Farn 1H 65
Barnes Dr. BL4: Farn 6D 48
BARNES GREEN 2H 87
Barnes Ho. BL4: Farn 1H 65
(off Hesketh Wlk.)
Barnes Mdws. OL15: L'ough 2A 16
Barnes St. BL4: Farn 1F 65
Barnes Ter. BL4: Kea 2C 66
Barneswell St. M40: Man 6E 89
Barnet Rd. BL1: Bolt 3A 32

Barnett Av. M20: Man 3F 131
Barnett Ct. OL10: H'ood 4G 39
Barnett Dr. M3: Sal 3D 4 (3B 100)
Barnfield M41: Urm 6D 110
Barnfield Av. SK6: Rom 6B 136
Barnfield Cl. BL7: Eger 1C 18
M5: Sal 4F 99
M26: Rad 4G 51
Barnfield Cres. M33: Sale 4H 127
Barnfield Dr. BL5: W'ton 6A 46
M28: Wors 5F 81
Barnfield Ho. M3: Sal 4G 5
Barnfield Ri. OL2: Shaw 4G 43
Barnfield Rd. M19: Man 5A 132
M27: Ward 1F 83
SK14: Hyde 2F 121
Barnfield Rd. E. SK3: Stoc 1H 157
Barnfield Rd. W. SK3: Stoc 1F 157
Barnfield St. M34: Dent 3D 118
OL10: H'ood 3A 40
OL12: Roch 1H 27
Barnfield Wlk. WA15: Tim 6C 140
(off Merefield Rd.)
Barn Fold OL4: Lees 4C 76
Barngate Dr. OL5: Mos 3G 93
Barngate Rd. SK8: Gat 5E 143
Barn Gro. M34: Aud 6E 105
Barnham Wlk. M23: Wyth 3E 141
Barnhill Av. M25: Pres 1H 85
Barnhill Dr. M25: Pres 1H 85
Barnhill Rd. M25: Pres 6H 69
Barnhill St. M14: Man 3D 114
Barnley Cl. M44: Irl 4F 109
Barnsdale Cl. BL2: Ain 4E 35
Barnsdale Dr. M8: Man 5E 87
Barnsfold Av. M14: Man 1G 131
Barnsfold Rd. SK6: Mar 2D 160
Barnside OL12: Whitw 1E 15
Barnside Av. M28: Walk 1A 82
Barnside Cl. BL9: Bury 3E 23
Barnside Way M35: Fail 5C 90
Barnsley St. SK1: Stoc 3B 146
Barns Pl. WA15: Haleb 5C 152
Barnstaple Dr. M40: Man 5G 87
Barnstead Av. M20: Man 4H 131
Barnston Av. M14: Man 5F 115
Barnston Cl. BL1: Bolt 1D 32
Barn St. BL1: Bolt 4E 175 (6C 32)
M26: Rad 3C 52
M45: White 2C 68
OL1: O'ham 4F 177 (3E 75)
Barnview Dr. M44: Irl 6D 108
Barn Wlk. M11: Man 6G 103
Barnway Wlk. M40: Man 1E 89
Barnwell Cl. M34: Aud 2E 119
Barnwood Cl. BL1: Bolt 4C 32
(off Barnwood Dr.)
Barnwood Dr. BL1: Bolt 4C 32
Barnwood Rd. M23: Wyth 2G 153
Barnwood Ter. BL1: Bolt 4C 32
(off Faraday Dr.)
Baroness Gro. M7: Sal 1A 100
Baron Fold M38: Lit H 4E 65
Baron Fold Cres. M38: Lit H 4D 64
Baron Fold Gro. M38: Lit H 4D 64
Baron Fold Rd. M38: Lit H 4D 64
(off Manchester Rd. W.)
Baron Grn. SK8: H Grn 6H 155
Baron Rd. SK14: Hyde 2D 136
Barons Ct. M35: Fail 5F 89
SK9: Wilm 3E 173
(off Swan St.)
Baron St. BL9: Bury 4D 36
(not continuous)
OL4: O'ham 5H 75
OL16: Roch 4C 178 (4H 27)
Baron Wlk. BL3: Lit L 4E 51
BARRACK HILL 1G 147
Barrack Hill SK6: Rom 1G 147
Barrack Hill Cl. SK6: Bred 6G 135
Barracks La. M33: Sale 3F 127
(off Banky La.)
Barrack St. M15: Man 4C 8 (6B 100)

Barra Dr. M41: Urm 2F **111**
Barrass St. M11: Man 6F **103**
Barratt Gdns. M24: Mid 4H **55**
Barrett Av. BL4: Kea 2B **66**
Barrett Cl. BL9: Bury 3G **37**
Barrett St. OL4: O'ham 4H **75**
Barrfield Rd. M6: Sal 1E **99**
Barr Hill Av. M6: Sal 6E **85**
Barrhill Cl. M15: Man 5E **9** (1C **114**)
Barrie Way BL1: Bolt 1F **33**
Barrington Av. M43: Droy 4H **103**
  SK8: Chea H 4C **156**
Barrington Cl. WA14: Alt 5F **139**
Barrington Rd. WA14: Alt 1B **174** (5F **139**)
Barrington St. M11: Man 3E **103**
Barrisdale Cl. BL3: Bolt 2F **47**
BARROW BRIDGE 1F **31**
Barrow Bri. BL1: Bolt 1F **31**
Barrowdene Ho. BL1: Bolt 1F **31**
  (off Bazley St.)
Barrowfield Rd. M22: Wyth 3G **153**
Barrowfields M24: Mid 5C **56**
Barrowfield Wlk. M24: Mid 6C **56**
Barrow Hill Rd. M8: Man 6D **86**
Barrow La. WA15: Hale 6B **152**
Barrow Mdw. SK8: Chea H 5A **156**
Barrows Ct. BL1: Bolt 5F **175** (1D **48**)
Barrowshaw Cl. M28: Walk 1G **81**
Barrow St. M3: Sal 5C **4** (4B **100**)
Barrule Av. SK7: H Gro 4E **159**
Barry Cl. M20: Man 3F **131**
Barry Cres. M28: Walk 6E **65**
Barry Lawson Cl. M8: Man 4D **86**
Barry Ri. WA14: Bow 3C **150**
Barry Rd. M23: Wyth 1H **141**
  SK5: Stoc 4H **133**
Barry St. OL1: O'ham 1H **75**
Barsham Dr. BL3: Bolt 2B **48**
Bar Ter. OL12: Whitw 2E **15**
Bartlam Pl. OL1: O'ham 3H **177**
Bartlemore St. OL1: O'ham 6G **59**
Bartlett Rd. OL2: Shaw 1G **59**
Bartlett St. M11: Man 6D **102**
Bartley Rd. M22: Nor 3A **142**
BARTON 5C **96**
Barton Aerodrome Vis. Cen. 6A **96**
Barton Arc. M3: Man 5H **5**
Barton Av. M41: Urm 5D **110**
Barton Bri. M30: Ecc 5F **97**
Barton Bus. Pk. M30: Ecc 4E **97**
Barton Cl. SK9: Wilm 5H **165**
Barton Ct. *M30: Ecc* *5F **97***
  (off Barton La.)
Barton Dock Rd. M32: Stre 1F **111**
  M41: Stre, Urm 1F **111**
Barton Emb. M30: Urm 6E **97**
Barton Fold SK14: Hyde 6B **120**
Barton Hall Av. M30: Ecc 4C **96**
Barton Ho. *M6: Sal* *1C **98***
  (off Moss Mdw. Rd.)
Barton La. M30: Ecc 5F **97**
Barton Moss Rd. M30: Ecc 1H **109**
Barton Pl. M4: Man 1A **6**
Barton Rd. BL4: Farn 2F **65**
  M24: Mid 1B **72**
  M27: Swin 4A **84**
  M28: Wors 6B **82**
  M30: Ecc 4E **97**
  M32: Stre 3H **111**
  M41: Urm 3E **111**
  SK4: Stoc 2A **144**
  SK16: Duk 1A **120**
Barton Sq. M2: Man 5G **5** (4D **100**)
Barton St. BL4: Farn 2A **66**
  M3: Man 2F **9** (5C **100**)
  OL1: O'ham 1D **74**
Barton Ter. M44: Irl 4G **109**
BARTON UPON IRWELL 5F **97**
Barton Wlk. BL4: Farn 2F **65**
Barway Rd. M21: Chor 6F **113**
Barwell Cl. SK5: Stoc 1H **133**
Barwell Rd. M33: Sale 4G **127**
Barwell Sq. BL4: Farn 5F **49**

Barwick Pl. M33: Sale 5A **128**
Barwood Lea BL0: Ram 4C **12**
Barwood Lea Mill BL0: Ram 3B **12**
Basechurch Wlk. *M12: Man* *1B **116***
  (off Skarratt Cl.)
Basford Rd. M16: Old T 4H **113**
Bashall St. BL1: Bolt 5A **32**
Basil Cl. OL16: Roch 5B **28**
Basildon Rd. M13: Man 2H **115**
Basil St. BL3: Bolt 2C **48**
  M14: Man 4G **115**
  OL16: Roch 5B **28**
  SK4: Stoc 6G **133**
Basle Cl. SK7: Bram 1G **157**
Baslow Av. M19: Man 5E **117**
Baslow Cl. SK13: Gam 6G **123**
Baslow Dr. SK7: H Gro 5F **159**
  SK8: H Grn 6G **155**
Baslow Fold *SK13: Gam* *6G **123***
  (off Castleton Cres.)
Baslow Grn. *SK13: Gam* *6G **123***
  (off Castleton Cres.)
Baslow Gro. SK5: Stoc 4H **133**
Baslow M. SK13: Gam 6G **123**
Baslow Rd. M32: Stre 4A **112**
  M34: Dent 1F **135**
  M43: Droy 6G **103**
Baslow St. SK1: Stoc 1A **146**
Baslow Way *SK13: Gam* *6G **123***
  (off Castleton Cres.)
Bassenthwaite Cl. M24: Mid 4H **55**
Basset Av. M6: Sal 6A **86**
Bassett Cl. OL12: Roch 6G **15**
Bassett Gdns. OL12: Roch 6G **15**
Bassett Way OL12: Roch 1G **27**
Bass La. BL9: Sum 6D **12**
Bass St. *BL2: Bolt* *6G **33***
  (off Dunstan St.)
  SK16: Duk 5H **105**
Basten Dr. M7: Sal 5C **86**
Batchelor Cl. M21: Chor 2C **130**
Bates Cl. OL11: Roch 4F **41**
Bateson Dr. OL4: Spri 3D **76**
Bateson St. SK1: Stoc 1H **145**
Bateson Way OL8: O'ham . . .6G **177** (4F **75**)
Bates St. M13: Man 3B **116**
  SK16: Duk 5A **106**
Bath Cl. SK7: H Gro 3G **159**
Bath Cres. M16: Old T 2A **114**
  SK8: Chea H 1D **166**
Bath Pl. WA14: Alt 3F **151**
Bath St. BL1: Bolt 2F **175** (5D **32**)
  OL9: Chad 2B **74**
  OL9: O'ham 4C **74**
  OL12: Roch 2A **28**
  WA14: Alt 3F **151**
Batley St. M9: Man 3A **88**
  OL5: Mos *2F **93***
  (off Seel St.)
Batsmans Dr. M27: Clif 5G **67**
Battenberg Rd. BL1: Bolt 5A **32**
Battersbay Gro. SK7: H Gro 3E **159**
Battersby Cl. SK2: Stoc 5E **147**
Battersby St. BL9: Bury 2B **38**
  M11: Man 6G **103**
  OL11: Roch 5D **26**
Battersea Rd. SK4: Stoc 2A **144**
Battey La. SK9: Wilm 3A **172**
Batty St. M8: Man 6G **87**
Baum, The OL16: Roch 2B **178** (3H **27**)
Baxendale St. BL1: Bolt 1C **32**
Baxter Gdns. M23: Wyth 4G **141**
Baxter Pk. Tennis Club 6D **142**
Baxter Rd. M33: Sale 5B **128**
Baxter St. OL8: O'ham 1B **90**
Baybutt St. M26: Rad 4C **52**
Baycliffe Wlk. *M8: Man* *5D **86***
  (off Felthorpe Dr.)
Baycroft Gro. M23: Wyth 2G **141**
Baydon Av. M7: Sal 5D **86**
Bayfield Gro. M40: Man 2C **88**
Bayley Cl. SK14: Hyde 2C **120**
Bayley Ct. BL1: Bolt 5B **32**

Bayleyfield SK14: Hyde 3B **120**
Bayley Ind. Est. SK15: Stal 4D **106**
Bayley St. SK15: Stal 3C **106**
Baynard Wlk. *M9: Man* *5F **71***
  (off Crab La.)
Baysdale Av. BL3: Bolt 3F **47**
Baysdale Dr. OL2: O'ham 2C **58**
Baysdale Wlk. M11: Man 4B **102**
Bayston Wlk. *M12: Man* *1B **116***
  (off Kempley Cl.)
Bay St. OL9: O'ham 2D **74**
  OL10: H'ood 2F **39**
  OL12: Roch 2A **28**
Bayswater Av. M40: Man 1E **103**
Bayswater St. BL3: Bolt 5A **48**
Baythorpe St. BL1: Bolt 2D **32**
Bay Tree Av. M28: Wors 6C **82**
Baytree Av. M34: Dent 3G **119**
  OL9: Chad 1G **73**
Baytree Dr. SK6: Bred 5F **135**
Baytree Gro. BL0: Ram 1B **22**
Baytree La. M24: Mid 1F **73**
Baytree Wlk. OL12: Whitw 4A **14**
Baywood St. M9: Man 3H **87**
Bazaar St. M6: Sal 1G **99**
Bazley Rd. M22: Nor 2B **142**
Bazley St. BL1: Bolt 1F **31**
BBC Broadcasting House . . .3B **10** (6E **101**)
Beacomfold SK6: Comp 6F **137**
Beacon Dr. M23: Wyth 3G **153**
Beaconfield Av. SK14: Hyde 5C **120**
Beacon Gro. OL8: O'ham 5A **76**
Beacon Rd. M17: T Pk 6G **97**
  SK6: Rom 2G **147**
Beaconsfield M14: Man 2G **131**
Beaconsfield Rd. WA14: B'ath 4F **139**
Beaconsfield St. BL3: Bolt 1B **48**
Beaconsfield Ter. SK15: C'ook 4B **94**
Beacon Vw. SK6: Mar 3D **148**
Beadham Dr. M9: Man 4E **71**
Beadle Av. OL12: Roch 4D **16**
Beaford Rd. M22: Wyth 5B **154**
Beagle Wlk. M22: Wyth 5C **154**
Bealbank Cl. OL16: Miln 2G **43**
Beal Cl. SK4: Stoc 6H **131**
Beal Cres. OL16: Roch 2C **28**
  (not continuous)
Bealcroft Cl. OL16: Miln 4E **29**
Bealcroft Wlk. OL16: Miln 4E **29**
Beale Gro. M21: Chor 1H **129**
Bealey Av. M26: Rad 2E **53**
  M26: Rad 3D **52**
Bealey Cl. M18: Man 2D **116**
Bealey Dr. BL9: Bury 6D **36**
Bealey Ind. Est. M26: Rad 2D **52**
Bealey Row M26: Rad 3C **52**
Beal La. OL2: Shaw 1H **59**
Beal Ter. OL16: Miln 5F **29**
Beal Vw. OL2: Shaw 6B **44**
Beal Wlk. M45: White 1A **70**
Beaminster Av. SK4: Stoc 6B **132**
Beaminster Cl. SK4: Stoc 6B **132**
Beaminster Dr. *SK4: Stoc* *6B **132***
  (off Priestnall Rd.)
Beaminster Rd. SK4: Stoc 6B **132**
Beaminster Wlk. *M13: Man* 2G **115**
  (off Lauderdale Cres.)
Beamish Cl. M13: Man 5E **11** (1G **115**)
Beamsley Dr. M22: Wyth 3H **153**
Beanfields M28: Wors 6B **82**
Beanfield Ter. M28: Wors 6B **82**
Bean Leach Av. SK2: Stoc 5F **147**
Bean Leach Dr. SK2: Stoc 5F **147**
Bean Leach Rd. SK2: Stoc 1E **159**
  SK7: H Gro 1E **159**
Beard Rd. M18: Man 3E **117**
Beard St. M43: Droy 4H **103**
  OL2: O'ham 4E **59**
Beardwood Rd. M9: Man 5H **71**
Bearswood Cl. SK14: Hyde 6D **120**
Beathwaite Dr. SK7: Bram 4E **157**
Beatrice Av. M18: Man 3H **117**
  SK8: Chea H 3B **156**

Beatrice Rd. BL1: Bolt 5A **32**
  M28: Wors 4D **82**
Beatrice St. BL4: Farn 1G **65**
  M27: Swin 2F **83**
  M34: Dent 4E **119**
  OL11: Roch 4F **27**
Beatrice Wignall St.
  M43: Droy 5A **104**
Beatrix Dr. SK13: Had 4G **123**
Beattock Cl. M15: Man 4D **8** (4B **100**)
Beauchamp St.
  OL6: A Lyme 4D **174** (1A **106**)
Beaufont Dr. OL4: O'ham 4A **76**
Beaufort Av. M20: Man 4E **131**
  M27: Swin 4F **83**
  M33: Sale 6C **128**
Beaufort Chase SK9: Wilm 6B **166**
Beaufort Cl. SK9: A Edg 4H **173**
  SK14: Hat 5A **122**
Beaufort Rd. M33: Sale 6C **128**
  OL6: A Lyme 2B **106**
  SK2: Stoc 1D **158**
  SK14: Hat 5A **122**
Beaufort St. M3: Man 2E **9** (5C **100**)
  M25: Pres 5A **70**
  M30: Ecc 2D **96**
  OL12: Roch 2E **27**
Beaufort Way SK14: Hat 6A **122**
             (off Beaufort Rd.)
Beaulieu WA15: Hale 3H **151**
Beauly Cl. BL0: Ram 1A **22**
Beaumaris Cl. M12: Man 1B **116**
Beaumaris Cres. SK7: H Gro 5C **158**
Beaumonds Way
  OL11: Roch 5C **26**
Beaumont Chase BL3: Bolt 4F **47**
Beaumont Cl. OL15: L'ough 4F **17**
Beaumont Ct. BL1: Bolt 5D **30**
  SK9: Hand 2G **165**
              (off Clay La.)
Beaumont Dr. BL3: Bolt 2E **47**
Beaumont Pl. SK15: Stal 1D **106**
Beaumont Rd. BL1: Bolt 6D **30**
  BL3: Bolt 6D **30**
  BL6: Los 6D **30**
  M21: Chor 2H **129**
Beaumont St. OL6: A Lyme 2A **106**
Beauvale Av. SK2: Stoc 4C **146**
Beaver Dr. BL9: Bury 3H **53**
Beaver Ho. SK1: Stoc 3B **146**
Beaver St. M1: Man 2A **10** (5E **101**)
Beaver Wlk. SK14: Hat 6H **121**
Bebbington Cl. M33: Sale 6F **129**
Bebbington St. M11: Man 4E **103**
Beccles Rd. M33: Sale 2B **140**
Beckenham Cl. BL8: Bury 4B **36**
Beckenham Rd. M8: Man 4E **87**
Becket Av. M7: Sal 5C **86**
Becket Mdws. OL4: O'ham 3H **75**
Becket Mdw. St.
  OL4: O'ham 3H **75**
  OL4: Lees 2C **76**
Beckfield Rd. M23: Wyth 6G **141**
Beckfoot Dr. M13: Man 4A **116**
Beckford St. M40: Man 6A **88**
Beck Gro. M28: Walk 2A **82**
  OL2: Shaw 5B **44**
Beckhampton Cl.
  M13: Man 6F **11** (2G **115**)
Beck Ho. SK14: Hat 6H **121**
Beckley Av. M25: Pres 1G **85**
Beckley Cl. OL2: O'ham 2H **59**
Beckside SK5: Stoc 6A **118**
Beck St. M11: Man 6G **103**
Beckton Gdns. M22: Wyth 2A **154**
Becontree Av. M34: Dent 3G **119**
Becontree Dr. M23: Wyth 4D **140**
Bedells La. SK9: Wilm 3D **172**
Bede St. BL1: Bolt 3A **32**
Bedfont Wlk. M9: Man 2A **88**
           (off Hemsley St. Sth.)

Bedford Av. M16: W Ran 5B **114**
  M27: Swin 4G **83**
  M28: Wors 2G **81**
  M33: Sale 1D **140**
  OL2: Shaw 6F **43**
  SK14: Hyde 4C **120**
Bedford Ct. M7: Sal 2B **86**
  WA15: Tim 5C **140**
Bedford Dr. WA15: Tim 4C **140**
Bedford Gro. M44: Cad 3A **124**
Bedford M. M16: Old T 4G **113**
  M30: Ecc 2G **97**
  M41: Urm 3E **111**
Bedfordshire Cl. OL9: Chad 4B **74**
Bedford St. BL1: Bolt 5B **32**
  BL7: Eger 1B **18**
  BL9: Bury 1G **37**
  M25: Pres 4A **70**
  OL6: A Lyme 3A **106**
  OL10: H'ood 3A **40**
  SK5: Stoc 1G **133**
            (not continuous)
Bedford Wlk. M34: Dent 5F **119**
Bedlington Cl. M23: Wyth 5E **141**
Bednal Av. M40: Man 1A **102**
Bedwell St. M16: W Ran 4D **114**
Bedworth Cl. BL2: Bolt 2F **49**
Beechacre BL0: Ram 4D **12**
Beech Av. BL3: Lit L 5D **50**
  BL4: Farn 1E **65**
  BL4: Kea 4D **66**
  M6: Sal .1E **99**
  M22: Nor 3B **142**
  M26: Rad 1H **67**
  M28: Wors 5E **81**
  M32: Stre 6E **113**
  M34: Dent 3D **118**
  M41: Urm 5E **111**
  M43: Droy 4H **103**
  M44: Irl .4G **109**
  M45: White 2F **69**
  OL1: Chad 5A **58**
  OL3: G'fld 3D **78**
  OL4: O'ham 1B **76**
  SK3: Stoc 5H **145**
  SK6: Mar 5B **148**
  SK7: H Gro 3E **159**
  SK8: Gat 1F **155**
  SK13: Glos 6H **123**
  WA15: Tim 3B **140**
Beech Cl. BL2: Bolt 5G **19**
  M25: Pres 6A **70**
  M31: Part 6D **124**
  OL12: Whitw 4A **14**
  SK9: A Edg 6E **173**
Beech Cotts. SK9: A Edg 6G **173**
Beech Ct. M6: Sal 2G **99**
  M8: Man 2D **86**
  M14: Man 1G **131**
  M21: Chor 6F **113**
  M33: Sale 5H **127**
  SK9: Wilm 3G **173**
Beech Cres. SK12: Poy 3E **169**
Beechcroft M25: Pres 6A **70**
Beechcroft Av. BL2: Bolt 1A **50**
Beechcroft Cl.
  M40: Man 2G **7** (2H **101**)
Beechcroft Gro. BL2: Bolt 1A **50**
Beechdale Cl. M40: Man 3E **89**
Beecher Wlk. M9: Man 5H **87**
          (off Kelvington Dr.)
Beeches, The BL1: Bolt 5B **18**
  M20: Man 5D **130**
  M30: Ecc 2H **97**
  OL5: Mos 2A **94**
  OL6: A Lyme 3B **106**
          (off Crawford M.)
  OL10: H'ood 3G **39**
  OL12: Whitw 4A **14**
  SK6: Rom 1H **147**
  SK8: Chea H 4D **156**
  WA14: Bow 3E **161**
Beeches End SK14: Hyde 1E **121**

Beechfield OL4: Gras 4H **77**
  OL11: Roch 5A **26**
  SK9: Wilm 3D **172**
           (off Albert Rd.)
  WA14: Alt 2E **151**
Beechfield Av. M26: Rad 6C **52**
  M38: Lit H 4E **65**
  M41: Urm 4C **110**
  SK9: Wilm 4B **172**
Beechfield Cl. M33: Sale 1H **139**
  OL4: Spri 3D **76**
  OL11: Roch 5A **26**
Beechfield Ct. BL9: Bury 6E **37**
Beechfield Dr. BL9: Bury 6E **37**
Beechfield M. SK14: Hyde 4E **121**
Beechfield Rd. BL1: Bolt 3H **31**
  M27: Swin 6G **83**
  OL16: Miln 6E **29**
  SK3: Stoc 1H **157**
  SK8: Chea H 5D **156**
  SK9: A Edg 6G **173**
  SK13: Had 4G **123**
Beechfield St. M8: Man 5E **87**
Beech Gro. BL8: G'mount 2A **22**
  M6: Sal .1E **99**
  M14: Man 2H **131**
  M33: Sale 5H **127**
  M38: Lit H 4C **64**
  OL7: A Lyme 4F **105**
  SK9: Wilm 3D **172**
  SK15: Stal 5D **106**
Beech Gro. Cl. BL9: Bury 1H **37**
Beech Hill Rd. OL4: Gras 3H **77**
Beech Holme Gro. SK2: Stoc 3C **146**
Beech Ho. BL5: W'ton 4A **46**
  M20: Man 5C **130**
  M22: Shar 5C **142**
          (off Lauriston Cl.)
  M30: Ecc 4D **96**
           (off New La.)
  OL2: Shaw 2H **59**
Beech Ho. Gdns. WA15: Tim 3A **140**
Beech Hurst Cl. M16: W Ran 5B **114**
Beechlands WA14: Alt 2D **150**
Beech La. OL4: Gras 4H **77**
  SK6: Rom 1A **148**
  SK9: Wilm 3D **172**
Beech Lawn WA14: Alt 1E **151**
Beech M. M21: Chor 1G **129**
  SK2: Stoc 6A **146**
Beech Mt. M9: Man 3H **87**
  OL7: A Lyme 5G **91**
Beechpark Av. M22: Nor 4A **142**
Beech Range M19: Man 6C **116**
Beech Rd. M21: Chor 1G **129**
  M33: Sale 5D **128**
  SK2: Stoc 5H **145**
  SK3: Stoc 5G **145**
  SK6: H Lan 6D **160**
  SK8: Chea H 4D **156**
  SK9: A Edg 6E **173**
  WA15: Hale 2G **151**
Beech St. BL1: Bolt 3D **32**
  BL9: Bury 3H **37**
  BL9: Sum 6C **12**
  M24: Mid 1B **72**
  M26: Rad 6C **52**
  M27: Swin 4H **83**
  M30: Ecc 4D **96**
  M35: Fail 3G **89**
  OL1: O'ham 2G **75**
  OL11: Roch 5F **27**
  OL16: Miln 1H **43**
  SK14: Hyde 4B **120**
           (off John St.)
Beech Tree Bank M25: Pres 5G **69**
Beechurst Rd. SK8: Chea H 6D **144**
Beech Vw. SK14: Hyde 5E **121**
Beech Vs. M33: Sale 5D **128**
          (off Carlyn Av.)
Beechville BL6: Los 6A **30**
Beech Wlk. M24: Mid 3B **72**
  M32: Stre 6C **112**

Beechway SK6: H Lan 6D 160
SK9: Wilm 4D 172
Beechwood BL9: Bury 1G 53
OL2: Shaw 5B 44
WA14: Bow 4D 150
Beechwood Av. BL0: Ram 3D 12
M21: Chor 2A 130
M41: Urm 4A 110
OL15: L'ough 6G 17
SK5: Stoc 5H 133
SK6: Rom 1A 148
SK15: H'rod 1G 107
Beechwood Ct. BL8: Tot 6A 22
M20: Man 6E 131
M25: Pres 6B 70
Beechwood Dr. M28: Wors 5D 82
M33: Sale 5E 127
OL2: O'ham 1C 58
OL5: Mos 1G 93
SK6: Mar 5E 149
SK9: Wilm 1H 173
SK14: Hyde 6D 120
Beechwood Gdns. M14: Man .1H 131
(off Ladybarn La.)
Beechwood Gro. M9: Man 4A 88
SK8: Chea H 5C 156
Beechwood La. SK15: H'rod 1G 107
Beechwood Rd. M25: Pres 6B 70
OL8: O'ham 1F 91
Beechwood St. BL3: Bolt 4D 48
Beechy Sq. OL1: O'ham 2G 75
(off Egerton St.)
Beede St. M11: Man 5D 102
Beedon Av. BL3: Lit L 3C 50
Beehive Grn. BL5: W'ton 6B 46
Beehive St. OL8: O'ham 6F 75
Beeley St. M6: Sal 6H 85
SK14: Hyde 5C 120
Beenham Cl. M33: Sale 6E 127
Beesley Grn. M28: Wors 3B 82
Beeston Av. M7: Sal 5H 85
WA15: Tim 5H 139
Beeston Cl. BL1: Bolt 5E 19
Beeston Gro. M45: White 2H 69
SK3: Stoc 6G 145
Beeston Rd. M33: Sale 5G 127
SK9: Hand 2H 165
Beeston St. M9: Man 3A 88
Beetham Twr. M3: Man 2F 9
Beeth St. M11: Man 6F 103
Beever St. M16: Old T 2A 114
OL1: O'ham 3H 177 (2G 75)
Begley Cl. SK6: Rom 2F 147
Begonia Av. BL4: Farn 6F 49
Begonia Wlk. M12: Man 1B 116
(off Clowes St.)
Beightons Wlk. OL12: Roch 5F 15
Belayse Cl. BL1: Bolt 2H 31
Belbeck St. BL8: Bury 3C 36
Belbeck St. Sth. BL8: Bury 3C 36
Belcroft Cl. M22: Nor 3C 142
Belcroft Dr. M38: Lit H 3C 64
Belcroft Gro. M38: Lit H 4C 64
Belding Av. M40: Man 2H 89
Beldon Rd. M9: Man 5F 71
Belfairs Cl. OL7: A Lyme 4H 91
BELFIELD .3C 28
Belfield Cl. OL16: Roch 3C 28
Belfield Ho. WA14: Bow 3E 151
Belfield La. OL16: Roch 4D 28
(Brocklebank Rd.)
OL16: Roch 4C 28
(Newbold Hall Dr.)
Belfield Lawn OL16: Roch 3D 28
Belfield Mill La. OL16: Roch 3D 28
Belfield Old Rd. OL16: Roch 3C 28
Belfield Rd. M20: Man 6F 131
M25: Pres 6C 70
OL16: Roch 3B 28
SK5: Stoc 4H 117
Belford Av. M34: Dent 4A 118
Belford Dr. BL3: Bolt 3C 48

Belford Rd. M32: Stre 4D 112
Belford Wlk. M23: Wyth 5G 141
Belfort Dr. M5: Sal 2A 8 (5H 99)
Belfry Cl. SK9: Wilm 1G 173
Belgate Cl. M12: Man 3C 116
Belgian Ter. OL2: O'ham 3F 59
Belgium St. OL11: Roch 4A 26
Belgrave Av. M14: Man 4A 116
M35: Fail 3B 90
M41: Urm 4A 110
OL8: O'ham 5G 75
SK6: Mar 5D 148
Belgrave Bungs. M26: Rad 3H 51
Belgrave Cl. M26: Rad 3A 52
Belgrave Ct. M34: Dent 3D 118
(off Belgrave St.)
OL8: O'ham 4F 75
Belgrave Cres. M30: Ecc 2H 97
SK2: Stoc 1B 158
Belgrave Dr. M26: Rad 3A 52
Belgrave Gdns. BL1: Bolt 3C 32
(off Gladstone St.)
Belgrave Ind. Est. OL8: O'ham 6G 75
Belgrave Rd. M33: Sale 5A 128
M40: Man 2G 89
M44: Cad 4B 124
OL8: O'ham 5F 75
WA14: Bow 2E 151
Belgrave St. BL1: Bolt 3C 32
(off Gladstone St.)
M26: Rad 3H 51
M34: Dent 3D 118
OL10: H'ood 4G 39
(not continuous)
OL12: Roch 2F 27
Belgrave St. Sth. BL1: Bolt 4C 32
Belgrave Ter. M40: Man 5A 88
Belgravia Gdns. M21: Chor 1G 129
WA15: Hale 5G 151
Belgravia Ho. WA14: Alt 2F 151
(off Brown St.)
Belgravia M. OL2: Shaw 6A 44
Belhaven Rd. M8: Man 1D 86
Belhill Gdns. M6: Sal 2F 99
Bellairs St. BL3: Bolt 4A 48
Bellam Ct. M27: Ward 2E 83
Bella St. BL3: Bolt 3A 48
Bell Clough Rd. M43: Droy 2B 104
Bell Cres. M11: Man 5A 102
(not continuous)
Belldale Cl. SK4: Stoc 1C 144
Belle Isle Av. OL12: Whitw 3E 15
Bellerby Cl. M45: White 1E 69
Belleville Av. M22: Wyth 5C 154
BELLE VUE 3E 117
Belle Vue Av. M12: Man 2B 116
Belle Vue Greyhound Stadium 2D 116
Belle Vue Leisure Cen. 3C 116
Belle Vue Station (Rail) 2E 117
Belle Vue St. M12: Man 1C 116
Belle Vue Ter. BL9: Bury . . .5A 176 (4E 37)
Bellew St. M11: Man 5A 102
Bellfield Av. OL8: O'ham 1F 91
SK8: Chea H 4D 156
Bellfield Cl. M9: Man 1G 87
Bellfield Vw. BL1: Bolt 2E 33
Bellingham Cl. BL8: Bury 3H 35
OL2: Shaw 5H 43
Bellis Cl. M12: Man 4A 102
Bell La. BL9: Bury 2G 37
OL16: Miln 4H 29
Bell Mdw. Dr. OL11: Roch 6B 26
Bellott St. M8: Man 5E 87
Bellott Wlk. OL1: O'ham 1E 75
(off Crompton St.)
Bellpit Cl. M28: Wors 4G 81
Bellscroft Av. M40: Man 4D 88
Bellshill Cres. OL16: Roch 2C 28
(not continuous)
Bell St. M43: Droy 3B 104
OL1: O'ham 2G 75
OL16: Roch 2B 178 (3H 27)
Bell Ter. M30: Ecc 5E 97

BELMONT .4H 173
Belmont Av. M6: Sal 2A 98
M27: Clif 4F 67
M34: Dent 3D 118
OL4: Spri 2D 76
Belmont Cl. SK4: Stoc 6G 133
Belmont Ct. SK4: Stoc 6G 133
Belmont Dr. BL8: Bury 4A 36
SK6: Mar B 2F 149
Belmont Rd. BL1: Bolt 3A 18
M26: Rad 6A 52
M33: Sale 3A 128
SK7: Bram 2G 167
SK8: Gat 5F 143
WA15: Hale 3G 151
Belmont Shop. Cen. SK4: Stoc 1G 145
Belmont St. M5: Sal 4D 98
(off Foster St.)
M16: Old T 2B 114
M30: Ecc 2F 97
OL1: O'ham 1E 177 (1E 75)
OL4: Lees 4C 76
SK4: Stoc 6F 133
Belmont Ter. M31: C'ton 3H 125
Belmont Vw. BL2: Bolt 1B 34
Belmont Wlk. M13: Man 5E 11
Belmont Way OL9: Chad 1C 74
OL12: Roch 1G 27
SK4: Stoc 1F 145
Belmore Av. M8: Man 2D 86
Belper Rd. M30: Ecc 5D 96
SK4: Stoc 2B 144
Belper St. OL6: A Lyme 1H 105
Belper Wlk. M18: Man 1E 117
(off Peacock Cl.)
Belper Way M34: Dent 1G 135
(off Heanor Av.)
Belroy Ct. M25: Pres 6H 69
Belsay Cl. OL7: A Lyme 6F 91
Belsay Dr. M23: Wyth 1G 153
Belstone Av. M23: Wyth 2G 153
Belstone Cl. SK7: Bram 3H 157
Belsyde Wlk. M9: Man 4A 88
(off Craigend Dr.)
Belthorne Av. M9: Man 1C 88
Belton Av. OL16: Roch 2C 28
Beltone Cl. M32: Stre 6B 112
Belton Wlk. M8: Man 5E 87
(off Cranlington Dr.)
OL9: O'ham 3D 74
Belvedere Av. BL8: G'mount 2A 22
SK5: Stoc 5H 117
Belvedere Ct. M25: Pres 6G 69
Belvedere Dr. SK6: Bred 6C 134
SK16: Duk 5C 106
Belvedere Gdns. SK4: Stoc 5D 132
(off Heaton Moor Rd.)
Belvedere Hgts. BL1: Bolt 6E 31
(off The Rowans)
Belvedere Ri. OL1: O'ham 4B 60
Belvedere Rd. M6: Sal 2G 99
M14: Man 1A 132
Belvedere Sq. M22: Wyth 2D 154
Belvoir Av. M19: Man 5C 116
SK7: H Gro 5E 159
Belvoir Mdws. OL16: Roch 5E 17
Belvoir St. BL2: Bolt 6G 33
OL12: Roch 2E 27
Belvor Av. M34: Aud 6E 105
Belwood Rd. M21: Chor 2H 129
Bembridge Cl. M14: Man 5G 115
Bembridge Dr. BL3: Bolt 2H 49
Bembridge Rd. M34: Dent 1H 135
Bempton Cl. SK2: Stoc 6G 147
Bemrose Av. WA14: Alt 5E 139
Benbecula Way M41: Urm 2E 111
Benbow Av. M12: Man 2B 116
Benbow St. M33: Sale 4B 128
Benbrierley Wharf M35: Fail 3H 89
Benbrook Gro. SK9: Wilm 5H 165
(off Barton Cl.)
Bench Carr OL12: Roch 2G 27

Benches La.—Betley Rd.

Benches La. SK6: Mar B 6H 137
BENCHILL 6B 142
Benchill Av. M22: Wyth 6B 142
Benchill Ct. M22: Wyth 1C 154
Benchill Ct. Rd. M22: Wyth 1C 154
Benchill Cres. M22: Wyth 6A 142
Benchill Dr. M22: Wyth 6B 142
Benchill Rd. M22: Wyth 5A 142
Bendall St. M11: Man 5G 103
Ben Davies Ct. SK6: Rom 6A 136
Bendemeer M41: Urm 4E 111
Bendix Ct. *SK14: Hyde 5C 120*
(off Mottram Rd.)
Bendix St. M4: Man 3C 6 (3F 101)
(not continuous)
Benedict Cl. *M7: Sal 6A 86*
(off Cromwell Gro.)
Benedict Dr. SK16: Duk 1B 120
Benfield Av. M40: Man 1E 89
Benfield St. OL10: H'ood 3H 39
Benfleet Cl. M12: Man 1C 116
Benfold Wlk. M24: Mid 4H 55
Bengain M7: Sal 5B 86
Bengal La. OL6: A Lyme 1A 106
(not continuous)
Bengal Sq. OL6: A Lyme 1A 106
Bengal St. M4: Man 3D 6 (3F 101)
SK3: Stoc 5E 179 (3G 145)
Benhale Wlk. *M8: Man 5E 87*
(off Tamerton Dr.)
Benham Cl. M20: Man 6G 131
Benin Wlk. *M40: Man 6E 89*
(off Marlinford Dr.)
Benja Fold SK7: Bram 1F 167
Benjamin St. OL7: A Lyme 4G 105
(not continuous)
Benjamin Wilson Ct.
M7: Sal 1D 4
Benmore Cl. OL10: H'ood 3E 39
Benmore Rd. M9: Man 5B 72
Bennett Cl. SK3: Stoc 3E 145
Bennett Dr. M7: Sal 5C 86
Bennett M. *SK14: Hyde 2B 120*
(off Harding St.)
Bennett Rd. M8: Man 2D 86
Bennett's La. BL1: Bolt 3A 32
Bennett St. M12: Man 1A 116
M26: Rad 3F 51
M32: Stre 5C 112
OL7: A Lyme 4F 105
(not continuous)
SK3: Stoc 3E 145
SK14: Holl 2F 123
SK14: Hyde 2A 120
SK15: Stal 4E 107
Benny La. M43: Droy 2C 104
Benson Cl. M7: Sal 6C 86
Benson St. BL9: Bury 4G 37
Benson Wlk. SK9: Wilm 5H 165
Ben St. M11: Man 3D 102
Bentcliffe Way M30: Ecc 4H 97
Bentfield Cres. OL16: Miln 1G 43
Bentfield Ind. Units OL9: Chad 3B 74
Bent Fold Dr. BL9: Bury 6G 53
BENTGATE 2F 43
Bentgate Cl. OL16: Miln 1G 43
Bentgate St. OL16: Miln 2G 43
Benthall Wlk. M34: Dent 1E 135
Bentham Cl. *BL4: Farn 6H 49*
(off Bentley St.)
BL8: Bury 2G 35
Bent Hill Sth. BL3: Bolt 3G 47
Bentinck Bus. Cen. OL6: A Lyme 6A 174
Bentinck Cl. WA14: Alt 3A 174 (1E 151)
Bentinck Ho.
OL6: A Lyme 6A 174 (3G 105)
Bentinck Ind. Est. M15: Man 4C 8
Bentinck Rd. WA14: Alt 1E 151
Bentinck St. BL1: Bolt 4H 31
BL4: Farn 6G 49
M15: Man 4C 8 (6B 100)
OL6: A Lyme 5A 174 (2G 105)
(not continuous)
Bentinck St.
OL7: A Lyme 6B 174 (3H 105)
OL8: O'ham 5F 75
OL12: Roch 2E 27
Bentinck Ter. OL6: A Lyme 6A 174
Bent La. M8: Man 4D 86
M25: Pres 5A 70
Bent Lanes M41: Urm 2B 110
(not continuous)
Bentley Av. M24: Mid 2F 57
Bentley Cl. M26: Rad 3D 52
Bentley Ct. BL4: Farn 6H 49
M7: Sal 3C 86
Bentley Fold BL8: Bury 1H 35
Bentley Hall Rd. BL8: Bury 1E 35
Bentley La. BL9: Bury 2F 23
Bentley M. OL12: Roch 1G 27
Bentley Rd. M7: Sal 3C 86
M21: Chor 6G 113
M34: Dent 4F 119
Bentleys, The SK5: Stoc 6H 133
Bentley St. BL2: Bolt 2G 49
BL4: Farn 6H 49
OL1: O'ham 1H 75
OL9: Chad 2B 74
OL12: Roch 1F 27
Bentmeadows OL12: Roch 2G 27
Benton Dr. SK6: Mar B 3G 149
Benton St. M9: Man 4B 88
Bents Av. M41: Urm 6B 110
SK6: Bred 6F 135
Bents Farm Cl. OL15: L'ough 4F 17
Bentside Rd. SK12: Dis 2H 171
Bent Spur Rd. BL4: Kea 4C 66
Bent St. BL4: Kea 2A 66
M8: Man 1E 101
Bent Ter. M41: Urm 3E 111
Bentworth Wlk. *M9: Man 4A 88*
(off Broadwell Dr.)
Benville Wlk. *M40: Man 5D 88*
(off Harold Priestnall Cl.)
Benwick Ter. *BL1: Bolt 3C 32*
(off Boardman St.)
Benyon St. OL4: Lees 3C 76
Berberis Wlk. M33: Sale 3E 127
Beresford Av. BL3: Bolt 2H 47
Beresford Ct. M20: Man 5E 131
SK9: A Edg 5G 173
(off Brown St.)
Beresford Cres. OL4: O'ham 1B 76
SK5: Stoc 4G 117
Beresford Rd. M13: Man 4B 116
M32: Stre 3E 113
Beresford St. M14: Man 4D 114
M35: Fail 4G 89
OL4: O'ham 1B 76
OL16: Miln 1H 43
Bergman Wlk. *M40: Man 5D 88*
(off Harmer Cl.)
Berigan Cl. M12: Man 2A 116
Berisford Cl. WA15: Tim 4G 139
Berkeley Av. M14: Man 3A 116
M32: Stre 3A 112
OL9: Chad 6H 73
Berkeley Cl. SK2: Stoc 3C 146
SK14: Hyde 6B 120
Berkeley Ct. M7: Sal 2C 86
M20: Man 6D 130
Berkeley Cres. M26: Rad 2E 51
SK14: Hyde 6B 120
Berkeley Dr. OL2: O'ham 5D 58
OL16: Roch 1B 42
Berkeley Ho. *BL1: Bolt 6A 32*
(off Westgate Av.)
Berkeley Rd. BL1: Bolt 1C 32
SK7: H Gro 2F 159
Berkeley St. OL2: O'ham 2D 58
OL6: A Lyme 5A 174 (2G 105)
Berkley Av. M19: Man 6C 116
Berkley Wlk. OL15: L'ough 4F 17
Berkshire Cl. OL9: Chad 4B 74
Berkshire Ct. BL9: Bury 6F 37
Berkshire Dr. M44: Cad 4A 124
Berkshire Pl. OL9: O'ham 4C 74
Berkshire Rd. M40: Man 1H 7 (2H 101)
Berlin Rd. SK3: Stoc 5F 145
Berlin St. BL3: Bolt 1A 48
Bermondsay St. *M5: Sal 5H 99*
(off St Joseph's Dr.)
Bernard Gro. BL1: Bolt 3A 32
Bernard St. M9: Man 3H 87
OL12: Roch 6G 15
Bernard Walker Ct. SK6: Comp 1F 149
Berne Cl. OL9: Chad 3C 74
SK7: Bram 1G 157
Bernice Av. OL9: Chad 3B 74
Bernice St. BL1: Bolt 3A 32
Berriedale Cl. M16: W Ran 5B 114
Berrie Gro. *M19: Man 1D 132*
(off Henderson St.)
Berrington Wlk. BL2: Bolt 4E 33
Berry Brow M40: Man 1F 103
OL3: G'fld 4D 78
Berry Cl. SK9: Wilm 4D 172
Berrycroft La. SK6: Rom 6G 135
Berryfield Gdns. WA14: W Tim 3F 139
Berry St. M1: Man 2D 10 (5F 101)
M27: Pen 1H 83
M30: Ecc 5D 96
OL3: G'fld 4D 78
SK15: Stal 5G 107
Bertha Rd. OL16: Roch 4C 28
Bertha St. BL1: Bolt 3B 32
M11: Man 6D 102
OL2: Shaw 2H 59
Bertie St. OL11: Roch 1F 41
Bertram St. M12: Man 1C 116
M33: Sale 5E 129
Bertrand Rd. BL1: Bolt 6A 32
Bert St. BL3: Bolt 4H 47
(not continuous)
Berwick Av. M41: Urm 5A 112
M45: White 2G 69
SK4: Stoc 6H 131
Berwick Cl. M28: Wors 4D 80
OL10: H'ood 4E 39
Berwick St. OL16: Roch 5B 28
Berwyn Av. M9: Man 4G 71
M24: Mid 1E 73
SK8: Chea H 6D 144
Berwyn Cl. OL8: O'ham 6E 75
Beryl Av. BL8: Tot 4H 21
Beryl St. BL1: Bolt 2D 32
BESOM HILL 2D 60
Besom La. SK15: Mill 2H 107
Bessemer Rd. M44: Irl 3D 124
Bessemer St. M11: Man 6E 103
Bessemer Way
OL1: O'ham 2F 177 (2E 75)
BESSES O' TH' BARN 2G 69
Besses o' th' Barn Station (Metro)
2G 69
Bessybrook Cl. BL6: Los 1C 46
Besthill Cotts. SK13: Char 6D 122
BESWICK 5B 102
Beswick Dr. M35: Fail 5A 90
Beswicke Royds St. OL16: Roch 2C 28
Beswicke St. OL12: Roch 3G 27
OL15: L'ough 4H 17
Beswick Row M4: Man 2A 6 (2E 101)
Beswicks La. SK9: A Edg 6A 172
Beswick St. M4: Man 4G 7 (3H 101)
M43: Droy 4B 104
OL2: O'ham 5E 59
Beta Av. M32: Stre 6C 112
Beta St. BL1: Bolt 1E 175 (5C 32)
Bethany La. OL16: Miln 1A 44
Bethel Av. M35: Fail 4G 89
Bethel Grn. OL15: L'ough 2A 16
Bethel St. OL10: H'ood 3G 39
Bethesda Ho. M7: Sal 3C 86
Bethesda St. OL8: O'ham 5F 75
Bethnall Dr. M14: Man 6E 115
Betjeman Pl. OL2: Shaw 6B 44
Betleymere Rd. SK8: Chea H 1B 156
Betley Rd. SK5: Stoc 6H 117

Betley St. M1: Man 1E **11** (5G **101**)
M26: Rad 3C **52**
OL10: H'ood 4G **39**
Betnor Av. SK1: Stoc 2B **146**
Betony Cl. OL12: Roch 6F **15**
Betsham St. M15: Man 2D **114**
Bettwood Dr. M8: Man 1D **86**
Betula Gro. M7: Sal 4B **86**
(off Bk. Hilton St.)
Betula M. OL11: Roch 2H **25**
Beulah St. M11: Man 6E **103**
Bevan Cl. M12: Man 6H **7** (4A **102**)
Bevendon Sq. M7: Sal 5C **86**
Beveridge St. M14: Man 4E **115**
Beverley Av. M34: Dent 5G **119**
M41: Urm 3G **111**
Beverley Cl. M45: White 6H **53**
OL6: A Lyme 5H **91**
Beverley Flats OL10: H'ood 3G **39**
(off Wilton St.)
Beverley Rd. OL16: Roch 3A **28**
BL1: Bolt 5H **31**
BL3: Lit L 4B **50**
M27: Pen 4C **84**
SK2: Stoc 3C **146**
Beverley St. M9: Man 2A **88**
Beverley Wlk. OL8: O'ham 4E **75**
SK6: Rom 2G **147**
Beverly Rd. M14: Man 2H **131**
Beverston OL11: Roch 6A **178** (5G **27**)
Beverston Dr. M7: Sal 5C **86**
Bevill Sq. M3: Sal 3E **5** (3C **100**)
BEVIS GREEN 3F **23**
Bevis Grn. BL9: Bury 3F **23**
Bewick St. BL2: Bolt 2F **33**
Bewley St. OL8: O'ham 1D **90**
Bewley Wlk. M40: Man 5C **88**
Bexhill Av. WA15: Tim 5H **139**
Bexhill Cl. BL3: Lit L 4E **51**
Bexhill Dr. M13: Man 4A **116**
Bexhill Rd. SK3: Stoc 1G **157**
Bexhill Wlk. OL9: Chad 3B **74**
Bexington Rd. M16: W Ran 4C **114**
Bexley Cl. M41: Urm 3D **110**
Bexley Dr. BL8: Bury 4B **36**
M38: Lit H 5G **65**
Bexley Ho. BL1: Bolt 4C **32**
(off Kenton Cl.)
Bexley Sq. M3: Sal 4D **4** (3B **100**)
Bexley St. OL9: O'ham 4C **74**
Bexley Wlk. M40: Man 5D **88**
(off John Foran Cl.)
Beyer Cl. M18: Man 2E **117**
Bibby La. M19: Man 3B **132**
(not continuous)
Bibby St. BL9: Bury 2F **53**
SK14: Hyde 2B **120**
Bibury Av. M22: Wyth 2H **153**
Bickerdike Av. M12: Man 4D **116**
Bickerdyke Ct. M12: Man 4D **116**
Bickershaw Dr. M28: Walk 1G **81**
(not continuous)
Bickerstaffe Cl. OL2: Shaw 1G **59**
Bickerton Ct. OL9: Chad 6B **74**
Bickerton Dr. SK7: H Gro 4A **158**
Bickerton Rd. WA14: Alt 6D **138**
Bickley Gro. M29: Ast 5A **80**
Biddall Dr. M23: Wyth 5H **141**
Biddisham Wlk. M40: Man 6H **87**
(off Thornton St. Nth.)
Biddulph Av. SK2: Stoc 6C **146**
Bideford Dr. BL2: Bolt 1C **50**
Bideford Rd. M23: Wyth 3F **141**
OL11: Roch 2D **40**
SK2: Stoc 2C **146**
Bidford Cl. M29: Tyld 2A **80**
Bidston Av. M14: Man 5F **115**
Bidston Cl. BL8: Bury 3A **36**
OL2: Shaw 1B **60**
Bidston Dr. SK9: Hand 5A **166**
Bidworth La. SK13: Gam 6F **123**
Biggin Gdns. OL10: H'ood 6A **40**
Bigginwood Wlk. M40: Man 4C **88**

Bignor St. M8: Man 5E **87**
Bilbao St. BL1: Bolt 5A **32**
Bilberry St. OL16: Roch 5A **28**
(not continuous)
Bilbrook St. M4: Man 1C **6** (2F **101**)
Billberry Cl. M45: White 1H **69**
Billing Av. M12: Man 3F **11** (6G **101**)
Billinge Cl. BL1: Bolt 1F **175** (5D **32**)
Billington Rd. M27: Pen 3E **85**
Bill La. M45: White 1F **69**
Bill Williams Cl. M11: Man 5E **103**
Billy La. M27: Clif 1H **83**
Billy Meredith Cl. M14: Man 4E **115**
Billy's La. SK8: Chea H 4C **156**
Billy Whelan Wlk. M40: Man 6E **89**
(off Tommy Taylor Cl.)
Bilsland Wlk. M40: Man 6E **89**
(off Orford Rd.)
Bilson Dr. SK3: Stoc 4D **144**
Bilson Sq. OL16: Miln 6G **29**
(off Newhey St.)
Bilton Wlk. M8: Man 3G **87**
(off Nunthorpe Dr.)
Binbrook Wlk. BL3: Bolt 3D **48**
(off Lever St.)
Bincombe Wlk. M13: Man 2G **115**
(off Carmoor Rd.)
Bindloss Av. M30: Ecc 2H **97**
Bindon Wlk. M9: Man 4H **87**
(off Carisbrook St.)
Bingham Dr. M23: Wyth 5F **141**
Bingham St. M27: Swin 3H **83**
Bingley Cl. M11: Man 5B **102**
Bingley Dr. M41: Urm 3B **110**
Bingley Rd. OL16: Roch 4C **28**
Bingley Sq. OL16: Roch 4C **28**
Bingley Ter. OL16: Roch 4C **28**
Bingley Wlk. BL4: Farn 2H **65**
M7: Sal 3F **85**
Binns Nook Rd. OL12: Roch 1A **28**
Binns Pl. M4: Man 5D **6** (4F **101**)
Binns St. SK15: Stal 4C **106**
Binn's Ter. OL15: L'ough 3H **17**
(off Lodge St.)
Binsley Cl. M44: Irl 6E **109**
Binstead Cl. M14: Man 4A **116**
Birbeck St. OL5: Mos 1G **93**
SK15: Stal 4D **106**
BIRCH 3G **55**
Birchacre Gro. M14: Man 2H **131**
Birchall Cl. SK16: Duk 6B **106**
Birchall Grn. SK6: Wood 4F **135**
Birchall Way M15: Man 6H **9** (1D **114**)
Birch Av. BL8: Tot 6A **22**
M6: Sal 1E **99**
M16: Old T 3G **113**
M24: Mid 2C **72**
M33: Sale 6B **128**
(off Hazel Av.)
M35: Fail 5H **89**
M44: Cad 4B **124**
M45: White 3F **69**
OL1: Chad 5A **58**
OL8: O'ham 1D **90**
OL12: Roch 5D **16**
SK4: Stoc 5D **132**
SK6: Rom 1B **148**
SK9: Wilm 3C **172**
Birch Cl. OL12: Whitw 3E **15**
Birch Ct. M13: Man 4A **116**
OL10: H'ood 4A **40**
(off Twin St.)
SK6: Mar 6C **148**
SK16: Duk 5B **106**
(off Birch La.)
Birch Cres. OL16: Miln 2G **43**
Birchdale WA14: Bow 3E **151**
Birchdale Av. SK8: H Grn 3F **155**
Birch Dr. M27: Pen 3B **84**
OL4: Lees 4C **76**
SK7: H Gro 3C **158**
Birchenall St. M40: Man 3B **88**
Birchen Bower Wlk. BL8: Tot 6H **21**

Birchenlea St. OL9: Chad 6A **74**
Birches, The M33: Sale 4G **127**
OL5: Mos 2F **93**
Birches End OL12: Whitw 4E **15**
Birchfield BL2: Bolt 5A **20**
OL7: A Lyme 5F **105**
Birchfield Av. BL9: Bury 4C **38**
Birchfield Dr. M28: Wors 4E **81**
OL11: Roch 6E **27**
Birchfield Gro. BL3: Bolt 3E **47**
Birchfield M. SK14: Hyde 5B **120**
Birchfield Rd. SK3: Stoc 4C **144**
Birchfields OL4: O'ham 5D **76**
WA15: Hale 1H **151**
Birchfields Av. M13: Man 4A **116**
M14: Man 4A **116**
Birchfields Rd. M13: Man 4A **116**
M14: Man 4A **116**
Birchfold M38: Lit H 5F **65**
Birchfold Cl. M38: Lit H 5F **65**
Birchgate Wlk. BL3: Bolt 2D **48**
Birch Gro. BL0: Ram 6A **12**
M14: Man 4H **115**
M25: Pres 3G **69**
M34: Aud 1F **119**
M34: Dent 4E **119**
WA15: Tim 6E **141**
Birchgrove Cl. BL3: Bolt 5G **47**
Birch Hall Cl. OL4: O'ham 5C **76**
Birch Hall La. M13: Man 5A **116**
Birch Hill Cres. OL12: Roch 5E **17**
Birch Hill La. OL12: W'le 6D **16**
Birch Hill Wlk. OL15: L'ough 4F **17**
Birch Ho. SK7: Bram 2G **167**
Birch Ind. Est. OL10: H'ood 2E **55**
Birchington Rd. M14: Man 1E **131**
Birchin La. M4: Man 5B **6** (4E **101**)
Birchinlee Av. OL2: O'ham 4B **58**
Birchin Pl. M4: Man 5B **6**
Birch La. M13: Man 4A **116**
SK16: Duk 5B **106**
(not continuous)
Birchlea WA15: Alt 1H **151**
Birch Lea BL9: Bury 6F **37**
Birchleaf Gro. M5: Sal 3C **98**
Birch Mill Bus. Cen. OL10: H'ood 2G **55**
Birch Mt. OL12: Roch 5E **17**
Birch Polygon M14: Man 4H **115**
Birch Rd. BL4: Kea 3B **66**
M8: Man 2F **87**
M24: Mid 5E **57**
M27: Swin 6F **83**
M28: Walk 2H **81**
M31: C'ton 5B **126**
M31: Part 6B **124**
OL3: Upp 2E **79**
OL12: W'le 6C **16**
SK8: Gat 6E **143**
SK12: Poy 5F **169**
WA14: D Mas 5B **126**
Birch St. BL2: Bolt 1F **49**
BL9: Bury 1C **176** (1F **37**)
M12: Man 1C **116**
M26: Rad 2E **53**
M43: Droy 5B **104**
OL7: A Lyme 4E **105**
OL10: H'ood 4H **39**
OL12: W'le 6C **16**
SK15: H'rod 6G **93**
Birch Ter. SK14: Hyde 5A **120**
Birch Tree Av. SK7: H Gro 4G **159**
Birchtree Cl. WA14: Bow 4E **151**
Birch Tree Ct. M22: Wyth 2B **154**
Birch Tree Dr. M22: Wyth 2B **154**
Birchvale Cl. M15: Man 5F **9** (1C **114**)
SK12: Poy 4E **169**
Birch Vw. OL12: Roch 5D **16**
Birch Vs. OL12: Whitw 4E **15**
Birchway SK6: H Lan 6D **160**
SK7: Bram 6F **157**
Birchwood M43: Droy 2B **104**
OL9: Chad 2G **73**

Birchwood Cl.—Blantyre Rd.

Birchwood Cl. SK4: Stoc 2C **144**
Birchwood Cres. SK14: Hyde 1E **121**
Birchwood Dr. M40: Man 5H **87**
SK9: Wilm 1G **173**
Birchwood Rd. M24: Mid 1E **73**
Birchwood Way SK16: Duk 1B **120**
Bird Hall Av. SK8: Chea H 1E **157**
Birdhall Gro. M19: Man 1C **132**
Bird Hall La. SK3: Stoc 4D **144**
Bird Hall Rd. SK8: Chea H 6D **144**
Birdlip Dr. M23: Wyth 2G **153**
Birkby Dr. M24: Mid 5A **56**
Birkdale Av. M45: White 3D **68**
OL2: O'ham 5E **59**
Birkdale Cl. OL10: H'ood 5H **39**
SK7: Bram 6A **158**
SK14: Hyde 2C **120**
Birkdale Dr. BL8: Bury 3B **36**
M33: Sale 1G **139**
Birkdale Gdns. BL3: Bolt 2B **48**
Birkdale Gro. M30: Ecc 3H **97**
SK5: Stoc 4H **133**
Birkdale Pl. M33: Sale 3H **127**
Birkdale Rd. OL16: Roch 1C **42**
SK5: Stoc 4G **133**
Birkdale St. M8: Man 4E **87**
Birkenhills Dr. BL3: Bolt 2E **47**
Birkett Cl. BL1: Bolt 5B **18**
Birkett Dr. BL1: Bolt 5B **18**
Birkinbrook Cl. M45: White 6G **53**
Birkleigh Wlk. BL2: Bolt 1A **50**
BIRKS 1D **76**
Birks Av. OL4: Lees 1D **76**
Birks Dr. BL8: Bury 5B **22**
Birkworth Ct. SK2: Stoc 5D **146**
Birley Cl. WA15: Tim 4H **139**
Birley Ct. M5: Sal 3F **99**
Birley Flds. M15: Man 6G **9** (2D **114**)
Birley Pk. M20: Man 6D **130**
Birley St. BL1: Bolt 1C **32**
BL9: Bury 6F **23**
OL12: Roch 2A **28**
Birling Dr. M23: Wyth 1H **153**
Birnam Gro. OL10: H'ood 4E **39**
Birshaw Cl. OL2: Shaw 2H **59**
Birstall Wlk. M23: Wyth 5G **141**
Birtenshaw Cres. BL7: Bro X 4F **19**
BIRTLE 5D **24**
Birtle Dr. M29: Ast 4A **80**
BIRTLE GREEN 5C **24**
Birtle Moor BL9: Bury 6C **24**
Birtle Rd. BL9: Bury 4C **24**
Birtles, The M22: Wyth 2B **154**
Birtles Av. SK5: Stoc 4H **117**
Birtles Cl. SK8: Chea 6C **144**
SK16: Duk 1A **120**
Birtlespool Rd. SK8: Chea H 1B **156**
Birtles Way *SK9: Hand* *2H* ***165***
(off Sandiway Rd.)
Birt St. M40: Man 1G **7** (1H **101**)
Birwood Rd. M8: Man 1F **87**
Biscay Cl. M11: Man 4B **102**
Bishop Cl. OL7: A Lyme 6G **91**
Bishopdale Cl. OL2: O'ham 2D **58**
Bishopgate St. OL9: Chad 3A **74**
Bishop Marshall Cl.
M40: Man 6H **87**
Bishop Marshall Way
M24: Mid 3H **55**
Bishop Rd. M6: Sal 1B **98**
M41: Urm 5H **109**
Bishopsbridge Cl. BL3: Bolt 3D **48**
Bishops Cl. BL3: Bolt 5E **49**
SK8: Chea 6C **144**
WA14: Bow 4D **150**
Bishops Cnr. *M15: Man* *6G* ***9***
(off Stretford Rd.)
Bishopscourt M7: Sal 3A **86**
Bishopsgate M2: Man 1H **9** (5D **100**)
Bishopsgate Wlk.
OL16: Roch 1C **42**
Bishops Mdw. M24: Mid 4H **55**
Bishops M. M33: Sale 3G **127**
Bishops Rd. BL3: Bolt 5E **49**
M25: Pres 6A **70**
Bishop St. M24: Mid 2F **73**
OL16: Roch 2B **28**
SK1: Stoc 2A **146**
Bishops Wlk. *OL7: A Lyme* *4G* ***105***
(off Hertford St.)
Bishopton Cl. M19: Man 6E **117**
Bisley Av. M23: Wyth 5F **141**
Bisley St. OL8: O'ham 3D **74**
Bismarck St. OL4: O'ham 4G **75**
Bispham Av. BL2: Bolt 6B **34**
SK5: Stoc 5H **117**
Bispham Cl. BL8: Bury 4H **35**
Bispham Gro. M7: Sal 4C **86**
Bispham St. BL2: Bolt 5G **33**
Bittern Cl. OL11: Roch 4B **26**
SK12: Poy 4A **168**
Bittern Dr. M43: Droy 2C **104**
Blackbank St. BL1: Bolt 3D **32**
(not continuous)
Blackberry Cl. WA14: B'ath 3D **138**
Blackberry La. SK5: Stoc 2B **134**
Black Brook Rd. SK4: Stoc 2F **133**
Blackburn Gdns. M20: Man 5E **131**
Blackburn Pl. M5: Sal 6A **4** (4A **100**)
Blackburn Rd. BL0: Eden 1G **13**
BL1: Bolt 1C **32**
BL7: Bel, Bolt 1B **18**
BL7: Eger 1C **32**
Blackburn St. M3: Sal 2C **4** (2B **100**)
M16: Old T 2A **114**
M25: Pres 5A **70**
M26: Rad 4A **52**
Blackcap Cl. M28: Wors 4F **81**
Blackcarr Rd. M23: Wyth 5H **141**
Blackchapel Dr. OL16: Roch 2B **42**
Black Clough OL2: Shaw 6B **44**
Blackcroft Cl. M27: Swin 3G **83**
Black Dad La. OL11: Roch 3E **25**
Blackden Wlk. SK9: Wilm 6H **165**
Blackdown Gro. OL8: O'ham 6E **75**
Blackett St. M12: Man 2G **11** (5H **101**)
Blackfield La. M7: Sal 3A **86**
Blackfields *M7: Sal* *3B* ***86***
(off Bury New Rd.)
Blackford Av. BL9: Bury 3F **53**
BLACKFORD BRIDGE 3E **53**
Blackford Rd. M19: Man 2D **132**
Blackford Wlk. M40: Man 1G **7**
Black Friar Ct. M3: Sal 1D **4**
Blackfriars Rd. M3: Sal 2D **4** (2B **100**)
Blackfriars St. M3: Man 3D **100**
M3: Sal 4G **5** (3D **100**)
Blackhill Cl. M13: Man 4D **10** (6F **101**)
Black Horse St. BL4: Farn 2A **66**
Blackhorse St. BL1: Bolt 4E **175** (6C **32**)
BLACK LANE 1H **51**
Blackleach Country Pk. 4H **65**
Blackleach Country Pk. Nature Reserve
. . . . 4H **65**
Blackleach Country Pk. Vis. Cen. 5H **65**
Blackleach Dr. M28: Walk 4H **65**
Blackledge St. BL3: Bolt 3A **48**
BLACKLEY 2A **88**
Blackley Cemetery & Crematorium
M9: Man 5E **71**
Blackley Cl. BL9: Bury 5G **53**
Blackley Health Studio 1H **87**
Blackley New Rd. M9: Man 6D **70**
Blackley Pk. Rd. M9: Man 2H **87**
Blackley St. M16: Old T 6B **8** (2A **114**)
M24: Mid 2F **71**
Black Lion Pas. SK1: Stoc 4H **179**
Blacklock St. M8: Man 1D **100**
Blackmore Rd. M32: Stre 2B **112**
Black Moss Cl. M26: Rad 4F **51**
Black Moss Ct. M26: Rad 3F **51**
Black Moss Rd. WA14: D Mas 4A **138**
Blackpits Rd. OL11: Roch 2H **25**
Blackpool St. M11: Man 3E **103**
Blackrock OL5: Mos 5G **93**
Blackrock St. M11: Man 4B **102**
Blackrod Dr. BL8: Bury 4H **35**
Blacksail Wlk. OL1: O'ham 6G **59**
Blackshaw Ho. BL3: Bolt 1A **48**
Blackshaw La. BL3: Bolt 1A **48**
OL2: O'ham 3F **59**
SK9: A Edg 5F **173**
Blackshaw Row *BL3: Bolt* *2A* ***48***
(off Blackshaw La.)
Blackshaw St. SK3: Stoc . . 4F **179** (3G **145**)
Blacksmith La. OL11: Roch 1D **40**
Blackstock St. M13: Man 3G **115**
Blackstone Av. OL16: Roch 3C **28**
Blackstone Ho. SK2: Stoc 6D **146**
Blackstone Rd. SK2: Stoc 6D **146**
Blackstone Wlk. *M9: Man* *5H* ***87***
(off Carisbrook St.)
Blackthorn Av. M19: Man 2C **132**
Blackthorn Cl. OL12: Roch 1G **27**
Blackthorne Cl. BL1: Bolt 4G **31**
Blackthorne Dr. M33: Sale 1F **139**
Blackthorne Rd. SK14: Hyde 3C **136**
Blackthorn M. OL12: Roch 1G **27**
Blackthorn Rd. OL8: O'ham 3D **90**
Blackthorn Wlk. *M31: Part* *6C* ***124***
(off Wood La.)
Blackwin St. M12: Man 1C **116**
Blackwood Dr. M23: Wyth 3D **140**
Blackwood St. BL3: Bolt 3E **49**
Bladen Cl. SK8: Chea H 1C **156**
Blair Av. M38: Lit H 5F **65**
M41: Urm 5A **110**
Blair Cl. M33: Sale 2E **139**
OL2: Shaw 6H **43**
SK7: H Gro 5C **158**
Blairhall Av. M40: Man 4C **88**
Blair La. BL2: Bolt 4H **33**
Blairmore Dr. BL3: Bolt 2E **47**
Blair Rd. M16: W Ran 6C **114**
Blair St. BL4: Kea 3D **66**
BL7: Bro X 3D **18**
M16: Old T 2B **114**
OL12: Roch 2F **27**
Blakedown Wlk. *M12: Man* *2A* ***116***
(off Cochrane Av.)
Blake Dr. SK2: Stoc 4E **147**
Blakefield Dr. M28: Walk 2A **82**
Blake Gdns. BL1: Bolt 3A **32**
Blakeley La. WA16: Mob 6F **163**
Blakelock St. OL2: Shaw 6H **43**
Blakemere Av. M33: Sale 6E **129**
Blakemore Wlk. M12: Man 4A **102**
Blake St. BL1: Bolt 3B **32**
BL7: Bro X 4E **19**
OL16: Roch 3A **28**
Blakeswell Cl. M41: Urm 4H **109**
Blakey Cl. BL3: Bolt 3F **47**
Blakey St. M12: Man 3C **116**
Blanchard St. M15: Man 2C **114**
Blanche St. OL12: Roch 1A **28**
Blanche Wlk. OL1: O'ham 2G **75**
Bland Cl. M35: Fail 4G **89**
Blandford Av. M28: Wors 3B **82**
Blandford Cl. BL8: Bury 6D **22**
Blandford Ct.
OL6: A Lyme 5A **174** (2G **105**)
SK15: Stal 3E **107**
Blandford Dr. M40: Man 1F **89**
Blandford Ho. SK15: Stal 3E **107**
Blandford Ri. BL6: Los 4A **30**
Blandford Rd. M6: Sal 6H **85**
M30: Ecc 3D **96**
SK4: Stoc 1D **144**
Blandford St.
OL6: A Lyme 5A **174** (2G **105**)
SK15: Stal 3E **107**
Bland Rd. M25: Pres 1H **85**
Bland St. BL9: Bury 2C **176** (2F **37**)
M16: W Ran 3C **114**
Blanefield Cl.
M21: Chor 2C **130**
Blantyre Av. M28: Walk 1A **82**
Blantyre Ho. M15: Man 3E **9**
Blantyre Rd. M27: Swin 5B **84**

202 A-Z Manchester

Blantyre St. M15: Man 3D **8** (6B **100**)
  M27: Swin 3F **83**
  M30: Ecc 2C **96**
Blanwood Dr. M8: Man 4F **87**
Blaven Cl. SK3: Stoc 6H **145**
Blaze Moss Bank SK2: Stoc 6D **146**
Bleackley St. BL8: Bury 1C **36**
Bleadale Cl. SK9: Wilm 5H **165**
Bleak Hey Rd. M22: Wyth 3D **154**
Bleakholt Rd. BL0: Ram 4H **13**
Bleakley St. M45: White 6E **53**
Bleaklow Wlk. *SK13: Gam* *6G 123*
  (off Castleton Cres.)
Bleak St. BL2: Bolt 3F **33**
Bleasby St. OL4: O'ham 2A **76**
Bleasdale Cl. BL9: Bury 4G **53**
Bleasdale Rd. BL1: Bolt 3F **31**
  M22: Wyth 3G **153**
Bleasdale St. OL2: O'ham 2D **58**
Bleasefell Chase M28: Wors 6E **81**
Bleatarn Rd. SK1: Stoc 4B **146**
Bledlow Cl. M30: Ecc 2G **97**
Blencarn Wlk. *M9: Man* *5H 87*
  (off Ravelston Dr.)
Blendworth Cl. *M8: Man* *4D 86*
  (off Broomfield Dr.)
Blenheim Av. M16: W Ran 5B **114**
  OL1: O'ham 4B **60**
Blenheim Cl. BL9: Bury 2F **53**
  OL10: H'ood 3A **40**
  SK9: Wilm 2G **173**
  SK12: Poy 3F **169**
  WA14: Bow 3F **151**
Blenheim Ct. *M9: Man* *4E 71*
  (off Deanswood Dr.)
Blenheim Rd. BL2: Bolt 6H **33**
  M16: Old T 4G **113**
  SK8: Chea H 3D **156**
Blenheim St. OL4: O'ham 6B **60**
  OL12: Roch 2E **27**
Blenheim Way OL6: A Lyme 1C **106**
Blenmar Cl. M26: Rad 2C **52**
Bleriot St. BL3: Bolt 4B **48**
Bletchley St. SK4: Stoc 2A **144**
Blethyn St. BL3: Bolt 5H **47**
Blinco Rd. M41: Urm 6H **111**
Blind La. M12: Man 3H **11** (6H **101**)
Blindsill Rd. BL4: Farn 2F **65**
Blisworth Av. M30: Ecc 5G **97**
Blisworth Cl. M4: Man 5H **7** (4H **101**)
Blithfield Wlk. M34: Dent 5E **119**
Block La. OL9: Chad 4B **74**
Blocksage St. SK16: Duk 6B **106**
Blodwell St. M6: Sal 3F **99**
Blofield Ct. *BL4: Farn* *1H 65*
  (off Mary St.)
Blomley St. OL11: Roch 3E **41**
Bloomfield Cl. SK8: Chea H 6A **156**
Bloomfield Dr. BL9: Bury 4H **53**
  M8: Sal 6C **86**
  M28: Wors 4E **81**
Bloomfield Rd. BL4: Farn 3H **65**
Bloomfield St. BL1: Bolt 2C **32**
Bloomsbury Gro. WA15: Tim 5A **140**
Bloomsbury La. WA15: Tim 5A **140**
Bloom St. BL0: Ram 5A **12**
  M1: Man 2A **10** (5E **101**)
  M3: Sal 4E **5** (3C **100**)
  OL9: O'ham 4E **177** (3E **75**)
  SK3: Stoc 3E **145**
Blossom Pl. OL16: Roch 2C **178** (3H **27**)
Blossoms Hey SK8: Chea H 4A **156**
Blossoms Hey Wlk. SK8: Chea H ...4A **156**
Blossoms La. SK7: W'ford 5C **166**
Blossoms St. SK2: Stoc 5H **145**
Blossom St. M3: Sal 3F **5**
  M4: Man 4D **6** (3F **101**)
Bloxham Wlk. M9: Man 6B **72**
Blucher St. M5: Sal 6A **4** (4A **100**)
  M12: Man 1A **116**
  OL7: A Lyme 5G **91**
Blue Bell Av. M40: Man 2C **88**
Bluebell Cl. SK14: Hyde 2D **120**

Bluebell Dr. OL11: Roch 2D **40**
Bluebell Gro. SK8: Chea 1H **155**
Bluebell Way SK9: Wilm 6G **165**
Blueberry Av. M40: Man 1E **89**
Blueberry Bus. Pk. OL16: Roch ...4D **28**
Blueberry Dr. O2: Shaw 6B **44**
Blueberry Rd. WA14: Bow 3C **150**
Blue Chip Bus. Pk. WA14: B'ath ...4E **139**
Bluefields OL2: Shaw 5B **44**
Blue Ribbon Wlk. M27: Swin 2A **84**
Bluestone Dr. SK4: Stoc 6A **132**
Bluestone Rd. M34: Dent 5A **118**
  M40: Man 3C **88**
Bluestone Ter. M34: Dent 5A **118**
Blundell Cl. BL9: Bury 4H **53**
Blundell St. BL1: Bolt 3E **175** (6C **32**)
Blundering La. SK15: Stal 1H **121**
Blunn St. OL8: O'ham 5F **75**
Blyborough Cl. M6: Sal 1E **99**
Blyth Av. M23: Wyth 1A **142**
  OL15: L'ough 6F **17**
Blyth Cl. WA15: Tim 5D **140**
Blythe Av. SK7: Bram 1E **167**
Blyton St. M15: Man 2F **115**
Blyton Way M34: Dent 1F **135**
Boad St. M1: Man 1D **10** (5E **101**)
Boardale Dr. M24: Mid 6A **56**
Boardman Cl. BL1: Bolt 3C **32**
  SK5: Stoc 5H **133**
Boardman Fold Cl. M24: Mid 4C **72**
Boardman Fold Rd. M24: Mid 4B **72**
Boardman La. M24: Mid 1F **71**
Boardman Rd. M8: Man 1D **86**
Boardman St. BL1: Bolt 3C **32**
  M30: Ecc 4G **97**
Board St. BL3: Bolt 1B **48**
  (not continuous)
  OL6: A Lyme 1B **106**
Boar Grn. Cl. M40: Man 4E **89**
Boarhurst Farm *OL3: G'fld* *4E 79*
  (off Boarhurst La.)
Boarshaw Clough M24: Mid 5D **56**
Boarshaw Clough Way M24: Mid ...5D **56**
Boarshaw Crematorium M24: Mid ...5E **57**
Boarshaw Cres. M24: Mid 5E **57**
Boarshaw La. M24: Mid 4F **57**
Boarshaw Rd. M24: Mid 6C **56**
BOARSHURST 4E **79**
Boarshurst Bus. Pk. OL3: G'fld ...3D **78**
Boarshurst La. OL3: G'fld 4D **78**
Boat La. M22: Nor 2C **142**
  M44: Irl 5F **109**
  OL3: Dig 2F **63**
Boat La. Ct. M22: Nor 2C **142**
Boatmans Row M29: Ast 6A **80**
Boatman's Wlk. OL7: A Lyme 4G **105**
Boatyard, The M32: Stre 5E **113**
Bobbin Wlk. OL4: O'ham 3G **75**
Bob Massey Cl. M11: Man 4E **103**
Bob's La. M44: Cad 5B **124**
Boddens Hill Rd. SK4: Stoc 2C **144**
Boddington Rd. M30: Ecc 4B **96**
Bodiam Rd. BL8: G'mount 2H **21**
Bodley St. M11: Man 3E **103**
Bodmin Cl. OL2: O'ham 4G **59**
Bodmin Cres. SK5: Stoc 4B **134**
Bodmin Dr. SK7: Bram 6G **157**
Bodmin Rd. M29: Ast 3A **80**
  M33: Sale 4F **127**
Bodmin Wlk. M23: Wyth 6G **141**
Bodney Wlk. M9: Man 6F **71**
Bodyline Health & Fitness Cen ...4A **128**
Body Work Gymnasium 4H **51**
B of the Bang 4B **102**
Bogart Cl. *M6: Sal* *1E 99*
  (off Monroe Cl.)
Boggart Hole Clough 1A **88**
Bognor Rd. SK3: Stoc 1G **157**
Bohemia Cotts. *SK15: Stal* *3F 107*
  (off Cocker Hill)
Bolam Cl. M23: Wyth 2F **141**
Boland Dr. M14: Man 1H **131**
Bolbury Cres. M27: Pen 3D **84**

Bolderod Pl. OL1: O'ham 1G **75**
Bolderstone Pl. SK2: Stoc 1E **159**
Bold St. BL1: Bolt 5F **175** (6D **32**)
  BL9: Bury 2G **37**
  M15: Man 2C **114**
  M16: W Ran 3C **114**
  WA14: Alt 2F **151**
Bolesworth Cl. M21: Chor 1F **129**
Boleyn Ct. OL10: H'ood 4G **39**
BOLHOLT 1A **36**
Bolholt Ind. Est. BL8: Bury 1B **36**
Bolholt Ind. Pk. BL8: Bury 1A **36**
Bolholt Ter. BL8: Bury 1B **36**
Bolivia St. M5: Sal 3C **98**
Bollen Wood Cl. SK9: Wilm 6F **165**
Bollin Av. WA14: Bow 5D **150**
Bollin Cl. BL4: Kea 3D **66**
  SK9: Wilm 1E **173**
Bollin Ct. M15: Man 6C **8**
  M33: Sale *1B 140*
  (off Bollin Dr.)
  SK9: Wilm 3F **173**
  WA14: Bow 4D **150**
Bollin Dr. M33: Sale 1B **140**
  WA14: Tim 3G **139**
Bollings Yd. BL1: Bolt 5G **175** (1D **48**)
Bollington Rd. M40: Man 3G **7** (3H **101**)
  SK4: Stoc 4F **133**
Bollington St. OL7: A Lyme 4G **105**
Bollin Hill SK9: Wilm 1D **172**
Bollin Ho. *M7: Sal* *6A 86*
  (off Victoria Lodge)
Bollin Link SK9: Wilm 2E **173**
Bollin Sq. WA14: Bow 4D **150**
Bollin Wlk. M45: White 5A **54**
  SK5: Stoc 4H **133**
  SK9: Wilm 2E **173**
Bollin Way M45: White 5A **54**
Bollinway WA15: Hale 5A **152**
Bollinwood Chase SK9: Wilm 2G **173**
Bolney Wlk. *M40: Man* *1H 101*
  (off Collyhurst St.)
Bolshaw Farm La. SK8: H Grn ...1G **165**
Bolshaw Rd. SK8: H Grn 1F **165**
Bolt Mdw. OL3: G'fld 5C **78**
BOLTON 4F **175** (6D **32**)
Bolton Av. M19: Man 1H **143**
  SK8: Chea H 1D **166**
Bolton Cl. M25: Pres 1F **85**
  SK12: Poy 3D **168**
Bolton Ent. Cen. BL3: Bolt 1A **48**
Bolton Excel Leisure Cen.
  ....6H **175** (1E **49**)
Bolton Ga. Retail Pk.
  BL1: Bolt 1G **175** (4E **33**)
Bolton Lads & Girls Club *6C 32*
  (off Spa Rd.)
Bolton Little Theatre *6C 32*
Bolton Museum, Art Gallery & Aquarium
  ....4F **175** (6D **32**)
Bolton Retail Pk. BL3: Bolt ...6F **175** (1D **48**)
Bolton Rd. BL2: Bolt 6G **19**
  BL3: Bolt 5H **49**
    (Manchester Rd.)
  BL3: Bolt 5D **46**
    (Snydale Way)
  BL4: Farn 5H **49**
  BL4: Kea 2A **66**
  BL5: W'ton 6A **46**
  BL8: Bury 5A **36**
  BL8: Haw 1D **20**
  BL9: Bury 3A **176** (5A **36**)
  M6: Sal 5C **84**
  M26: Rad 3F **51**
  M27: Pen 1H **83**
  M28: Walk 5H **65**
  OL11: Roch 1C **40**
Bolton Rd. Ind. Est. BL5: W'ton ...6A **46**
Bolton Rd. Nth. BL0: Ram 1C **12**
Bolton Rd. W. BL0: Ram 1H **21**
  BL8: Haw, Ram, Bury 1H **21**
Bolton Station (Rail) 6G **175** (1D **48**)
Bolton Steam Mus. 5A **32**

Bolton St.—Boundary Pk. Rd.

Bolton St. BL0: Ram 4B **12**
BL9: Bury 3A **176** (3E **37**)
M26: Rad 4H **51**
OL4: O'ham 3H **75**
(not continuous)
SK5: Stoc 2G **133**
Boltons Yd. OL3: Upp 1D **78**
Bolton Technology Exchange
BL1: Bolt 6B **32**
Bombay Ho. *M1: Man 5E **101***
(off Whitworth St.)
Bombay Rd. SK3: Stoc 4E **145**
Bombay Sq. M1: Man 2B **10**
Bombay St. M1: Man 2B **10** (5E **101**)
(not continuous)
OL6: A Lyme 1B **106**
Bonar Cl. SK3: Stoc 3E **145**
Bonar Rd. SK3: Stoc 3E **145**
Boncarn Dr. M23: Wyth 1G **153**
Bonchurch Wlk. M18: Man 1D **116**
Bondmark Rd. M18: Man 1E **117**
Bond St. BL0: Eden 3H **13**
BL9: Bury 3G **37**
M3: Sal 3F **5** (3C **100**)
M12: Man 2E **11** (5G **101**)
M34: Dent 4F **119**
OL12: Roch 1A **28**
SK15: Stal 2E **107**
Bond St. Ind. Est.
M12: Man 2E **11** (5G **101**)
Bongs Rd. SK2: Stoc 5F **147**
(not continuous)
Bonhill Wlk. *M11: Man 3D **102***
(off Coghlan Cl.)
Bonington Ri. SK6: Mar B 3F **149**
Bonis Cres. SK2: Stoc 1C **158**
Bonny Brow St. M24: Mid 2F **71**
Bonnyfields SK6: Rom 1H **147**
Bonsall Bank *SK13: Gam 5G **123***
(off Melandra Castle Rd.)
Bonsall Cl. *SK13: Gam 5G **123***
(off Melandra Castle Rd.)
Bonsall Fold *SK13: Gam 5G **123***
(off Rowsley Cl.)
Bonsall St. M15: Man 6G **9** (1D **114**)
Bonscale Cres. M24: Mid 4A **56**
Bonville Chase WA14: Alt 1C **150**
Bonville Rd. WA14: Alt 6C **138**
Boodle St.
OL6: A Lyme 4B **174** (2H **105**)
Bookham Wlk. *M9: Man 3A **88***
(off Swainsthorpe Dr.)
Boond St. M4: Man 5G **7** (4H **101**)
Boonfields BL7: Bro X 3E **19**
Booth Av. M14: Man 2H **131**
Booth Bri. Cl. M24: Mid 2G **71**
Boothby Ct. *M27: Swin 2F **83***
(off Boothby Rd.)
Boothby Rd. M27: Swin 2G **83**
Boothby St. SK2: Stoc 1C **158**
Booth Clibborn Ct. *M7: Sal 3B **86***
(off Park La.)
Booth Cl. BL8: Tot 6A **22**
SK15: Stal 4D **106**
Boothcote M34: Aud 1D **118**
Booth Dr. M41: Urm 2B **110**
Boothfield M30: Ecc 2C **96**
Boothfield Av. M22: Wyth 5B **142**
Boothfield Dr. M22: Wyth 5B **142**
Boothfield Rd. M22: Wyth 5A **142**
Boothfields BL8: Bury 2C **36**
Booth Hall Dr. BL8: Tot 6H **21**
Booth Hall Rd. M9: Man 6C **72**
Booth Hill La. OL1: O'ham 6E **59**
Booth Ho. Trad. Est. OL9: O'ham 3C **74**
Boothman Ct. M30: Ecc 2H **97**
Booth Rd. BL3: Lit L 5D **50**
M16: Old T 4A **114**
M33: Sale 3B **128**
M34: Aud 6A **104**
SK9: Wilm 6E **165**
WA14: Alt 1E **151**
Boothroyden Cl. M24: Mid 2G **71**
Boothroyden Rd. M9: Man 3G **71**
M24: Mid 2G **71**
Boothroyden Ter. M9: Man 3G **71**
BOOTH'S BANK 5F **81**
Boothsbank Av. M28: Wors 5F **81**
Booth's Hall Gro. M28: Wors 5F **81**
Booths Hall Paddock
M28: Wors 6F **81**
Booth's Hall Rd. M28: Wors 5F **81**
Boothshall Way M28: Wors 6E **81**
BOOTHSTOWN 6D **80**
Boothstown Dr. M28: Wors 6E **81**
Booth St. BL1: Bolt 2A **32**
BL8: Tot 5H **21**
M2: Man 6H **5** (4D **100**)
M3: Sal 4G **5** (3D **100**)
M24: Mid 3F **73**
M34: Dent 2F **119**
M35: Fail 4G **89**
OL4: Lees 3C **76**
OL6: A Lyme 6B **174** (3H **105**)
OL9: O'ham 3E **177** (3E **75**)
SK3: Stoc 6F **179** (4G **145**)
SK14: Holl 2E **123**
SK14: Hyde 6C **120**
SK15: Stal 5D **106**
Booth St. E. M13: Man 5C **10** (1F **115**)
Booth St. W. M15: Man 6A **10** (1E **115**)
Booth Way BL8: Tot 6H **21**
Boothway M30: Ecc 3H **97**
Boothwood Stile BL8: Holc 6A **12**
Boot La. BL1: Bolt 4D **30**
Bootle St. M2: Man 6G **5** (4D **100**)
Bordale Av. M9: Man 4B **88**
Bordan St. M11: Man 5B **102**
Borden Way BL9: Bury 1G **53**
Border Brook La. M28: Wors 5E **81**
Border Mill Fold OL5: Mos 2H **93**
Bordesley Av. M38: Lit H 3E **65**
Bordley Wlk. M23: Wyth 2E **141**
Bordon Rd. SK3: Stoc 4D **144**
Boringdon Cl. M40: Man 5D **88**
Borland Av. M40: Man 2F **89**
Bornmore Ind. Cen. BL8: Bury 2C **36**
Borough Arc. SK14: Hyde 4B **120**
Borough Av. M26: Rad 2D **52**
M27: Pen 2A **84**
Borough Rd. M50: Sal 4D **98**
WA15: Alt 3C **174** (1G **151**)
Borough St. SK15: Stal 4E **107**
Borrans, The M28: Wors 6D **80**
Borron St. SK1: Stoc 1A **146**
Borrowdale Av. BL1: Bolt 5G **31**
SK8: Gat 1F **155**
Borrowdale Cl. OL2: O'ham 1D **58**
Borrowdale Cres. M20: Man 5C **130**
OL7: A Lyme 6F **91**
Borrowdale Dr. BL9: Bury 4G **53**
OL11: Roch 1D **40**
Borrowdale Rd. M24: Mid 5H **55**
SK2: Stoc 4B **146**
Borrowdale Ter. *SK15: Stal 1E **107***
(off Springs La.)
Borsden St. M27: Ward 1F **83**
Borth Av. SK2: Stoc 4B **146**
Borth Wlk. M23: Wyth 5F **141**
Borwell St. M18: Man 1F **117**
Boscobel Rd. BL3: Bolt 5F **49**
Boscombe Av. M30: Ecc 5E **97**
Boscombe Dr. SK7: H Gro 3C **158**
Boscombe St. M14: Man 5F **115**
SK5: Stoc 5H **117**
Boscow Rd. BL3: Lit L 5C **50**
Bosden Av. SK7: H Gro 2E **159**
Bosden Cl. SK1: Stoc 4H **179**
SK9: Hand 2H **165**
Bosden Fold SK1: Stoc 4H **179** (3H **145**)
Bosden Fold Rd. SK7: H Gro 1E **159**
Bosden Hall Rd. SK7: H Gro 2E **159**
Bosdin Rd. E. M41: Urm 6A **110**
Bosdin Rd. W. M41: Urm 6A **110**
Boslam Wlk. M4: Man 4F **7**
Bosley Av. M20: Man 1E **131**
Bosley Cl. SK9: Wilm 5H **165**
Bosley Dr. SK12: Poy 4G **169**
Bosley Rd. SK3: Stoc 3C **144**
Bossall Av. M9: Man 5A **72**
Bossington Cl. SK2: Stoc 3C **146**
Bostock Wlk. M13: Man 4D **10**
Boston Cl. M35: Fail 2H **89**
SK7: Bram 6F **157**
Boston Ct. M50: Sal 5E **99**
Boston St. BL1: Bolt 4C **32**
M15: Man 2D **114**
OL8: O'ham 5F **75**
SK14: Hyde 5C **120**
Boston Wlk. M34: Dent 6G **119**
Boswell Av. M34: Aud 4D **104**
Boswell Way M24: Mid 3F **57**
Bosworth Cl. M45: White 1A **70**
Bosworth Sq. *OL11: Roch 1F **41***
(off Bosworth St.)
Bosworth St. M11: Man 5C **102**
OL11: Roch 1F **41**
Botanical Av. M16: Old T 2G **113**
Botanical Ho. M16: Old T 2G **113**
Botany Cl. OL10: H'ood 2F **39**
Botany La. OL6: A Lyme 1A **106**
Botany Rd. M30: Ecc 1C **96**
SK6: Wood 3G **135**
Botesworth Grn. OL16: Miln 6G **29**
Botha Cl. M11: Man 6F **103**
Botham Cl. M15: Man 2D **114**
Botham Ct. *M30: Ecc 2D **96***
(off Worsley Rd.)
Bothwell Rd. M40: Man 2E **7** (2G **101**)
Bottesford Av. M20: Man 4D **130**
Bottomfield Cl. OL1: O'ham 6G **59**
Bottomley Side M9: Man 1G **87**
BOTTOM OF WOODHOUSES 6A **90**
BOTTOM O' TH' BROW 2F **39**
BOTTOM O'TH' MOOR
BL2 2A **34**
BL6 2A **30**
Bottom o' th' Moor BL2: Ain 4D **34**
BL2: Bolt 3H **33**
BL6: Hor 2A **30**
OL1: O'ham 2G **75**
OL4: O'ham 2G **75**
BOTTOMS 2H **93**
Bottoms Fold OL5: Mos 3H **93**
Bottoms Hall Cotts. BL8: Tot 2F **21**
Bottoms Mill Rd. SK6: Mar B 6F **149**
Bottom St. SK14: Hyde 4D **120**
Boulden Dr. BL8: Bury 6C **22**
Boulder Dr. M23: Wyth 3G **153**
Boulderstone Rd. SK15: Stal 6E **93**
Boulevard, The M20: Man 3C **130**
(not continuous)
SK7: H Gro 3E **159**
SK14: Holl 2F **123**
Bouley Wlk. *M12: Man 1C **116***
(off Conquest Cl.)
Boulters Cl. M24: Mid 4B **56**
Boundary, The M27: Clif 5F **67**
Boundary Cl. OL5: Mos 5G **93**
(not continuous)
SK6: Wood 4A **136**
Boundary Cotts. SK15: C'ook 4A **94**
Boundary Ct. *M28: Wors 3F **81***
(off Morston Cl.)
SK4: Stoc 2C **132**
SK8: Chea 6G **143**
Boundary Dr. BL2: Bolt 2C **50**
Boundary Edge BL0: Eden 2H **13**
Boundary Gdns. *BL1: Bolt 3C **32***
(off Portland St.)
OL1: O'ham 6E **59**
Boundary Grn. M34: Dent 2E **119**
Boundary Gro. M33: Sale 6F **129**
Boundary Ind. Est.
BL2: Bolt 6C **34**
Boundary La. M15: Man 5A **10** (1E **115**)
Boundary Pk. 5D **58**
Boundary Pk. Rd.
OL1: O'ham 6C **58**

Boundary Rd. M23: Wyth 1F 153
   M27: Swin 2H 83
   M44: Irl 4F 109
   SK8: Chea 5B 144
Boundary St. BL1: Bolt 3B 32
   M12: Man 2C 116
   OL11: Roch 6A 178 (5G 27)
   OL15: L'ough 3G 17
Boundary St. E. M13: Man . . .4B 10 (6E 101)
Boundary St. W.
   M15: Man 5A 10 (1E 115)
Boundary Trad. Est.
   M44: Irl 4G 109
Boundary Wlk.
   OL11: Roch 6A 178 (6G 27)
Bourdon St. M40: Man 2H 7 (2H 101)
Bourget St. M7: Sal 3D 86
Bournbrook Av. M38: Lit H 3E 65
Bourne Av. M27: Swin 4D 83
Bourne Dr. M40: Man 2D 88
Bourne Ho. M5: Sal 3F 99
   (off Amersham St.)
Bournelea Av. M19: Man 3B 132
Bourne Rd. OL2: Shaw 5G 43
Bourne St. OL9: Chad 1B 90
   SK4: Stoc 5G 133
   SK9: Wilm 3C 172
Bourne Wlk. BL1: Bolt 4C 32
   (off Charnock Dr.)
Bournville Av. SK4: Stoc 5G 133
Bournville Dr. BL8: Bury 3A 36
Bournville Gro. M19: Man 6E 117
Bourton Cl. BL8: Bury 2B 36
Bourton Ct. M29: Tyld 2B 80
Bourton Dr. M18: Man 3D 116
Bowden Cl. OL11: Roch 5F 41
   SK14: Hat 6A 122
Bowden Cricket, Hockey & Squash Club
   . . . . .4E 151
Bowden La. SK6: Mar 4C 148
Bowden Rd. M27: Swin 4A 84
Bowden St. M34: Dent 4E 119
   SK7: H Gro 2E 159
BOWDON 3D 150
Bowdon Av. M14: Man 6D 114
Bowdon Ct. M16: Old T 2G 113
Bowdon Ho. SK3: Stoc 5E 179 (3G 145)
Bowdon Ri. WA14: Bow 3F 151
Bowdon Rd. WA14: Alt 2E 151
Bowdon St. SK3: Stoc 5E 179 (3G 145)
   (not continuous)
Bowen Cl. SK7: Bram 2H 167
Bowen St. BL1: Bolt 4H 31
Bower Av. OL12: Roch 5D 16
   SK4: Stoc 6E 133
   SK7: H Gro 4D 158
Bower Ct. SK14: Hyde 2E 121
Bowercup Fold SK15: C'ook 1H 107
Bowerfield Av. SK7: H Gro 5D 158
Bowerfield Cres. SK7: H Gro 5D 158
BOWER FOLD 5F 107
Bower Fold 5G 107
Bower Fold SK15: Stal 5G 107
Bowerfold La. SK4: Stoc 1E 145
   (not continuous)
Bower Gdns. SK15: Stal 5H 107
Bower Gro. SK15: Stal 3G 107
Bower Rd. WA15: Hale 4G 151
Bowers Av. M41: Urm 3D 110
Bowers St. M14: Man 2A 132
Bower St. BL9: Bury 2A 38
   M7: Sal 4C 86
   M40: Man 6B 88
   OL1: O'ham 2H 75
   SK5: Stoc 5H 117
Bower Ter. M43: Droy 2C 104
Bowery Av. SK8: Chea H 1B 168
Bowes Cl. BL8: Bury 6B 22
Bowes St. M14: Man 4D 114
Bowfell Circ. M41: Urm 4D 110
Bowfell Dr. SK6: H Lan 5C 160
Bowfell Gro. M9: Man 5F 71
Bowfell Rd. M41: Urm 5C 110

Bowfield Wlk. M40: Man 6E 89
   (off Langcroft Dr.)
Bowgreave Av. BL2: Bolt 6B 34
BOWGREEN 4C 150
Bow Grn. M. WA14: Bow 3D 150
Bow Grn. Rd. WA14: Bow 4B 150
Bowgreen Wlk. M15: Man 6D 8
Bowker Av. M34: Dent 1H 135
Bowker Bank Av. M8: Man 1D 86
Bowker Bank Ind. Est. M8: Man 6E 71
Bowker Cl. OL11: Roch 2A 26
Bowker Ct. M7: Sal 5B 86
Bowkers Row BL1: Bolt . . .4G 175 (6D 32)
Bowker St. M7: Sal 5B 86
   M26: Rad 4A 52
   M28: Walk 6F 65
   SK14: Hyde 4C 120
Bowker Va. Gdns. M9: Man 6D 70
Bowker Vale Stop (Metro) 6D 70
Bowlacre Rd. SK14: Hyde 3B 136
Bowland Av. M18: Man 3A 118
Bowland Cl. OL2: Shaw 6E 43
   OL6: A Lyme 4A 92
   SK2: Stoc 6E 147
Bowland Ct. M33: Sale 5B 128
Bowland Dr. BL1: Bolt 3E 31
Bowland Gro. OL16: Miln 1F 43
Bowland Rd. M23: Wyth 5F 141
   M34: Dent 4B 118
   SK6: Wood 4H 135
   SK13: Glos 6H 123
Bow La. M2: Man 6H 5 (4D 100)
   OL10: H'ood 3H 39
   WA14: Bow 5C 150
BOWLEE .6G 55
Bowlee Cl. BL9: Bury 6G 53
Bowlers Leisure Cen. 1A 112
Bowler St. M19: Man 1D 132
   OL2: Shaw 6H 43
Bowlers Wlk. OL12: Roch 1H 27
Bowley Av. M22: Wyth 3G 153
Bowling Cl. BL1: Bolt 6C 18
Bowling Grn. BL0: Eden 2G 13
Bowling Grn. Cl. OL9: Chad 5A 74
Bowling Grn. Ct. M16: W Ran 3B 114
Bowling Grn. Ct. OL10: H'ood 3H 39
   SK14: Hyde 5B 120
Bowling Grn. Way OL11: Roch 4B 26
Bowling Rd. M18: Man 4G 117
Bowling St. OL9: Chad 1B 90
Bowman Cres. OL6: A Lyme 2B 106
Bowmeadow Grange M12: Man 3B 116
Bowmead Wlk. M8: Man 5D 86
   (off Ermington Dr.)
Bowmont Cl. SK8: Chea H 1C 156
Bowness Av. M44: Cad 5B 124
   OL12: Roch 2E 27
   SK4: Stoc 3G 133
   SK8: Chea H 4D 156
Bowness Ct. M24: Mid 5H 55
Bowness Dr. M33: Sale 4H 127
Bowness Rd. BL3: Bolt 3B 48
   BL3: Lit L 3B 50
   M24: Mid 6G 55
   OL7: A Lyme 1F 105
   WA15: Tim 6D 140
Bowness St. M11: Man 6H 103
   M32: Stre 4D 112
Bowness Wlk. OL2: O'ham 3E 59
   (off Shaw St.)
Bowring St. M7: Sal 6A 86
   (off Croft St.)
Bowscale Cl. M13: Man 3B 116
Bowstone Hill Rd. BL2: Bolt 6D 20
Bow St. BL1: Bolt 3G 175 (6D 32)
   M2: Man 5G 5 (4D 100)
   OL1: O'ham 3H 177 (2F 75)
   OL6: A Lyme 5C 174 (2H 105)
   OL11: Roch 2F 41
   SK3: Stoc 3E 145
   SK16: Duk 3A 106
Bow Vs. WA14: Bow 3D 150

Bowyer Gdns. BL3: Bolt 4F 47
Boxgrove Rd. M33: Sale 4H 127
Boxgrove Wlk. M8: Man 5E 87
   (off Brentfield Av.)
Boxhill Dr. M23: Wyth 2G 141
Box St. BL0: Ram 3D 12
   OL15: L'ough 4G 17
Boxtree Av. M18: Man 3F 117
Box Wlk. M31: Part 6C 124
Box Works, The M15: Man . . .3D 8 (6B 100)
Boyd St. M12: Man 6C 102
Boyd's Wlk. SK16: Duk 6A 106
Boyer St. M16: Old T 2H 113
Boyle St. BL1: Bolt 4G 31
   M8: Man 5F 87
Boysnope Cres. M30: Ecc 3G 109
Boysnope Wharf M30: Ecc 3H 109
Brabant Rd. SK8: Chea H 3D 156
Brabham Cl. M21: Chor 1H 129
Brabham M. M27: Swin 4F 83
Brabyns Av. SK6: Rom 6B 136
Brabyns Brow SK6: Mar 4E 149
Brabyns Pk. Recreation Cen. 3E 149
Brabyns Rd. SK14: Hyde 2C 136
Bracadale Dr. SK3: Stoc 6G 145
Bracewell Cl. M12: Man 2C 116
Bracken Av. M28: Walk 6A 66
Bracken Cl. BL1: Bolt 5B 18
   M33: Sale 4E 127
   M43: Droy 3C 104
   OL4: Spri 3D 76
   OL10: H'ood 5H 39
   SK6: Mar B 4G 149
   SK14: Holl 1F 123
Bracken Dr. M23: Wyth 6H 141
Brackenfield Wlk. WA15: Tim 5D 140
   (off Aimson Rd. E.)
Brackenhall Ct. OL10: H'ood 3E 39
   (off Todd St.)
Brackenhill Ter. M34: Dent 2G 135
   (off Wordsworth Rd.)
Brackenhurst Av. OL5: Mos 2A 94
Brackenlea Fold OL12: Roch 1D 26
Brackenlea Pl. SK3: Stoc 6F 145
Bracken Lodge OL2: O'ham 6E 59
Brackenside SK5: Stoc 6A 118
Bracken Trade Pk. BL9: Bury 2E 53
Brackenwood Cl. OL2: O'ham 5C 58
Brackenwood Dr. SK8: Chea 1H 155
Brackenwood M. SK9: Wilm 1H 173
Brackley Av. M15: Man 4C 8 (6B 100)
   M44: Cad 3B 124
Brackley Ct. M22: Nor 3B 142
Brackley Dr. M24: Mid 4C 72
Brackley Lodge M30: Ecc 2H 97
Brackley Rd. BL5: O Hul 6G 47
   M30: Ecc 1F 97
   SK4: Stoc 5F 133
Brackley Sq. OL1: O'ham 1G 75
   (off St Stephens St.)
Brackley St. BL4: Farn 1H 65
   (not continuous)
   M28: Walk 5G 65
   OL1: O'ham 1G 75
Bracondale Av. BL1: Bolt 3H 31
Bradbourne Cl. BL3: Bolt 2D 48
Bradburn Av. M30: Ecc 4F 97
Bradburn Cl. M30: Ecc 4F 97
Bradburn Gro. M30: Ecc 4F 97
Bradburn Rd. M44: Irl 2C 124
Bradburn St. M30: Ecc 4F 97
Bradburn Wlk. M8: Man 5F 87
   (off Moordown Cl.)
Bradbury Av. WA14: Alt 6C 138
Bradbury's La. OL3: G'fld 5E 79
Bradbury St. M26: Rad 5A 52
   OL7: A Lyme 1G 105
   SK14: Hyde 6C 120
Bradbury Wlk. OL2: O'ham 3E 59
   (off Shaw St.)
Bradda Mt. SK7: Bram 3A 158
Braddan Av. M33: Sale 6C 128
Bradden Cl. M5: Sal 4G 99

Braddocks Cl.—Branksome Av.

Braddocks Cl. OL12: Roch ... 5D **16**
Braddon Av. M41: Urm ... 5F **111**
Braddon Rd. SK6: Wood ... 4G **135**
Braddon St. M11: Man ... 4E **103**
Brade Cl. M11: Man ... 5E **103**
Bradfield Av. M6: Sal ... 3C **98**
Bradfield Cl. SK5: Stoc ... 5G **117**
Bradfield Rd. M32: Stre ... 5A **112**
M41: Urm ... 5H **111**
BRADFORD ... 3C **102**
Bradford Av. BL3: Bolt ... 4F **49**
Bradford Ct. M40: Man ... 2E **89**
Bradford Cres. BL3: Bolt ... 3E **49**
Bradford Pk. Dr. BL2: Bolt ... 1F **49**
Bradford Rd. BL3: Bolt ... 5E **49**
BL4: Bolt, Farn ... 6E **49**
M30: Ecc ... 6G **83**
M40: Man ... 4G **7** (3H **101**)
Bradford St. BL2: Bolt ... 5H **175** (1E **49**)
BL4: Farn ... 2H **65**
(not continuous)
OL1: O'ham ... 1E **75**
Bradford Ter. BL9: Bury ... 6A **176** (4D **36**)
Bradgate Av. SK8: H Grn ... 4H **155**
Bradgate Cl. M22: Nor ... 3C **142**
Bradgate Rd. M33: Sale ... 1B **140**
WA14: Alt ... 6C **138**
Bradgate St. *OL7: A Lyme ... 3G* ***105***
(off Park St.)
OL7: A Lyme ... 4G **105**
(Victoria St.)
Bradgreen Rd. M30: Ecc ... 2E **97**
Brading Wlk. M22: Wyth ... 5C **154**
Bradley Av. M7: Sal ... 4H **85**
Bradley Cl. M34: Aud ... 6E **105**
WA15: Tim ... 4G **139**
Bradley Dr. BL9: Bury ... 5H **53**
BRADLEY FOLD ... 1D **50**
Bradley Fold OL4: Lees ... 3C **76**
SK15: Stal ... 3F **107**
Bradley Fold Cotts. BL2: Bolt ... 1D **50**
Bradley Fold Rd. BL2: Ain, Bolt ... 5E **35**
Bradley Fold Trad. Est.
BL2: Bolt ... 1E **51**
Bradley Grn. Rd. SK14: Hyde ... 1D **120**
Bradley Ho. OL8: O'ham ... 6G **177** (4F **75**)
Bradley La. BL2: Bolt ... 2D **50**
M32: Stre ... 2A **128**
OL16: Miln ... 1H **43**
Bradley's Ct. M1: Man ... 5C **6**
Bradley Smithy Cl. OL12: Roch ... 1G **27**
Bradley St. M1: Man ... 4C **6**
OL16: Miln ... 1H **43**
Bradney Cl. M9: Man ... 5F **71**
Bradnor Rd. M22: Shar ... 4B **142**
BRADSHAW ... 6G **19**
Bradshaw Av. M20: Man ... 2F **131**
M35: Fail ... 6G **89**
M45: White ... 5E **53**
Bradshaw Brow BL2: Bolt ... 1G **33**
BRADSHAW CHAPEL ... 6H **19**
Bradshaw Cres. SK6: Mar ... 4E **149**
Bradshaw Fold Av. M40: Man ... 6F **73**
Bradshawgate BL1: Bolt ... 4G **175** (6D **32**)
BL2: Bolt ... 4G **175** (1D **48**)
Bradshaw Hall Dr. BL2: Bolt ... 5G **19**
Bradshaw Hall Fold BL2: Bolt ... 5H **19**
Bradshaw Hall La. SK8: H Grn ... 5H **155**
(not continuous)
Bradshaw La. M32: Stre ... 1D **128**
Bradshaw Mdws. BL2: Bolt ... 5H **19**
Bradshaw Mill *BL2: Bolt ... 6G* ***19***
(off Maple St.)
Bradshaw Rd. BL2: Bolt ... 6H **19**
BL7: Tur ... 6H **19**
BL8: Tot ... 5E **21**
SK6: Mar ... 4D **148**
Bradshaw St. *BL4: Farn ... 2H* ***65***
(off Longcauseway)
M7: Sal ... 5C **86**
M24: Mid ... 2E ***73***
(off Shawbury St.)
M26: Rad ... 4H **51**
Bradshaw St. OL1: O'ham ... 3H **177** (2F **75**)
OL10: H'ood ... 3A **40**
(not continuous)
OL16: Roch ... 3A **28**
Bradstock Rd. M16: W Ran ... 4C **114**
Bradstone Rd. M8: Man ... 6D **86**
Bradwell Av. M20: Man ... 3D **130**
M32: Stre ... 4A **112**
Bradwell Dr. SK8: H Grn ... 6G **155**
Bradwell Fold *SK13: Gam ... 6G* ***123***
(off Buxton M.)
Bradwell Lea *SK13: Gam ... 6G* ***123***
(off Buxton M.)
Bradwell Pl. BL2: Bolt ... 4F **33**
Bradwell Rd. SK7: H Gro ... 5E **159**
Bradwell Ter. *SK13: Gam ... 6G* ***123***
(off Buxton M.)
Bradwell Wlk. *M41: Urm ... 4H* ***109***
(off Padbury Cl.)
Bradwen Av. M8: Man ... 2E **87**
Bradwen Cl. M34: Dent ... 6G **119**
Braemar Av. M32: Stre ... 5A **112**
M41: Urm ... 6C **110**
Braemar Ct. M9: Man ... 4E **71**
Braemar Dr. BL9: Bury ... 3B **38**
M33: Sale ... 1E **139**
Braemar Gdns. BL3: Bolt ... 2E **47**
Braemar Gro. OL10: H'ood ... 4E **39**
Braemar La. M28: Wors ... 5F **81**
Braemar Rd. M14: Man ... 1A **132**
SK7: H Gro ... 2F **159**
Braemore Cl. OL2: Shaw ... 5E **43**
Braemore Dr. SK14: B'tom ... 6B **122**
Brae Side OL8: O'ham ... 1E **91**
Braeside *M32: Stre ... 6A* ***112***
(off Urmston La.)
Braeside Cl. SK2: Stoc ... 5F **147**
Braeside Gro. BL3: Bolt ... 2E **47**
Braewood Cl. BL9: Bury ... 2A **38**
Bragenham St. M18: Man ... 2E **117**
Brailsford Av. SK13: Gam ... 5G **123**
Brailsford Cl. *SK13: Gam ... 5G* ***123***
(off Hathersage Cres.)
Brailsford Gdns. *SK13: Gam ... 5G* ***123***
(off Hathersage Cres.)
Brailsford Grn. *SK13: Gam ... 5G* ***123***
(off Melandra Castle Rd.)
Brailsford M. SK13: Gam ... 5G **123**
Brailsford Rd. BL2: Bolt ... 2G **33**
M14: Man ... 1A **132**
Braintree Rd. M22: Wyth ... 5B **154**
Braithwaite Rd. M24: Mid ... 3H **55**
Brakehouse Cl. OL16: Miln ... 5E **29**
Brakenhurst Dr. M7: Sal ... 5D **86**
Brakenlea Dr. M9: Man ... 1G **87**
Brakesmere Gro.
M28: Walk ... 5D **64**
Braley St. M12: Man ... 3D **10** (6F **101**)
Bramah Edge Ct. SK13: Tin ... 1H **123**
Bramall Cl. BL9: Bury ... 5H **53**
Bramall Ct. M3: Sal ... 2D **4** (2B **100**)
Bramall Hall ... 4F **157**
Bramall St. SK14: Hyde ... 3B **120**
Bramber Way *OL9: Chad ... 3B* ***74***
(off Petworth Rd.)
Bramble Av. M5: Sal ... 3A **8** (6A **100**)
OL4: O'ham ... 6B **60**
Bramble Cl. OL15: L'ough ... 4F **17**
Bramble Ct. SK15: Mill ... 1H **107**
Bramble Cft. BL6: Los ... 4A **46**
Bramble Wlk. M22: Wyth ... 3A **154**
M33: Sale ... 4E **127**
Bramblewood OL9: Chad ... 1G **73**
Brambling Cl. M34: Aud ... 3C **104**
SK2: Stoc ... 6G **147**
Bramcote Av. BL2: Bolt ... 2F **49**
M23: Wyth ... 5H **141**
Bramdean Av. BL2: Bolt ... 6A **20**
Bramfield Wlk. M15: Man ... 4D **8**
BRAMHALL ... 2G **167**
Bramhall Av. BL2: Bolt ... 1B **34**
Bramhall Cen., The
SK7: Bram ... 1F **167**
Bramhall Cl. M33: Sale ... 6E **129**
OL16: Miln ... 5E **29**
SK16: Duk ... 1B **120**
WA15: Tim ... 5D **140**
BRAMHALL GREEN ... 3H **157**
Bramhall La. SK2: Stoc ... 5H **145**
SK3: Stoc ... 5H **145**
Bramhall La. Sth. SK7: Bram ... 1G **167**
Bramhall Lane Tennis Club ... 5F **157**
BRAMHALL MOOR ... 2C **158**
Bramhall Moor Ind. Est.
SK7: H Gro ... 3B **158**
Bramhall Moor La. SK7: H Gro ... 4A **158**
Bramhall Mt. SK2: Stoc ... 6H **145**
BRAMHALL PARK ... 4E **157**
Bramhall Pk. Gro. SK7: Bram ... 4E **157**
Bramhall Pk. Rd. SK7: Bram ... 4E **157**
Bramhall Pk. Tennis Club ... 3F **157**
Bramhall Recreation Cen. ... 5A **158**
Bramhall Station (Rail) ... 1G **167**
Bramhall St. BL3: Bolt ... 4F **49**
M18: Man ... 2G **117**
Bramhall Wlk. M34: Dent ... 6F **119**
Bramham Rd. SK6: Mar ... 1E **161**
Bramhope Wlk. M9: Man ... 4H **87**
Bramley Av. M19: Man ... 1C **132**
M32: Stre ... 5B **112**
Bramley Cl. M27: Swin ... 5E **83**
SK7: Bram ... 1G **167**
SK9: Wilm ... 5A **172**
Bramley Cres. SK4: Stoc ... 2D **144**
Bramley Dr. BL8: Bury ... 5C **22**
SK7: Bram ... 1G **167**
Bramley Meade M7: Sal ... 4C **86**
Bramley Rd. BL1: Bolt ... 5D **18**
OL11: Roch ... 3A **26**
SK7: Bram ... 1G **167**
Bramley St. M7: Sal ... 1C **100**
Brammay Dr. BL8: Tot ... 6G **21**
Brampton Rd. BL3: Bolt ... 5H **47**
SK7: Bram ... 3H **157**
Brampton Wlk. *M40: Man ... 5D* ***88***
(off Harold Priestnall Cl.)
Bramway SK6: H Lan ... 6D **160**
SK7: Bram ... 6E **157**
Bramwell Dr. M13: Man ... 5E **11** (1G **115**)
Bramwell St. SK1: Stoc ... 3B **146**
Bramwood Ct. SK7: Bram ... 1G **167**
Bramworth Av. BL0: Ram ... 3B **12**
Brancaster Rd. M1: Man ... 3B **10** (6E **101**)
Branch Cl. BL8: Bury ... 1A **176** (2D **36**)
Branch Rd. OL15: L'ough ... 1E **29**
Brancker St. BL5: W'ton ... 6C **46**
Brandforth Gdns. BL5: W'ton ... 5A **46**
Brandforth Rd. M8: Man ... 3G **87**
Brandish Cl. M13: Man ... 2H **115**
Brandle Av. BL8: Bury ... 1C **36**
Brandlehow Dr. M24: Mid ... 5G **55**
BRANDLESHOLME ... 5C **22**
Brandlesholme Cl. BL8: Bury ... 1D **36**
Brandlesholme Rd. BL8: G'mount ... 2H **21**
Brandon Av. M22: Nor ... 3A **142**
M30: Ecc ... 6A **84**
M34: Dent ... 4H **117**
SK8: H Grn ... 4F **155**
Brandon Brow *OL1: O'ham ... 1E* ***75***
(off Sunfield Rd.)
Brandon Cl. BL8: Bury ... 6D **22**
SK9: Wilm ... 5H **165**
Brandon Cres. OL2: Shaw ... 5G **43**
Brandon Rd. M6: Sal ... 1B **98**
Brandon St. BL3: Bolt ... 3B **48**
OL16: Miln ... 5E **29**
Brandram Rd. M25: Pres ... 5A **70**
Brandsby Gdns. M5: Sal ... 5G **99**
Brandwood OL1: Chad ... 6G **57**
Brandwood Av. M21: Chor ... 5B **130**
Brandwood Cl. M28: Wors ... 3E **81**
Brandwood St. BL3: Bolt ... 3A **48**
(not continuous)
Branfield Av. SK8: H Grn ... 4H **155**
Brankgate Ct. M20: Man ... 4E **131**
Branksome Av. M25: Pres ... 5G **69**

Branksome Dr. M6: Sal 6A **84**
  M9: Man 4F **71**
  SK8: H Grn 4H **155**
Branksome Rd. SK4: Stoc 2D **144**
Bransby Av. M9: Man 5A **72**
Branscombe Dr. M33: Sale 4E **127**
Branscombe Gdns. BL3: Bolt 2H **49**
(off Bembridge Dr.)
Bransdale Av. OL2: O'ham 3C **58**
Bransdale Cl. BL3: Bolt 3F **47**
Bransford Rd. M11: Man 5G **103**
  M41: Urm 3E **111**
Branson St. M40: Man 4H **7** (3H **101**)
Branson Wlk. WA15: Tim 5D **140**
Branston Rd. M40: Man 1F **89**
Brantfell Gro. BL3: Bolt 5B **34**
Brantingham Ct. M16: W Ran 6C **114**
Brantingham Rd. M21: Chor 6H **113**
Brantwood Cl. OL2: O'ham 3C **58**
Brantwood Dr. BL2: Bolt 5B **34**
Brantwood Rd. M7: Sal 3B **86**
  SK4: Stoc 5E **133**
  SK8: Chea H 4B **156**
Brantwood Ter. M9: Man 4B **88**
Brassey St. M24: Mid 6C **56**
  OL6: A Lyme 1H **105**
Brassica Cl. M30: Ecc 1C **96**
Brassington Av. M5: Sal 5H **99**
  M21: Chor 2H **129**
Brassington Cres. SK13: Gam 5F **123**
Brassington Rd. SK4: Stoc 5A **132**
Brathay Cl. BL2: Bolt 3B **34**
  M45: White 1A **70**
Brattice Dr. M27: Pen 3C **84**
Brattray Dr. M24: Mid 4A **56**
Braunston Cl. M30: Ecc 5G **97**
Braxton Wlk. *M9: Man* *3A **88***
(off Hillier St.)
Bray Av. M30: Ecc 2D **96**
Braybrook Dr. BL1: Bolt 6D **30**
Bray Cl. SK8: Chea H 3A **156**
Brayford Rd. M22: Wyth 4B **154**
Brayshaw Cl. OL10: H'ood 4F **39**
Brayside Rd. M19: Man 5H **131**
  M20: Man 5H **131**
Braystan Gdns. SK8: Gat 5F **143**
Braystones Cl. WA15: Tim 5D **140**
Brayston Fold M24: Mid 1G **71**
Brayton Av. M20: Man 1G **143**
  M33: Sale 3F **127**
Brazennose St. M2: Man 6G **5** (4D **100**)
Brazil St. M1: Man 1B **10** (5E **101**)
Brazley Av. BL3: Bolt 4F **49**
Breach Ho. La. WA16: Mob 5A **162**
Bread St. M18: Man 1G **117**
Brean Wlk. M22: Wyth 4A **154**
Brechin Wlk. *M11: Man* *4E **103***
(off Bob Massey Cl.)
Brechin Way OL10: H'ood 4E **39**
Breckland Cl. SK15: Stal 3H **107**
Breckland Dr. BL1: Bolt 5D **30**
Breckles Pl. *BL3: Bolt* *2B **48***
(off Emblem St.)
Breck Rd. M30: Ecc 3D **96**
Brecon Av. M19: Man 2B **132**
  M34: Dent 6F **119**
  M41: Urm 4H **109**
  SK8: Chea H 4A **156**
Brecon Cl. OL2: O'ham 1C **58**
  SK12: Poy 3F **169**
Brecon Cres. OL6: A Lyme 5H **91**
Brecon Dr. BL9: Bury 6E **37**
Brecon Towers SK5: Stoc 2C **134**
BREDBURY 6G **135**
Bredbury Dr. BL4: Farn 1A **66**
BREDBURY GREEN 1G **147**
Bredbury Grn. SK6: Rom 1G **147**
Bredbury Pk. Ind. Est. SK6: Bred 3E **135**
(Ashton Rd.)
  SK6: Bred 3D **134**
(Stuart Rd.)
Bredbury Pk. Way SK6: Bred 4E **135**

Bredbury Rd. M14: Man 5F **115**
Bredbury Station (Rail) 5F **135**
Bredbury St. OL9: Chad 3B **74**
  SK14: Hyde 2B **120**
Brede Wlk. M23: Wyth 2D **140**
Bredon Way OL8: O'ham 6F **75**
Breezehill Cotts. *OL5: Mos* *2A **94***
(off Duke St.)
Breeze Hill Rd. OL4: O'ham 4B **76**
Breeze Mt. M25: Pres 1H **85**
BREIGHTMET 6B **34**
Breightmet Dr. BL2: Bolt 6A **34**
Breightmet Fold BL2: Bolt 5B **34**
Breightmet Fold La. BL2: Bolt 5B **34**
Breightmet Hill BL2: Bolt 4A **34**
Breightmet Ind. Est. BL2: Bolt 5B **34**
Breightmet St. BL2: Bolt 5G **175** (1D **48**)
Brellafield Dr. OL2: Shaw 4F **43**
Brenbar Cres. OL12: Whitw 4B **14**
Brenchley Dr. M23: Wyth 1G **141**
Brendon Av. M23: Wyth 2C **140**
Brendall Cl. SK2: Stoc 6G **147**
Brendon Av. M40: Man 4C **88**
  SK5: Stoc 3H **133**
Brendon Dr. M34: Aud 4D **104**
Brendon Hills OL2: O'ham 4C **58**
Brenley Wlk. *M9: Man* *3H **87***
(off Alfred St.)
Brennan Cl. M15: Man 6A **10** (2E **115**)
Brennan Ct. OL8: O'ham 1C **90**
Brennock Cl. M11: Man 5B **102**
Brentbridge Rd. M14: Man 1F **131**
Brent Cl. BL2: Bolt 2D **50**
  SK12: Poy 3B **168**
Brentfield Av. M8: Man 5D **86**
Brentford Av. BL1: Bolt 3H **31**
Brentford Rd. SK5: Stoc 3H **133**
Brentford St. M9: Man 4A **88**
Brent Ho. *BL1: Bolt* *4C **32***
(off Enfield Cl.)
Brent Moor Rd. SK7: Bram 2A **158**
Brentnall St. SK1: Stoc 6G **179** (3H **145**)
Brentnor Rd. M40: Man 1E **89**
Brenton Av. M33: Sale 5A **128**
Brenton Bus. Complex
  BL9: Bury *3G **37***
(off Bond St.)
Brent Rd. M23: Wyth 1G **141**
  SK4: Stoc 2E **145**
Brentwood M6: Sal 2E **99**
  M33: Sale 5A **128**
  M41: Urm 6B **110**
Brentwood Av. M28: Wors 5D **82**
  M41: Urm 5F **111**
  M44: Cad 3B **124**
  WA14: Tim 4G **139**
Brentwood Cl. OL15: L'ough 6F **17**
  SK5: Stoc 4C **134**
  SK15: Stal 3G **107**
Brentwood Ct. M25: Pres 6F **69**
  M30: Ecc 2H **97**
Brentwood Cres. WA14: Alt 5G **139**
Brentwood Dr. BL4: Farn 5G **49**
  M30: Ecc 1F **97**
  SK8: Gat 6F **143**
Brentwood Rd. M27: Swin 5F **83**
Brentwood St. M16: W Ran 3D **114**
Brereton Cl. WA14: Bow 4E **151**
Brereton Ct. SK8: Chea H 4A **156**
Brereton Dr. M28: Wors 4B **82**
Brereton Gro. M44: Cad 3C **124**
Brereton Rd. M30: Ecc 4B **96**
  SK9: Hand 4A **166**
Breslyn St. M3: Man 2H **5**
Bretherton St. M43: Droy 5A **104**
Bretland Gdns. SK14: Hat 6A **122**
Bretland Wlk. M22: Wyth 2D **154**
Breton Ho. *SK2: Stoc* *5A **146***
(off Canada St.)
Brettargh St. M6: Sal 1G **99**
Bretton Ct. BL4: Kea 3D **66**
Bretton Wlk. M22: Wyth 5B **154**
Brett Rd. M28: Wors 5E **81**

Brett St. M22: Nor 2C **142**
(not continuous)
Brewers Grn. SK7: H Gro 2D **158**
Brewer St. M1: Man 5C **6** (4F **101**)
Brewerton Rd. OL4: O'ham 4A **76**
Brewery St. SK1: Stoc 1H **179** (1H **145**)
(not continuous)
  WA14: Alt 2B **174** (1F **151**)
Brewery Yd. M3: Sal 4F **5** (3C **100**)
Brewster St. M9: Man 3H **87**
  M24: Mid 5C **56**
Brian Av. M43: Droy 2C **104**
Brian Farrell Dr. SK16: Duk 1C **120**
Brian Redhead Ct.
  M15: Man 4E **9** (6C **100**)
Brian Rd. BL4: Farn 5E **49**
Brian Statham Way M16: Old T 3G **113**
Brian St. OL11: Roch 3D **40**
Briar Av. OL4: O'ham 6B **60**
  SK7: H Gro 3F **159**
Briar Cl. M33: Sale 5E **127**
  M41: Urm 4C **110**
  OL12: Roch 2C **26**
Briar Cres. M22: Shar 6C **142**
Briardale Wlk. WA14: W Tim 2E **139**
Briardene M34: Dent 3G **119**
Briardene Gdns. M22: Wyth 1C **154**
Briarfield BL7: Eger 1B **18**
Briarfield Rd. BL4: Farn 6E **49**
  M20: Man 3H **131**
  M28: Wors 4B **82**
  OL3: Dob 5C **62**
  SK4: Stoc 3G **133**
  SK8: Chea H 2D **156**
  WA15: Tim 6C **140**
Briarfields Hall M15: Man 5A **10**
Briar Gro. OL9: Chad 6B **58**
  SK6: Wood 4G **135**
Briar Hill Av. M38: Lit H 5C **64**
Briar Hill Cl. M38: Lit H 5C **64**
Briar Hill Ct. M6: Sal 2G **99**
Briar Hill Gro. M38: Lit H 5C **64**
Briar Hill Way *M6: Sal* *2G **99***
(off Salford Shop. City)
Briar Hollow SK4: Stoc 2D **144**
Briarlands Av. M33: Sale 1H **139**
Briarlands Cl. SK7: Bram 1G **167**
Briar Lea Cl. *BL3: Bolt* *3C **48***
(off Aldsworth Dr.)
Briarlea Gdns. M19: Man 4A **132**
Briarley Gdns. SK6: Wood 3A **136**
Briarmere Wlk. OL9: Chad 2C **74**
Briars Mt. SK4: Stoc 1C **144**
Briarstead Cl. SK7: Bram 6F **157**
Briar St. BL2: Bolt 6H **33**
  OL11: Roch 5F **27**
Briarthorn Cl. SK6: Mar 2D **160**
Briarwood SK9: Wilm 2F **173**
Briarwood Av. M23: Wyth 3E **141**
  M43: Droy 2G **103**
Briarwood Chase SK8: Chea H 4D **156**
Briarwood Cres. SK6: Mar 2E **161**
Briary Dr. M29: Ast 3A **80**
Brice St. SK16: Duk 5H **105**
Brickbridge Rd. SK6: Mar 6E **149**
Brickfield Rd. Nth. SK6: Mar 6E **149**
Brickfield St. OL16: Roch 1B **28**
Brickground OL12: Roch 1G **25**
Brickhill La. WA15: Alt 3B **162**
Brickkiln Row WA14: Bow 4E **151**
Brickley St. M3: Man 1A **6** (2E **101**)
Bricknell Wlk. M22: Wyth 2D **154**
Brick St. BL9: Bury 2G **37**
  M4: Man 4B **6**
Bridcam St. M8: Man 6E **87**
Briddon St. M3: Man 1G **5** (2D **100**)
Brideoak St. M8: Man 5E **87**
  OL4: O'ham 1C **76**
Bridestowe Av. SK14: Hat 4G **121**
Bridestowe Wlk. SK14: Hat 4G **121**
Bride St. BL1: Bolt 3C **32**
Bridge Apartments, The
  M3: Sal 4F **5** (4C **100**)

Bridge Av. SK6: Wood 4G **135**
Bridge Bank Rd. OL15: L'ough 6F **17**
Bridge Cl. M26: Rad 5B **52**
  M31: Part 6E **125**
Bridgecrest Cl. SK8: Chea H 3D **156**
Bridge Dr. SK8: Chea 1H **155**
  SK9: Hand 4H **165**
Bridge End OL3: Del 3B **62**
Bridgefield Av. SK9: Wilm 6G **165**
Bridgefield Cl. SK6: H Lan 6C **160**
Bridgefield Cres. OL4: Spri 3D **76**
Bridgefield Dr. BL9: Bury 3A **38**
Bridgefield St. M26: Rad 4B **52**
  OL11: Roch 4F **27**
  SK1: Stoc 2F **179** (2G **145**)
Bridgefold Wlk. M26: Rad 4B **52**
Bridgefold Rd. OL11: Roch 4E **27**
Bridgefoot Cl. M28: Wors 6E **81**
Bridgeford Ct. *M32: Stre* 1D **128**
  (off Highfield Rd.)
Bridgeford St. M15: Man 6B **10** (1E **115**)
Bridge Gro. WA15: Tim 4H **139**
Bridge Hall Dr. BL9: Bury 3A **38**
Bridge Hall Fold BL9: Bury 3A **38**
Bridge Hall Ind. Est. BL9: Bury 3A **38**
Bridge Hall La. BL9: Bury 3A **38**
Bridge Ho. M1: Man 6D **6**
Bridge La. SK7: Bram 4H **157**
Bridgelea Rd. M20: Man 3F **131**
Bridgeman Ho. BL4: Farn 2H **65**
Bridgeman Pl. BL2: Bolt 5H **175** (1E **49**)
Bridgeman St. BL3: Bolt 6F **175** (3B **48**)
  BL4: Farn 6H **49**
Bridgemere Cl. M26: Rad 2H **51**
Bridge Mills BL0: Eden 2H **13**
Bridge Mills Bus. Pk.
  M6: Sal .6F **85**
Bridgend Cl. M12: Man 1C **116**
  SK8: Chea H 1E **157**
Bridgenorth Av. M41: Urm 5H **111**
Bridgenorth Dr. OL15: L'ough 6F **17**
Bridge Rd. BL9: Bury 5A **176** (4D **36**)
  M23: Wyth 4C **140**
Bridges Av. BL9: Bury 1F **53**
Bridges Ct. BL3: Bolt 5F **175**
Bridgeside Bus. Cen.
  SK6: Bred 3D **134**
Bridge St. BL0: Ram 3C **12**
  BL1: Bolt 2F **175** (5D **32**)
  BL4: Farn 6A **50**
  BL9: Bury 1G **37**
  M3: Man, Sal 5F **5** (4C **100**)
  M24: Mid 1C **72**
  M26: Rad 1D **66**
  M27: Pen 3A **84**
  M34: Aud 6F **105**
  M43: Droy 5G **103**
  OL1: O'ham 4H **177** (3G **75**)
  OL2: Shaw 5A **44**
  OL3: Upp 2D **78**
  OL4: Spri 3D **76**
  OL10: H'ood 3F **39**
  OL11: Roch 4E **41**
  OL12: Roch 6C **16**
  OL12: Whitw 4A **14**
  OL16: Miln 5F **29**
  SK1: Stoc 1G **179** (1H **145**)
  SK15: Stal 4D **106**
  SK16: Duk 1G **119**
Bridge St. Brow
  SK1: Stoc 1G **179** (1H **145**)
Bridge St. W. M3: Sal 5F **5** (4C **100**)
Bridges Way M34: Dent 2F **135**
Bridge Ter. BL9: Bury 3A **38**
Bridge Trad. Est. BL8: Bury 3D **36**
Bridgewater Cen., The
  M41: Urm 6G **97**
Bridgewater Circ. M41: Urm 1F **111**
Bridgewater Cl. SK8: H Grn 6G **155**
Bridgewater Ct. M32: Stre 4E **113**
Bridgewater Gdns.
  M28: Walk 5H **65**
  (off Fereday St.)

Bridgewater Hall 2H **9** (5D **100**)
Bridgewater Ho. M1: Man 2A **10**
  M15: Man 2A **10**
Bridgewater Pl. M4: Man 5A **6** (4E **101**)
Bridgewater Rd. M27: Swin 4B **84**
  M28: Walk 1G **81**
  M28: Wors 4D **80**
  WA14: Alt 4F **139**
Bridgewater St. BL1: Bolt 1B **48**
  BL4: Farn 1H **65**
  M3: Man 2E **9** (5C **100**)
  (not continuous)
  M3: Sal 1E **5** (2C **100**)
  M30: Ecc 3D **96**
  M32: Stre 5E **113**
  M33: Sale 4B **128**
  M38: Lit H 5F **65**
  OL1: O'ham 1G **75**
Bridgewater Viaduct
  M3: Man 3F **9** (6C **100**)
Bridgewater Vw. *M30: Ecc* 1E **97**
  (off Anson St.)
Bridgewater Wlk. *M28: Walk* 6H **65**
  (off Ellesmere Shop. Cen.)
Bridgewater Way
  M16: Old T 6A **8** (2G **113**)
Bridgeway SK6: Mar 5C **148**
Bridgewood Lodge OL10: H'ood 3F **39**
Bridgnorth Rd. M9: Man 6E **71**
Bridle Cl. M41: Urm 5A **110**
  M43: Droy 2C **104**
Bridle Ct. SK7: W'ford 5H **167**
Bridle Fold M26: Rad 3A **52**
Bridle Rd. M25: Pres 2B **70**
  SK7: W'ford 4H **167**
Bridle Way SK7: W'ford 5H **167**
Bridlington Av. M6: Sal 2C **98**
Bridlington Cl. M40: Man 5E **89**
Bridport Av. M40: Man 3F **89**
Bridson La. BL2: Bolt 4H **33**
Bridson St. M5: Sal 4E **99**
  OL4: O'ham 2A **76**
Brief St. BL2: Bolt 4G **33**
Brien Av. WA14: Alt 4F **139**
Briercliffe Cl. M18: Man 1E **117**
Briercliffe Rd. BL3: Bolt 2A **48**
Brierfield Dr. BL9: Bury 3E **23**
Brierfields M35: Fail 4A **90**
Brierholme Av. BL7: Eger 2C **18**
Brierley Av. M35: Fail 4H **89**
  M45: White 5E **53**
Brierley Cl. M34: Dent 6E **119**
  OL6: A Lyme 5E **93**
Brierley Dr. M24: Mid 2C **72**
Brierley Rd. E. M27: Swin 2G **83**
Brierley Rd. W. M27: Swin 2G **83**
Brierleys Pl. OL15: L'ough 3G **17**
Brierley St. BL9: Bury 5E **37**
  OL8: O'ham 6F **75**
  OL9: Chad 1C **74**
  OL10: H'ood 3H **39**
  SK15: Stal 4F **107**
  SK16: Duk 4B **106**
Brierley Wlk. OL9: Chad 1C **74**
Brierton Dr. M22: Wyth 4H **153**
Brierwood BL2: Bolt 4F **33**
Brierwood Cl. OL2: O'ham 6E **59**
Briery Av. BL2: Bolt 5H **19**
Brigade Dr. M32: Stre 4C **112**
Brigade St. BL1: Bolt 6A **32**
Brigadier Cl. M20: Man 3F **131**
Brigantine Cl. *M5: Sal* 5G **99**
  (off Jennings Av.)
Briggs Cl. M33: Sale 2E **139**
Briggs Fold BL7: Eger 1C **18**
Briggs Fold Cl. BL7: Eger 1C **18**
Briggs Fold Rd. BL7: Eger 1C **18**
Briggs Rd. M32: Stre 3F **113**
Briggs St. M3: Sal 2D **4** (2B **100**)
Brigham St. M11: Man 5E **103**
Bright Circ. M41: Urm 1G **111**
Brightgate Way M32: Stre 2A **112**
Brightman St. M18: Man 1G **117**

Brighton Av. BL1: Bolt 4G **31**
  M7: Sal .5C **86**
  M19: Man 2B **132**
  M41: Urm 4A **110**
  SK5: Stoc 5H **117**
Brighton Cl. SK8: Chea H 1E **157**
Brighton Ct. M5: Sal 6H **99**
Brighton Gro. M14: Man 5H **115**
  M33: Sale 4A **128**
  M41: Urm 5A **110**
  SK14: Hyde 6C **120**
Brighton Pl. M13: Man 6C **10** (2F **115**)
Brighton Range M18: Man 3H **117**
Brighton Rd. OL4: Scout 6E **61**
  SK4: Stoc 2E **145**
Brighton Rd. Ind. Est. SK4: Stoc 2E **145**
Brighton St. BL9: Bury 2H **37**
  M4: Man 1B **6** (2E **101**)
Bright Rd. M30: Ecc 3G **97**
Brightstone Wlk. *M13: Man* 3A **116**
  (off Clarence Rd.)
Bright St. BL7: Eger 1B **18**
  BL9: Bury 2G **37**
  M26: Rad 3C **52**
  M43: Droy 4B **104**
  OL6: A Lyme 3B **106**
  OL8: O'ham 4D **74**
  OL9: Chad 5A **74**
  OL16: Roch 6A **28**
Brightwater Cl. M45: White 1G **69**
Brightwell Wlk. *M4: Man* 4C **6**
  (off Oak St.)
Brigsteer Wlk. *M40: Man* 6H **87**
  (off Bishop Marshall Cl.)
Brigstock Av. M18: Man 2E **117**
Briksdal Way BL6: Los 6C **30**
Brimelows Bldgs. *M29: Ast* 6A **80**
  (off Higher Grn. La.)
Brimelow St. SK6: Bred 6C **134**
Brimfield Av. M29: Tyld 2A **80**
Brimfield Wlk. *M40: Man* 5E **89**
  (off Bridlington Cl.)
Brimmy Cft. La. OL3: Dens 2G **45**
Brimpton Wlk. *M8: Man* 5D **86**
  (off Kilmington Dr.)
Brimrod La. OL11: Roch 6F **27**
Brimscombe Av. M22: Wyth 3A **154**
Brindale Ho. SK5: Stoc 5C **134**
Brindale Rd. SK5: Stoc 5C **134**
Brindle Cl. M6: Sal 1F **99**
BRINDLE HEATH 1F **99**
Brindle Heath Ind. Est. M6: Sal 1G **99**
Brindle Heath Rd. M6: Sal 1F **99**
Brindlehurst Dr. M29: Ast 4A **80**
Brindle Pl. M15: Man 6A **10** (1D **114**)
Brindle Way OL2: Shaw 6B **44**
Brindley Av. M9: Man 4F **71**
  M33: Sale 3C **128**
  SK6: Mar 5D **148**
  M30: Ecc 5F **97**
Brindley Cl. BL4: Farn 1F **65**
  M30: Ecc 5F **97**
Brindley Dr. M28: Wors 5E **81**
Brindley Gro. *SK9: Wilm* 5A **166**
  (off Picton Dr.)
Brindley Lodge *M27: Swin* 5G **83**
  (off Worsley Rd.)
Brindley Rd. M16: Old T 2H **113**
Brindley St. BL1: Bolt 1D **32**
  M27: Pen 1H **83**
  M28: Walk 1H **81**
  (not continuous)
  M28: Wors 5D **80**
  M30: Ecc 2D **96**
Brinell Dr. M44: Irl 3C **124**
Brinkburn Rd. SK7: H Gro 2G **159**
Brinklow Cl. M11: Man 6G **103**
Brinkshaw Av. M22: Wyth 2C **154**
Brinks La. BL2: Bolt 6C **34**
Brinksway BL1: Bolt 6C **30**
  SK3: Stoc 3E **145**
Brinksway Trad. Est. SK4: Stoc 2E **145**
Brinksworth Cl. BL2: Bolt 5C **34**
BRINNINGTON 3C **134**

Brinnington Cres. SK5: Stoc 5B 134
Brinnington Ri. SK5: Stoc 5B 134
Brinnington Rd. SK1: Stoc 6A 134
    SK5: Stoc 6A 134
Brinnington Station (Rail) 3C 134
Brinsop Sq. M12: Man 1D 116
Brinston Wlk. *M40: Man* *4C 88*
                (off Whitehill Dr.)
Brinsworth Dr. M8: Man 5E 87
Briony Av. WA15: Hale 3C 152
Briony Cl. OL2: O'ham 5E 59
Brisbane Cl. SK7: Bram 2H 167
Brisbane Rd. SK7: Bram 2H 167
Brisbane St. M15: Man 2F 115
Briscoe La. M40: Man 2B 102
Briscoe M. BL3: Bolt 3E 49
Briscoe St. OL1: O'ham 1G 177 (1F 75)
Briscoe Wlk. M24: Mid 5G 55
Bristol Av. BL2: Bolt 4G 33
    M19: Man 1D 132
    OL6: A Lyme 5H 91
Bristol Cl. SK8: H Grn 6G 155
Bristol Ct. M7: Sal 2C 86
Bristol St. M7: Sal 4C 86
Bristowe St. M11: Man 2F 103
Britain St. BL9: Bury 1E 53
Britannia Av. OL2: Shaw 1A 60
Britannia Bus. Pk. BL2: Bolt 3E 33
Britannia Cl. M26: Rad 4A 52
Britannia Ind. Est. OL10: H'ood 3G 39
Britannia Mills M15: Man 3C 8 (6B 100)
Britannia Rd. M33: Sale 4B 128
Britannia St. M6: Sal 5G 85
    OL1: O'ham 2G 75
    OL10: H'ood 3F 39
Britannia Way BL2: Bolt 3E 33
Britnall Av. M12: Man 2A 116
Briton St. OL2: O'ham 5E 59
    OL16: Roch 3A 28
Britton Ho. M4: Man 1A 6
Britwell Wlk. *M8: Man* *3G 87*
               (off Mawdsley Dr.)
Brixham Av. SK8: Chea H 6B 156
Brixham Dr. M33: Sale 3F 127
Brixham Rd. M16: Old T 3H 113
Brixham Wlk. SK7: Bram 6G 157
Brixton Av. M20: Man 3E 131
Brixworth Wlk. *M9: Man* *6A 72*
             (off Greendale Dr.)
Broach St. BL3: Bolt 3C 48
Broad Acre OL12: Roch 1A 26
Broadacre SK15: Stal 1A 122
Broadacre Pl. SK9: A Edg 6A 172
Broadacre Rd. M18: Man 4G 117
BROADBENT 6H 59
Broadbent Av. OL6: A Lyme 5A 92
    SK16: Duk 5B 106
Broadbent Cl. OL2: O'ham 2G 59
    SK15: C'ook 5A 94
Broadbent Dr. BL9: Bury 1C 38
Broadbent Gro. SK14: Hat 6A 122
Broadbent Rd. OL1: O'ham 5A 60
Broadbent St. M27: Swin 4F 83
    SK14: Hyde 3B 120
BROADBOTTOM 6C 122
Broadbottom Rd. SK14: Mot 6B 122
Broadbottom Station (Rail) 6C 122
BROAD CARR 1E 93
Broadcarr La. OL4: O'ham 1E 93
    OL5: Mos 1E 93
Broad Ees Dole Nature Reserve 2D 128
BROADFIELD 4E 39
Broadfield Cl. M34: Dent 5G 119
Broadfield Distribution Cen.
    OL10: H'ood 4F 39
Broadfield Dr. OL15: L'ough 6F 17
Broadfield Gro. SK5: Stoc 4G 117
Broadfield Rd. M14: Man 5E 115
    SK5: Stoc 4G 117
Broadfield Stile
    OL16: Roch 5A 178 (5G 27)
Broadfield St. OL10: H'ood 4E 39
    OL16: Roch 5B 178 (5H 27)

Bradford Rd. BL3: Bolt 2F 47
Broadgate BL3: Bolt 2F 47
    M24: Mid 3F 73
    OL3: Dob 6A 62
    OL9: Chad 5G 73
             (not continuous)
Broadgate Ho. BL3: Bolt 2F 47
Broadgate Mdw. M27: Swin 5H 83
Broadgate Wlk. *M9: Man* *3A 88*
       (off Augustine Webster Cl.)
Broadgreen Gdns. BL4: Farn 5H 49
BROADHALGH 4C 26
Broadhalgh Av. OL11: Roch 4C 26
Broadhalgh Rd. OL11: Roch 5C 26
Broadhaven Rd. M40: Man 1H 7
Broadhead Rd. M45: White 6H 53
BROADHEATH 4E 139
Broadheath Cl. BL5: W'ton 6A 46
Broad Hey SK6: Rom 6B 136
Broadhill Cl. SK7: Bram 3A 158
Broadhill Rd. M19: Man 3A 132
    SK15: Stal 1E 107
Broadhurst M34: Dent 2G 119
Broadhurst Av. M27: Clif 6H 67
    OL1: Chad 6B 58
Broadhurst Ct. BL3: Bolt 3B 48
Broadhurst Gro. OL6: A Lyme 5A 92
Broadhurst St. BL3: Bolt 3B 48
    M26: Rad 2H 51
    SK3: Stoc 4G 145
Broad Ing OL12: Roch 2E 27
Broadlands Av. OL10: H'ood 5C 38
Broadlands Cres. OL10: H'ood 5C 38
Broadlands Rd. M28: Wors 5E 83
Broadlands Wlk. *M40: Man* *5C 88*
             (off Halliford Rd.)
Broadlands Way OL10: H'ood 5C 38
Broad La. OL3: Del 1A 62
    OL16: Roch 2B 42
    WA15: Hale 5B 152
Broadlea M41: Urm 4E 111
Broadlea Gro. OL12: Roch 1E 27
Broadlea Rd. M19: Man 4A 132
BROADLEY 4E 15
Broadley Av. M22: Wyth 1B 154
Broadley Vw. OL12: Whitw 4E 15
Broadlink M24: Mid 3F 73
Broad Mdw. BL7: Bro X 3F 19
Broadmeadow Av. M16: W Ran 6D 114
Broadmoss Dr. M9: Man 6C 72
Broadmount Ter. *OL9: O'ham* *5B 74*
            (off Devon Rd.)
BROAD OAK 5D 82
Broadoak Av. M22: Wyth 6A 142
    M28: Wors 4D 80
Broadoak Ct. M8: Man 5F 87
Broad Oak Cres. OL6: A Lyme 1G 91
Broadoak Dr. M22: Wyth 6B 142
Broad Oak Ind. Pk. M17: T Pk 6H 97
Broad Oak La. BL9: Bury 2A 38
    M20: Man 3G 143
           (Morningside Dr.)
    M20: Man 3F 143
           (Parrs Wood Rd.)
BROADOAK PARK 5E 83
Broad Oak Pk. M30: Ecc 1F 97
Broad Oak Rd. BL3: Bolt 5E 49
    M28: Wors 5D 82
Broadoak Rd. M22: Wyth 1A 154
    OL6: A Lyme 6H 91
    OL11: Roch 5A 26
    SK7: Bram 3G 157
Broadoaks BL9: Bury 2B 38
Broadoak Sports Cen.
    Ashton-under-Lyne 5A 92
Broad Oak Sports Cen.
    Bury 3A 38
Broadoaks Rd. M33: Sale 5A 128
    M41: Urm 6D 110
Broad Oak Ter. BL9: Bury 2C 38
Broad o' th' La. BL1: Bolt 1C 32
             (not continuous)

Broad Rd. M33: Sale 4C 128
Broad Shaw La. OL16: Roch 3D 42
             (not continuous)
Broadstone Av. OL4: O'ham 3D 60
Broadstone Cl. M25: Pres 6G 69
    OL12: Roch 2C 26
Broadstone Hall Rd. Nth.
    SK4: Stoc 3F 133
Broadstone Hall Rd. Sth.
    SK4: Stoc 3F 133
    SK5: Stoc 3F 133
Broadstone Ho. SK5: Stoc 2G 133
Broadstone Rd. BL2: Bolt 6H 19
    SK4: Stoc 3F 133
    SK5: Stoc 3F 133
Broad St. BL9: Bury 4B 176 (3E 37)
    M6: Sal 5D 84
             (not continuous)
    M24: Mid 2G 71
Broadview Ct. OL16: Roch 2C 42
Broad Wlk. SK9: Wilm 1C 172
Broadwalk M6: Sal 2G 99
Broadway BL4: Farn 6E 49
    M28: Walk, Wors 2G 81
    M31: Part 5E 125
    M33: Sale 4A 128
    M35: Fail 4F 89
    M40: Man 4F 89
    M41: Urm 3C 110
    M43: Droy 6A 104
    M44: Irl 6E 109
    M50: Sal 5D 98
    OL2: O'ham 5C 58
    OL9: Chad 6G 73
    SK2: Stoc 4C 146
    SK7: Bram 3H 157
    SK8: Chea 1G 155
    SK9: Wilm 3E 173
    SK14: Hyde 1H 119
    SK16: Duk, Hyde 1H 119
    WA15: Hale 5A 152
Broadway, The SK6: Bred 5E 135
Broadway Av. SK8: Chea 6H 143
Broadway Cl. M41: Urm 2E 111
Broadway Ind. Est. M50: Sal 5G 99
    SK14: Hyde 1H 119
Broadway Leisure Cen. 1G 89
Broadway M. WA15: Hale 4B 152
Broadway Nth. M43: Droy 5A 104
Broadway Station (Metro) 5F 99
Broadway St. OL8: O'ham 5F 75
Broadwell Dr. M9: Man 4A 88
Broadwood BL6: Los 6C 30
Broadwood Cl. SK12: Dis 6D 160
Brocade Cl. M3: Sal 2C 4 (2B 100)
Broche Cl. OL11: Roch 2D 40
Brock, The OL2: Shaw 5F 43
Brock Av. BL2: Bolt 6B 34
Brock Cl. M11: Man 6F 103
Brockenhurst Dr. BL2: Bolt 2B 34
Brockford Dr. M9: Man 4A 72
Brockholes SK13: Glos 6H 123
Brocklebank Rd. M14: Man 1G 131
    OL16: Roch 4D 28
Brocklehurst Av. BL9: Bury . .6D 176 (4F 37)
Brocklehurst St. M9: Man 3C 88
Brocklehurst Wlk. M14: Man 5F 115
Brock St. M1: Man 5D 6 (4F 101)
Brockton Wlk. M8: Man 3E 87
Brockway OL16: Roch 2C 42
Brocton Ct. M7: Sal 2B 86
Brodick Dr. BL2: Bolt 1B 50
Brodick St. M40: Man 3B 88
Brodie Cl. M30: Ecc 3D 96
Brogan St. M18: Man 2F 117
Brogden Dr. SK8: Gat 6F 143
Brogden Gro. M33: Sale 6A 128
Brogden Ter. M33: Sale 5A 128
Bromborough Av. M20: Man 1E 131
Bromfield OL12: Roch 1B 178 (3H 27)
Bromleigh Av. M9: Man 2H 87
Bromleigh Av. SK8: Gat 5F 143

Bromley Av. M41: Urm 6A 110
  OL2: O'ham 1C 58
Bromley Cres. OL6: A Lyme 5H 91
BROMLEY CROSS 3F 19
Bromley Cross Rd. BL7: Bro X 4F 19
Bromley Cross Station (Rail) 4F 19
Bromley Rd. M33: Sale 1C 140
Bromley St. M4: Man 1C 6 (2F 101)
  M34: Dent 3F 119
  OL9: Chad 6A 74
Bromlow St. M11: Man 4E 103
Brompton Av. BL3: Bolt 3B 90
Brompton Rd. M14: Man 5F 115
  M32: Stre 4H 111
  SK4: Stoc 1C 144
Brompton St. OL4: O'ham 4G 75
Brompton Ter. SK16: Duk 4H 105
                (off Queen St.)
Brompton Way SK9: Hand 2H 165
Bromsgrove Av. M30: Ecc 3E 97
Bromshill Dr. M7: Sal 5C 86
Bromwich Dr. M9: Man 4H 87
Bromwich St. BL2: Bolt 1E 49
Bronington Cl. M22: Nor 4C 142
Bronte Av. BL9: Bury 1F 53
Bronte Cl. BL1: Bolt 4B 32
  OL1: O'ham 3B 60
  OL12: Roch 1C 26
Bronte St. M15: Man 2E 115
Bronville Cl. OL1: Chad 6C 58
Brook, The OL15: L'ough 2A 16
Brookash Rd. M22: Wyth 5E 155
Brook Av. M19: Man 5D 116
  M27: Swin 4H 83
  M43: Droy 4H 103
  OL2: Shaw 5H 43
  OL3: Upp .1E 79
  SK4: Stoc 4F 133
  WA15: Tim 5G 139
Brook Bank BL2: Bolt 2H 33
Brookbank Cl. M24: Mid 2D 72
BROOK BOTTOM 1F 93
Brookbottom BL2: Bolt 5A 20
Brookbottom Rd. M26: Rad 1H 51
Brook Bldg., The BL7: Eger 1B 18
Brookburn Rd. M21: Chor 2G 129
Brook Bus. Complex
  M12: Man 6B 102
Brook Cl. M45: White 1H 69
  WA15: Tim 5G 139
Brookcot Rd. M23: Wyth 4F 141
Brook Ct. M7: Sal 2A 86
Brookcroft Av. M22: Wyth 6B 142
Brookcroft Rd. M22: Wyth 6B 142
Brookdale OL12: Roch 6G 15
Brookdale Av. M34: Aud 6D 104
  M34: Dent 5H 119
  M40: Man 1F 103
  SK6: Mar 1E 161
Brookdale Cl. BL1: Bolt 3D 32
  SK6: Bred 6F 135
Brookdale Cotts. SK2: Stoc 4F 147
Brookdale Ct. M33: Sale 2C 140
Brookdale Pk. Cvn. Site
  M38: Lit H 4F 65
Brookdale Ri. SK7: Bram 4H 157
Brookdale Rd. SK7: Bram 4H 157
  SK8: Gat .6D 142
Brookdale St. M35: Fail 4G 89
Brookdean Cl. BL1: Bolt 2A 32
Brookdene Rd.
  BL9: Bury .6G 53
  M19: Man 3A 132
Brook Dr. M29: Ast 5A 80
  M45: White 1H 69
  SK6: Mar 1D 160
Brooke Av. SK9: Hand 3H 165
Brooke Ct. SK9: Hand 4A 166
Brooke Dr. SK9: Hand 3H 165
Brooke Pk. SK9: Hand 3A 166
Brookes St. M24: Mid 5D 56
Brooke Way SK9: Hand 3H 165
BROOKFIELD 4H 123

Brookfield M25: Pres 5H 69
  OL2: Shaw 4G 43
  SK13: Gam, Had 4G 123
Brookfield Av. BL2: Ain 4E 35
             (not continuous)
  M6: Sal 2C 98
  M21: Chor 2A 130
  M41: Urm 5C 110
  OL2: O'ham 4D 58
  SK1: Stoc 4A 146
  SK6: Bred 5G 135
  SK12: Poy 3C 168
  WA15: Tim 3H 139
Brookfield Bus. Cen. SK8: Chea 6A 144
Brookfield Cl. M25: Pres 5H 69
  SK1: Stoc 4A 146
Brookfield Ct. M18: Man 3F 117
  M19: Man 1B 132
Brookfield Cres. SK8: Chea 1H 155
Brookfield Dr. M27: Swin 2G 83
  M28: Wors 5D 80
  OL15: L'ough 3E 17
  WA15: Tim 4A 140
Brookfield Gdns. M22: Wyth 5A 142
Brookfield Gro. M18: Man 3F 117
  OL6: A Lyme 3B 106
Brookfield Ho. SK8: Chea 1H 155
Brookfield Ind. Est. SK13: Had 4G 123
Brookfield Rd. BL9: Bury 3E 23
  M8: Man .2E 87
  M30: Ecc .1D 96
  SK8: Chea 6A 144
Brookfields OL5: Mos 1G 93
Brookfield St. BL2: Bolt 6F 33
  OL8: O'ham 6G 177 (4F 75)
Brookfield Ter. SK7: H Gro 2F 159
Brookfold M35: Fail 3G 89
Brookfold La. BL2: Bolt 1B 34
  SK14: Hyde 5F 121
Brookfold Rd. SK4: Stoc 3F 133
Brook Gdns. BL2: Bolt 1A 34
  OL10: H'ood 3G 39
BROOK GREEN 3G 117
Brook Grn. La. M18: Man 4H 117
Brook Gro. M44: Irl 5E 109
Brookhead Av. M20: Man 2D 130
Brookhead Dr. SK8: Chea 6C 144
Brook Hey SK14: Hyde 4H 119
Brook Hey Av. BL3: Bolt 4D 48
Brook Hey Cl. OL12: Roch 5D 16
Brookheys Rd WA14: D Mas 1A 138
Brookheys Rd. M31: C'ton 5A 126
             (not continuous)
Brookhill Cl. OL3: Dig 2E 63
Brookhill St. M40: Man 2A 102
Brook Ho. M15: Man 4C 8
  M23: Wyth 4D 140
             (off Bridge Rd.)
Brookhouse Av. BL4: Farn 3G 65
  M30: Ecc .4C 96
Brook Ho. Cl. BL2: Bolt 2A 34
Brookhouse Cl. BL8: G'mount 3G 21
Brookhouse Mill La. BL8: G'mount . . .3H 21
Brookhurst La. M38: Lit H 3C 64
Brookhurst Rd. M18: Man 3F 117
Brookland Av. BL4: Farn 2G 65
Brookland Cl. M44: Irl 5D 108
Brookland Gro. BL1: Bolt 3G 31
BROOKLANDS 1B 140
Brooklands OL12: W'le 5C 16
Brooklands, The OL10: H'ood 3G 39
Brooklands Av. M20: Man 3E 131
  M34: Dent 5D 118
  OL9: Chad 4B 74
  OL5: Mos .1F 93
  SK4: Stoc 4F 133
Brooklands Cl. M8: Man 1D 86
  M33: Sale 1B 140
  OL11: Roch 5E 27
Brooklands Cres. M33: Sale 6B 128
Brooklands Dr. M43: Droy 2C 104
  OL4: Grot 3F 77

Brooklands Ho. M33: Sale 6B 128
         (off Brooklands Rd.)
Brooklands Pde. OL4: Grot 3F 77
Brooklands Pl. M33: Sale 6A 128
Brooklands Rd. BL0: Ram 1A 22
  M8: Man .1C 86
  M25: Pres 1C 86
  M27: Swin 5F 83
  M33: Sale 6B 128
  SK5: Stoc 5G 117
  SK7: H Gro 4E 159
Brooklands Sports Club 1B 140
Brooklands Station (Metro) 6A 128
Brooklands Sta. App. M33: Sale 6A 128
Brookland St. M24: Mid 6C 56
  OL2: O'ham 2D 58
Brookland St. OL16: Roch 2B 42
Brook La. BL9: Bury 3G 53
  OL3: Dob .5B 62
  OL4: Lees .3C 76
  OL8: O'ham 5G 75
             (not continuous)
  OL16: Roch 2B 42
  SK9: A Edg 6B 172
  WA15: Tim 5G 139
Brooklawn Dr. M20: Man 5F 131
  M25: Pres 3A 70
Brookleigh Rd. M20: Man 3H 131
Brooklet Cl. OL4: Spri 4D 76
Brook Lodge SK8: Chea 1H 155
Brooklyn Av. M16: W Ran 5A 114
  M41: Urm 5A 110
  OL15: L'ough 2G 17
  OL16: Roch 5D 16
Brooklyn Ct. M20: Man 2G 131
Brooklyn Cres. SK8: Chea 6H 143
Brooklyn Pl. SK8: Chea 5H 143
Brooklyn Rd. SK2: Stoc 5C 146
  SK8: Chea 6H 143
Brooklyn St. BL1: Bolt 4C 32
  OL1: O'ham 6A 60
Brook Mdw. BL5: W'ton 6A 46
Brook Mill BL7: Bolt 4D 18
Brook Rd. M14: Man 2G 131
  M41: Urm 4C 110
  SK4: Stoc 4E 133
  SK8: Chea 5H 143
Brooks Av. M26: Rad 1H 51
  SK7: H Gro 2D 158
  SK14: Hyde 6C 120
BROOKSBOTTOMS 6C 12
Brooksbottoms Cl. BL0: Ram 5C 12
Brooks Dr. M35: Fail 5G 89
  SK8: Chea 3G 155
  WA15: Hale, Tim 1D 152
  WA15: Haleb 5D 152
  WA15: Tim 4D 140
Brooks End OL11: Roch 2A 26
Brook Shaw St. BL9: Bury 1G 37
Brookshaw St. BL9: Bury 1F 37
             (not continuous)
  M11: Man 4C 102
Brook Side OL4: O'ham 3B 76
Brookside M20: Man 1D 142
  OL5: Mos .2F 93
Brookside Av. BL4: Farn 2G 65
  M43: Droy 2C 104
  OL4: Grot 3F 77
  SK2: Stoc 4E 147
  SK12: Poy 4E 169
Brookside Bus. Pk. M24: Mid 3F 73
Brookside Cl. BL0: Ram 6A 12
  BL2: Bolt .6H 19
  SK8: Chea 1H 155
  SK13: Had 3H 123
  SK14: Hyde 4E 121
Brookside Ct. M19: Man 5C 116
Brookside Cres. BL8: G'mount 2G 21
  M24: Mid .3E 73
  M28: Walk 6A 66
Brookside Dr. M7: Sal 2B 86
  SK14: Hyde 4E 121
Brookside La. SK6: H Lan 6C 160

Brookside Miniature Railway 6F 159
Brookside Railway Mus. 6F 159
Brookside Rd. BL2: Bolt 5H 33
   M33: Sale 1A 140
   M40: Man 2C 88
   SK8: Gat 5E 143
Brookside Ter. OL3: Del 3A 62
                                    (off High St.)
   SK9: A Edg 6B 172
Brookside Vs. SK8: Gat 5E 143
                              (off Pendlebury Rd.)
Brookside Wlk. M26: Rad 6H 35
Brooksmouth BL8: Bury 3D 36
Brook's Pl. OL12: Roch 3G 27
Brook's Rd. M16: Old T 4A 114
Brooks St. SK1: Stoc 6H 179 (4H 145)
Brookstone Cl. M21: Chor 3B 130
Brook St. BL1: Bolt 3F 175 (6D 32)
   BL4: Farn 6A 50
   BL5: W'ton 6A 46
   BL9: Bury 1G 37
                              (not continuous)
   M1: Man 3B 10 (6F 101)
   M26: Rad 4B 52
                                   (Rectory La.)
   M26: Rad 2C 66
                              (Stoneclough Rd.)
   M27: Swin 3F 83
   M33: Sale 4C 128
   M35: Fail 5F 89
   OL1: O'ham 2G 75
   OL2: O'ham 4D 58
   OL9: Chad 1B 74
   OL12: W'le 6C 16
   OL15: L'ough 4H 17
   SK7: H Gro 3E 159
   SK8: Chea 5B 144
   SK14: Hyde 4C 120
Brook Ste.
   OL6: A Lyme 6A 174 (3G 105)
Brook St. Ind. Est. SK1: Stoc 6H 179
Brook St. W. OL6: A Lyme 3G 105
Brook Ter. M12: Man 4B 116
   M41: Urm 3E 111
   OL16: Miln 1A 44
Brookthorn Cl. SK2: Stoc 6F 147
Brookthorpe Av. M19: Man 3A 132
Brookthorpe Mdws. BL8: Bury 2A 36
Brookthorpe Rd. BL8: Bury 2A 36
Brook Vw. SK9: A Edg 6D 172
Brookville Flats OL12: Whitw 4A 14
Brook Wlk. BL8: Bury 5A 22
   M34: Dent 1F 135
Brookwater Cl. BL8: Tot 5H 21
Brookway OL4: Gras 3A 78
   OL4: Lees 4C 76
   OL15: L'ough 5G 17
   WA15: Tim 4H 139
Brookway Cl. M19: Man 5A 132
Brookway Cl. M23: Wyth 4F 141
Brookway Retail Pk.
   M23: Wyth 3E 141
Brookwood Av. M8: Man 3G 87
   M33: Sale 6G 127
Brookwood Cl. M34: Dent 2G 135
Broom Av. M7: Sal 3C 86
   M19: Man 1D 132
   SK5: Stoc 3H 133
Broom Cres. M6: Sal 2C 98
Broomcroft Rd. M20: Man 1F 143
Broomedge M7: Sal 3B 86
Broome Gro. M35: Fail 5H 89
Broomehouse Av. M44: Irl 1C 124
Broome St. OL9: O'ham 3D 74
Broomfield M27: Pen 5D 84
Broomfield Cl. BL2: Ain 4E 35
   SK5: Stoc 3H 133
   SK9: Wilm 1H 173
Broomfield Ct. M20: Man 5E 131
   WA15: Hale 2G 151
                              (off Broomfield La.)
Broomfield Cres. M24: Mid 6H 55
   SK2: Stoc 1A 158

Broomfield Dr. M8: Man 4D 86
   SK5: Stoc 3H 133
Broomfield La. WA15: Hale 3G 151
Broomfield Rd. BL3: Bolt 3A 48
   SK4: Stoc 5E 133
Broomfields M34: Dent 2G 119
Broomfield Sq. OL11: Roch 6H 27
Broomfield Ter. OL16: Miln 1H 43
Broomgrove La. M34: Dent 3G 119
Broomhall Rd. M9: Man 4E 71
   M27: Pen .5D 84
Broomhill Dr. SK7: Bram 4F 157
Broomhurst Av. OL8: O'ham 5D 74
Broomhurst Hall M20: Man 1F 143
Broom La. M7: Sal 4B 86
   M19: Man 1D 132
Broomleigh Wlk. M40: Man 3A 88
                               (off Sequoia St.)
Brownslow Wlk. M13: Man 4D 10
   M2: Man 6H 5 (4D 100)
   M6: Sal 4F 99
   M24: Mid .5C 56
   M26: Rad .1H 51
   M34: Aud 2E 119
                               (off Denton Rd.)
   M35: Fail .4G 89
   OL1: O'ham 2G 75
   OL9: Chad 1A 74
   OL10: H'ood 2H 39
   OL15: L'ough 4H 17
   SK1: Stoc 1F 179 (2G 145)
   SK9: A Edg 5G 173
   WA14: Alt 2F 151
Brownsville Rd. SK4: Stoc 4D 132
Brownville Gro. SK16: Duk 6C 106
Brownwood Av. SK1: Stoc 2B 146
Brownwood Cl. M33: Sale 2C 140
Brows Av. M23: Wyth 1G 141
Browsholme Ct. BL5: W'ton 5A 46
                              (off Abbeylea Dr.)
Browsholme Ho. BL1: Bolt 6A 32
Browside Cl. OL16: Roch 6D 16
Brow St. OL11: Roch 1A 42
Brow Wlk. M9: Man 6H 71
Broxton Av. BL3: Bolt 4H 47
Broxton St. M40: Man 2B 102
Broxwood Cl. M18: Man 2F 117
                                   (off Kirk St.)
Broyne Cl. M11: Man 5B 102
Bruce St. OL11: Roch 1E 41
Bruce Wlk. M11: Man 6F 103
                                  (off Brock Cl.)
Brundage Rd. M22: Wyth 3B 154
Brundett Pl. M33: Sale 5H 127
Brundrett's Rd. M21: Chor 1H 129
Brundrett St. SK1: Stoc 3A 146
Brunel Av. M5: Sal 4H 99
Brunel Cl. M32: Stre 5E 113
Brunel St. BL1: Bolt 2B 32
Brunel Wlk. M12: Man 1B 116
                               (off Skarratt Cl.)
Brun La. OL3: Dig 1G 63
Bruno St. M9: Man 5F 71
Brunstead Cl. M23: Wyth 5D 140
BRUNSWICK 6E 11 (1G 115)
Brunswick Ct. BL1: Bolt 2E 175 (5C 32)
Brunswick Rd. M20: Man 3G 131
   WA14: Alt 4F 139
Brunswick Sq. OL1: O'ham 4F 147
Brunswick St. BL9: Bury 1C 176 (2F 37)
   M13: Man 6C 10 (1F 115)
   M32: Stre 1D 128
   OL1: O'ham 4F 177 (3E 75)
   OL2: Shaw 6H 43
   OL5: Mos .3H 93
   OL10: H'ood 3G 39
                              (not continuous)
   OL16: Roch 3A 28
   SK16: Duk 4A 106
Brunton Rd. SK5: Stoc 3H 133
Brunt St. M14: Man 4F 115

Brownlea Av. SK16: Duk 6A 106
Brownley Ct. M22: Wyth 6C 142
Brownley Ct. Rd. M22: Wyth 6B 142
Brownley Rd. M22: Shar 5C 142
Brown Lodge Dr. OL15: L'ough 6F 17
Brown Lodge St. OL15: L'ough 6F 17
Brownlow Av. OL2: O'ham 4G 59
Brownlow Cen. BL1: Bolt 4C 32
                              (off Brownlow Way)
Brownlow Cl. SK12: Poy 5E 169
BROWNLOW FOLD 3H 31
Brownlow Way BL1: Bolt 4C 32
Brownrigg Cl. M24: Mid 6G 55
Brown's La. SK9: Wilm 1H 173
                              (not continuous)
Brownslow Wlk. M13: Man 4D 10
Broseley Av. M20: Man 6H 131
Broseley Rd. M16: Old T 5G 113
Brosscroft Village SK13: Had 1H 123
Brotherdale Cl. OL2: O'ham 2D 58
Brotherod Hall Rd. OL12: Roch 1E 27
Brotherton Cl. M15: Man 4C 8 (1B 114)
Brotherton Dr. M3: Sal 3D 4 (3B 100)
Brougham St. M28: Walk 6G 65
Brough St. M11: Man 6G 103
Broughton Av. M38: Lit H 4F 65
Broughton Bri. M7: Sal 2B 100
Broughton Grn. Sq. M7: Sal 4B 86
Broughton La. M7: Sal 6B 86
                              (not continuous)
   M8: Man .6B 86
BROUGHTON M. M33: Sale 6C 128
BROUGHTON PARK 3B 86
Broughton Rd. M6: Sal 1G 99
   SK5: Stoc 5H 133
Broughton Rd. E. M6: Sal 1H 99
Broughton St. BL1: Bolt 2B 32
   M8: Man .6D 86
Broughton Trade Cen. M7: Sal 1B 100
Broughton Vw. M6: Sal 2H 99
Broughville Dr. M20: Man 3G 143
Brow, The M9: Man 1H 87
Brow Av. M24: Mid 3D 72
Browbeck OL1: O'ham 2F 177 (2E 75)
Browfield Av. M5: Sal 6H 99
Browfield Way OL2: O'ham 6E 59
Browmere Dr. M20: Man 5D 130
Brownacre St. M20: Man 3F 131
Brown Bank Rd. OL15: L'ough 6F 17
Brownbank Wlk. M15: Man 2D 114
                               (off Arnott Cres.)
Browncross St. M3: Sal 5F 5 (4C 100)
Brown Edge Rd. OL4: O'ham 5C 76
Brownhill Countryside Cen. 6C 62
Brownhill Dr. OL4: Aus 2E 77
Brownhill La. OL3: Upp 6D 62
Brownhills Cl. BL8: Tot 6A 22
Brownhill Vw. OL12: Roch 2G 27
Browning Av. M43: Droy 4A 104
Browning Cl. BL1: Bolt 4B 32
Browning Rd. M24: Mid 5D 56
   M27: Swin 3G 83
   OL1: O'ham 6H 59
   SK5: Stoc .6F 117
Browning St. M3: Sal 4D 4 (3B 100)
   M15: Man 6D 8 (1B 114)
Brown La. SK8: H Grn 4E 155

Bruntwood Av.—Burford Rd.

Bruntwood Av. SK8: H Grn 4E 155
Bruntwood Cotts. SK8: Chea 3A 156
Bruntwood La. SK8: Chea 1A 156
SK8: H Grn 4A 156
Bruntwood Pk. 3H 155
BRUSHES 2H 107
Brushes Av. SK15: Stal 2H 107
Brushes Rd. SK15: Stal 2H 107
Brussels Rd. SK3: Stoc 5F 145
Bruton Av. M32: Stre 6B 112
Brutus Wlk. *M7: Sal* *5C 86*
(off Bradshaw St.)
Bryan Rd. M21: Chor 5H 113
Bryan St. OL4: O'ham 6A 60
Bryant Cl. M13: Man 6F 11 (2G 115)
Bryant's Acre BL1: Bolt 6D 30
Bryantsfield BL1: Bolt 1D 46
Bryceland Cl.
M12: Man 2H 11 (5A 102)
Bryce St. BL3: Bolt 2C 48
SK14: Hyde 3B 120
Brydges Rd. SK6: Mar 6C 148
Brydon Av. M12: Man 3F 11 (6G 101)
Brydon Cl. M6: Sal 3F 99
Bryndale Gro. M33: Sale 2H 139
Brynden Av. M20: Man 4G 131
Bryn Dr. SK5: Stoc 4H 133
Brynford Av. M9: Man 4E 71
Bryngs Dr. BL2: Bolt 1B 34
Brynhall Cl. M26: Rad 2G 51
Brynheys M38: Lit H 4E 65
Brynheys Cl. M38: Lit H 4E 65
Bryn Lea Ter. BL1: Bolt 1F 31
Brynorme Rd. M8: Man 1E 87
Brynton Rd. M13: Man 4A 116
(not continuous)
Bryn Wlk. BL1: Bolt 1F 175
Bryone Dr. SK2: Stoc 6B 146
Bryony Cl. M22: Wyth 4A 154
M28: Walk 5H 65
Bryson Wlk. M18: Man 2E 117
Buccleuch Lodge M20: Man 4D 130
Buchanan St. BL0: Ram 3B 12
M27: Pen 2H 83
Buchan St. M11: Man 3D 102
Buckden Rd. SK4: Stoc 2F 133
Buckden Wlk. M23: Wyth 1F 141
Buckfast Av. OL8: O'ham 5A 76
Buckfast Cl. M21: Chor 6H 113
SK8: Chea H 1D 166
SK12: Poy 2D 168
WA15: Hale 3B 152
Buckfast Rd. M24: Mid 4B 56
M33: Sale 3F 127
Buckfast Wlk. M7: Sal 5C 86
Buckfield Av. M5: Sal 6H 99
Buckhurst Rd. BL9: Bury 5G 13
M19: Man 6C 116
Buckingham Av. M6: Sal 3D 98
M34: Dent 5H 119
M45: White 2G 69
Buckingham Bingo
Manchester 2H 143
Middleton 1B 72
Old Trafford 2H 113
Walkden 5G 65
Buckingham Dr. BL8: Bury 5B 36
SK16: Duk 6D 106
Buckingham Gro. WA14: Tim 2H 139
Buckingham Rd. M21: Chor 5H 113
M25: Pres 1H 85
M27: Clif 1A 84
M32: Stre 3F 113
M43: Droy 4G 103
M44: Cad 3A 124
SK4: Stoc 4D 132
(not continuous)
SK8: Chea H 3C 156
SK9: Wilm 3C 172
SK12: Poy 4D 168
SK15: Stal 2E 107
Buckingham Rd. W.
SK4: Stoc 5C 132
Buckinghamshire Pk. Cl.
OL2: Shaw 5H 43
Buckingham St. M5: Sal 4F 99
OL16: Roch 3A 28
SK2: Stoc 5A 146
Buckingham Way *SK2: Stoc* *5H 145*
(off Windsor St.)
WA15: Tim 4A 140
Buckland Av. M9: Man 6E 71
Buckland Gro. SK14: Hyde 1E 137
Buckland Rd. M6: Sal 1D 98
Buck La. M33: Sale 3G 127
Buckle Ho. M30: Ecc 3G 97
BUCKLEY 6B 16
Buckley Av. M18: Man 3E 117
Buckley Barn Ct. *OL11: Roch* *4E 41*
(off Heape St.)
Buckley Brook St. OL12: Roch 1B 28
Buckley Bldgs. OL5: Mos 2A 94
Buckley Chase OL16: Miln 6E 29
Buckley Cl. SK14: Hyde 2C 136
Buckley Dr. OL3: Dens 4G 45
SK6: Rom 2G 147
Buckley Farm La. OL12: Roch 6B 16
Buckley Flds. OL12: Roch 1A 28
Buckley Hall Ind. Est. OL12: Roch 6B 16
Buckley Hill La. OL16: Miln 6E 29
Buckley La. BL4: Farn 3F 65
M45: White 6E 69
OL12: Roch 6B 16
Buckley Mill *OL3: Upp* *1D 78*
(off Mortimer St.)
Buckley Rd. M18: Man 3D 116
OL4: O'ham 1B 76
OL12: Roch 1B 28
Buckley Rd. Ind. Est. OL12: Roch 1A 28
Buckley Sq. BL4: Farn 3G 65
Buckley St. BL9: Bury 1C 176 (2F 37)
M11: Man 5F 103
M26: Rad 4A 52
M34: Aud 6D 104
M43: Droy 5A 104
OL2: Shaw 6A 44
OL3: Upp 1D 78
OL4: Lees 4C 76
OL9: Chad 2A 74
OL10: H'ood 2A 40
OL16: Roch 1D 178 (3A 28)
SK5: Stoc 5G 117
SK15: Stal 5D 106
Buckley Ter. OL12: Roch 6B 16
Buckley Vw. OL12: Roch 6B 16
BUCKLEY WELLS 4D 36
BUCKLEY WOOD 5A 58
Bucklow Av. M14: Man 5F 115
M31: Part 6D 124
Bucklow Cl. OL4: O'ham 3C 60
SK14: Mot 6B 122
Bucklow Dr. M22: Nor 3C 142
Bucklow Vw. WA14: Bow 2C 150
Bucknell Ct. M40: Man 1E 7 (1G 101)
Buckstones Rd. OL1: O'ham 4A 44
OL2: Shaw 4A 44
Buckthorn Cl. BL5: W'ton 5A 46
M21: Chor 3B 130
WA15: Tim 6E 141
Buckthorn La. M30: Ecc 4B 96
Buckton Cl. OL3: Dig 2E 63
Buckton Dr. SK15: C'ook 6A 94
BUCKTON VALE 6A 94
Buckton Va. M. SK15: C'ook 4B 94
Buckton Va. Rd. SK15: C'ook 5A 94
SK15: Mill 1H 107
Buckton Vw. SK15: C'ook 4B 94
Buckwood Cl. SK7: H Gro 2G 159
Budding Vw. M4: Man 1A 6
Buddleia Gro. *M7: Sal* *5B 86*
(off Bk. Hilton St.)
Bude Av. M29: Ast 3A 80
M41: Urm 1D 126
SK5: Stoc 4B 134
Bude Cl. SK7: Bram 6H 157
Bude Ter. SK16: Duk 4H 105
Bude Wlk. M23: Wyth 6H 141
Budsworth Av. M20: Man 2F 131
Budworth Gdns. M43: Droy 4B 104
Budworth Rd. M33: Sale 6E 129
Budworth Wlk. SK9: Wilm 6A 166
BUERSIL 2B 42
Buersil Av. OL16: Roch 1B 42
BUERSIL HEAD 4B 42
Buersil St. OL16: Roch 2B 42
Buerton Av. M9: Man 4E 71
Buffalo Ct. M50: Sal 5E 99
Buffoline Trad. Est. M19: Man 6D 116
Bugle St. M1: Man 2F 9 (5C 100)
Buildbase Way SK3: Stoc 5D 144
Buile Dr. M9: Man 5B 72
Buile Hill Av. M38: Lit H 5F 65
Buile Hill Dr. M5: Sal 2D 98
Buile Hill Gro. M38: Lit H 4F 65
Buile Ho. M6: Sal 2E 99
Buile St. M7: Sal 4C 86
Bulford Av. M22: Wyth 3H 153
Bulkeley Bus. Cen. SK8: Chea 6B 144
Bulkeley Rd. SK8: Chea 5A 144
SK9: Hand 4G 165
SK12: Poy 4E 169
Bulkeley St. SK3: Stoc 5E 179 (3F 145)
Bullcote Grn. OL2: O'ham 3G 59
Bullcote La. OL1: O'ham 3G 59
Bullcroft Dr. M29: Ast 5A 80
Buller M. BL8: Bury 5B 36
Buller Rd. M13: Man 5B 116
Buller St. BL3: Bolt 5G 49
BL8: Bury 4B 36
M43: Droy 5B 104
OL4: O'ham 1B 76
Bullfinch Dr. BL9: Bury 6A 24
Bullfinch Wlk. M21: Chor 2B 130
Bull Hill Cres. M26: Rad 1B 68
Bullock St. SK1: Stoc 4H 145
Bullows Rd. M38: Lit H 3D 64
Bulrush Cl. M28: Walk 4H 65
Bulteel St. BL3: Bolt 5A 48
M28: Wors 5C 80
M30: Ecc 2D 96
Bulwer St. OL16: Roch 3A 28
Bungalows, The SK7: H Gro 1F 159
BUNKERS HILL 3G 147
Bunkers Hill M45: White 6D 68
SK6: Rom 2H 147
Bunkers Hill Rd. SK14: Hat 6A 122
Bunsen St. M1: Man 5C 6 (4F 101)
Bunting M. M28: Wors 3F 81
Bunyan Cl. OL1: O'ham 3C 60
Bunyan St. OL12: Roch 1C 178 (2H 27)
(not continuous)
Bunyard St. M8: Man 5F 87
Burbage Bank *SK13: Gam* *5G 123*
(off Edale Cres.)
Burbage Gro. *SK13: Gam* *5G 123*
(off Edale Cres.)
Burbage Rd. M23: Wyth 3G 153
Burbage Way *SK13: Gam* *5G 123*
(off Edale Cres.)
Burbridge Cl. M11: Man 4A 102
Burchall Fld. OL16: Roch 4B 28
Burdale Dr. M6: Sal 1B 98
Burdale Wlk. M23: Wyth 2F 141
Burder St. OL8: O'ham 1C 90
Burdett Av. OL12: Roch 2B 26
Burdett Way *M12: Man* *2A 116*
(off Chipstead Av.)
Burdith Av. M14: Man 5E 115
Burdon Av. M22: Wyth 2C 154
Burford Av. M16: W Ran 5B 114
M41: Urm 3G 111
SK7: Bram 2E 167
Burford Cl. SK9: Wilm 4B 172
Burford Cres. SK9: Wilm 4B 172
Burford Dr. BL3: Bolt 2C 48
M16: W Ran 5B 114
M27: Swin 1G 83
Burford Gro. M33: Sale 2G 139
Burford Rd. M16: W Ran 5B 114

212 A-Z Manchester

Burford Wlk.—Butler Green

Burford Wlk. *M16: W Ran* *5B* ***114***
(off Burford Rd.)
Burgess Av. OL6: A Lyme 6A **92**
Burgess Dr. M35: Fail 4H **89**
Burghley Av. OL4: O'ham 3B **76**
Burghley Cl. M26: Rad 2D **50**
SK15: Stal 3E **107**
Burghley Dr. M26: Rad 2D **50**
Burgin Wlk. M40: Man 6G **87**
Burgundy Dr. BL8: Tot 4H **21**
Burke St. BL1: Bolt 3B **32**
Burkitt St. SK14: Hyde 5C **120**
Burland Cl. M7: Sal 6C **86**
Burleigh Cl. SK7: H Gro 4A **158**
Burleigh Ct. M32: Stre 3E **113**
Burleigh Ho. *M15: Man* *2F* ***115***
(off Dilworth St.)
Burleigh M. M21: Chor 3H **129**
Burleigh Rd. M32: Stre 4E **113**
Burleigh St. M15: Man 2F **115**
Burlescombe Cl. WA14: Alt 5D **138**
Burley Ct. SK4: Stoc 1E **145**
Burlin Ct. M16: W Ran 4B **114**
Burlington Av. OL8: O'ham 5E **75**
Burlington Cl. SK4: Stoc 1A **144**
Burlington Ct. WA14: Alt 6F **139**
Burlington Dr. SK3: Stoc 1H **157**
Burlington Gdns. SK3: Stoc 1H **157**
Burlington Ho. OL6: A Lyme 5A **174**
Burlington M. SK3: Stoc 1H **157**
Burlington Rd. M20: Man 2G **131**
M30: Ecc 1G **97**
WA14: Alt 1B **174** (6F **139**)
Burlington St.
M15: Man 6B **10** (2E **115**)
OL6: A Lyme 6A **174** (3G **105**)
OL7: A Lyme 3F **105**
OL11: Roch 1A **42**
Burlington St. E. M15: Man . .6C **10** (2E **115**)
Burman St. M11: Man 6H **103**
M43: Droy 5H **103**
Burnaby St. BL3: Bolt 2B **48**
OL8: O'ham 4C **74**
OL11: Roch 1E **41**
BURNAGE .4A **132**
Burnage Av. M19: Man 1B **132**
Burnage Hall Rd. M19: Man 2A **132**
Burnage La. M19: Man 1H **143**
Burnage Range M19: Man 6C **116**
Burnage Station (Rail) 5H **131**
Burn Bank OL3: G'fld 4A **78**
Burnbray Av. M19: Man 3A **132**
Burnby Wlk. M23: Wyth 2F **141**
Burndale Dr. BL9: Bury 4G **53**
BURNDEN 3F **49**
Burnden Ind. Est. BL3: Bolt 3F **49**
Burnden Pk. BL3: Bolt 2E **49**
Burnden Rd. BL3: Bolt 2F **49**
BURNEDGE .3D **42**
Burnedge Cl. OL12: Whitw 3B **14**
Burnedge Fold Rd. OL4: Gras 3H **77**
Burnedge La. OL4: Gras 3G **77**
Burnedge M. OL4: Gras 3H **77**
Burnell Cl. M40: Man 2G **7** (2H **101**)
Burnell Ct. OL10: H'ood 6H **39**
Burnet Cl. OL16: Roch 1C **42**
Burnett Av. M5: Sal 5H **99**
Burnett Cl. M40: Man 6H **87**
Burnfield Rd. M18: Man 4F **117**
SK5: Stoc 4H **117**
Burnham Av. BL1: Bolt 4G **31**
SK5: Stoc 6H **117**
Burnham Cl. SK8: Chea H 3B **156**
Burnham Dr. M19: Man 1B **132**
M41: Urm 4E **111**
Burnham Rd. M34: Dent 4A **118**
Burnham Wlk. *BL4: Farn* *6H* ***49***
(off Bentley St.)
Burnleigh Ct. BL5: O Hul 6F **47**
BURNLEY BROW 1E **75**
Burnley La. OL1: Chad 5A **58**
OL9: Chad 5A **58**
(not continuous)
Burnley Rd. BL0: Eden 1G **13**
BL9: Bury 3E **23**
(not continuous)
Burnley St. M35: Fail 3A **90**
OL9: Chad 2B **74**
Burnmoor Rd. BL2: Bolt 5B **34**
Burnsall Av. M45: White 1D **68**
Burnsall Gro. OL2: O'ham 3D **58**
Burnsall Wlk. M22: Wyth 3G **153**
Burns Av. BL9: Bury 1F **53**
M27: Swin 2F **83**
SK8: Chea 5B **144**
Burns Cl. M11: Man 4B **102**
OL1: O'ham 2C **60**
Burns Ct. OL11: Roch 5A **26**
Burns Cres. SK2: Stoc 4E **147**
Burns Fold SK16: Duk 6E **107**
Burns Gdns. M25: Pres 6F **69**
Burns Gro. M43: Droy 3A **104**
Burnside BL0: Ram 3G **13**
OL2: Shaw 5B **44**
SK13: Had 3H **123**
SK15: Stal 6H **107**
WA15: Haleb 6D **152**
Burnside Av. M6: Sal 6B **84**
SK4: Stoc 3G **133**
Burnside Cl. M26: Rad 6H **35**
OL10: H'ood 4H **39**
SK6: Bred 6F **135**
SK15: Stal 6H **107**
Burnside Cres. M24: Mid 4A **56**
Burnside Dr. M19: Man 3A **132**
Burnside Rd. BL1: Bolt 3H **31**
OL16: Roch 5C **28**
SK8: Gat 6E **143**
Burns Rd. M34: Dent 2G **135**
M38: Lit H 4F **65**
Burns St. OL10: H'ood 4H **39**
Burnthorp Av. M9: Man 6F **71**
Burnthorpe Cl. OL11: Roch 5A **26**
Burntwood Wlk. *M9: Man* *3A* ***88***
(off Princedom St.)
Burran Rd. M22: Wyth 5B **154**
Burrows Av. M21: Chor 3H **129**
BURRS 5D **22**
Burrs Activity Cen. 5D **22**
Burrs Cl. BL8: Bury 5C **22**
Burrs Country Pk. 5D **22**
Burrs Country Pk. Cvn. Club Site
BL8: Bury 5D **22**
Burrs Lea Cl. BL9: Bury 5E **23**
Burrswood Av. BL9: Bury 5E **23**
Burrwood Dr. SK3: Stoc 6F **145**
Burslem Av. M20: Man 1E **131**
Burstead St. M18: Man 6G **103**
Burstock St. M4: Man 1C **6** (2F **101**)
Burston St. M18: Man 1E **117**
Burtinshaw St. M18: Man 2F **117**
Burton Av. BL8: Bury 1H **35**
M20: Man 3F **131**
WA15: Tim 2A **140**
Burton Dr. SK12: Poy 3D **168**
Burton Gro. M28: Wors 4E **83**
Burton M. M20: Man 4D **130**
Burton Pl. M15: Man 3C **8** (6B **100**)
Burton Rd. M20: Man 5D **130**
Burton St. M24: Mid 1B **72**
(not continuous)
M40: Man 1F **101**
OL4: Lees 4C **76**
SK4: Stoc 6G **133**
Burton Wlk. M3: Sal 3D **4** (3B **100**)
SK4: Stoc *6G* ***133***
(off Heskith St.)
Burtonwood Ct. M24: Mid 6B **56**
Burtree St. M12: Man 1C **116**
Burwell Cl. BL3: Bolt 3B **48**
OL12: Roch 6F **15**
Burwell Gro. M23: Wyth 4F **141**
BURY 4B **176** (3E **37**)
Bury & Bolton Rd.
BL8: Bury 5A **36**
M26: Ain, Bury, Rad 6E **35**
Bury & Rochdale Old Rd.
BL9: Bury 1D **38**
OL10: H'ood 1D **38**
Bury Art Gallery, Mus. & Archives
. . . . .4B **176** (3E **37**)
Bury Av. M16: W Ran 5A **114**
Bury Bolton Street Station
East Lancashire Railway
. . . . .4A **176** (3E **37**)
Bury Bus. Cen. BL9: Bury 2G **37**
Bury FC 6F **37**
BURY GROUND 2A **176** (3D **36**)
Bury Ind. Est. BL2: Bolt 6B **34**
Bury New Rd. BL0: Ram 3D **12**
BL1: Bolt 2H **175** (5E **33**)
BL2: Ain, Bolt 6C **34**
BL2: Bolt 2H **175** (5E **33**)
BL9: Bury, H'ood 3A **38**
M7: Sal .4B **86**
M8: Man 1G **5** (4B **86**)
M25: Pres 4G **69**
M45: White 6E **53**
OL10: H'ood 3A **38**
Bury Old Rd. BL0: Ram 3H **13**
BL2: Ain, Bolt 4C **34**
BL2: Bolt 3H **175** (6E **33**)
(not continuous)
BL9: Bury 4B **38**
(Heap Brow)
BL9: Bury 5F **13**
(Nangreaves)
M7: Sal .1B **86**
M8: Man 2C **86**
M25: Pres 1B **86**
M45: Pres, White 2F **69**
OL10: H'ood 4B **38**
Bury Pl. M11: Man 3E **103**
Bury Rd. BL0: Eden 2G **13**
BL2: Bolt 6F **33**
BL7: Edg 1B **20**
BL8: Tot 5H **21**
BL9: Bury 3B **52**
M26: Rad 3B **52**
OL11: Roch 6A **26**
Bury Station (Metro) 4B **176** (3E **37**)
Bury St. M3: Sal 3F **5** (3C **100**)
M26: Rad 3C **52**
OL5: Mos 3G **93**
OL10: H'ood 3F **39**
SK5: Stoc 6H **133**
Bury Transport Mus. 3A **176** (3E **37**)
Bushell St. BL3: Bolt 3H **47**
Bushey Dr. M23: Wyth 6G **141**
Busheyfield Cl.
SK14: Hyde 2B **120**
Bushfield Wlk. *M23: Wyth* *4E* ***141***
(off Sandy La.)
Bushgrove Wlk. *M9: Man* *4H* ***71***
(off Claygate Dr.)
Bushmoor Wlk. M13: Man 2H **115**
Bushnell Wlk. *M9: Man* *4A* ***72***
(off Claygate Dr.)
Bush St. M40: Man 6A **88**
Bushton Wlk. *M40: Man* *6G* ***87***
(off Ribblesdale Dr.)
Bushway Wlk. *M8: Man* *5F* ***87***
(off Appleford Dr.)
Bus. & Technology Cen.
M30: Ecc 3E **97**
BUSK 1C **74**
Busk Rd. OL9: Chad 1C **74**
(not continuous)
Busk Wlk. OL9: Chad 1C **74**
Butcher La. M23: Wyth 4D **140**
(not continuous)
OL2: O'ham 2C **58**
Bute Av. OL8: O'ham 6F **75**
Bute St. BL1: Bolt 4H **31**
M40: Man 3B **88**
M50: Sal 4D **98**
Butler Ct. M32: Stre 6D **112**
M40: Man 2F **7**
BUTLER GREEN 5A **74**

Butler Grn. OL9: Chad 5A **74**
Butler La. M4: Man 2F **7** (2G **101**)
Butler St. BL0: Ram 5A **12**
   M4: Man 2F **7** (2G **101**)
Butley St. SK7: H Gro 1E **159**
Butman St. M18: Man 1H **117**
Buttercup Av. M38: Lit H 6D **64**
Buttercup Dr. OL4: O'ham 5B **60**
   OL11: Roch 2D **40**
   SK3: Stoc 6F **145**
Butterfield Cl. SK8: Chea H 4D **156**
Butterhouse La. OL3: Dob 5E **63**
Butler La. M3: Man 5G **5** (4D **100**)
Butterley Cl. SK16: Duk 6D **106**
Buttermere Av. M22: Wyth 3H **153**
   M27: Swin 5H **83**
   OL10: H'ood 5H **39**
Buttermere Cl. BL3: Lit L 3B **50**
   M32: Stre 4C **112**
Buttermere Dr. BL0: Ram 2B **12**
   M24: Mid 5A **56**
   WA15: Haleb 1D **162**
Buttermere Gro. OL2: O'ham 6D **42**
Buttermere Rd. BL4: Farn 1C **64**
   M31: Part 6C **124**
   OL4: O'ham 1B **76**
   OL7: A Lyme 1F **105**
   SK8: Gat 2F **155**
Buttermere Ter. SK15: Stal 2E **107**
(off Springs La.)
Buttermill Cl. M44: Irl 4F **109**
Butterstile Av. M25: Pres 1F **85**
Butterstile Cl. M25: Pres 2F **85**
Butterstile La. M25: Pres 1F **85**
Butterwick Cl. M12: Man 4D **116**
Butterworth Cl. OL16: Miln 6G **29**
BUTTERWORTH HALL 6G **29**
Butterworth Hall OL16: Miln 6G **29**
Butterworth La. OL9: Chad 6G **73**
Butterworth Pl. OL15: L'ough 3G **17**
Butterworth St. M11: Man 5C **102**
   M24: Mid 2E **73**
   M26: Rad 3B **52**
   OL4: O'ham 2A **76**
   OL9: Chad 1B **74**
   OL15: L'ough 4G **17**
Butterworth Way OL3: G'fld 4D **78**
Buttery Ho. La.
   WA15: Haleb 3E **153**
Butt Hill Av. M25: Pres 6H **69**
Butt Hill Cl. M25: Pres 6H **69**
Butt Hill Dr. M25: Pres 6H **69**
Butt Hill Rd. M25: Pres 6H **69**
Butt La. OL5: Mos 5F **77**
Button Hole OL2: Shaw 6B **44**
Button La. M23: Wyth 1G **141**
Buttress St. M18: Man 1E **117**
Butts, The OL16: Roch 3B **178** (4H **27**)
Butts Av, The OL16: Roch 3B **178**
Butts La. OL3: Del 3H **61**
Buxted Rd. OL1: O'ham 6H **59**
Buxton Av. M20: Man 3D **130**
   OL6: A Lyme 5D **92**
Buxton Cl. SK13: Gam 5G **123**
(off Buxton M.)
Buxton Ct. SK2: Stoc 5A **146**
Buxton Cres. M33: Sale 2D **140**
   OL16: Roch 1B **42**
Buxton La. M43: Droy 5G **103**
   SK6: Mar 6C **148**
Buxton M. SK13: Gam 6G **123**
Buxton Old Rd. SK12: Dis 1H **171**
Buxton Pl. OL8: O'ham 6F **177** (4E **75**)
Buxton Rd. M32: Stre 4A **112**
   SK2: Stoc 5A **146**
   SK6: H Lan 4F **159**
   SK7: H Gro 4F **159**
   SK12: Dis 4F **159**
(Hartington Rd.)
   SK12: Dis 1H **171**
(Market St.)
Buxton Rd. W.
   SK12: Dis 1E **171**

Buxton St. BL8: Bury 3C **36**
   M1: Man 2D **10** (5F **101**)
   OL10: H'ood 4H **39**
   OL12: Whitw 2B **14**
   SK7: H Gro 2D **158**
   SK8: Gat 6E **143**
Buxton Ter. SK14: Holl 1F **123**
Buxton Wlk. SK13: Gam 6G **123**
(off Buxton M.)
Buxton Way M34: Dent 1F **135**
Buxworth Rd. WA14: W Tim 2E **139**
Bycroft Wlk. M40: Man 1F **103**
(off Eastmoor Dr.)
Bye Rd. BL0: Ram 2E **13**
Bye St. M34: Aud 6F **105**
Byfield Rd. M22: Wyth 1A **154**
Byland Av. OL4: O'ham 5B **76**
   SK8: Chea H 1D **166**
Byland Cl. BL1: Bolt 3C **32**
Byland Gdns. M26: Rad 3G **51**
Bylands Cl. SK12: Poy 3D **168**
Bylands Fold SK16: Duk 1B **120**
Byland Wlk. M22: Wyth 4B **154**
Byng Av. M44: Cad 5B **124**
Byng St. BL4: Farn 1H **65**
   OL10: H'ood 5A **40**
Byre Cl. M33: Sale 6G **129**
Byroe Ct. WA14: Alt 5F **139**
Byrom Av. M19: Man 6E **117**
Byrom Ct. M43: Droy 4H **103**
Byrom Pde. M19: Man 6E **117**
Byrom Pl. M3: Man 6F **5**
Byrom St. BL8: Bury 1B **36**
   M3: Man 1F **9** (5C **100**)
   M5: Sal 5G **99**
   M16: Old T 3B **114**
   WA14: Alt 2F **151**
Byron Av. M25: Pres 6F **69**
   M26: Rad 3F **51**
   M27: Swin 3G **83**
   M43: Droy 3A **104**
Byron Dr. SK8: Chea 5B **144**
Byron Gro. SK5: Stoc 6G **117**
Byron Ho. OL8: O'ham 1B **90**
(off Grammar School Rd.)
Byron Rd. BL8: G'mount 1H **21**
   M24: Mid 5D **56**
   M32: Stre 4E **113**
   M34: Dent 1F **135**
Byrons Dr. WA15: Tim 5A **140**
Byron St. M30: Ecc 3F **97**
   OL2: O'ham 3E **59**
   OL8: O'ham 1B **90**
Byron Wlk. BL4: Farn 3F **65**
   OL2: O'ham 3E **59**
(off Shaw St.)
Byrth Rd. OL8: O'ham 3F **91**
Bywell Wlk. M8: Man 4D **86**
(off Levenhurst Rd.)

C

Cabin La. OL4: O'ham 4D **60**
Cablestead Wlk. M11: Man 5C **102**
(off Dapple Gro.)
Cable St. BL1: Bolt 1G **175** (5D **32**)
   M3: Sal 3F **5** (3C **100**)
   M4: Man 3C **6** (3F **101**)
Cabot Pl. SK5: Stoc 5H **133**
Cabot St. M13: Man 5D **10** (1F **115**)
Caddington Rd. M21: Chor 2A **130**
CADISHEAD 4C **124**
Cadishead Way M30: Ecc 6F **109**
   M44: Cad, Irl 6B **124**
Cadishead Way Circ. M44: Cad 6A **124**
Cadleigh Wlk. M40: Man 4C **88**
(off Shelderton Cl.)
Cadmium Wlk. M18: Man 3E **117**
Cadnam Dr. M22: Wyth 2D **154**
Cadogan Pl. M7: Sal 2C **86**
Cadogan St. M14: Man 3E **115**
Cadum Wlk. M13: Man 5E **11**

Caen Av. M40: Man 6E **73**
Caernarvon Cl. BL8: G'mount 2H **21**
Caernarvon Dr. SK7: H Gro 4C **158**
Caernarvon Way M34: Dent 6F **119**
Caesar St. OL11: Roch 3A **42**
Cairn Dr. M6: Sal 6A **86**
   OL11: Roch 5A **26**
Cairngorm Dr. BL3: Bolt 3E **47**
Cairns Pl. OL6: A Lyme 6B **92**
Cairnwell Rd. OL9: Chad 1H **73**
Caister Av. M45: White 2G **69**
Caister Cl. M41: Urm 6G **109**
Caistor Cl. M16: W Ran 1C **130**
Caistor St. SK1: Stoc 6B **134**
Caistor Wlk. OL1: O'ham 2G **177**
Caithness Cl. M23: Wyth 1G **153**
Caithness Dr. BL3: Bolt 1E **47**
Caithness Rd. OL11: Roch 6A **26**
Cajetan Ho. M24: Mid 4B **72**
Cakebread St. M12: Man 3E **11** (6G **101**)
Calamanco Way M44: Irl 1E **125**
Calbourne Cres. M12: Man 4D **116**
Calcot Wlk. M23: Wyth 5F **141**
Calcutta Rd. SK3: Stoc 4E **145**
Caldbeck Av. BL1: Bolt 4F **31**
   M33: Sale 4E **129**
Caldbeck Dr. BL4: Farn 2C **64**
   M24: Mid 6A **56**
Caldecott Rd. M9: Man 4E **71**
Calder Av. M22: Nor 3B **142**
   M44: Irl 6D **108**
   OL15: L'ough 2G **17**
CALDER BANK 3B **110**
Calderbank Av. M41: Urm 3A **110**
Calderbeck Way M22: Shar 5C **142**
CALDERBROOK 2A **16**
Calderbrook Ct. SK8: Chea H 1D **156**
Calderbrook Dr. SK8: Chea H 1C **156**
Calderbrook Rd. OL15: L'ough 3G **17**
Calderbrook Ter. OL15: L'ough 3A **16**
Calderbrook Wlk. M9: Man 4H **87**
(off Grangewood Dr.)
Calderbrook Way OL4: O'ham 4H **75**
Calder Cl. BL9: Bury 3G **23**
   SK5: Stoc 4A **134**
   SK12: Poy 5D **168**
Calder Ct. M41: Urm 3A **110**
Calder Cres. M45: White 5H **53**
Calderdale Ct. OL2: O'ham 2C **58**
(off Denbydale Way)
Calder Dr. BL4: Kea 4D **66**
   M27: Swin 2G **83**
   M28: Walk 1E **81**
Calder Flats OL10: H'ood 3G **39**
(off Wilton St.)
Calder Gdns. OL15: L'ough 3G **17**
Calder Gro. OL2: Shaw 5G **43**
Calder Ho. M7: Sal 6A **86**
CALDERMOOR 3G **17**
Calder Rd. BL3: Bolt 4C **48**
CALDERSHAW 1D **26**
Caldershaw Bus. Cen. OL12: Roch . . .1D **26**
Caldershaw Cen., The OL12: Roch . . .1D **26**
Caldershaw La. OL12: Roch 1C **26**
Caldershaw Rd. OL12: Roch 2C **26**
Calder St. OL16: Roch 1B **28**
Caldervale Av. M21: Chor 5A **130**
Calder Wlk. M24: Mid 5G **55**
   M45: White 5H **53**
Calder Way M45: White 5H **53**
Calderwood Cl. BL8: Tot 5H **21**
Caldey Rd. M23: Wyth 6E **141**
Caldon Cl. M30: Ecc 5F **97**
Caldwell Cl. SK5: Stoc 6H **117**
Caldy Dr. BL0: Ram 6A **12**
Caldy Rd. M6: Sal 1D **98**
   SK9: Hand 4H **165**
Caledon Av. M40: Man 3C **88**
Caledonian Dr. M30: Ecc 5G **97**
Caledonia St. BL3: Bolt 2A **48**
   M26: Rad 3C **52**
(not continuous)
Caledonia Way M32: Stre 2A **112**

CALE GREEN 5H 145
Cale Grn. SK2: Stoc 5H 145
Cale Grn. Cl. SK2: Stoc 5H 145
Cale St. SK2: Stoc 4H 145
Caley St. BL1: Bolt 3F 31
   M1: Man 2A 10
Calf Hey OL15: L'ough 3F 17
Calf Hey Cl. M26: Rad 4F 51
Calf Hey Head OL12: Whitw 1F 15
Calf Hey La. OL12: Whitw 1F 15
Calf Hey Nth. OL11: Roch 1A 42
Calf Hey Rd. OL2: Shaw 5B 44
Calf Hey Sth. OL11: Roch 1A 42
Calf La. OL5: Mos 5A 78
Calgarth Dr. M24: Mid 4H 55
Calgary St. M18: Man 2E 117
Calico Cl. M3: Sal 2C 4 (2B 100)
Calico Cres. SK15: C'ook 5B 94
Callaghan Wlk. OL10: H'ood 4G 39
Calland Av. SK14: Hyde 4D 120
Callander Sq. OL10: H'ood 4D 38
Callender St. BL0: Ram 3B 12
Calliards La. OL15: L'ough 5F 17
Calliard's Rd. OL16: Roch 5E 17
Callingdon Rd. M21: Chor 4B 130
Callington Cl. SK14: Hat 5A 122
Callington Dr. SK14: Hat 5A 122
Callington Wlk. *SK14: Hat* 5A 122
                          (off Callington Dr.)
Callis Rd. BL3: Bolt 1A 48
Callum Wlk. M13: Man 6E 11
Calluna M20: Man 5E 131
Calne Wlk. M23: Wyth 6G 141
Calow Cl. SK13: Gam 5G 123
Calow Grn. SK13: Gam 6G 123
Caltha St. BL0: Ram 3B 12
Calthorpe Av. M9: Man 4G 87
Calton Av. M7: Sal 4G 85
Calvary Ct. SK3: Stoc 3F 145
Calve Cft. Rd. M22: Wyth 3C 154
Calver Av. M30: Ecc 5E 97
Calver Bank *SK13: Gam* 5G 123
                              (off Eyam La.)
Calver Cl. M41: Urm 4H 109
   SK13: Gam 5G 123
                       (off Hathersage Cres.)
Calver Fold *SK13: Gam* 5F 123
                              (off Calver M.)
Calver Hey Cl. BL5: W'ton 5C 46
Calverleigh Cl. BL3: Bolt 5G 47
Calverley Av. M19: Man 2B 132
Calverley Cl. SK9: Wilm 1F 173
Calverley Rd. SK8: Chea 6C 144
Calverley Way OL12: Roch 5G 15
Calver M. SK13: Gam 5F 123
Calver Pl. *SK13: Gam* 5G 123
                       (off Hathersage Cres.)
Calverton Dr. M40: Man 4E 89
Calvert Rd. BL3: Bolt 4C 48
Calvert St. M5: Sal 3D 98
Calvin Wlk. M34: Dent 1G 135
   SK8: Chea H 4A 156
Calvine Wlk. M40: Man 1F 7
Calvin St. BL1: Bolt 4D 32
Cambeck Cl. M45: White 6H 53
Cambeck Wlk. M45: White 6G 53
Cambell Rd. M30: Ecc 3D 96
Camberley Cl. BL8: Tot 6A 22
   SK7: Bram 6A 158
Camberley Dr. OL11: Roch 5B 26
Cambert La. M18: Man 2E 117
                                (Garratt Way)
   M18: Man 2F 117
                             (Wellington St.)
Camberwell Dr. OL7: A Lyme 5G 91
Camberwell St. M8: Man 1E 101
   OL8: O'ham 5E 75
Camberwell Way OL2: O'ham 3C 58
Camborne St. M14: Man 5F 115
Cambourne Dr. BL3: Bolt 2G 47
Cambourne Rd. SK14: Hat 4A 122
Cambo Wlk. SK4: Stoc 6B 132
Cambrai Cres. M30: Ecc 1C 96

Cambrian Dr. OL2: O'ham 4C 58
   OL16: Miln 5G 29
Cambrian Rd. SK3: Stoc 3B 44
Cambrian St. M40: Man 3H 7 (3A 102)
Cambria Sq. *BL3: Bolt* 2A 48
                           (off Cambria St.)
Cambria St. BL3: Bolt 2A 48
   OL4: O'ham 2B 76
Cambridge Av. M16: W Ran 5A 114
   OL11: Roch 5C 26
   SK9: Wilm 2C 172
Cambridge Cl. BL4: Farn 6D 48
   M33: Sale 6F 127
Cambridge Dr. BL3: Lit L 3D 50
   M34: Dent 4A 118
   SK6: Wood 4A 136
Cambridge Gro. M30: Ecc 3H 97
   M45: White 1G 69
Cambridge Hall *M13: Man* 4A 10
                          (off Rudcroft Cl.)
Cambridge Ho. M15: Man 4A 10
Cambridge Ind. Est.
   M7: Sal 1E 5 (1C 100)
Cambridge Rd. M9: Man 2H 87
   M35: Fail 6H 89
   M41: Urm 6D 110
   M43: Droy 2H 103
   SK4: Stoc 4E 133
   SK8: Gat 5F 143
   WA15: Hale 3G 151
Cambridge St. M1: Man 3H 9 (6D 100)
                           (not continuous)
   M7: Sal 1C 100
   M15: Man 4A 10 (6E 101)
   OL7: A Lyme 4F 105
   OL9: O'ham 4B 74
   SK2: Stoc 5A 146
   SK15: Stal 3E 107
   SK16: Duk 4A 106
Cambridge Ter. *SK2: Stoc* 5A 146
                            (off Russell St.)
   SK15: Mill 1H 107
Camdale Wlk. *M8: Man* 5D 86
                          (off Felthorpe Dr.)
Camden Av. M40: Man 1E 103
Camden Cl. BL2: Ain 4E 35
Camden Ho. *BL1: Bolt* 4C 32
                             (off Kenton Cl.)
Camden St. OL5: Mos 6H 77
Camelford Cl. M15: Man 6A 10 (1E 115)
Camelia Rd. M9: Man 4G 87
Camellia Cl. BL1: Bolt 6H 31
Cameron Cl. OL2: O'ham 1D 58
Cameron Ho. BL8: Bury 3C 36
   M38: Lit H 4C 64
Cameron St. BL1: Bolt 6B 18
   BL8: Bury 3C 36
   M1: Man 2G 9 (5D 100)
Caminada Ho. M15: Man 6D 8
Camley Wlk. *M8: Man* 5F 87
                          (off Appleford Dr.)
Camomile Wlk. *M31: Part* 6D 124
                           (off Wychelm Rd.)
Campania St. OL2: O'ham 5E 59
Campanula Wlk. *M8: Man* 5E 87
                           (off Magnolia Dr.)
Campbell Cl. BL8: Bury 1G 35
Campbell Ct. BL4: Farn 5G 49
Campbell Ho. BL4: Farn 6F 49
Campbell Rd. BL3: Bolt 5G 47
   M13: Man 5B 116
   M27: Swin 5G 83
   M33: Sale 6H 127
Campbell St. BL4: Farn 5F 49
   OL12: Roch 1G 27
   SK5: Stoc 6H 117
Campbell Wlk. *BL4: Farn* 5G 49
                          (off Campbell Ct.)
Campbell Way M28: Walk 6G 65
Campden Way SK9: Hand 3H 165
Campfield Av. M3: Man 2F 9
Campion Wlk. M11: Man 5B 102

Campion Way M34: Dent 1G 135
   OL12: Roch 6E 15
Camponia Gdns. M7: Sal 6B 86
Camp St. BL8: Bury 2C 36
   M3: Man 1F 9 (5C 100)
   M7: Sal 1A 100
   OL6: A Lyme 4C 174 (2H 105)
Camrose Gdns. *BL1: Bolt* 4C 32
                            (off Woking Ter.)
Camrose Wlk. *M13: Man* 2H 115
                         (off Winterford Av.)
Cams Acre Cl. M26: Rad 4G 51
Cams La. M26: Rad 5G 51
                            (not continuous)
Canada St. BL1: Bolt 3A 32
   M40: Man 1A 102
   SK2: Stoc 5A 146
Canal Bank M30: Ecc 2E 97
Canal Circ. M30: Ecc 4A 98
Canal Rd. WA14: Tim 4G 139
Canal Side BL3: Lit L 6C 50
   M30: Ecc 2E 97
Canalside M26: Rad 4H 51
Canalside Cl. OL5: Mos 5A 78
Canalside Ind. Est. OL16: Roch 6B 28
Canalside Nth. M17: T Pk 2E 113
Canal Side Wlk. OL7: A Lyme 4H 105
Canal St. M1: Man 1B 10 (5E 101)
   M5: Sal 5B 4 (4A 100)
   M43: Droy 4A 104
   OL9: Chad 6B 74
   OL10: H'ood 5A 40
   OL11: Roch 6A 28
   OL15: L'ough 4H 17
   SK1: Stoc 3H 179 (2H 145)
   SK6: Mar 5E 149
   SK14: Hyde 4A 120
   SK15: Stal 4E 107
Canal Wharf SK4: Stoc 6G 133
Canary Way M27: Pen 4E 85
Canberra Rd. SK7: Bram 2G 167
Canberra St. M11: Man 4E 103
Canberra Way OL11: Roch 2A 42
Candahar St. BL3: Bolt 4E 49
Candleford Pl. SK2: Stoc 1E 159
Candleford Rd. M20: Man 3F 131
Candlestick Pk. BL9: Bury 1B 38
Candy La. SK10: Adl 6C 168
Canisp Cl. OL9: Chad 6H 57
Canley Cl. SK1: Stoc 5H 179 (3H 145)
Canmore Cl. BL3: Bolt 4G 47
Cannel Ct. M28: Wors 4F 81
Canning Dr. BL1: Bolt 3C 32
Canning St. BL1: Bolt 3D 32
   BL9: Bury 1D 176 (1F 37)
   SK4: Stoc 1G 145
Cannock Dr. SK4: Stoc 1C 144
Cannon Ct. *M3: Man* 4H 5
                          (off Cateaton St.)
Cannon Gro. BL3: Bolt 1B 48
Cannon St. BL0: Ram 5A 12
   BL3: Bolt 1B 48
   M3: Sal 3C 4 (3B 100)
   M26: Rad 2H 51
   M30: Ecc 3G 97
   OL9: O'ham 3E 177
   SK14: Holl 2E 123
Cannon St. Nth. BL3: Bolt 1B 48
Cannon Wlk. M34: Dent 5E 119
Cann St. BL8: Tot 3F 21
Canon Dr. WA14: Bow 4D 150
Canon Flynn Ct. OL16: Roch 4C 28
Canon Grn. Ct. M3: Sal 3E 5
Canon Grn. Dr. M3: Sal 2E 5 (2C 100)
Canon Hussey Ct. M3: Sal 5C 4
Canons Cl. BL1: Bolt 3H 31
Canons Gro. M40: Man 6A 88
Canonsleigh Cl. M8: Man 6C 86
Canon St. BL9: Bury 1G 37
   OL16: Roch 1B 28
Canonsway M27: Swin 3G 83
Canon Tighe Ct. OL9: Chad 2A 74
Cansfield Cl. BL4: Kea 3C 66

Canterbury Cl. OL11: Roch 4C 26
  SK16: Duk 1B 120
Canterbury Cres. M24: Mid 5F 57
Canterbury Dr. BL8: Bury 1D 36
  M25: Pres 1A 86
Canterbury Gdns. M5: Sal 3A 98
Canterbury Grange SK9: Wilm . . .2E 173
Canterbury Gro. BL3: Bolt 4B 48
Canterbury Rd. M41: Urm 4D 110
  SK1: Stoc 2B 146
  WA15: Hale 2C 152
Canterbury St. OL6: A Lyme 1A 106
Canterfield Cl. M43: Droy 3D 104
Cantley Wlk. *M8: Man* *5E 87*
                (off Dinnington Dr.)
Cantrell St. M11: Man 4D 102
Canute Ct. M32: Stre 4E 113
Canute Rd. M32: Stre 4E 113
Canute St. BL2: Bolt 4G 33
  M26: Rad 4G 51
Cape Gdns. OL2: Shaw 1H 59
Capella Dr. M11: Man 5B 102
Capella Wlk. M7: Sal 1A 100
Capenhurst Cl. M23: Wyth 1F 153
  SK12: Poy 3F 169
Capesthorne Cl. SK7: H Gro 5F 159
Capesthorne Dr. OL2: Shaw 6F 43
Capesthorne Rd. SK6: H Lan 6C 160
  SK7: H Gro 5F 159
  SK9: Wilm 4B 172
  SK16: Duk 1B 120
  WA15: Tim 5D 140
Capesthorne Wlk. M34: Dent 5E 119
Cape St. M20: Man 2G 131
Capital Ho. M50: Sal 6G 99
Capital Quay M50: Sal 6G 99
Capital Rd. M11: Man 6H 103
Capitol Cl. BL1: Bolt 2G 31
Capricorn Dr. M9: Man 6D 72
Capricorn Way *M6: Sal* *1A 100*
                  (off Gemini Rd.)
Capstan St. M9: Man 3A 88
Capstone Dr. SK6: Mar 5C 148
Captain Clarke Rd. SK14: Hyde 2H 119
CAPTAIN FOLD 2A 40
Captain Fold OL10: H'ood 2A 40
Captain Fold Rd. M38: Lit H 4C 64
Captain Lees Gdns. BL5: W'ton 6A 46
Captain Lees Rd. BL5: W'ton 6A 46
Captain's Clough Rd. BL1: Bolt 3G 31
Captain Wlk. *M5: Sal* *5H 99*
             (off Robert Hall St.)
Capton Cl. SK7: Bram 3A 158
Caradoc Av. M8: Man 5F 87
Carberry Ct. SK8: Chea H 3C 156
Carberry Rd. M18: Man 2F 117
Cardale Wlk. *M9: Man* *4H 87*
             (off Conran St.)
Carden Av. M27: Swin 4F 83
  M41: Urm 5A 110
Cardenbrook Gro. SK9: Wilm 5H 165
           (off Rookerypool Cl.)
Carder Cl. M27: Swin 4H 83
Carders Ct. OL11: Roch 2D 40
Cardew Av. M22: Wyth 1D 154
Cardiff Cl. OL8: O'ham 1B 90
Cardiff St. M7: Sal 4C 86
Cardiff Wlk. M34: Dent 6F 119
Cardigan Dr. BL9: Bury 6E 37
Cardigan Rd. OL8: O'ham 1B 90
Cardigan St. M6: Sal 4E 99
  M26: Rad 1H 51
  OL2: O'ham 3E 59
  OL12: Roch 6G 15
Cardigan Ter. M14: Man 3D 114
Cardinal M. M24: Mid 5H 55
Cardinal St. M8: Man 5F 87
  OL1: O'ham 3H 177 (2G 75)
Cardinal Vaughan Ct.
  OL11: Roch 6B 178 (5H 27)
Carding Gro. M3: Sal 2E 5 (2C 100)
Cardus St. M19: Man 6C 116

Cardwell Gdns. *BL1: Bolt* *3C 32*
               (off Canning Dr.)
Cardwell Rd. M30: Ecc 4C 96
Cardwell St. OL8: O'ham 6F 75
Caremine Av. M19: Man 5D 116
Carey Cl. M7: Sal 1D 4 (1B 100)
Carey Wlk. *M15: Man* *2D 114*
             (off Wellhead Cl.)
Carfax Fold OL12: Roch 1D 26
Carfax St. M18: Man 2F 117
Cargate Wlk. M8: Man 5D 86
Carib St. M15: Man 2D 114
Carill Av. M9: Man 2B 88
  M40: Man 2B 88
Carill Dr. M14: Man 1H 131
Carina Pl. M7: Sal 1B 4 (1A 100)
Cariocca Bus. Pk.
  M12: Man 5G 11 (1H 115)
  M40: Man 1H 7 (2H 101)
Carisbrook Av. M41: Urm 6E 111
  M45: White 3G 69
Carisbrook Dr. M27: Swin 5A 84
Carisbrooke Av. SK7: H Gro 4D 158
Carisbrooke Dr. BL1: Bolt 2D 32
Carisbrook St. M9: Man 4H 87
Carlburn St. M11: Man 3F 103
Carleton Rd. SK12: Poy 3A 170
Carley Fold BL3: Bolt 3F 47
Carley Gro. M9: Man 5G 71
Carlford Gro. M25: Pres 6F 69
Carlin Ga. WA15: Tim 5A 140
Carling Dr. M22: Wyth 3C 154
Carlingford Cl. SK3: Stoc 6G 145
Carlisle Cl. BL3: Lit L 5C 50
  M45: White 2H 69
  SK6: Rom 2G 147
Carlisle Cres. OL6: A Lyme 4A 92
Carlisle Dr. M44: Irl 5E 109
  WA14: Tim 3G 139
Carlisle St. BL7: Bro X 3E 19
  M27: Pen 1H 83
  OL9: O'ham 5C 74
               (not continuous)
  OL12: Roch 6H 15
  SK3: Stoc 5E 179 (3G 145)
  SK9: A Edg 5G 173
Carlisle Way M34: Dent 6F 119
Carloon Rd. M23: Wyth 2H 141
Carlow Dr. M22: Wyth 3C 154
Carl St. BL1: Bolt 3B 32
Carlton Av. BL3: Bolt 3G 47
  M14: Man 4F 115
  M16: Old T 3H 113
  M25: Pres 1C 86
  M45: White 6D 52
  OL4: O'ham 6B 60
  SK6: Rom 6B 136
  SK7: Bram 2F 167
  SK8: Chea H 2B 156
  SK9: Wilm 5G 165
Carlton Cl. BL2: Bolt 2A 34
  M28: Wors 2G 81
Carlton Ct. M25: Pres 2G 85
  WA15: Hale 4B 152
Carlton Cres. M41: Urm 6F 111
  SK1: Stoc 1A 146
Carlton Dr. M25: Pres 1C 86
  SK8: Gat 5E 143
Carlton Flats *OL10: H'ood* *3G 39*
             (off St James St.)
Carlton Gdns. BL4: Farn 6H 49
Carlton Ho. M16: W Ran 4A 114
Carlton Mans. M16: W Ran 4B 114
Carlton Pl. BL4: Farn 6H 49
  M45: White 2C 68
  SK7: H Gro 4G 159
Carlton Range M18: Man 3H 117
Carlton Rd. BL1: Bolt 5G 31
  M6: Sal 1E 99
  M16: W Ran 4B 114
  M28: Wors 2G 81
  M33: Sale 3A 128
  M41: Urm 6E 111

Carlton Rd. OL6: A Lyme 6A 92
  SK4: Stoc 1C 144
  SK14: Hyde 4E 121
  WA15: Hale 4B 152
Carlton Springs *OL6: A Lyme* *1H 105*
              (off Turner La.)
Carlton St. BL2: Bolt 5H 175 (1D 48)
  BL4: Farn 6H 49
  BL9: Bury 5F 37
  M16: Old T 3A 114
  M30: Ecc 2F 97
Carlton Way OL2: O'ham 5D 58
  WA3: G'ook 4A 124
Carlyle Cl. M8: Man 5E 87
Carlyle St. BL9: Bury 3A 176 (2D 36)
Carlyn Av. M33: Sale 5D 128
Carmel Av. M5: Sal 2A 8 (5A 100)
Carmel Cl. M5: Sal 2A 8 (5A 100)
Carmel Ct. M8: Man 1D 86
  M9: Man 2A 88
Carmenna Dr. SK7: Bram 6H 157
Carmichael Cl. M31: Part 6C 124
Carmichael St. SK3: Stoc 3F 145
Carmine Fold M24: Mid 5B 56
Carmona Dr. M25: Pres 5G 69
Carmona Gdns. M7: Sal 2A 86
Carmoor Rd. M13: Man 2G 115
Carna Rd. SK5: Stoc 5G 117
Carnarvon St. M3: Man 1H 5 (2D 100)
  M7: Sal 4C 86
  OL8: O'ham 1B 90
  SK1: Stoc 3A 146
Carnation Rd. BL4: Farn 6E 49
  OL4: O'ham 5C 76
Carnegie Av. M19: Man 6D 116
Carnegie Cl. M33: Sale 6F 127
Carnforth Av. OL9: Chad 3A 74
  OL11: Roch 6F 41
Carnforth Dr. BL8: G'mount 1A 22
  M33: Sale 6A 128
Carnforth Rd. SK4: Stoc 3F 133
  SK8: Chea H 1E 157
Carnforth Sq. OL11: Roch 6F 41
Carnforth St. M14: Man 4F 115
Carnoustie BL3: Bolt 4G 47
Carnoustie Cl. M40: Man 4E 89
  SK9: Wilm 1G 173
Carnoustie Dr. BL0: Ram 4A 12
  SK8: H Grn 4G 155
Carnwood Cl. M40: Man 1F 103
Carolina Way M50: Sal 4E 99
Caroline St. BL3: Bolt 3B 48
  M7: Sal 1C 100
  M44: Irl 1D 124
  OL6: A Lyme 2A 106
  SK3: Stoc 4F 145
               (not continuous)
  SK15: Stal 4E 107
Carpenters Ct. SK9: A Edg 5G 173
Carpenters La. M4: Man 4B 6 (3E 101)
Carpenters Wlk. M43: Droy 4H 103
Carpenters Way OL16: Roch 1B 42
CARR
  OL3, Bury 2B 12
  OL3, Oldham 2E 63
  SK15 .4B 94
Carradale Dr. M33: Sale 4E 127
Carradale Wlk. *M40: Man* *5C 88*
             (off Halliford Rd.)
Carr Av. M25: Pres 1F 85
CARR BANK 3F 23
Carr Bank BL0: Ram 2B 12
Carr Bank Av. BL0: Ram 2B 12
  M9: Man 6D 70
Carr Bank Dr. BL0: Ram 2B 12
Carr Bank Rd. BL0: Ram 2B 12
CARRBROOK .5B 94
Carrbrook Cl. SK15: C'ook 5A 94
Carrbrook Cres. SK15: C'ook 5A 94
Carrbrook Dr. OL2: O'ham 6E 59
Carrbrook Rd. SK15: C'ook 4B 94
               (not continuous)

Carrbrook Ter.—Castleton Grn.

Carrbrook Ter. M26: Rad . . . 3C **52**
Carr Brow SK6: H Lan . . . 6E **161**
Carr Cl. SK1: Stoc . . . 3B **146**
Carrfield SK14: Hyde . . . 3B **120**
Carrfield Av. M38: Lit H . . . 5C **64**
SK3: Stoc . . . 1A **158**
WA15: Tim . . . 5D **140**
Carrfield Cl. M38: Lit H . . . 5C **64**
Carrfield Gro. M38: Lit H . . . 5C **64**
Carr Fold BL0: Ram . . . 2B **12**
Carrgate Rd. M34: Dent . . . 6H **119**
Carrgreen Cl. M19: Man . . . 4B **132**
Carr Gro. OL16: Miln . . . 5G **29**
Carr Head OL3: Dig . . . 1E **63**
Carrhill Quarry Cl. OL5: Mos . . . 1G **93**
Carrhill Rd. OL5: Mos . . . 1G **93**
Carrhouse La. SK14: Gam, Holl . . . 3E **123**
(not continuous)
Carr Ho. Rd. OL4: Spri . . . 2D **76**
Carriage Dr. M40: Man . . . 6H **87**
OL15: L'ough . . . 2H **17**
Carriage Dr., The SK13: Had . . . 3H **123**
Carriages, The WA14: Alt . . . 1E **151**
Carriage St. M16: Old T . . . 2B **114**
Carrick Gdns. M22: Wyth . . . 1B **154**
M24: Mid . . . 3B **56**
Carrie St. BL1: Bolt . . . 5H **31**
Carrigart M25: Pres . . . 6H **69**
Carrill Gro. M19: Man . . . 6C **116**
Carrill Gro. E. M19: Man . . . 6C **116**
CARRINGTON . . . **3A 126**
Carrington Barn SK6: Mar . . . 4D **160**
Carrington Bus. Pk. M31: C'ton . . . 3G **125**
Carrington Cl. OL16: Roch . . . 6D **16**
Carrington Dr. BL3: Bolt . . . 3D **48**
Carrington Fld. St.
SK1: Stoc . . . 6H **179** (4H **145**)
Carrington Ho. *M6: Sal* . . . *1C* ***98***
(off Moss Mdw. Rd.)
Carrington La. M31: C'ton . . . 2B **126**
M33: Sale . . . 2B **126**
Carrington Rd. M14: Man . . . 1G **131**
M41: Urm . . . 1A **126**
SK1: Stoc . . . 6A **134**
Carrington Spur M33: Sale . . . 3E **127**
M41: Urm . . . 3E **127**
Carrington St. M27: Pen . . . 2B **84**
OL9: Chad . . . 6B **74**
Carrington Ter. *M27: Pen* . . . *2B* ***84***
(off Carrington St.)
Carr La. OL3: Dig . . . 2E **63**
OL3: G'fld . . . 3D **78**
SK9: A Edg . . . 6A **172**
SK15: C'ook . . . 4B **94**
Carr Lea OL4: Lyd . . . 3G **77**
Carr Mdw. OL16: Miln . . . 1A **44**
Carrmel Ct. *OL3: Del* . . . *4B* ***62***
(off Oldham Rd.)
Carr Mill M. SK9: Wilm . . . 6F **165**
Carrock Wlk. M24: Mid . . . 6F **55**
Carron Av. M9: Man . . . 2B **88**
Carron Gro. BL2: Bolt . . . 6B **34**
Carr Ri. SK15: C'ook . . . 4B **94**
Carr Rd. M44: Irl . . . 5F **109**
WA15: Hale . . . 3B **152**
Carrs Av. SK8: Chea . . . 5C **144**
Carrs Ct. SK9: Wilm . . . 2E **173**
Carrsdale Dr. M9: Man . . . 1G **87**
Carrsfield Rd. M22: Shar . . . 5C **142**
Carrslea Cl. M26: Rad . . . 2G **51**
Carrs Rd. SK8: Chea . . . 5B **144**
Carr St. BL0: Ram . . . 2B **12**
M27: Swin . . . 4F **83**
OL6: A Lyme . . . 6B **92**
Carrsvale Av. M41: Urm . . . 4D **110**
Carrswood Rd. M23: Wyth . . . 3C **140**
Carruthers Cl.
OL10: H'ood . . . 2B **40**
Carruthers St. M4: Man . . . 4G **7** (3H **101**)
CARR WOOD . . . **4H 25**
Carrwood WA15: Haleb . . . 6B **152**
Carr Wood Av. SK7: Bram . . . 5G **157**
Carrwood Hey BL0: Ram . . . 5A **12**
Carrwood Rd. SK7: Bram . . . 4F **157**
SK9: Wilm . . . 6D **164**
Carsdale Rd. M22: Wyth . . . 5C **154**
Carslake Av. BL1: Bolt . . . 5A **32**
Carslake Rd. M40: Man . . . 6H **87**
Carson Rd. M19: Man . . . 1C **132**
Carstairs Av. SK2: Stoc . . . 1A **158**
Carstairs Cl. M8: Man . . . 4D **86**
Car St. OL1: O'ham . . . 2G **75**
Carswell Cl. M29: Tyld . . . 2A **80**
Carter Cl. M34: Dent . . . 5F **119**
Carter Pl. SK14: Hyde . . . 2B **120**
Carter St. BL3: Bolt . . . 3E **49**
BL4: Kea . . . 2A **66**
M7: Sal . . . 6B **86**
OL5: Mos . . . 3G **93**
SK14: Hyde . . . 2B **120**
SK15: Stal . . . 3F **107**
Carthage St. OL8: O'ham . . . 5F **75**
Carthorpe Arch M5: Sal . . . 4F **99**
Cartleach Gro. M28: Walk . . . 1E **81**
Cartleach La. M28: Walk . . . 1D **80**
Cartmel OL12: Roch . . . 1B **178**
Cartmel Av. OL16: Miln . . . 1F **43**
SK4: Stoc . . . 3F **133**
Cartmel Cl. BL3: Bolt . . . 5D **46**
BL9: Bury . . . 4G **53**
OL8: O'ham . . . 6D **74**
SK7: H Gro . . . 2C **158**
SK8: Gat . . . 2G **155**
Cartmel Cres. BL2: Bolt . . . 3G **33**
OL9: Chad . . . 1H **89**
Cartmel Dr. WA15: Tim . . . 5D **140**
Cartmel Gro. M28: Wors . . . 4D **82**
Cartmell Ct. M9: Man . . . 5C **72**
Cartmel Wlk. *M9: Man* . . . *4H* ***87***
(off Shiredale Dr., not continuous)
M24: Mid . . . 5A **56**
Cartridge Cl. M22: Wyth . . . 2D **154**
Cartridge St. OL10: H'ood . . . 3G **39**
Cartwright Rd. M21: Chor . . . 1F **129**
Cartwright St. M34: Aud . . . 1F **119**
SK14: Hyde . . . 2E **121**
Carver Av. M25: Pres . . . 4A **70**
Carver Cl. M16: Old T . . . 2H **113**
Carver Dr. SK6: Mar . . . 6C **148**
Carver Rd. SK6: Mar . . . 6C **148**
WA15: Hale . . . 3G **151**
Carver St. M16: Old T . . . 2H **113**
Carver Theatre . . . **6D 148**
Carver Wlk. *M15: Man* . . . *2D* ***114***
(off Wellhead Cl.)
Carville Rd. M9: Man . . . 6D **72**
Casablanca Health and Fitness Cen.
. . . ***4E 107***
(off Armentieres Sq.)
Cascade Dr. M7: Sal . . . 6C **86**
Cashel Ct. M27: Ward . . . 2E **83**
Cashgate Ct. OL8: O'ham . . . 6D **74**
Cashmere Rd. SK3: Stoc . . . 4E **145**
Cashmore Wlk. M12: Man . . . 6H **11**
Caspian Rd. M9: Man . . . 6D **72**
WA14: B'ath . . . 5C **138**
Cassandra Ct. M5: Sal . . . 2B **8** (5A **100**)
Cass Av. M5: Sal . . . 5G **99**
Cassidy Cl. M4: Man . . . 3D **6** (3F **101**)
Cassidy Ct. M50: Sal . . . 5E **99**
Cassidy Gdns. M24: Mid . . . 3H **55**
Casson Ga. OL12: Roch . . . 2G **27**
Casson St. M35: Fail . . . 4H **89**
Casterton Way M28: Wors . . . 6E **81**
Castle Av. M34: Dent . . . 5E **119**
OL11: Roch . . . 6A **178** (5G **27**)
Castlebrook Cl. BL9: Bury . . . 3H **53**
Castle Cl. M43: Droy . . . 3B **104**
Castle Cotts. SK15: C'ook . . . 3B **94**
Castle Ct. BL2: Bolt . . . 3H **175**
OL6: A Lyme . . . 4H **91**
Castle Courts M5: Sal . . . 4H **99**
Castle Cft. BL2: Bolt . . . 2H **33**
(not continuous)
Castlecroft Ct. BL9: Bury . . . 3A **176**
Castlecroft M. BL9: Bury . . . 3A **176** (3E **37**)
Castlecroft Rd. BL9: Bury . . . 3A **176** (3E **37**)
Castledene Av. M6: Sal . . . 2E **99**
Castle Farm Dr. SK2: Stoc . . . 6B **146**
Castle Farm La. SK2: Stoc . . . 5B **146**
(not continuous)
CASTLEFIELD . . . **2E 9 (5C 100)**
Castlefield Av. M7: Sal . . . 3C **86**
Castlefield Gallery . . . **3F 9**
Castleford Cl. *BL1: Bolt* . . . *5B* ***32***
(off Gaskell St.)
Castleford St. OL1: Chad . . . 6C **58**
Castleford Wlk. *M21: Chor* . . . *2B* ***130***
(off Arrowfield Rd.)
Castlegate M15: Man . . . 3E **9** (6C **100**)
Castle Gro. BL0: Ram . . . 1A **22**
CASTLE HALL . . . **4F 107**
Castle Hall Cl. SK15: Stal . . . 4F **107**
Castle Hall Ct. SK15: Stal . . . 4E **107**
Castle Hall Vw. SK15: Stal . . . 4E **107**
Castle Hey Cl. BL9: Bury . . . 4A **54**
CASTLE HILL
BL2 . . . **2F 33**
SK6 . . . **2E 135**
WA14 . . . **5B 150**
WA15 . . . **3F 163**
Castle Hill SK6: Bred . . . 2E **135**
Castle Hill Cres.
OL11: Roch . . . 5A **178** (5G **27**)
Castle Hill Dr. *M9: Man* . . . *1G* ***87***
(off Marshbrook Dr.)
Castlehill Ind. Pk. SK6: Bred . . . 4F **135**
Castle Hill Mobile Home Pk.
SK6: Wood . . . 3F **135**
Castle Hill Rd. BL9: Bury . . . 3A **24**
(not continuous)
M25: Pres . . . 1B **86**
Castle Hill St. BL2: Bolt . . . 3F **33**
Castle Irwell Student Village
M6: Sal . . . 6H **85**
Castle La. OL5: Mos, Stal . . . 3A **94**
SK15: C'ook, Mos . . . 3A **94**
Castle Leisure Cen. . . . **3A 176 (3E 37)**
Castlemere Dr. OL2: Shaw . . . 5B **44**
Castlemere Rd. M9: Man . . . 6G **71**
Castlemere St.
OL11: Roch . . . 5A **178** (5G **27**)
Castlemere Ter.
OL11: Roch . . . 6A **178** (5H **27**)
Castle M. *BL4: Farn* . . . *2H* ***65***
(off Castle St.)
Castle Mill La. WA15: Alt . . . 6H **151**
Castlemill St. OL1: O'ham . . . 2H **75**
Castlemoor Av. M7: Sal . . . 3H **85**
Castle Pk. Ind. Est. OL1: O'ham . . . 2H **75**
Castle Quay M15: Man . . . 3E **9** (6C **100**)
Castlerea Cl. M30: Ecc . . . 5F **97**
Castlerigg Cl. SK4: Stoc . . . 2F **133**
Castlerigg Dr. M24: Mid . . . 4G **55**
OL2: O'ham . . . 1C **58**
Castle Rd. BL9: Bury . . . 4A **54**
Castleshaw Cen. . . . **1C 62**
Castle Shaw Rd. SK2: Stoc . . . 6D **146**
Castle St. BL2: Bolt . . . 4H **175** (6E **33**)
BL4: Farn . . . 2H **65**
BL9: Bury . . . 3B **176** (3E **37**)
BL9: Sum . . . 1D **22**
M3: Man . . . 2E **9** (5C **100**)
M24: Mid . . . 2F **73**
M30: Ecc . . . 3H **97**
SK3: Stoc . . . 6E **179** (4F **145**)
SK13: Had . . . 3H **123**
SK14: Hyde . . . 4D **120**
SK15: Stal . . . 4E **107**
Castle Ter. SK15: C'ook . . . 4B **94**
CASTLETON . . . **4E 41**
Castleton Av. M32: Stre . . . 3B **112**
Castleton Bank *SK13: Gam* . . . *6G* ***123***
(off Castleton Cres.)
Castleton Ct. M34: Dent . . . 1G **135**
Castleton Cres. SK13: Gam . . . 6G **123**
Castleton Dr. SK6: H Lan . . . 1D **170**
Castleton Grn. *SK13: Gam* . . . *6G* ***123***
(off Castleton Cres.)

Castleton Gro. OL6: A Lyme 5D 92
  SK13: Gam 6G 123
    (off Castleton Cres.)
Castleton Rd. M7: Sal 2C 86
  OL2: O'ham 5C 42
  SK7: H Gro 4E 159
Castleton Rd. Sth. OL11: Roch 2F 41
Castleton Station (Rail) 3E 41
Castleton St. BL2: Bolt 3F 33
  OL9: O'ham 3C 74
  WA14: B'ath 4E 139
Castleton Swimming Pool 2E 41
Castleton Ter. SK13: Gam 6G 123
Castleton Wlk. M11: Man 4B 102
    (off Burns Cl.)
Castleton Water Activity Cen. 3E 41
Castleton Way M34: Dent 1G 135
Castle Wlk. OL6: A Lyme 4H 91
  SK15: Stal 4E 107
    (off Crossfield Cl.)
Castle Way M27: Clif 1A 84
Castleway M6: Sal 1E 99
  OL11: Roch 4D 40
  WA15: Haleb 6C 152
Castlewood Gdns. SK2: Stoc 6C 146
Castlewood Rd. M7: Sal 3G 85
Castlewood Sq. BL2: Bolt 4G 33
Castle Yd. SK1: Stoc 1G 179 (1H 145)
Catalan Sq. M3: Man 2E 9
Catchdale Cl. M9: Man 4G 71
Catches Cl. OL11: Roch 3D 26
Catches La. OL11: Roch 2D 26
Cateaton St. BL9: Bury 1C 176 (2F 37)
  M3: Man 4H 5 (3D 100)
Caterham Av. BL3: Bolt 5F 47
Caterham St. M4: Man 6H 7 (4H 101)
Catesby Rd. M16: W Ran 4B 114
Catfield Wlk. M15: Man 4D 8
Catford Rd. M23: Wyth 6F 141
Cathedral App. M3: Sal ...3H 5 (3D 100)
Cathedral Cl. SK16: Duk 1B 120
Cathedral Gates M3: Man 4H 5
Cathedral Rd. OL9: Chad 6H 57
Cathedral St. M4: Man 4H 5 (3D 100)
Cathedral Yd. M3: Man 4H 5
Catherine Ho. SK4: Stoc 1B 144
Catherine St. M8: Man 2C 86
  M27: Swin 4E 83
  SK6: Rom 2F 147
  WA14: Bow 2E 151
Catherine St. BL3: Bolt 5H 47
  BL9: Bury 1E 53
  M11: Man 6G 103
  M30: Ecc 2C 96
  OL4: Lees 3C 76
  SK7: H Gro 1E 159
  SK14: Hyde 4B 120
Catherine St. E. M34: Dent 4D 118
Catherine St. W. M34: Dent 4D 118
Catherston Rd. M16: W Ran 4C 114
CATLEY LANE HEAD 5C 14
Catlow La. M4: Man 4B 6
Catlow St. M7: Sal 1C 100
Caton Cl. BL9: Bury 5E 37
Caton St. OL16: Roch 5C 178 (5H 27)
Cato St. BL0: Ram 5A 12
Catskowl Cl. M18: Man 4F 117
Catterall Cres. BL2: Bolt 5H 19
Catterick Av. M20: Man 6G 131
  M33: Sale 1E 139
Catterick Dr. BL3: Lit L 4C 50
Catterick Rd. M20: Man 6G 131
Catterwood Dr. SK6: Comp 1F 149
Catterwood Rd. SK6: Comp 1F 149
Cattlin Way OL8: O'ham 1C 90
Cauldale Cl. M24: Mid 4H 55
Causeway, The OL9: Chad 4F 73
  WA14: Alt 2B 174 (1F 151)
Causeway Cl. OL4: O'ham 3C 60
Causey Dr. M24: Mid 4H 55
Cavalier St. M40: Man 4H 7 (3H 101)
Cavanagh Cl. M13: Man 6G 11 (1H 115)
Cavan Cl. SK3: Stoc 4B 144

Cavannah Ct. OL1: O'ham 4C 60
    (off Northgate La.)
Cavell St. M1: Man 5C 6
Cavell Way M5: Sal 4G 99
  M6: Sal 3G 99
Cavendish Av. M20: Man 3D 130
  M27: Clif 6C 68
Cavendish Ct. M7: Sal 2B 86
  M9: Man 4E 71
    (off Deanswood Dr.)
  M32: Stre 3E 113
    (off Nansen Cl.)
  M41: Urm 5G 111
    (off Cavendish Rd.)
  SK4: Stoc 1B 144
Cavendish Gdns. BL3: Bolt 4A 48
Cavendish Gro. M30: Ecc 2G 97
Cavendish Hall M15: Man 4A 10
Cavendish Ho. M30: Ecc 2G 97
    (not continuous)
  OL6: A Lyme 3H 105
    (off Cavendish St.)
Cavendish Ind. Est.
  OL6: A Lyme 2G 105
Cavendish M. SK9: Wilm 4D 172
Cavendish Mill OL6: A Lyme 3H 105
Cavendish Pl. M11: Man 3C 102
  M27: Pen 3A 84
    (off Bridge St.)
Cavendish Rd. M7: Sal 2A 86
  M20: Man 3D 130
  M28: Wors 5D 82
  M30: Ecc 2G 97
  M32: Stre 3E 113
  M41: Urm 5G 111
  OL11: Roch 2G 41
  SK4: Stoc 1B 144
  SK7: H Gro 4D 158
  WA14: Bow 2E 151
Cavendish St. M15: Man 5A 10 (1E 115)
  OL6: A Lyme 5A 174 (2G 105)
  OL8: O'ham 5F 177 (3E 75)
Cavendish Ter. M21: Chor 1H 129
    (off Wilbraham Rd.)
Cavendish Way OL2: O'ham 5C 58
Cavenham Gro. BL1: Bolt 5A 32
Cavenham Wlk. M9: Man 4G 87
    (off Mannington Dr.)
Caversham Dr. M9: Man 3A 88
Cawdor Av. BL4: Farn 5F 49
Cawdor Ct. BL4: Farn 5G 49
Cawdor Ho. M30: Ecc 5F 97
    (off Enfield Cl.)
Cawdor Pl. WA15: Tim 5C 140
Cawdor Rd. M14: Man 6G 115
Cawdor St. BL4: Farn 5F 49
  M15: Man 4C 8 (6B 100)
  M27: Swin 3F 83
  M28: Walk 1A 82
  M30: Ecc 4E 97
Cawdor Wlk. BL4: Farn 5G 49
    (off Cawdor St.)
Cawley Av. M25: Pres 1F 85
Cawley Ter. M9: Man 4E 71
Cawood Ho. SK5: Stoc 3C 134
Cawood Sq. SK5: Stoc 2C 134
Cawston St. M8: Man 5E 87
    (off Cranlington Dr.)
Cawthorne Ct. M27: Ward 2F 83
Caxton Rd. M14: Man 6F 115
Caxton St. M3: Sal 4F 5 (3C 100)
  OL10: H'ood 3H 39
  OL11: Roch 3C 40
Caygill St. M3: Man 3F 5 (3C 100)
Cayley St. OL16: Roch 4B 28
Caythorpe St. M14: Man 4E 115
Cayton St. M12: Man 4C 116
Ceal, The SK6: Comp 1F 149
Cecil Av. M33: Sale 6G 127
Cecil Ct. SK3: Stoc 3D 144
  WA15: Hale 3G 151
Cecil Dr. M41: Urm 5A 110
Cecil Gro. M18: Man 2F 117

Cecilia Ct. Nth. BL3: Bolt 3E 49
    (off Cecilia St.)
Cecilia Ct. Sth. BL3: Bolt 3E 49
    (off Cecilia St.)
Cecilia St. BL3: Bolt 3E 49
Cecil Rd. M9: Man 4H 71
  M30: Ecc 4G 97
  M32: Stre 6C 112
  WA15: Hale 3G 151
Cecil St. BL2: Bolt 6F 33
  BL9: Bury 5C 176 (4F 37)
  M15: Man 2F 115
  M28: Walk 6H 65
  OL2: O'ham 3C 58
  OL5: Mos 3G 93
  OL7: A Lyme 4G 105
  OL8: O'ham 4E 75
  OL11: Roch 6H 27
  OL15: L'ough 4F 17
  SK3: Stoc 6E 179
  SK15: Stal 4F 107
  SK16: Duk 5H 105
Cecil Wlk. OL7: A Lyme 4G 105
    (off Cecil St.)
Cecil Walker Ho. M31: Part 5E 125
Cedar Av. BL3: Lit L 5D 50
  M45: White 3F 69
  OL6: A Lyme 6B 92
  OL10: H'ood 2G 39
  SK7: H Gro 3E 159
  SK15: Stal 6G 107
  WA14: Alt 1E 151
Cedar Bank Cl. OL16: Roch 4D 28
Cedar Cl. SK12: Poy 4E 169
Cedar Ct. M14: Man 6G 115
  M25: Pres 4G 69
    (off Longfield Cen.)
  SK8: Chea H 3C 156
    (off Vaudrey Dr.)
  WA15: Tim 6B 140
    (off Edenhurst Dr.)
Cedar Cres. BL0: Ram 2C 12
  OL9: Chad 1B 74
Cedar Dr. M27: Clif 5F 67
  M41: Urm 6E 111
  M43: Droy 3C 104
Cedar Gro. BL4: Farn 1F 65
  M14: Man 1H 131
  M25: Pres 3G 69
  M34: Dent 4E 119
  OL2: O'ham 1D 58
  OL2: Shaw 1H 59
  SK4: Stoc 4E 133
  SK16: Duk 5D 106
Cedar Ho., The
  SK15: Mill 1H 107
    (off Bramble Cl.)
Cedar La. OL4: Gras 3H 77
  OL16: Miln 2G 43
Cedar Lawn SK8: Chea H 3C 156
    (off Vaudrey Dr.)
Cedar M. OL7: A Lyme 6H 91
Cedar Pl. M7: Sal 1A 100
Cedar Rd. M24: Mid 1E 73
  M31: Part 6C 124
  M33: Sale 3F 127
  M35: Fail 5H 89
  SK2: Stoc 1B 158
  SK6: Mar 1C 160
  SK8: Gat 6E 143
  WA15: Hale 2G 151
Cedars, The BL1: Bolt 5D 18
Cedars Rd. M22: Wyth 2B 154
Cedar St. BL9: Bury 2G 37
    (not continuous)
  OL4: O'ham 2A 76
    (not continuous)
  OL6: A Lyme 1B 106
  OL12: Roch 2H 27
  SK14: Hyde 2C 120
Cedar Technology Cen.
  WA14: B'ath 4D 138

Cedar Vw. OL6: A Lyme 1B **106**
(off Cedar St.)
Cedarway SK9: Wilm 5C **172**
Cedarwood SK12: Poy 3E **169**
Cedarwood Av. SK4: Stoc 2C **144**
Cedarwood Cl. M22: Nor 3C **142**
Cedar Wood Ct. BL1: Bolt 6G **31**
Cedric Rd. M8: Man 1C **86**
    OL4: O'ham 2A **76**
Cedric St. M11: Sal 3E **99**
Celandine Cl. OL15: L'ough 3F **17**
Celia St. M8: Man 3G **87**
Cellini Sq. BL1: Bolt 4B **32**
Celtic St. SK1: Stoc 3A **146**
Cemetery La. BL9: Bury 5G **37**
Cemetery Rd. BL0: Ram 5A **12**
    BL2: Bolt 6F **33**
    BL4: Kea 6B **50**
    M5: Sal 4E **99**
    M26: Rad 3H **51**
    (not continuous)
    M34: Aud 1F **119**
    M34: Dent 6F **119**
    M35: Fail 5H **89**
    M43: Droy 4H **103**
    OL2: O'ham 2C **58**
    OL5: Mos 4H **93**
Cemetery Rd. Nth. M27: Swin 1G **83**
Cemetery Rd. Sth. M27: Swin 2G **83**
Cemetery St. M24: Mid 6C **56**
Cenacle Ho. M16: W Ran 5C **114**
    (off Alexandra Rd. Sth.)
Cennick Cl. OL4: O'ham 3B **76**
Centaur Cl. M27: Clif 1H **83**
Centaur Way M8: Man 4D **86**
    (off Narburth Dr.)
Centenary Circ. M30: Ecc 4A **98**
Centenary Ct. BL3: Bolt 3D **48**
Centenary Way M17: T Pk 4B **98**
    M30: Ecc 4A **98**
Central Art Gallery
    Ashton-under-Lyne 6B **174**
Central Av. BL0: Ram 3G **13**
    BL1: Bolt 1E **49**
    BL4: Farn 1E **65**
    BL9: Bury 6D **36**
    M6: Sal 5E **85**
    M19: Man 5C **116**
    M27: Clif 1D **84**
    M28: Walk 4G **65**
    M33: Sale 2F **139**
    OL3: G'fld 4D **78**
    OL15: L'ough 3H **17**
Central Cl. BL1: Bolt 4C **32**
Central Ct. Apartments M3: Sal . . .4D **4**
Central Dr. BL9: Bury 3F **23**
    M8: Man 2F **87**
    M27: Swin 4B **84**
    M41: Urm 5F **111**
    SK5: Stoc 4H **133**
    SK6: Rom 6A **136**
    SK7: Bram 3F **157**
    SK8: H Grn 5H **155**
Central Ho. M9: Man 4A **72**
Central Leisure Cen. 3D **178** (4A **28**)
Central Pk. Est. M17: T Pk 1B **112**
Central Pl. SK9: Wilm 2E **173**
    (off Station Rd.)
Central Retail Pk.
    BL2: Bolt 6H **175** (1D **48**)
    M4: Man 5E **7** (4G **101**)
Central Rd. M20: Man 4E **131**
    M23: Wyth 1F **153**
    M31: Part 6D **124**
Central St. BL0: Ram 3B **12**
    BL1: Bolt 3E **175** (6C **32**)
    M2: Man 6H **5** (4D **100**)
Central Way WA14: Alt . . .2A **174** (1F **151**)
Centre Gdns. BL1: Bolt 4B **32**
Centre Pk. Rd. BL1: Bolt 4B **32**
Centrepoint M17: T Pk 2A **112**
Centre Retail Pk., The
    OL2: O'ham 5B **58**

Centre Va. Cl. OL15: L'ough 2H **17**
Centurion Gro. M7: Sal 5C **86**
Century Gdns.
    OL12: Roch 1B **178** (3H **27**)
Century Lodge BL4: Farn 1G **65**
Century Mill Ind. Est. BL4: Farn 1F **65**
Century Pk. Ind. Est.
    WA14: B'ath 5C **138**
Century St. M3: Man 2F **9** (5C **100**)
Cestrian St. BL3: Bolt 4D **48**
Ceylon St. M40: Man 5C **88**
    OL4: O'ham 4B **76**
Chadbury Cl. BL6: Los 4C **46**
CHADDERTON 2B **74**
Chadderton Dr. BL9: Bury 5G **53**
CHADDERTON FOLD 5H **57**
Chadderton Fold OL1: Chad 5H **57**
    (not continuous)
Chadderton Hall Rd. OL1: Chad 6H **57**
    OL9: Chad 6H **57**
Chadderton Hgts. OL1: Chad 4H **57**
Chadderton Ind. Est. M24: Mid 4E **73**
CHADDERTON PARK 1H **73**
Chadderton Pk. Rd. OL9: Chad 6H **57**
Chadderton Pct. OL9: Chad 2B **74**
Chadderton Sports Cen. 2B **74**
Chadderton St. M4: Man . . .3C **6** (3F **101**)
Chadderton Way
    OL1: O'ham 5C **58**
    OL9: O'ham 1E **177** (1D **74**)
    (off Windcroft Cl.)
Chaddesley Wlk. M11: Man 5C **102**
    (off Windcroft Cl.)
Chaddock La. M28: Wors 5D **80**
    M29: Ast 5B **80**
Chaddock Level, The M28: Wors 6E **81**
CHADKIRK .3H **147**
Chadkirk Chapel 2A **148**
Chadkirk Ind. Est. SK6: Rom 3H **147**
Chadkirk M. SK6: Rom 1A **148**
Chadkirk Rd. SK6: Rom 2H **147**
Chads Theatre 4D **156**
Chadvil Rd. SK8: Chea 6G **143**
Chadwell Rd. SK2: Stoc 4E **147**
Chadwick Cl. M14: Man 4F **115**
    (off Union Pl.)
    OL10: Miln 6G **29**
    SK9: Wilm 6G **165**
Chadwick Fold BL9: Bury 4F **23**
    OL10: H'ood 3B **40**
Chadwick Hall Rd. OL11: Roch 5D **26**
Chadwick La. OL10: H'ood 3B **40**
    OL11: Roch 3D **40**
    OL16: Roch 3C **42**
Chadwick Rd. M30: Ecc 3G **97**
    M41: Urm 5H **111**
Chadwicks Cl. SK15: Stal 2D **106**
Chadwick St. BL2: Bolt 1E **49**
    BL3: Lit L 4D **50**
    BL9: Bury 1C **38**
    M27: Swin 3H **83**
    OL6: A Lyme 3C **106**
    OL11: Roch 4F **27**
    OL16: Roch 4E **29**
    SK1: Stoc 5G **179** (3H **145**)
    SK6: Mar 6D **148**
Chadwick Ter. OL12: Roch 5F **15**
Chadwick Wlk. M27: Swin 3H **83**
    (off Chadwick St.)
Chaffinch Cl. M22: Shar 6D **142**
    M43: Droy 2C **104**
    OL4: O'ham 5B **76**
Chaffinch Dr. BL9: Bury 1A **38**
CHAIN BAR 6E **73**
Chain Bar La. SK14: Mot 5B **122**
Chain Bar Way SK14: Mot 5B **122**
Chainhurst Wlk. M13: Man 5E **11**
Chain Rd. M9: Man 3H **71**
Chain St. M1: Man 6A **6** (4E **101**)
Chain Wlk. M9: Man 4A **72**
Chalcombe Grange M12: Man 3B **116**
Chale Cl. M40: Man 2G **7** (2H **101**)
Chale Dr. M24: Mid 3E **73**
Chale Grn. BL2: Bolt 2A **34**

Chalfont Av. M41: Urm 5G **111**
    (off Gladstone Rd.)
Chalfont Cl. OL8: O'ham 5H **75**
Chalfont Dr. M8: Man 4E **87**
    M28: Walk 3A **82**
Chalfont Ho. M5: Sal 3F **99**
    (off Amersham St.)
Chalfont St. BL1: Bolt 3D **32**
    (not continuous)
Chalford Rd. M23: Wyth 1G **153**
Challenor Sq. M12: Man 1C **116**
    (off Polesworth Cl.)
Challinor St. BL1: Bolt 5H **31**
Challum Dr. OL9: Chad 1A **74**
Chamber Hall Cl.
    OL8: O'ham 5D **74**
Chamberhall St.
    BL9: Bury 1B **176** (2E **37**)
Chamber Ho. Dr. OL11: Roch 2D **40**
Chamber House Urban Farm 2C **40**
Chamberlain Dr. SK9: Wilm 6H **165**
Chamberlain Gdns.
    SK6: Bred 5F **135**
Chamberlain Rd. SK15: H'rod 6G **93**
Chamberlain St. BL3: Bolt 1B **48**
Chamber Rd. OL2: Shaw 6G **43**
    OL8: O'ham 6F **177** (6C **74**)
Chambers, The M33: Sale 4A **128**
    (off York Rd.)
Chambers Ct. SK14: Mot 4C **122**
Chambersfield Ct. M5: Sal 4F **99**
Champagnole Ct. SK16: Duk 4H **105**
    (off Hill St.)
Champness Hall
    OL16: Roch 4C **178** (4H **27**)
Champneys Wlk. M9: Man 5H **87**
    (off Penerley Dr.)
Chancel Av. M5: Sal 2A **8** (5A **100**)
Chancel Cl. SK16: Duk 1A **120**
Chancel La. SK9: Wilm 1E **173**
Chancellor La.
    M12: Man 2G **11** (5H **101**)
Chancel M. SK1: Stoc 2H **179** (2A **146**)
Chancel Pl. M1: Man 6E **7**
    OL16: Roch 4B **178** (4H **27**)
Chancery Cl. M29: Ast 3A **80**
Chancery La. BL1: Bolt 4G **175** (6D **32**)
    (not continuous)
    M2: Man 6H **5** (4E **101**)
    OL2: Shaw 6A **44**
    OL3: Dob 5C **62**
Chancery Pl. M2: Man 6H **5**
Chancery St. OL4: O'ham 3A **76**
    OL9: Chad 1C **74**
Chandlers Point M50: Sal 5G **99**
Chandlers Row M28: Wors 6C **82**
Chandley Ct. SK1: Stoc 6H **179**
Chandley St. SK8: Chea 5H **143**
Chandos Gro. M5: Sal 3D **98**
Chandos Hall M1: Man 2C **10**
Chandos Rd. M21: Chor 6A **114**
    M25: Pres 1H **85**
    SK4: Stoc 3D **132**
Chandos Rd. Sth.
    M21: Chor 1A **130**
Chandos St. OL2: Shaw 6A **44**
Change Way M3: Sal 2E **5** (2C **100**)
Channing Ct. OL16: Roch 5B **28**
Channing Sq. OL16: Roch 5B **28**
Channing St. OL16: Roch 5B **28**
Chanters, The M28: Wors 4G **81**
Chanters Cl. M9: Man 5G **71**
Chantler's Av. BL8: Bury 3A **36**
Chantry Cl. SK5: Stoc 2G **133**
    SK12: Dis 2H **171**
Chantry Rd. SK12: Dis 1H **171**
Chantry Wlk. M8: Man 4D **86**
    (off Lanfield Dr.)
Chapel All. BL1: Bolt 3F **175** (6D **32**)
Chapel Cl. BL9: Bury 3H **53**
    SK16: Duk 5A **106**
Chapel Cotts. SK9: Wilm 6A **164**

Chapel Ct. M26: Rad 3H 51
   (off Ainsworth Rd.)
  M33: Sale 3G 127
   (off Green La.)
  SK6: Mar 6D 148
   (off Chadwick St.)
  SK9: Wilm 3D 172
  SK14: Hyde 6A 120
  WA14: Alt 3A 174 (1F 151)
Chapel Cft. OL2: O'ham 3D 58
Chapel Dr. OL6: A Lyme 6C 92
  WA15: Haleb 6C 152
CHAPEL FIELD 6C 52
Chapelfield M26: Rad 6C 52
Chapelfield Cl. SK15: Mill 1H 107
Chapelfield Dr. M28: Walk 6F 65
Chapel Fld. Rd. M34: Dent 4F 119
Chapelfield Rd. M12: Man . .2F 11 (5G 101)
Chapel Flds. SK6: Mar 6D 148
   (off Church La.)
Chapelfield St. BL1: Bolt 2C 32
Chapel Gdns. BL8: G'mount 2F 21
  M34: Aud 1F 119
   (off Guide La.)
Chapel Ga. OL16: Miln 5F 29
Chapel Grn. M34: Dent 4F 119
Chapel Gro. M26: Rad 1A 68
  M41: Urm 5G 111
Chapel Hill OL15: L'ough 3H 17
  SK16: Duk 5A 106
Chapel Hill Dr. M9: Man 6G 71
Chapel Ho. SK5: Stoc 1G 133
Chapel Ho's. OL12: Whitw 1B 14
   (off Oak Cl.)
  SK2: H Gro 1C 158
  SK6: Mar 6E 149
Chapel La. BL8: Holc 3A 12
  M9: Man 5F 71
  M31: Part 6D 124
  M32: Stre 6C 112
  M33: Sale 3G 127
  OL2: O'ham 3D 58
  OL11: Roch 3F 25
  SK9: Wilm 3C 172
  SK13: Had 2H 123
  WA15: Haleb 5B 152
Chapel Mdw. M28: Wors 4F 81
Chapel Pl. BL2: Bolt 2G 49
  BL3: Bolt 2G 49
  M41: Urm 5F 97
Chapel Rd. M22: Nor 3B 142
  M25: Pres 2F 85
  M27: Swin 4E 83
  M33: Sale 4B 128
  M44: Irl 6E 109
  OL3: G'fld 3C 78
  OL8: O'ham 5E 73
  SK9: A Edg 5G 173
Chapel St. BL1: Bolt 2G 175
  BL3: Lit L 4D 50
  BL4: Farn 1A 66
  BL7: Eger 1B 18
  BL8: Tot 4G 21
  M3: Sal 4C 4 (3B 100)
  M19: Man 6C 116
  M24: Mid 2G 71
   (Manchester Old Rd.)
  M24: Mid 1B 72
   (Wood St., not continuous)
  M25: Pres 5G 69
  M26: Rad 2D 66
  M27: Pen 2A 84
  M28: Wors 5D 80
  M30: Ecc 4E 97
  M34: Aud 1F 119
  M43: Droy 4B 104
  OL2: O'ham 3D 58
  OL2: Shaw 6H 43
  OL3: Upp 1D 78
   (not continuous)
  OL4: Lees 3C 74
  OL5: Mos 2G 93
  OL6: A Lyme 5D 174 (2A 106)

Chapel St. OL10: H'ood 3H 39
  OL11: Roch 1A 42
  OL12: Whitw 1E 15
  OL12: W'le 5C 16
  OL15: L'ough 1B 16
  SK4: Stoc 1H 143
  SK6: Wood 4H 135
  SK7: H Gro 2E 159
  SK8: Chea 6H 143
  SK9: A Edg 5G 173
  SK14: Hyde 5B 120
  SK15: Stal 3E 107
  SK16: Duk 5H 105
Chapel Ter. BL0: Ram 1F 13
  M20: Man 2F 131
Chapeltown Rd. BL7: Bro X 4F 19
  M26: Rad 6A 52
Chapeltown St. M1: Man . . .1D 10 (5F 101)
Chapel Vw. SK16: Duk 5A 106
Chapelvw. Cl. SK14: Hyde 2C 136
Chapel Wlk. M24: Mid 2G 71
   (off Chapel St.)
  M25: Pres 2G 85
  M30: Ecc 3H 97
   (off Cambridge Gro.)
  M45: White 6H 53
  SK6: Mar 5D 148
  SK13: Had 2H 123
  SK15: Stal 4F 107
Chapel Walks M2: Man 5H 5 (4D 100)
  M33: Sale 4B 128
  SK8: Chea H 1D 166
Chapelway Gdns. OL2: O'ham 1D 58
Chaplin Cl. M6: Sal 1E 99
Chapman Ct. SK14: Hat 1C 158
Chapman Gallery 3A 4 (3H 99)
Chapman M. M18: Man 2F 117
Chapman Rd. SK14: Hat 6A 122
Chapman St. BL1: Bolt 4H 31
  M18: Man 1F 117
Chappell Rd. M43: Droy 3A 104
Chapter St. M40: Man 1B 102
Charcoal La. WA14: Bow 2A 150
Charcoal Rd. WA14: Bow 1A 150
Charcoal Woods WA14: Bow 2C 150
Charcon Wlk. OL2: O'ham 3E 59
Chard Dr. M22: Wyth 4B 154
Chardin Av. SK6: Mar B 3G 149
Chard St. M26: Rad 4A 52
Charges St. OL7: A Lyme 4F 105
Chariot St. M11: Man 5F 103
Charlbury Av. M25: Pres 6C 70
  SK5: Stoc 3H 133
Charlbury Way OL2: O'ham 2G 59
Charlecote Rd. SK12: Poy 3F 169
Charles Av. M34: Aud 6A 104
  SK6: Mar 4A 148
Charles Ct. BL1: Bolt 1G 175 (5D 32)
  WA15: Tim 5B 140
   (off Thorley La., not continuous)
Charles Halle Rd. M15: Man 2E 115
Charles Holden St. BL1: Bolt 1B 48
Charles La. OL16: Miln 6G 29
Charles M. OL16: Miln 6G 29
Charles Morris Cl. M35: Fail 4A 90
Charles Morris Ho. M35: Fail 4A 90
Charles Shaw Cl. OL4: O'ham 6B 60
Charles St. BL1: Bolt 2G 175 (5D 32)
  BL4: Farn 6A 50
  BL4: Kea 2A 66
  BL7: Eger 2G 19
  BL9: Bury 1D 176 (2F 37)
  M1: Man 3A 10 (6E 101)
  M6: Sal 1F 99
   (not continuous)
  M27: Swin 2F 83
  M34: Dent 2F 119
  M43: Droy 4G 103
  M44: Cad 3C 124
  M45: White 2F 69
  OL2: O'ham 3D 58
  OL7: A Lyme 6B 174 (3H 105)
  OL9: O'ham 3C 74

Charles St. OL10: H'ood 5A 40
  OL15: L'ough 4G 17
  SK1: Stoc 6H 179 (4H 145)
   (not continuous)
  SK7: H Gro 2D 158
  SK16: Duk 5H 105
Charleston Cl. M33: Sale 1F 139
Charleston Sq. M41: Urm 4D 110
Charleston St. OL8: O'ham 5F 75
CHARLESTOWN
  M6 .6H 85
  M9 . . . . .6C 72
Charlestown Ct. OL6: A Lyme 1H 105
Charlestown Ind. Est.
  OL6: A Lyme 1H 105
Charlestown Rd. M9: Man 1H 87
Charlestown Rd. E. SK2: Stoc 2A 158
Charlestown Rd. W. SK3: Stoc 2H 157
Charlestown Way
  OL6: A Lyme 4A 174 (2G 105)
Charles Whittaker St.
  OL12: Roch 2B 26
Charlesworth Av. BL3: Bolt 4F 49
  M34: Dent 1F 135
Charlesworth St. M11: Man 5B 102
  SK1: Stoc 6G 179 (4H 145)
Charley Av. M7: Sal 1B 100
Charlock Sq. WA14: B'ath 3D 138
Charlock Wlk. M31: Part 6D 124
   (off Central Rd.)
Charlotte La. OL4: Gras 4A 78
Charlotte Pl. WA15: Hale 2H 151
Charlotte St. BL0: Ram 4B 12
  BL1: Bolt 3C 32
  M1: Man 6A 6 (4E 101)
  OL16: Roch 1A 42
  SK1: Stoc 6B 134
  SK8: Chea 6H 143
Charlton Av. M25: Pres 6H 69
  M30: Ecc 4F 97
  SK14: Hyde 3E 121
Charlton Ct. M25: Pres 6H 69
Charlton Dr. M27: Ward 1F 83
  M33: Sale 5C 128
Charlton Fold M28: Walk 4G 65
Charlton Pl. M12: Man 3D 10 (6F 101)
Charlton Rd. M19: Man 6D 116
Charminster Dr. M8: Man 3F 87
Charminster M. M27: Swin 5H 83
Charmouth Wlk. M22: Wyth 2D 154
Charnley Cl. M33: Sale 5A 128
  M40: Man 2A 102
Charnley Grange BL6: Los 6B 30
Charnley St. M45: White 1F 69
Charnock Dr. BL1: Bolt 4C 32
Charnville Rd. SK8: Gat 6D 142
Charnwood SK6: H Lan 6D 160
Charnwood Av. M34: Dent 4B 118
Charnwood Cl. M28: Walk 1G 81
  OL2: Shaw 5E 43
  OL6: A Lyme 4A 92
Charnwood Cres. SK7: H Gro 5D 158
Charnwood Rd. M9: Man 4H 71
  SK6: Wood 4A 136
Charter Av. M26: Rad 5C 52
Charter Cl. M33: Sale 6F 127
Charter Ho. M30: Ecc 4H 97
Charter Rd. WA15: Alt 3C 174 (1G 151)
Charter St. M3: Man 1H 5 (2D 100)
  OL1: O'ham 1G 75
  OL16: Roch 1A 42
Chartist Ho. SK14: Hyde 5C 120
Chartwell Cl. M5: Sal 3F 99
Chartwell Dr. M23: Wyth 4E 141
Chase, The BL1: Bolt 6G 31
  M28: Wors 6C 82
Chasefield WA14: Bow 3C 150
Chaseley Fld. Mans. M6: Sal 1E 99
Chaseley Rd. M6: Sal 1E 99
  OL12: Roch 3G 27
Chase St. M4: Man 1B 6 (2E 101)
Chasetown Cl. M23: Wyth 5D 140

Chasewood M19: Man 6C **116**
(off Motherwell Av.)
Chassen Av. M41: Urm 5C **110**
Chassen Ct. M41: Urm 6D **110**
Chassen Rd. BL1: Bolt 6H **31**
M41: Urm 5D **110**
Chassen Road Station (Rail) 6D **110**
Chataway Rd. M8: Man 3G **87**
Chatburn Av. OL11: Roch 5F **41**
Chatburn Ct. OL2: Shaw 5H **43**
Chatburn Gdns. OL10: H'ood 3D **38**
Chatburn Rd. BL1: Bolt 2F **31**
M21: Chor 1A **130**
Chatburn Sq. OL11: Roch 5F **41**
Chatcombe Rd. M22: Wyth 3G **153**
Chatfield Rd. M21: Chor 1H **129**
Chatford Cl. M7: Sal 1E **5** (1C **100**)
Chatham Ct. M20: Man 3E **131**
Chatham Gdns. BL3: Bolt 2B **48**
Chatham Gro. M20: Man 3E **131**
Chatham Ho. SK3: Stoc 5E **179**
Chatham Pl. BL3: Bolt 2B **48**
Chatham Rd. M16: Old T 4A **114**
M18: Man 4G **117**
Chatham St. M1: Man 6C **6** (4F **101**)
SK3: Stoc 5E **179** (3F **145**)
SK14: Hyde 2C **136**
Chatley Rd. M30: Ecc 4B **96**
Chatley St. M3: Man 1A **6** (1D **100**)
Chatswood Av. SK2: Stoc 5H **145**
Chatsworth Av. M25: Pres 5H **69**
Chatsworth Cl. BL9: Bury 2G **53**
M41: Urm 5G **111**
M43: Droy 2F **103**
OL2: Shaw 5B **44**
WA15: Tim 6C **140**
Chatsworth Ct. M9: Man 4E **71**
(off Deanswood Dr.)
SK2: Stoc 6A **146**
Chatsworth Cres. M32: Stre 4H **111**
(off Chatsworth Rd.)
Chatsworth Gro. BL3: Lit L 3C **50**
M16: W Ran 5B **114**
Chatsworth M. SK7: Bram 3F **157**
Chatsworth Rd. M18: Man 2E **117**
M26: Rad 2F **51**
M28: Wors 5D **82**
M30: Ecc 1H **97**
M32: Stre 4H **111**
M43: Droy 3G **103**
SK6: H Lan 1D **170**
SK7: H Gro 4F **159**
SK8: Chea H 6D **144**
SK9: Wilm 5B **172**
Chatsworth St. OL4: O'ham 4A **76**
OL12: Roch 6G **15**
CHATTERTON 3F **13**
Chatterton BL0: Ram 3F **13**
Chatterton Cl. M20: Man 3G **131**
Chatterton Old La. BL0: Ram 3F **13**
Chatterton Rd. BL0: Ram 3F **13**
Chattock St. M16: W Ran 4C **114**
Chatton Cl. BL8: Bury 3H **35**
Chatwell Ct. OL16: Miln 1A **44**
Chatwood Rd. M40: Man 1F **89**
Chaucer Av. M26: Rad 3G **51**
M34: Dent 2G **135**
M43: Droy 4A **104**
SK5: Stoc 1F **133**
Chaucer M. SK1: Stoc 2B **146**
Chaucer Ri. SK16: Duk 6E **107**
Chaucer Rd. M24: Mid 5D **56**
Chaucer St. BL1: Bolt 3B **32**
OL1: O'ham 4F **177** (3E **75**)
OL2: O'ham 2E **59**
OL11: Roch 3E **41**
Chaumont Way
OL6: A Lyme 5C **174** (2H **105**)
Chauncy Rd. M40: Man 3G **89**
Chaytor Av. M40: Man 4D **88**
CHEADLE 5A **144**
Cheadle Av. M7: Sal 4G **85**
Cheadle Ct. SK8: Chea H 4A **156**

Cheadle Grn. SK8: Chea 5A **144**
CHEADLE HEATH 4C **144**
CHEADLE HULME 3C **156**
Cheadle Hulme Recreation Cen. 6D **156**
Cheadle Hulme Station (Rail) 3D **156**
Cheadle Old Rd. SK3: Stoc 4E **145**
Cheadle Pl. SK8: Chea 5B **144**
Cheadle Pools & Target Fitness Cen.
. . . . .1A **156**
Cheadle Rd. SK8: Chea 1A **156**
Cheadle Royal Bus. Pk.
SK8: Chea 2G **155**
Cheadle Sq. BL1: Bolt 4E **175** (6C **32**)
Cheadle St. M11: Man 5F **103**
Cheadle Wood SK8: Chea H 5A **156**
Cheam Cl. M11: Man 6D **102**
Cheam Rd. WA15: Tim 3H **139**
Cheapside M2: Man 5H **5** (4D **100**)
M24: Mid 6C **56**
OL1: O'ham 3F **177** (2E **75**)
SK14: Hyde 4C **120**
Cheapside Sq. BL1: Bolt 4F **175** (6D **32**)
Cheddar St. M18: Man 2F **117**
Cheddington Cl. SK8: Chea H 6C **156**
Cheddleton Rd. WA14: W Tim 3E **139**
Chedlee Dr. SK8: Chea H 5A **156**
Chedlin Dr. M23: Wyth 1G **153**
Chedworth Cres. M38: Lit H 3E **65**
Chedworth Dr. M23: Wyth 5H **141**
Chedworth Gro. BL3: Bolt 2C **48**
(off Parrot St.)
Cheeky Chimps Activity Cen. 3C **76**
Cheeryble St. M11: Man 6H **103**
(not continuous)
M43: Droy 5H **103**
Cheesden Wlk. M45: White 6A **54**
Cheetham Av. M24: Mid 6D **56**
Cheetham Fold Rd. SK14: Hyde 1B **136**
Cheetham Gdns. SK15: Stal 4F **107**
CHEETHAM HILL 4D **86**
Cheetham Hill OL2: Shaw 1H **59**
OL12: Whitw 2B **14**
Cheetham Hill Rd.
M4: Man 1A **6** (2E **101**)
M8: Man 1A **6** (3D **86**)
SK15: Stal 1B **120**
SK16: Duk 1B **120**
Cheetham Pde. M8: Man 3D **86**
Cheetham Pk. Cen. M8: Man 6D **86**
Cheetham Pl. SK6: Bred 5F **135**
Cheethams Cres. OL2: O'ham 3G **59**
Cheetham St. M24: Mid 1B **72**
M26: Rad 4C **52**
M35: Fail 3A **90**
(not continuous)
M40: Man 6A **88**
OL1: O'ham 2H **75**
OL2: Shaw 1A **60**
OL16: Roch 2B **178** (3H **27**)
Cheetham Wlk. SK14: Hyde 4C **120**
Cheetwood Rd. M8: Man 1D **100**
Cheetwood St. M8: Man 1C **100**
Chelbourne Dr. OL8: O'ham 1B **90**
Chelburn Cl. SK2: Stoc 6D **146**
Chelburn Ct. SK3: Stoc 5G **145**
Chelburn Vw. OL15: L'ough 2A **16**
Cheldon Wlk. M40: Man 5E **89**
(off Bridlington Cl.)
Chelford Av. BL1: Bolt 6C **18**
Chelford Cl. M13: Man 2H **115**
M24: Mid 5E **57**
WA15: Alt 5G **139**
Chelford Dr. M27: Swin 1G **83**
M29: Ast 5A **80**
Chelford Gro. SK3: Stoc 6E **145**
Chelford Ho. SK3: Stoc 6H **147**
Chelford Rd. M16: Old T 4A **114**
M33: Sale 1E **141**
SK9: A Edg, N Ald 5F **173**
SK9: Hand 2H **165**
Chellow Cl. OL5: Mos 2F **93**
Chellow Dene OL5: Mos 2F **93**

Chell St. M12: Man 3B **116**
Chelmer Cl. BL5: W'ton 6A **46**
Chelmer Gro. OL10: H'ood 2E **39**
Chelmsford Av. M40: Man 1D **102**
Chelmsford Rd. SK3: Stoc 3E **145**
Chelmsford St.
OL8: O'ham 6E **177** (4E **75**)
Chelmsford Wlk. M34: Dent 6G **119**
(off Kendal Av.)
Chelsea Av. M26: Rad 3F **51**
Chelsea Cl. OL2: Shaw 6H **43**
Chelsea Rd. BL3: Bolt 4B **48**
M40: Man 6E **89**
M41: Urm 6G **109**
Chelsea St. BL9: Bury 2F **53**
OL11: Roch 6F **27**
Chelsfield Gro. M21: Chor 1B **130**
Chelston Av. M40: Man 1F **89**
Chelston Dr. SK8: H Grn 1G **165**
Cheltenham Cres. M7: Sal 3C **86**
Cheltenham Dr. M33: Sale 5C **128**
Cheltenham Grn. M24: Mid 3C **72**
Cheltenham Rd. M21: Chor 5H **113**
M24: Mid 3C **72**
SK3: Stoc 4C **144**
Cheltenham St. M6: Sal 1H **99**
OL1: O'ham 6H **59**
OL11: Roch 1F **41**
Chelt Wlk. M22: Wyth 3H **153**
Chelwood Cl. BL1: Bolt 4B **18**
Chelwood Dr. M43: Droy 3H **103**
Chelwood M. BL6: Los 6B **30**
Chelworth Mnr. SK7: Bram 4E **157**
Chendre Cl. M27: Pen 1H **83**
Chendre Rd. M9: Man 6D **72**
Cheney Cl. M11: Man 6F **103**
Chepstow Av. M33: Sale 6E **127**
Chepstow Cl. OL11: Roch 3B **26**
Chepstow Dr. OL1: O'ham 6H **59**
SK7: H Gro 3G **159**
Chepstow Ho. M1: Man 2H **9**
Chepstow Rd. M21: Chor 6G **113**
M27: Clif 1A **84**
Chepstow St. M1: Man 2H **9** (5D **100**)
(not continuous)
Chepstow St. Sth.
M1: Man 2H **9** (5D **100**)
CHEQUERBENT 6B **46**
Chequers Rd. M21: Chor 1H **129**
Cherington Cl. M23: Wyth 1H **141**
SK9: Hand 4B **166**
Cherington Dr. M29: Tyld 2A **80**
Cherington Rd. SK8: Chea 1G **155**
Cheriton Av. M33: Sale 4C **128**
Cheriton Cl. SK14: Hat 5H **121**
Cheriton Dr. BL2: Bolt 6A **34**
Cheriton Ri. SK2: Stoc 5G **147**
Cheriton Rd. M41: Urm 4H **109**
Cherrington Dr. OL11: Roch 5F **41**
Cherry Av. BL9: Bury 2A **38**
M11: Man 6F **103**
OL6: A Lyme 5H **91**
OL8: O'ham 6A **76**
Cherry Cl. BL9: Bury 6G **37**
SK2: Stoc 4E **147**
CHERRY CLOUGH 2F **45**
Cherry Ct. M33: Sale 5A **128**
WA15: Tim 4C **140**
(off Whitley Pl.)
Cherry Cft. SK6: Rom 2C **148**
(not continuous)
Cherry Dr. M27: Swin 3A **84**
Cherry Gdns. BL1: Bolt 5F **31**
Cherry Gro. OL2: O'ham 1C **58**
OL11: Roch 3C **26**
SK15: Stal 5E **107**
Cherry Hall Dr. OL2: Shaw 6E **43**
Cherry Hinton OL1: O'ham 1D **74**
(off Cottam St.)
Cherry Holt Av. SK4: Stoc 5B **132**
Cherry La. M33: Sale 1E **139**
OL3: Dens 2F **45**
Cherry Orchard Cl. SK7: Bram 4F **157**

Cherry St. M25: Pres 4A 70
Cherryton Wlk.
  M13: Man 6E 11 (1G 115)
CHERRY TREE 1C 148
Cherry Tree Av. BL4: Farn 1D 64
  SK12: Poy 4F 169
Cherry Tree Ct. SK6: Rom 1C 148
  SK9: Wilm 1H 173
  WA15: Tim 6B 140
Cherry Tree Dr. M6: Sal 3G 99
  SK2: Stoc 1C 158
Cherry Tree Dr. SK7: H Gro 5F 159
Cherry Tree Est. SK6: Rom 2D 148
Cherry Tree La. BL8: Bury 4C 36
  SK2: Stoc 6C 146
  SK6: Rom 1C 148
  WA14: Tim 6A 150
Cherry Tree Rd. M23: Wyth 2F 141
  SK8: Chea H 4B 156
Cherry Tree Wlk. M32: Stre 6C 112
  OL5: Mos 2F 93
Cherry Tree Way BL2: Bolt 1F 33
Cherry Wlk. M31: Part 6B 124
  SK8: Chea H 5E 157
Cherrywood OL9: Chad 2F 73
Cherrywood Cl. M28: Wors 2F 81
Chertsey Cl. M18: Man 2G 117
  OL2: Shaw 5H 43
Chervil Cl. M14: Man 1G 131
Cherwell Av. OL10: H'ood 2E 39
Cherwell Cl. M45: White 1G 69
  OL8: O'ham 2C 90
  SK8: Chea H 6C 156
Cherwell Ct. OL10: H'ood 2F 39
                 (off Peel La.)
Cherwell Rd. BL5: W'ton 5A 46
CHESHAM 1F 37
Chesham Av. BL1: Bolt 3C 32
  M22: Wyth 1A 154
  M41: Urm 4A 110
  OL11: Roch 6F 41
Chesham Cl. SK9: Wilm 5C 172
Chesham Cres. BL9: Bury 2G 37
Chesham Fold Rd. BL9: Bury 2H 37
Chesham Ho. M5: Sal 4F 99
           (off Amersham St.)
Chesham Ind. Est. BL9: Bury 1G 37
Chesham Pl. WA14: Bow 3E 151
Chesham Rd. BL9: Bury 1F 37
  M30: Ecc 1H 97
  OL4: O'ham 3A 76
  SK9: Wilm 5C 172
Chesham St. BL3: Bolt 5H 47
Chesham Woods Local Nature Reserve
  . . . . .6G 23
Cheshill Ct. M7: Sal 5D 86
Cheshire Cl. M32: Stre 6B 112
Cheshire Ct. BL0: Ram 3D 12
Cheshire Gdns. M14: Man 6E 115
Cheshire Rd. M31: Part 6B 124
  SK15: C'ook 6A 94
Cheshires, The OL5: Mos 2H 93
Cheshire Sq. SK15: C'ook 6A 94
Cheshire St. OL5: Mos 3H 93
Chesney Av. OL9: Chad 1G 89
Chesshyre Av. M4: Man 5H 7 (3H 101)
Chessington Ri. M27: Clif 4H 68
Chester Av. BL3: Lit L 3D 50
  M33: Sale 2D 138
  M41: Urm 4G 111
  M45: White 5G 69
  OL11: Roch 5C 26
  SK15: Stal 2H 107
  SK16: Duk 6C 106
  WA15: Hale 3H 151
Chester Cl. BL3: Lit L 3D 50
  M44: Cad 4B 124
  SK9: Wilm 6A 166
Chester Dr. BL0: Ram 5A 12
Chesterfield Gro.
  OL6: A Lyme 2B 106
Chesterfield St. OL4: O'ham 3H 75
Chesterfield Way M34: Dent 1G 135

Chestergate SK1: Stoc 2F 179 (2G 145)
  SK3: Stoc 3E 179 (2F 145)
             (not continuous)
Chester Pl. OL2: O'ham 3D 58
Chester Rd. M15: Man 6A 8 (6B 100)
  M16: Old T 6A 8 (2H 113)
  M29: Tyld 3B 80
  M32: Stre 1C 128
  SK7: H Gro 6D 158
  SK7: W'ford 6F 167
  SK12: Poy 6F 167
  WA14: Rost 6A 150
Chester's Cft. Pk. Home Est.
  SK8: Chea H 2C 166
Chester Sq. OL6: A Lyme 3G 105
Chester St. BL9: Bury 1G 37
  M1: Man 6E 101
  M15: Man 4H 9 (6D 100)
  M25: Pres 4G 69
  M27: Swin 4G 83
  M34: Dent 5F 119
  OL9: O'ham 4C 74
  SK3: Stoc 2F 145
Chesterton Dr. BL3: Bolt 2E 47
Chesterton Gro. M43: Droy 3A 104
Chesterton Rd. M23: Wyth 3D 140
  OL1: O'ham 5H 59
Chester Wlk. BL1: Bolt 3C 32
           (off Halliwell Rd.)
Chester Walks SK6: Rom 2G 147
            (not continuous)
Chestnut Av. BL8: Tot 6A 22
  BL9: Bury 3H 37
  M21: Chor 1H 129
  M28: Walk 1H 81
  M43: Droy 2G 103
  M44: Cad 4B 124
  M45: White 2F 69
  SK8: Chea 6A 144
Chestnut Cl. BL3: Bolt 3H 47
  OL4: O'ham 1B 76
  SK9: Wilm 1H 173
  SK15: Stal 5E 107
Chestnut Ct. BL9: Bury 5F 23
  SK7: Bram 3F 157
Chestnut Cres. OL8: O'ham 1G 91
Chestnut Dr. BL9: Bury 4F 23
  M33: Sale 2F 139
  SK12: Poy 4F 169
Chestnut Fold M26: Rad 3A 52
Chestnut Gdns. M34: Dent 5E 119
  OL10: H'ood 4G 39
Chestnut Gro. M26: Rad 1A 68
  M35: Fail 5H 89
  SK14: Hyde 1E 121
Chestnut Pl. OL16: Roch 3B 28
Chestnut Rd. M30: Ecc 1C 96
Chestnut St. OL9: Chad 6H 73
Chestnut Vs. SK4: Stoc 1E 145
Chestnut Wlk. M31: Part 6B 124
Chestnut Way OL15: L'ough 4E 17
Chesworth Cl. SK1: Stoc 5G 179
Chesworth Ct. M43: Droy 4H 103
Chesworth Fold
  SK1: Stoc 5G 179 (3H 145)
Chetwyn Av. BL7: Bro X 4E 19
  OL2: O'ham 3C 58
Chetwynd Av. M41: Urm 5E 111
Chetwynd Cl. M33: Sale 3G 127
Chevassut St. M15: Man 5E 9 (1C 114)
Chevin Gdns. SK7: Bram 6A 158
Chevington Dr. M9: Man 5H 87
  SK4: Stoc 6H 131
Chevington Gdns. BL1: Bolt 2C 32
            (off Walley St.)
Cheviot Av. OL2: O'ham 4C 58
  OL8: O'ham 6E 75
  SK8: Chea H 3B 156
Cheviot Cl. BL0: Ram 5C 12
  BL1: Bolt 6B 18
  BL8: Bury 2A 36
  M6: Sal .2E 99
  M24: Mid 1F 73

Cheviot Cl. OL9: Chad 4A 74
  OL16: Miln 4G 29
  SK4: Stoc 6F 133
Cheviot Ct. OL8: O'ham 5E 75
Cheviot Rd. SK7: H Gro 4B 158
Cheviots Rd. OL2: Shaw 5G 43
Cheviot St. M3: Man 1H 5 (2D 100)
Chevithorne Cl. WA14: Alt 5D 138
Chevril Cl. M15: Man 5A 10 (1E 115)
Chevron Cl. M6: Sal 3H 99
  OL11: Roch 2D 40
Chevron Pl. WA14: Alt 4F 139
Chew Brook Dr. OL3: G'fld 4D 78
CHEW MOOR 3C 46
Chew Moor La. BL5: Bolt, W'ton 5A 46
  BL6: Los 4A 46
Chew Rd. OL3: G'fld 6G 79
Chew Va. OL3: G'fld 4D 78
  SK16: Duk 6D 106
Chew Valley Rd. OL3: G'fld 3C 78
Chicago Av. M90: Man A 6H 153
Chichester Bus. Cen. OL16: Roch . . .4A 28
Chichester Cl. M33: Sale 6F 127
  OL15: L'ough 6F 17
Chichester Cres. OL9: Chad 6A 58
Chichester Rd. M15: Man 2C 114
               (Bold St.)
  M15: Man 6G 9 (1D 114)
           (Old Birley St.)
  SK6: Rom 1A 148
Chichester Rd. Sth.
  M15: Man 2C 114
Chichester St. OL16: Roch 4A 28
Chichester Way M34: Dent 6G 119
           (off Trowbridge Rd.)
Chicken La. SK5: Stoc 5H 117
Chidlow Av. M20: Man 2E 131
Chidwall Rd. M22: Wyth 3H 153
Chief St. OL4: O'ham 3G 75
Chiffon Way M3: Sal 2C 4 (2B 100)
Chigwell Cl. M22: Wyth 6C 142
Chilcombe Wlk. M9: Man 4A 72
          (off Crossmead Dr.)
Chilcote Av. M33: Sale 5G 127
Childwall Cl. BL3: Bolt 5C 48
Chilham Rd. M28: Walk 1A 82
  M30: Ecc 1H 97
Chilham St. BL3: Bolt 4H 47
  M27: Swin 5G 83
Chill Factore 1E 111
Chillington Wlk. M34: Dent 6E 119
Chiltern Av. M41: Urm 4A 110
  SK8: Chea H 3B 156
Chiltern Cl. BL0: Ram 5C 12
  M28: Walk 3A 82
  OL2: Shaw 5F 43
  SK7: H Gro 4B 158
Chiltern Dr. BL2: Bolt 6G 33
  BL8: Bury 1B 36
  M27: Swin 5H 83
  OL2: O'ham 3C 58
  SK2: Stoc 1A 158
  WA15: Hale 3H 151
Chiltern Gdns. M33: Sale 2C 140
Chiltern Rd. BL0: Ram 5C 12
Chiltern Way M29: Ast 3A 80
Chilton Av. OL9: Chad 3A 74
Chilton Dr. M24: Mid 2E 73
Chilworth St. M14: Man 5F 115
Chime Bank M8: Man 5F 87
Chimes Ct. OL4: Grot 4F 77
China La. M1: Man 6C 6 (4F 101)
Chinese Arts Cen. 4B 6
Chingford Wlk. M13: Man 3B 116
            (off Bates St.)
Chinley Av. M32: Stre 3A 112
  M40: Man 3C 88
Chinley Cl. M33: Sale 6D 128
  SK4: Stoc 6D 132
  SK7: Bram 2G 157
Chinley St. M6: Sal 6H 85
  OL1: O'ham 1H 75

Chinwell Vw.—Church St.

Chinwell Vw. *M19: Man* *6C* ***116***
(off Carrill Gro. E.)
Chip Hill Rd. BL3: Bolt 3F **47**
Chippendale Pl. OL6: A Lyme 6C **92**
Chippenham Av. SK2: Stoc 4D **146**
Chippenham Ct. M4: Man 4G **7** (3H **101**)
Chippenham Rd. M4: Man 4F **7** (3G **101**)
Chipping Fold OL16: Miln 6F **29**
Chipping Rd. BL1: Bolt 3F **31**
Chipping Sq. M12: Man 3B **116**
Chipstead Av. M12: Man 2A **116**
Chirmside St. BL8: Bury 4B **36**
Chirton Wlk. *M40: Man* *4C* ***88***
(off Webdale Dr.)
Chiseldon Av. M22: Wyth 3C **154**
Chiselhurst St. M8: Man 4E **87**
Chisholm Ct. *M24: Mid* *6B* ***56***
(off Cross St.)
Chisholme Cl. BL8: G'mount 1G **21**
Chisholm St. M11: Man 6F **103**
Chisledon Av. M7: Sal 5D **86**
Chisledon Cl. *BL3: Bolt* *2C* ***48***
(off Bantry St.)
Chislehurst Av. M41: Urm 4E **111**
Chislehurst Cl. BL8: Bury 4B **36**
Chiswick Dr. M26: Rad 2D **50**
Chiswick Rd. M20: Man 6G **131**
Chisworth Cl. SK7: Bram 2G **157**
Chisworth St. BL2: Bolt 2F **33**
Chisworth Wlk. *M34: Dent* *1G* ***135***
(off Matlock Av.)
Choir St. M7: Sal 1C **100**
Chokeberry Cl. WA14: B'ath 3D **138**
Cholmondeley Av. WA14: Tim 2G **139**
Cholmondeley Rd. M6: Sal 1B **98**
Chomlea WA14: Alt 1D **150**
Chomlea Mnr. M6: Sal 1C **98**
Choral Gro. M7: Sal 6C **86**
Chorlegh Grange *SK9: A Edg* *5G* ***173***
(off Chapel Rd.)
Chorley Cl. BL8: Bury 4H **35**
Chorley Hall Cl. SK9: A Edg 5F **173**
Chorley Hall La. SK9: A Edg 5F **173**
Chorley New Rd. BL1: Bolt 6D **30**
BL6: Los 5A **30**
Chorley Old Rd. BL1: Bolt 3F **31**
BL6: Hor 2A **30**
Chorley Rd. M27: Ward 2F **83**
M33: Sale 1E **141**
Chorley St. BL1: Bolt 5C **32**
M32: Stre 3F **113**
Chorley Wood Av. M19: Man 3B **132**
Chorlton Brook M30: Ecc 6F **83**
Chorlton Brook Ho. *SK8: Chea* *5A* ***144***
(off Stockport Rd.)
Chorlton Ct. *M16: Old T* *4A* ***114***
(off Up. Chorlton Rd.)
CHORLTON-CUM-HARDY 1G **129**
Chorlton Dr. SK8: Chea 5A **144**
Chorlton Ees Nature Reserve 2F **129**
CHORLTON FOLD 6F **83**
Chorlton Fold M30: Ecc 6F **83**
(not continuous)
SK6: Wood 4A **136**
Chorlton Grn. M21: Chor 1G **129**
Chorlton Gro. SK1: Stoc 4B **146**
Chorlton Leisure Cen. 6H **113**
Chorlton Mill M1: Man 3H **9**
Chorlton Pk. 2A **130**
Chorlton Pl. M21: Chor 6H **113**
Chorlton Point *M21: Chor* *1G* ***129***
(off Wilbraham Rd.)
Chorlton Rd. M15: Man 6D **8** (3B **114**)
M16: Old T 4D **8** (3B **114**)
Chorlton St. M1: Man 1B **10** (5E **101**)
M16: Old T 6A **8** (2A **114**)
CHORLTON UPON MEDLOCK 3H **115**
Chorlton Vw. *M21: Chor* *1G* ***129***
(off Whitelow Rd.)
CHORLTONVILLE 3A **130**
Chorlton Water Pk. 5H **129**
Chretien Rd. M22: Nor 1B **142**
Christchurch Av. M5: Sal 4A **4** (3H **99**)
Christchurch Cl. BL2: Bolt 2B **34**
Christchurch Ct. OL9: O'ham 4C **74**
Christ Church La. BL2: Bolt 2B **34**
Christchurch Rd. M33: Sale 4E **127**
Christie Flds. Office Pk.
M21: Chor 4B **130**
Christie Rd. M32: Stre 4E **113**
Christie St. SK1: Stoc 4A **146**
Christie St. Ind. Est. SK1: Stoc 4A **146**
Christie Way M21: Chor 4B **130**
Christine St. OL2: Shaw 6H **43**
(not continuous)
Christleton Av. SK4: Stoc 4F **133**
Christleton Way *SK9: Hand* *2H* ***165***
(off Spath La.)
Christopher Acre OL11: Roch 2A **26**
Christopher St. M5: Sal 4G **99**
M40: Man 1F **103**
Christy Cl. SK14: Hyde 4A **120**
Chronnell Dr. BL2: Bolt 5A **34**
Chudleigh Cl. SK7: Bram 2A **158**
WA14: Alt 5D **138**
Chudleigh Rd. M8: Man 1E **87**
Chulsey Ga. La. BL6: Los 3A **46**
Chulsey St. BL3: Bolt 3H **47**
Church Av. BL3: Bolt 3A **48**
M6: Sal 3D **98**
M24: Mid 1F **57**
M34: Dent 1G **135**
M40: Man 6E **89**
SK9: Sty 5E **165**
SK14: Hyde 1D **136**
Church Bank BL1: Bolt 3H **175** (6E **33**)
WA14: Bow 3D **150**
Churchbank SK15: Stal 3H **107**
Church Brow M24: Mid 6C **56**
SK14: Hyde 6B **120**
SK14: Mot 4C **122**
WA14: Bow 3D **150**
Church Cl. BL0: Ram 4B **12**
M26: Rad 1D **66**
M34: Aud *6F* ***105***
(off Ashworth Av.)
SK9: Hand 4H **165**
Church Coppice WA15: Hale 3H **151**
Church Ct. BL0: Eden 1G **13**
BL9: Bury 2G **37**
SK16: Duk 4H **105**
WA15: Hale 4G **151**
Church Cft. BL9: Bury 3H **53**
Churchdale Rd. M9: Man 5F **71**
Church Dr. M25: Pres 5G **69**
Churches, The OL6: A Lyme 3A **106**
Churchfield M21: Chor 1G **129**
Churchfield Cl. M26: Rad 6H **51**
Churchfield Rd. M6: Sal 6D **84**
Church Flds. OL3: Dob 5C **62**
Churchfields M33: Sale 3F **127**
M34: Aud 6E **105**
WA14: Bow 4D **150**
Churchfield Wlk. *M11: Man* *5C* ***102***
(off Pitman Cl.)
Churchgate BL1: Bolt 3G **175** (6D **32**)
M41: Urm 6G **111**
SK1: Stoc 2H **179** (2H **145**)
Churchgate Bldgs.
M1: Man 1E **11** (5G **101**)
Church Grn. M6: Sal 2F **99**
M26: Rad 3D **52**
Church Gro. M30: Ecc 4G **97**
SK7: H Gro 3E **159**
Churchill Av. BL2: Ain 4F **35**
M16: W Ran 5B **114**
Churchill Cl. OL10: H'ood 5A **40**
Churchill Ct. M6: Sal 3F **99**
Churchill Cres. SK5: Stoc 6G **117**
SK6: Mar 4B **148**
Churchill Dr. BL3: Lit L 5E **51**
BL4: Farn 6C **48**
Churchill Pl. M30: Ecc 1E **97**
Churchill Rd.
WA14: B'ath 4F **139**
Churchill St. BL2: Bolt 6G **33**
OL4: O'ham 5H **177** (3G **75**)
OL11: Roch 3E **27**
OL12: Roch 2E **27**
SK4: Stoc 6F **133**
Churchill St. E. OL4: O'ham 3G **75**
Churchill Way M6: Sal 3G **99**
M17: T Pk 6C **98**
Church La. BL0: Eden 1G **13**
BL9: Bury 6B **24**
M7: Sal 2H **85**
M9: Man 4A **88**
(Kingscliffe St.)
M9: Man 3H **87**
(Water St.)
M19: Man 3B **132**
M25: Pres 5G **69**
M33: Sale 3G **127**
M45: White 1E **69**
OL1: O'ham 3G **177** (2F **75**)
OL3: Upp 6F **63**
OL5: Mos 2H **93**
OL16: Roch 4B **178** (4H **27**)
SK6: Mar 5D **148**
SK6: Rom 1A **148**
SK7: W'ford 5E **167**
SK9: A Edg 4G **173**
Churchley Cl. SK3: Stoc 5C **144**
Churchley Rd. SK3: Stoc 4C **144**
Church Lodge SK4: Stoc 1A **144**
Church Mnr. SK4: Stoc 5D **132**
Church Mdw. BL9: Bury 2H **53**
OL3: G'fld 4A **78**
SK14: Hyde 4A **120**
Church Mdw. Gdns.
SK14: Hyde 4A **120**
Church Mdws. BL2: Bolt 2B **34**
Church M. BL8: Bury 4C **36**
M26: Rad 6C **52**
M34: Dent 4E **119**
Church Pas. OL1: O'ham 3G **177** (2F **75**)
Church Pl. OL10: H'ood 3H **39**
Church Ri. *BL2: Bolt* *6G* ***33***
(off Tonge Old Rd.)
Church Rd. BL0: Ram 1E **13**
BL1: Bolt 3F **31**
BL4: Farn, Kea 1A **66**
M22: Nor 2B **142**
M24: Mid 2F **73**
M26: Rad 1C **66**
M28: Walk 6H **65**
M29: Ast 5A **80**
M30: Ecc 3H **97**
M33: Sale 5D **128**
M41: Urm 6B **110**
OL2: Shaw 1H **59**
OL3: G'fld 4A **78**
OL3: Upp 1D **78**
OL16: Roch 5B **28**
SK4: Stoc 1E **179** (1F **145**)
SK8: Chea H 5D **156**
SK8: Gat 6E **143**
SK9: Hand 3H **165**
SK9: Wilm 5B **172**
SK14: Holl 3F **123**
Church Rd. E. M33: Sale 5D **128**
Church Rd. W. M33: Sale 5D **128**
Churchside BL4: Farn 2F **65**
Churchside Cl. M9: Man 1H **87**
Church Sq. SK16: Duk 4H **105**
Church Stile
OL16: Roch 4B **178** (4H **27**)
Churchstoke Wlk. M23: Wyth 4E **141**
Churchston Av. SK7: Bram 3A **158**
Church St. BL0: Ram 3C **12**
BL2: Ain 4E **35**
BL2: Bolt 6H **19**
BL3: Lit L 4B **50**
BL4: Farn 1A **66**
BL4: Kea 2A **66**
BL8: Bury 1H **35**
BL9: Bury 2G **37**
M4: Man 4B **6** (3E **101**)

Church St. M24: Mid 5C **56**
    M27: Pen 3B **84**
    M27: Swin 3G **83**
    M30: Ecc 3G **97**
    (not continuous)
    M32: Stre 6C **112**
    *M34: Aud 6E **105**
    (off Ryecroft La.)*
    M35: Fail 3H **89**
    M43: Droy 4A **104**
    OL1: O'ham 3G **177** (2F **75**)
    OL2: O'ham 3D **58**
    OL3: Del 3A **62**
    OL4: Lees 4C **76**
    OL6: A Lyme 6C **174** (3H **105**)
    OL10: H'ood 3H **39**
    OL11: Roch 5G **27**
    OL12: Whitw 1E **15**
    OL15: L'ough 4G **17**
    OL16: Miln 1H **43**
    *OL16: Roch 6D **16**
    (off Laycock St.)*
    SK4: Stoc 6G **133**
    (not continuous)
    SK6: Bred 4G **135**
    SK6: Mar 5D **148**
    SK8: Chea 5H **143**
    SK9: Wilm 2E **173**
    SK13: Had 3H **123**
    SK14: Hyde 6B **120**
    SK15: Stal 3E **107**
    SK16: Duk 4H **105**
    WA14: Alt 1B **174** (6F **139**)
Church St. E. M26: Rad 4C **52**
    (not continuous)
    OL4: O'ham 1C **76**
Church St. Ind. Est.
    M24: Mid 5C **56**
Church St. W. M26: Rad 4B **52**
    (off Stamford St.)
Church Ter. *M33: Sale 3A **128***
    OL1: O'ham 3G **177** (2F **75**)
    OL12: W'le 5C **16**
    OL16: Miln 6G **29**
    SK4: Stoc 1F **145**
    SK9: Hand 3H **165**
Churchtown Av. BL2: Bolt 6B **34**
Church Vw. M35: Fail 3H **89**
    M44: Irl 5E **109**
    OL12: Roch 1A **26**
    SK9: Sty 5E **165**
    SK14: Hyde 6B **120**
    SK14: Mot 4C **122**
    WA14: Bow 4D **150**
Church Wlk. BL4: Farn 1G **65**
    BL8: G'mount 2F **21**
    M27: Clif 6H **67**
    OL2: O'ham 3D **58**
    SK9: Wilm 3C **172**
    SK15: Stal 2E **107**
    WA14: Alt 1A **174** (6F **139**)
Churchwood Rd. M20: Man 6F **131**
Churnet St. M40: Man 6H **87**
Churning Ter. M44: Irl 4F **109**
Churston Av. M9: Man 5A **72**
Churton Av. M14: Man 5F **115**
    M33: Sale 6H **127**
Churton Rd. M18: Man 4E **117**
Churwell Av. SK4: Stoc 5B **132**
Cicero St. M9: Man 3A **88**
    OL1: O'ham 6G **59**
Cilder's Villa OL4: Grot 5F **77**
Cinder Hill BL9: Bury 5H **23**
Cinder Hill La. M24: Mid 3A **58**
    OL1: Chad 3A **58**
Cinder La. BL1: Bolt 2F **31**
Cinder St. M4: Man 3E **7** (3G **101**)
Cineworld
    Ashton-under-Lyne 2F **105**
    Bolton 2E **33**
    Manchester 2H **143**
    Stockport 4F **179**
Cinnabar Dr. M24: Mid 5B **56**

Cinnamon Cl. M22: Nor 3C **142**
    *OL12: Roch 3F **27**
    (off Spotland Rd.)*
Cinnamon St. OL12: Roch 3F **27**
Cipher St. M4: Man 2E **7** (2G **101**)
Circle, The M32: Stre 3H **111**
Circle Sth. M17: T Pk 1E **113**
Circuit, The M20: Man 4F **131**
    SK3: Stoc 5E **145**
    SK8: Chea H 6C **156**
    SK9: A Edg 6E **173**
    SK9: Wilm 4A **172**
Circular Rd. M20: Man 4F **131**
    M25: Pres 1H **85**
    M34: Dent 5E **119**
Cirencester Cl. M38: Lit H 3E **65**
Ciss La. M41: Urm 5G **111**
Citadel, The SK1: Stoc 4G **179**
Citrus Way M6: Sal 3G **99**
CITY, THE 5D **118**
City Airport Manchester 6A **96**
City Av. M34: Dent 5E **119**
City Course Trad. Est.
    *M11: Man 6C **102**
    (off Whitworth St.)*
City Ct. Trad. Est. M4: Man . .3E **7** (3G **101**)
City Gdns. M34: Dent 5D **118**
City Lofts Salford Quays M50: Sal . . .6E **84**
City of Manchester Stadium 4B **102**
City Pk. M16: Old T 6A **8** (2H **113**)
City Point M3: Sal 4E **5** (3C **100**)
    M32: Stre 2F **113**
City Rd. M15: Man 6B **8** (1A **114**)
    M28: Wors 3E **81**
City Rd. E. M15: Man 3G **9** (6D **100**)
City Sth. M15: Man 3G **9** (6D **100**)
City Tower M1: Man 6B **6** (4E **101**)
City Wlk. M27: Pen 3B **84**
Clacton Wlk. M13: Man 5E **11**
Clague St. M11: Man 3C **102**
Claife Av. M40: Man 1D **88**
CLAMMERCLOUGH 1A **66**
Clammerclough Rd. BL4: Kea 1A **66**
Clandon Av. M30: Ecc 4D **96**
Clapgate SK6: Rom 2F **147**
Clapgate Rd. OL11: Roch 2A **26**
Clapham St. M40: Man 3E **89**
Clara Gorton Ct. *OL16: Roch 5B **28**
    (off Ethel St.)*
Clara St. OL9: O'ham 5C **74**
    OL11: Roch 6H **27**
    OL12: Whitw 4B **14**
Clare Av. SK9: Hand 4G **165**
Clarebank BL1: Bolt 6F **31**
Clare Cl. BL8: Bury 6D **22**
Clare Ct. BL4: Farn 6D **48**
    SK1: Stoc 2A **146**
Claremont Av. M20: Man 4E **131**
    SK4: Stoc 4E **133**
    SK6: Mar 5A **148**
    WA14: W Tim 3F **139**
Claremont Ct. *BL1: Bolt 4C **32**
    (off Faraday Dr.)*
Claremont Dr. M38: Lit H 4F **65**
    WA14: W Tim 3F **139**
Claremont Gdns. OL6: A Lyme 6C **92**
Claremont Gro. M20: Man 6E **131**
    WA15: Hale 2G **151**
Claremont Range M18: Man 3H **117**
Claremont Rd. M6: Sal 6D **84**
    M16: W Ran 4C **114**
    M33: Sale 4B **128**
    OL11: Roch 4E **27**
    OL16: Miln 6E **29**
    SK2: Stoc 6B **146**
    SK8: Chea H 5C **156**
Claremont St. M35: Fail 3H **89**
    OL6: A Lyme 1B **106**
    OL8: O'ham 1F **91**
    OL9: Chad 6C **58**

Clarence Arc.
    OL6: A Lyme 6C **174** (3H **105**)
Clarence Av. M17: T Pk 6H **97**
    M45: White 2G **69**
    OL8: O'ham 5D **74**
Clarence Cl. BL9: Bury 1G **37**
Clarence Ct. *BL1: Bolt 5C **32**
    (off Back La.)*
    SK9: Wilm 3D **172**
Clarence Ho. *SK15: Stal 5C **106**
    (off High St.)*
Clarence Rd.
    M13: Man 4A **116**
    M27: Swin 4E **83**
    OL6: A Lyme 1A **106**
    SK4: Stoc 4D **132**
    WA15: Hale 2H **151**
Clarence St. BL1: Bolt 2F **175** (5D **32**)
    (not continuous)
    BL4: Farn 6A **50**
    M2: Man 6H **5** (4D **100**)
    M7: Sal 1A **100**
    OL2: O'ham 4G **59**
    OL12: Roch 1F **27**
    SK14: Hyde 3C **120**
    SK15: Stal 4C **106**
Clarendon Av. SK4: Stoc 6D **132**
    WA15: Alt 6G **139**
Clarendon Cotts. SK9: Sty 4E **165**
Clarendon Cres. M30: Ecc 2H **97**
    M33: Sale 4D **128**
Clarendon Gro. BL2: Bolt 1F **49**
Clarendon Ind. Est.
    SK14: Hyde 4C **120**
Clarendon Pl. *M30: Ecc 3H **97**
    (off Wellington Rd.)*
    SK14: Hyde 5B **120**
Clarendon Rd. BL2: Bolt 6G **33**
    M16: W Ran 5A **114**
    M27: Swin 3H **83**
    M30: Ecc 2H **97**
    M33: Sale 5D **128**
    M34: Aud 6A **104**
    M34: Dent 5H **119**
    M41: Urm 4A **110**
    M44: Irl 2C **124**
    SK7: H Gro 2F **159**
    SK14: Hyde 4B **120**
Clarendon Rd. W.
    M21: Chor 5H **113**
Clarendon St. BL3: Bolt 2C **48**
    BL9: Bury 1G **37**
    M15: Man 5G **9** (1D **114**)
    (not continuous)
    M45: White 1F **69**
    OL5: Mos 3H **93**
    OL16: Roch 1B **42**
    SK5: Stoc 6H **133**
    SK14: Hyde 4B **120**
    (Clarke Way, not continuous)
    SK14: Hyde 5B **120**
    (Market St.)
    SK16: Duk 5G **105**
    (not continuous)
Clarendon Wlk. *M5: Sal 3G **99**
    (off Cavell Way)*
Clare Rd. M19: Man 1C **132**
    SK5: Stoc 5H **133**
Clare St. M1: Man 3D **10** (6F **101**)
    M34: Dent 3E **119**
Claribel St. M11: Man 5A **102**
Claridge Rd. M21: Chor 5G **113**
Clarion St. M4: Man 2E **7** (2G **101**)
Clark Av. M18: Man 2G **117**
Clarke Av. M5: Sal 6H **99**
Clarke Brow M24: Mid 6C **56**
Clarke Cres. M38: Lit H 3B **64**
    WA15: Hale 2B **152**
Clarke Ind. Est.
    M32: Stre 2H **111**
Clarkes Cft. BL9: Bury 2A **38**
Clarke's Hill M45: White 2B **68**
Clarke's La. OL12: Roch 3F **27**

Clarke St. BL1: Bolt 5A **32**
   BL4: Farn 2A **66**
   OL7: A Lyme 5F **105**
   OL10: H'ood 3H **39**
   OL16: Roch 1B **28**
   WA14: B'ath 4F **139**
Clarkethorn Ter. SK5: Stoc 6G **133**
Clarke Way SK14: Hyde 4B **120**
Clarksfield Rd. OL4: O'ham 3A **76**
Clarksfield St. OL4: O'ham 3A **76**
Clark's Hill M25: Pres 5G **69**
Clarkson Cl. M24: Mid 2G **71**
   M34: Dent 5D **118**
Clarkwell Cl. OL1: O'ham 1E **177**
Clatford Wlk. M9: Man 4H **87**
   (off Carisbrook St.)
Claude Av. M27: Swin 3F **83**
Claude Rd. M21: Chor 2G **129**
Claude St. M8: Man 2E **87**
   M27: Swin 3F **83**
   M30: Ecc 2D **96**
Claudia Sq. SK15: C'ook 6A **94**
Claughton Av. BL2: Bolt 6B **34**
   M28: Wors 3G **81**
Claughton Rd. BL8: Bury, Tot 6H **21**
Claverham Wlk. M23: Wyth 4E **141**
   (off Sandy La.)
Claverton Rd. M23: Wyth 6E **141**
Claxton Av. M9: Man 6H **71**
Clay Bank M43: Droy 4H **103**
Claybank BL8: Tot 3F **21**
Claybank Dr. BL8: Tot 4F **21**
Claybank St. OL10: H'ood 2G **39**
Claybank Ter. OL5: Mos 5A **78**
Claybarn M. M44: Irl 5F **109**
Claybrook Wlk. M11: Man 4C **102**
   (off Sledmere Cl.)
Clayburn St. M15: Man 5F **9** (1C **114**)
Claycourt Av. M30: Ecc 1D **96**
Clay Cft. Ter. OL15: L'ough 2G **17**
Claydon Dr. M26: Rad 2D **50**
Clayfield Dr. OL11: Roch 3B **26**
Claygate Dr. M9: Man 4H **71**
Clayhill Wlk. M9: Man 2A **88**
Clayland Cl. SK14: Holl 3F **123**
Clayland St. SK14: Holl 3F **123**
Clay La. M23: Wyth 1F **153**
   OL11: Roch 3H **25**
   SK9: Sty 3F **165**
   SK9: Wilm 5A **172**
   WA15: Hale, Tim 1C **152**
Claymere Av. OL11: Roch 3A **26**
Claymoor OL1: O'ham 2F **177**
Claymore St. BL3: Bolt 4D **48**
   M18: Man 1G **117**
Clay St. BL7: Bro X 4E **19**
   (not continuous)
   OL8: O'ham 5E **75**
   OL15: L'ough 4F **17**
Claythorpe Wlk. M8: Man 6C **70**
CLAYTON 4E **103**
Clayton Arms Sports Hall, The 5C **58**
Clayton Av. BL2: Bolt 2G **49**
   M20: Man 5F **131**
CLAYTON BRIDGE 1G **103**
Claytonbrook Rd. M11: Man 4E **103**
Clayton Cl. BL8: Bury 4H **35**
   M15: Man 2C **114**
Clayton Ct. M11: Man 6E **103**
Clayton Hall Rd. M11: Man 3E **103**
Clayton Ind. Est. M11: Man 4F **103**
Clayton La. M11: Man 5D **102**
Clayton La. Sth. M11: Man 6C **102**
Claytons Cl. OL4: Spri 2D **76**
Clayton St. BL2: Bolt 2F **49**
   M11: Man 2D **102**
   M34: Dent 5F **119**
   M35: Fail 4H **89**
   OL9: Chad 6A **74**
   OL12: Roch 1B **28**
   SK16: Duk 5B **106**
Clayton Va. M11: Man 2E **103**
Cleabarrow Dr. M28: Wors 6E **81**

Cleadon Av. M18: Man 3E **117**
Cleadon Dr. Sth. BL8: Bury 6C **22**
Clearwater Dr. M20: Man 4D **130**
Cleavley St. M30: Ecc 3D **96**
Clee Av. M13: Man 5B **116**
Cleethorpes Av. M9: Man 6F **71**
Cleeve Rd. M23: Wyth 1G **141**
   OL4: O'ham 3A **76**
Cleeve Way SK8: Chea H 1D **166**
CLEGG HALL 1E **29**
Clegg Hall Rd. OL15: L'ough 1E **29**
   OL16: Roch 1D **28**
Clegg Pl. OL6: A Lyme 1B **106**
Clegg's Av. OL12: Whitw 3A **14**
   (off Clegg St.)
Clegg's Bldgs. BL1: Bolt 5C **32**
Clegg's La. M38: Lit H 4E **65**
Cleggs La. Ind. Site
   M38: Lit H 3F **65**
Clegg St. BL2: Bolt 6G **33**
   M43: Droy 4H **103**
   M45: White 2F **69**
   OL1: O'ham 4G **177** (3F **75**)
   (not continuous)
   OL4: O'ham 5H **177** (3F **75**)
   OL4: Spri 3E **77**
   OL12: Whitw 3A **14**
   OL15: L'ough 3F **17**
   OL16: Miln 6G **29**
   SK6: Bred 6F **135**
Cleggswood Av. OL15: L'ough 6G **17**
Cleggs Yd. OL15: L'ough 4F **17**
Clelland St. BL4: Farn 2A **66**
Clematis Wlk. M27: Ward 1G **83**
Clement Cl. M11: Man 6H **103**
   (off Toxteth St.)
   OL16: Roch 5B **28**
Clementina St.
   OL12: Roch 1B **178** (2H **27**)
   (not continuous)
Clementine Cl. M6: Sal 1B **98**
   (off Coconut Gro.)
Clement Pl. OL12: Roch 3G **27**
   (off Clement Royds St.)
   OL15: L'ough 4H **17**
   (off Halifax Rd.)
Clement Rd. SK6: Mar B 4F **149**
Clement Royds St.
   OL12: Roch 1A **178** (3G **27**)
   (not continuous)
Clement Stott Cl. M9: Man 5B **72**
Clement St. OL9: O'ham 6B **74**
   SK4: Stoc 6G **133**
Cleminson St. M3: Sal 4C **4** (3B **100**)
Clemshaw Cl. OL10: H'ood 4G **39**
Clerewood Av. SK8: H Grn 6F **155**
Clerke St. BL9: Bury 3C **176** (3F **37**)
Clerk's Ct. M5: Sal 3B **98**
Clevedon Av. M41: Urm 5A **112**
Clevedon Rd. OL9: Chad 6A **58**
Clevedon St. M9: Man 4A **88**
Cleveland Av. M6: Sal 2C **98**
   M19: Man 5D **116**
   SK14: Hyde 5A **120**
Cleveland Cl. BL0: Ram 6C **12**
   M27: Clif 1A **84**
Cleveland Dr. OL16: Miln 5G **29**
Cleveland Gdns. BL3: Bolt 3H **47**
Cleveland Gro. OL2: O'ham 4C **58**
Cleveland Rd. M8: Man 2F **87**
   SK4: Stoc 5C **132**
   WA15: Hale 2H **151**
Clevelands Cl. OL2: Shaw 5G **43**
Cleveland St. BL3: Bolt 3H **47**
Cleveleys Av. BL2: Bolt 5G **33**
   BL9: Bury 5E **37**
   M21: Chor 2A **130**
   OL16: Roch 2B **42**
   SK8: H Grn 4F **155**
Cleveleys Gro. M7: Sal 4C **86**
Cleves Ct. OL10: H'ood 4G **39**
Cleworth Hall La. M29: Tyld 2A **80**
Cleworth Rd. M24: Mid 5B **56**

Cleworth St. M15: Man 4C **8** (6B **100**)
Cleworth Wlk. M15: Man 4C **8**
Clibran St. M8: Man 5F **87**
Clifden Dr. M22: Wyth 3C **154**
CLIFF, THE 4B **86**
Cliff Av. BL9: Sum 1C **22**
   M7: Sal 5A **86**
Cliffbrook Gro. SK9: Wilm 5H **165**
   (off Bosley Cl.)
Cliff Cres. M7: Sal 4B **86**
Cliff Dale SK15: Stal 5D **106**
Cliffdale Dr. M8: Man 2E **87**
Cliffe St. OL15: L'ough 1B **16**
Cliff Grange M7: Sal 4B **86**
Cliff Gro. SK4: Stoc 5D **132**
Cliff Hill OL2: Shaw 4B **44**
Cliff Hill Rd. OL2: Shaw 4B **44**
Cliffmere Cl. SK8: Chea H 2B **156**
Cliff Mt. BL0: Ram 2B **12**
Clifford Av. M34: Dent 2E **119**
   WA15: Tim 5B **140**
Clifford Ct. M15: Man 2C **114**
   (off Chorlton Rd.)
   SK2: Stoc 6B **146**
Clifford Lamb St. M9: Man 1D **88**
Clifford Rd. BL3: Bolt 5G **47**
   SK9: Wilm 3C **172**
   SK12: Poy 3C **168**
Clifford St. M13: Man 5C **10** (1F **115**)
   M27: Pen 3B **84**
   M30: Ecc 5D **96**
   OL11: Roch 6H **27**
Cliff Rd. BL9: Bury 2F **53**
   SK9: Wilm 1E **173**
Cliff Side SK9: Wilm 1E **173**
Cliff St. OL16: Roch 2B **28**
CLIFTON 6H **67**
Clifton Av. M14: Man 1H **131**
   M29: Ast 5A **80**
   M30: Ecc 2F **97**
   OL4: O'ham 4H **75**
   SK8: H Grn 3E **155**
   WA15: Alt 6G **139**
Clifton Cl. M16: Old T 2B **114**
   OL4: O'ham 4H **75**
   OL10: H'ood 4G **39**
Clifton Country Pk. Local Nature Reserve
   . . . . .4G **67**
Clifton Ct. BL4: Farn 5F **49**
   M27: Clif 5G **67**
   SK4: Stoc 5C **132**
Clifton Cres. OL4: O'ham 4G **59**
Clifton Dr. M27: Clif 1C **84**
   M27: Ward 2F **83**
   SK6: Mar 4C **148**
   SK8: Gat 6D **142**
   SK8: H Grn 3E **155**
   SK9: Wilm 5B **172**
CLIFTON GREEN 6A **68**
Clifton Gro. M16: Old T 2B **114**
   (off Hamilton St.)
   M27: Ward 1F **83**
Clifton Holmes OL3: Del 2A **62**
Clifton Ho. M30: Ecc 2F **97**
   (off Clifton Rd.)
Clifton House Arboretum 4F **67**
Clifton Ho. Rd. M27: Clif 4F **67**
   (not continuous)
Clifton Ind. Est.
   M27: Clif 6B **68**
CLIFTON JUNCTION 6C **68**
Clifton Lodge SK2: Stoc 6A **146**
Clifton Pk. Rd.
   SK2: Stoc 6A **146**
Clifton Pl. M25: Pres 4G **69**
Clifton Rd. M21: Chor 1A **130**
   M24: Mid 1F **57**
   M25: Pres 5E **69**
   M30: Ecc 2F **97**
   M33: Sale 6B **128**
   M41: Urm 5C **110**
   SK4: Stoc 6C **132**
Clifton Station (Rail) 1C **84**

Clifton St. BL1: Bolt 5C **32**
  BL4: Farn 5F **49**
  BL4: Kea 2B **66**
  BL9: Bury 1F **37**
  M16: Old T 2B **114**
    (not continuous)
  M29: Tyld 3C **80**
  M35: Fail 2A **90**
  M40: Man 2B **102**
  OL3: G'fld 4D **78**
  OL6: A Lyme 2G **105**
  OL11: Roch *6A 28*
    (off Well St.)
  OL16: Miln 5F **29**
  SK9: A Edg 5G **173**
Clifton Vw. M27: Clif 5G **67**
Clifton Vs. BL5: Bolt 2A **90**
Cliftonville Dr. M6: Sal 5B **84**
  M27: Swin 5A **84**
Cliftonville Rd. OL16: Roch 5C **42**
Clifton Vis. Cen. 4G **67**
Clifton Wlk. M24: Mid 4H **55**
Climax Works SK5: Stoc 5G **117**
Climb Rochdale 4C **178**
Clinton Av. M14: Man 5D **114**
Clinton Gdns. M14: Man 5E **115**
Clinton Ho. *M5: Sal* *4F 99*
    (off Amersham St.)
Clinton St. OL6: A Lyme 1B **106**
Clinton Wlk. OL4: O'ham 3G **75**
Clippers Quay M50: Sal 1G **113**
Clipsley Cres. OL4: O'ham 3D **60**
Cliston Wlk. SK7: H Gro 3A **158**
Clito St. M9: Man 3B **88**
Clive Av. M45: White 6E **53**
Clivedale Pl. BL1: Bolt 4G **175** (6D **32**)
Cliveley Wlk. M27: Pen 3B **84**
Clive Lloyd Ct. M32: Stre 4E **113**
Clively Av. M27: Clif 2B **84**
Clive Rd. M35: Fail 4G **89**
Clive St. BL1: Bolt 4G **175** (6D **32**)
  M4: Man 2C **6** (2F **101**)
  OL7: A Lyme 6G **91**
  OL8: O'ham 1D **90**
    (not continuous)
Clivewood Wlk. *M12: Man* *1A 116*
    (off Bennett St.)
Clivia Gro. *M7: Sal* *5B 86*
    (off Bk. Hilton St.)
Cloak St. M1: Man 3B **10** (6E **101**)
Clockhouse Av. M43: Droy 2G **103**
Clockhouse M. M43: Droy 2G **103**
Clock St. OL9: Chad 1B **90**
Clock Tower Cl. M28: Walk 6D **64**
  SK14: Hyde 6C **120**
Clock Tower Ct. OL16: Miln 6G **29**
Cloister Cl. SK16: Duk 1A **120**
Cloister Rd. SK4: Stoc 1H **143**
Cloisters, The M33: Sale 5D **128**
  OL16: Roch 2B **28**
  SK8: Chea 6C **144**
Cloister St. BL1: Bolt 3A **32**
  M9: Man 3B **88**
Clondberry Cl. M29: Tyld 2C **80**
Clopton Wlk. M15: Man 5F **9** (1C **114**)
    (Birchvale Cl.)
  M15: Man 6F **9**
    (Rolls Cres.)
Close, The BL2: Bolt 2F **33**
  BL8: Bury 5C **22**
  M24: Mid 4D **56**
  M34: Dent 3D **118**
  SK6: Mar B 2F **149**
  SK15: Stal 1D **106**
    (not continuous)
  WA14: Alt 6E **139**
Closes Farm BL3: Bolt 5H **47**
Clothorn Rd. M20: Man 5F **131**
Cloudberry Wlk. M31: Part 6D **124**
Cloudstock Gro. M38: Lit H 4C **64**

CLOUGH
  OL2 . . . . .1B **60**
  OL15 .2G **17**
Clough OL2: Shaw 1B **60**
Clough, The BL1: Bolt 6E **31**
  OL7: A Lyme 5H **91**
  SK5: Stoc 3B **134**
Clough Av. M33: Sale 2F **139**
  SK6: Mar B 5G **149**
  SK9: Wilm 5F **165**
Clough Bank M9: Man 1H **87**
  OL15: L'ough 1G **17**
Cloughbank M26: Rad 2E **67**
Clough Cl. OL4: Gras 3A **78**
Clough Ct. M24: Mid 5D **56**
Clough Dr. M25: Pres 5F **69**
Clough End Rd. SK14: Hat 6A **122**
Cloughfield Av. M5: Sal 2A **8** (5H **99**)
Clough Flats *OL10: H'ood* *3G 39*
    (off St James St.)
Clough Fold M26: Rad 2D **66**
Clough Fold Rd. SK14: Hyde 6A **120**
Clough Ga. OL8: O'ham 1D **90**
  SK14: Hyde 1C **136**
Cloughgate Ho. *OL8: O'ham* *1D 90*
    (off Hollins Rd.)
Clough Gro. M45: White 5D **52**
Clough Head *OL15: L'ough* *1A 16*
    (off Higher Calderbrook Rd.)
Clough La. M25: Pres 5F **69**
  OL4: Gras 3H **77**
  OL10: H'ood 1G **39**
Clough Mdw. BL1: Bolt 1D **46**
  SK6: Wood 4A **136**
Clough Mdw. Rd. M26: Rad 4G **51**
Clough Pk. Av. OL4: Gras 3A **78**
Clough Rd. M9: Man 3B **88**
  M24: Mid 5C **56**
  M35: Fail 4A **90**
  M43: Droy 3A **104**
  OL2: Shaw 1B **60**
  OL15: L'ough 1G **17**
Cloughs Av. OL9: Chad 1F **73**
Clough Side M9: Man 2B **88**
Cloughside SK6: Mar B 4G **149**
Clough St. BL4: Kea 2B **66**
  M24: Mid 5D **56**
  M26: Rad 6C **52**
  M40: Man 1E **103**
  OL12: W'le 6C **16**
Clough Ter. OL15: L'ough 2G **17**
Cloughton Wlk. *M40: Man* *6F 89*
    (off Terence St.)
Clough Top Rd. M9: Man 1C **88**
Clough Wlk. SK5: Stoc 3B **134**
Clove Av. M18: Man 1G **117**
Clovelly Av. OL8: O'ham 1C **90**
Clovelly Rd. M21: Chor 1A **130**
  M27: Swin 4E **83**
  SK2: Stoc 3C **146**
Clovelly St. M40: Man 6F **89**
  OL11: Roch 2D **40**
Clover Av. SK3: Stoc 6F **145**
Cloverbank Av. M19: Man 5H **131**
Clover Cres. OL8: O'ham 6B **76**
Clover Ct. M33: Sale 2D **140**
Cloverdale Sq. BL1: Bolt 4G **31**
Cloverfield Wlk. *M28: Walk* *6H 65*
    (off Malvern Gro.)
CLOVER HALL 2C **28**
Clover Hall Cres. OL16: Roch 2C **28**
Cloverley M33: Sale 1B **140**
Cloverley Dr. WA15: Tim 1A **152**
Clover Rd. SK6: Rom 6C **136**
  WA15: Tim 6A **140**
Clover St. OL12: Roch 2A **178** (3G **27**)
Clover Vw. OL16: Roch 4C **28**
Clowes St. M3: Sal 4F **5** (3C **100**)
  M12: Man 1B **116**
    (not continuous)
  OL9: Chad 1B **90**
Clubhouse Cl. OL2: Shaw 1H **59**
  OL11: Roch 4C **26**

Club St. M11: Man 6H **103**
Club Theatre 2F **151**
Clumber Cl. SK12: Poy 4E **169**
Clumber Rd. M18: Man 3H **117**
  SK12: Poy 4E **169**
Clunton Av. BL3: Bolt 3H **47**
Clutha Rd. SK3: Stoc 1H **157**
Clwyd Av. SK3: Stoc 4F **145**
Clyde Av. M45: White 3F **69**
Clyde Cl. OL16: Roch 5B **28**
Clyde Rd. M20: Man 5D **130**
  M26: Rad 2H **51**
  M29: Ast 4A **80**
  SK3: Stoc 4E **145**
Clydesdale Gdns. M11: Man 4C **102**
Clydesdale Ri. OL3: Dig 2F **63**
Clydesdale St. OL8: O'ham 5E **75**
Clyde St. BL1: Bolt 3C **32**
  OL1: O'ham 6A **60**
  OL7: A Lyme 5F **105**
Clyde Ter. M26: Rad 2H **51**
Clyffe M. M5: Sal 6H **99**
Clyne Ct. *M32: Stre* *3F 113*
    (off Adlington Dr.)
Clyne St. M32: Stre 2F **113**
Clysbarton Ct. SK7: Bram 4F **157**
Coach La. OL11: Roch 6A **26**
Coach Rd. M29: Ast 5A **80**
  SK14: Holl 2C **122**
Coal Bank Fold OL11: Roch 2H **25**
Coalbrook Wlk. M12: Man 1H **11**
Coalburn St. M12: Man 1C **116**
Coal Pit La. OL8: O'ham 4C **90**
Coalshaw Grn. Rd. OL9: Chad 6A **74**
Coatbridge St. M11: Man 4E **103**
Cobalt Av. M41: Urm 1H **111**
Cobalt Way M24: Mid 3F **73**
Cobb Cl. M8: Man 6C **70**
Cobbett's Way SK9: Wilm 5C **172**
Cobble Bank M9: Man 6H **71**
Cobblestones OL3: Del 4B **62**
Cobden Cen., The *M50: Sal* *4F 99*
    (off Vere St.)
Cobden Lodge *OL11: Roch* *3E 41*
    (off Tudor Hall St.)
Cobden Mill Ind. Est.
  BL4: Farn 6G **49**
Cobden St. BL1: Bolt 2B **32**
  BL7: Eger 1B **18**
  BL9: Bury 2G **37**
  M6: Sal 1F **99**
  M9: Man 3A **88**
  M26: Rad 1H **51**
  OL4: O'ham 6B **60**
  OL6: A Lyme 3B **106**
  OL9: Chad 2B **74**
  OL10: H'ood 4H **39**
Coberley Av. M41: Urm 3B **110**
Cob Hall Rd. M32: Stre 6C **112**
Cobham Av. BL3: Bolt 4B **48**
  M40: Man 1E **89**
Coblers Hill OL3: Del 2B **62**
Cobourg St. M1: Man 1C **10** (5F **101**)
Coburg Av. M7: Sal 1B **100**
Cochrane Av. M12: Man 2A **116**
Cochrane St. BL3: Bolt 2D **48**
COCKBROOK 2A **106**
Cock Brow SK14: Hyde 2G **137**
Cock Clod St. M26: Rad 4C **52**
Cockcroft Rd. M5: Sal 3A **4** (3H **99**)
Cockcroft St. M9: Man 2H **87**
COCKER HILL 3E **107**
Cocker Hill SK15: Stal 3E **107**
Cocker Mill La. OL2: O'ham 2F **59**
Cockers La. SK15: Stal 5H **107**
Cocker St. M38: Lit H 5E **65**
Cockey Moor Rd. BL2: Ain 4F **35**
  BL8: Bury 4F **35**
Cock Hall La. OL12: Whitw 4A **14**
Cockhall La. OL12: Whitw 4A **14**
Cocklinstones BL8: Bury 2B **36**
Cocksfoot Dr. OL5: Mos 3A **94**

Coconut Gro.—Condor Wlk.

|---|---|
Coconut Gro. M6: Sal	.3H 99
Codale Dr. BL2: Bolt	.4B 34
Coddington Av. M11: Man	.5G 103
Cody Ct. M50: Sal	.5E 99
Coe St. BL3: Bolt	.2D 48
Coghlan Cl. M11: Man	.3D 102
Coin St. OL2: O'ham	.3E 59
Coke St. M7: Sal	.3D 86
Coke St. W. M7: Sal	.3D 86
Colborne Av. M30: Ecc	.3D 96
SK5: Stoc	.4H 117
SK6: Rom	.1A 148
Colbourne Av. M8: Man	.2D 86
Colbourne Gro. SK14: Hat	.4A 122
Colbourne Way SK14: Hat	.4A 122
Colby Wlk. M40: Man	.4C 88
Colchester Av. BL2: Bolt	.5A 34
M25: Pres	.1A 86
Colchester Cl. M23: Wyth	.2E 141
Colchester Dr. BL4: Farn	.6E 49
Colchester Pl. SK4: Stoc	.6D 132
Colchester Wlk. OL1: O'ham	.2G 177
Colclough Cl. M40: Man	.5D 88
Coldalhurst La. M29: Ast	.5A 80
Coldfield Dr. M23: Wyth	.5F 141
Cold Greave Cl. OL16: Miln	.1A 44
COLD HURST	.1E 177 (1E 75)
COLDHURST HOLLOW	.1G 177 (1F 75)
Coldhurst Hollow Est. OL1: O'ham	.6F 59
Coldhurst St. OL1: O'ham	.1E 177 (1E 75)
Coldhurst St. W. OL1: O'ham	.1E 75
(off Trafalgar St.)	
Coldstream Av. M9: Man	.5H 71
Coldwall Ind. Est. OL12: Roch	.3F 27
Colebrook Dr. M40: Man	.5C 88
Colebrook Rd. WA15: Tim	.5A 140
Coleby Av. M16: Old T	.3A 114
M22: Wyth	.4D 154
Coledale Dr. M24: Mid	.5G 55
Coleford Gro. BL1: Bolt	.1C 48
Colemore Av. M20: Man	.6H 131
Colenso Ct. BL2: Bolt	.6G 33
Colenso Gro. SK4: Stoc	.6D 132
Colenso Rd. BL2: Bolt	.6H 33
Colenso St. OL8: O'ham	.6D 74
Colenso Way M14: Man	.1A 6 (2E 101)
Coleport Cl. SK8: Chea H	.4C 156
Coleridge Av. M24: Mid	.4E 57
M26: Rad	.4G 51
Coleridge Cl. SK5: Stoc	.6G 117
Coleridge Rd. BL8: G'mount	.1H 21
M16: Old T	.4A 114
OL1: O'ham	.3B 60
OL15: L'ough	.1F 29
SK5: Stoc	.6G 117
Coleridge St. M40: Man	.1E 103
Coleridge Way SK5: Stoc	.6G 117
Colesbourne Cl. M38: Lit H	.3E 65
Coleshill St. M40: Man	.1H 7 (2A 102)
Colesmere Wlk. M40: Man	.2F 89
Cole St. M40: Man	.3B 88
Colgate Cres. M14: Man	.1F 131
Colgate La. M5: Sal	.1G 113
Colgrove Av. M40: Man	.1E 89
Colina Dr. M7: Sal	.6C 86
M8: Man	.6C 86
Colindale Av. M9: Man	.5A 72
Colindale Cl. BL3: Bolt	.2A 48
(off Langshaw Wlk.)	
Colin Murphy Rd.	
M15: Man	.4E 9 (1C 114)
Colin Rd. SK4: Stoc	.5G 133
Colinton Cl. BL1: Bolt	.4B 32
Colinwood Cl. BL9: Bury	.4F 53
Coll Dr. M41: Urm	.2F 111
College Av. M43: Droy	.5H 103
OL8: O'ham	.6D 74
College Bank Way	
OL12: Roch	.3A 178 (4G 27)
College Cl. SK2: Stoc	.5A 146
SK9: Wilm	.1C 172
College Ct. OL12: Roch	.4F 27
SK4: Stoc	.6C 132

College Cft. M30: Ecc	.3H 97
College Dr. M16: W Ran	.5A 114
College Ho. SK4: Stoc	.5D 132
WA14: Bow	.4E 151
College Land M3: Man	.5G 5 (4D 100)
College Rd.	
M16: W Ran	.4A 114
M30: Ecc	.3A 98
(off St Mary's Rd.)	
OL8: O'ham	.5D 74
OL12: Roch	.3A 178 (4F 27)
College Way BL3: Bolt	.1B 48
Collegiate Way M27: Clif	.6H 67
Collen Cres. BL8: Bury	.5C 22
Collett St. OL1: O'ham	.1A 76
Colley St. M32: Stre	.2F 113
OL16: Roch	.2B 28
Collie Av. M6: Sal	.6A 86
Collier Av. OL16: Miln	.4F 29
Collier Cl. SK14: Hat	.6A 122
Collier Hill OL8: O'ham	.6D 74
Collier Hill Av. OL8: O'ham	.6C 74
Collier's Ct. OL11: Roch	.4B 42
Collier St. M3: Man	.2F 9 (5C 100)
M3: Sal	.3F 5 (3C 100)
M6: Sal	.5F 85
M26: Rad	.4B 52
M27: Swin	.4G 83
Collier Wlk. SK14: Hat	.6A 122
Colliery St. M11: Man	.4C 102
(not continuous)	
Collin Av. M18: Man	.3E 117
Collingburn Av. M5: Sal	.6H 99
Collingburn Ct. M5: Sal	.6H 99
Colling Cl. M44: Irl	.6E 109
Collinge Av. M24: Mid	.1E 73
Collinge St. BL8: Bury	.1B 36
M24: Mid	.2F 73
OL2: Shaw	.6H 43
OL10: H'ood	.3G 39
Collingham Rd. WA14: W Tim	.2E 139
Collingham St. M8: Man	.1F 101
Colling St. BL0: Ram	.4B 12
Collington Cl. M12: Man	.2C 116
Collingwood Av. M43: Droy	.2G 103
Collingwood Cl. SK12: Poy	.4G 169
Collingwood Dr. M27: Swin	.4B 84
Collingwood Rd. M19: Man	.6B 116
Collingwood St. OL11: Roch	.5E 41
Collingwood Way	
OL1: O'ham	.1G 177 (1F 75)
Collins St. BL8: Bury	.1H 35
Collins Way OL9: Chad	.6C 74
Collop Dr. OL10: H'ood	.6A 40
Coll's La. OL3: Del	.3H 61
Colman Gdns. M5: Sal	.6H 99
Colmore Dr. M9: Man	.5C 72
Colmore Gro. BL2: Bolt	.1F 33
Colmore St. BL2: Bolt	.2F 33
Colne St. OL11: Roch	.4F 41
Colonial Rd. SK2: Stoc	.5A 146
Colshaw Cl. E. M26: Rad	.3H 51
Colshaw Cl. Sth. M26: Rad	.3H 51
Colshaw Dr. SK9: Wilm	.6H 165
Colshaw Rd. M23: Wyth	.6G 141
Colshaw Wlk. SK9: Wilm	.6H 165
(off Howty Cl.)	
Colson Dr. M24: Mid	.2B 72
Colsterdale Cl. OL2: O'ham	.2E 59
Colt Hill La. OL3: Upp	.1B 78
Coltishall Ho. SK8: Chea	.6C 144
Coltness Wlk. M40: Man	.6E 89
(off Marlinford Dr.)	
Coltsfoot Dr. WA14: B'ath	.3D 138
Columbia Av. M18: Man	.3H 117
Columbia Rd. BL1: Bolt	.5A 32
Columbia St. OL8: O'ham	.5F 75
Columbine Cl. OL12: Roch	.6E 15
Columbine St. M11: Man	.6F 103

Columbine Wlk. M31: Part	.6D 124
(off Central Rd.)	
Columbus Way M50: Sal	.5D 98
Colville Dr. BL8: Bury	.4B 36
WA15: Tim	.5A 140
Colville Rd. OL1: O'ham	.6D 58
Colwell Av. M32: Stre	.5B 112
Colwell Wlk. M9: Man	.4F 71
Colwick Av. WA14: Alt	.5G 139
Colwith Av. BL2: Bolt	.4A 34
Colwood Wlk. M8: Man	.5D 86
(off Kilmington Dr.)	
Colwyn Av. M14: Man	.1A 132
M24: Mid	.3C 72
Colwyn Cres. SK5: Stoc	.4H 133
Colwyn Gro. BL1: Bolt	.4B 32
Colwyn Rd. M27: Swin	.5E 83
SK7: Bram	.5G 157
SK8: Chea H	.4A 156
Colwyn St. M6: Sal	.2F 99
OL7: A Lyme	.5G 91
OL9: O'ham	.2D 74
OL11: Roch	.3D 40
Colwyn Ter. OL7: A Lyme	.5G 91
(off Colwyn St.)	
Colyton Wlk. M22: Wyth	.2D 154
Combe Cl. M11: Man	.2D 102
Combermere Av. M20: Man	.2E 131
Combermere Cl. SK8: Chea H	.1B 156
Combermere St. SK16: Duk	.4A 106
Combs Bank SK13: Gam	.5F 123
(off Brassington Cres.)	
Combs Fold SK13: Gam	.5F 123
(off Brassington Cres.)	
Combs Gdns. SK13: Gam	.6F 123
(off Brassington Cres.)	
Combs Gro. SK13: Gam	.5F 123
(off Brassington Cres.)	
Combs Lea SK13: Gam	.6F 123
(off Brassington Cres.)	
Combs M. SK13: Gam	.6F 123
Combs Ter. SK13: Gam	.6F 123
(off Brassington Cres.)	
Combs Way SK13: Gam	.5F 123
(off Brassington Cres.)	
Comer Ter. M33: Sale	.5A 128
Commerce Way M17: T Pk	.3C 112
Commercial Av. SK8: Chea H	.2A 166
Commercial Brow SK14: Hyde	.3C 120
Commercial Rd. SK7: H Gro	.2D 158
Commercial St. M15: Man	.3F 9 (6C 100)
SK14: Hyde	.4C 120
Common La. M31: C'ton	.4F 125
Common Side Rd. M28: Wors	.4D 80
Community St. OL7: A Lyme	.4F 105
Como St. BL3: Bolt	.3A 48
(off Randal St.)	
Como Wlk. M18: Man	.1D 116
Compass St. M11: Man	.6E 103
COMPSTALL	.1F 149
Compstall Av. M14: Man	.5F 115
COMPSTALL BROW	.1D 148
Compstall Gro. M18: Man	.1G 117
Compstall Mills Est. SK6: Comp	.1F 149
Compstall Rd. SK6: Mar B	.1E 149
SK6: Rom	.1A 148
(not continuous)	
Compton Cl. M41: Urm	.6G 109
Compton Dr. M23: Wyth	.3G 153
Compton Fold OL2: Shaw	.5A 44
Compton St. SK15: Stal	.4F 107
Compton Way M24: Mid	.2E 73
Comrie Wlk. M23: Wyth	.6G 141
Comus St. M5: Sal	.1A 8 (5A 100)
Concastrian Ind. Est. M9: Man	.4G 87
Concert La. M2: Man	.6A 6 (4E 101)
Concord Bus. Pk. M22: Wyth	.4C 154
Concord Pl. M6: Sal	.6G 85
Concord Way SK16: Duk	.5B 106
Condor Cl. M43: Droy	.2C 104
Condor Pl. M6: Sal	.6G 85
Condor Wlk. M13: Man	.6D 10

Conduit St.—Coppice St.

Conduit St. OL1: O'ham 4B 60
OL6: A Lyme 6D 174 (3A 106)
SK13: Tin 1H 123
Coney Grn. M26: Rad 2A 52
Coney Green Sports Cen. 3B 52
Coney Gro. M23: Wyth 4G 141
Coneymead SK15: Stal 1E 107
Congham Rd. SK3: Stoc 3E 145
Congleton Av. M14: Man 5E 115
Congleton Cl. SK9: A Edg 6G 173
Congleton Rd.
SK9: A Edg, N Ald 5G 173
Congou St. M1: Man 1E 11 (5G 101)
Congreave St. OL1: O'ham 1E 177 (1E 75)
Conifer Wlk. M31: Part 6C 124
Coningsby Dr. M9: Man 3H 87
Conisber Cl. BL7: Eger 2C 18
Conisborough
OL11: Roch 6A 178 (5G 27)
Conisborough Pl. M45: White 2H 69
Coniston Av. BL4: Farn 2C 64
M9: Man 3H 87
M33: Sale 1C 140
M38: Lit H 4E 65
M45: White 1F 69
OL8: O'ham 6D 74
SK14: Hyde 3A 120
Coniston Cl. BL0: Ram 1C 12
BL3: Lit L 3C 50
M34: Dent 5B 118
OL9: Chad 2A 74
Coniston Ct. *M22: Shar 5C 142*
(off Downes Way)
Coniston Dr. BL9: Bury 6E 37
M24: Mid 5A 56
SK9: Hand 3G 165
SK15: Stal 2E 107
Coniston Gro. M38: Lit H 5E 65
OL2: O'ham 1D 58
OL7: A Lyme 1G 105
OL10: H'ood 4H 39
Coniston Hall *M13: Man 3H 115*
(off Hathersage Rd.)
Coniston Ho. *M28: Walk 1A 82*
(off Holyoake Rd.)
Coniston Rd. M27: Swin 4H 83
M31: Part 5C 124
M32: Stre 4C 112
M41: Urm 1A 126
SK5: Stoc 3H 133
SK6: H Lan 5B 160
SK8: Gat 5F 143
Coniston St. BL1: Bolt 2D 32
M6: Sal 1H 99
M40: Man 6E 89
Coniston Wlk. WA15: Tim 6D 140
Conival Way OL9: Chad 6A 58
Conmere Sq. M15: Man 4H 9 (6D 100)
Connaught Av. M19: Man 2B 132
M45: White 2G 69
OL16: Roch 2B 42
Connaught Cl. SK9: Wilm 1F 173
Connaught Sq. BL2: Bolt 3F 33
Connaught St. BL8: Bury 4B 36
OL8: O'ham 5F 177 (3E 75)
Connel Cl. BL2: Bolt 1B 50
Connell Rd. M23: Wyth 5G 141
Connell Way OL10: H'ood 2B 40
Connery Cres. OL6: A Lyme 5B 92
Connie St. M11: Man 5E 103
Conningsby Cl. BL7: Bro X 3D 18
Connington Av. M9: Man 2H 87
Connington Cl.
OL2: O'ham 3C 58
Connor Way SK8: Gat 1D 154
Conquest Cl. M12: Man 1C 116
Conrad Cl. OL1: O'ham 3C 60
Conran St. M9: Man 4H 87
Consett Av. M23: Wyth 5G 141
Consort Av. OL2: O'ham 1C 58
Consort Cl. SK16: Duk 1A 120
Consort Pl. WA14: Bow 3D 150
Constable Cl. BL1: Bolt 4B 32
Constable Dr. SK6: Mar B 3F 149
SK9: Wilm 1H 173
Constable Ho. M34: Dent 4F 119
Constable St. M18: Man 1G 117
Constable Wlk. M34: Dent 2G 135
OL1: O'ham 4B 60
Constance Gdns. M5: Sal 4F 99
Constance Rd. BL3: Bolt 2A 48
M31: Part 6D 124
Constance St. M15: Man 3F 9 (6C 100)
Constantine Ct. M5: Sal 2A 4 (2H 99)
Constantine Rd.
OL16: Roch 3B 178 (4H 27)
Constantine St.
OL4: O'ham 3B 76
Constellation Trad. Est.
M26: Rad 1H 51
Consul St. M22: Nor 2C 142
Contact Theatre 2F 115
Convamore Rd. SK7: Bram 6F 157
Convent Gro. OL11: Roch 6F 27
Convent St. OL4: O'ham 5A 76
Conway Av. BL1: Bolt 4G 31
M27: Clif 6B 68
M44: Irl 1D 124
M45: White 2F 69
Conway Cen., The SK5: Stoc 5G 133
Conway Cl. BL0: Ram 3B 12
M16: Old T 4G 113
M24: Mid 2C 72
M45: White 2F 69
OL10: H'ood 2E 39
Conway Cres. BL8: G'mount 1H 21
Conway Dr. BL9: Bury 3B 38
SK7: H Gro 4C 158
SK15: Stal 2E 107
WA15: Tim 5C 140
Conway Gro. OL9: Chad 6H 57
Conway Rd. M33: Sale 6D 128
M41: Urm 3F 111
SK8: Chea H 3A 156
Conway St. BL4: Farn 2H 65
SK5: Stoc 5G 133
Conway Towers SK5: Stoc 2C 134
Conyngham Rd. M14: Man 3H 115
COOKCROFT 2D 76
Cooke St. BL4: Farn 2A 66
M34: Dent 4E 119
M35: Fail 3H 89
SK7: H Gro 2D 158
Cook St. BL9: Bury 4D 176 (3F 37)
M3: Sal 4F 5 (3C 100)
M30: Ecc 3E 97
M34: Aud 1F 119
OL4: O'ham 2A 76
OL16: Roch 2B 28
SK3: Stoc 2G 145
SK14: Hyde 2D 120
Cook Ter. OL16: Roch 2B 28
SK16: Duk 4H 105
(off Hill St.)
Coomassie St. M6: Sal 2F 99
M26: Rad 4A 52
OL10: H'ood 3G 39
Coombes Av. SK6: Mar 6D 148
SK14: Hyde 6D 120
Coombes St. SK2: Stoc 6B 146
Co-operation St. M35: Fail 2H 89
Co-operative St. M6: Sal 3F 99
M26: Rad 3A 52
M38: Lit H 3C 64
OL2: Shaw 6H 43
OL3: Upp 1D 78
OL4: Spri 3D 76
SK7: H Gro 2E 159
SK12: Dis 1H 171
Cooper Fold M24: Mid 3C 56
Cooper Ho. M15: Man 6A 10
Cooper La. M9: Man 4H 71
M24: Mid 4B 56
Coopers Brow SK1: Stoc 2G 179
Cooper's Fold
SK8: Chea H 1B 166
Cooper St. BL9: Bury 3B 176 (3E 37)
M2: Man 6H 5 (4D 100)
(not continuous)
M32: Stre 6D 112
OL4: Spri 2E 77
OL12: Roch 5D 16
SK1: Stoc 6H 179 (4H 145)
SK7: H Gro 2F 159
SK16: Duk 4H 105
Coopers Wlk. OL16: Roch 1C 28
Coop St. BL1: Bolt 1C 32
M4: Man 3C 6 (3F 101)
Copage Dr. SK6: Bred 5G 135
COPE BANK 3A 32
Cope Bank BL1: Bolt 3A 32
Cope Bank E. *BL1: Bolt 4A 32*
(off Valletts La.)
Cope Bank W. BL1: Bolt 3H 31
Cope Cl. M11: Man 6G 103
Copeland Av. M27: Clif 2C 84
Copeland Cl. M24: Mid 6G 55
Copeland M. BL1: Bolt 6G 31
Copeland St. SK14: Hyde 2B 120
Copeman Cl. M13: Man 6E 11 (1G 115)
Copenhagen Sq. OL16: Roch 3A 28
Copenhagen St. M40: Man 5C 88
OL16: Roch 3A 28
(not continuous)
Cope St. BL1: Bolt 4A 32
Copgrove Rd. M21: Chor 2H 129
Copgrove Wlk. M22: Wyth 6C 154
COPLEY 3G 107
Copley Av. SK15: Stal 3G 107
Copley Leisure Cen. 3G 107
Copley Pk. M. SK15: Stal 3G 107
Copley Rd. M21: Chor 5G 113
Copley St. OL2: Shaw 5A 44
Copperas La. M43: Droy 5G 103
(not continuous)
Copperas St. M4: Man 4B 6 (3E 101)
Copperbeech Cl. M22: Nor 2C 142
Copper Beech Dr. SK13: Gam 6G 123
SK15: Stal 2H 107
Copper Beech Mnr. *SK13: Gam 6G 123*
(off Orchard Dr.)
Copperfield Ct. WA14: Alt 2E 151
Copperfield Rd. SK8: Chea H 2D 166
SK12: Poy 5D 168
Copperfields BL6: Los 4B 46
SK9: Wilm 1F 173
SK12: Poy 5D 168
(off Weller Av.)
Copper La. M45: White 2B 68
Copper Pl. M14: Man 6E 115
Copperways M20: Man 4F 131
COPPICE 5E 75
Coppice, The BL0: Ram 5A 12
BL2: Bolt 6H 19
M9: Man 1C 88
M24: Mid 4D 72
M25: Pres 5G 69
M28: Wors 6E 83
(Chatsworth Rd.)
M28: Wors 3B 82
(Old Clough La.)
SK7: Bram 1G 167
SK12: Poy 5G 169
WA15: Haleb 5B 152
Coppice Av. M33: Sale 1F 139
SK12: Dis 1E 171
Coppice Cl. BL5: W'ton 4A 46
SK6: Wood 5H 135
SK12: Dis 1E 171
Coppice Ct. SK8: H Grn 5F 155
Coppice Dr. M22: Nor 2B 142
OL12: Whitw 2E 15
Coppice Ho. SK12: Poy 5C 168
Coppice Ind. Est. *OL8: O'ham 4D 74*
(off Windsor Rd.)
Coppice La. SK12: Dis 1E 171
Coppice Rd. SK12: Poy 4G 169
Coppice St. BL9: Bury 2H 37
OL8: O'ham 4D 74

Coppice Wlk.—Cottesmore Cl.

Coppice Wlk. M34: Dent 5D **118**
Coppice Way SK9: Hand 3A **166**
Coppingford Cl. OL12: Roch 1C **26**
Copping St. M12: Man 1B **116**
Coppins, The SK9: Wilm 5B **172**
Coppleridge Dr. M8: Man 2E **87**
Copplestone Ct. M27: Ward 2E **83**
Copplestone Dr. M33: Sale 4E **127**
Coppy Bri. Dr. OL16: Roch 3D **28**
Cop Rd. OL1: O'ham 3A **60**
Copse, The BL7: Tur 1G **19**
SK6: Mar B 3G **149**
WA15: Haleb 6D **152**
Copse Av. M22: Wyth 2C **154**
Copse Dr. BL9: Bury 5F **23**
Copse Wlk. OL15: L'ough 4F **17**
Copson St. M20: Man 2F **131**
Copster Av. OL8: O'ham 6E **75**
COPSTER HILL 6E **75**
Copster Hill Rd. OL8: O'ham 6E **75**
Copster Pl. OL8: O'ham 6E **75**
Copthall La. M8: Man 3D **86**
(not continuous)
Copthorne Cl. OL10: H'ood 5H **39**
Copthorne Cres. M13: Man 5A **116**
Copthorne Dr. BL2: Bolt 1A **50**
Copthorne Wlk. BL8: Tot 6H **21**
Coptic Rd. OL9: Chad 1H **73**
Coptrod Head Cl. OL12: Roch 5G **15**
Coptrod Rd. OL11: Roch 3F **27**
Coral Av. SK8: Chea H 4C **156**
Coral M. OL2: O'ham 4E **59**
Coral Rd. SK8: Chea H 4C **156**
Coral St. M13: Man 4E **11** (6G **101**)
Coram St. M18: Man 1H **117**
Corbar Rd. SK2: Stoc 6A **146**
Corbel Ho. *M30: Ecc* *2F* ***97***
(off Clifton Rd.)
Corbel Way M30: Ecc 2F **97**
Corbett St. M11: Man 4C **102**
OL16: Roch 3B **28**
Corbett Way OL3: Dens 4G **45**
Corbridge Wlk. *M8: Man* *5F* ***87***
(off Appleford Dr.)
Corbrook Rd. OL9: Chad 6G **57**
Corby St. M12: Man 1C **116**
Corcoran Cl. OL10: H'ood 2G **39**
Corcoran Dr. SK6: Rom 1D **148**
Corda Av. M22: Nor 3B **142**
Corday La. M25: Pres 1B **70**
Cordingley Av. M43: Droy 5H **103**
Cordova Av. M34: Dent 4H **117**
Corelli St. M40: Man 1B **102**
Corfe Cl. M41: Urm 6G **109**
Corfe Cres. SK7: H Gro 4C **158**
Corgi Heritage Cen. The ***3H 39***
(off York St.)
Corinthian Av. M7: Sal 6A **86**
Corinth Wlk. *M28: Walk* *1H* ***81***
(off Bridgewater Rd.)
Corkland Cl. OL6: A Lyme 3C **106**
Corkland Rd. M21: Chor 1H **129**
Corkland St. OL6: A Lyme 3C **106**
Corks La. SK12: Dis 2H **171**
Cork St. BL9: Bury 3G **37**
M12: Man 1H **11** (5H **101**)
OL6: A Lyme 5D **174** (2A **106**)
Corless Fold M29: Ast 6A **80**
Corley Av. SK3: Stoc 4B **144**
Corley Wlk. M11: Man 4B **102**
Cormallen Gro. M35: Fail 4A **90**
Cormorant Cl. M28: Walk 6G **65**
Cormorant Wlk.
M12: Man *1C* ***116***
(off Flamingo Cl.)
Cornall St. BL8: Bury 2C **36**
CORNBROOK 3C **8** (6B **100**)
Cornbrook Arches
M15: Man 4B **8** (6A **100**)
Cornbrook Cl. OL12: W'le 6C **16**
Cornbrook Ct. M15: Man 6C **8** (1B **114**)
Cornbrook Gro.
M16: Old T 6C **8** (2B **114**)
Cornbrook Pk. Rd.
M15: Man 5B **8** (1A **114**)
Cornbrook Rd.
M16: Old T 4B **8** (6A **100**)
Cornbrook Stop (Metro) **4B 8 (6A 100)**
Cornbrook St. M16: Old T 6C **8** (2B **114**)
(not continuous)
Cornbrook Way M16: Old T 2B **114**
Corn Cl. M13: Man 2G **115**
Cornell St. M4: Man 3D **6** (3F **101**)
Corner Brook BL6: Los 4A **46**
Corner Cft. SK9: Wilm 5D **172**
Cornerhouse Art Gallery **2A 10 (5E 101)**
Corner St. OL6: A Lyme 3A **106**
Cornfield Cl. BL9: Bury 4F **23**
M33: Sale *6F* ***129***
(off Pimmcroft Way)
Cornfield Dr. M22: Wyth 2A **154**
Cornfield Rd. SK6: Rom 6C **136**
Cornfield St. OL16: Miln 6F **29**
Cornford Av. M18: Man 4D **116**
Cornhey Rd. M33: Sale 1E **139**
Cornhill Av. M41: Urm 4D **110**
Corn Hill La. M34: Aud 2A **118**
Cornhill Rd. M41: Urm 3D **110**
Cornhill St. OL1: O'ham 5B **60**
Cornish Cl. M22: Wyth 5B **154**
Cornish Way OL2: O'ham 4F **59**
Cornishway M22: Wyth 4A **154**
Cornishway Ind. Est. *M22: Wyth* *5B* ***154***
(off Cornishway)
Cornlea Dr. M28: Wors 4G **81**
Corn Mill Cl. OL12: Roch 5C **16**
Corn Mill Dr. BL4: Farn 2A **66**
Corn Mill La. SK15: Stal 4F **107**
Corn St. M35: Fail 5E **89**
OL4: O'ham *2G* ***75***
(off Lees Rd.)
Cornwall Av. M19: Man 1D **132**
Cornwall Cl. SK6: H Lan 6C **160**
Cornwall Ct. M18: Man 1F **117**
Cornwall Cres. OL3: Dig 3D **62**
SK5: Stoc 3C **134**
Cornwall Dr. BL9: Bury 5F **37**
Cornwall Ho. M3: Sal 5D **4**
Cornwall Rd. M43: Droy 2A **104**
M44: Cad 4B **124**
SK8: H Grn 5F **155**
Cornwall St. M11: Man 6F **103**
M30: Ecc 4E **97**
OL9: O'ham 4B **74**
Cornwall St. Ind. Est. *M11: Man* *6F* ***103***
(off Cornwall St.)
Cornwell Cl. SK9: Wilm 1G **173**
Cornwood Cl. *M8: Man* *4D* ***86***
(off Narbuth Dr.)
Corona Av. OL8: O'ham 6D **74**
SK14: Hyde 4C **120**
Coronation Av. OL10: H'ood 5A **40**
SK14: Hyde 6C **120**
SK16: Duk 6D **106**
Coronation Gdns. M26: Rad 3G **51**
(not continuous)
Coronation Rd. M26: Rad 2G **51**
M35: Fail 5G **89**
M43: Droy 2H **103**
OL6: A Lyme 5A **92**
Coronation Sq. BL3: Lit L 4D **50**
M12: Man 2F **11** (5G **101**)
M34: Aud 6D **104**
Coronation St. BL1: Bolt 4F **175** (6D **32**)
M3: Man 1E **9** (5C **100**)
M5: Sal 1A **8** (5H **99**)
M11: Man 5E **103**
M27: Pen 2H **83**
M34: Dent 4D **118**
OL1: O'ham 2G **75**
SK5: Stoc 5G **133**
Coronation Vs. OL12: Whitw 3B **14**
Coronation Wlk. M26: Rad 2G **51**
Coronet Way M50: Sal 4B **98**
Corporation Cotts.
M31: C'ton 3G **125**
Corporation Rd. M30: Ecc 3H **97**
M34: Aud, Dent 2D **118**
OL11: Roch 5F **27**
(not continuous)
Corporation St. BL1: Bolt 3F **175** (6D **32**)
M3: Man 4H **5** (3D **100**)
M4: Man 4H **5** (3D **100**)
M24: Mid 1C **72**
SK1: Stoc 1H **179** (1H **145**)
SK14: Hyde 5B **120**
SK15: Stal 4E **107**
Corporation Yd. SK5: Stoc 1H **133**
Corran Cl. M30: Ecc 3D **96**
Corrie Cl. M34: Dent 6F **119**
Corrie Cres. BL4: Kea 4F **67**
Corrie Dr. BL4: Kea 5F **67**
Corrie Rd. M27: Clif 6A **68**
Corrie St. M38: Lit H 5E **65**
Corrie Way SK6: Bred 4E **135**
Corrigan St. M18: Man 1G **117**
Corringham Rd. M19: Man 2E **133**
Corring Way BL1: Bolt 1F **33**
Corrin Rd. BL2: Bolt 2F **49**
Corris Av. M9: Man 4E **71**
Corry St. OL10: H'ood 3A **40**
Corson St. BL3: Bolt 5H **49**
Corston Wlk. M40: Man 6D **88**
Corwen Cl. OL8: O'ham 1B **90**
Cosgrove Cres. M35: Fail 6G **89**
Cosgrove Rd. M35: Fail 6G **89**
Cosham Rd. M22: Wyth 2D **154**
Cosmo Bingo **4E 97**
Costabeck Wlk. *M40: Man* *1F* ***103***
(off Stansfield St.)
Costobadie Cl. SK14: Mot 4B **122**
Costobadie Way *SK14: Mot* *4B* ***122***
(off Ashworth La.)
COSTON PARK **5C 116**
Cotaline Cl. OL11: Roch 2D **40**
Cotefield Av. BL3: Bolt 4D **48**
Cotefield Cl. SK6: Mar 6D **148**
Cotefield Rd. M22: Wyth 3H **153**
COTE GREEN **2F 149**
Cote Grn. La. SK6: Mar B 2F **149**
Cote Grn. Rd. SK6: Mar B 2F **149**
Cote La. OL5: Mos 6A **78**
OL15: L'ough 3F **17**
Cote Royd *OL6: A Lyme* *2B* ***106***

Cotford Rd. BL1: Bolt 6D **18**
Cotham St. M3: Man 1G **5** (1D **100**)
Cotman Dr. SK6: Mar B 3G **149**
Cotswold Av. M41: Urm 4B **110**
OL2: Shaw 5F **43**
OL9: Chad 4A **74**
SK7: H Gro 4B **158**
Cotswold Cl. BL0: Ram 5C **12**
M25: Pres 4A **70**
Cotswold Cres. BL8: Bury 2A **36**
OL16: Miln 4G **29**
Cotswold Dr. M6: Sal 2F **99**
OL2: O'ham 4B **58**
Cotswold Rd. SK4: Stoc 6F **133**
Cottage Cft. BL2: Bolt 6H **19**
Cottage Gdns. SK6: Bred 6D **134**
Cottage Gro. SK9: Wilm 4B **172**
Cottage La. SK13: Gam 5G **123**
Cottage Lawns SK9: A Edg 4H **173**
Cottages, The OL4: Scout 6F **61**
Cottage Wlk. M43: Droy 2H **103**
OL12: Roch 5E **15**
Cottam Cres. SK6: Mar B 4F **149**
Cottam Gro. M27: Swin 4A **84**
Cottam St. BL8: Bury 2C **36**
OL1: O'ham 1D **74**
Cottenham La. M3: Sal 1F **5** (2C **100**)
M7: Sal 1E **5** (1C **100**)
Cottenham St. M13: Man 5D **10** (1F **115**)
Cotterdale Cl. M16: W Ran 5B **114**
Cotteril Cl. M23: Wyth 2C **140**
Cotterill St. M6: Sal 3G **99**
Cotter St. M12: Man 3E **11** (6G **101**)
Cottesmore Cl. OL12: Whitw 3E **15**

Cottesmore Dr. M8: Man 3G 87
Cottesmore Gdns.
　WA15: Haleb 5C 152
Cottingham Dr. OL6: A Lyme 1A 106
Cottingham Rd.
　M12: Man 6H 11 (1A 116)
Cottingley Cl. BL1: Bolt 6B 18
Cotton Bldg., The BL7: Eger 1B 18
　(off Deakins Mill Way)
Cotton Cl. SK14: Hyde 6C 120
Cottonfield Rd. M20: Man 3G 131
Cottonfields BL7: Bolt 4D 18
Cotton Fold OL16: Roch 5C 28
Cotton Hill M20: Man 4G 131
Cotton La. M20: Man 3G 131
　OL11: Roch 1E 41
Cotton Mill Cres. OL9: O'ham ...5B 74
Cotton St. BL1: Bolt 3B 32
　M4: Man 4D 6 (3F 101)
Cotton St. E.
　OL6: A Lyme 6A 174 (3G 105)
Cotton St. W. OL6: A Lyme 3G 105
Cotton Tree Cl. OL4: O'ham 1B 76
Cotton Tree Cl. SK14: Hyde 5B 120
　(off Reynold St.)
Cotton Tree St.
　SK4: Stoc 2E 179 (2G 145)
Cottonwood Dr. M33: Sale 4E 127
Cottrell Rd. WA15: Haleb 6D 152
Coucill Sq. BL4: Farn 1A 66
Coulsden Dr. M9: Man 6H 71
Coulthart St.
　OL6: A Lyme 5C 174 (2H 105)
Coulthurst St. BL0: Ram 3B 12
Coulton Cl. OL4: O'ham 1G 75
Coulton Wlk. M5: Sal 3F 99
Councillor La. SK8: Chea 5B 144
Councillor St. M12: Man 4A 102
Countess Av. SK8: Chea H 2A 166
Countess Gro. M7: Sal 1B 100
Countess La. M26: Rad 2F 51
Countess Pl. M25: Pres 5A 70
Countess Rd. M20: Man 6F 131
Countess St. OL6: A Lyme 3B 106
　SK2: Stoc 6A 146
Counthill Dr. M8: Man 1C 86
Counthill Rd. OL4: O'ham 6B 60
　(not continuous)
Counting Ho. Rd. SK12: Dis 2H 171
Count St. OL16: Roch 6A 28
County Av. OL6: A Lyme 1C 106
COUNTY END 4D 76
County End Bus. Pk. OL4: Lees ...3D 76
County End Ter. OL4: Spri 3D 76
　(off Oldham Rd.)
County Rd. M28: Walk 5E 65
County St. M2: Man 6H 5
　OL8: O'ham 1C 90
Coupland Cl. OL4: O'ham 3D 60
　OL12: Whitw 1E 15
Coupland St. M15: Man 6A 10 (2E 115)
　OL12: Whitw 1E 15
Coupland St. E.
　M15: Man 6B 10 (1E 115)
Courier St. M18: Man 1G 117
Course Vw. OL4: O'ham 6C 76
Court, The M25: Pres 6H 69
Court Dr. M40: Man 1G 103
Courteney Pl. WA14: Bow 4C 150
Courtfield Av. M9: Man 5H 71
Courthill St. SK1: Stoc 3A 146
Courthouse Way OL10: H'ood 3H 39
　(off Woodland St.)
Courtney Grn. SK9: Wilm 5H 165
Court St. BL2: Bolt 4H 175 (6E 33)
　OL3: Upp 1D 78
Courts Vw. M33: Sale 4C 128
Courtyard, The BL1: Bolt 4D 32
　M7: Sal 3A 86
　SK6: Bred 4G 135
　(off Rodney Dr.)
　SK14: Holl 2F 123
Courtyard Dr. M28: Walk 6E 65

Cousin Flds. BL7: Bro X 4G 19
Covall Wlk. M8: Man 5F 87
　(off Hawkeshead Rd.)
Cove, The WA15: Hale 2H 151
Covell Rd. SK12: Poy 2D 168
Covent Gdns. SK1: Stoc 3G 179 (2H 145)
Coventry Av. SK3: Stoc 4B 144
Coventry Gro. OL9: Chad 6A 58
Coventry Rd. M26: Rad 2H 51
Coverdale Av. BL1: Bolt 5G 31
　OL2: O'ham 2C 58
Coverdale Cl. OL10: H'ood 4G 39
Coverdale Cres.
　M12: Man 5H 11 (1H 115)
Cover Dr. OL11: Roch 3D 40
Coverham Av. OL4: O'ham 5B 76
Coverhill Rd. OL4: Grot 4F 77
Covert Rd. M22: Shar 6C 142
　OL4: O'ham 6B 76
Covington Pl. SK9: Wilm 3E 173
Cowan St. M40: Man 4H 7 (3H 101)
Cowburn St. M3: Man 1H 5 (2D 100)
　OL10: H'ood 4A 40
Cowdals Rd. BL6: Los 3B 46
Cowesby St. M14: Man 4E 115
COWHILL 3B 74
Cowhill La. OL6: A Lyme ...4D 174 (2A 106)
Cowhill Trad. Est. OL6: A Lyme ...1A 106
　(off Tramway Rd.)
Cowie St. OL2: Shaw 5H 43
Cow La. BL3: Bolt 5H 47
　M5: Sal 6B 4 (4A 100)
　M33: Sale 3E 129
　M35: Fail 4G 89
　OL4: O'ham 2A 76
　SK2: Stoc 1D 158
　(not continuous)
　SK7: Stoc 1D 158
　SK9: Wilm 2F 173
　WA14: D Mas 6A 138
　WA15: Alt 6H 151
Cow Lees BL5: W'ton 6A 46
Cowley Rd. BL1: Bolt 6D 18
Cowley St. M40: Man 5E 89
Cowling St. M7: Sal 3F 85
　OL8: O'ham 5F 91
COWLISHAW 1G 59
Cowlishaw OL2: Shaw 2G 59
COWLISHAW BROW 4D 136
Cowlishaw La. OL2: Shaw 2G 59
Cowlishaw Rd. SK6: Rom 4D 136
　SK14: Hyde, Stoc 4D 136
Cowm Pk. Way OL12: Whitw 3A 14
Cowm Pk. Way Sth. OL12: Whitw ...1E 15
Cowm Top La. OL11: Roch 2G 41
Cowper St. M24: Mid 1F 73
　OL6: A Lyme 4D 174 (2A 106)
Cowper Wlk. M11: Man 4B 102
　(off Newcombe Cl.)
COX GREEN 2D 18
Cox Grn. Cl. BL7: Eger 1C 18
Coxton Rd. M22: Wyth 4C 154
Coxwold Gro. BL3: Bolt 5A 48
　(off Maltby Dr.)
Crabbe St. M4: Man 1B 6 (2E 101)
Crab La. M9: Man 5F 71
Crabtree Av. SK12: Dis 2H 171
　WA15: Haleb 6D 152
Crabtree Ct. SK12: Dis 1H 171
　(off Buxton Old Rd.)
Crabtree La. M11: Man 5F 103
　(not continuous)
Crabtree Rd. OL1: O'ham 1H 75
Craddock Rd. M33: Sale 1C 140
Craddock St. OL5: Mos 6G 93
Cradley Av. M11: Man 5F 103
Crag Av. BL9: Sum 1D 22
Cragg Fold BL9: Sum 1D 22
Cragg Pl. OL15: L'ough 4H 17
Cragg Rd. OL1: Chad 5H 57
　(not continuous)
Crag La. BL9: Sum 1D 22
Cragside Way SK9: Wilm 3F 173

Craig Av. BL8: Bury 4B 36
　M41: Urm 4C 110
Craig Cl. SK4: Stoc 2D 144
Craigend Dr. M9: Man 4A 88
Craighall Av. M19: Man 1B 132
Craighall Rd. BL1: Bolt 5C 18
Craigie St. M8: Man 6D 86
Craiglands OL16: Roch 3B 42
Craiglands Av. M40: Man 5C 88
Craigmore Av. M20: Man 5B 130
Craignair Ct. M27: Pen 4B 84
Craig Rd. M18: Man 3E 117
　SK4: Stoc 2B 144
Craig Wlk. OL8: O'ham 4E 75
Craigweil Av. M20: Man 6H 131
Craigwell Rd. M25: Pres 1C 86
Craigwell Wlk. M13: Man 4C 10
Crail Pl. OL10: H'ood 4D 38
Cramer St. M40: Man 6B 88
Crammond Cl. M40: Man 5F 89
Cramond Cl. BL1: Bolt 4B 32
Cramond Wlk. BL1: Bolt 4B 32
　(off Cramond Cl.)
Crampton Dr. WA15: Haleb 5C 152
Crampton La. M31: C'ton 2H 125
Cranage Av. SK9: Hand 2H 165
　(off Spath La.)
Cranage Rd. M19: Man 1D 132
Cranark Cl. BL1: Bolt 6G 31
Cranberry Cl. WA14: B'ath 3D 138
Cranberry Dr. BL3: Bolt 3F 47
　M34: Dent 4D 118
Cranberry Rd. M31: Part 6D 124
Cranberry St. OL4: O'ham 3H 75
Cranborne Cl. BL6: Los 4A 30
Cranbourne Av. SK8: Chea H ...3D 156
Cranbourne Cl. OL7: A Lyme 1G 105
　WA15: Tim 5A 140
Cranbourne Ct. SK4: Stoc 5D 132
Cranbourne Rd. M16: Old T 3A 114
　M21: Chor 1H 129
　OL6: A Lyme 1G 105
　OL7: A Lyme 1G 105
　OL11: Roch 5A 26
　SK4: Stoc 5D 132
Cranbourne St. M5: Sal 6A 4 (4H 99)
Cranbourne Ter. OL6: A Lyme ...6H 91
Cranbrook Cl. BL1: Bolt 4D 32
　(off Lindfield Dr.)
Cranbrook Dr. M25: Pres 1A 86
Cranbrook Gdns. OL7: A Lyme ...1H 105
Cranbrook Pl. OL4: O'ham 3A 76
Cranbrook Rd. M18: Man 4G 117
　M30: Ecc 1C 96
Cranbrook St. M26: Rad 2C 52
　OL4: O'ham 3H 75
　OL7: A Lyme 1G 105
Cranbrook Wlk. OL9: Chad 3A 74
Crandon Ct. M27: Pen 2A 84
Crandon Dr. M20: Man 3G 143
Cranesbill Cl. M22: Wyth 4A 154
Crane St. BL3: Bolt 4H 47
　M12: Man 2F 11 (5G 101)
Cranfield Cl. M40: Man 3H 7 (3H 101)
Cranford Av. M20: Man 5H 131
　M32: Stre 4F 113
　M33: Sale 3C 128
　M45: White 5E 53
Cranford Cl. M27: Swin 5B 84
　M45: White 5E 53
Cranford Dr. M44: Irl 4D 108
Cranford Gdns. M41: Urm 4A 110
　SK6: Mar 3D 148
Cranford Ho. M30: Ecc 2H 97
　(off Half Edge La.)
Cranford Rd. M41: Urm 4A 110
　SK9: Wilm 6E 165
Cranford St. BL3: Bolt 5A 48
Cranham Cl. BL8: Bury 2B 36
Cranham Cl. M38: Lit H 3E 65
Cranham Rd. M22: Wyth 3G 153
Cranleigh Av. SK4: Stoc 5B 132

Cranleigh Cl.—Croftside Way

Cranleigh Cl. OL4: O'ham .6B 60
Cranleigh Dr. M28: Walk .3A 82
M33: Sale .2C 140
(Ashstead Rd.)
M33: Sale .4A 128
(Ashton La.)
SK7: H Gro .5G 159
SK8: Chea .5B 144
Cranlington Dr. M8: Man .5D 86
Cranmer Ct. OL10: H'ood .4G 39
Cranmere Av. M19: Man .5E 117
Cranmere Dr. M33: Sale .1F 139
Cranmer Rd. M20: Man .5F 131
Cranshaw St. M29: Tyld .2B 80
Cranston Dr. M20: Man .3F 143
M33: Sale .6E 129
Cranston Gro. SK8: Gat .6D 142
Cranswick St. M14: Man .4E 115
Crantock Dr. SK8: H Grn .5G 155
SK15: Stal .2H 107
Crantock St. M12: Man .4D 116
Cranwell Ct. M43: Droy .5B 104
(off Williamson La.)
Cranwell Dr. M19: Man .5A 132
Cranworth St. SK15: Stal .4F 107
Craston Rd. M13: Man .5A 116
Crathie Ct. BL1: Bolt .4H 31
Craunton Ho. M30: Ecc .3H 97
Craven Av. M5: Sal .5H 99
Craven Dr. M5: Sal .1G 113
WA14: B'ath .3E 139
Craven Gdns. OL11: Roch .6G 27
Cravenhurst Av. M40: Man .1D 102
Craven Pl. BL1: Bolt .3E 31
M11: Man .3E 103
Craven Rd. SK5: Stoc .3H 133
WA14: B'ath .4E 139
(not continuous)
Craven St. BL9: Bury .2H 37
M5: Sal .6B 4 (4A 100)
M43: Droy .4A 104
OL1: O'ham .6E 59
OL6: A Lyme .6B 92
Craven Ter. M33: Sale .5C 128
Cravenwood OL6: A Lyme .5D 92
Cravenwood Ri. BL5: W'ton .5A 46
(off Abbeylea Dr.)
Cravenwood Rd. M8: Man .3E 87
SK5: Stoc .5G 117
Crawford Av. BL2: Bolt .1F 49
M28: Wors .3B 82
Crawford M. OL6: A Lyme .3B 106
Crawford Sq. OL10: H'ood .4E 39
Crawford St. BL2: Bolt .1F 49
M30: Ecc .2F 97
M40: Man .6E 89
OL6: A Lyme .3B 106
OL16: Roch .6A 28
Crawley Av. M22: Wyth .2B 154
M30: Ecc .2A 98
Crawley Cl. M29: Tyld .2A 80
Crawley Gro. SK2: Stoc .5B 146
Crawley Way OL9: Chad .3A 74
Cray, The OL16: Miln .5E 29
Craydon St. M11: Man .5E 103
Crayfield Rd. M19: Man .1D 132
Crayford Rd. M40: Man .1D 102
Cray Wlk. M13: Man .4C 10
Creaton Way M24: Mid .3G 55
Creden Av. M22: Wyth .2D 154
Crediton Cl. M15: Man .6H 9 (2D 114)
WA14: Alt .5D 138
Crediton Dr. BL2: Bolt .6C 34
Crediton Ho. M6: Sal .2A 98
Creel Cl. M9: Man .5F 71
Cremer Ho. M30: Ecc .3H 97
Cresbury St. M12: Man .3G 11 (6H 101)
Crescent, The BL2: Bolt .1B 34
BL3: Lit L .5D 50
BL7: Bro X .3E 19
BL9: Bury .2G 37
M5: Sal .4A 4 (3H 99)
M19: Man .6C 116
Crescent, The M24: Mid .1A 72
M25: Pres .5H 69
M26: Rad .2F 51
M28: Wors .6C 82
M41: Urm .4B 110
M43: Droy .4H 103
M44: Irl .4F 109
OL2: Shaw .1G 59
OL5: Mos .2F 93
OL12: Whitw .1E 15
SK3: Stoc .6H 145
SK6: Bred .5D 134
SK8: Chea .5H 143
SK15: Stal .1H 121
WA14: Alt .6C 138
WA15: Tim .4H 139
Crescent Av. BL1: Bolt .5B 32
BL4: Farn .3G 65
M8: Man .3E 87
M25: Pres .1H 85
M27: Pen .3C 84
Crescent Cl. SK3: Stoc .6A 146
SK16: Duk .4A 106
Crescent Ct. M21: Chor .6F 113
(off Alderfield Rd.)
M33: Sale .6B 128
Crescent Dr. M8: Man .2F 87
M38: Lit H .4F 65
Crescent Gro. M19: Man .6C 116
M25: Pres .1H 85
SK8: Chea .5G 143
Crescent Pk. SK4: Stoc .1E 145
Crescent Range M14: Man .4G 115
Crescent Rd. BL3: Bolt .3E 49
BL4: Kea .3B 66
M8: Man .3D 86
OL9: Chad .1G 89
OL11: Roch .1D 40
SK1: Stoc .6B 134
SK8: Chea .5G 143
SK9: A Edg .4H 173
SK16: Duk .4A 106
WA14: Alt .5C 138
WA15: Hale .3G 151
Crescent St. M8: Man .3G 87
Crescent Vw. SK16: Duk .4A 106
(off Peel St.)
Crescent Way SK3: Stoc .6A 146
Cresgarth Ho. SK3: Stoc .1A 158
Cressfield Way M21: Chor .2B 130
Cressingham Rd. BL3: Bolt .3G 47
M32: Stre .6B 112
Cressington Cl. M5: Sal .3E 99
(off Cedric St.)
Cresswell Gro. M20: Man .4E 131
Crest, The M43: Droy .6A 104
Crestfold M38: Walk .5E 65
Crest Lodge SK7: Bram .3H 157
Crest St. M3: Man .2A 6 (2D 100)
Crestwood Wlk. M40: Man .5G 87
(off Barnstaple Dr.)
Crete St. OL8: O'ham .5F 75
Crewe Rd. M23: Wyth .3E 141
Crib Fold OL3: Dob .5C 62
Crib La. OL3: Dob .5C 62
Criccieth Rd. SK3: Stoc .4C 144
Criccieth St. M16: W Ran .3D 114
Cricketfield La. M28: Walk .6G 65
Cricket Gro., The
M21: Chor .3H 129
Crickets La. OL6: A Lyme .2A 106
(not continuous)
Crickets La. Nth.
OL6: A Lyme .5D 174 (2A 106)
Cricket St. BL3: Bolt .2B 48
M34: Dent .3G 119
Cricket Vw. OL16: Miln .6F 29
Cricklewood Rd. M22: Wyth .3A 154
CRIMBLE .1A 40
Crimble La.
OL10: H'ood, Roch .1A 40
OL11: Roch .6A 26
Crimble St. OL12: Roch .3F 27
Crime La. M35: O'ham .4D 90
OL8: O'ham .4D 90
CRIME VIEW .4D 90
Crimsworth Av. M16: Old T .5H 113
Crinan Sq. OL10: H'ood .4D 38
Crinan Wlk. M40: Man .1G 7
Crinan Way BL2: Bolt .1B 50
Cringlebarrow Cl. M28: Wors .6D 80
Cringle Cl. BL3: Bolt .3E 47
Cringle Dr. SK8: Chea .1G 155
Cringleford Cl. M12: Man .2B 116
Cringle Hall Rd. M19: Man .1B 132
Cringle Rd. M19: Man .2D 132
Cripple Ga. La. OL11: Roch .4G 41
Crispin Rd. M22: Wyth .5C 154
Critchley Cl. SK14: Hyde .6D 120
Criterion St. SK5: Stoc .5H 117
Croal St. BL1: Bolt .1B 48
Croal Wlk. M45: White .6H 53
Croasdale Av. M14: Man .1F 131
Croasdale Cl. OL2: O'ham .2E 59
Croasdale St. BL1: Bolt .4D 32
(not continuous)
Crocker Wlk. M9: Man .3A 88
(off Kingscliffe St.)
Crocus Dr. OL2: O'ham .2G 59
Crocus St. BL1: Bolt .1D 32
Crocus Wlk. M7: Sal .5B 86
(off Hilton St. Nth.)
Croft, The BL1: Bolt .1F 175
BL9: Bury .1G 53
OL8: O'ham .1E 91
SK2: Stoc .5B 146
SK13: Had .1H 123
Croft Acres BL0: Ram .3G 13
Croft Av. M25: Pres .1D 70
Croft Bank M7: Sal .6A 86
M18: Man .2G 117
OL12: Whitw .3B 14
SK15: Mill .1H 107
Croft Brow OL8: O'ham .1E 91
Croft Cl. WA15: Haleb .1C 162
Croft Dell BL1: Bolt .2G 31
Croft Dr. BL8: Tot .5G 21
Croft Edge OL3: G'fld .4C 78
Crofters, The M33: Sale .6F 129
Crofters Brook M26: Rad .3C 52
Crofters Grn. SK9: Wilm .3C 172
Crofters Hall Wlk. M40: Man .4D 88
(off Duncombe Dr.)
Crofters Wlk. BL2: Bolt .5G 19
Croft Ga. BL2: Bolt .1A 34
Croft Gates Rd. M24: Mid .2H 71
Croft Gro. M38: Lit H .4D 64
Crofthead OL15: L'ough .2H 17
Croft Head Dr. OL16: Miln .4F 29
Croft Hey BL0: Ram .3G 13
Crofthill Ct. OL12: Roch .5D 16
Croft Hill Rd. M40: Man .2C 88
Croft Ind. Est. BL9: Bury .2G 53
Croftlands BL0: Ram .6A 12
Croftlands Rd. M22: Wyth .1C 154
Croft La. BL3: Bolt .2F 49
BL9: Bury .2G 53
M26: Rad .3C 52
Croftleigh Cl. M45: White .5E 53
Crofton Av. WA15: Tim .2A 140
Crofton St. M14: Man .4F 115
M16: Old T .3B 114
OL8: O'ham .6E 75
(not continuous)
Croft Rd. M33: Sale .1D 140
SK8: Chea H .3D 156
SK9: Wilm .5B 172
Croft Row OL5: Mos .2H 93
Crofts OL2: Shaw .5C 44
CROFTS BANK .3E 111
Crofts Bank Rd. M41: Urm .3E 111
Croft Side BL3: Bolt .2A 50
Croftside Av. M28: Walk .6A 66
Croftside Cl. M28: Walk .6A 66
Croftside Gro. M28: Walk .6A 66
Croftside Way SK9: Wilm .3F 173

Croft Sq. OL12: Roch 6C **16**
Croft St. BL3: Bolt 3F **49**
  BL9: Bury 3G **37**
  M7: Sal 6A **86**
  M11: Man 4D **102**
  M35: Fail 2A **90**
  M38: Lit H 4D **64**
  OL12: Roch 6C **16**
  SK14: Hyde 5A **120**
  SK15: Stal 3F **107**
Croich Bank BL8: Haw 1D **20**
Croich Grn. BL8: Haw 1D **20**
Cromar Rd. SK7: H Gro 2F **159**
Cromarty Av. OL9: Chad 6H **73**
Cromarty Sq.
  OL10: H'ood 4E **39**
Cromarty Wlk. *M11: Man 4B 102*
  (off Biscay Cl.)
Crombie Av. M22: Nor 4B **142**
Crombouke Fold
  M28: Wors 4F **81**
Cromdale Av. BL1: Bolt 5H **31**
  SK7: H Gro 2F **159**
Cromer Av. BL2: Bolt 4G **33**
  M20: Man 3F **131**
  M34: Dent 4A **118**
Cromer Ind. Est. M24: Mid 6D **56**
Cromer Rd. BL8: Bury 6D **22**
  (not continuous)
  M33: Sale 6C **128**
  SK8: Chea 5A **144**
Cromer St. M11: Man 4F **103**
  M24: Mid 6D **56**
  OL2: Shaw 6H **43**
  OL12: Roch 1A **178** (2G **27**)
  SK1: Stoc 1B **146**
Cromford Av. M32: Stre 4B **112**
Cromford Bank *SK13: Gam 5F 123*
  (off Grassmoor Cres.)
Cromford Bus. Cen.
  OL1: O'ham 1H **75**
Cromford Cl. BL1: Bolt 4C **32**
  SK13: Gam 5F 123
  (off Grassmoor Cres.)
Cromford Fold *SK13: Gam 5F 123*
  (off Grassmoor Cres.)
Cromford Gdns. BL1: Bolt 3D **32**
Cromford Grn. *SK13: Gam 5F 123*
  (off Grassmoor Cres.)
Cromford Gro. *SK13: Gam 5F 123*
  (off Grassmoor Cres.)
Cromford Lea *SK13: Gam 5F 123*
  (off Grassmoor Cres)
Cromford Pl. *SK13: Gam 5F 123*
  (off Grassmoor Cres.)
Cromford St. OL1: O'ham 1G **75**
Cromford Way
  SK13: Gam 5F **123**
Cromhall Wlk. *M8: Man 5E 87*
  (off Starmoor Dr.)
Cromhurst St. M8: Man 3E **87**
Cromley St. SK6: H Lan 1C **170**
Cromley Rd. SK2: Stoc 2A **158**
  SK6: H Lan 6C **160**
Crompton Av. BL2: Bolt 5A **34**
  OL16: Roch 2B **42**
Crompton Cl. BL1: Bolt 1E **33**
  M26: Rad 1B **68**
  SK6: Mar 4D **148**
Crompton Ct. BL3: Lit L 4E **51**
CROMPTON FOLD 5B **44**
Crompton Fold *BL8: Bury 1B 36*
  (off Dorning St.)
Crompton Ga. OL2: Shaw 5G **43**
Crompton Ho. M27: Swin 3G **83**
Crompton Lodge Cvn. Pk.
  BL4: Bolt 4A **50**
Crompton Pl. BL1: Bolt 4F **175** (6D **32**)
  M26: Rad 4B **52**
Crompton Pool 1H **59**
Crompton Rd. BL6: Los 5A **30**
  M19: Man 2C **132**
  M26: Rad 1C **66**

Crompton St. BL1: Bolt 1H **175** (5E **33**)
  BL4: Farn 2A **66**
  BL9: Bury 3B **176** (3E **37**)
  M27: Swin 3G **83**
  M28: Walk 1B **82**
  M38: Lit H 4B **64**
  OL1: O'ham 1E **75**
  OL2: O'ham 4E **59**
  OL2: Shaw 6H **43**
  OL6: A Lyme 1C **106**
  OL9: Chad 2C **74**
  (not continuous)
Crompton Va. BL2: Bolt 5H **33**
Crompton Way BL1: Bolt 1D **32**
  BL2: Bolt 1D **32**
  OL2: Shaw 1H **59**
Cromwell Av. M16: W Ran 5A **114**
  SK5: Dent 5A **118**
  SK6: Mar 4B **148**
  SK8: Gat 5E **143**
Cromwell Bri. M6: Sal 6A **86**
Cromwell Ct. *M6: Sal 1H 99*
  (off Cromwell Rd.)
  M44: Irl 2C **124**
  OL1: O'ham 5G **177**
Cromwell Gro. M7: Sal 6A **86**
  M19: Man 6C **116**
Cromwell Range M14: Man 5H **115**
Cromwell Rd. M6: Sal 1G **99**
  M25: Pres 5A **70**
  M27: Swin 2G **83**
  M30: Ecc 3E **97**
  M32: Stre 6E **113**
  M44: Irl 2C **124**
  M45: White 5D **52**
  OL2: Shaw 1C **58**
  SK6: Bred 3D **134**
  SK7: Bram 1F **167**
Cromwell St. BL1: Bolt 1B **48**
  OL1: O'ham 5G **177** (3F **75**)
  OL10: H'ood 4H **39**
  SK4: Stoc 6F **133**
Crondale Wlk. M13: Man 6E **11**
Crondall St. M14: Man 4E **115**
Cronkeyshaw Av. OL12: Roch 1G **27**
Cronkeyshaw Rd. OL12: Roch 2G **27**
Cronshaw Ind. Est. OL11: Roch 6D **178**
Cronshaw St. M19: Man 1D **132**
Crookhill Dr. M8: Man 4D **86**
Crookilley Way SK1: Stoc 6A **134**
  SK6: Bred 6A **134**
Crook St. BL3: Bolt 6F **175** (1D **48**)
  M26: Rad 4B **52**
  OL16: Roch 2D **178** (3A **28**)
  SK14: Hyde 5B **120**
Croom Wlk. M40: Man 3H **7**
Crosby Av. M28: Walk 1B **82**
Crosby Rd. BL1: Bolt 5H **31**
  M6: Sal 6D **84**
  M26: Rad 6G **35**
  M40: Man 6F **89**
Crosby St. OL12: Roch 1C **14**
  SK2: Stoc 6G **179** (4H **145**)
Crosfield Av. BL9: Sum 1C **22**
Crosfield Gro. M18: Man 3F **117**
Crosland Ind. Est. SK6: Bred 5E **135**
Cross, The BL8: Bury 1H **35**
  SK13: Had 2H **123**
Cross Av. M25: Pres 3G **69**
Crossacres Rd. M22: Wyth 2B **154**
Cross Bank M25: Pres 2H **115**
CROSS BANK ....
Crossbank Av. OL4: Lees 2D **76**
  OL4: Lees 2H **115**
Crossbank Ho. *OL9: O'ham 3D 74*
  (off Manchester St.)
Crossbank St.
  OL8: O'ham 5E **177** (3E **75**)
  (not continuous)
Crossbank Way M24: Mid 6B **56**
Crossbill Brow WA14: W Tim 2E **139**
Crossbridge Rd. SK14: Hyde 5E **121**
Crossbrook Way OL16: Miln 6G **29**
Crossby Cl. M24: Mid 4B **72**

Cross Cliffe SK14: Hyde 1A **136**
Crosscliffe St. M16: W Ran 3D **114**
Crossdale Rd. BL2: Bolt 5A **34**
  M9: Man 5B **72**
Crossefield Rd. SK8: Chea H 2C **156**
Crossen St. BL3: Bolt 2G **49**
Crossfell Av. M9: Man 4F **71**
Crossfield Cl. M34: Dent 5G **119**
  OL2: Shaw 4A **44**
  OL12: W'le 5C **16**
  SK15: Stal 4E **107**
Cross Fld. Dr. M26: Rad 4G **51**
Crossfield Dr. M27: Swin 2G **83**
  M28: Wors 4B **82**
Crossfield Gro. SK2: Stoc 1B **158**
  SK6: Mar B 2F **149**
Crossfield Pl. OL11: Roch 6A **28**
  OL12: W'le 6C **16**
  SK9: Hand 3H **165**
  WA15: Hale 3B **152**
Crossfields BL7: Bro X 3F **19**
Crossfield St. BL9: Bury 3F **53**
Crossford Cl. M33: Sale 3B **128**
Crossford Dr. BL3: Bolt 3E **47**
Crossford St. M32: Stre 6D **112**
Crossgate Av. M22: Wyth 5B **142**
Crossgate M. SK4: Stoc 1A **144**
Crossgates Rd. OL16: Miln 4F **29**
Cross Glebe St.
  OL6: A Lyme 5D **174** (2A **106**)
Cross Gro. WA15: Tim 3H **139**
Crosshill St. M16: W Ran 3D **114**
Crosshill Wlk. BL3: Bolt 2E **47**
Cross Hope St. OL6: A Lyme 1B **106**
Cross Keys St. M4: Man 3C **6** (3F **101**)
Cross Knowle Vw. M41: Urm 3B **110**
Crossland Rd. M21: Chor 1G **129**
  M43: Droy 3B **104**
Crosslands M25: Pres 6G **69**
Crosslands Rd. M28: Wors 5D **80**
Cross La. BL8: Holc 4A **12**
  M5: Sal 4G **99**
  M18: Man 2F **117**
  M26: Rad 3C **52**
  M43: Droy 1D **104**
  SK6: Mar 6C **148**
  SK9: Wilm 6B **166**
Cross La. E. M31: Part 6D **124**
Cross La. W. M31: Part 6D **124**
Crosslee Rd. M9: Man 5B **72**
Cross Lees OL12: Roch 6A **16**
Crossley Ct. *M4: Man 5H 7*
  (off Pollard St.)
Crossley Cres. OL6: A Lyme 5B **92**
Crossley Est. OL9: Chad 3B **74**
Crossley Pk. SK4: Stoc 2D **132**
Crossley Rd. M19: Man 2B **132**
  M33: Sale 3A **128**
  SK4: Stoc 2B **132**
Crossley St. BL3: Lit L 3C **50**
  M18: Man 1D **116**
  OL2: O'ham 5E **59**
  OL2: Shaw 6A **44**
  OL16: Miln 5E **29**
  SK15: Stal 3D **106**
  SK16: Duk 4B **106**
Crossmead Dr. M9: Man 4A **72**
Crossmeadow Cl. OL11: Roch 3C **26**
Crossmoor Cres. SK6: Rom 1A **148**
Crossmoor Dr. BL2: Bolt 5F **33**
Crossmoor Gro. SK6: Rom 1A **148**
Cross Ormrod St. BL3: Bolt 1B **48**
Cross Rd. M21: Chor 1H **129**
  SK8: H Grn 6F **155**
Cross St. BL0: Ram 3C **12**
  BL1: Bolt 1G **175** (5D **32**)
  BL3: Lit L 4D **50**
  BL4: Farn 6H **49**
  BL4: Kea 4D **66**
  BL7: Bro X 4E **19**
  BL9: Bury 3C **176** (3F **37**)
  (not continuous)

Cross St.—Cunningham Way

Cross St. M2: Man 6H 5 (4D 100)
M3: Sal 3F 5 (3C 100)
M16: Old T 2B 114
M24: Mid 1B 72
(not continuous)
M26: Rad 4B 52
M27: Clif 1D 84
M28: Wors 4E 83
M32: Stre 5D 112
M33: Sale 4B 128
M34: Dent 2E 119
M41: Urm 6E 111
M45: White 6E 53
OL4: Lees 3C 76
OL4: O'ham 2H 75
OL4: Spri 3E 77
OL5: Mos 1G 93
OL6: A Lyme 6A 174 (3G 105)
OL10: H'ood 4A 40
OL11: Roch 3F 41
OL16: Roch 4D 28
SK13: Had 2H 123
SK14: B'tom 6C 122
(off Gorsey Brow)
SK14: Holl 3F 123
SK14: Hyde 5B 120
SK15: Mill 1H 107
WA14: Alt 2B 174 (1F 151)
Crosswaite Rd. SK2: Stoc 5D 146
Crossway M20: Man 6F 131
M43: Droy 6A 104
SK2: Stoc 1A 158
SK7: Bram 2G 167
Crossway Rd. M33: Sale 2H 139
Crossways OL8: O'ham 2G 91
SK7: Bram 4E 157
Croston Cl. SK9: A Edg 5H 173
Croston Cl. Rd. BL9: Bury 1A 24
(not continuous)
Crostons Ct. *BL8: Bury 2D 36*
(off Crostons Rd.)
Crostons Rd. BL8: Bury 2D 36
Croston St. BL3: Bolt 3A 48
Croston Wlk. M11: Man 4A 102
Croton St. SK4: Stoc 1A 144
Croughton Cl. M11: Man 6F 103
Crowbank Wlk. *M40: Man 6C 88*
(off Bower St.)
Crowborough Wlk.
M15: Man 2D 114
(off Arnott Cres.)
Crowbrook Gro. *SK9: Wilm 6H 165*
(off Colshaw Dr.)
CROWCROFT PARK 5D 116
Crowcroft Rd. M12: Man 4C 116
M13: Man 4C 116
Crowden Rd. M40: Man 1D 88
CROWHILL 1F 105
Crow Hill SK15: C'ook 6A 94
Crowhill Cotts. OL7: A Lyme 1G 105
Crow Hill Nth. M24: Mid 3B 72
Crowhill Rd. OL7: A Lyme 1F 105
Crow Hill Sth. M24: Mid 3B 72
Crow Hill Vw. OL4: O'ham 5D 76
Crowhurst Wlk. *M23: Wyth 4E 141*
(off Sandy La.)
Crowland Gdns. SK8: Chea H 1D 166
Crowland Rd. BL2: Bolt 3G 33
M23: Wyth 2F 153
Crow La. BL0: Ram 3C 12
Crowley La. OL4: O'ham 6B 60
Crowley Rd. M9: Man 3B 88
WA15: Tim 5B 140
Crown Bus. Cen. M35: Fail 3H 89
Crown Ct. SK7: H Gro 2D 158
Crowneast St. OL11: Roch 4E 27
Crown Gdns. OL16: Roch 6B 28
Crowngreen Rd. M30: Ecc 4G 97
Crown Hill OL5: Mos 3H 93
Crownhill Ct. M43: Droy 3A 104
Crownhill Dr. M43: Droy 3A 104
Crown Ho. *M22: Shar 5C 142*
(off Lauriston Cl.)
Crown Ind. Est. M4: Man 3E 7 (3G 101)
SK5: Stoc 4G 117
WA14: Tim 4G 139
Crown La. M4: Man 2B 6 (2E 101)
Crown M. BL8: Haw 1E 21
SK2: Stoc 1C 158
Crown Passages
WA15: Hale 3G 151
CROWN POINT 4F 119
(junc. of A57 with A6017)
Crown Point Av. M40: Man 6E 89
Crown Point Nth. Shop. Pk.
M34: Dent 3E 119
Crown Point Sth. Ind. Pk.
M34: Dent 4F 119
Crown Rd. OL10: H'ood 3F 39
Crown Royal Ind. Pk.
SK1: Stoc 5H 179 (3A 146)
Crown Sq. M3: Man 6F 5 (4C 100)
Crown St. BL1: Bolt 3G 175 (6D 32)
M3: Sal 3E 5 (3C 100)
M15: Man 3E 9 (6C 100)
M34: Dent 3E 119
M35: Fail 3H 89
M40: Man 6E 89
OL2: Shaw 6H 43
OL6: A Lyme 6B 174 (3H 105)
OL16: Roch 6B 28
SK6: Bred 5F 135
SK6: Mar 2D 160
CROW OAK 6C 52
Crowsdale Pl. SK2: Stoc 1E 159
Crowshaw Dr. OL12: Roch 6G 15
Crows Nest BL3: Bolt 2B 50
Crowswood Dr. SK15: C'ook 6H 93
Crowther Av. M5: Sal 5G 99
Crowther Ct. OL15: L'ough 5E 17
Crowther St. M18: Man 2G 117
OL15: L'ough 4E 17
OL16: Roch 1B 42
SK1: Stoc 3G 179 (2H 145)
Crowthorn Dr. M23: Wyth 3G 153
Crowthorn Rd.
OL7: A Lyme 4F 105
SK4: Stoc 2F 133
Crowton Av. M33: Sale 1F 139
Croxdale Cl. OL7: A Lyme 6E 91
Croxdale Wlk. *M9: Man 4H 71*
(off Claygate Dr.)
Croxton Av. OL16: Roch 3B 28
Croxton Cl. M33: Sale 1F 139
SK6: Mar 6C 148
Croxton Wlk. M13: Man 5E 11
Croyde Cl. BL2: Bolt 2B 34
M22: Wyth 6D 154
Croydon Av. OL2: O'ham 1C 58
OL11: Roch 6F 41
Croydon Ct. M5: Sal 5H 99
Croydon Dr. M40: Man 1E 103
Croydon Ho. *BL1: Bolt 4C 32*
(off Kenton Cl.)
Croydon Sq. OL11: Roch 5F 41
Crummock Cl. BL3: Lit L 4B 50
Crummock Dr. M24: Mid 4A 56
Crummock Gro. BL4: Farn 2C 64
Crummock Rd. SK8: Gat 2F 155
CRUMPSALL 1D 86
CRUMPSALL GREEN 1E 87
Crumpsall La. M8: Man 2D 86
Crumpsall Stop (Metro) 2E 87
Crumpsall St. BL1: Bolt 3C 32
Crumpsall Va. M9: Man 1G 87
Crumpsall Way M8: Man 2F 87
Crundale Rd. BL1: Bolt 5E 19
Cruttenden Rd.
SK2: Stoc 1C 158
Cryer St. M43: Droy 1C 104
Crystal Ho. M16: W Ran 4B 114
Cuba Ind. Est. BL0: Ram 1C 12
Cube 1A 10
Cube, The M11: Man 3B 102
Cubley Rd. M7: Sal 3C 86
Cuckoo Gro. M25: Pres 3H 69
Cuckoo La. BL9: Bury 3A 38
(not continuous)
M25: Pres 3H 69
M45: White 3H 69
Cuckoo Nest M25: Pres 2H 69
Cuddington Av. M20: Man 1E 131
Cuddington Cres. SK3: Stoc 5F 145
Cuddington Way *SK9: Hand 2H 165*
(off Pickmere Rd.)
Cudworth Rd. M9: Man 4E 71
Cuerdon Wlk. M22: Nor 3C 142
Culand St. M12: Man 1A 116
Culbert Av. M20: Man 6G 131
CULCHETH .6E 89
Culcheth Av. SK6: Mar 5D 148
Culcheth La. M40: Man 6E 89
Culcheth Rd. WA14: Alt 2F 151
Culcombe Wlk. *M13: Man 2G 115*
(off Corn Cl.)
Culford Cl. M12: Man 2A 116
Culgaith Wlk. *M9: Man 4H 87*
(off Ruskington Dr.)
Culham Cl. *BL1: Bolt 3B 32*
(off Raglan St.)
Cullen Gro. M9: Man 6B 72
Cullercoats Wlk. M12: Man 4D 116
Culmere Rd. M22: Wyth 4B 154
Culmington Cl. M15: Man 6E 9 (2C 114)
Culross Av. BL3: Bolt 1E 47
M40: Man 2G 89
Culvercliffe Wlk. M3: Man 1F 9
Culverden Wlk. M6: Sal 5F 85
Culver Rd. SK3: Stoc 6F 145
Culvert St. OL4: O'ham 6C 60
OL16: Roch 3B 42
Culverwell Dr. M5: Sal 3H 99
Cumber Cl. SK9: Wilm 5A 172
Cumber Dr. SK9: Wilm 5A 172
Cumberland Av. M27: Clif 1H 83
M44: Cad 5A 124
OL10: H'ood 3E 39
SK5: Stoc 5C 134
SK16: Duk 5C 106
Cumberland Cl. BL9: Bury 1E 53
Cumberland Dr. OL1: O'ham 6D 58
OL2: O'ham 6D 58
WA14: Bow 5C 150
Cumberland Gro. OL7: A Lyme 1H 105
Cumberland Point M27: Clif 1A 84
Cumberland Rd. M9: Man 2H 87
M33: Sale 1C 140
M41: Urm 6E 111
OL11: Roch 3H 41
Cumberland St. M7: Sal 1B 100
SK15: Stal 3D 106
Cumber La. SK9: Wilm 4A 172
Cumbermere La. M29: Tyld 1A 80
Cumbrae Gdns. M5: Sal 4D 98
Cumbrae Rd. M19: Man 6E 117
Cumbria Ct. M25: Pres 2G 85
Cumbrian Cl. M13: Man 5D 10 (1G 115)
OL2: Shaw 5F 43
Cumbria Wlk. M6: Sal 1H 99
Cummings St. OL8: O'ham 1C 90
Cunard Cl. M13: Man 5E 11 (1G 115)
Cundall Wlk. M23: Wyth 2F 141
Cundey St. BL1: Bolt 4A 32
Cundiff Ct. M19: Man 6E 117
Cundiff Rd. M21: Chor 3H 129
(not continuous)
Cundy St. SK14: Hyde 3C 120
Cunliffe Av. BL0: Ram 5A 12
Cunliffe Brow BL1: Bolt 3H 31
Cunliffe Dr. M33: Sale 6C 128
OL2: Shaw 6B 44
Cunliffe St. BL0: Ram 2C 12
M26: Rad 4C 52
SK3: Stoc 3E 145
SK14: Hyde 3A 120
Cunningham Dr. BL9: Bury 6H 53
M22: Wyth 5E 155
Cunningham Way
OL1: O'ham 1G 177 (1F 75)

Curate Ct. *SK1:* Stoc 2A *146*
     (off Curate St.)
Curate St. SK1: Stoc 2A **146**
Curlew Cl. OL11: Roch 4B **26**
Curlew Dr. M44: Irl 3E **109**
Curlew Rd. OL4: O'ham 5C **76**
Curlew Wlk.
    M12: Man 2A **116**
Curlew Way SK13: Glos 6H **123**
Currier La.
    OL6: A Lyme 3A **106**
Curtain Theatre 6B **178** (5H **27**)
Curtels Cl. M28: Wors 4E **83**
Curtis Gro. SK13: Had 2H **123**
Curtis Rd. SK4: Stoc 1C **144**
Curtis St. BL3: Bolt 5A **48**
    M19: Man 6E **117**
Curzon Ashton FC 1E **105**
Curzon Av. M14: Man 3A **116**
Curzon Cl. OL11: Roch 3H **41**
Curzon Dr. WA15: Tim 5B **140**
Curzon Grn. SK2: Stoc 3D **146**
Curzon M. SK9: Wilm 4D **172**
Curzon Rd. BL1: Bolt 6A **32**
    M7: Sal 4B **86**
    M32: Stre 4A **112**
    M33: Sale 4B **128**
    OL6: A Lyme 1B **106**
    OL11: Roch 3H **41**
    SK2: Stoc 4D **146**
    SK8: H Grn 6F **155**
    SK12: Poy 5E **169**
Curzon St. OL1: O'ham . . .3G **177** (2F **75**)
    OL5: Mos 2G **93**
Curzon Urmston Cinema 4D **110**
Cutacre La. BL5: O Hul 3B **64**
CUTGATE 3C **26**
Cutgate Cl. M23: Wyth 2E **141**
Cutgate Rd. OL12: Roch 2D **26**
Cutgate Shop. Pct.
    OL11: Roch 3D **26**
Cuthbert Av. M19: Man 5D **116**
Cuthbert Bus. Cen.
    M11: Man 6E *103*
    (off Ashton Old Rd.)
Cuthbert Mayne Ct.
    OL16: Roch 5A **178** (5G **27**)
Cuthbert Rd. SK8: Chea 5A **144**
Cuthbert St. BL3: Bolt 5H **47**
Cuthill Wlk. *M40: Man* 1F *103*
    (off Eastmoor Dr.)
Cutland St. M40: Man 5C **88**
Cutland Way OL15: L'ough 5G **17**
Cut La. OL12: Roch 2B **26**
CUTLER HILL 4B **90**
Cutler Hill Rd. M35: Fail 4B **90**
Cutler St. OL9: Chad 2C **74**
Cutnook La. M44: Irl 2D **108**
Cutter Cl. M5: Sal 5G **99**
Cycle St. M11: Man 5D **102**
Cyclone St. M11: Man 5B **102**
Cygnus Av. M7: Sal 1B **4** (2A **100**)
Cymbal Ct. SK5: Stoc 6H **133**
Cynthia Dr. SK6: Mar 6D **148**
Cypress Av. OL9: Chad 1B **74**
Cypress Cl. SK3: Stoc 3E **145**
Cypress Gdns.
    OL16: Roch 4D **28**
Cypress Gro. BL4: Kea 2B **66**
    M34: Dent 4G **119**
Cypress Oaks
    SK15: Mill, Stal 2H **107**
Cypress Pl. M4: Man 1A **6** (2E **101**)
Cypress Rd. M30: Ecc 1C **96**
    M43: Droy 2A **104**
    OL4: O'ham 1B **76**
Cypress St. M9: Man 4H **87**
    M24: Mid 1E **73**
Cypress Wlk. M33: Sale 3E **127**
Cypress Way SK6: H Lan 6E **161**
Cyprus Cl. M5: Sal 4F **99**
    OL4: O'ham 4B **76**
Cyprus St. M32: Stre 5D **112**

Cyril St. BL3: Bolt 2E **49**
    M14: Man 4F **115**
    OL2: Shaw 6A **44**
Cyrus St. M40: Man 4H **7** (3H **101**)

D

Daccamill Dr. M27: Swin 5H **83**
Dacre Av. M16: W Ran 5H **113**
Dacre Cl. M24: Mid 6F **55**
Dacre Rd. OL11: Roch 1H **41**
DACRES 5C **78**
Dacres Av. OL3: G'fld 5B **78**
Dacres Dr. OL3: G'fld 5B **78**
Dacres Rd. OL3: G'fld 5B **78**
Daffodil Cl. OL12: Roch 6G **15**
Daffodil Rd. BL4: Farn 6E **49**
Daffodil St. BL1: Bolt 6D **18**
Dagenham Rd. M14: Man 3G **115**
Dagenham Rd. Ind. Est.
    M14: Man 4G *115*
    (off Dagenham Rd.)
Dagmar St. M28: Walk 5G **65**
Dagnall Av. M21: Chor 3H **129**
Dahlia Cl. M19: Man 3B **132**
    OL12: Roch 6F **15**
Daimler St. M8: Man 5E **87**
Dain Cl. SK16: Duk 5B **106**
Daine Av. M23: Wyth 2H **141**
Dainton St. M12: Man 3H **11** (6H **101**)
Daintry Cl. M15: Man 5G **9** (1D **114**)
Daintry Rd. OL9: O'ham 2C **74**
Dairybrook Gro. *SK9: Wilm* 6A *166*
    (off Lyngard Cl.)
Dairydale Cl. M44: Irl 4F **109**
Dairyground Rd. SK7: Bram 6G **157**
Dairy Ho. La. SK8: Chea H 4C **166**
    (not continuous)
Dairyhouse La.
    WA14: B'ath, D Mas 5C **138**
Dairy Rd. SK7: Bram 3D **166**
Dairy St. OL9: Chad 2B **74**
Daisy Av. BL4: Farn 6E **49**
    M13: Man 3A **116**
Daisy Bank M40: Man 6E **89**
    SK14: Hyde 1A **136**
Daisy Bank Av. M6: Sal 5C **84**
    M27: Pen 5C **84**
Daisy Bank Hall M14: Man 3H **115**
Daisy Bank La. SK8: H Grn 4E **155**
Daisy Bank Rd. M14: Man 3H **115**
Daisy Bank Vs. *M14: Man* 3H *115*
    (off Hope Rd.)
DAISYFIELD .4B **36**
Daisyfield BL8: Bury 5C **36**
Daisyfield Cl. M22: Wyth 4A **154**
Daisyfield Ct. BL8: Bury 4C **36**
Daisyfield Wlk. *M28: Walk* 6H *65*
    (off Cecil St.)
Daisy Hill Cl. M33: Sale 5E **129**
Daisy Hill Ct. *OL4: O'ham* 1C *100*
    (off Howard St.)
Daisy Hill Rd. OL5: Mos 2H **93**
Daisy M. SK3: Stoc 1F **157**
DAISY NOOK 5D **90**
Daisy Nook Country Pk. 5D **90**
Daisy St. BL3: Bolt 3A **48**
    BL8: Bury 3C **36**
    OL9: Chad 1A **74**
    OL9: O'ham 2D **74**
    OL12: Roch 3G **27**
    SK1: Stoc 4H **145**
Daisy Way SK6: H Lan 6D **160**
Dakerwood Cl. M40: Man 6E **89**
Dakota Av. M50: Sal 5E **99**
Dakota Sth. M50: Sal 5F **99**
Dalbeattie St. M9: Man 3A **88**
Dalberg St. M12: Man 4G **11** (6H **101**)
Dalbury Dr. M40: Man 6G **87**
Dalby Av. M27: Swin 4G **83**
Dalby Gro. SK1: Stoc 2A **146**
DALE 2B **62**

Dale Av. M30: Ecc 2E **97**
    OL5: Mos 6A **78**
    SK7: Bram 5H **157**
Dalebank M. M27: Clif 4F **67**
Dalebeck Cl. M45: White 1H **69**
Dalebeck Wlk. M45: White 1A **70**
Dale Brook Av. SK16: Duk 1B **120**
Dalebrook Ct. SK4: Stoc 2E **145**
Dalebrook Rd. M33: Sale 2C **140**
Dale Ct. M34: Dent 5F **119**
Dale End OL8: O'ham 1G **91**
Dalefields OL3: Del 3B **62**
Daleford Sq. M13: Man 4E **11**
Dalegarth Av. BL1: Bolt 6C **30**
Dale Gro. M44: Cad 3C **124**
    OL7: A Lyme 4G **91**
    WA15: Tim 4H **139**
Dalehead Cl. M18: Man 1H **117**
Dalehead Dr. OL2: Shaw 6B **44**
Dale Ho. M24: Mid 6E **57**
    OL2: Shaw 1H **59**
    SK1: Stoc 1G **179**
Dale Ho. Fold SK12: Poy 3G **169**
Dale La. OL3: Del 2B **62**
Dale Lee BL5: W'ton 6A **46**
Dale Rd. M24: Mid 5D **56**
    SK6: Mar 3C **148**
Dales Av. M8: Man 1D **86**
    M45: White 6D **52**
DALES BROW 5F **83**
Dales Brow BL1: Bolt 5D **18**
    M27: Swin 5G **83**
Dales Brow Av. OL7: A Lyme 6G **91**
Dalesfield Cres. OL5: Mos 2A **94**
Dales Gro. M28: Walk 2B **82**
Dales La. M45: White 6E **53**
Dalesman Dr. M9: Man 3B **88**
Dalesman Dr. OL1: O'ham 4B **60**
Dalesman Wlk. M15: Man 5A **10**
Dales Pk. Dr. M27: Swin 5F **83**
Dale Sq. OL2: O'ham 3F **59**
Dale St. BL0: Ram 1C **12**
    BL4: Farn 6A **50**
    BL8: Bury 1C **36**
    M1: Man 5B **6** (4E **101**)
    M24: Mid 2D **72**
    M26: Rad 5A **52**
    M27: Swin 5G **83**
    M45: White 6E **53**
    OL2: Shaw 1H **59**
    OL6: A Lyme 5E **93**
    OL16: Miln 5F **29**
    OL16: Roch 4C **28**
    SK3: Stoc 5F **145**
    SK15: Stal 4D **106**
Dale St. E. OL6: A Lyme . . .6A **174** (3G **105**)
Dale St. Ind. Est. M26: Rad 5A **52**
Dale St. W.
    OL6: A Lyme 6A **174** (3G **105**)
Daleswood Av. M45: White 6D **52**
Dale Vw. M34: Dent 2G **135**
    OL15: L'ough 1F **29**
    SK14: Hyde 1B **136**
    SK14: Mot 4C **122**
Dalham Av. M9: Man 1C **88**
Dalkeith Av. SK5: Stoc 2H **133**
Dalkeith Gro. BL3: Bolt 2F **47**
Dalkeith Rd. SK5: Stoc 2H **133**
Dalkeith Sq. OL10: H'ood 4E **39**
Dalkeith St. M18: Man 1D **116**
Dalley Av. M7: Sal 1C **4** (1B **100**)
Dallimore Rd. M23: Wyth 5E **141**
Dalmahoy Cl. M40: Man 3E **89**
Dalmain Cl. M8: Man 5D **86**
Dalmeny Ter. OL11: Roch 1H **41**
Dalmorton Rd. M21: Chor 1B **130**
Dalny St. M19: Man 6D **116**
Dalston Av. M35: Fail 3B **90**
Dalston Dr. M20: Man 1G **143**
    SK7: Bram 2E **167**

Dalston Gdns. BL1: Bolt 3C **32**
   (off Gladstone St.)
Dalton Av. M14: Man 5E **115**
   M27: Clif 6C **68**
   M32: Stre 3H **111**
   M45: White 2G **69**
   OL16: Roch 4D **28**
Dalton Bldgs. OL5: Mos 1H **93**
Dalton Cl. BL0: Ram 5A **12**
   OL16: Roch 4D **28**
Dalton Ct. M40: Man 1F **101**
   SK4: Stoc 5E **133**
Dalton Dr. M27: Pen 4D **84**
Dalton Ellis Hall M14: Man 3H **115**
   (off Conyngham Rd.)
Dalton Gdns. M41: Urm 4D **110**
Dalton Gro. SK4: Stoc 5E **133**
Dalton Rd. M9: Man 4H **71**
   M24: Mid 2F **71**
Dalton St. BL8: Bury 3B **36**
   (not continuous)
   M4: Man 1D **6** (1F **101**)
   M30: Ecc 2F **97**
   M33: Sale 3C **128**
   M35: Fail 3G **89**
   M40: Man 1D **6** (1F **101**)
   OL1: O'ham 2H **75**
   OL9: Chad 2B **74**
Daltry St. OL1: O'ham 1G **75**
Dalveen Av. M41: Urm 3E **111**
Dalveen Dr. WA15: Tim 4H **139**
Dalymount Cl. BL2: Bolt 3F **33**
Damask Av. M3: Sal 3C **4** (3B **100**)
Dame Hollow SK8: H Grn 6H **155**
Dameral Cl. M8: Man 5F **87**
Damery Ct. SK7: Bram 5G **157**
Damery Rd. SK7: Bram 5G **157**
Dame St. OL9: O'ham 1D **74**
Dam Head Dr. M9: Man 6A **72**
Damien St. M12: Man 5D **116**
Damson Grn. M24: Mid 1F **73**
Damson Wlk. M31: Part 6B **124**
   (off Wood La.)
Dan Bank SK6: Mar 5A **148**
Danbury Wlk. M23: Wyth 3D **140**
Danby Cl. SK14: Hyde 3D **120**
Danby Ct. OL1: O'ham 1E **75**
   (off Bradford St.)
Danby Pl. SK14: Hyde 3D **120**
Danby Rd. BL3: Bolt 4C **48**
   SK14: Hyde 3D **120**
Danby Wlk. M9: Man 2A **88**
   (off Polworth Rd.)
Dancehouse, The 3A **10**
Dane Av. M31: Part 5D **124**
   SK3: Stoc 3C **144**
DANE BANK 5B **118**
Dane Bank M24: Mid 1D **72**
Dane Bank Dr. SK12: Dis 1H **171**
Danebank M. M34: Dent 5B **118**
Danebank Wlk. M13: Man 4D **10**
Danebridge Cl. BL4: Farn 1A **66**
   (off Peel St.)
DANEBROOK 2H **171**
Dane Cl. SK7: Bram 2F **157**
Danecroft BL3: Lit L 4D **50**
Dane Dr. SK9: Wilm 3G **173**
Danefield Cl. SK8: H Grn 5H **155**
Danefield Rd. M33: Sale 3C **128**
Dane Hill Cl. SK12: Dis 2H **171**
Daneholme Rd. M19: Man 4A **132**
Dane Ho. M33: Sale 5C **128**
   (off Northenden Rd.)
Dane M. M33: Sale 3B **128**
Dane Rd. M33: Sale 5A **128**
   M34: Dent 5A **118**
Dane Rd. Ind. Est. M33: Sale 3C **128**
Dane Road Station (Metro) 3C **128**
Danes, The M8: Man 2D **86**
Danesbury Ri. SK8: Chea 6H **143**
Danesbury Rd. BL2: Bolt 1F **33**
Daneshill M25: Pres 3H **69**

Daneshill Dr. M23: Wyth 1G **153**
   (off Chedlin Dr.)
Danes La. OL12: Whitw 1C **14**
Danesmoor Dr. BL9: Bury 1G **37**
Danesmoor Rd. M20: Man 4E **131**
Danes Rd. M14: Man 5H **115**
Dane St. BL3: Bolt 3A **48**
   M11: Man 6G **103**
   OL4: O'ham 2A **76**
   OL5: Mos 6H **77**
   OL11: Roch 4G **27**
   OL12: Roch 4A **178** (4G **27**)
Danesway M25: Pres 1B **86**
   M27: Pen 4C **84**
Danesway Ct. BL1: Bolt 3B **32**
Danesway Dr. OL12: Whitw 2E **15**
Daneswood Av. M9: Man 5B **72**
   OL12: Whitw 2E **15**
Daneswood Cl. OL12: Whitw 1D **14**
Daneswood Fold OL12: Whitw 1D **14**
Danett Cl. M12: Man 1D **116**
Dane Wlk. SK5: Stoc 5H **133**
Danforth Gro. M19: Man 1D **132**
Daniel Adamson Av. M31: Part 6B **124**
Daniel Adamson Rd. M50: Sal 5D **98**
Daniel Ct. M31: Part 5D **124**
Daniel Fold OL12: Roch 6D **14**
Daniel's La. SK1: Stoc 1G **179**
Daniel St. OL1: O'ham 1H **75**
   OL2: O'ham 4G **59**
   OL10: H'ood 3F **39**
   OL12: Whitw 3B **14**
   SK7: H Gro 3E **159**
Daniel St. Ind. Est. OL12: Whitw 3B **14**
   (off Daniel St.)
Danisher La. OL8: O'ham 3F **91**
Dannywood Cl. SK14: Hyde 1A **136**
Danson St. M40: Man 2A **102**
Dantall Av. M9: Man 6C **72**
Dante Cl. M30: Ecc 1A **98**
Danty St. SK16: Duk 4H **105**
Danube, The M15: Man 3F **9**
Danwood Cl. M34: Dent 5A **120**
Dapple Gro. M11: Man 5C **102**
Darbishire St. BL1: Bolt 1H **175** (4E **33**)
Darby Rd. M44: Irl 3E **125**
Darbyshire Cl. BL1: Bolt 5A **32**
Darbyshire Ho. WA15: Tim 4C **140**
   (off Oakleigh Ct.)
Darbyshire St. M26: Rad 4A **52**
Darbyshire Wlk. M26: Rad 4B **52**
DARCY LEVER 2H **49**
Darcy Wlk. M14: Man 3E **115**
Darden Cl. SK4: Stoc 6A **132**
Daresbury Av. M41: Urm 3H **109**
   WA15: Alt 6G **139**
Daresbury Cl. M33: Sale 6F **129**
   SK3: Stoc 6F **145**
   SK9: Wilm 1F **173**
Daresbury Rd. M21: Chor 6F **113**
Daresbury St. M8: Man 3E **87**
   (not continuous)
Darfield Wlk. M40: Man 2G **7**
Dargai St. M11: Man 4F **103**
Dargle Rd. M33: Sale 3B **128**
Darian Av. M22: Wyth 5A **154**
Dark La. M12: Man 2G **11** (5H **101**)
   OL3: Del 1A **62**
   OL3: Upp 1C **78**
   OL5: Mos 1H **93**
   (not continuous)
   SK6: Bred 6D **134**
   WA14: D Mas 6H **125**
Dark Lane Nature Reserve 1A **138**
Darlbeck Wlk. M21: Chor 4A **130**
Darley Av. BL4: Farn 6A **50**
   M20: Man 5C **130**
   M21: Chor 3H **129**
   (not continuous)
   M30: Ecc 5E **97**
   SK8: Gat 6F **143**
Darley Ct. BL1: Bolt 3A **32**
Darley Gro. BL4: Farn 6A **50**

DARLEY PARK 3A **114**
Darley Rd. M16: Old T 4A **114**
   OL11: Roch 1H **41**
   SK7: H Gro 6F **159**
Darley St. BL1: Bolt 4B **32**
   BL4: Farn 1A **66**
   M11: Man 4B **102**
   M32: Stre 3D **112**
   M33: Sale 5B **128**
   SK4: Stoc 6E **133**
Darley Ter. BL1: Bolt 4B **32**
   (off Peterhead Cl.)
Darlington Cl. BL8: Bury 6B **22**
Darlington Rd. M20: Man 3E **131**
   OL11: Roch 2H **41**
Darlington St. E. M29: Tyld 2A **80**
Darliston Av. M9: Man 4E **71**
Darlton Wlk. M9: Man 3A **88**
   (off Sequoia St.)
Darnall Av. M20: Man 1E **131**
Darnbrook Dr. M22: Wyth 4H **153**
Darncombe Cl. M16: W Ran 3D **114**
DARN HILL 4D **38**
Darnley Av. M28: Wors 2F **81**
Darnley St. M16: Old T 3B **114**
Darnton Gdns. OL6: A Lyme 2C **106**
Darnton Rd. OL6: A Lyme 1C **106**
   SK15: Stal 1C **106**
Darras Rd. M18: Man 4E **117**
Darrell Wlk. M8: Man 5F **87**
Dart Cl. OL9: Chad 1H **73**
Dartford Av. M30: Ecc 3D **96**
   SK5: Stoc 2B **134**
Dartford Cl. M12: Man 6H **11** (1H **115**)
Dartford Rd. M41: Urm 6E **111**
Dartington Cl. M23: Wyth 5D **140**
   SK7: Bram 2H **157**
Dartmouth Cl. OL8: O'ham 5F **75**
Dartmouth Cres. SK5: Stoc 4C **134**
Dartmouth Rd. M21: Chor 1A **130**
   M45: White 2G **69**
Dartnall Cl. SK12: Dis 1E **171**
Darton Av. M40: Man 2H **7** (2H **101**)
Darvel Cl. BL2: Bolt 1B **50**
Darwell Av. M30: Ecc 5E **97**
Darwen Rd. BL7: Eger 2C **18**
Darwen St. M16: Old T 6A **8** (2A **114**)
Darwin Gro. SK7: Bram 1G **167**
Darwin St. BL1: Bolt 3B **32**
   OL4: O'ham 4A **76**
   OL7: A Lyme 3G **105**
   SK14: Hyde 2E **121**
Dashwood Rd. M25: Pres 4G **69**
Dashwood Wlk. M12: Man 1C **116**
   (off Radbourne Cl.)
Datchet Ter. OL11: Roch 1H **41**
DAUBHILL 4A **48**
Dauntesy Av. M27: Pen 4D **84**
Davehall Av. SK9: Wilm 2D **172**
Davenfield Gro. M20: Man 6F **131**
   (off Davenfield Rd.)
Davenfield Rd. M20: Man 6F **131**
Davenham Rd. M33: Sale 3G **127**
   SK5: Stoc 5H **117**
   SK9: Hand 3H **165**
Davenhill Rd. M19: Man 1C **132**
DAVENPORT 6H **145**
Davenport Av. M20: Man 2F **131**
   M26: Rad 1H **51**
   SK9: Wilm 5B **172**
Davenport Dr. SK6: Wood 3H **135**
Davenport Fold BL2: Bolt 2C **34**
Davenport Fold Rd. BL2: Bolt 1C **34**
Davenport Gdns. BL1: Bolt 2E **175**
DAVENPORT GREEN
   SK9 . . . . .5B **172**
   WA15 .3E **153**
Davenport La. WA14: B'ath 4E **139**
Davenport Lodge SK3: Stoc 6H **145**
DAVENPORT PARK 1A **158**
Davenport Pk. Rd. SK2: Stoc 6A **146**
Davenport Rd. SK7: H Gro 2D **158**
Davenport Station (Rail) 6H **145**

Davenport St. BL1: Bolt 2E 175 (5C 32)
M34: Aud 5E 105
M43: Droy 4G 103
Davenport Ter. M9: Man 3A 88
Daventry Rd. M21: Chor 1B 130
OL11: Roch 1H 41
Daventry Way OL11: Roch 2H 41
Daveyhulme St. OL12: Roch 2B 28
Daveylands SK9: Wilm 3G 173
Davey La. SK9: A Edg 4G 173
David Brow BL3: Bolt 5G 47
David Cl. M34: Dent 6G 119
David Cuthbert Ct.
    M11: Man 6E 103
        (off Greenside St.)
David Lewis Cl. OL16: Roch 5C 28
David Lloyd Leisure
    Bolton 6B 32
    Cheadle 3G 155
    Urmston 6E 97
David M. M14: Man 2G 131
David Pegg Wlk. M40: Man 6D 88
        (off Roger Byrne Cl.)
David's Farm Cl. M24: Mid 2D 72
Davids La. OL4: Spri 2D 76
Davidson Dr. M24: Mid 3D 72
David's Rd. M43: Droy 3G 103
David St. BL8: Bury 2C 36
        (not continuous)
    M34: Dent 5G 119
    OL1: O'ham 4F 177 (3E 75)
    OL12: Roch 2H 27
    SK5: Stoc 1G 133
David St. Nth. OL12: Roch 2H 27
Davies Av. SK8: H Grn 1F 165
Davies Cl. M32: Stre 6D 112
        (off Cyprus St.)
    SK6: Rom 1H 147
        (off Metcalfe Dr.)
Davies Rd. M31: Part 6E 125
    SK6: Bred 6D 134
Davies Sq. M14: Man 3E 115
Davis St. BL4: Kea 2C 66
    OL1: O'ham 1D 74
    OL7: A Lyme 4F 105
Davis Hall M14: Man 3H 115
        (off Daisy Bank Hall)
Davis St. M30: Ecc 4G 97
Davy Av. M27: Clif 1D 84
DAVYHULME 4E 111
Davyhulme Circ. M41: Urm 3E 111
Davyhulme Millennium Pk. 2A 110
Davyhulme Rd. M32: Stre 4C 112
    M41: Urm 3A 110
Davyhulme Rd. E. M32: Stre 4D 112
Davylands M41: Urm 2B 110
Davy St. M40: Man 1D 6 (1F 101)
Daw Bank SK3: Stoc 3E 179 (2G 145)
Dawes St. BL3: Bolt 5F 175 (1D 48)
Dawley Cl. BL3: Bolt 1A 48
        (off Blackshaw La.)
Dawley Flats OL10: H'ood 3G 39
        (off St James St.)
Dawlish Av. M43: Droy 3G 103
    OL9: Chad 6H 57
    SK5: Stoc 4C 134
    SK8: Chea H 5B 156
Dawlish Cl. SK7: Bram 6G 157
    SK14: Hat 4A 122
    WA3: Rix 6A 124
Dawlish Rd. M21: Chor 1A 130
    M33: Sale 4G 127
Dawnay St. M11: Man 6D 102
Dawn St. OL2: Shaw 1H 59
Dawson La. BL1: Bolt 6C 32
Dawson Rd. SK8: H Grn 5H 155
    WA14: B'ath 4F 139
Dawson St. BL9: Bury 1G 37
    M3: Man 2C 8 (5B 100)
    M3: Sal 3G 5 (3D 100)
    M27: Pen 3A 84
    OL4: Lees 4C 76
    OL4: O'ham 3B 76

Dawson St. OL10: H'ood 3G 39
    OL12: Roch 1B 178 (3H 27)
    SK1: Stoc 6B 134
    SK14: Hyde 6C 120
Day Dr. M35: Fail 5H 89
Day Gro. SK14: Mot 4C 122
Daylesford Cl. SK8: Chea 1H 155
Daylesford Cres. SK8: Chea 1H 155
Daylesford Rd. SK8: Chea 1H 155
Daytona Karting 1E 113
Deacon Av. M27: Swin 2G 83
Deacon Cl. WA14: Bow 4D 150
Deacons Cl. SK1: Stoc 2H 179 (2A 146)
Deacons Cres. BL8: Tot 6A 22
Deacon's Dr. M6: Sal 5D 84
Deacon St. OL16: Roch 2B 28
Deakins Bus. Pk. BL7: Eger 2B 18
Deakins Mill Way BL7: Eger 1B 18
Deal Av. SK5: Stoc 4B 134
Deal Cl. M40: Man 6F 89
Dealey Rd. BL3: Bolt 3G 47
Deal Sq. SK14: Hyde 5C 120
Deal St. BL3: Bolt 4D 48
    BL9: Bury 3H 37
        (not continuous)
    SK14: Hyde 5C 120
Deal Wlk. OL9: Chad 3A 74
Dean Av. M16: Old T 4H 113
    M40: Man 5D 88
Dean Bank Av. M19: Man 1B 132
Dean Bank Dr. OL16: Roch 4B 42
Dean Brook Cl. M40: Man 4D 88
Dean Cl. BL0: Eden 2G 13
    BL4: Farn 1D 64
    M15: Man 6C 8 (1B 114)
    M31: Part 5D 124
    SK9: Wilm 6G 165
Dean Ct. BL1: Bolt 1G 175 (5D 32)
    M15: Man 6C 8
    OL11: Roch 1H 41
    SK16: Duk 4H 105
        (off Hill St.)
Dean Dr. SK9: Wilm 6G 165
    WA14: Bow 4D 150
DEANE .2F 47
Deane Av. BL3: Bolt 2H 47
    SK8: Chea 6B 144
    WA15: Tim 6A 140
Deane Chu. Clough
    BL3: Bolt 2G 47
Deane Chu. La. BL3: Bolt 3H 47
Deane Cl. M45: White 2D 68
Deane Rd. BL3: Bolt 5E 175 (2A 48)
Deanery Ct. M8: Man 4E 87
Deanery Gdns. M7: Sal 3B 86
Deanery Way SK1: Stoc 1F 179 (1H 145)
Deane Wlk. BL3: Bolt 1C 48
Dean Hall M14: Man 3H 115
        (off Daisy Bank Hall)
Dean La. M40: Man 5D 88
    SK7: H Gro 5D 158
Dean Lane Station (Rail) 5D 88
Dean Moor Rd. SK7: H Gro 3A 158
Dean Rd. M3: Sal 2F 5 (2C 100)
    M18: Man 3G 117
    M44: Cad 3C 124
    SK9: Hand 4A 166
DEAN ROW 6B 166
Dean Row Rd. SK9: Wilm 6G 165
DEANS .4G 83
Deanscourt Av. M27: Swin 4G 83
Deansgate BL1: Bolt 4E 175 (6C 32)
    M3: Man 3F 9 (6C 100)
        (not continuous)
    M26: Rad 4B 52
Deansgate, The M14: Man 1H 131
Deansgate La. WA14: Tim 4G 139
    WA15: Tim 4G 139
Deansgate M. M3: Man 2F 9
Deansgate Quay M3: Man 2F 9
Deansgate Station (Rail) 2F 9 (5C 100)
Deanshut Rd. OL8: O'ham 1G 91
Deans Rd. M27: Swin 4G 83

Deans Rd. Ind. Est. M27: Swin 4G 83
Dean St. M1: Man 5C 6 (4F 101)
    M26: Rad 4H 51
    M35: Fail 4F 89
    OL5: Mos 2F 93
    OL6: A Lyme 5A 174 (2G 105)
    OL16: Roch 2B 28
    SK15: Stal 4E 107
Deansway M27: Swin 3G 83
Deanswood Dr. M9: Man 4E 71
Dean Ter. OL6: A Lyme 1A 92
Dean Wlk. M24: Mid 5H 55
Deanwater Cl. M13: Man 4D 10 (6F 101)
Deanwater Ct. M32: Stre 1C 128
    SK8: H Grn 6H 155
Deanway M40: Man 3C 88
    M41: Urm 5H 109
    SK9: Wilm 6G 165
Deanway Technology Cen.
    SK9: Hand 4H 165
Deanway Trad. Est. SK9: Hand 4H 165
Dearden Av. M38: Lit H 4E 65
Dearden Clough BL0: Eden 3H 13
Dearden Fold BL0: Eden 3H 13
    BL8: Bury 4C 36
Deardens St. BL8: Bury 4C 36
Dearden St. BL3: Lit L 3C 50
    M15: Man 5F 9 (1C 114)
    OL15: L'ough 3H 17
    SK15: Stal 3E 107
Dearman's Pl. M3: Sal 4F 5 (3C 100)
Dearnalay Way OL9: Chad 5B 74
Dearncamme Cl. BL2: Bolt 6F 19
Dearne Dr. M32: Stre 5E 113
DEARNLEY 5E 17
Dearnley Cl. OL15: L'ough 5E 17
Dearnley Pas. OL15: L'ough 5E 17
DEBDALE 3H 117
Debdale Av. M18: Man 3H 117
Debdale La. M18: Man 3H 117
Debdale Outdoor Cen. 3G 117
Debdale Pk. 3H 117
Debenham Av. M40: Man 1E 103
Debenham Ct. BL4: Farn 2H 65
Debenham Rd. M32: Stre 6A 112
De Brook Cl. M41: Urm 6A 110
Dee Av. WA15: Tim 6D 140
Dee Dr. BL4: Kea 4C 66
Deepcar St. M19: Man 5C 116
Deepdale OL4: O'ham 3B 76
Deepdale Av. M20: Man 1E 131
    OL2: O'ham 5C 42
    OL16: Roch 5C 28
Deepdale Cl. SK5: Stoc 6H 117
Deepdale Ct. M9: Man 6D 72
Deepdale Dr. M27: Pen 4D 84
Deepdale Rd. BL2: Bolt 4B 34
Deepdene St. M12: Man 1B 116
Deeping Av. M16: W Ran 5B 114
Deep La. OL15: L'ough 2H 29
    OL16: Miln 4H 29
Deeplish Cott. OL11: Roch 6H 27
        (off Clifford St.)
Deeplish Rd. OL11: Roch 6H 27
Deeplish St. OL11: Roch 6H 27
Deeply Va. La. BL9: Bury 1A 24
Deeracre Av. SK2: Stoc 5C 146
Deerfold Cl. M18: Man 2F 117
Deerhurst Dr. M8: Man 5D 86
Dee Rd. M29: Ast 4A 80
Deeroak Cl. M18: Man 1D 116
Deerpark Rd. M16: W Ran 4C 114
Deerwood Va. SK14: Hat 6A 122
Defence St. BL3: Bolt 1B 48
Deganwy Gro. SK5: Stoc 4H 133
Degas Cl. M7: Sal 3H 85
Deighton Av. M20: Man 1E 131
Delacourt Rd. M14: Man 1E 131
Delafield Av. M12: Man 5C 116
Delahays Av. M28: Wors 4A 82
Delaford Cl. SK3: Stoc 1G 157
Delaford Wlk. M40: Man 1F 103
        (off Eastmoor Dr.)

Delahays Dr. WA15: Hale 3B **152**
Delahays Range M18: Man 3H **117**
Delahays Rd. WA15: Hale 3A **152**
Delaheyes Lodge WA15: Tim 6B **140**
Delaine Rd. M20: Man 3G **131**
Delamere Av. M6: Sal 5C **84**
   M27: Clif 1B **84**
   M32: Stre 5D **112**
              (not continuous)
   M33: Sale 6E **129**
   M45: White 1D **68**
   OL2: Shaw 5B **44**
Delamere Cl. SK6: Wood 4A **136**
   SK7: H Gro 2G **159**
   SK15: C'ook 5A **94**
Delamere Ct. M9: Man 4E **71**
Delamere Gdns. BL1: Bolt 2B **32**
              (off Harvey St.)
Delamere Lodge SK7: H Gro 3D **158**
             (off Chester Rd.)
Delamere Rd. M19: Man 1D **132**
   M34: Dent 5B **118**
   M41: Urm 5B **110**
   OL16: Roch 1C **42**
   SK2: Stoc 1B **158**
   SK7: H Gro 2G **159**
   SK8: Gat 6F **143**
   SK9: Hand 3H **165**
Delamere St. BL9: Bury 6G **23**
   M11: Man 6H **103**
   OL6: A Lyme 5C **174** (3H **105**)
   OL8: O'ham 4H **75**
Delamer Rd. WA14: Bow 2E **151**
Delaunays Rd. M8: Man 2E **87**
   M9: Man 2E **87**
   M33: Sale 5H **127**
Delaware Wlk. M9: Man 4H **87**
Delbooth Av. M41: Urm 3A **110**
Delft Wlk. M6: Sal 6G **85**
Delfur Rd. SK7: Bram 6H **157**
Delhi Rd. M44: Irl 1D **124**
Dell, The BL2: Bolt 6G **19**
   WA14: Hale 5G **151**
Dellar St. OL12: Roch 2E **27**
Dell Av. M27: Pen 4D **84**
Dell Cl. OL4: Spri 4D **76**
Dellcot Cl. M6: Sal 6B **84**
   M25: Pres 1B **86**
Dellcot La. M28: Wors 6B **82**
Dell Gdns. OL12: Roch 1D **26**
Dellhide Cl. OL4: Spri 3E **77**
Dell Rd. OL12: Whitw 4E **15**
Dell Rd. OL12: Roch 5D **14**
Dell Side SK6: Bred 6E **135**
Dellside Gro. M28: Walk 6A **66**
Dell Side Way OL12: Roch 1E **27**
Dell St. BL2: Bolt 6G **19**
DELPH 3B **62**
Delph Av. BL7: Eger 1B **18**
Delph Brook Way BL7: Eger 1B **18**
DELPH HILL 3E **31**
Delph Hill BL1: Bolt 3E **31**
Delph Hill Cl. BL1: Bolt 3E **31**
Delphi Av. M28: Walk 1H **81**
Delph La. BL2: Bolt 4E **35**
   OL3: Del 2B **62**
Delph New Rd. OL3: Del, Dob 5A **62**
Delph Rd. OL3: Dens 6G **45**
Delph St. BL3: Bolt 2B **48**
   OL16: Miln 5F **29**
Delside Av. M40: Man 3C **88**
Delta Cl. OL2: O'ham 5C **58**
Delta Point M34: Aud 6E **105**
Delta Rd. M34: Aud 6E **105**
Delta Wlk. M40: Man 4C **88**
Delves Av. WA14: W Tim 2F **139**
Delvino Wlk. M14: Man 3E **115**
Delwood Gdns. M22: Wyth 1B **154**
De Massey Cl. SK6: Wood 3H **135**
Demesne Cl. SK15: Stal 4G **107**
Demesne Cres. SK15: Stal 4G **107**
Demesne Dr. SK15: Stal 3G **107**
Demesne Rd. M16: W Ran 5C **114**

Demmings, The SK8: Chea 6B **144**
Demmings Ind. Est. SK8: Chea 6B **144**
Demmings Rd. SK8: Chea 6B **144**
Dempsey Dr. BL9: Bury 5H **53**
Denbigh Cl. SK7: H Gro 5C **158**
Denbigh Dr. OL2: Shaw 1F **59**
Denbigh Pl. M5: Sal 3G **99**
Denbigh Rd. BL2: Bolt 2F **49**
   M27: Clif 1A **84**
   M34: Dent 6F **119**
Denbigh St. OL5: Mos 3H **93**
   OL8: O'ham 6F **75**
   SK4: Stoc 6F **133**
Denbigh Wlk. M15: Man 6F **9**
Denbury Dr. WA14: Alt 6D **138**
Denbury Grn. SK7: H Gro 4A **158**
Denbury Wlk. M9: Man 5G **87**
           (off Mannington Dr.)
Denbydale Way OL2: O'ham 3C **58**
             (not continuous)
Denby La. SK4: Stoc 5F **133**
Denby Rd. SK16: Duk 6A **106**
Dencombe Rd. M13: Man 3B **116**
Dene Bank BL2: Bolt 6G **19**
Dene Brow M34: Dent 1H **135**
Dene Ct. SK4: Stoc 1E **145**
Dene Dr. M24: Mid 2B **72**
Denefield Cl. SK6: Mar B 2F **149**
Denefield Pl. M30: Ecc 2H **97**
Deneford Rd. M20: Man 1E **143**
Dene Hollow SK5: Stoc 6A **118**
Dene Ho. SK4: Stoc 2A **144**
Denehurst Rd. OL11: Roch 3D **26**
Dene Pk. M20: Man 1E **143**
Dene Rd. M20: Man 6E **131**
Dene Rd. W. M20: Man 6D **130**
Denes, The SK5: Stoc 6H **117**
Deneside M40: Man 5H **87**
Deneside Cres. SK7: H Gro 2F **159**
Deneside Wlk. M9: Man 2A **88**
             (off Dalbeattie St.)
Dene St. BL2: Bolt 6G **19**
Denesway M33: Sale 6G **127**
             (not continuous)
Deneway SK4: Stoc 1E **145**
   SK6: H Lan 5D **160**
   SK7: Bram 6E **157**
Deneway Cl. SK4: Stoc 1E **145**
Deneway M. SK4: Stoc 1E **145**
Denewell Av. M13: Man 6G **11** (1H **115**)
Denewood Ct. SK9: Wilm 3D **172**
Denham Cl. BL1: Bolt 6E **19**
Denham Dr. M44: Irl 6E **109**
   SK7: Bram 6F **157**
Denham St. M13: Man 3H **115**
   M26: Rad 2H **51**
Den Hill Dr. OL4: Spri 3D **76**
Denhill Rd. M15: Man 3D **114**
Denholme Rd. OL11: Roch 1H **41**
Denholm Rd. M20: Man 3G **143**
Denhurst Rd. OL15: L'ough 3H **17**
Denis Av. M16: W Ran 5C **114**
Denison Rd. M14: Man 4G **115**
   SK7: H Gro 5E **159**
Denison St. M14: Man 4G **115**
Deniston Rd. SK4: Stoc 4D **132**
Den La. OL3: Upp 6D **62**
   OL4: Spri 2D **76**
Denman Wlk. M8: Man 5D **86**
            (off Ermington Dr.)
Denmark Rd. M15: Man 2E **115**
   M33: Sale 3B **128**
Denmark St. OL4: O'ham 2H **75**
   OL9: Chad 1C **74**
   OL16: Roch 3A **28**
   WA14: Alt 3B **174** (1F **151**)
Denmark Way OL9: Chad 1C **74**
Denmore Rd. M40: Man 6E **73**
Denning Pl. M27: Clif 1H **83**
Dennington Dr. M41: Urm 3E **111**
Dennis Ho. SK4: Stoc 5D **132**
Dennison Av. M20: Man 2F **131**
Dennison Rd. SK8: Chea H 5D **156**

DENSHAW 4H **45**
Denshaw Av. M34: Dent 2D **118**
Denshaw Cl. M19: Man 6A **132**
Denshaw Fold OL3: Dens 4H **45**
Denshaw Rd. OL3: Del 6G **45**
Densmore St. M35: Fail 4H **89**
Denson Rd. WA15: Tim 3B **140**
Denstone Av. M30: Ecc 2G **97**
   M33: Sale 6G **127**
   M41: Urm 4E **111**
Denstone Cres. BL2: Bolt 3H **33**
Denstone Rd. M6: Sal 6D **84**
   M41: Urm 4E **111**
   SK5: Stoc 6H **117**
Denstone Wlk. M9: Man 4A **72**
            (off Woodmere Dr.)
Dent Cl. SK5: Stoc 3C **134**
Dentdale Cl. BL1: Bolt 1D **46**
Dentdale Wlk. M22: Wyth 5A **154**
DENTON 4F **119**
Denton Bus. Pk. M34: Dent 4D **118**
Denton Ct. M34: Dent 2E **119**
Denton Ent. Cen. M34: Dent 4F **119**
             (off Pitt St.)
Denton Hall Farm Rd. M34: Dent 5C **118**
Denton La. OL9: Chad 4A **74**
Denton Rd. BL2: Bolt 1D **50**
   M34: Aud 2E **119**
Denton St Lawrence's Church 4F **119**
             (off Town La.)
Denton Station (Rail) 3C **118**
Denton St. BL9: Bury 1F **37**
   OL10: H'ood 4G **39**
   OL12: Roch 2H **27**
Denton Swimming Pool 4E **119**
Denton Ter. M34: Aud 1E **119**
Denver Av. M40: Man 1H **7** (2H **101**)
Denver Dr. WA15: Tim 3A **140**
Denver Rd. OL11: Roch 1H **41**
Denville Cres. M22: Wyth 2C **154**
Denyer Ter. SK16: Duk 4H **105**
             (off Hill St.)
Denzell Gdns. WA14: Bow 2C **150**
Depleach Rd. SK8: Chea 6H **143**
             (not continuous)
Deptford Av. M23: Wyth 2G **153**
De Quincey Cl. WA14: W Tim 2F **139**
De Quincey Rd. WA14: W Tim 2F **139**
Deramore Cl. OL6: A Lyme 2C **106**
Deramore St. M14: Man 4F **115**
Derby Av. M6: Sal 3E **99**
Derby Cl. M44: Cad 4A **124**
Derby Ct. BL9: Bury 6F **23**
   M33: Sale 6C **128**
   OL9: O'ham 4C **74**
Derby Gro. M19: Man 6D **116**
Derby Ho. M15: Man 2F **115**
            (off Dilworth St.)
Derby Range SK4: Stoc 5D **132**
Derby Rd. M5: Sal 4E **99**
   M6: Sal 4E **99**
   M14: Man 2G **131**
   M26: Rad 1C **66**
   M33: Sale 3G **127**
   M41: Urm 4F **111**
   M45: White 3G **69**
   OL6: A Lyme 2B **106**
   SK4: Stoc 5E **133**
   SK14: Hyde 3C **120**
Derbyshire Av. M32: Stre 4A **112**
Derbyshire Cres. M32: Stre 4B **112**
Derbyshire Grn. M32: Stre 5D **112**
Derbyshire Gro. M32: Stre 4B **112**
Derbyshire La. M32: Stre 5C **112**
Derbyshire La. W.
   M32: Stre 4A **112**
Derbyshire Rd. M33: Sale 5C **128**
   M40: Man 1F **103**
   SK12: Poy 2A **170**
Derbyshire Rd. Sth.
   M33: Sale 6C **128**
Derbyshire Row BL1: Bolt 2C **32**
Derbyshire St. M11: Man 5E **103**

Derby St. BL0: Ram 3D 12
  BL3: Bolt 6E 175 (3B 48)
  BL5: W'ton 6A 46
  M8: Man 6C 86
  M25: Pres 5G 69
  M34: Dent 4D 118
    (not continuous)
  M35: Fail 2H 89
  OL5: Mos 3H 93
  OL7: A Lyme 6G 91
  OL9: Chad 6B 74
  OL9: O'ham 4C 74
  OL10: H'ood 3F 39
  OL11: Roch 6A 28
  SK3: Stoc 3F 145
  SK6: Mar 5D 148
  WA14: Alt 6G 139
Derby Ter. M34: Aud 5D 104
Derby Way SK6: Mar 5D 148
Dereham Cl. BL8: Bury 6D 22
Derg St. M6: Sal 3F 99
Derker Station (Rail) 1G 75
Derker St. OL1: O'ham 1G 75
Dermot Murphy Cl. M20: Man 3D 130
Dernford Av. M19: Man 4B 132
Derrick Walker Ct.
  OL11: Roch 6F 27
Derry Av. M22: Wyth 1C 154
Derry St. OL1: O'ham 4G 177 (3F 75)
Derville Wlk. M9: Man 3H 87
    (off Alderside Rd.)
Derwen Rd. SK3: Stoc 4G 145
Derwent Av. M21: Chor 4B 130
  M43: Droy 4G 103
  M45: White 1H 69
  OL7: A Lyme 1G 105
  OL10: H'ood 4H 39
  OL16: Miln 5H 29
  WA15: Tim 6D 140
Derwent Cl. BL3: Lit L 4B 50
  M21: Chor 4B 130
  M28: Walk 1F 81
  M31: Part 5D 124
  M34: Dent 5B 118
  M45: White 1H 69
Derwent Dr. BL4: Kea 4D 66
  BL9: Bury 6D 36
  M33: Sale 1A 140
  OL2: Shaw 5G 43
  OL9: Chad 2A 74
  OL15: L'ough 1F 29
  SK7: Bram 2E 167
  SK9: Hand 2G 165
Derwent Rd. BL4: Farn 1D 64
  M24: Mid 4A 56
  M32: Stre 4D 112
  M41: Urm 5A 110
  SK6: H Lan 5C 160
Derwent St. M5: Sal 2B 8 (5A 100)
  M8: Man 5G 87
  M43: Droy 4F 103
  OL12: Roch 2H 27
Derwent St. Ind. Est.
  M5: Sal 2B 8 (6A 100)
Derwent Ter. SK15: Stal 1E 107
Derwent Wlk. M45: White 1H 69
  OL4: O'ham 2B 76
Desford Av. M21: Chor 6A 114
Design St. BL3: Bolt 3H 47
Desmond Rd. M22: Wyth 1C 154
Destructor St. M27: Swin 2G 83
De Trafford Ho. M30: Ecc 4F 97
    (off Fintry Gro.)
De Trafford M. SK9: Wilm 5H 165
    (off Colshaw Dr.)
De Traffords, The M44: Irl 4F 109
Dettingen St. M6: Sal 5D 84
Deva Cen. M3: Sal 4E 5 (3C 100)
Deva Cl. SK7: H Gro 4D 158
  SK12: Poy 3B 168
Deva Ct. M16: Old T 6B 8 (2A 114)
Devaney Wlk. M34: Dent 6E 119
Deva Sq. OL9: O'ham 4C 74

Devas St. M15: Man 2F 115
    (not continuous)
Deverill Av. M18: Man 3H 117
Devine Cl. M3: Sal 3C 4 (3B 100)
  OL2: O'ham 1D 58
Devisdale Ct. WA14: Alt 2D 150
Devisdale Grange WA14: Bow 2D 150
Devisdale Rd. WA14: Alt 1D 150
Devoke Av. M28: Walk 1A 82
Devoke Gro. BL4: Farn 1C 64
Devoke Rd. M22: Wyth 3H 153
Devon Av. M19: Man 1B 132
  M45: White 6E 53
Devon Cl. BL3: Lit L 3D 50
  M6: Sal 2A 98
  OL2: Shaw 6F 43
  SK5: Stoc 5C 134
Devon Dr. BL2: Ain 4E 35
  OL3: Dig 3D 62
Devonia Ho. OL16: Roch 2B 42
Devon M. M45: White 6E 53
Devonport Cres. OL2: O'ham 3F 59
Devon Rd. M31: Part 6C 124
  M35: Fail 5G 89
  M41: Urm 6A 110
  M43: Droy 2A 104
  M44: Cad 4B 124
Devonshire Cl. M41: Urm 5G 111
  OL10: H'ood 3E 39
Devonshire Ct. BL1: Bolt 5H 31
  M7: Sal 3B 86
  M33: Sale 6D 128
    (off Derbyshire Rd. Sth.)
  SK2: Stoc 6A 146
Devonshire Dr. M28: Wors 5C 80
  SK9: A Edg 4H 173
Devonshire Pk. Rd. SK2: Stoc 6A 146
Devonshire Pl. M25: Pres 4G 69
Devonshire Point M30: Ecc 3G 97
Devonshire Rd. BL1: Bolt 4G 31
  M6: Sal 2A 98
  M21: Chor 1A 130
  M28: Walk 3G 65
  M30: Ecc 3G 97
  OL11: Roch 3H 41
  SK4: Stoc 1D 144
  SK7: H Gro 5F 159
  WA14: Alt 5F 139
Devonshire St. M7: Sal 5B 86
  M12: Man 6G 11 (1H 115)
Devonshire St. E. M35: Fail 6F 89
Devonshire St. Nth.
  M12: Man 4H 11 (6H 101)
Devonshire St. Sth.
  M13: Man 6G 11 (2H 115)
Devon St. BL2: Bolt 6E 33
  BL4: Farn 5H 49
  BL9: Bury 5F 37
  M27: Pen 1H 83
  OL9: O'ham 5B 74
    (not continuous)
  OL11: Roch 6B 178 (5H 27)
Dewar Cl. M11: Man 4C 102
Dewberry Cl. M27: Swin 1G 83
  M29: Tyld 2C 80
Dewes Av. M27: Clif 1B 84
Dewey St. M11: Man 6F 103
Dewhirst Rd. OL12: Roch, W'le 5H 15
Dewhirst Way OL12: Roch 5H 15
Dewhurst Clough Rd.
  BL7: Eger 1B 18
Dewhurst Ct. BL7: Eger 1B 18
Dewhurst Rd. BL2: Bolt 2A 34
Dewhurst St. M8: Man 1D 100
  OL10: H'ood 3A 40
De Wint Av. SK6: Mar B 3F 149
Dew Mdw. Cl. OL12: Roch 1G 27
Dewsnap Bri. SK16: Duk 1A 120
Dewsnap Cl. SK16: Duk 1A 120
Dewsnap La. SK14: Mot 1B 122
  SK16: Duk 1A 120
Dewsnap Way SK14: Hat 5A 122
    (off Stockport Rd.)

Dew Way OL9: O'ham 2D 74
Dexter Rd. M9: Man 4E 71
Deyne Av. M14: Man 3G 115
  M25: Pres 5H 69
Deyne St. M6: Sal 3E 99
Dial Ct. BL4: Farn 1H 65
Dial Pk. Rd. SK2: Stoc 1D 158
Dial Rd. SK2: Stoc 6C 146
  WA15: Haleb 5C 152
Dialstone La. SK2: Stoc 4C 146
Dialstone Recreation Cen. 5D 146
Diamond Cl. OL6: A Lyme 1B 106
Diamond St. OL6: A Lyme 1B 106
  SK2: Stoc 5A 146
Diamond Ter. SK6: Mar 1D 160
Dibden Wlk. M23: Wyth 6G 141
Dicken Grn. OL11: Roch 1H 41
Dicken Grn. La. OL11: Roch 1H 41
Dickens Cl. SK8: Chea H 2D 166
Dickens La. SK12: Poy 4D 168
Dickenson Rd. M14: Man 4G 115
Dickens Rd. M30: Ecc 4F 97
Dickens St. OL1: O'ham 3C 60
Dickinson Cl. BL1: Bolt 4C 32
    (off Dickinson St.)
Dickinson St. BL1: Bolt 4C 32
  M1: Man 1H 9 (5E 101)
  M3: Sal 1F 5 (1C 100)
  OL4: O'ham 2H 75
Dickinson Ter. BL1: Bolt 4C 32
    (off Dickinson St.)
Dickins St. OL10: H'ood 3F 39
Didcot Rd. M22: Wyth 4A 154
Didley Sq. M12: Man 6C 102
DIDSBURY 6F 131
Didsbury Ct. M20: Man 5F 131
Didsbury Pk. M20: Man 1F 143
Didsbury Rd. SK4: Stoc 1H 143
Didsbury Sports Cen. & Swimming Pool
  . . . . .1F 143
Digby Rd. OL11: Roch 1H 41
Digby Wlk. M11: Man 4B 102
    (off Albert St.)
Dig Gate La. OL16: Miln 2E 43
DIGGLE 3E 63
DIGGLE EDGE 1G 63
Diggle Mill Cotts.
  OL3: Dig 3H 63
Diggles La. OL11: Roch 5A 26
    (Hawthorn Rd.)
  OL11: Roch 4B 26
    (Swift Rd.)
Diggle St. OL2: Shaw 1H 59
Diggle Wlk. SK15: C'ook 5A 94
    (off Friezland Cl.)
Diglea OL3: Dig 2F 63
Digsby Ct. M20: Man 5F 131
Dijon St. BL3: Bolt 3A 48
Dilham Ct. BL1: Bolt 5A 32
Dillicar Wlk. M9: Man 4H 87
    (off Ravelston Dr.)
Dillmoss Wlk. M15: Man 6D 8
Dillon Dr. M12: Man 2A 116
Dilworth Cl. OL10: H'ood 3D 38
Dilworth Ct. SK2: Stoc 6E 147
Dilworth Ho. M15: Man 2F 115
    (off Dilworth St.)
Dilworth St. M15: Man 2F 115
Dimora Dr. M27: Pen 5D 84
Dingle, The SK7: Bram 4E 157
  SK14: Hyde 3C 136
Dingle Av. M34: Dent 5H 119
  OL2: Shaw 4A 44
  SK9: A Edg 6A 172
Dingle Bank Rd. SK7: Bram 3F 157
Dinglebrook Gro. SK9: Wilm 6A 166
    (off Malpas Cl.)
Dingle Cl. M26: Rad 6B 52
  SK6: Rom 1B 148
Dingle Dr. M43: Droy 2B 104
Dingle Gro. SK8: Gat 5D 142
Dingle Hollow SK6: Rom 1C 148
Dingle Rd. M24: Mid 3A 72

Dingle Ter.—Dove Bank Rd.

Dingle Ter. OL6: A Lyme 1H **91**
Dingle Wlk. BL1: Bolt 1F **175**
Dinglewood SK7: Bram 4E **157**
Dinmore Ct. *SK2: Stoc 6D 146*
(off Lisburne La.)
Dinmor Rd. M22: Wyth 4A **154**
Dinnington Dr. M8: Man 5D **86**
Dinorwic Cl. M8: Man 1E **87**
Dinsdale Cl. M40: Man 3H **7**
Dinsdale Dr. BL3: Bolt 2B **48**
Dinslow Wlk. *M8: Man 4D 86*
(off Winterford Rd.)
Dinting Av. M20: Man 2E **131**
Dinting La. SK13: Glos 6H **123**
Dinting La. Ind. Est. SK13: Glos 5H **123**
Dinting Lodge Ind. Est.
SK13: Had 5H **123**
Dinting Rd. SK13: Glos, Had 5H **123**
Dinting Station (Rail) 5H **123**
DINTING VALE 6H **123**
Dinting Va.
SK13: Gam, Glos, Had 5G **123**
Dinting Va. Bus. Pk. SK13: Gam 5G **123**
Dinton Ho. *M5: Sal 4F 99*
(off Buckingham St.)
Dinton St. M15: Man 4B **8** (6A **100**)
Dipper Dr. WA14: W Tim 2E **139**
Dipton Wlk. *M8: Man 5G 87*
(off Lanhill Dr.)
Dirty La. OL4: Scout 6F **61**
Dirty Leech OL12: W'le 3H **15**
Discovery Pk. SK4: Stoc 3D **132**
DISLEY 1H **171**
Disley Av. M20: Man 3D **130**
Disley Ho. SK3: Stoc 6E **179**
Disley Station (Rail) 1G **171**
Disley St. OL11: Roch 1E **41**
Disley Wlk. M34: Dent 6G **119**
Distaff Rd. SK12: Poy 3B **168**
Ditton Brook BL5: W'ton 6A **46**
Ditton Mead Cl. OL12: Roch 1B **28**
Ditton Wlk. M23: Wyth 5F **141**
Division St. BL3: Bolt 3D **48**
OL12: Roch 1B **28**
Dixon Av. M7: Sal 5C **86**
Dixon Cl. M33: Sale 1D **140**
Dixon Closes OL11: Roch 4A **26**
Dixon Ct. SK8: Chea 6H **143**
Dixon Dr. M27: Clif 5G **67**
Dixon Fold M45: White 6E **53**
OL11: Roch 5A **26**
Dixon Grn. Dr. BL4: Farn 6F **49**
Dixon Rd. M34: Dent 6H **119**
Dixon St. M6: Sal 5F **85**
M24: Mid 5C **56**
M40: Man 5D **88**
(not continuous)
M44: Irl 1D **124**
OL1: O'ham 1F **177** (1E **75**)
OL4: Lees 1C **76**
OL6: A Lyme 1B **106**
OL11: Roch 1F **41**
Dobb Hedge Cl. WA15: Haleb 1C **162**
Dobbin Dr. OL11: Roch 2H **41**
Dobbinetts La. M23: Wyth 1D **152**
WA15: Hale 1D **152**
Dob Brook Cl. M40: Man 5E **89**
DOBCROSS 5C **62**
Dobcross Cl. M13: Man 5C **116**
Dobcross New Rd. OL3: Dob 6C **62**
Dobfield Rd. OL16: Roch 3D **28**
Dobhill St. BL4: Farn 1H **65**
Dobroyd Ho. *OL4: O'ham 1C 76*
(off Huddersfield Rd.)
Dobroyd St. M8: Man 3E **87**
Dobson Ct. M40: Man 1D **102**
Dobson Rd. BL1: Bolt 6A **32**
Dobson St. BL1: Bolt 3B **32**
Dock Office M50: Sal 6G **99**
Doctor Dam Cotts. OL12: Roch 1G **25**
Doctor Fold La. OL10: H'ood 1F **55**
Doctor La. OL4: Scout 6G **61**
DOCTOR LANE HEAD 6G **61**
Doctor La. Head Cotts. OL4: Scout . . .6G **61**
Doctors La. BL9: Bury 3A **176** (3D **36**)
Dodd Cft. OL16: Roch 2B **42**
Doddington La. M5: Sal 5G **99**
Doddington Wlk. M34: Dent 6F **119**
Dodd St. M5: Sal 3D **98**
Dodge Fold SK2: Stoc 5E **147**
Dodge Hill SK4: Stoc 1F **179** (1G **145**)
Dodgson St. OL16: Roch 5A **28**
Doe Brow M27: Clif 5G **67**
Doefield Av. M28: Wors 3G **81**
Doe Hey Gro. BL4: Farn 5F **49**
Doe Hey Rd. BL3: Bolt 5F **49**
DOFFCOCKER 4G **31**
Doffcocker La. BL1: Bolt 4F **31**
Doffcocker Lodge Local Nature Reserve
. . . . .4E **31**
Dogford Rd. OL2: O'ham 2D **58**
DOG HILL .6C **44**
Dog Hill La. OL2: Shaw 6C **44**
Dolbey St. M5: Sal 4E **99**
Dolefield M3: Man 5F **5** (4C **100**)
D'Oliveira Ct. M24: Mid 5A **56**
Dollond St. M9: Man 2A **88**
Dolman Wlk. *M8: Man 5D 86*
(off Felthorpe Dr.)
Dolphin Pl. M12: Man 4F **11** (6G **101**)
Dolphin St. M12: Man 4F **11** (6G **101**)
Dolwen Wlk. *M40: Man 5D 88*
(off Harold Priestnall Cl.)
Doman St. BL3: Bolt 2D **48**
Dombey Rd. SK12: Poy 5D **168**
Dome, The *M41: Urm 1F 111*
(off The Trafford Cen.)
Domestic App. M90: Man A 6A **154**
Domett St. M9: Man 1G **87**
Dominic Cl. M23: Wyth 2E **141**
Donald Av. SK14: Hyde 6D **120**
Donald St. M1: Man 2B **10** (5E **101**)
Dona St. SK1: Stoc 3A **146**
(not continuous)
Don Av. M6: Sal 3C **98**
Doncaster Av. M20: Man 2E **131**
Doncaster Cl. BL3: Lit L 4B **50**
Doncasters Cl. OL1: O'ham 4B **60**
Doncaster Wlk. OL1: O'ham 2G **177**
Donhead Wlk. *M13: Man 6F 11*
(off Lauderdale Cres.)
Donkey La. SK9: Wilm 4D **172**
Donleigh St. M40: Man 5F **89**
Donnington OL11: Roch 6A **178** (5G **27**)
Donnington Av. SK8: Chea 5B **144**
Donnington Gdns. M28: Walk 6H **65**
Donnington Rd. M18: Man 2G **117**
M26: Rad 2E **51**
Donnison St. M12: Man 1B **116**
Donovan St. M40: Man 1G **101**
Don St. BL3: Bolt 4B **48**
M24: Mid 6E **57**
Doodson Av. M44: Irl 5E **109**
Doodson Sq. BL4: Farn 1H **65**
Dooley La. SK6: Mar 4H **147**
Dooley's La. SK9: Wilm 5A **164**
Dorac Av. SK8: H Grn 6G **155**
Dora St. BL0: Ram 5A **12**
Dorchester Av. BL2: Bolt 4A **34**
M25: Pres 1A **86**
M34: Dent 6F **119**
M41: Urm 4H **111**
Dorchester Cl. SK9: Wilm 1G **173**
WA15: Hale 2C **152**
Dorchester Ct. M33: Sale 1B **140**
SK8: Chea H 4D **156**
Dorchester Dr. M23: Wyth 2E **141**
OL2: O'ham 5D **58**
Dorchester Gro. OL10: H'ood 5G **39**
Dorchester Pde. *SK7: H Gro 4B 158*
(off Jackson's La.)
Dorchester Rd. M27: Swin 5H **83**
SK7: H Gro 4B **158**
Dorclyn Av. M41: Urm 5F **111**
Dorfield Cl. SK6: Bred 6E **135**
Doric Av. SK6: Bred 6D **134**
Doric Cl. M11: Man 4B **102**
Doris Av. BL2: Bolt 6H **33**
Doris Rd. SK3: Stoc 3E **145**
Doris St. M24: Mid 5C **56**
Dorking Av. M40: Man 1D **102**
Dorking Cl. BL1: Bolt 3D **32**
SK1: Stoc 4B **146**
Dorlan Av. M18: Man 3H **117**
Dorland Gro. SK2: Stoc 4B **146**
Dorman St. *M11: Man 6F 103*
(off Lees St.)
Dormer St. BL1: Bolt 2D **32**
Dorning Rd. M27: Swin 4A **84**
Dorning St. BL4: Kea 1B **66**
BL8: Bury 1B **36**
M30: Ecc .4F **97**
Dornton Wlk. *M8: Man 5D 86*
(off Dudley St.)
Dorothy Rd. SK7: H Gro 2F **159**
Dorothy St. BL0: Ram 4B **12**
M7: Sal 4D **86**
Dorrian M. BL1: Bolt 6F **31**
Dorrington Rd. M33: Sale 5F **127**
SK3: Stoc 4C **144**
Dorris St. BL3: Bolt 4A **48**
M19: Man 1D **132**
Dorrit Cl. SK12: Poy 5E **169**
Dorset Av. BL4: Farn 1G **65**
M14: Man 5E **115**
M34: Aud 5C **104**
OL2: Shaw 6F **43**
OL3: Dig .3E **63**
SK5: Stoc 4C **134**
SK7: Bram 3F **157**
SK8: Chea H 6E **145**
Dorset Cl. BL4: Farn 1G **65**
OL10: H'ood 4E **39**
Dorset Dr. BL9: Bury 5G **37**
Dorset Rd. M19: Man 6E **117**
M35: Fail 5H **89**
M43: Droy 2H **103**
M44: Cad 4B **124**
WA14: Alt 6D **138**
Dorset St. BL2: Bolt 4H **175** (6E **33**)
M27: Pen .1H **83**
M32: Stre 6D **112**
OL6: A Lyme 2B **106**
OL9: O'ham 4C **74**
OL11: Roch 6B **178** (5H **27**)
Dorsey St. M4: Man 4C **6** (3F **101**)
Dorstone Cl. M40: Man 1F **103**
Dorwood Av. M9: Man 4G **71**
Dougall Wlk. *M12: Man 1C 116*
(off Bridgend Cl.)
Doughty Av. M30: Ecc 2H **97**
Dougill St. BL1: Bolt 4H **31**
Douglas Av. BL8: Bury 3B **36**
M32: Stre 4D **112**
Douglas Cl. M45: White 5A **54**
Douglas Grn. M6: Sal 6G **85**
Douglas Rd. M28: Wors 4E **83**
SK3: Stoc 1G **157**
SK7: H Gro 2E **159**
Douglas Sq. *OL10: H'ood 4D 38*
(off Dundee Cl.)
Douglas St. BL0: Ram 3B **12**
BL1: Bolt 6C **18**
M7: Sal 5B **86**
M27: Swin 4A **84**
M35: Fail .4A **90**
M40: Man 4C **88**
OL1: O'ham 1G **75**
OL6: A Lyme 2B **106**
SK14: Hyde 5C **120**
Douglas Wlk. M33: Sale 4E **127**
M45: White 5A **54**
Douglas Way M45: White 6A **54**
Doulton St. M40: Man 3E **89**
Dounby Av. M30: Ecc 2D **96**
Douro St. M40: Man 6B **88**
Douthwaite Dr. SK6: Rom 2C **148**
DOVE BANK 3C **50**
Dove Bank Rd. BL3: Lit L 3C **50**

A-Z Manchester 239

Dovebrook Cl.—Duke St.

Dovebrook Cl. SK15: C'ook 4A **94**
Dovecote M43: Droy 2D **104**
Dovecote Bus. & Technology Pk.
M33: Sale 5F **129**
Dovecote Cl. BL7: Bro X 3F **19**
Dovecote La. M38: Lit H 6C **64**
OL4: Lees 2D **76**
Dovecote M. M21: Chor 1G **129**
Dovedale Av. M20: Man 2E **131**
M25: Pres 6C **70**
M30: Ecc .2G **97**
M41: Urm 5F **111**
M43: Droy 3G **103**
Dovedale Cl. SK6: H Lan 6C **160**
Dovedale Ct. *M24: Mid 5A* ***56***
(off Grisdale Dr.)
Dovedale Dr. OL12: W'le 6D **16**
Dovedale Rd. BL2: Bolt 4B **34**
SK2: Stoc 4D **146**
Dovedale St. M35: Fail 4G **89**
Dove Dr. BL9: Bury 1H **37**
M44: Irl .4E **109**
Dovehouse Cl. M45: White 1D **68**
Doveleys Rd. M6: Sal 1D **98**
Dover Cl. BL8: G'mount 2A **22**
Dovercourt Av. SK4: Stoc 6B **132**
Dover Gro. BL3: Bolt 2B **48**
Doveridge Gdns. M6: Sal 2F **99**
Dove Rd. BL3: Bolt 3H **47**
Dover Pk. M41: Urm 3F **111**
Dover Rd. M27: Clif 1A **84**
Dover St. BL4: Farn 5G **49**
M13: Man 6C **10** (1F **115**)
M30: Ecc .3D **96**
OL9: O'ham 4C **74**
OL16: Roch 1B **28**
SK5: Stoc 2G **133**
DOVE STONE 6G **79**
Dovestone Cres.
SK16: Duk 6D **106**
Dove Stone Sailing Club 6G **79**
Dovestone Wlk. M40: Man 2G **89**
Doveston Gro. M33: Sale 3B **128**
Doveston Rd. M33: Sale 3B **128**
Dove St. BL1: Bolt 1D **32**
OL4: O'ham 3A **76**
OL11: Roch 4F **27**
Dove Wlk. BL4: Farn 1D **64**
M8: Man 6F **87**
Dovey Cl. M29: Ast 4A **80**
Dow Fold BL8: Bury 2H **35**
Dowland Cl. M23: Wyth 1F **141**
Dow La. BL8: Bury 2H **35**
Dowling St. OL11: Roch 6B **178** (5H **27**)
Downcast Way *M27: Pen 3D* ***84***
(off Shearer Way)
Downes Way M22: Shar 5C **142**
Downesway SK9: A Edg 5F **173**
Downfield Cl. BL0: Ram 3A **12**
Downfields SK5: Stoc 6A **118**
Downgate Wlk. *M8: Man 5E* ***87***
(off Tamerton Dr.)
Down Grn. Rd. BL2: Bolt 2A **34**
Downhall Grn. BL1: Bolt 1F **175** (5D **32**)
Downham Av. BL2: Bolt 5G **33**
Downham Chase WA15: Tim 5B **140**
Downham Cl. OL2: O'ham 5C **58**
Downham Cres. M25: Pres 6B **70**
Downham Gdns. M25: Pres 6C **70**
Downham Gro. M25: Pres 6C **70**
Downham Rd. OL10: H'ood 3E **39**
SK4: Stoc 4F **133**
Downham Wlk. M23: Wyth 3E **141**
Downhill Cl. OL1: O'ham 6E **59**
Downing Cl. OL7: A Lyme 5F **91**
Downing St. M1: Man 3D **10** (6F **101**)
M13: Man 4E **11**
OL7: A Lyme 5F **91**
Downing St. Ind. Est.
M12: Man 3D **10** (6F **101**)
Downley Cl. OL12: Roch 1D **26**
Downley Dr. M4: Man 4F **7** (3G **101**)
Downs, The M24: Mid 3D **72**
Downs, The M25: Pres 1G **85**
SK8: Chea 2H **155**
WA14: Alt 3A **174** (2E **151**)
Downs Dr. WA14: Tim 3G **139**
Downshaw Rd. OL7: A Lyme 5G **91**
Dowry Pk. Ests. OL4: Lees 2C **76**
Dowry Rd. OL4: Lees 2C **76**
Dowry St. OL8: O'ham 6F **75**
Dowson Rd. SK14: Hyde 2B **136**
Dowson St. BL2: Bolt 4H **175** (6E **33**)
Dow St. SK14: Hyde 2B **120**
Doyle Av. SK6: Bred 6D **134**
Doyle Cl. OL1: O'ham 3C **60**
Doyle Rd. BL3: Bolt 4E **47**
Drake Av. BL4: Farn 2H **65**
M22: Wyth 3H **153**
M44: Cad 3C **124**
Drake Cl. OL1: O'ham 1F **75**
Drake Ct. SK5: Stoc 5G **133**
Drake Rd. OL15: L'ough 2A **16**
WA14: B'ath 3D **138**
Drake St. OL11: Roch 5A **178** (5G **27**)
OL16: Roch 3C **178** (4H **27**)
Draxford Ct. SK9: Wilm 3E **173**
Draycott St. BL1: Bolt 3C **32**
Draycott St. E. BL1: Bolt 3D **32**
Drayfields M43: Droy 3D **104**
Drayford Cl. M23: Wyth 1F **141**
Drayton Cl. BL1: Bolt 3B **32**
M33: Sale 1F **139**
SK9: Wilm 6H **165**
Drayton Dr. SK8: H Grn 6F **155**
Drayton Gro. WA15: Tim 1A **152**
Drayton Mnr. M20: Man 3F **143**
Drayton St. M15: Man 6E **9** (2C **114**)
Drayton Wlk. *M16: Old T 2B* ***114***
(off Fernleigh Dr.)
Drefus Av. M11: Man 3E **103**
Dresden St. M40: Man 3E **89**
Dresser Cen., The M11: Man 6D **102**
Drewett St. M40: Man 1A **102**
Driffield St. M14: Man 4E **115**
M30: Ecc .5E **97**
Drinkwater Rd. M25: Pres 2F **85**
Driscoll St. M13: Man 4B **116**
Drive, The BL0: Eden 2G **13**
BL9: Bury .6F **23**
M7: Sal 2A **86**
M20: Man 6G **131**
M25: Pres 5H **69**
M33: Sale 2G **139**
SK5: Stoc 5B **134**
SK6: Bred 6D **134**
SK6: Mar 5C **148**
SK8: Chea H 1E **157**
WA15: Haleb 5D **152**
Droitwich Rd. M40: Man 1G **7** (1H **101**)
Dronfield Rd. M6: Sal 1D **98**
M22: Nor 3B **142**
Droughts La. M25: Pres 1C **70**
DROYLSDEN 4A **104**
Droylsden FC
(Butchers Arms Ground) 4A **104**
Droylsden Little Theatre *. 3B* ***104***
(off Market St.)
Droylsden Rd. M34: Aud 4B **104**
M40: Man .5E **89**
Drummond St. BL1: Bolt 1C **32**
Drury La. OL9: Chad 6A **74**
Drury St. M19: Man 6C **116**
Dryad Cl. M27: Pen 1H **83**
Drybrook Cl. M13: Man 2A **116**
Dryburgh Av. BL1: Bolt 2B **32**
Dry Clough La. OL3: Upp 2C **78**
Dryclough Wlk. OL2: O'ham 4E **59**
Dryden Av. M27: Swin 4F **83**
SK8: Chea 5B **144**
Dryden Cl. SK6: Mar 1D **160**
SK16: Duk 6F **107**
Dryden Rd. M16: Old T 4A **114**
Dryden St. M13: Man 6E **11** (1G **115**)
Dryden Way *M34: Dent 1G* ***135***
(off Spenser Av.)
Drygate Wlk. *M9: Man 4A* ***88***
(off Craigend Dr.)
Dryhurst Dr. SK12: Dis 1H **171**
Dryhurst La. SK12: Dis 1H **171**
Dryhurst Wlk. M15: Man 6A **10** (1E **115**)
Drymoss OL8: O'ham 2G **91**
Drysdale Vw. *BL1: Bolt 1C* ***32***
(off Broad O' Th' La.)
Drywood Av. M28: Wors 6C **82**
Drywood Cotts. OL10: H'ood 3G **55**
Ducal St. M4: Man 1C **6** (2F **101**)
Duchess Pk. Cl. OL2: Shaw 5H **43**
Duchess Rd. M8: Man 3F **87**
Duchess St. OL2: Shaw 5G **43**
Duchess Wlk. BL3: Bolt 3H **47**
Duchy Av. BL5: O Hul 6G **47**
M28: Walk 3H **81**
Duchy Cvn. Pk. M6: Sal 6F **85**
Duchy Rd. M6: Sal 5E **85**
Duchy St. M6: Sal 2F **99**
SK3: Stoc 4F **145**
Ducie Av. BL1: Bolt 6A **32**
Ducie Ct. M15: Man 2F **115**
Ducie St. BL0: Ram 2B **12**
M1: Man 6C **6** (4F **101**)
M26: Rad .2H **51**
M45: White 1F **69**
OL8: O'ham 1F **91**
Duckshaw La. BL4: Farn 1H **65**
Duckworth Rd. M25: Pres 6F **69**
Duckworth St. BL3: Bolt 3A **48**
BL9: Bury .1G **37**
(not continuous)
OL2: Shaw 6A **44**
Duddon Av. BL2: Bolt 4B **34**
Duddon Cl. M45: White 1H **69**
Duddon Wlk. M24: Mid 5A **56**
Dudley Av. BL2: Bolt 4G **33**
M45: White 1F **69**
Dudley Cl. M15: Man 2C **114**
Dudley Ct. M16: W Ran 4B **114**
Dudley Rd. M16: W Ran 5B **114**
M27: Pen .2H **83**
M33: Sale 3C **128**
M44: Cad 5B **124**
WA15: Tim 4B **140**
Dudley St. M7: Sal 4C **86**
M8: Man 5D **86**
M30: Ecc .4E **97**
OL4: O'ham 3B **76**
Dudlow Wlk. M15: Man 6D **8**
Dudwell Cl. BL1: Bolt 3A **32**
Duerden St. BL3: Bolt 5G **47**
Duffield Ct. *M15: Man 2E* ***115***
(off Brennan Cl.)
M24: Mid .4B **72**
Duffield Gdns. M24: Mid 4B **72**
Duffield Rd. M6: Sal 6D **84**
M24: Mid .4B **72**
Duffins Cl. OL12: Roch 6F **15**
Dufton Wlk. M22: Wyth 4C **154**
M24: Mid .5A **56**
Dugdale Av. M9: Man 5A **72**
Duke Av. SK8: Chea H 1B **166**
Duke Ct. M16: Old T 2B **114**
Dukefield St. M22: Nor 3C **142**
Duke Pl. M3: Man 2E **9** (5C **100**)
Duke Rd. BL2: Ain 4E **35**
SK14: Hyde 2D **120**
Duke's Av. BL3: Lit L 3C **50**
Dukes Ct. *M30: Ecc 3G* ***97***
(off Wellington Rd.)
Dukes Platting OL6: A Lyme 6D **92**
Duke's Ter. SK16: Duk 4H **105**
Duke St. BL0: Ram 5A **12**
BL1: Bolt 1E **175** (5C **32**)
(not continuous)
M3: Man 2E **9** (5C **100**)
M3: Sal 3G **5** (3D **100**)
M7: Sal 6B **86**
M26: Rad .5B **52**
M28: Walk .1D **82**
M29: Ast 5A **80**

Duke St. M30: Ecc 1E 97
M34: Dent 4E 119
M35: Fail 4A 90
M38: Lit H 4E 65
OL2: Shaw 1A 60
OL5: Mos 2A 94
OL6: A Lyme 5C 174 (2H 105)
OL10: H'ood 3F 39
OL12: Roch 1C 178 (2H 27)
(not continuous)
OL15: L'ough 4G 17
SK1: Stoc 3G 179 (2H 145)
SK9: A Edg 4H 173
SK15: Stal 4D 106
Duke St. Nth. BL1: Bolt 1E 175 (5C 32)
(Prince St.)
BL1: Bolt 1E 175 (5C 32)
(School Hill)
Dukes Wlk. WA15: Hale 2H 151
Duke's Wharf M28: Wors 6B 82
DUKINFIELD 4H 105
Dukinfield Crematorium
SK16: Duk 4B 106
DUKINFIELD HALL 6G 105
Dukinfield Rd. SK14: Hyde 2A 120
Dukinfield Swimming Pool 6B 106
Dulford Wlk. M13: Man 2G 115
(off Plymouth Gro.)
Dulgar St. M11: Man 5C 102
Dulverton Gdns. BL3: Lit L 5C 50
Dulverton St. M40: Man 5D 88
Dulwich Cl. M33: Sale 6F 127
Dulwich St. M4: Man 1C 6 (2F 101)
Dumbarton Cl. SK5: Stoc 3H 133
Dumbarton Dr. OL10: H'ood 4E 39
Dumbarton Rd. SK5: Stoc 2H 133
Dumbell St. M27: Pen 1H 83
Dumber La. M33: Sale 3H 127
Dumers Cl. M26: Rad 3D 52
Dumers La. BL9: Bury 3D 52
M26: Rad 3D 52
Dumfries Av. OL3: Dens 3G 45
Dumfries Dr. OL3: Dens 3G 45
Dumfries Hollow OL10: H'ood 2B 40
Dumfries Wlk. OL10: H'ood 4E 39
DUMPLINGTON 6E 97
Dumvilles Brow SK1: Stoc 2G 179
Dunbar Av. M23: Wyth 2G 153
Dunbar Dr. BL3: Bolt 4C 48
Dunbar Gro. OL10: H'ood 5D 38
Dunbar St. OL1: O'ham 1E 177 (1E 75)
Dunblane Av. BL3: Bolt 2E 47
SK4: Stoc 1F 145
Dunblane Gro. OL10: H'ood 5E 39
Duncan Edwards Ct. M40: Man 2F 99
(off Eddie Colman Cl.)
Duncan Edwards Ho. M6: Sal 2F 99
(off Florin Gdns.)
Duncan Edwards Ter. M6: Sal 2F 99
(off Doveridge Gdns.)
Duncan Rd. M13: Man 4B 116
(not continuous)
Duncan St. M5: Sal 1A 8 (5A 100)
M7: Sal 5A 86
SK16: Duk 1A 120
Dunchurch Cl. BL6: Los 1D 46
Dunchurch Rd. M33: Sale 5G 127
Dun Cl. M3: Sal 3C 4 (3B 100)
Duncombe Cl. SK7: Bram 2A 158
Duncombe Dr. M40: Man 4D 88
Duncombe Rd. BL3: Bolt 4C 48
Duncombe St. M7: Sal 5C 86
Duncote Gro. OL2: O'ham 2F 59
Dundee M30: Ecc 3G 97
(off Monton La.)
Dundee Cl. OL10: H'ood 4D 38
Dundee La. BL0: Ram 3B 12
Dundonald Rd. M20: Man 6G 131
SK8: Chea H 6C 156
Dundonald St. SK2: Stoc 5H 145
Dundraw Cl. M24: Mid 6F 55
Dundrennan Cl. SK12: Poy 2D 168
Dunecroft M34: Dent 3G 119

Dunedin Dr. M6: Sal 6F 85
Dunedin Rd. BL8: G'mount 1H 21
Dunelm Dr. M33: Sale 2D 140
Dungeon Wlk. SK9: Wilm 2E 173
Dunham Ho. WA14: Bow 2B 150
Dunham Lawn WA14: Alt 1D 150
DUNHAM MASSEY 6A 138
Dunham M WA14: Bow 4B 150
Dunham Ri. WA14: Alt 1E 151
Dunham Rd. M31: C'ton 5H 125
SK9: Hand 2H 165
SK16: Duk 1B 120
WA14: Alt, Bow 2A 174 (4B 150)
Dunham St. M15: Man 6F 9 (1C 114)
OL4: Lees 1C 76
DUNHAM TOWN 1A 150
Dunkeld Gdns. M23: Wyth 5G 141
Dunkeld Rd. M23: Wyth 5F 141
Dunkerley Av. M35: Fail 4H 89
Dunkerleys Cl. M8: Man 3D 86
(off Grangeforth Rd.)
Dunkerley St. OL2: O'ham 3D 58
OL4: O'ham 1A 76
OL7: A Lyme 6G 91
Dunkery Rd. M22: Wyth 4B 154
Dunkirk Cl. M34: Dent 5A 118
Dunkirk La. SK14: Hyde 2H 119
Dunkirk Ri. OL12: Roch 3A 178 (3G 27)
Dunkirk Rd. M45: White 6F 53
Dunkirk St. M43: Droy 4B 104
Dunley Cl. M12: Man 2C 116
Dunlin Cl. BL2: Bolt 6H 175 (2E 49)
OL11: Roch 4B 26
SK2: Stoc 6G 147
SK12: Poy 3A 168
Dunlin Dr. M44: Irl 4E 109
Dunlin Wlk. WA14: B'ath 3D 138
(off Barlow Rd.)
Dunlop Av. OL11: Roch 2G 41
Dunlop St. M3: Man 5C 5 (4D 100)
Dunmail Cl. M29: Ast 5A 80
Dunmail Dr. M24: Mid 4A 56
Dunmaston Av. WA15: Tim 4D 140
Dunmere Wlk. M9: Man 5G 87
(off Hendham Va.)
Dunmore Rd. SK8: Gat 5F 143
Dunmow Ct. SK2: Stoc 6E 147
Dunmow Wlk. M23: Wyth 1G 141
Dunnerdale Wlk. M18: Man 2E 117
(off Beyer Cl.)
Dunnisher Rd. M23: Wyth 1H 153
Dunnock Cl. SK2: Stoc 6F 147
Dunollie Rd. M33: Sale 6E 129
Dunoon Cl. OL10: H'ood 4E 39
Dunoon Dr. BL1: Bolt 6A 18
Dunoon Rd. SK5: Stoc 2H 133
Dunoon Wlk. M9: Man 4H 87
(off Kingsbridge Rd.)
Dunrobin Cl. OL10: H'ood 5E 39
DUNSCAR 3C 18
Dunscar Bri. BL7: Eger 3C 18
Dunscar Cl. M45: White 2D 68
Dunscar Fold BL7: Eger 3C 18
Dunscar Grange BL7: Bro X 3D 18
Dunscar Ind. Est.
BL7: Eger 3C 18
Dunscar Sq. BL7: Eger 3C 18
Dunsfold Dr. M23: Wyth 3D 140
Dunsford Ct. OL4: Spri 3D 76
(off Lauren Cl.)
Dunsley Av. M40: Man 1F 89
Dunsmore Cl. M16: W Ran 3B 114
Dunsop Dr. BL1: Bolt 2F 31
Dunstable OL12: Roch 1B 178
Dunstable St. M19: Man 6D 116
Dunstall Rd. M22: Shar 6C 142
Dunstan St. M40: Man 3C 88
Dunstan St. BL2: Bolt 6G 33
Dunstar Av. M34: Aud 6E 105
Dunster Av. M9: Man 5A 72
M27: Clif 1B 84
OL11: Roch 6G 27
SK5: Stoc 4C 134

Dunster Cl. OL9: Chad 5A 74
SK7: H Gro 4C 158
Dunster Dr. M41: Urm 6G 109
Dunster Pl. M28: Wors 4D 80
Dunster Rd. M28: Wors 4D 80
Dunsters Av. BL8: Bury 6C 22
Dunsterville Ter. OL11: Roch 6G 27
(off New Barn La.)
Dunston St. M11: Man 5E 103
Dunton Grn. SK5: Stoc 3B 134
Dunton Towers SK5: Stoc 3B 134
(off Dunton Grn.)
Dunvegan Rd. SK7: H Gro 4F 159
Dunwood Av. OL2: Shaw 5A 44
Dunwood Pk. Courts OL2: Shaw 4A 44
Dunworth St. M14: Man 4F 115
Dura Bank OL12: Whitw 4B 14
Durant St. M4: Man 2C 6 (2F 101)
Durban Cl. OL2: Shaw 1G 59
Durban Rd. BL1: Bolt 6C 18
Durban St. OL7: A Lyme 4E 105
OL8: O'ham 6C 74
OL11: Roch 3E 41
Durden M. OL2: Shaw 1H 59
Durham Av. M41: Urm 4G 111
Durham Cl. BL3: Lit L 3D 50
M27: Clif 1H 83
SK6: Rom 2G 147
SK16: Duk 1B 120
Durham Cres. M35: Fail 5A 90
Durham Dr. BL0: Ram 6A 12
BL9: Bury 5G 37
OL6: A Lyme 3B 92
Durham Gro. M44: Cad 3A 124
Durham Ho. SK3: Stoc 5E 179 (3G 145)
Durham Rd. M6: Sal 1C 98
Durhams Pas. OL15: L'ough 4G 17
Durham St. BL1: Bolt 3D 32
M9: Man 4A 88
M26: Rad 2C 52
M43: Droy 5A 104
OL9: O'ham 5C 74
(not continuous)
OL11: Roch 6C 178 (5H 27)
SK5: Stoc 5G 117
Durham St. Bri. OL11: Roch 6A 28
Durham Wlk. M34: Dent 6F 119
(off Lancaster Rd.)
OL10: H'ood 3E 39
Durley Av. M8: Man 4F 87
WA15: Tim 4B 140
Durling St. M12: Man 4F 11 (6G 101)
Durnford Av. M41: Urm 5A 112
Durnford Cl. OL12: Roch 1H 25
Durnford St. M24: Mid 6B 56
Durnford Wlk. M22: Wyth 2H 153
Durrington Wlk. M40: Man 6E 73
(off Moston La.)
Dutton St. M3: Man 1H 5 (2D 100)
Duty St. BL1: Bolt 2C 32
Duxbury Av. BL2: Bolt 6A 20
BL3: Lit L 2C 50
Duxbury Dr. BL9: Bury 3A 38
Duxbury St. BL1: Bolt 2B 32
(off Winter St.)
Duxford Lodge M8: Man 1D 86
Duxford Wlk. M40: Man 6E 73
(off Moston La.)
Dyche St. M4: Man 3B 6 (2F 101)
Dyche St. Trad. Est.
M4: Man 2C 6
Dye Ho. La. OL16: Roch 6C 16
Dye La. SK6: Rom 1H 147
Dyers Ct. OL15: L'ough 3G 17
Dyer St. M5: Sal 3B 8 (6A 100)
Dymchurch Av. M26: Rad 2E 67
Dymchurch St. M40: Man 1E 103
Dysarts Cl. OL5: Mos 6A 78
Dysart St. OL6: A Lyme 3B 106
SK2: Stoc 6B 146
Dyserth Gro. SK5: Stoc 5H 133
Dyson Cl. BL4: Farn 1H 65
Dyson Gro. OL4: Lees 1D 76

Dyson Ho. BL4: Farn 1H **65**
(off Hesketh Wlk.)
Dyson St. BL4: Farn 2H **65**
OL5: Mos 2G **93**
Dystelegh Rd. SK12: Dis 1H **171**

E

Eades St. M6: Sal 2G **99**
Eadington St. M8: Man 2E **87**
Eafield Av. OL16: Miln 4F **29**
Eafield Cl. OL16: Miln 4F **29**
Eafield Rd. OL15: L'ough 6E **17**
OL16: Roch 2C **28**
Eagar St. M40: Man 5E **89**
Eagle Cl. M15: Man 2C **114**
(off Dudley Cl.)
OL3: Del 2B **62**
Eagle Dr. M6: Sal 6G **85**
Eagle Fold SK14: Hyde 1E **121**
Eagles Nest M25: Pres 6G **69**
Eagle St. BL2: Bolt 3H **175** (6E **33**)
M4: Man 3B **6** (3E **101**)
OL9: O'ham 4E **177** (3F **75**)
OL16: Roch 5D **178** (5A **28**)
Eagle Technology Pk.
OL11: Roch 1A **42**
Eagle Way OL11: Roch 1A **42**
EAGLEY 4D **18**
Eagley Bank BL1: Bolt 5D **18**
Eagley Brook Way BL1: Bolt 2D **32**
Eagley Brow BL1: Bolt 5D **18**
(not continuous)
Eagley Ct. BL7: Bro X 4E **19**
Eagley Dr. BL8: Bury 4A **36**
Eagley Vw. BL8: Bury 4A **36**
Eagley Way BL1: Bolt 4D **18**
Ealees Rd. OL15: L'ough 4H **17**
Ealing Av. M14: Man 5G **115**
Ealinger Way M27: Pen 1H **83**
Ealing Ho. BL1: Bolt 4C **32**
(off Enfield Cl.)
Ealing Pl. M19: Man 3C **132**
Ealing Rd. SK3: Stoc 3F **145**
Eames Av. M26: Rad 1C **66**
Eamont Wlk. M9: Man 4H **87**
(off Ruskington Dr.)
Earby Gro. M9: Man 6B **72**
Earle Ct. OL7: A Lyme 4F **105**
(off Graham St.)
Earle Rd. SK7: Bram 3G **157**
Earlesdon Cres. M38: Lit H 3E **65**
Earlesfield Cl. M33: Sale 1F **139**
Earle St. OL7: A Lyme 3F **105**
Earl Rd. BL0: Ram 3B **12**
SK4: Stoc 5E **133**
SK8: Chea H 3A **166**
SK9: Hand 3A **166**
Earlscliffe Ct. WA14: Alt 1D **150**
Earl's Lodge M35: Fail 5F **89**
Earlston Av. M34: Dent 4A **118**
Earl St. BL0: Ram 3D **12**
M7: Sal 1B **100**
M25: Pres 5A **70**
M34: Dent 3A **118**
OL5: Mos 2F **93**
OL10: H'ood 3G **39**
OL11: Roch 5E **41**
SK3: Stoc 3F **145**
Earls Way M35: Fail 5F **89**
Earlswood Rd. OL8: O'ham 6E **75**
Earlswood Wlk. BL3: Bolt 3D **48**
M18: Man 1E **117**
(off Briercliffe Cl.)
Earl Ter. SK16: Duk 4H **105**
Earl Wlk. M12: Man 1B **116**
Early Bank SK15: Stal 5G **107**
Early Bank Rd. SK14: Hyde 1F **121**
SK15: Hyde, Stal 5F **107**
Earnshaw Av. OL12: Roch 6G **15**
SK1: Stoc 2B **146**
Earnshaw Cl. OL7: A Lyme 6F **91**

Earnshaw Clough OL5: Mos 3A **94**
Earnshaw St. BL3: Bolt 4H **47**
SK14: Holl 3F **123**
Easby Cl. SK8: Chea H 1D **166**
SK12: Poy 2D **168**
Easby Rd. M24: Mid 4B **56**
Easedale Cl. M41: Urm 4B **110**
Easedale Rd. BL1: Bolt 5G **31**
Easington Wlk. M40: Man 5C **88**
Easingwold WA14: Alt 2A **174**
East Av. M19: Man 2B **132**
M45: White 5E **53**
SK8: H Grn 4G **155**
SK15: Stal 2E **107**
(not continuous)
Eastbank St. BL1: Bolt 3D **32**
Eastbourne Gro. BL1: Bolt 5G **31**
Eastbourne St. OL8: O'ham 5H **75**
OL11: Roch 6B **178** (6H **27**)
Eastbrook Av. M26: Rad 3C **52**
Eastburn Av. M40: Man 1F **7** (2G **101**)
E. Central St. M27: Swin 4B **84**
Eastchurch Cl. BL4: Farn 2H **65**
E. Church Way OL10: H'ood 6B **40**
Eastcombe Av. M7: Sal 4H **85**
Eastcote Av. M11: Man 5G **103**
Eastcote Rd. SK5: Stoc 4H **133**
Eastcote Wlk. BL4: Farn 6A **50**
(off Darley St.)
East Cl. Wlk. M13: Man 5E **11** (1G **115**)
East Cres. M24: Mid 2B **72**
Eastdale Pl. WA14: B'ath 4F **139**
EAST DIDSBURY 2G **143**
East Didsbury Station (Rail) 2G **143**
E. Downs Rd. SK8: Chea H 3B **156**
WA14: Bow 3E **151**
East Dr. BL9: Bury 3H **53**
M6: Sal 6E **85**
M21: Chor 6F **113**
M27: Swin 4B **84**
M34: Dent 2D **160**
Easterdale OL4: O'ham 3A **76**
Eastern Av. M27: Clif 6D **68**
(not continuous)
Eastern By-Pass
M11: Man 5F **103**
(Crabtree La.)
M11: Man 3E **103**
(Stanton St.)
Eastern Circ. M19: Man 3C **132**
Eastfield M6: Sal 1E **99**
Eastfield Av. M24: Mid 2C **72**
M40: Man 2H **7** (2A **102**)
Eastfields M26: Rad 2G **51**
Eastford Sq. M40: Man 1G **101**
(off Sand St.)
Eastgarth Wlk. M9: Man 6A **72**
(off Greendale Dr.)
Eastgate OL12: Whitw 2D **14**
Eastgate St. OL7: A Lyme 4G **105**
OL16: Roch 2C **178** (3H **27**)
E. Grange Av. M11: Man 2E **103**
East Gro. M13: Man 2G **115**
Eastgrove Av. BL1: Bolt 5C **18**
Eastham Av. BL9: Bury 5E **23**
M14: Man 6F **115**
Eastham Way M38: Lit H 4F **65**
SK9: Hand 4H **165**
(off Redesmere Rd.)
Easthaven Av. M11: Man 3E **103**
E. Hill St. OL4: O'ham 3G **75**
Eastholme Dr.
M19: Man 2D **132**
Easthope Cl. M20: Man 2F **131**
E. Lancashire Crematorium
M26: Rad 1A **52**
East Lancashire Railway
Bury Bolton Street Station
............4A **176** (3E **37**)
Heywood Station 4A **40**
Irwell Vale Station 1F **13**
Ramsbottom Station 3C **12**
Summerseat Station 1C **22**

E. Lancashire Rd.
M27: Pen, Sal, Swin 3E **83**
M28: Swin, Walk, Wors 4D **80**
M29: Ast 6A **80**
East Lea M34: Dent 4G **119**
Eastleigh Av. M7: Sal 3C **86**
Eastleigh Dr. M40: Man 1G **7** (2H **101**)
Eastleigh Gro. BL1: Bolt 5C **32**
(off Vernon St.)
Eastleigh Rd. M25: Pres 6C **70**
SK8: H Grn 4F **155**
E. Lynn Dr. M28: Walk 6C **66**
East Meade BL3: Bolt 5C **48**
M21: Chor 2H **129**
M25: Pres 1B **86**
M27: Swin 5G **83**
East Moor M28: Wors 4E **81**
Eastmoor Dr. M40: Man 1F **103**
Eastmoor Gro. BL3: Bolt 5H **47**
E. Newton St. M4: Man 2F **7**
Eastnor Cl. M15: Man 6C **8** (1B **114**)
Easton Cl. M24: Mid 2E **73**
Easton Dr. SK8: Chea 6C **144**
Easton Rd. M43: Droy 3G **103**
E. Ordsall La. M3: Sal 6C **4** (4B **100**)
M5: Sal 6C **4** (4B **100**)
Eastover SK6: Rom 3G **147**
Eastpark Cl. M13: Man 5F **11** (1G **115**)
E. Philip St. M3: Sal 1F **5** (2C **100**)
East Rd. M12: Man 4C **116**
M18: Man 4D **116**
M90: Man A 6A **154**
SK15: C'ook 5A **94**
Eastry Av. SK5: Stoc 3B **134**
Eastside Valley M4: Man 6G **7**
East St. BL0: Eden 1G **13**
BL9: Sum 5D **176** (4F **37**)
M26: Rad 4B **52**
M34: Aud 6F **105**
OL6: A Lyme 1B **106**
OL12: W'le 6C **16**
OL15: L'ough 4H **17**
OL16: Roch 4D **28**
(Hartley St., not continuous)
OL16: Roch 1D **178** (3A **28**)
(North St.)
E. Tame Bus. Pk. SK14: Hyde 1E **121**
E. Union St. M16: Old T 6B **8** (1A **114**)
East Va. SK6: Mar 6E **149**
East Vw. BL0: Ram ......1B **12** & 4F **13**
BL9: Sum 6C **12**
M24: Mid 1B **72**
M33: Sale 6B **128**
OL12: Whitw 1B **14**
Eastville Gdns. M19: Man 4A **132**
Eastward Av. SK9: Wilm 3C **172**
East Way BL1: Bolt 2F **33**
Eastway M24: Mid 6B **56**
M33: Sale 1G **139**
M41: Urm 4A **110**
OL2: Shaw 1H **59**
Eastwood M14: Man 6G **115**
Eastwood Av. M28: Walk 6E **65**
M40: Man 2H **89**
M41: Urm 5F **111**
M43: Droy 4G **103**
Eastwood Cl. BL3: Bolt 4G **47**
BL9: Bury 3H **37**
Eastwood Ct. BL9: Bury 3H **37**
Eastwood Dr. SK3: Stoc 6F **145**
Eastwood Educational Nature Reserve
............5F **107**
Eastwood Rd. M40: Man 2G **89**
Eastwood St. M34: Aud 6D **104**
OL15: L'ough 4H **17**
Eastwood Ter. BL1: Bolt 5F **31**
Eastwood Vw. SK15: Stal 4F **107**
Eaton Cl. M27: Pen 1H **83**
SK8: Chea H 2B **156**
SK12: Poy 4G **169**
SK16: Duk 1A **120**
Eaton Ct. WA14: Bow 4E **151**

Eaton Dr. OL7: A Lyme 1F **105**
  SK9: A Edg 4F **173**
  WA15: Tim 3A **140**
Eaton Rd. M8: Man 2D **86**
  M33: Sale 5A **128**
  WA14: Bow 4E **151**
Eaves La. OL9: Chad 4A **74**
Ebbdale Cl. SK1: Stoc 5H **179** (3H **145**)
Ebberstone St. M14: Man 5E **115**
Ebden St. M1: Man 2C **10**
Ebenezer Cl. M15: Man 4H **9** (6D **100**)
Ebnall Wlk. M14: Man 2H **131**
Ebor Cl. OL2: Shaw 5G **43**
Ebor Ho. M32: Stre 6F **113**
Ebor Rd. M22: Wyth 1C **154**
Ebor St. OL15: L'ough 4H **17**
Ebsworth St. M40: Man 3B **88**
Ebury St. M26: Rad 3H **51**
ECCLES 3H **97**
Eccles Bri. Rd. SK6: Mar 6D **148**
Eccles Cl. M11: Man 5E **103**
Eccles Crematorium M30: Ecc 5B **96**
Eccles Dr. M27: Swin 5H **83**
Eccles Fold M30: Ecc 3G **97**
Eccleshall St. M11: Man 4D **102**
          (not continuous)

Eccles New Rd.
  M5: Ecc, Sal 3A **98**
  M50: Ecc, Sal 3A **98**
Eccles Old Rd. M6: Sal 2B **98**
Eccles Rd. M27: Swin 5H **83**
Eccles Station (Metro) 3H **97**
Eccles Station (Rail) 3H **97**
Eccleston Av. BL2: Bolt 4F **33**
  M14: Man 6F **115**
  M27: Swin 4F **83**
Eccleston Cl. BL8: Bury 4A **36**
Eccleston Pl. M7: Sal 3A **88**
Eccleston Rd. SK3: Stoc 1G **157**
Eccleston St. M35: Fail 3A **90**
Eccleston Way SK9: Hand 3H **165**
         (off Henbury Rd.)
Eccups La. SK9: Wilm 6A **164**
Echo St. M1: Man 2C **10** (5F **101**)
Eckersley Cl. M23: Wyth 5F **141**
Eckersley Rd. BL1: Bolt 2C **32**
Eckersley St. BL3: Bolt 3A **48**
Eckford St. M8: Man 5F **87**
Eclipse Cl. OL16: Roch 4C **28**
Edale Av. M34: Aud 6D **104**
  M34: Dent 1F **135**
  M40: Man 3C **88**
  M41: Urm 6D **110**
  SK5: Stoc 6A **118**
Edale Bank SK13: Gam 5G **123**
Edale Cl. M44: Irl 6E **109**
  SK7: H Gro 4E **159**
  SK8: H Grn 6H **155**
  SK13: Gam 5G **123**
  WA14: Bow 4E **151**
Edale Cres. SK13: Gam 5G **123**
Edale Fold SK13: Gam 5G **123**
         (off Edale Cl.)
Edale Gro. M33: Sale 1G **139**
  OL6: A Lyme 5E **93**
Edale Rd. BL3: Bolt 3G **47**
  BL4: Farn 2G **65**
  M32: Stre 4B **112**
Edale St. M6: Sal 6H **85**
Edbrook Wlk. M13: Man 2H **115**
Eddie Colman Cl.
  M40: Man 6D **88**
Eddie Colman Ct. M6: Sal 2G **99**
        (off Belvedere Rd.)
Eddisbury Av. M20: Man 1D **130**
  M41: Urm 3H **109**
Edditch Gro. BL2: Bolt 6G **33**
Eddystone Cl. M5: Sal 4G **99**
Eden Av. BL0: Eden 2G **13**
  BL1: Bolt 2C **32**
  SK6: H Lan 6C **160**
Edenbridge Dr. M26: Rad 2D **66**

Edenbridge Rd. M40: Man 1D **102**
  SK8: Chea H 1D **156**
Eden Cl. M15: Man 6A **10** (1E **115**)
  OL10: H'ood 2E **39**
  SK1: Stoc 3A **146**
  SK9: Wilm 4B **172**
Eden Ct. BL0: Eden 3G **13**
  M19: Man 1C **132**
Edendale Dr. M22: Wyth 4B **154**
EDENFIELD 2H **13**
Edenfield Av. M21: Chor 5B **130**
Edenfield Ct. SK14: Hyde 6C **120**
Edenfield La. M28: Wors 1B **96**
Edenfield Rd. M25: Pres 6C **70**
  OL11: Roch 3C **26**
  OL12: Roch 1E **25**
Edenfield St. OL12: Roch 2E **27**
Eden Gro. BL1: Bolt 2C **32**
Edenhall Av. M19: Man 1B **132**
Edenham Wlk. M40: Man 1F **89**
        (off Enstone Dr.)
Edenhurst Dr. WA15: Tim 6B **140**
Edenhurst Rd. SK2: Stoc 5B **146**
Eden La. BL0: Ram 3G **13**
Eden Lodge BL1: Bolt 2C **32**
        (off Eden St.)
Eden Pk. Rd. SK8: Chea H 5A **156**
Eden Pl. M33: Sale 4B **128**
  SK8: Chea 5H **143**
Edensor Dr. WA15: Hale 2C **152**
Eden St. BL0: Eden 3G **13**
  BL1: Bolt 2C **32**
  BL9: Bury 3C **176** (3F **37**)
  OL1: O'ham 2F **177** (2E **75**)
  OL12: Roch 3F **27**
Edenvale M28: Wors 4E **81**
Eden Way OL2: Shaw 5G **43**
Edenwood Rd. BL0: Ram 4G **13**
Edgar St. BL0: Ram 4B **12**
  BL3: Bolt 6E **175** (1C **48**)
  OL16: Roch 1C **28**
Edgar St. W. BL0: Ram 4B **12**
Edgbaston Dr. M16: Old T 4G **113**
EDGE, THE 1B **90**
Edge, The M3: Sal 4G **5** (3C **100**)
Edgecote Cl. M22: Shar 5D **142**
Edgedale Av. M19: Man 4A **132**
Edge End OL3: Dob 4C **62**
Edgefield Av. M9: Man 5A **72**
Edge Fold BL4: Farn 1A **64**
Edge Fold Cres. M28: Walk 3H **81**
Edgefold Ind. Est. BL4: Farn 6A **48**
Edge Fold Rd. M28: Walk, Wors 2H **81**
Edge Grn. M28: Wors 3G **81**
Edge Hill Av. OL2: O'ham 4E **59**
Edgehill Chase SK9: Wilm 2H **173**
Edgehill Cl. M5: Sal 3F **99**
Edge Hill Rd. M32: Stre 6E **113**
  OL2: O'ham 4E **59**
Edgehill Rd. M6: Sal 2C **98**
Edgehill St. M4: Man 4B **6**
Edge La. BL1: Hor 1D **30**
  BL6: Hor 1C **30**
  M32: Stre 6D **112**
  M43: Droy 3F **103**
  SK14: Mot 3A **122**
        (not continuous)
Edge La. OL1: O'ham 1G **75**
Edge La. St. OL2: O'ham 3E **59**
EDGELEY .4E **145**
Edgeley Fold SK3: Stoc 4E **145**
Edgeley Pk. 6E **179** (4G **145**)
Edgeley Rd. M41: Urm 1C **126**
  SK3: Stoc 4C **144**
Edgemoor WA14: Bow 3C **150**
Edgemoor Cl. M26: Rad 2G **51**
  OL4: O'ham 6B **60**
Edgemoor Dr. OL11: Roch 6B **26**
Edge St. M4: Man 4B **6** (3E **101**)
Edge Vw. OL1: Chad 6G **57**
Edgeview Wlk. M13: Man 4D **10**
Edge Wlk. SK15: Stal 4F **107**

Edgeware Av. M25: Pres 5D **70**
Edgeware Rd. M30: Ecc 1C **96**
  OL9: Chad 6G **73**
Edgewater M5: Sal 3D **98**
Edgeway SK9: Wilm 4E **173**
Edgeworth Av. BL2: Ain 4F **35**
Edgeworth Dr. M14: Man 2A **132**
  M23: Bolt 3B **48**
Edgmont Av. BL3: Bolt 3B **48**
Edgware Rd. M40: Man 1D **102**
Edgworth Cl. OL10: H'ood 3E **39**
Edgworth Dr. BL8: Bury 4A **36**
Edilom Rd. M8: Man 1C **86**
Edinburgh M30: Ecc 3G **97**
        (off Monton St.)
Edinburgh Cl. M33: Sale 6F **127**
  SK8: Chea 5B **144**
Edinburgh Dr. SK6: Wood 5A **136**
Edinburgh Ho. M3: Sal 5D **4**
        (off Rocket St.)
Edinburgh Rd. BL3: Lit L 5C **50**
Edinburgh Sq. M40: Man 1A **102**
        (off Giltbrook Av.)
Edinburgh Way OL11: Roch 1F **41**
Edington OL12: Roch 1B **178**
Edison Rd. M30: Ecc 4E **97**
Edison St. M11: Man 6G **103**
Edith Av. M14: Man 4E **115**
Edith Cavell Cl. M11: Man 4E **103**
Edith Cliff Wlk. M40: Man 2H **89**
Edith St. BL0: Ram 1E **13**
  BL1: Bolt 1A **48**
  BL4: Farn 2H **65**
  OL8: O'ham 6F **75**
Edith Ter. SK6: Comp 1F **149**
Edleston Gro. SK9: Wilm 6A **166**
        (off Picton Dr.)
Edlin Cl. M12: Man 3A **116**
Edlingham OL11: Roch 6A **178** (5G **27**)
Edlington Wlk. M40: Man 5E **89**
Edmonds St. M24: Mid 6D **56**
Edmonton Ct. SK2: Stoc 1A **158**
Edmonton Rd. M40: Man 1C **102**
  SK2: Stoc 1A **158**
Edmund Cl. SK4: Stoc 6G **133**
Edmunds Fold OL15: L'ough 3F **17**
Edmunds Pas. OL15: L'ough 2G **17**
Edmund St. M6: Sal 2E **99**
  M26: Rad 3C **52**
  M35: Fail 3H **89**
  M43: Droy 4A **104**
  OL2: Shaw 6A **44**
  OL12: Roch 1A **178** (3F **27**)
  OL16: Miln 5F **29**
Edna St. SK14: Hyde 6B **120**
Edson Rd. M8: Man 6D **70**
Edstone Cl. BL3: Bolt 3F **47**
Edward Av. M6: Sal 2C **98**
  M21: Chor 2F **129**
  OL15: L'ough 6E **17**
  SK6: Bred 6E **135**
Edward Charlton Rd. M16: Old T . . .5G **113**
Edward Ct. WA14: B'ath 4D **138**
Edward Grant Ct. M9: Man 2A **88**
Edward M. OL9: O'ham 4C **74**
Edward Onyon Ct. M6: Sal 3E **99**
Edward Pilkington Memorial Cotts.
  M27: Clif 6H **67**
Edward Rd. M9: Man 4H **71**
  OL2: Shaw 1G **59**
Edwards Cl. SK6: Mar 6C **148**
Edwards Ct. M22: Wyth 2B **154**
  SK7: H Gro 5E **159**
Edwards Dr. M45: White 1H **69**
Edward St. BL3: Bolt 2B **48**
  BL4: Farn 5F **49**
  BL9: Bury 5D **176** (4F **37**)
  M7: Sal 1F **5** (1C **100**)
  M9: Man 3A **88**
  M24: Mid 5C **56**
  M25: Pres 4G **69**
  M26: Rad 1D **66**
        (Market St.)

Edward St. M26: Rad 5B **52**
(Stand La.)
M33: Sale 5E **129**
M34: Aud 6D **104**
M34: Dent 3F **119**
M43: Droy 5A **104**
OL6: A Lyme 3C **106**
OL9: Chad 1A **74**
OL9: O'ham 3C **74**
OL12: Roch 5D **16**
OL12: Whitw 3B **14**
OL16: Roch 3A **28**
SK1: Stoc 4G **179** (3H **145**)
SK6: Mar B 2E **149**
SK14: Hyde 4A **120**
(not continuous)
SK16: Duk 1A **120**
Edward Sutcliffe Cl. M14: Man 5E **115**
Edwards Way SK6: Mar 6C **148**
Edwin Rd. M11: Man 4A **102**
Edwin St. BL9: Bury 4B **176** (3E **37**)
SK1: Stoc 3B **146**
Edwin Waugh Gdns. OL12: Roch 6F **15**
Edzell Wlk. M11: Man 4E **103**
(off Kincraig Cl.)
Eeasbrook M41: Urm 6F **111**
Egbert St. M40: Man 4C **88**
EGERTON 1B **18**
Egerton Cl. OL10: H'ood 4H **39**
Egerton Ct. M14: Man 3G **115**
(off Up. Park Rd.)
M21: Chor 1F **129**
M28: Wors 3C **82**
M34: Dent 3G **119**
(off Margaret Rd.)
SK3: Stoc 1A **158**
Egerton Cres. M20: Man 2F **131**
OL10: H'ood 4G **39**
Egerton Dr. M33: Sale 4B **128**
WA15: Hale 3A **152**
Egerton Gro. M28: Walk 6H **65**
Egerton Ho. M5: Sal 6G **99**
(off Elmira Way)
M15: Man 3D **8**
SK4: Stoc 5C **132**
Egerton Lodge BL7: Eger 2C **18**
M34: Dent 3G **119**
(off Margaret Rd.)
Egerton M. M43: Droy 5A **104**
EGERTON PARK 4D **82**
Egerton Pk. M28: Wors 4D **82**
Egerton Pk. Art College Sports Hall
. . . . .3E **119**
(off Boundary Grn.)
Egerton Pl. OL2: Shaw 1G **59**
Egerton Rd. M14: Man 1H **131**
M28: Walk 6H **65**
M30: Ecc 1F **97**
M45: White 2F **69**
SK3: Stoc 6A **146**
SK9: Wilm 6F **165**
WA15: Hale 2A **152**
Egerton Rd. Nth. M16: W Rar 5A **114**
SK4: Stoc 4E **133**
Egerton Rd. Sth. M21: Chor 1A **130**
SK4: Stoc 4E **133**
Egerton St. BL4: Farn 6G **49**
M3: Sal 5D **4** (4B **100**)
M15: Man 3D **8** (6B **100**)
M24: Mid 2G **71**
M25: Pres 5A **70**
M30: Ecc 3D **96**
M34: Dent 2D **118**
M43: Droy 4B **104**
OL1: O'ham 3H **177** (2F **75**)
OL5: Mos 1G **93**
OL6: A Lyme 2A **106**
OL10: H'ood 4G **39**
OL15: L'ough 4H **17**
Egerton Ter. M14: Man 2H **131**
Egerton Va. BL7: Eger 1B **18**
Egerton Wlk. M28: Walk 6H **65**
(off Ellesmere Shop. Cen.)

Eggington St. M40: Man 6G **87**
Egham Ct. BL2: Bolt 4F **33**
(off Horsa St.)
Egham Ho. BL3: Bolt 5H **47**
Egmont St. M6: Sal 5E **85**
M8: Man 3E **87**
OL5: Mos 3G **93**
Egmont Ter. SK15: Stal 5F **107**
(off Spring Bank)
Egremont Av. M20: Man 2E **131**
Egremont Cl. M45: White 6G **53**
Egremont Ct. M7: Sal 3A **86**
(off Bury New Rd.)
Egremont Gro. SK3: Stoc 3D **144**
Egremont Rd. OL16: Miln 1E **43**
Egret Dr. M44: Irl 4E **109**
Egyptian St. BL1: Bolt 1F **175** (4D **32**)
Egypt La. M25: Pres 6B **54**
Eida Way M17: T Pk 5C **98**
Eight Acre M45: White 2C **68**
Eighth Av. OL8: O'ham 2D **90**
Eighth St. M17: T Pk 1D **112**
(not continuous)
Eighth St. W. M17: T Pk 1C **112**
Eileen Gro. M14: Man 5G **115**
Eileen Gro. W. M14: Man 5F **115**
Elaine Av. M9: Man 1D **88**
Elbain Wlk. M40: Man 4H **87**
(off Orford Rd.)
Elberton Wlk. M8: Man 4D **86**
(off Highshore Dr.)
Elbe St. M12: Man 2F **11** (5G **101**)
Elbow St. M19: Man 6C **116**
Elbut La. BL9: Bury 6D **24**
Elcho Ct. WA14: Bow 3D **150**
Elcho Rd. WA14: Bow 2D **150**
Elcot Cl. M40: Man 6G **87**
Elderberry Cl. OL3: Dig 2E **63**
Elderberry Wlk.
M31: Part 6C **124**
(off Wood La.)
Elderberry Way SK9: Wilm 1H **159**
Elder Cl. BL8: Tot 6H **21**
SK2: Stoc 3D **146**
Eldercot Gro. BL3: Bolt 3G **47**
Eldercot Rd. BL3: Bolt 3G **47**
Elder Ct. SK4: Stoc 6D **132**
Eldercroft Rd. WA15: Tim 6C **140**
Elder Dr. BL3: Bolt 2A **50**
Elderfield Dr. SK6: Bred 5F **135**
Elder Gro. M40: Man 1H **89**
Elder Mt. Rd. M9: Man 1H **87**
Elder Rd. OL4: Lees 3C **76**
Elder St. OL16: Roch 6B **28**
Elderwood OL9: Chad 2G **73**
Eldon Cl. M34: Aud 6E **105**
Eldon Pl. M30: Ecc 4E **97**
Eldon Pct. OL8: O'ham 6F **177**
Eldon Rd. M44: Irl 5E **109**
SK3: Stoc 4E **145**
Eldon St. BL2: Bolt 4F **33**
BL9: Bury 1F **37**
OL8: O'ham 6G **177** (4F **75**)
Eldon St. Est.
OL8: O'ham 6G **177**
Eldridge Dr. M40: Man 6C **88**
Eldroth Av. M22: Wyth 2B **154**
Eleanor Rd. M21: Chor 1G **129**
OL2: O'ham 4E **59**
Eleanor St. BL1: Bolt 6E **19**
OL1: O'ham 1D **74**
Electo St. M11: Man 6G **103**
Electric Pk. M17: T Pk 2C **112**
Elevator Rd. M17: T Pk 1E **113**
Eleventh St. M17: T Pk 1C **112**
Elf Mill Cl. SK3: Stoc 5G **145**
Elf Mill Ter. SK3: Stoc 5G **145**
Elford Gro. M18: Man 3A **118**
Elgar St. M12: Man 3C **116**
Elgin Av. M20: Man 6H **131**
Elgin Dr. M33: Sale 6E **129**
Elgin Rd. OL4: O'ham 4A **76**
SK16: Duk 1A **120**

Elgin St. BL1: Bolt 3A **32**
OL7: A Lyme 1G **105**
(not continuous)
SK15: Stal 4F **107**
Elgol Cl. SK3: Stoc 6H **145**
Elgol Ct. OL10: H'ood 4E **39**
Elgol Dr. BL3: Bolt 1E **47**
Elham Cl. M26: Rad 2E **67**
Eliot Rd. M30: Ecc 4F **97**
Eliot Wlk. M24: Mid 4E **57**
Elishaw Row M5: Sal 4F **99**
Elisie St. BL0: Ram 5A **12**
Eli St. OL9: Chad 6A **74**
Elitex Ho. M7: Sal 1C **100**
Eliza Ann St. M30: Ecc 4F **97**
M40: Man 1G **101**
Elizabethan Way OL16: Miln 5F **29**
Elizabeth Av. M34: Dent 2E **119**
OL2: O'ham 4D **58**
OL9: Chad 6A **74**
SK1: Stoc 5H **179** (3H **145**)
SK12: Dis 2H **171**
SK15: Stal 3E **107**
Elizabeth Cl. M32: Stre 5D **112**
Elizabeth Ct. M14: Man 2H **131**
M18: Man 4H **117**
(off Reddish La.)
SK4: Stoc 1E **145**
Elizabeth Gro. OL2: Shaw 6H **43**
Elizabeth Ho. SK4: Stoc 2D **144**
Elizabeth Rd. M31: Part 5D **124**
Elizabeth Slinger Rd. M20: Man 5C **130**
Elizabeth St. BL0: Eden 2G **13**
M8: Man 5D **86**
M25: Pres 5A **70**
M26: Rad 4A **52**
M27: Pen 2H **83**
M34: Dent 4D **118**
M45: White 2F **69**
OL6: A Lyme 1H **105**
OL10: H'ood 3G **39**
OL11: Roch 2E **41**
SK14: Hyde 4B **120**
Elizabeth St. Ind. Est. M34: Dent 4H **117**
(off Grey St.)
Elizabeth Yarwood Ct.
M13: Man 5D **10** (1F **115**)
Eliza St. BL0: Ram 3D **12**
M15: Man 5E **9** (1C **114**)
Elkanagh Gdns. M6: Sal 2F **99**
Elkstone Av. M38: Lit H 3E **65**
Elladene Pk. M21: Chor 1A **130**
Ellanby Cl. M14: Man 4F **115**
Elland Cl. BL9: Bury 5H **53**
Ellaston Dr. M41: Urm 5F **111**
Ellastone Rd. M6: Sal 1C **98**
Ellbourne Rd. M9: Man 6E **71**
ELLENBROOK 3G **81**
Ellenbrook Cl. M12: Man 1D **116**
Ellenbrook Rd. M22: Wyth 5B **154**
M28: Wors 3F **81**
(not continuous)
Ellenbrook St. M12: Man 1D **116**
Ellendale Grange M28: Wors 3F **81**
Ellen Gro. BL4: Kea 4E **67**
Ellenhall Cl. M9: Man 3H **87**
Ellenor Dr. M29: Ast 4A **80**
Ellenroad App. OL16: Miln 1G **43**
Ellenroad St. OL16: Miln 1G **43**
Ellenroad The World's Largest Working
Steam Mill Engine 1G **43**
Ellenrod Dr. OL12: Roch 1C **26**
Ellenrod La. OL12: Roch 1C **26**
Ellenshaw Cl. OL12: Roch 1C **26**
Ellens Pl. OL15: L'ough 6F **17**
Ellen St. BL1: Bolt 2A **32**
(not continuous)
M43: Droy 5B **104**
OL9: O'ham 1D **74**
SK4: Stoc 6F **133**
Ellen Wilkinson Cres.
M12: Man 2C **116**
Elleray Cl. BL3: Lit L 4E **51**

Elleray Rd.—Elton Bank

Elleray Rd. M6: Sal 6D **84**
M24: Mid 4B **72**
Ellerbeck Cl. BL2: Bolt 6G **19**
Ellerbeck Cres. M28: Wors 3G **81**
Ellerby Av. M27: Clif 6A **68**
Ellerslie Ct. M14: Man 4G **115**
Ellesmere Av. M28: Walk 6G **65**
M30: Ecc 2G **97**
OL6: A Lyme 4A **92**
SK6: Mar 5D **148**
Ellesmere Circ. M41: Urm 6F **97**
Ellesmere Cl. M38: Lit H 5F **65**
SK16: Duk 6C **106**
Ellesmere Dr. SK8: Chea 6C **144**
Ellesmere Gdns. BL3: Bolt 4B **48**
Ellesmere Grn. M30: Ecc 2G **97**
Ellesmere Ho. *M30: Ecc 2H **97***
(off Sandwich Rd.)
ELLESMERE PARK **1G 97**
Ellesmere Pk. *M30: Ecc 1A **98***
(off Park Rd.)
Ellesmere Rd. BL3: Bolt 4A **48**
M21: Chor 6A **114**
M30: Ecc 1G **97**
SK3: Stoc 4C **144**
WA14: Alt 5F **139**
Ellesmere Rd. Nth. SK4: Stoc 4E **133**
Ellesmere Rd. Sth. M21: Chor 1A **130**
Ellesmere Shop. Cen. M28: Walk 6H **65**
Ellesmere Sports Club **3H 81**
Ellesmere St. BL3: Bolt 1B **48**
BL4: Farn 1H **65**
M15: Man 4C **8** (6B **100**)
M27: Pen 2A **84**
M27: Swin 4F **83**
M29: Ast 6A **80**
M30: Ecc 4F **97**
(not continuous)
M35: Fail 3H **89**
M38: Lit H 6F **65**
OL11: Roch 6B **178** (6H **27**)
Ellesmere Ter. M14: Man 2H **131**
Ellesmere Wlk. BL4: Farn 1H **65**
Ellingham Cl. M11: Man 4B **102**
Elliot Sq. OL1: O'ham 1G **75**
Elliott Av. SK14: Hyde 2B **120**
Elliott Dr. M33: Sale 5G **127**
Elliott St. BL1: Bolt 2A **32**
BL4: Farn 2G **65**
OL4: Lees 3C **76**
OL12: Roch 1D **178** (3A **28**)
Ellis Bank Wlk. *M13: Man 4D **10***
(off Deanwater Cl.)
Ellis Cres. M28: Walk 6F **65**
Ellis Dr. M8: Man 2F **87**
Ellis Fold OL12: Roch 6A **14**
Ellisland Wlk. *M40: Man 5C **88***
(off Colebrook Dr.)
Ellis La. M24: Mid 1F **71**
Ellison Cl. SK14: Holl 2F **123**
Ellison Ho. *OL7: A Lyme 4G **105***
(off Park St.)
Ellis St. BL0: Ram 4B **12**
BL3: Bolt 2B **48**
BL8: Bury 3B **36**
M7: Sal 1C **100**
M15: Man 6F **9** (1C **114**)
SK14: Hyde 4D **120**
Elliston Sq. *M12: Man 1C **116***
(off Bridgend Cl.)
Ellonby Ri. BL6: Los 2C **46**
Ellon Wlk. *M11: Man 4E **103***
(off Edith Cavell Cl.)
Ellor St. M6: Sal 2F **99**
Ellwood Rd. SK1: Stoc 2B **146**
Elly Clough OL2: O'ham 4C **58**
Elm Av. M26: Rad 1H **67**
Elmbank Av. M20: Man 5C **130**
Elmbank Rd. M24: Mid 1E **73**
Elm Beds Cvn. Pk. SK12: Poy 5A **170**
Elm Beds Rd. SK12: Poy 5A **170**
Elmbridge Wlk. BL3: Bolt 2B **48**
M40: Man 5C **88**
Elm Cl. M31: Part 6D **124**
SK12: Poy 4F **169**
SK14: Mot 3C **122**
Elm Ct. SK1: Stoc 3B **146**
Elm Cres. M28: Wors 4C **82**
SK9: A Edg 4H **173**
Elmdale Av. SK8: H Grn 3F **155**
Elmdale Wlk. M15: Man 5A **10**
Elm Dr. M32: Stre 6B **112**
Elmfield Av. M22: Nor 3C **142**
Elmfield Cl. SK9: A Edg 4H **173**
Elmfield Ct. *SK3: Stoc 6H **145***
(off Elmfield Rd.)
Elmfield Dr. SK6: Mar 5C **148**
Elmfield Ho. *SK3: Stoc 6H **145***
(off Plumley Cl.)
Elmfield Rd. M34: Aud 5C **104**
SK3: Stoc 6H **145**
SK9: A Edg 4H **173**
Elmfield St. BL1: Bolt 2D **32**
(Blackburn Rd.)
BL1: Bolt 3D **32**
(Pendlebury St.)
M8: Man 5E **87**
Elmgate Gro. M19: Man 6C **116**
Elm Gro. BL4: Farn 1F **65**
BL7: Bro X 3E **19**
M20: Man 6F **131**
M25: Pres 3G **69**
M27: Ward 2D **82**
M33: Sale 3B **128**
M34: Dent 2D **118**
M41: Urm 5G **111**
M43: Droy 3F **103**
OL4: Grot 3F **77**
OL6: A Lyme 6A **92**
OL11: Roch 6G **27**
OL12: W'le 4C **16**
OL16: Miln 2G **43**
SK9: A Edg 4G **173**
*SK9: Hand 4G **165***
(off Sagars Rd.)
SK14: Hyde 5D **120**
Elmham Wlk. M40: Man 1F **7**
Elmhurst Dr. M19: Man 4B **132**
Elmira Way M5: Sal 6G **99**
Elmlea WA15: Alt 1H **151**
Elmley Cl. SK2: Stoc 6G **147**
Elmore Wood OL15: L'ough 3E **17**
Elm Pk. Ct. M20: Man 5F **131**
Elmpark Ga. OL12: Roch 6D **14**
Elmpark Gro. OL12: Roch 6D **14**
Elmpark Va. OL12: Roch 6D **14**
Elmpark Vw. OL12: Roch 6D **14**
Elmpark Way OL12: Roch 6D **14**
Elmridge Dr. WA15: Haleb 5C **152**
Elm Rd. BL3: Lit L 5D **50**
BL4: Kea 4B **66**
M20: Man 5E **131**
OL8: O'ham 2D **90**
SK6: H Lan 6D **160**
SK8: Gat 6E **143**
WA15: Hale 2G **151**
Elm Rd. Sth. SK3: Stoc 4C **144**
Elms, The M45: White 5F **53**
OL5: Mos 2F **93**
OL15: L'ough 5F **17**
Elms Cl. M45: White 5F **53**
Elmscott Wlk. *M13: Man 2H **115***
(off Bletchley Cl.)
Elmsdale Av. M9: Man 4H **71**
Elms Farm M45: White 5F **53**
Elmsfield Av. OL11: Roch 2A **26**
Elmsleigh Ct. M30: Ecc 2H **97**
Elmsleigh Rd. SK8: H Grn 3E **155**
Elmsmere Rd. M20: Man 6H **131**
Elms Rd. M45: White 6F **53**
SK4: Stoc 4D **132**
SK15: Stal 2H **107**
Elms Sq. M45: White 6E **53**
Elms St. M45: White 6E **53**
Elmstead Av. M20: Man 3E **131**
Elmstead Ho. M27: Swin 4H **83**
Elmsted Cl. SK8: Chea H 2D **156**
Elmstone Cl. M9: Man 1G **87**
Elmstone Gro. *BL1: Bolt 4D **32***
(off Kentford Rd.)
Elm St. BL0: Eden 2H **13**
BL0: Ram 3D **12**
BL4: Farn 6H **49**
BL9: Bury 3H **37**
M24: Mid 6E **57**
M27: Swin 2G **83**
M30: Ecc 4F **97**
M35: Fail 3H **89**
OL10: H'ood 3H **39**
OL12: Roch 2H **27**
OL12: Whitw 3B **14**
OL15: L'ough 1F **29**
SK6: Bred 5F **135**
Elmsway SK6: H Lan 1C **170**
SK7: Bram 6E **157**
WA15: Haleb 5B **152**
Elmswood Av. M14: Man 5D **114**
Elmswood Dr. SK14: Hyde 4E **121**
Elmsworth Av. M19: Man 6D **116**
Elmton Rd. M9: Man 6A **72**
Elm Tree Cl. M35: Fail 4B **90**
SK15: Stal 5E **107**
Elm Tree Dr. M22: Wyth 2B **154**
SK16: Duk 6D **106**
Elmtree Dr. SK4: Stoc 1D **144**
Elm Tree Rd. SK6: Bred 6C **134**
(not continuous)
Elmwood M28: Wors 6C **82**
M33: Sale 5E **127**
Elmwood Ct. M32: Stre 1C **128**
Elmwood Dr. OL2: O'ham 2C **58**
Elmwood Gro. BL1: Bolt 5A **32**
BL4: Farn 3H **65**
M9: Man 4B **88**
Elmwood Lodge M20: Man 5E **131**
Elmwood Pk. SK15: Stal 2H **107**
Elrick Wlk. *M11: Man 4D **102***
(off Emily Beavan Cl.)
Elsa Rd. M19: Man 6E **117**
Elsdon Dr. M18: Man 1F **117**
Elsdon Gdns. BL2: Bolt 4F **33**
Elsdon Rd. M13: Man 5B **116**
Elsfield Cl. *BL1: Bolt 3B **32***
(off Raglan St.)
Elsham Cl. BL1: Bolt 6C **18**
Elsham Dr. M28: Walk 6F **65**
Elsham Gdns. M18: Man 3D **116**
Elsie St. BL4: Farn 1G **65**
M9: Man 3A **88**
Elsinore Av. M44: Irl 6D **108**
Elsinore Bus. Cen. M16: Old T 3G **113**
Elsinore Cl. M35: Fail 4B **90**
Elsinore Rd. M16: Old T 3G **113**
Elsinore St. BL2: Bolt 2F **33**
Elsma Rd. M40: Man 1G **103**
Elsmore Rd. M14: Man 6E **115**
Elson Dr. SK14: Hyde 2B **136**
Elson St. BL8: Bury 1B **36**
Elstead Wlk. M9: Man 6F **71**
Elsted Rd. OL3: G'fld 4A **78**
Elstree Av. M40: Man 1D **102**
Elstree Ct. M41: Urm 5F **111**
Elswick Av. BL3: Bolt 2H **47**
M21: Chor 4B **130**
SK7: Bram 6G **157**
Elsworth Cl. M26: Rad 6B **52**
Elsworth Dr. BL1: Bolt 1D **32**
Elsworth St. M3: Man 1A **6** (2E **101**)
Elterwater Cl. BL8: Bury 1B **36**
M24: Mid 4H **55**
Elterwater Rd. BL4: Farn 2C **64**
Eltham Av. SK2: Stoc 6C **146**
Eltham Dr. M41: Urm 3E **111**
Eltham St. M19: Man 5C **116**
ELTON **3C 36**
Elton Av. BL4: Farn 1D **64**
M19: Man 1C **132**
Elton Bank *SK13: Gam 6F **123***
(off Brassington Cres.)

Elton Brook Cl.—Errwood Cres.

Elton Brook Cl. BL8: Bury 2B **36**
Elton Cl. M45: White 1G **69**
SK9: Wilm 6A **166**
*SK13: Gam 6F **123***
(off Brassington Cres.)
Elton Dr. SK7: H Gro 5D **158**
Elton Ho. BL8: Bury 3B **36**
Elton Lea *SK13: Gam 6F **123***
(off Brassington Cres.)
Elton Lofts *BL8: Bury 3C **36***
(off Fairy St.)
Elton Pl. *SK13: Gam 6F **123***
(off Brassington Cres.)
Elton Rd. M33: Sale 1G **139**
Elton Sailing Club 5C 36
Elton Sq. Ho. BL8: Bury 4C **36**
Elton St. BL2: Bolt 3H **175** (6E **33**)
M7: Sal 1D **4** (2B **100**)
M32: Stre 2F **113**
OL11: Roch 4E **41**
Elton's Yd. M7: Sal 1D **4** (2B **100**)
Elton Va. Rd. BL8: Bury 3B **36**
Elvate Cres. M8: Man 6D **86**
Elverdon Cl. M15: Man 2C **114**
Elverston St. M22: Nor 2C **142**
Elverston Way OL9: Chad 1C **74**
Elvey St. M40: Man 6B **88**
Elvington Cres. M28: Wors 3G **81**
Elvira Cl. M35: Fail 4B **90**
Elwick Cl. M16: W Ran 4D **114**
Elworth Way *SK9: Hand 3H **165***
(off Delamere Rd.)
Elwyn Av. M22: Nor 4B **142**
Ely Av. M32: Stre 4H **111**
Ely Cl. M28: Wors 3F **81**
Ely Cres. M35: Fail 6H **89**
Ely Dr. BL8: Bury 1D **36**
M29: Ast 4A **80**
Ely Gdns. M41: Urm 5G **111**
Ely Gro. *BL1: Bolt 4C **32***
(off Kentford Rd.)
Elysian Flds. M6: Sal 2B **98**
Elysian St. M11: Man 5E **103**
Ely St. OL9: O'ham 4B **74**
Embankment Bus. Pk. SK4: Stoc 2B **144**
Embassy Wlk. M18: Man 3F **117**
Ember St. M11: Man 3F **103**
Embla Wlk. BL3: Bolt 3E **49**
Emblem St. BL3: Bolt 2B **48**
Embleton Cl. BL2: Bolt 4A **34**
Embleton Wlk. *M18: Man 1E **117***
(off Peacock Cl.)
Embsay Cl. BL1: Bolt 6B **18**
Emerald Dr. OL1: O'ham 4C **60**
Emerald Rd. M22: Wyth 6D **154**
Emerald St. BL1: Bolt 2D **32**
M34: Dent 4E **119**
Emerson Av. M30: Ecc 2A **98**
Emerson Dr. M24: Mid 6B **56**
Emerson Ho. M30: Ecc 3H **97**
Emerson St. M5: Sal 3D **98**
Emery Av. M21: Chor 3A **130**
Emery Cl. SK4: Stoc 5C **132**
WA14: Alt 4F **139**
Emery Ct. SK4: Stoc 2B **144**
Emily Beavan Cl. M11: Man 4D **102**
Emily Cl. M35: Fail 2A **90**
Emily Pl. M43: Droy 4H **103**
Emley St. M19: Man 6D **116**
Emlyn Gro. SK8: Chea 5C **144**
Emlyn St. BL4: Farn 6G **49**
M27: Swin 3F **83**
M28: Walk 6H **65**
Emmanuel Cl. *BL3: Bolt 2B **48***
(off Emblem St.)
Emmanuel Ct. OL6: A Lyme 1H **105**
Emmanuel Pl. *BL3: Bolt 2B **48***
(off Emblem St.)
Emma St. OL8: O'ham 6F **75**
OL12: Roch 2A **178** (3G **27**)
Emmaus Wlk. M6: Sal 2F **99**
Emmeline Grange M6: Sal 3E **99**
Emmerson St. M27: Pen 2H **83**
Emmett St. E. M40: Man 6A **88**
Emmott Cl. OL10: H'ood 3G **39**
Emmott Way OL1: O'ham 5G **177** (3F **75**)
Empire Rd. BL2: Bolt 6A **34**
SK16: Duk 1A **120**
Empire St. M3: Man 1D **100**
Empress Av. SK6: Mar 6D **148**
Empress Bus. Cen.
M16: Old T 6B **8** (1A **114**)
Empress Ct. M15: Man 6B **8** (1A **114**)
Empress Dr. SK4: Stoc 5F **133**
Empress St. BL1: Bolt 4H **31**
M8: Man 3D **86**
M16: Old T 6A **8** (1A **114**)
Emsworth Cl. BL2: Bolt 4E **33**
Emsworth Dr. M33: Sale 2C **140**
Ena St. BL3: Bolt 4E **49**
OL1: O'ham 6A **60**
Enbridge St. M5: Sal 5G **99**
Encombe Pl. M3: Sal 4C **4** (3B **100**)
Endcott Cl. M18: Man 1D **116**
Enderby Rd. M40: Man 2E **89**
Ending Rake OL12: Whitw 5E **15**
Endon Dr. M21: Chor 1D **130**
Endon St. BL1: Bolt 4H **31**
Endsleigh Rd. M20: Man 3G **131**
Endsley Av. M28: Wors 2G **81**
Energis Fitness Club 6H 165
Energy St. M40: Man 2A **102**
Enfield Av. M19: Man 3C **132**
OL8: O'ham 6E **75**
Enfield Cl. BL1: Bolt 4C **32**
BL9: Bury 2F **53**
M30: Ecc 5F **97**
OL11: Roch 3A **26**
Enfield Dr. M11: Man 3E **103**
Enfield Ho. *M30: Ecc 5F **97***
(off Enfield Cl.)
Enfield Rd. M27: Swin 5G **83**
M30: Ecc 1F **97**
Enfield St. *M28: Walk 4H **65***
(off Worsley Rd. Nth.)
SK14: Hyde 2C **136**
Enford Av. M22: Wyth 3G **153**
Engal Cl. BL0: Ram 4A **12**
Engell Cl. M18: Man 2F **117**
Engels Ho. *M30: Ecc 5F **97***
(off Trafford Rd.)
ENGINE FOLD 6F 65
Engine Fold Rd. M28: Walk 6E **65**
Engine La. M29: Tyld 6A **64**
Engine St. OL9: Chad 5B **74**
England St. OL6: A Lyme 6D **174** (2A **106**)
Engledene BL1: Bolt 5B **18**
Englefield Gro. *M18: Man 3F **117***
(off Milkwood Gro.)
Enid Cl. M7: Sal 6B **86**
Ennerdale Av. BL2: Bolt 4B **34**
(not continuous)
M21: Chor 5B **130**
M27: Swin 5H **83**
OL2: O'ham 6C **42**
Ennerdale Cl. BL3: Lit L 4B **50**
Ennerdale Dr. BL9: Bury 5G **53**
M33: Sale 4G **127**
SK8: Gat 2F **155**
WA15: Tim 3A **140**
Ennerdale Gdns. BL2: Bolt 4A **34**
Ennerdale Gro. BL4: Farn 1C **64**
OL7: A Lyme 6F **91**
Ennerdale Rd. M24: Mid 5B **56**
M31: Part 6C **124**
M32: Stre 4C **112**
OL11: Roch 1D **40**
SK1: Stoc 4B **146**
SK6: Wood 5H **135**
Ennerdale Ter. SK15: Stal 2E **107**
Ennis Cl. M23: Wyth 6E **141**
Ennismore Av. M30: Ecc 3A **98**
Enstone Dr. M40: Man 2F **89**
Enstone Way M29: Tyld 2A **80**
Enterprise Cen. Two *SK3: Stoc 2F **145***
(off Chester St.)
Enterprise Ho. M50: Sal 6G **99**
Enterprise Trad. Est. M17: T Pk 5A **98**
Enticott Rd. M44: Cad 4A **124**
Entron Ho. OL2: Shaw 6F **43**
Entwisle Av. M41: Urm 3D **110**
Entwisle Rd. OL16: Roch 2D **178** (4A **28**)
Entwisle Row BL4: Farn 1H **65**
Entwisle St. BL4: Farn 6H **49**
M27: Ward 2F **83**
OL16: Miln 5E **29**
Entwistle St. BL2: Bolt 5F **33**
Enver Rd. M8: Man 3F **87**
Enville Rd. M6: Sal 5E **85**
M40: Man 2D **88**
WA14: Bow 2E **151**
Enville St. M9: Man 6H **71**
M34: Aud 6F **105**
OL6: A Lyme 4D **174** (2A **106**)
Enys Wlk. M6: Sal 6G **85**
Epping Cl. OL6: A Lyme 4A **92**
OL9: Chad 1G **73**
Epping Dr. M33: Sale 4E **127**
Epping Rd. M34: Dent 5B **118**
Epping St. M15: Man 5H **9** (1D **114**)
Eppleworth Ri. M27: Clif 6A **68**
Epsley Cl. M15: Man 6A **10** (1E **115**)
Epsom Av. M19: Man 3B **132**
M33: Sale 1E **139**
SK9: Hand 3A **166**
Epsom Cl. OL11: Roch 3B **26**
SK7: H Gro 3F **159**
Epsom M. *M7: Sal 5B **86***
(off Rigby St.)
Epsom Wlk. *OL9: Chad 2C **74***
(off Garforth St.)
Epworth Ct. SK4: Stoc 6D **132**
Epworth Gro. *BL3: Bolt 4A **48***
(off Maltby Dr.)
Epworth St. M1: Man 6F **7** (4G **101**)
Equitable St. OL4: O'ham 1B **76**
OL11: Roch 6D **178** (5A **28**)
OL16: Miln 6F **29**
Era St. BL2: Bolt 6A **34**
M33: Sale 5B **128**
Ercall Av. M12: Man 1A **116**
Erica Av. OL4: O'ham 3D **60**
Erica Cl. SK5: Stoc 1A **134**
Erica Dr. M19: Man 5A **132**
Eric Brook Cl. M14: Man 4E **115**
Eric Bullows Cl. M22: Wyth 4A **154**
Eric St. M5: Sal 4F **99**
OL4: O'ham 2A **76**
OL15: L'ough 3G **17**
Erin Cl. OL9: Chad 4B **74**
Erindale Wlk. *M40: Man 5H **87***
(off Barnstaple Dr.)
Erin St. M11: Man 6G **103**
Erith Cl. SK5: Stoc 3B **134**
Erith Rd. OL4: O'ham 3A **76**
Erlesdene WA14: Bow 2D **150**
Erlesmere Av. M34: Dent 3G **119**
Erlesmere Cl. OL4: O'ham 3D **60**
Erlington Av. M16: Old T 5H **113**
Ermen Rd. M30: Ecc 5E **97**
Ermington Ct. OL10: H'ood 4G **39**
Ermington Dr. M8: Man 5D **86**
Erneley Cl. M12: Man 4D **116**
Ernest St. BL1: Bolt 1B **48**
(not continuous)
M25: Pres 5F **69**
SK2: Stoc 5A **146**
SK8: Chea 5G **143**
Ernest Ter. OL12: Roch 2B **28**
Ernlouen Av. BL1: Bolt 5G **31**
ERNOCROFT 1H 149
Ernocroft Gro. M18: Man 1G **117**
Ernocroft Rd. SK6: Mar B 2F **149**
Erringdon Cl. SK2: Stoc 5D **146**
Errington Cl. BL3: Bolt 2F **47**
Errington Dr. M7: Sal 1B **100**
Errol Av. M9: Man 4E **71**
M22: Wyth 1A **154**
Errwood Cres. M19: Man 1C **132**

246 A-Z Manchester

Errwood Pk. Works SK4: Stoc 3D 132
Errwood Rd. M19: Man 4B 132
Erskine Cl. BL3: Bolt 2E 47
Erskine Rd. M9: Man 4A 72
  M31: Part 6D 124
Erskine St. M15: Man 6D 8 (1B 114)
  SK6: Comp 6F 137
Erwin St. M40: Man 5D 88
Eryngo St. SK1: Stoc 2A 146
Escott St. M16: W Ran 4D 114
Esher Dr. M33: Sale 2C 140
Esk Av. BL0: Eden 1G 13
Esk Cl. M41: Urm 3C 110
Eskdale SK8: Gat 1G 155
Eskdale Av. BL2: Bolt 3B 34
  M20: Man 2E 131
  OL2: O'ham 6D 42
  OL3: G'fld 4D 78
  OL8: O'ham 5D 74
  OL11: Roch 1D 40
  SK6: Wood 4H 135
  SK7: Bram 2E 167
Eskdale Cl. BL9: Bury 4G 53
Eskdale Dr. M24: Mid 4B 56
  WA15: Tim 4C 140
Eskdale Gro. BL4: Farn 1D 64
Eskdale Ho. M13: Man 3A 116
Eskdale M. OL3: G'fld 4D 78
Eskdale Ter. SK15: Stal 1E 107
Eskrick St. BL1: Bolt 4B 32
Esmond Rd. M8: Man 4E 87
Esmont Dr. M24: Mid 4A 56
Esplanade, The
  OL16: Roch 4A 178 (4G 27)
Esporta Health & Fitness
  Bolton 2D 32
  Denton 4C 118
  Middleton 5F 55
  Salford Quays 6F 99
Essex Av. BL9: Bury 4C 38
  M20: Man 5F 131
  M43: Droy 2A 104
  SK3: Stoc 3D 144
Essex Cl. M35: Fail 6H 89
  OL2: Shaw 5F 43
Essex Dr. BL9: Bury 5F 37
Essex Gdns. M44: Cad 5A 124
Essex Pl. M27: Clif 1H 83
           (off Cumberland Av.)
Essex Rd. M18: Man 3H 117
  SK5: Stoc 4C 134
Essex St. M2: Man 6H 5 (4D 100)
  OL11: Roch 6B 178 (5H 27)
Essex Way M16: Old T 60 8 (2B 114)
Essington Dr. M40: Man 5H 87
Essington Wlk. M34: Dent 6E 119
Essoldo Cl. M18: Man 2E 117
Estate St. OL8: O'ham 5F 75
Estate St. Sth. OL8: O'ham 5F 75
Est Bank Rd. BL0: Ram 6A 12
           (not continuous)
Esther St. OL4: O'ham 2B 76
  OL15: L'ough 4F 17
           (off Bamford St.)
Estonfield Dr. M41: Urm 5H 111
Eston St. M13: Man 3H 115
Eswick St. M11: Man 4E 103
Etchells Rd. SK8: H Grn 4H 155
  WA14: W Tim 3F 139
Etchells St. SK1: Stoc 2G 179 (2H 145)
Etchell St. M40: Man 6G 87
Ethel Av. M9: Man 4H 71
  M27: Pen 3B 84
Ethel Cl. OL16: Roch 5B 28
Ethel St. BL3: Bolt 1B 48
  OL8: O'ham 6F 75
  OL12: Whitw 3B 14
  OL16: Roch 5B 28
Ethel Ter. M19: Man 6C 116
Etherley Cl. M44: Irl 5E 109

Etherow Av. M40: Man 1H 89
  SK6: Rom 1C 148
Etherow Country Pk. 1G 149
Etherow Country Pk. Local Nature Reserve
  ....6G 137
Etherow Country Park Vis. Cen. 1F 149
Etherow Ct. SK14: Hyde 5C 120
           (off Ridling La.)
Etherow Ind. Est. SK13: Had 2G 123
           (not continuous)
Etherow Way SK13: Had 2G 123
Etherstone St. M8: Man 3G 87
Eton Av. OL8: O'ham 6E 75
Eton Cl. M16: Old T 2B 114
  OL11: Roch 5D 26
Eton Ct. M16: Old T 2B 114
           (off Eton Cl.)
Eton Dr. SK8: Chea 3H 155
Eton Hill Ind. Est. M26: Rad 2D 52
Eton Hill Rd. M26: Rad 2C 52
Eton Pl. M26: Rad 4H 51
Eton Vale Sports Club 3A 36
Eton Way Nth. M26: Rad 2C 52
Eton Way Sth. M26: Rad 2C 52
Etruria Cl. M13: Man 2A 116
Ettington Cl. BL8: Bury 2A 36
Ettrick Cl. M11: Man 6F 103
Euan Pl. M33: Sale 5C 128
           (off Montague Rd.)
Euclid Cl. M11: Man 4A 102
Europa Bus. Pk. SK3: Stoc 5D 144
Europa Circ. M17: T Pk 2D 112
Europa Ga. M17: T Pk 2D 112
Europa Ho. BL9: Bury 1C 176 (2F 37)
Europa Trad. Est. M26: Rad 2D 66
Europa Way M17: T Pk 2D 112
  M26: Rad 2C 66
  SK3: Stoc 5D 144
Eustace St. BL3: Bolt 4E 49
  OL9: Chad 6B 58
Euston Av. M9: Man 6C 72
Euxton Cl. BL8: Bury 4A 36
Evans Cl. M20: Man 6E 131
Evans Rd. M30: Ecc 4C 96
Evans St. M3: Sal 2F 5 (2C 100)
  M24: Mid 1D 72
  OL1: O'ham 1G 177 (1F 75)
  OL6: A Lyme 1B 106
Evan St. M40: Man 6A 88
Evanton Wlk. M9: Man 4A 88
           (off Nethervale Dr.)
Eva Rd. SK3: Stoc 4C 144
Eva St. M14: Man 4G 115
  OL12: Roch 1A 28
Evelyn St. M14: Man 1H 131
  OL1: O'ham 6H 59
Evenholme Flats WA14: Bow 3D 150
Evening St. M35: Fail 3H 89
Evenly Cl. M11: Man 1G 117
Eventhall Ho. M25: Pres 2G 85
Everard Cl. M28: Wors 2G 81
Everard St. M5: Sal 3B 8 (6A 100)
Everbrom Rd. BL3: Bolt 5G 47
Everdingen Wlk. OL1: O'ham 4B 60
Everest Av. OL7: A Lyme 6H 91
Everest Cl. SK14: Hyde 3E 121
  SK16: Duk 4H 105
Everest Rd. SK14: Hyde 3E 121
Everest St. OL11: Roch 3A 42
Everett Ct. M20: Man 3F 131
           (off Aldborough St.)
Everett Rd. M20: Man 3E 131
Everglade OL8: O'ham 2G 91
Evergreen M. M7: Sal 4B 86
Evergreen Wlk. M33: Sale 3E 127
           (off Epping Dr.)
Everleigh Cl. BL2: Bolt 6A 20
Everleigh Dr. M7: Sal 5D 86
Eversden Ct. M7: Sal 1C 100
Eversham Av. SK4: Stoc 6D 132
Everside Cl. M28: Walk 4G 65
Everside Dr. M8: Sal 6C 86
Eversley Ct. M33: Sale 1B 140

Eversley Rd. M20: Man 6E 131
Everton Rd. OL8: O'ham 6D 74
  SK5: Stoc 5H 117
Everton St. M27: Swin 3G 83
Every St. BL0: Ram 3D 12
  BL9: Bury 1C 176 (1F 37)
  M4: Man 6G 7 (4H 101)
Evesham Av. M23: Wyth 4D 140
Evesham Cl. BL3: Bolt 1B 48
           (off Punch St.)
  M24: Mid 4D 72
Evesham Dr. BL4: Farn 5F 49
  SK9: Wilm 5G 165
Evesham Gdns. M24: Mid 4C 72
Evesham Gro. M33: Sale 5E 129
  OL6: A Lyme 4A 92
Evesham Rd. M9: Man 1C 88
  M24: Mid 4C 72
  SK8: Chea 1C 156
Evesham Wlk. BL3: Bolt 2B 48
           (off Stanway Cl.)
  M24: Mid 4D 72
  OL8: O'ham 4E 75
Eveside Cl. SK8: Chea H 1D 156
Eve St. OL8: O'ham 1F 91
Evington Av. M11: Man 6A 104
Ewan Fields 5D 120
Ewan St. M18: Man 1F 117
Ewart Av. M5: Sal 4G 99
Ewart Ct. SK13: Had 2H 123
           (off Wesley St.)
Ewart St. BL1: Bolt 3C 32
Ewhurst Av. M27: Swin 5F 83
Ewing Cl. M8: Man 2E 87
Ewood OL8: O'ham 3G 91
Ewood Dr. BL8: Bury 5A 36
Ewood Ho. M30: Ecc 3H 97
Exbourne Rd. M22: Wyth 4A 154
Exbridge Wlk. M40: Man 1F 103
           (off Stansfield Rd.)
Exbury OL12: Roch 1A 178
Exbury St. M14: Man 1H 131
Excalibur Way M44: Irl 2C 124
Excelsior Gdns. OL10: H'ood 5B 40
Excelsior Ter. OL15: L'ough 6F 17
           (off Barke St.)
Exchange Ct. M4: Man 4A 6
Exchange Quay M5: Sal 1G 113
Exchange Quay Station (Metro) 1G 113
Exchange Sq. M3: Man 4H 5 (3D 100)
Exchange St. BL0: Eden 2G 13
  BL1: Bolt 4F 175 (6D 32)
  M2: Man 5H 5 (4D 100)
  OL4: O'ham 2H 75
           (off Gravel Walks)
  SK3: Stoc 3E 179 (2G 145)
Exeter Av. BL2: Bolt 3F 33
  BL4: Farn 6D 48
  M26: Rad 2G 51
  M30: Ecc 1A 98
  M34: Dent 6F 119
Exeter Cl. SK8: Chea H 5B 156
  SK16: Duk 1B 120
Exeter Ct. M14: Man 2G 131
           (off Wilmslow Rd.)
  M24: Mid 6B 56
  OL6: A Lyme 4B 92
Exeter Dr. M44: Irl 5F 109
  OL6: A Lyme 4B 92
Exeter Gro. OL11: Roch 6C 178
Exeter Rd. M41: Urm 3F 111
  SK5: Stoc 4C 134
Exeter St. M6: Sal 3E 99
           (off Langton St.)
  OL11: Roch 6C 178 (6H 27)
Exeter Wlk. SK7: Bram 6H 157
Exford Cl. M40: Man 2G 7 (2H 101)
  SK5: Stoc 3H 133
Exford Dr. BL2: Bolt 1C 50
Exhall Cl. M38: Lit H 3E 65
Exmoor Cl. OL6: A Lyme 4A 92
Exmoor Wlk. M23: Wyth 2G 153
Exmouth Av. SK5: Stoc 4C 134
Exmouth Pl. OL16: Roch 2B 42

Exmouth Rd. M33: Sale 4F **127**
Exmouth Sq. OL16: Roch 2A **42**
Exmouth St. OL16: Roch 2A **42**
Express Trad. Est. BL4: Farn 3A **66**
Eyam Cl. SK13: Gam 4F **123**
             (off Eyam M.)
Eyam Fold SK13: Gam 5F **123**
          (off Haddon M.)
Eyam Gdns. SK13: Gam 5F **123**
             (off Eyam M.)
Eyam Grn. SK13: Gam 5F **123**
     (off Grassmoor Cres.)
Eyam Gro. SK2: Stoc 6D **146**
  SK13: Gam 5F **123**
     (off Grassmoor Cres.)
Eyam La. SK13: Gam 5F **123**
Eyam Lea SK13: Gam 5G **123**
             (off Eyam M.)
Eyam M. SK13: Gam 5G **123**
Eyam Rd. SK7: H Gro 5E **159**
Eycott Dr. M24: Mid 6H **55**
Eyebrook Rd. WA14: Bow 3B **150**
Eynford Av. SK5: Stoc 3B **134**
Eyre St. M15: Man 6A **10** (2E **115**)

F

Faber St. M4: Man 1B **6** (2E **101**)
FACIT 3B **14**
Factory Brow M24: Mid 2G **71**
Factory La. M5: Sal 5C **4**
  M9: Man 2G **87**
Factory St. BL0: Ram 2C **12**
  M24: Mid 1B **72**
  M26: Rad 4B **52**
FAILSWORTH 4H **89**
Failsworth Ind. Est. M35: Fail 5E **89**
Failsworth Pct. M35: Fail 4H **89**
Failsworth Rd. M35: Fail 4B **90**
Failsworth Sports Cen. 4A **90**
Failsworth Station (Rail) 3G **89**
Fairacres BL2: Bolt 2A **34**
Fairacres Rd. SK6: H Lan 5C **160**
Fairbairn Apartments
  M4: Man 4D **6**
Fairbank M43: Droy 5H **103**
Fairbank Av. M14: Man 3F **115**
Fairbank Dr. M24: Mid 5H **55**
Fairbottom St.
  OL1: O'ham 3H **177** (2F **75**)
Fairbottom Wlk. M43: Droy 5A **104**
          (off Wood Sq.)
Fairbourne Av. SK9: A Edg 6E **173**
  SK9: Wilm 5C **172**
Fairbourne Cl. SK9: Wilm 5C **172**
Fairbourne Dr. SK9: Wilm 5C **172**
  WA15: Tim 2B **140**
Fairbourne Rd. M19: Man 6E **117**
  M34: Dent 5E **119**
Fairbourne Wlk. OL1: O'ham 6A **60**
Fairbrook Dr. M6: Sal 3E **99**
Fairbrother St. M5: Sal 4A **8** (6A **100**)
Fairburn Cl. M41: Urm 3C **110**
Fairclough St. BL3: Bolt 3D **48**
  M11: Man 3C **102**
Fairfax Av. M20: Man 5F **131**
  WA15: Tim 5A **140**
Fairfax Cl. SK6: Mar 4B **148**
Fairfax Dr. OL15: L'ough 6F **17**
  SK9: Wilm 5C **172**
Fairfax Rd. M25: Pres 4G **69**
FAIRFIELD
  BL9 .2B **38**
  M43 .5A **104**
Fairfield Av. M43: Droy 5A **104**
  SK6: Bred 5G **135**
  SK8: Chea H 3B **156**
Fairfield Ct. M14: Man 3H **115**
  M43: Droy 5H **103**
Fairfield Dr. BL9: Bury 2B **38**
Fairfield Ho. M43: Droy 4A **104**
     (off Manchester Rd.)

Fairfield Rd. BL4: Farn 2G **65**
  M11: Man 6G **103**
  M24: Mid 6A **56**
  M43: Droy 5G **103**
  M44: Cad 4A **124**
  WA15: Tim 6C **140**
Fairfields BL7: Eger 3D **18**
  OL8: O'ham 1E **91**
Fairfield Sq. M43: Droy 5A **104**
        (not continuous)
Fairfield Station (Rail) 6A **104**
Fairfield St. M1: Man 1C **10** (5F **101**)
  M6: Sal 6D **84**
  M12: Man 2G **11** (5H **101**)
Fairfield Vw. M34: Aud 6A **104**
Fairford Cl. SK5: Stoc 4H **133**
Fairford Dr. BL3: Bolt 2C **48**
Fairford Way SK5: Stoc 4H **133**
  SK9: Wilm 6G **173**
Fairham Wlk. M4: Man 6H **7** (4H **101**)
Fairhaven Av. BL5: W'ton 6B **46**
  M21: Chor 1H **129**
  M45: White 2D **68**
Fairhaven Cvn. Pk.
  SK14: Hyde 5A **122**
Fairhaven Cl. SK7: Bram 5H **157**
Fairhaven Rd. BL1: Bolt 2D **32**
Fairhaven St. M12: Man 1B **116**
Fairhills Ind. Est. M44: Irl 1D **124**
Fairhills Rd. M44: Irl 1D **124**
Fairholme Av. M41: Urm 6E **111**
Fairholme Cvn. Pk. M8: Man 1F **101**
Fairholme Rd. M20: Man 3G **131**
  SK4: Stoc 6E **133**
Fairhope Av. M6: Sal 1B **98**
Fairhope Ct. M6: Sal 2C **98**
       (off Fairhope Av.)
Fairhurst Dr. M28: Walk 1D **80**
Fairisle Cl. M11: Man 4B **102**
Fairlands Pl. OL11: Roch 3B **42**
Fairlands Rd. BL9: Bury 4F **23**
  M33: Sale 1H **139**
Fairlands St. OL11: Roch 3B **42**
Fairlands Vw. OL11: Roch 3B **42**
Fairlawn SK4: Stoc 6F **133**
Fairlawn Cl. M14: Man 3E **115**
Fairlea M34: Dent 5G **119**
Fairlea Av. M20: Man 1G **143**
Fairlee Av. M34: Aud 4C **104**
Fairleigh Av. M6: Sal 2C **98**
Fairless Rd. M30: Ecc 4F **97**
Fairlie Av. BL3: Bolt 2F **47**
Fairlie Dr. WA15: Tim 3B **140**
Fairman St. M16: W Ran 4D **114**
Fairmead Rd. M23: Wyth 2A **142**
Fairmile Dr. M20: Man 3G **143**
Fairmount Av. BL2: Bolt 5A **34**
Fairmount Rd. M27: Swin 5D **82**
Fairoak Ct. BL3: Bolt 2B **48**
Fair Oak Rd. M19: Man 4B **132**
Fairstead Wlk. M11: Man 6H **103**
Fair St. BL3: Bolt 5A **48**
  M1: Man 6E **7** (4G **101**)
  M27: Pen 2A **84**
Fairthorne Grange OL7: A Lyme 4F **105**
      (off Bennett St.)
Fairview Av. M19: Man 5B **116**
  M34: Dent 6A **118**
Fairview Cl. OL9: Chad 1G **73**
  OL12: Roch 1G **25**
  SK6: Mar 4D **148**
Fairview Dr. SK6: Mar 4D **148**
Fairview Rd. M34: Dent 5A **118**
  WA15: Tim 6C **140**
Fair Vw. Ter. OL15: L'ough 3A **16**
Fairway M25: Pres 1B **86**
  M27: Pen 4C **84**
  M43: Droy 5A **104**
  OL11: Roch 4D **40**
  OL12: Whitw 2E **15**
  OL16: Miln 5G **29**
  SK7: Bram 1F **167**
  SK8: Gat 1F **155**

Fairway, The M40: Man 4E **89**
  SK2: Stoc 4D **146**
Fairway Av. BL2: Bolt 1C **34**
  M23: Wyth 4D **140**
Fairway Ct. M34: Dent 3B **118**
Fairway Cres. OL2: O'ham 1D **58**
Fairway Dr. M33: Sale 1G **139**
Fairway Ho. SK4: Stoc 5C **132**
Fairway Rd. BL9: Bury 4G **53**
  OL4: O'ham 5C **76**
Fairways, The M45: White 3F **69**
  OL2: O'ham 2D **58**
Fairwood Rd. M23: Wyth 4D **140**
Fairy La. M8: Man 6C **86**
  M33: Sale 5F **129**
Fairy St. BL8: Bury 3C **36**
Fairywell Cl. SK9: Wilm 6H **165**
Fairywell Dr. M33: Sale 2A **140**
Fairywell Rd. WA15: Tim 3B **140**
Faith St. BL1: Bolt 4G **31**
Falcon Av. M41: Urm 5G **111**
Falcon Bus. Cen. OL9: Chad 1C **74**
Falcon Cl. BL9: Bury 1H **37**
  M50: Sal 4C **98**
  OL12: Roch 1H **25**
Falcon Ct. M7: Sal 2B **86**
  M15: Man 2C **114**
  M50: Sal 5D **98**
Falcon Cres. M27: Clif 1B **84**
Falcon Dr. M24: Mid 4A **56**
  M38: Lit H 4E **65**
  M44: Irl 3F **109**
  OL9: Chad 1C **74**
Falcon Ho. BL9: Bury 1G **37**
Falcon St. BL1: Bolt 1F **175** (5D **32**)
  OL8: O'ham 6F **177** (4E **75**)
Falcon's Vw. OL8: O'ham 6E **75**
Falconwood Chase M28: Wors 5F **81**
Falconwood Way M11: Man 5B **102**
Falfield Dr. M8: Man 6F **87**
Falinge Fold OL12: Roch 2F **27**
Falinge Mnr. M. OL12: Roch 2G **27**
Falinge M. OL12: Roch 2A **178** (3G **27**)
Falinge Rd. OL12: Roch 1A **178** (2F **27**)
Falkirk Dr. BL2: Bolt 1B **50**
Falkirk St. OL4: O'ham 2A **76**
Falkirk Wlk. M23: Wyth 3G **153**
Falkland Av. M40: Man 1H **101**
  OL11: Roch 3E **27**
Falkland Cl. OL4: O'ham 3C **60**
Falkland Ho. M14: Man 6G **115**
Falkland Rd. BL2: Bolt 6C **34**
Fall Bank SK4: Stoc 3F **133**
Fall Birch Rd. BL6: Los 5A **30**
Fallons Rd. M28: Ward 2E **83**
Fallow Av. M18: Man 5F **117**
FALLOWFIELD 1G **131**
Fallowfield Av. M5: Sal 5H **99**
Fallowfield Dr. OL12: Roch 1F **27**
Fallow Flds. Dr. SK5: Stoc 6A **118**
Fallowfield Shop. Cen. M14: Man . . .6A **116**
Fallows, The OL9: Chad 4A **74**
Falls Grn. Av. M40: Man 5C **88**
Falls Gro. SK8: H Grn 2E **155**
Falmer Cl. BL8: Bury 5C **22**
  M18: Man 1H **117**
Falmer Dr. M22: Wyth 4A **154**
Falmouth Av. M33: Sale 4F **127**
  M41: Urm 4A **110**
Falmouth Cres. SK5: Stoc 4C **134**
Falmouth Rd. M44: Irl 5F **109**
Falmouth St. M40: Man 1B **102**
  OL8: O'ham 5F **75**
  OL11: Roch 6A **28**
Falsgrave Cl. M40: Man 6C **88**
Falshaw Dr. BL9: Bury 2E **23**
Falside Wlk. M40: Man 6E **89**
Falstaff M. SK6: Bred 6G **135**
     (off Thomas St.)
Falston Av. M40: Man 1F **89**
Falstone Av. BL0: Ram 5C **12**
Falterley Rd. M23: Wyth 3F **141**
Fancroft Rd. M22: Wyth 6A **142**

Fane Wlk.—Fernhill

Fane Wlk. M9: Man .6F 71
Faraday Av. M8: Man .5E 87
M27: Clif .1D 84
Faraday Dr. BL1: Bolt .4C 32
Faraday Ri. OL12: Roch .2D 26
Faraday St. M1: Man .4C 6 (4F 101)
Farcroft Av. M26: Rad .1C 52
Farcroft Cl. M23: Wyth .3F 141
SK2: Stoc .4E 147
Far Cromwell Rd. SK6: Bred .2D 134
Fardale OL2: Shaw .1H 59
Farden Dr. M23: Wyth .3D 140
Farewell Cl. OL11: Roch .3E 41
Far Hey Cl. M26: Rad .4G 51
Farholme OL2: O'ham .5C 58
Faringdon OL11: Roch .6A 178 (5G 27)
Faringdon Wlk. BL3: Bolt .2C 48
Farland Pl. BL3: Bolt .2F 47
Farlands Dr. M20: Man .4F 143
Farlands Ri. OL16: Roch .2C 42
Far La. M18: Man .3F 117
Farleigh Cl. BL5: W'ton .5A 46
Farley Av. M18: Man .3A 118
Farley Ct. SK8: Chea H .2B 156
Farley Rd. M33: Sale .1C 140
Farley Way SK5: Stoc .6G 117
Farman St. BL3: Bolt .4B 48
Farm Av. M32: Stre .3A 112
Farm Cl. BL8: Tot .5H 21
SK4: Stoc .3E 133
Farmers Cl. M33: Sale .6G 129
Farmer St. SK4: Stoc .6F 133
Farmfield M33: Sale .3G 127
Farmfold SK9: Sty .3D 164
Farm Hill M25: Pres .4E 69
Farmlands Wlk. OL1: O'ham .3A 60
Farm La. M25: Pres .1C 70
M28: Wors .6B 82
SK12: Dis .1E 171
SK14: Hyde .1B 136
Farm Rd. OL8: O'ham .3C 90
Farmside Av. M44: Irl .4E 109
Farm Side Pl. M19: Man .6C 116
Farmstead Cl. M35: Fail .5C 90
Farm St. M35: Fail .5F 89
OL1: Chad .6B 58
OL10: H'ood .5A 40
Farm Wlk. OL15: L'ough .4F 17
OL16: Roch .2C 28
WA14: Bow, D Mas .3A 150
Farmway M24: Mid .2C 72
Farm Yd. M19: Man .6C 116
Farn Av. SK5: Stoc .5G 117
Farnborough Av. OL4: O'ham .3B 76
Farnborough Rd. BL1: Bolt .5C 18
M40: Man .1G 7 (2H 101)
Farncombe Cl. *M23: Wyth .4D 140*
(off Petersfield Dr.)
Farndale Sq. M28: Walk .6G 65
Farndale Wlk. *M9: Man .3A 88*
(off Caversham Dr.)
Farndon Av. SK7: H Gro .1F 159
Farndon Cl. M33: Sale .6E 129
Farndon Dr. WA15: Tim .5A 140
Farndon Rd. SK5: Stoc .5G 117
Farnham Av. M9: Man .4H 71
Farnham Cl. *BL1: Bolt .4C 32*
(off Bk. Ashford Wlk.)
SK8: Chea H .6C 156
Farnham Dr. M44: Irl .6E 109
Farnhill Wlk. M23: Wyth .2E 141
Farnley Cl. OL12: Roch .1B 26
Farnsworth Av. OL7: A Lyme .6H 91
Farnsworth Cl. OL7: A Lyme .6H 91
FARNWORTH .1H 65
Farnworth & Kearsley By-Pass
BL4: Farn, Kea .5H 49
Farnworth Dr. M14: Man .5G 115
Farnworth Leisure Cen. .1H 65
Farnworth Station (Rail) .6A 50
Farnworth St. BL3: Bolt .3A 48
OL10: H'ood .3G 39
Farrand Rd. OL8: O'ham .1B 90
Farrant Ho. M12: Man .3C 116
Farrant Rd. M12: Man .3C 116
Farrar Rd. M43: Droy .5H 103
Farrell St. M7: Sal .1E 5 (2C 100)
Farrer Rd. M13: Man .4B 116
Far Ridings SK6: Rom .6B 136
Farrier Cl. M33: Sale .6F 129
Farriers La. OL11: Roch .1D 40
Farringdon Dr. M26: Rad .3G 51
Farringdon St. M6: Sal .2E 99
Farrington Av. M20: Man .2E 131
Farrowdale Av. OL2: Shaw .1H 59
Farrow St. OL2: Shaw .1H 59
(not continuous)
Farrow St. E. *OL2: Shaw .1H 59*
(off Market St.)
Farr St. SK3: Stoc .3F 145
Farwood Cl. *M16: Old T .2A 114*
(off Stanley Rd.)
Fastnet St. M11: Man .5C 102
Fatherford Cl. OL3: Dig .2F 63
Faulkenhurst M. OL1: Chad .6C 58
Faulkenhurst St. OL1: Chad .6C 58
Faulkner Dr. WA15: Tim .1B 152
Faulkner Rd. M32: Stre .5E 113
Faulkner St. BL3: Bolt .2C 48
M1: Man .1A 10 (5E 101)
OL16: Roch .3C 178 (4H 27)
Faversham Brow *OL1: O'ham .1E 75*
(off Sunfield Rd.)
Faversham St. M40: Man .4D 88
Fawborough Rd. M23: Wyth .2F 141
Fawcett St. BL2: Bolt .6F 33
Fawley Av. SK14: Hyde .6B 120
Fawley Gro. M22: Wyth .1B 154
Fawns Keep SK9: Wilm .2G 173
SK15: Stal .1A 122
Fay Av. M9: Man .6D 72
Fay Gdns. SK13: Had .3G 123
Faywood Dr. SK6: Mar .5E 149
Fearn Dene OL12: Roch .1D 26
Fearneyside BL3: Lit L .4B 50
Fearnhead Cl. BL4: Farn .1A 66
Fearnhead St. BL3: Bolt .3A 48
Fearn St. OL10: H'ood .3G 39
Featherstall Brook Vw.
OL15: L'ough .4G 17
(off William St.)
Featherstall Ho. *OL9: O'ham .4C 74*
(off Featherstall Rd. Sth.)
Featherstall Rd. OL15: L'ough .4F 17
Featherstall Rd. Nth. OL1: O'ham .2D 74
OL9: O'ham .2D 74
Featherstall Rd. Nth. Rdbt.
OL9: O'ham .1D 74
(off Featherstall Rd. Nth.)
Featherstall Rd. Sth. OL9: O'ham .4C 74
Featherstall Sq. OL15: L'ough .4G 17
Federation St. M4: Man .3A 6 (3E 101)
M25: Pres .4F 69
Feldom Rd. M23: Wyth .1F 141
Fellbridge Cl. BL5: W'ton .6A 46
Fellbrigg Cl. M18: Man .4E 117
Fellfoot Cl. M28: Wors .6D 80
Fellfoot Mdw. BL5: W'ton .5A 46
Felling Wlk. *M14: Man .4F 115*
(off Gt. Western St.)
Fellpark Rd. M23: Wyth .1G 141
Fells Gro. M28: Walk .2B 82
Fellside BL2: Bolt .2C 34
OL1: O'ham .2F 177 (2E 75)
Fellside Cl. BL8: G'mount .2H 21
Fellside Gdns. OL15: L'ough .2F 17
Fellside Grn. SK15: Stal .2E 107
Fell St. BL8: Bury .3C 36
Felltop Ct. OL4: Lyd .4G 77
Felltop Dr. SK5: Stoc .1A 134
Felsham Cl. BL4: Farn .6G 49
Felskirk Rd. M22: Wyth .5A 154
Felsted BL1: Bolt .5E 31
Felt Ct. M34: Dent .5C 118
Feltham St. M12: Man .1C 116
Felthorpe Dr. M8: Man .5D 86
Felton Av. M22: Wyth .2B 154
Felton Cl. BL9: Bury .2G 53
Felton Wlk. BL1: Bolt .3C 32
Fencegate Av. SK4: Stoc .4F 133
Fence St. SK2: Stoc .1D 158
Fenchurch Av. M40: Man .1E 103
Fencot Dr. M12: Man .3C 116
Fenella St. M13: Man .3A 116
Fenham Cl. M40: Man .6G 87
Fenmore Av. M18: Man .4D 116
Fennel St. M4: Man .3H 5 (3D 100)
Fenners Cl. BL3: Bolt .4B 48
Fenney St. M7: Sal .6B 86
Fenney St. E. M7: Sal .5C 86
Fenn St. M15: Man .5E 9 (1C 114)
FENNY HILL .5H 75
Fenside Rd. M22: Shar .6C 142
Fenstock Wlk. *M40: Man .1F 103*
(off Assheton Rd.)
Fentewan Wlk. SK14: Hat .4A 122
Fenton Av. SK7: H Gro .1C 158
Fenton M. OL11: Roch .6G 27
Fenton St. BL8: Bury .2C 36
M12: Man .2C 116
OL2: Shaw .2H 59
OL4: O'ham .3H 75
OL11: Roch .6G 27
Fenwick Dr. M24: Mid .6H 55
SK4: Stoc .6A 132
Fenwick St. M15: Man .5A 10 (1E 115)
OL12: Roch .4G 27
Ferdinand St. M40: Man .1H 101
Fereday St. M28: Walk .5H 65
Ferguson Ct. M19: Man .1B 132
Ferguson Gdns. OL12: Roch .6H 15
Ferguson Way OL4: O'ham .6B 60
Fernacre M33: Sale .4C 128
Fernally St. SK14: Hyde .5C 120
Fern Av. M41: Urm .5C 110
FERN BANK .4G 107
Fern Bank M40: Man .4E 89
SK15: Stal .5G 107
Fernbank M26: Rad .1A 68
Fern Bank Cl. SK15: Stal .5G 107
Fern Bank Ct. *SK14: Hyde .1C 136*
(off Fern Bank St.)
Fern Bank Dr. M23: Wyth .3E 141
Fern Bank St. SK14: Hyde .1C 136
Fernbray Av. M19: Man .5H 131
Fernbrook Wlk. *M8: Man .4D 86*
(off Highshore Dr.)
Fern Cl. M24: Mid .1F 73
OL4: Spri .3D 76
SK6: Mar .5D 148
Fern Clough BL1: Bolt .6F 31
Fernclough Rd. M9: Man .4H 87
Fern Comn. OL2: Shaw .6H 43
Fern Cott. OL4: Grot .4E 77
Fern Cres. SK15: Stal .5G 107
Ferndale *SK9: Hand .4H 165*
(off Station Rd.)
SK14: Hyde .1E 121
Ferndale Av. M45: White .2C 68
OL16: Roch .5C 42
SK2: Stoc .1B 158
Ferndale Cl. OL4: O'ham .5B 76
Ferndale Gdns. M19: Man .3A 132
Ferndale Rd. M33: Sale .1B 140
Ferndene Gdns. M20: Man .4F 131
Ferndene Rd. M20: Man .4F 131
M25: Pres .2A 70
M45: White .2A 70
Ferndown Av. OL9: Chad .2F 73
SK7: H Gro .4C 158
Ferndown Dr. M44: Irl .4E 109
Ferndown Rd. BL2: Bolt .2A 34
M23: Wyth .3D 140
Ferney Fld. Rd.
OL9: Chad .2H 73
Ferngate Dr. M20: Man .3F 131
FERN GROVE .1A 38
Ferngrove BL9: Bury .6H 23
FERNHILL .1C 176 (1F 37)

Fernhill—First Av.

Fernhill OL4: Gras 3A 78
OL4: O'ham 5B 76
SK6: Mel 5F 149
Fernhill Av. BL3: Bolt 3G 47
Fernhill Cvn. Pk. BL9: Bury 1E 37
Fernhill Dr. M18: Man 3D 116
FERNHILL GATE 4G 47
Fern Hill La. OL12: Roch 6C 14
Fernhills BL7: Eger 1C 18
Fernhill St. BL9: Bury 1C 176 (2F 37)
Fernholme Ct. OL8: O'ham 5C 74
Fern Ho. M23: Wyth 1G 153
Fernhurst Gro. BL1: Bolt 4C 32
(off Lindfield Dr.)
Fernhurst Rd. M20: Man 4G 131
Fernhurst St. OL1: Chad 6C 58
Fernie St. M4: Man 1A 6 (2E 101)
Fern Isle Cl. OL12: Whitw 3D 14
Fern Lea SK14: Holl 1F 123
Fernlea SK4: Stoc 4E 133
SK8: H Grn 4F 155
WA15: Hale 4H 151
Fernlea Av. OL1: Chad 6C 58
Fernlea Cl. OL12: Roch 1D 26
SK13: Had 3G 123
Fernlea Cres. M27: Swin 4G 83
Fernleaf St. M14: Man 3E 115
Fern Lea Gro. M38: Lit H 5D 64
Fernlea Lodge BL4: Farn 2A 66
(off Longcauseway)
Fernleigh Av. M19: Man 6E 117
Fernleigh Dr. M16: Old T 2A 114
Fernley Av. M34: Dent 5G 119
Fernley Rd. SK2: Stoc 5B 146
Fern Lodge Dr. OL6: A Lyme 6B 92
Ferns, The SK14: Hyde 2E 121
Ferns Gro. BL1: Bolt 6H 31
Fernside M26: Rad 2D 66
Fernside Av. M20: Man 4H 131
Fernside Ct. M26: Rad 3E 67
Fernside Gro. M28: Walk 5A 66
Fernside Way OL12: Roch 1C 26
Fernstead BL3: Bolt 1A 48
Fern St. BL0: Ram 2D 12
(not continuous)
BL3: Bolt 1A 48
BL4: Farn 6A 50
BL9: Bury 1C 176 (2F 37)
M4: Man 1A 6 (1E 101)
OL8: O'ham 4D 74
OL9: Chad 1A 74
OL11: Roch 5F 27
OL12: W'le 6C 16
Fernthorpe Av. OL3: Upp 6E 63
Fern Vw. WA15: Tim 6E 141
Fernview Dr. BL0: Ram 2A 22
Fernwood SK6: Mar B 4F 149
Fernwood Av. M18: Man 4F 117
Fernwood Gro. SK9: Wilm 1F 173
Ferrand Lodge OL15: L'ough 2H 17
Ferrand Rd. OL15: L'ough 3H 17
Ferring Wlk. OL9: Chad 3B 74
Ferris St. M11: Man 5F 103
Ferrous Way M44: Irl 3D 124
Ferryhill Rd. M44: Irl 5E 109
Ferrymasters Way M44: Irl 6E 109
Ferry Rd. M44: Irl 5E 109
(not continuous)
Ferry St. M11: Man 5A 102
Festival Village M41: Urm 1G 111
(off The Trafford Cen.)
Fettler Cl. M27: Swin 5H 83
Fewston Cl. BL1: Bolt 6C 18
Fiddick Ct. M6: Sal 3F 99
(off Newport St.)
Fiddlers La. M44: Irl 4F 109
Field Bank Gro. M19: Man 6E 117
Fieldbrook Wlk. BL5: W'ton 6A 46
Field Cl. SK6: Mar 6B 148
SK7: Bram 3F 167
Fieldcroft OL11: Roch 4D 26
Fielden Av. M21: Chor 6H 113
Fielden Ct. M21: Chor 4B 130
FIELDEN PARK 5D 130
Fielden Rd. M20: Man 5D 130
Fielden St. OL15: L'ough 2B 16
(off Todmorden Rd.)
OL15: L'ough 1E 29
(Lit. Clegg Rd.)
Fielders Way M27: Clif 5G 67
Fieldfare Av. M40: Man 1D 102
Fieldfare Way OL7: A Lyme 4G 91
Fieldhead Av. BL8: Bury 3A 36
M29: Ast 6A 80
OL11: Roch 4D 26
Fieldhead M. SK9: Wilm 1H 173
Fieldhead Rd. SK9: Wilm 1H 173
Fieldhouse Ind. Est. OL12: Roch 1H 27
Fieldhouse La. SK6: Mar 5E 149
Fieldhouse Rd. OL12: Roch 1H 27
Fielding Av. SK12: Poy 5E 169
Fielding Ind. Est. M34: Dent 5C 118
Fielding St. M24: Mid 5C 56
(not continuous)
M30: Ecc 4E 97
Fieldings Wharf M43: Droy 5A 104
(off Market St.)
Field La. OL6: A Lyme 6B 92
Field Pl. M20: Man 6F 131
(off Crossway)
Field Rd. M33: Sale 3G 127
OL16: Roch 4D 28
Fields, The SK6: Rom 2G 147
Fields Cres. SK14: Holl 1F 123
Fieldsend Cl. SK15: Stal 5H 107
Fields End Fold M30: Ecc 3G 109
Fields Farm Cl. SK14: Hat 5H 121
Fields Farm Rd. SK14: Hat 6G 121
Fields Farm Wlk. SK14: Hat 5H 121
(off Fields Farm Rd.)
Fields Gro. SK14: Holl 2F 123
Fieldside Cl. SK7: Bram 3F 167
Fields New Rd. OL9: Chad 5A 74
Field St. M6: Sal 3F 99
M18: Man 1G 117
M35: Fail 4G 89
M43: Droy 5H 103
OL11: Roch 1A 42
SK6: Bred 6F 135
SK14: Hyde 2B 120
Fieldsway OL8: O'ham 1E 91
Field Va. Dr. SK5: Stoc 6A 118
Fieldvale Rd. M33: Sale 2G 139
Field Vw. Wlk. M14: Man 5D 114
Field Wlk. M31: Part 6C 124
WA15: Hale 2B 152
Fieldway OL16: Roch 2B 42
Fife Av. OL9: Chad 5H 73
Fifield Cl. OL8: O'ham 6G 75
Fifth Av. BL1: Bolt 6H 31
BL3: Lit L 3B 50
BL9: Bury 1B 38
M11: Man 3E 103
M17: T Pk 2C 112
OL8: O'ham 1C 90
SK16: Duk 5G 105
Fifth St. BL1: Bolt 1F 31
M17: T Pk 2C 112
Filbert St. OL1: O'ham 6A 60
Filby Wlk. M40: Man 1A 102
Fildes St. M24: Mid 2F 73
Filey Av. M16: W Ran 5B 114
M41: Urm 3C 110
Filey Dr. M6: Sal 5D 84
Filey Rd. M14: Man 1H 131
SK2: Stoc 4C 146
Filey St. OL16: Roch 6C 16
Filleigh WA14: Bow 3C 150
Filton Av. BL3: Bolt 2B 48
Filton Wlk. M9: Man 5G 87
(off Westmere Dr.)
Finance St. OL15: L'ough 4E 17
Finborough Cl. M16: W Ran 3C 114
Finchale Dr. WA15: Hale 4B 152
Finch Av. BL4: Farn 2D 64
Finchcroft OL1: O'ham 2E 177 (2E 75)
Finchley Av. M40: Man 1E 103
Finchley Cl. BL8: Bury 4B 36
Finchley Gro. M40: Man 2C 88
Finchley Rd. M14: Man 1F 131
WA15: Hale 2G 151
Finchwood Rd. M22: Shar 6C 142
Findon Rd. M23: Wyth 5G 141
Finger Post BL3: Lit L 3C 50
Finghall Rd. M41: Urm 5D 110
Finland Rd. SK3: Stoc 4F 145
Finlan Rd. M24: Mid 2F 57
Finlay St. BL4: Farn 1H 65
Finney Cl. SK9: Wilm 5G 165
Finney Dr. M21: Chor 2G 129
SK9: Wilm 5G 165
FINNEY GREEN 6H 165
Finney La. SK8: H Grn 4E 155
Finney St. BL3: Bolt 3D 48
Finningley Rd. M9: Man 3F 71
Finny Bank Rd. M33: Sale 3A 128
Finsbury Av. M40: Man 1E 103
Finsbury Cl. OL8: O'ham 5H 75
Finsbury Rd. SK5: Stoc 1G 133
Finsbury St. OL11: Roch 6F 27
Finsbury Way SK9: Hand 5A 166
Finstock Cl. M30: Ecc 4D 96
Fintry Gro. M30: Ecc 4F 97
Fir Av. SK7: Bram 5G 157
Firbank M25: Pres 5A 70
Firbank Cl. OL7: A Lyme 3F 105
Firbank Rd. M23: Wyth 6G 141
OL2: O'ham 1D 58
Firbarn Cl. OL16: Roch 4D 28
Firbeck Dr. M4: Man 3G 7 (3H 101)
Fir Cl. SK7: H Gro 2E 159
SK12: Poy 4E 169
Fircroft Ct. SK3: Stoc 1H 157
Fircroft Rd. OL8: O'ham 1G 91
Firdale Av. M40: Man 2G 89
Firdale Wlk. OL9: Chad 2C 74
Firdon Wlk. M9: Man 4A 88
(off Nethervale Dr.)
Firecrest Cl. M28: Wors 3F 81
Firefly Cl. M3: Sal 5C 4
Fire Sta. Sq. M5: Sal 4A 4 (3A 100)
Fire Sta. Yd. OL11: Roch 6C 178 (5H 27)
Firethorn Av. M19: Man 3B 132
Firethorn Dr. SK14: Hyde 5E 121
Firethorn Wlk. M33: Sale 4E 127
(off Lavender Cl.)
Firfield Gro. M28: Walk 6B 66
FIRGROVE 4D 28
Fir Gro. M19: Man 6C 116
OL9: Chad 1B 74
Firgrove Av. OL16: Roch 3D 28
Firgrove Bus. Pk. OL16: Roch 2D 28
Firgrove Gdns. OL16: Roch 3D 28
Fir La. OL2: O'ham 1D 58
Fir Rd. BL4: Farn 1F 65
M27: Swin 5G 83
M34: Dent 4G 119
SK6: Mar 6C 148
SK7: Bram 4G 157
Firs, The SK9: Wilm 4D 172
WA14: Bow 3D 150
Firs Av. M16: Old T 5H 113
M35: Fail 4G 89
OL6: A Lyme 6H 91
Firsby Av. SK6: Bred 5F 135
Firsby St. M19: Man 6C 116
(off Barlow Rd.)
Firs Cl. SK8: Gat 2E 155
Firs Gro. SK8: Gat 1E 155
Firs Rd. M33: Sale 5F 127
(not continuous)
SK8: Gat 2E 155
First Av. BL3: Lit L 3C 50
BL8: Tot 5H 21
M11: Man 3F 103
M17: T Pk 2D 112
M27: Swin 6F 83
M29: Ast 6A 80
OL8: O'ham 1D 90

First Av. SK12: Poy 6D **168**
  SK15: C'ook 6A **94**
Fir St. BL0: Ram 2D **12**
  BL1: Bolt 3D **32**
  BL9: Bury 3G **37**
  M6: Sal 3F **99**
  M16: Old T 3A **114**
  (off Worthington St.)
  M26: Rad 5B **52**
  M30: Ecc 4F **97**
  M35: Fail 4G **89**
  M40: Man 1G **7** (1H **101**)
  M44: Cad 3A **124**
  OL2: O'ham 1D **58**
  OL10: H'ood 4A **40**
  SK4: Stoc 1E **179** (1G **145**)
First St. BL1: Bolt 1F **31**
Firsway M33: Sale 6E **127**
FIRSWOOD 4G **113**
Firswood Dr. M27: Swin 5G **83**
  OL2: O'ham 1C **58**
  SK14: Hyde 4E **121**
Firswood Mt. SK8: Gat 1E **155**
Firth Cl. M7: Sal 5B **86**
Firth Rd. M20: Man 4G **131**
Firth St. OL1: O'ham 4G **177** (3F **75**)
Fir Tree Av. M28: Wors 6F **81**
  OL8: O'ham 1F **91**
Firtree Av. M33: Sale 5E **127**
Fir Tree Cl. SK16: Duk 5D **106**
Fir Tree Cres. SK16: Duk 5D **106**
Fir Tree Dr. SK14: Hyde 2C **120**
Fir Tree La. SK16: Duk 6D **106**
Firvale Av. SK8: H Grn 4F **155**
Firwood Av. BL4: Farn 2G **65**
  M41: Urm 5A **112**
  (not continuous)
Firwood Cl. SK2: Stoc 3C **146**
Firwood Ct. M30: Ecc 2G **97**
Firwood Cres. M26: Rad 6B **52**
FIRWOOD FOLD 2G **33**
Firwood Fold BL2: Bolt 2G **33**
Firwood Gro. BL2: Bolt 3F **33**
Firwood Ind. Est. BL2: Bolt 2G **33**
Firwood La. BL2: Bolt 2F **33**
  (not continuous)
Firwood Pk. OL9: Chad 1G **73**
Firwood Stables *BL2: Bolt* *2G 33*
  (off Ashdown Dr.)
Fiscal Way M35: Fail 4G **89**
Fishbourne Sq. *M14: Man* *4G 115*
  (off Claremont Rd.)
Fishbrook Ind. Est. BL4: Kea 2B **66**
Fisherfield OL12: Roch 2B **26**
Fishermans Wharf
  BL3: Bolt 2D **48**
Fishermore Rd. M41: Urm 5A **110**
Fisher St. OL1: O'ham 1H **177** (1F **75**)
FISHPOOL 6C **176** (5F **37**)
Fishwick St. OL16: Roch 5A **28**
Fistral Av. SK8: H Grn 5G **155**
Fistral Cres. SK15: Stal 2H **107**
Fitchfield Wlk. *M28: Walk* *6H 65*
  (off Malvern Gro.)
Fit City
  Broughton Cen. **6B 86**
  Broughton Pool **5B 86**
  Cadishead **4B 124**
  Clarendon **3G 99**
  Eccles *4H 97*
  (off Barton La.)
  Irlam **6E 109**
  Ordsall **6G 99**
  Pendlebury **2G 83**
  Worsley **1G 81**
Fitness First
  Bolton **5G 175**
  Gorton **3G 117**
  Manchester Central **1H 9**
  Moston **6E 73**
  Rochdale **1G 41**
  Whitefeld **6G 53**
Fitton Av. M21: Chor 3H **129**

Fitton Cres. M27: Clif 6H **67**
FITTON HILL 1G **91**
Fitton Hill Rd. OL8: O'ham 5G **75**
Fitton Hill Shop. Pct. OL8: O'ham 1G **91**
Fitton St. OL2: O'ham 3F **59**
  OL2: Shaw 6F **43**
  OL16: Roch 3A **28**
Fitzgeorge St. M40: Man 6G **87**
Fitzgerald Cl. M25: Pres 1F **85**
Fitzgerald Ct. M34: Dent 1G **135**
Fitzgerald Way *M6: Sal* *2F 99*
  (off Salford Shop. City)
Fitzhugh St. BL1: Bolt 6E **19**
Fitzroy St. M43: Droy 5B **104**
  OL7: A Lyme 5F **105**
  SK15: Mill 1H **107**
Fitzwarren Ct. M6: Sal 3F **99**
Fitzwarren St. M6: Sal 2F **99**
Fitzwilliam Ct. M14: Man 3G **115**
Fitzwilliam St. M7: Sal 1D **4** (1B **100**)
Five Fold Ind. Pk. OL9: O'ham 3D **74**
Five Quarters M26: Rad 2G **51**
Fiveways M43: Droy 3H **103**
Fiveways Pde. SK7: H Gro 5E **159**
Flag Cft. Dr. M23: Wyth 6H **141**
Flagგwood Av. SK6: Mar 4B **148**
Flagship Av. *M5: Sal* *5H 99*
  (off St Joseph's Dr.)
Flake La. OL2: O'ham 2D **58**
Flamborough Wlk. *M14: Man* *3F 115*
  (off Gateshead Cl.)
Flamingo Cl. M12: Man 1C **116**
Flamingo Vs. *M44: Irl* *4E 109*
  (off Robin Dr.)
Flamstead Av. M23: Wyth 5E **141**
Flannel St. OL12: Roch 3A **28**
Flash *SK15: C'ook* *4B 94*
  (off Carisbrook Rd.)
Flash Cotts. OL4: O'ham 5E **77**
Flashfields M25: Pres 2F **85**
Flash St. M40: Man 5E **89**
Flatley St. M15: Man 6A **10** (1E **115**)
Flavian Wlk. *M11: Man* *5D 102*
  (off Herne St.)
Flaxcroft Rd. M22: Wyth 2H **153**
Flaxfield Av. SK15: Stal 3H **107**
Flaxman Ri. OL1: O'ham 3A **60**
Flaxpool Cl. M16: W Ran 3C **114**
  (not continuous)
Flax St. BL0: Ram 5A **12**
  M3: Sal 2D **4** (2B **100**)
Flaxwood Wlk. M22: Wyth 2H **153**
Fleece St. *OL4: O'ham* *2H 75*
  (off Honduras St.)
  OL16: Roch 3B **178** (4H **27**)
Fleeson St. M14: Man 4G **115**
Fleet St. M18: Man 1H **117**
  OL4: O'ham 2A **76**
  OL6: A Lyme 6A **174** (3G **105**)
  (not continuous)
  OL11: Roch 5F **41**
  SK14: Hyde 3C **120**
Fleetwood Rd. M28: Walk 6E **65**
Fleming Cl. OL12: Roch 4D **16**
Fleming Pl. OL9: O'ham 3D **74**
Fleming Rd. M22: Wyth 3B **154**
Flemish Rd. M34: Dent 5H **119**
Fletcher Av. M27: Clif 6A **68**
FLETCHER BANK 3D **12**
Fletcher Cl. OL9: O'ham 3D **74**
  OL10: H'ood 3H **39**
Fletcher Ct. *M26: Rad* *5B 52*
  (off New Rd.)
  M26: Rad 1D **66**
  (Stoneclough Ri.)
Fletcher Dr. SK12: Dis 1D **170**
  WA14: Bow 4E **151**
FLETCHER FOLD 1F **53**
Fletcher Fold BL9: Bury 1F **53**
Fletcher Fold Rd. BL9: Bury 1F **53**
Fletcher Moss Botanical Gdns. 2F **143**
Fletchers Pas. OL15: L'ough 3G **17**
Fletcher Sq. M1: Man 6E **7**

Fletcher's Rd. OL15: L'ough 6E **17**
Fletchers Sq. *OL15: L'ough* *3H 17*
  (off Barehill St.)
Fletcher St. BL3: Bolt 6E **175** (2C **48**)
  BL3: Lit L 4D **50**
  BL4: Farn 1H **65**
  BL9: Bury 3G **37**
  M26: Rad 3C **52**
  M40: Man 6B **88**
  OL6: A Lyme 5D **174** (2A **106**)
  OL11: Roch 6A **28**
  OL15: L'ough 3G **17**
  SK1: Stoc 2G **179** (2H **145**)
Fletsand Rd. SK9: Wilm 3F **173**
Fletton Cl. OL12: Roch 1G **27**
Fletton M. OL12: Roch 1G **27**
Flexbury Wlk. *M40: Man* *1F 103*
  (off Eastmoor Dr.)
Flint Cl. M11: Man 3D **102**
  SK7: H Gro 4C **158**
Flint Gro. M44: Cad 3A **124**
Flint St. M43: Droy 3B **104**
  OL1: O'ham 1A **76**
  SK3: Stoc 6F **179** (3G **145**)
Flitcroft Ct. BL3: Bolt 3D **48**
Flitcroft St. OL4: O'ham 5A **76**
FLIXTON 6B **110**
Flixton Rd. M31: Man 6H **11** (2H **115**)
  M31: C'ton 1A **126**
  M41: Urm 6B **110**
  (not continuous)
Flixton Station (Rail) 6B **110**
Floatshall Rd. M23: Wyth 5F **141**
Floats Rd. M23: Wyth 5E **141**
Flora Dr. M7: Sal 1B **100**
Floral Ct. M7: Sal 5B **86**
Flora St. BL3: Bolt 3B **48**
  M9: Man 6G **71**
  OL1: O'ham 2F **177** (2E **75**)
Florence Av. BL1: Bolt 1D **32**
Florence Ct. SK3: Stoc 5D **144**
Florence Pk. Ct. M20: Man 5G **131**
Florence St. BL3: Bolt 3B **48**
  M30: Ecc 4D **96**
  M33: Sale 3B **128**
  M35: Fail 3H **89**
  M43: Droy 5B **104**
  OL16: Roch 5B **28**
  SK4: Stoc 1F **179** (1G **145**)
Florence Way SK14: Holl 2F **123**
Florian Ho. OL1: O'ham 2G **177** (2F **75**)
Florida St. OL8: O'ham 6E **177** (4E **75**)
Florin Gdns. M6: Sal 2F **99**
Florist St. SK3: Stoc 6F **179** (4G **145**)
Flowery Bank OL8: O'ham 5H **75**
Flowery Fld. SK2: Stoc 1A **158**
Flowery Fld. Grn. SK14: Hyde 3A **120**
Flowery Fld. Ind. Pk.
  SK14: Hyde 2B **120**
Flowery Field Station (Rail) 2B **120**
Floyd Av. M21: Chor 3A **130**
Floyer Rd. M9: Man 5A **72**
Flynn Ct. *M6: Sal* *1E 99*
  (off Monroe Cl.)
Foden La. SK7: W'ford 4F **167**
Foden Wlk. SK9: Wilm 1H **165**
FOGGBROOK 5F **147**
Foggbrook Cl. SK2: Stoc 5F **147**
Fogg La. BL3: Bolt 3H **49**
Fog La. M19: Man 5H **131**
  M20: Man 5F **131**
Fog Lane Pk. 5G **131**
Fold, The M9: Man 6H **71**
  M41: Urm 4C **110**
  OL2: O'ham 3G **59**
Fold Av. M43: Droy 3B **104**
Fold Cres. SK15: C'ook 5B **94**
Fold Gdns. OL12: Roch 6D **14**
Fold Grn. OL9: Chad 4A **74**
FOLD HEAD 1D **14**
Fold M. BL9: Bury 5F **23**
  SK7: H Gro 2E **159**

Fold Rd. M26: Rad 2E 67
Folds Rd. BL1: Bolt 2G 175 (5D 32)
Fold St. BL1: Bolt 4G 175 (6D 32)
  BL9: Bury 3D 36
  M40: Man 3C 88
  OL10: H'ood 2A 40
Fold Vw. BL7: Eger 2C 18
  OL8: H'ham 1G 91
Fold Way OL7: A Lyme 2F 105
Foleshill Av. M9: Man 4H 87
Foley Gdns. OL10: H'ood 6A 40
Foley Wlk. M22: Wyth 5C 154
Foliage Cres. SK5: Stoc 5B 134
Foliage Gdns. SK5: Stoc 4C 134
Foliage Rd. SK5: Stoc 5B 134
Folkestone Rd. M11: Man 3F 103
Folkestone Rd. E. M11: Man 3F 103
Folkestone Rd. W. M11: Man 3E 103
Follows St. M18: Man 1F 117
Folly La. M27: Swin 6F 83
Folly Vw. M27: Swin 5F 83
Folly Wlk. OL12: Roch 2H 27
Fonthill Gro. M33: Sale 2H 139
Fontwell Cl. M16: Old T 4A 114
Fontwell La. OL1: O'ham 6G 59
Fontwell Rd. BL3: Lit L 5C 50
Fontwell Wlk. M40: Man 1F 89
Foot Mill Cres. OL12: Roch 1F 27
Foot O' Th' Rake BL0: Ram 3B 12
                    (off Milton St.)
Foot Wood Cres. OL12: Roch 1F 27
Forber Cres. M18: Man 4F 117
Forbes Cl. M33: Sale 1D 140
  SK1: Stoc 3B 146
Forbes Pk. SK7: Bram 6F 157
Forbes Rd. SK1: Stoc 2B 146
Forbes St. SK6: Bred 5F 135
Fordbank Rd. M20: Man 1E 143
Forde Cl. M24: Mid 5C 56
Ford Gdns. OL11: Roch 5D 26
Ford Gro. SK14: Mot 3C 122
Fordham Gro. BL1: Bolt 5A 32
Ford La. M6: Sal 1G 99
  M20: Man 1E 143
  M22: Nor 2C 142
Ford Lodge M20: Man 1F 143
Ford's La. SK7: Bram 1F 167
Ford St. M3: Sal 4D 4 (3B 100)
  M12: Man 5G 11 (6H 101)
  M26: Rad .1C 66
  SK3: Stoc 2F 145
  SK16: Duk 1A 120
Ford Way SK14: Mot 3C 122
Forebay Dr. M44: Irl 6F 109
Foreland Cl. M40: Man 6H 87
Forest Cl. SK16: Duk 1A 120
Forest Ct. M41: Urm 4H 109
Forest Dr. M33: Sale 1G 139
  WA15: Tim 5H 139
Forester Dr. SK15: Stal 4E 107
Forester Hill Av. BL3: Bolt 4E 49
                  (Newport Rd.)
  BL3: Bolt 4D 48
                  (Rishton Av.)
Forester Hill Cl. BL3: Bolt 4D 48
Foresters Grn. M17: T Pk 1E 113
            (off Wharfside Way)
Forest Gdns. M31: Part 6B 124
Forest Range M19: Man 6C 116
Forest Rd. BL1: Bolt 2H 31
Forest St. M30: Ecc 1C 96
  OL6: A Lyme 1A 106
  OL8: O'ham 1F 91
Forest Vw. OL12: Roch 1F 27
Forest Way BL7: Bro X 5G 19
Forfar St. BL1: Bolt 6C 18
Forge Ind. Est.
  OL4: O'ham 2H 75
Forge St. OL4: O'ham 2H 75
Formby Av. M21: Chor 2B 130
Formby Dr. SK8: H Grn 5F 155
Formby Rd. M6: Sal 6E 85
Forrester Dr. OL2: Shaw 5B 44

Forrester Ho. M12: Man 1C 116
             (off Blackwin St.)
Forrester St. M28: Wors 3C 82
Forrest Rd. M34: Dent 6H 119
Forshaw Av. M18: Man 1H 117
Forshaw St. M34: Dent 3D 118
Forston Wlk. M8: Man 5F 87
Forsythia Wlk. M31: Part 6C 124
             (off Blossom Rd.)
Forsyth St. OL12: Roch 1A 26
Fortescue St. SK2: Stoc 4D 146
Forth Pl. M26: Rad 2H 51
Forth Rd. M26: Rad 2H 51
Forton Av. BL2: Bolt 6A 34
Fortran Cl. M5: Sal 4G 99
Fortrose Av. M9: Man 6F 71
Fortuna Gro. M19: Man 1B 132
Fortune St. BL3: Bolt 3F 49
Fortyacre Dr. SK6: Bred 6E 135
Forum Gro. M7: Sal 6C 86
Forum Leisure Cen. 2A 154
Forum Sq. M22: Wyth 2B 154
              (off Ainley Rd.)
Fosbrook Av. M20: Man 5G 131
Foscarn Dr. M23: Wyth 6H 141
Fossgill Av. BL2: Bolt 6G 19
Foster Cl. BL9: Bury 1B 38
Foster La. BL2: Bolt 4B 34
            (not continuous)
Foster St. M5: Sal 4D 98
  M26: Rad .4H 51
  M34: Dent 4F 119
  OL4: O'ham 2A 76
Foster Ter. BL1: Bolt 4C 32
            (off Barnwood Dr.)
Fotherby Dr. M9: Man 6H 71
Fothergill Grange
  SK8: Chea H 5C 156
Foulds Av. BL8: Bury 3A 36
Foundry, The M1: Man 3H 9
Foundry La. M4: Man 4C 6 (3B 101)
Foundry St. BL3: Bolt 2D 48
  BL3: Lit L .6F 50
  BL9: Bury 4D 176 (3F 37)
  M26: Rad .4H 51
  OL8: O'ham 5E 177 (3E 75)
  OL10: H'ood 3G 39
  SK16: Duk 5A 106
            (not continuous)
Fountain Av. WA15: Hale 3B 152
Fountain Cl. SK12: Poy 3D 168
Fountain Pl. M45: White 2F 69
  SK12: Poy 3D 168
             (off Chester Rd.)
Fountains Av. BL2: Bolt 4G 33
Fountains Cl. M29: Ast 4A 80
Fountain Sq. M27: Swin 3H 83
         (off Swinton Shop. Cen.)
  SK12: Dis 1H 171
             (off Market St.)
Fountains Rd. M32: Stre 4H 111
  SK7: Bram 1D 166
  SK8: Chea H 1D 166
Fountain St. BL8: Bury 4C 36
  BL9: Bury 3G 37
  M2: Man 6A 6 (4E 101)
  M24: Mid 1B 72
  M30: Ecc .5E 97
  OL1: O'ham 3F 177 (2E 75)
  OL6: A Lyme 1C 106
  SK14: Hyde 4D 120
Fountain St. Nth. BL9: Bury 3G 37
Fountains Wlk. OL9: Chad 4A 74
  SK16: Duk 1A 120
Fouracres Rd. M23: Wyth 6F 141
FOUR LANE ENDS 6F 21
FOURLANE ENDS 6H 169
Four Lanes SK14: Mot 3C 122
Four Lanes Way
  OL11: Roch 1G 25
Four Stalls End
  OL15: L'ough 5G 17

Fourth Av. BL1: Bolt 6H 31
  BL3: Lit L .3B 50
  BL9: Bury 1A 38
  M11: Man 2E 103
  M17: T Pk 2C 112
  M27: Swin 6F 83
  OL8: O'ham 2C 90
  OL9: Chad 4A 74
  SK5: C'ook 5A 94
Fourth St. BL1: Bolt 1F 31
Fourways M17: T Pk 1A 112
Fourways Wlk. M40: Man 1D 88
Fovant Cres. SK5: Stoc 6G 117
Fowey Wlk. M23: Wyth 6G 141
  SK14: Hat 4A 122
Fowler Av. M18: Man 6H 103
Fowler St. OL8: O'ham 6C 74
Fownhope Av. M33: Sale 6H 127
Fownhope Rd. M33: Sale 6H 127
Foxall Cl. M24: Mid 2G 71
Foxall St. M24: Mid 2G 71
Fox Bank Ct. SK3: Stoc 3F 145
Foxbank St. M13: Man 3A 116
Fox Bench Cl. SK7: Bram 1E 167
Foxbench Wlk. M21: Chor 3B 130
Fox Cl. WA15: Tim 5H 139
Foxcroft St. OL15: L'ough 4F 17
Foxdale St. M11: Man 4E 103
Foxdenton Dr. M32: Stre 4H 111
Foxdenton La. M24: Mid 3G 73
  OL9: Chad 3G 73
Foxdenton Wlk. M34: Dent 6E 119
Foxendale Wlk. BL3: Bolt 2D 48
            (off Fletcher St.)
Foxfield Cl. BL8: Bury 6B 22
Foxfield Dr. OL8: O'ham 2C 90
Foxfield Rd. M23: Wyth 2F 153
Foxfold Cl. M28: Wors 4D 80
Foxford Wlk. M22: Wyth 3C 154
Foxglove Ct. OL12: Roch 6F 15
Foxglove Dr. BL9: Bury 2B 38
  WA14: B'ath 3E 139
Foxglove La. SK15: Stal 2E 107
Foxglove Wlk. M31: Part 6D 124
            (off Cross La. W.)
Foxhall Rd. M34: Dent 3D 118
  WA15: Tim 5G 139
Foxham Wlk. M7: Sal 5C 86
Foxhill OL2: Shaw 5E 43
  WA14: Alt 4C 138
Foxhill Chase SK2: Stoc 6G 147
Fox Hill Cl. SK4: Stoc 1C 144
Fox Hill Dr. SK15: Stal 5G 107
Foxhill Pk. SK15: Stal 5G 107
Fox Hill Rd. OL11: Roch 5F 41
Foxhill Rd. M30: Ecc 4B 96
Foxholes Cl. OL12: Roch 2A 28
Foxholes Rd. OL12: Roch 2A 28
  SK14: Hyde 1A 136
Foxlair Ct. M22: Wyth 2H 153
Foxlair Rd. M22: Wyth 2H 153
Foxland Rd. SK8: Gat 1F 155
Foxley Cl. M43: Droy 5G 103
Foxley Gro. BL3: Bolt 1B 48
Foxley Wlk. M12: Man 2C 116
Fox Pk. Rd. OL8: O'ham 1C 90
FOX PLATT .2G 93
Fox Platt Rd. OL5: Mos 2F 93
Fox Platt Ter. OL5: Mos 3G 93
Fox St. BL9: Bury 1D 176 (2F 37)
  M30: Ecc .3H 97
  OL8: O'ham 1C 90
  OL10: H'ood 3G 39
  OL16: Miln 5E 29
  OL16: Roch 3B 28
  SK3: Stoc 3F 145
Foxton St. M24: Mid 2G 71
Foxton Wlk. M23: Wyth 2G 153
Foxwell Wlk. M8: Man 5F 87
            (off Moordown Cl.)
Foxwood Dr. OL5: Mos 1H 93
  SK14: Hyde 3C 120

Foxwood Gdns. M19: Man 4A **132**
Foynes Cl. M40: Man 6H **87**
Frame, The M11: Man 3C **102**
Framingham Rd. M33: Sale 6A **128**
Framley Rd. M21: Chor 2D **130**
Frampton Cl. M24: Mid 2D **72**
Fram St. M6: Sal 3E **99**
   M9: Man .3B **88**
Frances Av. SK8: Gat 5E **143**
Francesca Wlk. *M18: Man* *1F* **117**
   (off Briercliffe Cl.)
Frances St. BL1: Bolt 3B **32**
   M13: Man .5D **10**
   OL1: O'ham 6G **59**
   OL16: Roch 6D **16**
   SK3: Stoc 4F **179** (3G **145**)
   SK8: Chea 5A **144**
   SK14: Hyde 4A **120**
Frances St. W. SK14: Hyde 4A **120**
Francis Av. M28: Walk 1B **82**
   M30: Ecc 3G **97**
Francis Rd. M20: Man 4G **131**
   M44: Irl 1D **124**
Francis St. BL4: Farn 6H **49**
   M3: Man 1G **5** (2D **100**)
   M29: Tyld .3B **80**
   M30: Ecc 2F **97**
   M34: Dent .1H **135**
   M35: Fail 4H **89**
   M44: Cad .4C **124**
Francis Ter. *SK16: Duk* *4A* **106**
   (off Astley St.)
Francis Thompson Dr.
   OL6: A Lyme 4B **174**
Frandley Wlk. M13: Man 3D **10**
Frankby Cl. M27: Pen 4C **84**
Frank Cowin Ct. *M7: Sal* *1B* **100**
   (off Fitzwilliam St.)
Frank Fold OL10: H'ood 3E **39**
Frankford Av. BL1: Bolt 3A **32**
Frankford Sq. BL1: Bolt 3A **32**
FRANK HILL 1F **177** (1E **75**)
Frank Hulme Ho. M32: Stre 6E **113**
Frankland Cl. M11: Man 3D **102**
Franklin Cl. OL1: O'ham 1F **177** (1E **75**)
Franklin St. M30: Ecc 3F **97**
   OL1: O'ham 1F **177** (1E **75**)
Franklyn Av. M41: Urm 5A **110**
Franklyn Cl. M34: Dent 5A **118**
Franklyn Rd. M18: Man 1G **117**
   M43: Droy 4A **104**
Franklyn Ter. *OL15: L'ough* *4G* **17**
   (off Church Rd.)
Frank Perkins Way M44: Irl 2D **124**
Frank Price Ct. M22: Wyth 2A **154**
Frank St. BL1: Bolt 3B **32**
   BL9: Bury 5D **176** (4F **37**)
   M1: Man .3A **10**
   M6: Sal 1G **99**
   M35: Fail .4G **89**
   SK14: Hyde 5C **120**
Frank Swift Wlk. *M14: Man* *4E* **115**
   (off Fred Tilson Cl.)
Frankton Rd. M45: White 2F **69**
Franton Rd. M11: Man 3D **102**
Fraser Av. M33: Sale 6E **129**
Fraser Ho. *BL1: Bolt* *4B* **32**
   (off Kirkhope Dr.)
Fraser Pl. M17: T Pk 3C **112**
Fraser Rd. M8: Man 2D **86**
Fraser St. M27: Pen 2A **84**
   OL2: Shaw 5G **43**
   OL6: A Lyme 2A **106**
   OL16: Roch 1B **42**
Fraternitas Ter. M43: Droy 2G **103**
Frecheville Ct. BL9: Bury 6B **176** (4E **37**)
Frecheville Pl. M22: Bury 5B **176** (4E **37**)
Freckleton Av. M21: Chor 5B **130**
Freckleton Dr. BL8: Bury 4H **35**
Freda Wlk. *M11: Man* *4B* **102**
   (off Doric Cl.)
Frederick Av. OL2: Shaw 2H **59**

Frederick Ct. BL4: Farn 1A **66**
   SK15: A Lyme *3C* **106**
   (off Clarence St.)
Frederick Rd. M6: Sal 2H **99**
   M7: Sal 2H **99**
Frederick St. BL0: Ram 4B **12**
   BL4: Farn .1H **65**
   M3: Sal 4E **5** (3C **100**)
   M34: Dent .2E **119**
   OL6: A Lyme 3C **106**
   OL8: O'ham 4C **74**
   OL9: Chad .1B **74**
   OL15: L'ough 3G **17**
Frederick Ter. *M9: Man* *2H* **87**
   (off Slack Rd.)
Fred Tilson Cl. M14: Man 4E **115**
Freehold St. OL11: Roch 6A **178** (6G **27**)
Freelands M29: Tyld 2A **80**
Freeland Wlk. *M11: Man* *5E* **103**
   (off Eccles Cl.)
Freeman Av. OL6: A Lyme 2B **106**
Freeman Rd. SK16: Duk 1A **120**
Freeman Sq. M15: Man 6A **10** (1E **115**)
Freemantle Av. M18: Man 4F **117**
Freemantle St. SK3: Stoc 3E **145**
Freesia Av. M38: Lit H 6D **64**
Freestone Cl. BL8: Bury . . .1A **176** (2D **36**)
FREETOWN .1G **37**
Freetown Bus. Pk. BL9: Bury 1G **37**
Freetown Cl. M14: Man 3E **115**
Freetrade St. OL11: Roch 6A **178** (6G **27**)
French Av. OL1: O'ham 6A **60**
   SK15: Stal .4G **107**
French Barn La. M9: Man 6G **71**
FRENCHES .3D **78**
Frenches Ct. OL3: G'fld 3C **78**
French Gro. BL3: Bolt 2H **49**
French St. OL6: A Lyme 1B **106**
   SK15: Stal .4G **107**
Frensham Wlk. M23: Wyth 1F **153**
Fresca Rd. OL1: O'ham 3B **60**
Freshfield M9: Man 5C **72**
   SK8: H Grn 4F **155**
Freshfield Av. BL3: Bolt 5B **48**
   (not continuous)
   M25: Pres .3A **70**
   SK14: Hyde 6B **120**
Freshfield Cl. M35: Fail 5A **90**
   SK6: Mar B 2F **149**
Freshfield Gro. BL3: Bolt 5D **48**
Freshfield Rd. SK4: Stoc 1B **144**
Freshfields M26: Rad 2F **51**
Freshfield Wlk. M11: Man 3E **103**
Freshford Wlk. M22: Wyth 4H **153**
Freshpool Way M22: Shar 5C **142**
Freshwater Dr. M34: Dent 1H **135**
   OL6: A Lyme 1C **106**
Freshwater St. M18: Man 1G **117**
Freshwinds Ct. OL4: O'ham 5B **76**
Fresnel Cl. SK14: Hyde 1F **121**
Frew Ho. M40: Man 1D **88**
Frewland Av. SK3: Stoc 1H **157**
Freya Gro. M5: Sal 2A **8** (5A **100**)
Friarmere Rd. OL3: Del 2A **62**
Friars Cl. M29: Tyld 2B **80**
   SK9: Wilm .1B **172**
   WA14: Bow 4D **150**
Friar's Ct. M5: Sal 3B **98**
Friars Cres. OL11: Roch 3H **41**
Friar's Rd. M33: Sale 5B **128**
Friendship Av. M18: Man 3G **117**
Friendship Sq. SK14: Holl 2F **123**
Frieston OL12: Roch 1A **178**
Frieston Rd. WA14: Tim 3G **139**
FRIEZLAND .4C **78**
Friezland Cl. SK15: C'ook 5A **94**
Friezland La. OL3: G'fld 5C **78**
Frimley Gdns. M22: Wyth 2B **154**
Frinton Av. M40: Man 6F **73**
Frinton Cl. M33: Sale 2H **139**
Frinton Rd. BL3: Bolt 4H **47**
Frobisher Cl. M13: Man 2H **115**
Frobisher Pl. SK5: Stoc 5G **133**

Frobisher Rd. OL15: L'ough 2A **16**
Frodesley Wlk. *M12: Man* *1B* **116**
   (off Wenlock Way)
Frodsham Av. SK4: Stoc 6E **133**
Frodsham Rd. M33: Sale 1E **141**
Frodsham St. M14: Man 4F **115**
Frodsham Way SK9: Hand 3A **166**
Frogley St. BL2: Bolt 2F **33**
Frogmore Av. SK14: Hyde 2C **136**
Frome Av. M41: Urm 6D **110**
   SK2: Stoc 6C **146**
Frome Cl. M29: Ast 5A **80**
Frome Dr. M8: Man 4F **87**
Frome St. OL4: O'ham 3A **76**
Frostlands St. M16: W Ran 4C **114**
Frost St. M4: Man 5H **7** (4H **101**)
   OL8: O'ham 5E **75**
Froxmer St. M18: Man 1E **117**
Froxmer St. Ind. Est. *M18: Man* *1E* **117**
   (off Froxmer St.)
Fuchsia Gro. *M7: Sal* *5B* **86**
   (off Hilton St. Nth.)
Fulbeck Wlk. M7: Sal 6C **86**
Fulbrook Dr. SK8: Chea H 1C **166**
Fulbrook Way M29: Tyld 2A **80**
Fulford St. M16: Old T 3A **114**
Fulham Av. M40: Man 6D **88**
Fulham St. OL4: O'ham 3A **76**
Fullerton Rd. SK4: Stoc 1D **144**
Full Pot La. OL11: Roch 3A **26**
FULLWOOD .1A **60**
Fulmar Cl. SK12: Poy 3A **168**
Fulmar Dr. M33: Sale 1E **139**
   SK2: Stoc 6F **147**
Fulmards Cl. SK9: Wilm 2F **173**
Fulmar Gdns. OL11: Roch 4B **26**
Fulmead Wlk. *M8: Man* *5D* **86**
   (off Kilmington Dr.)
Fulmer Dr. M4: Man 3F **7** (3G **101**)
Fulmere Ct. M27: Swin 5F **83**
Fulneck Sq. M43: Droy 5A **104**
Fulshaw Av. SK9: Wilm 3D **172**
Fulshaw Ct. SK9: Wilm 4D **172**
FULSHAW PARK 3C **172**
Fulshaw Pk. SK9: Wilm 5D **172**
Fulshaw Pk. Sth. SK9: Wilm 5C **172**
Fulshaw Wlk. M13: Man 4D **10**
Fulstone M. SK2: Stoc 5B **146**
Fulton Ct. *M15: Man* *2E* **115**
   (off Boundary La.)
Fulwood Av. M9: Man 5B **72**
Fulwood Cl. BL8: Bury 4H **35**
Furbarn La. OL11: Roch 3H **25**
Furbarn Rd. OL11: Roch 4H **25**
Furberry Ct. OL4: Grot 4F **77**
FUR LANE 3E **79**
Furlong Rd. M22: Wyth 2H **153**
Furnace St. SK14: Hyde 3A **120**
   SK16: Duk 4H **105**
Furness Av. BL2: Bolt 3F **33**
   M45: White 1G **69**
   OL7: A Lyme 4D **90**
   OL8: O'ham 6A **76**
   OL10: H'ood 2G **39**
   OL15: L'ough 3G **17**
Furness Cl. OL16: Miln 5E **29**
   SK12: Poy .3C **168**
Furness Flds. SK14: Hyde 3E **137**
Furness Gro. SK4: Stoc 2D **144**
Furness Quay M50: Sal 6G **99**
Furness Rd. BL1: Bolt 6H **31**
   M14: Man .6G **115**
   M24: Mid 4B **56**
   M41: Urm .4F **111**
   SK8: Chea H 1E **167**
Furness Sq. BL2: Bolt 3F **33**
Furnival Cl. M34: Dent 5A **118**
Furnival Rd. M18: Man 1E **117**
Furnival St. SK5: Stoc 5H **117**
Furrow Dr. M30: Ecc 1D **96**
Furrows, The M32: Stre 3B **112**
Furrow Sports Cen. 5G **55**
Further Fld. OL11: Roch 2H **25**

Further Hgts. Rd. OL12: Roch 1H 27
Further Hey Cl. OL4: Lees 2C 76
Further La. SK14: Hat 4A 122
Further Pits OL11: Roch 4E 27
Furtherwood Rd.
   OL1: O'ham 6C 58
Furzegate OL16: Roch 2B 42
Furze La. OL4: O'ham 6B 60
                              (not continuous)
Furze Wlk. M31: Part 6E 125
Fusion (1-9) M5: Sal 6B 4 (4A 100)
Fyfield Wlk. M8: Man 5F 87
                           (off Moordown Cl.)
Fylde Av. BL2: Bolt 6A 34
   SK8: H Grn 5G 155
Fylde Ct. M32: Stre 1C 128
                            (off Highfield Rd.)
Fylde Rd. SK4: Stoc 1C 144
Fylde St. BL3: Bolt 5H 49
Fylde St. E. BL3: Bolt 5H 49

G

Gable Av. SK9: Wilm 2D 172
Gable Ct. M34: Dent 4F 119
Gable Dr. M24: Mid 6A 56
Gables, The M33: Sale 6B 128
                           (Framingham Rd.)
   M33: Sale 4C 128
                                 (Irlam Rd.)
Gable St. BL2: Bolt 6H 19
   M11: Man 5B 102
Gabriels, The OL2: Shaw 6F 43
Gabriels Ter. M24: Mid 2E 73
Gaddum Rd. M20: Man 6G 131
   WA14: Bow 4C 150
Gadwall Cl. M28: Wors 3H 81
Gail Av. SK4: Stoc 1F 145
Gail Cl. M35: Fail 6G 89
   SK9: A Edg 4H 173
Gainford Av. SK8: Gat 1F 155
Gainford Gdns. M40: Man 2D 88
Gainford Rd. SK5: Stoc 6H 117
Gainford Wlk. BL3: Bolt 3C 48
Gainsboro Rd. M34: Aud 4D 104
Gainsborough Av. BL3: Bolt 4A 48
   M20: Man 4G 131
   M32: Stre 4F 113
   OL8: O'ham 5E 75
   SK6: Mar B 3F 149
Gainsborough Cl. SK9: Wilm 1G 173
Gainsborough Dr. OL11: Roch 2G 41
   SK8: Chea 5B 144
Gainsborough Ho. M33: Sale 6H 127
Gainsborough Rd. BL0: Ram 2B 22
   OL9: Chad 6G 57
Gainsborough St. M7: Sal 4C 86
Gainsborough Wlk. M34: Dent 6E 119
                              (not continuous)
   SK14: Hyde 2C 120
Gairloch Av. M32: Stre 5B 112
Gair Rd. SK5: Stoc 5H 133
Gair St. SK14: Hyde 3B 120
Gaitskell Cl. M12: Man 4A 102
Gala Bingo
   Ashton-under-Lyne . . .4B 174 (2H 105)
   Belle Vue 2D 116
   Manchester 3A 88
   Salford 2G 99
   Stockport 2H 179 (2A 146)
   Wythenshawe 3B 154
Galbraith Rd. M20: Man 6G 131
Galbraith Way OL11: Roch 3A 26
GALE .2H 17
Gale Cl. OL15: L'ough 2H 17
Gale Dr. M24: Mid 5H 55
Gale Rd. M25: Pres 6F 69
Gales Ter. OL11: Roch 6G 27
Gale St. SL10: H'ood 3F 39
   OL12: Roch 6H 15
Galgate Cl. BL8: Bury 4H 35
   M15: Man 4E 9 (6C 100)

Galindo St. BL2: Bolt 1G 33
Galland St. OL4: O'ham 2B 76
Gallery, The M3: Sal 4G 5
   M16: W Ran 4C 114
Gallery Oldham 4H 177
Galloway Cl. BL3: Bolt 2E 47
   OL10: H'ood 5D 38
Galloway Dr. M27: Clif 5H 67
Galloway Rd. M27: Swin 5F 83
Gallowsclough Rd. SK15: Mat 1A 122
Galston St. M11: Man 5C 102
Galsworthy Av. M8: Man 5E 87
Galvin Rd. M9: Man 6F 71
Galway St. OL1: O'ham 4G 177 (3F 75)
Galway Wlk. M23: Wyth 3F 153
Gambleside Cl. M28: Wors 3F 81
Gambrel Bank Rd. OL6: A Lyme 5H 91
Gambrel Gro. OL6: A Lyme 5H 91
GAMESLEY 5G 123
Gamesley Community & Sports Cen.
   . . . . .5G 123
Game St. OL4: O'ham 4A 76
Games Wlk. M22: Wyth 4H 153
Gamma Wlk. M11: Man 3D 102
                        (off John Heywood St.)
Gandy La. OL12: Roch 5F 15
Gan Eden M7: Sal 3C 86
Gantock Wlk. M14: Man 4G 115
                           (off Stenbury Cl.)
Ganton Av. M45: White 2D 68
Garbo Ct. M6: Sal 1E 99
                             (off Monroe Cl.)
Garbrook Av. M9: Man 4G 71
Garden Av. M32: Stre 4D 112
   M43: Droy 3B 104
Garden City BL0: Ram 1A 22
Garden Cl. OL15: L'ough 6F 17
Garden Ct. BL0: Ram 2C 12
                             (off Garden St.)
   OL16: Roch 3D 28
Gardeners Way OL7: A Lyme 3E 105
Gardenfold Ho. M43: Droy 3B 104
                               (off Fold Av.)
Garden La. M3: Man 5G 5 (4D 100)
   M3: Sal 3F 5 (3C 100)
                              (not continuous)
   M28: Wors 5E 81
   OL16: Roch 2D 178 (3A 28)
   WA14: Alt 1B 174 (6F 139)
Garden M. OL15: L'ough 4H 17
                           (off Industry St.)
Garden Row OL10: H'ood 1F 39
   OL12: Roch 1F 27
Gardens, The BL1: Bolt 5D 18
   M30: Ecc 1A 98
Garden St. BL0: Ram 3C 12
   BL4: Kea 1A 66
   BL8: Tot 4H 21
   BL9: Sum 6C 12
   M4: Man 4A 6 (3E 101)
   M30: Ecc 4G 97
   M34: Aud 1F 119
   OL1: O'ham 2G 75
   OL4: Spri 4D 76
   OL10: H'ood 2G 39
   OL16: Miln 1H 43
   SK2: Stoc 6C 146
   SK14: Hyde 3C 120
Garden Ter. OL2: O'ham 6C 42
   SK6: Mar 4F 161
Garden Vs. SK8: H Grn 6F 155
Garden Wlk. M31: Part 6C 124
   M34: Dent 4G 119
   OL6: A Lyme 1A 106
Garden Wall Cl. M5: Sal . . .2A 8 (5A 100)
Garden Way OL15: L'ough 1F 29
Gardner Grange SK5: Stoc 5C 134
Gardner Ho. M30: Ecc 4G 97
                            (off Church St.)
Gardner Rd. M25: Pres 5F 69
Gardner St. M6: Sal 2G 99
   M12: Man 1D 116
Garfield Av. M19: Man 6D 116

Garfield Cl. OL11: Roch 3A 26
Garfield Gro. BL3: Bolt 2B 48
Garfield St. BL3: Bolt 4A 48
   SK1: Stoc 1A 146
Garforth Av. M4: Man 3F 7 (3G 101)
Garforth Cres. M43: Droy 2B 104
Garforth Ri. BL1: Bolt 6G 31
Garforth St. OL9: Chad 2C 74
Gargrave Av. BL1: Bolt 3F 31
Gargrave St. M7: Sal 3F 85
   OL4: O'ham 3H 75
Garland Rd. M22: Wyth 2C 154
Garlick St. M18: Man 2F 117
   OL9: O'ham 4E 177 (3E 75)
                              (not continuous)
   SK14: Hyde 4D 120
Garnant Cl. M9: Man 3B 88
                           (off Gillford Av.)
Garner Av. WA15: Tim 2A 140
Garner Cl. WA14: Bow 3F 151
Garner Dr. M5: Sal 2D 98
   M29: Ast 6A 80
   M30: Ecc 2E 97
Garners La. SK3: Stoc 6F 145
Garnett St. BL0: Ram 3B 12
   BL1: Bolt 2C 32
   OL1: O'ham 1H 75
   SK1: Stoc 3G 179 (2H 145)
Garratt Way M18: Man 2E 117
Garret Gro. OL2: Shaw 6A 44
Garrett Hall Rd. M28: Wors 4C 80
Garrett La. M29: Ast 4B 80
Garrett Wlk. SK3: Stoc 3E 145
Garrick Cl. WA14: Alt 5F 139
Garron Wlk. M22: Wyth 3G 153
Garrowmore Wlk. M9: Man 6A 72
                          (off Greendale Dr.)
Garsdale Cl. BL9: Bury 6G 37
Garsdale La. BL1: Bolt 6D 30
Garsden Wlk. M23: Wyth 1F 153
Garside Gro. BL1: Bolt 3A 32
Garside Hey Rd. BL8: Bury 5B 22
Garside St. BL1: Bolt 6C 32
   M34: Dent 5F 119
   SK14: Hyde 6C 120
Garstang Av. BL2: Bolt 1A 50
Garstang Dr. BL8: Bury 4H 35
Garstang Ho. M15: Man 2F 115
Garston Cl. SK4: Stoc 6E 133
Garston St. BL9: Bury 1G 37
Garswood Dr. BL8: Bury 5B 22
Garswood Rd. BL3: Bolt 5C 48
   M14: Man 5D 114
Garth, The M5: Sal 3D 98
Garth Av. WA15: Tim 5G 139
Garth Hgts. SK9: Wilm 3F 173
Garthland Rd. SK7: H Gro 2F 159
Garthorne Cl. M16: W Ran 3B 114
Garthorp Rd. M23: Wyth 2E 141
Garth Rd. M22: Wyth 1B 154
   SK2: Stoc 4C 146
   SK6: Mar 5E 149
Garthwaite Av. OL8: O'ham 6E 75
Gartland Wlk. M8: Man 3G 87
Gartside St. M3: Man 6F 5 (4C 100)
                              (not continuous)
   OL3: Del 3A 62
   OL4: O'ham 4H 75
   OL7: A Lyme 4E 105
Garwick Rd. BL1: Bolt 2H 31
Garwood St. M15: Man 4G 9 (6C 100)
Gascoyne St. M14: Man 4F 115
Gaskell Cl. OL15: L'ough 3G 17
Gaskell Ri. OL1: O'ham 2C 60
Gaskell Rd. M30: Ecc 4G 97
   WA14: Alt 5F 139
Gaskell St. BL1: Bolt 5B 32
   M27: Pen 1H 83
   M40: Man 6E 89
   SK16: Duk 5H 105
Gaskell Swimming Pool 2G 39
                  (in Heywood Sports Complex)
Gaskill St. OL10: H'ood 3E 39

Gas St. BL1: Bolt 4E **175** (6C **32**)
(not continuous)
BL4: Farn 1H **65**
OL6: A Lyme 5B **174** (2H **105**)
OL10: H'ood 3H **39**
OL11: Roch 4A **178** (4G **27**)
SK4: Stoc 2E **179** (2G **145**)
SK4: Holl 2F **123**
Gaston Wlk. M9: Man 4H **71**
(off Claygate Dr.)
Gatcombe M. M26: Rad 2H **51**
SK9: Wilm 3D **172**
Gatcombe Sq. M14: Man 4H **115**
(off Rusholme Gro.)
Gateacre Wlk. M23: Wyth 3E **141**
Gate Cen., The SK6: Bred 3E **135**
Gatefield Cl. M26: Rad 4G **51**
GATE FOLD 1H **33**
Gate Fold BL2: Bolt 6H **19**
Gatehead Cft. OL3: Del 4B **62**
Gatehead M. OL3: Del 4B **62**
Gatehead Rd. OL3: Del 4B **62**
Gatehouse Ct. BL9: Bury 3A **38**
(off Bridgefield Dr.)
Gatehouse Rd. M28: Walk 5E **65**
Gate Keeper Fold OL7: A Lyme . . .4G **91**
Gatemere Cl. M28: Wors 3F **81**
Gates, The BL2: Bolt 2C **34**
Gatesgarth Rd. M24: Mid 5G **55**
Gateshead Cl. M14: Man 3F **115**
Gateside Wlk. M9: Man 4A **72**
(off Crossmead Dr.)
Gates Shop. Cen., The
BL1: Bolt 3G **175** (6D **32**)
Gate St. M11: Man 5E **103**
OL11: Roch 6H **27**
SK16: Duk 1G **119**
Gateway, The M6: Sal 1G **99**
(off Broughton Rd.)
M40: Man 5B **88**
Gateway Cres. OL9: Chad 4F **73**
Gateway Ho. M1: Man 6D **6**
Gateway Ind. Est. M1: Man . .6D **6** (4F **101**)
Gateway Rd. M18: Man 1E **117**
Gateways, The M27: Pen 2H **83**
Gathill Cl. SK8: Chea H 4B **156**
Gathurst St. M18: Man 1G **117**
GATLEY 6F **143**
Gatley Av. M14: Man 6E **115**
Gatley Brow OL1: O'ham 1E **75**
(off Sunfield Rd.)
Gatley Cl. M29: Tyld 2A **80**
Gatley Ct. M22: Nor 4C **142**
Gatley Grn. SK8: Gat 6E **143**
Gatley Rd. M33: Sale 6E **129**
SK8: Gat 6F **143**
Gatley Station (Rail) 5F **143**
Gatling Av. M12: Man 5D **116**
Gatwick Av. M23: Wyth 5H **141**
Gavel Wlk. M24: Mid 6A **56**
Gavin Av. M5: Sal 4G **99**
Gawsworth Av. M20: Man 2G **143**
Gawsworth Cl. OL2: Shaw 6F **43**
SK3: Stoc 6F **145**
SK7: Bram 2G **167**
SK12: Poy 5F **169**
WA15: Tim 5D **140**
Gawsworth Ct. M9: Man 4E **71**
(off Deanswood Dr.)
Gawsworth M. SK8: Gat 6F **143**
Gawsworth Pl. M22: Wyth 4D **154**
Gawsworth Rd. M33: Sale 2E **141**
Gawsworth Way M34: Dent 6G **119**
SK9: Hand 3A **166**
Gawthorne Cl. SK7: H Gro 3C **158**
Gawthorpe Cl. BL9: Bury 2G **53**
Gaydon Rd. M33: Sale 5F **127**
GAYTHORN 3G **9** (6D **100**)
Gaythorne St. BL1: Bolt 2D **32**
Gaythorn St. M5: Sal 5B **4** (4A **100**)
Gayton Wlk. M40: Man 1F **89**
Gaywood Wlk. M40: Man 5G **87**
(off Westmount Cl.)

Geddington Rd. WA14: W Tim 3E **139**
GEE CROSS 2C **136**
Gee Cross Fold SK14: Hyde 2C **136**
Gee La. M30: Ecc 2D **96**
OL8: O'ham 1B **90**
Gee St. SK3: Stoc 4F **145**
Gelder Clough Pk. OL11: Roch 6G **25**
Gelder Wood Country Pk. 5G **25**
Gellfield La. OL3: Upp 6F **63**
Gemini Rd. M6: Sal 1A **100**
Gendre Rd. BL7: Eger 3C **18**
Geneva Rd. SK7: Bram 2F **157**
Geneva Ter. OL11: Roch 3E **27**
Geneva Wlk. M8: Man 5F **87**
(off Moordown Cl.)
OL9: Chad 3C **74**
Genista Gro. M7: Sal 5B **86**
(off Hilton St. Nth.)
Geoff Bent Wlk. M40: Man 6D **88**
(off Roger Byrne Cl.)
Geoffrey St. BL0: Ram 5A **12**
BL9: Bury 1G **37**
George Barton St. BL2: Bolt 4F **33**
George Wood Gdns. M27: Pen 5G **25**
George Ct. SK16: Duk 4H **105**
(off Hill St.)
George Halstead Ct. M8: Man 2E **87**
(off Station Rd.)
George H Carnall Leisure Cen. 3G **111**
George La. SK6: Bred 5G **135**
George Leigh St. M4: Man . . .4D **6** (3F **101**)
George Mann Cl. M22: Wyth 4A **154**
George Parr Rd. M15: Man . . .6G **9** (1D **114**)
George Richards Way
WA14: B'ath 4D **138**
George Rd. BL0: Ram 4B **12**
George's Cl. SK12: Poy 4E **169**
Georges La. BL6: Hor 1A **30**
George Sq. OL1: O'ham 4F **177** (3E **75**)
George's Rd. M33: Sale 6B **128**
SK4: Stoc 2F **145**
George's Rd. E. SK12: Poy 4E **169**
George's Rd. W. SK12: Poy 4D **168**
George St. BL4: Farn 2F **65**
BL9: Bury 4D **176** (3F **37**)
M1: Man 1H **9** (5D **100**)
M25: Pres 2H **85**
M26: Rad 4H **51**
M30: Ecc 4E **97**
M34: Dent 4G **119**
M35: Fail 3H **89**
M41: Urm 5G **111**
M44: Irl 4F **109**
M45: White 5D **53**
OL1: O'ham 4F **177** (3E **75**)
OL2: Shaw 4A **44**
OL5: Mos 2G **93**
OL6: A Lyme 5D **174** (2A **106**)
OL9: Chad 2A **74**
OL10: H'ood 2F **39**
OL12: Whitw 2E **15**
OL15: L'ough 3H **17**
OL16: Roch 2D **178** (3A **28**)
(Ball St.)
OL16: Roch 6D **16**
(Greenfield La.)
OL16: Roch 5F **169**
(Rochdale Rd.)
SK1: Stoc 2A **146**
SK6: Comp 1F **149**
SK9: A Edg 5G **173**
SK15: Stal 3E **107**
WA14: Alt 3A **174** (1F **151**)
George St. E. SK1: Stoc 3B **146**
George St. Nth. M7: Sal 3D **86**
George St. Sth. M7: Sal 3C **86**
George St. W. SK1: Stoc 3B **146**
George Ter. M30: Ecc 3F **97**
(off Byron St.)
George Thomas Ct. M9: Man 3H **87**
Georgette Dr. M3: Sal 2F **5** (2D **100**)
Georgia Av. M20: Man 4D **130**
Georgiana St. BL4: Farn 5F **49**
Georgina Ct. BL3: Bolt 4H **47**

Georgina St. BL3: Bolt 5H **47**
Gerald Av. M8: Man 3E **87**
Gerald Rd. M6: Sal 6G **85**
Germain Cl. M9: Man 4G **71**
Germans Bldgs. SK2: Stoc 5A **146**
Gerrard Av. WA15: Tim 3A **140**
Gerrard Cl. OL7: A Lyme 4F **105**
Gerrards, The SK14: Hyde 2B **136**
Gerrards Cl. M44: Irl 5E **109**
Gerrards Gdns. SK14: Hyde 2C **136**
Gerrards Hollow SK14: Hyde 2B **136**
Gerrard St. BL4: Kea 1A **66**
M6: Sal 2H **99**
OL11: Roch 3A **42**
SK15: Stal 4F **107**
Gerrardswood SK14: Hyde 2B **136**
Gerry Wheale Sq. M14: Man 4E **115**
Gertrude Cl. M5: Sal 5G **99**
Gervis Cl. M40: Man 6H **87**
Ghyll Gro. M28: Walk 2A **82**
Giant's Seat M26: Rad 3G **67**
Giants Seat Gro. M27: Pen 3D **84**
Gibble Gabble SK14: B'tom 6C **122**
(off King St.)
Gibbon Av. M22: Wyth 3B **154**
Gibbon St. BL3: Bolt 2B **48**
M11: Man 3C **102**
Gibb Rd. M28: Wors 4D **82**
Gibbs Cl. OL3: G'fld 4E **63**
Gibbs St. M3: Sal 5C **4** (4B **100**)
Gib La. M23: Wyth 4H **141**
Gib La. Cotts. M23: Wyth 4A **142**
(off Gib La.)
Gibraltar La. M34: Dent 1H **135**
Gibraltar St. BL3: Bolt 1B **48**
OL4: O'ham 4B **76**
Gibsmere Cl. WA15: Tim 5D **140**
Gibson Av. M18: Man 6H **103**
Gibson Gro. M28: Walk 6E **65**
Gibson La. M28: Walk 6E **65**
Gibson Pl. M3: Man 1A **6** (2E **101**)
Gibsons Rd. SK4: Stoc 5D **132**
Gibson St. BL2: Bolt 4G **33**
OL4: O'ham 3A **76**
OL16: Roch 3C **28**
Gibson Ter. OL7: A Lyme 5G **105**
Gibson Way WA14: B'ath 3E **139**
Gidlow St. M18: Man 1G **117**
Giffard Wlk. SK7: Bram 3A **158**
Gifford Av. M9: Man 5B **72**
GIGG 6G **37**
Gigg Lane 6F **37**
Gigg La. BL9: Bury 6E **37**
Gilbert Bank SK6: Bred 5H **135**
Gilbert Ho. M5: Sal 6G **99**
(off Elmira Way)
Gilbert Rd. WA15: Hale 4G **151**
Gilbert St. BL0: Ram 4F **13**
M6: Sal 4F **99**
(off Hodge La.)
M15: Man 3F **9** (6C **100**)
M28: Walk 1G **81**
M30: Ecc 5D **96**
Gilbrook Way OL16: Roch 3B **42**
Gilchrist Rd. M44: Irl 3C **124**
Gilda Brook Rd. M30: Ecc, Sal 4A **98**
Gilda Brook Rdbt. M30: Ecc 3A **98**
Gilda Cres. Rd. M30: Ecc 2A **98**
Gilda Rd. M28: Wors 4C **80**
Gildenhall M35: Fail 4A **90**
Gilderdale Cl. OL2: Shaw 5H **43**
Gilderdale St. BL3: Bolt 3E **49**
Gildersdale Dr. M9: Man 4D **70**
Gildridge Rd. M16: W Ran 6C **114**
Gilesgate M14: Man 4G **115**
(off Viscount St.)
Giles St. M12: Man 3C **116**
GILLBENT 1B **166**
Gillbent Rd. SK8: Chea H 1C **166**
Gillbrook Rd. M20: Man 6F **131**
Gillemere Gro. OL2: Shaw 6A **44**

Gillers Grn. M28: Walk 6G **65**
Gillford Av. M9: Man 3B **88**
Gillingham Rd. M30: Ecc 3D **96**
Gillingham Sq. *M11: Man* *5B 102*
                 (off Glyneath Cl.)
Gill St. M9: Man 3B **88**
  SK1: Stoc 6B **134**
Gillwood Dr. SK6: Rom 2F **147**
Gilman Cl. M9: Man 1G **87**
Gilman St. M9: Man 1G **87**
Gilmerton Dr. M40: Man 6E **89**
Gilmore Dr. M25: Pres 4F **67**
Gilmore St. SK3: Stoc 6F **179** (4G **145**)
Gilmour St. M24: Mid 1C **72**
Gilmour Ter. M9: Man 2B **88**
                (not continuous)
GILNOW 1B **48**
Gilnow Gdns. BL1: Bolt 1A **48**
Gilnow Gro. BL1: Bolt 1B **48**
Gilnow La. BL3: Bolt 1A **48**
Gilnow Mill Ind. Est.
  BL1: Bolt 1A **48**
GILNOW PARK 6H **31**
Gilnow Rd. BL1: Bolt 1A **48**
Gilpin Pl. M41: Urm 6H **111**
Gilpin Wlk. M24: Mid 6A **56**
Giltbrook Av. M40: Man 1H **101**
Gilwell Dr. M23: Wyth 1F **153**
Gilwood Gro. M24: Mid 3B **56**
Gin Cft. La. BL0: Eden 1H **13**
Gingham Ct. *M26: Rad* *3C 52*
             (off Butterworth St.)
Gingham Pk. M26: Rad 2G **51**
Gipsey Moth Cl.
  WA15: Tim 6D **140**
Gipsy La. OL11: Roch 2E **41**
              (not continuous)
Gird La. SK6: Mar B 3H **149**
Girton St. BL2: Bolt 6H **33**
  M7: Sal 1C **100**
Girton Wlk. M40: Man 2F **89**
Girvan Av. M40: Man 1F **89**
Girvan Cl. BL3: Bolt 4A **48**
Girvan Wlk. OL10: H'ood 4D **38**
Gisborne Dr. M6: Sal 6G **85**
Gisburn Av. BL1: Bolt 3E **31**
Gisburn Dr. BL8: Bury 2G **35**
  OL11: Roch 2A **42**
Gisburne Av. M40: Man 1F **89**
Gissing Wlk. M9: Man 5H **87**
Givendale Dr. M8: Man 1E **87**
Givvons Fold OL4: O'ham 6B **60**
Glade, The BL1: Bolt 4B **32**
  SK4: Stoc 2C **144**
Glade Brow OL4: Grot 3E **77**
Gladeside Dr. M22: Wyth 1A **154**
Gladeside Rd. M22: Wyth 1A **154**
Glade St. BL1: Bolt 6A **32**
Gladewood Cl. SK9: Wilm 1F **173**
Glade Wood Dr. M35: Fail 3B **90**
Gladstone Bus. Pk.
  OL4: O'ham 3H **75**
Gladstone Cl. *BL1: Bolt* *3C 32*
             (off Gladstone St.)
  M15: Man 3C **114**
Gladstone Ct. *BL4: Farn* *6G 49*
             (off Gladstone Pl.)
  OL7: A Lyme *3G 105*
             (off Margaret St.)
  SK4: Stoc 6D **132**
Gladstone Cres. OL11: Roch 2H **41**
Gladstone Gro. SK4: Stoc 6C **132**
Gladstone Ho. *OL12: W'le* *6C 16*
           (off Old School Pl.)
Gladstone M. *SK4: Stoc* *6G 133*
             (off Short St.)
Gladstone Mill *SK15: Stal* *3F 107*
           (off Warrington St.)
Gladstone Pl. BL4: Farn 6G **49**
Gladstone Rd. BL4: Farn 6G **49**
  M30: Ecc 3G **97**
  M41: Urm 5G **111**
  WA14: Alt 5F **139**

Gladstone St. BL1: Bolt 3C **32**
  BL9: Bury 2H **37**
  M27: Pen 3A **84**
  OL4: O'ham 3H **75**
  SK2: Stoc 1C **158**
  SK13: Had 3H **123**
Gladstone Ter. Rd. OL3: G'fld 5C **78**
Gladville Dr. SK8: Chea 5C **144**
Gladwyn Av. M20: Man 5C **130**
Gladys St. BL3: Bolt 5H **49**
  M16: Old T 3A **114**
Glaisdale OL4: O'ham 3B **76**
Glaisdale Cl. BL2: Bolt 3F **33**
Glaisdale Dr. BL2: Bolt 3F **33**
Glaisdale St. BL2: Bolt 3F **33**
Glaister La. BL2: Bolt 4H **33**
Glamis Av. M11: Man 2D **102**
  M32: Stre 5A **112**
  OL10: H'ood 5A **40**
Glamorgan Pl. OL9: O'ham 4C **74**
Glandon Dr. SK8: Chea H 5E **157**
Glanford Av. M9: Man 6E **71**
Glanton Wlk. *M40: Man* *2F 89*
             (off Enstone Dr.)
Glanvor Rd. SK3: Stoc 3E **145**
Glass Box Gallery 2H **99**
Glasshouse St. M4: Man . .2E **7** (2G **101**)
Glasson Wlk. OL9: Chad 3A **74**
Glass St. BL4: Farn 2A **66**
Glastonbury OL12: Roch 1A **178**
Glastonbury Av. SK8: Chea H 1D **166**
  WA15: Hale 3B **152**
Glastonbury Dr. SK12: Poy 3D **168**
Glastonbury Gdns. M26: Rad 2G **51**
Glastonbury Rd. M29: Ast 4A **80**
  M32: Stre 4H **111**
Glaswen Gro. SK5: Stoc 5H **133**
Glazebrook Cl. OL10: H'ood 4G **39**
Glazebrook La. WA3: G'ook 4A **124**
Glazebury Dr. BL5: W'ton 5A **46**
  M23: Wyth 6H **141**
Glazedale Av. OL2: O'ham 3C **58**
Glaze Wlk. M45: White 5A **54**
Gleave Cl. WA15: Alt 3C **174** (1G **151**)
Gleaves Av. BL2: Bolt 1C **34**
Gleaves Rd. M30: Ecc 4G **97**
Gleave St. BL1: Bolt 2G **175** (5D **32**)
  M33: Sale 3B **128**
Glebe Ho. *M24: Mid* *5C 56*
            (off Rochdale Rd.)
Glebeland Rd. BL3: Bolt 2H **47**
Glebelands Rd. M23: Wyth 5F **141**
  M25: Pres 4G **69**
  M33: Sale 3G **127**
Glebe La. OL1: O'ham 3C **60**
Glebe Rd. M41: Urm 5E **111**
Glebe St. BL2: Bolt 5H **175** (1E **49**)
  M26: Rad 4B **52**
  M34: Dent 3G **119**
  OL2: Shaw 1H **59**
  OL6: A Lyme 5D **174** (2A **106**)
  OL9: Chad 6A **74**
  SK1: Stoc 2A **146**
Gleden St. M40: Man 3H **7** (3A **102**)
             (not continuous)
Gledhall St. SK15: Stal 3E **107**
Gledhill Av. M5: Sal 6G **99**
Gledhill Cl. OL2: Shaw 4G **43**
Gledhill St. M20: Man 2F **131**
Gledhill Way BL7: Bro X 3E **19**
Glemsford Cl. M40: Man 5D **88**
Glen, The BL1: Bolt 6E **31**
  M24: Mid 3D **72**
Glenacre Gdns. M18: Man 3G **117**
Glenarm Wlk. M22: Wyth 3C **154**
Glenart M30: Ecc 2G **97**
Glen Av. BL3: Bolt 2H **47**
  BL4: Kea 3D **66**
  M9: Man 2A **88**
  M27: Swin 3F **83**
  M28: Wors 3C **82**
  M33: Sale 3A **128**
Glenavon Dr. OL2: Shaw 5F **43**
  OL12: Roch 6F **15**

Glenbarry Cl. M13: Man 6D **10** (1F **115**)
Glenbarry St. M12: Man 2H **11** (5H **101**)
Glenbeck Rd. M45: White 6E **53**
Glenboro Av. BL8: Bury 3B **36**
Glenboro Ct. *BL8: Bury* *4C 36*
             (off Glenboro Av.)
Glen Bott St. BL1: Bolt 3B **32**
Glenbourne Pk. SK7: Bram 2F **167**
Glenbrook Gdns. BL4: Farn 5H **49**
Glenbrook Rd. M9: Man 4E **71**
Glenburn St. BL3: Bolt 4B **48**
Glenby Av. M22: Wyth 2D **154**
Glenby Est. OL9: Chad 3C **74**
Glencar Dr. M40: Man 1F **89**
Glencastle Rd. M18: Man 2E **117**
             (not continuous)
Glencoe BL2: Bolt 6F **33**
Glencoe Cl. OL10: H'ood 4D **38**
Glencoe Dr. BL2: Bolt 1B **50**
  M33: Sale 1E **139**
Glencoe Pl. OL11: Roch 4F **27**
Glencoe St. OL8: O'ham 1C **90**
Glen Cotts. BL1: Bolt 3E **31**
Glencoyne Dr. BL1: Bolt 5B **18**
Glencross Av. M21: Chor 5G **113**
Glendale M27: Clif 1B **84**
Glendale Av. BL9: Bury 4F **53**
  M19: Man 3B **132**
Glendale Cl. M28: Wors 4D **80**
  OL10: H'ood *3H 39*
            (off Prince St.)
Glendale Ct. OL8: O'ham 5F **75**
Glendale Dr. BL3: Bolt 1F **47**
Glendale Rd. M28: Wors 4D **80**
  M30: Ecc 2A **98**
Glendene Av. M43: Droy 2C **104**
  SK7: Bram 2F **167**
Glenden Foot OL12: Roch 1F **27**
Glendevon Cl. BL3: Bolt 2F **47**
  M22: Wyth 6A **142**
Glendevon Pl. M45: White 2H **69**
Glendinning St. M6: Sal 3E **99**
Glendon Ct. OL1: O'ham 3C **60**
Glendon Cres. OL6: A Lyme 4H **91**
Glendore M5: Sal 3C **98**
Glendower Dr. M40: Man 6G **87**
Gleneagles BL3: Bolt 4F **47**
Gleneagles Av. M11: Man 3E **103**
  OL10: H'ood 5H **39**
Gleneagles Cl. SK7: Bram 6A **158**
  SK9: Wilm 1G **173**
Gleneagles Rd. M41: Urm 3A **110**
  SK8: H Grn 4G **155**
Gleneagles Way BL0: Ram 4B **12**
Glenfield WA14: Alt 1D **150**
Glenfield Cl. OL4: O'ham 3B **76**
Glenfield Dr. SK12: Poy 4D **168**
Glenfield Rd. SK4: Stoc 5F **133**
Glenfield Sq. BL4: Farn 5F **49**
Glenfyne Rd. M6: Sal 6D **84**
Glen Gdns. OL12: Roch 1H **27**
Glengarth OL3: Upp 2D **78**
Glengarth Dr. BL1: Bolt 1C **46**
  BL6: Los 1C **46**
Glen Gro. M24: Mid 2E **73**
  OL2: O'ham 2D **58**
Glenham Ct. *M15: Man* *3C 114*
             (off Moss La. W.)
Glenhaven Av. M41: Urm 5E **111**
Glenholme Rd. SK7: Bram 6F **157**
Glenhurst Rd. M19: Man 4A **132**
Glenilla Av. M28: Wors 4A **82**
Glenlea Dr. M20: Man 3F **143**
Glenluce Wlk. BL3: Bolt 2E **47**
Glenmay Ct. M32: Stre 5C **112**
Glen Maye M33: Sale 5C **128**
Glenmere Cl. M25: Pres 3F **69**
Glenmere Rd. M20: Man 3G **143**
Glenmoor Rd. SK1: Stoc 2A **146**
Glen Morag Gdns.
  OL11: Roch 5C **26**
Glenmore Av. BL4: Farn 5E **49**
  M20: Man 5C **130**

Glenmore Bungs. SK16: Duk 6A 106
  (off Glenmore Gro.)
Glenmore Cl. BL3: Bolt 2E 47
  OL11: Roch 6A 26
Glenmore Dr. M8: Man 4F 87
  M35: Fail 3B 90
Glenmore Gro. SK16: Duk 5A 106
Glenmore Rd. BL0: Ram 1H 21
Glenmore St. BL9: Bury 5A 176 (4E 37)
Glenmuir Cl. M44: Irl 5E 109
Glenolden St. M11: Man 3F 103
Glenpark Wlk. M9: Man 4A 88
  (off Craigend Dr.)
Glenridding Cl. OL1: O'ham 6G 59
Glenridge Cl. BL1: Bolt 3D 32
Glen Ri. WA15: Tim 6A 140
Glen Rd. OL4: O'ham 3A 76
Glen Royd OL12: Roch 2E 27
Glensdale Dr. M40: Man 2G 89
Glenshaw Way OL9: Chad 5A 74
Glenshee Dr. BL3: Bolt 2F 47
Glenside Av. M18: Man 4F 117
Glenside Dr. BL3: Bolt 5D 48
  SK6: Wood 4H 135
  SK9: Wilm 3F 173
Glenside Gdns. M35: Fail 4A 90
Glenside Gro. M28: Walk 6A 66
Glen St. BL0: Ram 2B 12
  M50: Sal 6G 99
Glenthorn Av. M9: Man 3H 71
Glenthorne Dr. OL7: A Lyme 1G 105
Glenthorne St. BL1: Bolt 4C 32
  (off Nebraska St.)
Glenthorn Gro. M33: Sale 6B 128
Glen Trad. Est. OL4: O'ham 3B 76
Glentress M. BL1: Bolt 5G 31
Glentrool M. BL1: Bolt 6G 31
Glent Vw. SK15: Stal 1E 107
Glent Wakefield Rd. SK15: Stal 2F 107
Glentwood WA14: Hale 4G 151
Glenvale Cl. M26: Rad 4B 52
Glen Vw. OL2: O'ham 2D 58
  OL12: Whitw 3A 14
Glenville Cl. SK8: Chea H 6B 156
Glenville Rd. M8: Man 6D 86
Glenville Ter. M43: Droy 2G 103
  (off Greenside La.)
Glenville Wlk. SK15: Stal 4E 107
  (off Forester Dr.)
Glenville Way M34: Dent 5G 119
Glenwood Av. SK14: Hyde 2B 120
Glenwood Cl. M26: Rad 5B 52
Glenwood Dr. M9: Man 4A 88
  M24: Mid 5E 57
Glenwood Gro. SK2: Stoc 2B 158
Glenwyn Av. M9: Man 5A 72
Globe Cl. M16: Old T 2B 114
Globe Ind. Est. M26: Rad 4B 52
Globe La. BL7: Eger 1B 18
  SK16: Duk 6G 105
Globe La. Ind. Est. SK16: Duk 1H 119
Globe Pk. OL16: Roch 5B 28
Globe Sq. SK16: Duk 6G 105
Globe St. OL4: O'ham 2H 75
GLODWICK 4H 75
Glodwick OL4: O'ham 4H 75
GLODWICK BROOK 5F 75
Glodwick Rd. OL4: O'ham 4H 75
Glodwick Swimming Pool 3H 75
Glossop Rd. SK6: Mar B 3F 149
  SK13: Char, Gam 6F 123
Glossop Ter. M40: Man 6F 73
Gloster St. BL2: Bolt 6E 33
Gloucester Av. M19: Man 1D 132
  M45: White 1G 69
  OL10: H'ood 5G 39
  OL12: Roch 5D 16
  SK6: Mar 5D 148
Gloucester Cl. OL6: A Lyme 3B 92
  OL3: Dig 3E 63
Gloucester Ho. M7: Sal 5A 86
  (off Bk. Duncan St.)

Gloucester Pl. M6: Sal 2G 99
Gloucester Ri. SK16: Duk 6E 107
Gloucester Rd. M6: Sal 1C 98
  M24: Mid 3C 72
  M34: Dent 5A 118
  M41: Urm 5F 111
  M43: Droy 2A 104
  SK8: H Grn 6G 155
  SK12: Poy 3D 168
  SK14: Hyde 1C 136
Gloucester St. M1: Man 3H 9 (6D 100)
  M5: Sal 2A 8 (5A 100)
  M6: Sal 1G 99
  SK3: Stoc 4F 145
Gloucester St. Nth. OL9: O'ham 4C 74
Gloucester St. Sth. OL9: O'ham 4C 74
Glover Av. M8: Man 5F 87
Glover Cen. OL5: Mos 3H 93
Glover Cl. M7: Sal 3D 86
Glover Dr. SK14: Hyde 5C 120
Glover Fld. M7: Sal 5B 86
Glyn Av. WA15: Hale 3A 152
Glyneath Cl. M11: Man 5B 102
Glynis Cl. SK3: Stoc 5H 145
Glynne St. BL4: Farn 1G 65
Glynn Gdns. M20: Man 5B 130
Glynrene Dr. M27: Ward 2E 83
Glynwood Pk. BL4: Farn 6G 49
G Mex Cen. 2G 9 (5D 100)
G Mex Stop (Metro) 2G 9 (5D 100)
Gnat Bank Fold OL11: Roch 6B 26
Goadsby St. M4: Man 3B 6 (3E 101)
GOATS 4B 44
Goats Ga. Ter. M45: White 5D 52
Godbert Av. M21: Chor 4A 130
Goddard La. SK13: Had 1H 123
Goddard Rd. SK13: Had 3H 123
Goddard St. OL8: O'ham 5F 75
Godfrey Av. M43: Droy 2F 103
Godfrey Mill SK14: Hyde 4C 120
Godfrey Range M18: Man 3H 117
Godfrey Rd. M6: Sal 6C 84
Godlee Dr. M27: Swin 4G 83
GODLEY 4D 120
Godley Cl. M11: Man 5E 103
Godley Ct. SK14: Hyde 5D 120
  (off Mottram Rd.)
GODLEY GREEN 6E 121
GODLEY HILL 5F 121
Godley Hill SK14: Hyde 5F 121
Godley Hill Rd. SK14: Hyde 4F 121
Godley Station (Rail) 4E 121
Godley St. SK14: Hyde 3D 120
Godmond Hall Dr. M28: Wors 6D 80
Godolphin Cl. M30: Ecc 1H 97
Godson St. OL1: O'ham 1F 177 (6E 59)
Godwin St. M18: Man 1G 117
Goit Pl. OL16: Roch 3C 178 (4H 27)
Golborne Av. M20: Man 2D 130
Golborne Dr. M2: Shaw 5H 43
Golborne Ho. OL2: Shaw 5H 43
  (off Cowie St.)
GOLBURN CLOUGH 2D 78
Goldbrook Cl. OL10: H'ood 4A 40
Goldcraft Cl. OL10: H'ood 4A 40
Goldcrest Cl. M22: Shar 6D 142
  M28: Wors 4F 81
Goldenhill Av. M11: Man 2E 103
Golden Sq. M30: Ecc 4F 97
  (off Golden St.)
Golden St. M30: Ecc 4F 97
  OL2: Shaw 5C 44
Goldfinch Dr. BL9: Bury 1A 38
Goldfinch Way M43: Droy 2C 104
Goldie Av. M22: Wyth 4D 154
Goldrill Av. BL2: Bolt 5B 34
Goldrill Gdns. BL2: Bolt 5B 34
Goldsmith Av. M5: Sal 3D 98
  OL1: O'ham 3C 60
Goldsmith Rd. SK5: Stoc 6F 117
Goldsmith St. BL3: Bolt 3B 48
Goldsmith Way M34: Dent 2G 135
  (off Wordsworth Rd.)

Goldstein Rd. BL6: Los 3B 46
Gold St. M1: Man 6B 6 (4E 101)
Goldsworth Rd. OL1: O'ham 4B 60
Goldsworthy Rd. M41: Urm 4A 110
Goldwick Wlk. M23: Wyth 2E 141
Golf Rd. M33: Sale 5F 129
  WA15: Hale 2H 151
Golfview Dr. M30: Ecc 1F 97
Gollinrod BL9: Bury 5D 12
Gomer Wlk. M8: Man 5G 87
  (off Smedley Rd.)
Goodacre SK14: Hyde 1F 121
Gooden St. OL10: H'ood 4A 40
Goodhope Mill OL6: A Lyme 6A 174
Goodier Ho. Fold SK14: Hyde 3D 120
  (off Victoria St.)
Goodiers Dr. M5: Sal 5G 99
Goodier St. M33: Sale 5A 128
  M40: Man 1B 102
Goodier Vw. SK14: Hyde 2D 120
Good Intent OL16: Miln 6G 29
Goodison Cl. BL9: Bury 4H 53
Goodlad St. BL8: Bury 1B 36
Goodman St. M9: Man 3A 88
Goodrich OL11: Roch 6A 178 (5G 27)
Goodridge Av. M22: Wyth 4A 154
Goodrington Rd. SK9: Hand 4A 166
Goodshaw Rd. M28: Wors 3G 81
Good Shepherd Cl. OL16: Roch 3B 28
Goodwill Cl. M27: Swin 4H 83
Goodwin Cl. OL9: Chad 5C 74
Goodwin St. BL1: Bolt 2H 175 (5C 33)
Goodwood Av. M23: Wyth 3D 140
  M33: Sale 5E 127
Goodwood Cl. BL3: Lit L 4B 50
Goodwood Ct. M7: Sal 5B 86
Goodwood Cres. WA15: Tim 5C 140
Goodwood Dr. M27: Pen 4B 84
  OL1: O'ham 6H 59
Goodwood Rd. SK6: Mar 6C 148
Goodworth Wlk. M40: Man 4D 88
  (off Egbert St.)
Goole St. M11: Man 5C 102
Goose Cote Hill BL7: Eger 1C 18
Goose Grn. WA14: Alt 3B 174 (1F 151)
Goosehouse Grn. SK6: Rom 6B 136
Goose La. OL12: Roch 1B 178 (3H 27)
Goosetrey Cl. SK9: Wilm 6A 166
Goostrey Av. M20: Man 1E 131
Gordon Av. BL3: Bolt 2A 48
  M19: Man 6D 116
  M33: Sale 3B 128
  OL4: O'ham 3H 75
  OL9: Chad 6A 74
  SK7: H Gro 2D 158
Gordon Pl. M20: Man 4F 131
Gordon Rd. M27: Swin 5E 83
  M30: Ecc 2F 97
Gordon St. BL9: Bury 1A 176 (1E 37)
  M7: Sal 1B 100
  M16: Old T 2B 114
  M18: Man 1G 117
  OL2: Shaw 6A 44
  (not continuous)
  OL4: Lees 4C 76
  OL4: Spri 3E 77
  OL6: A Lyme 1B 106
  OL9: Chad 5H 73
  OL11: Roch 6A 28
  OL16: Miln 1H 43
  SK4: Stoc 1G 145
  SK14: Hyde 5C 120
  SK15: Stal 4F 107
Gordon Ter. M9: Man 3A 88
  (off Kingscliffe St.)
  SK15: Stal 3E 107
Gordon Way OL10: H'ood 4D 38
Gore Av. M5: Sal 3D 98
  M35: Fail 4B 90
Gorebrook Ct. M12: Man 3C 116
Gore Cl. BL9: Bury 4A 38
Gore Cres. M5: Sal 2D 98
Goredale Av. M18: Man 4G 117

Gore Dr. M5: Sal 2D 98
Gorelan Rd. M18: Man 2F 117
Gore St. M1: Man 6C 6 (4F 101)
  M3: Sal 5E 5 (4C 100)
  M6: Sal 2G 99
    (off Up. Gloucester St.)
Goring Av. M18: Man 1F 117
Gorrells Cl. OL11: Roch 2F 41
Gorrells Way OL11: Roch 2F 41
Gorrells Way Ind. Est. OL11: Roch ..2F 41
Gorse, The WA14: Bow 5D 150
Gorse Av. M32: Stre 4F 113
  M43: Droy 3C 104
  OL5: Mos 2A 94
  OL8: O'ham 6A 76
  SK6: Mar 5C 148
Gorse Bank BL9: Bury 2A 38
Gorse Bank Rd. WA15: Haleb ...6C 152
Gorse Cres. M32: Stre 4F 113
Gorse Dr. M32: Stre 4F 113
  M38: Lit H 3D 64
Gorsefield Cl. M26: Rad 3A 52
Gorsefield Dr. M27: Swin 4H 83
Gorsefield Hey SK9: Wilm 1H 173
Gorse Hall Cl. SK16: Duk 6D 106
Gorse Hall Dr. SK15: Stal 4E 107
Gorse Hall Rd. SK16: Duk 6C 106
GORSE HILL 3E 113
Gorselands SK8: Chea H 2D 166
Gorse La. M32: Stre 4F 113
Gorse Pit BL9: Bury 2A 38
Gorse Rd. M27: Swin 5G 83
  M28: Walk 1A 82
  OL16: Miln 5G 29
Gorses BL9: Bury 1E 39
Gorses Mt. BL2: Bolt 2G 49
Gorse Sq. M31: Part 6B 124
Gorses Rd. BL2: Bolt 2H 49
Gorse St. M32: Stre 4E 113
  OL9: Chad 5H 73
Gorseway SK5: Stoc 5B 134
Gorsey Av. M22: Wyth 6A 142
Gorsey Bank Rd. SK3: Stoc 3C 144
Gorsey Brow M41: Urm 5H 111
  SK1: Stoc 3H 179 (2A 146)
  SK6: Rom 1G 147
  SK14: B'tom 6C 122
Gorsey Clough Wlk. BL8: Tot 6H 21
Gorsey Dr. M22: Wyth 1A 154
Gorseyfields M43: Droy 5A 104
Gorsey Hill St. OL10: H'ood 4H 39
Gorsey Intakes SK14: B'tom 6C 122
Gorsey La. OL6: A Lyme 5D 92
  WA14: Alt 6D 138
Gorsey Mt. St. SK1: Stoc 2A 146
    (Hall St.)
  SK1: Stoc 3H 179 (2H 145)
    (Up. Brook St.)
Gorsey Rd. M22: Wyth 1A 154
  SK9: Wilm 2C 172
Gorsey Way OL6: A Lyme 5C 92
Gorston Wlk. M22: Wyth 5A 154
Gort Cl. BL9: Bury 6G 53
GORTON 3F 117
Gorton Cres. M34: Dent 5C 118
Gorton Cross Cen. M18: Man 2F 117
Gorton Gro. M28: Walk 4G 65
Gorton Ind. Est. M18: Man 1E 117
Gorton La. M12: Man 1C 116
  M18: Man 1C 116
Gorton Mkt. M18: Man 2F 117
Gorton Parks M18: Man 1E 117
Gorton Rd. M11: Man 6B 102
  M12: Man 6B 102
  SK5: Stoc 1H 133
Gorton Station (Rail) 1F 117
Gorton St. BL2: Bolt 5H 175 (1E 49)
  BL4: Farn 2F 65
  M3: Sal 3G 5 (3D 100)
  M30: Ecc 4C 96
  OL7: A Lyme 4F 105
  OL9: Chad 3B 74
  OL10: H'ood 3A 40

Gortonvilla Wlk. *M12:* Man 1B **116**
    (off Clowes St.)
Gosforth Cl. BL8: Bury 6C 22
  OL1: O'ham 6G 59
Gosforth Wlk. M23: Wyth 2F 141
Goshen La. BL9: Bury 1F 53
Goshen Sports Cen. 1G 53
Gosport Sq. M7: Sal 6B 86
Gosport Wlk. *M8:* Man 5C **87**
    (off Smeaton St.)
Goss Hall St. OL4: O'ham 3A 76
Gotha Wlk. M13: Man 5F 11
Gotherage Cl. SK6: Rom 1C 148
Gotherage La. SK6: Rom 2C 148
Gothic Cl. SK6: Rom 1D 148
Gough St. *OL10:* H'ood 3A **40**
    (off Adelaide St. E.)
  SK3: Stoc 2F 145
Goulden Rd. M20: Man 3E 131
Goulden St. M4: Man 3C 6 (3F 101)
  M6: Sal 3E 99
Goulder Rd. M18: Man 4G 117
Gould St. M4: Man 1B 6 (2F 101)
  M34: Dent 4E 119
  OL1: O'ham 1H 75
Gourham Dr. SK8: Chea H 3B 156
Govan St. M22: Nor 2C 142
Govind Ruia Ct. M16: W Ran 5C 114
Gowan Dr. M24: Mid 6H 55
Gowanlock's St. BL1: Bolt 3C 32
Gowan Rd. M16: W Ran 6C 114
Gower Av. SK7: H Gro 2C 158
Gower Ct. SK14: Hyde 1C 136
Gower Rd. SK4: Stoc 5F 133
  SK14: Hyde 6B 120
Gowers St. OL16: Roch 3B 28
Gowland St. BL1: Bolt 5B 32
  BL4: Farn 6G 49
  M27: Pen 2A 84
  OL1: O'ham 2G 75
  OL8: A Lyme 2A 106
Gowran Pk. OL4: O'ham 3B 76
Gowy Cl. SK9: Wilm 6A 166
Goya Ri. OL1: O'ham 3B 60
Goyt Av. SK6: Mar 1D 160
Goyt Cres. SK1: Stoc 6B 134
  SK6: Bred 6F 135
Goyt Mill SK6: Mar 1D 160
Goyt Rd. SK1: Stoc 6B 134
  SK6: Mar 1D 160
  SK12: Dis 2H 171
Goyt Valley Rd. SK6: Bred 6F 135
Goyt Valley Wlk.
  SK6: Bred 6F 135
Goyt Vw. SK6: Rom 1F 147
Goyt Wlk. M45: White 5H 53
Grace St. OL12: Roch 1A 28
Grace Wlk. M4: Man 6H 7 (4H 101)
Gracie Av. OL1: O'ham 6H 59
Gradwell St. SK3: Stoc ...4E 179 (3F 145)
Grafton Av. M30: Ecc 1A 98
Grafton Ct. *M15:* Man 2B **114**
    (off Chorlton Rd.)
  OL16: Roch 5B **28**
    (off Basil St.)
Graftons, The WA14: Alt 3A 174
Grafton St. BL1: Bolt 5B 32
  BL9: Bury 5F 37
  M13: Man 2F 115
  M35: Fail 3A 90
  OL1: O'ham 3C 60
  OL6: A Lyme 3B 106
    (not continuous)
  OL16: Roch 5B 28
  SK4: Stoc 6G 133
  SK14: Hyde 4B 120
  SK15: Mill 2H 107
  WA14: Alt 3B 174 (1F 151)
Graham Cres. M44: Cad 5A 124
Graham Dr. SK12: Dis 6G 161

Graham Rd. M6: Sal 1C 98
  SK1: Stoc 3B 146
Graham St. BL1: Bolt 1F 175 (5D 32)
  M11: Man 5C 102
  OL7: A Lyme 4F 105
Grainger Av. M12: Man 4C 116
GRAINS BAR 1E 61
Grains Rd. OL1: O'ham, Shaw ...6A 44
  OL2: O'ham, Shaw 6A 44
  OL3: Del 2E 61
Grain Vw. M5: Sal 5G 99
Gralam Cl. M33: Sale 2E 141
Grammar School Rd. OL8: O'ham ..1B 90
Grampian Cl. OL9: Chad 4A 74
Grampian Way OL2: Shaw 5G 43
Granada M. M16: W Ran 6C 114
Granada Rd. M34: Dent 4H 117
Granada Studios 1E 9 (5C 100)
Granada TV Cen. 6E 5 (4C 100)
Granary La. M28: Wors 1B 96
Granary M. SK12: Poy 4E 169
Granary Way M33: Sale 1H 139
Granby Ho. M1: Man 2B 10
Granby Rd. M27: Swin 4E 83
  M32: Stre 6D 112
  SK2: Stoc 6B 146
  SK8: Chea H 5D 156
  WA15: Tim 2B 140
Granby Row M1: Man 2B 10 (5E 101)
    (not continuous)
Granby St. BL8: Bury 1H 35
  OL9: Chad 6A 74
Granby Village M1: Man 2B 10
Grandale M. M14: Man 4G 115
Grand Central Pools 3F 179 (2G 145)
Grand Central Sq.
  SK1: Stoc 3F 179 (2G 145)
Grandidge St. OL11: Roch 6G 27
Grand Stand OL2: Shaw 5C 44
Grand Union Way M30: Ecc 5F 97
Granford Cl. WA14: Alt 4F 139
GRANGE 1B 62
Grange, The M14: Man 4G 115
  OL1: O'ham 1H 75
  SK3: Stoc 4E **145**
    (off Edgeley Rd.)
  SK14: Hyde 6D 120
Grange Arts Cen. 2E 177 (2E 75)
Grange Av. BL3: Lit L 4E 51
  M19: Man 1B 132
  M27: Swin 1F 83
  M30: Ecc 1F 97
  M32: Stre 5D 112
  M34: Dent 5H 119
  M41: Urm 5A 110
  OL8: O'ham 5C 74
  OL16: Miln 1F 43
  SK4: Stoc 4F 133
  SK8: Chea H 2B 156
  WA15: Hale 3A 152
  WA15: Tim 4B 140
Grange Cl. SK14: Hyde 6D 120
Grange Ct. BL8: Bury 3B 36
  OL8: O'ham 5D 74
  WA14: Bow 4E 151
Grange Cres. M41: Urm 6E 111
Grange Dr. M9: Man 6B 72
  M30: Ecc 1F 97
Grangeforth Rd. M8: Man 3D 86
Grange Gdns. M30: Ecc 2G 97
Grange Gro. M45: White 1F 69
Grange La. M20: Man 1F 143
  OL3: Del 1B 62
Grange Mnr. BL7: Bro X 3G 19
Grange Mill Wlk. M40: Man 5D 88
Grange Pk. Av.
  OL6: A Lyme 5D 92
  SK8: Chea 6H 143
  SK9: Wilm 1D 172
Grange Pk. Rd. BL7: Bro X 5G 19
  M9: Man 6B 72
  SK8: Chea 6H 143
Grange Pl. M44: Cad 4B 124

Grange Rd. BL3: Bolt 2H 47
   BL4: Farn 6E 49
   BL7: Bro X 4G 19
   BL8: Bury 3B 36
   M21: Chor 5G 113
   M24: Mid 1F 57
   M28: Wors 4C 80
   M30: Ecc 1B 96
   M33: Sale 5H 127
   M41: Urm 6E 111
   OL12: Whitw 2B 14
   SK7: Bram 2H 157
   WA14: Bow 4E 151
   WA15: Tim 4B 140
Grange Rd. Nth. SK14: Hyde 5D 120
Grange Rd. Sth. SK14: Hyde 6D 120
Grange St. M6: Sal 3E 99
   M35: Fail 5F 89
   OL9: O'ham 2E 177 (2E 75)
Grangethorpe Dr. M19: Man 2A 132
Grangethorpe Rd. M14: Man 5G 115
   M41: Urm 6E 111
Grange Wlk. M24: Mid 5A 56
Grangeway SK9: Hand 3G 165
Grangewood BL7: Bro X 4G 19
Grangewood Dr. M9: Man 4H 87
Granite Ct. M25: Pres 4G 69
   (off Longfield Cen.)
Granite St. OL1: O'ham 1H 75
Gransden Dr. M8: Man 5G 87
Granshaw St. M40: Man 2A 102
Gransmoor Av. M11: Man 6H 103
Gransmoor Rd. M11: Droy 5H 103
   M11: Man 6H 103
Grantchester Pl. BL4: Farn 6D 48
Grantchester Way BL2: Bolt 4A 34
Grant Cl. M9: Man 1H 87
Grantham Cl. BL1: Bolt 4C 32
Grantham Ct. M34: Dent 6F 119
   (off Stockport Rd.)
Grantham Dr. BL8: Bury 6D 22
Grantham Rd. SK4: Stoc 1E 145
Grantham St. M14: Man 4E 115
   OL4: O'ham 4G 75
Grant M. BL0: Ram 2B 12
Grants Entry BL0: Ram 3B 12
   (off Young St.)
Grants La. BL0: Ram 3C 12
Grant St. BL4: Farn 5F 49
   OL11: Roch 3F 41
Granville Av. M7: Sal 3C 86
   M16: W Ran 5A 114
Granville Cl. OL9: Chad 2C 74
Granville Ct. M16: W Ran 4A 114
   OL16: Miln 2H 43
Granville Gdns. M20: Man 1E 143
Granville Rd. BL3: Bolt 4A 48
   M14: Man 1G 131
   M34: Aud 4B 104
   M41: Urm 4G 111
   SK8: Chea H 6D 144
   SK9: Wilm 4C 172
   WA15: Tim 5C 140
Granville St. BL4: Farn 5H 49
   M27: Swin 3H 83
   M28: Walk 6G 65
   (not continuous)
   M30: Ecc 2F 97
   OL1: O'ham 6E 59
   OL6: A Lyme 3B 106
   OL9: Chad 1C 74
Granville Wlk. OL9: Chad 1C 74
Graphite Way SK13: Had 2G 123
Grasdene Av. M9: Man 6A 72
Grasmere Av. BL3: Lit L 3C 50
   BL4: Farn 2D 64
   M27: Ward 1E 83
   M41: Urm 6A 110
   M45: White 2C 68
   OL10: H'ood 5H 39
   SK4: Stoc 3G 133
Grasmere Cl. SK15: Stal 1E 107
Grasmere Ct. BL9: Bury 6G 37

Grasmere Cres. M30: Ecc 2D 96
   SK6: H Lan 4C 160
   SK7: Bram 5G 157
Grasmere Dr. BL9: Bury 6G 37
Grasmere Gro. OL7: A Lyme 1F 105
Grasmere Rd. M27: Swin 5H 83
   M31: Part 6C 124
   M32: Stre 4D 112
   M33: Sale 1C 140
   OL2: O'ham 1C 58
   OL4: O'ham 3A 76
   SK8: Gat 2F 155
   SK9: A Edg 5G 173
   WA15: Tim 5C 140
Grasmere St. BL1: Bolt 3D 32
   M12: Man 4D 116
   OL12: Roch 2H 27
Grasmere Wlk. M24: Mid 5B 56
Grason Av. SK9: Wilm 6G 165
GRASSCROFT 4G 77
Grasscroft SK5: Stoc 3C 134
Grasscroft Cl. M14: Man 5D 114
GRASSCROFT CLOUGH 3A 78
Grasscroft Rd. SK15: Stal 4E 107
Grassfield Av. M7: Sal 5A 86
Grassholme Dr. SK2: Stoc 5G 147
Grassingham Gdns.
   M6: Sal .2F 99
Grassington Av. M40: Man 2C 88
Grassington Ct. BL8: Bury 1H 35
Grassington Dr. BL9: Bury 4B 38
Grassington Pl. BL2: Bolt 4E 33
Grassland Ri. M38: Lit H 5C 64
Grass Mead M34: Dent 1G 135
Grassmoor Cres.
   SK13: Gam 5F 123
Grathome Wlk. BL3: Bolt 3C 48
   (off Belford Dr.)
Gratrix Av. M5: Sal 4A 8 (6H 99)
Gratrix La. M33: Sale 6F 129
Gratrix St. M18: Man 3G 117
Gratten Ct. M28: Walk 5G 65
Gravel Bank Rd. SK6: Wood 3H 135
GRAVEL HOLE 5D 58
Gravel La. M3: Sal 4F 5 (3D 100)
   SK9: Wilm 5B 172
Gravel Walks OL4: O'ham 2H 75
Gravenmoor Dr. M7: Sal 5C 86
Graver La. M40: Man 6F 89
   (not continuous)
Graves St. M26: Rad 1H 51
Gray Cl. SK14: Mot 4B 122
Graymar Rd. M38: Lit H 5E 65
Graymarsh Dr. SK12: Poy 5E 169
Grayrigg Wlk. M9: Man 4H 87
   (off Ruskington Dr.)
Graysands Rd. WA15: Hale 2H 151
Grayson Av. M45: White 1G 69
Grayson Rd. M38: Lit H 5F 65
Grayson Way OL3: G'fld 3D 78
Grayston Ct. SK6: Mar 4E 149
Gray St. BL1: Bolt 1E 175 (5C 32)
Gray St. Nth. BL1: Bolt 1E 175 (5C 32)
Graythorpe Wlk. M5: Sal 4G 99
Graythorp Wlk. M14: Man 4F 115
   (off Whickham Cl.)
Graythwaite Rd. BL1: Bolt 3F 31
Grazing Dr. M44: Irl 4F 109
Greame St. M16: W Ran 4D 114
   (not continuous)
Gt. Ancoats St. M4: Man 4C 6 (3F 101)
Gt. Arbor Way M24: Mid 6B 56
Gt. Bent Cl. OL12: Roch 5D 16
Gt. Boys Cl. M29: Tyld 2C 80
Gt. Bridgewater St.
   M1: Man 2F 9 (5D 100)
Gt. Cheetham St. E. M7: Sal 5C 86
Gt. Cheetham St. W.
   M7: Sal .6A 86
Gt. Clowes St. M7: Sal 1D 4 (5B 86)
Gt. Cowes St. M3: Sal 1D 4 (2B 100)
Gt. Ducie St. M3: Man 1G 5 (2D 100)

Gt. Egerton St.
   SK1: Stoc 2E 179 (1G 145)
   SK4: Stoc 2E 179 (2G 145)
Greater Manchester Fire Service Mus.
   . . . . .5C 178 (5H 27)
Greater Manchester Police Mus.
   . . . . .5C 6 (4F 101)
Greatfield Rd. M22: Wyth 2H 153
Great Flatt OL12: Roch 2D 26
Gt. Gable Cl. OL1: O'ham 1G 75
Gt. Gates Cl. OL11: Roch 1H 41
Gt. Gates Rd. OL11: Roch 2A 42
Gt. George St. M3: Sal 4C 4 (3B 100)
   OL16: Roch 5B 178 (5H 27)
   (not continuous)
Gt. Hall Cl. M26: Rad 3A 52
Gt. Heaton Cl. M24: Mid 2G 71
Great Holme BL3: Bolt 3D 48
GREAT HORROCKS 1E 101
GREAT HOWARTH 5B 16
Great Howarth OL12: Roch 5B 16
Gt. Howarth Rd. OL12: Roch 5B 16
Gt. Jackson St. M15: Man . . .3E 9 (6C 100)
Gt. John St. M3: Man 1E 9 (5C 100)
Gt. Jones St. M12: Man 1C 116
Great Lee OL12: Roch 6F 15
Gt. Lee Wlk. OL12: Roch 6F 15
GREAT LEVER 4D 48
Gt. Marlborough St.
   M1: Man 3A 10 (6E 101)
Gt. Marld Cl. BL1: Bolt 3F 31
Great Meadow OL2: Shaw 5F 43
Gt. Moor St. BL1: Bolt 5F 175 (1D 48)
   BL3: Bolt 5F 175 (1D 48)
   SK2: Stoc 6B 146
Gt. Newton St. M40: Man 6E 89
Gt. Norbury St. SK14: Hyde 4A 120
Great Northern 1G 9 (5C 100)
Gt. Northern Sq. Amphitheatre
   M3: Man .1G 9
Gt. Oak Dr. WA15: Alt 2C 174 (1G 151)
Gt. Portwood St.
   SK1: Stoc 1H 179 (1H 145)
Gt. Southern St. M14: Man 4F 115
Greatstone Apartments M32: Stre . . .4E 113
   (off Portland Rd.)
Gt. Stone Cl. M26: Rad 4F 51
Gt. Stone Rd. M16: Old T 4G 113
   M32: Stre 3F 113
Gt. Stones Cl. BL7: Eger 1C 18
Great Underbank
   SK1: Stoc 2F 179 (2H 145)
Gt. Western St. M16: W Ran 3C 114
GREAVE 3D 25
Greave SK6: Rom 5B 136
Greave Av. OL11: Roch 3D 26
GREAVEFOLD 5B 136
Greave Fold SK6: Rom 5A 136
Greave Pk. OL3: Upp 2D 78
Greave Rd. SK1: Stoc 3C 146
Greaves Av. M35: Fail 5F 89
Greaves Rd. SK9: Wilm 2A 172
Greaves St. OL1: O'ham 3G 177 (2F 75)
   OL2: Shaw 6A 44
   OL4: Lees 3D 76
   OL5: Mos 1G 93
Grebe Cl. SK12: Poy 3B 168
Grebe Wlk. SK2: Stoc 1G 159
Grecian Cres. BL3: Bolt 3D 48
Grecian St. M7: Sal 6A 86
Grecian St. Nth. M7: Sal 6A 86
Grecian Ter. M7: Sal 6A 86
   (off Albert Pk. Rd.)
Gredle Cl. M41: Urm 5H 111
Greeba Rd. M23: Wyth 5E 141
Greek St. M1: Man 4C 10
   SK3: Stoc 5F 179 (3G 145)
Green, The BL8: G'mount 2H 21
   M27: Clif 1B 84
   M28: Wors 6B 82
   M31: Part 5D 124
   OL8: O'ham 6G 75
   OL11: Roch 2E 41

Green, The—Greenroom Theatre

Green, The SK4: Stoc 6E **133**
SK6: Mar 2E **161**
SK8: Chea H 5B **156**
SK9: Hand 4A **166**
SK14: Hyde 1E **121**
SK15: Mill 1H **107**
WA15: Tim 4B 140
(off Whitley Gdns.)
Greenacre SK8: H Grn 6G **155**
Greenacre Cl. BL0: Ram 2E **13**
Greenacre La. M28: Wors 1B **96**
Green Acre Pk. BL1: Bolt 4D **32**
GREENACRES **2A 76**
Greenacres Ct. OL12: Roch 5D **16**
Greenacres Dr. M19: Man 5A **132**
GREENACRES HILL **1A 76**
GREENACRES MOOR **1A 76**
Greenacres Rd. OL4: O'ham 2H **75**
Green & Slater Homes SK4: Stoc 6C **132**
Green Av. BL3: Bolt 4F **49**
M27: Swin 4H **83**
M38: Lit H 4C **64**
Green Bank BL2: Bolt 2A **34**
BL4: Farn 6G **49**
SK4: Stoc 2F **133**
Greenbank *OL12: Whitw 4E 15*
(off Tonacliffe Rd.)
SK13: Had 2H **123**
Greenbank Av. M27: Swin 5F **83**
OL3: Upp 6E **63**
SK4: Stoc 1A **144**
SK8: Gat 6E **143**
Greenbank Cres. SK6: Mar 6D **148**
Greenbank Dr. OL15: L'ough 6F **17**
Greenbank Ho. *WA14: Bow 2F 151*
(off Albert Sq.)
Greenbank Rd. BL3: Bolt 2H **47**
(not continuous)
M6: Sal 2E **99**
M26: Rad 2H **51**
M33: Sale 4G **127**
OL12: Roch 2H **27**
(not continuous)
SK6: Mar B 2F **149**
SK8: Gat 5E **143**
Greenbank Ter. M24: Mid 6E **57**
SK4: Stoc 1F **179**
Greenbeech Cl. SK6: Mar 4C **148**
Greenbooth Cl. SK16: Duk 6D **106**
Greenbooth Rd. OL12: Roch 1H **25**
Green Bri. Cl. OL11: Roch 1H **41**
Greenbridge La. OL3: G'fld 4C **78**
Greenbrook Bus. Pk. BL9: Bury 1G **37**
Greenbrook Cl. BL9: Bury 1G **37**
Greenbrook St. BL9: Bury 1G **37**
Greenbrow Rd. M23: Wyth 6G **141**
(not continuous)
Green Bldg., The M1: Man 3H **9**
Greenburn Dr. BL2: Bolt 3A **34**
Green Cl. SK8: Gat 5E **143**
Green Clough OL15: L'ough 3B **16**
Greencourt Dr. M38: Lit H 5D **64**
Green Courts WA14: Bow 2D **150**
Greencourts Bus. Pk.
M22: Wyth 5E **155**
Green Cft. SK6: Rom 6B **136**
Greencroft Mdw. OL2: O'ham 2F **59**
Greencroft Rd. M30: Ecc 1D **96**
Greencroft Way M7: Sal 4B **86**
OL16: Roch 6D **16**
Greendale Dr. M9: Man 6A **72**
M26: Rad 6B **52**
Greendale Gro. M34: Dent 1H **135**
Green Dr. BL6: Los 6C **30**
M19: Man 6B **116**
SK9: Wilm 5H **165**
WA15: Tim 4A **140**
GREEN END **4B 132**
Green End M34: Dent 1H **135**
Green End Rd. M19: Man 4A **132**
GREENFIELD **3D 78**
Greenfield Av. M30: Ecc 5C **96**
M41: Urm 5F **111**
Greenfield Cl. BL5: W'ton 6A **46**
BL8: Bury 4A **36**
SK3: Stoc 5G **145**
WA15: Tim 5C **140**
Greenfield Ct. OL10: H'ood 4H **39**
Greenfield La. OL2: Shaw 1H **59**
OL11: Roch 1A **42**
OL16: Roch 6D **16**
Greenfield Rd. M38: Lit H 5E **65**
Greenfield Station (Rail) **3C 78**
Greenfield St. M34: Aud 6D **104**
OL11: Roch 1A **42**
SK13: Had 1H **123**
SK14: Hyde 5B **120**
Greenfield Ter. M41: Urm 5A **110**
Greenfield Vw. OL16: Roch 6D **16**
Greenfinch Gdns. WA14: W Tim 2D **138**
Green Fold M18: Man 1H **117**
Greenfold Av. BL4: Farn 2F **65**
Greenford Cl. SK8: Chea H 1D **156**
Greenford Rd. M8: Man 4E **87**
Green Gables Cl. SK8: H Grn 4F **155**
Greengage M13: Man 6F **11** (1G **115**)
GREEN GATE **2C 42**
GREENGATE **6D 16**
Green Ga. WA15: Haleb 1D **162**
Greengate M3: Sal 2G **5** (2D **100**)
M24: Man 6E **73**
SK14: Hyde 1B **136**
Greengate Cl. BL9: Bury 3A **38**
OL12: Roch 5D **16**
Greengate E. M40: Man 6E **73**
Greengate Ind. Est. M24: Mid 4E **73**
Greengate La. BL2: Bolt 5B **34**
M25: Pres 5G **69**
Greengate Rd. M34: Dent 3G **119**
Greengate Rdbt. M40: Man 6E **73**
Greengate St. OL4: O'ham 3G **75**
(not continuous)
Greengate W. M3: Sal 2E **5** (2C **100**)
Greengrove Bank OL16: Roch 6C **16**
Greenhalgh Moss La. BL8: Bury 6B **22**
Greenhalgh St. M35: Fail 5E **89**
SK4: Stoc 1F **179** (1G **145**)
Green Hall M. SK9: Wilm 3E **173**
Greenham Rd. M23: Wyth 1F **141**
Greenhaven Cl. M28: Walk 6B **66**
Greenhead Fold SK6: Rom 2G **147**
Greenhead Wlk. *BL3: Bolt 4C 48*
(off Settle St.)
GREENHEYS
M15 . . . . **2E 115**
M38 . . . . **3C 64**
Greenheys BL2: Bolt 2A **34**
M43: Droy 3A **104**
Greenheys Bus. Cen. *M15: Man 2E 115*
(off Pencroft Way)
Greenheys Cres. BL8: G'mount 2G **21**
Greenheys La. M15: Man 2D **114**
Greenheys La. W. M15: Man 2C **114**
Greenheys Rd. M38: Lit H 3C **64**
GREEN HILL
M24 . . . . **2F 73**
OL2 . . . . **4E 43**
Green Hill M25: Pres 5G **69**
Greenhill Av. BL3: Bolt 2H **47**
BL4: Farn 3G **65**
M33: Sale 3A **128**
OL2: Shaw 4E **43**
OL12: Roch 3G **27**
Greenhill Cotts. OL5: Mos 1H **93**
Greenhill La. BL3: Bolt 3F **47**
Greenhill Pas. OL1: O'ham 4H **177**
Green Hill Pl. SK3: Stoc 4F **145**
Green Hill Rd. SK14: Hyde 4D **120**
Greenhill Rd. BL8: Bury 4A **36**
M8: Man 4E **87**
M24: Mid 2E **73**
WA15: Tim 5C **140**
Green Hill St. SK3: Stoc 4F **145**
Green Hill Ter. SK3: Stoc 4F **145**
Greenhill Ter. M24: Mid 2E **73**
Greenhill Terraces OL4: O'ham 3G **75**
Greenhill Wlk. SK12: Dis 1H **171**
Green Hollow Fold SK15: C'ook 6H **93**
Greenholme Cl. M40: Man 2F **89**
Greenhow St. M43: Droy 5H **103**
Greenhurst Cres. OL8: O'ham 1G **91**
Greenhurst La. OL6: A Lyme 5C **92**
Greenhurst Rd. OL6: A Lyme 4B **92**
Greenhythe Rd. SK8: H Grn 1G **165**
Greening Rd. M19: Man 5D **116**
Greenland Rd. BL3: Bolt 5D **48**
BL4: Farn 5E **49**
Greenlands Cl. SK8: Chea H 5A **156**
Greenland St. M6: Sal 3E **99**
M8: Man 4D **86**
Green La. BL1: Bolt 3G **175** (6D **32**)
BL3: Bolt 4D **48**
BL4: Kea 2C **66**
M18: Man 1F **117**
M24: Mid 2F **73**
(Grimshaw La.)
M24: Mid 5D **56**
(Hilton Fold La.)
M30: Ecc 3E **97**
M33: Sale 3G **127**
M35: Fail 1G **103**
M44: Cad 4C **124**
M45: White 6F **53**
OL3: Del 3A 62
(off Church St.)
OL4: O'ham 5D **60**
OL5: Mos 5F **77**
OL6: A Lyme 6H **91**
OL8: O'ham 1D **90**
OL10: H'ood 3A **40**
OL12: Roch 1A **178** (3G **27**)
SK4: Stoc 6D **132**
SK6: Rom 2H **147**
SK7: H Gro 2D **158**
SK9: A Edg 6F **173**
SK9: Wilm 2E **173**
SK12: Dis 2G **171**
SK12: Poy 3A **170**
SK13: Had 3H **123**
SK14: Holl 1F **123**
SK14: Hyde 5E **121**
(Mottram Rd.)
SK14: Hyde 5E **121**
(St Paul's Hill Rd.)
WA15: Tim 2B **152**
(not continuous)
Green La. Ind. Est. SK4: Stoc 1F **145**
Green La. Nth. WA15: Tim 6B **140**
Greenlaw Ct. M16: Old T 2A **114**
Greenlea Av. M18: Man 4F **117**
Greenleach La. M28: Wors 3A **82**
Greenleaf Cl. M28: Wors 5D **80**
Greenleas BL6: Los 1C **46**
Greenlees St. OL12: Roch . . . 1B **178** (3H **27**)
Greenleigh Cl. BL1: Bolt 6B **18**
Greenmans OL3: G'fld 6C **78**
Greenmans La. OL3: G'fld 6C **78**
Green Mdw. OL12: Roch 5D **16**
Green Mdws. SK6: Mar 4D **148**
Green Mdws. Dr. SK6: Mar 3D **148**
Green Mdws. Wlk. M22: Wyth 4C **154**
GREENMOUNT **2H 21**
Greenmount Cl. BL8: G'mount 1H **21**
Greenmount Ct. BL1: Bolt 5G **31**
Greenmount Dr. BL8: G'mount 1H **21**
OL10: H'ood 6B **40**
Greenmount La. BL1: Bolt 4F **31**
Greenmount Pk. BL4: Kea 2C **66**
Greenoak M26: Rad 2E **67**
Greenoak Dr. M28: Walk 4G **65**
M33: Sale 2C **140**
Greenock Cl. BL3: Bolt 2E **47**
Greenock Dr. OL10: H'ood 4D **38**
Green Pk. Cl. BL8: G'mount 2H **21**
Greenpark Rd. M22: Nor 2B **142**
Green Pk. Vw. OL1: O'ham 5B **60**
Green Pastures SK4: Stoc 2H **143**
Green Rd. M31: Part 6C **124**
Greenroom Theatre **2H 9** (**6D 100**)

Greenroyd Av. BL2: Bolt 3A 34
Greenroyde OL11: Roch 6G 27
Greens, The OL12: Whitw 4A 14
Greensbridge Gdns.
  BL5: W'ton 6A 46
Greenshank Cl. OL11: Roch 4B 26
GREENSIDE 3H 103
Greenside BL2: Ain 4E 35
  BL4: Farn 6G 49
  M28: Wors 6C 82
  SK4: Stoc 2C 144
Greenside Cl. BL4: Kea 3B 66
  OL4: O'ham 5B 60
  SK16: Duk 5E 107
Greenside Ct. M30: Ecc 2F 97
Greenside Cres. M43: Droy 3H 103
Greenside Dr. BL8: G'mount 3G 21
  M44: Irl .6D 108
  WA14: Hale 4G 151
Greenside La. M43: Droy 2G 103
Greenside Pl. M34: Dent 1G 135
Greenside Shop. Cen. M43: Droy 4A 104
Greenside St. BL2: Ain 4E 35
  M11: Man 4D 102
Greenside Trad. Cen. M43: Droy . . .3A 104
Greenside Vw. SK14: Hyde 2E 121
Greenside Way M24: Mid 4E 73
Greenson Dr. M24: Mid 2A 72
Greenstead Av. M8: Man 3E 87
Greenstone Dr. M6: Sal 6F 85
Green St. BL0: Eden 2H 13
  BL4: Farn 6G 49
  BL8: Bury 1B 36
                 (Goodlad St.)
  BL8: Bury 1H 35
                 (Neston Rd.)
  M14: Man 2H 131
  M24: Mid 6D 56
  M26: Rad 4A 52
  M30: Ecc 5D 96
  M32: Stre 1C 128
  OL8: O'ham 3D 74
  SK3: Stoc 5H 145
  SK9: A Edg 5G 173
  SK14: Hyde 6C 120
Greensway Shop. Cen. OL2: Shaw . . .6H 43
              (off Milnrow Rd.)
Greenthorne Av. SK4: Stoc 2F 133
Greenthorn Wlk. M15: Man 2D 114
             (off Botham Cl.)
Green Tree Gdns. SK6: Rom 1H 147
Greenvale OL11: Roch 3H 25
Greenvale Ct. SK8: Chea 5G 143
Greenvale Dr. SK8: Chea 5G 143
Green Vw. M7: Sal 4B 86
Green Vw. Chase OL4: Grot 4F 77
Greenview Dr. M20: Man 3G 143
  OL11: Roch 3C 26
Green Villa Pk. SK9: Wilm 5B 172
Green Wlk. M16: W Ran 5A 114
  M31: Part 6C 124
  M32: Stre 5B 112
  SK8: Gat 5E 143
  SK14: Mot 5B 122
  WA14: Bow 2C 150
  WA15: Tim 4H 139
Green Walks M25: Pres 6A 70
Greenwatch Cl. M30: Ecc 4E 97
Greenwater Mdw. SK14: Holl 2F 123
Green Way BL1: Bolt 2F 33
  SK14: Mot 5B 122
Greenway M22: Nor 3C 142
  M24: Mid 4B 72
  OL2: Shaw 4F 43
  OL11: Roch 4D 40
  SK6: Rom 2C 148
  SK7: Bram 1F 167
  SK9: Wilm 3E 173
  SK14: Hyde 6B 120
  WA14: Alt 6C 138
Greenway Av. M19: Man 1D 132
Green Way Cl. BL1: Bolt 1E 33

Greenway Cl. BL8: Bury 2B 36
  M33: Sale 6G 127
Greenway Dr. OL5: Mos 1G 93
Greenway M. BL0: Ram 5C 12
Greenway Rd. SK8: H Grn 6G 155
  WA15: Tim 3H 139
Greenways M40: Man 2F 89
  OL7: A Lyme 5F 91
Greenwich Cl. M40: Man 1F 103
  OL11: Roch 5B 26
Greenwood Av. M27: Clif 2B 84
  M28: Walk 6G 65
  OL6: A Lyme 5A 92
             (not continuous)
  SK2: Stoc 5C 146
Greenwood Bus. Cen. M5: Sal 5G 99
Greenwood Cl. M28: Wors 4C 80
  WA15: Tim 6D 140
Greenwood Dr. SK9: Wilm 1G 173
Greenwood Gdns. SK6: Bred 6F 135
Greenwood Pl. M30: Ecc 1G 97
  OL15: L'ough 4H 17
            (off Hare Hill Rd.)
Greenwood Rd. M22: Wyth 2H 153
Greenwoods La. BL2: Bolt 1B 34
Greenwood St. BL4: Farn 1H 65
  M6: Sal .1F 99
  OL4: O'ham 1A 76
             (not continuous)
  OL4: Spri 4D 76
  OL8: O'ham 2F 91
  OL15: L'ough 4H 17
  OL16: Roch 4C 178 (4H 27)
  WA14: Alt 2A 174 (1F 151)
Greenwood Va. BL1: Bolt 2D 32
             (off Beryl St.)
  BL1: Bolt 2C 32
           (off Blackburn Rd.)
Greer St. M11: Man 5E 103
Greetland Dr. M9: Man 5B 72
Gregge St. OL10: H'ood 4A 40
             (not continuous)
Gregg M. SK9: Wilm 5F 165
Gregory Av. BL2: Bolt 5A 34
  SK6: Rom 2A 148
Gregory St. M12: Man 1B 116
  OL8: O'ham 6C 74
  SK14: Hyde 2C 120
Gregory Way SK5: Stoc 3H 133
Gregson Fld. BL3: Bolt 3C 48
             (not continuous)
Gregson Rd. SK5: Stoc 3G 133
Gregson St. OL1: O'ham . . .4H 177 (3F 75)
Greg St. SK5: Stoc 4G 133
Greg St. Ind. Est. SK4: Stoc 4G 133
Grelley Wlk. M14: Man 4F 115
            (off Ellanby Cl.)
Grendale Av. SK1: Stoc 2B 146
  SK7: H Gro 4E 159
Grendale Dr. M16: Old T 2A 114
Grendon Av. OL8: O'ham 5E 75
Grendon St. BL3: Bolt 4A 48
Grendon Wlk. M12: Man 1C 116
             (off Birch St.)
Grenfell Rd. M20: Man 6E 131
Grenham Av. M15: Man . . .5C 8 (1B 114)
Grenville Rd. SK7: H Gro 2C 158
Grenville St. SK3: Stoc 3F 145
  SK15: Mill 1H 107
  SK16: Duk 5A 106
Grenville Ter. OL6: A Lyme 3B 106
Grenville Wlk. OL15: L'ough 2A 16
Gresford Cl. M21: Chor 1G 129
Gresham Cl. M45: White 2D 68
Gresham Dr. OL9: O'ham 2C 74
Gresham St. BL1: Bolt 2D 32
  M34: Dent 3F 119
Gresham Wlk. SK4: Stoc 6G 133
            (off Hesketh St.)
Gresham Way M33: Sale 2A 140
Gresty Av. M22: Wyth 4D 154
Greswell St. M34: Dent 3F 119
Greta Av. SK8: H Grn 1G 165

Greton Cl. M13: Man 3A 116
Gretton Cl. OL2: O'ham 3F 59
Greville St. M13: Man 3A 116
Grey Cl. SK6: Bred 5G 135
Greyfriars Ct. M3: Sal 1E 5 (2C 100)
Greyfriars Rd. M22: Wyth 3H 153
Greyhound Dr. M6: Sal 6A 86
Grey Knotts M28: Wors 6E 81
Greylag Cres. M28: Wors 3H 81
Greylands Cl. M33: Sale 5H 127
Greylands Rd. M20: Man 3G 143
Grey Mare La. M11: Man 4B 102
Greymont Rd. BL9: Bury 5F 23
Grey Rd. WA14: Alt 6D 138
Greysham Ct. M16: W Ran 5C 114
Greystoke Av. M19: Man 6E 117
  M33: Sale 6B 128
  WA15: Tim 5D 140
Greystoke Cres. M45: White 5E 53
Greystoke Dr. BL1: Bolt 5B 18
  M24: Mid 5H 55
  SK9: A Edg 4G 173
Greystoke La. M35: Fail 5F 89
Greystoke St. SK1: Stoc 2A 146
Greystone Av. M21: Chor 1D 130
Greystone Cl. BL5: W'ton 5A 46
Greystone Wlk. SK4: Stoc 2F 133
Grey St. M12: Man 1A 116
  M24: Mid 6B 56
  M25: Pres 5A 70
  M26: Rad 4B 52
  M34: Dent 4D 118
  OL6: A Lyme 6D 174 (3A 106)
  SK15: Stal 4G 107
Greyswood Av. M8: Man 4D 86
Greytown Cl. M6: Sal 6F 85
Greywood Av. BL9: Bury 3H 37
Grierson St. BL1: Bolt 2C 32
  M16: W Ran 3C 114
Griffe La. BL9: Bury 4A 54
Griffin Cl. BL9: Bury 1G 37
Griffin Gro. M19: Man 1C 132
Griffin Ho. BL9: Bury 1G 37
Griffin La. SK8: H Grn 6H 155
Griffin Rd. M35: Fail 4F 89
Griffin St. M7: Sal 5A 86
Griffiths Cl. M7: Sal 1D 4 (1B 100)
Griffiths St. M40: Man 6E 89
Grimes Cotts. OL12: Roch 2B 26
Grimes St. OL12: Roch 2B 26
Grime St. BL0: Ram 5A 12
Grimscott Cl. M9: Man 2B 88
Grimshaw Av. M35: Fail 3A 90
Grimshaw Cl. SK6: Bred 5G 135
Grimshaw La. M24: Mid 1D 72
  M40: Man 6B 88
Grimshaw St. M35: Fail 3G 89
  SK1: Stoc 2A 146
Grimstead Cl. M23: Wyth 5E 141
Grindall Av. M40: Man 1D 88
Grindleford Gdns. SK13: Gam 5G 123
            (off Buxton M.)
Grindleford Gro. SK13: Gam 5G 123
           (off Edale Cres.)
Grindleford Lea SK13: Gam 5G 123
           (off Edale Cres.)
Grindleford Wlk. M21: Chor 4B 130
  SK13: Gam 5G 123
            (off Buxton M.)
Grindle Grn. M30: Ecc 5E 97
Grindleton Av. M22: Wyth 2B 154
Grindley Av. M21: Chor 4B 130
Grindlow St. M13: Man 2A 116
Grindon Av. M7: Sal 4G 85
Grindrod St. M26: Rad 3A 52
Grindsbrook Rd.
  M26: Rad 6H 35
Grinton Av. M13: Man 5A 116
Grisdale Dr. M24: Mid 5A 56
Grisdale Rd. BL3: Bolt 2A 48
Grisebeck Way
  OL1: O'ham 2F 177 (2E 75)
Grisedale Av. OL2: O'ham 5C 42

Grisedale Cl. M18: Man 3E 117
   M24: Mid .4H 55
Grisedale Rd. OL11: Roch 1D 40
Gristlehurst La. BL9: Bury 6D 24
   OL10: H'ood 6D 24
Gritley Wlk. M22: Wyth 4A 154
Grizebeck Cl. M18: Man 1E 117
Grizedale Cl. BL1: Bolt 3F 31
   SK15: C'ook 4B 94
Grizedale Rd. SK6: Wood 5H 135
Groby Ct. WA14: Alt 2A 174 (1E 151)
Groby Pl. WA14: Alt 1A 174 (6E 139)
Groby Rd. M21: Chor 1H 129
   M34: Aud 6E 105
   WA14: Alt 1D 150
Groby Rd. Nth. M34: Aud 5D 104
Groby St. OL8: O'ham 6G 75
   SK15: Stal 4G 107
Groom St. M1: Man 3C 10
Grosvenor Av. M45: White 1E 69
Grosvenor Casino
   Bolton 5E 175 (1C 48)
   Manchester 1C 100
   Salford 2C 8 (5B 100)
Grosvenor Cl. M28: Walk 4G 65
   SK9: Wilm 5D 172
Grosvenor Ct. M7: Sal 3B 86
   M16: W Ran 4C 114
   M33: Sale 4H 127
   OL7: A Lyme 4G 105
   SK8: Chea 5H 143
Grosvenor Cres. SK14: Hyde 6A 120
Grosvenor Dr. M28: Walk 4G 65
   SK12: Poy 4C 168
Grosvenor Gdns. M7: Sal 1B 100
   M22: Shar 5C 142
   SK15: Stal 4E 107
Grosvenor Ho. M16: W Ran 6C 114
                 (off Arnold Rd.)
   M33: Sale 5H 127
            (off Grosvenor Sq.)
   OL7: A Lyme 4G 105
                 (off Park St.)
Grosvenor Ho. M. M8: Man 1D 86
Grosvenor Ho. Sq. SK15: Stal 4E 107
Grosvenor Ind. Est.
   OL7: A Lyme 4G 105
Grosvenor Lodge SK7: H Gro 4B 158
           (off Dorchester Rd.)
Grosvenor Pl. M13: Man . . .4B 10 (6E 101)
   OL7: A Lyme 4G 105
Grosvenor Rd. M16: W Ran 5B 114
   M27: Swin 4B 84
   M28: Walk 4G 65
   M30: Ecc 2C 96
   M33: Sale 4H 127
   M41: Urm 5E 111
   M45: White 6E 53
   SK4: Stoc 6C 132
              (not continuous)
   SK6: Mar 4D 148
   SK8: Chea H 1E 157
   SK14: Hyde 6B 120
   WA14: Alt 1C 174 (6G 139)
Grosvenor Sq. M7: Sal 1B 100
   M15: Man 4B 10 (6E 101)
   M33: Sale 5A 128
   OL3: Upp 1D 78
               (off Watergate)
   SK15: Stal 4E 107
Grosvenor St. BL2: Bolt 6H 175 (1E 49)
   BL3: Lit L 3C 50
   BL4: Kea 1A 66
   BL9: Bury 6C 176 (5F 37)
   M1: Man 4B 10 (6E 101)
   M25: Pres 5A 70
   M26: Rad 3H 51
   M27: Pen 1H 83
   M32: Stre 5D 112
   M34: Dent 3D 118
   OL7: A Lyme 4F 105
               (not continuous)

Grosvenor St. OL10: H'ood 4G 39
   OL11: Roch 4E 41
   SK1: Stoc 5G 179 (3H 145)
   SK7: H Gro 2D 158
   SK15: Stal 4E 107
Grosvenor Way OL2: O'ham 5D 58
GROTTON .4F 77
Grotton Hollow OL4: Grot 3E 77
Grotton Mdws. OL4: Grot 4F 77
Grove, The BL2: Bolt 2F 49
   BL3: Lit L 4D 50
   M20: Man 2F 143
   M30: Ecc 4H 97
   M33: Sale 6B 128
   M41: Urm 6B 110
   OL2: Shaw 1G 59
   OL3: Dob 6B 62
   SK2: Stoc 6F 179 (4G 145)
   SK8: Chea H 5H 143
   SK13: Had 3H 123
   WA14: Alt 6F 139
Grove Arc. SK9: Wilm 2E 173
Grove Av. M35: Fail 6G 89
   SK9: Wilm 2D 172
Grove Bank OL4: Gras 4A 78
Grove Cl. M14: Man 4G 115
Grove Cotts. OL3: Dig 1F 63
   OL15: L'ough 3A 16
Grove Ct. M33: Sale 5D 128
   SK7: H Gro 2E 159
Grove Hill M28: Wors 5D 80
Grove Ho. M15: Man 2F 115
   SK4: Stoc 2A 144
Grove La. M20: Man 6F 131
   SK8: Chea H 1C 166
   WA15: Hale 2A 152
   WA15: Tim 4H 139
Grove M. M28: Walk 6H 65
            (off Malvern Gro.)
Grove Pk. .2C 166
Grove Pk. M33: Sale 5H 127
Grove Rd. M24: Mid 5D 56
   OL3: Upp 2D 78
   SK15: Mill 1H 107
   WA15: Hale 2G 151
Grove St. BL1: Bolt 3B 32
   BL4: Kea 1A 66
   M7: Sal .6C 86
   M43: Droy 5H 103
   OL3: G'fld 4D 78
   OL7: A Lyme 6E 91
   OL10: H'ood 3A 40
   OL11: Roch 6G 27
   SK7: H Gro 2E 159
   SK9: Wilm 2E 173
   SK16: Duk 4B 106
Grove Ter. OL4: O'ham 1C 76
Grove Way SK9: Wilm 2E 173
Grovewood Cl. OL7: A Lyme 6E 91
Grundey St. SK7: H Gro 3E 159
Grundy Av. M25: Pres 1E 85
Grundy Cl. BL9: Bury 4G 37
Grundy La. BL9: Bury 4G 37
Grundy Rd. BL4: Kea 2A 66
Grundy's Cl. M29: Ast 6A 80
Grundy St. BL3: Bolt 3B 48
               (off High St.)
   M28: Walk 1B 82
   OL10: H'ood 5A 40
   SK4: Stoc 1A 144
Guardian Cl. OL12: Roch 1G 27
Guardian Ct. M33: Sale 4A 128
Guardian Lodge SK8: Gat 6E 143
Guardian M. M23: Wyth 2C 140
Guernsey Cl. M19: Man 3C 132
Guest Rd. M25: Pres 3G 69
Guest St. M4: Man 5G 7 (4H 101)
GUIDE BRIDGE 5F 105
Guide Bridge Station (Rail) 5F 105
Guide Bridge Theatre 5E 105
Guide Bri. Trad. Est. OL7: A Lyme . .5E 105

Guide La. M34: Aud 5F 105
Guide Post Sq. M13: Man . . .6G 11 (1H 115)
Guide St. M50: Sal 4C 98
Guido St. BL1: Bolt 3B 32
   M35: Fail 4G 89
Guild Av. M28: Walk 1H 81
Guildford Av. SK8: Chea H 1C 166
Guildford Cl. SK1: Stoc 4B 146
Guildford Dr. OL6: A Lyme 4A 92
Guildford Gro. M24: Mid 4E 57
Guildford Rd. BL1: Bolt 3H 31
   M6: Sal 1B 98
   M19: Man 5D 116
   M41: Urm 3G 111
   SK16: Duk 6E 107
Guildford St. OL5: Mos 2H 93
Guildhall Cl. M15: Man 2E 115
Guild St. BL7: Bro X 4F 19
Guilford Rd. M30: Ecc 4D 96
Guinness Circ. M17: T Pk 5A 98
Guinness Ho. OL16: Roch 5B 28
Guinness Rd. M17: T Pk 5H 97
Guinness Rd. Trad. Est. M17: T Pk . . .5H 97
Guiseley Cl. BL9: Bury 3E 23
Gullane Cl. M40: Man 4E 89
Gull Cl. SK12: Poy 4B 168
Gulvain Pl. OL9: Chad 1H 73
Gunson Ct. M40: Man 2F 7 (2G 101)
Gunson St. M40: Man 2F 7 (2G 101)
Gun St. M4: Man 4D 6 (3F 101)
Gurner Av. M5: Sal 6H 99
Gurney St. M4: Man 5H 7 (4H 101)
Gutter End BL9: Bury 3C 176 (3F 37)
Gutter La. BL0: Ram 2B 12
Guy Fawkes St. M5: Sal 6H 99
Guywood Cotts. SK6: Rom 6A 136
Guywood La. SK6: Rom 6A 136
Gwelo St. M11: Man 3C 102
Gwenbury Av. SK1: Stoc 2B 146
Gwendor Av. M8: Man 6D 70
Gwladys St. SK15: C'ook 5A 94
Gwynant Pl. M20: Man 2G 131
Gwyneth Morley Ct. SK9: Hand 4H 165
Gylden Cl. SK14: Hyde 1F 121
Gypsy La. SK2: Stoc 5C 146
             (not continuous)
Gypsy Wlk. SK2: Stoc 5C 146
Gyte's La. M19: Man 5E 117

H

Habergham Cl. M28: Wors 4G 81
Hacienda, The M1: Man 2G 9
Hackberry Cl. WA14: B'ath 3D 138
Hacken Bri. Rd. BL3: Bolt 3H 49
Hacken La. BL3: Bolt 3G 49
Hackford Cl. BL1: Bolt 5A 32
   BL8: Bury 6D 22
Hacking St. BL9: Bury 3G 37
   M7: Sal .5C 86
   M25: Pres 5G 69
Hackle St. M11: Man 3E 103
Hackleton Cl. M4: Man 5H 7 (4H 101)
Hackness Rd. M21: Chor 1F 129
Hackney Av. M40: Man 1E 103
Hackney Cl. M26: Rad 2A 52
Hackwood Wlk. M8: Man 4D 86
           (off Levenhurst Rd.)
Haddington Dr. M9: Man 6A 72
Haddon Av. M40: Man 2H 89
Haddon Cl. BL9: Bury 2G 53
   SK6: H Lan 1C 170
   SK9: A Edg 4F 173
Haddon Grn. SK13: Gam 5F 123
          (off Grassmoor Cres.)
Haddon Gro. M33: Sale 6A 128
   SK5: Stoc 2G 133
   WA15: Tim 4H 139
Haddon Hall Rd. M43: Droy 3G 103
Haddon Ho. M5: Sal 2D 98
Haddon Lea SK13: Gam 5F 123
          (off Grassmoor Cres.)

Haddon M. SK13: Gam 5F **123**
Haddon Rd. M21: Chor 4B **130**
M28: Wors 5E **83**
M30: Ecc 5D **96**
SK7: H Gro 4E **159**
SK8: H Grn 6G **155**
Haddon St. M6: Sal 6H **85**
M32: Stre 3D **112**
OL11: Roch 6G **27**
Haddon Way M34: Dent 6G **119**
OL2: Shaw 5A **44**
Hadfield Av. OL9: Chad 5B **74**
Hadfield Cl. M14: Man 4H **115**
Hadfield Cres. OL6: A Lyme 6C **92**
Hadfield Ind. Est. SK13: Had 1H **123**
Hadfield Rd. SK13: Had 3G **123**
Hadfields Av. SK14: Holl 2F **123**
Hadfield St. M7: Sal 5C **86**
M16: Old T 6B **8** (1A **114**)
OL8: O'ham 6E **75**
SK16: Duk 6G **105**
Hadfield Ter. OL6: A Lyme 6C **92**
Hadleigh Cl. BL1: Bolt 5E **19**
Hadleigh Grn. BL6: Los 3B **46**
Hadley Av. M13: Man 5A **116**
Hadley Cl. SK8: Chea H 4B **156**
Hadley St. M6: Sal 6H **85**
Hadlow Grn. SK5: Stoc 3B **134**
Hadlow Wlk. *M40: Man* 2A **102**
(off Sabden Cl.)
Hadrian Ho. OL1: O'ham 2G **177** (2F **75**)
Hadwin St. BL1: Bolt 1F **175** (4D **32**)
Hafton Rd. M7: Sal 5H **85**
Hag End Brow BL2: Bolt 2G **49**
HAGGATE 4C **58**
Haggate Cres. OL2: O'ham 4C **58**
Hagg Bank La. SK12: Dis 6H **161**
Hagley Rd. M5: Sal 1G **113**
Hags, The BL9: Bury 2G **53**
HAGUE, THE 5E **123**
Hague Ct. M20: Man 4E **131**
Hague Ho. OL8: O'ham 6G **177**
Hague Pl. SK15: Stal 3E **107**
Hague Rd. M20: Man 4E **131**
SK14: B'tom 6D **122**
Hague St. OL4: O'ham 1C **76**
OL6: A Lyme 1A **106**
Haig Av. M44: Cad 5A **124**
Haig Ct. BL8: Bury 4B **36**
Haigh Av. SK4: Stoc 4G **133**
Haigh Hall Cl. BL0: Ram 5B **12**
Haigh La. OL1: Chad 6G **57**
Haigh Lawn WA14: Alt 2D **150**
Haigh Pk. SK4: Stoc 4G **133**
Haigh St. OL11: Roch 6D **178** (5A **28**)
Haig Rd. BL8: Bury 3B **36**
M32: Stre 4D **112**
Haile Dr. M28: Wors 5D **80**
Hailsham Cl. BL8: Bury 4C **22**
Hail St. BL0: Ram 5A **12**
Hailwood St. OL11: Roch 1G **41**
Halbury Gdns. OL9: Chad 3A **74**
Halbury Wlk. *BL1: Bolt* 3D **32**
(off Fairhaven Rd.)
Halcyon Cl. OL12: Roch 1D **26**
Haldane Rd. M5: Sal 4G **99**
Haldene Wlk. *M8: Man* 5D **86**
(off Felthorpe Dr.)
Haldon Rd. M20: Man 4H **131**
HALE . . . .
3G 151
Hale Av. SK12: Poy 5D **166**
Hale Bank Av. M20: Man 2D **130**
HALEBARNS 5C **152**
Hale Ct. WA14: Alt 3F **151**
Hale Grn. Ct. WA15: Hale 2A **152**
Hale La. M35: Fail 3G **89**
Hale Low Rd. WA15: Hale 2H **151**
HALE MOSS 2H **151**
Hale Rd. SK4: Stoc 6E **133**
WA14: Alt 2F **151**
WA15: Hale 2F **151**

Hales Cl. M43: Droy 2H **103**
Halesden Rd. SK4: Stoc 4F **133**
Hale Station (Rail) 3F **151**
Halesworth Wlk.
M40: Man 1G **101**
(off Talgarth Rd.)
Haletop M22: Wyth 3B **154**
Hale Vw. *WA14: Alt* 3F **151**
(off Ashley Rd.)
Hale Wlk. SK8: Chea 1C **156**
Haley Cl. SK5: Stoc 1H **133**
Haley St. M8: Man 4F **87**
HALF ACRE 3A **70**
Half Acre M26: Rad 1G **51**
Half Acre Dr. OL11: Roch 5E **27**
Half Acre La. OL11: Roch 5D **26**
Half Acre M. OL11: Roch 5D **26**
Half Acre Rd. OL11: Roch 5D **26**
Halfacre Rd. M22: Wyth 1A **154**
Half Edge La. M30: Ecc 2G **97**
Half Lea Grange
M30: Ecc 2G **97**
(off Half Edge La.)
Half Moon La. SK2: Stoc 5D **146**
Half Moon St. M2: Man 5H **5**
Halfpenny Bri. Ind. Est.
OL11: Roch 6D **178** (5A **28**)
Half St. M3: Sal 2F **5** (2C **100**)
Halifax Rd. OL12: Roch 2B **28**
OL15: L'ough 4H **17**
OL16: Roch 2B **28**
Halifax St. OL6: A Lyme 1H **105**
Hallacres La.
SK8: Chea H 5A **156**
Hallam Mill *SK2: Stoc* 5A **146**
(off Hallam St.)
Hallam Rd. M40: Man 6D **88**
Hallams Pas. SK2: Stoc 5A **146**
Hallam St. M26: Rad 3D **52**
SK2: Stoc 5A **146**
Hallas Gro. M23: Wyth 2H **141**
Hall Av. M14: Man 4H **115**
M33: Sale 3G **127**
SK15: H'rod 6G **93**
WA15: Tim 4H **139**
Hall Bank M30: Ecc 3E **97**
Hall Bank Ho. OL3: G'fld 4B **78**
Hallbottom St. SK14: Hyde 2D **120**
Hallbridge Gdns. BL1: Bolt 2E **33**
Hall Cl. SK14: Mot 2C **122**
Hall Coppice, The BL7: Eger 1B **18**
Hallcroft M31: Part 5D **124**
Hallcroft Gdns. OL16: Miln 5E **29**
Hall Dr. M24: Mid 2B **72**
SK14: Mot 2C **122**
Hall Farm Av. M41: Urm 4D **110**
Hall Farm Cl. SK7: H Gro 2G **159**
Hall Grn. Cl. SK16: Duk 4A **106**
Hall Grn. Rd. SK16: Duk 4A **106**
Hall Gro. M14: Man 4H **115**
SK8: Chea 5G **143**
Halliday Ct. OL15: L'ough 5E **17**
Halliday Rd. M40: Man 1D **102**
Halliford Rd. M40: Man 5C **88**
Hallington Cl. BL3: Bolt 2D **48**
HALL I' TH' WOOD 1F **33**
Hall i' th' Wood La. BL1: Bolt 1E **33**
Hall i' th' Wood La. BL2: Bolt 2F **33**
Hall i' th' Wood Mus. 1E **33**
Hall i' th' Wood Station (Rail) 2F **33**
HALLIWELL 3B **32**
Halliwell Av. OL8: O'ham 6E **75**
Halliwell Ind. Est. BL1: Bolt 2B **32**
Halliwell La. M8: Man 4D **86**
Halliwell Rd. BL1: Bolt 2A **32**
M25: Pres 2F **85**

Halliwell St. *BL1: Bolt* 3B **32**
(off Hobart St.)
OL12: Roch 3G **27**
(not continuous)
OL16: Miln, Roch 4E **29**
Halliwell St. W. M8: Man 4D **86**
Hallkirk Wlk. M40: Man 1F **89**
Hall La. BL4: Farn 5H **49**
(not continuous)
M23: Wyth 5H **141**
M31: Part 5D **124**
SK6: Wood 3H **135**
(not continuous)
Hall Lee Dr. BL5: W'ton 6A **46**
Hall Mdw. SK8: Chea H 4A **156**
Hall Moss La. SK7: Bram 2D **166**
Hall Moss Rd. M9: Man 6C **72**
Hall Pool Dr. SK2: Stoc 4E **147**
Hall Rd. M14: Man 4H **115**
OL6: A Lyme 6A **92**
SK7: Bram 4F **157**
SK9: Hand 4A **166**
SK9: Wilm 2D **172**
WA14: Bow 4E **151**
Hallroyd Brow OL1: O'ham 1F **177**
(off Halls Way)
Halls Barn *OL3: G'fld* 3D **78**
(off Halls Way)
Halls Cotts. OL3: G'fld 3D **78**
Hall's Pl. OL4: Spri 3D **76**
Hallstead Gro. M38: Lit H 5C **64**
Hallstead Gro. M38: Lit H 5C **64**
Hall St. BL3: Bolt 5H **49**
BL4: Bolt 5H **49**
BL8: Bury 6G **21**
(Parkgate)
BL8: Bury 1C **36**
(Rowans St.)
BL9: Sum 1C **22**
M1: Man 1H **9** (5D **100**)
M24: Mid 1C **72**
M26: Rad 1H **51**
M27: Pen 1H **83**
M35: Fail 5F **89**
OL2: O'ham 3D **58**
OL4: O'ham 2H **75**
(off Gravel Wlks.)
OL6: A Lyme 3C **106**
OL10: H'ood 4A **40**
OL12: Whitw 1E **15**
SK1: Stoc 2A **146**
SK8: Chea 5H **143**
SK14: Hyde 4H **119**
Hallsville Rd. M19: Man 6E **117**
Halls Way OL3: G'fld 3D **78**
Hallsworth Rd. M30: Ecc 4C **96**
Hallview Way M28: Walk 6D **64**
Hallwood Av. M6: Sal 1C **98**
Hallwood Rd. M23: Wyth 5G **141**
SK9: Hand 4H **165**
Hallworth Av. M34: Aud 4B **104**
Hallworth Rd. M8: Man 3F **87**
Halmore Rd. M40: Man 3G **7** (3H **101**)
Halsall Cl. BL9: Bury 5F **23**
Halsall Dr. BL3: Bolt 5C **48**
Halsbury Cl. M12: Man 1A **116**
Halsey Cl. OL9: Chad 1G **89**
Halsey Wlk. *M8: Man* 4D **86**
(off Greysworth Av.)
Halshaw La. BL4: Kea 2B **66**
Halsmere Dr. M9: Man 6A **72**
Halstead Av. M6: Sal 1D **98**
M21: Chor 2G **129**
Halstead Dr. M44: Irl 6F **109**
Halstead Gro. SK8: Gat 1D **154**
Halstead St. BL2: Bolt 6E **33**
BL9: Bury 6G **23**
Halstead Wlk. BL9: Bury 6G **23**
Halstock Wlk. *M40: Man* 6H **87**
(off Foreland Cl.)
Halstone Av. SK9: Wilm 5B **172**
Halston St. M15: Man 6F **9** (1C **114**)
Halter Cl. M26: Rad 2A **52**

Halton Bank M6: Sal 1F **99**
Halton Dr. WA15: Tim 2B **140**
Halton Flats OL10: H'ood 3G **39**
(off Meadow Cl.)
Halton Ho. M5: Sal 4F **99**
(off Amersham St.)
Halton Rd. M11: Man 3E **103**
Halton St. BL2: Bolt 6F **33**
SK14: Hyde 4D **120**
Halvard Av. BL9: Bury 5F **23**
Halvard Ct. BL9: Bury 5F **23**
Halvis Gro. M16: Old T 4H **113**
Hamble Cft. M26: Rad 1D **66**
(off Stoneclough Ri.)
Hambleden Cl. BL3: Bolt 2F **47**
Hambleton Cl. BL8: Bury 4H **35**
Hambleton Dr. M33: Sale 4F **127**
Hambleton Rd. SK8: H Grn 5G **155**
Hambridge Cl. M8: Man 4E **87**
Hamel St. BL3: Bolt 4B **48**
SK14: Hyde 2D **120**
Hamer Ct. OL16: Roch 2B **28**
Hamer Dr. M16: Old T 2B **114**
Hamer Hall Cres. OL12: Roch 1B **28**
Hamer Hill M9: Man 6G **71**
Hamer La. OL16: Roch 2B **28**
Hamer St. BL0: Ram 1B **22**
BL2: Bolt 4F **33**
M26: Rad 3C **52**
Hamer Ter. BL9: Sum 6C **12**
(off Waterside Rd.)
Hamerton Rd. M40: Man 1G **101**
Hamer Va. OL12: Roch 1B **28**
Hamilcar Av. M30: Ecc 3G **97**
Hamilton Av. M30: Ecc 4G **97**
M44: Cad 5B **124**
OL2: O'ham 4B **58**
Hamilton Cl. BL8: Bury 2B **36**
M25: Pres 6G **69**
Hamilton Ct. BL3: Lit L 4D **50**
(off Heywood St.)
M33: Sale 5B **128**
Hamilton Cres. SK4: Stoc 2D **144**
Hamilton Gro. M16: Old T 2B **114**
(off Hamilton St.)
Hamilton Ho. WA14: Alt . . .1B **174** (6F **139**)
Hamilton Lodge M14: Man 4G **115**
Hamilton M. M25: Pres 6G **69**
M30: Ecc 2D **96**
Hamilton Rd. M13: Man 4B **116**
M25: Pres 6G **69**
M29: Ast 5B **80**
M45: White 1E **69**
Hamilton Sq. SK4: Stoc 1G **145**
Hamilton St. BL1: Bolt 6C **18**
BL9: Bury 1F **37**
M7: Sal 4B **86**
M16: Old T 2B **114**
M27: Swin 2F **83**
M30: Ecc 2D **96**
OL4: O'ham 3G **75**
OL7: A Lyme 4F **105**
SK15: Stal 3D **106**
Hamilton Way OL10: H'ood 4C **38**
Hamlet, The BL6: Los 5B **30**
Hamlet Dr. M33: Sale 3G **127**
Hammerstone Rd. M18: Man 1E **117**
Hammer St. OL10: H'ood 3F **39**
Hammett Rd. M21: Chor 1G **129**
Hammond Av. SK4: Stoc 4G **133**
Hammond Ct. SK4: Stoc 4G **133**
Hammond Flats OL10: H'ood 3G **39**
(off Meadow Cl.)
Hamnet Cl. BL1: Bolt 6E **19**
Hamnett St. M11: Man 4F **103**
M43: Droy 4F **103**
SK14: Hyde 4B **120**
Hamon Rd. WA15: Alt . . .3C **174** (1G **151**)
Hampden Cl. M30: Ecc 3F **97**
Hampden Cres. M18: Man 2E **117**
(not continuous)
Hampden Gro. M30: Ecc 3F **97**

Hampden Rd. M25: Pres 5H **69**
M33: Sale 6A **128**
OL2: Shaw 1B **60**
Hampden St. OL10: H'ood 4H **39**
OL11: Roch 5C **178**
Hampshire Cl. BL9: Bury 5G **37**
SK5: Stoc 4C **134**
Hampshire Ho. SK5: Stoc 4C **134**
Hampshire Rd. M43: Droy 2A **104**
OL9: Chad 4B **74**
SK5: Stoc 4C **134**
Hampshire Wlk. M8: Man 5F **87**
(off Appleford Dr.)
Hampson Cl. M30: Ecc 4D **96**
Hampson Cres. SK9: Hand 3G **165**
Hampson Fold M26: Rad 3H **51**
Hampson Mill La. BL9: Bury 2F **53**
Hampson Pl. OL6: A Lyme 5C **92**
Hampson Rd. M32: Stre 5C **112**
Hampson Sq. M26: Rad 3A **52**
(off Water St.)
Hampson St. M5: Sal 6B **4** (4A **100**)
M26: Rad 3A **52**
M27: Pen 2A **84**
M30: Ecc 4D **96**
M33: Sale 5D **128**
M40: Man 1H **101**
M43: Droy 3A **104**
SK1: Stoc 3B **146**
Hampstead Av. M41: Urm 6A **110**
Hampstead Dr. M45: White 6E **53**
SK2: Stoc 6C **146**
Hampstead La. SK2: Stoc 6C **146**
Hampton Ct. SK9: Hand 2H **165**
(off Wilmslow Rd.)
Hampton Gro. BL9: Bury 5F **23**
SK8: Chea H 3A **156**
WA14: Tim 2H **139**
Hampton Ho. M33: Sale 5C **128**
(off Northenden Rd.)
Hampton M. SK3: Stoc 1H **157**
Hampton Rd. BL3: Bolt 4E **49**
M21: Chor 6F **113**
M35: Fail 3A **90**
M41: Urm 6F **111**
M44: Cad 5B **124**
Hampton St. OL8: O'ham 5D **74**
Hamsell Cl. M13: Man 4E **11** (6G **101**)
Hamsell Rd. M13: Man 4E **11** (6G **101**)
Hancock Cl. M14: Man 4F **115**
Hancock St. M32: Stre 1D **128**
Handel Av. M41: Urm 5C **110**
Handel M. M33: Sale 5C **128**
Handel St. BL1: Bolt 2B **32**
OL12: Whitw 1D **14**
Handford Ho. M41: Urm 5G **111**
(off Cavendish Rd.)
HANDFORTH 3H **165**
Handforth By-Pass SK8: Chea H 6A **166**
SK9: Chea, Wilm 6A **166**
Handforth Dean SK9: Hand 3A **166**
Handforth Gro. M13: Man 6A **116**
Handforth Rd. SK5: Stoc 4H **133**
SK9: Wilm 5A **166**
Handforth Station (Rail) 4H **165**
Handley Av. M14: Man 6F **115**
Handley Cl. SK3: Stoc 6E **145**
Handley Gdns. BL1: Bolt 6H **31**
Handley Rd. SK7: Bram 2G **157**
Handley St. BL9: Bury 5F **37**
OL12: Roch 2F **27**
Hands La. OL11: Roch 4C **26**
Handsworth St.
M12: Man 3H **11** (6H **101**)
Hanging Birch M24: Mid 2F **71**
Hanging Bri. M3: Man 4H **5**
(off Cateaton St.)
HANGING CHADDER 6C **42**
Hanging Chadder La. OL2: O'ham . . .6C **42**
Hanging Lees Cl. OL16: Miln 1A **44**
Hani Cl. M8: Man 2D **86**
Hani Wells Bus. Pk. M19: Man 2D **132**
Hankinson Cl. M31: Part 6D **124**

Hankinson Way M6: Sal 2G **99**
Hanley Cl. M24: Mid 4C **72**
SK12: Dis 2H **171**
Hanlith M. M19: Man 1B **132**
Hanlon St. M8: Man 2D **86**
Hannah Baldwin Cl. M11: Man 5B **102**
Hannah Brown Ho. WA15: Hale 2G **151**
(off Finchley Rd.)
Hannah Lodge M20: Man 5E **131**
(off Palatine Rd.)
Hannah St. M12: Man 5C **116**
Hannerton Rd. OL2: Shaw 5B **44**
Hannet Rd. M22: Wyth 3B **154**
Hanover Bus. Pk. WA14: B'ath 4D **138**
Hanover Cl. BL3: Bolt 2H **47**
(off Greenbank Rd.)
M28: Wors 5D **82**
OL7: A Lyme 4G **105**
Hanover Cres. M14: Man 3H **115**
Hanover Gdns. M7: Sal 3C **86**
Hanover Ho. BL3: Bolt 4A **48**
M14: Man 1H **131**
(off Ladybarn La.)
OL8: O'ham 5E **177**
Hanover Rd. WA14: B'ath 4D **138**
Hanover St. BL1: Bolt 4E **175** (6C **32**)
M4: Man 3A **6** (3E **101**)
OL5: Mos 2G **93**
OL11: Roch 3E **41**
OL15: L'ough 4G **17**
SK15: Stal 3D **106**
Hanover St. Nth. M34: Aud 5E **105**
Hanover St. Sth. M34: Aud 5E **105**
Hanover Towers SK5: Stoc 6H **133**
Hansby Cl. OL1: O'ham 6E **59**
Hansdon Cl. M8: Man 5E **87**
Hansen Wlk. M22: Wyth 3A **154**
Hanslope Wlk. M9: Man 3A **88**
(off Swainsthorpe Dr.)
Hanson Cl. M24: Mid 6C **56**
Hanson Cl. Ind. Est. M24: Mid 6C **56**
Hanson M. SK1: Stoc 1B **146**
Hanson Rd. M40: Man 4C **88**
Hanson St. BL9: Bury 1F **37**
M24: Mid 6C **56**
OL4: O'ham 2A **76**
Hanworth Cl. M13: Man 4D **10** (6F **101**)
Hapsford Wlk. M40: Man 6C **88**
Hapton Av. M32: Stre 6D **112**
Hapton Pl. SK4: Stoc 6G **133**
Hapton St. M19: Man 6C **116**
Harbern Cl. M30: Ecc 1F **97**
Harborne Wlk. BL8: G'mount 3H **21**
Harboro Cl. M33: Sale 6H **127**
Harboro Gro. M33: Sale 5H **127**
Harboro Rd. M33: Sale 4G **127**
Harboro Way M33: Sale 5H **127**
Harbour City Station (Metro) 5F **99**
Harbour Farm Rd. SK14: Hyde 1C **120**
Harbour La. OL16: Miln 6F **29**
Harbour La. Nth. OL16: Miln 5F **29**
Harbourne Av. M28: Wors 3G **81**
Harbourne Cl. M28: Wors 3G **81**
Harburn Wlk. M22: Wyth 5C **154**
Harbury Cl. BL3: Bolt 4G **47**
Harbury Cres. M22: Wyth 6A **142**
Harcles Dr. BL0: Ram 1B **22**
Harcombe Rd. M20: Man 3G **131**
Harcourt Av. M41: Urm 6H **111**
Harcourt Cl. M41: Urm 6H **111**
Harcourt Ind. Cen. M28: Walk 4H **65**
Harcourt Rd. M33: Sale 3A **128**
WA14: Alt 5F **139**
Harcourt St. BL4: Farn 5H **49**
M28: Walk 4H **65**
M32: Stre 4E **113**
OL1: O'ham 1H **75**
SK5: Stoc 1H **133**
Harcourt St. Sth. M28: Walk 4H **65**
Hardberry Pl. SK2: Stoc 5E **147**
Hardcastle Av. M21: Chor 3A **130**
Hardcastle Cl. BL2: Bolt 5G **19**
Hardcastle Gdns. BL2: Bolt 5G **19**

Hardcastle Rd. SK3: Stoc . . .6E **179** (4F **145**)
Hardcastle St. BL1: Bolt 3D **32**
   OL1: O'ham 3H **177** (2G **75**)
Harden Dr. BL2: Bolt 3H **33**
Harden Hills OL2: Shaw 5B **44**
HARDEN PARK 4G **173**
Harden Pk. SK9: A Edg 6D **172**
Hardfield Rd. M24: Mid 4C **72**
Hardfield St. OL10: H'ood 3H **39**
Hardicker St. M19: Man 2D **132**
Hardie Av. BL4: Farn 2F **65**
Harding St. M3: Sal 3G **5**
   M4: Man 5G **7** (4H **101**)
   M6: Sal 1G **99**
   SK1: Stoc .2B **146**
   SK14: Hyde 2B **120**
Hardman Av. M25: Pres 1B **86**
   SK6: Bred .6G **135**
Hardman Blvd. M3: Man 6F **5** (4C **100**)
Hardman Fold BL3: Bolt 5F **49**
Hardman La. M35: Fail 3G **89**
Hardman Rd. SK5: Stoc 1H **133**
Hardmans BL7: Bro X 4D **18**
Hardman's La. BL7: Bro X 3D **18**
Hardman's M. M45: White 3F **69**
Hardman Sq. M3: Man 6F **5** (4C **100**)
Hardman's Rd. M45: White 3F **69**
Hardman St. BL4: Farn 2A **66**
   BL9: Bury 1C **176** (1F **37**)
               (not continuous)
   M3: Man 6F **5** (4C **100**)
   M26: Rad .1H **51**
   M35: Fail 4F **89**
   OL9: Chad .6B **74**
   OL10: H'ood 3H **39**
   OL16: Miln .6G **29**
   SK3: Stoc .2F **145**
               (not continuous)
Hardon Gro. M13: Man 5B **116**
Hardrush Fold M35: Fail 5A **90**
Hardshaw Cl. M13: Man . . .5D **10** (1F **115**)
Hardsough La. BL0: Eden 1G **13**
Hardwick Cl. M26: Rad 2D **50**
   SK6: H Lan 1D **170**
Hardwicke Rd. SK12: Poy 3F **169**
Hardwicke St. OL11: Roch 1G **41**
Hardwick Rd. M31: Part 6E **125**
Hardwick St. OL7: A Lyme 3F **105**
Hardwood Cl. M8: Man 4E **87**
Hardy Av. M21: Chor 1G **129**
Hardy Cl. OL11: Roch 2H **41**
   SK16: Duk 5A **106**
Hardy Dr. SK7: Bram 6F **157**
   WA15: Tim 4H **139**
Hardy Farm M21: Chor 3H **129**
Hardy Gro. M27: Swin 6F **83**
   M28: Wors .3B **82**
Hardy La. M21: Chor 3H **129**
Hardy Mill Rd. BL2: Bolt 1B **34**
Hardy St. M30: Ecc 5D **96**
   OL4: O'ham 4G **75**
   OL6: A Lyme 5C **92**
Hardywood Rd. M34: Dent 2G **135**
Harebell Av. M38: Lit H 6D **64**
Harebell Cl. OL12: Roch 6F **15**
Harecastle Av. M30: Ecc 5G **97**
Haredale Dr. M8: Man 5F **87**
Hare Dr. BL9: Bury 3H **53**
Harefield Av. OL11: Roch 6A **28**
Harefield Dr. M20: Man 1E **143**
   OL10: H'ood 3B **40**
   SK9: Wilm .4D **172**
Harefield Rd. SK9: Hand 3A **166**
Harehill Cl. M13: Man 3D **10** (6F **101**)
Hare Hill Ct. OL15: L'ough 3H **17**
Hare Hill Rd. OL15: L'ough 3G **17**
   SK14: Hat .4G **121**
Hare Hill Wlk. SK14: Hat 4G **121**
Hareshill Bus. Pk. OL10: H'ood 5F **39**
Hareshill Rd. OL10: H'ood 5F **39**
Hare St. M4: Man 4B **6**
   OL11: Roch 6C **178** (6H **27**)

Harewood SK14: B'tom 6C **122**
Harewood Av. M33: Sale 5F **127**
   OL11: Roch 1H **25**
Harewood Cl. OL11: Roch 1H **25**
Harewood Ct. M9: Man 4E **71**
            (off Deanswood Dr.)
   M33: Sale .6C **128**
Harewood Dr. OL2: O'ham 2C **58**
   OL11: Roch 1G **25**
Harewood Gro. SK5: Stoc 1G **133**
Harewood Rd. M44: Irl 5F **109**
   OL2: Shaw .5A **44**
   OL11: Roch 1G **25**
Harewood Wlk. M34: Dent 6G **119**
             (off Tatton Rd.)
Harewood Way M27: Clif 1H **83**
   OL11: Roch 1G **25**
Harford Cl. SK7: H Gro 4A **158**
Hargate Av. OL12: Roch 1C **26**
Hargate Cl. BL9: Sum 1C **22**
Hargate Dr. M44: Irl 4E **109**
   WA15: Hale 4A **152**
Hargrave Cl. M9: Man 3C **72**
Hargreaves Ho. BL3: Bolt 5E **175** (1C **48**)
Hargreaves Rd. WA15: Tim 5C **140**
Hargreaves St. BL1: Bolt 3C **32**
   M4: Man 1B **6** (2E **101**)
   OL1: O'ham 2G **177** (2F **75**)
   OL9: O'ham 3C **74**
   OL11: Roch 1E **41**
Harkerside Cl. M21: Chor 1A **130**
Harkness St. M12: Man 4F **11** (6G **101**)
Harland Dr. M8: Man 4F **87**
Harland Way OL12: Roch 1C **26**
Harlech Av. M45: White 3H **69**
Harlech Dr. SK7: H Gro 4C **158**
Harleen Gro. SK2: Stoc 4D **146**
Harlesden Cres. BL3: Bolt 2A **48**
            (off Langshaw Wlk.)
Harley Av. BL2: Ain 4F **35**
   BL2: Bolt 2A **34**
   M14: Man .4A **116**
Harley Cl. M24: Mid 6B **56**
Harley Rd. M24: Mid 6B **56**
   M33: Sale .4B **128**
Harley St. M11: Man 5F **103**
   OL6: A Lyme 4C **174** (2H **105**)
Harling Rd. M22: Shar 4B **142**
Harlington Cl. M23: Wyth 4D **140**
            (off Petersfield Dr.)
Harlow Dr. M18: Man 4F **117**
Harlyn Av. SK7: Bram 6H **157**
Harmer Cl. M40: Man 6C **88**
Harmol Gro. OL7: A Lyme 5F **91**
Harmony Sq. M13: Man 6H **11** (2H **115**)
Harmony St. OL4: O'ham 5H **177** (3G **75**)
   OL16: Miln .5F **29**
Harmsworth Dr. SK4: Stoc 4D **132**
Harmsworth St. M6: Sal 3E **99**
Harold Av. M18: Man 3H **117**
   SK16: Duk 5B **106**
Haroldene St. BL2: Bolt 3F **33**
Harold Lees Rd. OL10: H'ood 2B **40**
Harold Priestnall Cl. M40: Man 5D **88**
Harold St. BL1: Bolt 3B **32**
   M16: Old T 6B **8** (1A **114**)
   M24: Mid 6A **56**
   M25: Pres 5F **69**
   M35: Fail 4G **89**
   OL9: O'ham 2D **74**
   OL16: Roch 1C **28**
   SK1: Stoc .3B **146**
Harper Ct. SK3: Stoc 6F **179** (4G **145**)
Harper Fold Rd. M26: Rad 4F **51**
HARPER GREEN 6F **49**
Harper Green Community Leisure Cen.
   . . . . .6F **49**
Harper Grn. Rd. BL4: Farn 5F **49**
Harper Ho. M19: Man 6B **116**
Harper Mill OL6: A Lyme 2A **106**
Harper Pl. OL6: A Lyme 2A **106**
Harper Rd. M22: Shar 4C **142**
Harper's La. BL1: Bolt 3H **31**

Harper Sq. OL2: Shaw 6A **44**
Harper St. BL4: Farn 5F **49**
   OL8: O'ham 5E **75**
   OL11: Roch 6G **27**
   SK3: Stoc 6E **179** (4G **145**)
Harpford Cl. BL2: Bolt 2C **50**
Harpford Dr. BL2: Bolt 2C **50**
Harp Ind. Est. OL11: Roch 3F **41**
Harp Rd. M17: T Pk 5A **98**
Harp St. M11: Man 6G **103**
Harp Trad. Est. M17: T Pk 5A **98**
HARPURHEY 4H **87**
Harpurhey Leisure Cen. 3A **88**
Harpurhey Pools 2H **87**
Harpurhey Rd. M8: Man 3G **87**
   M9: Man 3G **87**
Harridge, The OL12: Roch 6E **15**
Harridge Av. OL12: Roch 6E **15**
   SK15: Stal 3H **107**
Harridge Bank OL12: Roch 6E **15**
Harridge St. OL12: Roch 6E **15**
Harrier Cl. M22: Shar 6C **142**
   M28: Wors .3H **81**
Harriet St. BL3: Bolt 5H **47**
   M28: Walk .5H **65**
             (not continuous)
   M44: Cad .4C **124**
Harriett St. M4: Man 3F **7** (3G **101**)
   OL16: Roch 4D **178** (4A **28**)
Harringay Rd. M40: Man 6D **88**
Harrington Cl. BL9: Bury 6G **37**
Harrington Rd. WA14: Alt 6D **138**
Harrington St. M18: Man 2G **117**
Harris Av. M34: Dent 4B **118**
   M41: Urm .2F **111**
Harris Cl. M34: Dent 4B **118**
   OL10: H'ood 4C **38**
Harris Dr. BL9: Bury 5H **53**
   SK14: Hyde 3E **121**
Harrison Av. M19: Man 5D **116**
Harrison Cl. OL12: Roch 2B **26**
Harrisons Dr. SK6: Wood 4A **136**
Harrison St. BL0: Ram 2C **12**
   M4: Man 6G **7** (4H **101**)
   M7: Sal 1D **4** (1B **100**)
   M30: Ecc 5D **96**
   M38: Lit H .5E **65**
   OL1: O'ham 4G **177** (3F **75**)
   SK1: Stoc 6H **179** (4H **145**)
   SK14: Hyde 1D **136**
   SK15: Stal .3D **106**
Harris St. BL3: Bolt 1C **48**
   M8: Man 1C **100**
Harrogate Av. M25: Pres 1B **86**
Harrogate Cl. M11: Man 6G **103**
Harrogate Dr. SK5: Stoc 1G **133**
Harrogate Rd. SK5: Stoc 1G **133**
Harrogate Sq. BL8: Bury 4H **35**
Harroll Ga. M27: Swin 4A **84**
Harrop Ct. OL3: Dig 2F **63**
Harrop Ct. Rd. OL3: Dig 2F **63**
HARROP DALE .2F **63**
HARROP EDGE 2A **122**
Harrop Edge La. OL3: Dig 3C **62**
Harrop Edge Rd. SK14: Mot 3A **122**
Harrop Fold OL8: O'ham 2G **91**
Harrop Fold School Sports Hall 5E **65**
            (off Longshaw Dr.)
HARROP GREEN 2F **63**
Harrop Grn. La. OL3: Dig 2E **63**
HARROP RIDGE 1F **63**
Harrop Rd. WA15: Hale 3G **151**
Harrop St. BL3: Bolt 3G **47**
   M18: Man .1H **117**
   M28: Walk .6F **65**
   SK1: Stoc 6H **179** (4A **146**)
   SK15: Stal .3E **107**
Harrow Av. M19: Man 3C **132**
   OL8: O'ham 6D **74**
   OL11: Roch 5C **26**
Harrowby Ct. BL4: Farn 1F **65**
Harrowby Dr. M40: Man 6H **87**
Harrowby Fold BL4: Farn 1G **65**

Harrowby La. BL4: Farn 1G **65**
Harrowby Rd. BL1: Bolt 3F **31**
  BL3: Bolt 4G **47**
  M27: Swin 4G **83**
Harrowby St. BL4: Farn 1F **65**
Harrow Cl. BL9: Bury 2F **53**
  SK9: Wilm 1G **173**
Harrowdene Wlk. *M9: Man* *3H 87*
  (off Alderside Rd.)
Harrow Dr. M33: Sale 1A **140**
  SK8: Chea 3G **155**
Harrow M. OL2: Shaw 6H **43**
Harrow Rd. BL1: Bolt 5H **31**
  M33: Sale 1A **140**
Harrow St. M8: Man 2F **87**
  OL11: Roch 3B **42**
Harrycroft Rd. SK6: Wood 4H **135**
Harryfields SK14: B'tom 6B **122**
Harry Hall Gdns. M7: Sal 1B **4** (1A **100**)
Harry Piggott Ct. M9: Man 6G **71**
Harry Rd. SK5: Stoc 1H **133**
Harry Rowley Cl. M22: Wyth 4A **154**
Harry St. OL2: O'ham 5E **59**
  OL9: O'ham 3C **74**
  OL11: Roch 2D **40**
Harry Thorneycroft Wlk.
  M11: Man *5A 102*
  (off Rylance St.)
Harrytown SK6: Rom 1G **147**
Harry Whitehead St. BL9: Bury 5F **23**
Hart Av. M33: Sale 6F **129**
  M43: Droy 4B **104**
Hart Ct. OL5: Mos 1F **93**
Hart Dr. BL9: Bury 3H **53**
Harter St. M1: Man 1A **10** (5E **101**)
Hartfield Cl. M13: Man 5E **11** (1G **115**)
Hartfield Wlk. BL2: Bolt 5G **33**
Hartford Av. OL10: H'ood 3F **39**
  SK4: Stoc 3F **133**
  SK9: Wilm 4C **172**
Hartford Cl. OL10: H'ood 2F **39**
Hartford Dr. BL8: Bury 5A **22**
Hartford Gdns. WA15: Tim 6D **140**
Hartford Grange BL8: O'ham 5D **74**
Hartford Ind. Est. OL9: O'ham 3C **74**
Hartford Rd. M33: Sale 1F **139**
  M41: Urm 3G **111**
Hartford Sq. OL9: O'ham 3C **74**
Hartford St. M34: Dent 2E **119**
Hartford Wlk. *M9: Man* *5G 87*
  (off Mannington Dr.)
Hart Hill Dr. M6: Sal 2D **98**
Harthill St. M8: Man 6D **86**
Hartington Cl. M41: Urm 5G **111**
Hartington Ct. OL2: O'ham 3E **59**
Hartington Dr. M11: Man 2D **102**
  SK7: H Gro 5E **159**
Hartington Rd. BL1: Bolt 6A **32**
  M21: Chor 1H **129**
  M30: Ecc 2C **96**
  SK2: Stoc 6D **146**
  SK6: H Lan 6C **160**
  SK7: Bram 1G **167**
  SK8: H Grn 5H **155**
  SK12: Dis 6C **160**
  WA14: B'ath 4F **139**
Hartington St. M14: Man 4D **114**
Hartis Av. M7: Sal 5C **86**
Hartland Av. M41: Urm 5A **112**
Hartland Cl. M29: Ast 3A **80**
  SK2: Stoc 3C **146**
  SK12: Poy 2D **168**
Hartland Ct. *BL1: Bolt* *2C 32*
  (off Blackburn Rd.)
Hartland St. OL10: H'ood 3H **39**
Hartlebury OL11: Roch 6A **178** (5G **27**)
Hartlepool Cl. M14: Man 4F **115**
Hartley Av. M25: Pres 6A **70**
Hartley Gro. M44: Irl 3F **109**
Hartley Hall Gdns.
  M16: W Ran 6C **114**
Hartley La. OL11: Roch 1G **41**
Hartley Pl. OL16: Roch 4D **28**

Hartley Rd. M21: Chor 6G **113**
  WA14: Alt 6E **139**
Hartley St. M40: Man 3B **88**
  OL10: H'ood 3H **39**
  OL12: Roch 2D **26**
  OL12: W'le 6C **16**
  OL15: L'ough 4G **17**
  OL16: Roch 4D **28**
  SK3: Stoc 3F **145**
  SK15: Mill 2H **107**
Hartley Ter. OL11: Roch 2G **41**
  OL15: L'ough *4G 17*
  (off William St.)
Hart Mill Cl. OL5: Mos 1F **93**
Harton Av. M18: Man 4E **117**
Harton Cl. OL2: Shaw 1G **59**
Hart Rd. M14: Man 5E **115**
Hartshead Av. OL6: A Lyme 5A **92**
  SK15: Stal 2E **107**
Hartshead Cl. M11: Man 6A **104**
Hartshead Cres. M35: Fail 5C **90**
HARTSHEAD GREEN 3D **92**
Hartshead High School Sports Hall
  . . . .*4C 92*
  (off Greenhurst Rd.)
Hartshead Rd. OL6: A Lyme 5A **92**
Hartshead St. OL4: Lees 4C **76**
Hartshead Vw. SK14: Hyde 6D **120**
Hartsop Dr. M24: Mid 5G **55**
Hartspring Av. M27: Swin 4A **84**
Hart St. M1: Man 1A **10** (5E **101**)
  (Abingdon St.)
  M1: Man 6B **6** (4E **101**)
  (Minshull St.)
  M29: Tyld 3A **80**
  M43: Droy 3A **104**
  WA14: Alt 6G **139**
Hartswood Av. M34: Dent 3G **119**
Hartswood Rd. M20: Man 3H **131**
Hartwell Cl. BL2: Bolt 3G **33**
  M11: Man 5B **102**
Hartwell Gro. SK3: Stoc 1H **157**
Harty Ho. *M30: Ecc* *3G 97*
  (off Monton La.)
Harvard Cl. SK6: Wood 4A **136**
Harvard Gro. M6: Sal 2C **98**
Harvard Rd. M18: Man 2D **116**
Harvard St. OL11: Roch 1A **42**
Harvest Cl. M6: Sal 6E **85**
  M33: Sale 6G **129**
Harvest Pk. BL1: Bolt 5A **32**
Harvey Cl. M11: Man 5C **102**
Harvey St. BL1: Bolt 2B **32**
  BL8: Bury 2C **36**
  OL12: Roch 1B **28**
  SK1: Stoc 2H **179** (2H **145**)
Harvin Gro. M34: Dent 5G **119**
Harwell Rd. WA14: W Tim 2E **139**
Harwich Cl. M19: Man 6D **116**
  SK5: Stoc 3C **134**
Harwin Cl. OL12: Roch 6F **15**
HARWOOD 1B **34**
Harwood Ct. M6: Sal 1H **99**
  SK4: Stoc 1A **144**
Harwood Cres. BL8: Tot 4G **21**
Harwood Dr. BL8: Bury 4A **36**
Harwood Gdns. *OL10: H'ood* *4H 39*
  (off Mount St.)
Harwood Gro. BL2: Bolt 4F **33**
Harwood Ho. BL8: Tot 4G **21**
HARWOOD LEE 6A **20**
Harwood Mdw. BL2: Bolt 2B **34**
Harwood Pk. OL10: H'ood 4H **39**
Harwood Rd. BL8: Tot 1E **35**
  M19: Man 3A **132**
  SK4: Stoc 1A **144**
Harwood St. OL15: L'ough 4F **17**
  SK4: Stoc 6G **133**
Harwood Va. BL2: Bolt 2A **34**
Harwood Va. Ct. BL2: Bolt 2A **34**
Harwood Wlk. BL8: Tot 4G **21**
Haseley Cl. M26: Rad 2D **50**
  SK12: Poy 2E **169**

Haselhurst Wlk. M23: Wyth 1F **141**
Hasguard Cl. BL1: Bolt 5F **31**
Haslam Brow BL9: Bury 6A **176** (5E **37**)
Haslam Ct. BL3: Bolt 2H **47**
  M7: Sal .2B **86**
Haslam Hall M. BL1: Bolt 6E **31**
Haslam Hey Cl. BL8: Bury 3H **35**
Haslam Rd. SK3: Stoc 5G **145**
Haslam St. BL3: Bolt 2B **48**
  BL9: Bury 1G **37**
  M24: Mid 2E **73**
  OL12: Roch 3F **27**
Haslemere Av. WA15: Haleb 1C **162**
Haslemere Dr. SK8: Chea H 4C **156**
Haslemere Rd. M20: Man 3H **131**
  M41: Urm 6D **110**
Haslington Rd. M22: Wyth 3C **154**
Hasper Av. M20: Man 2E **131**
Hassall Av. M20: Man 2D **130**
Hassall St. M26: Rad 2E **53**
  SK15: Stal 4F **107**
Hassall Way *SK9: Hand* *2A 166*
  (off Spath La.)
Hassop Av. M7: Sal 4G **85**
Hassop Cl. M11: Man 4A **102**
Hassop Rd. SK5: Stoc 6A **118**
Hastings Av. M21: Chor 1G **129**
  M45: White 2H **69**
Hastings Cl. M45: White 2H **69**
  SK1: Stoc 4B **146**
  SK8: Chea H 4E **157**
Hastings Dr. M41: Urm 4A **110**
Hastings Rd. BL1: Bolt 5H **31**
  M25: Pres 4A **70**
  M30: Ecc 1C **96**
Hastings St. OL11: Roch 6H **27**
Haston Cl. SK5: Stoc 5H **133**
Hasty La. WA15: Ring 6E **153**
  (not continuous)
Hatchett Rd. M22: Wyth 4B **154**
Hatchley St. M13: Man 6G **11** (2H **115**)
Hatchmere Cl. SK8: Chea H 1B **156**
  WA15: Tim 5D **140**
Hateley Rd. M16: Old T 5G **113**
Hatfield Av. M19: Man 3B **132**
Hatfield Rd. BL1: Bolt 4A **32**
Hatford Cl. M29: Tyld 2A **80**
Hathaway Cl. SK8: H Grn 6F **155**
Hathaway Dr. BL1: Bolt 6E **19**
Hathaway Gdns. SK6: Bred 6F **135**
Hathaway Rd. BL9: Bury 4G **53**
Hatherleigh Wlk. BL2: Bolt 2B **50**
Hatherley Rd. M20: Man 3H **131**
HATHERLOW 1H **147**
Hatherlow SK6: Rom 1G **147**
Hatherlow Cl. BL5: W'ton 5A **46**
Hatherlow Hgts. SK6: Rom 2G **147**
Hatherlow La. SK7: H Gro 3D **158**
Hatherop Cl. M30: Ecc 4D **96**
Hathersage Av. M6: Sal 2D **98**
Hathersage Cres. SK13: Gam 5G **123**
Hathersage Rd. M13: Man 3G **115**
Hathersage St. OL9: O'ham 3C **74**
Hathersage Way M34: Dent 1G **135**
HATHERSHAW 6G **75**
Hathershaw La. OL8: O'ham 6F **75**
Hathershaw Sports Cen. 1F **91**
Hatherton Ct. M28: Walk 3H **65**
Hatro Ct. M41: Urm 6A **112**
Hatters Ct. SK1: Stoc 5H **179** (3H **145**)
HATTERSLEY 6A **20**
Hatters Ct. SK1: Stoc 6A **122**
  (off Hattersley Rd. E.)
Hattersley Ind. Est. SK14: Hat 6H **121**
Hattersley Rd. E. SK14: Hat 6A **122**
Hattersley Rd. W. SK14: Hat 5G **121**
Hattersley Station (Rail) 6G **121**
Hattersley Wlk. *SK14: Hat* *4G 121*
  (off Wardle Brook Av.)
Hatter St. M4: Man 3C **6**
Hatton Av. M7: Sal 1C **4** (2B **100**)
Hattonfold M33: Sale 2C **140**
Hatton Gro. BL1: Bolt 6E **19**

Hattons Ct. M32: Stre 4C 112
Hattons Rd. M17: T Pk 1B 112
Hatton St. M12: Man 4C 116
  SK1: Stoc 1F 179 (1G 145)
  SK4: Stoc 1F 179 (1G 145)
Hatton Ter. SK16: Duk 4H 105
  (off Queen St.)
Hat Works (The Mus. of Hatting)
  . . . . .3F 179 (2G 145)
HAUGH 1A 44
Haugh Fold OL16: Miln 1A 44
Haugh Hill Rd. OL4: O'ham 4C 60
Haugh La. OL16: Miln 1A 44
Haugh Sq. OL16: Miln 1A 44
Haughton Cl. SK6: Wood 3G 135
HAUGHTON DALE 2G 135
Haughton Dale Local Nature Reserve
  . . . . .2H 135
Haughton Dr. OL12: Nor 2B 142
HAUGHTON GREEN 1H 135
Haughton Grn. Rd. M34: Dent 1G 135
Haughton Hall Rd. M34: Dent 4G 119
Haughton St. M34: Aud 2F 119
  SK14: Hyde 6C 120
Havana Cl. M11: Man 4B 102
Haveley Rd. M22: Wyth 6A 142
Havelock Dr. M7: Sal 1C 4 (1B 100)
Havelock St. OL8: O'ham 6G 177 (4F 75)
Haven, The BL3: Lit L 4C 50
  (off Independent St.)
  WA15: Hale 2H 151
Havenbrook Gro. BL0: Ram 6A 12
Haven Cl. M26: Rad 2F 51
  OL4: Gras 3H 77
  SK7: H Gro 4C 158
Haven Dr. M43: Droy 3G 103
Haven La. OL4: O'ham 4C 60
Havenscroft Av. M30: Ecc 5F 97
Havenside Cl. OL4: O'ham 4C 60
Haven St. M6: Sal 4E 99
Havercroft Pk. BL1: Bolt 5D 30
Haverfield Rd. M9: Man 6A 72
Haverford St. M12: Man 1B 116
Havergate Walks SK2: Stoc 1F 159
Haverhill Gro. BL2: Bolt 3F 33
  (off Scawfell Av.)
Haversham Rd. M8: Man 1C 86
Havers Rd. M18: Man 2G 117
Havisham Cl. BL6: Los 3B 46
Hawarden Av. M16: W Ran 5A 114
Hawarden Rd. WA14: Alt 5F 139
Hawarden St. BL1: Bolt 6C 18
Haw Clough La. OL3: G'fld 3E 79
Hawdraw Grn. SK2: Stoc 5E 147
Hawes Av. BL4: Farn 1C 64
  M14: Man 2A 132
  M27: Swin 4H 83
Hawes Cl. BL8: Bury 6B 22
  SK2: Stoc 5A 146
Haweswater Cl. M34: Dent 5A 118
Haweswater Cres. BL9: Bury 2H 53
Haweswater Dr. M24: Mid 5A 56
Haweswater M. M24: Mid 5A 56
Hawfinch Gro. M28: Wors 3H 81
Hawick Gro. OL10: H'ood 4C 38
Hawk Cl. BL9: Bury 1H 37
Hawker Av. BL3: Bolt 4B 48
Hawkeshead Rd. M8: Man 5F 87
  (not continuous)
Hawke St. SK15: Stal 4G 107
HAWK GREEN 2D 160
Hawk Grn. Cl. SK6: Mar 2D 160
Hawk Grn. Rd. SK6: Mar 2D 160
Hawkhurst Rd. M13: Man 4B 116
Hawkinge Vw. OL10: H'ood 6B 40
Hawkins St. SK5: Stoc 5G 133
Hawkins Way OL15: L'ough 2A 16
Hawkridge Dr. M23: Wyth 1F 141
Hawk Rd. M44: Irl 4E 109
HAWKSHAW 1D 20
Hawkshaw Cl. BL8: Haw 1D 20
Hawkshaw Ct. M5: Sal 4G 99
Hawkshaw La. BL8: Haw 1D 20

Hawkshead Dr. BL3: Bolt 4G 47
  M24: Mid 6A 56
  OL2: O'ham 1D 58
Hawkshead Rd. OL2: Shaw 5G 43
Hawksheath Cl. BL7: Eger 2D 18
Hawksley Ct. OL8: O'ham 6C 74
  (off Maple St.)
Hawksley Ind. Est.
  OL8: O'ham 6C 74
Hawksley St. OL8: O'ham 6C 74
Hawksmoor Dr. OL2: Shaw 5H 43
Hawkstone Av. M43: Droy 2G 103
  M45: White 2D 68
Hawkstone Cl. BL2: Bolt 2A 34
Hawkswick Dr. M23: Wyth 1G 141
Hawk Yd. OL3: G'fld 4F 79
Hawk Yd. La. OL3: G'fld 4F 79
Hawley Dr. WA15: Haleb 5B 152
Hawley Grn. OL12: Roch 1F 27
Hawley La. WA15: Haleb 5B 152
Hawley St. M19: Man 1D 132
Haworth Av. BL0: Ram 1B 22
Haworth Ct. M26: Rad 4B 52
  (off Haworth Wlk.)
Haworth Dr. M32: Stre 4H 111
Haworth Rd. M18: Man 3E 117
Haworth St. BL8: Bury 1G 35
  M26: Rad 4B 52
  OL1: O'ham 6E 59
Haworth Wlk. M26: Rad 4B 52
Hawsworth Cl. M15: Man 2F 115
Hawthorn Apartments
  M26: Rad 3B 52
  (off Bury Rd.)
Hawthorn Av. BL0: Eden 3G 13
  BL0: Ram 1A 22
  BL8: Bury 1C 36
  M26: Rad 6B 52
  M28: Walk 2A 82
  M30: Ecc 2F 97
  M41: Urm 6H 111
  SK6: Mar 5B 148
  SK9: Wilm 2D 172
  WA15: Tim 4H 139
Hawthorn Bank BL2: Bolt 1A 34
  SK13: Had 3H 123
Hawthorn Cl. M29: Tyld 2B 80
  WA15: Tim 4H 139
Hawthorn Ct. SK6: Bred 6D 134
Hawthorn Cres. BL8: Tot 4H 21
  OL2: Shaw 1H 59
  OL8: O'ham 1F 91
Hawthornden M20: Man 5D 130
  (off Palatine Rd.)
Hawthorn Dr. M6: Sal 1B 98
  M19: Man 2B 132
  M27: Pen 4C 84
  M44: Cad 4B 124
  SK15: Stal 5D 106
Hawthorne Av. BL4: Farn 1F 65
Hawthorne Dr. M28: Wors 4C 82
Hawthorne Gro. OL9: Chad 1B 74
  SK6: Bred 5E 135
  SK12: Poy 3A 170
Hawthorne Rd. BL3: Bolt 2H 47
Hawthorne St. BL3: Bolt 2H 47
Hawthorn Grn.
  SK9: Wilm 2D 172
  (off Kennerley's La.)
Hawthorn Gro.
  OL7: A Lyme 4F 105
  SK4: Stoc 6D 132
  SK7: Bram 1E 167
  SK9: Wilm 2E 173
  SK14: Holl 1F 123
  SK14: Hyde 6B 120
Hawthorn La. M21: Chor 1F 129
  M32: Stre 1D 128
  M33: Sale 3F 127
  OL16: Miln 1G 43
  SK9: Wilm 2D 172
Hawthorn Lodge SK3: Stoc 1H 157
Hawthorn Pk. SK9: Wilm 2D 172

Hawthorn Rd. BL4: Kea 4D 66
  M32: Stre 1D 128
  (off Hancock St.)
  M34: Dent 3B 118
  M40: Man 2G 89
  M43: Droy 3C 104
  (not continuous)
  OL8: O'ham 1B 90
  OL11: Roch 5A 26
  SK4: Stoc 1B 144
  SK8: Gat 6E 143
  WA15: Hale 2G 151
Hawthorn Rd. Sth. M43: Droy 3C 104
Hawthorns, The M34: Aud 1D 118
  M34: Dent 3B 118
  (off Hawthorn Rd.)
  OL4: O'ham 3E 61
Hawthorn St. M18: Man 2G 117
  M34: Aud 1E 119
  SK9: Wilm 3D 172
Hawthorn Ter. SK4: Stoc 6D 132
  (off Hawthorn Gro.)
  SK9: Wilm 3D 172
Hawthorn Vw. SK9: Wilm 2D 172
Hawthorn Wlk. M31: Part 6C 124
  OL15: L'ough 4F 17
  SK9: Wilm 2D 172
Hawthorpe Gro. OL3: Upp 1D 78
Haxby Rd. M18: Man 4F 117
Hayburn Av. M23: Wyth 4H 141
Hayburn Rd. SK2: Stoc 3C 146
Haycock Cl. SK15: Stal 6H 107
Hay Cft. SK8: Chea H 5A 156
Hayden Ct. M40: Man 6H 87
  (off Sedgeford Rd.)
Haydn Av. M14: Man 3F 115
Haydock Av. M33: Sale 1D 138
Haydock Cl. M32: Stre 3F 113
Haydock Dr. M28: Wors 5F 81
  SK7: H Gro 3F 159
  WA15: Tim 6B 140
Haydock La. BL7: Bro X 3F 19
  (Chapeltown Rd.)
  BL7: Bro X 3E 19
  (Hospital Rd.)
Haydock M. M7: Sal 5B 86
  (off Rigby St.)
Haydock St. BL1: Bolt 1F 175 (5D 32)
  (not continuous)
Haydock Wlk. OL9: Chad 2C 74
  (off Middleton Rd.)
Haye's Rd. M44: Cad 4C 124
  (not continuous)
Hayeswater Circ. M41: Urm 4E 111
Hayeswater Rd. M41: Urm 4E 111
Hayfield Av. M29: Ast 5A 80
  SK6: Bred 5G 135
Hayfield Cl. BL8: G'mount 2H 21
  M12: Man 6A 102
  M24: Mid 4E 57
  OL4: O'ham 3D 60
Hayfield Rd. M6: Sal 1B 98
  SK6: Bred 5G 135
Hayfield St. M33: Sale 4A 128
Hayfield Wlk. M34: Dent 1G 135
  WA15: Tim 5C 140
Haygrove Wlk. M9: Man 3H 87
  (off Alfred St.)
Hay Ho. OL4: O'ham 1C 76
  (off Huddersfield Rd.)
Hayle Rd. OL1: O'ham 3B 60
Hayley St. M13: Man 3A 116
Hayling Cl. BL8: Bury 5C 22
Hayling Rd. M33: Sale 4G 127
Haymaker Ri. OL12: W'le 6C 16
Haymans Wlk. M13: Man . . .4D 10 (6F 101)
Haymarket, The BL9: Bury . . .4B 176 (3F 37)
Haymarket St. BL9: Bury 4B 176 (3E 37)
  M13: Man 6F 11 (2G 115)
Haymill Av. M38: Lit H 3E 65
Haymond Cl. M6: Sal 5G 85
Haynes St. BL3: Bolt 4H 47
  OL12: Roch 1C 178 (3H 27)

Haysbrook Av. M28: Walk 5D 64
Haysbrook Cl. OL7: A Lyme 4G 91
Haythorp Av. M22: Wyth 2C 154
Hayward Av. BL3: Lit L 4E 51
Hayward St. BL8: Bury 2C 36
Haywood Community Leisure Cen.
. . . . .5A 48
Hazel Av. BL0: Ram 2B 22
   BL8: Tot .6A 22
   BL9: Bury 3H 37
   M16: W Ran 5B 114
   M26: Rad 1C 66
   M27: Swin 4A 84
   M33: Sale 6B 128
   M38: Lit H 4C 64
   OL6: A Lyme 5C 92
   OL16: Miln 2G 43
   SK6: Rom 1B 148
   SK8: Chea H 6A 144
Hazelbadge Cl. SK12: Poy 3C 168
Hazelbadge Rd. SK12: Poy 3C 168
Hazelbank Av. M20: Man 2F 131
Hazelbottom Rd. M8: Man 4F 87
Hazel Cl. M43: Droy 3C 104
   SK6: Mar 1C 160
Hazel Cl. M16: W Ran 4B 114
                                    (off Dudley Rd.)
Hazelcroft SK9: A Edg 6G 173
Hazelcroft Gdns.
   SK9: A Edg 6G 173
Hazeldean Ct. SK9: Wilm 6H 165
Hazel Dene Cl. BL9: Bury 6F 37
Hazeldene Rd. M40: Man 2G 89
Hazel Dr. M22: Wyth 5E 155
   SK2: Stoc 5D 146
   SK12: Poy 4F 169
Hazelfields BL8: Wors 4D 82
Hazel Gdns. SK8: Chea H 4D 156
                                    (off Hazel Rd.)
HAZEL GROVE 3D 158
Hazel Gro. BL4: Farn 1F 65
   M5: Sal 3C 98
   M26: Rad 1H 67
   M41: Urm 5G 111
   OL9: Chad 1B 74
Hazel Grove Pool and Target Fitness Cen.
. . . . .4A 158
Hazel Grove Recreation Cen.
. . . . .5C 158
Hazel Grove Station (Rail) 3D 158
Hazelhall Cl. M28: Wors 4D 82
Hazel Hall Cotts. BL0: Ram 2B 22
Hazel Hall La. BL0: Ram 2B 22
HAZELHURST
   BL0 . . . . .4B 12
   M27 . . . . .4E 83
   OL6 . . . . .5D 92
Hazelhurst Cl. BL0: Ram 5B 12
   BL1: Bolt .3C 32
Hazelhurst Dr. M24: Mid 3B 56
Hazelhurst Fold M28: Wors 4E 83
Hazelhurst M. OL9: Chad 6A 74
Hazelhurst Rd. M28: Wors 4D 82
   OL6: A Lyme 5D 92
   SK15: Stal 1E 107
Hazel La. OL8: O'ham 1D 90
Hazelmere Av. M30: Ecc 1D 96
Hazel Mt. BL7: Eger 1C 18
Hazel Rd. M24: Mid 6D 56
   M45: White 1H 69
   SK8: Chea H 4D 156
   SK15: Stal 2G 107
   WA14: Alt 6F 139
Hazel St. BL0: Ram 5A 12
   M34: Aud 1E 119
   SK7: H Gro 2E 159
Hazel Ter. M9: Man 5H 71
Hazel Vw. SK6: Mar 2D 160
Hazel Wlk. M31: Part 6C 124
Hazelwell M33: Sale 6B 128
Hazelwood OL9: Chad 1G 73
Hazelwood Av. BL2: Bolt 2A 34
Hazelwood Cl. SK14: Hyde 5E 121

Hazelwood Ct. M41: Urm 4F 111
Hazelwood Dr. BL9: Bury 4F 23
   M34: Aud 1F 119
Hazelwood Rd. BL1: Bolt 3H 31
   M22: Wyth 5B 154
   SK2: Stoc 1A 158
   SK7: H Gro 3E 159
   SK9: Wilm 1F 173
   WA15: Hale 3G 151
Hazlemere BL4: Kea 2C 66
Headingley Dr. M16: Old T 4G 113
Headingley Rd. M14: Man 2H 131
Headingley Way BL3: Bolt 4B 48
Headlands Dr. M25: Pres 2G 85
Headlands Rd. SK7: Bram 4H 157
Headlands St. OL12: Roch 2G 27
HEADY HILL 3D 38
Heady Hill Ct. OL10: H'ood 4E 39
Heady Hill Ct. OL10: H'ood 3E 39
Heady Hill Rd. OL10: H'ood 3E 39
Heald Av. M14: Man 4F 115
Heald Cl. OL12: Roch 6E 15
   OL15: L'ough 6G 17
   WA14: Bow 3E 151
Heald Dr. OL12: Roch 6E 15
   WA14: Bow 3E 151
HEALD GREEN 5F 155
Heald Grn. Ho. M22: Wyth 5E 155
Heald Green Station (Rail) 5E 155
Heald Gro. M14: Man 3F 115
   SK8: H Grn 4E 155
Heald La. OL15: L'ough 6G 17
Heald Pl. M14: Man 3F 115
Heald Rd. WA14: Bow 3E 151
HEALDS GREEN 4H 57
Healds Grn. OL1: Chad 4H 57
Healdwood Rd. SK6: Wood 5A 136
                                    (not continuous)
HEALEY 4E 15
Healey Av. OL10: H'ood 2A 40
   OL12: Roch 5E 15
Healey Bottoms OL12: Roch 6D 14
Healey Cl. M7: Sal 3A 86
   M23: Wyth 1F 141
Healey Dell OL12: Roch 5D 14
Healey Dell Nature Reserve 5D 14
Healey Dell Nature Reserve Vis. Cen.
. . . . .5D 14
Healey Gro. OL12: Whitw 4E 15
Healey Hall M. OL12: Roch 5E 15
Healey La. OL12: Roch 5G 15
Healey Stones OL12: Roch 5G 15
Healey St. OL16: Roch 5A 178 (5G 27)
Healing St. OL11: Roch 6A 28
Heanor Av. M34: Dent 1G 135
HEAP BRIDGE 4A 38
Heap Brow Rd. BL9: Bury 4B 38
Heape St. OL11: Roch 4E 41
Heapfold OL12: Roch 1D 26
Heaplands BL8: G'mount 2H 21
Heapriding Bus. Pk.
   SK3: Stoc 2F 145
Heap Rd. OL12: Roch 1H 25
Heaps Farm Ct. SK15: Stal 5H 107
Heap St. BL3: Bolt 3C 48
   BL9: Bury .4B 38
   M26: Rad .4B 52
   M45: White 2F 69
   OL4: O'ham 2A 76
Heapworth Av. BL0: Ram 3B 12
Heapy Cl. BL8: Bury 4H 35
Heath, The M24: Mid 3D 72
   OL7: A Lyme 5G 91
Heath Av. BL0: Ram 2B 22
   M7: Sal 1B 4 (1A 100)
   M41: Urm 4G 111
Heathbank Rd. M9: Man 5G 71
   SK3: Stoc 4D 144
   SK8: Chea H 6B 156
Heath Cl. BL3: Bolt 5H 47
Heathcote Av. SK4: Stoc 6E 133
Heathcote Gdns.
   SK6: Rom 2C 148

Heathcote Rd. M18: Man 3E 117
Heath Cotts. BL1: Bolt 5B 18
Heath Cres. SK2: Stoc 6H 145
Heather Av. M43: Droy 3C 104
   M44: Cad .3B 124
   OL2: Shaw 5B 44
Heather Bank BL8: Tot 4G 21
Heather Brow SK15: Stal 6H 107
Heather Cl. OL4: O'ham 6C 60
   OL10: H'ood 5H 39
Heather Ct. SK4: Stoc 4F 133
   WA14: Bow 2D 150
Heatherdale Dr. M8: Man 5E 87
Heatherfield BL1: Bolt 6A 18
                                    (not continuous)
Heatherfield Ct. SK9: Wilm 1H 173
Heather Gro. M43: Droy 5B 104
   SK14: Holl 1F 123
Heatherlands OL12: Whitw 1B 14
Heather Lea M34: Dent 5G 119
Heather Rd. WA14: Hale 4G 151
   WA15: Hale 4G 151
Heathers, The SK2: Stoc 1B 158
Heatherside SK5: Stoc 6A 118
   SK15: Stal 3H 107
Heatherside Rd. BL0: Ram 2B 12
Heather St. M11: Man 3D 102
Heather Wlk. M31: Part 6C 124
                                    (off Gorse Sq.)
Heather Way OL3: Dig 3E 63
   SK6: Mar 5C 148
Heatherway M14: Man 3F 115
                                    (off Parkfield St.)
   M33: Sale 4F 127
Heath Farm La. M31: Part 6E 125
Heathfield BL2: Bolt 1B 34
   BL4: Farn .6A 50
   M28: Wors 6B 82
   SK9: Wilm 4D 172
Heathfield Av. M34: Dent 5D 118
   SK4: Stoc 4E 133
   SK8: Gat .6F 143
Heathfield Cl. M33: Sale 5F 129
Heathfield Ct. BL3: Bolt 4G 47
                                    (off Linnyshaw Cl.)
Heathfield Dr. BL3: Bolt 5H 47
   M27: Swin 4A 84
   M29: Tyld 2B 80
Heathfield Rd. BL9: Bury 4F 53
   M45: White 4F 53
   SK2: Stoc 5H 145
HEATHFIELDS 1E 79
Heathfields Rd. OL3: Upp 1E 79
Heathfields Sq. OL3: Upp 1E 79
Heathfield St. M40: Man 6E 89
Heathland Rd. M7: Sal 3H 85
Heathlands Dr. M25: Pres 2G 85
Heathlands Village M25: Pres 2G 85
Heathland Ter.
   SK3: Stoc 6F 179 (4G 145)
Heathlea Cl. BL1: Bolt 5C 18
Heath Rd. OL12: W'le 6C 16
   SK2: Stoc 5H 145
   WA14: Hale 3F 151
   WA15: Tim 3H 139
Heathside Gro. M28: Walk 6A 66
Heathside Pk. Rd. SK3: Stoc 3B 144
Heathside Rd. M20: Man 4G 131
   SK3: Stoc 4C 144
Heath St. M8: Man 4D 86
   OL11: Roch 5F 27
Heath Vw. M7: Sal 3G 85
   WA14: Alt 2F 151
                                    (off Tipping St.)
Heathway Av. M11: Man 3F 103
Heathwood OL3: Upp 1E 79
Heathwood Rd. M19: Man 5A 132
Heatley Cl. M34: Dent 5B 118
Heatley Rd. OL16: Roch 5D 28
Heatley Way SK9: Hand 3H 165
                                    (off Delamere Rd.)
HEATON 5G 31

Heaton Av.—Hereford Gro.

Heaton Av. BL1: Bolt .4F **31**
BL2: Bolt .6A **20**
BL3: Lit L .3C **50**
BL4: Farn .1G **65**
SK7: Bram .2F **157**
HEATON CHAPEL .4E **133**
Heaton Chapel Station (Rail) .4E **133**
Heaton Cl. BL9: Bury .2G **53**
SK4: Stoc .6C **132**
Heaton Ct. BL9: Bury .6F **37**
M25: Pres .6A **70**
M33: Sale .5C **128**
SK4: Stoc .5D **132**
Heaton Ct. Gdns. BL1: Bolt .6E **31**
Heaton Dr. BL9: Bury .2G **53**
Heaton Fold BL9: Bury .5E **37**
Heaton Gdns. SK4: Stoc .5E **133**
Heaton Grange BL1: Bolt .6G **31**
Heaton Grange Dr. BL1: Bolt .6G **31**
Heaton Gro. BL9: Bury .6F **37**
Heaton Hall .4C **70**
Heaton La. SK4: Stoc .2E **179** (2F **145**)
HEATON MERSEY .1A **144**
Heaton Mersey Ind. Est.
SK4: Stoc .2A **144**
HEATON MOOR .5D **132**
Heaton Moor Rd. SK4: Stoc .6D **132**
HEATON NORRIS .1F **145**
HEATON PARK .5A **70**
Heaton Pk. .4C **70**
Heaton Pk. Bowling Pavilion .3A **70**
Heaton Pk. Farm Cen. .4B **70**
Heaton Pk. Horticultural Cen. .4B **70**
Heaton Pk. Rd. M9: Man .4E **71**
Heaton Pk. Rd. W. M9: Man .4E **71**
Heaton Park Station (Metro) .5A **70**
Heaton Pk. Tramway Mus. .4D **70**
Heaton Rd. BL2: Bolt .2D **50**
BL6: Los .2C **46**
M20: Man .2G **131**
SK4: Stoc .6E **133**
Heatons Gro. BL5: W'ton .5A **46**
Heatons Sports Club .6D **132**
Heaton St. M7: Sal .4C **86**
M24: Mid .2F **71**
M25: Pres .5H **69**
M34: Dent .4D **118**
OL16: Miln .6G **29**
Heaton Towers *SK4: Stoc .1G **145***
(off Wilkinson Rd.)
HEAVILEY .5A **146**
Heaviley Gro. SK2: Stoc .5A **146**
Hebble Butt Cl. OL16: Miln .5E **29**
Hebble Cl. BL2: Bolt .6F **19**
Hebburn Dr. BL8: Bury .6C **22**
Hebburn Wlk. *M14: Man .3F **115***
(off Gt. Western St.)
Hebden Av. M6: Sal .2C **98**
SK6: Bred .5G **135**
Hebden Ct. BL1: Bolt .5C **32**
Hebden Wlk. *M15: Man .2D **114***
(off Arnott Cres.)
Hebers Ct. M24: Mid .4B **56**
Heber St. M26: Rad .4A **52**
Hebron St. OL2: O'ham .4G **59**
Hector Av. OL16: Roch .3B **28**
Hector Rd. M13: Man .4B **116**
Heddon Cl. SK4: Stoc .6A **132**
Heddon Wlk. *M8: Man .5G **87***
(off Smedley Rd.)
Hedgelands Wlk. *M33: Sale .4E **127***
(off Epping Dr.)
Hedge Rows OL12: Whitw .4A **14**
Hedge Rows, The SK14: Hyde .4E **121**
Hedges St. M35: Fail .3A **90**
Hedley St. BL1: Bolt .3A **32**
Hedley Wlk. *M8: Man .4D **86***
(off Halliwell La.)
Heginbottom Cres.
OL6: A Lyme .6A **92**
HEIGHTS .1A **62**
Heights Av. OL12: Roch .1G **27**
Heights Cl. OL12: Roch .1G **27**
Heights Ct. OL12: Roch .2G **27**
Heightside *WA15: Tim .6B **140***
(off Edenhurst Dr.)
Heights La. OL1: Chad .5H **57**
OL3: Del .6H **45**
OL12: Roch .1A **178** (1G **27**)
Helena St. M6: Sal .6C **84**
Helen St. BL4: Farn .1H **65**
M7: Sal .6A **86**
M30: Ecc .5D **96**
Helensville Av. M6: Sal .6F **85**
Helga St. M40: Man .1H **101**
Helias Cl. M28: Walk .6D **64**
Hellidon Cl. M12: Man .5G **11** (1H **115**)
Helmclough Way M28: Wors .3G **81**
Helmet St. M1: Man .2F **11** (5G **101**)
Helmsdale M28: Walk .1G **81**
Helmsdale Av. BL3: Bolt .1F **47**
Helmsdale Cl. BL0: Ram .5A **12**
Helmshore Av. OL4: O'ham .4C **60**
Helmshore Ho. *OL2: Shaw .5H **43***
(off Helmshore Way)
Helmshore Rd. BL8: Holc .1A **12**
Helmshore Wlk.
M13: Man .4D **10** (6F **101**)
Helmshore Way OL2: Shaw .5H **43**
Helsby Cl. OL4: Spri .3E **77**
Helsby Gdns. BL1: Bolt .1D **32**
Helsby Rd. M33: Sale .1E **141**
Helsby Wlk. M12: Man .1H **11** (5H **101**)
Helsby Way SK9: Hand .3H **165**
Helston Cl. M44: Irl .5F **109**
SK7: Bram .6H **157**
SK14: Hat .6H **121**
Helston Dr. OL2: O'ham .3F **59**
Helston Gro. SK8: H Grn .5G **155**
Helston Wlk. SK14: Hat .6H **121**
Helston Way M29: Ast .3A **80**
Helton Wlk. M24: Mid .6G **55**
Helv[illegible] M2[illegible] Mid .5H **55**
Helvellyn Wlk. OL1: O'ham .6G **59**
Hembury Av. M19: Man .3B **132**
Hembury Cl. M24: Mid .5D **56**
Hemlock Av. OL8: O'ham .6E **75**
Hemming Dr. M30: Ecc .4G **97**
Hemmington Dr. M9: Man .4H **87**
Hemmons Rd. M12: Man .5D **116**
Hempcroft Rd. WA15: Tim .6C **140**
Hempshaw Bus. Cen. SK1: Stoc .4B **146**
Hempshaw La.
SK1: Stoc .6H **179** (4H **145**)
(not continuous)
SK2: Stoc .4C **146**
Hemsby Cl. BL3: Bolt .3G **47**
Hemsley St. M9: Man .2A **88**
Hemsley St. Sth. M9: Man .3A **88**
Hemswell Cl. M6: Sal .1E **99**
Hemsworth Rd. BL1: Bolt .5B **32**
M18: Man .4F **117**
Henbury Dr. SK6: Wood .3H **135**
Henbury La. SK8: Chea H .1B **166**
Henbury Rd. SK9: Hand .3H **165**
Henbury St. M14: Man .4E **115**
SK2: Stoc .1C **158**
Henderson Av. M27: Pen .2H **83**
Henderson St. M19: Man .1D **132**
OL12: Roch .1B **28**
OL15: L'ough .4G **17**
Henderville St. OL15: L'ough .3G **17**
Hendham Cl. SK7: H Gro .3A **158**
Hendham Dr. WA14: Alt .6D **138**
Hendham Va. M9: Man .4G **87**
Hendham Va. Ind. Est. M8: Man .4G **87**
Hendon Dr. BL9: Bury .2F **53**
SK3: Stoc .4C **144**
Hendon Gro. OL10: H'ood .6A **40**
Hendon Rd. M9: Man .5G **71**
Hendriff Pl. OL12: Roch .2H **27**
Henfield Wlk. *M22: Wyth .2A **154***
(off Cornfield Dr.)
Hen Fold Rd. M29: Ast .4A **80**
Hengist St. BL2: Bolt .6G **33**
M18: Man .3F **117**
Henley Av. M16: Old T .4H **113**
M44: Irl .3C **124**
SK8: Chea H .3A **156**
Henley Cl. BL8: Bury .5B **36**
Henley Dr. OL7: A Lyme .1F **105**
WA15: Tim .4H **139**
Henley Grange SK8: Chea .6G **143**
Henley Gro. BL3: Bolt .4A **48**
Henley Pl. M19: Man .3C **132**
Henley St. OL1: O'ham .1D **74**
OL9: Chad .6A **74**
OL12: Roch .1A **178** (2G **27**)
Henley Ter. OL11: Roch .6G **27**
Henlow Wlk. M40: Man .1F **89**
Hennicker St. M28: Walk .2H **81**
Henniker Rd. BL3: Bolt .5G **47**
Henniker St. M27: Swin .5G **83**
Hennon St. BL1: Bolt .4B **32**
Henrietta St. BL3: Bolt .3H **47**
M16: Old T .3A **114**
OL6: A Lyme .4C **174** (1H **105**)
Henry Herman St. BL3: Bolt .4G **47**
Henry Lee St. BL3: Bolt .4A **48**
Henry Sq. OL6: A Lyme .6A **174**
Henry St. BL0: Ram .2D **12**
BL2: Bolt .6H **175** (1E **49**)
M4: Man .4C **6** (3F **101**)
(not continuous)
M16: Old T .2A **114**
M24: Mid .1B **72**
M25: Pres .4A **70**
M30: Ecc .4E **97**
M34: Dent .1H **135**
M35: Fail .4H **89**
M43: Droy .4A **104**
OL11: Roch .5B **178** (5H **27**)
OL12: W'le .5C **16**
OL15: L'ough .6F **17**
SK1: Stoc .3B **146**
SK14: Hyde .5B **120**
Henshaw Ct. M16: Old T .3H **113**
Henshaw La. OL9: Chad .1H **89**
Henshaw St. M32: Stre .5D **112**
OL1: O'ham .3F **177** (2E **75**)
Henshaw Wlk. *BL1: Bolt .3C **32***
(off Hargreaves St.)
M13: Man .4D **10**
Henson Gro. WA15: Tim .1A **152**
Henthorn St. OL1: O'ham .1G **75**
OL2: Shaw .1H **59**
Henton Wlk. M40: Man .1F **7**
Henty Cl. M30: Ecc .4D **96**
Henwick Hall Av. BL0: Ram .5B **12**
Henwood Rd. M20: Man .4G **131**
Hepburn Ct. *M6: Sal .1E **99***
(off Monroe Cl.)
Hepley Rd. SK12: Poy .4G **169**
Hepple Cl. SK4: Stoc .6B **132**
Heppleton Rd. M40: Man .2F **89**
Hepple Wlk. OL7: A Lyme .6E **91**
Heptonstall Wlk. *M18: Man .2E **117***
(off Hampden Cres.)
Hepton St. OL1: O'ham .1E **177** (1E **75**)
Hepworth St. SK14: Hyde .2C **136**
Heraldic Ct. M6: Sal .6G **85**
Herbert St. BL3: Lit L .4D **50**
M8: Man .6D **86**
M25: Pres .5F **69**
M26: Rad .2H **51**
M32: Stre .5D **112**
M34: Dent .3G **119**
M43: Droy .4H **103**
OL4: O'ham .6B **60**
OL9: Chad .2B **74**
SK3: Stoc .4F **145**
Hereford Cl. OL2: Shaw .6F **43**
OL6: A Lyme .4B **92**
Hereford Cres. BL3: Lit L .3D **50**
Hereford Dr. BL9: Bury .5F **37**
M25: Pres .6A **70**
M27: Swin .5H **83**
SK9: Hand .4A **166**
Hereford Gro. M41: Urm .5E **111**

Hereford Rd.—Higham St.

Hereford Rd. BL1: Bolt .5H **31**
M30: Ecc .6A **84**
SK5: Stoc .4C **134**
SK8: Chea .1C **156**
Hereford St. BL1: Bolt .3D **32**
M33: Sale .5B **128**
(not continuous)
OL9: O'ham .4B **74**
OL11: Roch .6A **28**
Hereford Wlk. *M34: Dent .6F **119***
(off Norwich Av.)
SK6: Rom .2G **147**
Hereford Way M24: Mid .6E **57**
SK15: Stal .6H **107**
Herevale Grange M28: Wors .4F **81**
Herevale Hall Dr. BL0: Ram .5B **12**
Heristone Av. M34: Dent .4F **119**
Heritage Gdns. M20: Man .1F **143**
*SK4: Stoc .5E **133***
(off Heaton Moor Rd.)
Heritage Pk. OL16: Roch .4A **28**
Heritage Wharf *OL7: A Lyme .4G **105***
(off Portland Pl.)
Herle Dr. M22: Wyth .4A **154**
Hermitage Av. SK6: Rom .1D **148**
Hermitage Ct. *WA15: Hale .2A **152***
(off Bancroft Rd.)
Hermitage Gdns. SK6: Rom .1D **148**
Hermitage Rd. M8: Man .2E **87**
WA15: Hale .2H **151**
Hermon Av. OL8: O'ham .5E **75**
Herne St. M11: Man .5C **102**
Heron Av. BL4: Farn .1D **64**
SK16: Duk .6C **106**
Heron Ct. M6: Sal .2B **98**
SK3: Stoc .6E **179**
Herondale Cl. M40: Man .6D **88**
Heron Dr. M34: Aud .4C **104**
M44: Irl .4E **109**
SK12: Poy .4A **168**
Heron La. OL5: Mos .6H **77**
Heron St. M15: Man .2C **114**
M27: Pen .2A **84**
OL8: O'ham .5C **74**
SK3: Stoc .3F **145**
Heron's Way BL2: Bolt .6H **175** (1E **49**)
Herries St. OL6: A Lyme .1B **106**
Herriots Bus. Pk. SK16: Duk .6G **105**
Herristone Rd. M8: Man .1E **87**
Herrod Av. SK4: Stoc .4G **133**
Herschel St. M40: Man .3C **88**
Hersey St. M6: Sal .3E **99**
Hersham Wlk. *M9: Man .3A **88***
(off Hemsley St. Sth.)
Hertford Gro. M44: Cad .3A **124**
Hertford Ind. Est. OL7: A Lyme .4G **105**
Hertford Rd. M9: Man .2H **87**
Hertfordshire Pk. Cl.
OL2: Shaw .5H **43**
Hertford St. OL7: A Lyme .4G **105**
Hesford Av. M9: Man .4B **88**
Hesketh Av. BL1: Bolt .6D **18**
M20: Man .6E **131**
OL2: Shaw .2G **59**
Hesketh Ho. *BL4: Farn .1H **65***
(off Hesketh Wlk.)
Hesketh Pl. *SK7: H Gro .1D **158***
(off Fenton Av.)
Hesketh Rd. M33: Sale .6H **127**
OL16: Roch .4C **28**
Hesketh St. SK4: Stoc .5G **133**
(All Saints' Rd.)
SK4: Stoc .6G **133**
(Belmont St.)
Hesketh Wlk. BL4: Farn .1H **65**
M24: Mid .5A **56**
Hessel St. M50: Sal .4D **98**
Hester Wlk. M15: Man .6H **9**
Heston Av. M13: Man .5A **116**
Heston Dr. M41: Urm .4E **111**
Heswall Av. M20: Man .2F **131**
Heswall Dr. BL8: Bury .6G **21**
Heswall Rd. SK5: Stoc .6H **117**
Heswall St. BL2: Bolt .6B **34**
Hetherington Wlk. *M12: Man .3C **116***
(off Norman Gro.)
Hethorn St. M40: Man .6E **89**
Hetton Av. M13: Man .5A **116**
Heversham Av. OL2: Shaw .6B **44**
Heversham Wlk. *M18: Man .1E **117***
(off Grizebeck Cl.)
Hewart Cl. M40: Man .1G **101**
Hewart Dr. BL9: Bury .2A **38**
Hewitt Av. M34: Dent .4H **117**
Hewitt St. M15: Man .3F **9** (6C **100**)
Hewlett Ct. BL0: Ram .1A **22**
Hewlett Rd. M21: Chor .6G **113**
Hewlett St. BL2: Bolt .4H **175** (6E **33**)
Hexham Av. BL1: Bolt .4F **31**
Hexham Cl. M33: Sale .6F **127**
OL9: Chad .2C **74**
SK2: Stoc .6E **147**
Hexham Rd. M18: Man .4E **117**
Hexon Cl. M6: Sal .2E **99**
Hexworth Wlk. SK7: Bram .3A **158**
Hey, The OL2: Shaw .5B **44**
Hey Bottom La. OL12: W'le .4H **15**
Heybrook OL16: Roch .2B **28**
Heybrook Cl. M45: White .1A **70**
Heybrook Rd. M23: Wyth .6H **141**
Heybrook St. OL16: Roch .3B **28**
Heybrook Wlk. M45: White .1A **70**
Heybury Cl. M11: Man .5B **102**
Hey Cres. OL4: Lees .2D **76**
Hey Cft. M45: White .2C **68**
Heycrofts Vw. BL0: Eden .2G **13**
Heyden Bank *SK13: Gam .5F **123***
(off Grassmoor Cres.)
Heyden Fold *SK13: Gam .5F **123***
(off Grassmoor Cres.)
Heyden Ter. SK13: Gam .5F **123**
Heyes Av. WA15: Tim .4B **140**
Heyes Dr. WA15: Tim .4B **140**
Heyes La. SK9: A Edg .4G **173**
WA15: Tim .4B **140**
Heyes Leigh WA15: Tim .4B **140**
Heyes Ter. *WA15: Tim .3B **140***
(off The Old Orchard)
Hey Flake La. OL3: Del .1A **62**
Heyford Av. M40: Man .1F **89**
Hey Head OL2: Shaw .5C **44**
Hey Head Cotts. BL2: Bolt .6D **20**
Hey Head La. OL15: L'ough .1H **17**
HEYHEADS .4A **94**
Heyheads New Rd. SK15: C'ook .4A **94**
Hey Hill Cl. OL2: O'ham .2G **59**
Heyland Rd. M23: Wyth .5G **141**
Hey La. OL3: Upp .6E **63**
Heylee *OL7: A Lyme .5F **105***
(off South St.)
Heyridge Dr. M22: Nor .2B **142**
HEYROD .6G **93**
Heyrod Fold SK15: H'rod .6G **93**
Heyrod Hall Est. SK15: H'rod .1G **107**
Heyrod St. M1: Man .1E **11** (5G **101**)
SK15: C'ook .6H **93**
Heyrose Wlk. M15: Man .6D **8**
Heys, The M25: Pres .4H **69**
OL6: A Lyme .1B **106**
SK5: Stoc .6A **118**
Heys Av. M23: Wyth .2G **141**
M27: Ward .1E **83**
SK6: Rom .6C **136**
Heysbank Rd. SK12: Dis .1H **171**
Heys Cl. OL16: Miln .6H **29**
Heys Cl. Nth. M27: Ward .1E **83**
Heys Ct. SK3: Stoc .3D **144**
Heyscroft Rd. M20: Man .3G **131**
SK4: Stoc .1C **144**
Heys Farm Cotts. SK6: Rom .6C **136**
Heysham Av. M20: Man .2D **130**
Heyshaw Wlk. M23: Wyth .2F **141**
HEYSIDE .4G **59**
Heyside OL2: O'ham .4G **59**
Heyside Av. OL2: O'ham .4G **59**
Heyside Cl. SK15: C'ook .5A **94**
Heyside Way BL9: Bury .5D **176** (4F **37**)
Heys La. OL10: H'ood .3E **39**
SK6: Rom .6C **136**
Heys Rd. M25: Pres .4G **69**
OL6: A Lyme .2B **106**
Heys St. BL8: Bury .3D **36**
Hey St. OL16: Roch .3B **28**
Heys Vw. M25: Pres .5H **69**
Heythrop Cl. M45: White .6E **53**
Hey Top OL3: G'fld .5F **79**
HEYWOOD .3H **39**
Heywood Av. M27: Clif .1B **84**
OL4: Aus .1E **77**
Heywood Cl. SK9: A Edg .4H **173**
Heywood Ct. M24: Mid .2E **71**
Heywood Distribution Pk.
OL10: H'ood .5C **38**
Heywood Fold Rd. OL4: Spri .2D **76**
Heywood Gdns. BL3: Bolt .3C **48**
M25: Pres .5H **69**
Heywood Gro. M33: Sale .3A **128**
Heywood Hall Rd. OL10: H'ood .2H **39**
Heywood Ho. *M6: Sal .2C **98***
(off Edgehill Rd.)
OL8: O'ham .6G **177** (4F **75**)
Heywood Ind. Pk. OL10: H'ood .5E **39**
Heywood La. OL4: Aus .2E **77**
Heywood M. *BL3: Lit L .4D **50***
(off Heywood St.)
M25: Pres .5H **69**
Heywood Old Rd. M24: Mid .5E **55**
OL10: H'ood .5E **55**
Heywood Pk. Vw. BL3: Bolt .3C **48**
Heywood Rd. M25: Pres .4H **69**
M33: Sale .6B **128**
OL11: Roch .3D **40**
SK9: A Edg .4H **173**
Heywood's Hollow BL1: Bolt .2D **32**
Heywood Sports Complex .2G **39**
Heywood Station
East Lancashire Railway .4A **40**
Heywood St. BL1: Bolt .1F **175** (5D **32**)
BL3: Lit L .4D **50**
BL9: Bury .4G **37**
M8: Man .4E **87**
M27: Swin .3G **83**
M35: Fail .4F **89**
OL4: O'ham .1C **76**
Heywood Way M6: Sal .2F **99**
Heyworth Av. SK6: Rom .6B **136**
Heyworth St. *M5: Sal .4E **99***
(off Bridson St.)
Hibbert Av. M34: Dent .2E **119**
SK14: Hyde .6C **120**
Hibbert Cres. M35: Fail .4A **90**
Hibbert La. SK6: Mar .6D **148**
Hibbert St. BL1: Bolt .3D **32**
M14: Man .4G **115**
OL4: Lees .2C **76**
SK4: Stoc .4G **133**
SK5: Stoc .4G **133**
Hibernia St. BL3: Bolt .2A **48**
Hibernia Way M32: Stre .2A **112**
Hibson Av. OL12: Roch .1H **25**
Hibson Cl. OL12: W'le .6C **16**
Hickenfield Rd. SK14: Hyde .2D **120**
Hicken Pl. SK14: Hyde .2D **120**
Hickton Dr. WA14: Alt .5D **138**
Hidden Gem
Manchester St Mary's Catholic Church .6G **5**
HIGGINSHAW .5G **59**
Higginshaw La.
OL1: O'ham .5G **59**
OL2: O'ham .5G **59**
Higginshaw Rd.
OL1: O'ham .1H **177** (6F **59**)
Higginson Rd. SK5: Stoc .2G **133**
Higgs Cl. OL4: O'ham .2B **76**
Higham Cl. OL2: O'ham .2G **59**
Higham Cotts. SK14: Hyde .1F **137**
Higham La. SK14: Hyde .1D **136**
Higham St. SK8: Chea H .4C **156**

270 A-Z Manchester

Higham Vw. *M6: Sal* 2G **99**
      (off Broad St.)
High Ash Gro. M34: Aud 6D **104**
High Av. BL2: Bolt 5A **34**
High Bank BL7: Bro X 4D **18**
    BL8: Bury .5C **36**
    M18: Man 2G **117**
    M34: Dent 5B **118**
    WA14: Alt 1A **174** (6F **139**)
    WA15: Hale 3A **152**
Highbank M27: Pen 4C **84**
High Bank Av. SK15: Stal 6H **107**
High Bank Cl. M44: Cad 3B **124**
High Bank Cres. M25: Pres 6A **70**
Highbank Cres. OL4: Gras 4A **78**
Highbank Dr. M20: Man 3F **143**
High Bank Gro. M25: Pres 6A **70**
High Bank La. BL6: Los 6B **30**
High Bank Rd. BL9: Bury 4F **53**
    M27: Pen .3B **84**
    M43: Droy 6H **103**
    SK14: Hyde 4D **120**
Highbank Rd. OL16: Miln 1A **44**
High Bankside
    SK1: Stoc 2G **179** (2H **145**)
High Bank St. BL2: Bolt 6G **33**
High Barn Cl. OL11: Roch 6G **27**
Highbarn Ho. OL2: O'ham *3E* **59**
    (off High Barn St.)
High Barn La. OL12: Whitw 4A **14**
    (Hall Fold)
    OL12: Whitw 1A **14**
    (Kiln Bank La.)
High Barn Rd. M24: Mid 2C **72**
    OL2: O'ham 3F **59**
High Barn St. OL2: O'ham 3E **59**
High Beeches BL2: Bolt 2D **50**
High Bent Av. SK8: Chea H 1C **166**
High Birch Ter. OL11: Roch 1D **40**
Highbridge Cl. BL2: Bolt 1C **50**
Highbrook Gro. BL1: Bolt *4C* **32**
    (off Lindfield Dr.)
High Brow M38: Lit H 6C **64**
Highbury SK4: Stoc 1B **144**
Highbury Av. M41: Urm 5A **110**
    M44: Irl 6E **109**
Highbury Ct. M25: Pres 4H **69**
Highbury Rd. M16: W Ran 6C **114**
    SK4: Stoc 3E **133**
Highbury Way OL2: O'ham 1D **58**
Highclere Av. M7: Sal 5D **86**
    M8: Man .5D **86**
Highclere Rd. M8: Man 1D **86**
Highcliffe Rd. M9: Man 6E **71**
Highclove La. M28: Wors 6D **80**
Highcrest Av. SK8: Gat 6D **142**
Highcrest Gro. M29: Tyld 2B **80**
Highcroft BL1: Bolt 2E **33**
    SK14: Hyde 2C **136**
Highcroft Av. M20: Man 5C **130**
Highcroft Rd. SK6: Rom 6A **136**
Highcroft Way OL12: Roch 5H **15**
HIGH CROMPTON 5E **43**
Highdales Rd. M23: Wyth 6H **141**
Highdown Wlk. M9: Man *3A* **88**
    (off Augustine Webster Cl.)
High Elm Dr. WA15: Haleb 5C **152**
High Elm Rd. WA15: Haleb 5C **152**
High Elms SK8: Chea H 2D **166**
Higher Ainsworth Rd. M26: Rad 6G **35**
Higher Alt Hill OL6: A Lyme 2A **92**
Higher Ardwick M12: Man 4F **11** (6G **101**)
Higher Arthurs OL3: G'fld 3D **78**
Higher Bank Rd. OL15: L'ough 6H **17**
HIGHER BANKS 2H **161**
Higher Barlow Row
    SK1: Stoc 4H **179** (3H **145**)
Higher Barn Rd. SK13: Had 3G **123**
HIGHER BARROWSHAW 5B **58**
Higher Bents La. SK6: Bred 6F **135**
HIGHER BLACKLEY 5F **71**
HIGHER BOARSHAW 5E **57**

Higher Bri. St. BL1: Bolt 1F **175** (4D **32**)
HIGHER BROUGHTON 5B **86**
Higher Bury St. SK4: Stoc 1F **145**
Higher Calderbrook OL15: L'ough . . .2A **16**
Higher Calderbrook Rd.
    OL15: L'ough 2A **16**
Higher Cambridge St.
    M15: Man 5A **10** (1E **115**)
Higher Carr La. OL3: G'fld 2D **78**
Higher Chatham St.
    M15: Man 5A **10** (1E **115**)
Higher Cleggswood Av.
    OL15: L'ough 6G **17**
Higher Clough Cl. BL3: Bolt 3G **47**
Higher Count Hill OL4: O'ham 5C **60**
Higher Cft. M30: Ecc 5E **97**
    M45: White 3C **68**
Higher Crossbank OL4: Lees 1D **76**
Higher Cross La. OL3: Upp 2E **79**
HIGHER CRUMPSALL 2E **87**
Higher Darcy St. BL2: Bolt 2G **49**
Higher Dean St. M26: Rad 4G **51**
HIGHER DISLEY 2H **171**
Higher Downs WA14: Alt 2E **151**
Higher Dunscar BL7: Eger 2C **18**
Higher Fold M24: Mid 4D **56**
Higherfold Farm SK6: H Lan 4C **160**
Higher Fold La. BL0: Ram 2E **13**
Higher Fullwood OL1: O'ham 3B **60**
HIGHER GAMESLEY 6F **123**
HIGHER GREEN 6A **80**
Higher Grn. OL6: A Lyme 1B **106**
Higher Grn. La. M29: Ast 6A **80**
HIGHER HARTSHEAD 2D **92**
Higher Henry St. SK14: Hyde 5B **120**
Higher Hillgate
    SK1: Stoc 4H **179** (3H **145**)
Higher Ho. Cl. OL9: Chad 5A **74**
HIGHER HURST 5C **92**
HIGHER HYDEGREEN 6B **94**
Higher Kinders OL3: G'fld 3D **78**
Higher La. M45: White 1E **69**
    SK12: Dis 6H **171**
Higher Lime Rd. OL8: O'ham 3C **90**
Higher Lodge OL11: Roch 1G **25**
Higher Lomax La. OL10: H'ood 3E **39**
Higher Lydgate Pk. OL4: Gras 3G **77**
Higher Mkt. St. BL4: Farn 1A **66**
Higher Mdws. M19: Man 1E **133**
Higher Moulding BL9: Bury 6C **24**
Higher Newtons OL5: Mos 1H **93**
HIGHER OGDEN 1C **44**
HIGHER OPENSHAW 6H **103**
Higher Ormond St. M15: Man 5B **10**
Higher Oswald St. M4: Man *3B* **6**
    (off Goadsby St.)
Higher Pk. OL2: Shaw 3A **44**
Higher Pit La. M26: Rad 5F **35**
HIGHER PYNTON 4A **170**
Higher Ridings BL7: Bro X 3D **18**
Higher Ri. OL2: Shaw 4G **43**
Higher Rd. M41: Urm 5F **111**
Higher Row BL9: Bury 2H **37**
HIGHER RUSHCROFT 5F **43**
Higher Shady La. BL7: Bro X 4F **19**
Higher Shore Rd. OL15: L'ough 2E **17**
HIGHER STAKE HILL 3G **57**
HIGHER SUMMERSEAT 2B **22**
Higher Summerseat BL0: Ram 1B **22**
Higher Swan La. BL3: Bolt 3B **48**
Higher Turf La. OL4: Scout 1F **77**
Higher Turf Pk. OL2: O'ham 4E **59**
Higher Wharf St. OL7: A Lyme 3H **105**
Higher Wheat La. OL16: Roch 3C **28**
HIGHER WOODHILL 6D **22**
Higher Wood St. M24: Mid 6B **56**
    (not continuous)
Higher York St. M13: Man . . .5C **10** (1F **115**)
HIGHFIELD .1D **64**
Highfield M20: Man 1F **143**
    M33: Sale 6C **128**
    SK8: Chea 2G **155**

Highfield Av. BL2: Bolt 2C **34**
    M26: Rad 6C **52**
    M28: Wors 3C **80**
    M33: Sale 6C **128**
    OL10: H'ood 3E **39**
    SK6: Rom 1F **147**
Highfield Cl. M32: Stre 1C **128**
    SK3: Stoc 1H **157**
    SK14: Hyde 1D **120**
Highfield Ct. BL4: Farn 2F **65**
    M25: Pres 4H **69**
    SK14: Mot 3C **122**
Highfield Cres. SK9: Wilm 6G **165**
Highfield Dr. BL4: Farn 1E **65**
    M24: Mid .2B **72**
    M27: Pen .4C **84**
    M30: Ecc .1F **97**
    M41: Urm 4E **111**
    OL2: O'ham 5E **59**
    OL5: Mos 3G **93**
Highfield Est. SK9: Wilm 6G **165**
Highfield Gdns. SK14: Holl 2F **123**
    SK14: Hyde 4D **120**
Highfield Glen OL6: A Lyme 6D **92**
    (off Highfield La.)
Highfield Ho. BL4: Farn 1D **64**
    SK3: Stoc 6H **145**
Highfield La. BL9: Bury 4F **53**
    M45: White 4F **53**
Highfield Mdw. OL5: Mos *3G* **93**
    (off Highfield Dr.)
Highfield Pk. SK4: Stoc 1B **144**
Highfield Pk. Rd. SK6: Bred 5E **135**
Highfield Parkway SK7: Bram 3F **167**
Highfield Pl. M18: Man 3H **117**
    (off Debdale La.)
    M25: Pres 4G **69**
Highfield Range M18: Man 3H **117**
Highfield Rd. BL0: Eden 3G **13**
    BL1: Bolt .3H **31**
    BL4: Farn .1C **64**
    M6: Sal 2F **99**
    M19: Man 6E **117**
    M25: Pres 3G **69**
    M30: Ecc .1F **97**
    M32: Stre 1C **128**
    M38: Lit H 4D **64**
    OL11: Roch 2A **26**
    OL16: Miln 5G **29**
    SK6: Mar .5D **148**
    SK6: Mel .5F **149**
    SK7: Bram 2H **157**
    SK7: H Gro 3G **159**
    SK8: Chea H 3A **156**
    SK12: Poy 3A **170**
    WA15: Hale 3A **152**
    WA15: Tim 6B **140**
Highfield Rd. Ind. Est. M38: Lit H 4D **64**
Highfield St. BL4: Kea 3C **66**
    M8: Man .4D **86**
    M24: Mid .1D **72**
    M34: Aud 1F **119**
    M34: Dent 2E **119**
    OL9: O'ham 2D **74**
    (not continuous)
    SK3: Stoc 3E **145**
    SK16: Duk 4H **105**
Highfield St. W. SK16: Duk 4H **105**
Highfield Ter. M9: Man 3H **87**
    OL4: O'ham 5B **60**
    OL7: A Lyme 4F **91**
High Gables BL1: Bolt 5H **31**
Highgate BL3: Bolt 5C **46**
Highgate Av. M41: Urm 3C **110**
Highgate Cen. SK6: Bred 6F **135**
Highgate Cres. M18: Man 4F **117**
High Ga. Dr. OL2: O'ham 6C **42**
Highgate Dr. M38: Lit H 4C **64**
Highgate La. M38: Lit H 4C **64**
    OL12: Whitw 3E **15**
Highgate Rd. WA14: Alt 1D **150**
High Gates M33: Sale 4E **129**
Highgrove M33: Sale 2A **140**
Highgrove, The BL1: Bolt 4D **30**

Highgrove Cl. BL1: Bolt 2D 32
Highgrove Ct. M9: Man 4E 71
Highgrove M. SK9: Wilm 3D 172
High Gro. Rd. OL3: G'fld 4A 78
　　OL4: Gras .4A 78
　　SK8: Chea 6G 143
High Ho's. BL1: Bolt 5B 18
High Hurst Cl. M24: Mid 1G 71
High Knowls OL4: O'ham 5E 77
Highland M. SK6: Rom 5A 136
Highland Rd. BL7: Bro X 3F 19
Highlands OL2: O'ham 4C 58
　　　　　　　　　　　　　　　(not continuous)
　　OL15: L'ough 6G 17
Highlands, The OL5: Mos 2F 93
Highlands Dr. SK2: Stoc 5F 147
Highlands Ho. OL5: Mos 2F 93
　　　　　　　　　　　　　　　　(off Old Brow)
Highlands Rd. OL2: O'ham 4C 58
　　OL2: Shaw 5F 43
　　OL11: Roch 6A 26
　　SK2: Stoc 5F 147
Highland Vw. OL5: Mos 1G 93
　　　　　　　　　　　　　　(off Quickedge Rd.)
Highland Wlk. M40: Man 5F 89
HIGH LANE 6C 160
High La. M21: Chor 1G 129
　　SK6: Wood 4H 135
High Lawn WA14: Bow 3E 151
High Lea SK8: Chea 6G 143
　　SK9: A Edg 5H 173
High Lee Ho. M33: Sale 4D 128
　　　　　　　　　　　　　　　　(off Broad Rd.)
High Lee La. OL4: O'ham 4F 61
High Legh Rd. M11: Man 5F 103
High Level Rd.
　　OL11: Roch 6C 178 (5H 27)
High Mdw. M27: Swin 4B 84
　　SK8: Chea H 5A 156
Highmeadow M26: Rad 6H 51
High Mdws. BL7: Bro X 3F 19
　　SK6: Rom 6A 136
Highmead St. M18: Man 2F 117
Highmead Wlk. M16: Old T 2B 114
　　　　　　　　　　　　　　　　(off Hamer Dr.)
High Moor Cres. OL4: O'ham 6C 60
Highmoor Vw. OL4: O'ham 6C 60
Highmore Dr. M9: Man 6A 72
High Mt. BL2: Bolt 2A 34
Highnam Wlk. M22: Wyth 4G 153
High Peak Rd. OL6: A Lyme 5E 93
　　OL12: Whitw 3E 15
High Peak St. M40: Man 5D 88
High Rid La. BL6: Los 5A 30
Highshore Dr. M8: Man 4D 86
High Stile La. OL3: Dob 5F 63
High Stile St. BL4: Kea 2A 66
Highstone Dr. M8: Man 5G 87
High St. BL3: Bolt 2B 48
　　BL3: Lit L .4D 50
　　BL8: Bury 2H 35
　　M4: Man 5A 6 (4E 101)
　　M24: Mid .5C 56
　　　　　　　　　　　　　　　(not continuous)
　　M28: Walk 6G 65
　　M43: Droy 4A 104
　　OL1: O'ham 3G 177 (2F 75)
　　　　　　　　　　　　　　　(not continuous)
　　OL2: O'ham 3D 58
　　OL2: Shaw 1H 59
　　OL3: Del .3B 62
　　OL3: Upp 6D 62
　　OL4: Lees 3C 76
　　OL5: Mos 1H 93
　　OL10: H'ood 3F 39
　　OL12: Roch 2B 178 (3H 27)
　　OL15: L'ough 4F 17
　　SK1: Stoc 2G 179 (2H 145)
　　SK7: H Gro 3F 159
　　SK8: Chea 5H 143
　　SK14: Hyde 4D 120
　　SK15: Stal 5C 106
　　WA14: Alt 2A 174 (1F 151)

Hightgate Ho. OL8: O'ham 1D 90
　　　　　　　　　　　　　　　　(off Marple Cl.)
Highthorne Grn. OL2: O'ham 5C 42
HIGHTOWN .4C 86
High Vw. M25: Pres 6H 69
High Vw. St. BL1: Bolt 5C 18
　　BL3: Bolt .2A 48
Highview Wlk. M9: Man 6A 72
High Wardle La. OL12: W'le 1H 15
Highwood OL11: Roch 2A 26
Highwood Cl. BL2: Bolt 4B 34
High Wood Fold SK6: Mar B 3G 149
Highworth St. BL3: Bolt 2C 48
　　　　　　　　　　　　　　　　(off Parrot St.)
Highworth Dr. M40: Man 1F 89
Higson Av. M21: Chor 2H 129
　　M30: Ecc .5E 97
　　SK6: Rom 1F 147
Hilary Av. OL8: O'ham 2F 91
　　SK8: H Grn 5H 155
Hilary Cl. SK4: Stoc 1F 145
Hilary Gro. BL4: Farn 2G 65
Hilary Rd. M22: Wyth 4A 154
Hilary St. OL11: Roch 4F 41
Hilberry Ho. OL5: Mos 6A 78
Hilbre Av. OL2: O'ham 5D 58
Hilbre Rd. M19: Man 1B 132
Hilbre Way SK9: Hand 3A 166
Hilbury Av. M9: Man 2H 87
Hilda Av. BL8: Tot 5H 21
　　SK8: Chea 6A 144
Hilda Gro. SK5: Stoc 5H 133
Hilda Rd. SK14: Hyde 2B 136
Hilda St. BL3: Bolt 3E 49
　　OL9: O'ham 2D 74
　　　　　　　　　　　　　　　(not continuous)
　　OL10: H'ood 3H 39
　　SK5: Stoc 5H 133
Hilden Ct. M16: W Ran 3B 114
Hilden St. BL2: Bolt 1E 49
Hilditch Cl. M23: Wyth 5H 141
Hiley Rd. M30: Ecc 5B 96
Hillam Cl. M41: Urm 6H 111
Hillary Av. OL7: A Lyme 6H 91
Hillary Rd. SK14: Hyde 2E 121
Hill Bank Cl. SK15: C'ook 6H 93
Hillbank Cl. BL1: Bolt 2A 32
Hillbank St. M24: Mid 1F 57
Hill Barn La. OL3: Dig 4F 63
Hillbrook Av. M40: Man 1D 88
Hillbrook Grange SK7: Bram 1F 167
Hillbrook Rd. SK1: Stoc 3C 146
　　SK7: Bram 1F 167
Hillbrow Wlk. M8: Man 4D 86
　　　　　　　　　　　　　　　(off Highshore Dr.)
Hillbury Rd. SK7: Bram 4H 157
Hill Carr WA14: Alt 1D 150
Hill Cl. OL4: O'ham 4A 76
Hillcote Wlk. M18: Man 1D 116
　　　　　　　　　　　　　　　　(off Marjorie Cl.)
Hill Cot Rd. BL1: Bolt 6D 18
Hill Ct. M. SK6: Rom 1H 147
Hillcourt Rd. SK6: H Lan 6C 160
　　SK6: Rom 6A 136
Hillcourt St. M1: Man 4B 10 (6E 101)
Hill Cres. M9: Man 6E 71
Hillcrest M6: Sal 2A 98
　　M24: Mid .4B 56
　　SK14: Hyde 2D 136
Hillcrest Av. OL10: H'ood 2E 39
　　SK4: Stoc 1C 144
Hillcrest Cres. OL10: H'ood 2E 39
Hillcrest Dr. M19: Man 2E 133
　　M34: Dent 6H 119
Hillcrest Rd. M25: Pres 1F 85
　　M29: Tyld .3B 80
　　OL11: Roch 3E 41
　　　　　　　　　　　　　　　(not continuous)
　　SK2: Stoc 5C 146
　　SK7: Bram 4H 157
Hill Cft. SK2: Stoc 5E 147
Hillcroft OL8: O'ham 2G 91
Hillcroft Cl. M8: Man 3E 87

Hillcroft Rd. WA14: Alt 6C 138
Hilldale Av. M9: Man 5H 71
Hill Dr. SK9: Hand 4A 166
Hillel Ho. M15: Man 2E 115
Hill End SK6: Rom 5B 136
Hillend SK14: Mot 6C 122
Hill End La. SK14: Mot 6B 122
Hillend Pl. M23: Wyth 1G 141
Hill End Rd. OL3: Del 2B 62
Hillend Rd. M23: Wyth 1G 141
Hill Farm Cl. OL8: O'ham 6G 75
Hillfield M5: Sal 3D 98
Hillfield Cl. M13: Man 2H 115
Hillfield Dr. BL2: Bolt 4F 33
　　M28: Wors 4E 81
Hillfield Wlk. BL2: Bolt 4F 33
Hillfoot Wlk. M15: Man 5D 8
Hillgate Av. M5: Sal 6H 99
Hillgate Bus. Cen. SK1: Stoc 5H 179
Hillgate St. OL6: A Lyme 1A 106
Hillhead Wlk. M8: Man 5E 87
　　　　　　　　　　　　　　　(off Barnsdale Dr.)
Hillhouse Ct. OL11: Roch 2D 40
Hillier St. M9: Man 3A 88
Hillier St. Nth. M9: Man 3A 88
Hillingdon Cl. OL8: O'ham 3B 90
Hillingdon Dr. M9: Man 1D 88
Hillingdon Ho. BL1: Bolt 4C 32
　　　　　　　　　　　　　　　(off Enfield Cl.)
Hillingdon Rd. M32: Stre 6E 113
　　M45: White 2C 68
Hillington Rd. M33: Sale 5G 127
　　SK3: Stoc 3E 145
Hillkirk Dr. OL12: Roch 6E 15
Hillkirk St. M11: Man 4A 102
Hill La. BL2: Bolt 5E 33
　　M9: Man 6H 71
Hillman Cl. M40: Man 6H 87
Hill Mt. SK16: Duk 5E 107
Hillock, The BL2: Bolt 5E 35
Hill Ri. BL0: Ram 4A 12
　　SK6: Rom 1H 147
　　WA14: Alt 6C 138
Hillsborough Dr. BL9: Bury 5H 53
Hill's Ct. BL8: Bury 1B 36
Hillsdale Gro. BL2: Bolt 2A 34
Hill Side BL1: Bolt 6F 31
Hillside Av. BL4: Farn 2F 65
　　BL7: Bro X 2F 19
　　M7: Sal 3G 85
　　M28: Walk 5G 65
　　M45: White 5E 53
　　OL2: O'ham 2E 59
　　OL2: Shaw 6B 44
　　OL3: Dig 3D 62
　　OL4: Grot .4E 77
　　OL4: O'ham 2E 59
　　SK14: Hyde 3D 136
　　SK15: C'ook 5B 94
Hillside Cl. BL2: Bolt 6A 20
　　BL3: Bolt .5D 46
　　M40: Man .2C 88
　　SK7: Bram 6A 158
　　SK12: Dis 1H 171
　　SK13: Had 4G 123
Hillside Ct. BL1: Bolt 6F 31
　　M25: Pres .6G 69
Hillside Cres. BL9: Bury 5F 23
　　OL6: A Lyme 6D 92
Hillside Dr. M24: Mid 6D 56
　　M27: Pen .5D 84
Hillside Gdns. BL9: Sum 1C 22
Hillside Gro. SK6: Mar B 2F 149
Hillside Ho. BL1: Bolt 6F 31
Hillside Rd. BL0: Ram 4A 12
　　SK2: Stoc 4D 146
　　SK6: Wood 4H 135
　　SK14: Hyde 4A 136
　　WA15: Hale 2A 152
Hillside St. BL3: Bolt 2B 48
Hillside Vw. M34: Dent 2G 135
　　OL16: Miln 5G 29
Hillside Wlk. OL12: Roch 5F 15

Hillside Way OL12: Whitw 4A **14**
Hills La. BL9: Bury, White 5A **54**
Hillspring Rd. OL4: Spri 3E **77**
Hillstone Av. OL12: Roch 5E **15**
Hillstone Cl. BL8: G'mount 1H **21**
Hill St. BL8: Bury 1H **35**
  BL9: Sum 6C **12**
  M7: Sal .5B **86**
             (not continuous)
  M20: Man 2F **131**
  M24: Mid 4C **56**
  M26: Rad 3H **51**
                  6B **52**
  M26: Rad 6B **52**
               (Ainsworth Rd.)
               (Rupert St.)
  OL2: Shaw 1A **60**
  OL4: O'ham 2H **75**
  OL7: A Lyme 3G **105**
  OL10: H'ood 3G **39**
  OL16: Roch 4D **178** (4A **28**)
  SK6: Rom 1H **147**
  SK14: Hyde 1D **136**
  SK16: Duk 4H **105**
  WA14: B'ath 3E **139**
HILL TOP
  M28 . . . . .4H **65**
  SK9 . . . . .1F **173**
Hill Top BL1: Bolt 2B **32**
  BL3: Lit L 3C **50**
  OL1: Chad 5H **57**
  SK6: Rom 6H **135**
  WA15: Hale 5A **152**
Hilltop OL12: Whitw 4E **15**
Hill Top Av. M25: Pres 5H **69**
  SK8: Chea H 4D **156**
  SK9: Wilm 1E **173**
Hilltop Av. M9: Man 6H **71**
  M45: White 1H **69**
Hill Top Ct. SK8: Chea H 4D **156**
Hilltop Ct. M8: Man 1D **86**
  M14: Man 6H **115**
  M28: Walk 5H **65**
               (off Fereday St.)
Hill Top Dr. OL11: Roch 3G **41**
  WA15: Hale 4A **152**
Hilltop Dr. BL8: Tot 5G **21**
  OL2: O'ham 5E **59**
  SK6: Mar 5A **148**
Hilltop Gro. M45: White 1H **69**
Hill Top La. OL3: Del 2F **61**
Hill Top Rd. M28: Walk 5H **65**
Hill Vw. OL3: Del *3B 62*
           (off St Annes Sq.)
  OL15: L'ough 2B **16**
  SK15: Stal 1H **121**
Hill Vw. Cl. OL1: O'ham 5A **60**
Hill Vw. Ct. BL1: Bolt 1C **32**
Hill Vw. Rd. BL1: Bolt 1C **32**
Hillview Rd. M34: Dent 6A **118**
Hillwood Av. M8: Man 6D **70**
Hillyard St. BL8: Bury 2C **36**
Hilly Cft. BL7: Bro X 3D **18**
Hilmarton Cl. BL2: Bolt 6A **20**
Hilrose Av. M41: Urm 5H **111**
Hilson Ct. M43: Droy 4A **104**
Hilton Arc. OL1: O'ham 3G **177**
Hilton Av. M41: Urm 5F **111**
Hilton Bank M28: Walk 6F **65**
Hilton Ct. SK3: Stoc 4E **179** (3G **145**)
Hilton Cres. M25: Pres 1H **85**
  M28: Wors 5F **81**
  OL6: A Lyme 6A **92**
Hilton Dr. M25: Pres 1H **85**
  M44: Cad 4A **124**
Hilton Fold La. M24: Mid 6D **56**
Hilton Gro. M28: Walk 6F **65**
  SK12: Poy 3D **168**
Hilton Ho. SK1: Stoc 3G **179** (1H **145**)
Hilton La. M25: Pres 2F **85**
  M28: Walk 1F **81**
Hilton Lodge
  M25: Pres 1H **85**
HILTON PARK 1H **85**

Hilton Rd. BL9: Bury 4C **176** (3F **37**)
  M22: Shar 6C **142**
  SK7: Bram 4H **157**
  SK12: Dis 6F **161**
  SK12: Poy 2A **170**
              (not continuous)
Hiltons Cl. OL8: O'ham 4E **75**
Hiltons Farm Cl. M34: Aud 1E **119**
Hilton Sq. M27: Pen 3A **84**
Hilton St. BL2: Bolt 6G **33**
  BL9: Bury 1F **37**
  M1: Man 5C **6** (4F **101**)
  M4: Man 4B **6** (3E **101**)
  M7: Sal .5B **86**
  M24: Mid 5B **56**
  M38: Lit H 5E **65**
  OL1: O'ham 1A **76**
  SK3: Stoc 3F **145**
Hilton St. Nth. M7: Sal 5B **86**
Hilton Wlk. M24: Mid 1G **71**
Himley Rd. M11: Man 2E **103**
Hincaster Wlk. M18: Man 2E **117**
          (off Hampden Cres.)
Hinchcombe Cl. M38: Lit H *3E 65*
            (off Haymill Av.)
Hinchley Rd. M9: Man 1D **88**
Hinchley Way M27: Pen 1H **83**
Hinckley St. M11: Man 5B **102**
Hindburn Cl. M45: White 6H **53**
Hindburn Dr. M28: Wors 3E **81**
Hindburn Wlk. M45: White 6H **53**
Hinde St. M40: Man 3C **88**
Hindhead Wlk. M40: Man 1F **103**
          (off Thaxmead Dr.)
Hind Hill St. OL10: H'ood 4H **39**
Hindle Dr. OL2: O'ham 4C **58**
Hindle St. M26: Rad 4A **52**
Hindle Ter. OL3: Del 3B **62**
Hindley Av. M22: Wyth 3H **153**
Hindley Cl. OL7: A Lyme 4F **105**
Hindley St. OL7: A Lyme 4F **105**
             (not continuous)
  SK1: Stoc 5H **179** (3H **145**)
Hindsford Cl. M23: Wyth 2D **140**
Hinds La. BL8: Bury 5C **36**
  M26: Bury, Rad 6C **36**
Hind St. BL2: Bolt 6H **33**
Hinkler Av. BL3: Bolt 4C **48**
Hinstock Cres. M18: Man 2F **117**
Hinton OL12: Roch 1A **178** (3H **27**)
Hinton Cl. OL11: Roch 5A **26**
Hinton Gro. SK14: Hyde 1E **137**
Hinton M. SK1: Stoc 2B **146**
Hinton St. M4: Man 2D **6** (2F **101**)
  OL8: O'ham 6G **177** (4F **75**)
Hipley Cl. SK6: Bred 4G **135**
Hirons La. OL4: Spri 4E **77**
Hirst Av. M28: Walk 4G **65**
Hitchen Cl. SK16: Duk 6D **106**
Hitchen Dr. SK16: Duk 6D **106**
Hitchen St. M13: Man 6G **11** (2G **115**)
Hives, The M17: T Pk 6B **98**
Hive St. OL8: O'ham 1B **90**
HMP Buckley Hall
  OL12: Roch 6A **16**
HMP Forest Bank M27: Pen 2E **85**
HMP Manchester
  M3: Man 1G **5** (1D **100**)
HMP Styal SK9: Sty 5E **165**
Hobart Cl. SK7: Bram 3H **167**
Hobart St. BL1: Bolt 3B **32**
  M18: Man 2F **117**
Hob Hill SK15: Stal 4D **106**
Hob Mill Ri. OL5: Mos 5A **78**
Hobson Cl. M34: Aud 1E **119**
Hobson Cres. M34: Aud 1E **119**
Hobson Moor Rd.
  SK14: Mot 1B **122**
Hobson St. M11: Man 6A **104**
  M35: Fail .5E **89**
  OL1: O'ham 4G **177** (3F **75**)
  SK5: Stoc 5H **117**

Hockenhull Cl. M22: Wyth 3C **154**
Hockerley Cl. M33: Sale 4F **127**
HOCKLEY 4F **169**
Hockley Cl. SK12: Poy 4G **169**
Hockley Paddock SK12: Poy 4F **169**
Hockley Rd. M23: Wyth 6F **141**
  SK12: Poy 4G **169**
Hodder Av. OL15: L'ough 3F **17**
Hodder Bank SK2: Stoc 6E **147**
Hodder Way M45: White 1A **70**
              (not continuous)
Hoddesdon St. M8: Man 4F **87**
Hodge Clough Rd.
  OL1: O'ham 3A **60**
Hodge La. M5: Sal 4F **99**
Hodge Rd. M28: Walk 1H **81**
  OL1: O'ham 4B **60**
Hodge St. M9: Man 2B **88**
Hodgson Dr. WA15: Tim 3A **140**
Hodgson St. M8: Man 6D **86**
  OL6: A Lyme 6A **174** (3G **105**)
Hodnet Av. M41: Urm 6A **110**
Hodnet Wlk. M34: Dent 6E **119**
Hodnet Rd. M27: Swin 1G **83**
Hodson St. M3: Sal 3E **5** (3C **100**)
Hogarth Ri. OL1: O'ham 3B **60**
Hogarth Rd. OL11: Roch 2H **41**
  SK6: Mar B 3F **149**
Hogarth Wlk. M8: Man *5G 87*
           (off Smeaton St.)
Hoggs Bri. Cl. M27: Pen 3D **84**
Holbeach Cl. BL8: Bury 6D **22**
Holbeck Av. OL12: Roch 5F **15**
Holbeck Gro. M14: Man 3A **116**
Holbeton Cl. M8: Man 6C **86**
  SK7: Bram 2H **157**
Holborn Av. M26: Rad 3F **51**
  M35: Fail .4B **90**
Holborn Dr. M8: Man 6F **87**
Holborn Gdns. OL11: Roch 6F **27**
Holborn Sq. OL11: Roch 6F **27**
Holborn St. OL11: Roch 6F **27**
Holbrook Av. M38: Lit H 3E **65**
Holbrook St. M1: Man 2B **10**
HOLCOMBE 3A **12**
Holcombe Av. BL8: Bury 3B **36**
HOLCOMBE BROOK 1G **21**
Holcombe Brook BL0: Ram *6A 12*
          (off Redisher Cft.)
Holcombe Brook Sports Club 1H **21**
Holcombe Cl. BL4: Kea 3C **66**
  M6: Sal .3G **99**
  OL4: Spri 2E **77**
  WA14: Alt 5D **138**
Holcombe Cres. BL0: Ram 1A **22**
Holcombe Cres. BL4: Kea 3C **66**
Holcombe Gdns. M19: Man 4A **132**
Holcombe Lee BL0: Ram 5A **12**
Holcombe M. BL0: Ram 6A **12**
Holcombe Old Rd. BL8: Holc 4A **12**
Holcombe Pct. BL0: Ram 1H **21**
Holcombe Rd. BL3: Lit L 4B **50**
  BL8: Ram, Tot 4A **12**
  M14: Man 2A **132**
Holcombe Vw. Cl. OL4: O'ham 5B **60**
Holcombe Village BL8: Holc 3A **12**
Holcombe Wlk. SK4: Stoc 2F **133**
Holden Av. BL0: Ram 4A **12**
  BL1: Bolt .5C **18**
  BL9: Bury 1C **38**
  M16: W Ran 6C **114**
Holden Clough Dr.
  OL7: A Lyme 4G **91**
HOLDEN FOLD 4C **58**
Holden Fold La. OL2: O'ham 5C **58**
            (not continuous)
Holden Gallery 4B **10**
Holden Rd. M7: Sal 2B **86**
Holden St. OL6: A Lyme 1A **106**
            (not continuous)
  OL8: O'ham 6F **75**
  OL12: Roch 1A **28**

Holder Av. BL3: Lit L 2D **50**
Holderness Dr. OL2: O'ham 5C **58**
Holdgate Cl. M15: Man 2C **114**
Holdsworth St. M27: Swin 4F **83**
Holebottom OL6: A Lyme 5A **92**
Hole Ho. Fold SK6: Rom 1H **147**
Holford Av. M14: Man 5F **115**
Holford Ct. M34: Dent 4F **119**
Holford Wlk. OL16: Roch 4D **28**
Holgate St. OL4: O'ham 6C **60**
Holhouse La. BL8: G'mount 1H **21**
Holiday La. SK2: Stoc 5F **147**
Holkar Mdws. BL7: Bro X 3F **19**
Holker Cl. M13: Man 2H **115**
SK12: Poy 3F **169**
Holker Way M34: Dent 6G **119**
(off Two Trees La.)
Holkham Cl. M4: Man 4F **7** (3G **101**)
Holland Av. SK15: Stal 3E **107**
Holland Cl. OL3: Del 3A **62**
SK12: Poy 4E **169**
Holland Ct. M8: Man 1D **86**
M26: Rad 3C **52**
SK1: Stoc 6H **179** (4A **146**)
Holland Gro. OL6: A Lyme 5H **91**
Holland Pk. SK7: Bram 6F **157**
Holland Ri. OL12: Roch ...2A **178** (3G **27**)
Holland Rd. M8: Man 1D **86**
SK7: Bram 6G **157**
SK14: Hyde 2D **120**
Holland St. BL1: Bolt 1D **32**
M6: Sal 6G **85**
M26: Rad 3C **52**
M34: Dent 3D **118**
M40: Man 3G **7** (3H **101**)
OL10: H'ood 3H **39**
OL12: Roch 2A **178** (4G **27**)
OL16: Roch 5D **16**
Holland St. E. M34: Dent 3D **118**
Holland St. W. M34: Dent 3D **118**
Holland Wlk. M6: Sal 6G **85**
Hollies, The BL2: Bolt 5B **34**
M6: Sal 2B **98**
M20: Man 6D **130**
M27: Swin 4B **84**
(Manchester Rd.)
M27: Swin 5F **83**
(Moorfield Cl.)
OL8: O'ham 5D **74**
SK4: Stoc 6D **132**
SK8: Gat 6F **143**
Hollies Ct. M33: Sale 5B **128**
Hollies Dr. SK6: Mar 6E **149**
Hollies La. SK9: Wilm 2H **173**
Hollin Bank SK4: Stoc 2F **133**
Hollin Cres. OL3: G'fld 5A **78**
Hollliney Rd. M22: Wyth 4D **154**
HOLLINGWORTH
OL15 ....6G **17**
SK14 ....2E **123**
Hollingworth Av. M40: Man 1H **89**
Hollingworth Cl. SK1: Stoc 4G **179**
Hollingworth Dr. SK6: Mar 2D **160**
Hollingworth Lake Cvn. Pk.
OL15: L'ough 2H **29**
Hollingworth Lake Country Pk. 1H **29**
Hollingworth Lake Nature Reserve . .1H **29**
Hollingworth Lake Sailing Club 1G **29**
Hollingworth Lake Vis. Cen. 6H **17**
Hollingworth Lake Water Activity Cen.
..........................6G **17**
Hollingworth Rd. OL15: L'ough 5H **17**
SK6: Bred 5E **135**
Hollingworth St. OL9: Chad 6B **74**
Hollinhall St. OL4: O'ham 2E **76**
Hollin Hey Rd. BL1: Bolt 2E **31**
Hollinhey Ter. SK14: Holl 2E **123**
Hollin Ho. M24: Mid 4C **56**
Hollinhurst Dr. BL6: Los 6C **30**
Hollinhurst Rd. M26: Rad 5C **52**
Hollin La. M24: Mid 2A **56**
OL11: Roch 5A **26**
SK9: Sty 1D **164**

HOLLINS
BL9 ....2G **53**
M24 ....4C **56**
OL8 ....6C **74**
Hollins BL4: Farn 1B **64**
Hollins, The SK6: Mar 5D **148**
SK13: Gam 5F **123**
(off Hollins M.)
SK14: Hyde 2C **136**
Hollins Bank SK13: Gam 5F **123**
(off Brassington Cres.)
Hollins Brook Cl. BL9: Bury 2H **53**
Hollins Brook Way BL9: Bury 1H **53**
Hollins Brow BL9: Bury 3F **53**
Hollins Cl. BL9: Bury 3H **53**
SK13: Gam 5F **123**
(off Brassington Cres.)
Hollinsclough Cl. M22: Shar 6C **142**
Hollinscroft Av. WA15: Tim 6D **140**
Hollins Dr. M24: Mid 3A **56**
Hollins Fold SK13: Gam 5F **123**
(off Brassington Cres.)
Hollins Gdns. SK13: Gam 5F **123**
(off Hollins M.)
HOLLINS GREEN 1E **91**
Hollins Grn. M24: Mid 4C **56**
Hollins Grn. Gdns. SK6: Mar 5D **148**
(off Station Rd.)
Hollins Gro. SK6: Mar 5D **148**
M33: Sale 5A **128**
SK13: Gam 5F **123**
(off Brassington Cres.)
Hollins Hall of Residence BL2: Bolt ..1F **49**
(within University of Bolton,
Chadwick Campus)
Hollinshead M7: Sal 5C **86**
(off Wilmur Av.)
Hollins La. BL0: Ram 4H **13**
BL9: Bury 2G **53**
OL3: G'fld 4F **79**
OL5: Mos 2H **93**
SK6: Mar 5D **148**
SK6: Mar B 4F **149**
SK13: Gam 5F **123**
Hollins M. BL9: Bury 3A **54**
SK13: Gam 5F **123**
Hollins Mt. SK6: Mar B 3F **149**
Hollins Rd. OL4: Lees 1D **76**
OL8: O'ham 1B **90**
Hollins Sq. BL9: Bury 4H **53**
Hollins St. BL2: Bolt 1F **49**
OL4: Spri 3D **76**
SK15: Stal 5D **106**
Hollins Ter. SK6: Mar 5D **148**
HOLLINS VALE 1G **53**
Hollins Wlk. M22: Wyth 3B **154**
Hollins Way SK13: Gam 5F **123**
(off Hollins M.)
Hollinswood Rd. BL2: Bolt 1F **49**
M28: Wors 5F **81**
HOLLINWOOD 1C **90**
Hollinwood Av. M40: Man 6F **73**
OL9: Chad 6F **73**
Hollinwood Bus. Cen.
OL8: O'ham 2B **90**
Hollinwood La. SK6: Mar 3F **161**
(not continuous)
Hollinwood Rd. SK12: Dis 1H **171**
Hollinwood Station (Rail) 1A **90**
Holloway Dr. M28: Ward 2E **83**
Hollowbrook Way OL12: Roch 1F **27**
Hollow End SK5: Stoc 2B **134**
Hollow End Towers SK5: Stoc 2B **134**
Hollow Fld. OL11: Roch 2H **25**
Hollowgate M27: Swin 5E **83**
Hollow Mdws. M26: Rad 3E **67**
Hollows, The SK8: H Grn 4G **155**
Hollows Av. M21: Chor 4A **130**
Hollows Ct. SK14: Hyde 5C **120**
(off Ridling La.)

Hollows Farm Av. OL12: Roch 1F **27**
Hollowspell OL12: Roch 6C **16**
Hollow Va. Dr. SK5: Stoc 6H **117**
Holly Av. M28: Walk 1A **82**
M41: Urm 5D **110**
SK8: Chea 6H **143**
Holly Bank M33: Sale 6C **128**
M40: Man 4E **89**
OL2: O'ham 3D **58**
(off Church St.)
OL2: O'ham 1D **58**
(Fir La.)
OL6: A Lyme 3B **106**
SK14: Holl 2F **123**
Hollybank M43: Droy 2C **104**
SK15: Mill 1H **107**
Holly Bank Cl. M15: Man 5B **8** (1A **114**)
Holly Bank Cotts. M31: Part 5D **124**
(off Manchester Rd.)
SK6: Wood 4H **135**
(off High La.)
Holly Bank Ct. SK8: Chea H 4C **156**
Hollybank Dr. BL6: Los 6B **30**
Holly Bank Ind. Est. M26: Rad 4H **51**
Holly Bank Rd. SK9: Wilm 6F **165**
Holly Bank St. M26: Rad 4H **51**
Hollybrook OL1: Chad 4B **58**
Hollybrook Dr. SK6: Rom 1C **148**
Hollybush St. M18: Man 1G **117**
Holly Cl. WA15: Tim 5A **140**
Holly Ct. BL9: Bury 3G **37**
M20: Man 3F **131**
M44: Irl 4F **109**
SK3: Stoc 6G **145**
SK14: Hyde 5E **121**
Hollycroft Av. BL2: Bolt 2A **50**
M22: Wyth 5B **142**
Holly Dene Dr. BL6: Los 6B **30**
Holly Dr. M33: Sale 5A **128**
Hollyedge Dr. M25: Pres 1G **85**
Holly Fold M45: White 6F **53**
Hollygate, The SK3: Stoc 2F **145**
(off Chestergate)
Holly Grange SK7: Bram 2H **157**
WA14: Bow 3F **151**
Holly Gro. BL1: Bolt 4A **32**
BL4: Farn 1E **65**
M33: Sale 5D **128**
M34: Dent 4G **119**
OL3: Dig 4E **63**
OL3: Dob 5E **63**
OL4: Lees 1C **76**
OL9: Chad 1B **74**
SK15: Stal 5C **106**
Hollyhedge Av. M22: Wyth 6B **142**
Hollyhedge Ct. M22: Shar 6C **142**
Hollyhedge Ct. Rd. M22: Shar 6C **142**
Hollyhedge Rd. M22: Shar, Wyth ...6A **142**
M23: Wyth 6F **141**
Hollyhey Dr. M23: Wyth 2A **142**
Holly Ho. Dr. M41: Urm 5B **110**
Hollyhouse Dr. SK6: Wood 4G **135**
Hollyhurst M28: Wors 5D **82**
Holly La. OL8: O'ham 1C **90**
SK9: Sty 3C **164**
Holly Mill Cres. BL1: Bolt 1D **32**
Hollymount M16: Old T 3H **113**
Hollymount Av. SK2: Stoc 6C **146**
Hollymount Dr. OL4: O'ham 4C **60**
SK2: Stoc 6D **146**
Hollymount Gdns. SK2: Stoc 6D **146**
Holly Mt. La. BL8: G'mount 2F **21**
Hollymount Rd. SK2: Stoc 6C **146**
Holly Oak Gdns. OL10: H'ood 4G **39**
Holly Rd. M27: Swin 5F **83**
SK4: Stoc 4E **133**
SK6: H Lan 6D **160**
SK7: Bram 2G **167**
SK12: Poy 4E **169**
Holly Rd. Nth. SK9: Wilm 3D **172**
Holly Rd. Sth. SK9: Wilm 4D **172**
Holly Royde Cl. M20: Man 3F **131**

Holly St. BL1: Bolt 1D **32**
   BL8: Tot 5H **21**
   BL9: Bury 3G **37**
   BL9: Sum 6C **12**
   M11: Man 5A **102**
   M43: Droy 3F **103**
   OL12: W'le 6C **16**
   OL16: Roch 3B **42**
   SK1: Stoc 2A **146**
Hollythorn Av. SK8: Chea H 6D **156**
Holly Va. Cotts. SK6: Mar B 3H **149**
Holly Vw. M22: Shar 1C **154**
Holly Wlk. M31: Part 6B **124**
Hollyway M22: Nor 3C **142**
Hollywood BL1: Bolt 3H **31**
   WA14: Bow 3F **151**
Hollywood Bowl
   Ashton-under-Lyne 2F **105**
Hollywood Rd. BL1: Bolt 3H **31**
Hollywood Towers SK3: Stoc 3F **145**
           (off Hardman St.)
Hollywood Way SK4: Stoc 2F **145**
Holmbrook M29: Tyld 2A **80**
Holm Ct. M6: Sal 3G **99**
           (off Mulberry Rd.)
Holmcroft Rd. M18: Man 4F **117**
Holmdale Av. M19: Man 4A **132**
Holmdale Ct. M33: Sale 5C **128**
Holme Av. BL8: Bury 5C **22**
Holmebrook Wlk. M8: Man 5E **87**
           (off Heywood St.)
Holme Cres. OL2: O'ham 5C **58**
Holmecroft Chase BL5: W'ton 4A **46**
Holmefield M33: Sale 5B **128**
Holmefield Dr. SK8: Chea H 5D **156**
Holme Ho. OL15: L'ough 2B **16**
Holme Ho. St. OL15: L'ough 1B **16**
Holmepark Gdns. M28: Wors 6E **81**
Holme Rd. M20: Man 6D **130**
Holmes Cotts. BL1: Bolt 2A **32**
Holmes Ct. SK1: Stoc 3H **179**
Holmes Rd. OL12: Roch 4F **27**
Holmes St. BL3: Bolt 3E **49**
   OL12: Roch 6C **16**
           (Halifax Rd.)
   OL12: Roch 3F **27**
           (Primrose St.)
   SK2: Stoc 6F **179**
   SK8: Chea 5A **144**
Holme St. SK14: Hyde 5B **120**
Holmes Way M34: Dent 2F **135**
Holmeswood Cl. SK9: Wilm 1F **173**
Holmeswood Rd. BL3: Bolt 5B **48**
Holme Ter. OL15: L'ough 2B **16**
Holmfield Av. M9: Man 4B **88**
   M25: Pres 6A **70**
Holmfield Av. W. M9: Man 4B **88**
Holmfield Cl. SK4: Stoc 6F **133**
Holmfield Grn. BL3: Bolt 4F **47**
Holmfirth Rd. OL3: G'fld 4E **79**
Holmfirth St. M13: Man 3B **116**
Holmfoot Wlk. M9: Man 4H **87**
           (off Foleshill Av.)
Holmlea Rd. M43: Droy 3G **103**
Holmleigh Av. M9: Man 2A **88**
Holmpark Rd. M11: Man 6H **103**
Holmside Gdns. M19: Man 1A **132**
Holmwood WA14: Bow 2C **150**
Holmwood Ct. M20: Man 5F **131**
Holmwood Rd. M20: Man 4F **131**
Holroyd St. M11: Man 5C **102**
   OL16: Roch 4D **178** (4A **28**)
Holset Dr. WA14: Alt 6D **138**
Holset Wlk. SK7: H Gro 3A **158**
Holst Av. M8: Man 5E **87**
Holstein Av. OL12: Roch 5F **15**
Holstein St. M13: Man 2H **115**
Holtby St. M9: Man 2A **88**
Holthouse Rd. BL8: Tot 6G **21**
Holt La. M35: Fail 4B **90**
HOLT LANE END 4B **90**

Holt La. M. M35: Fail 4B **90**
HOLTS 5C **76**
Holts La. OL4: O'ham 5B **76**
   SK9: Sty 3D **164**
           (not continuous)
Holts Pas. OL15: L'ough 4G **17**
Holts Ter. OL12: Roch 1G **27**
Holt St. BL0: Ram 3D **12**
   BL3: Bolt 2B **48**
   M27: Clif 1H **83**
   M30: Ecc 5E **97**
   M34: Aud 5E **105**
   M40: Man 6B **88**
   OL4: O'ham 1A **76**
   OL12: Whitw 4A **14**
   OL15: L'ough 1B **16**
   OL16: Miln 6G **29**
   SK1: Stoc 5H **179** (3H **145**)
   WA14: B'ath 3E **139**
Holt St. W. BL0: Ram 4B **12**
HOLT TOWN 3A **102**
Holt Town M40: Man 4H **7** (3H **101**)
Holt Town Ind. Est. M11: Man 3A **102**
Holtwood Wlk. SK5: Stoc 2C **134**
Holway Wlk. M9: Man 4G **87**
         (off Hendham Va.)
Holwick Rd. M23: Wyth 1F **141**
Holwood Dr. M16: W Ran 1C **130**
Holybourne Wlk. M23: Wyth 3D **140**
Holy Harbour St. BL1: Bolt 3A **32**
Holyhurst Wlk. BL1: Bolt 3C **32**
           (off Rix St.)
Holyoake Rd. M28: Walk 1H **81**
Holyoake St. M43: Droy 3C **104**
Holyoak St. M40: Man 5E **89**
Holyrood Cl. M25: Pres 3A **70**
Holyrood Ct. M25: Pres 3H **69**
Holyrood Dr. M25: Pres 3A **70**
   M27: Swin 4F **83**
Holyrood Gro. M25: Pres 3A **70**
Holyrood Rd. M25: Pres 4A **70**
Holyrood St. M40: Man 1G **103**
   OL1: O'ham 6G **59**
Holywood St. M14: Man 4F **115**
Homebeck Ho. SK8: Gat 6E **143**
Homebury Dr. M11: Man 3D **102**
Home Dr. M24: Mid 2B **72**
Home Farm Av. SK14: Mot 6B **122**
Home Front Mus. (by appointment only)
           . . . . .4C **128**
           (off Broad Rd.)
Homelands Cl. M33: Sale 1H **139**
Homelands Rd. M33: Sale 1H **139**
Homelands Wlk. M9: Man 4H **87**
           (off Shiredale Dr.)
Homelaurel Ho. M33: Sale 1B **140**
Homelyme Ho. SK12: Poy 4F **169**
Homer Dr. SK6: Mar B 3F **149**
Homer St. M26: Rad 3G **51**
Homerton Rd. M40: Man 1D **102**
Homestead, The M33: Sale 4H **127**
Homestead Cl. M31: Part 5E **125**
Homestead Cres. M19: Man 6H **131**
Homestead Gdns. OL12: Roch 4D **16**
Homestead Rd. SK12: Dis 1G **171**
Homewood Av. M22: Nor 2B **142**
Homewood Rd. M22: Nor 2A **142**
Honduras St. OL4: O'ham 2H **75**
Hondwith Cl. BL2: Bolt 6G **19**
Honeybourne Cl. M29: Tyld 2A **80**
Honeycombe Cotts. SK8: Chea 6A **144**
           (off Oak Rd.)
Honey Hill OL4: Lees 4D **76**
Honey St. M8: Man 1F **101**
Honeysuckle Cl. M23: Wyth 2D **140**
   SK6: Wood 4G **135**
Honeysuckle Dr. SK15: Stal 3F **107**
Honeysuckle Wlk. M33: Sale 3F **127**
Honeysuckle Way OL12: Roch 6F **15**
Honeywell La. OL8: O'ham 6F **75**
Honeywood Cl. BL0: Ram 6A **12**
Honford Ct. SK9: Hand 4H **165**
Honford Rd. M22: Wyth 1A **154**

Hong Kong Av. M90: Man A 5G **153**
Honister Dr. M24: Mid 5B **56**
Honister Rd. M9: Man 4B **88**
Honister Way OL11: Roch 1D **40**
Honiton Av. SK14: Hat 5G **121**
Honiton Cl. OL9: Chad 6G **57**
   OL10: H'ood 5G **39**
Honiton Dr. BL2: Bolt 1C **50**
Honiton Gro. M26: Rad 2F **51**
Honiton Ho. M6: Sal 2A **98**
           (off Devon Cl.)
Honiton Wlk. SK14: Hat 1H **121**
           (off Honiton Av.)
Honiton Way WA14: Alt 5C **138**
Honor St. M13: Man 4B **116**
Honsham Wlk. M23: Wyth 2E **141**
Hood Cl. M29: Tyld 2B **80**
Hood Sq. OL4: Grot 4E **77**
Hood St. M4: Man 4D **6** (3F **101**)
Hood Wlk. M34: Dent 2G **135**
Hoole Cl. SK8: Chea 6C **144**
HOOLEY BRIDGE 1G **39**
Hooley Bri. Ind. Est. OL10: H'ood . . .1G **39**
HOOLEY BROW 2H **39**
Hooley Clough OL10: H'ood 1H **39**
HOOLEY HILL 6F **105**
Hooley Range SK4: Stoc 6D **132**
Hooper St. M12: Man 2H **11** (5H **101**)
   OL4: O'ham 3G **75**
   SK1: Stoc 3F **179** (2G **145**)
Hooton St. BL3: Bolt 4A **48**
   M40: Man 2B **102**
Hooton Way SK9: Hand 2H **165**
           (off Beeston Rd.)
Hopcroft Cl. M9: Man 3F **71**
Hope Av. BL2: Bolt 1F **49**
   M32: Stre 4B **112**
   M38: Lit H 5G **65**
   SK9: Hand 4G **165**
Hope Chapel OL6: A Lyme 1B **106**
           (off Curzon Rd.)
Hope Cl. BL2: Bolt 6A **20**
Hope Ct. OL12: Roch 1B **178**
Hopecourt Cl. M6: Sal 1C **98**
Hope Cres. M6: Sal 2C **98**
Hopedale Cl. M11: Man 4B **102**
Hopedale Rd. SK5: Stoc 3H **133**
Hopefield St. BL3: Bolt 3B **48**
Hopefold Dr. M28: Walk 1A **82**
HOPE GREEN 6D **168**
Hope Grn. Way SK10: Adl 5D **168**
Hope Hey La. M38: Lit H 4D **64**
Hopelea La. SK10: Adl 6D **168**
Hopelea St. M20: Man 2F **131**
Hope Pk. Cl. M25: Pres 6H **69**
Hope Pk. Rd. M25: Pres 6H **69**
Hope Rd. M14: Man 3H **115**
   M25: Pres 1G **85**
   M33: Sale 6B **128**
Hopes Carr SK1: Stoc 3H **179** (2H **145**)
Hope St. BL0: Ram 4B **12**
   BL4: Farn 1A **66**
   M1: Man 6B **6** (4E **101**)
   M5: Sal 5A **4** (4A **100**)
   M7: Sal .4B **86**
   M27: Pen 3A **84**
   M27: Swin 4F **83**
   M30: Ecc 3H **97**
   M34: Aud 2E **119**
   M38: Lit H 5E **65**
   OL1: O'ham 2H **75**
   OL2: Shaw 6H **43**
   OL6: A Lyme 1B **106**
   OL10: H'ood 5B **40**
   OL11: Roch 4E **41**
   OL12: Roch 1B **178** (3H **27**)
   SK4: Stoc 2F **145**
   SK7: H Gro 2D **158**
   SK16: Duk 5H **105**
           (not continuous)
Hope Ter. SK3: Stoc 5F **179** (3G **145**)
   SK16: Duk 5H **105**
           (off Hope St.)

Hopgarth Wlk.—Hoyle St.

Hopgarth Wlk. *M40: Man* *6F 89*
(off Terence St.)
Hopkin Av. OL1: O'ham 1H 75
Hopkins Bldgs. OL5: Mos 6A 78
Hopkins Fld. WA14: Bow 4D 150
Hopkinson Av. M34: Dent 2D 118
Hopkinson Cl. OL3: Upp 1D 78
Hopkinson Rd. M9: Man 4H 71
Hopkins St. M12: Man 4C 116
SK14: Hyde 3C 120
Hopkin St. OL1: O'ham 3H 177 (2F 75)
Hoppet La. M43: Droy 3C 104
Hopton Av. M22: Wyth 2C 154
Hopton Ct. M15: Man 5A 10
HOPWOOD 4A 40
Hopwood Av. M30: Ecc 2F 97
OL10: H'ood 5H 39
Hopwood Cl. BL9: Bury 4F 53
Hopwood Ct. M24: Mid 3C 56
OL2: Shaw 6F 43
Hopwood Ct. M. OL10: H'ood 5A 40
Hopwood Rd. M24: Mid 3C 56
Hopwood St. M27: Pen 3A 84
M40: Man 5D 88
Horace Barnes Cl. M14: Man 4E 115
Horace Gro. SK4: Stoc 5G 133
Horace St. BL1: Bolt 3B 32
(not continuous)
Horatio St. M18: Man 1H 117
Horbury Av. M18: Man 4F 117
Horbury Dr. BL8: Bury 3C 36
Horden Wlk. *OL2: O'ham* *3E 59*
(off Shaw St.)
Hordern Cl. SK13: Had 3H 123
Horeb St. BL3: Bolt 2B 48
Horest La. OL3: Dens 5F 45
Horley Cl. BL8: Bury 4C 22
Horlock Ct. M5: Sal 2A 4 (2H 99)
Hornbeam Cl. M33: Sale 4E 127
WA15: Tim 6E 141
Hornbeam Ct. M6: Sal 2G 99
Hornbeam Rd. M19: Man 5D 116
Hornbeam Way M4: Man 1A 6 (2E 101)
Hornby Av. M9: Man 4A 72
Hornby Dr. BL3: Bolt 5D 46
Hornby Lodge *M25: Pres* *6H 69*
(off Prestwich Pk. Rd. Sth.)
Hornby Rd. M32: Stre 3F 113
Hornby St. BL9: Bury 1C 176 (6F 23)
M8: Man 1D 100
M24: Mid 1C 72
OL8: O'ham 4D 74
OL10: H'ood 4H 39
Horncastle Cl. BL8: Bury 6D 22
Horncastle Rd. M40: Man 1D 88
Hornchurch Ct. M15: Man 5H 9
OL10: H'ood 6A 40
Hornchurch Ho. SK2: Stoc 5A 146
Hornchurch St. M15: Man . . . 6E 9 (1C 114)
Horne St. BL9: Bury 5E 37
Hornet Cl. OL11: Roch 2A 42
Horniman Ho. M13: Man 2F 115
Hornsea Cl. BL8: Bury 3H 35
OL9: Chad 6H 57
Hornsea Rd. SK2: Stoc 6G 147
Hornsea Wlk. *M11: Man* *4C 102*
(off Grey Mare La.)
Horridge Fold BL7: Eger 1C 18
Horridge Fold Av. BL5: O Hul 5F 47
Horridge St. BL8: Bury 1B 36
Horrobin BL7: Tur 1G 19
Horrobin Fold BL7: Tur 1G 19
Horrobin La. BL7: Tur 1G 19
HORROCKS FOLD 4A 18
Horrocks Fold Av. BL1: Bolt 5B 18
Horrocks St. BL3: Bolt 2G 47
M26: Rad 3C 52
Horrocks Woods 5A 18
Horsa St. BL2: Bolt 4F 33
Horsedge St.
OL1: O'ham 1G 177 (1F 75)
Horsefield Av. OL12: Whitw 3E 15
Horsefield Cl. M21: Chor 2C 130
Horseshoe La. BL7: Bro X 3E 19
M24: Mid 3H 73
SK9: A Edg 4G 173
Horsfield St. BL3: Bolt 3G 47
Horsfield Way SK6: Bred 3E 135
Horsforth La. OL3: G'fld 5C 78
Horsham Av. SK7: H Gro 4C 158
Horsham Cl. BL8: Bury 4C 22
Horsham St. M6: Sal 3E 99
Horstead Wlk. *M19: Man* *5C 116*
(off Deepcar St.)
Horticultural Cen. in Wythenshawe Pk., The
. . . . 3F 141
Horton Av. BL1: Bolt 5C 18
Horton Rd. M14: Man 5E 115
Horton Sq. OL2: Shaw 1H 59
Horton St. SK1: Stoc 6H 179 (4A 146)
Hortree Rd. M32: Stre 5E 113
Horwood Cres. M20: Man 4H 131
Hoscar Dr. M19: Man 2B 132
Hoskins Cl. M12: Man 2C 116
Hospital Av. M30: Ecc 3G 97
Hospital Rd. BL7: Bro X 3D 18
M23: Wyth 6E 141
M27: Pen 4B 84
Hotel Rd. M90: Man A 6A 154
Hotel St. BL1: Bolt 4F 175 (6D 32)
Hothersall Rd. SK5: Stoc 2H 133
Hothersall St. M7: Sal 1E 5
Hotspur Cl. M14: Man 1E 131
Hough Cl. OL8: O'ham 1G 91
Hough End Av. M21: Chor 3A 130
Hough End Cen., The M21: Chor 2C 130
Houghend Cres. M21: Chor 2C 130
Hough Fold Way BL2: Bolt 6H 19
Hough Hall Rd. M40: Man 3B 88
Hough Hill Rd. SK15: Stal 4E 107
(not continuous)
Hough La. BL7: Bro X 4D 18
M24: Mid 3H 57
M29: Tyld 3A 80
SK14: Hyde 2D 120
Hough Rd. M20: Man 2E 131
Hough St. BL3: Bolt 2G 47
M29: Tyld 3B 80
Houghton Av. OL8: O'ham 1D 90
Houghton Cl. OL16: Roch 5C 28
Houghton La. M27: Swin 6F 83
Houghton Rd. M8: Man 2E 87
Houghton St. BL3: Bolt 6E 175 (2C 48)
BL9: Bury 6A 176 (4E 37)
M27: Pen 5D 84
OL2: O'ham 5E 59
Hough Wlk. M7: Sal 1B 4 (2A 100)
(not continuous)
Houldsworth Av. WA14: Tim 4G 139
Houldsworth Sq. SK5: Stoc 2G 133
Houldsworth St. M1: Man . . . 4C 6 (3F 101)
M26: Rad 2H 51
SK5: Stoc 2G 133
Hounslow Ho. *BL1: Bolt* *4C 32*
(off Kenton Cl.)
Houseley Av. OL9: Chad 6A 74
Housesteads SK14: Hat 6H 121
Houson St. OL8: O'ham 6G 177 (4F 75)
Houston Pk. M50: Sal 4F 99
Hove Cl. BL8: G'mount 2H 21
Hoveden St. M8: Man 1D 100
Hove Dr. M14: Man 2A 132
Hove St. BL3: Bolt 2A 48
Hove St. Nth. BL3: Bolt 1A 48
Hovey Cl. M8: Man 4D 86
Hoviley SK14: Hyde 4C 120
Hovingham St. OL16: Roch 3B 28
Hovington Gdns. M19: Man 3A 132
Hovis St. M11: Man 5E 103
Howard Av. BL3: Bolt 3G 47
BL4: Kea 2B 66
M30: Ecc 2F 97
SK4: Stoc 3E 133
SK8: Chea H 4C 156
Howard Cl. SK6: Rom 1G 147
Howard Ct. OL6: A Lyme . . . 5D 174 (2A 106)
Howard Dr. WA15: Hale 4A 152
Howard Hill BL9: Bury 2G 53
Howardian Cl. OL8: O'ham 6E 75
Howard La. M34: Dent 3F 119
Howard Pl. OL16: Roch 2B 178 (3H 27)
SK14: Hyde *5B 120*
(off Rutherford Way)
Howard Rd. M22: Nor 2B 142
Howard's La. OL5: Mos 2A 94
Howard Spring Wlk.
M8: Man *3D 86*
(off Absalom Dr.)
Howard St. BL1: Bolt 4D 32
M5: Sal 5G 99
M8: Man 1D 100
M26: Rad 4B 52
M32: Stre 5D 112
M34: Aud 1F 119
M34: Dent 2E 119
OL2: Shaw 6G 43
OL4: O'ham 1C 76
OL7: A Lyme 1G 105
OL12: Roch 1A 178 (3H 27)
SK1: Stoc 1G 179 (1H 145)
SK15: Mill 1H 107
Howard Way OL15: L'ough 2A 16
Howarth Av. M28: Wors 4E 83
Howarth Cl. BL9: Bury 1F 53
M11: Man 4C 102
Howarth Ct. SK2: Stoc 6B 146
HOWARTH CROSS 1B 28
Howarth Cross St. OL16: Roch 1B 28
Howarth Dr. M44: Irl 6D 108
Howarth Farm Way
OL12: Roch 6C 16
Howarth Grn. OL12: Roch 6D 16
Howarth Knowl OL12: Roch 4C 16
Howarth Sq. OL16: Roch 3A 28
Howarth St. BL4: Farn 2H 65
M16: Old T 3A 114
OL15: L'ough 3H 17
Howbridge Cl. M28: Wors 3G 81
Howbro Dr. OL7: A Lyme 6E 91
Howbrook Wlk. M15: Man 6H 9
Howclough Cl. M28: Walk 1B 82
How Clough Dr. M28: Walk 1B 82
Howcroft Cl. BL1: Bolt 2E 175 (5C 32)
Howcroft St. BL3: Bolt 2B 48
Howden Cl. SK5: Stoc 5G 117
(not continuous)
Howden Rd. M9: Man 4G 71
Howe Dr. BL0: Ram 1B 22
Howell Cft. Nth.
BL1: Bolt 3F 175 (6D 32)
Howell Cft. Sth.
BL1: Bolt 4F 175 (6D 32)
Howells Av. M33: Sale 4B 128
Howell's Yd. BL1: Bolt 4F 175
Howe St. M7: Sal 4A 86
OL7: A Lyme 5F 105
Howgill Cres. OL8: O'ham 6E 75
Howgill St. M11: Man 4F 103
How La. BL9: Bury 5E 23
(not continuous)
How Lea Dr. BL9: Bury 5F 23
Howley Cl. M44: Irl 6F 109
Howsin Av. BL2: Bolt 1F 33
Howton Cl. M12: Man 3C 116
Howty Cl. SK9: Wilm 6H 165
Hoxton Cl. SK6: Bred 5G 135
Hoy Dr. M41: Urm 2F 111
Hoylake Cl. M40: Man 3F 89
Hoylake Rd. M33: Sale 1F 141
SK3: Stoc 3C 144
Hoyland Cl. M12: Man 1B 116
Hoyle Av. OL8: O'ham 6E 177 (4E 75)
Hoyles Ct. M26: Rad 3C 52
Hoyle's Ter. OL16: Miln 5E 29
Hoyle St. BL1: Bolt 1C 32
M12: Man 2F 11 (5G 101)
M24: Mid 3E 73
M26: Rad 6B 52
OL12: Whitw 2B 14

Hoyle St. Ind. Est.
M12: Man 3F 11
Hoyle Wlk. M13: Man 5E 11
Hubert Worthington Ho.
SK9: A Edg 5G 173
(off George St.)
Hucclecote Av. M22: Wyth 3A 154
Hucklow Av. M23: Wyth 3G 153
Hucklow Bank SK13: Gam 5F 123
(off Grassmoor Cres.)
Hucklow Cl. SK13: Gam 5F 123
(off Grassmoor Cres.)
Hucklow Fold SK13: Gam 5F 123
(off Grassmoor Cres.)
Hucklow Lanes SK13: Gam 5F 123
(off Grassmoor Cres.)
Hudcar La. BL9: Bury 1G 37
Huddart Cl. M5: Sal 1A 8 (5H 99)
Huddersfield Narrow Canal Sculpture Trail
. . . . .5A 78
Huddersfield Rd. OL1: O'ham 2H 75
OL3: Del 3B 62
OL3: Dens 3H 45
OL3: Dig 4D 62
OL4: Aus, Lees, O'ham, Scout . .2H 75
OL5: Mos 2A 94
OL16: Miln 1H 43
SK15: C'ook 6A 94
SK15: Mill, Stal 3F 107
Hudson Ct. M9: Man 6G 71
Hudson Rd. BL3: Bolt 4H 47
SK14: Hyde 2C 136
Hudson St. OL9: Chad 2A 90
Hudsons Wlk. OL11: Roch 4D 26
Hudswell Cl. M45: White 1E 69
Hughenden Ct. BL8: Tot 4H 21
Hughes Cl. BL9: Bury 2G 37
M35: Fail 3G 89
Hughes St. BL1: Bolt 3A 32
(Bennett's La.)
BL1: Bolt 3B 32
(Rushey Fold La.)
M11: Man 5A 102
Hughes Way M30: Ecc 4C 96
Hugh Fold OL4: Lees 4C 76
(off Hartshead St.)
Hughley Cl. OL2: O'ham 3F 59
Hugh Lupus St. BL1: Bolt 6E 19
Hugh Oldham Dr. M7: Sal 5A 86
Hugh St. OL16: Roch 2D 178 (3A 28)
Hughtrede St. OL16: Roch 2B 42
Hugo St. BL4: Farn 5F 49
M40: Man 4C 88
OL11: Roch 3F 41
Hulbert St. BL8: Bury 4C 36
M24: Mid 6D 56
Hull Mill La. OL3: Del 2B 62
Hull Sq. M3: Sal 3C 4 (3B 100)
Hully St. SK15: Stal 3D 106
HULME 6G 9 (1D 114)
Hulme Ct. M15: Man 4E 9
Hulme Dr. WA15: Tim 4C 140
Hulme Hall M14: Man 3G 115
Hulme Hall Av. SK8: Chea H 5C 156
Hulme Hall Cl. SK8: Chea H 4C 156
Hulme Hall Cres. SK8: Chea H 5C 156
Hulme Hall La. M40: Man 1A 102
Hulme Hall Rd.
M15: Man 4C 8 (6B 100)
SK8: Chea H 3C 156
Hulme High St. M15: Man 2D 114
Hulme Mkt. Hall M15: Man 2D 114
Hulme Pl. M5: Sal 5B 4 (4A 100)
Hulme Rd. BL2: Bolt 5A 20
M26: Rad 2E 67
M33: Sale 6D 128
M34: Dent 4B 118
SK4: Stoc 3F 133
Hulme's La. M34: Dent 1E 135
Hulmes Rd. M35: Fail 1H 103
M40: Man 1G 103
(not continuous)
Hulmes Ter. BL2: Ain 5E 35

Hulme St. BL1: Bolt 2G 175 (5D 32)
BL8: Bury 2D 36
M1: Man 4H 9 (6D 100)
M5: Sal 5B 4 (4A 100)
M15: Man 4H 9 (6D 100)
(Cambridge St.)
M15: Man 4F 9 (6C 100)
(Jackson St.)
OL6: A Lyme 1B 106
OL8: O'ham 5E 75
SK1: Stoc 4B 146
Hulmeswood Ter. M34: Dent 2G 135
(off Tennyson Av.)
Hulme Wlk. M15: Man 6F 9
Hulton Av. M28: Walk 6E 65
Hulton Cl. BL3: Bolt 3G 47
Hulton District Cen. M28: Walk 5E 65
Hulton Dr. BL3: Bolt 4G 47
Hulton La. BL3: Bolt 5G 47
Hulton St. M5: Sal 6G 99
M16: W Ran 3C 114
M34: Dent 3E 119
M35: Fail 4F 89
Humber Dr. BL9: Bury 4F 23
Humber Rd. M29: Ast 4A 80
OL16: Miln 5G 29
Humberstone Av.
M15: Man 4F 9 (1D 114)
Humber St. M8: Man 4F 87
M50: Sal 4D 98
Hume St. M19: Man 1D 132
OL16: Roch 5A 28
Humphrey Booth Gdns. M6: Sal 2E 99
Humphrey Cres. M41: Urm 5A 112
Humphrey La. M41: Urm 5A 112
Humphrey Pk. M41: Urm 5A 112
Humphrey Park Station (Rail) 4A 112
Humphrey Rd. M16: Old T 2H 113
SK7: Bram 2G 157
Humphrey St. M8: Man 3D 86
Humphries Ct. M40: Man 1G 101
Huncoat Av. SK4: Stoc 4F 133
Huncote Dr. M9: Man 2A 88
(off Hemsley St. Sth.)
Hungerford Wlk. M23: Wyth 4D 140
(off Butcher La.)
HUNGER HILL 4D 46
Hunger Hill OL12: W'le 6D 16
Hunger Hill Av. BL3: Bolt 5E 47
Hunger Hill La. OL12: Roch 6B 14
Hunmanby Av.
M15: Man 4G 9 (6D 100)
Hunstanton Dr. BL8: Bury 6D 22
Hunston Rd. M33: Sale 6H 127
Hunt Av. OL7: A Lyme 6H 91
Hunter Dr. M26: Rad 3A 52
Hunters Cl. SK6: Bred 6F 135
SK9: Wilm 6B 166
Hunters Ct. SK15: Stal 6H 107
SK16: Duk 6D 106
Hunters Grn. BL0: Ram 6A 12
HUNTERS HILL 1E 63
Hunters Hill BL9: Bury 3H 53
Hunters Hill La. OL3: Dig 1D 62
Hunters La. OL1: O'ham 3H 177 (2F 75)
OL16: Roch 2B 178 (3H 27)
Hunters Lodge SK9: Wilm 6B 166
(off Hunters Cl.)
Hunters M. M33: Sale 4A 128
SK9: Wilm 2F 173
Hunterston Av. M30: Ecc 3A 98
Hunters Vw. SK9: Hand 4G 165
Hunt Fold BL8: G'mount 2H 21
Hunt Fold Dr. BL8: G'mount 2H 21
Huntingdon Av. OL9: Chad 4B 74
Huntingdon Cres. SK5: Stoc 4C 134
Huntingdon Wlk. BL1: Bolt 3C 32
(off Draycott St.)
Huntingdon Way M34: Dent 6F 119
Huntingdon Av. M20: Man 2E 131
Hunt La. OL9: Chad 1H 73
Huntley Ho. BL9: Bury 1H 37
Huntley Mt. Rd. BL9: Bury 1H 37

Huntley Rd. M8: Man 1C 86
SK3: Stoc 4D 144
Huntley St. BL9: Bury 2H 37
Huntley Way OL10: H'ood 4C 38
Huntly Chase SK9: Wilm 2F 173
Hunt Rd. SK14: Hyde 2E 121
Huntroyde Av. BL2: Bolt 4G 33
Hunt's Bank M3: Man 3H 5 (3D 100)
Huntsham Cl. WA14: Alt 5D 138
Huntsman Dr. M44: Irl 2D 124
Huntsman Rd. M9: Man 3B 88
Huntspill Rd. WA14: W Tim 3E 139
Hunts Rd. M6: Sal 6D 84
Hunt St. M9: Man 2H 87
Hurdlow Av. M7: Sal 4G 85
Hurdlow Grn. SK13: Gam 6F 123
(off Brassington Cres.)
Hurdlow Lea SK13: Gam 6F 123
(off Brassington Cres.)
Hurdlow M. SK13: Gam 6F 123
Hurdlow Wlk. M9: Man 4H 87
Hurdlow Way SK13: Gam 6F 123
(off Brassington Cres.)
Hurdsfield Rd. SK2: Stoc 1C 158
Hurford Av. M18: Man 1F 117
Hurlbote Cl. SK9: Hand 2H 165
Hurley Dr. SK8: Chea H 3A 156
Hurlston Rd. BL3: Bolt 5B 48
HURST 6B 92
Hurst Av. M33: Sale 6E 127
SK8: Chea H 1E 167
Hurstbank Av. M19: Man 5H 131
Hurst Bank Rd. OL6: A Lyme 1C 106
Hurstbourne Av. M11: Man 2D 102
HURST BROOK 1A 106
Hurst Brook Cl. OL6: A Lyme 1A 106
Hurstbrook Dr. M32: Stre 5H 111
Hurst Ct. M23: Wyth 1F 153
OL6: A Lyme 6B 92
Hurst Cross OL6: A Lyme 6B 92
HURSTEAD .5D 16
Hurstead Cl. M8: Man 5E 87
Hurstead Cotts. OL12: Roch 5D 16
Hurstead Grn. OL12: Roch 5D 16
Hursted Rd. OL16: Miln 5F 29
Hurstfield Ind. Est. SK5: Stoc 3G 133
Hurstfield Rd. M28: Wors 3F 81
Hurst Fold M44: Irl 4F 109
Hurstfold Av. M19: Man 6H 131
Hurst Grn. Cl. BL8: Bury 5H 35
Hurst Gro. OL6: A Lyme 6C 92
Hurst Hall Dr. OL6: A Lyme 6C 92
Hursthead Rd. SK8: Chea H 6D 156
Hurstheads La. SK6: Rom 2H 147
Hurst Wlk. M13: Man 4D 10
Hurst Hill Cres. OL6: A Lyme 1B 106
HURST KNOLL 6A 92
Hurst Lea Ct. SK9: A Edg 4G 173
Hurst Mdw. OL6: A Lyme 6B 92
OL16: Roch 3B 42
Hurstmead Ter. M20: Man 1F 143
(off South Rd.)
HURST NOOK 5C 92
Hurst St. BL3: Bolt 4A 48
BL9: Bury 3G 37
(not continuous)
M28: Walk 3G 65
OL9: O'ham 2D 74
OL11: Roch 6A 28
(not continuous)
SK5: Stoc 2G 133
Hurstvale Av. SK8: H Grn 4F 155
Hurstville Rd. M21: Chor 3H 129
Hurst Wlk. M22: Wyth 3G 153
Hurstway Dr. M9: Man 6A 72
Hurstwood BL1: Bolt 6B 18
OL6: A Lyme 5D 92
Hurstwood Cl. OL8: O'ham 5A 76
Hurstwood Ct. BL3: Bolt 3F 49
Hurstwood Gro. SK2: Stoc 5F 147
Hus St. M43: Droy 5H 103
Husteads Av. OL3: Dob 6A 62
Husteads La. OL3: Dob 6A 62

Hutchins La. OL4: O'ham 6B 60
Hutchinson Rd. OL11: Roch 2H 25
Hutchinson St. M26: Rad 3C 52
  OL11: Roch 5E 27
Hutchinson Way M26: Rad 5H 51
Hutton Av. M28: Wors 5D 80
  OL6: A Lyme 3C 106
Hutton Ho. OL11: Roch 5B 178
Hutton Lodge M20: Man 2G 131
  (off Wilmslow Rd.)
Hutton Wlk. M13: Man 6E 11
Huxley Av. M8: Man 5E 87
Huxley Cl. SK7: Bram 6G 157
Huxley Dr. SK7: Bram 6G 157
Huxley St. BL1: Bolt 3A 32
  OL4: O'ham 4A 76
  WA14: B'ath 4F 139
Huxton Grn. SK7: H Gro 3A 158
Hyacinth Cl. SK3: Stoc 6F 145
Hyacinth Wlk. M31: Part 6C 124
  (off Redbrook Rd.)
HYDE 5B 120
HYDE, THE .2F 165
Hydebank M41: Rom 2B 148
Hyde Central Station (Rail) 5A 120
Hyde Dr. M28: Walk 1G 81
Hyde Festival Theatre 5B 120
Hyde Fold Cl. M19: Man 3B 132
Hyde Gro. M13: Man 2G 115
  M28: Walk .1G 81
  M33: Sale .5B 128
Hyde Ho. SK4: Stoc 4E 133
Hyde Leisure Pool 5D 120
Hyde North Station (Rail) 2A 120
Hyde Pk. Pl. OL16: Roch 4C 28
  (off Newbold Hall Dr.)
Hyde Pl. M13: Man 2G 115
Hyde Point SK14: Hyde 3A 120
Hyde Rd. M12: Man 4F 11 (6G 101)
  M24: Mid 3G 73
  M28: Walk .1G 81
  M34: Dent .3F 119
  SK6: Wood 4G 135
  SK14: Mot .4B 122
Hyde's Cross M4: Man 3A 6
Hyde Sq. M24: Mid 6A 56
Hydes Ter. SK15: Stal 3F 107
Hyde St. BL3: Bolt 4A 48
  M43: Droy .1C 104
  SK16: Duk .5B 106
Hyde United FC 5D 120
Hyde Way SK14: Mot 4B 122
Hydon Brook Wlk. OL11: Roch 1E 41
Hydra Cl. M7: Sal 1B 4 (2A 100)
Hydrangea Cl. M33: Sale 4E 127
Hyldavale Av. SK8: Gat 5F 143
Hylton Dr. OL7: A Lyme 6F 91
  SK8: Chea H 4E 157
Hyman Goldstone Wlk.
  M8: Man 4D 86
  (off Carstairs Cl.)
Hyndman Ct. M5: Sal 3D 98
  (off Sheader Dr.)
Hypatia St. BL2: Bolt 5F 33
Hythe Cl. M14: Man 4G 115
Hythe Rd. SK3: Stoc 3D 144
Hythe St. BL3: Bolt 3G 47
Hythe Wlk. OL9: Chad 3B 74

Ian Frazer Ct. OL11: Roch 1H 41
Ibberton Wlk. M9: Man 2B 88
  (off Carnaby St.)
Ibsley OL12: Roch 2A 178 (3G 27)
Ice Ho. Cl. M28: Walk 6D 64
Iceland St. M6: Sal 3E 99
Idonia St. BL1: Bolt 2B 32
Ilfco Ho. M14: Man 4G 115
Ilex Gro. M7: Sal 5B 86
Ilford St. M11: Man 3D 102
Ilfracombe Rd. SK2: Stoc 3D 146

Ilfracombe St. M40: Man 5F 89
Ilkeston Wlk. M34: Dent 1G 135
  M40: Man 5C 88
  (off Halliford Rd.)
Ilkley Cl. BL2: Bolt 6G 33
  OL9: Chad .3B 74
Ilkley Cres. SK5: Stoc 1G 133
Ilkley Dr. M41: Urm 3C 110
Ilkley St. M40: Man 2C 88
Ilk St. M11: Man 3D 102
Illingworth Av. SK15: Stal 4G 107
Ilona Dr. M7: Sal 3G 85
Ilminster OL11: Roch 6A 178 (5G 27)
Ilminster Wlk. M9: Man 4A 72
  (off Crossmead Dr.)
Ilthorpe Wlk. M40: Man 5C 88
Imax Cinema
  Manchester 3A 6
  (within The Printworks)
Imex Bus. Pk. M13: Man 4B 116
Imogen Ct. M5: Sal 2B 8 (5A 100)
Imperial Point M50: Sal 6F 99
Imperial Ter. M33: Sale 3A 128
  (off Woodfield Gro.)
Imperial War Mus. North 6E 99
Ina Av. BL1: Bolt 4F 31
Ince Cl. M20: Man 2F 131
  SK4: Stoc .6G 133
Ince St. SK4: Stoc 6G 133
Inchcape Dr. M9: Man 5F 71
Inchfield Cl. OL11: Roch 3A 26
Inchfield Rd. M40: Man 2C 88
Inchley Rd. M13: Man 4C 10 (6F 101)
Inchwood M. OL4: O'ham 3C 60
Incline Rd. OL8: O'ham 1B 90
Independent Ho. SK8: Chea 2G 155
Independent St. BL3: Lit L 4C 50
India Ho. M1: Man 2A 10 (5E 101)
India St. BL9: Sum 6C 12
Indigo St. M6: Sal 6F 85
Indigo Wlk. M6: Sal 6F 85
Indus Pl. M7: Sal 1B 4 (1A 100)
Industrial St. BL0: Ram 4F 13
Industry Rd. OL12: Roch 2H 27
Industry St. OL11: Roch 2A 26
  OL12: Whitw 3B 14
  OL15: L'ough 4H 17
Infant St. M25: Pres 5A 70
Infirmary St. BL1: Bolt 4G 175 (6D 32)
Ingham Rd. WA14: W Tim 3F 139
Inghams La. OL15: L'ough 4H 17
Ingham St. BL9: Bury 4G 37
  M40: Man .1G 103
  OL1: O'ham 2G 75
Inghamwood Cl. M7: Sal 4D 86
Ingleby Av. M9: Man 5B 72
Ingleby Cl. BL5: W'ton 5A 46
  OL2: Shaw .5G 43
Ingleby Ct. M32: Stre 6E 113
Ingleby Way OL2: Shaw 5G 43
Ingledene Av. M7: Sal 2C 86
Ingledene Ct. M7: Sal 2C 86
Ingledene Gro. BL1: Bolt 3G 31
Ingle Dr. SK2: Stoc 4C 146
Inglefield OL11: Roch 2B 26
Inglehead Cl. M34: Dent 5G 119
Ingle Nook Cl. M31: C'ton 3B 126
Ingle Rd. SK8: Chea 5C 144
Ingles Fold M28: Wors 3F 81
Inglesham Cl. M23: Wyth 5H 141
Ingleton Av. M8: Man 1F 87
Ingleton Cl. BL2: Bolt 1H 33
  OL2: O'ham 2D 58
  SK8: Chea .5G 143
Ingleton M. BL8: Bury 1B 36
Ingleton Rd. SK3: Stoc 4E 145
Inglewhite Cl. BL9: Bury 6D 36
Inglewood WA14: Alt 2D 150
Inglewood Cl. BL9: Bury 1A 38
  M31: Part .5C 124
  OL7: A Lyme 6F 91
Inglewood Hollow SK15: Stal 5G 107
Inglewood Rd. OL9: Chad 6G 57

Inglewood Wlk. M13: Man 5E 11
Inglis St. OL15: L'ough 3H 17
Ingoe Cl. OL10: H'ood 2B 40
Ingoldsby Av. M13: Man 3H 115
Ingram Dr. SK4: Stoc 6A 132
Ings Av. OL12: Roch 1D 26
Ings La. OL12: Roch 1D 26
Inkerman St. M40: Man 5H 87
  OL12: Roch 2H 27
  (off Industry Rd.)
  SK14: Hyde 3B 120
Ink St. OL16: Roch 3C 178 (4H 27)
Inman St. BL9: Bury 6A 176 (5E 37)
  M34: Dent .4F 119
Innes St. M12: Man 4D 116
Innis Av. M40: Man 6E 89
Institute of Gymnastics 2E 117
Institute St. BL1: Bolt 4G 175 (6E 33)
Instow Cl. OL9: Chad 6H 57
Intake La. OL3: G'fld 6B 78
International App. M90: Man A 6A 154
Invar Rd. M27: Swin 2F 83
Inverbeg Dr. BL2: Bolt 6C 34
Invergarry Wlk. M11: Man 4E 103
  (off Bob Massey Cl.)
Inverlael Av. BL1: Bolt 5H 31
Inverness Av. M9: Man 5C 72
Inverness Rd. SK16: Duk 6A 106
Inver Wlk. M40: Man 1F 89
Inwood Wlk. M8: Man 5G 87
  (off Smedley Rd.)
Inworth Wlk. M8: Man 4D 86
  (off Highshore Dr.)
Iona Pl. BL2: Bolt 3G 33
Iona Way M41: Urm 2F 111
Ionian Gdns. M7: Sal 6A 86
Ipswich St. OL11: Roch 6H 27
Ipswich Wlk. M12: Man 2A 116
  (off Chipstead Av.)
  M34: Dent .6G 119
  (off Lancaster Rd.)
Iqbal Cl. M12: Man 2C 116
Irby Wlk. SK8: Chea 1C 156
Ireby Cl. M24: Mid 5G 55
Iredine St. M11: Man 4E 103
Irene Av. SK14: Hyde 3C 120
Iris Av. BL4: Farn 6E 49
  BL4: Kea 4B 66
  (not continuous)
  M11: Man 5F 103
Iris St. BL0: Ram 3B 12
  OL8: O'ham 1F 91
Iris Wlk. M31: Part 6D 124
  (off Cross La. W.)
Irkdale St. M8: Man 5G 87
Irk St. M4: Man 1B 6 (2E 101)
Irk Va. Dr. OL1: Chad 6G 57
Irk Way M45: White 5H 53
IRLAM 4F 109
Irlam Av. M30: Ecc 4F 97
Irlam Ind. Est. M44: Irl 2C 124
Irlam Locks Circ. M44: Irl 6F 109
Irlam Rd. M33: Sale 4C 128
  M41: Urm 6F 109
IRLAMS O'TH' HEIGHT 5C 84
Irlam Sq. M6: Sal 6D 84
Irlam Station (Rail) 2C 124
Irlam St. BL1: Bolt 2C 32
  M40: Man 6A 88
Irlam Wharf Rd. M44: Irl 2E 125
Irmass Ind. Est. M17: T Pk 1D 112
Irma St. BL1: Bolt 2D 32
Iron St. M40: Man 2A 102
Irvin Dr. M22: Wyth 5E 155
Irvine Av. M28: Wors 5E 81
Irving Cl. SK2: Stoc 2A 158
Irving Ho. BL1: Bolt 3C 32
  (off Irving St.)
Irving St. BL1: Bolt 3C 32
  OL8: O'ham 1B 90
Irvin St. M40: Man 5E 89
Irwell Av. M30: Ecc 4H 97
  M38: Lit H .5F 65

Irwell Cl. M26: Rad 5B **52**
Irwell Gro. M30: Ecc 4H **97**
Irwell Ho. M15: Man 3D **8**
   M44: Irl 6F **109**
Irwell Pk. Way
   M30: Ecc .4H **97**
Irwell Pl. M5: Sal 4A **4** (3A **100**)
   M26: Rad 1D **66**
   M30: Ecc .4H **97**
Irwell Sq. M3: Man 5E **5** (4C **100**)
Irwell St. BL0: Ram 3C **12**
   BL9: Bury 4A **176** (3E **37**)
   M3: Sal 5E **5** (4C **100**)
   M6: Sal 5G **85**
   M8: Man 1F **5** (1C **100**)
   M26: Rad 1C **66**
      (Ford St.)
   M26: Rad .5B **52**
      (Stand La.)
IRWELL VALE 1F **13**
Irwell Vale Station
   East Lancashire Railway 1F **13**
Irwell Wlk. OL8: O'ham 6C **74**
Irwin Dr. SK9: Hand 2G **165**
Irwin Pl. SK8: Chea H 2B **156**
Irwin Rd. WA14: B'ath 3E **139**
Irwin St. M34: Dent 4E **119**
Isaac Cl. M5: Sal 5G **99**
Isaac St. BL1: Bolt 5A **32**
Isaac Way M4: Man 6G **7** (4H **101**)
Isabella Cl. M16: Old T 3A **114**
Isabella St. OL12: Roch 1H **27**
Isabel Wlk. BL3: Bolt 2B **48**
Isaiah St. OL8: O'ham 5F **75**
Isa St. BL0: Ram 5A **12**
Isca St. M11: Man 4B **102**
Isel Wlk. M24: Mid 5H **55**
Isherwood Cl. OL10: H'ood 4H **39**
Isherwood Dr. SK6: Mar 5B **148**
Isherwood Rd. M31: C'ton 3B **126**
Isherwood St. OL10: H'ood 4A **40**
   OL11: Roch 6D **178** (5A **28**)
Isis Cl. M7: Sal 3F **85**
Islington Rd. SK2: Stoc 1C **158**
Islington St. M3: Sal 4D **4** (4B **100**)
Islington Way M3: Sal 5C **4** (4B **100**)
Isobel Baillie Lodge
   M16: Old T 2B **114**
   (off Whitchurch Dr.)
Isobel Cl. *M16: W Ran* 3D **114**
   (off Crosshill St.)
   M30: Ecc .4D **96**
Ivanhoe Ct. BL3: Bolt 5G **49**
Ivanhoe St. BL3: Bolt 5G **49**
   OL1: O'ham 6A **60**
Iveagh Ct. OL16: Roch 5B **28**
Iver Ho. *M5: Sal* 4F **99**
   (off Amersham St.)
Ivor St. OL11: Roch 2D **40**
Ivy Bank OL5: Mos 2A **94**
   OL12: Whitw 2B **14**
Ivy Bank Cl. BL1: Bolt 6C **18**
Ivy Bank Rd. BL1: Bolt 6C **18**
Ivybridge M13: Man 2H **115**
Ivybridge Ho. BL3: Bolt 2A **48**
Ivy Cl. M43: Droy 2H **103**
   OL2: Shaw 6H **43**
Ivy Cotts. M34: Dent 2G **135**
   OL12: Roch 2F **27**
Ivy Ct. M21: Chor 2H **129**
Ivycroft SK13: Had 3G **123**
Ivy Dr. M24: Mid 2B **72**
Ivygreen Dr. OL4: Spri 3D **76**
Ivygreen Rd. M21: Chor 1F **129**
Ivy Gro. BL4: Farn 1F **65**
   BL4: Kea 2B **66**
   M38: Lit H .5D **64**
Ivy Leaf Sq. M7: Sal 5C **86**
Ivylea Rd. M19: Man 5A **132**
Ivy Lodge Cl. SK15: Mill 1H **107**
Ivy Rd. BL1: Bolt 4A **32**
   BL8: Bury .3B **36**
   SK12: Poy .4E **169**

Ivy St. BL0: Ram 1H **21**
   BL3: Bolt 3A **48**
   M30: Ecc 4F **97**
   M40: Man .3C **88**
Ivy Ter. OL15: L'ough 1B **16**
Ivy Wlk. M31: Part 6B **124**

J

J2 Bus. Pk. BL9: Bury 3A **38**
Jack Brady Cl. M23: Wyth 1E **153**
Jackdaw Rd. BL8: G'mount 1H **21**
Jackie Brown Wlk. *M40: Man* 6H **87**
   (off Thornton St. Nth.)
Jack La. M41: Urm 6G **109**
   (Dunster St.)
   M41: Urm .5G **111**
   (Falcon Av.)
   M43: Droy .3B **104**
   (not continuous)
Jack Lane Nature Reserve 1G **125**
Jack McCann Ct. *OL16: Roch* 3A **28**
   (off Trafalgar St.)
Jackman Av. OL10: H'ood 6H **39**
Jackson Av. SK16: Duk 5B **106**
Jackson Cl. BL8: Bury 2B **36**
   OL8: O'ham 6E **177** (4E **75**)
   WA15: Tim 4C **140**
Jackson Ct. M21: Chor 6F **113**
   M41: Urm .4C **110**
Jackson Cres. M15: Man 5E **9** (1C **114**)
Jackson Gdns. M34: Dent 5D **118**
Jackson M. OL4: O'ham 6B **60**
Jackson Pit OL1: O'ham 4F **177** (3E **75**)
Jackson's Brickworks Local Nature Reserve
   . . . . .1B **170**
Jacksons Edge Rd. SK6: Dis 6E **161**
   SK12: Dis .6E **161**
Jacksons La. SK7: H Gro 4A **158**
Jacksons Pl. OL16: Roch 3B **28**
Jackson's Row M2: Man 6G **5** (4D **100**)
Jackson St. BL3: Bolt 2B **48**
   BL4: Farn .1H **65**
   BL4: Kea 2B **66**
   M24: Mid 6D **56**
   M26: Rad 5B **52**
   M28: Walk .5G **65**
   M32: Stre .5C **112**
   M33: Sale .5D **128**
   M35: Fail 5F **89**
   M45: White 2F **69**
   OL4: O'ham 2H **75**
   OL4: Spri .3D **76**
   OL6: A Lyme 1H **105**
   OL12: W'le 6C **16**
   OL16: Roch 5B **28**
   SK8: Chea 5A **144**
   SK14: Hyde 5B **120**
   SK14: Mot 4C **122**
Jack St. BL2: Bolt 4G **33**
Jack Talbot Sports Cen. 2G **39**
   (in Heywood Sports Complex)
Jack Taylor Ct. OL12: Roch 2B **28**
Jacobite Cl. M7: Sal 2A **86**
Jacobsen Av. SK14: Hyde 3D **120**
Jacob's Ladder *OL5: Mos* 2G **93**
   (off Hanover St.)
James Andrew St. M24: Mid 6D **56**
James Bentley Wlk. *M40: Man* 6E **89**
   (off Lastingham St.)
James Brindley Basin
   M1: Man 6E **7** (4G **101**)
James Butterworth Ct. *OL16: Roch* . . .5B **28**
   (off James Butterworth St.)
James Butterworth St. OL16: Roch . . .5B **28**
James Cl. SK16: Duk 5C **106**
James Corbett Rd. M50: Sal 4C **98**
James Ct. *M18: Man* 2F **117**
   (off Wellington St.)
James Dr. SK14: Hyde 5C **120**
James Henry Av. M5: Sal 5H **99**

James Hill St. OL15: L'ough 4H **17**
James Leech St.
   SK3: Stoc 4F **179** (3G **145**)
James Leigh St. M1: Man 2A **10**
James Nasmyth Way M30: Ecc 3E **97**
Jameson Cl. M8: Man 6C **86**
Jameson St. OL11: Roch 3D **40**
James Rd. OL2: Shaw 5H **43**
James St. BL3: Lit L 4D **50**
   BL4: Kea 1B **66**
   BL7: Eger .1B **18**
   BL9: Bury 4G **37**
   M3: Sal 5C **4** (4B **100**)
   M25: Pres .4G **69**
   (not continuous)
   M26: Rad .6A **52**
   M33: Sale .5D **128**
   M34: Aud .5E **105**
   M34: Dent 3G **119**
   M35: Fail 3A **90**
   M40: Man 1H **7** (2H **101**)
   M43: Droy .3B **104**
   OL2: O'ham 2G **59**
   OL4: O'ham 6B **60**
   OL10: H'ood 2H **39**
   OL12: Roch 5C **16**
   (Wardle Rd.)
   OL12: Roch 3A **28**
   (Yorkshire St.)
   OL12: Whitw 3B **14**
   OL15: L'ough 5E **17**
   SK3: Stoc 6E **179** (4G **145**)
   SK6: Bred .4G **135**
   SK15: Stal .5C **106**
James St. Nth. M26: Rad 5B **52**
James St. Sth. OL9: Chad 2A **74**
Jammy La. OL9: Chad 3C **74**
Jane Barter Ho. *BL4: Farn* 1H **65**
   (off Hesketh Wlk.)
Jane St. OL9: Chad 3B **74**
   OL12: Roch 1A **178** (3G **27**)
Japan St. M7: Sal 3D **86**
Jardine Way OL9: Chad 5H **73**
Jarvis St. OL4: O'ham 3G **75**
   OL12: Roch 2H **27**
Jasmine Av. M43: Droy 3C **104**
Jasmine Cl. M23: Wyth 2E **141**
Jasmine Ct. BL3: Bolt 4C **48**
Jasmine Wlk. *M31: Part* 6D **124**
   (off Erskine Wlk.)
Jauncey St. BL3: Bolt 2A **48**
Jayton Av. M20: Man 3F **143**
Jean Cl. M19: Man 5C **116**
Jedburgh Av. BL1: Bolt 5H **31**
Jefferson Pl. M4: Man 1A **6**
Jefferson Way OL12: Roch 6H **15**
Jeffreys Dr. SK16: Duk 5B **106**
Jeffrey Wlk. *OL10: H'ood* 3E **39**
   (off Gaskill St.)
Jehlum Cl. M8: Man 4F **87**
Jellicoe Av. M44: Cad 3C **124**
Jenkin Hall OL1: Chad 5H **57**
Jenkinson St. M15: Man 5B **10** (1E **115**)
Jenkyn Wlk. *M11: Man* 4B **102**
   (off Newcombe Cl.)
Jennaby Wlk. BL1: Bolt 3C **32**
Jennings Av. M5: Sal 5G **99**
Jennings Cl. SK14: Hyde 2F **121**
Jennings St. SK3: Stoc 4F **145**
Jennison Cl. M18: Man 1D **116**
Jenny Beck Gro. *BL3: Bolt* 3C **48**
   (off Aldsworth Dr.)
JENNY GREEN 5E **109**
Jenny La. SK7: W'ford 4G **167**
Jenny Lind Cl. BL3: Bolt 5G **49**
Jenny St. OL8: O'ham 1C **90**
Jepheys Pl. OL12: Roch 2H **27**
Jepheys St. OL12: Roch 2H **27**
Jepson St. SK2: Stoc 5A **146**
JERICHO 1C **38**
Jericho Rd. BL9: Bury 1C **38**
Jermyn St. OL12: Roch 1D **178** (3A **28**)
Jerrold St. OL15: L'ough 4H **17**

Jersey Cl. M19: Man 2B **132**
Jersey Rd. SK5: Stoc 5H **133**
Jersey St. M4: Man 4D **6** (3F **101**)
   OL6: A Lyme 1H **105**
Jerusalem Pl. M2: Man 1G **9**
Jesmond Av. M25: Pres 1H **85**
Jesmond Dr. BL8: Bury 6C **22**
Jesmond Gro. SK8: Chea H 5D **156**
Jesmond Rd. BL1: Bolt 1H **31**
Jesmond Wlk. M9: Man 4H **71**
              (off Claygate Dr.)
Jessamine Av. M7: Sal 1B **100**
Jessel Cl. M13: Man 5E **11** (1G **115**)
Jessie St. BL3: Bolt 2A **48**
   M40: Man 5C **88**
Jessop Dr. SK6: Mar 3D **148**
Jessop Forge BL3: Lit L 4C **50**
Jessup St. M18: Man 2F **117**
Jethro St. BL2: Bolt 5G **33**
               (Ainsworth La.)
   BL2: Bolt .1G **33**
              (Bradshaw Brow)
Jetson St. M18: Man 1H **117**
Jevington Wlk. M13: Man . . .6F **11** (1G **115**)
Jewel Cl. M41: Urm 5D **110**
Jimmy McMullen Wlk. M14: Man . . .4E **115**
           (off Fred Tilson Cl.)
Jinnah Cl. M11: Man 5E **103**
   OL4: O'ham 4A **76**
JJB Fitness
   Oldham .5B **58**
JJB Fitness Club 4C **176** (3F **37**)
JJB Soccer Dome 1D **110**
JJ Thomson M. M14: Man 1H **131**
Joan Lestor Ho. M38: Lit H 6G **65**
Joan St. M40: Man 4C **88**
Jobling St. M11: Man 5B **102**
Jocelyn St. M40: Man 5A **88**
Joddrell St. M3: Man 6F **5** (4C **100**)
Joel La. SK14: Hyde 2C **136**
Johannesburg Dr. M23: Wyth 1F **153**
Johannesburg Gdns. M23: Wyth . . .1F **153**
John Ashworth St. OL12: Roch 2B **28**
John Av. SK8: Chea 6A **144**
John Beeley Av. M11: Man 5F **103**
John Booth St. OL4: Spri 4D **76**
John Boste Ct. BL3: Bolt 4G **49**
John Brown St. BL1: Bolt 5C **32**
John Clynes Av. M40: Man 1F **7**
John Cross St. BL3: Bolt 3C **48**
John Dalton St. M2: Man 6G **5** (4D **100**)
   SK13: Had 2G **123**
John Derby Ho. M16: Old T 3G **113**
John Foran Cl. M40: Man 5D **88**
John Gilbert Way M17: T Pk 2D **112**
John Grundy Ho. SK14: Hyde 5C **120**
           (off Reynold St.)
John Henry St. OL12: Whitw 1B **14**
John Heywood St. M11: Man 3D **102**
John Howarth Countryside Cen. 5E **91**
John Kemble Ct. OL11: Roch 1F **41**
John Kennedy Gdns. SK14: Mot 4C **122**
John Kennedy Rd. SK14: Mot 4B **122**
JOHN LEE FOLD 6D **56**
John Lee Fold M24: Mid 6C **56**
John Lester Ct. M6: Sal 2G **99**
           (off Belvedere Rd.)
John Lloyd Ct. M44: Irl 1D **124**
           (off Alexandra Gro.)
Johnny King Cl. M40: Man 6H **87**
John Paine St. M27: Pen 1H **83**
             (off Pott St.)
John Roberts Cl. OL11: Roch 6G **27**
John Robinson Wlk. M40: Man 4C **88**
           (off Shelderton Cl.)
Johns Cl. M21: Chor 1H **129**
John Shepley St. SK14: Hyde 5C **120**
John Smeaton Ct. M1: Man . . .6E **7** (4G **101**)
Johnson Av. OL1: O'ham 2C **60**
Johnsonbrook Rd.
   SK14: Duk, Hyde 2A **120**

JOHNSON FOLD 2F **31**
Johnson Fold Av. BL1: Bolt 3E **31**
Johnson Gro. M24: Mid 1A **72**
Johnson's Sq. M40: Man 1H **101**
Johnson St. BL1: Bolt 5G **175** (1D **48**)
   M3: Sal 4F **5** (3C **100**)
   M15: Man 6C **8** (1B **114**)
   M26: Rad 5B **52**
   M27: Pen 5D **84**
   OL11: Roch 1F **27**
             (off Burnaby St.)
Johnson Ter. SK16: Duk 4H **105**
             (off Hill St.)
John's Pl. SK6: Rom 1A **148**
Johnston OL12: Roch 1A **178** (3G **27**)
Johnston Av. OL15: L'ough 6F **17**
John Stone Ct. M32: Stre 4A **112**
John St. BL3: Lit L 4D **50**
   BL4: Farn 1A **66**
   BL7: Bro X 4E **19**
   BL9: Bury 2D **176** (2F **37**)
   M3: Sal 3F **5** (3C **100**)
   M4: Man 4B **6** (3E **101**)
   M7: Sal .1B **100**
             (not continuous)
   M25: Pres 1C **70**
   M27: Swin 3A **84**
   M28: Walk 5H **65**
   M30: Ecc 4D **96**
   M33: Sale 4B **128**
   M34: Dent 3F **119**
   M35: Fail 2H **89**
   M43: Droy 5H **103**
   M44: Cad 4C **124**
   OL2: O'ham 3D **58**
   OL2: Shaw 2G **59**
   OL4: Spri 3E **77**
   OL7: A Lyme 5F **105**
   OL8: O'ham 4E **177** (3E **75**)
   OL10: H'ood 3H **39**
             (not continuous)
   OL12: Whitw 3B **14**
   OL15: L'ough 4G **17**
   OL16: Roch 6C **16**
             (Halifax Rd.)
   OL16: Roch 2C **178** (3H **27**)
            (St Mary's Ga.)
   SK1: Stoc 4G **179** (3H **145**)
             (not continuous)
   SK6: Bred 4G **135**
   SK6: Comp 6F **137**
   SK6: Mar 6E **149**
   SK6: Rom 1A **148**
   SK7: H Gro 2D **158**
   SK14: Holl 3F **123**
   SK14: Hyde 4B **120**
             (not continuous)
   SK15: H'rod 6F **93**
   WA14: Alt 1F **151**
John St. W. OL7: A Lyme 5F **105**
John William St. M11: Man 4E **103**
   M30: Ecc 3H **97**
Joiner St. M4: Man 5B **6** (4E **101**)
   M5: Sal 5B **4** (4A **100**)
Join Rd. M33: Sale 5D **128**
Jolly Brows BL2: Bolt 2H **33**
Jonas St. M7: Sal 1E **5** (2C **100**)
   M9: Man 3A **88**
Jones Sq. SK1: Stoc 6H **179** (4A **146**)
Jones St. BL1: Bolt 1F **175** (5D **32**)
   M6: Sal .2F **99**
   M26: Rad 3B **52**
   OL1: O'ham 1G **75**
   OL2: O'ham 5D **58**
   OL16: Roch 5A **28**
   SK13: Had 2H **123**
Jonquil Dr. M28: Walk 1D **80**
Jopson St. M24: Mid 6D **56**
Jordan Av. OL2: Shaw 4A **44**
Jordan St. M15: Man 3F **9** (6C **100**)
Joseph Adamson Ind. Est.
   SK14: Hyde 5A **120**
Joseph Dean Ct. M40: Man 4C **88**

Josephine Dr. M27: Swin 4A **84**
Joseph Jennings Ct. OL7: A Lyme . . .5G **91**
Joseph Johnson M. M22: Nor 2C **142**
Joseph Mamlock Ho. M8: Man 2C **86**
Joseph St. BL4: Farn 6H **49**
   M24: Mid 6B **56**
   M26: Rad 5B **52**
   M30: Ecc 4D **96**
   M35: Fail 3H **89**
   OL12: Roch 1F **27**
   OL15: L'ough 3H **17**
   SK6: Mar 5E **149**
Joshua La. M24: Mid 2F **73**
Josslyn Rd. M5: Sal 2D **98**
Jo St. M5: Sal 4G **99**
Joule Cl. M5: Sal 5G **99**
Joules Ct. SK1: Stoc 3H **179** (2H **145**)
Joule St. M9: Man 2A **88**
Jowett St. OL1: O'ham 6A **60**
   SK5: Stoc 5H **133**
Jowett's Wlk. OL7: A Lyme 3F **105**
Jowkin La. OL11: Roch 4H **25**
Joyce St. M40: Man 4D **88**
Joynson Av. M7: Sal 1B **100**
Joynson St. M33: Sale 4B **128**
Joy Pl. OL12: Roch 1H **27**
Joy St. BL0: Ram 3B **12**
   OL12: Roch 1H **27**
JUBILEE 3A **44**
Jubilee OL2: Shaw 3A **44**
Jubilee Av. M26: Rad 6C **52**
   SK16: Duk 4C **106**
Jubilee Cl. M30: Ecc 2F **97**
Jubilee Cotts. M28: Walk 6G **65**
           *SK7: H Gro 3E **159***
             (off Brook St.)
Jubilee Ct. M16: Old T 3H **113**
   SK5: Stoc 5H **117**
            *SK9: Hand 2A **166***
             (off Chelford Rd.)
Jubilee Ho. BL1: Bolt 5E **175** (1C **48**)
Jubilee Pool 4B **32**
Jubilee Rd. M24: Mid 6D **56**
Jubilee Sq. M34: Dent 4E **119**
             (off Market St.)
Jubilee St. BL3: Bolt 4A **48**
   M6: Sal .3F **99**
   OL2: Shaw 1A **60**
   OL7: A Lyme 4F **105**
Jubilee Ter. M24: Mid 6D **56**
Jubilee Wlk. OL12: Whitw 2B **14**
Jubilee Way BL9: Bury 3A **176** (3D **36**)
Judith St. OL12: Roch 6E **15**
Judson Av. M21: Chor 3A **130**
Julian Ho. OL1: O'ham 2G **177** (2F **75**)
Julia St. M3: Man 1G **5** (2D **100**)
   OL12: Roch 2A **178** (3G **27**)
Julius St. M19: Man 1D **132**
July St. M13: Man 2H **115**
Jumbles Country Pk. 1H **19**
Jumbles Country Pk. Vis. Cen. 2H **19**
Jumbles Sailing Club 2H **19**
Jumping Jack's Adventure Land 4B **120**
           (off Dukinfield Rd.)
Junction 19 Ind. Pk. OL10: H'ood 4B **40**
Junction 22 Bus. Pk. OL9: Chad 2H **89**
Junction All. OL16: Roch 4C **178** (4H **27**)
Junction Ho. M1: Man 6D **6**
Junction Rd. BL3: Bolt 2F **47**
   SK1: Stoc 6G **179** (4H **145**)
             (not continuous)
Junction Rd. W. BL6: Los 2C **46**
Junction St. SK14: Hyde 2A **120**
Junction Works M1: Man 6D **6**
June Av. SK4: Stoc 1D **144**
June St. OL7: A Lyme 3G **105**
Juniper Bank SK5: Stoc 1A **134**
Juniper Cl. BL1: Bolt 4C **32**
   M33: Sale 3A **128**
   OL4: O'ham 3D **60**
Juniper Cres. M43: Droy 5H **103**
Juniper Dr. OL16: Roch 4D **28**
Jupiter Wlk. M40: Man 6C **88**

Jura Cl. SK16: Duk 5B **106**
Jura Dr. M41: Urm 2G **111**
Jura Gro. OL10: H'ood 4F **39**
Jurby Av. M9: Man 5H **71**
Jury St. M8: Man 1D **100**
Justin Cl. M13: Man 4C **10** (6F **101**)
Jutland Av. OL11: Roch 3E **27**
Jutland Ho. M1: Man 6D **6**
Jutland St. M1: Man 6D **6** (4F **101**)

K

Kale St. M13: Man 4D **10** (6F **101**)
Kalmia Gro. M7: Sal 5B **86**
Kansas Av. M50: Sal 5E **99**
Kara St. M6: Sal 3E **99**
Karmo Ind. Est. OL11: Roch 5F **27**
Karting 2000 . . . . .1E **117**
Kate St. BL0: Ram 3B **12**
Kathan Cl. OL16: Roch 4B **28**
Katherine Ct. M16: Old T 2A **114**
(off Humphrey Rd.)
Katherine Ho.
  OL6: A Lyme 5A **174** (2G **105**)
Katherine Rd. SK2: Stoc 6C **146**
Katherine St.
  OL6: A Lyme 6A **174** (2H **105**)
  OL7: A Lyme 3F **105**
Kathkin Av. M8: Man 1F **87**
Kathleen Gro. M14: Man 5H **115**
(off Stanley Av.)
Kathleen St. OL12: Roch 4F **27**
Kay Av. SK6: Bred 6D **134**
Kay Brow BL0: Ram 3C **12**
  OL10: H'ood 3G **39**
Kayes Av. SK1: Stoc 2B **146**
Kayfields BL2: Bolt 1A **34**
Kay Gdn. Shop. Cen.
  BL9: Bury 4B **176** (3E **37**)
Kayley Ind. Est. OL7: A Lyme 2F **105**
Kay Lodge M14: Man 1G **131**
(off Lombard Gro.)
Kays Gdns. M3: Sal 3D **4** (3B **100**)
Kay St. BL0: Eden 3G **13**
  BL1: Bolt 1G **175** (4D **32**)
(Croasdale St.)
  BL1: Bolt 2G **175** (5D **32**)
(St George's St.)
  BL3: Lit L .4C **50**
  BL9: Bury .2G **37**
(not continuous)
  BL9: Sum .6C **12**
  M6: Sal 5F **85**
  M11: Man .6B **102**
  OL10: H'ood 3G **39**
  OL11: Roch 6G **27**
  OL15: L'ough 1F **29**
  SK15: Stal .4E **107**
Kays Wood Rd. SK6: Mar 5B **148**
Keadby Cl. M30: Ecc 5F **97**
Keal Dr. M44: Irl 3E **109**
Keane Ct. M8: Man 4E **87**
Keane St. OL7: A Lyme 2G **105**
Kean Pl. M30: Ecc 4F **97**
KEARSLEY 3C **66**
Kearsley Community Leisure Cen.
  . . . . .3A **66**
Kearsley Dr. BL3: Bolt 4F **49**
Kearsley Grn. M26: Rad 3E **67**
Kearsley Hall Rd.
  M26: Rad .2E **67**
Kearsley Mt. Shop. Pct.
  BL4: Kea 3D **66**
Kearsley Rd. M8: Man 1E **87**
  M26: Rad .1E **67**
Kearsley Station (Rail) 2C **66**
Kearsley St. M30: Ecc 3D **96**
Kearsley Va. M26: Rad 1D **66**
Kearton Dr. M30: Ecc 4A **98**
Keary Cl. M18: Man 1F **117**
Keasdon Av. M22: Wyth 1B **154**
Keaton Cl. M6: Sal 1E **99**

Keats Av. M34: Dent 1G **135**
  M43: Droy .3A **104**
  OL12: Roch 1C **26**
Keats Cres. M26: Rad 3G **51**
Keats Fold SK16: Duk 6F **107**
Keats Ho. SK5: Stoc 1G **133**
Keats M. M23: Wyth 3C **140**
Keats Rd. BL8: G'mount 1H **21**
  M30: Ecc 4F **97**
  OL1: O'ham 6H **59**
Keats Wlk. BL1: Bolt 3C **32**
(off Irving St.)
Keb La. OL8: O'ham 3G **91**
Keble Av. OL8: O'ham 6E **75**
Kedington Cl. M40: Man 6G **87**
(off Ribblesdale Dr.)
Kedleston Av. M14: Man 3A **116**
Kedleston Grn. SK2: Stoc 4D **146**
Kedleston Wlk. M34: Dent 6F **119**
Keele Cl. M40: Man 1F **7** (2G **101**)
  SK2: Stoc .5B **146**
Keeley Cl. M40: Man 1E **103**
Keep, The BL1: Bolt 6E **31**
Keepers Dr. OL12: Roch 1A **26**
Keighley Av. M43: Droy 2A **104**
Keighley Cl. BL8: Bury 3H **35**
Keighley St. BL1: Bolt 3A **32**
Keilder M. BL1: Bolt 6G **31**
Keith Av. M33: Sale 4D **128**
Keith Wlk. M40: Man 2G **7** (2H **101**)
Kelboro Av. M18: Man 6D **104**
Kelbrook Cl. SK2: Stoc 6E **147**
Kelbrook Rd. M11: Man 5D **102**
Kelby Av. M23: Wyth 4H **141**
Kelday Wlk. M8: Man 5G **87**
(off Smedley Rd.)
Keld Cl. BL8: Bury 6B **22**
Keld Wlk. M18: Man 2E **117**
(off Hampden Cres.)
Kelfield Av. M23: Wyth 1G **141**
Kelham Wlk. M40: Man 2E **89**
Kellbrook Cres. M7: Sal 2H **85**
(not continuous)
Kellet's Row M28: Walk 4G **65**
Kellett St. BL1: Bolt 5D **18**
  OL16: Roch 3B **28**
Kellett Wlk. M11: Man 3D **102**
(off Trimdon Cl.)
Kelling Wlk. M15: Man 4D **8**
Kelmarsh Cl. M11: Man 6F **103**
Kelmscott Lodge M41: Urm 4D **110**
(off Cornhill Rd.)
Kelsall Cl. SK3: Stoc 5F **145**
Kelsall Dr. M43: Droy 2H **103**
  WA15: Tim .1C **140**
Kelsall Rd. SK8: Chea 6C **144**
Kelsall St. M12: Man 1B **116**
  M33: Sale .5B **128**
  OL9: O'ham 3D **74**
  OL16: Roch 2C **178** (3H **27**)
Kelsall Way SK9: Hand 2H **165**
(off Spath La.)
Kelsey Flats OL10: H'ood 3G **39**
(off Meadow Cl.)
Kelsey Wlk. M9: Man 4F **71**
Kelso Cl. OL8: O'ham 2F **91**
Kelson Av. OL7: A Lyme 6G **91**
Kelso Pl. M15: Man 3C **8** (6B **100**)
Kelstern Av. M13: Man 4A **116**
Kelstern Sq. M13: Man 4A **116**
Kelton Cl. SK5: Stoc 4H **133**
Kelvin Av. M24: Mid 3F **71**
  M33: Sale .5B **128**
Kelvindale Dr. WA15: Tim 4C **140**
Kelvin Gro. M8: Man 5E **87**
  SK15: Mill .1H **107**
Kelvington Dr. M9: Man 5H **87**
Kelvin St. M4: Man 4B **6**
  OL7: A Lyme 5E **105**
Kelwood Av. BL9: Bury 6B **24**
Kemball M30: Ecc 3H **97**
Kemble Av. M23: Wyth 2A **142**

Kemmel Av. M22: Shar 6C **142**
Kemnay Wlk. M11: Man 4E **103**
(off Edith Cavell Cl.)
Kemp Av. OL11: Roch 6F **27**
Kempley Cl. M12: Man 1B **116**
Kempnough Hall Rd. M28: Wors 4A **82**
Kemp Rd. SK6: Mar B 4G **149**
Kempsey Ct. OL9: Chad 2B **74**
Kempsey Wlk. M40: Man 2F **89**
(off Enstone Dr.)
Kempsford Cl. M23: Wyth 5H **141**
Kempster St. M7: Sal 1B **100**
Kempston Gdns. BL1: Bolt 3C **32**
(off Wolfenden St.)
Kemp St. M24: Mid 1B **72**
  SK14: Hyde 3C **120**
Kempton Av. BL3: Lit L 5C **50**
  M33: Sale .6F **127**
Kempton Cl. M43: Droy 3C **104**
  SK7: H Gro 4G **159**
Kempton Ct. M33: Sale 6E **127**
Kempton Ho. M7: Sal 5A **86**
(off Griffin St.)
Kempton Rd. M19: Man 1C **132**
Kempton Way OL9: Chad 2C **74**
Kemsing Wlk. M5: Sal 4G **99**
Kenchester Av. M11: Man 5F **103**
Kendal Av. M33: Sale 6C **128**
  M34: Dent .6G **119**
  M41: Urm .3A **110**
  OL7: A Lyme 1F **105**
  OL12: Roch 1A **26**
  SK14: Hyde 2A **120**
Kendal Cl. OL10: H'ood 5A **40**
  WA15: Tim .6D **140**
Kendal Ct. M22: Shar 5C **142**
(off Downes Way)
  M30: Ecc 4D **96**
(off New La.)
  SK15: Stal .2E **107**
Kendal Dr. BL9: Bury 6D **36**
  OL2: Shaw .6B **44**
  SK7: Bram .2E **167**
  SK8: Gat 1G **155**
Kendal Gdns. SK6: Wood 5H **135**
Kendal Gro. M28: Walk 1B **82**
  M45: White .1F **69**
Kendal Ho. SK15: Stal 2E **107**
Kendall Rd. M8: Man 6D **70**
Kendal Rd. BL0: Ram 1A **22**
  BL1: Bolt 5A **32**
  M6: Sal 6C **84**
  M28: Wors .4C **80**
  M32: Stre .4D **112**
Kendal Rd. W. BL0: Ram 1H **21**
Kendal Ter. SK16: Duk 4A **106**
(off Astley St.)
Kendal Wlk. M24: Mid 6A **56**
Kendon Gro. M34: Dent 4E **119**
Kendrew Rd. BL3: Bolt 3G **47**
Kendrew Wlk. M9: Man 2A **88**
(off Shepherd St.)
Kenford Wlk. M8: Man 5D **86**
(off Ermington Dr.)
Kenilworth OL11: Roch 6A **178** (5G **27**)
Kenilworth Av. M20: Man 4D **130**
  M27: Clif 6B **68**
  M45: White .3G **69**
  OL9: Chad .6G **57**
  SK8: Chea H 2C **156**
  SK9: Hand .4H **165**
Kenilworth Cl. M26: Rad 1H **51**
  OL4: O'ham 4D **76**
  SK6: Mar 3D **148**
Kenilworth Dr. SK7: H Gro 5D **158**
Kenilworth Gro. M34: Aud 5C **104**
Kenilworth Rd. M33: Sale 5G **127**
  M41: Urm .6G **109**
  OL16: Roch 5C **42**
  SK3: Stoc .4B **144**
Kenilworth Sq. BL1: Bolt 4H **31**
Kenion Rd. OL11: Roch 5D **26**
Kenion St. OL16: Roch 4C **178** (4H **27**)

Kenley Dr. OL10: H'ood 6B **40**
Kenley Lodge SK7: Bram 6F **157**
Kenley Wlk. *M8: Man* 5G **87**
   (off Gransden Dr.)
Kenmay Av. BL3: Bolt 2F **47**
Kenmere Gro. M40: Man 2D **88**
Kenmor Av. BL8: Bury 5A **36**
Kenmore Cl. M45: White 1H **69**
Kenmore Dr. WA15: Tim 2A **152**
Kenmore Gro. M44: Cad 3B **124**
Kenmore Rd. M22: Nor 4B **142**
  M33: Sale 2E **139**
  M45: White 1H **69**
Kenmore Way
  M45: White 1H **69**
Kennard Cl. M9: Man 2B **88**
Kennard Pl. WA14: Alt 5G **139**
Kennedy Dr. BL3: Lit L 4E **51**
  BL9: Bury 5H **53**
  M29: Ast .4B **80**
Kennedy Rd. M5: Sal 3C **98**
Kennedy Sq. SK14: Mot 4B **122**
Kennedy St. BL2: Bolt 6G **33**
  M2: Man 6H **5** (4D **100**)
  OL8: O'ham 4E **75**
Kennedy Way M34: Dent 5D **118**
  SK4: Stoc 1E **145**
Kennerley Ct. SK2: Stoc 6A **146**
Kennerley Lodge
  SK3: Stoc 6H **145**
Kennerley Rd. SK2: Stoc 6A **146**
Kennerley's La. SK9: Wilm 2D **172**
Kennet Cl. SK9: Wilm 5H **165**
Kennet Flats OL10: H'ood 3G **39**
   (off Meadow Cl.)
Kenneth Collis Ct.
  M22: Wyth 2A **154**
Kenneth Sq. M7: Sal 5C **86**
Kennett Dr. SK6: Bred 5F **135**
Kennett Rd. M23: Wyth 2G **153**
Kenninghall Rd. M22: Wyth 2B **154**
Kennington Av. M40: Man 1D **102**
Kennington Fold BL3: Bolt 4B **48**
Kenny Cl. OL4: Lees 4B **76**
Kenside St. M16: W Ran 4D **114**
Kensington, The M20: Man 4F **131**
Kensington Av. M14: Man 3H **115**
  M26: Rad 3F **51**
  OL2: O'ham 1C **58**
  OL6: A Lyme 1C **106**
  OL9: Chad 1G **73**
  SK14: Hyde 6C **120**
Kensington Cl.
  BL8: G'mount 2H **21**
  OL16: Miln 5G **29**
Kensington Ct. BL1: Bolt 6C **32**
  M7: Sal 3A **86**
  M34: Dent 3B **118**
  SK9: Wilm 3D **172**
  SK14: Hyde 6C **120**
Kensington Dr. BL8: Bury 5A **36**
  M5: Sal 2D **98**
Kensington Gdns.
  SK14: Hyde 6D **120**
  WA15: Hale 4H **151**
Kensington Gro. M34: Dent 3B **118**
  SK15: Stal 4E **107**
  WA14: Tim 3G **139**
Kensington Pl. BL1: Bolt 6C **32**
Kensington Rd. M21: Chor 5G **113**
  M35: Fail 3B **90**
  OL8: O'ham 5D **74**
  SK3: Stoc 4D **144**
Kensington St. M14: Man 4E **115**
  OL11: Roch 1G **41**
  SK14: Hyde 6C **120**
Kenslow Av. M8: Man 1D **86**
Kensworth Cl. BL1: Bolt 4B **32**
  M23: Wyth 5D **140**
Kensworth Dr. BL1: Bolt 4B **32**
Kent Av. M43: Droy 4G **103**
  OL9: Chad 3A **74**
  SK8: Chea H 6E **145**

Kent Cl. M28: Walk 1F **81**
  OL3: Dig .3E **63**
Kent Ct. BL1: Bolt 1E **175** (5C **32**)
  M14: Man 4G **115**
Kent Dr. BL4: Kea 3D **66**
  BL9: Bury 5F **37**
Kentford Dr. M40: Man 1G **101**
Kentford Gro. BL4: Farn 1G **65**
   (off Westminster St.)
Kentford Rd. BL1: Bolt 4C **32**
Kent Gro. M35: Fail 5G **89**
Kentmere Av. OL12: Roch 6B **16**
Kentmere Cl. SK8: Gat 2F **155**
Kentmere Ct. M9: Man 5C **72**
Kentmere Dr. M24: Mid 4A **56**
Kentmere Gro. BL4: Farn 2D **64**
Kentmere Rd. BL2: Bolt 4B **34**
  WA15: Tim 5D **140**
   (not continuous)
Kentmore Cl. M12: Man 6C **102**
  SK4: Stoc 1A **144**
Kenton Av. M18: Man 4E **117**
Kenton Cl. BL1: Bolt 4B **32**
  M34: Aud 6D **104**
Kenton Rd. OL2: Shaw 6G **43**
Kenton St. OL8: O'ham 4H **75**
Kent Rd. M31: Part 6C **124**
  M34: Dent 5A **118**
  M44: Cad 4A **124**
  SK3: Stoc 3D **144**
Kent Rd. E. M14: Man 4H **115**
Kent Rd. W. M14: Man 4G **115**
Kentsford Dr. M26: Rad 2D **50**
Kentstone Av. SK4: Stoc 6H **131**
Kent St. BL1: Bolt 1E **175** (5C **32**)
  M2: Man .5H **5**
  M7: Sal 1B **100**
  M27: Pen 1H **83**
  OL8: O'ham 5F **75**
  OL11: Roch 6B **178** (5H **27**)
Kentucky St. OL4: O'ham 3A **76**
Kent Wlk. OL10: H'ood 4E **39**
Kentwell Cl. SK16: Duk 6H **105**
Ken Ward Sports Cen., The 6H **121**
Kenwick Dr. M40: Man 1G **89**
Kenwood Av. M19: Man 3B **132**
  SK7: Bram 2F **167**
  SK8: Gat .5E **143**
  WA15: Hale 3H **151**
Kenwood Cl. M32: Stre 5E **113**
Kenwood Ct. M32: Stre 6E **113**
Kenwood La. M28: Wors 6B **82**
Kenwood Rd. BL1: Bolt 2H **31**
  M32: Stre 6E **113**
  OL1: O'ham 6C **58**
  SK5: Stoc 4G **117**
KENWORTHY 1H **141**
Kenworthy Av. OL6: A Lyme 6B **92**
Kenworthy Gdns. OL3: Upp 1D **78**
Kenworthy La. M22: Nor 1B **142**
Kenworthy St. OL16: Roch 4C **28**
  SK15: Stal 4E **107**
   (not continuous)
Kenworthy Ter. OL16: Roch 4C **28**
Kenwright St. M4: Man 3B **6** (3E **101**)
Kenwyn St. M40: Man 2A **102**
Kenyon Av. M33: Sale 1E **141**
  OL8: O'ham 6F **75**
  SK16: Duk 6C **106**
Kenyon Bus. Pk. BL3: Bolt 2C **48**
Kenyon Cl. SK14: Hyde 2D **120**
Kenyon Cres. BL9: Bury 5F **23**
KENYON FOLD 6A **26**
Kenyon Fold OL11: Roch 6A **26**
Kenyon Gro. M38: Lit H 5C **64**
Kenyon Ho. SK16: Duk 4H **105**
   (off Astley St.)
Kenyon La. M24: Mid 1E **73**
  M25: Pres 5A **70**
  M40: Man 3C **88**
  SK16: Duk 6C **106**
   (off Kenyon Av.)
Kenyon Rd. BL2: Bolt 2D **50**

Kenyon St. BL0: Ram 2C **12**
  BL9: Bury 2G **37**
  M18: Man 1G **117**
  M26: Rad 4B **52**
  OL6: A Lyme 5A **174** (2G **105**)
  OL10: H'ood 3G **39**
  SK16: Duk 5H **105**
Kenyon Ter. M38: Lit H 6C **64**
Kenyon Way M38: Tot 6H **21**
  M38: Lit H 5C **64**
Keppel Rd. M21: Chor 6H **113**
Keppel St. OL6: A Lyme 2A **106**
Kepplecove Mdw. M28: Wors 6D **80**
Kepwick Dr. M22: Wyth 4C **154**
Kerenhappuch St. BL0: Ram 4B **12**
Kerfield Wlk. M13: Man 4D **10**
Kerfoot Cl. M22: Nor 3C **142**
Kermoor Av. BL1: Bolt 5C **18**
Kerne Gro. M23: Wyth 2G **141**
Kerrera Dr. M5: Sal 4D **98**
Kerridge Dr. SK6: Bred 5F **135**
Kerrier Cl. M30: Ecc 3A **98**
   (off Kearton Dr.)
Kerris Cl. M22: Wyth 4C **154**
Kerr St. M9: Man 6H **71**
Kerry Gro. BL2: Bolt 5F **33**
Kerry Wlk. M23: Wyth 2F **153**
KERSAL 3G **85**
  M38: Lit H 5F **65**
Kersal Av. M27: Pen 3C **84**
  M38: Lit H 5F **65**
Kersal Bank M7: Sal 3A **86**
Kersal Bar M7: Sal 2A **86**
Kersal Cell M7: Sal 3F **85**
   (off White Water Dr.)
Kersal Cl. M7: Sal 2A **86**
  M25: Pres 2G **85**
Kersal Crag M7: Sal 2A **86**
KERSAL DALE 3A **86**
Kersal Dr. WA15: Tim 4C **140**
Kersal Gdns. M7: Sal 3G **85**
Kersal Hall Av. M7: Sal 3G **85**
Kersal Rd. M7: Sal 2G **85**
  M25: Pres 2G **85**
Kersal Va. M25: Pres 3F **85**
Kersal Va. Ct. M7: Sal 3G **85**
Kersal Va. Rd. M25: Pres 2F **85**
Kersal Way M7: Sal 4H **85**
Kerscott Rd. M23: Wyth 2E **141**
Kersh Av. M19: Man 1D **132**
Kershaw Av. BL3: Lit L 3C **50**
  M25: Pres 1F **85**
   (not continuous)
  M33: Sale 1D **140**
Kershaw Bus. Cen. BL3: Bolt 2B **48**
   (off Baldwin St.)
Kershaw Dr. OL9: Chad 6F **73**
Kershaw Gro. M34: Aud 5B **104**
Kershaw Hey OL5: Mos 4H **93**
Kershaw La. M34: Aud 5B **104**
Kershaw Rd. M35: Fail 4H **89**
Kershaw St. BL2: Bolt 6G **19**
  BL3: Bolt .2B **48**
  BL9: Bury 3G **37**
  M43: Droy 4H **103**
  OL2: O'ham 2D **58**
  OL2: Shaw 6H **43**
   (not continuous)
  OL7: A Lyme 5F **105**
  OL10: H'ood 3F **39**
  OL12: Roch 1B **178** (3H **27**)
Kershaw St. E. OL2: Shaw 6H **43**
Kershaw Wlk. M12: Man 6H **11**
Kershope Gro. M5: Sal 5G **99**
Kersley St. OL4: O'ham 3G **75**
Kerswell Wlk. M40: Man 6C **88**
   (off Troydale Dr.)
Kerwin Wlk. M11: Man 5C **102**
   (off Mill St.)
Kerwood Dr. OL2: O'ham 4E **59**
Kesteven Rd. M9: Man 4H **87**
Keston Av. M9: Man 6C **72**
  M43: Droy 4G **103**
Keston Cres. SK5: Stoc 3B **134**

Keston Rd. OL1: O'ham 6A **60**
Kestor St. BL2: Bolt 5E **33**
        (not continuous)
Kestrel Av. BL4: Farn 2D **64**
  M27: Clif 1B **84**
  M34: Aud 4C **104**
  M38: Lit H 4E **65**
  OL4: O'ham 4A **76**
Kestrel Cl. M45: White 3G **69**
  SK6: Mar 2E **161**
  SK14: Hyde 3C **120**
Kestrel Ct. M50: Sal 5D **98**
Kestrel Dr. BL9: Bury 1H **37**
  M44: Irl 4E **109**
Kestrel M. OL11: Roch 4B **26**
Kestrel Rd. M17: T Pk 5H **97**
Kestrel St. BL1: Bolt . . .2H **175** (5E **33**)
Kestrel Vw. SK13: Glos 6H **123**
Kestrel Wlk. M12: Man 1C **116**
       (off Flamingo Cl.)
Keswick Av. M34: Dent 3D **118**
  M41: Urm 6A **110**
  OL7: A Lyme 6F **91**
  OL8: O'ham 5G **75**
  OL9: Chad 2A **74**
  SK8: Gat 2F **155**
  SK14: Hyde 3A **120**
Keswick Cl. M13: Man 2H **115**
  M24: Mid 5H **55**
  M44: Cad 5B **124**
  SK15: Stal 1E **107**
Keswick Ct. M22: Shar 5C **142**
       (off Downes Way)
  M24: Mid 5H **55**
Keswick Dr. BL9: Bury 6D **36**
  SK7: Bram 2E **167**
Keswick Gro. M6: Sal 2F **99**
Keswick Rd. M28: Walk 1B **82**
  M32: Stre 4C **110**
  SK4: Stoc 2F **133**
  SK6: H Lan 5C **160**
       (not continuous)
  WA15: Tim 5D **140**
Keswick St. BL1: Bolt 3D **32**
  OL11: Roch 3D **40**
Kesworthy Cl. SK14: Hat 5A **122**
Ketley Wlk. M22: Wyth 2D **154**
Kettering Rd. M19: Man 5D **116**
Kettleshulme Wlk. SK9: Wilm 6A **166**
       (off Picton Dr.)
Kettleshulme Way SK12: Poy 5F **169**
Kettlewell Wlk. M18: Man 2E **117**
       (off Hampden Cres.)
Ketton Cl. M11: Man 6G **103**
Kevin Av. OL2: O'ham 1E **59**
Kevin Ct. SK2: Stoc 1B **158**
Kevin St. M19: Man 1C **132**
Kew Av. SK14: Hyde 6C **120**
Kew Dr. M41: Urm 3C **110**
  SK8: Chea H 3A **156**
Kew Gdns. M40: Man 2C **88**
Kew Rd. M35: Fail 3A **90**
  OL4: O'ham 3H **75**
       (not continuous)
  OL11: Roch 2A **42**
Key Ct. M34: Dent 1G **135**
Keyhaven Wlk. M40: Man 6H **87**
       (off Glendower Dr.)
Keymer St. M11: Man 3A **102**
Keynsham Rd. M11: Man 2D **102**
Keystone Cl. M6: Sal 1E **99**
Key W. Cl. M11: Man 4B **102**
Keyworth Wlk. M40: Man 1A **102**
       (off Kirkhaven Sq.)
Khartoum St. M11: Man 3F **103**
  M16: Old T 3B **114**
Khubsuret Ho.
  OL11: Roch 6A **178** (5G **27**)
Kibbles Brow BL7: Bro X 3F **19**
Kibboth Crew BL0: Ram 2B **12**
Kibworth Cl. M45: White 1D **68**
Kibworth Wlk. M9: Man 4A **72**
       (off Crossmead Dr.)

Kidacre Wlk. M40: Man 4C **88**
       (off Rudd St.)
Kidderminster Way OL9: Chad 6H **57**
Kidnall Wlk. M9: Man 2B **88**
Kid St. M24: Mid 6B **56**
Kiel Cl. M30: Ecc 5G **97**
Kielder Hill M24: Mid 3B **56**
Kielder Sq. M5: Sal 4F **99**
Kilbride Av. BL2: Bolt 1B **50**
Kilburn Av. M9: Man 4H **71**
Kilburn Cl. SK8: H Grn 6F **155**
Kilburn Ct. M14: Man 3H **115**
       (off Hope Rd.)
Kilburn Rd. M26: Rad 3F **51**
  SK3: Stoc 4E **145**
Kilburn St. OL1: O'ham 6A **60**
Kilcoby Av. M27: Pen 3D **84**
Kildale Cl. BL3: Bolt 3E **47**
Kildare Cres. OL11: Roch 3H **41**
Kildare Rd. M21: Chor 1B **130**
  M27: Swin 4G **83**
Kildare St. BL4: Farn 2G **65**
Kildonan Dr. BL3: Bolt 1F **47**
Killer St. BL0: Ram 3C **12**
Killon St. BL9: Bury 4G **37**
Kilmaine Dr. BL3: Bolt 2E **47**
Kilmane Av. M9: Man 6D **72**
Kilmarsh Wlk. M8: Man 4D **86**
       (off Halliwell La.)
Kilmington Dr. M8: Man 5D **86**
Kilmory Dr. BL2: Bolt 1B **50**
Kiln Bank OL12: Whitw 3A **14**
       (off Tong End)
Kiln Bank La. OL12: Whitw 3A **14**
Kilnbrook Cl. OL4: Grot 5F **77**
Kiln Brow BL7: Bro X 3G **19**
Kiln Cft. SK6: Rom 2F **147**
Kiln Cft. La. SK9: Hand 3A **166**
Kilner Cl. BL9: Bury 3H **53**
Kilnerdeyne Ter.
  OL16: Roch 5A **178** (5G **27**)
Kilner Wlk. M40: Man 1G **101**
       (off Talgarth Rd.)
Kiln Fld. BL7: Bro X 3D **18**
KILN GREEN 2F **63**
Kiln Hill Cl. OL1: Chad 5H **57**
Kiln Hill La. OL1: Chad 5H **57**
Kilnhurst Wlk. BL1: Bolt 5B **32**
       (off Wentbridge Rd.)
Kiln La. OL16: Miln 5F **29**
  SK13: Had 2H **123**
Kiln Mt. OL16: Miln 5F **29**
Kilnsey Wlk. M18: Man 2E **117**
       (off Hampden Cres.)
Kilnside Dr. M9: Man 4H **87**
Kiln St. BL0: Ram 4B **12**
  BL3: Lit L 4C **50**
Kiln Wlk. OL12: Roch 1G **27**
Kilnwick Cl. M18: Man 4D **116**
Kilphin, The OL16: Roch 5B **30**
Kilrush Av. M30: Ecc 5F **97**
Kilsby Cl. BL4: Farn 5F **49**
  BL6: Los 1D **46**
Kilsby Wlk. M40: Man 1H **7** (1H **101**)
Kilton Wlk. M40: Man 1F **7**
Kilvert Dr. M33: Sale 4H **127**
Kilworth Av. M33: Sale 6H **127**
Kilworth Dr. BL6: Los 2D **46**
Kilworth St. OL11: Roch 1F **41**
Kimberley Av. SK6: Rom 1H **147**
Kimberley Rd. BL1: Bolt 6C **18**
Kimberley St. M7: Sal 4C **86**
  OL8: O'ham 6C **74**
  SK3: Stoc 4G **145**
Kimberley Wlk. M15: Man 4D **8**
Kimble Cl. BL8: G'mount 1H **21**
Kimbolton Cl. M12: Man 6C **102**
Kinburn Rd. M19: Man 1H **143**
Kinbury Wlk. M40: Man 1G **101**
       (off Kingsfold Av.)
Kincardine Ct. M13: Man 5D **10**
Kincardine Rd.
  M13: Man 4C **10** (6F **101**)

Kincraig Cl. BL3: Bolt 3E **47**
  M11: Man 4E **103**
Kinder Av. OL4: O'ham 4B **76**
  OL6: A Lyme 5E **93**
Kinder Cl. SK3: Stoc 6E **179**
Kinder Dr. SK6: Mar 5E **149**
Kinder Fold SK15: Stal 1H **121**
Kinder Gro. SK6: Rom 1C **148**
Kinder Ho. M5: Sal 2D **98**
       (off Medway Cl.)
Kinders OL3: G'fld 4D **78**
Kinders Cl. M31: C'ton 3H **125**
Kinders Cres. OL3: G'fld 4D **78**
Kinders Fold OL15: L'ough 2F **17**
Kinders La. OL3: G'fld 4D **78**
Kinders M. OL3: G'fld 4D **78**
Kinder St. SK3: Stoc 6E **179** (4G **145**)
  SK15: Stal 3E **107**
Kinderton Av. M20: Man 2F **131**
Kinder Way M24: Mid 5B **56**
Kineton Wlk. M13: Man 6F **11**
       (off Lauderdale Cres.)
King Albert St. OL2: Shaw 6H **43**
       (not continuous)
Kingcombe Wlk. M9: Man 3A **88**
       (off Thornsett Cl.)
King Edward Rd. SK14: Hyde 2C **136**
King Edwards Bldgs. M7: Sal 3D **86**
       (off Bury Old Rd.)
King Edwards St. SK14: Hyde 1D **136**
King Edward St. M5: Sal 2A **8** (5H **99**)
  M19: Man 6D **116**
  M30: Ecc 3E **97**
Kingfisher Av. M34: Aud 4C **104**
Kingfisher Cl. M12: Man 2A **116**
Kingfisher Ct. M50: Sal 5D **98**
  OL12: Roch 5C **16**
Kingfisher Dr. BL4: Farn 2D **64**
  BL9: Bury 1H **37**
Kingfisher M. SK6: Mar 5E **149**
Kingfisher Rd. SK2: Stoc 1F **159**
King George Rd. SK14: Hyde 6C **120**
Kingham Dr. M4: Man 3F **7** (3G **101**)
Kingholm Gdns. BL1: Bolt 4B **32**
       (off Kirkhope Dr.)
King La. OL1: O'ham 3C **60**
       (Sholver La.)
  OL1: O'ham 2C **60**
       (Wells Rd.)
Kingmoor Av. M26: Rad 3B **52**
Kings Acre WA14: Bow 4C **150**
Kings Av. M8: Man 3E **87**
  M45: White 5E **53**
  SK8: Gat 1E **155**
Kingsbridge Av. BL2: Ain 5F **35**
  SK14: Hat 5G **121**
Kingsbridge Cl. SK6: Mar 4C **148**
Kingsbridge Ct. M9: Man 4G **87**
Kingsbridge Dr. SK16: Duk 6H **105**
Kingsbridge Ho. BL3: Bolt 2A **48**
Kingsbridge Rd. M9: Man 4G **87**
  OL8: O'ham 4H **75**
Kingsbridge Wlk. SK14: Hat 5G **121**
Kingsbrook Ct. M16: W Ran 1C **130**
       (off St Austell Rd.)
Kingsbrook Rd. M16: W Ran 1C **130**
Kingsbury Av. BL1: Bolt 4G **31**
Kingsbury Ct. BL1: Bolt 4G **31**
Kingsbury Ct. Lodge BL1: Bolt 4G **31**
       (off Kingsbury Av.)
Kingsbury Dr. SK9: Wilm 1G **173**
Kingsbury Rd. M11: Man 3E **103**
Kingscliffe St. M9: Man 3A **88**
Kings Cl. M18: Man 1H **117**
  M25: Pres 4A **70**
  SK7: Bram 3H **157**
  SK9: Wilm 3D **172**
Kings Ct. M6: Sal 1G **99**
       (off St Georges Way)
  SK5: Stoc 6H **133**
  WA14: Alt 3A **174**
Kingscourt Av. BL1: Bolt 3A **32**
King's Cres. M16: Old T 4H **113**

Kingsdale Cl. BL9: Bury 6G **37**
Kingsdale Rd. M18: Man 3A **118**
Kingsdown Dr. BL1: Bolt 4D **32**
Kingsdown Gdns. *BL1: Bolt* *4D 32*
               (off Kingsdown Dr.)
Kingsdown Rd. M22: Wyth 4A **154**
Kingsdown Wlk. SK5: Stoc 4B **134**
Kings Dr. M24: Mid 1A **72**
    SK4: Stoc 6C **132**
    SK6: Mar 4C **148**
    SK8: Chea H 2C **156**
Kingsfield Dr. M20: Man 1G **143**
Kingsfold Av. M40: Man 1G **101**
Kingsfold Cl. BL2: Bolt 1A **50**
Kingsford St. M5: Sal 3D **98**
Kingsgate BL1: Bolt 3E **175** (6C **32**)
Kingsgate Rd. M22: Wyth 4A **154**
Kings Gro. M32: Stre 4F **113**
    OL12: Roch 5C **16**
Kingsheath Av. M11: Man 2D **102**
Kingshill Rd. M21: Chor 1G **129**
Kingsholme Rd. M22: Wyth 3A **154**
Kingsland OL11: Roch 2E **41**
Kingsland Cl. M40: Man 1G **7** (2H **101**)
Kingsland Rd. BL4: Farn 6E **49**
    OL11: Roch 1D **40**
    SK3: Stoc 4C **144**
Kings La. M32: Stre 4F **113**
Kingslea Rd. M20: Man 4G **131**
Kingsleigh Rd. SK4: Stoc 6A **132**
Kingsley Av. M7: Sal 4G **85**
    M9: Man 4B **88**
    M32: Stre 4F **113**
    M41: Urm 5D **110**
    M45: White 2G **69**
    SK4: Stoc 5G **133**
    SK9: Wilm 5G **165**
Kingsley Cl. M34: Dent 6D **118**
    OL6: A Lyme 6D **92**
Kingsley Ct. M5: Sal 4G **99**
Kingsley Dr. OL4: Lees 2C **76**
    SK8: Chea H 2C **156**
Kingsley Gro. M34: Aud 5C **104**
Kingsley Rd. M22: Nor 3B **142**
    M24: Mid 5D **56**
    M27: Swin 2F **83**
    M28: Walk 5G **65**
    OL4: O'ham 3A **76**
    WA15: Tim 4B **140**
Kingsley St. BL1: Bolt 3B **32**
    BL8: Bury 3B **36**
Kings Lynn Cl. M20: Man 6F **131**
Kingsmead M. M9: Man 4G **71**
Kingsmere Av. M19: Man 6B **116**
Kingsmill Av. M19: Man 1D **132**
Kingsnorth Cl. *BL1: Bolt* *4D 32*
               (off Adisham Dr.)
Kingsnorth Rd. M41: Urm 3A **110**
Kings Pk. M17: T Pk 2B **112**
King Sq. OL8: O'ham 4F **177** (3E **75**)
Kings Reach Bus. Pk.
    SK4: Stoc 2E **145**
Kings Rd. M16: Old T 4G **113**
    M21: Chor 1A **130**
    M25: Pres 1A **86**
    M32: Stre 6E **113**
    M33: Sale 5H **127**
    M34: Aud 2A **118**
    M44: Irl 3C **124**
    OL2: Shaw 1G **59**
    OL6: A Lyme 1A **106**
    OL8: O'ham 6H **177** (4F **75**)
    OL9: Chad 6G **73**
    OL16: Roch 6B **28**
    SK6: Rom 6G **135**
    SK7: H Gro 2E **159**
    SK8: Chea H 2B **156**
    SK9: Wilm 1B **172**
Kings Ter. M32: Stre 4F **113**
    SK16: Duk *5A 92*
               (off Queen St.)
KINGSTON 4H **119**
Kingston Arc. SK14: Hat 5A **122**

Kingston Av. BL2: Bolt 4G **33**
    M20: Man 2F **143**
    OL1: O'ham 6H **59**
    OL9: Chad 5A **74**
Kingston Cl. BL8: Bury 5B **36**
    M7: Sal 3B **86**
    M33: Sale 6F **127**
    OL2: Shaw 5H **43**
    SK14: Hat 5A **122**
Kingston Ct. *M20: Man* *2F 143*
               (off Kingston Rd.)
Kingston Dr. M33: Sale 4D **128**
    M41: Urm 1D **126**
    OL2: O'ham 1C **58**
Kingston Gdns. SK14: Hyde 4H **119**
Kingston Gro. M9: Man 5B **72**
Kingston Hill SK8: Chea 1H **155**
Kingston M. M35: Fail 4B **90**
Kingston Mill SK3: Stoc 2F **145**
Kingston Pl. SK8: Chea H 3A **156**
Kingston Rd. M20: Man 2F **143**
    M26: Rad 1C **52**
    M35: Fail 4B **90**
    SK9: Hand 3G **165**
Kingston St. SK3: Stoc 2F **145**
King St. BL0: Ram 3C **12**
    BL1: Bolt 3E **175** (6C **32**)
    BL2: Bolt 6H **19**
    BL4: Farn 1H **65**
    BL7: Bro X 1D **18**
    M2: Man 5G **5** (4D **100**)
               (not continuous)
    M3: Sal 3F **5** (3C **100**)
    M6: Sal 6D **84**
    M7: Sal 4C **86**
    M24: Mid 6C **56**
    M26: Rad 5B **52**
    M30: Ecc 4H **97**
    M32: Stre 6D **112**
    M34: Aud 1F **119**
    M34: Dent 4F **119**
    M35: Fail 5F **89**
    M43: Droy 5A **104**
               (not continuous)
    OL3: Del 3B **62**
    OL5: Mos 2H **93**
    OL8: O'ham 5F **177** (3E **75**)
    OL9: O'ham 4F **177** (3E **75**)
    OL10: H'ood 4H **39**
    OL12: Whitw 4B **14**
    OL16: Roch 3B **178** (4H **27**)
    SK7: W'ford 6D **166**
    SK14: B'tom 6C **122**
    SK14: Holl 2F **123**
    SK14: Hyde 4B **120**
    SK15: Stal 3E **107**
    SK16: Duk 4H **105**
King St. E. OL11: Roch 6B **178** (6H **27**)
    SK1: Stoc 1G **179** (1H **145**)
King St. Rdbt. OL1: O'ham 3E **75**
    OL4: O'ham 3E **75**
    OL8: O'ham 3E **75**
King St. Sth. OL11: Roch 6A **178** (6G **27**)
               (not continuous)
King St. W.
    M3: Man . . . . .5G **5** & 3E **179** (4D **100**)
    SK3: Stoc 2E **179** (2G **145**)
Kings Vw. SK4: Stoc 2E **145**
Kings Wlk. *M43: Droy* *5A 104*
               (off King St.)
    OL6: A Lyme *6B 92*
               (off King's Rd.)
Kingsway BL4: Kea 3B **66**
    M19: Man 1H **143**
    M20: Man 4G **143**
    M24: Mid 3B **72**
    M27: Pen 5C **84**
    M28: Walk 3H **81**
    M32: Stre 6C **112**
    OL16: Roch 6B **28**
    SK6: Bred 6E **135**
    SK7: Bram 3H **157**
    SK8: Chea, H Grn 3H **155**

Kingsway SK8: Gat 5G **143**
    SK16: Duk 6C **106**
    WA14: Alt 1B **174** (6F **139**)
Kingsway Av. M19: Man 8B **116**
Kingsway Bldgs. M19: Man 4A **132**
Kingsway Cl. OL8: O'ham 4E **75**
Kingsway Cres. M19: Man 4A **132**
Kingsway Pk. M41: Urm 2E **111**
Kingsway Retail Pk. OL16: Roch . . .4D **28**
Kingsway Sth. SK8: Chea H 6A **156**
Kingsway W. Ind. Pk. OL16: Roch . .6B **28**
Kingswear Dr. BL1: Bolt 4A **32**
Kingswood Ct. *SK9: Wilm* *2E 173*
               (off Grove Av.)
Kingswood Gro. SK5: Stoc 6H **117**
Kingswood Rd. M14: Man 1H **131**
    M24: Mid 4B **56**
    M25: Pres 4F **69**
    OL8: O'ham 1D **96**
Kingthorpe Gdns. *BL3: Bolt* *3D 48*
               (off Lever St.)
King William Ent. Pk.
    M50: Sal 5G **99**
King William St. M30: Ecc 2C **96**
    M50: Sal 5G **99**
Kingwood Av. BL1: Bolt 5F **31**
Kinlett Wlk. M40: Man 1F **89**
Kinley Cl. *M12: Man* *1B 116*
               (off Clowes St.)
Kinley Rd. BL4: Farn 6D **48**
Kinloch Dr. BL1: Bolt 6H **31**
Kinloch Gdns. OL8: O'ham 5F **75**
Kinloch St. M11: Man 3C **102**
    OL8: O'ham 5G **75**
Kinmel Av. SK5: Stoc 5C **134**
Kinmel Wlk. M23: Wyth 5F **141**
Kinmount Wlk. *M9: Man* *5H 87*
               (off Lathbury Rd.)
Kinnaird Cres. SK1: Stoc 3B **146**
Kinnaird Rd. M20: Man 4G **131**
Kinnerley Gro. M28: Wors 2E **81**
Kinross *M30: Ecc* *3H 97*
               (off Peel St.)
Kinross Av. SK2: Stoc 2A **158**
Kinross Cl. BL0: Ram 1A **22**
Kinross Dr. BL3: Bolt 2F **47**
Kinross Rd. M14: Man 4A **116**
Kinsale Wlk. M23: Wyth 2F **153**
Kinsbury Cl. BL8: Bury 5A **22**
Kinsey Av. M23: Wyth 4F **141**
Kinsley Dr. M28: Walk 1G **81**
Kintore Av. SK7: H Gro 2F **159**
Kintore Wlk. *M40: Man* *6F 87*
               (off Ribblesdale Dr.)
Kintyre Av. M5: Sal 4D **98**
Kintyre Cl. *M11: Man* *4E 103*
               (off Coatbridge St.)
Kintyre Dr. BL3: Bolt 2E **47**
Kinver Cl. *BL3: Bolt* *4A 48*
               (off Woodbine Rd.)
Kinver Rd. M40: Man 1E **89**
Kipling Av. M34: Dent 2G **135**
    M43: Droy 2A **104**
Kipling Cl. SK2: Stoc 4F **147**
Kipling Rd. OL1: O'ham 5H **59**
Kipling St. M7: Sal 5B **86**
Kippax St. M14: Man 4F **115**
Kirby Av. M27: Swin 6F **83**
    OL9: Chad 6F **73**
Kirby Wlk. OL2: Shaw 5H **43**
Kirkbank St. OL9: O'ham 1D **74**
               (not continuous)
Kirkburn Vw. BL8: Bury 6C **22**
Kirkby Av. M33: Sale 1C **140**
    M40: Man 4D **88**
Kirkby Cl. BL9: Bury 6E **37**
Kirkby Dr. M33: Sale 1D **140**
Kirkby Rd. BL1: Bolt 5H **31**
Kirkdale Av. M40: Man 1F **89**
Kirkdale Dr. OL2: O'ham 2C **58**
Kirkebrook Rd. BL3: Bolt 3G **47**
Kirkfell Dr. M29: Ast 4A **80**
    SK6: H Lan 5C **160**

Kirkfell Wlk. OL1: O'ham 6F 59
(not continuous)
Kirkgate Cl. M40: Man 2F 7
Kirkhall La. BL1: Bolt 5A 32
Kirkhall Workshops BL1: Bolt 5A 32
(off Bilbao St.)
Kirkham Av. M18: Man 1F 117
Kirkham Cl. M34: Dent 4F 119
Kirkham Rd. SK8: H Grn 4G 155
KIRKHAMS .2H 69
Kirkham St. BL2: Bolt 4F 33
M5: Sal .4E 99
M38: Lit H 4E 65
OL9: O'ham 2E 177 (2D 74)
Kirkhaven Sq. M40: Man 1A 102
Kirkhill Grange BL5: W'ton 5A 46
Kirkhill Wlk. M40: Man 1F 89
(off Blandford Dr.)
KIRKHOLT 3H 41
Kirkholt Wlk. M9: Man 6A 72
(off Woodmere Dr.)
Kirkhope Dr. BL1: Bolt 4B 32
Kirkhope Wlk. BL1: Bolt 4B 32
Kirklands BL2: Bolt 3H 33
M33: Sale 1A 140
Kirklee Av. OL9: Chad 6A 58
Kirklee Rd. OL11: Roch 3F 41
Kirklees BL8: Tot 4A 22
Kirklees Cl. BL8: Tot 4A 22
Kirklees St. BL8: Tot 4H 21
Kirklees Wlk. M45: White 6H 53
Kirkley St. SK14: Hyde 6B 120
Kirklinton Dr. M9: Man 5H 87
Kirkman Av. M30: Ecc 5E 97
Kirkman Cl. M18: Man 3F 117
Kirkmanshulme La. M12: Man 3B 116
Kirkman St. BL9: Bury 4F 53
Kirk Rd. M19: Man 2D 132
Kirkstall OL12: Roch 1A 178 (3G 27)
Kirkstall Av. OL10: H'ood 2G 39
OL15: L'ough 3G 17
Kirkstall Cl. SK12: Poy 3D 168
Kirkstall Gdns. M26: Rad 2G 51
Kirkstall Rd. M24: Mid 4B 56
M41: Urm 4G 111
Kirkstall Sq. M13: Man 6E 11 (1G 115)
Kirkstead Cl. M11: Man 5C 102
Kirkstead Rd. SK8: Chea H 6E 157
Kirkstile Pl. M27: Clif 5G 67
Kirkstone Av. M28: Walk 2B 82
Kirkstone Cl. OL1: O'ham 6F 59
Kirkstone Dr. M24: Mid 5A 56
OL2: O'ham 1D 58
Kirkstone Rd. M40: Man 1E 89
SK14: Hyde 2A 120
Kirk St. M18: Man 2F 117
Kirktown Wlk. M11: Man 5E 103
(off Greenside St.)
Kirkwall Dr. BL2: Bolt 2F 49
Kirkway M9: Man 5C 72
M24: Mid 2C 72
OL11: Roch 3H 41
Kirkwood Dr. M40: Man 1G 101
Kirtley Av. M30: Ecc 2F 97
Kirtlington Cl. OL2: O'ham 2G 59
Kirton Lodge M25: Pres 5A 70
Kirton Wlk. M9: Man 4G 71
Kitchener Av. M44: Cad 5A 124
Kitchener St. BL3: Bolt 4F 49
BL8: Bury 4B 36
Kitchenr Way BL4: Farn 6D 48
Kitchen St. OL16: Roch 2D 178 (3A 28)
Kitepool St. M30: Ecc 1C 96
Kitter St. OL12: Roch 6B 16
Kittiwake Ct. SK2: Stoc 6F 147
KITT'S MOSS 1F 167
Kitt's Moss La. SK7: Bram 1F 167
Kitty Wheeldon Gdns. M33: Sale 4A 128
(off Ashton La.)
Kiveton Cl. M28: Walk 1G 81
Kiwi St. M6: Sal 3G 99
Knacks La. OL12: Roch 4C 14
Knaresborough Cl. SK5: Stoc 6G 117

Knarr Barn La. OL3: Dob 4H 61
Knarr La. OL3: Del 5A 62
(not continuous)
Kneller Wlk. OL1: O'ham 3B 60
Knight Cres. M24: Mid 3H 55
Knightley Wlk. M40: Man 6H 87
(off Thornton St. Nth.)
Knightsbridge SK1: Stoc . . .1G 179 (1H 145)
Knightsbridge Cl. M7: Sal 3B 86
SK9: Wilm 6H 165
Knightsbridge M.
M20: Man 5F 131
Knights Cl. M25: Pres 4H 69
Knights Ct. M5: Sal 3A 98
Knight St. BL1: Bolt 1F 175 (5D 32)
BL8: Bury 3C 36
M20: Man 1F 143
OL7: A Lyme 3F 105
SK14: Hyde 6D 120
Knightswood BL3: Bolt 4F 47
Knightswood Rd. M8: Man 4E 87
Kniveton Cl. M12: Man 1B 116
(off Kniveton Rd.)
Kniveton Rd. M12: Man 1B 116
Knivton St. SK14: Hyde 4D 120
Knob Hall Gdns.
M23: Wyth 2F 153
Knole Av. SK12: Poy 3F 169
Knoll, The OL2: Shaw 1A 60
OL5: Mos 2F 93
WA14: Alt 6D 138
Knoll St. M7: Sal 4B 86
OL11: Roch 2D 40
Knoll St. Ind. Pk. M7: Sal 4B 86
(off Knoll St.)
Knott Fold SK14: Hyde 1B 136
Knott Hill La. OL3: Del 4A 62
Knott Hill Local Nature Reserve
. . . . .4D 92
Knott La. BL1: Bolt 3F 31
SK14: Hyde 1B 136
KNOTT LANES 4E 91
Knott Lanes OL8: O'ham 3F 91
KNOTT MILL 4F 9 (6C 100)
Knowe Av. M22: Wyth 4B 154
Knowl Cl. BL0: Ram 5C 12
M34: Dent 5B 118
Knowldale Way M12: Man 2A 116
(off Dillon Dr.)
Knowle Av. OL7: A Lyme 1F 105
Knowle Dr. M25: Pres 1G 85
Knowle Grn. SK9: Hand 4G 165
Knowle Pk. SK9: Hand 4G 165
Knowle Rd. SK6: Mel 5G 149
Knowles Cl. M6: Sal 2B 98
Knowles Edge St. BL1: Bolt 3A 32
Knowles Pl. M15: Man 5H 9
Knowles St. BL1: Bolt 4E 33
M26: Rad 3A 52
Knowle Way SK14: Mot 5B 122
(off Chain Bar La.)
Knowl Hill Dr. OL12: Roch 1A 26
Knowl Hill Vw. OL10: H'ood 3E 39
Knowl Rd. OL16: Roch 5D 28
Knowls, The OL8: O'ham 2B 90
KNOWLS LANE 4D 76
Knowls La. OL4: O'ham 4D 76
Knowl St. OL8: O'ham 1C 90
SK15: Stal 3F 107
Knowl Syke St. OL12: W'le 5C 16
Knowl Top La. OL3: Upp 2F 79
Knowl Vw. BL8: Tot 5A 22
OL15: L'ough 1F 29
Knowsley Av. OL4: Spri 2E 77
Knowsley Av. M5: Sal 5H 99
M41: Urm 3E 111
OL4: Spri 2E 77
Knowsley Cres. SK1: Stoc 3B 146
Knowsley Dr. M27: Swin 6F 83
OL4: Spri 2E 77
Knowsley Grange
BL1: Bolt 6D 30
Knowsley Grn. OL4: Spri 2E 77

Knowsley Rd. BL1: Bolt 3H 31
BL2: Ain 4E 35
M45: White 1F 69
SK1: Stoc 3B 146
SK7: H Gro 5F 159
Knowsley Sq. BL1: Bolt 2F 175 (6D 32)
BL9: Bury 6A 176 (4E 37)
M8: Man 1D 100
OL12: Roch 1A 178 (3G 27)
Knowsley Ter. OL4: Spri 2E 77
SK1: Stoc 3B 146
(off Knowsley Rd.)
Knutsford Av. M16: Old T 3B 114
M33: Sale 5E 129
SK4: Stoc 2F 133
Knutsford Rd. M18: Man 2E 117
SK9: A Edg 6A 172
SK9: Wilm 6B 172
Knutsford St. M6: Sal 3E 99
Knutsford Vw. WA15: Haleb 5C 152
KNUTSHAW BRIDGE 4E 47
Knutshaw Cres. BL3: Bolt 5D 46
Knypersley Av. SK2: Stoc 4C 146
Krokus Sq. OL9: Chad 2A 74
Kyle Ct. SK7: H Gro 4F 159
Kylemore Av. BL3: Bolt 2H 47
Kylemore Pl. BL4: Farn 2G 65
Kyle Rd. SK7: H Gro 4F 159
Kynder St. M34: Dent 4F 119

L

Labrador Quay M50: Sal 6G 99
Labtec St. M27: Pen 2B 84
Laburnum Av. BL8: Tot 4H 21
M27: Swin 5G 83
M30: Ecc 5C 96
(off Wilfred Rd)
M34: Aud 4C 104
M35: Fail 5H 89
M45: White 3F 69
OL2: Shaw 1H 59
OL6: A Lyme 5A 92
OL9: Chad 6B 58
SK14: Hyde 1B 136
SK15: Stal 5D 106
SK16: Duk 5D 106
Laburnum Cl. WA15: Tim 6B 140
Laburnum Ct. BL8: Tot 4H 21
Laburnum Dr. BL9: Bury 6G 53
Laburnum Gro. M25: Pres 4G 69
M29: Tyld 2B 80
Laburnum Ho. OL2: Shaw 1H 59
Laburnum La. OL16: Miln 2G 43
WA15: Hale 5G 151
Laburnum Lodge BL2: Bolt 5B 34
Laburnum Pk. BL2: Bolt 6F 19
Laburnum Rd. BL4: Farn 1F 65
M18: Dent 4H 117
M18: Man 3F 117
M24: Mid 1E 73
M28: Walk 1A 82
M34: Dent 4H 117
M41: Urm 3D 110
M44: Cad 4B 124
OL8: O'ham 3C 90
Laburnum St. BL1: Bolt 5B 32
M6: Sal 3F 99
Laburnum Ter. OL11: Roch 1G 41
Laburnum Vs. OL8: O'ham 2G 91
(off Simkin Way)
Laburnum Wlk. M33: Sale 4E 127
(off Epping Dr.)
Laburnum Way OL15: L'ough 3F 17
SK3: Stoc 3D 144
Lacerta M. M7: Sal 1B 4 (2A 100)
Lacey Av. SK9: Wilm 6F 165
Lacey Cl. SK9: Wilm 6F 165
Lacey Ct. SK9: Wilm 6F 165
LACEY GREEN 6F 165
Lacey Grn. SK9: Wilm 1E 173
Lacey Gro. SK9: Wilm 6G 165

Lackford Dr. M40: Man 1F 7 (1G 101)
Lacrosse Av. OL8: O'ham 5C 74
Lacy Gro. M32: Stre 6D 112
Lacy St. M32: Stre 6D 112
  SK1: Stoc 4G 179 (3H 145)
Lacy Wlk. M12: Man 1H 11
Ladbrooke Cl. OL6: A Lyme 1A 106
Ladbrooke Rd. OL6: A Lyme 6A 92
Ladcastle Rd.
  OL3: Dob, Upp 6B 62
Ladhill La. OL3: G'fld 4D 78
LADYBARN 2H 131
Ladybarn Cres. M14: Man 2H 131
  SK7: Bram 1H 167
Ladybarn Ho. M14: Man 6H 115
Ladybarn La. M14: Man 1H 131
Ladybarn Mnr. SK7: Bram 5G 157
Ladybarn Rd. M14: Man 1H 131
Ladybower SK8: Chea H 1E 157
Ladybridge Av. M28: Man 3G 81
Lady Bri. Brow BL1: Bolt 6F 31
Ladybridge Community Leisure Cen. .3F 47
Lady Bri. La. BL1: Bolt 6F 31
  BL3: Bolt 1F 47
Ladybridge Ri. SK8: Chea H 2E 157
Ladybridge Rd.
  SK8: Chea H 3D 156
Ladybrook Av. WA15: Tim 4B 140
Ladybrook Ct. SK8: Chea H 2D 156
  (off Ladybridge Rd.)
Ladybrook Gro. SK9: Wilm 5H 165
Ladybrook Rd. SK7: Bram 4E 157
Ladyfield St. SK9: Wilm 2E 173
Ladyfield Ter. SK9: Wilm 2E 173
Lady Harriet Wlk. M28: Walk 6G 65
  (off Ellesmere Shop. Cen.)
Ladyhill Vw. M28: Wors 3G 81
LADY HOUSE 1E 43
Ladyhouse Cl. OL16: Miln 6G 29
Ladyhouse La. OL16: Miln 6F 29
  (not continuous)
Lady Kelvin Rd. WA14: Alt 5E 139
Ladylands Av. M11: Man 3E 103
Ladymeadow Cl. BL1: Bolt 2F 33
Ladymere Dr. M28: Wors 3F 81
Lady Rd. OL4: Lees 3C 76
Ladys Cl. SK12: Poy 3E 169
Ladyshore Cl. M5: Sal 4F 99
Ladyshore Rd. BL3: Lit L 5E 51
Lady's Incline SK12: Poy 3E 169
Ladysmith, The OL6: A Lyme 6D 92
Ladysmith Av. BL9: Bury 6G 23
Ladysmith Cen.
  OL6: A Lyme 5C 174 (2H 105)
Ladysmith Dr. OL6: A Lyme 6D 92
Ladysmith Rd. M20: Man 6G 131
  OL6: A Lyme 6D 92
  SK15: Stal 1E 107
Ladysmith St. OL8: O'ham 6C 74
  SK3: Stoc 6F 179 (4G 145)
Ladythorn Av. SK6: Mar 6E 149
Ladythorn Cres. SK7: Bram 1H 167
Ladythorne Av. M25: Pres 1G 85
Ladythorne Ct. M25: Pres 1G 85
  (off Ladythorne Dr.)
Ladythorne Dr. M25: Pres 1G 85
Ladythorn Gro. SK7: Bram 1H 167
Ladythorn Rd. SK7: Bram 6G 157
Ladywell Av. M38: Lit H 5E 65
Ladywell Cl. SK7: H Gro 3A 158
Ladywell Gro. M38: Lit H 4E 65
Ladywell Station (Metro) 3A 98
Ladywell Trad. Est. M50: Sal 3B 98
LA Fitness
  Sale .1B 140
Lagan Wlk. M22: Wyth 3C 154
Lagos Cl. M14: Man 3E 115
Laindon Rd. M14: Man 3A 116
Lainton Ct. SK3: Stoc 3E 145
Lake Bank OL15: L'ough 6G 17
Lake Dr. M24: Mid 2B 72
Lake Ho. M15: Man 4C 8 (6B 100)
Lakeland Ct. M24: Mid 5H 55

Lakeland Cres. BL9: Bury 1E 53
Lakeland Dr. OL2: O'ham 5C 42
Lakelands Dr. BL3: Bolt 2F 47
Lakenheath Dr. BL1: Bolt 5D 18
Lake Rd. M17: T Pk 6C 98
  M34: Dent 3F 119
  SK15: Stal 1D 106
Lake Side OL15: L'ough 1G 29
  SK13: Had 1H 123
Lakeside BL9: Bury 2F 53
  SK8: Chea 2G 155
Lakeside Av. BL3: Bolt 5E 49
  M28: Walk 4H 65
  OL7: A Lyme 1F 105
Lakeside Bldg. SK8: Chea 2G 155
Lakeside Cl. M18: Man 1H 117
Lakeside Ct. M7: Sal 2B 86
Lakeside Dr. SK12: Poy 2E 169
Lakeside Grn. SK2: Stoc 5C 146
Lakeside Ri. M9: Man 6E 71
Lakeside Rd. SK6: Mar 5E 149
  SK16: Duk 5A 106
Lake St. BL3: Bolt 2D 48
  OL11: Roch 6B 178 (5H 27)
  SK2: Stoc 6B 146
Lakes Vw. SK15: Stal 1D 106
Lakewood SK16: Duk 5H 105
Lake Vw. M9: Man 1C 88
  OL15: L'ough 2F 17
Lakin St. M40: Man 4C 88
Laleham Grn. SK7: Bram 2F 157
Lamb Cl. M12: Man 2B 116
Lamb Ct. M3: Sal 4E 5 (3C 100)
Lambert Dr. M33: Sale 3F 127
Lambert Hall M1: Man 2C 10
  (off Granby Row)
Lamberton Dr. M23: Wyth 5E 141
Lambert St. OL7: A Lyme 4F 105
Lambeth Av. M35: Fail 3B 90
Lambeth Gro. SK6: Wood 4G 135
Lambeth Rd. M40: Man 1E 103
  SK5: Stoc 2H 133
Lambeth Ter. OL11: Roch 6D 27
Lamb La. M3: Sal 4E 5 (3C 100)
Lambourn Cl. BL3: Bolt 2C 48
  (off Parrot St.)
  SK12: Poy 3D 168
Lambourne Cl. M22: Wyth 5B 154
Lambourne Gro. OL16: Miln 6F 29
Lambourn Rd. M41: Urm 3H 109
Lambrook Wlk. M40: Man 1F 103
  (off Eastmoor Dr.)
Lambs Fold SK4: Stoc 4F 133
Lambton Rd. M21: Chor 1B 130
  M28: Wors 4E 83
Lambton St. BL3: Bolt 5A 48
  M30: Ecc 1D 96
Lamburn Av. M40: Man 1F 89
Lamb Wlk. M34: Dent 2G 119
  (off Wordsworth Rd.)
Lamerton Way SK9: Wilm 5A 166
Lamorna Cl. M7: Sal 3H 85
Lamphey Cl. BL1: Bolt 5D 30
Lamplight Way M27: Pen 4E 85
Lamport Cl. M1: Man 3C 10 (6F 101)
Lamport Ct. M1: Man 3C 10
Lampson St. M8: Man 1C 100
Lamzeus Cl. WA14: Alt 4F 139
Lamsholme Cl. M19: Man 5C 116
Lanark Av. M22: Nor 3B 142
Lanark Cl. OL10: H'ood 4D 38
  SK7: H Gro 3G 159
Lanbury Dr. M8: Man 4D 86
Lancashire Aero Club 6A 96
Lancashire County Cricket Club Mus.
  . . . . .3G 113
Lancashire County Cricket Ground
  . . . . .3F 113
Lancashire Ct. OL9: O'ham 4C 74
LANCASHIRE HILL 6G 133
Lancashire Hill SK4: Stoc 6G 133
  SK5: Stoc 6G 133

Lancaster Av. BL0: Ram 5A 12
  BL4: Farn 6D 48
  M24: Mid 2E 73
  M35: Fail 4G 89
  M41: Urm 4G 111
  M45: White 2G 69
  SK15: Stal 2E 107
Lancaster Cl. BL1: Bolt 4H 175 (6E 33)
  SK6: Rom 2G 147
  SK7: H Gro 5D 158
Lancaster Ct. M19: Man 1B 132
  M40: Man 1D 102
Lancaster Dr. BL3: Lit L 3D 50
  BL9: Bury 3F 23
  M25: Pres 1A 86
Lancaster Ho. M1: Man 2B 10
  OL2: O'ham 2D 58
  SK3: Stoc 5E 179
Lancaster Lodge M27: Swin 5B 84
Lancaster Rd. M6: Sal 5B 84
  M20: Man 6E 131
  M34: Dent 6F 119
  M43: Droy 2H 103
  M44: Cad 4A 124
  SK9: Wilm 6A 166
Lancaster Sq. OL2: O'ham 2D 58
Lancaster St. M26: Rad 4G 51
  OL5: Mos 2F 93
  OL9: Chad 5A 74
  SK1: Stoc 1A 146
Lancaster Ter. BL1: Bolt 3C 32
  (off Boardman St.)
  OL11: Roch 1H 25
Lancaster Wlk. BL1: Bolt 3C 32
  (off Halliwell Rd.)
Lancelot Rd. M22: Wyth 3D 154
Lancelyn Dr. SK9: Wilm 1G 173
Lanchester Dr. BL3: Bolt 2B 48
Lanchester St. M40: Man 2A 102
Lancing Av. M20: Man 6H 131
Lancing Wlk. OL9: Chad 3A 74
Landau Dr. M28: Walk 6D 64
Landcross Rd. M14: Man 6G 115
Landells Wlk. M40: Man 6C 88
  (off Peckford Dr.)
Lander Gro. M9: Man 6B 72
Landkey Cl. M23: Wyth 1F 141
Land La. SK9: Wilm 3F 173
  (not continuous)
Landmark, The M26: Rad 5B 52
  (off New Rd.)
Landmark Ct. BL1: Bolt 4F 31
Landmark Ho. SK8: Chea H 3D 156
Landor Cl. M34: Dent 4H 117
Landore Cl. M26: Rad 3B 52
Landos Ct. M40: Man 2F 7 (2G 101)
Landos Rd. M40: Man 2F 7 (2G 101)
Landrace Dr. M28: Wors 5F 81
Landsberg Rd. M35: Fail 3B 90
Landsberg Ter. M35: Fail 3B 90
Landseer Dr. SK6: Mar B 4F 149
Landseer St. OL4: O'ham . . .6H 177 (4G 75)
  (not continuous)
Lands End Rd. M24: Mid 2F 71
LANDSLOW GREEN 1D 122
Landstead Dr. M40: Man 3H 7 (3A 102)
Lane, The BL1: Bolt 6D 30
LANE BOTTOM 1C 44
Lane Brow OL4: Grot 4F 77
Lane Dr. OL4: Grot 4F 77
LANE END
  OL3 . . . . .6B 78
  OL10 .6B 40
Lane End M30: Ecc 4H 97
  OL10: H'ood 5B 40
Lane End Cl. M35: Fail 5A 90
Lane End Rd. M19: Man 5H 131
LANE ENDS
  SK6, Marple Bridge 2G 149
  SK6, Romiley 6B 136
Lane Ends SK6: Rom 6B 136
Lanegate SK14: Hyde 1B 136
Lane Head Rd. OL4: O'ham 5D 76

Lane Mdw. OL2: Shaw 1G 59
Lanesfield Wlk. M8: Man 3G 87
(off Stakeford Dr.)
LANE SIDE 6B 44
Laneside Av. OL2: Shaw 6B 44
Laneside Cl. OL15: L'ough 3G 17
Laneside Dr. SK7: Bram 4A 158
Laneside Wlk. OL16: Miln 4F 29
Lanfield Dr. M8: Man 4D 86
Langbourne Cl. M26: Rad 1D 66
Langcliffe Pl. M26: Rad 1E 67
Langcliffe Wlk. M18: Man 2E 117
(off Hampden Cres.)
Langcroft Dr. M40: Man 6E 89
Langdale Av. M19: Man 1D 132
OL8: O'ham 5D 74
OL16: Roch 5C 42
Langdale Cl. M34: Dent 6E 119
SK8: H Lan 5C 160
SK8: Gat 2G 155
WA15: Tim 6G 139
Langdale Ct. M8: Man 5F 87
Langdale Dr. BL9: Bury 4G 53
M24: Mid 4B 56
M28: Walk 2B 82
Langdale Hall M14: Man 4G 115
(off Upper Pk. Rd.)
Langdale M. BL9: Bury 6F 23
Langdale Rd. M14: Man 3H 115
M31: Part 6C 124
M32: Stre 4C 112
M33: Sale 2G 139
SK4: Stoc 3E 133
SK6: Wood 4H 135
SK7: Bram 2E 167
Langdale St. BL3: Bolt 4C 48
BL4: Farn 2G 65
Langdale Ter. SK15: Stal 1E 107
(off Springs La.)
Langden Cl. OL2: Shaw 5G 43
Langdon Cl. BL1: Bolt 5B 32
Langfield Av. M16: W Ran 4B 114
Langfield Cres. M43: Droy 3C 104
Langford Dr. M44: Irl 6E 109
Langford Gdns. BL3: Bolt 3C 48
(off Aldsworth Dr.)
Langford Rd. M20: Man 3E 131
SK4: Stoc 5E 133
Langford St. M34: Dent 4F 119
Langham Cl. BL1: Bolt 5E 19
Langham Ct. M20: Man 5D 130
M32: Stre 3A 112
Langham Gro. WA15: Tim 3B 140
Langham Rd. M6: Sal 3F 99
OL8: O'ham 5E 75
SK4: Stoc 2D 144
WA14: Bow 3D 150
Langham St. OL7: A Lyme 6G 91
Langham St. Ind. Est.
OL7: A Lyme 6G 91
Langholm Dr. BL2: Bolt 1B 50
Langholme Cl. M15: Man 4D 8 (6B 100)
Langholme Pl. M30: Ecc 3D 96
Langholme Way OL10: H'ood 4D 38
Langland Cl. M9: Man 5A 72
(off Leconfield Dr.)
M19: Man 6F 117
Langland Dr. M30: Ecc 4C 96
LANGLEY 6A 56
Langley Av. M24: Mid 3A 56
M25: Pres 4H 69
OL4: Grot 4F 77
SK7: H Gro 4B 158
Langley Cl. M41: Urm 5G 111
Langley Ct. M7: Sal 2C 86
Langley Cres. M25: Pres 3H 69
Langley Dr. BL3: Bolt 2A 48
M28: Wors 5D 80
SK9: Hand 4A 166
Langley Gdns. M25: Pres 3H 69
Langley Grange M25: Pres 3H 69

Langley Gro. M25: Pres 3H 69
Langley Hall Rd. M25: Pres 3H 69
Langley Ho. M24: Mid 4C 56
Langley La. M24: Mid 3G 55
OL10: H'ood 3G 55
Langley Rd. M6: Sal 3F 85
M14: Man 6G 115
M25: Pres 4G 69
M27: Pen 3F 85
M33: Sale 6G 127
Langley Rd. Sth. M6: Sal 5F 85
Langness St. M11: Man 4E 103
Lango St. M16: Old T 2A 114
(off Howarth St.)
Langport Av. M12: Man 6H 11 (1A 116)
Langroyd Wlk. M8: Man 4D 86
(off Highshore Dr.)
Langsett Av. M6: Sal 2C 98
SK13: Gam 6F 123
(off Wardlow M.)
Langsett Grn. SK13: Gam 6F 123
(off Wardlow M.)
Langsett Gro. SK13: Gam 6F 123
(off Wardlow M.)
Langsett La. SK13: Gam 6F 123
Langsett Lea SK13: Gam 6F 123
(off Youlgreave Cres.)
Langsett Ter. SK13: Gam 6F 123
(off Youlgreave Cres.)
Langshaw Rd. BL3: Bolt 2A 48
Langshaw St. M6: Sal 4F 99
M16: Old T 3A 114
Langshaw Wlk. BL3: Bolt 2A 48
Langside Av. M9: Man 5A 72
Langside Dr. BL3: Bolt 3E 47
Langston Grn. SK7: H Gro 4A 158
Langston St. M3: Man 1G 5 (2D 100)
Langthorne St. M19: Man 1D 132
Langthorne Wlk. BL3: Bolt 1E 47
(off Deane Rd.)
Langton Cl. M35: Fail 3B 90
Langton St. M6: Sal 3E 99
M24: Mid 1C 72
OL10: H'ood 2H 39
Langton Ter. OL11: Roch 1G 41
Langtree Cl. M28: Wors 3F 81
Langworthy Av. M38: Lit H 5F 65
Langworthy Rd. M6: Sal 1F 99
M40: Man 4C 88
Langworthy Station (Metro) 4E 99
Lanhill Dr. M8: Man 5G 87
Lankro Way M30: Ecc 4H 97
Lanley Cl. BL3: Lit L 4D 50
Lanreath Wlk. M8: Man 5F 87
(off Moordown Cl.)
Lansbury Ho. M16: W Ran 4B 114
(off Whalley Rd.)
Lansdale Gdns. M19: Man 4A 132
Lansdale St. BL4: Farn 1A 66
M28: Walk 4H 65
M30: Ecc 5C 96
Lansdown Cl. SK8: Chea H 6E 157
Lansdowne Av. M34: Aud 4C 104
SK6: Rom 1B 148
Lansdowne Cl. BL0: Ram 4B 12
BL2: Bolt 4F 33
Lansdowne Ct. OL9: Chad 3B 74
Lansdowne Dr. M28: Wors 3G 81
Lansdowne Ho. M20: Man 1F 143
(off Wilmslow Rd.)
Lansdowne Rd. BL2: Bolt 3F 33
M8: Man 2E 87
M30: Ecc 3F 97
M33: Sale 3A 128
M41: Urm 1A 126
OL9: Chad 3C 74
WA14: Alt 5F 139
Lansdowne Rd. Nth. M41: Urm 6A 110
Lansdowne St. OL11: Roch 4E 27
Lapwing Cen. 3C 134
Lapwing Cl. OL11: Roch 4A 26
SK15: Stal 1E 107
Lapwing Ct. M20: Man 4E 131

Lapwing La. M20: Man 4E 131
OL7: A Lyme 4D 104
SK5: Stoc 2B 134
Larch Av. M26: Rad 6B 52
M27: Swin 5E 83
M32: Stre 6D 112
SK8: Chea H 4C 156
Larch Cl. M23: Wyth 3C 140
M35: Fail 5H 89
SK6: Mar 6C 148
SK12: Poy 4F 169
Larches, The OL5: Mos 2H 93
Larch Gdns. M8: Man 6E 87
Larch Gro. M27: Ward 1D 82
OL4: Lees 1C 76
OL9: Chad 1B 74
Larch Ho. M14: Man 3G 115
(off Rusholme Pl.)
Larchlea WA15: Alt 1H 151
Larch Rd. M30: Ecc 1C 96
M31: Part 6C 124
M34: Dent 4G 119
Larch St. BL9: Bury 3H 37
OL8: O'ham 4D 74
Larchview Rd. M24: Mid 1E 73
Larchway OL16: Roch 4D 28
SK6: H Lan 6D 160
SK7: Bram 6E 157
Larchwood OL9: Chad 1G 73
SK8: Chea 5H 143
Larchwood Av. M9: Man 4B 88
Larchwood Cl. M33: Sale 5E 127
Larchwood Dr. SK9: Wilm 1H 173
Larchwood St. BL1: Bolt 3D 32
Larden Wlk. M8: Man 5D 86
(off Greyswood Av.)
Largs Wlk. M23: Wyth 5F 141
Larke Ri. M20: Man 6D 130
Larkfield Av. M38: Lit H 4D 64
Larkfield Cl. BL8: G'mount 1H 21
OL7: A Lyme 4H 91
Larkfield Gro. BL2: Bolt 5F 33
M38: Lit H 4D 64
Larkfield M. M38: Lit H 4D 64
Larkhall Ri. M22: Shar 6C 142
LARK HILL
M24 . . . . .1C 72
M29 . . . . .6A 80
LARKHILL 3A 108
Lark Hill BL4: Farn 2H 65
SK3: Stoc 3E 145
Larkhill SK15: Stal 6E 93
Larkhill Cl. WA15: Tim 5B 140
Larkhill Ct. M24: Mid 1C 72
Lark Hill La. OL3: Del, Dig 3C 62
Lark Hill Pl. OL12: Roch 2G 27
Lark Hill Rd. OL3: Dob 5B 62
SK3: Stoc 3E 145
Larkhill Rd. SK8: Chea H 6E 145
Larkhill Wlk. M8: Man 5F 87
(off Appleford Dr.)
Lark M. OL3: G'fld 5E 79
Larkside Av. M28: Walk 6A 66
Larkspur Cl. BL1: Bolt 2F 33
Larks Ri. M43: Droy 2D 104
Lark St. BL1: Bolt 2G 175 (5D 32)
BL4: Farn 2H 65
OL1: O'ham 4B 60
Larkswood Dr. SK2: Stoc 6F 147
Larkwood Cl. SK15: C'ook 4A 94
Larmuth Av. M21: Chor 3A 130
Larne Av. M32: Stre 5C 112
SK3: Stoc 4D 144
Larne St. M11: Man 5C 102
Larwood Av. SK4: Stoc 2D 144
Lascar Av. M5: Sal 5G 99
Laser Quest & The Rock 1F 111
Lashbrook Cl. M40: Man 1H 101
Lassell Fold SK14: Hyde 1F 121
Lassell St. M11: Man 6H 103
(not continuous)
Lastingham St. M40: Man 5E 89
Latchford St. OL7: A Lyme 1G 105

Latchmere Rd.—Leckenby Cl.

Latchmere Rd. M14: Man ... 1G **131**
Latham Cl. SK6: Bred ... 4F **135**
Latham St. BL1: Bolt ... 3D **32**
M11: Man ... 6H **103**
Lathbury Rd. M9: Man ... 5H **87**
M40: Man ... 5H **87**
Lathom Gro. M33: Sale ... 6E **129**
Lathom Hall Av. OL4: Spri ... 2E **77**
Lathom Rd. M20: Man ... 2H **131**
M44: Irl ... 1D **124**
Lathom St. BL9: Bury ... 1G **37**
Latimer St. OL4: O'ham ... 3G **75**
Latin St. OL16: Roch ... 5A **178** (5G **27**)
Latrigg Cres. M24: Mid ... 5G **55**
Latrobe St. M43: Droy ... 5A **104**
Lauderdale Cres.
M13: Man ... 6F **11** (1G **115**)
Launceston Cl. OL8: O'ham ... 5A **76**
SK7: Bram ... 6H **157**
Launceston Rd. M26: Rad ... 2F **51**
Laundry St. M6: Sal ... 1F **99**
Laura St. BL9: Sum ... 1C **22**
Laureate's Pl. OL4: Spri ... 2F **77**
Laureate Way M34: Dent ... 2G **135**
Laurel Av. BL3: Bolt ... 2A **50**
M14: Man ... 5E **115**
OL9: Chad ... 1F **73**
SK8: Chea ... 6H **143**
Laurel Bank SK14: Hyde ... 1A **136**
SK15: Stal ... 5F **107**
Laurel Bank Gdns. M9: Man ... 6H **71**
Laurel Ct. BL1: Bolt ... 1F **175**
M20: Man ... 3F **131**
OL16: Roch ... 5B ***28***
(off Vavasour St.)
SK4: Stoc ... 5D **132**
Laurel Dr. M38: Lit H ... 5E **65**
WA15: Tim ... 1B **152**
Laurel End La. SK4: Stoc ... 6C **132**
Laurel Grn. M34: Dent ... 5G **119**
Laurel Gro. M5: Sal ... 3C **98**
Laurel Ho. M6: Sal ... 1B **98**
SK4: Stoc ... 5D **132**
Laurel Rd. SK4: Stoc ... 5D **132**
Laurels, The OL5: Mos ... 2H **93**
SK6: H Lan ... 5D **160**
Laurels Dr. OL15: L'ough ... 6F **17**
Laurel St. BL1: Bolt ... 6A **32**
BL8: Tot ... 5H **21**
BL9: Bury ... 3H **37**
M24: Mid ... 1F **73**
OL4: O'ham ... 3H **75**
SK4: Stoc ... 1E **179** (1G **145**)
Laurel Trad. Est. OL2: O'ham ... 5G **59**
Laurel Wlk. M31: Part ... 6C **124**
Laurel Way SK7: Bram ... 5E **157**
Laurence Cl. M12: Man ... 1D **116**
Laurence Lowry Ct. *M27: Pen ... 2H* ***83***
(off Lowry Dr.)
Lauren Cl. OL4: Spri ... 3D **76**
Lauria Ter. BL2: Ain ... 4F **35**
Laurie Pl. *OL12: Roch ... 2H* ***27***
(off Duke St.)
Laurieston Ct. SK8: Chea ... 6G **143**
Lauriston Cl. M22: Shar ... 5C **142**
Lauriston Gallery, The ... *4B* ***128***
(within Waterside Arts Cen.)
Lausanne Rd. M20: Man ... 2F **131**
SK7: Bram ... 2G **157**
Lavender Cl. M23: Wyth ... 2E **141**
M33: Sale ... 4E **127**
Lavender Rd. BL4: Farn ... 6E **49**
OL4: O'ham ... 5C **76**
Lavenders Brow
SK1: Stoc ... 2H **179** (2H **145**)
Lavender St. M26: Rad ... 4F **51**
Lavender Wlk. M31: Part ... 6C **124**
Lavenham Av. M11: Man ... 4F **103**
Lavenham Bus. Pk. *OL9: O'ham ... 3C* ***74***
(off Parsons St.)
Lavenham Cl. BL9: Bury ... 4F **53**
SK7: H Gro ... 4E **159**
Laverton Cl. BL9: Bury ... 4C **38**
Lavington Av. SK8: Chea ... 5C **144**
Lavington Gro. M18: Man ... 3F **117**
Lavinia St. M30: Ecc ... 3D **96**
Lavister Av. M19: Man ... 6H **131**
Lawefield Cres. M27: Clif ... 4F **67**
Lawers Av. OL9: Chad ... 1A **74**
Lawfield Ct. SK7: Bram ... 3F **157**
Lawflat OL12: W'le ... 6C **16**
Lawler Av. M5: Sal ... 1H **113**
Lawnbank Cl. M24: Mid ... 6A **56**
Lawn Closes OL8: O'ham ... 6A **76**
Lawndale Cl. M26: Rad ... 5B **52**
Lawndale Dr. M28: Wors ... 3F **81**
Lawn Dr. M27: Swin ... 4G **83**
WA15: Tim ... 5G **139**
Lawnfold SK13: Had ... 3G **123**
Lawngreen Av. M21: Chor ... 2G **129**
Lawnhurst Av. M23: Wyth ... 3F **141**
Lawnhurst Trad. Est.
SK3: Stoc ... 6D **144**
Lawns, The SK9: Wilm ... 5B **172**
WA14: Bow ... 2E **151**
Lawnside M. M20: Man ... 4E **131**
Lawn St. BL1: Bolt ... 4B **32**
Lawnswood OL11: Roch ... 2E **41**
Lawnswood Dr. M27: Swin ... 5B **84**
M29: Tyld ... 2B **80**
Lawnswood Pk. Rd. M27: Swin ... 5A **84**
Lawrence Cl. OL12: Roch ... 2C **26**
Lawrence Pl. SK12: Poy ... 5D **168**
Lawrence Rd. M41: Urm ... 4A **110**
SK7: H Gro ... 2E **159**
WA14: Alt ... 5E **139**
Lawrence St. BL9: Bury ... 3F **53**
SK1: Stoc ... 3F **179** (2G **145**)
Lawrie Av. BL0: Ram ... 4B **12**
Lawson Av. SK8: Gat ... 6F **143**
Lawson Cl. M24: Mid ... 3C **56**
M28: Wors ... 4E **83**
Lawson Dr. WA15: Tim ... 5A **140**
Lawson Gro. M33: Sale ... 3A **128**
Lawson Rd. BL1: Bolt ... 3A **32**
Lawson St. BL1: Bolt ... 1C **32**
M9: Man ... 1G **87**
OL1: O'ham ... 1G ***75***
(off Mortimer St.)
Lawson Wlk. M34: Dent ... 1F **135**
Laws Ter. OL15: L'ough ... 4F **17**
Law St. OL11: Roch ... 1E **41**
Lawton Av. SK7: Bram ... 5G **157**
Lawton Cl. SK6: Rom ... 2F **147**
Lawton Fold OL4: Grot ... 2F **77**
Lawton Moor Rd. M23: Wyth ... 2G **141**
Lawton Rd. SK4: Stoc ... 5E **133**
Lawton Sq. OL3: Del ... 3B **62**
Lawton St. M11: Man ... 6F **103**
M43: Droy ... 3B **104**
OL3: Del ... 3A ***62***
(off King St.)
OL12: Roch ... 1D **178** (2A **28**)
SK14: Hyde ... 4C ***120***
(off Hopkins St.)
SK15: Stal ... 4F **107**
Laxey Cl. OL9: Chad ... 4B **74**
Laxey St. M40: Man ... 4D **88**
Laxfield Dr. M41: Urm ... 4H **109**
Laxford Gro. BL3: Bolt ... 1E **47**
Layard St. OL6: A Lyme ... 2G **105**
Laycock Av. BL2: Bolt ... 2F **33**
SK15: Mill ... 1H **107**
Laycock Cres. M35: Fail ... 4H **89**
Laycock Dr. SK16: Duk ... 6E **107**
Laycock Gro. M35: Fail ... 4H **89**
Laycock St. OL16: Roch ... 6D **16**
Laycock Way M34: Dent ... 2F **135**
Layfield Cl. BL8: Tot ... 3F **21**
Laystall St. M1: Man ... 5D **6** (4F **101**)
Laythe Barn Cl. OL16: Miln ... 5E **29**
Layton Av. SK14: Hyde ... 4A **120**
Layton Cl. SK1: Stoc ... 3A **146**
Layton Dr. BL4: Kea ... 3B **66**
SK6: Rom ... 6A **136**
Layton St. M40: Man ... 3H **7** (3H **101**)
Lazonby Wlk. *M13: Man ... 3B* ***116***
(off Bates St.)
Leabank St. M19: Man ... 6C **116**
Leabrook Dr. M40: Man ... 3G **89**
Leaburn Dr. M19: Man ... 5A **132**
Leach Cl. OL16: Roch ... 1C **28**
Leaches Rd.
BL0: Eden, Ram ... 1D **12**
(not continuous)
Leach M. M25: Pres ... 5F **69**
Leach St. BL3: Bolt ... 2C **48**
BL4: Farn ... 6A **50**
M18: Man ... 1D **116**
M25: Pres ... 5F **69**
OL2: O'ham ... 2G **59**
OL2: Shaw ... 1A **60**
OL16: Miln ... 6F **29**
OL16: Roch ... 5B **28**
Leach Wlk. OL4: O'ham ... 1C **76**
Leaconfield Dr. M28: Wors ... 4B **82**
Lea Ct. M35: Fail ... 4G **89**
SK4: Stoc ... 5D **132**
Leacroft Av. BL2: Bolt ... 2H **49**
Leacroft Rd. M21: Chor ... 4B **130**
Leadale Ri. OL4: Spri ... 3E **77**
Leader Williams Rd. M44: Irl ... 6D **108**
Lea Dr. M9: Man ... 6B **72**
Leafield M29: Tyld ... 2A **80**
Leafield Av. M20: Man ... 5H **131**
Lea Fld. Cl. M26: Rad ... 4G **51**
Leafield Dr. M28: Wors ... 5E **81**
SK8: Chea H ... 1B **166**
Leafield Rd. SK12: Dis ... 1G **171**
Leaford Av. M34: Dent ... 3D **118**
Leaford Cl. M34: Dent ... 3D **118**
Leaf St. BL2: Bolt ... 2G **49**
M15: Man ... 5G **9** (1D **114**)
SK5: Stoc ... 2G **133**
Leaf Ter. OL12: Roch ... 5F **15**
Lea Ga. BL2: Bolt ... 6H **19**
Leagate M41: Urm ... 6G **111**
Lea Ga. Cl. BL2: Bolt ... 6H **19**
League St. OL16: Roch ... 6A **28**
Leaholme Cl. M40: Man ... 6F **89**
Leah St. OL15: L'ough ... 4H **17**
Leak St. M16: Old T ... 5B **8**
Leamington Av. BL9: Bury ... 3E **23**
M20: Man ... 5D **130**
Leamington Ct. SK5: Stoc ... 2G **133**
Leamington Ho. *M15: Man ... 2F* ***115***
(off Denmark Rd.)
Leamington Rd. M30: Ecc ... 2D **96**
M41: Urm ... 4D **110**
SK5: Stoc ... 2G **133**
(not continuous)
Leamington St. M11: Man ... 6F **103**
OL4: O'ham ... 1A **76**
OL12: Roch ... 1A **178** (3G **27**)
Leamore Wlk. *M9: Man ... 6A* ***72***
(off Leconfield Dr.)
Lea Mt. Dr. BL9: Bury ... 1B **38**
Leam St. OL6: A Lyme ... 1B **106**
Leander Cl. M9: Man ... 1A **88**
M26: Rad ... 1G **51**
Leander Dr. OL11: Roch ... 4F **41**
Lea Rd. SK4: Stoc ... 5D **132**
SK8: H Grn ... 4F **155**
Leas, The WA15: Hale ... 2B **152**
Leaside Av. OL1: Chad ... 5B **58**
Leaside Cl. OL12: Roch ... 1F **27**
Leaside Dr. M20: Man ... 4H **131**
Leaside Gro. M28: Walk ... 6A **66**
Leaside Way SK9: Wilm ... 3F **173**
Leaton Av. M23: Wyth ... 5G **141**
Leavale Cl. M38: Lit H ... 5D **64**
Leavengreave Ct.
OL12: Whitw ... 1B **14**
Lea Vw. OL2: O'ham ... 4C **58**
Leaway OL12: W'le ... 6C **16**
Le Bas Ho. M20: Man ... 3D **130**
Lecester Rd. M8: Man ... 5F **87**
Leckenby Cl. *M28: Wors ... 5E* ***81***
(off Border Brook La.)

Leconfield Dr.—Lewes Wlk.

Leconfield Dr. M9: Man . . . 5A 72
Leconfield Rd. M30: Ecc . . . 1B 96
LECTURERS CLOSE . . . 6F 175 (1D 48)
Lecturers Cl.
BL3: Bolt . . . 6F 175 (2D 48)
Ledbroke Cl. M5: Sal . . . 5H 99
Ledburn Cl. M15: Man . . . 5D 8 (1B 114)
Ledburn Ct. M15: Man . . . 5D 8
Ledbury Av. M41: Urm . . . 4E 111
Ledbury Cl. M24: Mid . . . 3C 72
Ledbury Rd. M35: Fail . . . 1G 103
Ledbury Wlk. M9: Man . . . 6G 71
Ledge Ley SK8: Chea H . . . 5A 156
Ledsham Av. M9: Man . . . 4E 71
Ledson Rd. M23: Wyth . . . 6F 141
Ledward La. WA14: Bow . . . 3D 150
Lee Av. BL3: Bolt . . . 4B 48
WA14: B'ath . . . 4D 138
Leech Av. OL6: A Lyme . . . 6C 92
Leech Brook Av. M34: Aud . . . 1E 119
Leech Brook Cl. M34: Aud . . . 1E 119
Leech St. SK14: Hyde . . . 4D 120
SK15: Stal . . . 4E 107
Lee Cl. M44: Irl . . . 6D 108
Lee Ct. M22: Nor . . . 3C 142
Lee Cres. M32: Stre . . . 4E 113
Lee Cross OL3: Dig . . . 3F 63
Lee Dale Cl. M34: Dent . . . 5G 119
Leedale St. M12: Man . . . 5C 116
Leeds Cl. BL9: Bury . . . 4H 53
Lee Flds. OL3: Upp . . . 1D 78
Leefields Cl. OL3: Upp . . . 1D 78
Lee Fold M29: Ast . . . 4A 80
Leegate Cl. SK4: Stoc . . . 5B 132
Leegate Dr. M9: Man . . . 5B 72
Leegate Gdns. SK4: Stoc . . . 5B 132
Leegate Ho. SK4: Stoc . . . 5C 132
Leegate Rd. SK4: Stoc . . . 5B 132
(not continuous)
Leegrange Rd. M9: Man . . . 2A 88
Lee Gro. BL4: Farn . . . 1D 64
Leek St. M26: Rad . . . 4G 51
Leemans Hill St. BL8: Tot . . . 6A 22
Lee Rd. M9: Man . . . 3A 88
LEES . . . 3C 76
Lees Av. M34: Dent . . . 5E 119
LEESBROOK . . . 3B 76
Lees Brook Pk. OL4: O'ham . . . 3B 76
Lees Cotts. BL7: Tur . . . 1G 19
Lee's Ct.
SK1: Stoc . . . 3G 179 (2H 145)
LEESFIELD . . . 4B 76
Leesfield OL6: A Lyme . . . 1H 105
Lees Gro. OL4: O'ham . . . 4B 76
Lees Hall Ct. M14: Man . . . 1H 131
Lees Hall Cres. M14: Man . . . 1H 131
Lees Ho. OL4: Lees . . . 2C 76
Lee Side OL3: Dig . . . 4F 63
(not continuous)
Leeside SK4: Stoc . . . 2C 144
Lees New Rd. OL4: O'ham . . . 1B 92
Lees Pk. Av. M43: Droy . . . 3C 104
Lees Pk. Way M43: Droy . . . 3C 104
Lees Rd. OL4: O'ham . . . 2G 75
OL5: Mos . . . 6F 77
OL6: A Lyme . . . 5B 92
SK7: Bram . . . 2F 167
Lees Sq. OL6: A Lyme . . . 2A 106
Lees St. M11: Man . . . 6F 103
M24: Mid . . . 2F 73
M27: Pen . . . 2H 83
M43: Droy . . . 3B 104
OL2: Shaw . . . 6H 43
(not continuous)
OL5: Mos . . . 1G 93
OL6: A Lyme . . . 1H 105
OL8: O'ham . . . 3G 91
SK15: Stal . . . 3E 107
Lees St. E. *OL2: Shaw . . . 6A 44*
(off Lees St.)
Lees St. Ent. Trad. Est.
M18: Man . . . 1G 117
Leestone Rd. M22: Shar . . . 5C 142
Lee St. BL9: Bury . . . 3F 23
M24: Mid . . . 4B 56
OL3: Upp . . . 1D 78
OL8: O'ham . . . 6E 177 (3D 74)
OL15: L'ough . . . 3H 17
SK1: Stoc . . . 3G 179 (2H 145)
Leesway OL4: Lees . . . 4C 76
Leesway Dr. M34: Dent . . . 5G 119
Leeswood Av. M21: Chor . . . 3A 130
Leewood M27: Clif . . . 5F 67
Leewood Ct. SK4: Stoc . . . 6D 132
Left Bank M3: Man . . . 5F 5 (4C 100)
Le Gendre St. BL2: Bolt . . . 3F 33
(not continuous)
Legh Cl. SK12: Poy . . . 3E 169
Legh Ct. M33: Sale . . . 6D 128
Legh Dr. M34: Aud . . . 4B 104
SK6: Wood . . . 3H 135
Leghorn Wlk. *M11: Man . . . 4B 102*
(off Yeoman Wlk.)
Legh Rd. M7: Sal . . . 3B 86
M33: Sale . . . 6E 129
SK12: Dis . . . 1E 171
Legh St. M7: Sal . . . 4B 86
M30: Ecc . . . 4E 97
Legion Gro. M7: Sal . . . 5C 86
Legwood Ct. M41: Urm . . . 5E 111
Leicester Av. M7: Sal . . . 3D 86
M34: Dent . . . 6F 119
M43: Droy . . . 2H 103
WA15: Tim . . . 3A 140
Leicester Ct. M7: Sal . . . 2C 86
Leicester Rd. M7: Sal . . . 5C 86
M33: Sale . . . 4B 128
M35: Fail . . . 6A 90
M45: White . . . 6D 52
WA15: Hale . . . 3G 151
Leicester St. OL4: O'ham . . . 3H 75
OL7: A Lyme . . . 1H 105
OL11: Roch . . . 6A 28
SK5: Stoc . . . 5H 117
Leicester Wlk. *M7: Sal . . . 5C 86*
(off Brighton Av.)
Leigh Av. M27: Swin . . . 6F 83
SK6: Mar . . . 6C 148
Leighbrook Rd. M14: Man . . . 1F 131
Leigh Cl. BL8: Tot . . . 4G 21
Leigh Cotts. WA15: Tim . . . 1C 152
Leigh Fold SK14: Hyde . . . 2C 120
Leigh La. BL8: Bury . . . 2A 36
Leigh Rd. M28: Wors . . . 5E 81
(not continuous)
SK9: Wilm . . . 4A 172
WA15: Hale . . . 3G 151
Leigh St. BL4: Farn . . . 1H 65
BL8: Bury . . . 1H 35
OL10: H'ood . . . 3F 39
OL16: Roch . . . 4D 28
SK14: Hyde . . . 5C 120
Leighton Av. BL1: Bolt . . . 5H 31
OL15: L'ough . . . 1F 29
Leighton Dr. SK6: Mar B . . . 3G 149
Leighton Rd. M16: Old T . . . 3A 114
Leighton St. M40: Man . . . 3C 88
Leinster Rd. M27: Swin . . . 4G 83
Leinster St. BL4: Farn . . . 1G 65
Leith Av. M33: Sale . . . 5E 129
Leith Pl. OL8: O'ham . . . 1E 91
Leith Rd. M33: Sale . . . 5E 129
Le Mans Cres. BL1: Bolt . . . 4F 175 (6D 32)
Lemnos St. OL1: O'ham . . . 2G 75
Lemonpark Ind. Est. OL10: H'ood . . . 5A 40
Lena St. BL1: Bolt . . . 3D 32
M1: Man . . . 6C 6 (4F 101)
Len Cox Wlk. M4: Man . . . 4C 6
Lenfield La. OL1: O'ham . . . 6E 59
Leng Rd. M40: Man . . . 6F 89
Lenham Av. *M30: Ecc . . . 3D 96*
(off Dover St.)
Lenham Cl. SK5: Stoc . . . 3B 134
Lenham Gdns. BL2: Bolt . . . 1A 50
Lenham Towers SK5: Stoc . . . 3B 134
Lenham Wlk. M22: Wyth . . . 5B 154
Lennox Gdns. BL3: Bolt . . . 2F 47
Lennox Ho. OL6: A Lyme . . . 4D 174 (1H 105)
Lennox St. M34: Aud . . . 1E 119
OL6: A Lyme . . . 4D 174 (2A 106)
Lennox Wlk. OL10: H'ood . . . 4D 38
Lenora St. BL3: Bolt . . . 3H 47
Lenten Gro. OL10: H'ood . . . 6H 39
Lenthall Wlk. *M8: Man . . . 4D 86*
(off Crookhill Dr.)
Lentmead Dr. M40: Man . . . 2C 88
Lenton Gdns. M22: Shar . . . 6C 142
Lentworth Dr. M28: Walk . . . 4G 65
Leominster Dr. M22: Wyth . . . 2C 154
Leominster Rd. M24: Mid . . . 3D 72
Leonardin Cl. OL2: Shaw . . . 5F 43
Leonard St. BL3: Bolt . . . 4C 48
OL11: Roch . . . 4E 41
Leonard Way OL2: O'ham . . . 4F 59
Leopold Av. M20: Man . . . 4E 131
Leopold Ct. OL11: Roch . . . 4F 27
Leopold St. OL11: Roch . . . 4F 27
Lepp Cres. BL8: Bury . . . 5C 22
Leroy Dr. M9: Man . . . 1H 87
Lerryn Dr. SK7: Bram . . . 4F 157
Lesley Rd. M32: Stre . . . 6A 112
Leslie Av. BL9: Bury . . . 4F 53
OL9: Chad . . . 6B 74
Leslie Gro. WA15: Tim . . . 5A 140
Leslie Hough Way M6: Sal . . . 1A 4 (1H 99)
Leslie St. BL2: Bolt . . . 4F 33
M14: Man . . . 4F 115
Lester Rd. M38: Lit H . . . 4C 64
Lester St. M32: Stre . . . 5D 112
Letchworth Av. OL11: Roch . . . 6A 28
Letchworth St. M14: Man . . . 4F 115
Letham St. OL8: O'ham . . . 1F 91
Levedale Rd. M9: Man . . . 5A 72
Leven Cl. BL4: Kea . . . 3D 66
Levenhurst Rd. M8: Man . . . 4D 86
Levens Cl. SK8: Gat . . . 1F 155
Levens Dr. BL2: Bolt . . . 4A 34
LEVENSHULME . . . 6C 116
Levenshulme Rd. M18: Man . . . 3F 117
Levenshulme Station (Rail) . . . 6C 116
Levenshulme Swimming Pools . . . 6D 116
Levenshulme Ter. *M19: Man . . . 6C 116*
(off Stockport Rd.)
Levenshulme Trad. Est.
M19: Man . . . 5E 117
Levens Rd. SK7: H Gro . . . 3C 158
Levens St. M6: Sal . . . 6H 85
M40: Man . . . 4C 88
Levens Wlk. OL9: Chad . . . 4A 74
Leven Wlk. M23: Wyth . . . 5G 141
M45: White . . . 1A 70
Lever Av. M27: Clif . . . 1B 84
Lever Bri. Pl. BL3: Bolt . . . 2H 49
Lever Chambers BL1: Bolt . . . 5F 175
Lever Ct. M7: Sal . . . 3G 85
Lever Dr. BL3: Bolt . . . 3C 48
LEVER EDGE . . . 4C 48
Lever Edge La. BL3: Bolt . . . 5A 48
Leverett Cl. WA14: Alt . . . 6C 138
Lever Gdns. BL3: Lit L . . . 4C 50
Lever Gro. BL2: Bolt . . . 2E 49
Lever Hall Rd. BL2: Bolt . . . 6H 33
Leverhulme Av. BL3: Bolt . . . 4E 49
Lever Shop. Pde. BL3: Bolt . . . 3C 48
Lever St. BL0: Ram . . . 3C 12
BL2: Bolt . . . 2E 49
BL3: Bolt . . . 3C 48
(not continuous)
BL3: Lit L . . . 3C 50
M1: Man . . . 5B 6 (4F 101)
M24: Mid . . . 6C 56
M26: Rad . . . 2H 51
OL10: H'ood . . . 2H 39
SK7: H Gro . . . 3D 158
Lever Wlk. M24: Mid . . . 2B 72
Levington Dr. OL8: O'ham . . . 3G 91
Levi St. BL1: Bolt . . . 4F 31
Lewes Av. M34: Dent . . . 6F 119
Lewes Wlk. OL9: Chad . . . 3B 74

Lewis Av.—Linby St.

Lewis Av. M9: Man 2A 88
M41: Urm 2F 111
Lewis Dr. OL10: H'ood 4D 38
Lewisham Av. M40: Man 1D 102
Lewisham Cl. OL2: O'ham 1C 58
Lewisham Ho. *BL1: Bolt 4C 32*
(off Kenton Cl.)
Lewis Rd. M43: Droy 3G 103
SK5: Stoc 6H 117
Lewis St. M30: Ecc 4F 97
M40: Man 1H 7 (2H 101)
OL2: Shaw 2H 59
OL10: H'ood 2A 40
SK14: Hyde 4C 120
Lewtas St. M30: Ecc 4G 97
Lexton Av. M8: Man 1F 87
Leybourne Av. M19: Man 5D 116
Leybourne M. *M7: Sal 5C 86*
(off Gt. Cheetham St. E.)
Leybourne St. BL1: Bolt 3C 32
Leybrook Rd. M22: Wyth 2A 154
Leyburn Av. M32: Stre 4C 112
M41: Urm 6C 110
OL2: O'ham 3D 58
Leyburn Cl. M45: White 1E 69
Leyburne Rd. SK2: Stoc 5D 146
Leyburn Gro. *BL4: Farn 6H 49*
(off Spring St.)
SK6: Rom 1A 148
Leyburn Ho. M13: Man 3H 115
Leyburn Rd. M40: Man 1E 89
Leycett Dr. M23: Wyth 2G 141
Leycroft St. M1: Man 1D 10 (5F 101)
Leyden Wlk. M23: Wyth 1G 153
Ley Dr. OL10: H'ood 6A 40
Leyfield Av. SK6: Rom 1A 148
Leyfield Ct. SK6: Rom 1A 148
Leyfield Rd. OL16: Miln 5D 28
Ley Hey Av. SK6: Mar 4D 148
Ley Hey Ct. SK6: Mar 4D 148
LEY HEY PARK 4C 148
Ley Hey Rd. SK6: Mar 4D 148
Leyland Av. M20: Man 6H 131
M44: Irl 3F 109
SK8: Gat 5F 143
Leyland St. BL9: Bury 3F 53
SK4: Stoc 2E 179 (2G 145)
Ley La. SK6: Mar B 2G 149
Ley Rd. M29: Ast 5A 80
(not continuous)
Leys Rd. WA14: Tim 3G 139
Leyton Av. M40: Man 4D 88
Leyton Cl. BL4: Farn 6D 48
Leyton Dr. BL9: Bury 2F 53
Leyton St. OL12: Roch 1H 27
Leywell Dr. OL1: O'ham 4B 60
Leywell Rd. M9: Man 3B 88
Library La. OL9: O'ham 1D 74
Library Theatre *1H 9*
(off St Peter's Sq.)
Library Wlk. M2: Man 6H 5
Libra St. *BL1: Bolt 3B 32*
(off Darwin St.)
Lichens Cres. OL8: O'ham 6G 75
Lichfield Av. BL2: Bolt 3F 33
M29: Ast 4A 80
OL6: A Lyme 4B 92
SK5: Stoc 2G 133
WA15: Hale 2C 152
Lichfield Cl. BL4: Farn 6E 49
M26: Rad 2F 51
OL3: Dens 3G 45
Lichfield Dr. BL8: Bury 1D 36
M8: Man 4F 87
M25: Pres 1A 86
M27: Swin 5H 83
OL9: Chad 6A 58
Lichfield Rd. M26: Rad 2F 51
M30: Ecc 1H 97
M41: Urm 3F 111
Lichfield St. M6: Sal 6G 85
Lichfield Ter. OL16: Roch 1C 42
Lichfield Wlk. SK6: Rom 2G 147
Lidbrook Wlk. M12: Man 1A 116
Liddington Hall Dr. BL0: Ram 5B 12
Lidgate Gro. *BL4: Farn 1G 65*
(off Westminster St.)
M20: Man 6E 131
Lidgett Cl. M38: Lit H 4G 65
Lidiard St. M8: Man 2E 87
Lieutenant Wlk. *M5: Sal 5H 99*
(off Tatton St.)
Liffey Av. M22: Wyth 2C 154
Lifton Av. M40: Man 1A 102
Light Alders La. SK12: Dis 6E 161
Lightbirches La. OL5: Mos 1F 93
Lightborne Rd. M33: Sale 5F 127
Lightbounds Rd. BL1: Bolt 2F 31
Lightbourne Av. M27: Swin 4H 83
LIGHTBOURNE GREEN 4H 83
Lightbowne Rd. M40: Man 5C 88
Lightburn Av. OL15: L'ough 5E 17
Lightburne Av. BL1: Bolt 6H 31
Lightfoot Wlk. *M11: Man 4B 102*
(off Newcombe Cl.)
Lighthorne Av. SK3: Stoc 4B 144
Lighthorne Gro. SK3: Stoc 4B 144
Lighthorne Rd. SK3: Stoc 4B 144
Lighthouse OL15: L'ough 2A 16
Light Oaks Rd. M6: Sal 1B 98
Lightwood M28: Wors 3F 81
Lightwood Cl. BL4: Farn 6A 50
Lignum Av. OL9: Chad 1B 74
Lilac Av. BL9: Bury 6D 36
M27: Swin 3A 84
OL16: Miln 2G 43
SK14: Hyde 1B 136
Lilac Ct. M6: Sal 3G 99
Lilac Gro. M25: Pres 3G 69
M40: Man 2C 88
OL9: Chad 1B 74
Lilac La. OL8: O'ham 1D 90
Lilac Rd. OL11: Roch 3H 41
WA15: Hale 2A 152
Lilac St. SK2: Stoc 5H 145
Lilac Vw. Cl. OL2: Shaw 1A 60
Lilac Wlk. M31: Part 6C 124
Lila St. M9: Man 4B 88
Lilburn Cl. BL0: Ram 5C 12
Liley St. OL16: Roch 4A 28
Lilford Cl. M12: Man 1C 116
Lilian St. M16: Old T 3A 114
Lillian Gro. SK5: Stoc 1H 133
Lilly St. BL1: Bolt 5B 32
SK14: Hyde 1D 136
Lilmore Av. M40: Man 5E 89
Lilstock Wlk. *M9: Man 6A 72*
(off Woodmere Dr.)
Lily Av. BL4: Farn 6F 49
Lily Cl. SK3: Stoc 6F 145
LILY HILL 5F 53
Lily Hill St. M45: White 5E 53
Lily La. M9: Man 4B 88
LILY LANES 3B 92
Lily Lanes OL5: Mos 3C 92
OL6: A Lyme 3C 92
Lily St. M24: Mid 1E 73
M30: Ecc 4D 96
OL1: O'ham 6E 59
OL2: O'ham 3F 59
OL16: Miln 5F 29
Lily Thomas Ct. M11: Man 6F 103
Lima St. BL9: Bury 2H 37
Lime Av. M27: Swin 5E 83
M41: Urm 5D 110
M45: White 2F 69
Lime Bank St.
M12: Man 2H 11 (5H 101)
Limebrook Cl. M11: Man 6G 103
Lime Cl. M6: Sal 2G 99
SK16: Duk 1B 120
Lime Ct. M6: Sal 2G 99
Lime Cres. M16: Old T 3H 113
Limeditch Rd. M35: Fail 2A 90
LIME FIELD 1A 72
LIMEFIELD 5F 23
Limefield M24: Mid 1A 72
OL5: Mos 1F 93
OL16: Roch 4E 29
Limefield Av. BL4: Farn 6H 49
Limefield Brow BL9: Bury 4F 23
Limefield Cl. BL1: Bolt 1H 31
Limefield Ct. M7: Sal 2B 86
Limefield Rd. BL1: Bolt 1G 31
BL9: Bury 4F 23
M7: Sal 2B 86
M26: Rad 4F 51
Limefield Ter. M19: Man 6C 116
Lime Gdns. M24: Mid 1A 72
SK16: Duk 5H 105
LIME GATE 2C 90
Lime Ga. OL8: O'ham 1C 90
Lime Grn. OL8: O'ham 2D 90
Lime Grn. Pde. *OL8: O'ham 2D 90*
(off Lime Grn.)
Lime Grn. Rd. OL8: O'ham 3C 90
Lime Gro. BL0: Ram 2D 12
BL9: Bury 4F 23
M15: Man 6C 10 (2F 115)
M16: Old T 3H 113
M20: Man 6E 131
M25: Pres 3G 69
M28: Walk 2H 81
M34: Dent 3F 119
OL2: O'ham 1D 58
OL6: A Lyme 6A 92
OL10: H'ood 2G 39
OL15: L'ough 3F 17
SK8: Chea 5H 143
SK15: Stal 5C 106
WA15: Tim 4B 140
LIMEHURST 5G 91
Limehurst WA14: Alt 1E 151
Limehurst Av. M20: Man 1D 130
OL7: A Lyme 5G 91
Limehurst Ct. OL8: O'ham 2D 90
Limehurst Rd.
OL7: A Lyme 5G 91
Lime Kiln La. SK6: Mar 6E 149
Limekiln La. M12: Man 2G 11 (5H 101)
Lime Kilns, The M28: Wors 6C 82
Lime La. M35: Fail 4C 90
OL8: O'ham 2C 90
(not continuous)
Lime Pl. *SK16: Duk 5H 105*
(off Railway St.)
Lime Rd. M32: Stre 6D 112
Limers Ga. OL12: W'le 4H 15
Limerston Dr. M40: Man 6B 88
Limes, The OL5: Mos 2F 93
(The Birches)
OL5: Mos 2A 94
(Winterford Rd.)
SK3: Stoc 4F 145
Limesdale Cl. BL2: Bolt 2D 50
LIME SIDE 2D 90
Limeside Rd. OL8: O'ham 1C 90
Limestead Av. M8: Man 3E 87
Lime St. BL4: Farn 1A 66
BL9: Bury 5F 23
M30: Ecc 4F 97
OL1: Chad 6C 58
OL11: Roch 1E 41
SK6: Bred 5E 135
SK16: Duk 5H 105
(not continuous)
Lime Tree Cl. M41: Urm 6G 111
Lime Tree Gro. M35: Fail 4B 90
Limetrees Rd. M24: Mid 1B 72
Limetree Wlk. *M11: Man 4B 102*
(off Albert St.)
Lime Wlk. M31: Part 6B 124
SK9: Wilm 6H 165
(off Malpas Cl.)
Limewood Mdw.
M29: Ast 5A 80
Limley Gro. M21: Chor 2A 130
Linacre Av. BL3: Bolt 5C 48
Linby St. M15: Man 4E 9 (6C 100)

Lincoln Av. BL3: Lit L 4C 50
  M19: Man 6D 116
  M32: Stre 4H 111
  M34: Dent 6F 119
  M43: Droy 2A 104
  M44: Cad 5A 124
  SK8: H Grn 6F 155
Lincoln Cl. OL6: A Lyme 3B 92
  OL11: Roch 6D 178 (5A 28)
Lincoln Ct. Ind. Est.
  OL11: Roch 6D 178 (5A 28)
Lincoln Ct. M7: Sal 2C 86
  M40: Man 1D 102
Lincoln Dr. BL9: Bury 5F 37
  M25: Pres 1A 86
  OL15: L'ough 6G 17
  WA15: Tim 6B 140
Lincoln Grn. SK5: Stoc 3B 134
Lincoln Gro. BL2: Bolt 1B 34
  M13: Man 2G 115
  M33: Sale 5E 129
Lincoln Leach Ct. OL11: Roch 6H 27
Lincoln Minshull Cl. M23: Wyth 1F 141
Lincoln Pl. M1: Man 3A 10
Lincoln Ri. SK6: Rom 2G 147
Lincoln Rd. BL1: Bolt 5H 31
  M24: Mid 4E 73
  M27: Swin 4G 83
  M35: Fail 5A 90
  SK9: Wilm 6A 166
Lincoln Sq. M2: Man 6G 5
  (off Brazennose St.)
Lincoln St. M13: Man 3B 116
  M30: Ecc 4E 97
  OL9: O'ham 4B 74
  OL11: Roch 6D 178 (5A 28)
Lincoln Towers
  SK1: Stoc 4H 179 (3H 145)
Lincoln Wlk. OL10: H'ood 3E 39
Lincombe Rd. M22: Wyth 5A 154
Linda Dr. SK7: H Gro 3D 158
Lindale SK14: Hyde 2A 120
Lindale Av. BL1: Bolt 5F 31
  BL9: Bury 4G 53
  M40: Man 1F 89
  M41: Urm 4B 110
  OL2: O'ham 5C 42
  OL9: Chad 3A 74
Lindale Cl. M28: Wors 4C 80
Lindale Dr. M24: Mid 4A 56
Lindale Ri. OL2: Shaw 6B 44
Lindale Rd. M28: Wors 4C 80
Lindbury Av. SK2: Stoc 4C 146
Linden Av. BL0: Ram 3D 12
  BL3: Lit L 2C 50
  M6: Sal .5E 85
  M27: Swin 4F 83
  M33: Sale 5H 127
  M34: Aud 6D 104
  OL4: O'ham 1B 76
  WA15: Alt 6G 139
Linden Cl. BL0: Ram 3G 13
  M34: Dent 4G 119
Linden Dr. M5: Sal 5G 99
Linden Gro. M14: Man 1H 131
  M44: Cad 4B 124
  SK2: Stoc 1B 158
  SK7: Bram 3F 167
Linden Lea M33: Sale 1B 140
Linden M. M28: Wors 5D 80
Linden Pk. M19: Man 1B 132
Linden Rd. M20: Man 5E 131
  M28: Wors 5D 80
  M34: Dent 4G 119
  SK8: Chea H 2C 156
  SK15: Stal 6H 107
Linden Wlk. BL2: Bolt 6F 19
Linden Way M43: Droy 5G 103
  SK6: H Lan 6E 161
Lindenwood OL9: Chad 1G 73
Lindeth Av. M18: Man 3F 117
Lindfield Dr. BL1: Bolt 4C 32
Lindfield Est. Nth. SK9: Wilm 3D 172

Lindfield Est. Sth. SK9: Wilm 3C 172
Lindfield Rd. SK5: Stoc 6H 117
Lindinis Av. M6: Sal 3G 99
Lindisfarne OL12: Roch 1A 178
Lindisfarne Dr. M33: Sale 2B 140
Lindisfarne Dr. SK12: Poy 3D 168
Lindisfarne Pl. BL2: Bolt 3G 33
Lindisfarne Rd.
  OL7: A Lyme 6E 91
Lindley Gro. SK3: Stoc 6F 145
Lindley St. BL3: Lit L 4D 50
  BL4: Kea .3D 66
Lindleywood Rd. M14: Man 1A 132
Lindon Av. M34: Dent 5D 118
Lindop Rd. WA15: Hale 4H 151
Lindow Cl. BL8: Bury 5B 22
Lindow Common Local Nature Reserve
  . . . . .2B 172
Lindow Ct. M33: Sale 6F 129
  (off Northenden Rd.)
  SK6: Bred 6D 134
  SK9: Wilm 1B 172
Lindow Fold Dr. SK9: Wilm 5A 172
Lindow La. SK9: Wilm 2B 172
LINDOW MOSS 2A 172
Lindow Pde. SK9: Wilm 3C 172
Lindow Rd. M16: Old T 5H 113
Lindow St. M33: Sale 6F 129
Lindrick Av. M45: White 3D 68
Lindrick Cl. M40: Man 4E 89
Lindrick Ter. BL3: Bolt 2B 48
Lindsay Av. M19: Man 6B 116
  M27: Swin 4G 83
  SK8: Chea H 4D 156
Lindsay Cl. OL4: O'ham 5B 60
Lindsay Rd. M19: Man 1B 132
Lindsay St. SK15: Stal 3F 107
Lindsell Rd. WA14: W Tim 3E 139
Lindsgate Dr. WA15: Tim 4B 140
Lindside Wlk. M9: Man 6A 72
  (off Woodmere Dr.)
Lind St. M40: Man 4H 7 (3A 102)
Lindum Av. M16: Old T 3A 114
Lindum Ct. OL10: H'ood 3A 40
Lindum St. M14: Man 4F 115
Lindwall Cl. M23: Wyth 1H 141
Lindy Av. M27: Clif 6H 67
Linear Walkway M30: Ecc 2F 97
Linebank Grn. WA14: Alt 5G 139
  (off Grosvenor Rd.)
Linehan Cl. SK4: Stoc 1H 143
Lineholme OL2: O'ham 5C 58
Linen Ct. M3: Sal 2C 4 (2B 100)
Lines Rd. M43: Droy 4B 104
  M44: Irl .1D 124
Linfield Cl. BL2: Bolt 1H 33
Linfield St. M11: Man 4D 102
Linford Av. M40: Man 1E 89
Lingard Cl. M34: Aud 5C 104
Lingard La. SK6: Bred 4D 134
Lingard Rd. M22: Nor 2B 142
Lingard St. SK5: Stoc 1H 133
Lingard Ter. M34: Aud 5C 104
Lingcrest Cl. M19: Man 2E 133
Lingdale Rd. SK8: Chea H 3B 156
Lingdale Wlk. M40: Man 4C 88
Lingfield M16: W Ran 4D 114
  (off Whalley Rd.)
Lingfield Av. M33: Sale 1D 138
  SK7: H Gro 3F 159
Lingfield Cl. BL4: Farn 2G 65
  BL8: Bury 4C 22
Lingfield Rd. M11: Man 3E 103
Lingfield Wlk. OL9: Chad 2C 74
  (off Kempton Way)
Lingholme Dr. M24: Mid 5G 55
Lingmell Cl. BL1: Bolt 5F 31
  M24: Mid .5F 55
  M41: Urm 3B 110
Lingmoor Cl. M24: Mid 5G 55
Lingmoor Rd. BL1: Bolt 4F 31
Lingmoor Wlk. M15: Man 6H 9
Lings Wlk. M22: Wyth 4C 154

Linguard Bus. Pk.
  OL16: Roch 5D 178 (5A 28)
Linhope Cl. SK4: Stoc 6A 132
Liniden Cres. BL8: Tot 6H 21
Link, The OL2: Shaw 5F 43
  SK5: Stoc 3C 134
  SK9: Hand 4H 165
Link Av. M41: Urm 6A 112
Linkfield Dr. M28: Wors 5D 80
Link La. OL8: O'ham 1E 91
Link Rd. M33: Sale 2F 139
  OL4: Spri .2D 76
Links, The M40: Man 4E 89
  SK14: Hyde 1E 121
Links Av. M35: Fail 6H 89
Links Cres. M25: Pres 1C 86
Links Dr. BL6: Los 6B 30
Linksfield M34: Dent 2F 119
Linkside Av. OL2: O'ham 2D 58
Links Pl. OL6: A Lyme 5C 92
Links Ri. M41: Urm 3C 110
Links Rd. BL2: Bolt 1C 34
  BL6: Los .6B 30
  OL10: H'ood 5H 39
  SK6: Mar .1D 160
  SK6: Rom 6B 136
  SK9: Wilm 6B 172
Links Vw. M25: Pres 2G 85
  OL11: Roch 5D 26
Links Vw. Ct. M45: White 2D 68
Links Way OL9: Chad 1C 74
Linksway M25: Pres 1B 86
  M27: Swin 5A 84
  SK8: Gat .1E 155
Linksway Cl. SK4: Stoc 4C 132
Linksway Dr. BL9: Bury 4G 53
Linkwang Ind. Est. M24: Mid 1D 72
Linley Dr. OL4: O'ham 5B 76
Linley Gro. BL0: Ram 1A 22
Linley Rd. M33: Sale 4B 128
  SK8: Chea H 5D 156
Linley St. M26: Rad 2E 53
Linnell Dr. OL11: Roch 3A 26
Linnet Cl. M34: Aud 4C 104
  SK2: Stoc 6F 147
Linnet Dr. BL9: Bury 1H 37
  M44: Irl .4E 109
Linnet Hill OL11: Roch 5E 27
Linnets Wood M. M28: Walk 6A 66
Linnett Cl. M12: Man 3B 116
Linney La. OL2: Shaw 6A 44
Linney Rd. SK7: Bram 3F 157
Linn St. M8: Man 2E 87
LINNYSHAW 6A 66
Linnyshaw Cl. BL3: Bolt 4G 47
Linnyshaw Ind. Est. M28: Walk 6B 66
Linnyshaw La. M28: Walk 5A 66
Linsford Ct. BL3: Bolt 5G 47
Linslade Gdns. BL3: Bolt 2C 48
  (off Derby St.)
Linslade Ho. M5: Sal 4F 99
  (off Buckingham St.)
Linslade Wlk. M9: Man 4H 87
  (off Carisbrook St.)
Linstead Dr. M8: Man 5D 86
Linthorpe Wlk. BL3: Bolt 3H 47
Linton Av. RI 9: Bury 6F 23
  M34: Dent 4A 118
Linton Cl. M4: Man 1G 11 (5H 101)
Linton Rd. M33: Sale 3C 128
Linton Va. M26: Rad 1D 66
Linton Wlk. M7: Sal 3F 85
  (not continuous)
Linwood Gro. M12: Man 5C 116
Linwood St. M35: Fail 5E 89
Lion Brow M9: Man 1H 87
Lion Fold La. M9: Man 6H 71
Lions Dr. M27: Swin 4A 84
Lion St. M9: Man 1H 87
Lisbon St. OL12: Roch 2E 27
Lisburn Av. M21: Chor 6A 114
  M33: Sale 6A 128
Lisburne Av. SK2: Stoc 5D 146

Lisburne Cl. SK2: Stoc 5D 146
Lisburne Ct. SK2: Stoc 5D 146
Lisburne La. SK2: Stoc 6C 146
Lisburn Rd. M40: Man 3C 88
Liscard Av. M14: Man 6F 115
Lisetta Av. OL4: O'ham 4H 75
Liskeard Av. OL2: O'ham 4F 59
Liskeard Cl. OL16: Roch 2D 28
Liskeard Dr. SK7: Bram 6H 157
Lisle St. OL12: Roch 1D 178 (2A 28)
Lismore Av. BL3: Bolt 2F 47
    SK3: Stoc 4D 144
Lismore Rd. SK16: Duk 6B 106
Lismore Wlk. M22: Wyth 5C 154
Lismore Way M41: Urm 2F 111
Lissadel Science Pk. M6: Sal 2H 99
Lissadel St. M6: Sal 1G 99
Lisson Gro. WA15: Hale 3G 151
Lister Rd. M24: Mid 3F 71
Lister St. BL3: Bolt 4H 47
Liston St. SK16: Duk 5C 106
Litcham Cl. M1: Man 3C 10 (6F 101)
Litchfield Ct. M24: Mid 2F 71
Litchfield Dr. M28: Wors 4C 82
Litherland Av. M22: Wyth 3C 154
Litherland Rd. BL3: Bolt 5C 48
    M33: Sale 6E 129
Little 66 BL9: Bury 6H 37
Lit. Ancoats St. M1: Man 4C 6 (3F 101)
Littlebank St. OL4: O'ham 3H 75
LITTLE BOLTON 4B 98
Lit. Bolton Ter. M5: Sal 3C 98
LITTLEBOROUGH 4H 17
Littleborough Coach House & Heritage Cen.
    . . . . .4H 17

Littleborough Ind. Est.
    OL15: L'ough 4G 17
Littleborough Sports Cen. 2H 17
Littleborough Station (Rail) 4H 17
Littlebourne Wlk. BL1: Bolt 5E 19
Littlebrook Cl. SK8: Chea H 1E 157
    SK13: Had 3H 123
Lit. Brook Rd. M33: Sale 2E 139
Little Brow BL7: Bro X 4E 19
LITTLE CLEGG 1F 29
Lit. Clegg Rd. OL15: L'ough 1F 29
Littledale St. OL12: Roch 3G 27
    (not continuous)
Lit. David St. M1: Man 1B 10 (5E 101)
Lit. Ees La. M33: Sale 3H 127
Lit. Egerton St. SK1: Stoc 1F 179
Little Fields SK14: Mot 3C 122
Little Flatt OL12: Roch 2D 26
LITTLE GREEN 6E 57
Littlegreen Gdns. M6: Sal 2F 99
Littleham Wlk. M18: Man 2E 117
    (off Hampden Cres.)
Lit. Harwood Lee BL2: Bolt 2H 33
Littlehaven Cl. M12: Man 2A 116
Lit. Heath La. WA14: D Mas 6A 138
Lit. Hey St. OL2: O'ham 3G 59
Littlehills Cl. M24: Mid 6A 56
Lit. Holme St. M4: Man 5H 7 (3H 101)
Lit. Holme Wlk. BL3: Bolt 3D 48
Lit. Howarth Way OL12: Roch 5C 16
LITTLE HULTON 4E 65
Lit. John St. M3: Man 1E 9 (4C 100)
Little La. M9: Man 5F 71
LITTLE LEVER 4D 50
Little Lever Leisure Cen. 4B 50
Lit. Lever St. M1: Man 5C 6 (4F 101)
    (not continuous)
Little Mdw. Rd. WA14: Bow 4D 150
Little Mdws. BL7: Bro X 4D 18
Lit. Moor Clough BL7: Eger 1C 18
Little Moor Cotts. SK1: Stoc 3B 146
    (off Hampson St.)
Littlemoor Ho. OL4: O'ham 1A 76
Littlemoor La. OL3: Dig 3D 62
    OL4: O'ham 1A 76
Littlemoor Rd. SK14: Mot 5C 122
LITTLEMOSS 3C 104
Littlemoss Bus. Pk. M43: Droy 2C 104

Lit. Moss La. M27: Clif 1H 83
Littlemoss Rd. M43: Droy 2C 104
Lit. Nelson St. M4: Man . . .2B 6 (2E 101)
Lit. Oak Cl. OL4: Lees 3C 76
LITTLE PARK 1B 72
Lit. Peter St. M15: Man 3F 9 (6C 100)
Lit. Pitt St. M1: Man 5D 6
Lit. Quay St. M3: Man 6G 5 (4D 100)
Littler Av. M21: Chor 4A 130
Littlers Point M17: T Pk 2D 112
Lit. Stones Rd. BL7: Eger 1C 18
Littleton Rd. M6: Sal 3F 85
    M7: Sal 3F 85
Little Town OL8: O'ham 5C 74
Little Underbank
    SK1: Stoc 2G 179 (2H 145)
LITTLEWOOD 6F 23
Littlewood OL2: O'ham 3G 59
    (off Oldham Rd.)
Littlewood Av. BL9: Bury 6F 23
Littlewood Rd. M22: Wyth 1A 154
Littlewood St. M6: Sal 3E 99
Litton Bank SK13: Gam 6G 123
    (off Riber Bank)
Littondale Cl. OL2: O'ham 2E 59
Litton Fold SK13: Gam 6G 123
    (off Litton M.)
Litton Gdns. SK13: Gam 6G 123
Litton M. SK13: Gam 6G 123
Liverpool Cl. SK5: Stoc 2G 133
Liverpool Rd. M3: Man 1D 8 (5B 100)
    M30: Ecc 2H 109
    M44: Cad, Irl 6A 124
Liverpool Road Steam Railway . . .5C 100
    (off Liverpool Rd.)
Liverpool St. M5: Sal 3D 98
    M6: Sal 5A 4 (3E 99)
    SK5: Stoc 2G 133
Liverstudd Av. SK5: Stoc 1H 133
Liverton Ct. M9: Man 4F 71
    (off Liverton Dr.)
Liverton Dr. M9: Man 4F 71
Livesey St. M4: Man 1E 7 (2G 101)
    M19: Man 1D 132
    OL1: O'ham 1A 76
Livingstone Av. M22: Wyth 3H 153
Livingstone Av. OL5: Mos 2F 93
Livingstone Pl. M16: Old T 2H 113
    (off Carver St.)
Livingstone St. OL4: Lees 4C 76
    OL4: Spri 3E 77
Livsey Cl. BL1: Bolt 1F 175 (4D 32)
Livsey La. BL0: H'ood 3E 39
Livsey St. M45: White 1F 69
    OL16: Roch 4D 178 (4A 28)
Lizard St. M1: Man 5C 6
Lizmar Ter. M9: Man 3B 88
Llanberis Rd. SK8: Chea H 4A 156
Llanfair Rd. SK3: Stoc 3E 145
Lloyd Av. SK8: Gat 5E 143
Lloyd Ct. M12: Man 1B 116
    (off Kelsall St.)
Lloyd Rd. M19: Man 2D 132
Lloyds Ct. WA14: Alt 3A 174 (1F 151)
Lloyd's Gdns. WA14: Alt 2F 151
Lloyd Sq. WA14: Alt 3A 174 (1F 151)
Lloyd St. M2: Man 6G 5 (4D 100)
    (not continuous)
    M43: Droy 4H 103
    OL10: H'ood 4H 39
    OL11: Roch 1F 41
    OL12: Whitw 4A 14
    SK4: Stoc 6F 133
    (not continuous)
    WA14: Alt 3A 174 (1F 151)
    WA15: Alt 3B 174 (1F 151)
Lloyd St. Nth. M14: Man 3E 115
    M15: Man 3E 115
Lloyd St. Sth. M14: Man 6E 115
Lloyd Wright Av. M11: Man 5A 102
L & M Bus. Pk. WA14: Alt 5E 139
LOBDEN 2G 15

Lobden Cres. OL12: Whitw 2E 15
Lobelia Av. BL4: Farn 6E 49
Lobelia Wlk. M31: Part 6C 124
    (off Redbrook Av.)
Lobley Cl. OL12: Roch 1B 28
Lochawe Cl. OL10: H'ood 4E 39
Lochinver Gro. OL10: H'ood 4E 39
Lochmaddy Cl. SK7: H Gro 4F 159
Lock Bldg., The M1: Man . . .2H 9 (5D 100)
Lock Cl. OL10: H'ood 5A 40
Lockes Yd. M1: Man 3H 9
Lockett Gdns. M3: Sal 3D 4 (3B 100)
Lockett St. M6: Sal 6G 85
    M8: Sal 1C 100
Lockhart Cl. M12: Man 2C 116
Lockhart St. OL16: Roch 6B 28
Lockingate St. OL6: A Lyme 5H 91
Locking Ga. Ri. OL4: O'ham 6C 60
Lock Keepers M. M27: Pen 3D 84
Locklands La. M44: Irl 5E 109
Lock La. BL3: Bolt 3C 46
    BL6: Los 3C 46
    M31: Part 6B 124
Lock Rd. WA14: Alt 5E 139
Locks, The M44: Irl 6F 109
Lock Side SK15: Stal 3F 107
    (off Mottram Rd.)
Lockside SK6: Mar 5E 149
Lockside Vw. OL5: Mos 6A 78
    SK15: Stal 3F 107
Locksley Cl. SK4: Stoc 1E 145
Lockton Cl. M1: Man 3D 10 (6F 101)
    SK5: Stoc 3G 133
Lockton Cl. M1: Man 3C 10
Lock Vw. M26: Rad 1D 66
Lockwood St. M12: Man 4D 116
Loddon Wlk. M9: Man 3A 88
    (off Hillier St.)
Lodge, The SK13: Had 1H 123
Lodge Av. M41: Urm 5G 111
Lodge Bank SK13: Had 1H 123
Lodge Bank Rd. OL15: L'ough 6F 17
Lodge Brow M26: Rad 5B 52
Lodge Cl. SK16: Duk 6C 106
Lodge Ct. SK4: Stoc 1B 144
Lodge Dr. M29: Ast 5A 80
Lodge Farm Cl. SK7: Bram 3G 157
Lodge Fold M43: Droy 3B 104
Lodge Grn. SK16: Duk 6C 106
Lodge La. OL3: Del 2A 62
    (not continuous)
    SK14: Hyde 3B 120
    SK16: Duk 5B 106
Lodge M. BL0: Ram 3C 12
Lodgepole Cl. M30: Ecc 5B 96
Lodge Rd. M26: Rad 5B 52
Lodges, The M28: Wors 3C 82
Lodgeside Cl. M43: Droy 3B 104
Lodge St. BL0: Ram 1E 13
    (Bye Rd.)
    BL0: Ram 3C 12
    (Kay Brow)
    M24: Mid 6C 56
    M40: Man 6A 88
    OL7: A Lyme 4F 105
    OL12: W'le 6C 16
    OL15: L'ough 3H 17
    SK14: Hyde 2C 120
Lodge Vw. BL2: Bolt 5E 33
    (not continuous)
    M43: Droy 3B 104
Loen Cres. BL1: Bolt 2A 32
Loganberry Av. M6: Sal 2G 99
Logan St. BL1: Bolt 6C 18
Logwood Av. BL8: Bury 2D 36
Loisine Cl. OL11: Roch 2D 40
Lok Fu Gdns. M8: Man 6C 86
Lomas Cl. M19: Man 6A 132
Lomas La. OL6: A Lyme 5A 174 (2G 105)
Lomas St. M24: Mid 6D 56
    M35: Fail 2A 90
    SK3: Stoc 6E 179 (4F 145)

Lomax's Bldgs. BL2: Bolt . . .5G **175** (1D **48**)
Lomax St. BL1: Bolt 3C **32**
  BL4: Farn 6G **49**
  BL8: G'mount 2H **21**
  BL9: Bury 2G **37**
  M1: Man 5E **7** (4G **101**)
  M26: Rad 5A **52**
  M45: White 5E **53**
  OL12: Roch 1C **178** (2H **27**)
  OL15: L'ough 2G **17**
Lombard Cl. SK6: Bred 5F **135**
Lombard Gro. M14: Man 1G **131**
Lombard St. OL1: O'ham 2F **177** (2E **75**)
  OL12: Roch 3F **27**
Lombardy St. M6: Sal 2G **99**
  WA15: Hale 2A **152**
Lomond Av. M32: Stre 4D **112**
  WA15: Hale 2A **152**
Lomond Cl. SK2: Stoc 2A **158**
Lomond Dr. BL8: Bury 1B **36**
Lomond Lodge M8: Man 1D **86**
Lomond Pl. BL3: Bolt 1E **47**
Lomond Rd. M22: Wyth 3D **154**
  SK8: H Grn 3E **155**
Lomond Ter. OL16: Roch 1C **42**
London Pl. SK1: Stoc 3G **179** (2H **145**)
London Rd. M1: Man 6C **6** (5F **101**)
  OL1: O'ham 6H **59**
  SK7: H Gro 2D **158**
  SK9: A Edg 5G **173**
  SK10: Adl 6C **168**
London Rd. Nth. SK12: Poy 3E **169**
London Rd. Sth. SK12: Poy 5D **168**
London Sq. SK1: Stoc 3G **179** (2H **145**)
London St. BL3: Bolt 3C **48**
  M6: Sal 1H **99**
  M45: White 2F **69**
Longacres Dr. OL12: Whitw 4B **14**
Longacres La. OL12: Whitw 3B **14**
Longacres Rd. WA15: Haleb 6C **152**
Longacre St. M1: Man 1E **11** (4G **101**)
Longbow Ct. M7: Sal 6B **86**
Longbridge Rd. M17: T Pk 1A **112**
Longcauseway BL4: Farn 2H **65**
Longcliffe Wlk. BL1: Bolt 3D **32**
                (off Hibbert St.)
Longcrag Wlk. M15: Man 2E **115**
                (off Botham Cl.)
Longcroft Dr. WA14: Alt 1D **150**
Longcroft Gro. M23: Wyth 4G **141**
  M34: Aud 5B **104**
Long Cft. La. SK8: Chea H 5A **156**
Longdale Cl. OL2: O'ham 3C **58**
Longdale Dr. SK14: Mot 4C **122**
Longdale Gdns. SK14: Mot 4C **122**
Longdell Wlk. M9: Man 3A **88**
          (off Dalbeattie St.)
Longden Av. OL4: O'ham 4C **60**
Longden Ct. SK7: Bram 2G **167**
Longdendale Recreation Cen. 4B **122**
Longden Rd. M12: Man 5C **116**
Longden St. BL1: Bolt 5A **32**
Longfellow Av. BL3: Bolt 4H **47**
Longfellow Cres. OL3: O'ham 3B **60**
Longfellow Wlk. M34: Dent 2G **135**
         (off Wordsworth Rd.)
Longfield BL9: Bury 6G **23**
  M25: Pres 4G **69**
Longfield Av. M41: Urm 6E **111**
  SK8: H Grn 6G **155**
  WA15: Tim 5C **140**
Longfield Cen. M25: Pres 4G **69**
Longfield Cl. SK14: Hyde 1C **120**
Longfield Cotts. M41: Urm 5D **110**
         (off Stamford Rd.)
Longfield Cres. OL4: O'ham 6A **60**
Longfield Dr. M41: Urm 5D **110**
Longfield Gdns. M44: Cad 5B **124**
Longfield La. OL4: O'ham 6B **60**
Longfield Pk. OL2: Shaw 1G **59**
Longfield Rd. BL3: Bolt 5G **47**
  M23: Wyth 3F **141**
  OL2: Shaw 1G **59**
  OL11: Roch 3E **27**

Longford Av. BL1: Bolt 3A **32**
  M32: Stre 5E **113**
Longford Cl. M32: Stre 4E **113**
Longford Cotts. M32: Stre 5F **113**
Longford Ho. M21: Chor 5F **113**
Longford Pk. 5F **113**
Longford Pl. M14: Man 3A **116**
Longford Rd. M21: Chor 6G **113**
  M32: Stre 4E **113**
  SK5: Stoc 6H **117**
Longford Rd. W. M19: Man 6F **117**
  SK5: Stoc 6F **117**
Longford St. M18: Man 1F **117**
  OL10: H'ood 3H **39**
Longford Trad. Est. M32: Stre 4D **112**
Longford Wharf M32: Stre 5E **113**
Long Grain Pl. SK2: Stoc 6D **146**
Longham Cl. M11: Man 4A **102**
  SK7: Bram 4F **157**
Long Hey WA15: Hale 2A **152**
Longhey Rd. M22: Wyth 6B **142**
Long Hill OL11: Roch 1F **41**
Longhill Wlk. M40: Man 5C **88**
          (off Halliford Rd.)
Longhirst Cl. BL1: Bolt 2H **31**
Longhope Rd. M22: Wyth 2H **153**
Longhurst La. SK6: Mar B 4F **149**
Longhurst Rd. M9: Man 5F **71**
Longlands Dr. SK14: Hyde 4F **121**
Long La. BL2: Bolt 2H **49**
  BL9: Bury 4E **23**
  OL3: Dob 5C **62**
  OL3: G'fld 3F **79**
  OL9: Chad 6H **73**
  SK12: Dis 3H **171**
Longlevens Rd. M22: Wyth 3A **154**
Longley Dr. M28: Wors 5D **82**
Longley La. M22: Nor 3B **142**
Longley Rd. M28: Walk 1H **81**
Longley St. OL1: O'ham 5G **177**
  OL2: Shaw 2H **59**
Long Marl Dr. SK9: Hand 3B **166**
Longmead Av. SK7: H Gro 3D **158**
Longmeade Gdns. SK9: Wilm 3F **173**
Long Meadow BL7: Bro X 4G **19**
  SK14: Hyde 1D **120**
Longmeadow SK8: Chea H 6E **157**
Longmeadow Gro. M34: Dent 5E **119**
Long Mdw. Pas. SK14: Hyde 4B **120**
Longmead Rd. M6: Sal 6D **84**
Longmead Way M24: Mid 6D **56**
Longmere Av. M22: Wyth 2B **154**
Long Millgate M3: Man 3H **5** (3D **100**)
Longnor Grn. SK13: Gam 5F **123**
        (off Brassington Cres.)
Longnor M. SK13: Gam 5F **123**
Longnor Rd. SK7: H Gro 5E **159**
  SK8: H Grn 6H **155**
Longnor Way SK13: Gam 5F **123**
        (off Brassington Cres.)
Longport Av. M20: Man 2E **131**
Longridge BL7: Bro X 3G **19**
Longridge Av. SK15: Stal 1E **107**
Longridge Cres. BL1: Bolt 3F **31**
Longridge Dr. BL8: Bury 5A **36**
  OL10: H'ood 3D **38**
Long Row SK15: C'ook 4B **94**
Long Rushes OL2: Shaw 5F **43**
Longshaw Av. M27: Pen 2A **84**
Longshaw Dr. M28: Walk 5E **65**
Longshaw Ford Rd. BL1: Bolt 1F **31**
Longshut La. SK1: Stoc 6H **179** (4H **145**)
Longshut La. W.
  SK2: Stoc 6G **179** (4H **145**)
Long Sides Rd. WA15: Haleb 6C **152**
LONG SIGHT 5E **59**
LONGSIGHT 3C **116**
Longsight Bk. BL2: Bolt 6A **20**
Longsight Ind. Est. M12: Man 3B **116**
Longsight La. BL2: Bolt 2H **33**
           (not continuous)
  SK8: Chea H 2B **166**
Longsight Lodge BL2: Bolt 1A **34**

Longsight Rd. BL0: Ram 6A **12**
  BL8: G'mount 6A **12**
  M18: Man 4D **116**
Longsight Shop. Cen. M22: Man 3B **116**
Longsons, The SK5: Stoc 6H **133**
         (off Lancashire Hill)
Longson St. BL1: Bolt 4E **33**
Long St. M18: Man 1G **117**
  M24: Mid 6C **56**
  M27: Swin 4H **83**
Longthwaite Cl. M24: Mid 5H **55**
Longton Av. M20: Man 4E **131**
Longton Rd. M6: Sal 6C **84**
  M9: Man 4G **71**
Longton St. BL9: Bury 3F **53**
Longtown Gdns. BL1: Bolt 3C **32**
        (off Gladstone St.)
Longview Dr. M27: Ward 2E **83**
Long Wlk. M31: Part 6B **124**
Longwall Av. M28: Wors 3F **81**
Longwood Av. SK2: Stoc 5B **146**
  SK6: Rom 6C **136**
Long Wood Rd. M17: T Pk 1B **112**
  M22: Wyth 2C **154**
Long Wood Rd. Est. M17: T Pk 1B **112**
Longworth Cl. M41: Urm 6A **110**
Longworth Clough BL7: Eger 1B **18**
Longworth La. BL7: Eger 1A **18**
Longworth Rd. BL7: Bel, Bolt, Eger . .1A **18**
Longworth St. BL2: Bolt 6G **33**
  M3: Man 1F **9** (5C **100**)
Lonsdale Av. M27: Swin 6F **83**
  M41: Urm 3D **110**
  OL16: Roch 6B **28**
  SK5: Stoc 4H **117**
Lonsdale Ct. M24: Mid 2E **73**
Lonsdale Gro. BL4: Farn 1G **65**
        (off Westminster St.)
Lonsdale Rd. BL1: Bolt 5H **31**
  M19: Man 5D **116**
  OL8: O'ham 1C **90**
Lonsdale St. BL8: Bury 3C **36**
  M40: Man 5E **89**
Loom St. M4: Man 4D **6** (3F **101**)
Loonies Ct. SK1: Stoc 3G **179** (3H **145**)
Lord Byron Sq. M50: Sal 4F **99**
Lord Derby Rd. SK14: Hyde 4B **136**
Lord Kitchener Ct. M33: Sale 3B **128**
Lord La. M35: Fail 1G **103**
Lord La. M. M35: Fail 5H **89**
Lord Napier Dr. M5: Sal 6H **99**
Lord Nth. St. M40: Man 1A **102**
Lord's Av. M5: Sal 3D **98**
Lordsfield Av. OL7: A Lyme 1H **105**
Lord's Fold BL1: Bolt 3F **31**
        (off New Church Rd.)
Lord Sheldon Way
  OL6: A Lyme 4A **174** (4D **104**)
  OL7: A Lyme 4D **104**
Lordship Cl. M9: Man 2B **88**
Lordsmead St. M15: Man . . .5D **8** (1B **114**)
Lord Sq. OL16: Roch 3B **178** (4H **27**)
Lord's Stile La. BL7: Bro X 3E **19**
Lords St. M44: Cad 4A **124**
Lord St. BL3: Lit L 4D **50**
  BL4: Kea 1A **66**
  BL9: Bury 4D **176** (3F **37**)
             (Cecil St.)
  BL9: Bury . . . .
           (Waterfold La.)
  M3: Man 1H **5** (1D **100**)
  M4: Man 1A **6** (2E **101**)
  M7: Sal 1A **100**
  M24: Mid 5C **56**
  M26: Rad 4A **52**
  M34: Dent 3A **118**
  OL1: O'ham 1G **177** (1F **75**)
         (not continuous)
  OL6: A Lyme 1H **105**
  OL15: L'ough 4H **17**
  SK1: Stoc 3F **179** (2H **145**)
  SK14: Holl 3F **123**
  SK15: Duk, Stal 5D **106**

Lord St. SK16: Duk 5C **106**
Loretto Rd. M41: Urm 6H **111**
Lorgill Cl. SK3: Stoc 1H **157**
Loring St. M40: Man 6E **89**
Lorland Rd. SK3: Stoc 4D **144**
Lorna Gro. SK8: Gat 5D **142**
Lorna Rd. SK8: Chea H 3D **156**
Lorna Way M44: Irl 1F **125**
Lorne Av. OL2: O'ham 4B **58**
Lorne Gro. M41: Urm 5G **111**
  SK3: Stoc 5G **145**
Lorne Rd. M14: Man 1G **131**
Lorne St. BL1: Bolt 3F **175** (6D **32**)
  BL4: Farn 5G **49**
  M30: Ecc 5D **96**
  OL5: Mos 2G **93**
  OL8: O'ham 5E **75**
  OL10: H'ood 3H **39**
  OL12: Roch 6B **16**
Lorne Way OL10: H'ood 4D **38**
Lorraine Cl. OL10: H'ood 5A **40**
Lorraine Rd. WA15: Tim 6A **140**
Lorton Cl. M24: Mid 5G **55**
  M28: Wors 5D **80**
Lorton Gro. BL2: Bolt 5B **34**
LOSTOCK 1C **46**
Lostock Av. M19: Man 6D **116**
  M33: Sale 5E **129**
  M41: Urm 4D **110**
  SK7: H Gro 4B **158**
  SK12: Poy 3B **168**
Lostock Circ. M41: Urm 3H **111**
Lostock Cl. OL10: H'ood 2F **39**
Lostock Ct. M32: Stre 3H **111**
  SK9: Hand 3H **165**
Lostock Dr. BL9: Bury 5F **23**
Lostock Gro. M32: Stre 4B **112**
LOSTOCK HALL FOLD 6A **30**
Lostock Hall Rd. SK12: Poy 4B **168**
LOSTOCK JUNCTION 2D **46**
Lostock Junc. La. BL6: Los 1C **46**
Lostock Pk. Dr. BL6: Los 6A **30**
Lostock Rd. M5: Sal 3E **99**
  M41: Urm 3E **111**
  SK9: Hand 3H **165**
  SK12: Poy 5D **168**
Lostock Station (Rail) 1C **46**
Lostock Wlk. M45: White 6A **54**
Lothian Av. M30: Ecc 2D **96**
Lottery Row BL1: Bolt 4G **175** (6D **32**)
Lottery St. SK3: Stoc 2F **145**
Lottie St. M27: Pen 3A **84**
Loughborough Cl. M33: Sale 6F **127**
Loughfield M41: Urm 5C **110**
Loughrigg Av. OL2: O'ham 5C **42**
Loughrigg Cl. M29: Ast 4A **80**
Louisa St. BL1: Bolt 3C **32**
  M11: Man 5E **103**
  M28: Walk 5H **65**
Louis Av. BL9: Bury 1F **37**
Louise Cl. OL12: Roch 6C **16**
Louise Gdns. OL12: Roch 6C **16**
Louise St. OL12: Roch 6B **16**
  (not continuous)
Louvaine Av. BL1: Bolt 1F **31**
Louvaine Cl. M18: Man 1G **117**
Louvain St. M35: Fail 4G **89**
Lovalle St. BL1: Bolt 4A **32**
Lovat Rd. BL2: Bolt 6B **34**
Love La. BL0: Eden, Ram 4H **13**
  SK4: Stoc 1G **145**
Lovell Ct. M8: Man 1D **86**
Lovell Dr. SK14: Hyde 3D **120**
Lovers La. OL4: Gras 3G **77**
Lovett Wlk. M22: Nor 3C **142**
Low Bank OL12: Roch 6C **16**
Lowbrook Av. M9: Man 6D **72**
Lowbrook La. OL4: Wat 6D **60**
Lowcock St. M7: Sal 1E **5** (1C **100**)
Lowcroft Cres. OL9: Chad 1H **73**
LOW CROMPTON 6F **43**
Low Crompton Rd. OL2: O'ham 1E **59**

Lowcross Rd. M40: Man 5C **88**
Lowe Grn. OL2: O'ham 5D **58**
Lwr. Albion St. M1: Man . . .2C **10** (5F **101**)
Lwr. Alma St. SK16: Duk 4H **105**
Lwr. Alt Hill OL6: A Lyme 3A **92**
LOWER ARTHURS 3D **78**
Lwr. Bamford Cl. M24: Mid 5C **56**
Lowerbank M34: Dent 2F **119**
Lwr. Bank Cl. SK13: Had 4H **123**
Lwr. Bank St. BL9: Bury . . .3A **176** (3E **37**)
Lwr. Bank St. SK13: Had 3G **123**
Lower Beechwood OL11: Roch 6F **27**
Lower Beestow OL5: Mos 5G **93**
Lower Bennett St. SK14: Hyde 3A **120**
Lwr. Bents La. SK6: Bred 5F **135**
Lower Birches OL4: O'ham 5D **76**
LOWER BREDBURY 1D **146**
Lwr. Bridgeman St.
  BL2: Bolt 6H **175** (1E **49**)
Lower Broadacre SK15: Stal 1A **122**
Lwr. Brooklands Pde. M8: Man 1C **86**
  (off Counthill Dr.)
Lwr. Brook La. M28: Wors 6C **82**
LOWER BROUGHTON 1B **4** (1C **100**)
Lwr. Broughton Rd. M7: Sal . . .1C **4** (6A **86**)
Lwr. Bury St. SK4: Stoc 1F **145**
Lwr. Byrom St. M3: Man 1E **9** (5C **100**)
Lower Calderbrook OL15: L'ough 2A **16**
  (off Calderbrook Rd.)
Lwr. Carr La. OL3: G'fld 3D **78**
Lower Carrs OL6: A Lyme 6B **92**
  SK1: Stoc 3H **179** (1H **145**)
Lower Chatham St.
  M1: Man 3A **10** (6E **101**)
  M15: Man 4A **10** (6E **101**)
Lower Chesham BL9: Bury 2H **37**
  (off Chesham Cres.)
Lower Crimble OL11: Roch 1A **40**
  (not continuous)
Lower Cft. M45: White 3C **68**
Lowercroft Ind. Pk. BL8: Bury 2H **35**
Lowercroft Rd. BL8: Bury 3G **35**
Lower Crossbank OL4: Lees 1D **76**
LOWER CRUMPSALL 3G **87**
Lwr. Darcy St. BL2: Bolt 2G **49**
Lower Dingle OL1: O'ham 3A **60**
Lwr. Edge Av. M1: Man . . .1F **177** (1E **75**)
Lowerfield Dr. SK2: Stoc 6F **147**
Lowerfields OL3: Dob 6C **62**
  OL8: O'ham 5H **75**
Lower Fields Ri. OL2: Shaw 1A **58**
LOWER FOLD 6E **15**
Lower Fold BL2: Bolt 1B **34**
  M34: Dent 4G **119**
  SK6: Mar B 3F **149**
Lower Fold Av. OL2: O'ham 3G **59**
Lowerfold Cl. OL12: Roch 5E **15**
Lwr. Fold Cotts. SK6: H Lan 6B **160**
Lowerfold Cres. OL12: Roch 5E **15**
Lowerfold Dr. OL12: Roch 5E **15**
Lowerfold Way OL12: Roch 5E **15**
Lwr. Frenches Dr. OL3: G'fld 4C **78**
Lower Gate OL16: Roch 3B **178**
Lwr. Goodwin Cl. BL2: Bolt 2A **34**
Lwr. Goodwin Fold BL2: Bolt 2A **34**
  (off Lwr. Goodwin Cl.)
Lower Grn. M24: Mid 4B **72**
  OL6: A Lyme 1A **106**
  OL12: Roch 2E **27**
Lower Hague SK22: N Mil 5H **161**
LOWER HEALEY 6G **15**
Lwr. Healey La. OL12: Roch 6G **15**
Lwr. Hey La. OL5: Mos 6A **78**
Lower Higham Vis. Cen. 1E **137**
Lower Hillgate
  SK1: Stoc 2G **179** (2H **145**)
LOWER HINDS 5D **36**
Lower Ho. Dr. BL6: Los 6C **30**
Lower Ho. St. OL1: O'ham 1H **75**
Lower Ho. Wlk. BL7: Bro X 3E **19**
Lwr. Hyde Grn. SK15: Mill 6A **94**
LOWER IRLAM 1D **124**
Lwr. Jowkin La. OL11: Roch 4H **25**

LOWER KERSAL 5H **85**
Lwr. Knoll Rd. OL3: Dig 2E **63**
Lower Knotts BL2: Bolt 5B **20**
Lower La. OL16: Miln 6D **28**
  OL16: Roch 2C **42**
Lower Lea SK12: Dis 1G **171**
Lwr. Lime Rd. OL8: O'ham 3C **90**
Lower Marlands BL7: Bro X 3D **18**
Lower Mead BL7: Eger 2D **18**
Lwr. Mdw. Rd. SK9: Hand 3A **166**
Lwr. Moat Cl. SK4: Stoc 6G **133**
Lwr. Monton Rd. M30: Ecc 3G **97**
LOWER MOOR 1C **44**
Lwr. Ormond St. M1: Man . . .3A **10** (6E **101**)
  M15: Man 4A **10** (6E **101**)
Lwr. Park Cres. SK12: Poy 1C **168**
Lwr. Park Rd. M14: Man 3G **115**
  SK12: Poy 2B **168**
LOWER PLACE 1A **42**
LOWER POOLS 3G **31**
Lower Pools BL1: Bolt 3F **31**
Lwr. Rawson St. BL4: Farn 6A **50**
Lower Rd. BL0: Ram 1D **12**
LOWER ROE CROSS 2B **122**
LOWER RUSHCROFT 4G **43**
Lwr. Rushcroft OL2: Shaw 5H **43**
Lwr. Seedley Rd. M6: Sal 2E **99**
Lwr. Sheriff St.
  OL12: Roch 2A **178** (3G **27**)
Lower Standrings OL11: Roch 3C **26**
  (off Bagslate Moor Rd.)
Lower Stones OL3: Del 4A **62**
Lower St. BL4: Farn 2G **65**
  OL16: Roch 1A **42**
Lwr. Strines Rd. SK6: Mar 6E **149**
LOWER SUMMERSEAT 2C **22**
Lwr. Sutherland St. M27: Swin 3G **83**
Lower Tenterfield OL11: Roch 1H **25**
  (off Hutchinson Rd.)
Lwr. Tong BL7: Bro X 4D **18**
Lwr. Turf La. OL4: Scout 2E **77**
Lwr. Tweedale St.
  OL11: Roch 6B **178** (5H **27**)
Lwr. Vickers St. M40: Man . . .2H **7** (2H **101**)
Lwr. Victoria St. OL9: Chad 2B **74**
Lwr. Wharf St.
  OL6: A Lyme 6C **174** (3H **105**)
Lwr. Wheat End OL16: Roch 3B **28**
Lwr. Woodhill Rd. BL8: Bury 2D **36**
  (not continuous)
Lowerwood La. BL2: Bolt 4F **33**
Lwr. Wrigley Grn. OL3: Dig 4E **63**
Lowes, The WA14: Bow 4D **150**
Lowes Rd. BL9: Bury 5F **23**
Lowestead Rd. M11: Man 3E **103**
Lowestoft St. M14: Man 5F **115**
Lowe St. M26: Rad 3H **51**
  M34: Dent 4H **119**
  SK1: Stoc 3G **179** (2H **145**)
Loweswater Rd. BL4: Farn 2C **64**
  SK8: Gat 2F **155**
Loweswater Ter. SK15: Stal 1E **107**
  (off Ullswater Ter.)
Lowfell Wlk. M18: Man 4F **117**
Lowfield Av. M43: Droy 2H **103**
  OL6: A Lyme 6D **92**
Lowfield Gro. SK2: Stoc . . .6G **179** (4H **145**)
Lowfield Rd. SK2: Stoc . . .6G **179** (5G **145**)
  SK3: Stoc 5G **145**
Lowfield Wlk. M9: Man 6A **72**
  (off Normanton Dr.)
Lowgill Wlk. M18: Man 2E **117**
  (off Beyer Cl.)
Low Gro. La. OL3: G'fld 4A **78**
Low Hill OL12: Roch 6C **16**
Lowhouse Cl. OL16: Miln 4G **29**
Lowick Av. BL3: Bolt 4E **49**

Lowick Cl. SK7: H Gro 3D 158
Lowick Grn. SK6: Wood 4F 135
Lowland Gro. OL7: A Lyme 5G 91
Lowland Rd. SK2: Stoc 1B 158
Lowlands Cl. M24: Mid 4E 73
Low Lea Rd. SK6: Mar B 4F 149
Low Mdws. OL2: O'ham 1D 58
Lowndes Cl. SK2: Stoc 5B 146
Lowndes La. SK2: Stoc 4B 146
Lowndes St. BL1: Bolt 5H 31
Lowndes Wlk. M13: Man 6E 11
Lownorth Rd. M22: Wyth 5C 154
Lowood Av. M41: Urm 3B 110
Lowood Cl. OL16: Miln 5F 29
Lowrey Wlk. M9: Man 4A 88
                (off Craigend Dr.)
Low Rd. OL4: Wat 6E 61
Lowry, The 6E 99
Lowry Ct. M14: Man 1G 131
Lowry Ct. M45: White 5D 52
            SK14: Mot 3C 122
Lowry Dr. M27: Pen 2H 83
            SK6: Mar B 3F 149
Lowry Gro. SK14: Mot 4B 122
Lowry Ho. M30: Ecc 3G 97
              (off Monton La.)
Lowry Lodge M16: Old T 2B 114
              (off Hamer Dr.)
Lowry Outlet Mall M50: Sal 6F 99
Lowry Wlk. BL1: Bolt 4B 32
Lows, The OL4: O'ham 4H 75
              (not continuous)
LOW SIDE 5A 76
Lowside Av. BL1: Bolt 1C 46
            SK6: Wood 4A 136
Lowside Dr. OL4: O'ham 4H 75
Low's Pl. OL12: Roch 1A 28
Lowstern Cl. BL7: Eger 2C 18
Lowther Av. M18: Man 4D 116
              OL2: O'ham 5C 42
              WA15: Tim 5A 140
Lowther Cl. M25: Pres 6G 69
Lowther Ct. M25: Pres 6F 69
Lowther Cres. M24: Mid 6A 56
Lowther Gdns. M41: Urm 4H 109
Lowther Rd. M8: Man 2E 87
              M25: Pres 6F 69
              OL11: Roch 1G 41
Lowther St. BL3: Bolt 5E 49
Lowthorpe St. M14: Man 5E 115
Lowton Av. M9: Man 4B 88
Lowton Rd. M33: Sale 1F 139
Lowton St. M26: Rad 3A 52
Low Wood Cl. SK7: Bram 4E 157
Low Wood Rd. M34: Dent 3A 118
Loxford Cl. M15: Man 5H 9
Loxford St. M15: Man 5H 9 (1D 114)
Loxham St. BL3: Bolt 5H 49
Loxley Chase BL1: Bolt 3C 32
Loxley Wlk. M40: Man 1A 102
              (off Filby Wlk.)
Loynd St. BL0: Ram 3D 12
Lubeck St. M9: Man 3A 88
Lucas Rd. BL4: Farn 1E 65
Lucas St. BL9: Bury 2G 37
              OL4: O'ham 2H 75
Lucas Wlk. M11: Man 5B 102
Lucerne Cl. OL9: Chad 3C 74
Lucerne Rd. SK7: Bram 2G 157
Lucien Cl. M12: Man 2A 116
Luciol Cl. M29: Tyld 2A 80
Lucknow St. OL11: Roch 6H 27
Lucy St. BL1: Bolt 4G 31
              M7: Sal 6B 86
              M15: Man 6C 8 (1B 114)
              SK3: Stoc 5E 179 (3G 145)
Ludford Gro. M33: Sale 1H 139
Ludgate Hill M4: Man 2C 6 (2F 101)
Ludgate Rd. M40: Man 1E 103
              OL11: Roch 3A 42
Ludgate St. M4: Man 2B 6 (2E 101)
Ludlow Av. M27: Clif 1A 84
              M45: White 3H 69

Ludlow Pk. OL4: O'ham 3B 76
              (off Lees Brook Pk.)
Ludlow Rd. SK2: Stoc 3C 146
Ludlow Towers SK5: Stoc 2C 134
Ludwell Wlk. M8: Man 5E 87
              (off Barnsdale Dr.)
Lugano Rd. SK7: Bram 2G 157
Luke Fold SK15: Stal 5H 107
Luke Kirby Ct. M27: Pen 2H 83
Luke Rd. M43: Droy 4B 104
Luke Wlk. M8: Man 5F 87
              (off Appleford Dr.)
Lullington Cl. M22: Wyth 4A 154
Lullington Rd. M6: Sal 1D 98
Lulworth Av. M41: Urm 5B 110
Lulworth Cl. BL8: Bury 5C 22
Lulworth Cres. M35: Fail 3B 90
Lulworth Gdns. M23: Wyth 3F 141
Lulworth Rd. BL3: Bolt 4G 47
              M24: Mid 5C 56
              M30: Ecc 2E 97
Lumb Carr Av. BL0: Ram 5A 12
Lumb Carr Rd. BL8: Holc 6A 12
Lumb Cl. SK7: Bram 1G 167
Lumber La. M28: Wors 3A 82
Lumb Ho. SK7: Bram 1G 167
Lumb La. M34: Aud 4C 104
              (not continuous)
              M43: Droy 2C 104
              (not continuous)
              OL7: Droy 2C 104
              SK7: Bram 1G 167
Lumley Cl. M14: Man 3F 115
Lumn Hollow SK14: Hyde 5C 120
              (not continuous)
Lumn Rd. SK14: Hyde 5C 120
Lumn's La. M27: Clif 1C 84
Lumn St. BL9: Bury 2F 23
Lumsdale Rd. M32: Stre 3A 112
Lumsden St. BL3: Bolt 2C 48
Lum St. BL1: Bolt 2H 175 (5E 33)
Lunar Wlk. BL1: Bolt 1A 48
Luna St. M4: Man 4C 6 (3F 101)
Lundale Wlk. M40: Man 5C 88
              (off Craiglands Av.)
Lund Av. M26: Rad 1B 68
Lund St. M16: Old T 6A 8 (1A 114)
Lundy Av. M21: Chor 4A 130
Lune Cl. M45: White 1G 69
Lune Gro. OL10: H'ood 2E 39
Lune St. OL8: O'ham 5E 75
Lune Wlk. M43: Droy 5B 104
              (off Ellen St.)
              M45: White 1G 69
Lune Way SK5: Stoc 4H 133
Lune Av. M18: Man 1H 117
Lupin Av. BL4: Farn 6E 49
Lupin Cl. OL1: O'ham 4C 60
Lupton St. M34: Dent 3F 119
Lurden Wlk. OL9: Chad 5A 74
Lurgan Av. M33: Sale 6C 128
Lutener Av. WA14: W Tim 3E 139
Luton Dr. M23: Wyth 1G 153
Luton Rd. SK5: Stoc 1H 133
Luton St. BL3: Bolt 3C 49
              BL8: Bury 4B 36
Luxhall Wlk. M40: Man 1D 102
Luxor Gro. M34: Dent 4H 117
LUZLEY 4F 93
LUZLEY BROOK 3F 59
Luzley Brook Rd. OL2: O'ham ..2G 59
Luzley Rd. OL5: Mos 3F 93
              OL6: A Lyme, Mos ...6F 93
              SK15: Stal 2F 107
Lyceum Pas. OL16: Roch ...3B 178 (4H 27)
Lyceum Pl. M15: Man 4A 10 (6E 101)
Lychgate Ct. BL2: Bolt 5A 34
              OL4: O'ham 5C 76
Lychgate M. M21: Chor 1G 129
              SK4: Stoc 1A 144
Lychwood SK6: Mar 5D 148

Lydbrook Cl. BL1: Bolt 1C 48
Lydden Av. M11: Man 2F 103
Lydford OL11: Roch 6A 178 (5G 27)
Lydford Gdns. BL2: Bolt 2B 50
Lydford St. M6: Sal 1H 99
Lydford Wlk. M13: Man 6F 11
LYDGATE 3G 77
Lydgate Av. BL2: Bolt 5A 34
Lydgate Cl. M34: Dent 6H 119
              M45: White 6G 53
              SK15: C'ook 5A 94
Lydgate Dr. OL4: O'ham 4A 76
Lydgate Fold OL4: Lyd 4G 77
Lydgate Rd. M33: Sale 1C 140
              M43: Droy 2G 103
Lydgate Wlk. M45: White 6G 53
Lydiate Cl. BL3: Bolt 4D 48
Lydiat La. SK9: A Edg 6G 173
Lydney Av. SK8: H Grn 6G 155
Lydney Rd. M41: Urm 4H 109
Lyefield Wlk. OL16: Roch 5B 28
Lyme Av. SK9: Wilm 6F 165
Lyme Clough Way M24: Mid 3B 56
Lyme Ct. SK7: H Gro 2D 158
              SK14: Hyde 4C 120
Lymefield Ct. SK2: Stoc 4D 146
Lymefield Dr. M28: Wors 4E 81
Lymefield Gro. SK2: Stoc 5B 146
Lyme Gro. M33: Sale 6C 128
              M43: Droy 4H 103
              SK2: Stoc ...6G 179 (4H 145)
              SK6: Mar 6D 148
              SK6: Rom 1B 148
              WA14: Alt 3A 174 (1E 151)
Lyme Hall 6E 171
Lyme Ho. SK4: Stoc 2A 144
Lyme Lea Cl. SK8: Chea H 5D 156
Lyme Pk. 6E 171
Lyme Pk. Country Pk. 5E 171
Lyme Pl. SK16: Duk 5H 105
Lyme Rd. SK7: H Gro 4E 159
              SK12: Dis 6E 161
              SK12: Poy 4A 170
Lymes, The WA14: Bow 4E 151
Lyme St. SK4: Stoc 1A 144
              SK7: H Gro 2D 158
Lyme Ter. SK16: Duk 4H 105
Lyme Vw. Ct. SK6: Rom 1B 148
Lymewood Dr. SK9: Wilm 1H 173
              SK12: Dis 1F 171
Lymington Cl. M24: Mid 4D 72
Lymington Dr. M23: Wyth 2D 140
Lymm Cl. M28: Walk 6E 65
              SK3: Stoc 5F 145
Lymm Rd. WA14: Lit B 5A 150
Lymm Wlk. SK8: Chea 1C 156
Lyncombe Cl. SK8: Chea H 1D 166
Lyndale Av. M27: Swin 5F 83
              SK5: Stoc 4H 117
Lyndale Dr. OL15: L'ough 3G 17
Lyndene Av. M28: Wors 3C 82
Lyndene Ct. OL10: H'ood 2G 39
Lyndene Gdns. SK8: Gat 5F 143
Lyndene Rd. M22: Wyth 6B 142
Lyndhurst Av. M25: Pres 6C 70
              M33: Sale 6H 127
              M34: Dent 4E 119
              M41: Urm 3E 111
              M44: Irl 4F 109
              OL6: A Lyme 6H 91
              OL9: Chad 4H 73
              OL11: Roch 5F 41
              SK6: Bred 5F 135
              SK7: H Gro 4C 158
Lyndhurst Cl. SK9: Wilm 4A 172
Lyndhurst Dr. WA15: Hale 3A 152
Lyndhurst Gdns. M24: Mid 1A 72
Lyndhurst Rd. M20: Man 5E 131
              M32: Stre 5B 112
              OL8: O'ham 6D 74
              SK5: Stoc 5G 117
Lyndhurst St. M6: Sal 3E 99
Lyndhurst Vw. SK16: Duk 4A 106

Lyndon Cl. BL8: Tot 5H 21
  OL4: Scout 1F 77
Lyndon Cft. OL8: O'ham 5C 74
Lyndon Rd. M44: Irl 6D 108
Lyne Edge Cres. SK16: Duk 6D 106
Lyne Edge Rd. SK16: Duk 6E 107
Lyneham Wlk. M7: Sal 5D 86
            (off Highclere Av.)
Lyne Vw. SK14: Hyde 1D 120
Lyngard Cl. SK9: Wilm 6A 166
Lyngarth Ho. WA14: Alt 5G 139
           (off Grosvenor Rd.)
Lyngate Cl. SK1: Stoc 3A 146
Lyn Gro. OL10: H'ood 2E 39
Lynham Dr. OL10: H'ood 5H 39
Lynmouth Av. M20: Man 3E 131
  M41: Urm 1D 126
  OL2: O'ham 4C 58
  OL8: O'ham 6F 75
  SK5: Stoc 2G 133
Lynmouth Cl. M26: Rad 3C 52
  OL9: Chad 6G 57
Lynmouth Ct. M25: Pres 6F 69
Lynmouth Gro. M25: Pres 6F 69
Lynn Av. M33: Sale 3C 128
Lynn Dr. M43: Droy 3C 103
Lynnfield Ho. WA14: Alt 6F 139
Lynn St. OL9: O'ham 5C 74
Lynnwood Dr. OL11: Roch 3C 26
Lynnwood Rd. M19: Man 1H 143
Lynroyle Way OL11: Roch 2F 41
Lynside Wlk. M22: Wyth 6B 154
Lynsted Av. BL3: Bolt 4E 49
Lynthorpe Av. M44: Cad 3B 124
Lynthorpe Rd. M40: Man 1F 89
Lynton Av. M27: Pen 2H 83
  M41: Urm 5G 109
  M44: Cad 3C 124
  OL2: O'ham 4C 58
  OL8: O'ham 1C 90
  OL11: Roch 2D 40
  SK14: Hat 5G 121
Lynton Cl. OL9: Chad 6H 57
Lynton Ct. SK9: A Edg 4G 173
Lynton Cres. M28: Walk 3H 81
Lynton Dr. M19: Man 2B 132
  M25: Pres 3A 70
  SK6: H Lan 5C 160
Lynton Gro. WA15: Tim 6H 139
Lynton La. SK9: A Edg 4G 173
Lynton Lea M26: Rad 3C 52
Lynton M. SK9: A Edg 4G 173
Lynton Pk. Rd. SK8: Chea H 5B 156
Lynton Rd. BL3: Bolt 5A 48
  M21: Chor 6G 113
  M27: Pen 2H 83
  M29: Tyld 3B 80
  SK4: Stoc 4E 133
  SK8: Gat 6G 143
Lynton St. M14: Man 5F 115
Lynton Ter. M26: Rad 2D 66
Lyntonvale Av. SK8: Gat 5F 143
Lynton Wlk. SK14: Hat 5G 121
Lyn Town Trad. Est. M30: Ecc 3F 97
Lynway Dr. M20: Man 4F 131
Lynway Gro. M24: Mid 5D 56
Lynwell Rd. M30: Ecc 3F 97
Lynwood SK9: Wilm 3D 172
  WA15: Hale 5A 152
Lynwood Av. BL3: Bolt 5F 49
  M16: W Ran 5A 114
  M30: Ecc 3F 97
Lynwood Cl. OL7: A Lyme 4G 91
Lynwood Ct. M8: Man 1D 86
Lynwood Dr. OL4: O'ham 1B 76
Lynwood Gro. BL2: Bolt 1H 33
  M33: Sale 4C 128
  M34: Aud 4C 104
  SK4: Stoc 3E 133
Lyon Av. M28: Wors 3C 82
Lyon Ind. Est. WA14: B'ath 4D 138
Lyon Rd. BL4: Kea 3A 66
  WA14: B'ath 4E 139

Lyon Rd. Ind. Est. BL4: Kea 3A 66
Lyons Dr. BL8: Bury 4A 36
Lyon's Fold M33: Sale 3B 128
Lyons Rd. M17: T Pk 6A 98
Lyon St. M27: Swin 4G 83
  OL2: Shaw 6H 43
Lyon Way SK5: Stoc 3G 133
Lyra Pl. M7: Sal 1B 4 (2A 100)
Lyric Theatre 6E 99
            (in The Lowry)
Lysander Cl. M14: Man 1F 131
Lytham Av. M21: Chor 2A 130
Lytham Cl. OL6: A Lyme 5C 92
Lytham Ct. OL6: A Lyme 5C 92
Lytham Dr. OL10: H'ood 4G 39
  SK7: Bram 6A 158
Lytham Rd. M14: Man 6A 116
  M41: Urm 5G 109
  SK8: H Grn 4F 155
Lytham St. OL12: Roch 6G 15
  SK3: Stoc 5H 145
Lytherton Av. M44: Cad 5B 124
Lyth St. M14: Man 2H 131
Lytton Av. M8: Man 5E 87
Lytton Rd. M43: Droy 3A 104
Lytton St. BL1: Bolt 3B 32

M

Mabel Av. BL3: Bolt 4E 49
  M28: Wors 4C 82
Mabel Rd. M35: Fail 2A 90
Mabel's Brow BL4: Kea 2A 66
Mabel St. BL1: Bolt 5A 32
  M40: Man 6F 89
  OL12: Roch 1F 27
Mabfield Rd. M14: Man 6G 115
Mabledon Cl. SK8: H Grn 5H 155
Mabs Cl. OL6: A Lyme 3B 106
Macauley St. OL2: O'ham 3E 59
Macauley Cl. SK16: Duk 6E 107
Macauley Rd. M16: Old T 5H 113
  SK5: Stoc 6F 117
Macauley St. OL11: Roch 3F 41
Macauley Way M34: Dent 1G 135
Mc Bride Riverside Pk. M24: Mid . . .1B 72
McCall Wlk. M11: Man 3D 102
            (off Trimdon Cl.)
Macclesfield Rd. SK7: H Gro 6F 159
  SK9: A Edg 5G 173
  SK9: Wilm 2F 173
McConnell Rd. M40: Man 4C 88
McCready Dr. M5: Sal 5H 99
Macdonald Av. BL4: Farn 2E 65
Macdonald Rd. M44: Irl 2C 124
Macdonald St. OL8: O'ham 5F 75
McDonna St. BL1: Bolt 2A 32
McDonough Cl. OL8: O'ham 6G 75
McDowall Wlk. M8: Man 1F 87
Macefin Av. M21: Chor 5B 130
McEvoy St. BL1: Bolt 3D 32
Macfarren St. M12: Man 4C 116
McGinty Pl. M1: Man 2A 10
Macintosh Mills M15: Man . .3H 9 (6D 100)
McKean St. BL3: Bolt 3E 49
Mackenzie Gro. BL1: Bolt 1B 32
Mackenzie Ind. Pk. SK3: Stoc 5D 144
Mackenzie Rd. M7: Sal 5H 85
Mackenzie St. BL1: Bolt 6B 18
  M12: Man 4C 116
Mackenzie Wlk. OL1: O'ham 2C 60
Mackeson Dr. OL6: A Lyme 1C 106
Mackeson Rd. OL6: A Lyme 1C 106
McKie Cl. OL8: O'ham 6G 75
Mackintosh Way
  OL1: O'ham 2G 177 (2F 75)
Mackworth St. M15: Man 2C 114
McLaren Ct. M21: Chor 6G 113
Maclaren Dr. M8: Man 2C 86
McLean Dr. M44: Irl 3E 109
Maclure Rd. OL11: Roch 5C 178 (5H 27)
Macnair Ct. SK6: Mar 6E 149

Macnair M. SK6: Mar 6E 149
McNaught St. OL16: Roch 5B 28
Mconnel Apartments M4: Man 4D 6
Madams Wood Rd.
  M28: Walk 6D 64
Maddison Rd. M43: Droy 5H 103
Madeira Pl. M30: Ecc 3D 96
Madeley Cl. WA14: Hale 5G 151
Madeley Dr. OL9: Chad 3B 74
Madeley Gdns. BL1: Bolt 3C 32
          (off Hargreaves St.)
  OL12: Roch 2F 27
Maden's Sq. OL15: L'ough 4H 17
Maden Vw. OL11: Roch 5E 41
Maden Wlk. OL9: Chad 1B 74
Madison Apartments
  M16: Old T 2H 113
Madison Av. M34: Aud 5C 104
  SK8: Chea H 3C 156
Madison Gdns. BL5: W'ton 5A 46
  M35: Fail 4G 89
Madison Pk. BL5: W'ton 5A 46
Madison St. M18: Man 1G 117
Madras Rd. SK3: Stoc 4E 145
Mafeking Av. BL9: Bury 6G 23
Mafeking Rd. BL2: Bolt 6A 34
Mafeking St. OL8: O'ham 6C 74
Magdala St. OL1: O'ham 1E 75
  OL10: H'ood 5A 40
Magda Rd. SK2: Stoc 6C 146
Magenta Av. M44: Irl 3C 124
Magna Carta Ct. M6: Sal 5B 84
Magnetic Ho. M50: Sal 6F 99
Magnolia Cl. M31: Part 6C 124
          (off Redbrook Rd.)
  M33: Sale 4E 127
Magnolia Ct. M6: Sal 3G 99
  M33: Sale 3E 127
          (off Magnolia Cl.)
Magnolia Dr. M8: Man 5E 87
Magnum Cen. OL16: Roch 5A 28
Magpie Cl. M43: Droy 2C 104
Magpie La. OL4: O'ham 5B 76
Magpie Wlk. M11: Man 4B 102
          (off Newcombe Cl.)
Maher Gdns. M15: Man 3C 114
Mahogany Wlk. M33: Sale 4E 127
          (off Epping Dr.)
Mahood St. SK3: Stoc 4F 145
Maida St. M12: Man 5D 116
Maiden Cl. OL7: A Lyme 5G 91
Maiden M. M27: Swin 4H 83
Maidford Cl. M4: Man 5H 7 (4H 101)
  M32: Stre 5E 113
Maidstone Av. M21: Chor 6G 113
Maidstone M. M21: Chor 6G 113
Maidstone Rd. SK4: Stoc 6H 131
Maidstone Wlk. M34: Dent 6G 119
         (off Worcester Av.)
Main Av. M17: T Pk 2C 112
  M19: Man 2B 132
Main Dr. WA14: D Mas 2A 150
Maine Rd. M14: Man 4E 115
          (not continuous)
Mainhill Wlk. M40: Man 6E 89
          (off Marlinford Dr.)
Mainprice Cl. M6: Sal 2F 99
Main Rd. M27: Clif 6C 68
  OL9: O'ham 2C 74
Main St. M35: Fail 3H 89
  SK14: Hyde 3B 120
Mainwaring Dr. SK9: Wilm 1G 173
Mainwaring Ter. M23: Wyth 1G 141
Mainway M24: Mid 3B 72
Mainway E. M24: Mid 3E 73
Mainwood Rd. WA15: Tim 6C 140
Mainwood Sq. M13: Man 4D 10
Maismore Rd. M22: Wyth 4G 153
Maitland Av. M21: Chor 4A 130
Maitland Cl. OL12: Roch 6C 16
Maitland St. SK1: Stoc 4B 146
Maitland Wlk. OL9: Chad 1B 74
Maizefield Cl. M33: Sale 5F 129

Major St. BL0: Ram 3B **12**
　M1: Man 1A **10** (5E **101**)
　OL16: Miln 5F **29**
Major Wlk. M5: Sal 5H **99**
　(off Robert Hall St.)
Makants Cl. M29: Tyld 3C **80**
Makant St. BL1: Bolt 2A **32**
Makepeace Wlk. M8: Man 1C **86**
Makin Ct. OL10: H'ood 4H **39**
Makinson La. BL6: Hor 1A **30**
Makinson Yd. BL1: Bolt 3E **175**
Makin St. M1: Man 2A **10** (5E **101**)
Makkah Cl. Man 6C **88**
Malaga Av. M90: Man A 6H **153**
Malakoff St. SK15: Stal 5C **106**
Malbern Ind. Est. M34: Dent 3D **118**
Malbrook Wlk. M13: Man 5E **11**
Malby St. OL1: O'ham 1G **177** (1F **75**)
Malcolm Av. M27: Clif 6A **68**
Malcolm Dr. M27: Clif 1A **84**
Malcolm St. OL11: Roch 2F **41**
Malden Gro. M23: Wyth 4G **141**
Maldon Cl. BL3: Lit L 4C **50**
　SK2: Stoc 5G **147**
Maldon Cres. M27: Swin 5H **83**
Maldon Dr. M30: Ecc 1G **97**
Maldon St. OL11: Roch 6C **178** (6H **27**)
Maldwyn Av. BL3: Bolt 5H **47**
　M8: Man 1E **87**
Malford Dr. M8: Man 5D **86**
Malgam Dr. M20: Man 3F **143**
Malham Cl. OL2: O'ham 3D **58**
Malham Cl. SK2: Stoc 5D **146**
Malham Dr. M45: White 1G **69**
Malham Gdns. *BL3: Bolt* *4A 48*
　(off Maltby Dr.)
Malimson Bourne *M7: Sal* *5B 86*
　(off Hilton St. Nth.)
Mall, The BL9: Bury 4C **176** (3F **37**)
　M30: Ecc 3H **97**
　M33: Sale 5B **128**
　SK14: Hyde 5B **120**
　SK15: Stal 1A **122**
Mallaig Wlk. *M11: Man* *5E 103*
　(off Brigham St.)
Mallard Cl. OL8: O'ham 1D **90**
　SK2: Stoc 6G **147**
　SK16: Duk 6C **106**
Mallard Ct. M50: Sal 5D **98**
　SK8: H Grn 5G **155**
Mallard Cres. SK12: Poy 3A **168**
Mallard Grn. WA14: B'ath 3D **138**
Mallards Reach SK6: Rom 1H **147**
Mallard St. M1: Man 3A **10** (5E **101**)
Mallett Cres. BL1: Bolt 3F **31**
Malley Gdns. OL5: Mos 3H **93**
Malley Wlk. *M9: Man* *6A 72*
　(off Greendale Dr.)
Malling Rd. M23: Wyth 1G **153**
Mallison St. BL1: Bolt 2D **32**
Mallory Av. OL7: A Lyme 6H **91**
Mallory Ct. WA14: Bow 2E **151**
Mallory Rd. SK14: Hyde 2E **121**
Mallory Wlk. M23: Wyth 3D **140**
Mallow Cft. OL16: Roch 1C **42**
Mallowdale M28: Wors 3F **81**
Mallowdale Av. M14: Man 1F **131**
Mallowdale Cl. BL1: Bolt 6D **30**
Mallowdale Rd. SK2: Stoc 6E **147**
Mallow St. M15: Man 5E **9** (1C **114**)
Mallow Wlk. *M31: Part* *6D 124*
　(off Broom Rd.)
Malmesbury Cl. SK12: Poy 3D **168**
Malmesbury Rd. SK8: Chea H 1D **166**
Malpas Cl. SK8: Chea 1C **156**
　SK9: Wilm 6H **165**
Malpas Dr. WA14: Tim 3G **139**
Malpas St. M12: Man 1C **116**
　OL1: O'ham 2H **177** (2F **75**)
Malpas Wlk. *M16: Old T* *2B 114*
　(off Clifton Cl.)
Malsham Rd. M23: Wyth 1F **141**
Malta Cl. M24: Mid 2F **73**

Malta St. M4: Man 6G **7** (4H **101**)
　OL4: O'ham 3B **76**
Maltby Ct. OL4: Lees 4D **76**
Maltby Dr. BL3: Bolt 4A **48**
Maltby Rd. M23: Wyth 5F **141**
Malton Av. BL3: Bolt 3G **47**
　M21: Chor 1H **129**
　M45: White 5F **53**
Malton Cl. M45: White 5F **53**
　OL9: Chad 6H **57**
Malton Dr. SK7: H Gro 6D **158**
　WA14: Alt 5C **138**
Malton Rd. M28: Wors 4C **80**
　SK4: Stoc 5C **132**
Malton St. OL8: O'ham 4D **74**
Malt St. M15: Man 4C **8** (6B **100**)
Malus Ct. M6: Sal 2G **99**
Malvern Av. BL1: Bolt 4G **31**
　BL9: Bury 6F **23**
　M41: Urm 4D **110**
　M43: Droy 3C **104**
　OL6: A Lyme 4A **92**
　SK8: Gat 6D **142**
Malvern Cl. BL4: Farn 1D **64**
　M25: Pres 4A **70**
　M27: Pen 5D **84**
　OL2: O'ham 4C **58**
　OL2: Shaw 5F **43**
　OL16: Miln 4G **29**
　SK4: Stoc 6F **133**
Malvern Dr. M27: Pen 5D **84**
　WA14: Alt 6D **138**
Malvern Gro. M6: Sal 2C **98**
　M20: Man 3E **131**
　M28: Walk 6H **65**
Malvern Row M15: Man 6C **8**
Malvern St. M15: Man 6C **8** (1B **114**)
　OL8: O'ham 4D **74**
Malvern St. E. OL11: Roch 4E **27**
Malvern St. W. OL11: Roch 4E **27**
Manby Rd. M18: Man 3D **116**
Manby Sq. M18: Man 3D **116**
Mancentral Trad. Est.
　M5: Sal 5D **4** (4B **100**)
MANCHESTER 5A **6** (4D **100**)
Manchester Airport Eastern Link Rd.
　SK7: Bram 1A **166**
　SK8: Chea H 1A **166**
　SK9: Hand 1A **166**
Manchester Airport Station (Rail)
　. .6H **153**
Manchester Apollo 5F **11** (1G **115**)
Manchester Aquatics Cen.
　. . . . . .4B **10** (6F **101**)
Manchester Art Gallery 6A **6** (4E **101**)
Manchester Bus. Pk. M22: Wyth . . .5B **154**
Manchester Cathedral 3H **5** (3D **100**)
Manchester Cathedral Vis. Cen. 4H **5**
Manchester Chambers
　OL1: O'ham 3F **177** (2E **75**)
Manchester City FC 3B **102**
Manchester Climbing Cen. 6B **102**
Manchester Craft & Design Cen.
　. . . . .*4B 6*
　(off Oak St.)
Manchester Crematorium
　M21: Chor 3A **130**
Manchester Evening News Arena
　. . . . . .2H **5** (2D **100**)
Manchester Fort Shop. Pk.
　M8: Man 6E **87**
Manchester Ind. Cen.
　M3: Man 1D **8** (5B **100**)
　(not continuous)
Manchester Ind. Pk.
　M40: Man 6B **88**
MANCHESTER INTERNATIONAL AIRPORT
　. .1H **163**
Manchester Intl. Bus. Cen.
　M22: Wyth 6E **155**
Manchester International Convention Cen.
　. . . . . .1G **9** (5D **100**)

Manchester Jewish Mus. 1E **101**
Manchester Leisure Sports
　Development Cen., The 3E **115**
Manchester Maccabi Community &
　Sports Club 6B **70**
Manchester Metropolitan University
　All Saints Building 6E **101**
　Aytoun Building 1B **10** (5F **101**)
　Bellhouse Building *4A 10*
　(off Lwr. Ormond St.)
　Chatham Building 5B **10** (1E **115**)
　Didsbury Campus 1F **143**
　Elizabeth Gaskell Campus 3G **115**
　Geoffrey Manton Building *1E 115*
　(off Rosamond Rd. W.)
　Grosvenor Building 5A **10**
　Hollings Campus 5H **115**
　John Dalton Building
　. . . . . .3A **10** (6E **101**)
　Loxford Tower 4A **10**
　Mabel Tylecote Building 4A **10**
　St Augustine's *4A 10*
　(off Lower Chatham St.)
Manchester Mus., The 6B **10** (1F **115**)
Manchester New Rd.
　M24: Mid 4A **72**
　M31: Part 6D **124**
Manchester Old Rd.
　BL9: Bury 6A **176** (4E **37**)
　M24: Mid 2F **71**
　M31: C'ton 3H **125**
Manchester Rd. BL0: Ram 3E **13**
　BL2: Bolt 5H **175** (1E **49**)
　BL3: Bolt 1E **49**
　BL4: Kea, Swin 3C **66**
　BL5: Bolt, W'ton 5A **46**
　BL9: Bury 4B **176** (3E **37**)
　(Angouleme Way, not continuous)
　BL9: Bury 3E **13**
　(Whalley Rd.)
　M16: W Ran 6H **113**
　M21: Chor 6H **113**
　(Barlow Moor Rd.)
　M21: Chor 1G **129**
　(Wilbraham Rd.)
　M27: Pen, Swin 4A **84**
　M27: Ward 1D **82**
　M28: Walk 1H **81**
　M29: Ast 5A **80**
　M29: Tyld 2A **80**
　M31: C'ton, Part 5D **124**
　M34: Aud 6A **104**
　M34: Dent 3A **118**
　(not continuous)
　M43: Droy 4G **103**
　OL2: Shaw 2G **59**
　OL3: G'fld 5G **93**
　OL5: Mos 5G **93**
　OL7: A Lyme 3F **105**
　OL8: O'ham 1B **90**
　OL9: O'ham 1B **90**
　OL10: H'ood 2G **55**
　OL11: Roch 6A **178** (2E **41**)
　OL16: Roch 5A **178** (6F **27**)
　SK4: Stoc 4E **133**
　SK8: Chea 3H **143**
　SK9: Wilm 2E **173**
　SK13: Tin 1G **123**
　SK14: Holl 1G **123**
　SK14: Hyde 4H **119**
　WA1: Rix 6A **124**
　WA14: Alt, B'ath, Tim 5F **139**
Manchester Rd. E. M38: Lit H 5E **65**
Manchester Rd. Nth.
　M34: Dent 3C **118**
Manchester Rd. Sth.
　M34: Dent 4C **118**
Manchester Rd. W. M38: Lit H 3B **64**
Manchester Rugby Club 1C **166**
Manchester St Mary's Catholic Church
　Hidden Gem 6G **5**
Manchester Science Pk.
　M15: Man 2E **115**

Manchester St.
M16: Old T 6B **8** (2A **114**)
OL1: O'ham 4F **177** (3E **75**)
OL8: O'ham 4D **74**
(not continuous)
OL9: O'ham 4E **177** (3E **75**)
OL10: H'ood, Mid 3H **39**
Manchester St. Rdbt.
OL9: O'ham 4E **177**
Manchester Tennis Cen. 3B **102**
Manchester United FC 2F **113**
Manchester United Mus. & Tour . . .*2F 113*
Manchester Velodrome
(National Cycling Cen.) 3C **102**
Manchet St. OL11: Roch 4D **40**
Mancroft Av. BL3: Bolt 3B **48**
Mancroft Ter. BL3: Bolt 3B **48**
Mancroft Wlk. M1: Man 3C **10**
Mancunian Rd. M34: Dent 1G **135**
Mancunian Way M1: Man . .3B **10** (6E **101**)
M15: Man 4E **9** (6C **100**)
Mandalay Gdns. SK6: Mar 4B **148**
Mandale Pk. 6F **27**
Mandarin Grn. WA14: B'ath 3D **138**
Mandarin Wlk. *M6: Sal* *2H 99*
(off Milton Pl.)
Mandeville St. M19: Man 1D **132**
Mandeville Ter. BL8: Haw 1D **20**
Mandley Cl. BL3: Lit L 2C **50**
Mandley Pk. Av. M7: Sal 4C **86**
Mandon Cl. M26: Rad 2G **51**
Manesty Cl. M24: Mid 5G **55**
Manet Cl. M7: Sal 3H **85**
Mangle St. M1: Man 5C **6** (4F **101**)
Mango Pl. M6: Sal 3G **99**
Manifold Dr. SK6: H Lan 1D **170**
Manifold St. M6: Sal 6H **85**
Manilla Wlk. *M11: Man* *4B 102*
(off Abernant Cl.)
Manipur St. M11: Man 5B **102**
Manley Av. M27: Clif 5G **67**
Manley Cl. BL9: Sum 1C **22**
Manley Cres. BL5: W'ton 6B **46**
Manley Gro. SK7: Bram 1G **167**
SK14: Mot 4B **122**
MANLEY PARK 5A **114**
Manley Rd. M16: W Ran 6H **113**
M21: Chor 6H **113**
M33: Sale 2G **139**
OL8: O'ham 5E **75**
OL11: Roch 2E **41**
(not continuous)
Manley Row BL5: W'ton 6B **46**
Manley St. M7: Sal 5B **86**
Manley Way SK14: Mot 4C **122**
Manningham Rd. BL3: Bolt 2H **47**
Mannington Dr. M9: Man 4G **87**
Mannock St. OL8: O'ham 3D **74**
Manns, The OL3: G'fld 4B **78**
Manor Av. BL3: Lit L 4E **51**
M16: W Ran 5B **114**
M33: Sale 4F **127**
M41: Urm 6F **111**
Manor Cl. M34: Dent 5H **119**
OL4: Gras 4A **78**
OL9: Chad 1C **74**
SK8: Chea H 5E **157**
SK9: Wilm 1B **172**
Manor Cotts. OL5: Mos 1G **93**
Manor Ct. BL2: Bolt 1H **33**
M32: Stre 6B **112**
M33: Sale 5F **127**
SK1: Stoc *2A 146*
(off Hall St.)
Manordale Wlk. *M40: Man* *5G 87*
(off Westmount Cl.)
Manor Dr. M21: Chor 5B **130**
OL2: O'ham 4E **59**
Mnr. Farm Cl. OL7: A Lyme 5F **91**
Mnr. Farm Ri. OL4: O'ham 2B **76**
Manorfield Cl. BL1: Bolt 4G **31**

Manor Gdns. SK9: Wilm 2G **173**
Manor Ga. Rd. BL2: Bolt 5C **34**
Mnr. Hill Rd. SK6: Mar 4D **148**
Manorial Dr. M38: Lit H 4C **64**
Manor Ind. Est. M32: Stre 1C **128**
Manor Lodge M27: Pen 3D **84**
SK8: Chea H 4E **157**
Mnr. Mill Cl. OL16: Roch 6D **16**
Manor Pk. M41: Urm 6F **111**
Manor Rd. M6: Sal 1D **98**
M19: Man 5D **116**
M24: Mid 3B **72**
M27: Swin 5H **83**
M29: Ast 5A **80**
M32: Stre 6B **112**
M33: Sale 4B **128**
M34: Aud 6B **104**
M34: Dent 5H **119**
M43: Droy 4G **103**
OL2: Shaw 6G **43**
OL4: O'ham 5A **76**
SK5: Stoc 4B **134**
SK6: Mar 4D **148**
SK6: Wood 4H **135**
SK7: Bram 4E **157**
SK8: Chea H 4E **157**
SK9: Wilm 1B **172**
SK14: Hyde 2C **122**
WA15: Alt 3C **174** (1G **151**)
Manor St. BL0: Ram 2B **12**
BL1: Bolt 3G **175** (6D **32**)
BL4: Farn 2G **65**
BL4: Kea 4D **66**
BL9: Bury 3G **37**
M12: Man 3E **11** (5G **101**)
M24: Mid 5C **56**
M34: Aud 6F **105**
OL2: O'ham 5G **59**
OL5: Mos 1G **93**
Manor Vw. SK6: Wood 4H **135**
Manor Wlk. *M34: Aud* *6F 105*
(off Mt. Pleasant St.)
Manor Yd. *OL3: Upp* *1D 78*
(off Wade Row)
Manse, The OL5: Mos 3G **93**
Mansfield Av. BL0: Ram 1B **22**
M9: Man 5H **71**
M34: Dent 3D **118**
Mansfield Cl. M34: Dent 2D **118**
OL7: A Lyme 4F **105**
Mansfield Cres. M34: Dent 3D **118**
Mansfield Dr. M9: Man 5A **72**
Mansfield Grange OL11: Roch 5E **27**
Mansfield Gro. BL1: Bolt 3H **31**
Mansfield Rd. M9: Man 5H **71**
M41: Urm 6D **110**
OL5: Mos 2A **94**
OL8: O'ham 4H **75**
OL11: Roch 4A **26**
SK14: Hyde 6C **120**
Mansfield St. OL7: A Lyme 5E **105**
Mansfield Vw. OL5: Mos 2A **94**
Mansford Dr. M40: Man 6B **88**
Manshaw Cres. M34: Aud 6A **104**
Manshaw Rd. M11: Man 6A **104**
Manson Av. M45: White 4E **53**
Mansion Ho., The WA14: Alt 4F **139**
Manson Av. M15: Man 4C **8** (6B **100**)
Manstead Wlk. M40: Man . .3H **7** (3A **102**)
Manston Dr. SK8: Chea H 3D **156**
Manston Lodge SK2: Stoc 6B **146**
Manswood Dr. M8: Man 4E **87**
Mantell Wlk. *M40: Man* *4F 89*
(off Bower St.)
Manthorpe Av. M28: Wors 4C **82**
Mantley La. OL3: Dens 6E **45**
Manton Av. M9: Man 1D **88**
M34: Dent 4A **118**
Manton Cl. M7: Sal 5D **86**
Manton Ho. SK5: Stoc 5B **134**
Manvers St. SK5: Stoc 6G **133**
Manwaring St. M35: Fail 3G **89**
Manway Bus. Pk. WA14: Tim 3G **139**

Maple Av. BL1: Bolt 4H **31**
BL9: Bury 3H **37**
M21: Chor 1H **129**
M30: Ecc 1C **96**
M32: Stre 6D **112**
M34: Aud 4B **104**
M34: Dent 4E **119**
M45: White 2F **69**
SK6: Mar 1D **160**
SK8: Chea H 3B **156**
SK12: Poy 4F **169**
SK15: Stal 5D **106**
Maple Bank WA14: Bow 2D **150**
Maple Cl. BL4: Kea 4B **66**
M6: Sal 2F **99**
M24: Mid 1F **73**
M33: Sale 5E **127**
OL2: Shaw 5F **43**
OL9: Chad 6B **58**
SK2: Stoc 5B **146**
Maple Ct. M16: Old T 3H **113**
SK4: Stoc 5E **133**
Maplecroft SK1: Stoc 3B **146**
Mapledon Rd. M9: Man 3B **88**
Maple Dr. WA15: Tim 6E **141**
Maplefield Dr. M28: Wors 4F **81**
Maple Gro. BL0: Ram 4D **12**
BL8: Tot 6A **22**
M25: Pres 3G **69**
M28: Walk 3H **81**
M35: Fail 6G **89**
M40: Man 1G **89**
Maple Ho. M14: Man 3G **115**
SK14: Hyde 1D **136**
Maple Rd. BL4: Farn 1E **65**
M23: Wyth 3C **140**
M27: Swin 5G **83**
M31: Part 6C **124**
OL9: Chad 6B **58**
SK7: Bram 2G **167**
SK9: A Edg 6E **173**
Maple Rd. W. M23: Wyth 3C **140**
Maple St. BL2: Bolt 6G **19**
BL3: Bolt 2B **48**
OL8: O'ham 6C **74**
OL11: Roch 5F **27**
Maple Wlk. BL3: Bolt 2A **50**
M23: Wyth 3C **140**
Maplewood Cl. M9: Man 1G **87**
OL2: O'ham 5C **58**
Maplewood Ct. M7: Sal 4B **86**
Maplewood Gdns. BL1: Bolt 3C **32**
Maplewood Gro. SK15: Stal 2G **107**
Maplewood Ho. *BL1: Bolt* *4C 32*
(off Prospect St.)
Maplewood Rd. SK9: Wilm 1H **173**
Mapley Av. M22: Nor 3B **142**
Maplin Cl. M13: Man 4E **11** (1H **115**)
Maplin Dr. SK2: Stoc 6G **147**
Maranatha Ct. M30: Ecc 5D **97**
Marble St. M2: Man 5A **6** (4E **101**)
OL1: O'ham 1H **75**
Marbury Av. M14: Man 6F **115**
Marbury Cl. M41: Urm 4H **109**
SK3: Stoc 4C **144**
Marbury Dr. WA14: Tim 2G **139**
Marbury Rd. SK4: Stoc 3F **133**
SK9: Wilm 6F **165**
Marcer Rd. M40: Man 3G **7** (3H **101**)
March Av. SK4: Stoc 1D **144**
Marchbank Dr. SK8: Chea 5G **143**
March Dr. BL8: Bury 6D **22**
Marchers M. M30: Ecc 4D **96**
Marches Cl. OL2: O'ham 3H **59**
Marchioness St. M18: Man 4H **117**
Marchmont Cl. M13: Man . .6G **11** (1H **115**)
March St. OL16: Roch 4A **28**
Marchwood Av. M21: Chor 6B **114**
Marcliffe Dr. M19: Man 6E **117**
OL11: Roch 5D **26**
Marcliffe Ind. Est. SK7: H Gro 4E **159**
Marcliff Gro. SK4: Stoc 1D **144**
Marcroft Pl. OL11: Roch 1A **42**

Marcus Garvey Ct.—Marmion Dr.

Marcus Garvey Ct. M16: W Ran 5C **114**
Marcus Gro. M14: Man 4G **115**
Marcus St. BL1: Bolt 4H **31**
Mardale Av. M20: Man 4G **131**
M27: Ward 1E **83**
M41: Urm 4B **110**
OL2: O'ham 5C **42**
Mardale Cl. BL2: Bolt 4B **34**
M25: Pres 2A **70**
OL4: O'ham 1B **76**
SK15: Stal 2E **107**
Mardale Dr. BL2: Bolt 4B **34**
M24: Mid 6A **56**
SK8: Gat 5F **143**
Mardale Rd. M27: Swin 5F **83**
Marden Rd. M23: Wyth 6G **141**
Mardyke OL12: Roch 2A **178** (3G **27**)
Marfield Av. OL9: Chad 4A **74**
Marfield Ct. M41: Urm 6A **110**
Marford Cl. M22: Wyth 5B **142**
Marford Cres. M33: Sale 1H **139**
Margaret Ashton Cl. M9: Man 4B **88**
Margaret Av. OL16: Roch 4C **28**
Margaret Ho.
OL6: A Lyme 6A **174** (3G **105**)
Margaret Rd. M34: Dent 3G **119**
M43: Droy 3G **103**
Margaret Sands St.
M15: Man 6C **8** (1B **114**)
Margaret St. BL9: Bury 5D **176** (4F **37**)
OL2: Shaw 1H **59**
OL6: A Lyme 6A **174** (2G **105**)
OL7: A Lyme 3G **105**
OL8: O'ham 1B **90**
OL10: H'ood 3F **39**
SK5: Stoc 2G **133**
Margaret Ter. OL6: A Lyme 6A **174**
Margaret Ward Ct.
*OL11: Roch 6A **28***
(off Wellfield St.)
Margate Av. M40: Man 6D **88**
Margate Rd. SK5: Stoc 2H **133**
Margrove Chase BL6: Los 2C **46**
Margrove Cl. M35: Fail 4C **90**
Margrove Rd. M6: Sal 1C **98**
Margroy Cl. OL12: Roch 1A **28**
Marguerita Rd. M40: Man 1F **103**
(not continuous)
Marham Cl. M21: Chor 3C **130**
Maria St. BL1: Bolt 3C **32**
Marie Cl. M34: Dent 5F **119**
Marie St. M7: Sal 4C **86**
Marigold St. OL11: Roch 6H **27**
Marigold Ter. *M24: Mid 2F **73***
(off Sundew Pl.)
Mariman Dr. M8: Man 1E **87**
Marina Av. M34: Dent 6G **119**
Marina Cl. SK9: Hand 3H **165**
Marina Cres. M11: Man 2D **102**
Marina Dr. SK6: Mar 4A **148**
Marina Rd. M43: Droy 3B **104**
SK6: Bred 5E **135**
Marine Av. M31: Part 6B **124**
Marion St. BL3: Bolt 5G **49**
OL8: O'ham 6F **75**
Maritime Ct. M33: Sale 5H **127**
Marjorie Cl. M18: Man 1D **116**
Mark Av. M6: Sal 1H **99**
Markenfield Dr. OL2: Shaw 6F **43**
Market Av.
OL6: A Lyme 5C **174** (2H **105**)
Market Chambers *BL0: Ram 2C **12***
(off Ramsbottom La.)
Market Hall BL1: Bolt 3F **175** (6D **32**)
Market Pde. BL9: Bury 4C **176** (3F **37**)
Market Pl. BL0: Eden 2G **13**
BL0: Ram 2B **12**
BL1: Bolt 2F **175** (5D **32**)
BL4: Farn 1H **65**
BL9: Bury 3B **176** (3E **37**)
M22: Wyth 2B **154**
M24: Mid 6C **56**
M26: Rad 5B **52**
Market Pl. M27: Pen 2A **84**
M34: Dent 4E **119**
M43: Droy 4A **104**
OL1: O'ham 3F **177** (2E **75**)
OL2: O'ham 3D **58**
OL2: Shaw 1H **59**
*OL5: Mos 2G **93***
(off Market St.)
OL6: A Lyme 5C **174** (2H **105**)
OL10: H'ood 3H **39**
OL16: Roch 3B **178** (4H **27**)
SK1: Stoc 1G **179** (1H **145**)
(not continuous)
SK6: Comp 1E **149**
SK14: Hyde 5B **120**
(not continuous)
SK14: Mot 4C **122**
Market Pct. BL4: Farn 1H **65**
Market Sq. OL2: O'ham 3D **58**
WA14: Alt 2A **174**
(not continuous)
Market St. BL0: Eden 1G **13**
BL1: Bolt 3F **175** (6D **32**)
BL3: Lit L 4C **50**
BL4: Farn 6H **49**
BL8: Tot 4H **21**
BL9: Bury 5C **176** (4F **37**)
(Angouleme Way)
BL9: Bury 3B **176** (3E **37**)
(Bolton St., not continuous)
M2: Man 4H **5** (4D **100**)
M24: Mid 6B **56**
(not continuous)
M26: Rad 1D **66**
M27: Pen 2A **84**
M34: Dent 4E **119**
(not continuous)
M43: Droy 5A **104**
OL2: O'ham 3D **58**
OL2: Shaw 1H **59**
OL5: Mos 2G **93**
OL6: A Lyme 5C **174** (2H **105**)
OL10: H'ood 3G **39**
OL12: Whitw 4E **15**
SK6: Mar 6D **148**
SK12: Dis 1H **171**
SK14: Holl 2F **123**
SK14: Hyde 4B **120**
SK14: Mot 3C **122**
SK15: Stal 3E **107**
WA14: Alt 2A **174** (1F **151**)
Market Street Stop (Metro)
....................**5A 6 (4E 101)**
Market Wlk. M33: Sale 5B **128**
Market Way M6: Sal 2F **99**
OL16: Roch 2B **178** (3H **27**)
Markfield Av. M13: Man 6G **11** (2H **115**)
Markham Cl. M12: Man 1H **11** (5A **102**)
SK14: Hyde 1B **120**
Markham St. SK14: Hyde 1B **120**
Markington St. M14: Man 4E **115**
Mark Jones Wlk. *M40: Man 6D **88***
(off Mitchell St.)
MARKLAND HILL 5E 31
Markland Hill BL1: Bolt 5E **31**
Markland Hill Cl. BL1: Bolt 4F **31**
Markland Hill La. BL1: Bolt 4E **31**
Markland St. BL0: Ram 3B **12**
BL3: Bolt 5F **175** (1D **48**)
SK14: Hyde 6C **120**
(not continuous)
Markland Tops BL1: Bolt 4F **31**
Mark La. M4: Man 4A **6**
OL2: Shaw 1A **60**
Marks St. M26: Rad 4A **52**
Mark St. M28: Wors 4D **80**
OL9: O'ham 2D **74**
OL12: Roch 2B **28**
Mark Wood OL3: Del 3B **62**
MARLAND 1D 40
Marland Av. OL8: O'ham 2G **91**
OL11: Roch 1D **40**
SK8: Chea H 3B **156**
Marland Cl. OL11: Roch 6D **26**
Marland Cres. SK5: Stoc 1H **133**
Marland Fold OL11: Roch 1D **40**
Marland Fold La. OL8: O'ham 2F **91**
Marland Grn. OL11: Roch 1D **40**
Marland Hill Rd. OL11: Roch 6E **27**
Marland Old Rd. OL11: Roch 1D **40**
Marland St. OL9: Chad 6A **74**
Marland Tops OL11: Roch 1D **40**
Marland Way M32: Stre 4D **112**
Marlborough Av. M16: W Ran 5A **114**
SK8: Chea H 3D **156**
SK9: A Edg 4H **173**
Marlborough Cl. BL0: Ram 6C **12**
M34: Dent 4F **119**
OL7: A Lyme 5E **105**
OL12: Whitw 2E **15**
SK6: Mar 4B **148**
Marlborough Ct. M9: Man 4E **71**
Marlborough Dr. M35: Fail 5G **89**
SK4: Stoc 5F **133**
Marlborough Gdns. BL4: Farn 1E **65**
Marlborough Gro. M43: Droy 3C **104**
Marlborough Rd. M7: Man, Sal 5D **86**
M7: Sal 5D **86**
M30: Ecc 1A **98**
M32: Stre 4C **112**
M33: Sale 5B **128**
M41: Urm 4B **110**
M44: Irl 4F **109**
OL2: O'ham 5E **59**
SK14: Hyde 1C **136**
WA14: Bow 3F **151**
Marlborough St. BL1: Bolt 5A **32**
OL4: O'ham 5H **177** (3G **75**)
OL7: A Lyme 5E **105**
(not continuous)
OL10: H'ood 5A **40**
OL12: Roch 2E **27**
Marlbrook Wlk. BL3: Bolt 3D **48**
Marlcroft Av. SK4: Stoc 1D **144**
Marlcroft Cl. M23: Wyth 4G **141**
Marld Cres. BL1: Bolt 3F **31**
Marle Av. OL5: Mos 2A **94**
Marle Cft. M45: White 3C **68**
Marle Earth Cotts. *OL5: Mos 2A **94***
(off Micklehurst Rd.)
Marle Ri. OL5: Mos 2A **94**
Marler Rd. SK14: Hyde 3C **120**
Marley Cl. WA15: Tim 4H **139**
Marley Dr. M33: Sale 3A **128**
Marleyer Cl. M40: Man 4E **89**
Marleyer Ri. SK6: Rom 3G **147**
Marley Rd. M19: Man 1D **132**
SK12: Poy 5E **169**
Marlfield Rd. OL2: Shaw 5E **43**
WA15: Haleb 6D **152**
Marlfield St. M9: Man 2A **88**
Marlhill Cl. SK2: Stoc 6E **147**
Marlhill Ct. SK2: Stoc 6E **147**
Marlinford Dr. M40: Man 6E **89**
Marloes WA14: Bow 3D **150**
Marlor Ct. OL10: H'ood 3F **39**
Marlor St. M34: Dent 3E **119**
Marlow Cl. BL2: Bolt 4B **34**
M41: Urm 3D **110**
SK8: Chea H 3B **156**
Marlow Dr. M27: Swin 5G **83**
M44: Irl 4E **109**
SK9: Hand 2G **165**
WA14: Bow 3B **150**
Marlowe Dr. M20: Man 5F **131**
Marlowe Wlk. M34: Dent 2F **135**
Marlowe Walks SK6: Bred 1E **147**
Marlow Ho. *M5: Sal 4F **99***
(off Hodge La.)
Marlow Rd. M9: Man 2B **88**
Marlton Wlk. *M9: Man 5A **72***
(off Leconfield Dr.)
Marlwood Rd. BL1: Bolt 3F **31**
Marlwood Way
OL2: O'ham 5C **58**
Marmion Dr. M21: Chor 1G **129**

Marne Av.—Matlock M.

Marne Av. M22: Shar 6C **142**
OL6: A Lyme 6D **92**
Marne Cres. OL11: Roch 3E **27**
Marnland Gro. BL3: Bolt 3E **47**
Maroon Rd. M22: Wyth 6D **154**
MARPLE **5D 148**
Marple Av. BL1: Bolt 1E **33**
MARPLE BRIDGE **4F 149**
Marple Cl. OL8: O'ham 1D **90**
Marple Ct. SK1: Stoc 6H **179** (4A **146**)
MARPLE DALE **3B 148**
Marple Gro. M32: Stre 4C **112**
Marple Hall Dr. SK6: Mar 4B **148**
Marple Old Rd. SK2: Stoc 5G **147**
Marple Packhorse Bridge **2F 161**
Marple Rd. SK2: Stoc 4D **146**
Marple Station (Rail) **4E 149**
Marple St. M15: Man 6D **8** (2B **114**)
Marple Swimming Pool **5D 148**
Marquis Av. BL9: Bury 1E **37**
Marquis Dr. SK8: H Grn 6H **155**
Marquis St. M19: Man 6F **117**
Marrick Av. SK8: Chea 6G **143**
Marriott St. M20: Man 3F **131**
SK1: Stoc 5H **179** (3H **145**)
Marryat Ct. *M12: Man* *1B 116*
(off Gregory St.)
Mars Av. BL3: Bolt 4A **48**
Marsden Cl. OL5: Mos 1F **93**
OL7: A Lyme 6E **91**
OL16: Roch 5C **42**
Marsden Dr. WA15: Tim 5C **140**
Marsden Ho. BL1: Bolt 3E **175**
Marsden Rd. BL1: Bolt 3E **175** (6C **32**)
SK6: Rom 6A **136**
Marsden's Sq. *OL15: L'ough* *3H 17*
(off Sutcliffe St.)
Marsden St. BL9: Bury 1C **176** (2F **37**)
M2: Man 5H **5** (4D **100**)
M24: Mid *2E 73*
(off Lancaster Av.)
M28: Walk 1D **82**
M28: Wors 4D **80**
M30: Ecc 2E **97**
SK13: Had *3H 123*
(off Queen St.)
Marsden Wlk. M26: Rad 3H **51**
Marsett Cl. OL12: Roch 2C **26**
Marsett Wlk. M23: Wyth 1F **141**
Marshall Ct. *OL1: O'ham* *1E 75*
(off Bradford St.)
OL6: A Lyme 3B **106**
Marshall Rd. M19: Man 6C **116**
Marshall Stevens Way
M17: T Pk 2B **112**
Marshall St. M4: Man 3C **6** (3F **101**)
M12: Man 5F **11** (1G **115**)
OL16: Roch 4C **28**
Marsham Cl. M13: Man 2A **116**
OL4: Grot 4F **77**
Marsham Dr. SK6: Mar 6E **149**
Marsham Rd. SK7: H Gro 4B **158**
Marshbrook Dr. M9: Man 1G **87**
Marshbrook Rd. M41: Urm 4E **111**
Marsh Cl. SK3: Stoc 5F **145**
Marshdale Rd. BL1: Bolt 5F **31**
Marshes Fold M28: Walk 1G **81**
Marshfield Rd. WA15: Tim 6C **140**
Marshfield St. M13: Man 6F **11** (1G **115**)
Marshfield Wlk. *M13: Man* *6F 11*
(off Lauderdale Cres.)
Marsh Fold La. BL1: Bolt 5A **32**
Marsh Head OL3: Dig 2G **63**
Marsh Hey Cl. M38: Lit H 3D **64**
Marsh La. BL3: Lit L 3D **50**
BL4: Farn 1E **65**
Marsh Lea OL3: Dig 2F **63**
Marsh Rd. BL3: Lit L 3C **50**
M38: Lit H 5F **65**
Marsh St. BL1: Bolt 3C **32**
M28: Walk 1B **82**
Marsland Av. WA15: Tim 3B **140**
Marsland Cl. M34: Dent 4B **118**
Marsland Rd. M33: Sale 6A **128**
SK6: Mar 4B **148**
WA15: Tim 5B **140**
MARSLANDS **5D 62**
Marslands OL3: Dig 4D **62**
Marsland St. SK1: Stoc 6H **133**
(not continuous)
SK7: H Gro 3D **158**
Marsland St. Ind. Est.
SK7: H Gro 3E **159**
Marsland St. Nth. M7: Sal 4D **86**
Marsland St. Sth. M7: Sal 4D **86**
Marsland Ter. SK1: Stoc 3B **146**
Mars St. OL9: O'ham 2C **74**
Marston Cl. M35: Fail 5C **90**
M45: White 1A **70**
Marston Dr. M44: Irl 5F **109**
Marston Ho. *M5: Sal* *4F 99*
(off Cypress Cl.)
Marston Rd. M7: Sal 3C **86**
M32: Stre 5F **113**
Martens Rd. M44: Irl 4C **124**
Marthall Dr. M33: Sale 1E **141**
Marthall Way SK9: Hand 2A **166**
Martham Dr. SK2: Stoc 5G **147**
Martha's Ter. OL16: Roch 6C **16**
Martha St. BL3: Bolt 3B **48**
OL1: O'ham 1D **74**
Martin Av. BL3: Lit L 4E **51**
BL4: Farn 2D **64**
OL4: O'ham 3A **76**
Martin Cl. M34: Dent 2F **119**
SK2: Stoc 6F **147**
Martindale Cl. OL2: O'ham 2E **59**
Martindale Cres. M12: Man 1A **116**
M24: Mid 4H **55**
Martindale Gdns. *BL1: Bolt* *3C 32*
(off Jennaby Wlk.)
Martin Dr. M44: Irl 3E **109**
Martingale Cl. M26: Rad 2A **52**
Martingale Ct. M8: Man 4E **87**
Martingale Way M43: Droy 2D **104**
Martin Gro. BL4: Kea 2B **66**
Martin Ho. M14: Man 4H **115**
Martin La. OL12: Roch 2D **26**
Martin Rd. M27: Clif 1B **84**
Martinsclough BL6: Los 1C **46**
Martinscroft Rd. M23: Wyth 6H **141**
Martins Fld. OL12: Roch 2B **26**
Martin St. BL9: Bury 2B **38**
M5: Sal 3E **99**
M34: Aud 6F **105**
SK14: Hyde 5C **120**
Martlesham Wlk. M4: Man 4B **6**
Martlet Av. SK12: Dis 1G **171**
Martlet Cl. M14: Man 6F **115**
Martlett Av. OL11: Roch 4A **26**
Martock Av. M22: Wyth 2C **154**
Marton Av. BL2: Bolt 5G **33**
M20: Man 1G **143**
Marton Grange M25: Pres 6B **70**
Marton Grn. SK3: Stoc 6F **145**
Marton Gro. SK4: Stoc 3G **133**
Marton Pl. M33: Sale 5A **128**
Marton Way *SK9: Hand* *2A 166*
(off Spath La.)
Marvic Ct. M13: Man 4A **116**
Marwood Cl. M26: Rad 1C **66**
WA14: Alt 5D **138**
Marwood Dr. M23: Wyth 2F **153**
Mary Close Pk., The (Bowling Green)
....**4E 15**
(off Market St.)
Maryfield Ct. M16: W Ran 1C **130**
Mary France St.
M15: Man 5E **9** (1C **114**)
Mary Hulton Ct. BL5: W'ton 6A **46**
Maryland Av. BL2: Bolt 6H **33**
Marylon Dr. M22: Nor 3C **142**
Maryport Dr. WA15: Tim 4D **140**
Mary St. BL0: Ram 4B **12**
BL4: Farn 2H **65**
BL9: Bury 5F **23**
Mary St. M3: Man 1F **5** (2D **100**)
M34: Dent 3G **119**
M43: Droy 4B **104**
OL10: H'ood 3G **39**
OL16: Roch 5D **16**
SK1: Stoc 1H **179** (1A **146**)
SK8: Chea 5H **143**
SK14: Hyde 4A **120**
SK16: Duk 4H **105**
Masboro St. M8: Man 4D **86**
Masbury Cl. BL1: Bolt 4C **18**
Masefield Av. M25: Pres 6F **69**
M26: Rad 3G **51**
Masefield Cl. SK16: Duk 6F **107**
Masefield Cres. M43: Droy 4A **104**
Masefield Dr. BL4: Farn 2F **65**
SK4: Stoc 1C **144**
Masefield Gro. SK5: Stoc 6G **117**
Masefield Rd. BL3: Lit L 3D **50**
M43: Droy 4A **104**
OL1: O'ham 5H **59**
Mason Clough BL1: Bolt 6D **18**
Mason Gdns. BL3: Bolt 1C **48**
Mason Row BL7: Eger 1B **18**
Mason St. BL7: Eger 2C **18**
BL9: Bury 3G **37**
M4: Man 3C **6** (3F **101**)
OL7: A Lyme 4F **105**
OL10: H'ood 3F **39**
OL16: Roch 4C **178** (4H **27**)
Massey Av. M35: Fail 3B **90**
OL6: A Lyme 5A **92**
Massey Cft. OL12: Whitw 1E **15**
Massey Rd. M33: Sale 5E **129**
WA15: Alt 3C **174** (1G **151**)
Massey St. BL9: Bury 2H **37**
M5: Sal 5B **4** (4A **100**)
SK1: Stoc 3G **179** (2H **145**)
SK9: A Edg 5G **173**
Massey Wlk. M22: Wyth 4D **154**
Massie St. SK8: Chea 5H **143**
Masson Pl. M4: Man 1A **6**
Matchmoor La. BL6: Hor 1A **30**
Matham Wlk. M15: Man 4A **10**
Mather Av. M25: Pres 2A **86**
M30: Ecc 3G **97**
M45: White 5F **53**
Mather Cl. M45: White 6F **53**
Mather Fold Cotts.
BL7: Eger 2C **18**
Mather Fold Rd. M28: Wors 2F **81**
Mather Rd. BL9: Bury 4F **23**
M30: Ecc 3G **97**
Mather St. BL3: Bolt 6E **175** (1C **48**)
BL4: Kea 1A **66**
M26: Rad 4A **52**
M35: Fail 4F **89**
Mather Way *M6: Sal* *2G 99*
(off Salford Shop. City)
Matisse Way M7: Sal 3H **85**
MATLEY **1H 121**
Matley Cl. SK14: Hyde 2F **121**
Matley Ct. SK14: Mot 1A **122**
Matley Grn. SK5: Stoc 3C **134**
Matley La. SK14: Hyde 2F **121**
SK15: Mat 2F **121**
Matley Pk. La. SK15: Stal 1H **121**
Matlock Av. M7: Sal 4G **85**
M20: Man 3D **130**
M34: Dent 1G **135**
M41: Urm 1D **126**
OL6: A Lyme 5D **92**
Matlock Bank *SK13: Gam* *6G 123*
(off Castleton Cres.)
Matlock Cl. BL4: Farn 6A **50**
M33: Sale 5C **128**
Matlock Dr. SK7: H Gro 5E **159**
Matlock Gdns. *SK13: Gam* *6G 123*
(off Castleton Cres.)
Matlock La. *SK13: Gam* *6G 123*
(off Castleton Cres.)
Matlock M. *WA14: Alt* *6G 139*
(off Renshaw St.)

Matlock Pl.—Meadow Ri.

Matlock Pl. *SK13: Gam* *6G* ***123***
(off Castleton Cres.)
Matlock Rd. M32: Stre 4A **112**
SK5: Stoc 6A **118**
SK8: H Grn 6G **155**
Matlock St. M30: Ecc 5E **97**
Matson Wlk. M22: Wyth 3G **153**
Matt Busby Cl. M27: Pen 4B **84**
Matterdale Ter. *SK15: Stal* *1E* ***107***
(off Ullswater Ter.)
Matthew Cl. OL8: O'ham 5A **76**
Matthew Moss La. OL11: Roch 1D **40**
Matthews Av. BL4: Kea 2B **66**
Matthews La. M12: Man 5C **116**
M18: Man 5E **117**
M19: Man 5C **116**
Matthew's St. M12: Man 6B **102**
Matthias Ct. M3: Sal 2C **4** (2B **100**)
Mattison St. M11: Man 6G **103**
Maudsley Cl. M7: Sal 5D **86**
Maudsley St. BL9: Bury 5A **176** (4E **37**)
Maud St. BL2: Bolt 6G **19**
OL12: Roch 1A **28**
Mauldeth Cl. SK4: Stoc 6C **132**
Mauldeth Ct. SK4: Stoc 6C **132**
Mauldeth Rd. M14: Man 2G **131**
M19: Man 3A **132**
(Broadhill Rd.)
M19: Man 5B **132**
(Leegate Rd.)
M20: Man 2G **131**
SK4: Stoc 1B **144**
Mauldeth Road Station (Rail) 3A **132**
Mauldeth Rd. W. M20: Man 1D **130**
M21: Chor 3A **130**
Maunby Gdns. M38: Lit H 6G **65**
Maureen Av. M8: Man 3E **87**
Maureen St. OL12: Roch 1A **28**
Maurice Cl. SK16: Duk 5C **106**
Maurice Dr. M6: Sal 1F **99**
Maurice Pariser Wlk. *M8: Man* *4D* ***86***
(off Squire Rd.)
Maurice St. M6: Sal 1F **99**
Maveen Ct. SK2: Stoc 1A **158**
Maveen Gro. SK2: Stoc 1A **158**
Mavis Gro. OL16: Miln 5G **29**
Mavis St. OL11: Roch 4E **41**
Mawdsley Dr. M8: Man 3G **87**
Mawdsley St. BL1: Bolt 4F **175** (6D **32**)
Maxton Ho. *BL4: Farn* *1A* ***66***
(off Bridgewater St.)
Maxwell Av. SK2: Stoc 6C **146**
Maxwell St. BL1: Bolt 1C **32**
BL9: Bury 2H **37**
Mayall St. OL5: Mos 2G **93**
Mayall St. E. OL4: O'ham 2A **76**
Mayan Av. M3: Sal 3C **4** (3B **100**)
May Av. SK4: Stoc 1E **145**
SK8: Chea H 1D **166**
Maybank St. BL3: Bolt 2B **48**
Mayberth Av. M8: Man 1E **87**
Maybreck Cl. BL3: Bolt 2A **48**
Maybrook Wlk. *M9: Man* *3H* ***87***
(off Alfred St.)
Mayburn Cl. M24: Mid 4E **73**
Maybury Cl. BL0: Ram 4B **12**
Maybury St. M18: Man 1G **117**
May Ct. M16: W Ran 4B **114**
Maycroft SK5: Stoc 3B **134**
Maycroft Av. M20: Man 4G **131**
May Dr. M19: Man 3B **132**
Mayer St. SK2: Stoc 4C **146**
Mayes Ct. *M14: Man* *2H* ***131***
(off Sheringham Rd.)
Mayes Gdns. M4: Man 6G **7** (4H **101**)
Mayes St. M4: Man 3A **6** (3E **101**)
(not continuous)
Mayfair M7: Sal 2A **86**
Mayfair, The M20: Man 4F **131**
Mayfair Av. M6: Sal 2B **98**
M26: Rad 3F **51**
M41: Urm 5D **110**
M45: White 2F **69**
Mayfair Cl. SK12: Poy 3E **169**
SK16: Duk 5D **106**
Mayfair Ct. M14: Man 1G **131**
WA15: Tim 4B **140**
(Park Rd.)
WA15: Tim 5B **140**
(Stockport Rd.)
Mayfair Cres. M35: Fail 3B **90**
Mayfair Dr. M33: Sale 1G **139**
M44: Irl 5E **109**
OL2: O'ham 5D **58**
Mayfair Gdns. *M45: White* *2F* ***69***
(off Bury New Rd.)
OL11: Roch 6F **27**
Mayfair Gro. M45: White 2G **69**
Mayfair Pk. M20: Man 5D **130**
Mayfair Rd. M22: Wyth 2C **154**
MAYFIELD 2B **28**
Mayfield BL2: Bolt 6H **19**
M26: Rad 5G **51**
Mayfield Av. BL3: Bolt 4F **49**
BL4: Farn 2G **65**
M27: Swin 5E **83**
M28: Walk 6H **65**
M32: Stre 6B **112**
M33: Sale 5E **129**
M34: Dent 2G **135**
OL4: Spri 2E **77**
SK5: Stoc 4H **133**
Mayfield Cl. BL0: Ram 1A **22**
WA15: Tim 5B **140**
Mayfield Gro. M18: Man 4H **117**
SK5: Stoc 4H **133**
SK9: Wilm 4B **172**
Mayfield Ind. Pk. M44: Irl 4G **109**
Mayfield Mans. M16: W Ran 4C **114**
Mayfield Rd. BL0: Ram 1A **22**
M7: Sal 2A **86**
M16: W Ran 4C **114**
OL1: O'ham 6H **59**
SK6: Mar B 2F **149**
SK7: Bram 3G **167**
WA15: Tim 5B **140**
Mayfield St. M34: Aud 2E **119**
OL16: Roch 2B **28**
(not continuous)
Mayfield Ter. OL16: Roch 2B **28**
Mayflower Av. M5: Sal 5G **99**
Mayford Rd. M19: Man 5C **116**
Maygate OL9: O'ham 1D **74**
May Gro. M19: Man 1D **132**
Mayhill Dr. M6: Sal 1A **98**
M28: Wors 3C **82**
Mayhurst Av. M21: Chor 6B **130**
Maynard Rd. WA14: W Tim 3E **139**
Mayorlowe Av. SK5: Stoc 5C **134**
Mayor's Rd. WA15: Alt 3C **174** (1G **151**)
Mayor St. BL1: Bolt 1B **48**
BL3: Bolt 1B **48**
BL8: Bury 2C **36**
OL9: O'ham 2C **74**
Mayo St. M12: Man 2G **11** (5H **101**)
May Pl. *OL11: Roch* *1A* ***42***
(off Oldham Rd.)
OL15: L'ough 5E **17**
Maypole, The *M6: Sal* *1G* ***99***
(off Broughton Rd.)
Maypool Dr. SK5: Stoc 3H **133**
May Rd. M16: W Ran 4B **114**
M27: Pen 5B **84**
SK8: Chea H 1D **166**
Maysmith M. M7: Sal 5B **86**
May St. BL2: Bolt 6E **33**
M26: Rad 4A **52**
M30: Ecc 1E **97**
M40: Man 6E **89**
(not continuous)
OL8: O'ham 5C **74**
OL10: H'ood 5A **40**
(not continuous)
Mayton St. M11: Man 5C **102**
Mayville Dr. M20: Man 4F **131**
May Wlk. M31: Part 6C **124**
Maywood SK9: Wilm 5B **172**
Maywood Av. M20: Man 3F **143**
Maze St. BL3: Bolt 2G **49**
(not continuous)
Meachin Av. M21: Chor 4A **130**
Mead, The M5: Sal 3D **98**
Meade, The BL3: Bolt 5C **48**
M21: Chor 2H **129**
SK9: Wilm 1F **173**
Meade Cl. M41: Urm 5E **111**
Meade Gro. M13: Man 4B **116**
Meade Hill Rd. M8: Man 6C **70**
M25: Pres 6C **70**
Meade Mnr. M21: Chor 2H **129**
Meadfoot Av. M25: Pres 6A **70**
Meadfoot Rd. M18: Man 1F **117**
Meadland Gro. BL1: Bolt 1D **32**
Meadon Av. M27: Clif 2B **84**
Meadow, The BL1: Bolt 6C **30**
OL3: Del 2B **62**
Meadow Av. WA15: Hale 2B **152**
Meadow Bank M21: Chor 2G **129**
SK4: Stoc 1D **144**
SK6: Bred 6F **135**
WA15: Tim 4A **140**
Meadowbank OL7: A Lyme 5G **91**
SK14: Holl 1F **123**
Meadowbank Cl. M35: Fail 5A **90**
OL4: O'ham 5C **76**
Meadow Bank Ct. M32: Stre 6B **112**
Meadowbank Rd. BL3: Bolt 5H **47**
Meadowbrook Cl. BL6: Los 4C **46**
BL9: Bury 1A **38**
Meadowbrook Way SK8: Chea H 1D **156**
Meadow Brow SK9: A Edg 4G **173**
Meadowburn Nook M30: Ecc 1D **96**
Meadow Cl. BL3: Lit L 5D **50**
M32: Stre 6E **113**
M34: Dent 2G **135**
OL5: Mos 6A **78**
OL10: H'ood 3G **39**
OL12: Roch 2C **26**
SK6: H Lan 5D **160**
SK6: Wood 4G **135**
SK9: Wilm 5B **172**
WA15: Hale 2B **152**
Meadow Cotts. OL12: Whitw 2B **14**
Meadow Ct. M6: Sal 2B **98**
M21: Chor 1F **129**
WA15: Hale 2C **152**
Meadow Cft. M45: White 3C **68**
SK7: H Gro 1E **159**
Meadowcroft M26: Rad 2H **51**
SK14: Mot 3C **122**
Meadowcroft Ho. OL11: Roch 5B **26**
Meadowcroft La. OL1: O'ham 6H **59**
OL11: Roch 5B **26**
Meadowfield BL6: Los 6B **30**
OL16: Roch 2B **42**
Meadowfield Cl. SK13: Had 4H **123**
Meadowfield Ct. SK14: Hyde 3B **120**
Meadowfield Dr. M28: Wors 5F **81**
Meadow Fold OL3: Upp 1E **79**
Meadowgate M28: Wors 3B **82**
M41: Urm 6F **111**
Meadowgate Rd. M6: Sal 2B **98**
Meadow Head Av.
OL12: Whitw 3F **15**
Meadow Head La. OL11: Roch 1E **25**
Meadow Hgts. *BL0: Ram* *3D* ***12***
(off Fir St.)
Meadow Ind. Est. M35: Fail 5E **89**
M35: Man 1G **103**
SK1: Stoc 6H **133**
Meadow La. BL2: Bolt 6C **34**
M28: Wors 6B **82**
M34: Dent 1G **135**
OL8: O'ham 1E **91**
SK12: Dis 1H **171**
SK16: Duk 5B **106**
Meadow Mill SK1: Stoc 6H **133**
Meadow Pk. BL0: Ram 1F **13**
Meadow Ri. OL2: Shaw 4G **43**

Meadow Rd. M7: Sal 1B **4** (2A **100**)
  M24: Mid 3A **72**
  M41: Urm 6F **111**
Meadows, The M24: Mid 3D **72**
  M25: Pres 5H **69**
  M26: Rad 2G **51**
  M44: Cad 3C **124**
  M45: White *2C 68*
                    (off Old Hall La.)
  OL3: Upp 2D **78**
  OL4: Grot 3E **77**
  OL12: Whitw 4A **14**
  SK6: Bred 5H **135**
  SK13: Had 3H **123**
Meadows Cl. SK7: H Gro 2E **159**
Meadowside OL16: Miln 1A **44**
  SK7: Bram 3E **157**
Meadowside Av. BL2: Bolt 5G **33**
  M22: Wyth 1B **154**
  M28: Walk 5A **66**
  M44: Irl 5E **109**
Meadowside Cl. M26: Rad 2A **52**
Meadowside Gro. M28: Walk 6A **66**
Meadows La. BL2: Bolt 2B **34**
Meadows Rd. M33: Sale 3C **128**
  SK4: Stoc 2E **133**
                  (not continuous)
  SK8: Chea H 5B **156**
  SK8: H Grn 4F **155**
Meadow St. SK2: Stoc 6C **146**
  SK14: Hyde 6C **120**
Meadowsweet La. M28: Walk 5D **64**
Meadow Vw. OL12: Roch 2C **26**
Meadow Wlk. BL4: Farn 1E **65**
  M31: Part 6C **124**
  OL15: L'ough 4F **17**
  SK6: Bred 6F **135**
Meadow Way BL8: Tot 5G **21**
  BL9: Sum 1C **22**
  M40: Man 2C **88**
  SK9: Wilm 5B **172**
  WA15: Hale 2B **152**
Meads, The OL9: Chad 3A **74**
Meads Ct. M27: Swin 3H **83**
Meadscroft Dr. SK9: A Edg 5F **173**
Meads Gro. BL4: Farn 1B **64**
  M29: Ast 5A **80**
Mead Way M34: Dent 1F **135**
Meadway BL0: Ram 4F **13**
  BL4: Kea 6B **50**
  BL9: Bury 1F **53**
  M29: Tyld 2B **80**
  M33: Sale 6G **127**
  OL9: Chad 1G **89**
  OL11: Roch 1E **41**
  SK6: H Lan 5D **160**
  SK7: Bram 2G **167**
  SK12: Poy 2B **168**
  SK15: Stal 1A **122**
  SK16: Duk 6C **106**
Meadway Cl. M33: Sale 1G **139**
Meadway Ct. SK7: Bram 2G **167**
Meadway Rd. SK8: Chea H 2D **156**
Mealhouse Brow SK1: Stoc 2G **179**
Mealhouse La.
  BL1: Bolt 3F **175** (6D **32**)
Meal St. SK4: Stoc 6G **133**
Meanwood Brow *OL12: Roch* *3F 27*
               (off Rooley Moor Rd.)
Meanwood Fold OL12: Roch 3F **27**
Mecca Bingo
  Bank Top 4E **177** (3E **75**)
  Bolton 5E **175** (1C **48**)
  Breightmet 6B **34**
  Rochdale 3D **178** (4A **28**)
  Sale .5A **128**
  West Gorton 1C **116**
Meddings Cl. SK9: A Edg 6G **173**
Medina Cl. SK8: Chea H 1D **156**
Medley St. OL12: Roch 2H **27**
Medlock Cl. BL4: Farn 1F **65**
Medlock Ct. M11: Man 6D **102**
  OL4: Lees 2C **76**

Medlock Dr. OL8: O'ham 2G **91**
Medlock Gates M35: Fail 1H **103**
Medlock Ho. M15: Man 3D **8**
Medlock Leisure Cen. 3B **104**
Medlock Rd. M35: Fail 1H **103**
Medlock St. M15: Man 3G **9** (6D **100**)
  M43: Droy 3A **104**
  OL1: O'ham 2G **75**
MEDLOCK VALE 1H **103**
Medlock Way M45: White 1A **70**
  OL4: Lees 3C **76**
Medtia Sq. OL1: O'ham 5G **177**
Medway, The OL10: H'ood 2F **39**
Medway Cl. M5: Sal 2D **98**
  OL8: O'ham 6C **74**
  SK9: Wilm 5H **165**
Medway Cres. WA14: Alt 5E **139**
Medway Dr. BL4: Kea 4D **66**
Medway Rd. M28: Wors 3F **81**
  OL2: Shaw 5G **43**
  OL8: O'ham 6C **74**
Medway Wlk. M40: Man 1G **7**
Meech St. M11: Man 5E **103**
Meek St. OL2: O'ham 5G **59**
Meerbrook Rd. SK3: Stoc 3C **144**
Mee's Sq. M30: Ecc 5F **97**
Megabowl
  Bury .1H **53**
  Stockport 4F **179** (3G **145**)
Megna Cl. OL9: O'ham 2D **74**
Melandra Castle Rd. SK13: Gam . . .6F **123**
Melandra Cres. SK14: Hat 5A **122**
Melandra Rd. SK13: Had 4F **123**
Melanie Dr. SK5: Stoc 1H **133**
Melba St. M11: Man 5G **103**
Melbecks Wlk. M23: Wyth 1F **141**
Melbourne Av. M32: Stre 5D **112**
  M90: Man A 5G **153**
  OL9: Chad 2A **74**
Melbourne Cl. OL11: Roch 3A **42**
Melbourne M. *M7: Sal* *6B 86*
                    (off Arrow St.)
  OL9: Chad 2B **74**
Melbourne Rd. BL3: Bolt 2H **47**
  OL11: Roch 3A **42**
  SK7: Bram 1G **167**
Melbourne St. M7: Sal 6C **86**
  M9: Man 3A **88**
  M15: Man 4F **9** (6C **100**)
  M27: Pen 3B **84**
  M34: Dent 5E **119**
  OL9: Chad 2B **74**
  SK5: Stoc 1H **133**
  SK15: Stal 3E **107**
Melbourne St. Nth. OL6: A Lyme 1A **106**
Melbourne St. Sth.
  OL6: A Lyme 4D **174** (1A **106**)
Melbury Av. M20: Man 5H **131**
Melbury Rd. SK8: Chea H 1D **166**
Meldon Rd. M13: Man 5A **116**
Meldreth Dr. M12: Man 3B **116**
Meldrum St. OL8: O'ham 5F **75**
Melford Av. M40: Man 2G **89**
Melford Gro. OL4: O'ham 3B **76**
Melford Rd. SK7: H Gro 4F **159**
Melfort Av. M32: Stre 6E **113**
Melia Ho. M4: Man 1B **6**
Meliden Cres. BL1: Bolt 4H **31**
  M22: Wyth 2C **154**
Melksham Cl. *M5: Sal* *3H 99*
                (off Culverwell Dr.)
Mellalieu St. M24: Mid 4A **56**
  OL2: O'ham 5E **59**
Melland Av. M21: Chor 4A **130**
Melland Rd. M18: Man 4E **117**
Mellands Ct. *M18: Man* *4F 117*
               (off Levenshulme Rd.)
Melland Sports Cen. 4E **117**
Meller Rd. M13: Man 5B **116**
Melling Av. OL9: Chad 6G **57**
  SK4: Stoc 3G **133**
Melling Rd. OL4: O'ham 3A **76**
Melling St. M12: Man 3C **116**

Mellington Av. M20: Man 3F **143**
Mellodew Dr. OL1: O'ham 3B **60**
MELLOR 5H **149**
Mellor Brow OL10: H'ood 3G **39**
Mellor Cl. BL1: Bolt 1B **48**
  OL6: A Lyme 3C **106**
Mellor Ct. SK2: Stoc 4E **147**
Mellor Dr. BL9: Bury 6D **36**
  M28: Wors 5G **81**
Mellor Gro. BL1: Bolt 4H **31**
Mellor Ho. *OL2: O'ham* *3E 59*
              (off Royton Hall Pk.)
Mellor Rd. OL6: A Lyme 1D **106**
  SK8: Chea H 4D **156**
Mellor Sports Club 5H **149**
Mellors Rd. M17: T Pk 6B **98**
Mellor St. M25: Pres 5F **69**
  M26: Rad 5B **52**
                (not continuous)
  M30: Ecc 4F **97**
  M32: Stre 3E **113**
  M35: Fail 5F **89**
  M40: Man 2G **7** (2H **101**)
  M43: Droy 4H **103**
  OL2: O'ham 2D **58**
  OL4: Lees 3C **76**
  OL8: O'ham *1C 90*
         (off Limeside Rd., not continuous)
  OL11: Roch 3F **27**
  OL12: Roch 3F **27**
Mellor Vw. SK12: Dis 1H **171**
Mellor Way OL9: Chad 5B **74**
Mellowstone Dr. M21: Chor 1D **130**
Melloy Pl. M8: Man 1E **101**
Melmerby Ct. M5: Sal 4F **99**
Melon Pl. M6: Sal 3H **99**
Melrose OL12: Roch 2A **178** (3G **27**)
Melrose Apartments *M13: Man* . . .*3G 115*
              (off Hathersage Rd.)
Melrose Av. BL1: Bolt 4G **31**
  BL8: Bury 2C **36**
  M20: Man 6G **131**
  M30: Ecc 1C **96**
  M33: Sale 5B **128**
  OL10: H'ood 6G **39**
  OL15: L'ough 2G **17**
  SK3: Stoc 4B **144**
Melrose Cl. M45: White 5F **53**
Melrose Ct. OL9: Chad 5A **74**
Melrose Cres. SK3: Stoc 1F **157**
                  (not continuous)
  SK12: Poy 2B **170**
  WA15: Hale 4B **152**
Melrose Gdns. M26: Rad 2G **51**
  M26: Rad 2G **51**
Melrose Rd. BL3: Lit L 4B **50**
  M26: Rad 2G **51**
Melrose St. BL9: Sum 1B **22**
  M40: Man 6E **89**
  OL1: O'ham 6H **59**
  OL11: Roch 4F **27**
Melsomby Rd. M23: Wyth 1G **141**
Meltham Av. M20: Man 3E **131**
Meltham Cl. SK4: Stoc 2A **144**
Meltham Pl. *BL3: Bolt* *3B 48*
             (off Bk. Willows La.)
Meltham Rd. SK4: Stoc 2A **144**
Melton Av. M34: Dent 4A **118**
  M41: Urm 4G **109**
Melton Cl. M28: Walk 1G **81**
  OL10: H'ood 4F **39**
Melton Dr. BL9: Bury 2G **53**
Melton Rd. M8: Man 2C **86**
Melton Row *M26: Rad* *3H 51*
               (off Melton St.)
Melton St. *M9: Man* *2B 88*
               (off Gilmour Ter.)
  M26: Rad 3H **51**
  OL10: H'ood 4F **39**
  SK5: Stoc 5H **133**
Melton Wlk. *M26: Rad* *3H 51*
               (off Melton St.)
Melton Way *M26: Rad* *3H 51*
               (off Melton St.)

Melverley Rd. M9: Man 4E **71**
Melville Cl. M11: Man 6G **103**
Melville Rd. BL4: Kea 3B **66**
  M32: Stre 4B **112**
  M44: Cad 4A **124**
Melville St. BL3: Bolt 3E **49**
  OL4: Lees 4C **76**
  OL6: A Lyme 4C **174** (2H **105**)
  OL11: Roch 4F **41**
Melvin Av. M22: Wyth 1C **154**
Melyncourt Dr. SK14: Hat 4A **122**
Memorial Rd. M28: Walk 1H **81**
Menai Gro. SK8: Chea 5C **144**
Menai Rd. SK3: Stoc 5G **145**
Menai St. BL3: Bolt 4H **47**
Mendip Av. M22: Wyth 1D **154**
Mendip Cl. BL2: Bolt 6C **34**
  OL2: O'ham 4C **58**
  OL9: Chad 4A **74**
  SK4: Stoc 6G **133**
  SK8: H Grn 6F **155**
Mendip Ct. SK4: Stoc 6G **133**
Mendip Cres. BL8: Bury 2B **36**
Mendip Dr. BL2: Bolt 1C **50**
  OL16: Miln 4G **29**
Mendip Rd. OL8: O'ham 6D **74**
Mendips Cl. OL2: Shaw 5F **43**
Menston Av. M40: Man 2G **89**
Mentmore Rd. OL16: Roch 3D **28**
Mentone Cres. M22: Wyth 1C **154**
Mentone Rd. SK4: Stoc 6D **132**
Mentor St. M13: Man 4B **113**
Menzies Ct. M21: Chor 6H **113**
          (off Ransfield Rd.)
Mercer La. OL11: Roch 3A **26**
Mercer Rd. M18: Man 2F **117**
Mercer's Rd. OL10: H'ood 6H **39**
Mercer St. M19: Man 6D **116**
  M43: Droy 3B **104**
Merchants Quay M50: Sal 1F **113**
Merchants Quay Ct. M30: Ecc 2E **97**
Mercian Mall
  OL6: A Lyme 5C **174** (2H **105**)
Mercian Way SK3: Stoc 6E **179** (4F **145**)
Mercia St. BL3: Bolt 2A **48**
Mercury Bldgs. M1: Man 6C **6**
Mercury Bus. Pk. M41: Urm 1H **111**
Mercury Way M41: Urm 2H **111**
Mere, The OL6: A Lyme 5C **92**
  SK8: Chea H 1C **156**
Mere Av. M6: Sal 3E **99**
  M24: Mid 3C **72**
  M43: Droy 5G **103**
Mere Bank Cl. M28: Walk 6G **65**
Merebank Cl. OL11: Roch 3A **26**
Merebrook Cl. M26: Rad 5B **52**
Mere Cl. BL9: Bury 2H **53**
  M33: Sale 6F **129**
  M34: Dent 5B **118**
Mereclough Av. M28: Walk 2B **82**
Meredew Av. M27: Swin 5G **83**
Meredith Ct. M15: Man 6A **10**
            (off Epsley Cl.)
Meredith St. BL3: Bolt 4D **48**
  M14: Man 2H **131**
Mere Dr. M20: Man 5F **131**
  M27: Clif 1A **84**
Merefield Av. OL11: Roch 6G **27**
Merefield Rd. WA15: Tim 6C **140**
Merefield St. OL11: Roch 6G **27**
Merefield Ter. OL11: Roch 6G **27**
Mere Fold M28: Walk 6F **65**
Mere Gdns. BL1: Bolt 5C **32**
Merehall Cl. BL1: Bolt 5C **32**
Merehall Dr. BL1: Bolt 5C **32**
Merehall St. BL1: Bolt 4B **32**
Mere Ho. M15: Man 4B **8** (6B **100**)
  SK4: Stoc 2A **144**
Mereland Av. M20: Man 5G **131**
Mere La.
  OL11: Roch 6B **178** (6H **27**)
Meremanor M28: Walk 2B **82**
Merepool Cl. SK6: Mar 4A **148**

Mere Side SK15: Stal 1D **106**
          (not continuous)
Mereside Cl. SK8: Chea H 1B **156**
Mereside Gro. M28: Walk 6A **66**
Mereside Wlk. M15: Man 6D **8**
Mere St. OL11: Roch 5B **178** (5H **27**)
Mere Wlk. BL1: Bolt 5C **32**
Merewood Av. M22: Wyth 5B **142**
Merewood Av. M22: Wyth 5B **142**
Meriden Cl. M26: Rad 1H **51**
Meriden Gro. BL6: Los 1D **46**
Meridian Cl. OL8: O'ham 6F **177**
Meridian Pl. M20: Man 5E **131**
Merinall Cl. OL16: Roch 4C **28**
Meriton Rd. SK9: Hand 3G **165**
Merlewood Av. M19: Man 2E **133**
  M34: Aud 4B **104**
  OL3: Upp 1D **78**
Merlewood Dr. M27: Swin 5E **83**
Merlin Cl. OL8: O'ham 3G **91**
          (not continuous)
  OL15: L'ough 1G **29**
  SK2: Stoc 5G **147**
Merlin Dr. M27: Clif 1B **84**
Merlin Gro. BL1: Bolt 4H **31**
Merlin Ho. M19: Man 5H **131**
Merlin Rd. M44: Irl 4E **109**
  OL16: Miln 5F **29**
Merlyn Av. M20: Man 5G **131**
  M33: Sale 3C **128**
  M34: Dent 5E **119**
Merlyn Ct. M20: Man 5G **131**
          (off Milden Cl.)
Merrick Av. M22: Wyth 1C **154**
Merrick St. OL10: H'ood 4A **40**
Merridale, The WA15: Hale 5A **152**
Merridale Rd. M40: Man 2E **89**
Merridge Wlk. M8: Man 5D **86**
         (off Brentfield Av.)
Merrill St. M4: Man 5H **7** (4H **101**)
Merriman St. M16: W Ran 3C **114**
Merrion St. BL4: Farn 5G **49**
Merrow Wlk. M1: Man 3C **10**
Merrybent Cl. SK2: Stoc 6D **146**
Merrybower Rd. M7: Sal 3C **86**
Merrydale Av. M30: Ecc 1G **97**
Merryman Hall OL16: Roch 1B **28**
Merseybank Av. M21: Chor 5B **130**
Mersey Bank Lodge
  SK13: Had 2H **123**
Mersey Bank Rd. SK13: Had 3H **123**
Mersey Cl. M45: White 6H **53**
Mersey Cl. M33: Sale 4E **129**
Mersey Cres. M20: Man 6B **130**
Mersey Dr. M31: Part 5E **125**
  M45: White 6H **53**
Mersey Ferries Terminal 6F **99**
Mersey Mdws. M20: Man 6D **130**
Mersey Rd. M20: Man 6D **130**
  M33: Sale 3B **128**
  SK4: Stoc 1B **144**
Mersey Rd. Ind. Est.
  M35: Fail 2B **90**
Mersey Rd. Nth. M35: Fail 2A **90**
Mersey Sq. M45: White 6H **53**
Mersey St. SK1: Stoc 2F **179** (2G **145**)
          (not continuous)
Mersey St. M11: Man 6G **103**
          (not continuous)
  SK1: Stoc 1A **146**
Mersey Valley Vis. Cen. 4F **129**
Mersey Vw. M41: Urm 1A **126**
Merseyside SK1: Stoc 2F **179** (2G **145**)
Merston Dr. M20: Man 3G **143**
Merton Av. OL8: O'ham 6D **74**
  SK6: Bred 5G **135**
  SK7: H Gro 5F **159**
Merton Cl. BL3: Bolt 2A **48**
Merton Dr. M43: Droy 4G **103**
Merton Gro. M29: Ast 5A **80**
  OL9: Chad 6F **73**
  WA15: Tim 5B **140**

Merton Rd. M25: Pres 4A **70**
  M33: Sale 4A **128**
  SK3: Stoc 3D **144**
  SK12: Poy 3B **168**
Merton St. BL8: Bury 2D **36**
Merton Wlk. M9: Man 4A **88**
         (off Nethervale Dr.)
Merville Av. M40: Man 2B **88**
Mervyn Rd. M7: Sal 5G **85**
Merwell Rd. M41: Urm 6A **110**
Merwood Av. SK8: H Grn 5H **155**
Merwood Gro. M14: Man 3A **116**
Meshaw Cl. M23: Wyth 1E **141**
Mesnefield Rd. M7: Sal 3G **85**
Mesne Lea Gro. M28: Wors 3A **82**
Mesne Lea Rd. M28: Walk 3A **82**
Met, The 3B **176**
Metal Box Way BL5: W'ton 5A **46**
Metcalfe Ct. M38: Lit H 5D **64**
  SK6: Rom 1H **147**
         (off Metcalfe Dr.)
Metcalfe Dr. SK6: Rom 1H **147**
Metcalfe St. OL16: Roch 4D **28**
Metcalf M. OL3: Upp 1D **78**
Metcalf Ter. BL2: Ain 4F **35**
Metfield Pl. BL1: Bolt 5A **32**
Metfield Wlk. M40: Man 1F **89**
Methodist Intl. Ho. M14: Man 3A **116**
         (off Daisy Bank Rd.)
Methuen St. M12: Man 4D **116**
Methwold St. BL3: Bolt 3A **48**
Metroplex Bus. Pk. M50: Sal 5E **99**
Mevagissey Wlk. OL4: O'ham 1A **76**
Mews, The BL1: Bolt 5H **31**
  M25: Pres 6H **69**
  M28: Wors 5A **82**
  M33: Sale 6C **128**
  M40: Man 2B **102**
  M45: White 1D **68**
  SK8: Gat 6F **143**
Mexborough St. OL4: O'ham 1B **76**
Meyer St. SK3: Stoc 5H **145**
Meyrick Rd. M6: Sal 2G **99**
Miall St. OL11: Roch 6C **178** (5H **27**)
Micawber Rd. SK12: Poy 5E **169**
Michael Ct. M19: Man 1H **143**
Michaels Hey Pde. M23: Wyth 3C **140**
Michael St. M24: Mid 1B **72**
Michael Wife La.
  BL0: Eden, Ram 1H **13**
         (not continuous)
Michigan Av. M50: Sal 5F **99**
Michigan Pk. M50: Sal 5F **99**
Mickleby Wlk. M40: Man 2F **7**
MICKLEHURST 2H **93**
Micklehurst Av. M20: Man 5C **130**
Micklehurst Grn. SK2: Stoc 6E **147**
Micklehurst Rd. OL5: Mos 3H **93**
Midbrook Wlk. M22: Wyth 3H **153**
         (off Plowden Rd.)
Middlebourne St. M6: Sal 3E **99**
Middlebrook Dr. BL6: Los 1C **46**
Middle Calderbrook OL15: L'ough 2A **16**
Middle Fld. OL11: Roch 2H **25**
Middlefield OL8: O'ham 3G **91**
Middlefields SK8: Chea H 1D **156**
Middlegate M40: Man 6F **73**
  OL8: O'ham 1E **91**
Middle Grn. OL6: A Lyme 1A **106**
Middleham St. M14: Man 5E **115**
MIDDLE HEALEY 5F **15**
Middle Hill OL12: Roch 5H **15**
Middle Hillgate
  SK1: Stoc 3H **179** (2H **145**)
MIDDLE HULTON 6A **48**
Middle Newgate OL15: L'ough 1G **17**
Middlesex Dr. BL9: Bury 5F **37**
Middlesex Rd. M9: Man 1H **87**
  SK5: Stoc 3B **134**
Middlesex Wlk. OL9: O'ham 3D **74**
Middlestone Dr. M9: Man 4H **87**
Middle St. OL12: Whitw 4A **14**
MIDDLETON .5C **56**

Middleton Av. M35: Fail 4H **89**
Middleton Cen. Ind. Est.
  M24: Mid 1B **72**
Middleton Cl. M26: Rad 6H **35**
Middleton Dr. BL9: Bury 4F **53**
Middleton Gdns. M24: Mid 1B **72**
MIDDLETON JUNCTION 3F **73**
Middleton Leisure Cen. 1C **72**
Middleton Old Rd. M9: Man 1H **87**
Middleton Rd. M8: Man 2D **86**
  M24: Mid 3E **71**
           (not continuous)
  OL1: Chad 6F **57**
  OL2: O'ham 4B **58**
  OL9: Chad 3E **177** (6F **57**)
           (not continuous)
  OL10: H'ood, Mid 5A **40**
  SK5: Stoc 5H **117**
Middleton Shop. Cen.
  M24: Mid 1B **72**
Middleton Swimming Baths 1C **72**
Middleton Vw. M24: Mid 1D **72**
Middleton Way M24: Mid 1B **72**
Middleway OL4: Grot 4F **77**
Middlewich Wlk. M18: Man 2E **117**
          (off Peacock Cl.)
MIDDLEWOOD 2A **170**
Middlewood Ct. OL9: Chad 1A **74**
Middlewood Dr. SK4: Stoc 2C **144**
Middlewood Grn. OL9: Chad 1A **74**
Middle Wood La. OL15: L'ough . . .3E **17**
Middlewood Rd. SK6: H Lan 6B **160**
  SK12: Poy 6H **159**
Middlewood Station (Rail) 1B **170**
Middlewood St. M5: Sal 6B **4** (4A **100**)
Middlewood Vw. SK6: H Lan 5B **160**
Middlewood Wlk. M9: Man 4H **87**
        (off Fernclough Rd.)
Midfield Ct. M7: Sal 4C **86**
Midford Av. M30: Ecc 3D **96**
Midford Dr. BL1: Bolt 4C **18**
Midford Wlk. M8: Man 5E **87**
        (off Barnsdale Dr.)
Midge Hall Dr. OL11: Roch 5C **26**
Midge Hill OL5: Mos 5H **77**
Midgley Av. M18: Man 1G **117**
Midgley Cres. OL6: A Lyme 1C **106**
Midgley Dr. OL16: Roch 3C **42**
Midgley St. M27: Swin 5F **83**
Midgrove OL3: Del 3B **62**
Midgrove La. OL3: Del 4B **62**
Midhurst Av. M40: Man 1D **102**
Midhurst Cl. BL1: Bolt 4C **32**
        (off Bk. Ashford Wlk.)
  SK8: Chea H 5B **156**
Midhurst St. OL11: Roch 6H **27**
Midhurst Way OL9: Chad 3B **74**
        (off Petworth Rd.)
Midland Cotts. SK7: H Gro 4A **160**
Midland Rd. SK5: Stoc 5H **117**
  SK7: Bram 1G **157**
Midland St. M12: Man 3H **11** (6H **101**)
Midland Ter. WA14: Alt 3F **151**
        (off Ashley Rd.)
Midland Wlk. SK7: Bram 2G **157**
        (not continuous)
Midlothian St. M11: Man 3D **102**
Midmoor Wlk. M9: Man 6A **72**
        (off Stockfield Dr.)
MID REDDISH 2H **133**
Midville Rd. M11: Man 2E **103**
MIDWAY 5D **168**
Midway SK8: Chea H 2D **166**
Midway Dr. SK12: Poy 5D **168**
Midway St. M12: Man 5C **116**
Midwood Hall M6: Sal 2F **99**
        (off Eccles Old Rd.)
Milan St. M7: Sal 5C **86**
Milbourne Rd. BL9: Bury 5F **23**
Milburn Av. M23: Wyth 1H **141**
Milburn Dr. BL2: Bolt 5B **34**
Milbury Dr. OL15: L'ough 1G **29**
Milden Cl. M20: Man 5G **131**

Mildred Av. M25: Pres 2A **86**
  OL2: O'ham 5E **59**
  OL4: Grot 4F **77**
Mildred St. M7: Sal 6A **86**
Mild St. M9: Man 6H **71**
MILE END 5B **146**
Mile End La. SK2: Stoc 6B **146**
Mile La. BL8: Bury 4H **35**
MILES PLATTING 2H **7** (2A **102**)
Miles Platting Swimming Pool &
  Fitness Cen. 1H **7** (2H **101**)
Miles St. BL1: Bolt 3B **32**
  BL4: Farn 1G **65**
  M12: Man 6C **102**
  OL1: O'ham 1H **75**
  SK14: Hyde 5D **120**
Milford Av. OL8: O'ham 1C **90**
Milford Brow OL4: Lees 2C **76**
Milford Cres. OL15: L'ough 3H **17**
Milford Dr. M19: Man 2D **132**
Milford Gro. SK2: Stoc 4C **146**
Milford Rd. BL2: Bolt 1B **34**
  BL3: Bolt 4C **48**
Milford St. M6: Sal 4E **99**
  M9: Man 5F **71**
  OL12: Roch 2H **27**
Milking Grn. Ind. Est.
  OL4: Lees 4D **76**
Milking La. BL3: Farn 5B **48**
Milkstone Pl. OL11: Roch . .6B **178** (5H **27**)
Milkstone Rd.
  OL11: Roch 5B **178** (5H **27**)
Milk St. BL0: Ram 4F **13**
  M2: Man 5A **6** (4E **101**)
  OL4: O'ham 2A **76**
  OL11: Roch 5B **178** (5H **27**)
  SK14: Hyde 5B **120**
Milkwood Gro. M18: Man 3F **117**
Mill, The SK15: Stal 4E **107**
Millais St. M40: Man 3C **88**
Millard St. OL9: Chad 2A **74**
Millard Wlk. M18: Man 3F **117**
Mill Bank M26: Rad 5B **52**
Millbank Cl. OL10: H'ood 3F **39**
Millbank Gdns. BL1: Bolt 4H **31**
        (off Ivy Rd.)
Millbank St. M1: Man 6E **7** (4G **101**)
  OL10: H'ood 3F **39**
Millbeck Ct. M24: Mid 5H **55**
Millbeck Gro. BL3: Bolt 3C **48**
        (off Roxalina St.)
Millbeck Rd. M24: Mid 5H **55**
Millbeck St. M15: Man 5A **10** (1E **115**)
Millbrae Gdns. OL2: Shaw 6F **43**
MILLBROOK 1H **107**
Millbrook SK14: Holl 1F **123**
Millbrook Av. M34: Dent 6D **118**
Millbrook Bank OL11: Roch 2H **25**
Millbrook Cl. OL2: Shaw 1B **60**
Millbrook Fold SK7: H Gro 5F **159**
Millbrook Gro. SK9: Wilm 6H **165**
        (off Bankside Cl.)
Millbrook Ho. BL4: Farn 1A **66**
        (off Lime St.)
Mill Brook Ind. Est. M23: Wyth . . .5E **141**
Millbrook Rd. M23: Wyth 2G **153**
Millbrook St. SK1: Stoc . . .4G **179** (3H **145**)
Millbrook Towers
  SK1: Stoc 4G **179** (3H **145**)
MILL BROW
  M28 . . . . .5E **81**
  SK6 . . . . .3H **149**
Mill Brow M9: Man 1G **87**
  M28: Wors 5B **82**
  OL1: Chad 5A **58**
  OL6: A Lyme 2A **92**
  SK6: Mar B 3H **149**
Mill Brow Rd. SK6: Mar B 3H **149**
Millbrow Ter. OL1: Chad 5A **58**
Mill Bldg., The BL7: Eger 2B **18**
Mill Ct. M41: Urm 5G **111**
Mill Ct. Dr. M26: Rad 1D **66**
Millcrest Cl. M28: Wors 6D **80**

Mill Cft. BL1: Bolt 5B **32**
  OL2: Shaw 1A **60**
Mill Cft. Cl. OL12: Roch 1G **25**
Millcroft La. OL3: Del 1B **62**
        (not continuous)
Milldale Cl. BL6: Los 6B **30**
Millennium Ct. BL3: Bolt 4H **47**
Millennium Ho. M16: Old T 6B **8**
  M34: Dent 5C **118**
Millennium Tower M50: Sal 5F **99**
Miller Hey OL5: Mos 4H **93**
Miller Ho. OL2: Shaw 2H **59**
Miller Mdw. Cl. OL2: Shaw 5A **44**
Miller Rd. OL8: O'ham 6E **75**
Millers Brook Cl. OL10: H'ood 2H **39**
Millers Cl. M33: Sale 6G **129**
Millers Ct. M5: Sal 3A **98**
  SK15: Stal 5D **106**
Miller St. BL1: Bolt 1C **32**
  BL9: Sum 1C **22**
  M4: Man 2A **6** (3E **101**)
  M26: Rad 1H **51**
  OL6: A Lyme 1H **105**
  OL10: H'ood 3H **39**
        (not continuous)
Millers Wharf SK15: Stal 3F **107**
Millett St. BL0: Ram 2D **12**
  BL9: Bury 3D **36**
Millett Ter. BL9: Bury 4C **24**
Millfield OL10: H'ood 3H **39**
        (off Hornby St.)
Millfield Ct. WA15: Hale 3G **151**
Millfield Dr. M28: Wors 5F **81**
Millfield Gro. OL16: Roch 5B **28**
Millfield Rd. BL2: Bolt 6C **34**
Millfield Wlk. M40: Man 1E **89**
        (off Pleasington Dr.)
Millfold OL12: Whitw 3B **14**
Mill Fold Gdns. OL15: L'ough 5G **17**
Mill Fold Rd. M24: Mid 1B **72**
Millford Av. M41: Urm 5A **110**
        (not continuous)
Millford Gdns. M41: Urm 5A **110**
MILLGATE 1B **14**
Mill Ga. OL8: O'ham 6D **74**
Millgate BL7: Eger 1B **18**
  OL3: Del 3B **62**
  OL16: Roch 1C **28**
  SK1: Stoc 1G **179** (1H **145**)
Mill Ga. Cen. BL9: Bury 3C **176** (3F **37**)
Millgate Cen. OL3: Del 3B **62**
Millgate La. M20: Man 3F **143**
        (Parrs Wood Rd.)
  M20: Man 2F **143**
        (Wilmslow Rd.)
Mill Grn. St. M12: Man 2G **11** (5H **101**)
Millhalf Cl. M11: Man 6E **9** (2C **114**)
Millhead Av. M40: Man 3A **102**
MILL HILL 3H **175** (6E **33**)
Mill Hill M38: Lit H 3C **64**
Mill Hill Av. SK12: Poy 6D **158**
Mill Hill Cvn. Pk. BL2: Bolt 5E **33**
Mill Hill Gro. SK14: Mot 5B **122**
Mill Hill Hollow SK12: Poy 6D **158**
Mill Hill St. BL2: Bolt 5E **33**
Mill Hill Way SK14: Mot 5B **122**
        (off Chain Bar La.)
Mill Ho. BL9: Bury 3F **23**
Millhouse Av. M23: Wyth 1G **153**
Mill Ho. Cl. OL12: Roch 5D **16**
Millhouse St. BL0: Ram 1E **13**
Millner Ct. SK2: Stoc 4D **146**
Milliners Wharf M4: Man . . .5G **7** (4H **101**)
Milling St. M1: Man 2H **9** (5D **100**)
Millington Rd. M17: T Pk 6C **98**
Millington Wlk. M15: Man 5D **8**
Mill La. BL6: Los 1A **46**
  BL8: Bury 1B **36**
  M22: Nor 2C **142**
  M34: Dent 6H **119**
  M35: Fail 4E **89**
  OL2: O'ham 3C **58**

Mill La. OL3: Dob 6H **61**
  OL5: Mos 1G **93**
  OL6: A Lyme 6B **174** (3H **105**)
  OL9: Chad 5C **74**
  SK5: Stoc 6H **117**
  SK6: Rom 4G **147**
  SK6: Wood *3G 135*
  (off Hyde Rd.)
  SK6: Wood 3G **135**
  (Lambeth Gro., not continuous)
  SK7: H Gro 5F **159**
  SK8: Chea 5H **143**
  (not continuous)
  SK8: Chea H 2D **156**
  SK14: Hyde 6H **119**
  WA15: Alt 3D **162**
Mill Nook OL12: Roch 6H **15**
Millom Av. M23: Wyth 2H **141**
Millom Cl. OL16: Roch 2C **28**
Millom Ct. WA15: Tim 5D **140**
Millom Dr. BL9: Bury 5G **53**
Millom Pl. SK8: Gat 2F **155**
Millow St. M4: Man 2A **6** (2E **101**)
Mill Pond Cl. OL2: Shaw 1H **59**
Millpool Cl. SK6: Wood 4H **135**
Millpool Wlk. *M9: Man* *3H 87*
  (off Alderside Rd.)
Millrise OL1: O'ham 1F **177**
Mill Rd. BL9: Bury 3F **23**
  SK9: Wilm 2E **173**
Mills Farm Cl. OL8: O'ham 2G **91**
MILLS HILL 1G **73**
Mills Hill Rd. M24: Mid 6F **57**
Mills Hill Station (Rail) 6F **57**
Millside *OL6: A Lyme* *2A 106*
  (off Mossley Rd.)
Mills St. OL10: H'ood 3F **39**
  OL12: Whitw 4B **14**
Millstone Cl. SK12: Poy 2F **169**
Millstone Ct. SK6: Bred 6G **135**
Millstone Rd. BL1: Bolt 4F **31**
Millstream La. M40: Man 2G **103**
Mill St. BL0: Ram 5A **12**
  BL1: Bolt 3H **175** (5E **33**)
  BL4: Farn 1G **65**
  BL7: Bro X 3D **18**
  BL8: Tot 4H **21**
  M6: Sal 1G **99**
  M11: Man 5C **102**
  (not continuous)
  M26: Rad 5B **52**
  (not continuous)
  M28: Wors 4E **81**
  M35: Fail 4E **89**
  OL2: O'ham 3D **58**
  OL3: Upp 1D **78**
  OL5: Mos 3G **93**
  OL15: L'ough 6F **17**
  SK6: Wood 4G **135**
  (not continuous)
  SK7: H Gro 2D **158**
  SK9: Wilm 2E **173**
  SK14: Hyde 2C **120**
  SK15: Stal 4G **107**
  WA14: Alt 6G **139**
Mill St. Ind. Est.
  BL1: Bolt 3H **175** (5E **33**)
Milltown Cl. M26: Rad 5B **52**
Milltown St. M26: Rad 5B **52**
Mill Vw. Ct. OL8: O'ham 6D **74**
Millwain Ho. SK4: Stoc 5C **132**
Millwall Cl. M18: Man 2F **117**
Millway WA15: Haleb 6C **152**
Millway Wlk. *M40: Man* *6E 89*
  (off Orford Rd.)
Millwell La. BL1: Bolt 3F **175**
Millwood Cl. SK8: Chea H 5A **156**
Millwood Ct. BL9: Bury 1F **53**
  OL2: O'ham 3D **58**
Millwood Ter. SK14: Hyde 5B **120**
Millwood Vw. SK15: Stal 3F **107**
Millwright St. M40: Man 6D **88**
Mill Yd. BL9: Bury 2G **37**

Milne Cl. M12: Man 1C **116**
  SK16: Duk 5A **106**
Milne Gro. OL16: Miln 6H **29**
Milner Av. BL9: Bury 6F **23**
  WA14: B'ath 4D **138**
Milner St. M16: Old T 3B **114**
  M26: Rad 4G **51**
  M27: Swin 3H **83**
  OL12: Whitw 1E **15**
Milne St. *M12: Man* *1C 116*
  (off Milne Cl.)
  OL1: O'ham 5G **59**
  OL2: Shaw 1H **59**
  OL9: Chad 2B **74**
  (Brook St.)
  OL9: Chad 6C **58**
  (Burnley La.)
  OL9: O'ham 4C **74**
  OL11: Roch 3E **41**
Milngate Cl. OL16: Roch 2C **42**
Milnholme BL1: Bolt 2H **31**
MILNROW 5E **29**
Milnrow Cl. M13: Man . . .3D **10** (6F **101**)
Milnrow Rd. OL2: Shaw 6H **43**
  OL15: L'ough 1F **29**
  OL16: Miln 6H **43**
  OL16: Roch 4C **178** (4A **28**)
Milnrow Station (Rail) 6F **29**
Milnthorpe Rd. BL2: Bolt 5A **34**
Milnthorpe St. M6: Sal 6H **85**
Milnthorpe Way M12: Man 1A **116**
Milsom Av. BL3: Bolt 4A **48**
Milstead Wlk. *M40: Man* *6C 88*
  (off Peckford Dr.)
Milston Wlk. *M8: Man* *5E 87*
  (off Barnsdale Dr.)
Milton Av. BL3: Bolt 4H **47**
  BL3: Lit L 3D **50**
  M5: Sal 3D **98**
  M43: Droy 4A **104**
  M44: Irl 3C **124**
  SK15: Mill 1H **107**
Milton Cl. M32: Stre 4E **113**
  SK6: Mar 1D **160**
  SK16: Duk 6F **107**
  (not continuous)
Milton Ct. M7: Sal 2C **86**
  M19: Man 5A **132**
  M30: Ecc 3F **97**
  SK7: Bram 1G **167**
Milton Cres. BL4: Farn 3F **65**
  SK8: Chea 6G **143**
Milton Dr. M33: Sale 3A **128**
  OL9: Chad 3A **74**
  SK12: Poy 3D **168**
  WA15: Tim 2A **140**
Milton Gro. M16: W Ran 5A **114**
  M33: Sale 3A **128**
Milton Lodge M16: W Ran 5A **114**
Milton Mt. *M18: Man* *3F 117*
  (off Old Hall Dr.)
Milton Pl. M6: Sal 2H **99**
Milton Rd. M25: Pres 4A **70**
  M26: Rad 3F **51**
  M27: Swin 2F **83**
  M32: Stre 4E **113**
  M34: Aud 4D **104**
  SK7: Bram 6G **157**
Milton St. BL0: Ram 3B **12**
  M7: Sal 1C **100**
  M24: Mid 6B **56**
  M30: Ecc 3F **97**
  OL2: O'ham 2E **59**
  OL5: Mos 1G **93**
  OL16: Roch 2C **178** (3H **27**)
  SK14: Hyde 3B **120**
Milton Vw. OL5: Mos 1G **93**
Milverton Av. SK14: Hat 6G **121**
Milverton Cl. BL6: Los 2D **46**
Milverton Dr. SK7: Bram 2D **166**
Milverton Rd. M14: Man 3H **115**
Milverton Wlk. SK14: Hat 5G **121**
Milwain Dr. SK4: Stoc 3E **133**

Milwain Rd. M19: Man 1B **132**
  M32: Stre 6C **112**
Mimosa Dr. M27: Pen 1H **83**
Mincing St. M4: Man 2B **6** (2E **101**)
Minden Cl. BL8: Bury 3B **36**
  M20: Man 5G **131**
Minden Pde. BL9: Bury 4C **176** (3F **37**)
Minden St. M6: Sal 5E **85**
Minehead Av. M20: Man 2D **130**
  M41: Urm 1D **126**
Miners M., The M28: Wors 4F **81**
Minerva Rd. BL4: Farn 6D **48**
  OL6: A Lyme 6D **174** (3A **106**)
Minerva Ter. *OL15: L'ough* *4G 17*
  (off William St.)
Mine St. OL10: H'ood 1G **39**
Minford Cl. M40: Man 6D **88**
Minnie St. BL3: Bolt 4H **47**
  OL12: Whitw 3B **14**
Minoan Gdns. M7: Man 6A **86**
Minorca Av. M11: Man 3F **103**
Minorca Cl. OL11: Roch 3A **26**
Minorca St. BL3: Bolt 3C **48**
Minor St. M35: Fail 3A **90**
  (not continuous)
  OL11: Roch 4E **41**
Minshull St. M1: Man 6B **6** (4E **101**)
Minshull St. Sth. M1: Man . .1C **10** (5F **101**)
Minsmere Cl. M8: Man 5E **87**
Minsmere Walks SK2: Stoc 6F **147**
Minstead Cl. SK14: Hyde 6E **121**
Minstead Wlk. M22: Wyth 3H **153**
Minster Cl. BL2: Bolt 3G **33**
  SK16: Duk 1B **120**
Minster Dr. M41: Urm 4C **110**
  SK8: Chea 6C **144**
  WA14: Bow 5C **150**
Minster Gro. M29: Ast 4A **80**
Minster Rd. BL2: Bolt 3G **33**
  M9: Man 3B **88**
Minster Way OL9: Chad 6A **58**
Minstrel Cl. M27: Swin 4G **83**
Minton Ct. *BL3: Bolt* *3G 47*
  (off Hough St.)
Minton St. M40: Man 3E **89**
  OL4: O'ham 4G **75**
Minto St. OL7: A Lyme 1G **105**
  (not continuous)
Mintridge Cl. M11: Man 6G **103**
Mint St. BL0: Ram 3F **13**
Mirabel St. M3: Man 2G **5** (2D **100**)
Miranda Ct. M5: Sal 2B **8** (5A **100**)
Mirfield Av. M9: Man 5H **71**
  OL8: O'ham 5E **75**
  SK4: Stoc 1D **144**
Mirfield Dr. M24: Mid 6B **56**
  M30: Ecc 1F **97**
  M41: Urm 3E **111**
Mirfield Rd. M9: Man 5H **71**
Miriam St. BL3: Bolt 3H **47**
  M35: Fail 5F **89**
Missenden Ho. *M5: Sal* *4F 99*
  (off Cyprus Cl.)
Mission St. OL10: H'ood 3G **39**
Missouri Av. M50: Salf 4E **99**
Misterton Wlk. *M23: Wyth* *3E 141*
  (off Sandy La.)
Mistletoe Gro. M3: Sal 2D **4**
Mistral Ct. M30: Ecc 2G **97**
Mitcham Av. M9: Man 6C **72**
Mitchell Cl. SK8: Gat 5D **142**
Mitchell Gdns. M22: Shar 6C **142**
MITCHELL HEY 4A **178** (4G **27**)
Mitchell Hey OL12: Roch 4G **27**
Mitchell Ho. *SK8: Gat* *5D 142*
  (off Mitchell Cl.)
Mitchells Quay M35: Fail 4G **89**
Mitchell St. BL8: Bury 1C **36**
  M30: Ecc 2E **97**
  M40: Man 6D **88**
  OL1: O'ham 1E **75**
  OL12: Roch 3F **27**
  OL16: Roch 6C **16**

Mitcheson Gdns. M6: Sal 2F 99
Mitford Ct. M14: Man 2G 131
Mitford Rd. M14: Man 2G 131
Mitford St. M32: Stre 6C 112
Mitre Rd. M13: Man 3B 116
Mitre St. BL1: Bolt 1C 32
   M35: Fail 3H 89
Mitton Cl. BL8: Bury 3G 35
   OL10: H'ood 3D 38
Mizpah Gro. BL8: Bury 3B 36
Mizzy Rd. OL12: Roch 2G 27
Moadlock SK6: Rom 5A 136
Moat Av. M22: Wyth 6A 142
Moat Gdns. M22: Wyth 1A 154
Moat Hall Av. M30: Ecc 5C 96
Moat Rd. M22: Wyth 1A 154
Moat Wlk. SK5: Stoc 2C 134
Mobberley Cl. M19: Man 5A 132
Mobberley Rd. BL2: Bolt 5H 33
   SK9: Wilm 6A 164
Moberly Hall M15: Man 6C 10
Mocha Pde. M7: Sal 1D 4 (2B 100)
Modbury Cl. SK7: H Gro 4A 158
Modbury Ct. M26: Rad 2C 66
Modbury Wlk. M8: Man 5E 87
   (off Brinsworth Dr.)
Mode Hill La. M45: White 1A 70
Mode Hill Wlk. M45: White 1A 70
Model Lodging Ho. M3: Sal 4E 5
Mode Wheel Circ. M17: T Pk 6C 98
Mode Wheel Ind. Est. M50: Sal 5D 98
Mode Wheel Rd. M50: Sal 4D 98
Mode Wheel Rd. Sth. M50: Sal 5D 98
Modwen Rd. M5: Sal 1H 113
Moelfre Dr. SK8: Chea H 6E 157
Moffat Cl. BL2: Bolt 1B 50
Moffat Ct. SK16: Duk 4H 105
Moggie La. SK10: Adl 6F 169
Moisant St. BL3: Bolt 4B 48
Moison Ho. SK2: Stoc 5A 146
   (off Canada St.)
Mold St. BL1: Bolt 2C 32
   OL1: O'ham 1F 177 (1E 75)
Molesworth St.
   OL16: Roch 3D 178 (4A 28)
Mollets Wood M34: Dent 2G 119
Mollington Rd. M22: Wyth 5C 154
Mollis Gro. OL1: O'ham 4C 60
Molyneux Rd. BL5: W'ton 6A 46
   M19: Man 6E 117
Molyneux St. OL12: Roch 3F 27
Mona Av. M32: Stre 4C 112
   SK8: H Grn 4H 155
Monaco Dr. M22: Nor 1B 142
Monarch Cl. M44: Irl 3C 124
   OL2: O'ham 5D 58
Mona Rd. OL9: Chad 4B 74
Monart Rd. M9: Man 2A 88
Mona St. M6: Sal 1G 99
   (off Gloucester St.)
   SK14: Hyde 5C 120
Mona Way M44: Irl 1F 125
Moncrieffe St. BL3: Bolt 6G 175 (1D 48)
   (not continuous)
Monde Trad. Est. M17: T Pk 1A 112
Mond Rd. M44: Irl 3F 109
Money Ash Rd. WA15: Alt 2F 151
Monfa Av. SK2: Stoc 1A 158
Monica Av. M8: Man 6D 70
Monica Ct. M30: Ecc 2H 97
Monica Gro. M19: Man 1B 132
Monks Cl. M8: Man 1F 87
   OL16: Miln 5E 29
Monks Ct. M5: Sal 3B 98
Monksdale Av. M41: Urm 5D 110
Monks Hall Gro. M30: Ecc 3H 97
Monks La. BL2: Bolt 3H 33
Monkswood OL1: O'ham . . .2E 177 (2E 75)
Monkton Av. M18: Man 4E 117
Monkwood Dr. M9: Man 3A 88
   (off Dalbeattie St.)
Monmouth Av. BL9: Bury 6F 23
   M33: Sale 4H 127

Monmouth Rd. SK8: Chea H 4D 156
Monmouth St. M18: Man 1G 117
   M24: Mid 1E 73
   OL9: O'ham 4C 74
   OL11: Roch 6B 178 (5H 27)
Monroe Cl. M6: Sal 1E 99
Monsal Av. M7: Sal 4G 85
   SK2: Stoc 4D 146
Monsall Cl. BL9: Bury 5G 53
Monsall Rd. M40: Man 5A 88
Monsall St. M40: Man 6H 87
   OL8: O'ham 6E 75
Mons Av. OL11: Roch 3E 27
Montague Bus. Pk. M16: Old T 3G 113
Montague Ct. M33: Sale 5C 128
   (off Montague Rd.)
Montague Ho. SK3: Stoc 2F 145
   (off East St.)
Montague Rd. M16: Old T 2G 113
   M33: Sale 5B 128
   OL6: A Lyme 3B 106
Montague St. BL3: Bolt 4H 47
Montague Way SK15: Stal 3E 107
Montagu Rd. SK2: Stoc 4D 146
Montagu St. SK6: Comp 1F 149
Montana Sq. M11: Man 6G 103
Montcliffe Cres. M16: W Ran 6D 114
Monteagle St. M9: Man 5F 71
Montford Ent. Cen. M50: Sal 4F 99
   (off Wynford Sq.)
Montford St. M50: Sal 4F 99
Montgomery OL11: Roch 6A 178 (5G 27)
Montgomery Dr. BL9: Bury 5H 53
Montgomery Ho. M16: W Ran 5D 114
   OL8: O'ham 2B 90
Montgomery Rd. M13: Man 5B 116
Montgomery St. OL8: O'ham 1B 90
   OL11: Roch 1E 41
   (off Manchester Rd.)
Montgomery Way M26: Rad 2E 51
Montmano Dr. M20: Man 3D 130
MONTON 1F 97
Monton Av. M30: Ecc 2G 97
Monton Bri. Ct. M30: Ecc 1E 97
Montondale M30: Ecc 2E 97
Montonfields Rd. M30: Ecc 2E 97
Monton Grn. M30: Ecc 1F 97
Monton La. M30: Ecc 3G 97
Montonmill Gdns. M30: Ecc 2E 97
Monton Rd. M30: Ecc 2F 97
   (not continuous)
   SK5: Stoc 5C 134
Monton St. BL3: Bolt 4C 48
   M14: Man 3E 115
   M26: Rad 4H 51
Montpellier M. M7: Sal 2C 86
Montpellior Rd. M22: Wyth 3B 154
Montreal St. M19: Man 6D 116
   OL8: O'ham 5F 75
Montrose M30: Ecc 3G 97
   (off Monton La.)
Montrose Av. BL0: Ram 1A 22
   BL2: Bolt 4G 33
   M20: Man 4E 131
   M32: Stre 5B 112
   SK2: Stoc 2A 158
   SK16: Duk 6A 106
Montrose Cres. M19: Man 6B 116
Montrose Dr. BL7: Bro X 4F 19
Montrose Gdns. OL2: O'ham 3F 59
Montrose St. OL11: Roch 5E 41
MONTSERRAT 3E 31
Montserrat Brow BL1: Bolt 3D 30
Montserrat Rd. BL1: Bolt 3E 31
Monyash Ct. SK13: Gam 6F 123
   (off Youlgreave Cres.)
Monyash Gro. SK13: Gam 6F 123
   (off Youlgreave Cres.)
Monyash Lea SK13: Gam 6F 123
   (off Ashford M.)
Monyash M. SK13: Gam 6F 123
Monyash Pl. SK13: Gam 6F 123
   (off Monyash M.)

Monyash Way SK13: Gam 6G 123
   (off Ashford M.)
Moon Gro. M14: Man 4H 115
Moon St. OL9: O'ham 2C 74
Moorbottom Rd. BL8: Holc 4A 12
Moorby Av. M19: Man 5A 132
Moorby St. OL1: O'ham 1G 75
Moorby Wlk. BL3: Bolt 2D 48
   (off Fletcher St.)
MOORCLOSE 2E 73
Moor Cl. M26: Rad 2G 51
Moorclose St. M24: Mid 1E 73
Moorclose Wlk. M9: Man 4H 87
   (off Conran St.)
Moorcock Av. M27: Pen 3B 84
Moorcot Ct. M23: Wyth 3F 141
Moor Cres. OL3: Dig 4D 62
Moorcroft BL0: Ram 3G 13
   OL11: Roch 2H 41
Moorcroft Dr. M19: Man 5B 132
Moorcroft Rd. M23: Wyth 2F 141
Moorcroft Sq. SK14: Hyde 1C 120
Moorcroft St. M43: Droy 5A 104
   OL8: O'ham 1C 90
Moorcroft Wlk. M19: Man 5A 132
Moordale Av. OL4: O'ham 6C 60
Moordale St. M20: Man 4E 131
Moordown Cl. M8: Man 5F 87
Moor Edge Rd. OL5: Mos 2B 94
Mooredge Ter. OL2: O'ham 5E 59
Moore Ho. M30: Ecc 5F 97
Moore St. M6: Sal 1E 99
   M34: Dent 6G 119
Moore End M22: Nor 3B 142
Moor End Av. M7: Sal 3A 86
Moor End Ct. M7: Sal 3A 86
Moore's Ct. BL1: Bolt 5A 32
Moore St. OL16: Roch 4C 178 (4H 27)
Moore Wlk. M34: Dent 2G 135
   (off Wordsworth Rd.)
Moorfield M7: Sal 2A 86
   (off Moor La.)
   M26: Rad 3G 51
   M28: Wors 4D 80
   (Crosslands Rd.)
   M28: Wors 3B 82
   (Old Clough La.)
Moorfield Av. M20: Man 2G 131
   M34: Dent 6G 119
   OL15: L'ough 2G 17
   SK15: Stal 6H 107
Moorfield Chase BL4: Farn 2H 65
Moorfield Cl. M27: Swin 5F 83
   M30: Ecc 3F 97
   M44: Irl 4F 109
Moorfield Dr. SK9: Wilm 4B 172
   SK14: Hyde 2D 120
Moorfield Gro. BL2: Bolt 4F 33
   M33: Sale 6D 128
   SK4: Stoc 5D 132
Moorfield Hamlet OL2: Shaw 6F 43
Moorfield Hgts. SK15: C'ook 4A 94
Moorfield M. OL2: Shaw 6H 43
Moorfield Pde. M41: Urm 4F 109
Moorfield Pl. OL12: Roch 2H 27
   (off Turner St.)
Moorfield Rd. M6: Sal 1D 98
   M20: Man 5D 130
   M27: Swin 5E 83
   M44: Irl 4F 109
   OL8: O'ham 1B 90
Moorfield St. M20: Man 2F 131
   (not continuous)
   SK14: Holl 2F 123
Moorfield Ter. SK14: Holl 2F 123
   SK15: C'ook 4A 94
Moorfield Vw. OL15: L'ough 3G 17
Moorfield Wlk. M41: Urm 5F 111
MOORGATE .5A 94
Moor Ga. BL2: Bolt 6H 19
Moorgate BL9: Bury 2D 176 (2F 37)
Moorgate Av. M20: Man 2D 130
   OL11: Roch 4C 26
Moorgate Cotts.
   SK15: C'ook 4B 94

Moorgate Ct. *BL2: Bolt* 4F *33*
   (off Starkie Rd.)
Moorgate Dr. M29: Ast 6A *80*
   SK15: C'ook 5A *94*
Moor Ga. La. OL15: L'ough 1E *17*
Moorgate M. SK5: C'ook 4A *94*
Moorgate Retail Pk.
   BL9: Bury 2D *176* (2F *37*)
Moorgate Rd. M26: Rad 5G *35*
   SK15: C'ook 4A *94*
Moorgate St. OL3: Upp 1D *78*
Moorhead St. M4: Man 2D *6* (2F *101*)
MOORHEY 3H *75*
Moorhey Ind. Est.
   OL4: O'ham 3H *75*
Moorhey Rd. M38: Lit H 3D *64*
Moorhey St. OL4: O'ham 3H *75*
Moor Hill OL11: Roch 3B *26*
Moorhill Ct. M7: Sal 2A *86*
Moorhouse Farm OL16: Miln 5E *29*
Moorhouse Fold OL16: Miln 5E *29*
Moorings, The M28: Wors 6C *82*
   OL5: Mos 6A *78*
   SK12: Dis 1H *171*
Moorings Pk. M17: T Pk 5B *98*
Moorland Av. M8: Man 1D *86*
   M33: Sale 6C *128*
   M43: Droy 4G *103*
   OL3: Del 4B *62*
   OL11: Roch 3B *26*
   OL12: Whitw 2E *15*
   OL16: Miln 5G *29*
Moorland Cres. OL12: Whitw 2E *15*
Moorland Dr. M38: Lit H 3E *65*
   SK8: Chea H 5B *156*
Moorland Fold SK15: Stal 6H *107*
Moorland Gro. BL1: Bolt 3G *31*
Moorland Ho. *M27: Swin* 4H *83*
   (off Worsley Rd.)
Moorland Rd. M20: Man 6F *131*
   SK2: Stoc 1A *158*
   (not continuous)
   SK15: C'ook 6A *94*
Moorlands Av. M41: Urm 4D *110*
Moorlands Cvn. Pk.
   OL3: Dens 2H *45*
Moorlands Cres. OL5: Mos 2H *93*
Moorlands Dr. OL5: Mos 6A *78*
Moorlands St. OL2: Shaw 6A *44*
Moorland St. OL12: Roch 2G *27*
Moorlands Vw. BL3: Bolt 5G *47*
Moorland Ter. OL12: Roch 2C *26*
Moor La. BL1: Bolt 5E *175* (1C *48*)
   BL3: Bolt 5E *175* (1C *48*)
   M7: Sal 3G *85*
   M23: Wyth 1G *141*
   M41: Urm 4C *110*
   OL3: Dob 5E *63*
   OL12: Roch 6B *14*
   SK7: W'ford 4F *167*
   SK9: Wilm 4A *172*
Moorlea M35: Fail 3H *89*
Moor Lodge SK4: Stoc 5D *132*
Moor Nook M33: Sale 6D *128*
Moor Pk. Av. OL11: Roch 3D *40*
Moor Pk. Rd. M20: Man 3G *143*
Moor Platt *M33: Sale* 6A *128*
   (off Derbyshire Rd. Sth.)
Moor Platt Cl. BL6: Hor 2A *30*
Moor Rd. BL8: Holc 1A *12*
   M23: Wyth 2E *141*
   OL15: L'ough 2A *16*
Moorsbrook Gro. *SK9: Wilm* 6A *166*
   (off Lyngard Cl.)
Moorsholme Av. M40: Man 4C *88*
MOORSIDE
   M28 .3E *83*
   OL4 .4C *60*
Moorside OL11: Roch 2H *41*
Moorside Av. BL1: Bolt 3G *31*
   BL2: Ain 4F *35*
   BL4: Farn 2F *65*
   M43: Droy 3C *104*

Moorside Ct. *M33: Sale* 5B *128*
   (off Sibson Rd.)
   M34: Dent 3F *119*
Moorside Cres.
   M43: Droy 3C *104*
Moorside Ho. *WA15: Tim* 4C *140*
   (off Oakleigh Ct.)
Moorside La. M34: Dent 3G *119*
   (not continuous)
Moorside Lodge
   M27: Swin 3F *83*
Moorside Rd. BL8: Tot 5G *21*
   M7: Sal 3A *86*
   M8: Man 2E *87*
   M27: Swin 4E *83*
   M41: Urm 4A *110*
   OL5: Mos 2A *94*
   SK4: Stoc 1C *144*
Moorside Station (Rail) 2F *83*
Moorside St. M43: Droy 3B *104*
Moorside Vw. BL8: Tot 5H *21*
   OL2: Shaw 5A *44*
   (off Small Brook Rd.)
Moorsley Dr. M9: Man 5B *72*
Moor St. BL9: Bury 1D *176* (2F *37*)
   M27: Swin 4H *83*
   M30: Ecc 4D *96*
   OL1: O'ham 2H *75*
   OL2: Shaw 1G *59*
   OL10: H'ood 3F *39*
Moors Vw. BL0: Ram 3B *12*
Moorton Av. M19: Man 2B *132*
Moorton Pk. M19: Man 2B *132*
Moortop Cl. M9: Man 4G *71*
Moor Top Pl. SK4: Stoc 6D *132*
Moor Vw. Cl. OL12: Roch 1B *26*
Moorville Rd. M6: Sal 6C *84*
Moor Way BL8: Haw 1D *20*
Moorway SK9: Wilm 4B *172*
Moorway Dr. M9: Man 5C *72*
Moorwood Dr. M33: Sale 6G *127*
   OL8: O'ham 5A *76*
Mora Av. OL9: Chad 6B *58*
Moran Cl. SK9: Wilm 5A *166*
Moran Wlk. M15: Man 6H *9*
Morar Dr. BL2: Bolt 6C *34*
Morar Rd. SK16: Duk 6B *106*
Mora St. M9: Man 3B *88*
Moravian Cl. SK16: Duk 4A *106*
Moravian Fld. M43: Droy 5A *104*
Moray Cl. BL0: Ram 5A *12*
Moray Rd. OL9: Chad 5A *74*
Morbourne Cl. M12: Man 1A *116*
Morden Av. M11: Man 3E *103*
Morecombe Cl. M40: Man 5D *88*
Morelands, The BL1: Bolt 6G *31*
Moresby Dr. M20: Man 3F *143*
Morestead Wlk. M40: Man 1F *7*
Moreton Av. M32: Stre 5D *112*
   M33: Sale 6G *127*
   M45: White 6F *53*
   (not continuous)
   SK7: Bram 2G *167*
Moreton Cl. SK16: Duk 1B *120*
Moreton Dr. BL8: Bury 2B *36*
   SK9: Hand 4A *166*
   SK12: Poy 3F *169*
Moreton Ho. *WA14: Alt* 1D *150*
   (off Groby Rd.)
Moreton La. SK2: Stoc 4C *146*
Moreton St. OL9: Chad 1H *73*
Moreton Wlk. SK2: Stoc 4C *146*
Morgan Pl. SK5: Stoc 5H *133*
Morgan St. OL15: L'ough 4H *17*
Morillon Rd. M44: Irl 3E *109*
Morland Rd. M16: Old T 3A *114*
MORLEY 5A *164*
Morley Av. M14: Man 6E *115*
   M27: Swin 5G *83*
MORLEY GREEN 6A *164*
Morley Grn. Rd.
   SK9: Wilm 6A *164*
Morley Rd. M26: Rad 3F *51*

Morley St. BL3: Bolt 1B *48*
   BL9: Bury 5F *37*
   M45: White 1F *69*
   OL4: O'ham 6C *60*
   OL16: Roch 2B *28*
Morley Way OL3: G'fld 4D *78*
Morna Wlk. M12: Man 1H *11* (5H *101*)
Morningside WA14: Alt 6D *138*
Morningside Cl. M43: Droy 6A *104*
   OL16: Roch 5B *28*
Morningside Dr. M20: Man 3G *143*
Mornington Av. SK8: Chea 1H *155*
Mornington Cl. *OL1: O'ham* 1E *75*
   (off Bradford St.)
Mornington Cres. M14: Man 1E *131*
Mornington Rd. BL1: Bolt 5H *31*
   M33: Sale 4D *128*
   OL11: Roch 3H *41*
   SK8: Chea 1H *155*
Morpeth Cl. M12: Man 2A *116*
   OL7: A Lyme 1E *105*
Morpeth St. M27: Swin 5G *83*
Morrell Rd. M22: Nor 3B *142*
Morris Fold Dr. BL6: Los 2B *46*
MORRIS GREEN 5A *48*
Morris Grn. BL3: Bolt 5A *48*
Morris Grn. Bus. Pk. *BL3: Bolt* 3A *48*
   (off Fearnhead St.)
Morris Grn. La. BL3: Bolt 4A *48*
Morris Grn. St. BL3: Bolt 5A *48*
Morris Gro. M41: Urm 1A *126*
Morris Hall *M14: Man* 3H *115*
   (off Daisy Bank Hall)
Morrison St. BL3: Bolt 4C *48*
Morrison Wlk. *M40: Man* 6C *88*
   (off Eldridge Dr.)
Morris St. BL1: Bolt 3H *175* (6E *33*)
   M20: Man 2F *131*
   M26: Rad 2E *53*
   OL4: O'ham 4G *75*
Morrowfield Av. M8: Man 4D *86*
Morse Rd. M40: Man 6D *88*
Morston Cl. M28: Wors 3F *81*
Mortar St. OL4: O'ham 1A *76*
   (not continuous)
Mort Ct. *BL1: Bolt* 2A *32*
   (off Halliwell Rd.)
Mortfield Gdns. BL1: Bolt 5B *32*
Mortfield La. BL1: Bolt 5B *32*
   (not continuous)
Mort Fold M38: Lit H 4E *65*
Mortimer Av. M9: Man 5A *72*
Mortimer St. OL1: O'ham 6G *59*
Mortlake Cl. M28: Walk 6D *64*
Mortlake Dr. M40: Man 6D *88*
Mort La. M29: Tyld 2C *80*
Morton Moss Ct. *BL3: Bolt* 3G *47*
   (off Higher Clough Cl.)
Morton St. M24: Mid 5C *56*
   M26: Rad 5B *52*
   M35: Fail 5E *89*
   SK4: Stoc 5G *133*
Morton Ter. *M34: Dent* 6G *119*
   (off Tatton Rd.)
   SK6: Wood 4H *135*
Mort St. BL4: Farn 1F *65*
Morven Av. SK7: H Gro 2F *159*
Morven Dr. M23: Wyth 6G *141*
Morven Gro. BL2: Bolt 2B *34*
Morville Rd. M21: Chor 6B *114*
Moschatel Wlk. M31: Part 6D *124*
Moscow Cl. SK3: Stoc 4F *145*
Moscow Rd. E. SK3: Stoc 4F *145*
Mosedale Cl. M23: Wyth 5E *141*
   M29: Ast 5A *80*
Mosedale Rd. M24: Mid 5H *55*
Moseldene Rd. SK2: Stoc 6D *146*
Moseley Ct. M19: Man 6B *116*
   SK8: Chea H 2B *156*
Moseley Grange SK8: Chea H 2B *156*
Moseley Rd. M14: Man 1H *131*
   M19: Man 1B *132*
   SK8: Chea H 2B *156*

Moseley St. SK3: Stoc 5E **179** (3G **145**)
MOSES GATE 5G 49
Moses Gate Country Pk. 3H **49**
Moses Gate Station (Rail) 5G 49
Moses Ga. Workshops
  BL3: Bolt 5H **49**
              (off Gladys St.)
Mosley Arc. *M1: Man* 6A **6**
              (off Parker St.)
Mosley Av. BL0: Ram 1B **22**
  BL9: Bury 6F **23**
Mosley Cl. WA15: Tim 4H **139**
MOSLEY COMMON 4D 80
Mosley Comn. Rd. M28: Wors 3C **80**
  M29: Tyld 3C **80**
Mosley Rd. M17: T Pk 3C 112
  WA15: Tim 5B **140**
Mosley St. M2: Man 1H **9** (4E **101**)
  M26: Rad 3H **51**
Mosley Street Stop (Metro)
  . . . . .6A **6** (4E **101**)
Moss, The M24: Mid 3D **72**
Mossack Av. M22: Wyth 4B **154**
Moss Av. OL16: Roch 5C **28**
Moss Bank M8: Man 3E **87**
  OL2: Shaw 1H **59**
            (off Queen St.)
  SK7: Bram 2E 167
Moss Bank Av. M43: Droy 3C **104**
Moss Bank Cl. BL1: Bolt 1B **32**
Mossbank Av. SK13: Had 3G **123**
Moss Bank Ct. M43: Droy 3C **104**
Moss Bank Gro. M27: Ward 1F **83**
Mossbank Gro. OL10: H'ood 2G **39**
Moss Bank Rd. M27: Ward 1F **83**
Moss Bank Trad. Est.
  M28: Walk 5A **66**
Moss Bank Way BL1: Bolt 4E **31**
Mossbray Av. M19: Man 5H **131**
Moss Bri. Rd. OL16: Roch 5B **28**
Moss Brook Ct. *M40: Man* 1G **101**
           (off Kentford Dr.)
Mossbrook Dr. M38: Lit H 3C **64**
Moss Brook Rd. M9: Man 4A **88**
Moss Cl. M26: Rad 2F **51**
Mossclough Ct. M9: Man 4A **88**
Moss Colliery Rd. M27: Clif 6G **67**
Moss Cft. Cl. M41: Urm 4A **110**
Mossdale Av. BL1: Bolt 6D **30**
Mossdale Rd. M23: Wyth 2F **141**
  M33: Sale 2G **139**
Mossdown Rd. OL2: O'ham 4G **59**
Mosses Ho. BL9: Bury 5C **176** (4F **37**)
Moss Farm Cl. M24: Mid 3D **72**
Mossfield Cl. BL9: Bury 2H **37**
  SK4: Stoc 1D **144**
Mossfield Ct. BL1: Bolt 1E **175** (5C **32**)
Mossfield Grn. M30: Ecc 3G **109**
Mossfield Rd. BL4: Farn 1F **65**
  BL4: Kea 4B **66**
  M27: Swin 1G **83**
  WA15: Tim 5D **140**
Moss Fold M29: Ast 4A **80**
  OL6: A Lyme 2A **106**
           (off Ripon St.)
Mossgate Rd. OL2: Shaw 5F **43**
Moss Grange Av.
  M16: W Ran 3B **114**
Moss Grn. M31: C'ton 3B **128**
MOSS GROVE 1D **90**
Moss Gro. OL2: Shaw 4E **43**
Moss Gro. Ct. *M15: Man* 3C **114**
        (off Moss La. W.)
Mossgrove Rd. WA15: Tim 4H **139**
Mossgrove St. OL8: O'ham 1D **90**
Mosshall Cl. M15: Man 6D **8** (1B **114**)
Moss Hall Rd. BL9: Bury 4B **38**
  OL10: H'ood, Mid 6D **38**
MOSS HEY 1A **60**
Moss Hey Dr. M23: Wyth 2H **141**
Mosshey St. OL2: Shaw 1A **60**
Moss Ho. La. *M28: Wors* 6D **80**
      (off Vicars Hall La.)

Moss Ho. Ter. M9: Man 2G **87**
Moss Ind. Est. OL16: Roch 6B **28**
Mossland Cl. OL10: H'ood 5H **39**
Mossland Gro. BL3: Bolt 5D **46**
Moss La. BL1: Bolt 3G **31**
  BL4: Kea 4D **66**
  M9: Mid 4C **72**
  M24: Mid 4B **72**
         (not continuous)
  M27: Ward 2F **83**
  M28: Walk 5A **66**
         (not continuous)
  M31: Part, Warb 6D **124**
  M33: Sale 6D **126**
          (Firsway)
  M33: Sale 6F **127**
         (Manor Av.)
  M41: Urm 2F **111**
  M44: Cad 4B **124**
  M45: White 1F **69**
  OL2: O'ham 4G **59**
  OL7: A Lyme 1D **104**
  OL12: Whitw 2D **14**
  OL16: Roch 5D **178** (5A **28**)
  SK7: Bram 2E **167**
  SK9: A Edg 5H **173**
  SK9: Sty 2B **164**
  WA14: Alt 2B **174** (1F **151**)
  WA15: Alt 2B **174** (1F **151**)
  WA15: Tim 4H **139**
Moss La. E. M15: Man 3D **114**
Moss Lane Ground 2H **151**
Moss La. Ind. Est. M45: White 6F **53**
  OL2: O'ham 4G **59**
Moss La. Trad. Est. M45: White 6G **53**
Moss La. W. M15: Man 3C **114**
Moss Lea BL1: Bolt 1B **32**
Mosslee Av. M8: Man 6D **70**
MOSSLEY 2A **94**
MOSSLEY BROW 3G **93**
MOSSLEY CROSS 2F **93**
Mossley Industrial Heritage Cen. . . .2G **93**
Mossley Rd. OL4: Gras 5H **77**
  OL6: A Lyme 2A **106**
Mossley Station (Rail) 2G **93**
Moss Lodge La. OL7: A Lyme 3D **104**
Moss Mnr. M33: Sale 6G **127**
Moss Mdw. Rd. M6: Sal 1C **98**
Mossmere Rd. SK8: Chea H 1C **156**
Moss Mill St. OL16: Roch 6B **28**
MOSS NOOK 6D **154**
Moss Nook Ind. Area
  M22: Wyth 5D **154**
Moss Pk. Rd. M32: Stre 5A **112**
Moss Pl. BL9: Bury 5E **37**
Moss Rd. BL4: Farn 2A **66**
  M32: Stre 3C **112**
  M33: Sale 5D **126**
  M44: Cad 6A **108**
  SK9: A Edg 4H **173**
Moss Rose SK9: A Edg 4H **173**
Moss Row BL9: Bury 5D **176** (4F **37**)
  OL11: Roch 2H **25**
Moss Shaw Way M26: Rad 2F **51**
         (not continuous)
MOSS SIDE 3E **115**
Moss Side BL8: Bury 6A **22**
Moss Side La. OL16: Miln 6C **28**
Moss Side Leisure Cen. 2D **114**
Moss Side Rd. M44: Cad 3B **124**
Moss St. BL4: Farn 6A **50**
  BL9: Bury 4B **176** (3E **37**)
  BL9: Sum 1D **22**
  M7: Sal 6B **86**
  M34: Aud 4B **104**
  M43: Droy 3B **104**
  OL4: O'ham 1C **76**
  OL10: H'ood 3G **39**
  OL16: Roch 5B **28**
  SK14: Holl 2F **123**
Moss St. E.
  OL6: A Lyme 5B **174** (2H **105**)
Moss St. W. OL7: A Lyme 3F **105**

Moss Ter. OL6: A Lyme . . .6A **174** (3G **105**)
  OL16: Roch 5B **28**
  SK9: Wilm 6B **166**
Moss Va. Cres. M32: Stre 3H **111**
Moss Va. Rd. M41: Urm 5G **111**
         (not continuous)
Moss Vw. M40: Man 1E **89**
Moss Vw. Rd. BL2: Bolt 5A **34**
  M31: Part 6E **125**
Moss Way M33: Sale 5G **127**
  OL7: A Lyme, Aud 4E **105**
Mossway M24: Mid 4B **72**
Mosswood Pk. M20: Man 3F **143**
Mosswood Rd. SK9: Wilm 4A **166**
Mossylea Cl. M24: Mid 4D **72**
MOSTON .3C **88**
Moston Bank Av. M9: Man 4A **88**
Moston Fairway Nature Reserve 3E **89**
Moston La. M9: Man 3A **88**
  M40: Man 3A **88**
         (Kenyon La.)
  M40: Man 1F **89**
         (Leyburn Rd.)
Moston La. E. M40: Man 1F **89**
Moston Rd. M24: Mid 4F **73**
Moston Station (Rail) 1F **89**
Moston St. M7: Sal 4D **86**
  SK5: Stoc 2H **133**
Mostyn Av. BL9: Bury 6F **23**
  M14: Man 1A **132**
  SK8: Chea H 4A **156**
Mostyn Rd. SK7: H Gro 4B **158**
Mostyn St. SK15: Duk, Stal 5D **106**
  SK16: Duk 5D **106**
Motcombe Farm Rd.
  SK8: H Grn 4F **155**
Motcombe Gro. SK8: H Grn 2E **155**
Motcombe Rd. SK8: H Grn 3E **155**
Motherwell Av. M19: Man 6C **116**
Mottershead Av. BL3: Lit L 3C **50**
Mottershead Rd. M22: Wyth 1A **154**
Mottram Av. M21: Chor 4A **130**
Mottram Cl. SK8: Chea 6C **144**
Mottram Dr. WA15: Tim 6A **140**
Mottram Fold SK1: Stoc . . .4G **179** (3H **145**)
  SK14: Mot 4C **122**
MOTTRAM IN LONGENDALE 3C **122**
Mottram Moor SK14: Holl, Mot 3C **122**
Mottram Old Rd. SK14: Hyde 1D **136**
  SK15: Stal 4G **107**
MOTTRAM RISE 6H **107**
Mottram Rd. M33: Sale 6E **129**
  SK9: A Edg 5H **173**
  SK14: B'tom 6B **122**
  SK14: Hat, Hyde 4C **120**
  SK15: Stal 4F **107**
Mottram St. SK1: Stoc 4H **179** (3H **145**)
         (Bamford St.)
  SK1: Stoc 4G **179** (3H **145**)
         (Millbrook St.)
Mottram Towers
  SK1: Stoc 4G **179** (3H **145**)
Mottram Vw. SK15: Stal 1A **122**
Mottram Way SK1: Stoc 4G **179**
Mough La. OL9: Chad 6F **73**
Moulding Moss BL9: Bury 5D **24**
Mouldsworth Av. M20: Man 2E **131**
  SK4: Stoc 3F **133**
Moulton St. M8: Man 1C **100**
Moulton St. Pct. M8: Man 1C **100**
Mount, The M7: Sal 3A **86**
  OL6: A Lyme 2B **106**
  SK5: Stoc 5B **134**
  WA14: Alt 1A **174** (6F **139**)
  WA15: Haleb 5C **152**
Mountain Ash OL12: Roch 6D **14**
Mountain Ash Cl. M33: Sale 4E **127**
  OL12: Roch 6D **14**
Mountain Gro. M28: Walk 5G **65**
Mountain St. M28: Walk 5G **65**
  M40: Man 1F **103**
  OL5: Mos 2G **93**
  SK1: Stoc 1A **146**

Mount Av.—Nansen St.

Mount Av. OL12: Roch 5E **17**
OL15: L'ough 2G **17**
Mountbatten Av. SK16: Duk 6D **106**
Mountbatten Cl. BL9: Bury 5H **53**
Mountbatten St. M18: Man 2E **117**
Mt. Carmel Ct. *M5: Sal 3A **8***
(off Mt. Carmel Cres.)
Mt. Carmel Cres. M5: Sal 3A **8** (6A **100**)
Mount Dr. M41: Urm 5H **111**
SK6: Mar 6D **148**
Mountfield M25: Pres 5H **69**
Mountfield Rd. SK3: Stoc 4E **145**
SK7: Bram 2G **167**
Mountfield Wlk. *BL1: Bolt 4C **32***
(off Kentford Rd., not continuous)
*M11: Man 4B **102***
(off Hopedale Cl.)
Mountfold M24: Mid 2D **72**
Mountford Av. M8: Man 1D **86**
Mount Gro. SK8: Gat 5D **142**
Mountheath Ind. Pk. M25: Pres 2H **85**
Mount La. OL3: Dob 1A **78**
Mount Pl. *OL12: Roch 3G **27***
(off Clements Royds St.)
Mt. Pleasant *BL3: Bolt 2G **49***
(off Lever Bri. Pl.)
BL9: Bury 6F **13**
M24: Mid 1G **71**
M25: Pres 1C **70**
SK2: Stoc 5F **147**
SK6: Wood 4H **135**
SK7: H Gro 2D **158**
SK9: Wilm 6B **172**
(Knutsford Rd.)
SK9: Wilm 6F **165**
(Styal Rd.)
SK14: Hyde 4E **121**
Mt. Pleasant Bus. Cen.
OL4: O'ham 2H **75**
Mt. Pleasant Ho. M27: Swin 3A **84**
Mt. Pleasant Rd. BL4: Farn 1D **64**
M34: Dent 5F **119**
Mt. Pleasant St. M34: Aud 6F **105**
(not continuous)
OL4: O'ham 2H **75**
OL6: A Lyme 1A **106**
(not continuous)
Mt. Pleasant Trad. Est.
*OL6: A Lyme 1A **106***
(off Pleasant St.)
Mt. Pleasant Wlk. M26: Rad 3A **52**
Mount Rd. M18: Man 2E **117**
M19: Man 2E **117**
M24: Mid 2B **72**
M25: Pres 2A **70**
SK4: Stoc 1E **145**
SK14: Hyde 3E **137**
Mountroyal Cl. SK14: Hyde 2D **120**
Mt. St Joseph's Rd. BL3: Bolt 2H **47**
Mountside BL7: Eger 3C **18**
Mountside Cl. OL12: Roch 1G **27**
Mountside Cres. M25: Pres 5F **69**
Mt. Sion Rd. M26: Rad 5F **51**
Mt. Skip La. M38: Lit H 5E **65**
Mountsorrel Rd. WA14: W Tim 3E **139**
Mount St. BL0: Ram 2B **12**
BL1: Bolt 4C **32**
M2: Man 1H **9** (5D **100**)
M3: Sal 3D **4** (3B **100**)
M27: Swin 4H **83**
M30: Ecc 5E **97**
M34: Dent 6H **119**
OL2: O'ham 4E **59**
OL10: H'ood 4H **39**
OL11: Roch 4E **41**
OL12: Roch 3G **27**
SK14: Hyde 5C **120**
Mount Ter. M43: Droy 2G **103**
WA14: Alt 2A **174**
Mount Vw. OL3: Upp 1C **78**
Mount Vw. Rd. OL2: Shaw 1B **60**
Mt. Zion Rd. BL9: Bury 2F **53**
Mousell St. M8: Man 1E **101**
Mouselow Cl. SK13: Had 4H **123**
Mowbray Av. M25: Pres 1A **86**
M33: Sale 6C **128**
Mowbray St. BL1: Bolt 4H **31**
OL1: O'ham 4H **177** (3F **75**)
OL7: A Lyme 3G **105**
OL11: Roch 2D **40**
SK1: Stoc 4H **179** (3H **145**)
Mowbray Wlk. M24: Mid 5A **56**
Mow Halls La. OL3: Dob 6C **62**
Moxley Rd. M8: Man 2C **86**
Moy Hill OL16: Miln 6H **29**
Moyse Av. BL8: Bury 6H **21**
Mozart Cl. M4: Man 3F **7** (3G **101**)
MUDD 5C **122**
Mudhurst La. SK12: Dis 6H **171**
Muirfield Av. SK6: Bred 5G **135**
Muirfield Cl. BL3: Bolt 4F **47**
M25: Pres 4H **69**
M40: Man 3E **89**
OL10: H'ood 4H **39**
SK9: Wilm 1G **173**
Muirfield Dr. M29: Ast 3A **80**
Muirhead Ct. M6: Sal 6G **85**
Mulberry Av. OL10: H'ood 6D **38**
Mulberry Cl. M26: Rad 5A **52**
OL10: H'ood 6D **38**
OL11: Roch 6G **27**
SK8: H Grn 6G **155**
Mulberry Ct. *M6: Sal 2G **99***
(off Mulberry Rd.)
M41: Urm 5G **111**
*WA14: Alt 5F **139***
(off Gaskell Rd.)
Mulberry Ho. OL3: Del 3B **62**
Mulberry M. SK4: Stoc 1E **179** (1F **145**)
Mulberry Mt. St.
SK3: Stoc 5F **179** (3G **145**)
Mulberry Rd. M6: Sal 3G **99**
Mulberry St. M2: Man 6G **5** (4D **100**)
OL6: A Lyme 5D **174** (2A **106**)
Mulberry Wlk. M33: Sale 3F **127**
M43: Droy 5G **103**
Mulberry Way
OL10: H'ood 6D **38**
Mule St. BL2: Bolt 5E **33**
Mulgrave Rd. M28: Wors 3C **82**
Mulgrave St. BL3: Bolt 5A **48**
M27: Swin 2F **83**
Mulgrove Wlk. *M9: Man 6A **72***
(off Haverfield Rd.)
Mullacre Rd. M22: Wyth 5B **142**
Mull Av. M12: Man 2B **116**
Mulliner St. *BL1: Bolt 4D **32***
(off Prospect St.)
Mullineux St. M28: Walk 1H **81**
Mullion Cl. M19: Man 5F **117**
Mullion Dr. WA15: Tim 4G **139**
Mullion Wlk. M8: Man 5F **87**
Mulmount Cl. OL8: O'ham 6C **74**
MUMPS 2G **75**
Mumps OL1: O'ham 2G **75**
Mumps M. *OL1: O'ham 2G **75***
(off Garden St.)
Mumps Rdbt. OL1: O'ham 2G **75**
OL4: O'ham 2G **75**
Munday St. M4: Man 5G **7** (4H **101**)
Municipal Cl. *OL10: H'ood 3H **39***
(off Hartland St.)
Munn Rd. M9: Man 4F **71**
Munro Av. M22: Wyth 3D **154**
Munslow Wlk. M9: Man 6B **72**
Munster St. M4: Man 2A **6** (2E **101**)
Muriel St. M7: Sal 6B **86**
OL10: H'ood 3A **40**
OL16: Roch 6B **28**
Murieston Rd. WA15: Hale 3G **151**
Murrayfield OL11: Roch 5A **26**
Murray Rd. BL9: Bury 4C **176** (3F **37**)
Murray St. M4: Man 4D **6** (3F **101**)
M7: Sal 5B **86**
Murrow Wlk. *M9: Man 3H **87***
(off Alderside Rd.)
Murton Ter. BL1: Bolt 1C **32**
Musabbir Sq. OL12: Roch 1D **178**
Musbury Av. SK8: Chea H 3D **156**
Muscle & Fitness Gymnasium *1H **83***
(off Station Rd.)
Musden Wlk. SK4: Stoc 2F **133**
Mus. of Science & Industry
1E **9** (5C **100**)
Mus. of the Manchester Regiment, The
5C **174** (2H **105**)
Mus. of Transport 5F **87**
Museum St. M2: Man 1G **9** (5D **100**)
Musgrave Gdns. BL1: Bolt 5A **32**
Musgrave Rd. BL1: Bolt 5H **31**
M22: Wyth 2B **154**
Muslin St. M5: Sal 6B **4** (4A **100**)
Muter Av. M22: Wyth 3D **154**
Mutual St. OL10: H'ood 2A **40**
Myerscroft Cl. M40: Man 2G **89**
Myrrh St. BL1: Bolt 2C **32**
Myrrh Wlk. *BL1: Bolt 2C **32***
(off Myrrh St.)
Myrtle Bank M25: Pres 2G **85**
Myrtle Cl. OL8: O'ham 4E **75**
Myrtle Gdns. BL9: Bury 3H **37**
Myrtle Gro. M25: Pres 1H **85**
M34: Dent 4H **117**
M43: Droy 3C **104**
M45: White 5D **52**
Myrtleleaf Gro. M5: Sal 3D **98**
Myrtle Pl. M7: Sal 1A **100**
Myrtle Rd. M24: Mid 5E **57**
M31: Part 6B **124**
Myrtle St. BL1: Bolt 5B **32**
M11: Man 5A **102**
*M16: Old T 3A **114***
(off Langshaw St.)
SK3: Stoc 3D **144**
Myrtle St. Nth. BL9: Bury 3H **37**
Myrtle St. Sth. BL9: Bury 3H **37**
My St. M5: Sal 4E **99**
Mytham Gdns. BL3: Lit L 5D **50**
Mytham Rd. BL3: Lit L 4D **50**
Mytholme Av. M44: Cad 6A **124**
Mythorn Wlk. *M40: Man 6C **88***
(off Harmer Cl.)
Mytton Rd. BL1: Bolt 1H **31**
Mytton St. M15: Man 2D **114**

N

Nabbs Fold BL8: G'mount 1H **21**
Nabbs Way BL8: G'mount 2A **22**
Nab La. SK6: Mar 3C **148**
Naburn Cl. SK5: Stoc 3C **134**
Naburn St. M13: Man 3H **115**
Nada Lodge *M8: Man 2D **86***
(off St Mary's Hall Rd.)
Nada Rd. M8: Man 2D **86**
Naden Vw. OL11: Roch 2H **25**
Naden Wlk. M45: White 1G **69**
Nadine St. M6: Sal 2E **99**
Nadin St. OL8: O'ham 6E **75**
Nailers Grn. *BL8: G'mount 2H **21***
(off Brandlesholme Rd.)
Nairn Cl. M40: Man 2H **7**
Nall Ga. OL16: Roch 3C **42**
Nall St. M19: Man 2D **132**
OL16: Miln 4E **29**
Nameplate Cl. M30: Ecc 3D **96**
Nancy St. M15: Man 5C **8** (1B **114**)
Nandywell BL3: Lit L 4D **50**
Nangreave Rd. SK2: Stoc 5A **146**
NANGREAVES 6F **13**
Nangreave St. M5: Sal 6C **4** (4B **100**)
Nan Nook Rd. M23: Wyth 2F **141**
Nansen Av. M30: Ecc 2E **97**
Nansen Cl. M32: Stre 3E **113**
Nansen Rd. SK8: Gat 1E **155**
Nansen St. M6: Sal 3E **99**
M11: Man 5A **102**
M32: Stre 4D **112**

A-Z Manchester 309

Nansmoss Rd. SK9: Wilm 6B 164
Nantes Ct. BL1: Bolt 3B 32
Nantwich Av. OL12: Roch 6H 15
Nantwich Cl. SK8: Chea 6C 144
Nantwich Rd. M14: Man 6E 115
Nantwich Wlk. BL3: Bolt 3C 48
Nantwich Way SK9: Hand 2A 166
(off Spath La.)
Napier Ct. M15: Man 6B 8
SK4: Stoc 6D 132
SK14: Hyde 6C 120
(off Napier St.)
Napier Grn. M5: Sal 6H 99
Napier Rd. M21: Chor 1H 129
M30: Ecc 2E 97
SK4: Stoc 6D 132
Napier St. M27: Swin 4F 83
OL2: Shaw 5H 43
SK7: H Gro 2D 158
SK14: Hyde 6C 120
Napier St. E. OL8: O'ham 4D 74
Napier St. W. OL8: O'ham 4C 74
Naples Rd. SK3: Stoc 5D 144
Naples St. M4: Man 2B 6 (2E 101)
NAR 4G 15
Narbonne Av. M30: Ecc 1A 98
Narborough Wlk. M40: Man 6G 87
(off Westmount Cl.)
Narbuth Dr. M8: Man 4D 86
Narcissus Wlk. M28: Walk 6D 64
NARROW GATE BROW 6D 42
Narrow La. SK10: Adl 6G 169
Narrows, The WA14: Alt 3A 174 (2E 151)
Narrow Wlk. WA14: Bow 3E 151
Naseby Av. M9: Man 5B 72
Naseby Ct. M25: Pres 4A 70
Naseby Pl. M25: Pres 5A 70
Naseby Rd. SK5: Stoc 1G 133
Naseby Wlk. M45: White 1A 70
Nash Rd. M17: T Pk 5G 97
Nash St. M15: Man 6E 9 (1C 114)
Nasmyth Av. M34: Dent 3G 119
Nasmyth Bus. Cen. M30: Ecc 2E 97
Nasmyth Rd. M30: Ecc 5E 97
Nasmyth St. M8: Man 6G 87
Nathan Dr. M3: Sal 3E 5 (3C 100)
Nathans Rd. M22: Wyth 1A 154
National Ind. Est.
OL7: A Lyme 3F 105
National Squash Cen. 3B 102
National Trad. Est.
SK7: H Gro 2C 158
Naunton Rd. M24: Mid 2D 72
Naunton Wlk. M9: Man 3A 88
(off Jonas St.)
Naval St. M4: Man 3E 7 (3G 101)
Nave Ct. M6: Sal 1F 99
Navenby Av. M16: Old T 3A 114
Navigation Ho. M1: Man 6D 6
Navigation Rd. WA14: Alt 4F 139
Navigation Road Station (Rail & Metro)
. . . . .5G 139
Navigation Trad. Est.
M40: Man 6B 88
Naylor Ct. M40: Man 1F 7 (2G 101)
Naylor St. M40: Man 1G 7 (2H 101)
OL1: O'ham 2F 177 (2E 75)
Nazeby Wlk. OL9: O'ham 4C 74
Naze Ct. OL1: O'ham 1E 75
(off Bradford St.)
Naze Wlk. SK5: Stoc 3C 134
Neal Av. OL6: A Lyme 2B 106
SK8: H Grn 5E 155
Neale Av. OL3: G'fld 4E 79
Neale Rd. M21: Chor 2G 129
NEAR BARROWSHAW 6B 60
Near Birches Pde.
OL4: O'ham 5C 76
Nearbrook Rd. M22: Wyth 1A 154
Nearcroft Rd. M23: Wyth 4G 141
Near Hey Cl. M26: Rad 4G 51
Nearmaker Av. M22: Wyth 1A 154

Nearmaker Rd. M22: Wyth 1A 154
Neary Way M41: Urm 2E 111
Neasden Gro. BL3: Bolt 2A 48
(off Langshaw Wlk.)
Neath Av. M22: Nor 4B 142
Neath Cl. M45: White 2A 70
SK12: Poy 2D 168
Neath Fold BL3: Bolt 4B 48
Neath St. OL9: O'ham 2D 74
Neden Cl. M11: Man 5D 102
Needham Av. M21: Chor 1H 129
Needham Cl. M45: White 2F 69
Needwood Cl. M40: Man 6H 87
Needwood Rd. SK6: Wood 4A 136
Neem Ho. M14: Man 5G 115
(off Rusholme Pl.)
Neenton Sq. M12: Man 1C 116
Neild St. M1: Man 2D 10 (5G 101)
OL8: O'ham 5E 75
Neill St. M7: Sal 1C 100
Neilson Cl. M24: Mid 2E 73
Neilson St. M23: Wyth 5G 141
Neilston Av. M40: Man 4D 88
Neilston Ri. BL1: Bolt 6C 30
Nell Carrs BL0: Ram 1E 13
Nellie St. OL10: H'ood 3F 39
Nell La. M21: Chor 2A 130
Nell St. BL1: Bolt 1D 32
Nelson Av. M30: Ecc 2F 97
SK12: Poy 4G 169
Nelson Bus. Cen. M34: Dent 3F 119
Nelson Cl. M15: Man 3C 114
SK12: Poy 4G 169
Nelson Ct. M40: Man 1H 101
(off Droitwich Rd.)
Nelson Dr. M43: Droy 3F 103
M44: Cad 3C 124
Nelson Fold M27: Pen 2A 84
Nelson Mandela Ct. M16: W Ran 4C 114
(off Range Rd.)
Nelson Pit Vis. Cen. 4B 170
Nelson Rd. M9: Man 4H 71
Nelson Sq. BL1: Bolt 4G 175 (6D 32)
Nelson St. BL3: Bolt 2E 49
BL3: Lit L 4D 50
BL4: Farn 1A 66
BL9: Bury 6C 176 (5F 37)
(not continuous)
M5: Sal 4E 99
M7: Sal 6B 86
M13: Man 2F 115
M24: Mid 2E 73
M29: Tyld 3A 80
M30: Ecc 3F 97
M32: Stre 6D 112
M34: Aud 1F 119
M34: Dent 3F 119
(not continuous)
M40: Man 1H 7 (2A 102)
OL4: Lees 4C 76
OL10: H'ood 4H 39
OL15: L'ough 4H 17
OL16: Roch 4B 178 (4H 27)
SK7: H Gro 1F 159
SK14: Hyde 5C 120
Nelson Way OL9: Chad 5B 74
Nelstrop Cres. SK4: Stoc 3F 133
Nelstrop Rd. SK4: Stoc 3E 133
SK4: Stoc 2E 133
Nelstrop Rd. Nth. M19: Man 6F 117
SK4: Stoc 2E 133
Nelstrop Wlk. M34: Stoc 3E 133
Nepaul Rd. M9: Man 2A 88
Neptune Gdns. M7: Sal 6A 86
Nero St. BL0: Ram 2E 13
Nesbit St. BL2: Bolt 2G 33
Nesfield Rd. M23: Wyth 1H 141
Neston Av. BL1: Bolt 6D 18
M20: Man 5G 131
M33: Sale 1E 141
Neston Cl. OL2: Shaw 6B 44
Neston Gro. SK3: Stoc 6F 145

Neston Rd. BL8: Bury 1H 35
OL16: Roch 1C 42
Neston St. M11: Man 6H 103
Neston Way SK9: Hand 4H 165
Neswick Wlk. M23: Wyth 1F 141
Netherbury Cl. M18: Man 4E 117
Nethercote Av. M23: Wyth 5H 141
Nethercroft OL11: Roch 2A 26
Nethercroft WA14: Alt 6E 139
Nethercroft Rd. WA15: Tim 6C 140
Netherfield Cl. OL8: O'ham 5C 74
Netherfield Rd. BL3: Bolt 5B 48
Netherfields SK9: A Edg 6G 173
Netherhey La. OL2: O'ham 5C 58
Nether Hey St. OL8: O'ham 4H 75
(not continuous)
Netherhouse Rd. OL2: Shaw 6G 43
Netherland St. M5: Sal 5G 99
NETHER LEES 4B 76
Netherlees OL4: Lees 4B 76
Netherlow Ct. SK14: Hyde 5C 120
(off Union St.)
Nether St. M12: Man 2E 11 (5G 101)
SK14: Hyde 1D 136
Netherton Gro. BL4: Farn 5F 49
Netherton Rd. M14: Man 6E 115
Nethervale Dr. M9: Man 4A 88
Netherwood M35: Fail 3B 90
Netherwood Rd. M22: Nor 4A 142
Netherwood Way BL5: W'ton 5A 46
Netley Av. OL12: Roch 6H 15
Netley Gdns. M26: Rad 3G 51
Netley Rd. M23: Wyth 1G 153
Nettlebarn Rd. M22: Wyth 6A 142
Nettleford Rd. M16: W Ran 1C 130
Nettleton Gro. M9: Man 2B 88
Nevada St. BL1: Bolt 4C 32
(off St Ann St.)
M13: Man 2H 115
Nevendon Dr. M23: Wyth 1F 153
Nevern Cl. BL1: Bolt 5F 31
Nevile Ct. M7: Sal 3H 85
Nevile Rd. M7: Sal 3H 85
Neville Cardus Wlk.
M14: Man 5G 115
(off Taylor St.)
Neville Cl. BL1: Bolt 2E 175 (5C 32)
Neville Dr. M44: Irl 3E 109
Neville St. OL9: Chad 2C 74
SK7: H Gro 2D 158
Nevill Rd. SK7: Bram 3G 157
Nevin Av. SK8: Chea H 4A 156
Nevin Cl. SK7: Bram 6A 158
Nevin Rd. M40: Man 2F 89
Nevis Gro. BL1: Bolt 6B 18
Nevis St. OL11: Roch 3A 42
Nevy Fold Av. BL6: Hor 2A 30
New Acre Ct. SK6: Rom 1H 147
(off Metcalfe Dr.)
New Allen St. M40: Man 2E 7 (2G 101)
NEWALL GREEN 1G 153
Newall Rd. M23: Wyth 2F 153
Newall St. OL9: Chad 1B 90
OL15: L'ough 3H 17
Newark Av. M14: Man 4F 115
M26: Rad 2E 51
Newark Pk. Way OL2: O'ham 6C 42
Newark Rd. M27: Clif 1B 84
OL12: Roch 6H 15
SK5: Stoc 4H 133
Newark Sq. OL12: Roch 6H 15
New Bailey St. M3: Sal 4E 5 (4C 100)
Newbank Chase OL9: Chad 1A 74
New Bank Cl. OL3: Dob 6B 62
Newbank Cl. M24: Mid 2E 73
New Bank St. M12: Man 1A 116
SK13: Had 2H 123
Newbank Twr. M3: Sal 1E 5 (2C 100)
New Barn OL3: Del 6G 45
New Barn Cl. OL2: Shaw 6G 43
New Barn La. OL11: Roch 6F 27
New Barn Rd. OL8: O'ham 1G 91
New Barns Av. M21: Chor 3A 130

New Barn St. BL1: Bolt 4H **31**
OL16: Roch 6A **28**
Newbarn St. OL2: Shaw 6G **43**
New Barton St. M6: Sal 6C **84**
Newbeck St. M4: Man 3B **6**
New Beech Rd. SK4: Stoc 1A **144**
(not continuous)
New Belvedere Cl. M32: Stre 5D **112**
Newberry Gro. SK3: Stoc 6F **145**
NEWBOLD 4C **28**
NEWBOLD BROW 3B **28**
Newbold Cl. SK16: Duk 5A **106**
Newbold Hall Dr. OL16: Roch 4C **28**
Newbold Hall Gdns.
OL16: Roch 4C **28**
Newbold Moss OL16: Roch 4B **28**
Newbold St. BL8: Bury 3C **36**
OL16: Roch 4C **28**
Newbold Wlk. M15: Man 5H **9**
Newboult Rd. SK8: Chea 5A **144**
Newbourne Cl. SK7: H Gro 2D **158**
Newbreak Cl. OL4: O'ham 1B **76**
Newbreak St. OL4: O'ham 1B **76**
New Bri. Gdns. BL9: Bury 2E **53**
Newbridge Gdns. BL2: Bolt 1A **34**
New Bri. La.
SK1: Stoc 2H **179** (2H **145**)
New Bri. St. M3: Sal 2G **5** (2D **100**)
Newbridge Vw. OL5: Mos 3H **93**
New Briggs Fold BL7: Eger 1C **18**
New Brighton Cotts.
OL12: Whitw 4B **14**
(off Ruth St.)
New Broad La. OL16: Roch 2C **42**
Newbrook Av. M21: Chor 6B **130**
New Bldgs. Pl. OL16: Roch 2B **178**
Newburn Av. M9: Man 5B **72**
NEW BURY 2F **65**
Newbury Av. M33: Sale 5E **127**
Newbury Cl. SK8: Chea H 1C **166**
Newbury Ct. WA15: Tim 4H **139**
(off Tulip Dr.)
Newbury Dr. M30: Ecc 2D **96**
M41: Urm 2E **111**
Newbury Gro. OL10: H'ood 5G **39**
Newbury Pl. M7: Sal 4B **86**
Newbury Rd. BL3: Lit L 6B **50**
SK8: H Grn 6F **155**
Newbury Wlk. BL1: Bolt 4C **32**
M9: Man 5H **87**
(off Ravelston Dr.)
OL9: Chad 2C **74**
(off Kempton Way)
Newby Cl. BL9: Bury 6G **37**
Newby Dr. M24: Mid 4B **56**
M33: Sale 6E **129**
SK8: Gat 5E **143**
WA14: Alt 5F **139**
Newby Rd. BL2: Bolt 4A **34**
SK4: Stoc 1E **145**
SK7: H Gro 3C **158**
Newby Rd. Ind. Est.
SK7: H Gro 3C **158**
Newcastle St. M15: Man 4H **9** (6D **100**)
(not continuous)
Newcastle Wlk. M34: Dent 6G **119**
(off Trowbridge Rd.)
New Cateaton St.
BL9: Bury 1D **176** (2F **37**)
New Cathedral St.
M1: Man 4H **5** (3D **100**)
New Century Ho. M34: Dent 4C **118**
New Chapel La. BL6: Hor 2A **30**
Newchurch OL8: O'ham 3G **91**
New Church Ct. M26: Rad 4A **52**
M45: White 2F **69**
(off Elizabeth St.)
New Church Rd. BL1: Bolt 3F **31**
New Church St. M26: Rad 4B **52**
Newchurch St. M11: Man 5B **102**
(off Blackrock St.)
OL11: Roch 4E **41**
Newchurch Wlk. M26: Rad 4B **52**

New City Rd. M28: Wors 3E **81**
Newcliffe Rd. M9: Man 5B **72**
New Coin St. OL2: O'ham 4B **58**
New College St. M3: Man . . .6E **5** (4C **100**)
Newcombe Cl. M11: Man 4B **102**
Newcombe Ct. M33: Sale 5B **127**
(off Beech Gro.)
Newcombe Dr. M38: Lit H 3D **64**
Newcombe Rd. BL0: Ram 2A **22**
Newcombe St. M3: Man 1H **5** (2D **100**)
New Ct. Dr. BL7: Eger 1B **18**
New Ct. St. M3: Man 6F **5** (4C **100**)
Newcroft M35: Fail 5B **90**
Newcroft Cres. M41: Urm 6H **111**
Newcroft Dr. M9: Man 2G **87**
M41: Urm 6A **112**
SK3: Stoc 5F **145**
Newcroft Rd. M41: Urm 6H **111**
New Cross M4: Man 4C **6** (3F **101**)
New Cross St. M5: Sal 3C **98**
M27: Swin 4A **84**
Newdale Rd. M12: Man 5D **116**
NEW DELPH .4B **62**
NEW EARTH .4A **76**
Newearth Rd. M28: Wors 3F **81**
New Earth St. OL4: O'ham 4A **76**
OL5: Mos 1H **93**
New Ellesmere App. M28: Walk 5G **65**
New Elm Rd. M3: Man 1D **8** (5B **100**)
New Field Cl. M26: Rad 4G **51**
OL16: Roch 4B **28**
Newfield Head La. OL16: Miln 6H **29**
Newfield Vw. OL16: Miln 5G **29**
(not continuous)
New Forest Rd. M23: Wyth 3C **140**
New Gartside St.
M3: Man 6E **5** (4C **100**)
Newgate OL16: Roch . . .3A **178** (4G **27**)
SK9: Wilm 2A **172**
Newgate Cotts. BL5: O Hul 6G **47**
Newgate Dr. M38: Lit H 3D **64**
Newgate Rd. M33: Sale 2D **138**
New George St. BL8: Bury 2C **36**
M4: Man 3B **6** (3E **101**)
New Grn. BL2: Bolt 5A **20**
New Hall Av. M7: Sal 3B **86**
SK8: H Grn 6F **155**
Newhall Av. BL2: Bolt 1D **50**
M30: Ecc 6C **96**
New Hall Cl. M33: Sale 5F **129**
New Hall Dr. M23: Wyth 1G **141**
New Hall La. BL1: Bolt 4G **31**
Newhall Pl. BL1: Bolt 5G **31**
New Hall Rd. BL9: Bury 1C **38**
M7: Sal 3B **86**
Newhall Rd. SK5: Stoc 5A **118**
Newham Av. M11: Man 3D **102**
Newham Dr. BL8: Bury 5B **36**
Newhart Gro. M28: Walk 1G **81**
Newhaven Av. M11: Man 6H **103**
Newhaven Bus. Pk. M30: Ecc 4G **97**
Newhaven Cl. BL8: Bury 4C **22**
SK8: Chea H 3E **157**
Newhaven Wlk. BL2: Bolt 4E **33**
New Herbert St. M6: Sal 6C **84**
NEWHEY 1H **43**
Newhey Av. M22: Wyth 6B **142**
New Hey Rd. SK8: Chea 5A **144**
Newhey Rd. M22: Wyth 1B **154**
OL16: Miln 6G **29**
(not continuous)
Newhey Station (Rail) 1H **43**
New Heys Way BL2: Bolt 5H **19**
New Holder St. BL1: Bolt 6C **32**
Newholme Ct. M32: Stre 5E **113**
Newholme Gdns. M28: Walk 6G **65**
Newholme Rd. M20: Man 4D **130**
Newhouse Cl. OL12: W'le 6C **16**
Newhouse Cres. OL11: Roch 3A **26**
Newhouse Rd. OL10: H'ood 5H **39**
New Ho's. OL4: Scout 1G **77**

Newhouse St. OL12: W'le 6C **16**
Newick Wlk. M9: Man 6A **72**
(off Leconfield Dr.)
Newington Av. M8: Man 6D **70**
Newington Ct. WA14: Bow 2E **151**
Newington Dr. BL1: Bolt 4D **32**
BL8: Bury 5A **36**
Newington Wlk. BL1: Bolt 4D **32**
(off Kentford Rd.)
New Islington M4: Man 4F **7** (3G **101**)
New Kings Head Yd.
M3: Sal 3G **5** (3D **100**)
Newlands M35: Fail 1G **103**
Newlands Av. BL2: Bolt 4B **34**
M30: Ecc 5B **96**
M44: Irl 5E **109**
M45: White 6E **53**
OL12: Roch 6H **15**
SK7: Bram 5H **157**
SK8: Chea H 6C **156**
Newlands Cl. OL12: Roch 6H **15**
SK8: Chea H 6C **156**
Newlands Dr. M20: Man 3G **143**
M25: Pres 4G **69**
M27: Pen 5C **84**
SK9: Wilm 4B **172**
SK13: Had 3H **123**
Newlands Rd. M23: Wyth 3F **141**
SK8: Chea 5H **143**
Newland St. M8: Man 2F **87**
Newlands Wlk. M24: Mid 3A **56**
New La. BL2: Bolt 4H **33**
M24: Mid 6C **56**
M30: Ecc 4D **96**
OL2: O'ham 3D **58**
New La. Ct. BL2: Bolt 3A **34**
New Lawns SK5: Stoc 6A **118**
Newlea Cl. BL1: Bolt 3A **32**
New Lees St. OL6: A Lyme 6B **92**
(not continuous)
New Lester Cl. M29: Tyld 2A **80**
New Lester Way M38: Lit H 5C **64**
Newlyn Av. SK15: Stal 2H **107**
Newlyn Cl. SK7: H Gro 4D **158**
Newlyn Dr. M33: Sale 2C **140**
SK6: Bred 6G **135**
Newlyn St. M14: Man 5F **115**
NEW MANCHESTER 2E **81**
New Mansion Ho. SK1: Stoc 6G **179**
Newman St.
OL6: A Lyme 5A **174** (2G **105**)
OL16: Roch 6C **16**
SK14: Hyde 4C **120**
New Mkt. M2: Man 5H **5** (4D **100**)
Newmarket Cl. M33: Sale 1D **138**
Newmarket Gro. OL7: A Lyme 6E **91**
New Mkt. La. M2: Man 5A **6** (4E **101**)
Newmarket M. M7: Sal 5B **86**
Newmarket Rd. BL3: Lit L 5C **50**
OL7: A Lyme 6E **91**
New Mdw. BL6: Los 6C **30**
New Medlock Ho.
M15: Man 4H **9** (6D **100**)
New Mill OL16: Roch 1D **28**
NEW MILLS .6A **162**
New Mill St. OL15: L'ough 4G **17**
Newmill Wlk. M8: Man 5E **87**
(off Brentfield Av.)
New Moor La. SK7: H Gro 2D **158**
New Moss Rd. M44: Cad 3B **124**
NEW MOSTON 2G **89**
New Mount St. M4: Man 2B **6**
Newnham St. BL1: Bolt 2D **32**
New Oak Cl. M35: Fail 3C **90**
New Pk. Rd. M5: Sal 6H **99**
Newpark Wlk. M8: Man 5E **87**
(off Tamerton Dr.)
Newport Av. SK5: Stoc 6G **133**
Newport M. BL4: Farn 2H **65**
(off Newport St.)
Newport Rd. BL3: Bolt 4E **49**
M21: Chor 6G **113**
M34: Dent 1H **135**

Newport St. BL1: Bolt 4F **175** (6D **32**)
  BL3: Bolt 5F **175** (1D **48**)
  BL4: Farn 2H **65**
  BL8: Tot 6A **22**
  M6: Sal 3E **99**
  M14: Man 4F **115**
  M24: Mid 6E **57**
  OL8: O'ham 4D **74**
Newquay Av. BL2: Ain 4F **35**
  SK5: Stoc 2G **133**
Newquay Dr. SK7: Bram 6H **157**
New Quay St. M3: Man 6E **5** (4C **100**)
New Radcliffe St.
  OL1: O'ham 3E **177** (2E **75**)
New Ridd Ri. SK14: Hyde 1B **136**
New Riven Ct. BL3: Lit L 4C **50**
New Rd. M26: Rad 5B **52**
  OL8: O'ham 5E **75**
  OL12: Whitw 1D **14**
  OL15: L'ough 5E **17**
  SK13: Tin 1H **123**
New Royd Av. OL4: Lees 1D **76**
Newry Rd. M30: Ecc 5G **97**
Newry St. BL1: Bolt 2B **32**
Newry Wlk. *M9: Man* *6F 71*
  (off Riverdale Rd.)
Newsham Cl. BL3: Bolt 2B **48**
Newsham Rd. SK3: Stoc 5G **145**
Newsham Wlk. M12: Man 4D **116**
Newshaw La. SK13: Had 4H **123**
Newsholme St. M8: Man 4D **86**
New Smithfield Mkt. M11: Man . . .6E **103**
New Springs BL1: Bolt 2H **31**
Newstead OL12: Roch 2A **178** (3G **27**)
Newstead Av. M20: Man 4H **131**
  OL6: A Lyme 4A **92**
Newstead Cl. SK12: Poy 2D **168**
Newstead Dr. BL3: Bolt 5G **47**
Newstead Gro. SK6: Bred 6F **135**
Newstead Rd. M41: Urm 4G **111**
Newstead St. WA15: Tim 4H **139**
New St. BL1: Bolt 5E **175** (1C **48**)
  BL8: Tot 5H **21**
  M26: Rad 5B **52**
  M27: Pen 2A **84**
  M30: Ecc 4E **97**
  M40: Man 1A **102**
  M43: Droy 5A **104**
  OL3: Upp 1D **78**
  OL4: Lees 3C **76**
  OL12: Roch 1G **27**
  OL15: L'ough 5F **17**
  OL16: Miln 6G **29**
  SK9: Wilm 4B **172**
  SK15: Stal 5E **107**
  WA14: Alt 3A **174** (1E **151**)
New Tame OL3: Del 6G **45**
New Tempest Rd. BL6: Los 3C **46**
New Ter. SK9: Wilm 1E **173**
  SK14: Hyde 2D **120**
  (Hamel St.)
  SK14: Hyde 6C **120**
  (Osborne Rd.)
New Thomas St. M6: Sal 1G **99**
NEWTON 3D **120**
Newton Av. M12: Man 3B **116**
  M20: Man 3E **131**
Newton Bus. Pk. SK14: Hyde 2E **121**
Newton Ct. *SK14: Hyde* *2B 120*
  (off Markham St.)
Newton Cres. M24: Mid 5H **55**
Newtondale Av. OL2: O'ham 3C **58**
Newton Dr. BL8: G'mount 2A **22**
Newton for Hyde Station (Rail) . . .3D **120**
New Tong Fld. BL7: Bro X 4D **18**
Newton Grn. SK14: Hyde 2D **120**
Newton Hall 3A **120**
Newton Hall Ct. SK14: Hyde 2A **120**
Newton Hall Rd.
  SK14: Hyde 2A **120**
NEWTON HEATH 5D **88**
Newton Moor Ind. Est.
  SK14: Hyde 2C **120**

Newtonmore Wlk. *M11: Man* *4D 102*
  (off Kincraig Cl.)
Newton Rd. M24: Mid 2F **71**
  M35: Fail 1G **103**
  M41: Urm 5E **111**
  SK9: Wilm 6E **165**
  WA14: Alt 4G **139**
Newton St. BL1: Bolt 3C **32**
  BL9: Bury 5F **23**
  M1: Man 5C **6** (4F **101**)
  M32: Stre 6D **112**
  M35: Fail 5E **89**
  M40: Man 5E **89**
  M43: Droy 2B **104**
  OL6: A Lyme 4D **174** (2A **106**)
  OL16: Roch 6B **28**
  SK3: Stoc 5E **179** (3G **145**)
  SK14: Hyde 4B **120**
  SK15: Stal 3D **106**
Newton Ter. *BL1: Bolt* *3C 32*
  (off Newton Wlk.)
  SK16: Duk *4H 105*
  (off Queen St.)
Newton Wlk. BL1: Bolt 3C **32**
NEWTON WOOD 1A **120**
Newton Wood Rd. SK16: Duk 1H **119**
NEW TOWN 1H **59**
NEWTOWN
  M4 . . . . .2F **101**
  M27 . . . . .1G **83**
  SK12 . . . . .4G **169**
Newtown Av. M34: Dent 5G **119**
Newtown Cl. M11: Man 5D **102**
  M27: Pen 1H **83**
Newtown Ct. M25: Pres 5A **70**
  M40: Man 1G **101**
Newtown M. M25: Pres 5A **70**
Newtown St. M25: Pres 5A **70**
  OL2: Shaw 1H **59**
New Union St. M4: Man 4E **7** (3G **101**)
New Vernon St.
  BL9: Bury 1D **176** (1F **37**)
New Viaduct St. M11: Man 3A **102**
Newville Dr. M20: Man 4H **131**
New Vine St. M15: Man 5G **9** (1D **114**)
New Wakefield St.
  M1: Man 3A **10** (6E **101**)
New Way OL12: Whitw 4A **14**
New Welcome St.
  M15: Man 5G **9** (1D **114**)
New William Cl. *M31: Part* *5D 124*
  (off Moss La.)
NEW WINDSOR 5A **4** (3H **99**)
New York BL3: Bolt 3F **47**
New York St. M1: Man 6A **6** (4E **101**)
  OL10: H'ood 3F **39**
  (not continuous)
New Zealand Rd. SK1: Stoc 2A **146**
Neyland Cl. BL1: Bolt 6F **31**
Ney St. OL7: A Lyme 5F **91**
Niagara St. SK2: Stoc 5A **146**
Nicholas Cft. M4: Man 4B **6** (3E **101**)
Nicholas Owen Cl. M11: Man 5E **103**
Nicholas Rd. OL8: O'ham 5E **75**
Nicholas St. BL2: Bolt 5E **33**
  M1: Man 6A **6** (4E **101**)
Nicholson Rd. SK14: Hyde 2A **120**
Nicholson Sq. SK16: Duk 5H **105**
Nicholson St. OL4: Lees 3C **76**
  OL11: Roch 6H **27**
  SK4: Stoc 1G **145**
Nichols St. *M6: Sal* *2H 99*
  (off Gerrard St.)
Nicker Brow OL3: Dob 5C **62**
Nicklebly Rd. SK12: Poy 4D **168**
Nick Rd. La. OL12: W'le 2H **15**
Nico Ditch M18: Man 5E **117**
Nicolas Rd. M21: Chor 6F **113**
Nicola St. BL7: Eger 3C **18**
Nield Rd. M34: Dent 4F **119**
Nields Brow WA14: Bow 3E **151**
Nield St. OL5: Mos 1F **93**
Nields Way SK6: Mel 1H **161**

Nigel Rd. M9: Man 4B **88**
Nigher Moss Av. OL16: Roch 4C **28**
Nightingale Cl. SK9: Wilm 6F **165**
Nightingale Dr. M34: Aud 3C **104**
Nightingale Gdns. M23: Wyth 2G **141**
Nightingale St. M3: Man 2G **5** (2D **100**)
Nightingales Wlk. BL3: Bolt 4D **48**
Nile, The M15: Man 3G **9**
Nile St. BL3: Bolt 2D **48**
  OL1: O'ham 1F **177** (1E **75**)
  OL7: A Lyme 5F **105**
  OL16: Roch 3A **28**
Nile Ter. M7: Sal 6B **86**
NIMBLE NOOK 4A **74**
Nimble Nook OL9: Chad 4A **74**
Nina Dr. M40: Man 6E **73**
Nine Acre Ct. *M5: Sal* *6H 99*
  (off Taylorson St.)
Nine Acre Dr. M5: Sal 6H **99**
Ninehouse La. BL3: Bolt 3D **48**
Ninfield Rd. M23: Wyth 1H **153**
Ninian Ct. M24: Mid 6B **56**
Ninian Gdns. M28: Walk 6H **65**
Ninth Av. OL8: O'ham 2D **90**
Nipper La. M45: White 6E **53**
Nisbet Av. M22: Wyth 2C **154**
Nithe Wlk. BL8: Bury 5A **22**
Niven St. M12: Man 3E **11** (6G **101**)
Nixon Rd. BL3: Bolt 4A **48**
Nixon Rd. Sth. BL3: Bolt 4A **48**
Nixon St. M35: Fail 4G **89**
  OL11: Roch 2D **40**
  SK3: Stoc 5F **179** (3G **145**)
NOB END 5C **50**
Noble Mdw. OL12: Roch 4D **16**
Noble St. BL3: Bolt 2C **48**
  OL8: O'ham 5F **75**
Noel Dr. M33: Sale 5D **128**
Noel St. BL1: Bolt 3E **175** (6C **32**)
Nolan St. M9: Man 4A **88**
No Limits Fitness Cen. 1D **160**
Nona St. M6: Sal 3E **99**
NOOK 6B **44**
Nook, The BL9: Bury 4B **38**
  M28: Wors 3B **82**
  M30: Ecc 2C **96**
  M41: Urm 6F **111**
  OL3: G'fld 5E **79**
  SK7: Bram 2F **167**
Nook Cotts. OL4: Aus 1E **77**
Nook Farm Av. OL12: Roch 6H **15**
Nook Flds. BL2: Bolt 2A **34**
Nook La. OL6: A Lyme 6B **92**
Nook Side OL12: Roch 6H **15**
Nook Ter. OL12: Roch 6H **15**
Noon Sun Cl. OL3: G'fld 5C **78**
Noon Sun St. OL12: Roch 2H **27**
Norbet Wlk. *M9: Man* *4A 88*
  (off Broadwell Dr.)
Norbreck Av. M21: Chor 2H **129**
  SK8: Chea 5C **144**
Norbreck Gdns. BL2: Bolt 5G **33**
Norbreck St. BL2: Bolt 5G **33**
Norburn Rd. M13: Man 5B **116**
Norbury Av. M6: Sal 6D **84**
  M33: Sale 5H **127**
  OL4: Gras 3G **77**
  SK6: Mar 5C **148**
  SK14: Hyde 5B **120**
Norbury Cl. *M40: Man* *1A 102*
  (off Giltbrook Av.)
Norbury Cres. SK7: H Gro 3D **158**
Norbury Dr. SK6: Mar 5C **148**
Norbury Gro. BL1: Bolt 1E **33**
  M27: Pen 2H **83**
  SK7: H Gro 3D **158**
Norbury Hollow Cvn. Site
  SK12: Poy 1A **170**
Norbury Hollow Rd. SK7: H Gro . . .5H **159**
Norbury Ho. OL4: O'ham 4H **75**
Norbury La. OL8: O'ham 6B **76**
Norbury M. SK6: Mar 5C **148**
NORBURY MOOR 5F **159**

Norbury St. M7: Sal 5C **86**
 OL16: Roch 1B **42**
 SK1: Stoc 3G **179** (2H **145**)
Norbury Way SK9: Hand 2H **165**
 (off Chelford Rd.)
Norcliffe Hall M. SK9: Sty 3B **164**
Norcliffe Wlk. M18: Man 3D **116**
Norcot Wlk. M15: Man 5D **8**
Norcross Cl. SK2: Stoc 6D **146**
Nordale Pk. OL12: Roch 1H **25**
Nordek Cl. OL2: O'ham 2D **58**
Nordek Dr. OL2: O'ham 2D **58**
NORDEN .2A **26**
Norden Av. M20: Man 3E **131**
Norden Cl. OL11: Roch 1G **25**
Norden Ct. BL3: Bolt 3C **48**
Norden Lodge OL11: Roch 3A **26**
Norden Rd. OL11: Roch 6H **25**
Nordens Dr. OL9: Chad 1H **73**
Nordens Rd. OL9: Chad 1H **73**
Nordens St. OL9: Chad 1A **74**
Norden Way OL11: Roch 1G **25**
Noreen Av. M25: Pres 4A **70**
Norfield Cl. SK16: Duk 5A **106**
Norfolk Av. M18: Man 3E **117**
 M34: Dent 4H **117**
 M43: Droy 2H **103**
 M45: White 1G **69**
 OL10: H'ood 3E **39**
 SK4: Stoc 3E **133**
Norfolk Cl. BL3: Lit L 3D **50**
 M44: Cad 4A **124**
 OL2: Shaw 6F **43**
 OL15: L'ough 3A **16**
Norfolk Cres. M35: Fail 5G **89**
Norfolk Dr. BL4: Farn 6H **49**
Norfolk Gdns. M41: Urm 4H **109**
 OL10: H'ood 2E **39**
Norfolk Ho. M7: Sal 2C **86**
 M33: Sale 5D **128**
Norfolk Rd. M18: Man 3E **117**
Norfolk St. M2: Man 5H **5** (4D **100**)
 M6: Sal 6G **85**
 M28: Walk 3H **65**
 OL9: O'ham 5B **74**
 (not continuous)
 OL11: Roch 5A **178** (5G **27**)
 SK14: Hyde 5B **120**
Norfolk Way OL2: O'ham 5D **58**
Norford Way OL11: Roch 3A **26**
Norgate St. M20: Man 6F **131**
Norlan Av. M34: Aud 6E **105**
Norland Wlk. M40: Man 6C **88**
 (off Bower St.)
Norleigh Rd. M22: Nor 3B **142**
Norley Av. M32: Stre 4F **113**
Norley Cl. OL1: Chad 5B **58**
Norley Dr. M19: Man 5E **117**
 M33: Sale 5E **129**
Norman Av. SK7: H Gro 2C **158**
Normandale Av. BL1: Bolt 4G **31**
Normandy Chase
 WA14: Alt 1D **150**
Normanby Gro. M27: Swin 2G **83**
Normanby Rd. M28: Wors 2G **81**
Normanby St. BL3: Bolt 5H **47**
 M14: Man 3E **115**
 M27: Swin 2G **83**
Norman Cl. M24: Mid 6E **57**
Normandy Cres.
 M26: Rad 4H **51**
Norman Gro. M12: Man 3B **116**
 SK5: Stoc 2G **133**
Norman Rd. M7: Sal 4C **86**
 M14: Man 5G **115**
 M33: Sale 6B **128**
 OL6: A Lyme 5A **92**
 OL11: Roch 5F **27**
 SK4: Stoc 6D **132**
 SK15: Stal 3D **106**
 WA14: Alt 5E **139**
Norman Rd. W. M9: Man 4B **88**
Norman's Pl. WA14: Alt 3A **174** (1F **151**)

Norman St. BL3: Bolt 3D **48**
 (off Rishton La.)
 BL9: Bury 1H **37**
 M12: Man 2D **116**
 M24: Mid 6D **56**
 M26: Rad 3D **52**
 (off Sandford St.)
 M35: Fail 2A **90**
 OL1: O'ham 1D **74**
 SK14: Hyde 5C **120**
Normanton Av. M6: Sal 2C **98**
Normanton Dr. M9: Man 5A **72**
Normanton Rd. SK3: Stoc 4C **144**
Norman Weall Ct. M24: Mid 5C **56**
Normington St. OL4: O'ham 2A **76**
Norreys Av. M41: Urm 4A **110**
Norreys St. OL16: Roch 2D **178** (3A **28**)
Norris Av. SK4: Stoc 2E **145**
NORRIS BANK 1E **145**
Norris Bank Ter. SK4: Stoc 2E **145**
NORRIS HILL 1D **144**
Norris Hill Dr. SK4: Stoc 1E **145**
Norris Rd. M33: Sale 1B **140**
Norris St. BL3: Bolt 2C **48**
 BL3: Lit L 4C **50**
 BL3: Farn 2H **65**
Norris Towers SK4: Stoc 1F **179**
Nortex Bus. Cen. BL1: Bolt 5B **32**
Northallerton Rd. M7: Sal 5G **85**
Northampton Rd. M40: Man 5B **88**
Northampton Way M34: Dent 6G **119**
 (off Leicester Av.)
North Av. BL4: Farn 1E **65**
 BL8: G'mount 2H **21**
 BL9: Bury 3H **53**
 M19: Man 2B **132**
 OL3: G'fld 4D **78**
 SK15: Stal 2E **107**
Northavon Cl. M30: Ecc 4A **98**
 (off Andoc Av.)
Nth. Back Rock BL9: Bury 3B **176**
 (not continuous)
Northbank Gdns. M19: Man 3A **132**
Northbank Ho. M28: Wors 6C **82**
Northbank Ind. Est. M44: Irl 4D **124**
Northbank Ind. Pk. M44: Irl 3D **124**
 (not continuous)
Northbank Wlk. M20: Man 6B **130**
Nth. Blackfield La. M7: Sal 3A **86**
Northbourne St. M6: Sal 3E **99**
Northbrook Av. M8: Man 5D **70**
Nth. Brook Rd. SK13: Had 3G **123**
Nth. Broughton St. M3: Sal 4E **5**
North Circ. M45: White 3G **69**
North City Shop. Cen. M9: Man 3A **88**
Nth. Clifden La. M7: Sal 5C **86**
Northcliffe Rd. SK2: Stoc 3C **146**
North Cl. SK13: Tin 1H **123**
Northcombe Rd. SK3: Stoc 6G **145**
Northcote Av. M22: Wyth 1B **154**
Northcote Rd. SK7: Bram 6H **157**
North Cres. M11: Man 2F **103**
North Cft. OL8: O'ham 6G **75**
Northdale Rd. M9: Man 4F **71**
Nth. Dean St. M27: Pen 2A **84**
Northdene Dr. OL11: Roch 5B **26**
Northdown Av. M15: Man 5C **8** (1B **114**)
 SK6: Wood 4A **136**
Nth. Downs Rd. SK8: Chea H 5F **43**
 SK8: Chea H 2B **156**
North Dr. M27: Swin 4B **84**
 M34: Aud 4C **104**
NORTHENDEN 2B **142**
Northenden Pde. M22: Nor 2B **142**
Northenden Rd. M33: Sale 4B **128**
 SK8: Gat 5E **143**
Northenden Vw. M20: Man 1F **143**
 (off South Rd.)
North End Rd. SK15: Stal 3F **107**
Northen Gro. M20: Man 5D **130**
Northerly Cres. M40: Man 6F **73**
Northern, The
 (Tennis & Squash Club) 5E **131**

Northern Av. M27: Clif 6C **68**
Northern Gro. BL1: Bolt 4A **32**
NORTHERN MOOR 2F **141**
Northfield Av. M40: Man 1H **89**
Northfield Dr. SK9: Wilm 1G **173**
Northfield Rd. BL9: Bury 5F **23**
 M40: Man 1H **89**
Northfield St. BL3: Bolt 2A **48**
Northfleet Rd. M30: Ecc 5B **96**
North Ga. OL8: O'ham 1E **91**
Northgate OL12: Whitw 2E **15**
Northgate La. OL1: O'ham 4C **60**
Northgate Rd. SK3: Stoc 3E **145**
Nth. George St. M3: Sal 2C **4** (3B **100**)
North Gro. M13: Man 2H **115**
 M28: Walk 6G **65**
 M41: Urm 5E **111**
Nth. Harvey St.
 SK1: Stoc 2H **179** (2H **145**)
Nth. Hill St. M3: Sal 2D **4** (2B **100**)
Northland Rd. BL1: Bolt 5D **18**
 M9: Man 6C **72**
Northlands M26: Rad 2G **51**
North La. OL12: Roch 1C **178** (3H **27**)
Northleach Cl. BL8: Bury 2B **36**
Northleigh Dr. M25: Pres 6B **70**
Northleigh Ho. M16: Old T 5H **113**
Northleigh Rd. M16: Old T 4H **113**
Nth. Lonsdale St. M32: Stre 4E **113**
Nth. Manchester Bus. Pk.
 M40: Man 5A **88**
North Meade M21: Chor 2H **129**
NORTH MOOR 2D **74**
Northmoor Rd. M12: Man 3C **116**
North Nook OL4: Aus 1D **76**
Northolme Gdns. M19: Man 4A **132**
Northolt Ct. M11: Man 3F **103**
Northolt Dr. BL3: Bolt 3D **48**
Northolt Fold OL10: H'ood 6A **40**
Northolt Rd. M23: Wyth 2F **141**
North Pde. M3: Man 5G **5**
 M33: Sale 1D **140**
 OL16: Miln 1A **44**
Nth. Phoebe St. M5: Sal 4H **99**
North Pl. SK1: Stoc 2G **179** (2H **145**)
Northpoint Ind. Est. SK16: Duk 1H **119**
NORTH REDDISH 6G **117**
Northridge Rd. M9: Man 3H **71**
North Ri. OL3: G'fld 4D **78**
 (not continuous)
North Rd. M11: Man 3D **102**
 M25: Pres 4F **69**
 M31: C'ton 5H **125**
 M34: Aud 3D **104**
 M43: Droy 3D **102**
 SK15: Stal 3F **107**
 WA15: Hale 5A **152**
Northside Av. M41: Urm 6B **110**
North Stage M50: Sal 5F **99**
Nth. Star Dr. M3: Sal 5C **4** (4B **100**)
Northstead Av. M34: Dent 5H **119**
North St. BL0: Ram 3F **13**
 M8: Man 6E **87**
 M24: Mid 5C **56**
 M26: Rad 3C **52**
 OL2: O'ham 3D **58**
 (not continuous)
 OL6: A Lyme 5A **174** (2H **105**)
 (Oldham Rd.)
 OL6: A Lyme 5A **174** (3G **105**)
 (Welbeck St. Nth.)
 OL10: H'ood 3F **39**
 OL12: Whitw 4A **14**
 OL15: L'ough 4H **17**
 (off East St.)
 OL16: Roch 1D **178** (3A **28**)
Northumberland Av.
 OL7: A Lyme 1H **105**
Northumberland Cl. M16: Old T 2A **114**
Northumberland Cres.
 M16: Old T 2A **114**
 (off Henry St.)

Northumberland Ho. OL9: O'ham 4C **74**
(off Milne St.)
Northumberland Rd.
M16: Old T 6B **8** (3A **114**)
SK5: Stoc 2B **134**
Northumberland St. M7: Sal 4B **86**
Northumberland Way M22: Shar 5C **142**
Northumbria St. BL3: Bolt 2A **48**
Northurst Dr. M8: Man 6D **70**
Nth. Vale Rd. WA15: Tim 5H **139**
North Vw. BL0: Ram 3F **13**
BL9: Sum 1B **22**
M45: White 5E **53**
OL5: Mos 2A **94**
SK3: Stoc 3B **14**
North Vw. Cl. OL4: Lyd 4G **77**
Northward Rd. SK9: Wilm 3C **172**
North Way BL1: Bolt 1F **33**
SK5: Stoc 3C **134**
SK14: Hyde 5C **120**
Northway M30: Ecc 3H **97**
M43: Droy 5A **104**
WA14: Alt 5G **139**
Nth. Western St. M1: Man . . .2E **11** (5G **101**)
M12: Man 3G **11** (6H **101**)
M19: Man 1C **132**
Northwold Dr. BL1: Bolt 5E **31**
M9: Man 6D **72**
Northwood BL2: Bolt 1H **33**
Northwood Cres. BL3: Bolt 2A **48**
Northwood Gro. M33: Sale 5B **128**
North Woodley M26: Rad 6C **52**
Norton Av. M12: Man 4D **116**
M33: Sale 3F **127**
M34: Dent 4A **118**
M41: Urm 3F **111**
Norton Grange M25: Pres 6B **70**
Norton Gro. SK4: Stoc 2D **144**
Norton Rd. M28: Wors 4C **80**
OL12: Roch 6H **15**
Norton St. BL1: Bolt 2D **32**
M1: Man 6F **7** (4G **101**)
M3: Sal 3G **5** (3D **100**)
M7: Sal 4C **86**
M16: Old T 3A **114**
M40: Man 1A **102**
Norview Dr. M20: Man 4F **143**
Norville Av. M40: Man 6F **73**
Norway Gro. SK5: Stoc 5H **133**
Norway St. BL1: Bolt 3B **32**
M6: Sal 3E **99**
M32: Stre 4E **113**
Norwell Rd. M22: Shar 6C **142**
Norwich Av. M34: Dent 6F **119**
OL9: Chad 6A **58**
OL11: Roch 4C **26**
Norwich Cl. OL6: A Lyme 3B **92**
SK16: Duk 6E **107**
Norwich Dr. BL8: Bury 2D **36**
Norwich Rd. M32: Stre 4H **111**
Norwich St. OL11: Roch 6A **28**
Norwick Cl. BL3: Bolt 3E **47**
Norwood M25: Pres 1H **85**
Norwood Av. M7: Sal 3A **82**
M20: Man 5H **131**
SK6: H Lan 6B **160**
SK7: Bram 2E **167**
SK8: Chea H 2C **156**
Norwood Cl. M28: Walk 3A **82**
OL2: Shaw 5G **43**
Norwood Ct. M32: Stre 6E **113**
(off Norwood Rd.)
Norwood Cres. OL2: O'ham 5E **59**
Norwood Dr. M27: Swin 4E **83**
WA15: Tim 6D **140**
Norwood Gro. BL1: Bolt 5B **32**
OL2: O'ham 5E **59**
Norwood Lodge M7: Sal 3A **86**
Norwood Pk. WA14: Alt 6E **139**
Norwood Rd. M32: Stre 6E **113**
SK2: Stoc 1B **158**
SK8: Gat 5F **143**
Nottingham Av. SK5: Stoc 3C **134**

Nottingham Cl. SK5: Stoc 4C **134**
Nottingham Dr. BL1: Bolt 4C **32**
M35: Fail 6A **90**
OL6: A Lyme 4H **91**
Nottingham Ter. SK5: Stoc 3C **134**
Nottingham Way
M34: Dent 6G **119**
Nowell Cl. M24: Mid 4C **56**
Nowell Ho. M24: Mid 4C **56**
Nowell Rd. M24: Mid 4C **56**
Nudger Cl. OL3: Dob 5B **62**
Nudger Grn. OL3: Dob 5B **62**
Nuffield Cl. BL1: Bolt 4H **31**
Nuffield Ho. BL1: Bolt 4H **31**
Nuffield Rd. M22: Wyth 1C **154**
Nugent Rd. BL3: Bolt 4C **48**
Nugget St. OL4: O'ham 3H **75**
No. 2 Passage SK3: Stoc 2F **145**
Nuneaton Dr. M40: Man 1G **7** (2H **101**)
Nuneham Av. M20: Man 2G **131**
Nunfield Cl. M40: Man 1D **88**
Nunnery Rd. BL3: Bolt 3H **47**
Nunthorpe Dr. M8: Man 3G **87**
Nursery Av. WA15: Hale 5G **151**
Nursery Brow M45: White 6B **52**
Nursery Cl. M33: Sale 5D **128**
SK2: Stoc 4D **146**
Nursery Dr. SK12: Poy 3D **168**
Nursery Gdns. OL16: Roch 3C **28**
Nursery Gro. M31: Part 5D **124**
Nursery La. SK3: Stoc 4C **144**
SK9: Wilm 3C **172**
Nursery Rd. M25: Pres 3G **69**
M35: Fail 4A **90**
M41: Urm 3C **110**
SK4: Stoc 1E **145**
SK8: Chea H 4B **156**
SK14: Hyde 4A **120**
Nursery St. M6: Sal 2F **99**
M16: W Ran 4D **114**
Nutbank La. M9: Mid 3A **72**
Nuthatch Av. M28: Wors 3H **81**
Nuthurst Rd. M40: Man 1E **89**
NUTSFORD VALE 3D **116**
Nutsford Va. M12: Man 3D **116**
Nut St. BL1: Bolt 3B **32**
NUTTALL 5C **12**
Nuttall Av. BL3: Lit L 4E **51**
M45: White 1F **69**
Nuttall Cl. BL0: Ram 4C **12**
Nuttall Hall Cotts. BL0: Ram 4D **12**
Nuttall Hall Rd. BL0: Ram 5D **12**
NUTTALL LANE 4C **12**
Nuttall La. BL0: Ram 4B **12**
Nuttall M. M45: White 1F **69**
Nuttall Sq. BL9: Bury 2F **53**
Nuttall St. BL9: Bury 4G **37**
M11: Man 6C **102**
M16: Old T 2A **114**
M44: Cad 3C **124**
OL8: O'ham 5H **75**
OL16: Roch 4D **178** (4A **28**)
Nutt La. M25: Pres 1C **70**
Nutwood Ct. SK5: Stoc 2G **133**
NW Regional Basketball Cen. 1A **134**

O

Oadby Cl. M12: Man 3C **116**
Oadby Pl. SK5: Stoc 5H **117**
Oak Av. BL0: Ram 1A **22**
BL3: Lit L 4D **50**
M21: Chor 1H **129**
M24: Mid 2C **72**
M44: Cad 4B **124**
M45: White 2F **69**
OL2: O'ham 1D **58**
SK4: Stoc 1D **144**
SK6: Rom 1A **148**
SK8: Chea H 3C **156**
SK9: Wilm 4C **172**
OAK BANK 1G **69**

Oak Bank M9: Man 3H **87**
M25: Pres 2F **85**
(Hilton La.)
M25: Pres 4G **69**
(Stanhope Av.)
SK9: A Edg 6D **172**
SK15: C'ook 4B **94**
Oak Bank Av. M9: Man 2B **88**
Oakbank Av. OL9: Chad 1G **73**
Oakbank Cl. M45: White 1H **69**
Oakbank Dr. BL1: Bolt 5B **18**
Oakbarton BL6: Los 3C **46**
Oakcliffe Rd. M23: Wyth 4G **141**
OL12: Roch 5C **16**
Oak Cl. OL12: Whitw 1B **14**
SK9: Wilm 3C **172**
SK14: Mot 3C **122**
Oak Coppice BL1: Bolt 6G **31**
Oak Cotts. SK9: Sty 3C **164**
Oak Ct. SK6: Bred 5G **135**
Oakcroft SK15: Stal 6H **107**
Oakcroft Way M22: Shar 5C **142**
Oakdale BL2: Bolt 1H **33**
Oakdale Cl. M45: White 1D **68**
Oakdale Ct. OL3: Del 4A **62**
WA14: Alt 6E **139**
Oakdale Dr. M20: Man 2G **143**
M29: Ast 5A **80**
SK8: H Grn 3F **155**
Oakdean Ct. SK9: Wilm 6F **165**
Oakden Dr. M34: Dent 5C **118**
Oakdene M27: Swin 5D **82**
Oakdene Av. SK4: Stoc 4F **133**
SK8: H Grn 5F **155**
Oak Dene Cl. OL3: G'fld 5C **78**
Oakdene Cres. SK6: Mar 4D **148**
Oakdene Gdns. SK6: Mar 4D **148**
Oakdene Rd. M24: Mid 1E **73**
SK6: Mar 5D **148**
WA15: Tim 3B **140**
Oakdene St. M9: Man 3B **88**
Oak Dr. M14: Man 6H **115**
M34: Dent 3A **118**
SK6: Mar 5B **148**
SK7: Bram 6E **157**
Oaken Bank Rd. OL10: H'ood 2B **56**
OAKEN BOTTOM 1H **49**
Oakenbottom Rd. BL2: Bolt 1H **49**
Oaken Clough OL7: A Lyme 5F **91**
Oakenclough OL1: O'ham 2F **177**
Oakenclough Cl. SK9: Wilm 5H **165**
Oaken Clough Dr. OL7: A Lyme 5F **91**
Oakenclough Dr. BL1: Bolt 3F **31**
Oaken Clough Ter. OL7: A Lyme . . .5F **91**
Oakenrod Hill OL11: Roch 4E **27**
Oakenrod Vs. OL11: Roch 4F **27**
Oakenshaw Av. OL12: Whitw 3E **15**
Oakenshaw Vw. OL12: Whitw 3E **15**
Oaken St. OL7: A Lyme 5G **91**
Oaker Av. M20: Man 5C **130**
Oakes St. BL4: Kea 2B **66**
Oakfield M25: Pres 5A **128**
M33: Sale 4A **128**
SK16: Duk 1C **120**
Oakfield Av. M16: Old T 4G **113**
M16: W Ran 4B **114**
M43: Droy 4H **103**
SK8: Chea 5A **144**
SK15: C'ook 5A **94**
Oakfield Cl. SK7: Bram 3G **167**
SK9: A Edg 6E **173**
Oakfield Ct. WA15: Tim 5H **139**
Oakfield Dr. M38: Lit H 4C **64**
Oakfield Gro. BL4: Farn 3G **65**
M18: Man 3F **117**
Oakfield Ho. WA15: Alt . . .2C **174** (1G **151**)
Oakfield M. M33: Sale 5A **128**
SK3: Stoc 6H **145**
Oakfield Rd. M20: Man 6E **131**
SK3: Stoc 6H **145**
SK9: A Edg 6E **173**
SK12: Poy 3F **169**
SK13: Had 4G **123**

Oakfield Rd. SK14: Hyde 2C 120
   WA15: Alt 1C 174 (6G 139)
Oakfield St. M8: Man 5E 87
   WA15: Alt 1C 174 (6G 139)
Oakfield Ter. OL11: Roch 3E 27
Oakfield Trad. Est.
   WA15: Alt 1C 174 (6G 139)
Oakfold Av. OL6: A Lyme 5B 92
Oakford Av. M40: Man 2F 7 (2G 101)
Oakford Cl. SK13: Had 3H 123
Oakford Wlk. BL3: Bolt 3A 48
Oak Gates BL7: Eger 2C 18
Oak Gro. M30: Ecc 4D 96
   OL6: A Lyme 5B 92
   SK8: Chea 6A 144
   SK12: Poy 3D 168
Oakham Av. M20: Man 1E 131
Oakham Cl. BL8: Bury 6E 23
Oakham M. M7: Sal 2A 86
Oakham Rd. M34: Dent 6G 119
Oak Hill OL15: L'ough 4F 17
Oakhill Cl. BL2: Bolt 6C 34
Oakhill Ct. M7: Sal 4C 86
Oakhill Trad. Est. M28: Walk 3G 65
Oakhill Way M8: Man 4D 86
                (off Greenland St.)
Oak Ho. M14: Man 6H 115
Oakhouse Dr. M21: Chor 2H 129
Oakhurst Chase SK9: A Edg 4G 173
Oakhurst Dr. SK3: Stoc 6D 144
Oakhurst Gdns. M25: Pres 5G 69
Oakington Av. M14: Man 4F 115
                  (off Heald Pl.)
Oakland Av. M6: Sal 1A 98
   M16: Old T 3G 113
   M19: Man 5A 132
   SK2: Stoc 5C 146
Oakland Ct. SK12: Poy 3D 168
Oakland Gro. BL1: Bolt 3G 31
Oakland Ho. M16: Old T 2G 113
Oaklands BL1: Bolt 6F 31
Oaklands, The OL11: Roch 4E 41
Oaklands Av. SK6: Mar B 3G 149
   SK8: Chea H 3C 156
Oaklands Cl. SK9: Wilm 6A 166
Oaklands Ct. OL4: G'fld 4B 78
Oaklands Dene SK14: Hyde 5E 121
Oaklands Dr. M25: Pres 5H 69
   M33: Sale 4A 128
   SK7: H Gro 4E 159
Oaklands Ho. M14: Man 6G 115
Oaklands Pk. OL4: G'fld 4A 78
Oaklands Rd. BL0: Ram 3G 13
   M7: Sal .4G 85
   M27: Swin 5F 83
   OL2: O'ham 5E 59
   OL3: G'fld 4B 78
   OL4: G'fld 4B 78
   SK14: Hyde 5E 121
Oakland Ter. OL11: Roch 4E 41
Oak La. M45: White 1H 69
   SK9: Wilm 3C 172
Oaklea M16: Old T 4A 114
           (off Up. Chorlton Rd.)
Oak Lea Av. SK9: Wilm 4D 172
Oaklea Rd. M33: Sale 4G 127
Oakleigh SK3: Stoc 1H 157
   SK4: Stoc 6D 132
          (off Heaton Moor Rd.)
Oakleigh Av. BL3: Bolt 5E 49
   M19: Man 2B 132
   WA15: Tim 4A 140
Oakleigh Cl. OL10: H'ood 6A 40
Oakleigh Ct. WA15: Tim 4C 140
Oakleigh Ho. M33: Sale 6G 127
Oakleigh M. M33: Sale 6G 127
Oakleigh Rd. SK8: Chea H 5A 156
Oakley Cl. M26: Rad 1A 68
   M40: Man 1A 104
Oakley Dr. OL1: O'ham 3B 60
Oakley Pk. BL1: Bolt 6F 31
Oakley St. OL15: L'ough 5E 17

Oakley Vs. SK4: Stoc 6D 132
Oak Lodge SK7: Bram 6H 157
Oakmere Av. M30: Ecc 1E 97
Oakmere Cl. M22: Wyth 1B 154
Oakmere Rd. SK8: Chea H 1B 156
   SK9: Hand 2H 165
Oak M. SK9: Wilm 6G 165
Oakmoor Dr. M7: Sal 3G 85
Oakmoor Rd. M23: Wyth 5G 141
Oakridge Wlk. M9: Man 4H 87
             (off Carisbrook St.)
Oak Rd. M7: Sal 5A 86
   M20: Man 4F 131
   M31: Part 6B 124
   M33: Sale 5D 128
   M35: Fail 5H 89
   OL8: O'ham 1C 90
   SK8: Chea 5A 144
   WA15: Hale 2G 151
Oaks, The SK8: H Grn 3E 155
   SK14: Hyde 4E 121
Oaks Av. BL2: Bolt 6G 19
Oaks Bus. Pk., The
   M23: Wyth 3E 141
Oakshaw Cl. M9: Man 1H 87
Oakshaw Dr. OL12: Roch 2C 26
Oakside Cl. SK8: Chea 5A 144
Oaks La. BL2: Bolt 6F 19
Oak St. BL0: Ram 4B 12
   M4: Man 4B 6 (3E 101)
             (not continuous)
   M24: Mid .2F 73
   M26: Rad 6C 52
   M27: Pen 2A 84
   M30: Ecc 4F 97
   M34: Aud 1F 119
   OL2: Shaw 6A 44
   OL10: H'ood 2F 39
   OL12: Whitw 1B 14
   OL15: L'ough 6F 17
             (Smithy Bri. Rd.)
   OL15: L'ough 4H 17
               (West Vw.)
   OL16: Miln 2G 43
   OL16: Roch 4B 178 (4H 27)
   SK3: Stoc 3D 144
   SK7: H Gro 2D 158
   SK14: Hyde 3C 120
Oak Ter. OL15: L'ough 1B 16
Oak Tree Cl. SK2: Stoc 3D 146
   SK14: Hyde 5E 121
Oaktree Cotts. SK8: Chea H 2B 156
Oak Tree Ct. SK8: Chea 6A 144
Oak Tree Cres. SK15: Stal 5E 107
Oak Tree Dr. SK16: Duk 6D 106
Oak Vw. OL12: Whitw 1B 14
Oak Vw. Rd. OL3: G'fld 4D 78
Oak Vs. SK15: C'ook 4B 94
Oakville Dr. M6: Sal 1A 98
Oakville Ter. M40: Man 2B 88
Oak Wlk. M34: Aud 1E 119
Oakway M20: Man 3G 143
   M24: Mid 3B 56
Oakwell Dr. BL9: Bury 4H 53
   M7: Sal 2C 86
Oakwell Mans. M7: Sal 2C 86
Oakwood M27: Clif 5G 67
   M33: Sale 5E 127
   OL9: Chad 2G 73
Oakwood Av. M27: Clif 5G 67
   M28: Walk 1B 82
   M34: Aud 6E 105
   M40: Man 2F 89
   SK8: Gat 6E 143
   SK9: Wilm 3B 172
Oakwood Cl. BL8: Bury 2B 36
Oakwood Ct. WA14: Bow 5D 150
Oakwood Dr. BL1: Bolt 5F 31
   M6: Sal 6B 84
   M28: Walk 1B 82
Oakwood Est. M5: Sal 4D 98
Oakwood Ho. M21: Chor 1A 130
Oakwood La. WA14: Bow 4C 150

Oakwood Rd. SK6: Rom 1A 148
   SK12: Dis 1H 171
Oakworth Cft. OL4: O'ham 3D 60
Oakworth Dr. BL1: Bolt 6B 18
Oakworth St. M9: Man 1G 87
Oatlands SK9: A Edg 6H 173
Oatlands Rd. M22: Wyth 4A 154
Oat St. SK1: Stoc 4A 146
Oban Av. M40: Man 1D 102
   OL1: O'ham 6H 59
Oban Cres. SK3: Stoc 1F 157
Oban Dr. M33: Sale 6E 129
Oban Gro. BL1: Bolt 6C 18
Oban St. BL1: Bolt 2B 32
Oberlin St. OL4: O'ham 2B 76
   OL11: Roch 6F 27
Oberon Cl. M30: Ecc 3F 97
         (off Shakespeare Cres.)
Occleston Cl. M33: Sale 2E 141
Occupiers La. SK7: H Gro 4G 159
Ocean Ho. M15: Man 2E 115
           (off Boundary La.)
Ocean St. WA14: B'ath 5D 138
Ocean St. Trad. Est.
   WA14: B'ath 5D 138
Ocean Wlk. M15: Man 6H 9
Ockendon Dr. M9: Man 4A 88
Octagon Ct. BL1: Bolt 4F 175 (6D 32)
Octagon Theatre 4F 175 (6D 32)
Octavia Dr. M40: Man 1E 103
Oddfellow Hall OL6: A Lyme 6B 174
Oddies Yd. OL12: Roch 1A 28
             (off Isabella St.)
Odell St. M11: Man 6D 102
Odeon Cinema
   Manchester 3A 6 (3E 101)
   Rochdale 1G 41
   The Trafford Cen. 1G 111
Odessa Av. M6: Sal 1B 98
Odette St. M18: Man 3E 117
OFFERTON 6E 147
Offerton Dr. SK2: Stoc 5D 146
Offerton Fold SK2: Stoc 4C 146
OFFERTON GREEN 5G 147
Offerton Grn. SK2: Stoc 5F 147
Offerton Ind. Est. SK2: Stoc 4C 146
Offerton La. SK2: Stoc 3B 146
Offerton Rd. SK2: H Gro 2G 159
   SK7: H Gro 2G 159
Offerton St. SK1: Stoc 1B 146
Off Green St. M24: Mid 6D 56
Off Grove Rd. SK15: Mill 1H 107
Off Kershaw St. OL2: Shaw 6H 43
           (off Kershaw St. E.)
Off Ridge Hill La. SK15: Stal 3D 106
           (off Ridge Hill La.)
Off Stamford St. SK15: Mill 1H 107
           (off Stamford St.)
Off Vaudrey La. M34: Dent 5G 119
Ogbourne Wlk. M13: Man 6F 11
          (off Lauderdale Cres.)
Ogden Cl. M45: White 6G 53
   OL10: H'ood 3E 39
Ogden Ct. SK14: Hyde 5C 120
             (off Frank St.)
Ogden Gdns. SK16: Duk 5C 106
Ogden Gro. SK8: Gat 1D 154
Ogden La. M11: Man 6F 103
   OL16: Miln 1B 44
Ogden Rd. M35: Fail 5H 89
   SK7: Bram 2E 167
Ogden Sq. SK16: Duk 5H 105
Ogden St. M20: Man 6F 131
   M24: Mid 1C 72
   M25: Pres 5A 70
   M27: Swin 4H 83
   OL4: O'ham 3B 76
   OL9: Chad 1B 74
   OL11: Roch 3E 41
Ogden Wlk. M45: White 1G 69
Ogmore Wlk. M40: Man 1E 89
Ogwen Dr. M25: Pres 4H 69
Ohio Av. M50: Sal 5F 99

O'Kane Ho. *M30: Ecc* 4F **97**
　　　　　　　　　　　(off Cawdor St.)
Okehampton Cl. M26: Rad 2E **51**
Okehampton Cres. M33: Sale 4F **127**
Okeover Rd. M7: Sal 3B **86**
Olaf St. BL2: Bolt 4F **33**
Olanyian Dr. M8: Sal 6C **86**
Old Bank Cl. SK6: Bred 6G **135**
Old Bank St. M2: Man 5H **5** (4D **100**)
Old Bank Vw. OL1: O'ham 3A **60**
Old Barn Pl. BL7: Bro X 3E **19**
Old Barton Rd. M41: Urm 6F **97**
Old Bent La. OL12: W'le 3H **15**
Old Birley St. M15: Man 6G **9** (2D **114**)
OLD BIRTLE 4C **24**
Old Boat Yd., The M28: Wors 6C **82**
Old Broadway M20: Man 4F **131**
Old Brook Cl. OL2: Shaw 5B **44**
Oldbrook Fold WA15: Tim 1B **152**
Old Brow OL5: Mos 3G **93**
　　　　　　　　　　　(Park St.)
　　OL5: Mos 2G **93**
　　　　　　　　　　　(Seel St.)
Old Brow Ct. OL5: Mos 3G **93**
Old Brow La. *OL16: Roch* 6C **16**
　　　　　　　　(off Wheelwright Dr.)
Oldbury Cl. M40: Man 2G **7** (2H **101**)
　　OL10: H'ood 6H **39**
Oldcastle Av. M20: Man 1E **131**
Old Chapel St. SK3: Stoc . . .5E **179** (4E **145**)
Old Church M. SK16: Duk 5C **106**
Old Church St. M40: Man 5D **88**
　　OL1: O'ham 3H **177** (2F **75**)
Old Clay Dr. OL12: Roch 5C **16**
Old Clough La. M28: Walk 2B **82**
　　　　　　　　　　(not continuous)
Oldcott Cl. M28: Wors 6D **80**
Old Ct. House, The M3: Sal 4C **4**
Old Ct. St. SK14: Hyde 5B **120**
Old Courtyard, The
　　M22: Shar 6C **142**
Old Croft OL4: Spri 3E **77**
Oldcroft M. SK1: Stoc 4B **146**
Old Crofts Bank M41: Urm 3E **95**
Old Cross St. OL6: A Lyme .5D **174** (2A **106**)
Old Dairy M. SK11: Roch 2A **120**
Old Delph Rd. OL11: Roch 2A **26**
Old Doctors St. BL8: Tot 4H **21**
Old Eagley M. BL1: Bolt 5D **18**
Old Edge La. OL2: O'ham 5E **59**
　　　　　　　　　　(not continuous)
Old Elm St. M12: Man 5F **11** (1G **115**)
Old Engine La. BL0: Ram 3D **12**
Oldershaw Dr. M9: Man 5H **87**
Old Farm Cres. M43: Droy 5H **103**
Old Farm Dr. SK2: Stoc 5F **147**
Old Farm M. SK8: Chea H 6E **157**
OLDFIELD BROW 5C **138**
Oldfield Dr. WA15: Tim 5H **139**
Oldfield Gro. M33: Sale 4C **128**
Oldfield La. WA14: D Mas 1A **150**
Oldfield M. WA14: Alt 6E **139**
Oldfield Rd. M5: Sal 3A **8** (6A **100**)
　　M25: Pres 2A **70**
　　M33: Sale 4C **128**
　　WA14: Alt 6C **138**
Oldfield St. M11: Man 4D **102**
Old Fold M30: Ecc 1E **97**
　　SK7: H Gro 1D **158**
Old Garden, The WA15: Tim 4B **140**
Old Gdns. St.
　　SK1: Stoc 4H **179** (3H **145**)
Oldgate Wlk. M15: Man 6D **8**
Old Grn. BL2: Bolt 5A **20**
　　BL8: G'mount 2H **21**
Old Ground St. BL0: Ram 3C **12**
Old Hall Cl. BL8: Bury 4B **22**
　　SK14: Mot 2C **122**
Old Hall Clough BL6: Los 6C **30**
　　　　　　　　　　(not continuous)
Old Hall Ct. M33: Sale 5E **129**
　　M45: White 2C **68**
Old Hall Cres. SK9: Hand 4A **166**

Old Hall Dr. M18: Man 3F **117**
　　SK2: Stoc 5E **147**
Old Hall Fold SK13: Had 2H **123**
Old Hall La. BL6: Bolt 4C **30**
　　M13: Man 5A **116**
　　M14: Man 6H **115**
　　M24: Man 3E **71**
　　M25: Pres 1D **70**
　　　　　　　　　　(not continuous)
　　M28: Wors 4A **82**
　　M45: White 2C **68**
　　SK6: Mel 6F **149**
　　SK7: W'ford 6F **167**
　　SK14: Mot 2C **122**
Old Hall M. BL1: Bolt 4D **30**
Old Hall Rd. M7: Man 2B **86**
　　M32: Stre 3A **112**
　　M33: Sale 5E **129**
　　M40: Man 4D **88**
　　M45: White 2C **68**
　　SK8: Gat 5E **143**
Old Hall Sq. SK13: Had 2H **123**
Old Hall St. BL4: Farn 2A **66**
　　M11: Man 6G **103**
　　M24: Mid 1B **72**
　　SK16: Duk 6G **105**
Old Hall St. Nth.
　　BL1: Bolt 3F **175** (6D **32**)
OLDHAM 3G **177** (2F **75**)
Oldham Athletic FC 5D **58**
Oldham B'way. Bus. Pk.
　　OL9: Chad 5G **73**
Oldham Bus. Cen. OL1: O'ham 5G **177**
Oldham Central Trad. Pk.
　　OL1: O'ham 1G **75**
Oldham Coliseum Theatre
　　. . . . . .3H **177** (2F **75**)
Oldham Ct. M40: Man 2F **7** (2G **101**)
Oldham Crematorium
　　OL8: O'ham 2C **90**
Oldham Dr. SK6: Bred 5G **135**
OLDHAM EDGE 1G **177** (1F **75**)
Oldham Ho. OL2: Shaw 1D **58**
Oldham Mumps Station (Rail) 3G **75**
Oldham RLFC 5D **58**
Oldham Rd. M4: Man 3D **6** (3F **101**)
　　M24: Mid 1C **72**
　　M35: Fail 6F **89**
　　M40: Man 3D **6** (3F **101**)
　　OL1: Dens, O'ham 1E **61**
　　OL2: O'ham 3E **59**
　　OL2: O'ham, Shaw 3H **59**
　　OL3: Del, Dob, O'ham 1G **77**
　　OL3: Dens 1E **61**
　　OL3: G'fld, Upp 2G **78**
　　OL4: Gras, G'fld, Grot, Lyd, Spri
　　. . . . . .3D **76**
　　OL4: Scout 1G **77**
　　OL6: A Lyme 4B **174** (2H **105**)
　　OL7: A Lyme 4A **174** (4G **91**)
　　OL11: Roch 1A **42**
　　　　　　　　　　(not continuous)
　　OL16: Roch 4C **178** (5A **28**)
Oldhams La. BL1: Bolt 6B **18**
　　　　　　　　　　(not continuous)
Oldham Sports Cen. 3G **177** (2F **75**)
Oldhams Ter. BL1: Bolt 6B **18**
Oldham St. M1: Man 5B **6** (4E **101**)
　　M5: Sal 6C **4** (4B **100**)
　　M34: Dent 5C **118**
　　M43: Droy 3B **104**
　　SK5: Stoc 2G **133**
　　SK14: Hyde 5B **120**
Oldham Way
　　OL1: O'ham 5G **177** (1D **74**)
　　OL4: O'ham 5G **177** (1D **74**)
　　OL8: O'ham 4E **177** (1D **74**)
　　OL9: O'ham 4E **177** (1D **74**)
Oldham Werneth Station (Rail) 3D **74**
Old Heyes Rd. WA15: Tim 3B **140**
Old Ho. Ter. OL6: A Lyme 6C **92**
Old Kays BL8: Tot 3G **21**

Old Kiln La. BL1: Bolt 3C **30**
　　OL4: Grot 5F **77**
Oldknow Rd. SK6: Mar 5E **149**
Old La. BL6: Hor 3A **30**
　　BL9: Bury 3F **23**
　　M11: Man 5F **103**
　　M38: Lit H 3D **64**
　　OL3: Dob 5D **62**
　　OL3: Upp 6F **63**
　　OL4: Aus 1E **77**
　　OL4: Gras 3A **78**
　　OL9: Chad 5B **74**
Old Lansdowne Rd.
　　M20: Man 5D **130**
Old Lees St. OL6: A Lyme 6B **92**
Old Links Cl. BL1: Bolt 3E **31**
Old Manor, The OL12: Roch 2G **27**
Old Market Pl.
　　WA14: Alt 1B **174** (6F **139**)
Old Market St. M9: Man 1G **87**
Old Meadow Dr. M34: Dent 2F **119**
Old Meadow La. WA15: Hale 2B **152**
Old Medlock St. M3: Man 1D **8** (5B **100**)
Old Mill Cl. M27: Pen 3B **84**
Old Mill Ho. OL4: Grot 4E **77**
Old Mill La. OL4: Grot 4E **77**
　　SK7: H Gro 5G **159**
Old Mills Hill M24: Mid 6F **57**
Old Mill St. M4: Man 5E **7** (4G **101**)
Oldmill St. OL12: Roch 1B **178** (3H **27**)
Old Moat La. M20: Man 2E **131**
Oldmoor Rd. SK6: Bred 4E **135**
Old Mount St. M4: Man 2B **6** (2F **101**)
Old Nans La. BL2: Bolt 3B **34**
Old Nursery Fold BL2: Bolt 1A **34**
Old Oak Cl. BL2: Bolt 2D **50**
Oak Oak Cotts. BL8: Haw 1G **21**
Old Oak Dr. M34: Dent 4G **119**
Old Oake Cl. M28: Walk 1A **82**
Old Oak St. M20: Man 6F **131**
Old Orchard SK9: Wilm 2D **172**
Old Orchard, The WA15: Tim 3B **140**
Old Pack Horse Rd. OL3: Del 1D **62**
Old Park La. M30: Urm 1E **111**
Old Parrin La. M30: Ecc 2D **96**
Old Pasture Cl. SK2: Stoc 4E **147**
Old Quarry La. BL7: Eger 2D **18**
Old Rectory Gdns. SK8: Chea 5H **143**
Old River Cl. M44: Irl 5E **109**
Old Rd. BL1: Bolt 1C **32**
　　M9: Man 1H **87**
　　M35: Fail 4G **89**
　　OL6: A Lyme 6D **92**
　　OL16: Roch 5E **17**
　　SK4: Stoc 6G **133**
　　SK8: Chea 5B **144**
　　SK9: Hand 4H **165**
　　SK9: Wilm 1E **173**
　　SK14: Hyde 2B **120**
　　SK14: Mot 1B **122**
　　SK15: Stal 5G **107**
　　SK16: Duk 4A **106**
　　　　　　　　　　(not continuous)
Old School Ct. *M9: Man* 1G **87**
　　　　　　　　(off Old School Dr.)
　　M30: Ecc 1F **97**
Old School Dr. M9: Man 1G **87**
Old School Ho., The
　　OL15: L'ough 3F **17**
Old School La. SK8: Chea H 5C **156**
　　　　　　　　　　(not continuous)
Old School M. *SK16: Duk* 5C **106**
　　　　　　　　(off Vicarage Dr.)
Old School Pl. OL12: W'le 6C **16**
Old School Rooms, The
　　BL1: Bolt 5G **175**
Old Shaw St. M5: Sal 5G **99**
Old Sq. OL6: A Lyme 5D **174** (2A **106**)
Old Stables, The M34: Aud 1F **119**
Old Station St. M30: Ecc 4E **97**
Oldstead Gro. BL3: Bolt 3F **47**
Oldstead Wlk. *M9: Man* 5H **87**
　　　　　　　　(off Kelvington Dr.)

Old St. OL4: O'ham 4B 76
    OL6: A Lyme 6A 174 (3G 105)
    SK15: Stal 3E 107
Old Swan Cl. BL7: Eger 1C 18
OLD TAME 5F 45
Old Tannery, The SK14: Hyde 1D 136
Old Thorn La. OL3: G'fld 3F 79
Old Towns Cl. BL8: Tot 4H 21
OLD TRAFFORD 6A 8 (2H 113)
Old Trafford Cricket Ground 4F 113
Old Trafford Football Ground 2F 113
Old Trafford Station (Metro) 3G 113
Old Vicarage Gdns. M28: Walk 6H 65
Old Vicarage Rd. BL6: Hor 2A 30
Oldway Wlk. M40: Man 6D 88
Old Wellington Rd. M30: Ecc 3F 97
Old Wells Cl. M38: Lit H 3E 65
Old Well Wlk. M33: Sale 1E 139
Old Wood La. BL2: Ain, Bolt 5C 34
Oldwood Rd. M23: Wyth 2G 153
Old Wool La. SK8: Chea H 1B 156
                  (Betleymere Rd.)
    SK8: Chea H 6B 144
                  (Pickmere Gdns.)
Old York St. M15: Man 5E 9 (1C 114)
Oleo Ter. M44: Irl 4G 109
Olga St. BL1: Bolt 3B 32
Olivant St. BL9: Bury 6A 176 (5E 37)
Olive Bank BL8: Bury 1B 36
Oliver Cl. OL15: L'ough 4F 17
Oliver Fold Cl. M28: Wors 5C 80
Olive Rd. WA15: Tim 3A 140
Oliver St. SK1: Stoc 5G 179 (3H 145)
Olive Shapley Av. M20: Man 6F 131
Olive Stanring Ho. OL15: L'ough 3H 17
Olive St. BL3: Bolt 3B 48
    BL8: Bury 3D 36
    M26: Rad 4C 52
    M35: Fail 3G 89
    OL10: H'ood 3A 40
    OL11: Roch 4E 41
Olive Wlk. M33: Sale 3E 127
                  (off Epping Dr.)
Olivia Cl. M5: Sal 2B 8 (5A 100)
Olivia Gro. M14: Man 4H 115
Olivier Ho. WA14: Alt 3B 174
Ollerbarrow Rd. WA15: Hale 3G 151
Ollerbrook Ct. BL1: Bolt 3D 32
Ollerenshaw Hall M14: Man 3H 115
                  (off Daisy Bank Hall)
Ollerton OL12: Roch 1A 178
Ollerton Av. M16: Old T 4A 114
    M33: Sale 3F 127
Ollerton Cl. M22: Nor 2C 142
Ollerton Ct. M16: Old T 5H 113
                  (off Manchester Rd.)
Ollerton Dr. M35: Fail 5H 89
Ollerton Rd. SK9: Hand 2H 165
Ollerton St. BL1: Bolt 5D 18
Ollerton Ter. BL1: Bolt 5D 18
Ollier Av. M12: Man 5C 116
Olmpic St. M11: Man 5A 102
Olney OL11: Roch 6A 178 (5G 27)
Olney Av. M22: Wyth 5B 142
Olney St. M13: Man 3H 115
Olsberg Cl. M26: Rad 3C 52
Olwen Av. M12: Man 2C 116
Olwen Cres. SK5: Stoc 1H 133
Olympia Cl. M44: Irl 5E 109
Olympia Trad. Est.
    M15: Man 3F 9 (6C 100)
Olympic Ct. M50: Sal 5F 99
Olympic Ho. M90: Man A 6A 154
Omega Circ. M44: Irl 3D 124
Omega Dr. M44: Irl 3D 124
Omer Av. M13: Man 5B 116
Omer Dr. M19: Man 2A 132
Onchan Av. OL4: O'ham 3H 75
One Ash Cl. OL12: Roch 1H 27
One Oak Ct. SK7: Bram 3E 157
One Oak La. SK9: Wilm 2H 173
Ongar Wlk. M9: Man 6F 71
Onslow Av. M40: Man 2G 89

Onslow Cl. OL1: O'ham 1E 177 (1E 75)
Onslow Rd. SK3: Stoc 3E 145
Onslow St. OL11: Roch 1E 41
Ontario Ho. M50: Sal 6G 99
Onward St. SK14: Hyde 5B 120
OOZEWOOD 1C 58
Oozewood Rd. OL2: O'ham 2A 58
Opal Cl. M14: Man 1H 131
Opal Gdns. M14: Man 3H 115
Opal Hall M15: Man 5A 10 (1E 115)
Opal St. M19: Man 1D 132
OPENSHAW 5D 102
Openshaw Fold. M27: Clif 1A 84
Openshaw Fold BL9: Bury 6D 36
Openshaw Fold Rd.
    BL9: Bury 5D 36
Openshaw La. M44: Cad 3C 124
                  (off Prospect Av.)
Openshaw Pl. BL4: Farn 1F 65
Openshaw St. BL9: Bury 4G 37
Openshaw Wlk. M11: Man 4E 103
                  (off Greenside St.)
Opera House 6F 5 (4C 100)
Oracle Ct. M28: Walk 1H 81
                  (off Sparta Av.)
Orama Av. M6: Sal 1A 98
Orama Mill OL12: Whitw 1E 15
Oram St. BL9: Bury 1G 37
                  (not continuous)
Orange Hill Rd. M25: Pres 4A 70
Orbital 24 M34: Dent 4D 118
Orbital Way M34: Dent 4D 118
Orbit Ho. M30: Ecc 4H 97
                  (off Albert St.)
Orchard, The OL8: O'ham 6A 76
    SK9: A Edg 6H 173
Orchard Av. BL1: Bolt 2D 32
    M18: Man 3G 117
                  (off Woodland Rd.)
    M28: Wors 4F 81
    M31: Part 5D 124
Orchard Brow OL2: Shaw 6F 43
                  (off Surrey Rd.)
Orchard Cl. SK8: Chea H 6E 157
    SK9: Wilm 4C 172
    SK12: Poy 4E 169
    SK2: Stoc 5D 146
    WA15: Tim 4B 140
Orchard Dr. SK9: Hand 5A 166
    SK13: Gam 6G 123
    WA15: Hale 2A 152
Orchard Gdns. BL2: Bolt 2B 34
    SK8: Gat 5D 142
Orchard Grn. SK9: A Edg 5H 173
Orchard Gro. M20: Man 4D 130
    OL2: Shaw 6G 43
Orchard Ind. Est. M6: Sal 1G 99
Orchard Pl. M33: Sale 4B 128
    SK12: Poy 3D 168
    WA15: Tim 4B 140
Orchard Ri. SK14: Hyde 2D 136
Orchard Rd. M35: Fail 4H 89
    SK6: Comp 1F 141
    WA15: Alt 1D 174 (6G 139)
Orchard Rd. E. M22: Nor 1B 142
Orchard Rd. W. M22: Nor 1B 142
Orchards, The OL2: Shaw 6G 43
    OL10: H'ood 3A 40
                  (off Orchard St.)
    SK3: Stoc 1H 157
Orchard St. BL4: Farn 2A 66
    M6: Sal 6G 85
                  (not continuous)
    M20: Man 4D 130
    OL10: H'ood 2A 40
    SK1: Stoc 3H 179 (2H 145)
    SK14: Hyde 5C 120
Orchard Trad. Est. M6: Sal 6F 85
Orchard Va. SK3: Stoc 5E 145
Orchard Wlk. BL8: G'mount 2H 21
                  (off Lomax St.)
Orchid Av. BL4: Farn 6F 49

Orchid Cl. M44: Irl 1C 124
    OL1: O'ham 6D 58
Orchid Dr. BL9: Bury 5G 37
Orchid St. M9: Man 4H 87
Orchid Way OL12: Roch 6F 15
Ordell Wlk. M9: Man 6A 72
Ordnance St. M30: Ecc 3F 97
ORDSALL 6H 99
Ordsall Av. M38: Lit H 5F 65
Ordsall District Cen. M5: Sal 5H 99
Ordsall Hall Mus. 1H 113
Ordsall La. M5: Sal 4A 8 (1G 113)
Oregon Av. OL1: O'ham 6E 59
Oregon Cl. M13: Man 5E 11 (1G 115)
Orford Av. SK12: Dis 1H 171
Orford Cl. SK6: H Lan 6C 160
Orford Rd. M25: Pres 4H 69
    M40: Man 6E 89
Organ Way SK14: Holl 2F 123
Oriel Av. OL8: O'ham 6E 75
Oriel Cl. OL9: Chad 4A 74
    SK2: Stoc 5B 146
Oriel Ct. M33: Sale 4B 128
Oriel Rd. M20: Man 5E 131
Oriel St. BL3: Bolt 2A 48
    OL11: Roch 6H 27
Orient, The M41: Urm 1F 111
                  (off The Trafford Cen.)
Orient Dr. OL7: A Lyme 2F 105
Orient Ho. M1: Man 2B 10
Orient Rd. M6: Sal 1A 98
Orient St. M7: Sal 4D 86
Oriole Dr. M28: Wors 3F 81
Oriole Ho. M19: Man 6H 131
Orion Bus. Pk. SK3: Stoc 6E 145
Orion Pl. M7: Sal 1A 100
Orion Trad. Est. M17: T Pk 5A 98
Orkney Cl. M23: Wyth 1G 153
    M26: Rad 3B 52
Orkney Dr. M41: Urm 2F 111
Orlanda Av. M6: Sal 1A 98
Orlanda Dr. M7: Sal 5D 86
Orlando St. BL2: Bolt 6H 175 (2E 49)
                  (not continuous)
    BL3: Bolt 2E 49
Orleans Way OL1: O'ham 2F 177 (2E 75)
Orley Wlk. OL1: O'ham 3B 60
Orme Av. M6: Sal 6B 84
    M24: Mid 2C 72
Orme Cl. M11: Man 4A 102
    M41: Urm 5H 111
Ormerod Av. OL2: O'ham 4E 59
Ormerod Cl. SK6: Rom 2F 147
Ormerod St. OL10: H'ood 4A 40
Ormeston Lodge M41: Urm 6F 111
Orme St. M11: Man 4A 102
    OL4: O'ham 4G 75
    SK9: A Edg 5G 173
Ormonde Av. M6: Sal 1B 98
Ormonde Ct. OL6: A Lyme 1A 106
Ormonde St. OL6: A Lyme 1A 106
Ormond St. BL3: Bolt 2H 49
    BL9: Bury 2G 37
Ormrods, The BL9: Bury 6D 24
Ormrod St. BL2: Bolt 1G 33
    BL3: Bolt 5E 175 (1C 48)
    BL4: Farn 1G 65
    BL9: Bury 3G 37
Ormsby Av. M18: Man 3D 116
Ormsby Cl. SK3: Stoc 1G 157
Ormsgill St. M15: Man 6G 9 (2D 114)
Orms Gill Pl. SK2: Stoc 5E 147
Ormskirk Av. M20: Man 3D 130
Ormskirk Cl. BL8: Bury 5H 35
Ormskirk Rd. SK5: Stoc 3H 133
Ornatus St. BL1: Bolt 6D 18
Ornsay Wlk. M11: Man 4E 103
                  (off Bob Massey Cl.)
Oronsay Gro. M5: Sal 4D 98
Orphanage St. SK4: Stoc 6G 133
Orpington Dr. BL8: Bury 4B 36
Orpington Rd. M9: Man 4A 88
                  (off Vernon St.)

Orrell St. BL8: Bury 2C 36
  M11: Man 5F 103
Orrel St. M6: Sal 3E 99
Orrishmere Rd. SK8: Chea H 2B 156
Orron St. OL15: L'ough 4G 17
Orsett Cl. M40: Man 1F 7 (2G 101)
Orthes Gro. SK4: Stoc 4F 133
Orton Av. M23: Wyth 2G 141
Orton Rd. M23: Wyth 2G 141
Orvietto Av. M6: Sal 1A 98
Orville Dr. M19: Man 2B 132
Orwell Av. M22: Wyth 5B 142
  M34: Dent 4A 118
Orwell Cl. BL8: Bury 1D 36
  SK9: Wilm 5H 165
Orwell Rd. BL1: Bolt 3H 31
Osborne Cl. BL8: Bury 5B 36
  SK9: Wilm 3G 173
Osborne Dr. M27: Pen 4C 84
Osborne Gro. BL1: Bolt 4A 32
  SK8: H Grn 2E 155
Osborne Ho. M26: Rad 4G 51
               (off Bolton Rd.)
  M30: Ecc 3E 97
          (off Queen Victoria St.)
Osborne Pl. SK13: Had 2H 123
Osborne Rd. M6: Sal 3A 98
  M9: Man .4A 88
  M19: Man 6B 116
  M34: Dent 3F 119
  OL8: O'ham 4D 74
  SK2: Stoc 6G 179 (4H 145)
  SK14: Hyde 6C 120
  WA15: Alt 1C 174 (6G 139)
Osborne St. M6: Sal 2F 99
  M20: Man 6E 131
  M40: Man 1E 7 (1G 101)
  OL2: Shaw 1H 59
  OL9: O'ham 1C 74
  OL10: H'ood 4H 39
  OL11: Roch 6G 27
  SK6: Bred 6D 134
Osborne Ter. M33: Sale 5B 128
  OL6: A Lyme 4D 174
Osborne Trad. Est. OL9: O'ham 1C 74
Osborne Wlk. M26: Rad 3G 51
Osbourne Cl. BL4: Farn 6H 49
Osbourne Pl. WA14: Alt 3A 174
Oscar St. BL1: Bolt 3A 32
  M40: Man 4C 88
Oscott Av. M38: Lit H 3E 65
Oscroft Cl. M8: Man 5D 86
Oscroft Wlk. M14: Man 2H 131
                (off Lyth St.)
Osman Ho. BL1: Bolt 1F 175
Osmond St. OL4: O'ham 2A 76
Osmund Av. BL2: Bolt 6H 33
Osprey Cl. M15: Man 2C 114
  SK16: Duk 6C 106
Osprey Ct. M15: Man 2C 114
              (off Osprey Cl.)
Osprey Dr. M43: Droy 2C 104
  M44: Irl .4E 109
  SK9: Wilm 1F 173
Osprey Ho. M50: Sal 5C 98
Ossington Wlk. M23: Wyth 1G 141
Ossory St. M14: Man 4F 115
Osterley Rd. M9: Man 6B 72
Ostlers Ga. M43: Droy 3D 104
Ostrich La. M25: Pres 6A 70
Oswald Cl. M6: Sal 6G 85
Oswald La. M21: Chor 6H 113
Oswald Rd. M21: Chor 6G 113
Oswald St. BL3: Bolt 3A 48
            (not continuous)
  M4: Man 6G 7 (4H 101)
                (Every St.)
  M4: Man 2A 6 (2E 101)
                (Miller St.)
  OL2: Shaw 5A 44
  OL9: O'ham 1D 74
  OL16: Roch 3A 28
  SK5: Stoc 4H 117

Oswestry Cl. BL8: G'mount 3G 21
Otago St. OL4: O'ham 6A 60
Othello Dr. M30: Ecc 3F 97
Otley Av. M6: Sal 2C 98
Otley Cl. OL9: Chad 3B 74
Otley Gro. SK3: Stoc 1F 157
Otmoor Way OL2: O'ham 3G 59
Otranto Av. M6: Sal 1B 98
Ottawa Cl. M23: Wyth 1F 153
Otterburn Ho. M30: Ecc 2G 97
Otterburn Pl. SK2: Stoc 5E 147
Otterbury Cl. BL8: Bury 3H 35
Otter Dr. M8: Bury 3H 53
  M8: Man .6C 86
Otterham Wlk. M40: Man 6F 89
Otterspool Rd. SK6: Rom 2H 147
Ottery Wlk. M40: Man 1F 89
Oulder Hill OL11: Roch 4D 26

Oulder Hill Community Complex
                    . . . . .3C 26

Oulder Hill Dr. OL11: Roch 4C 26
Oldfield Cl. OL16: Roch 5B 28
Oulton Av. M33: Sale 4E 129
Oulton St. BL1: Bolt 6E 19
Oulton Wlk. M40: Man 2H 7
Oundle Cl. M14: Man 4G 115
Ouse St. M50: Sal 4C 98
Outline Fitness & Leisure Cen. 2F 179
Outram Cl. SK6: Marp 1D 160
Outram Ho. M1: Man 6E 7
Outram M. OL3: Upp 6D 62
Outram Rd. SK16: Duk 1H 119
Outram Sq. M43: Droy 5A 104
Outrington Dr. M11: Man 5C 102
OUTWOOD .1H 67
Outwood Av. M27: Clif 5F 67
Outwood Dr. SK8: H Grn 5E 155
Outwood Gro. BL1: Bolt 6C 18
Outwood La. M90: Man A 5A 154
Outwood La. W. M90: Man A 5H 153
Outwood Rd. M26: Rad 6A 52
  SK8: H Grn 5F 155
Oval, The SK8: H Grn 5F 155
Oval Dr. SK16: Duk 6H 105
Oval Vw. SK6: Wood 4H 135
Over Ashberry WA14: W Tim 2D 138
Overbridge Rd. M3: Sal 1C 100
  M7: Sal 1F 5 (1C 100)
  M8: Man 1C 100
Overbrook Av. M40: Man 6H 87
Overbrook Dr. M25: Pres 6H 69
Overcombe Wlk. M40: Man 6G 87
           (off Glendower Dr.)
Overdale M27: Swin 5A 84
  SK6: Mar 5D 148
  WA14: Alt 6D 138
Overdale Cl. OL1: O'ham 6E 59

Overdale Crematorium
  BL1: Bolt 1G 47
Overdale Cres. M41: Urm 5B 110
Overdale Dr. BL1: Bolt 6G 31
Overdale Ho. M6: Sal 1B 98
Overdale Rd. M22: Wyth 6B 142
  SK6: Rom 2F 147
Overdell Dr. OL12: Roch 5E 15
Overdene Cl. BL6: Los 1B 46
Overens St. OL4: O'ham 2H 75
Overfield Way OL12: Roch 1H 27
Overgreen BL2: Bolt 2A 34
Overhill Dr. SK9: Wilm 2H 173
Overhill La. SK9: Wilm 2H 173
Overhill Rd. OL9: Chad 1H 73
  SK9: Wilm 2G 173
Overlea Dr. M19: Man 4A 132
Overlinks Dr. M6: Sal 6B 84
Overman Way M27: Pen 4E 85
Overstone Dr. M8: Man 4D 86
Overton Av. M22: Wyth 6B 142
Overton Cl. M26: Rad 6B 52
Overton Cres. M33: Sale 1F 139
  SK7: H Gro 1E 159
Overton La. BL1: Bolt 6D 30
Overton Rd. M22: Wyth 6B 142

Overton Way SK9: Hand 2H 165
Over Town La. OL12: Roch 1G 25
Overt St. OL11: Roch 6H 27
Overwood Rd. M22: Nor 3B 142
Ovington Wlk. M40: Man 6G 87
          (off Ribblesdale Dr.)
Owen Fold OL4: Lees 2D 76
Owenington Gro.
  M38: Lit H 4E 65
Owens Cl. OL9: Chad 1G 73
Owens Farm Dr. SK2: Stoc 4E 147
Owens Pk. M14: Man 6H 115
Owen St. M6: Sal 6G 85
  M30: Ecc 4D 96
  OL1: O'ham 4C 60
  SK3: Stoc 2F 145
OWLER BARROW 2A 36
Owlerbarrow Rd.
  BL8: Bury 2A 36
Owler La. OL9: Chad 6F 73
Owls Ga. OL4: Lees 3C 76
Owlwood Cl. M38: Lit H 6C 64
Owlwood Dr. M38: Lit H 6C 64
Oxbow Way M45: White 1G 69
Oxbridge Cl. M33: Sale 6F 127
Oxendale Dr. M24: Mid 6H 55
Oxendon Av. M11: Man 2D 102
Oxenholme Wlk. M18: Man 2F 117
             (off Borwell St.)
Oxenhurst Grn. SK2: Stoc 6E 147
Oxford Av. M33: Sale 5F 127
  M43: Droy 2H 103
  M45: White 1G 69
  OL11: Roch 5C 26
Oxford Cl. BL4: Farn 1D 64
Oxford Ct. M2: Man 1H 9 (5D 100)
  M15: Man 5H 9 (1D 114)
  M16: Old T 2B 114
              (off Globe Cl.)
Oxford Dr. M24: Mid 5E 57
  SK6: Wood 3A 136
Oxford Gro. BL1: Bolt 4A 32
            (not continuous)
  M44: Cad 3A 124
Oxford Ho. OL9: O'ham 3C 74
Oxford Pk. Community Sports Cen.
                    . . . . .5F 105
Oxford Pl. M14: Man 3G 115
  OL16: Roch 6A 28
Oxford Rd. BL3: Lit L 4B 50
  M1: Man 3A 10 (6E 101)
  M6: Sal .1A 98
  M13: Man 4B 10 (6E 101)
  M15: Man 6E 101
  SK14: Hyde 1C 136
  SK16: Duk 5B 106
  WA14: Alt 2F 151
Oxford Road Station (Rail)
                .3A 10 (6E 101)
Oxford St. BL1: Bolt 3F 175 (6D 32)
  BL9: Bury 4G 37
  M1: Man 1H 9 (5D 100)
  M16: Old T 2B 114
  M30: Ecc 4G 97
  OL2: Shaw 6H 43
  OL7: A Lyme 5F 105
  OL9: O'ham 4B 74
  SK15: Mill 1H 107
  SK15: Stal 4G 107
Oxford St. E. OL7: A Lyme 5F 105
Oxford St. W. OL7: A Lyme 5F 105
Oxford Wlk. M34: Dent 6G 119
             (off Worcester Av.)
Oxford Way OL12: Roch 1G 27
  SK4: Stoc 6F 133
Ox Ga. BL2: Bolt 6H 19
Ox Hey Cl. BL0: Ram 2C 12
Ox Hey La.
  OL3: Del, Dens 4H 45
Oxhill Wlk. M40: Man 1F 89
            (off Blandford Dr.)
Oxney Rd. M14: Man 3G 115
Ox St. BL0: Ram 4B 12

Oxted Wlk. M8: Man 5E **87**
(off Dinnington Dr.)
Oxton Av. M22: Wyth 1A **154**
Oxton St. M11: Man 6H **103**
Ozanam Ct. M7: Sal 4B **86**

P

PACIFIC QUAYS 5D **98**
Pacific Rd. WA14: B'ath 5C **138**
Pacific Way M50: Sal 5C **98**
Packer St. BL1: Bolt 3A **32**
OL16: Roch 3B **178** (4H **27**)
Pack Horse Yd. OL16: Roch 3B **178**
Packwood Chase
OL9: Chad 1H **73**
Padbury Cl. M41: Urm 4H **109**
Padbury Ho. M5: Sal 4F **99**
(off Cypress Cl.)
Padbury Wlk. M40: Man 6B **88**
(off Mansford Dr.)
Padbury Way BL2: Bolt 3H **33**
Padden Brook SK6: Rom 1H **147**
Padden Brook M. SK6: Rom 1H **147**
Paddington Av. M40: Man 6D **88**
Paddington Cl. M6: Sal 3G **99**
Paddison St. M27: Swin 4G **83**
Paddock, The BL0: Ram 2B **12**
M28: Wors 4A **82**
M45: White 2C **68**
OL3: G'fld 5B **78**
SK7: Bram 4F **157**
SK9: Hand 3H **165**
SK13: Had 2H **123**
SK14: Holl 2G **123**
WA15: Tim 1B **152**
Paddock Chase SK12: Poy 1F **169**
Paddock Ct. M35: Fail 6H **89**
Paddock Fld. M5: Sal 5H **99**
Paddock Head OL15: L'ough 5E **17**
Paddock La. M35: Fail 6H **89**
Paddock Rd. SK14: Hyde 1B **136**
Paddocks, The SK3: Stoc 1A **158**
Paddock St. M12: Man 3E **175** (6G **101**)
Paderborn Rd. BL1: Bolt 5E **175** (1C **48**)
Padiham Cl. BL9: Bury 6D **36**
Padstow Cl. SK14: Hat 4H **121**
Padstow Dr. SK7: Bram 6H **157**
Padstow St. M40: Man 2A **102**
Padstow Wlk. SK14: Hat 4H **121**
Padworth Wlk. M23: Wyth 3D **140**
Pagan St. OL16: Roch 2C **178** (3H **27**)
Paget St. M40: Man 6H **87**
OL6: A Lyme 1A **106**
Pagnall Ct. OL9: Chad 4B **74**
Paignton Av. M19: Man 1B **132**
SK14: Hat 5G **121**
Paignton Dr. M33: Sale 4F **127**
Paignton Gro. SK5: Stoc 2G **133**
Paignton Wlk. SK14: Hat 5G **121**
Pailin Dr. M43: Droy 3C **104**
Pailton Cl. BL6: Los 1D **46**
Painswick Pk. BL4: Farn 6H **49**
Paisley Pk. BL4: Farn 6H **49**
Paiton St. BL1: Bolt 6A **32**
Palace Ct. BL1: Bolt 2F **175** (5D **32**)
Palace Gdns. OL2: O'ham 5D **58**
Palace Rd. M33: Sale 4A **128**
OL6: A Lyme 6C **92**
Palace St. BL1: Bolt 2F **175** (5D **32**)
BL9: Bury 3G **37**
(not continuous)
OL9: O'ham 2C **74**
Palace Theatre 2A **10** (5E **101**)
Palatine Av. M20: Man 3F **131**
OL11: Roch 3C **26**
Palatine Cl. M44: Irl 6D **108**
Palatine Ct. M34: Dent 2E **119**
Palatine Cres. M20: Man 4F **131**
Palatine Dr. BL9: Bury 3F **23**
Palatine Ho. SK3: Stoc 5E **179**

Palatine M. M20: Man 3F **131**
M34: Dent 3E **119**
Palatine Rd. M22: Nor 2B **142**
OL11: Roch 3C **26**
Palatine St. BL0: Ram 3C **12**
BL1: Bolt 3F **175** (6D **32**)
M34: Dent 2E **119**
(not continuous)
OL16: Roch 4C **28**
Palatine Ter. OL11: Roch 3C **26**
Paley St. BL1: Bolt 3G **175** (6D **32**)
Palfrey Pl. M12: Man 4F **11** (6G **101**)
Palgrave Av. M40: Man 6H **87**
Palin Wood Rd. OL3: Del 2B **62**
Pall Mall M2: Man 5H **5** (4D **100**)
(not continuous)
Pall Mall Ct. M2: Man 5H **5**
Pallotine Wlk. OL11: Roch 6F **27**
Palma Av. M90: Man A 5G **153**
Palm Bus. Cen. OL9: Chad 3B **74**
Palm Cl. M33: Sale 4E **127**
Palmer Av. SK8: Chea 5B **144**
Palmer Cl. M8: Man 1F **87**
OL8: O'ham 5F **75**
Palmerston Av. M16: W Ran 5B **114**
Palmerston Cl. BL0: Ram 5B **12**
M34: Dent 4B **118**
Palmerstons Ct. BL1: Bolt 6G **31**
Palmerston Rd. M34: Dent 4B **118**
SK2: Stoc 2A **158**
Palmerston St. M12: Man . . .1G **11** (5H **101**)
Palmer St. M7: Sal 6A **86**
M33: Sale 5A **128**
SK16: Duk 4H **105**
Palm Gro. OL9: Chad 1B **74**
Palm St. BL1: Bolt 2D **32**
M13: Man 4B **116**
M43: Droy 3F **103**
OL4: O'ham 1A **76**
Pamir Dr. OL7: A Lyme 3F **105**
Pandora St. M20: Man 4E **131**
Panfield Rd. M22: Wyth 1A **154**
Pangbourne Av. M41: Urm 4G **111**
Pangbourne St. SK3: Stoc 5E **145**
Pankhurst Cen., The 2F **115**
Pankhurst Wlk. M14: Man 4F **115**
(off Ellanby Cl.)
Panmure St. OL8: O'ham 5F **75**
Pansy Rd. BL4: Farn 1E **65**
Paperhouse Cl. OL11: Roch 2H **25**
Paper Mill Rd. BL7: Bro X 4E **19**
Paprika Cl. M11: Man 6F **103**
Parade, The M27: Swin 3H **83**
SK6: Rom 2G **147**
SK9: A Edg 5G **173**
Parade Rd. M90: Man A 6A **154**
Paradise St. BL0: Ram 3C **12**
M34: Aud 6F **105**
SK13: Had 2H **123**
Paradise Wlk. M11: Man 6D **6**
Paradise Wharf M1: Man . . .6D **6** (4F **101**)
Paramel Av. BL3: Lit L 2D **50**
Parbold Av. M20: Man 3E **131**
Pardoner's Ct. M5: Sal 3B **98**
Pares Land Wlk.
OL16: Roch 5B **28**
(off McNaught St.)
Pargate Chase OL11: Roch 3C **26**
Parham Wlk. M9: Man 6A **72**
(off Stockfield Dr.)
Paris Av. M5: Sal 6H **99**
Parish Vw. M5: Sal 5H **99**
Parish Wlk. BL2: Ain 4F **35**
Paris St. BL3: Bolt 3H **47**
Park, The M32: Stre 3E **113**
OL3: G'fld 4E **79**
OL4: Gras 4H **77**
Park 66 BL9: Bury 1H **53**
Park Av. BL0: Ram 3D **12**
BL1: Bolt 1C **32**
M7: Sal 3D **86**
M16: Old T 2A **114**
M19: Man 6C **116**

Park Av. M25: Pres 5H **69**
M26: Rad 3D **52**
M27: Swin 4A **84**
M33: Sale 3A **128**
M35: Fail 3F **89**
M41: Urm 1E **111**
M45: White 3D **68**
OL9: Chad 6B **58**
SK3: Stoc 4B **144**
SK6: Rom 1A **148**
SK7: Bram 2F **167**
SK8: Chea H 4B **156**
SK9: Wilm 1F **173**
SK12: Poy 3E **169**
SK14: Hyde 3D **120**
WA14: Tim 3G **139**
WA15: Hale 4H **151**
Park Bank M5: Sal 3D **98**
PARK BRIDGE 1A **92**
Park Bridge Heritage Cen. 2A **92**
Park Bri. Rd. OL6: A Lyme 4G **91**
OL7: A Lyme 4G **91**
Parkbridge Wlk. M13: Man 5D **10**
Parkbrook Rd. M23: Wyth 4H **141**
Park Brow Cl. M21: Chor 1A **130**
Park Bungs. SK6: Mar 6D **148**
Park Cl. M45: White 3F **69**
OL9: Chad 6B **58**
SK15: Stal 2D **106**
WA14: Tim 3H **139**
Park Cotts. BL1: Bolt 2A **32**
OL2: Shaw 5F **43**
OL3: G'fld 4A **78**
Park Ct. M22: Wyth 2B **154**
M28: Walk 2A **82**
M33: Sale 4A **128**
OL11: Roch 5B **178** (5H **27**)
Park Cres. M. SK8: Chea 1A **156**
Park Cres. M14: Man 4G **115**
OL6: A Lyme 3C **106**
OL9: Chad 6H **57**
SK9: Wilm 6F **165**
Parkdale OL9: Chad 6B **58**
Parkdale Av. M18: Man 2E **117**
M34: Aud 6D **104**
Parkdale Rd. BL2: Bolt 4G **33**
Parkdene Cl. BL2: Bolt 1H **33**
Park Dr. M16: W Ran 5A **114**
M30: Ecc 1F **97**
SK4: Stoc 1D **144**
SK9: Wilm 6F **165**
SK14: Hyde 3B **120**
WA15: Hale 3H **151**
WA15: Tim 4A **140**
Parkend Rd. M23: Wyth 1G **153**
Parker Arc. M1: Man 6A **6**
(off Parker St.)
Parker St. BL9: Bury 3G **37**
M1: Man 6B **6** (4E **101**)
Parkfield M5: Sal 3D **98**
M24: Mid 1B **72**
M30: Ecc 3G **109**
M43: Droy 3A **104**
OL9: Chad 6A **58**
Parkfield Av. BL4: Farn 2F **65**
M14: Man 4F **115**
M25: Pres 6B **70**
M41: Urm 6D **110**
OL8: O'ham 1B **90**
SK6: Mar 5D **148**
Parkfield Cl. OL16: Roch 3B **42**
Parkfield Ct. WA14: Alt 1E **151**
Parkfield Dr. M24: Mid 1A **72**
M29: Tyld 2B **80**
Parkfield Est. M27: Swin 5A **84**
Parkfield Ind. Est. M24: Mid 1A **72**
Parkfield Rd. BL3: Bolt 4D **48**
OL4: Gras 3A **78**
SK8: Chea H 4B **156**
WA14: Alt 1E **151**
Parkfield Rd. Nth. M40: Man 1G **89**
Parkfield Rd. Sth. M20: Man 5E **131**
Parkfields SK15: Stal 2H **107**

Parkfield St. M14: Man 4F 115
(Claremont Rd.)
M14: Man 3F 115
(Moss La. E.)
OL16: Roch 3B 42
Parkgate BL8: Bury 6G 21
OL9: Chad 6B 58
Park Ga. Av. M20: Man 3F 131
Park Ga. Cl. SK6: Bred 4E 135
Parkgate Dr. BL1: Bolt 6D 18
M27: Swin 4A 84
SK2: Stoc 1B 158
Parkgate Rd. WA14: W Tim 3E 139
Park Gates Av. SK8: Chea H 4E 157
Park Gates Dr. SK8: Chea H 4E 157
Parkgate Way OL2: Shaw 6B 44
SK9: Hand 3H 165
(off Davenham Rd.)
Park Gro. M19: Man 5C 115
M26: Rad 3H 51
M28: Walk 3H 81
SK4: Stoc 5D 132
Park Hall M14: Man 4G 115
(off Thurloe St.)
Park Hill M25: Pres 2B 86
OL12: Roch 2H 27
Parkhill Av. M8: Man 1F 87
Park Hill Dr. M45: White 1E 69
Park Hill Rd. WA15: Hale 4A 152
Parkhills Cl. BL9: Bury 6D 176 (5F 37)
Parkhills Rd. BL9: Bury 6D 176 (5E 37)
Park Hill St. BL1: Bolt 5B 32
Park Ho. M23: Wyth 4C 140
(off Bridge Rd.)
M43: Droy 5A 104
Park Ho. Bri. Est. M6: Sal 4E 85
Park Ho. Bri. Rd. M6: Sal 5E 85
Parkhouse St. M11: Man 5D 102
Parkhouse St. Ind. Est.
M11: Man 5D 102
Parkhurst Av. M40: Man 2G 89
Parkin Cl. SK16: Duk 5A 106
Parkinson St. BL3: Bolt 2A 48
BL9: Bury 6F 23
Parkin St. M12: Man 4C 116
Parklake Av. M7: Sal 3C 86
Parklands M33: Sale 4C 128
(off Charlton Dr.)
M45: White 1E 69
(Higher La.)
M45: White 5F 53
(Well La.)
OL2: O'ham 6C 42
OL2: Shaw 5B 44
OL4: Gras 3A 78
SK6: Rom 6C 136
SK7: Bram 4G 157
SK9: Wilm 2F 173
WA14: Alt 1D 150
Parklands, The M26: Rad 2D 66
SK4: Stoc 5G 133
Parklands Cres. OL10: H'ood 5E 39
Parklands Dr. M33: Sale 1F 139
Parklands Ho. OL2: O'ham 6C 42
Parklands Rd. M23: Wyth 4F 141
Parklands Sports Cen. 2A 154
Parklands Way OL10: H'ood 5E 39
SK12: Poy 3E 169
PARK LANE 2D 68
Park Lane 3E 69
Park La. M6: Sal 6C 84
M7: Sal 3B 86
M27: Pen 4D 84
M28: Wors 4B 80
M45: White 2D 68
OL2: O'ham 2D 58
(not continuous)
OL3: G'fld 4E 79
OL8: O'ham 1F 91
OL16: Roch 2B 178 (3H 27)
SK1: Stoc 3B 146
SK12: Poy 3E 169
SK16: Duk 5A 106

Park La. WA15: Hale 4A 152
Park La. Ct. M7: Sal 3B 86
M45: White 2D 68
Park La. W. M27: Pen 4D 84
Park Lea Ct. M7: Sal 2C 86
Parkleigh Dr. M40: Man 1G 89
Park Lodge M7: Sal 3B 86
M16: W Ran 5C 114
M19: Man 6C 116
Park Lodge Cl. SK8: Chea 1A 156
Park Mdw. BL5: W'ton 6A 46
Park M. M16: W Ran 5A 114
M26: Rad 3C 52
Park Mill Ind. Est.
OL5: Mos 6H 77
Park Mt. SK8: Gat 6E 143
Parkmount Rd. M9: Man 2A 88
Park Pde. OL2: Shaw 4A 44
OL6: A Lyme 6A 174 (3G 105)
Park Pde. Ind. Est.
OL6: A Lyme 3G 105
Park Pl. M4: Man 1A 6 (2E 101)
M6: Sal 2A 98
M25: Pres 4A 70
SK4: Stoc 1B 144
Park Range M14: Man 4H 115
Park Ri. SK6: Rom 6A 136
SK15: Stal 2D 106
Park Rd. BL0: Ram 6A 12
BL1: Bolt 6A 32
BL3: Lit L 3B 50
BL5: W'ton 6B 46
BL9: Bury 1B 176 (1E 37)
M6: Sal 1A 98
M8: Man 6B 70
M24: Mid 1B 72
M25: Pres 6B 70
M28: Walk 2G 81
M30: Ecc 1A 98
(Ellesmere Pk.)
M30: Ecc 1F 97
(Monton)
M31: Part 6E 125
M32: Stre 3B 112
M33: Sale 3A 128
M34: Aud 5D 104
M34: Dent 4E 119
OL4: O'ham 5G 177 (3E 75)
OL8: O'ham 5G 177 (3E 75)
OL12: Roch 2A 28
OL15: L'ough 3H 17
SK4: Stoc 4D 132
SK6: Rom 6A 136
SK8: Chea 5A 144
SK8: Chea H 4E 157
SK8: Gat 5D 142
SK9: Wilm 2C 172
SK12: Dis 1D 170
SK14: Hyde 3B 120
SK16: Duk 4A 106
WA14: Bow 2C 150
WA14: Tim 3G 139
WA15: Hale 4G 151
WA15: Tim 3G 139
Park Rd. Nth. M41: Urm 4E 111
Park Rd. Sth. M41: Urm 5E 111
Park Row BL1: Bolt 5D 18
SK4: Stoc 2A 144
Park Seventeen M45: White 6F 53
Parkside M14: Man 6G 115
M24: Mid 3A 72
OL12: Whitw 3B 14
Park Side Av. OL2: Shaw 5A 44
Parkside Av. M7: Sal 3C 86
M28: Walk 2H 81
M30: Ecc 4E 97
M35: Fail 6G 89
Parkside Cl. M26: Rad 3D 52
SK6: H Lan 5B 160
Parkside Ind. Est.
OL2: O'ham 3E 59
Parkside La. SK6: Mel 5G 149
Parkside M. M45: White 6F 53

Parkside Rd. M14: Man 5D 114
M33: Sale 6D 128
Parkside St. BL2: Bolt 4G 33
Parkside Wlk. BL9: Bury 6D 176 (4F 37)
SK7: Bram 2G 157
(not continuous)
Parks Nook BL4: Farn 2G 65
Park Sq. M16: Old T 5G 113
OL6: A Lyme 1C 106
Parkstead Dr. M9: Man 5H 87
Parkstone Av. M18: Man 1H 117
M45: White 3D 68
Parkstone Cl. BL8: Bury 3H 35
Parkstone Dr. M27: Swin 5B 84
Parkstone La. M28: Wors 1B 96
Parkstone Rd. M44: Irl 4E 109
Park St. BL1: Bolt 5B 32
BL4: Farn 6H 49
M3: Man 1H 5 (2D 100)
M3: Sal 5C 4
M7: Sal 3B 86
M25: Pres 5A 70
M26: Rad 3C 52
M27: Swin 4A 84
M34: Dent 4D 118
M43: Droy 3C 104
OL2: O'ham 3E 59
OL2: Shaw 6H 43
OL5: Mos 3G 93
OL6: A Lyme 6B 174 (3G 105)
OL7: A Lyme 3G 105
OL8: O'ham 6E 177 (4E 75)
(not continuous)
OL10: H'ood 5A 40
OL16: Roch 5B 178 (5H 27)
SK1: Stoc 1G 179 (1H 145)
SK6: Bred 6F 135
SK15: Stal 4F 107
Parkway M9: Man 4F 71
M25: Pres 1A 86
M27: Pen 5C 84
Parks Yd. BL9: Bury 3B 176 (3E 37)
Park Ter. BL1: Bolt 4D 18
M45: White 2D 68
OL5: Mos 3G 93
OL10: H'ood 2H 39
Park Vw. BL1: Bolt 5D 18
(not continuous)
BL4: Farn 6H 49
BL4: Kea 2B 66
M9: Man 5G 87
M14: Man 3F 115
(Fairbank Av.)
M14: Man 2A 132
(Green St.)
M34: Aud 5D 104
OL2: Shaw 5E 43
OL6: A Lyme 1D 106
OL9: Chad 6A 58
OL15: L'ough 3H 17
SK1: Stoc 4B 146
SK3: Stoc 4B 144
SK6: Bred 6C 134
SK7: H Gro 5H 159
SK8: Gat 5E 143
Park Vw. Ct. M21: Chor 6F 113
M25: Pres 6H 69
SK6: Rom 1A 148
Parkview Ct. M32: Stre 6F 113
Park Vw. Rd. BL3: Bolt 3A 48
M25: Pres 6H 69
Parkville Rd. M20: Man 4G 131
Parkway M25: Pres 2A 70
Park Way M17: T Pk 3H 111
M32: Stre 3H 111
M41: Urm 3H 111
Parkway M34: Dent 4C 118
M38: Lit H 5C 64
OL9: Chad 5A 58
OL11: Roch 3D 26
SK3: Stoc 4B 144
SK7: Bram 3G 157
SK9: Wilm 3E 173

Parkway Bus. Cen. M14: Man 5D **114**
Parkway Circ. M17: T Pk 1A **112**
Parkway Four Ind. Est.
   M17: T Pk 1A **112**
Parkway Gro. M38: Lit H 5C **64**
Parkway Ind. Est. M17: T Pk 1A **112**
Parkway Trad. Est. M32: Stre 2A **112**
Parkwood BL7: Eger 1B **18**
Parkwood Cotts. OL1: O'ham 1D **70**
Parkwood Rd. M23: Wyth 4A **142**
Parlane St. M4: Man 1C **6** (2F **101**)
Parliament Pl. BL9: Bury . . .6A **176** (4E **37**)
Parliament St. BL9: Bury . . .6A **176** (4E **37**)
Parndon Dr. SK2: Stoc 4C **146**
Parnell Av. M22: Nor 3B **142**
Parnell Cl. M29: Ast 6A **80**
Parnham Cl. M26: Rad 2D **50**
Parrbrook Cl. M45: White 6G **53**
Parrbrook Wlk. M45: White 6H **53**
PARR BROW .4C **80**
Parr Cl. BL4: Farn 1F **65**
Parrenthorn Rd. M25: Pres 2A **70**
Parrfield Rd. M28: Wors 4C **82**
PARR FOLD .2G **81**
Parr Fold BL9: Bury 5H **53**
Parr Fold Av. M28: Wors 2G **81**
   (not continuous)
Parr Ho. OL8: O'ham 6G **177**
Parrin La. M30: Ecc 2D **96**
Parr La. BL9: Bury 6G **53**
Parrot St. BL3: Bolt 2C **48**
   M11: Man 4E **103**
Parrs Ct. M44: Irl 5D **108**
Parrs Mt. M. SK4: Stoc 1B **144**
Parr St. M11: Man 6G **103**
   M30: Ecc 4F **97**
Parrs Wood Av. M20: Man 1G **143**
Parrs Wood Ct. M20: Man 2G **143**
Parrs Wood Entertainment Cen. . . .2H **143**
Parrs Wood La. M20: Man 2G **143**
Parrs Wood Rd. M20: Man 3F **143**
Parrs Wood Sports Cen. 2H **143**
Parry Mead SK6: Bred 5G **135**
Parry Rd. M12: Man 3C **116**
Parry Wlk. OL6: A Lyme 1B **106**
Parslow Av. M8: Man 3E **87**
Parsonage M3: Man 5G **5** (4D **100**)
Parsonage Cl. BL9: Bury 2G **37**
   M5: Sal .2A **8**
Parsonage Ct. M20: Man 3F **131**
   SK4: Stoc 5D **132**
Parsonage Dr. M28: Walk 1G **81**
Parsonage Gdns. M3: Man 5G **5**
   SK6: Mar 1E **161**
Parsonage Grn. SK9: Wilm 2E **173**
   (off Alderley Rd.)
Parsonage La. M3: Man 4G **5**
Parsonage Rd. M20: Man 2G **131**
   M26: Rad 2E **67**
   M28: Walk 1G **81**
   M41: Urm 6A **110**
   (not continuous)
   SK4: Stoc 5D **132**
Parsonage St. BL9: Bury 2G **37**
   M8: Man 2D **86**
   M15: Man 2C **114**
   M26: Rad 3A **52**
   SK4: Stoc 1E **179** (1G **145**)
   SK14: Hyde 5B **120**
Parsonage Ter. OL16: Miln 5F **29**
   (off Parsonage Wlk.)
Parsonage Wlk. OL16: Miln 4F **29**
Parsonage Way SK8: Chea 6D **144**
Parson's Dr. M24: Mid 5B **56**
Parsons Fld. M6: Sal 6G **85**
Parsons La. BL9: Bury 3C **176** (3F **37**)
Parsons St. OL9: O'ham 3C **74**
Parsons Way M9: Man 4A **88**
Parth St. BL9: Bury 4B **38**
PARTINGTON 6E **125**
Partington Cl. BL4: Farn 6H **49**
Partington La. M27: Swin 4G **83**
Partington Leisure Cen. 6D **124**

Partington Pk. OL11: Roch 5E **41**
Partington Pl. M33: Sale 4B **128**
   (off School Rd.)
Partington Shop. Cen.
   M31: Part 6D **124**
Partington St. BL3: Bolt 5A **48**
   M28: Wors 4E **83**
   M30: Ecc 2F **97**
   (off Monton Rd.)
   M35: Fail 4H **89**
   M40: Man 6B **88**
   OL1: O'ham 2G **75**
   OL10: H'ood 3E **39**
   OL11: Roch 3D **40**
Partridge Av. M23: Wyth 5H **141**
Partridge Cl. M44: Irl 3E **109**
   OL11: Roch 4B **26**
Partridge Ct. SK2: Stoc 6B **146**
Partridge Ri. M43: Droy 2D **104**
Partridge Rd. M35: Fail 5C **90**
Partridge St. M32: Stre 2F **113**
Partridge Way OL9: Chad 1F **73**
Parvet Av. M43: Droy 2H **103**
Pascal St. M19: Man 1C **132**
Pass, The OL16: Roch 3A **28**
PASSMONDS 2D **26**
Passmonds Cres.
   OL11: Roch 3D **26**
Passmonds Way OL11: Roch 3D **26**
Pass St. OL9: O'ham 3D **74**
Paston Rd. M22: Shar 4B **142**
Pasture Cl. OL10: H'ood 4F **39**
Pasturefield Cl. M33: Sale 6F **129**
Pasture Fld. Rd. M22: Wyth 4D **154**
Pasturegreen Way M44: Irl 4F **109**
Pastures La. OL4: Scout 1F **77**
Patch Cft. Rd. M22: Wyth 4D **154**
Patchett St. M12: Man 1B **116**
Patch La. SK7: Bram 2F **167**
   (not continuous)
Patey St. M12: Man 4C **116**
Pathfield Wlk. M9: Man 3H **87**
   (off Smallfield Dr.)
Patience St. OL12: Roch 2E **27**
Patmos St. BL0: Ram 3D **12**
Paton Av. BL3: Bolt 4E **49**
Paton M. BL3: Bolt 4E **49**
Paton St. M1: Man 6C **6** (4F **101**)
   OL12: Roch 6F **15**
Patricia Dr. M28: Walk 1A **82**
Patrick Roddy Ct. M18: Man 2E **117**
PATRICROFT 4F **97**
Patricroft Bri. M30: Ecc 4E **97**
Patricroft Rd. M30: Ecc 3E **97**
Patricroft Station (Rail) 3E **97**
Patten St. M20: Man 3F **131**
Patterdale SK8: Chea 6G **143**
Patterdale Av. M41: Urm 3D **110**
   OL7: A Lyme 6F **91**
Patterdale Cl. OL1: O'ham 6G **59**
   OL11: Roch 2D **40**
   SK15: Stal 2E **107**
Patterdale Dr. BL9: Bury 6E **37**
   M24: Mid 5A **56**
Patterdale Rd. BL2: Bolt 1B **34**
   M22: Nor 3C **142**
   M31: Part 6C **124**
   OL7: A Lyme 6F **91**
   SK1: Stoc 4B **146**
   SK6: Wood 5H **135**
Patterdale Wlk. WA15: Tim 6D **140**
   (off Bowness Rd.)
Pattern Ho. SK15: Stal 3E **107**
Patterson Av. M21: Chor 6G **113**
Patterson St. BL3: Bolt 3G **47**
   M34: Dent 3F **119**
Patting Cl. M44: Irl 4G **109**
Pattishall Cl. M4: Man 6H **7** (4H **101**)
Pattison Cl. OL12: Roch 6E **15**
Patton Cl. BL9: Bury 5H **53**
Patton Ct. M7: Sal 1A **100**
Paul Ct. SK1: Stoc 2A **146**
   (off Hall St.)

Paulden Av. M23: Wyth 5H **141**
   OL4: O'ham 6C **60**
Paulden Dr. M35: Fail 4A **90**
Paulette St. BL1: Bolt 3C **32**
Paulhan Rd. M20: Man 5H **131**
Paulhan St. BL3: Bolt 4B **48**
Paul Row OL15: L'ough 2A **16**
Pavilion Cl. OL12: Roch 1H **27**
Pavilion Dr. OL6: A Lyme 6B **92**
Pavilion Lodge M16: Old T 4G **113**
   (off Edgbaston Dr.)
Pavilions, The M21: Chor 6A **114**
   SK8: Chea 1H **155**
Pavilion Wlk. M26: Rad 3H **51**
Paxford Pl. SK9: Wilm 4D **172**
Paxton Pl. M11: Man 5A **102**
Paythorne Grn. SK2: Stoc 6E **147**
Peabody St. BL3: Bolt 3C **48**
Peacefield SK6: Mar 6C **148**
Peacehaven Av. M11: Man 3E **103**
Peace St. BL3: Bolt 2B **48**
   M35: Fail 2A **90**
Peaceville Rd. M19: Man 6B **116**
Peach Bank M24: Mid 1C **72**
Peach Bank Ho. M24: Mid 1C **72**
Peach Rd. OL4: O'ham 6B **60**
Peach St. M25: Pres 4A **70**
Peach Tree Cl. M7: Sal 5D **86**
   (off Brakenhurst Dr.)
Peach Tree Ct. M6: Sal 3G **99**
Peacock Av. M6: Sal 6D **84**
Peacock Cl. M18: Man 1E **117**
   SK13: Had 3G **123**
Peacock Dr. SK8: H Grn 1F **165**
Peacock Gro. M18: Man 3F **117**
Peacock Way SK9: Hand 2H **165**
   (off Pickmere Rd.)
Peak Bank SK6: Rom 1G **147**
Peakdale Av. M8: Man 3F **87**
   SK8: H Grn 4F **155**
Peakdale Rd. M43: Droy 2G **103**
   SK6: Mar 1E **161**
   SK13: Had 4G **123**
Peaknaze Cl. M27: Pen 3B **84**
Peak St. BL1: Bolt 3B **32**
   M1: Man 6D **6** (4F **101**)
   OL9: O'ham 3C **74**
   SK1: Stoc 2A **146**
Peak Vw. SK13: Had 3H **123**
Peanock La. OL15: L'ough 1G **29**
Pear Av. BL9: Bury 2A **38**
Pear Cl. M24: Mid 3D **72**
Peardale Cl. M30: Ecc 5E **97**
Pear Ind. Est. SK6: Bred 1C **146**
Pearl Av. M7: Sal 2C **86**
Pearl Mill Cl. OL8: O'ham 5H **75**
Pearl St. M34: Dent 4E **119**
   OL11: Roch 3E **27**
   SK7: H Gro 1E **159**
Pearl Way SK14: Mot 4C **122**
Pearn Av. M19: Man 4B **132**
Pearn Rd. M19: Man 4B **132**
Pearson Cl. M31: Part 6E **125**
   OL16: Miln 4F **29**
Pearson Gro. OL4: Lees 3C **76**
Pearson Ho. M30: Ecc 5F **97**
Pearson St. BL9: Bury 2H **37**
   OL16: Roch 3C **28**
   SK5: Stoc 6H **133**
   SK16: Duk 1A **120**
Peart Av. SK6: Wood 3A **136**
Pear Tree Cl. M6: Sal 3G **99**
   SK6: Mar B 3F **149**
   SK13: Had 3G **123**
Pear Tree Ct. M6: Sal 3G **99**
Pear Tree Dr. BL4: Farn 2E **65**
   SK15: Stal 3F **107**
Pear Tree Gro. M29: Tyld 2B **80**
Pear Tree Pl. BL4: Farn 2E **65**
Pear Tree Wlk. M33: Sale 4E **127**
   (off Mountain Ash Cl.)

Peartree Wlk. M22: Wyth 1H 153
Peart St. M34: Dent 4E 119
Peary St. M4: Man 1D 6 (2F 101)
Peaslake Cl. SK6: Rom 1B 148
Peatfield Av. M7: Ward 1F 83
Peatfield Wlk. M15: Man 2D 114
(off Botham Cl.)
Pebble Cl. SK15: Stal 1E 107
Pebworth Cl. M24: Mid 4B 72
Peckford Dr. M40: Man 6C 88
Peckforton Cl. SK8: Gat 6E 143
Peckforton Wlk. SK9: Wilm 6A 166
(off Colshaw Dr.)
Peckmill Cl. SK9: Wilm 5A 166
Pedder St. BL1: Bolt 4A 32
Pedler Brow La. OL12: L'ough 3E 17
OL15: L'ough 3E 17
Pedley Wlk. M13: Man 3D 10
Pedthorpe Cl. BL2: Bolt 4F 33
Peebles Dr. M40: Man 1F 103
PEEL 5C 64
Peel Av. BL0: Ram 4A 12
M41: Urm 1F 111
(off The Trafford Cen.)
WA14: Hale 3F 151
Peel Bri. BL0: Ram 3C 12
PEEL BROW 2C 12
Peel Cen., The
SK1: Stoc 1H 179 (1A 146)
Peel Circ. M41: Urm 1G 111
Peel Cotts. BL8: Aff 3C 20
Peel Ct. SK2: Stoc 5A 146
(off Peel St.)
Peel Cross Rd. M5: Sal 4G 99
Peel Dr. M33: Sale 5E 129
M38: Lit H 5D 64
Peelgate Dr. SK8: H Grn 3E 155
PEEL GREEN 5D 96
Peel Grn. Rd. M30: Ecc 5D 96
Peel Grn. Trad. Est. M30: Ecc 5D 96
Peel Gro. M12: Man 3C 116
M28: Wors 3A 82
PEEL HALL 3D 154
Peel Hall Av. M29: Tyld 2A 80
Peel Hall Rd. BL5: Sum 1B 22
M22: Wyth 2C 154
Peel Ho. M30: Ecc 3H 97
M38: Lit H 6D 64
Peel Ind. Est. BL9: Bury 1B 176 (1E 37)
Peel La. M8: Man 1E 101
M28: Walk 6D 64
M29: Ast 6A 80
M38: Lit H 6D 64
OL10: H'ood 2F 39
Peel Mills BL9: Bury 1B 176 (2E 37)
Peel Moat Ct. SK4: Stoc 4E 133
Peel Moat Rd. SK4: Stoc 4D 132
Peel Moat Sports and Target Fitness Cen.
. . . . .4D 132
Peel Monument 4A 12
Peel Mt. BL0: Ram 5A 12
M6: Sal 1A 4 (2H 99)
Peel Pk. Cres. M38: Lit H 5D 64
Peel Rd. WA15: Hale 2G 151
Peel Sq. M18: Man 3F 117
Peel St. BL4: Farn 1A 66
M26: Rad 5B 52
M30: Ecc 3H 97
M34: Aud 1E 109
M34: Dent 3E 119
M35: Fail 5F 89
M43: Droy 5H 103
OL2: Shaw 6G 43
OL6: A Lyme 5B 174 (2H 105)
OL9: Chad 3B 74
OL10: H'ood 3F 39
OL12: Roch 1A 178 (3G 27)
OL15: L'ough 4H 17
SK2: Stoc 5H 145
SK14: Hyde 6C 120
SK15: Stal 4D 106
SK16: Duk 4A 106

Peel Ter. SK16: Duk 4H 105
(off Queen St.)
Peel Theatre 6B 176 (4E 37)
Peel Vw. BL8: Tot 5A 22
Peel Way BL9: Bury 3A 176 (3E 37)
Peelwood Av. M38: Lit H 4E 65
Peerglow Pk. Est. WA14: Tim 3G 139
Peers Cl. M41: Urm 3H 109
Peers St. BL8: Bury 3C 36
Pegamoid St. BL2: Bolt 4F 33
Pegasus Ct. M33: Sale 4D 128
(off Broad Rd.)
OL11: Roch 4E 27
Pegasus Sq. M7: Sal 1B 4
Pegwell Dr. M7: Sal 6C 86
Pekin St. OL6: A Lyme 1A 106
Pelham Pl. M8: Man 1F 87
Pelham St. BL3: Bolt 4A 48
OL7: A Lyme 5E 105
OL8: O'ham 1F 91
Pellowe Rd. OL8: O'ham 6E 75
Pelton Av. M27: Ward 1F 83
Pelton Wlk. M40: Man 6H 87
(off Pitsford Rd.)
Pemberton Ho. OL2: Shaw 5H 43
(off Napier St.)
Pemberton St. BL1: Bolt 1C 32
M16: Old T 3A 114
M38: Lit H 5F 65
OL11: Roch 3E 41
Pemberton Way OL2: Shaw 5H 43
Pembridge Fold M24: Mid 1E 73
Pembridge Rd. M9: Man 5B 72
Pembroke Av. M30: Ecc 3F 97
M33: Sale 4H 127
Pembroke Cl. M13: Man 6G 11 (1H 115)
Pembroke Ct. M27: Pen 3B 84
OL12: Roch 2H 27
(off Alma St.)
SK6: Rom 1F 147
SK7: H Gro 3E 159
Pembroke Dr. BL9: Bury 6E 37
OL4: O'ham 3C 60
Pembroke Gro. M44: Cad 3A 124
Pembroke Ho. SK3: Stoc 5E 179
Pembroke St. BL1: Bolt 5B 32
M6: Sal 4E 99
M7: Sal 5C 86
OL8: O'ham 3D 74
OL15: L'ough 3H 17
Pembroke Way M34: Dent 6G 119
(off Worcester Av.)
Pembry Cl. SK5: Stoc 4B 134
Pembury Cl. M22: Wyth 2A 154
Penarth Rd. BL3: Bolt 3H 47
M22: Nor 3B 142
Pencarrow Cl. M20: Man 6D 130
Pencombe Cl. M12: Man 2C 116
Pencroft Way M15: Man 2E 115
Pendeen Cl. M22: Wyth 4C 154
Pendennis OL11: Roch 6A 178 (5G 27)
Pendennis Av. BL6: Los 2D 46
Pendennis Cl. M26: Rad 2E 51
Pendennis Rd. SK4: Stoc 6E 133
Pendle Av. BL1: Bolt 5C 18
PENDLEBURY 3B 84
Pendlebury Cl. M25: Pres 1F 85
Pendlebury Ct. M27: Pen 2A 84
Pendlebury Fold BL3: Bolt 5D 46
Pendlebury Rd. M27: Swin, Pen 3H 83
SK8: Gat 5E 143
Pendlebury St. BL1: Bolt 2D 32
Pendlebury Towers SK5: Stoc 6H 133
Pendle Cl. BL8: Bury 2B 36
Pendle Ct. BL1: Bolt 2B 32
Pendlecroft Av. M27: Pen 4C 84
Pendle Gro. OL2: O'ham 4C 58
Pendle Ho. M34: Dent 5F 119
Pendle Rd. M34: Dent 5F 119
PENDLETON 2G 99
Pendleton Grn. M6: Sal 2F 99
(off Nursery St.)

Pendleton Ho. M6: Sal 2G 99
(off Broughton Rd.)
Pendleton Way M6: Sal 2F 99
Pendle Wlk. M40: Man 2G 7 (2H 101)
SK5: Stoc 4A 134
Pendleway M27: Pen 2A 84
Pendragon Pl. M35: Fail 4A 90
Pendrell Wlk. M9: Man 6A 72
(off Sanderstead Av.)
Penelope Rd. M6: Sal 6D 84
Penerley Dr. M9: Man 5H 87
Penfair Cl. M11: Man 4C 102
Penfield Cl. M1: Man 3C 10 (6F 101)
Penfold Wlk. M12: Man 1B 116
(off Witterage Cl.)
Pengham Wlk. M23: Wyth 2G 141
Pengwern Av. BL3: Bolt 3H 47
Penhale M. SK7: Bram 6H 157
Penhall Wlk. M40: Man 6C 88
(off Mansford Dr.)
Peninsula M7: Sal 4H 85
Penistone Av. M6: Sal 2C 98
M9: Man 6C 72
OL16: Roch 5C 28
Penketh Av. M18: Man 3D 116
Penmere Gro. M33: Sale 2G 139
Penmoor Chase SK7: H Gro 4B 158
Penmore Cl. OL2: Shaw 6A 44
Pennant Dr. M25: Pres 4G 69
Pennant Ind. Est. OL1: O'ham 1H 75
Pennant St. OL1: O'ham 1H 75
Pennell St. M11: Man 4F 103
Penn Grn. SK8: Chea H 4D 156
Penn Ho. Cl. SK7: Bram 5G 157
Pennine Av. OL9: Chad 4A 74
Pennine Bus. Pk. OL10: H'ood 5F 39
Pennine Cl. BL8: Bury 2B 36
M9: Man 5B 72
M27: Pen 2A 84
SK15: Stal 2H 107
Pennine Dr. OL6: A Lyme 1C 106
OL12: W'le 6C 16
OL16: Miln 4G 29
WA14: Alt 6D 138
Pennine Gro. OL6: A Lyme 5C 92
Pennine Pct. OL16: Miln 6F 29
Pennine Rd. SK6: Wood 3A 136
SK7: H Gro 4B 158
Pennine Ter. SK16: Duk 4A 106
(off Peel St.)
Pennine Va. OL2: Shaw 5A 44
Pennine Vw. M34: Aud 2E 119
OL2: O'ham 3E 59
OL5: Mos 2H 93
OL15: L'ough 1B 16
OL16: Roch 1D 178
SK15: H'rod 1G 107
Pennington Cl. M38: Lit H 5C 64
Pennington Rd. BL3: Bolt 4D 48
Pennington St. BL8: Bury 1G 35
M12: Man 5C 116
M28: Walk 1A 82
OL9: Chad 6B 74
Pennistone Cl. M44: Irl 4F 109
Pennon Cl. M7: Sal 5C 86
Penn St. BL4: Farn 1G 65
M40: Man 3B 88
OL8: O'ham 4D 74
OL10: H'ood 4A 40
OL16: Roch 2C 178 (3H 27)
Penny Black Chambers
M28: Wors 6B 82
(off Barton Rd.)
Penny Bri. La. M41: Urm 6C 110
(not continuous)
Penny Brook Fold SK7: H Gro 2F 159
Penny La. SK5: Stoc 1H 145
(not continuous)
Penny Mdw.
OL6: A Lyme 5D 174 (2A 106)
Pennymoor Dr. WA14: Alt 5D 138
Penrhos Av. SK8: Gat 6D 142

Penrhyn Av. M24: Mid 2C **72**
  SK8: Chea H 4A **156**
Penrhyn Cres. SK7: H Gro 5C **158**
Penrhyn Dr. M25: Pres 5H **69**
Penrhyn Rd. SK3: Stoc 3D **144**
Penrice Cl. M26: Rad 2F **51**
Penrice Fold M28: Wors 4F **81**
Penrith Av. BL1: Bolt 4G **31**
  M11: Man 2D **102**
  M28: Walk 1B **82**
  M33: Sale 1C **140**
  M45: White 2H **69**
  OL7: A Lyme 6F **91**
  OL8: O'ham 5C **74**
  SK5: Stoc 6H **117**
Penrith Cl. M31: Part 5C **124**
Penrith St. OL11: Roch 6H **27**
Penrod Pl. M6: Sal 1H **99**
Penrose Cl. M8: Man 5E **87**
Penrose Gdns. M24: Mid 6D **56**
Penrose St. BL2: Bolt 6G **33**
Penrose Wlk. M24: Mid 3C **56**
Penroy Av. M20: Man 6B **130**
Penroyson Cl. M12: Man 1B **116**
Penruddock Wlk. *M13: Man* *3B 116*
         (off Bates St.)
Penry Av. M44: Cad 3C **124**
Penryn Av. M33: Sale 2C **140**
  OL2: O'ham 3F **59**
Penryn Ct. M7: Sal 2B **86**
Pensarn Av. M14: Man 1A **132**
Pensarn Gro. SK5: Stoc 5H **133**
Pensby Cl. M27: Pen 4C **84**
Pensby Wlk. *M40: Man* *6H 87*
       (off Tollard Av.)
Pensford Ct. BL2: Bolt 5A **20**
Pensford Rd. M23: Wyth 2F **153**
Penshurst Rd. SK5: Stoc 3B **134**
Penshurst Rd. *M34: Dent* *6G 119*
      (off Two Trees La.)
Penthorpe Dr. OL2: O'ham 4F **59**
Pentland Av. M40: Man 1E **89**
Pentland Cl. SK7: H Gro 4B **158**
Pentlands, The OL2: Shaw 5F **43**
Pentlands Av. M7: Sal 6B **86**
Pentland Ter. BL1: Bolt 4C **32**
Pentland Way SK14: Hyde 1F **121**
Pentwyn Gro. M23: Wyth 4H **141**
Penwell Fold OL1: O'ham 6E **59**
Penydarren Vw. BL3: Bolt 5G **49**
Penzance St. M40: Man 2A **102**
Peoples History Mus. 5E **5**
Peover Av. M33: Sale 5E **129**
Peover Rd. SK9: Hand 2A **166**
Peover Wlk. SK8: Chea 6C **144**
Pepler Av. M23: Wyth 1H **141**
Peploe Wlk. M23: Wyth 2D **140**
Pepper Cl. M22: Wyth 5B **142**
Pepper Ct. SK9: Wilm 3D **172**
Pepperhill Rd. M16: W Ran 3D **114**
Peppermint Cl. OL16: Miln 1A **44**
Pepper Rd. SK7: H Gro 3B **158**
Percival Cl. M8: Man 5D **86**
Percival Rd. M43: Droy 4B **104**
Percival Wlk. OL2: O'ham 4E **59**
Percy Dr. M5: Sal 6H **99**
Percy Rd. M34: Dent 5E **119**
Percy St. BL0: Ram 4B **12**
  BL1: Bolt 3D **32**
  BL4: Farn 2A **66**
  BL9: Bury 2G **37**
  M15: Man 6D **8** (1B **114**)
  OL4: O'ham 2A **76**
  OL16: Roch 6B **28**
  SK1: Stoc 1G **179** (1H **145**)
  SK15: Stal 4F **107**
Peregrine Cres. M43: Droy 2C **104**
Peregrine Dr. M44: Irl 4E **109**
Peregrine Rd. SK2: Stoc 1F **159**
Peregrine St. M15: Man 2D **114**
Peregrine Vw. *M43: Droy* *2C 104*
        (off Bittern Dr.)
Perendale Ri. BL1: Bolt 1C **32**

Periton Wlk. *M9: Man* *6A 72*
      (off Leconfield Dr.)
Perivale Dr. OL8: O'ham 5H **75**
Perkins Av. M7: Sal 6C **86**
Pernham St. OL4: O'ham 2A **76**
Perrin St. SK14: Hyde 5B **120**
Perry Av. SK14: Hyde 3E **121**
Perry Cl. OL11: Roch 6F **27**
Perrygate Av. M20: Man 3E **131**
Perrymead M25: Pres 3A **70**
Perry Rd. WA15: Tim 5B **140**
Pershore OL12: Roch 2A **178** (3G **27**)
Pershore Rd. M24: Mid 4C **56**
Perth *M30: Ecc* *3E 97*
      (off Monton La.)
Perth Av. OL9: Chad 5A **74**
Perth Cl. SK7: Bram 2G **167**
Perth Rd. OL11: Roch 3B **42**
Perth St. BL3: Bolt 4A **48**
  M27: Swin 4F **83**
  OL2: O'ham 3G **59**
Peru St. M3: Sal 3C **4** (3B **100**)
Peterborough Cl.
  OL6: A Lyme 5H **91**
Peterborough Dr. BL1: Bolt 4D **32**
Peterborough St. M18: Man 1H **117**
Peterborough Wlk. *BL1: Bolt* *4C 32*
      (off Charnock Dr.)
  BL1: Bolt *4D 32*
      (off Peterborough Dr.)
Peterchurch Wlk. *M11: Man* *5E 103*
      (off Eccles Cl.)
Peterhead Cl. BL1: Bolt 4B **32**
Peterhead Wlk. M5: Sal 4G **99**
Peterhouse Gdns. SK6: Wood 5A **136**
Peterloo Ct. *M6: Sal* *3E 99*
      (off St Luke's Rd.)
Peterloo Ter. M24: Mid 5C **56**
Peter Moss Way M19: Man 6E **117**
Petersburg Rd. SK3: Stoc 5E **145**
Peters Ct. WA15: Tim 6D **140**
Petersfield Dr. M23: Wyth 4D **140**
Petersfield Wlk. *BL1: Bolt* *4D 32*
      (off Bk. Ashford Wlk.)
Peter St. BL9: Bury 1D **176** (2F **37**)
  M2: Man 1G **9** (5D **100**)
  M3: Man 1G **9** (5D **100**)
  M30: Ecc 4F **97**
  M34: Dent 4G **119**
  OL1: O'ham 4G **177** (3F **75**)
  SK1: Stoc 1A **146**
      (not continuous)
  SK7: H Gro 2D **158**
  SK13: Had 1H **123**
  WA14: Alt 2F **151**
Peterswood Cl. M22: Wyth 2H **153**
Peter Wood Gdns. M32: Stre 6A **112**
Petheridge Dr. M22: Wyth 4H **153**
PETRE BANK 3G **169**
Petrel Av. SK12: Poy 3B **168**
Petrel Cl. M43: Droy 2C **104**
  OL11: Roch 4B **26**
  SK3: Stoc 5F **145**
Petrel Ho. M19: Man 5H **131**
Petrie Ct. M6: Sal 1H **99**
Petrie St. OL12: Roch 1B **178** (2H **27**)
Petrock Wlk. *M40: Man* *6E 89*
      (off Gaskell St.)
Petts Cres. OL15: L'ough 3G **17**
Petunia Wlk. *M38: Lit H* *4D 64*
      (off Madams Wood Rd.)
Petworth Cl. M22: Shar 6C **142**
Petworth Rd. OL9: Chad 3B **74**
Pevensey Ct. M9: Man 1C **88**
Pevensey Rd. M6: Sal 6E **85**
Pevensey Wlk. OL9: Chad 3B **74**
Peveril Cl. M45: White 2A **70**
Peveril Cres. M21: Chor 5G **113**
Peveril Dr. SK7: H Gro 5F **159**
Peveril Rd. M5: Sal 3D **98**
  OL1: O'ham 6A **60**
  WA14: B'ath 4E **139**
Peveril St. BL3: Bolt 4H **47**

Peverill Ter. SK14: Hyde 1D **136**
Peversham Cl. M30: Ecc 1H **97**
Pewsey Rd. M22: Wyth 2D **154**
Pexhill Ct. SK4: Stoc 1C **144**
Pexwood OL1: Chad 6G **57**
Pheasant Cl. M28: Wors 5E **81**
Pheasant Dr. M21: Chor 2B **130**
Pheasant Ri. WA14: Bow 4F **151**
Phelan Cl. M40: Man 6G **87**
Phethean St. BL2: Bolt 6E **33**
  BL4: Farn 6G **49**
Philip Av. M34: Dent 2E **119**
Philip Dr. M33: Sale 1B **140**
Philip Godlee Lodge
  M20: Man 1F **143**
Philip Howard Ct. *BL4: Farn* *1G 65*
      (off Glynne St.)
Philips Av. BL4: Farn 2H **65**
Philips Ct. *M14: Man* *3H 115*
      (off Hope Rd.)
Philips Dr. M45: White 3D **68**
PHILIPS PARK 2C **102**
Philips Pk.
  Bank Bri. Rd. 2C **102**
  Philip's Pk. Rd. W. 4D **68**
Philips Pk. Rd. M11: Man 3A **102**
Philips Pk. Rd. E. M45: White 3E **69**
Philips Pk. Rd. W. M45: White 4C **68**
Philips Sports Cen. 2E **69**
Philip St. BL3: Bolt 2B **48**
  M30: Ecc 4F **97**
  OL4: O'ham 1A **76**
  OL11: Roch 6H **27**
Phillimore St. OL4: Lees 4C **76**
Phillip & Pauline Gordon Ho.
  M25: Pres 2H **85**
Phillips Pl. M45: White 2F **69**
Phillip Way SK14: Hat 6A **122**
Phipps St. M28: Walk 5G **65**
Phoebe St. *BL3: Bolt* *3A 48*
      (off Church Av.)
  M5: Sal 5G **99**
Phoenix, The M7: Sal 6B **86**
Phoenix Cl. OL10: H'ood 4B **40**
Phoenix Ct. SK4: Stoc 4G **133**
Phoenix Ind. Est. M35: Fail 3A **90**
Phoenix Pk. Ind. Est.
  OL10: H'ood 4B **40**
Phoenix Pl. OL4: Spri 3D **76**
Phoenix St. BL1: Bolt 1H **175** (5E **33**)
  BL4: Farn 2H **65**
  BL9: Bury 3A **176** (3E **37**)
  M2: Man 5A **6** (4E **101**)
  OL1: O'ham 4G **177** (3F **75**)
  OL4: Spri 3D **76**
  OL12: Roch 2E **27**
  OL15: L'ough 3H **17**
Phoenix Way M15: Man 6G **9** (2D **114**)
  M26: Rad 5A **52**
  M41: Urm 1G **111**
Phyllis St. M24: Mid 2E **73**
  OL12: Roch 2D **26**
Piccadilly M1: Man 5B **6** (4E **101**)
  SK1: Stoc 2G **179** (2H **145**)
Piccadilly Gdns. 5B **6** (4E **101**)
Piccadilly Gardens Stop (Metro)
  . . . . .6B **6** (4E **101**)
Piccadilly Pl. M1: Man 1C **10** (5F **101**)
Piccadilly Plaza M1: Man 6A **6**
Piccadilly Sth. M1: Man 6C **6** (4F **101**)
Piccadilly Station (Rail & Metro)
  . . . . .1D **10** (5F **101**)
Piccadilly Trad. Est.
  M1: Man 1F **11** (5G **101**)
PICCADILLY VILLAGE
  . . . . .6E **7** (4G **101**)
Piccard Cl. M40: Man 6H **87**
Pickering Cl. BL8: Bury 6B **22**
  M26: Rad 1C **66**
  M41: Urm 5D **110**
  WA15: Tim 4A **140**
Pickering St. M15: Man 2C **114**
Pickford Av. BL3: Lit L 4E **51**

Pickford Ct.—Plato St.

Pickford Ct. M15: Man 2C 114
SK16: Duk 5A 106
Pickford La. SK16: Duk 5A 106
Pickford M. *SK16: Duk 5A 106*
(off Pickford La.)
Pickford's Brow SK1: Stoc 2G 179
Pickford St. M4: Man 4D 6 (3F 101)
Pickford Wlk. OL2: O'ham 4E 59
Pickhill OL3: Upp 1D 78
Pickhill M. OL3: Upp 1D 78
Pickmere Av. M20: Man 1F 131
Pickmere Cl. M33: Sale 1F 141
M43: Droy 4B 104
SK3: Stoc 5E 145
Pickmere Gdns.
SK8: Chea H 6B 144
Pickmere M. OL3: Upp 1D 78
Pickmere Rd. SK9: Hand 2H 165
Pickmere Ter. SK16: Duk 4H 105
Pickup St. OL16: Roch 4D 178 (4A 28)
Pickwick Rd. SK12: Poy 4D 168
Picton Cl. M3: Sal 3E 5 (3C 100)
Picton Dr. SK9: Wilm 6A 166
Picton Sq. OL4: O'ham 3G 75
Picton St. M7: Sal 1D 4 (2B 100)
OL7: A Lyme 5G 91
Picton Wlk. *M16: W Ran 4D 114*
(off Bedwell St.)
Pierce St. OL1: O'ham 6A 60
Piercy Av. M7: Sal 1B 100
Piercy St. M4: Man 5G 7 (4H 101)
M35: Fail 4G 89
Piethorne Cl. OL16: Miln 1A 44
Pigeon St. M1: Man 5D 6 (4F 101)
Piggott St. BL4: Farn 2G 65
Pike Av. M35: Fail 5C 90
Pike Fold La. M9: Man 6G 71
Pike Mill Est. BL3: Bolt 3C 48
Pike Nook Workshops BL3: Bolt 2C 48
Pike Rd. BL3: Bolt 3B 48
Pike St. OL11: Roch 6H 27
Pike Vw. Cl. OL4: O'ham 4H 75
Pilgrim Dr. M11: Man 4B 102
Pilgrim Way OL1: O'ham 4B 60
Pilkington Dr. M45: White 5H 53
Pilkington Rd. BL4: Kea 3B 66
M9: Man 1C 88
M26: Rad 2H 51
Pilkington St. BL0: Ram 4B 12
BL3: Bolt 2C 48
M24: Mid 6D 56
Pilkington Way M26: Rad 4A 52
Pilling Fld. BL7: Eger 2C 18
Pilling St. BL8: Bury 2C 36
M34: Dent 4F 119
OL12: Roch 3F 27
Pilling Wlk. OL9: Chad 3A 74
Pilning St. BL3: Bolt 3E 49
Pilot Ind. Est. BL3: Bolt 3F 49
Pilot St. BL9: Bury 6D 176 (4G 37)
Pilsworth Cotts. BL9: Bury 2A 54
Pilsworth Ind. Est. BL9: Bury 6H 37
Pilsworth Rd. BL9: Bury 1G 53
(not continuous)
OL10: H'ood 6D 38
Pilsworth Rd. Ind. Est. BL9: Bury 1G 53
Pilsworth Way BL9: Bury 1G 53
Pimblett St. M3: Man 1H 5 (2D 100)
PIMHOLE 4G 37
Pimhole Fold BL9: Bury 4G 37
Pimhole Rd. BL9: Bury 3G 37
Pimlico Cl. *M7: Sal 5B 86*
(off Hilton St. Nth.)
Pimlott Gro. M25: Pres 1E 85
SK14: Hyde 2B 120
Pimlott Rd. BL1: Bolt 2F 33
Pimmcroft Way M33: Sale 6F 129
Pincher Wlk. *M11: Man 4E 103*
(off Edith Cavell Cl.)
Pinder Wlk. M15: Man 6H 9
Pineacre Cl. WA14: W Tim 2D 138
Pineapple St. SK7: H Gro 3E 159
Pine Av. M45: White 2F 69
Pine Cl. M34: Aud 1E 119
SK6: Mar 1C 160
Pine Ct. M20: Man 5E 131
SK7: Bram 3F 157
Pine Gro. BL4: Farn 1F 65
M14: Man 3A 116
M25: Pres 3G 69
M27: Swin 4F 83
M28: Wors 3A 82
M30: Ecc 1G 97
M33: Sale 3F 127
M34: Dent 4G 119
OL2: O'ham 1D 58
SK16: Duk 5D 106
Pinehurst Rd. M40: Man 6A 88
Pinelea WA15: Alt 1H 151
Pine Lodge SK7: Bram 6H 157
Pine Mdws. M26: Rad 3D 66
Pine Rd. M20: Man 5E 131
SK7: Bram 5H 157
SK12: Poy 4F 169
SK15: Stal 5C 106
Pines, The M33: Sale 1B 140
OL10: H'ood 3H 39
(off Pine St.)
Pine St. BL1: Bolt 3D 32
BL9: Bury 3H 37
M1: Man 6A 6 (4E 101)
M24: Mid 2E 73
M26: Rad 3B 52
OL6: A Lyme 1H 105
OL9: Chad 1A 74
OL10: H'ood 3H 39
OL15: L'ough 3H 17
OL16: Miln 2H 43
OL16: Roch 4B 28
SK6: Wood 4H 135
SK14: Hyde 2B 120
Pine St. Nth. BL9: Bury 2H 37
(not continuous)
Pine St. Sth. BL9: Bury 3H 37
Pinetop Cl. M21: Chor 3B 130
Pine Tree Rd. OL8: O'ham 2D 90
Pine Trees WA16: Mob 6A 162
Pinetree St. M18: Man 2E 117
Pine Wlk. *M31: Part 6C 124*
(off Wood La.)
Pineway OL4: Lees 3D 76
Pinewood M33: Sale 5F 127
OL9: Chad 2G 73
WA14: Bow 3C 150
Pinewood Cl. BL1: Bolt 3C 32
SK4: Stoc 6C 132
SK16: Duk 4A 106
Pinewood Ct. M33: Sale 4D 128
SK9: Wilm 6A 166
(off Brackenwood M.)
WA14: Hale 4G 151
Pinewood Cres. BL0: Ram 1B 22
Pinewood Rd. M21: Chor 2G 129
SK9: Wilm 1H 173
Pinewoods, The SK6: Wood 4H 135
Pinfold SK13: Had 3G 123
Pinfold Av. M9: Man 1C 88
Pinfold Cl. WA15: Haleb 6D 152
Pinfold Ct. *M32: Stre 6C 112*
(off Barton Rd.)
M45: White 1E 69
Pinfold Dr. M25: Pres 4F 69
SK8: Chea H 4C 156
Pinfold La. M45: White 1E 69
M90: Man A 1F 163
SK6: Rom 5B 136
Pinfold Rd. M28: Walk 2G 81
Pingate Dr. SK8: Chea H 1C 166
Pingate La. SK8: Chea H 1C 166
Pingate La. Sth. SK8: Chea H 1C 166
Pingle La. OL3: Del 2H 61
Pingot OL2: Shaw 4B 44
Pingot, The M44: Irl 4F 109
Pingot Av. M23: Wyth 2H 141
Pingot La. SK14: B'tom 6D 122
Pinhigh Pl. M6: Sal 5B 84
Pink Bank La. M12: Man 3C 116
(not continuous)
Pin Mill Brow M12: Man 1G 11 (5H 101)
Pinnacle Dr. BL7: Eger 1C 18
Pinner Fold SK15: Stal 2H 107
Pinner Pl. M19: Man 3C 132
Pinners Cl. BL0: Ram 2B 12
Pinnington La. M32: Stre 5D 112
Pinnington Rd. M18: Man 1F 117
Pintail Av. SK3: Stoc 5F 145
Pintail Cl. OL12: Roch 1D 26
Pioneer Ct. *OL7: A Lyme 4G 105*
(off Victoria St., not continuous)
Pioneer Rd. M27: Clif 1D 84
Pioneer St. M11: Man 2D 102
M24: Mid 2F 57
OL11: Roch 6D 178 (5A 28)
OL15: L'ough 4H 17
Pioneers Villa OL16: Miln 1C 44
Pioneers Yd. OL16: Miln 6F 29
Piperhill Av. M22: Nor 1B 142
Pipers Cl. OL11: Roch 3H 25
Pipers Ct. M44: Irl 4G 109
Pipewell Av. M18: Man 2E 117
Pipit Cl. M34: Aud 3C 104
Pirie Wlk. *M40: Man 5E 89*
(off Queensferry St.)
Pitcairn Ho. *M30: Ecc 4F 97*
(off Adelaide St.)
Pitchcombe Rd. M22: Wyth 3H 153
Pitcombe Cl. BL1: Bolt 4B 18
Pitfield Cotts. SK14: Hyde 4A 120
Pitfield Gdns. M23: Wyth 4F 141
Pitfield La. BL2: Bolt 2B 34
Pitfield St. BL2: Bolt 6F 33
Pit La. OL2: O'ham 5C 42
(not continuous)
Pitman Cl. M11: Man 5C 102
Pitmore Wlk. M40: Man 1F 89
PITSES 5B 76
Pits Farm Av. OL11: Roch 4E 27
Pitsford Rd. M40: Man 6A 88
Pitshouse OL12: Roch 1A 26
Pitshouse La. OL12: Roch 1A 26
Pit St. OL9: Chad 5B 74
Pittbrook St. M12: Man 3H 11 (6H 101)
Pitt St. M26: Rad 4G 51
M34: Dent 4F 119
OL4: O'ham 3G 75
OL10: H'ood 3G 39
OL12: Roch 1C 178 (3H 27)
SK3: Stoc 4E 179 (3F 145)
SK14: Hyde 4B 120
Pitt St. E. OL4: O'ham 4H 75
Pixmore Av. BL1: Bolt 1F 33
Place, The M1: Man 6D 6 (4F 101)
Place Rd. WA14: Alt 5E 139
Plain Pitt St. SK14: Hyde 2A 120
(not continuous)
Plainsfield St. M16: W Ran 3C 114
Plane Ct. M6: Sal 3G 99
Plane Rd. M35: Fail 6H 89
Plane St. OL4: O'ham 2A 76
Plane Tree Cl. SK6: Mar 6B 148
Plane Tree Rd. M31: Part 6B 124
Planetree Rd. WA15: Hale 3A 152
Planetree Wlk. M23: Wyth 3C 140
Planet Way M34: Aud 2E 119
Plantagenet Wlk. *M40: Man 1F 103*
(off Marguerita Rd.)
Plantagent St. OL5: Mos 6H 77
Plantation Av. M28: Walk 5G 65
Plantation Gro. BL9: Bury 3A 54
Plantation Ind. Est. OL6: A Lyme 3B 106
Plantation St. M18: Man 2G 117
OL6: A Lyme 3B 106
Plantation Vw. BL9: Sum 6C 12
Plant Cl. M33: Sale 4A 128
Plant Hill Rd. M9: Man 4G 71
Plasman Ind. Cen. M19: Man 6E 117
Plate St. OL1: O'ham 3H 177 (2F 75)
Platinum Rd. M41: Urm 2H 111
Plato St. OL9: O'ham 2D 74

Platt Av. OL6: A Lyme 5A **92**
Plattbrook Cl. M14: Man 6F **115**
Platt Cl. OL16: Miln 6G **29**
Platt Ct. M14: Man 5G **115**
Platt Fields Pk. 5G **115**
Platt Hall
  (The Gallery of Costume) 5G **115**
Platt Hill Av. BL3: Bolt 3G **47**
Platt Ho. *M5: Sal* *1G 113*
  (off Elmira Way)
Platting Gro. OL7: A Lyme 6F **91**
Platting La. OL11: Roch 1A **42**
Platting Rd. OL4: Lyd, Scout 1G **77**
Platt La. M14: Man 6E **115**
  OL3: Del, Dob 4B **62**
Platt Lane Complex 5F **115**
Platts Dr. M44: Irl 5E **109**
Platt St. OL4: Spri 3D **76**
  SK8: Chea 5A **144**
  SK16: Duk 6G **105**
Platt Wlk. M34: Dent 6E **119**
Playfair Cl. OL10: H'ood 6A **40**
Playfair St. BL1: Bolt 5D **18**
  M14: Man 3F **115**
Playgolf Manchester 1E **111**
Pleachway SK4: Stoc 1B **144**
Pleasant Cl. OL11: Roch 3E **41**
Pleasant Gdns. BL1: Bolt 2E **175** (5C **32**)
Pleasant Rd. M30: Ecc 4G **97**
Pleasant St. BL8: Bury 1H **35**
  M9: Man .4H **87**
  OL10: H'ood 1G **39**
  OL11: Roch 3D **40**
Pleasant Ter. *SK16: Duk* *4A 106*
  (off Peel St.)
PLEASANT VIEW 3B **42**
Pleasant Vw. M9: Man 5F **71**
  M26: Rad .1B **68**
  OL2: Shaw 1B **60**
  OL4: Lees .2D **76**
  SK6: Comp 6F **137**
Pleasant Way SK8: Chea H 1E **167**
Pleasingdon Dr. BL8: Bury 3G **35**
  M40: Man .1E **89**
Plevna St. BL2: Bolt 3H **175** (6E **33**)
Plodder La. BL4: Farn 1A **64**
  BL5: O Hul 6G **47**
Ploughbank Dr. M21: Chor 2B **130**
Plough Cl. M41: Urm 5G **109**
Ploughfields M28: Wors 6E **81**
Plough St. SK16: Duk 5B **106**
Plover Cl. OL11: Roch 4A **26**
Plover Dr. BL9: Bury 1H **37**
  M44: Irl 3E **109**
  WA14: B'ath 3D **138**
Plover Ter. M21: Chor 2B **130**
Plowden Cl. BL3: Bolt 4A **48**
Plowden Rd. M22: Wyth 3H **153**
Plowley Cl. M20: Man 1F **143**
Plucksbridge Rd. SK6: Mar 2F **161**
Plumbley Dr. M16: Old T 4A **114**
Plumbley St. M11: Man 6G **103**
Plumley Cl. M33: Sale 6F **129**
  SK3: Stoc 6H **145**
Plumley Rd. SK9: Hand 2H **165**
Plummer Av. M21: Chor 3H **129**
Plumpton Cl. OL2: O'ham 6E **59**
Plumpton Dr. BL9: Bury 5E **23**
Plumpton Rd. OL11: Roch 5B **42**
Plumpton Wlk. M13: Man 3B **116**
Plum St. OL8: O'ham 4D **74**
Plumtree Cl. M30: Ecc 3G **97**
Plunge Rd. BL0: Eden 2H **13**
Pluto Cl. M6: Sal 1A **100**
Plymouth Av. M13: Man 2A **116**
Plymouth Cl. OL6: A Lyme 4H **91**
Plymouth Dr. BL4: Farn 1D **64**
  SK7: Bram 6G **157**
Plymouth Gro.
  M13: Man 6E **11** (1G **115**)
  M26: Rad .2F **51**
  SK3: Stoc 4D **144**

Plymouth Gro. W. M13: Man 2A **116**
Plymouth Rd. M33: Sale 4F **127**
Plymouth St. OL8: O'ham 5F **75**
  (not continuous)
Plymouth Vw. M13: Man . . .6E **11** (1G **115**)
Plymouth Village *M13: Man* *2H 115*
  (off Plymouth Gro.)
Plymtree Cl. M8: Man 1C **86**
POBGREEN .6F **63**
Pobgreen La. OL3: Upp 6F **63**
Pochard Dr. SK12: Poy 3A **168**
  WA14: B'ath 4D **138**
Pochin St. M40: Man 1H **7** (2A **102**)
POCKET 1A **48**
Pocket Nook BL6: Los 4C **46**
Pocket Nook Rd. BL6: Los 4B **46**
Pocket Workshops, The
  BL3: Bolt .1A **48**
Pocklington Dr. M23: Wyth 4F **141**
Podsmead Rd. M22: Wyth 3H **153**
Point, The OL6: A Lyme 6D **174**
Point Retail Pk., The
  OL16: Roch 3D **178** (4A **28**)
Poise Brook Dr. SK2: Stoc 6F **147**
Poise Brook Rd. SK2: Stoc 6F **147**
Poise Cl. SK7: H Gro 2G **159**
Poland St. M4: Man 3E **7** (3G **101**)
  M34: Aud .5E **105**
Poland St. Ind. Est.
  M4: Man 3E **7** (3G **101**)
Polden Cl. OL8: O'ham 1E **91**
Polden Wlk. *M9: Man* *2B 88*
  (off Glen Av.)
Poleacre La. SK6: Wood 3A **136**
Polebrook Av. M12: Man 6H **11** (1H **115**)
Polefield App. M25: Pres 3H **69**
Polefield Circ. M25: Pres 3H **69**
Polefield Gdns. M25: Pres 3H **69**
Polefield Grange M25: Pres 3H **69**
Polefield Gro. M25: Pres 3H **69**
Polefield Hall Rd. M25: Pres 3H **69**
Polefield Rd. M9: Man 1H **87**
  M25: Pres .3A **70**
Pole La. BL9: Bury 4A **54**
  M35: Fail 3H **89**
Pole La. Ct. BL9: Bury 4A **54**
Pole St. BL2: Bolt 4F **33**
  OL7: A Lyme 1H **105**
Polesworth Cl. M12: Man 1C **116**
Police St. M2: Man 5G **5** (4D **100**)
  M6: Sal 2G **99**
  M30: Ecc .2F **97**
  WA14: Alt 1B **174** (6F **139**)
Pollard Ct. *OL1: O'ham* *1E 75*
  (off Bradford St.)
Pollard Gro. OL15: L'ough 3A **16**
Pollard Ho. BL3: Bolt 5H **47**
Pollards La. BL9: Sum 1C **22**
Pollard Sq. M31: Part 6E **125**
Pollard St. M4: Man 6F **7** (4G **101**)
Pollard St. E. M40: Man 4H **7** (3H **101**)
Pollen Cl. M33: Sale 1D **140**
Pollen Rd. WA14: Alt 5E **139**
Polletts Av. SK5: Stoc 3C **134**
Pollit Cft. SK6: Rom 2F **147**
Pollitt Av. OL6: A Lyme 6A **92**
Pollitt Cl. M12: Man 1B **116**
Pollitts Cl. M30: Ecc 3D **96**
Pollitt St. M26: Rad 4C **52**
Polly Grn OL12: Roch 6H **15**
Polo Rd. M17: T Pk 5A **98**
Polperro Cl. OL2: O'ham 3G **59**
Polperro Wlk. SK14: Hat 4H **121**
Polruan Rd. M21: Chor 5G **113**
Polruan Wlk. SK14: Hat 4H **121**
Polworth Rd. M9: Man 2A **88**
Polygon, The M7: Sal 5A **86**
  M30: Ecc .2G **97**
Polygon Av. M13: Man 6F **11** (1G **115**)
Polygon Rd. M8: Man 2D **86**
Polygon St.
  M13: Man 4F **11** (6G **101**)

Pomfret St. M6: Sal 6C **84**
  M12: Man .1C **116**
Pomona Cres. M5: Sal 6H **99**
Pomona Docks
  M16: Old T 5A **8** (1A **114**)
Pomona Station (Metro) 1H **113**
Pomona Strand
  M16: Old T 6A **8** (2G **113**)
  (not continuous)
Pomona St. OL11: Roch 6H **27**
Ponds Cl. M21: Chor 6H **113**
Pondwater Cl. M28: Walk 6D **64**
Ponsford Av. M9: Man 6C **72**
Ponsonby Rd. M32: Stre 4D **112**
Pontefract Cl. M27: Swin 4B **84**
Pool Bank St. M24: Mid 2F **71**
  (not continuous)
Poolcroft M33: Sale 6F **129**
Poole Cl. SK7: Bram 4F **157**
Pooley Cl. M24: Mid 6F **55**
Pool Fld. Cl. M26: Rad 4G **51**
Pool Fold M35: Fail 5A **90**
Pool Fold Cl. BL1: Bolt 3G **31**
Pool Ho. Rd. SK12: Poy 2A **170**
Pool Pl. BL1: Bolt 3G **31**
Pool St. BL1: Bolt 2E **175**
  OL8: O'ham 5F **75**
Pool Ter. BL1: Bolt 3G **31**
Poolton Rd. M9: Man 5F **71**
Poorfield St. OL8: O'ham 6F **177**
Poot Hall OL12: Roch 6H **15**
Pope Way *M34: Dent* *2G 135*
  (off Kipling Av.)
Poplar Av. BL1: Bolt 1D **32**
  BL2: Bolt 5G **19**
  BL9: Bury .2H **37**
  M19: Man .2D **132**
  OL4: Lyd 5G **77**
  OL8: O'ham 1D **90**
  OL12: Roch 2E **27**
  SK9: Wilm .4C **172**
  WA14: Alt .5G **139**
Poplar Cl. SK8: Gat 6F **143**
Poplar Ct. M34: Aud 1F **119**
  SK3: Stoc . . *.* *6H 145*
  (off Garners La.)
Poplar Dr. M25: Pres 1G **85**
Poplar Gro. BL0: Ram 2D **12**
  M18: Man .3F **117**
  M33: Sale .6B **128**
  M41: Urm .5G **111**
  M44: Cad .3B **124**
  OL6: A Lyme 6A **92**
  SK2: Stoc .1C **158**
Poplar Rd. M19: Man 6H **131**
  M27: Swin .4F **83**
  M28: Walk .2F **81**
  M30: Ecc .1G **97**
  M32: Stre .1C **128**
  SK16: Duk .6D **106**
Poplars, The BL8: Bury 5C **22**
  OL5: Mos .2A **94**
  WA14: Alt 2A **174** (1E **151**)
Poplars Rd. SK15: Stal 2H **107**
Poplar St. M24: Mid 2F **73**
  M34: Aud .6F **105**
  M35: Fail 5F **89**
  SK4: Stoc .1A **144**
Poplar Wlk. *M31: Part* *6B 124*
  (off Long Wlk.)
  M34: Aud *1F 119*
  (off Poplar St.)
  OL9: Chad .1B **74**
Poplar Way SK6: H Lan 6E **161**
Poplin Dr. M3: Sal 2F **5** (2C **100**)
Poppy Cl. M23: Wyth 2E **141**
  OL9: Chad .2F **73**
Poppyfield Vw. OL11: Roch 2A **26**
Poppythorn Ct. M25: Pres 4G **69**
Poppythorn La. M25: Pres 4G **69**
  (not continuous)
Porchester Dr. M26: Rad 2E **51**
Porchfield Sq. M3: Man 1F **9** (5C **100**)

Porlock Av.—Primary Cl.

Porlock Av. M34: Aud 5C 104
SK14: Hat 5G 121
Porlock Cl. SK1: Stoc 3C 146
Porlock Rd. M23: Wyth 5H 141
M41: Urm 1C 126
Porlock Wlk. SK14: Hat 5G 121
Porritt Cl. OL11: Roch 5A 26
Porritt St. BL9: Bury 1G 37
(not continuous)
Porritt Way BL0: Ram 2C 12
Portal Ct. M24: Mid 1E 73
Portal Gro. M34: Dent 6H 119
Portal Wlk. M9: Man 3H 87
(off Alderside Rd.)
Porter Dr. M40: Man 5H 87
Porter St. BL9: Bury 1F 37
OL9: O'ham 4C 74
Portfield Cl. BL1: Bolt 5F 31
Portfield Wlk. M40: Man 6D 88
(off Harmer Cl.)
Portgate Wlk. M13: Man 6G 11
Porthleven Cres. M29: Ast 3A 80
Porthleven Dr. M23: Wyth 5E 141
Porthtowan Wlk. SK14: Hat 4A 122
(off Underwood Rd.)
Portico Library & Gallery, The
6A 6 (4E 101)
Portinscale Cl. BL8: Bury 2B 36
Portland, The M14: Man 1H 131
Portland Arc. M1: Man 6B 6
(off Parker St.)
Portland Basin Mus. 4G 105
Portland Chambers
SK15: Stal 3F 107
(off Portland Pl.)
Portland Cl. SK7: H Gro 4B 158
Portland Ct. M20: Man 6F 131
Portland Cres. M13: Man 2H 115
Portland Gro. SK4: Stoc 5D 132
Portland Ho. M6: Sal 2A 98
OL6: A Lyme 6A 174 (3G 105)
SK6: Mar 6C 148
Portland Ind. Est. BL9: Bury 1G 37
(off Portland St.)
Portland Mill OL6: A Lyme 6A 174
Portland Pl. OL7: A Lyme 3G 105
SK15: Stal 3F 107
Portland Rd. M13: Man 4B 116
M27: Swin 4A 84
M28: Walk 4G 65
M30: Ecc 2H 97
M32: Stre 3E 113
WA14: Bow 2E 151
Portland St. BL1: Bolt 3C 32
BL9: Bury 1G 37
M1: Man 1A 10 (5E 101)
Portland St. Nth.
OL6: A Lyme 5A 174 (2G 105)
Portland St. Sth.
OL6: A Lyme 6A 174 (3G 105)
OL7: A Lyme 3G 105
Portland Ter. OL6: A Lyme 6A 174
Portloe Rd. SK8: H Grn 6F 155
Portman Rd. M16: W Ran 4C 114
Portman St. OL5: Mos 2G 93
Porton Wlk. M22: Wyth 4H 153
Portrea Cl. SK3: Stoc 6G 145
Portree Cl. M30: Ecc 3D 96
Portree Ct. OL10: H'ood 5E 39
Portrush Rd. M22: Wyth 3C 154
Portside Cl. M28: Wors 6F 81
Portslade Wlk. M23: Wyth 6F 141
Portsmouth Cl. M7: Sal 6B 86
Portsmouth St. M13: Man 6D 10 (2F 115)
(not continuous)
Port Soderick Av. M5: Sal 4G 99
Portstone Cl. M16: W Ran 3C 114
Port St. M1: Man 5C 6 (4F 101)
OL8: O'ham 5F 75
SK1: Stoc 1E 179 (2G 145)
SK14: Hyde 5B 120
(off Market St.)
Portugal Rd. M25: Pres 1H 85
Portugal St. BL2: Bolt 6F 33
M4: Man 3E 7 (3G 101)
(not continuous)
OL7: A Lyme 4F 105
Portugal St. E. M1: Man 1E 11 (5G 101)
Portville Rd. M19: Man 5C 116
Portway M22: Wyth 3H 153
PORTWOOD 6B 134
Portwood Ind. Est. SK1: Stoc 1B 146
(not continuous)
Portwood Pl. SK1: Stoc 1H 145
Portwood Wlk. M9: Man 4H 87
(off Shiredale Dr.)
Posnett St. SK3: Stoc 3E 145
Postal St. M1: Man 5C 6
Post Office St.
WA14: Alt 1B 174 (6F 139)
Potato Wharf M3: Man 2D 8 (5B 100)
POT GREEN 6A 12
Pot Hill OL6: A Lyme 1A 106
Pot Hill Sq. OL6: A Lyme 1A 106
Pot Ho. La. OL12: W'le 4H 15
Potter Ho. OL8: O'ham 6G 177
Potter Rd. SK13: Had 4G 123
Potter's La. M9: Man 4A 88
Potter St. BL9: Bury 2G 37
M26: Rad 3D 52
Pottery La. M11: Man 2B 116
M12: Man 2B 116
Pottinger St. OL7: A Lyme 4F 105
Pott St. M27: Pen 1H 83
M40: Man 6F 89
WA14: Alt 2A 174 (1F 151)
Poulton Av. BL2: Bolt 6A 34
Poulton St. M11: Man 6G 103
Poundswick La. M22: Wyth 2A 154
Powder Mill Cl. M44: Irl 6F 109
Powell Av. SK14: Hyde 4C 120
Powell Ho. BL9: Bury 1D 176
Powell St. BL8: Bury 4B 36
M11: Man 3F 103
M16: Old T 3A 114
Powerhouse Health & Fitness Cen. 4B 120
(off Borough Arc.)
Powerleague Soccer Cen.
Alexandra Pk. 1D 130
Ardwick 3G 11 (6H 101)
Norris Bank 2D 144
Powicke Dr. SK6: Rom 2F 147
Powis Rd. M41: Urm 6G 109
Pownall Av. M20: Man 1E 131
SK7: Bram 6H 157
Pownall Ct. SK9: Wilm 1B 172
POWNALL GREEN 6G 157
POWNALL PARK 1C 172
Pownall Pl. SK7: Bram 6G 157
(off Bramhall La. Sth.)
Pownall Rd. SK8: Chea H 4C 156
SK9: Wilm 1C 172
WA14: Alt 2F 151
Pownall St. SK7: H Gro 2D 158
Poynings Dr. M22: Wyth 4A 154
Poynt Chase M28: Wors 6F 81
Poynter St. M40: Man 2E 89
Poynter Wlk. OL1: O'ham 3B 60
POYNTON 3D 168
Poynton Cl. BL9: Bury 4G 37
Poynton Ind. Est. SK12: Poy 6E 169
Poynton Leisure Cen. 5F 169
Poynton Sports Club 3E 169
Poynton Station (Rail) 3C 168
Poynton St. M15: Man 6H 9 (1D 114)
Praed Rd. M17: T Pk 2C 112
Pratt Wlk. M11: Man 4B 102
(off Raglan Cl.)
Precinct, The SK2: Stoc 5D 146
SK3: Stoc 4F 145
SK8: Chea H 3D 156
SK14: Holl 2F 123
Precinct Cen. M13: Man 5B 10 (1E 115)
Preece Cl. SK14: Hyde 3E 121
Preesall Av. SK8: H Grn 5F 155
Preesall Cl. BL8: Bury 4H 35
Premier Rd. M8: Man 1D 100
Premier St. M16: Old T 3B 114
Prentice Wlk. M11: Man 4C 102
Prenton St. M11: Man 5G 103
Prenton Way BL8: Tot 6H 21
Presall St. BL2: Bolt 5G 33
Prescot Av. M29: Tyld 2B 80
Prescot Cl. BL9: Bury 4G 37
Prescot Rd. M9: Man 4H 87
WA15: Hale 3H 151
Prescott Ct. M28: Walk 6F 65
(off Prescott St.)
Prescott Rd. SK9: Wilm 6F 165
Prescott St. BL3: Bolt 3A 48
M28: Walk 6F 65
OL16: Roch 1C 28
Prescott Wlk. M34: Dent 6H 119
Press St. M11: Man 6F 103
Presswood Ct. M6: Sal 5C 84
(off Swinton Pk. Rd.)
Prestage St. M12: Man 5D 116
M16: Old T 2A 114
Prestbury Av. M14: Man 6D 114
WA15: Alt 5G 139
Prestbury Cl. BL9: Bury 4G 37
SK2: Stoc 1D 158
Prestbury Dr. OL1: O'ham 6D 58
SK6: Bred 6E 135
Prestbury Rd. BL1: Bolt 6E 19
Prestfield Rd. M45: White 2G 69
Presto Gdns. BL3: Bolt 3H 47
PRESTOLEE 1C 66
Prestolee Rd. BL3: Lit L 6C 50
M26: Rad 6C 50
Preston Av. M30: Ecc 2A 98
M44: Irl 2D 124
Preston Cl. M30: Ecc 2A 98
Preston Rd. M19: Man 1C 132
Preston St. BL3: Bolt 3F 49
M18: Man 1E 117
M24: Mid 1C 72
OL4: O'ham 3G 75
OL12: Roch 2E 27
Presto St. BL3: Bolt 3H 47
BL4: Farn 6A 50
PRESTWICH 4G 69
Prestwich Cl. SK2: Stoc 4B 146
Prestwich Forest Pk. 5C 68
Prestwich Hills M25: Pres 6G 69
PRESTWICH PARK 1F 85
Prestwich Pk. Rd. Sth. M25: Pres 6G 69
Prestwich Station (Metro) 4G 69
Prestwick Wlk. M40: Man 1E 89
(off Pleasington Dr.)
Prestwood Cl. BL1: Bolt 4B 32
Prestwood Dr. BL1: Bolt 4B 32
Prestwood Rd. BL4: Farn 6E 49
M6: Sal 1C 98
Pretoria Rd. BL2: Bolt 5A 34
OL8: O'ham 6C 74
Pretoria St. OL12: Roch 2E 27
PRETTYWOOD 3C 38
Price St. BL4: Farn 6H 49
BL9: Bury 4G 37
M4: Man 5H 7 (4H 101)
SK16: Duk 5A 106
PRICKSHAW 3D 14
Prickshaw La. OL12: Roch 3D 14
Pridmouth Rd. M20: Man 3G 131
Priest Av. SK8: Gat 1E 155
Priest Hill OL1: O'ham 2E 75
(off Henshaw St.)
Priest Hill St.
OL1: O'ham 3F 177 (2E 75)
Priestley Rd. M28: Ward 3E 83
Priestley Way OL2: Shaw 6B 44
Priestnall Ct. SK4: Stoc 6B 132
(off Priestnall Rd.)
Priestnall Recreation Cen. 6B 132
Priestnall Rd. SK4: Stoc 6B 132
Priest St. OL9: Chad 5B 74
Priestwood Av. OL4: O'ham 3D 60
Primary Cl. M44: Cad 4B 124

Primley Wlk. M9: Man 3A 88
(off Edward St.)
Primrose Av. BL4: Farn 6E 49
M28: Walk 1F 81
M41: Urm 5F 111
OL3: Upp 6E 63
SK6: Mar 5C 148
SK14: Hyde 2B 136
PRIMROSE BANK 6E 177 (4E 75)
Primrose Bank BL8: Tot 4G 21
M28: Walk 1F 81
OL3: G'fld 4D 78
OL8: O'ham 6E 177 (4E 75)
WA14: Bow 4E 151
Primrose Cl. BL2: Bolt 1C 34
M5: Sal 3F 99
Primrose Cotts. WA14: Bow 4E 151
(off Brickkiln Row)
Primrose Cres. SK14: Hyde 1B 136
Primrose Dr. BL9: Bury 1B 38
M43: Droy 2C 104
Primrose Hill Cotts. OL5: Mos 2A 94
(off Micklehurst Rd.)
OL10: H'ood 1C 40
Primrose Hill Ct. OL2: Shaw 5F 43
Primrose St. BL1: Bolt 1D 32
BL4: Kea 2A 66
M4: Man 3D 6 (3F 101)
OL12: Roch 3F 27
Primrose Ter. SK15: Stal 3F 107
Primrose Wlk.
OL8: O'ham 6F 177 (4E 75)
SK6: Mar 5C 148
Primula St. BL1: Bolt 1D 32
Prince Albert Av. M19: Man 5C 116
(off Belvoir Av.)
Prince Charlie St. OL1: O'ham 1H 75
Princedom St. M9: Man 3A 88
Prince Edward Av. M34: Dent 5F 119
OL4: O'ham 2A 76
Prince George St. OL1: O'ham 6A 60
Princemead Pl. M17: T Pk 2B 112
Prince of Wales Ind. Units
OL1: O'ham 6A 60
Prince Rd. SK12: Poy 2A 170
Princes Av. BL3: Lit L 3D 50
M20: Man 5G 131
M44: Irl 4G 109
SK6: Bred 6G 135
Prince's Bri. M3: Man 1D 8 (5B 100)
Princes Ct. BL0: Ram 3C 12
(off Silver St.)
M30: Ecc 2F 97
Princes Dr. M33: Sale 6D 128
SK6: Mar 4C 148
Prince's Incline SK12: Poy 3E 169
Princes Rd. M33: Sale 6C 128
SK4: Stoc 5C 132
SK6: Bred 6G 135
WA14: Alt 5F 139
Princess Av. BL4: Kea 3B 66
M25: Pres 1A 86
M34: Dent 4E 119
OL12: Roch 5C 16
SK8: Chea H 2C 156
Princess Cl. OL5: Mos 3A 94
OL10: H'ood 4H 39
SK16: Duk 5B 106
Princess Ct. M15: Man 5C 8
M25: Pres 6H 69
Princess Dr. M24: Mid 1A 72
Princess Gro. BL4: Farn 1H 65
Princess Pde. BL9: Bury 4C 176 (3F 37)
M14: Man 6D 114
Princess Parkway M22: Nor 3A 142
M23: Wyth 3A 142
Princess Rd. BL6: Los 6B 30
M14: Man 3D 114
M15: Man 5G 9 (1D 114)
M16: W Ran 3D 114
M20: Man 6B 130
M21: Chor 6B 130
M25: Pres 5A 70

Princess Rd. M41: Urm 4D 110
OL2: Shaw 1G 59
OL9: Chad 6G 73
OL16: Roch 4D 28
SK9: Wilm 4C 172
Princess St. BL1: Bolt 4G 175 (6D 32)
M1: Man 1A 10 (5E 101)
M2: Man 6H 5 (4D 100)
M6: Sal 1G 99
(off Cheltenham St.)
M15: Man 5B 8 (1A 114)
M26: Rad 4G 51
M27: Swin 4A 84
M30: Ecc 3E 97
M35: Fail 4G 89
OL4: Lees 3C 76
OL6: A Lyme 1B 106
OL12: Roch 1B 178 (3H 27)
OL12: Whitw 1E 15
(off Albert St.)
SK14: Hyde 5C 120
WA14: B'ath 3E 139
Prince's St. SK1: Stoc 2F 179 (2G 145)
Prince St. BL0: Ram 3C 12
BL1: Bolt 1E 175 (6C 32)
OL1: O'ham 2G 75
OL10: H'ood 3H 39
OL16: Roch 6A 28
Princes Wlk. SK7: Bram 6A 158
Princes Wood Rd. SK12: Poy 2A 170
Princethorpe Cl. BL6: Los 1D 46
Princeton Cl. M6: Sal 2C 98
Prince Way OL2: O'ham 1C 58
Prinknash Rd. M22: Wyth 3B 154
Printers Brow SK14: Holl 2G 123
Printers Cl. SK4: Stoc 1H 143
Printers Dr. SK15: C'ook 5C 94
Printers Fold SK14: Holl 2F 123
Printers La. BL2: Bolt 5G 19
Printers Pk. SK14: Holl 2G 123
Printer St. M11: Man 5F 103
OL1: O'ham 4G 177 (3F 75)
Printon Av. M9: Man 5F 71
Printworks, The M4: Man 3A 6 (3E 101)
Printworks La. M19: Man 6E 117
Printworks Rd. SK15: H'rod 2F 107
Prior St. OL8: O'ham 4H 75
Priory, The M7: Sal 5A 86
Priory Av. M7: Sal 5A 86
M21: Chor 1H 129
Priory Cl. M33: Sale 3D 128
OL8: O'ham 6D 74
SK16: Duk 1B 120
Priory Ct. M30: Ecc 3G 97
(off Abbey Gro.)
SK5: Stoc 1G 133
WA14: Bow 4E 151
(off Priory St.)
Priory Gdns. M20: Man 5F 131
Priory Gro. M7: Sal 5A 86
OL9: Chad 5A 74
Priory La. SK5: Stoc 1G 133
Priory Pl. BL2: Bolt 3G 33
M7: Sal 5A 86
Priory Rd. M27: Swin 2G 83
M33: Sale 4C 128
SK8: Chea 6C 144
SK9: Wilm 1B 172
WA14: Bow 5D 150
Priory St. WA14: Bow 5E 151
Pritchard St. M1: Man 2B 10 (5E 101)
M32: Stre 5D 112
Privet St. OL4: O'ham 6B 60
Proctor St. BL8: Bury 4C 36
Proctor Way M30: Ecc 6B 96
(not continuous)
Progress Av. M34: Aud 1F 119
Progressive Bus. Pk. M34: Aud 5E 105
Progress St. BL1: Bolt 4D 32
OL6: A Lyme 5A 174 (2G 105)
OL11: Roch 4E 41
Progress Way M34: Dent 5C 118
Promenade St. OL10: H'ood 3A 40

Propps Hall Dr. M35: Fail 5F 89
Prospect Av. BL2: Bolt 2B 34
BL4: Farn 2G 65
M44: Cad 3C 124
Prospect Ct. BL8: Tot 4H 21
Prospect Dr. M35: Fail 6H 89
WA15: Haleb 6D 152
Prospect Ho. M9: Man 4A 88
(off Church La.)
Prospect Pl. BL4: Farn 2G 65
M27: Swin 4A 84
(off Manchester Rd.)
OL6: A Lyme 6B 92
OL10: H'ood 2H 39
Prospect Rd. M44: Cad 3C 124
OL6: A Lyme 6C 92
OL9: O'ham 2C 74
SK16: Duk 4B 106
Prospect St. BL1: Bolt 4D 32
OL10: H'ood 4A 40
OL11: Roch 1G 41
OL15: L'ough 3H 17
Prospect Ter. BL8: Bury 1D 36
OL12: Roch 1G 25
Prospect Va. SK8: H Grn 4F 155
Prospect Vw. M27: Swin 4A 84
(off Manchester Rd.)
Prospect Vs. M9: Man 2B 88
Prosperity M29: Ast 3B 80
Protector Way M44: Irl 1D 124
Prout St. M12: Man 4C 116
Provender Cl. WA14: B'ath 3F 139
Providence Ho. OL4: O'ham 1C 76
(off Huddersfield Rd.)
Providence St. BL3: Bolt 6G 175 (2D 48)
M4: Man 5G 7 (4H 101)
M34: Aud 6F 105
OL6: A Lyme 1B 106
Provident Av. M19: Man 6E 117
Provident Cl. OL2: Shaw 6H 43
Provident Way WA15: Tim 4A 140
Provis Rd. M21: Chor 2H 129
Prubella Av. M34: Dent 2E 119
Pryce St. BL1: Bolt 4B 32
Pryme St. M15: Man 3E 9 (6C 100)
Pudding La. SK14: Hat 4G 121
(not continuous)
Puffin Av. SK12: Poy 3B 168
Puffingate Cl. SK15: C'ook 4A 94
Pugin Wlk. M9: Man 5H 87
(off Oldershaw Dr.)
Pulborough Cl. BL8: Bury 4B 22
Pulford Av. M21: Chor 5B 130
Pulford Rd. M33: Sale 1C 140
Pullman Cl. M19: Man 1D 132
Pullman Cl. BL2: Bolt 2E 49
Pullman Dr. M32: Stre 5H 111
Pullman St. OL11: Roch 6H 27
Pump St. OL9: O'ham 1B 90
Pump Yd. M4: Man 3A 6
Punch La. BL3: Bolt 5D 46
(not continuous)
BL3: O Hul 6D 46
Punch St. BL3: Bolt 1B 48
Purbeck Cl. M22: Wyth 4A 154
Purbeck Dr. BL6: Los 5A 30
BL8: Bury 5C 22
Purcell Cl. BL1: Bolt 4B 32
Purcell St. M12: Man 4C 116
Purdon St. BL9: Bury 5F 23
Purdy Ho. OL8: O'ham 6F 177 (4E 75)
Puritan Wlk. M40: Man 6G 87
(off Ribblesdale Dr.)
Purley Av. M23: Wyth 2H 141
Purley Dr. M44: Cad 4A 124
Purple St. BL1: Bolt 3G 175
Purslow Cl. M12: Man 4A 102
Purton Wlk. M9: Man 4A 88
(off Broadwell Dr.)
Putney Cl. OL1: O'ham 6E 59
Puzzletree Ct. SK2: Stoc 4C 146
Pymgate Dr. SK8: H Grn 3E 155
Pymgate La. SK8: H Grn 3E 155

Pym St. M30: Ecc 3F **97**
    M40: Man 3B **88**
    OL10: H'ood 4H **39**
Pyramid Ct. M7: Sal 5B **86**
Pyrus Cl. M30: Ecc 5B **96**
Pytha Fold Rd. M20: Man 4G **131**

Q

Quadrant, The M9: Man 6C **72**
    M43: Droy 4H **103**
    OL10: H'ood 3A **40**
    SK1: Stoc 2B **146**
    SK6: Rom 1G **147**
Quail Dr. M44: Irl 4E **109**
Quail St. OL4: O'ham 4A **76**
Quainton Ho. M5: Sal 4F **99**
    (off Amersham St.)
Quakersfield BL8: Tot 3G **21**
Quantock Cl. SK4: Stoc 1G **145**
Quantock Dr. OL8: O'ham 6F **75**
Quantock St. M16: W Ran 3C **114**
Quarlton Dr. BL8: Haw 1D **20**
Quarmby Rd. M18: Man 3H **117**
Quarry Bank Mill 4C **164**
Quarry Bank Rd. SK9: Sty 4C **164**
Quarry Clough SK15: Stal 5H **107**
Quarry Hgts. SK15: Stal 5D **106**
Quarry Hill OL12: Roch 6G **15**
Quarry La. OL3: Dob 6H **61**
    OL4: Scout 6H **61**
Quarrymans Vw. WA15: Tim 5B **140**
Quarry Pond Rd. M28: Walk 6D **64**
Quarry Ri. SK6: Rom 6H **135**
    SK15: Stal 5D **106**
Quarry Rd. BL4: Kea 2C **66**
    SK6: Rom 1H **147**
Quarry St. BL0: Ram 3D **12**
    (not continuous)
    M26: Rad 4B **52**
    OL12: Roch 2G **27**
    SK6: Wood 4H **135**
    SK15: Stal 4D **106**
Quarry Vw. OL12: Roch 6G **15**
Quarry Wlk. M11: Man **4B 102**
    (off Redfield Cl.)
Quay 5 M5: Sal 6H **99**
Quay Ct. M44: Irl 6F **109**
    (off Bankquay Ct.)
Quays, The M50: Sal 6F **99**
Quayside Cl. M28: Wors 6F **81**
Quays Reach M50: Sal 4E **99**
Quays Theatre 6E **99**
    (in The Lowry)
Quay St. M3: Man 6E **5** (4C **100**)
    M3: Sal 4F **5** (3C **100**)
    OL10: H'ood 4A **40**
Quayview M5: Sal 5G **99**
Quay W. M17: T Pk 1E **113**
Quebec Bldg. M3: Sal 3F **5**
Quebec Pl. BL3: Bolt 2A **48**
Quebec St. BL3: Bolt 2B **48**
    M34: Dent 3E **119**
    OL9: O'ham 1C **74**
Queen Alexandra Cl.
    M5: Sal 2A **8** (5A **100**)
Queen Anne Cl. BL9: Bury 3A **54**
Queen Anne Ct. SK9: Wilm 3F **173**
Queen Anne Dr. M28: Wors 4F **81**
Queenhill Dr. SK14: Hyde 2D **120**
Queenhill Rd. M22: Nor 2C **142**
Queens Av. BL3: Lit L 3C **50**
    BL7: Bro X 4E **19**
    M18: Man 2D **116**
    OL12: Roch 5C **16**
    SK6: Bred 6G **135**
Queensbrook BL1: Bolt 6C **32**
Queensbury Cl. BL1: Bolt 6B **18**
    SK9: Wilm 1G **173**
Queensbury Ct. M40: Man 2H **7**
Queensbury Pde.
    M40: Man 2H **7**

Queens Cl. M28: Walk 6H **65**
    M28: Wors 4D **80**
    SK4: Stoc 1C **144**
    SK14: Hyde 2C **136**
Queens Ct. M20: Man 5E **131**
    M40: Man 6H **87**
    M41: Urm 5H **109**
    SK4: Stoc 1C **144**
    SK6: Mar 5E **149**
    SK9: Wilm 3D **172**
    (off Queens Rd.)
Queenscroft M30: Ecc 2G **97**
Queens Dr. M25: Pres 1A **86**
    OL11: Roch 2G **41**
    SK4: Stoc 1C **144**
    SK8: Chea H 2C **156**
    SK14: Hyde 2D **136**
Queensferry St. M40: Man 5E **89**
Queens Gdns. SK8: Chea 5A **144**
Queensgate BL1: Bolt 5A **32**
    SK7: Bram 2G **167**
Queensgate Dr. OL2: O'ham 1C **58**
Queen's Gro. M12: Man 3C **116**
Queensland Rd. M18: Man 2D **116**
Queensmead Pl. M17: T Pk 2B **112**
Queens Pk. 5G **87**
Queens Pk. Mus. & Art Gallery 5G **87**
Queen's Pk. Rd. OL10: H'ood 1H **39**
Queens Pk. SK1: Bolt 5B **32**
Queens Pl. BL9: Sum 1C **22**
Queen Sq. OL6: A Lyme 2B **106**
Queens Rd. BL3: Bolt 3H **47**
    M8: Man 6E **87**
    M9: Man 5G **87**
    M33: Sale 4H **127**
    M40: Man 5H **87**
    M41: Urm 6F **111**
    OL6: A Lyme 6B **92**
    OL8: O'ham 6H **177** (4F **75**)
    OL9: Chad 2A **74**
    OL15: L'ough 4H **17**
    SK6: Bred 6G **135**
    SK7: H Gro 2E **159**
    SK8: Chea H 1B **156**
    (not continuous)
    SK9: Wilm 3D **172**
    WA15: Hale 2G **151**
Queen's Rd. Ter. OL15: L'ough 4H **17**
    (off Queen's Rd.)
Queens Ter. SK9: Hand 3H **165**
    SK16: Duk 4H **105**
Queenston Rd. M20: Man 5E **131**
Queen St. BL0: Ram 3B **12**
    BL1: Bolt 4E **175** (6C **32**)
    BL4: Farn 1H **65**
    BL8: Tot 6A **22**
    BL9: Bury 3G **37**
    M2: Man 6G **5** (4D **100**)
    M3: Sal 3F **5** (3C **100**)
    M6: Sal 6D **84**
    M24: Mid 1E **73**
    M26: Rad 5C **52**
    M34: Aud 1F **119**
    M34: Dent 3E **119**
    M35: Fail 4G **89**
    M38: Lit H 6F **65**
    OL1: O'ham 3H **177** (2F **75**)
    OL2: O'ham 3D **58**
    OL2: Shaw 1H **59**
    OL4: Spri 3D **76**
    OL5: Mos 2G **93**
    OL6: A Lyme 2A **106**
    OL10: H'ood 2H **39**
    OL12: Roch 1C **178** (3H **27**)
    OL15: L'ough 4H **17**
    SK6: Mar 5E **149**
    SK8: Chea 5B **144**
    SK13: Had 3H **123**
    SK14: Hyde 6C **120**
    SK15: Stal 3E **107**
    SK16: Duk 4H **105**
Queen St. Mills OL5: Mos 2H **93**
Queen St. W. M20: Man 2F **131**

Queens Vw. OL15: L'ough 6G **17**
Queen's Wlk. M43: Droy 4A **104**
Queensway BL4: Kea 4B **66**
    M19: Man 1H **143**
    M27: Clif 1A **84**
    M28: Wors 3F **81**
    M31: Part 5D **124**
    M41: Urm 3G **111**
    M44: Irl 5D **108**
    OL3: G'fld 3D **78**
    OL5: Mos 3H **93**
    OL11: Roch 3F **41**
    SK8: H Grn 5F **155**
    SK12: Poy 4D **168**
    SK16: Duk 6D **106**
Queensway Neighbourhood Cen.
     . . . . .6A **28**
Queen Victoria St. M30: Ecc 3E **97**
    OL11: Roch 1A **42**
Quenby St. M15: Man 4D **8** (6B **100**)
Quendon Av. M7: Sal 1C **100**
QUICK 5H **77**
QUICK EDGE 6G **77**
Quickedge La. OL4: Grot 5F **77**
Quickedge Rd. OL4: Lyd, Mos 1G **93**
    OL5: Mos 1G **93**
Quick Rd. OL5: Mos 5H **77**
Quick Vw. OL5: Mos 6A **78**
QUICKWOOD 1G **93**
Quickwood M34: Dent 3G **119**
    (off Herbert Sth.)
    OL5: Mos 1H **93**
    (off Roughtown Rd.)
Quill Ct. M44: Irl 3C **124**
    (off Magenta Av.)
Quilter Gro. M9: Man 1G **87**
Quince Ho. M6: Sal 2H **99**
    (off Milton Pl.)
Quinney Cres. M16: W Ran 3C **114**
Quinn St. M11: Man 4C **102**
Quinton OL12: Roch 2A **178** (3G **27**)
Quinton Wlk. M13: Man 5D **10**
Quintrell Brow BL7: Bro X 3E **19**

R

Rabbit La. SK14: Mot 1C **122**
Raby St. M14: Man 3D **114**
    M16: W Ran 3C **114**
Race, The SK9: Hand 5H **165**
Racecourse Pk. SK9: Wilm 3C **172**
Racecourse Rd. SK9: Wilm 2B **172**
Racecourse Wlk. M26: Rad 3H **51**
Racefield Hamlet OL1: Chad 3A **58**
Racefield Rd. WA14: Alt 1E **151**
Rachel Rosing Wlk. M8: Man 3D **86**
Rachel St. M12: Man 2F **11** (5G **101**)
Rackhouse Rd. M23: Wyth 2H **141**
Radbourne Cl. M12: Man 1C **116**
Radbourne Gro. BL3: Bolt 3F **47**
Radbourne Ho. BL2: Bolt 1F **49**
RADCLIFFE 4B **52**
Radcliffe Borough FC 3G **51**
Radcliffe Bri. M26: Rad 5A **52**
Radcliffe Moor Rd. BL2: Bolt 1D **50**
    M26: Bolt, Rad 1D **50**
Radcliffe New Rd. M45: White 5C **52**
Radcliffe Pk. Cres. M6: Sal 6C **84**
Radcliffe Pk. Rd. M6: Sal 6B **84**
Radcliffe Pool 4A **52**
Radcliffe Rd. BL2: Bolt 6F **33**
    BL3: Bolt 2H **49**
    BL9: Bury 6D **36**
    OL4: O'ham 5B **60**
Radcliffe Station (Metro) 4B **52**
Radcliffe St.
    OL1: O'ham 1G **177** (1F **75**)
    (not continuous)
    OL2: O'ham 3D **58**
    OL4: Spri 3E **77**
Radcliffe Vw. M5: Sal 6H **99**
    (off Ordsall Dr.)

Radclyffe St. M24: Mid 5C 56
  OL9: Chad 1B 74
Radclyffe Ter. M24: Mid 5C 56
Radelan Gro. M26: Rad 3F 51
Radford Cl. SK2: Stoc 4D 146
Radford Dr. M9: Man 3A 88
               (off Hemsley St. Sth.)
  M44: Irl 4E 109
Radford Ho. SK2: Stoc 4E 147
Radium St. M4: Man 3E 7 (3G 101)
Radlet Dr. WA15: Tim 3A 140
Radlett Wlk. M13: Man 2G 115
              (off Plymouth Gro.)
Radley Cl. BL1: Bolt 4G 31
  M33: Sale 6F 127
Radley St. M16: W Ran 4D 114
  M43: Droy 5G 103
Radnor Av. M34: Dent 4B 118
Radnor Ho. SK3: Stoc 5E 179
Radnormere Dr.
  SK8: Chea H 1B 156
Radnor St. M15: Man 2D 114
  M18: Man 3E 117
  M32: Stre 5D 112
  OL9: O'ham 4C 74
Radstock Cl. BL1: Bolt 4C 18
  M14: Man 6F 115
Radstock Rd. M32: Stre 5C 112
Radway M29: Tyld 2A 80
Raeburn Dr. SK6: Mar B 3F 149
Rae St. SK3: Stoc 3E 145
Raglan Av. M27: Clif 1B 84
  M45: White 2H 69
Raglan Cl. M11: Man 4B 102
Raglan Dr. WA14: Tim 3G 139
Raglan Rd. M32: Stre 4B 112
  M33: Sale 6H 127
Raglan St. BL1: Bolt 3B 32
  OL11: Roch 4E 41
  SK14: Hyde 5A 120
Raglan Wlk. M15: Man 6H 9
Ragley Cl. SK12: Poy 3F 169
Raikes Clough Ind. Est.
  BL3: Bolt 3G 49
Raikes La. BL3: Bolt 3F 49
Raikes La. Ind. Est.
  BL3: Bolt 3F 49
Raikes Rd. BL3: Bolt 2H 49
Raikes Way BL3: Bolt 2H 49
Railside Ter. M30: Ecc 3A 98
              (off St Mary's Rd.)
Railton Av. M16: W Ran 4B 114
Railton Ter. M9: Man 4B 88
Railway App. OL11: Roch 3E 41
Railway Bank SK14: Hyde 5A 120
           (off Bowling Grn. St.)
Railway Brow OL11: Roch 4E 41
Railway Cotts.
  SK6: Bred 5F 135
             (off Kennett Dr.)
Railway Rd. M32: Stre 2E 113
  M41: Urm 5F 111
  OL9: Chad 1A 90
  OL9: O'ham 3D 74
  SK1: Stoc 4F 179 (3G 145)
  SK6: Mar 5B 148
Railway St. BL0: Ram 3C 12
  BL4: Farn 6A 50
  BL9: Sum 1C 22
  M18: Man 1E 117
  M26: Rad 5A 52
  OL10: H'ood 4A 40
  OL15: L'ough 4H 17
  OL16: Miln 1H 43
  OL16: Roch 5D 178 (5A 28)
  SK4: Stoc 1E 179 (1G 145)
  SK14: Hyde 5B 120
  SK16: Duk 4H 105
  WA14: Alt 3A 174 (1F 151)
Railway St. Ind. Est.
  M18: Man 1F 117
Railway St. W. BL9: Sum 1B 22

Railway Ter. BL8: Bury 4C 36
  BL9: Sum 1C 22
  M21: Chor 5H 113
            (off Manchester Rd.)
  OL10: H'ood 4H 39
  SK12: Dis 1H 171
Railway Vw. OL2: Shaw 5A 44
  OL4: Spri 3D 76
  SK5: Stoc 5G 117
Raimond St. BL1: Bolt 2A 32
Rainbow Cl. M21: Chor 2H 129
Raincliff Av. M13: Man 5B 116
Raines Crest OL16: Miln 5G 29
Rainford Av. M20: Man 1E 131
  WA15: Tim 5A 140
Rainford Ho. BL1: Bolt 3C 32
             (off Haydock St.)
Rainford St. BL2: Bolt 5G 19
Rainforth St. M13: Man 4B 116
Rainham Dr. BL1: Bolt 4C 32
  M8: Man .4E 87
Rainham Gro. BL1: Bolt 4C 32
            (off Rainham Dr.)
Rainham Way OL9: Chad 3B 74
  SK5: Stoc 3B 134
Rainhill Wlk. M40: Man 1F 103
            (off Eastmoor Dr.)
Rainow Av. M43: Droy 4G 103
Rainow Dr. SK12: Poy 5G 169
Rainow Rd. SK3: Stoc 5E 145
Rainow Way SK9: Wilm 6A 166
            (off Malpas Cl.)
Rainsdale Flats OL10: H'ood 3G 39
            (off Meadow Cl.)
Rainshaw St. BL1: Bolt 1D 32
  OL2: O'ham 3D 58
  OL4: O'ham 1B 76
RAINSOUGH 2G 85
Rainsough Av. M25: Pres 2G 85
Rainsough Brow M25: Pres 2F 85
Rainsough Cl. M25: Pres 2G 85
Rainsough Hill M25: Pres 2F 85
Rainton Wlk. M40: Man 1F 89
            (off Enstone Dr.)
Rainwood OL9: Chad 1G 73
Raja Cl. M8: Man 4F 87
Rake Cl. M11: Roch 4H 25
Rake, The BL0: Ram 3B 12
Rake Fold BL0: Ram 3A 12
Rakehead Wlk. M15: Man 2A 116
            (off Botham Cl.)
Rake La. M27: Clif 6A 68
Rake St. BL9: Bury 1F 37
Rake Top OL12: Roch 2D 26
Rakewood Dr. OL4: O'ham 3C 60
Rakewood Rd. OL15: L'ough 6H 17
Raleigh Cl. M20: Man 4E 131
  OL1: O'ham 1G 177 (1F 75)
Raleigh Gdns. OL15: L'ough 2A 16
Raleigh St. M32: Stre 5D 112
  SK5: Stoc 5G 133
Ralli Courts M3: Sal 5E 5 (4C 100)
Ralli Quays M3: Sal 5E 5 (4C 100)
Ralph Av. SK14: Hyde 2C 136
Ralph Grn. St. OL9: O'ham 6B 74
Ralph Sherwin Ct. OL12: Roch 5D 16
Ralphs La. OL3: Dens 3H 45
  SK16: Duk 6A 106
Ralph St. BL1: Bolt 3B 32
  M11: Man 4F 103
  OL12: Roch 2A 28
Ralston Cl. M7: Sal 3D 86
Ralstone Av. OL8: O'ham 5F 75
Ramage Wlk. M12: Man 4A 102
Ramillies Av. SK8: Chea H 4D 156
Ramp Rd. E. M90: Man A 6A 154
Ramp Rd. Sth. M90: Man A 6A 154
            (off Outwood La.)
Ramp Rd. W. M90: Man A 6H 153
Ramsay Av. BL4: Farn 2E 65
Ramsay Pl. OL16: Roch 2D 178 (3A 28)
Ramsay St. BL1: Bolt 1C 32
  OL16: Roch 2D 178 (3A 28)

Ramsay Ter. OL16: Roch 2D 178 (3A 28)
RAMSBOTTOM 3C 12
Ramsbottom Heritage Cen. 2B 12
               (off Carr St.)
Ramsbottom La. BL0: Ram 2C 12
Ramsbottom Rd. BL7: Edg 1B 20
  BL8: Haw 1B 20
Ramsbottom Row M25: Pres 5G 69
Ramsbottom Station
  East Lancashire Railway 3C 12
Ramsbottom Swimming Pool 2C 12
Ramsbury Dr. M40: Man 1F 89
Ramsdale Rd. SK7: Bram 5G 157
Ramsdale St. OL9: Chad 2A 74
Ramsden Cl. OL1: O'ham 2E 177 (2E 75)
Ramsden Cres.
  OL1: O'ham 1E 177 (2E 75)
Ramsden Fold M27: Clif 1H 83
Ramsden Rd. OL12: W'le 4C 16
Ramsden St. BL3: Bolt 2H 49
  OL1: O'ham 1E 177 (2E 75)
  OL6: A Lyme 1H 105
Ramsey Av. M19: Man 6F 117
Ramsey Gro. BL8: Bury 3B 36
Ramsey St. M40: Man 4D 88
  OL1: O'ham 1H 75
  OL9: Chad 4B 74
Ramsgate Rd. M40: Man 1E 103
  SK5: Stoc 2H 133
Ramsgate St. M7: Sal 6C 86
Ramsgill Cl. M23: Wyth 2F 141
Ramsgreave Cl. BL9: Bury 6D 36
Ramsgte St. M8: Man 1C 100
Ram St. M38: Lit H 5D 64
Ramwell Gdns. BL3: Bolt 2B 48
Ramwells Brow BL7: Bro X 3D 18
Ramwells Ct. BL7: Bro X 2F 19
Ramwells M. BL7: Bro X 3F 19
          (off Windy Harbour La.)
Ranby Av. M9: Man 5B 72
Randale Dr. BL9: Bury 4G 53
Randall Wlk. M11: Man 4B 102
            (off Raglan Cl.)
Randal St. BL3: Bolt 3A 48
  SK14: Hyde 4C 120
Randerson St. M12: Man 3E 11
Randlesham St. M25: Pres 5A 70
Randolph Pl. SK3: Stoc 6F 179 (4G 145)
Randolph Rd. BL4: Kea 2B 66
Randolph St. BL3: Bolt 1B 48
  M19: Man 5D 116
  OL8: O'ham 1C 90
Rands Clough Dr. M28: Wors 5F 81
Rand St. OL1: O'ham 6B 60
Ranelagh Rd. M27: Pen 4C 84
Ranelagh St. M11: Man 3D 102
Raneley Gro. OL11: Roch 3A 42
Ranford Rd. M19: Man 1C 132
Range Dr. SK6: Wood 3A 136
Range Hall Ct. SK1: Stoc 2A 146
             (off Hall St.)
Range La. OL3: Dens 4H 45
Rangemore Av. M22: Nor 3C 142
Range Rd. M16: W Ran 4C 114
  SK3: Stoc 6F 179 (5G 145)
  SK15: Duk, Stal 5F 107
Range Stadium 1D 130
Range St. BL3: Bolt 3B 48
  M11: Man 5E 103
Rankin Cl. M15: Man 2C 114
Rankine Ter. BL3: Bolt 2B 48
Ranmore Av. M11: Man 5F 103
Rannoch Rd. BL2: Bolt 6B 34
Ransfield Rd. M21: Chor 6H 113
Ranulph Ct. M6: Sal 6D 84
             (off King St.)
Ranworth Av. SK4: Stoc 1B 144
Ranworth Cl. BL1: Bolt 5E 19
  M11: Man 5C 102
Raper St. OL4: O'ham 1A 76
Raphael St. BL1: Bolt 3B 32
Rappax Rd. WA15: Hale 5A 152
Rasbottom St. BL3: Bolt 2B 48

Raspberry La. M30: Irl 2F **109**
   M44: Irl 3D **108**
Rassbottom Brow SK15: Stal 3D **106**
Rassbottom Ind. Est.
   SK15: Stal 3D **106**
Rassbottom St. SK15: Stal 3D **106**
Rastell Wlk. M9: Man 6A **72**
   (off Ravenswood Dr.)
Ratcliffe Av. M44: Irl 5E **109**
Ratcliffe St. M19: Man 6D **116**
   M29: Tyld 2A **80**
   SK1: Stoc 5G **179** (3H **145**)
Ratcliffe Ter. OL5: Mos 3G **93**
Ratcliffe Towers
   SK1: Stoc 4G **179** (3H **145**)
Rathan Rd. M41: Urm 3E **111**
Rathbone Ct. OL16: Roch 4C **28**
Rathbourne Av. M9: Man 5H **71**
Rathen Rd. M20: Man 4F **131**
Rathmell Rd. M23: Wyth 1F **141**
Rathmore Av. M40: Man 6A **88**
Rathvale Dr. M22: Wyth 5A **154**
Rath Wlk. *M40: Man* 6E **89**
   (off Orford Rd.)
Rathybank Cl. BL1: Bolt 4A **32**
Rattenbury Ct. M6: Sal 6C **84**
Raveden Cl. BL1: Bolt 2A **32**
Raveley Av. M14: Man 1H **131**
Ravelston Dr. M9: Man 5H **87**
Raven Av. OL9: Chad 4A **74**
Raven Cl. M43: Droy 2C **104**
Raven Ct. *M15: Man* 2C **114**
   (off Dudley Cl.)
Ravendale Cl. OL12: Roch 2C **26**
Raven Dr. M44: Irl 4E **109**
Ravenfield Gro. *BL1: Bolt* 5B **32**
   (off Gaskell St.)
Ravenglass Dr. M24: Mid 4H **55**
Ravenhead Cl. M14: Man 1H **131**
Ravenhead Sq. SK15: C'ook 6A **94**
Ravenhurst *M7: Sal* 2C **86**
   (off Up. Park Rd.)
   M7: Sal 2C **86**
   (Bury Old Rd.)
Ravenhurst Dr. BL1: Bolt 1D **46**
Ravenna Av. M23: Wyth 4D **140**
Ravenoak Av. M19: Man 1E **133**
Ravenoak Dr. M35: Fail 3A **90**
Ravenoak Rd. SK2: Stoc 1A **158**
   SK8: Chea H 5D **156**
Raven Rd. BL3: Bolt 3G **47**
   WA15: Tim 2B **140**
Ravensbury St. M11: Man 3D **102**
Ravenscar Cres. M22: Wyth 5B **154**
Ravenscar Wlk. *BL4: Farn* 2H **65**
   (off Norris St.)
Ravens Cl. M25: Pres 1C **86**
Ravenscraig Rd. M38: Lit H 3F **65**
Ravensdale Gdns. M30: Ecc 2G **97**
Ravensdale Rd. BL1: Bolt 6D **30**
Ravensdale St. M14: Man 4G **115**
Ravensfield SK16: Duk 6D **106**
Ravensfield Ind. Est. SK16: Duk . . . 4G **105**
Ravens Holme BL1: Bolt 6E **31**
Ravenside Pk. OL9: Chad 4A **74**
Ravens Pl. M25: Pres 1C **86**
Ravenstonedale Dr. OL2: O'ham . . . 2E **59**
Ravenstone Dr. M33: Sale 4E **129**
Ravenstones Dr. OL3: Dig 4E **63**
Raven St. BL9: Bury 1F **37**
   M12: Man 2F **11** (5G **101**)
   OL11: Roch 2A **26**
Ravensway M25: Pres 1B **86**
Ravens Wood BL1: Bolt 6E **31**
Ravenswood M20: Man 5D **130**
Ravenswood Av. SK4: Stoc 2C **144**
Ravenswood Ct. SK3: Stoc 1H **157**
Ravenswood Dr. BL1: Bolt 6E **31**
   M9: Man 6A **72**
   SK8: Chea H 5D **156**
Ravenswood Rd. M32: Stre 2F **113**
   SK9: Wilm 5B **172**

Raven Ter. *SK16: Duk* 4A **106**
   (off Peel St.)
Raven Way *M6: Sal* 2F **99**
   (off Salford Shop. City)
Ravenwood OL9: Chad 2F **73**
Ravenwood Dr.
   M34: Aud 1E **119**
   WA15: Haleb 6C **152**
Ravine Av. M9: Man 4A **88**
   (not continuous)
Rawcliffe Av. BL2: Bolt 6B **34**
Rawcliffe St. M14: Man 4F **115**
Rawdon Cl. M19: Man 6D **116**
Rawlyn Rd. BL1: Bolt 3F **31**
Rawpool Gdns. M23: Wyth 4G **141**
Rawson Av. BL4: Farn 6A **50**
Rawson Rd. BL1: Bolt 4A **32**
Rawsons Rake BL0: Ram 3A **12**
Rawson St. BL4: Farn 6H **49**
Rawsthorne Av. BL0: Eden 3G **13**
   M18: Man 5F **117**
Rawsthorne St. BL1: Bolt 3C **32**
   M29: Tyld 3B **80**
Rawstron St. OL12: Whitw 4A **14**
Rayburn Way M8: Man 6E **87**
Raycroft Av. M9: Man 1C **88**
Raydon Av. *M40: Man* 6H **87**
   (off Sedgeford Rd.)
Raylees BL0: Ram 5C **12**
Rayleigh Av. M11: Man 6H **103**
Raymond Av. BL9: Bury 6F **23**
   OL9: Chad 5B **74**
Raymond Rd. M23: Wyth 1H **141**
Raymond St. M27: Pen 2H **83**
Rayner La. OL7: A Lyme 4D **104**
Rayners Cl. SK15: Stal 4D **106**
Rayner St. SK1: Stoc 3B **146**
Raynham Av. M20: Man 6F **131**
Raynham St. OL6: A Lyme 2A **106**
Raysonhill Dr. M9: Man 1G **87**
Reabrook Av. M12: Man 1B **116**
Reach, The M28: Walk 1A **82**
Read Cl. BL9: Bury 6D **36**
   OL2: Shaw 1H **59**
Reade Av. M41: Urm 6A **110**
Reade Ho. *M41: Urm* 6B **110**
   (off Flixton Rd.)
Reading Cl. M11: Man 5E **103**
Reading Dr. M33: Sale 5F **127**
Reading St. M6: Sal 6H **85**
Reading Wlk. M34: Dent 6F **119**
Readitt Wlk. *M11: Man* 3D **102**
   (off Coghlan Cl.)
Read St. SK14: Hyde 4A **120**
Read St. W. SK14: Hyde 4A **120**
Reaney Wlk. *M12: Man* 1C **116**
   (off Stonehurst Cl.)
Reather Wlk. M40: Man 1F **7**
Rebecca Cl. *OL16: Miln* 6F **29**
   (off Harbour La.)
Rebecca St. M8: Man 3E **87**
Recreation Rd. M35: Fail 2A **90**
Recreation St. BL2: Bolt 6A **20**
   BL3: Bolt 3C **48**
   M25: Pres 5A **70**
Rectory Av. M8: Man 2E **87**
   M25: Pres 5H **69**
Rectory Cl. M26: Rad 3D **52**
   M34: Dent 5G **119**
Rectory Ct. SK6: Mar 6D **148**
Rectory Flds. SK1: Stoc 2A **146**
Rectory Gdns. M25: Pres 5H **69**
Rectory Grn. M25: Pres 4G **69**
   SK1: Stoc 2H **179** (2A **146**)
Rectory Gro. M25: Pres 6H **69**
Rectory Hill BL9: Bury 1B **38**
Rectory La. BL9: Bury 1B **38**
   M25: Pres 4G **69**
   M26: Rad 4B **52**
Rectory Rd. M8: Man 2D **86**
Rectory St. M24: Mid 6B **56**
Redacre SK12: Poy 1F **169**
Redacre Rd. M18: Man 1G **117**

Red Bank BL9: Bury 5C **24**
   M4: Man 2A **6** (2E **101**)
   M8: Man 2A **6** (1E **101**)
Red Bank Rd. M26: Rad 2H **51**
Redbarn Cl. SK6: Bred 5F **135**
Redbourne Dr. M41: Urm 3B **110**
Redbrick Ct. OL7: A Lyme 4G **105**
Red Bri. BL2: Bolt 4C **34**
Redbridge Gro. *M21: Chor* 1G **129**
   (off Crossland Rd.)
Redbrook Av. M40: Man 6A **88**
Redbrook Cl. BL4: Farn 6A **50**
Redbrook Gro. *SK9: Wilm* 6H **165**
   (off Colshaw Dr.)
Redbrook Rd. M31: Part 6C **124**
   WA15: Tim 5D **140**
Red Brook St. OL11: Roch 4F **27**
Redbrow Hollow SK6: Comp 1E **149**
Redburn Rd. M23: Wyth 4H **141**
Redby St. M11: Man 6D **102**
Redcar Av. M20: Man 3F **131**
   M41: Urm 3C **110**
Redcar Cl. OL1: O'ham 6H **59**
   SK7: H Gro 4G **159**
Redcar Lodge *M27: Pen* 4C **84**
   (off Redcar Rd.)
Redcar Rd. BL1: Bolt 1H **31**
   BL3: Lit L 4C **50**
   M27: Pen 4C **84**
Redcar St. OL12: Roch 1A **178** (3G **27**)
Redcliffe Ct. M25: Pres 1H **85**
Redclyffe Av. M14: Man 4G **115**
Redclyffe Circ. M41: Urm 1E **111**
Redclyffe Rd. M20: Man 4E **131**
   M41: Urm 6F **97**
Redcot BL1: Bolt 6H **31**
Redcot Ct. M45: White 2C **68**
Redcote St. M40: Man 3C **88**
Redcourt Av. M20: Man 5F **131**
Redcroft Gdns. M19: Man 5A **132**
Redcroft Rd. M33: Sale 5G **127**
Redcross St. OL12: Roch . . . 1B **178** (2H **27**)
Redcross St. Nth. OL12: Roch 2G **27**
Reddaway Cl. M6: Sal 6G **85**
REDDISH 2G **133**
Reddish Cl. BL2: Bolt 5A **20**
REDDISH GREEN 2F **133**
Reddish La. M18: Man 3G **117**
Reddish Leisure Cen. 2G **133**
Reddish North Station (Rail) 5H **117**
Reddish Rd. SK5: Stoc 5H **133**
Reddish South Station (Rail) 2H **133**
REDDISH VALE 2A **134**
Reddish Vale Country Pk. 2B **134**
Reddish Vale Country Pk.
   Local Nature Reserve 1B **134**
Reddish Vale Farm 2A **134**
Reddish Va. Rd. SK5: Stoc 2H **133**
Reddish Vale Sports Cen.
   (NW Regional Basketball Cen.)
   . . . . 1A **134**
Reddish Vale Vis. Cen. 2B **134**
Reddyshore Brow OL15: L'ough 3A **16**
Redesmere Cl. M43: Droy 4B **104**
   WA15: Tim 5D **140**
Redesmere Dr. SK8: Chea H 1B **156**
   SK9: A Edg 5F **173**
Redesmere Pk. M41: Urm 1D **126**
Redesmere Rd. SK9: Hand 2H **165**
Redfearn Wood OL12: Roch 1D **26**
Redfern Av. M33: Sale 6E **129**
Redfern Cotts. OL11: Roch 2H **25**
Redfern Ho. SK6: Rom 1G **147**
Redfern St. M4: Man 3A **6** (3E **101**)
Redfern Way OL11: Roch 2H **25**
Redfield Cl. M11: Man 4B **102**
Redford Dr. SK7: Bram 3A **158**
Redford Rd. M8: Man 5D **70**
Redford St. BL8: Bury 2C **36**
Red Gables OL7: A Lyme 1G **105**
Redgate SK14: Hyde 1B **136**
Redgate La. M12: Man 1B **116**
   (not continuous)

Redgates Wlk. M21: Chor 6H **113**
(off Ransfield Rd.)
Redgate Way BL4: Farn 6D **48**
Redgrave Ho. WA14: Alt 3B **174**
Redgrave Pas. OL4: O'ham 1B **76**
Redgrave St. OL4: O'ham 1A **76**
Redgrave Wlk. M19: Man 6E **117**
Red Hall St. OL4: O'ham 3A **76**
Redhill Dr. SK6: Bred 6D **134**
Redhill Gro. BL1: Bolt 1E **175**
Redhill St. M4: Man 5D **6** (4F **101**)
Red Ho. La. WA14: D Mas 4A **138**
Redhouse La. SK6: Bred 5F **135**
SK12: Dis 1H **171**
Redington Cl. M28: Wors 5E **81**
Redisher Cft. BL0: Ram 6A **12**
Redisher La. BL8: Haw 1H **21**
Redland Av. SK5: Stoc 4H **133**
Redland Cl. OL15: L'ough 3H **17**
Redland Cres. M21: Chor 3H **129**
Red La. BL2: Bolt 4H **33**
(not continuous)
OL3: Dig 1E **63**
OL12: Roch 1B **28**
SK12: Dis 2F **171**
Red Lion St. M4: Man 4B **6** (3E **101**)
Redlynch Wlk. M8: Man 4E **87**
Redman Ga. BL2: Bolt 5D **20**
Redmans Cl. M30: Ecc 4D **96**
Redmere Dr. BL9: Bury 5G **37**
Redmere Gro. M14: Man 1G **131**
Redmire M. SK16: Duk 6D **106**
Redmires Ct. M5: Sal 4G **99**
Redmond Cl. M34: Aud 6E **105**
Redmoor Sq. M13: Man 3D **10**
Redmoss Row M27: Pen 3D **84**
Red Pike Wlk. OL1: O'ham 1G **75**
Redpoll Cl. M28: Wors 4F **81**
Red Rock La. M26: Rad 3F **67**
Red Rose Cres. M19: Man 2E **133**
Red Rose Gdns.
M33: Sale 3B **128**
M38: Walk 5E **65**
(off County Rd.)
Red Rose Retail Cen.
M5: Sal 1A **8** (4H **99**)
Red Row SK7: H Gro 5H **159**
Redruth St. M14: Man 5F **115**
Redscar Wlk. M24: Mid 6A **56**
Redshaw Av. BL2: Bolt 5F **19**
Redshaw St. M14: Man 6H **115**
Redstart Gro. M28: Wors 3H **81**
Redstone Rd. M19: Man 6H **131**
Redthorn Av. M19: Man 2B **132**
Redvale Dr. M7: Sal 5C **86**
REDVALES 6E **37**
Redvales Rd. BL9: Bury 6E **37**
Redvers St. OL1: O'ham 1D **74**
Redwater Cl. M28: Wors 5E **81**
Redwing Cen. M17: T Pk 1C **112**
Redwing Rd. BL8: G'mount 1H **21**
Redwood M33: Sale 5E **127**
OL9: Chad 2F **73**
Redwood Cl. BL3: Bolt 2A **50**
OL12: Roch 6D **14**
SK3: Stoc 3D **144**
Redwood Dr. M8: Man 6F **87**
M34: Aud 1E **119**
SK6: Bred 6F **135**
Redwood La. OL4: Lees 2C **76**
Redwood Pk. Gro.
OL16: Roch 4D **28**
Redwood Rd. OL3: Upp 2E **79**
Redwood St. M6: Sal 1F **99**
Reece Cl. SK16: Duk 5B **106**
Reeceton Gdns. BL1: Bolt 6H **31**
Reedbank Rd. M26: Rad 1A **68**
Reed Cl. BL4: Farn 1G **65**
Reed Ct. OL1: O'ham 1E **75**
(off Bradford St.)
Reedham Cl. BL1: Bolt 5A **32**

Reedham Wlk. M40: Man 1A **102**
(off Giltbrook Av.)
OL9: O'ham 5C **74**
Reed Hill OL16: Roch 2B **178** (3H **27**)
Reedley Dr. M28: Wors 3G **81**
Reedmace Cl. M28: Walk 2A **82**
Reedmaker Pl. M27: Swin 3F **83**
Reedshaw Bank SK2: Stoc 6D **146**
Reedshaw Rd. M9: Man 5G **87**
Reed St. M18: Man 1F **117**
OL1: O'ham 2G **75**
(off Hardcastle St.)
Reeman Cl. SK6: Bred 5G **135**
Reeman Ct. SK9: Wilm 5F **165**
Reeve Cl. SK2: Stoc 6F **147**
Reeve's Ct. M5: Sal 3A **98**
Reeves Rd. M21: Chor 2H **129**
Reevey Av. SK7: H Gro 3C **158**
Reform St. OL12: Roch 1B **178** (2H **27**)
Reform Wlk. M11: Man 5D **102**
Refuge St. OL2: Shaw 1H **59**
Regal Cl. M45: White 1H **69**
Regal Fold OL12: Roch 5B **16**
Regal Ind. Est. M12: Man 6C **102**
Regal Wlk. M40: Man 5E **89**
(off Lastingham St.)
Regan Av. M21: Chor 2B **130**
Regan St. BL1: Bolt 2B **32**
M26: Rad 5B **52**
Regatta Cl. OL9: Chad 6A **74**
Regatta St. M6: Sal 5F **85**
Regency Chambers BL9: Bury 4A **176**
Regency Cl. M40: Man 6H **87**
OL8: O'ham 5D **74**
Regency Ct. M33: Sale 5H **127**
OL11: Roch 4B **26**
SK2: Stoc 5A **146**
SK8: Chea H 3C **156**
SK15: Stal 3C **106**
(off Waterloo Rd.)
WA15: Hale 2C **152**
Regency Gdns. SK8: Chea H 5A **156**
SK14: Hyde 3D **120**
Regency Lodge M25: Pres 5G **69**
Regency Pk. SK9: Wilm 4C **172**
Regent Av. M14: Man 5E **115**
M38: Lit H 5G **65**
Regent Bank SK9: Wilm 4C **172**
Regent Bri. M5: Sal 5B **100**
Regent Cvn. Pk. M6: Sal 1F **99**
Regent Cinema
Marple 5D **148**
Regent Cl. OL10: H'ood 4F **39**
SK7: Bram 3F **167**
SK8: Chea H 1E **157**
SK9: Wilm 4C **172**
Regent Ct. M7: Sal 2B **86**
SK4: Stoc 4E **133**
WA14: Alt 2A **174** (1F **151**)
WA15: Haleb 5C **152**
(off Dial Rd.)
Regent Cres. M35: Fail 5G **89**
M41: Urm 1F **111**
(off The Trafford Cen.)
OL2: O'ham 5D **58**
Regent Dr. BL6: Los 6B **30**
M34: Dent 6D **118**
OL5: Mos 4H **93**
Regent Fold OL5: Mos 4H **93**
Regent Ho. M14: Man 4H **115**
SK4: Stoc 2E **179**
Regent Pl. M14: Man 3G **115**
Regent Retail Pk.
M5: Sal 1B **8** (5A **100**)
Regent Rd. BL6: Los 6B **30**
M5: Sal 1A **8** (4H **99**)
SK2: Stoc 5A **146**
WA14: Alt 2A **174** (1E **151**)
Regents, The SK9: Wilm 1F **173**
Regents Hill BL6: Los 1C **46**
Regents Pl. M5: Sal 4H **99**
Regent Sq. M5: Sal 2A **8** (5H **99**)
(not continuous)

Regent St. BL0: Ram 4A **12**
BL9: Bury 1F **37**
M24: Mid 5B **56**
M30: Ecc 3H **97**
M40: Man 6F **89**
OL1: O'ham 2G **75**
OL2: Shaw 6H **43**
(off Kershaw St. E.)
OL10: H'ood 4F **39**
OL12: Roch 1D **178** (2H **27**)
OL15: L'ough 4H **17**
Regent Trad. Est. M5: Sal 5C **4** (4B **100**)
Regent Wlk. BL4: Farn 1H **65**
Regina Av. SK15: Stal 3E **107**
Regina Ct. M6: Sal 2A **98**
Reginald Latham Ct. M40: Man 1H **7**
Reginald St. BL3: Bolt 5G **47**
M11: Man 6H **103**
M27: Swin 2F **83**
M30: Ecc 5C **96**
Reid Cl. M34: Dent 1G **135**
Reigate Cl. BL8: Bury 4B **36**
Reigate Rd. M41: Urm 1A **126**
Reilly St. M15: Man 5G **9** (1D **114**)
Reins Lee Av. OL8: O'ham 1G **91**
Reins Lee Rd. OL7: A Lyme 5G **91**
Reliance St. M40: Man 4E **89**
Reliance St. Ent. Pk.
M40: Man 5E **89**
Reliance Trad. Est. M40: Man 5E **89**
Rembrandt Wlk. OL1: O'ham 3B **60**
Rena Cl. SK4: Stoc 6F **133**
Rena Ct. SK4: Stoc 6F **133**
Rendel Cl. M32: Stre 5D **112**
Renfrew Dr. BL3: Bolt 4F **47**
Rennie Cl. M32: Stre 5E **113**
Renols Ho. M5: Sal 3B **8**
Renshaw Av. M30: Ecc 4F **97**
Renshaw Dr. BL9: Bury 2A **38**
Renshaw St. M30: Ecc 4F **97**
WA14: Alt 6G **139**
Renton Rd. BL3: Bolt 4H **47**
M22: Wyth 1B **154**
M32: Stre 5E **113**
Renwick Gro. BL3: Bolt 4A **48**
(off Maltby Dr.)
Repton Av. M34: Dent 4A **118**
M40: Man 2G **89**
M41: Urm 5H **109**
M43: Droy 2F **103**
OL8: O'ham 6D **74**
SK14: Hyde 4C **120**
Repton Cl. M33: Sale 6F **127**
Reservoir Gdns. M28: Walk 5H **65**
(off Worsley Rd. Nth.)
Reservoir Rd. SK3: Stoc 4F **145**
Reservoir St. M3: Sal 2F **5** (2C **100**)
M6: Sal 3F **99**
OL16: Roch 3C **28**
Residences, The M25: Pres 6A **70**
Retford Av. OL16: Roch 1B **42**
Retford Cl. BL8: Bury 6E **23**
Retford St. OL4: O'ham 4H **75**
Retiro St. OL1: O'ham 3H **177** (2F **75**)
Retley Pas. OL1: O'ham 3F **177**
Retreat, The M28: Wors 3B **82**
SK6: Rom 2A **148**
Reuben St. SK4: Stoc 5G **133**
Revers St. BL8: Bury 2D **36**
Reveton Grn. SK7: Bram 3A **158**
Rex Bldgs. SK9: Wilm 3E **173**
Rexcine Way SK14: Hyde 2E **121**
Rex Ct. OL4: Grot 3F **77**
Reynard Ct. M13: Man 3A **116**
Reynard Rd. M21: Chor 2H **129**
Reynard St. SK14: Hyde 4B **120**
Reynell Rd. M13: Man 5B **116**
Reyner St. M1: Man 1A **10**
OL6: A Lyme 3C **106**
Reynolds Dr. M18: Man 1F **117**
SK6: Mar B 3F **149**
Reynolds M. SK9: Wilm 1H **173**
Reynolds Rd. M16: Old T 3A **114**

Reynold St. SK14: Hyde 5B **120**
Rhine, The M15: Man 3G **9**
Rhine Cl. BL8: Tot 4H **21**
Rhine Dr. M8: Man 6C **86**
Rhiwlas Dr. BL9: Bury 5F **37**
Rhode Ho's. SK6: Mar 2D **160**
RHODES .2G **71**
Rhodes Av. OL3: Upp 6E **63**
OL4: Lees 4D **76**
RHODES BANK 4H **177** (3F **75**)
Rhodes Bank
OL1: O'ham 4H **177** (3F **75**)
Rhodes Bus. Pk. M24: Mid 2G **71**
Rhodes Cres. OL11: Roch 2H **41**
Rhodes Dr. BL9: Bury 5G **53**
RHODES GREEN 1F **71**
Rhodes Hill OL4: Lees 4D **76**
Rhodes St. OL1: O'ham . . .3H **177** (2G **75**)
OL2: Shaw 4G **59**
OL4: Lees 3D **76**
OL12: Roch 6B **16**
SK14: Hyde 4A **120**
Rhodes St. Nth. SK14: Hyde 4A **120**
Rhode St. BL8: Tot 5H **21**
Rhos Av. M14: Man 1A **132**
M24: Mid 2C **72**
SK8: Chea H 4B **156**
Rhos Dr. SK7: H Gro 4D **158**
Rhosleigh Av. BL1: Bolt 1C **32**
Rhyddings, The BL9: Bury 4C **24**
Rial Pl. M15: Man 6A **10**
Rialto Gdns. M7: Sal 5C **86**
Ribble Av. BL2: Bolt 6A **34**
OL9: Chad 6G **57**
OL15: L'ough 3F **17**
Ribble Dr. BL4: Kea 4C **66**
BL9: Bury 3F **23**
M28: Wors 5D **80**
M45: White 6G **53**
Ribble Gro. OL10: H'ood 2E **39**
Ribblehead Ct. M26: Rad 1E **67**
Ribble Rd. OL8: O'ham 6C **74**
Ribblesdale Cl. OL10: H'ood 6A **40**
Ribblesdale Dr. M40: Man 6G **87**
Ribblesdale Rd. BL3: Bolt 3B **48**
Ribble St. OL11: Roch 1G **41**
Ribbleton Cl. BL8: Bury 4H **35**
Ribble Wlk. *M43: Droy* 5A **104**
(off Ellen St.)
Ribchester Dr. BL9: Bury 6D **36**
Ribchester Gro. BL2: Bolt 4A **34**
Riber Bank SK13: Gam 6G **123**
Riber Cl. *SK13: Gam* 6G **123**
(off Baslow M.)
Riber Fold *SK13: Gam* 6G **123**
(off Baslow M.)
Riber Grn. *SK13: Gam* 6G **123**
(off Baslow M.)
Ribston St. M15: Man 6E **9** (1C **114**)
Rice St. M3: Man 1E **9** (5C **100**)
Richard Burch St.
BL9: Bury 1D **176** (2F **37**)
Richard Reynolds Ct. *M44: Cad* . . .3C **124**
(off Dean Rd.)
Richards Cl. M34: Aud 6E **105**
Richardson Cl. M45: White 6F **53**
Richardson Rd. M30: Ecc 3G **97**
Richardson St. M11: Man 6G **103**
SK1: Stoc 4A **146**
Richard St. BL0: Ram 2E **13**
M26: Rad 4H **51**
OL11: Roch 5C **178** (5H **27**)
SK1: Stoc 6H **133**
Richbell Cl. M44: Irl 2C **124**
Richborough Cl. M7: Sal 6C **86**
Richelieu St. BL3: Bolt 3E **49**
Richmal Ter. BL0: Ram 2B **12**
Richmond Av. M25: Pres 2A **86**
M41: Urm 5G **111**
OL2: Shaw 3D **58**
OL9: Chad 5A **74**
SK9: Hand 2H **165**
Richmond Cl. BL8: Tot 5H **21**

Richmond Cl. M33: Sale 6F **129**
M45: White 2D **68**
OL2: Shaw 2H **59**
OL5: Mos 3A **94**
OL16: Roch 2C **42**
SK15: Stal 4E **107**
SK16: Duk 1B **120**
Richmond Ct. M3: Sal 3C **4**
M9: Man 4E **71**
(off Deanswood Dr.)
M13: Man 3H **115**
M34: Aud 1E **119**
SK2: Stoc 6D **146**
WA14: Bow 3D **150**
Richmond Cres. OL5: Mos 3A **94**
Richmond Dr. M28: Wors 3E **83**
Richmond Gdns. BL3: Bolt 4F **49**
Richmond Grn. SK7: Bram 1H **167**
WA14: Bow 3D **150**
Richmond Gro. BL4: Farn 6E **49**
M13: Man 3H **115**
M30: Ecc 2G **97**
SK8: Chea H 3B **156**
Richmond Gro. E. M12: Man 2A **116**
Richmond Hill M3: Sal 2E **5**
SK14: Hyde 6D **120**
WA14: Bow 3D **150**
Richmond Hill Rd. SK8: Chea 6G **143**
Richmond Ho. *M27: Pen* 1H **83**
(off Berry St.)
SK15: Stal 4E **107**
(off Grosvenor St.)
Richmond Pk. M14: Man 6H **115**
Richmond Rd. M14: Man 1H **131**
M17: T Pk 6A **98**
M28: Wors 4C **80**
M34: Dent 4A **118**
M35: Fail 3A **90**
SK4: Stoc 1B **144**
SK6: Rom 6A **136**
SK16: Duk 1B **120**
WA14: Alt 1A **174** (6F **139**)
WA14: Bow 3D **150**
Richmond St. BL9: Bury 5E **37**
M1: Man 1B **10** (5E **101**)
M3: Sal 2E **5** (2C **100**)
M34: Aud 1E **119**
M43: Droy 3C **104**
OL6: A Lyme 2F **105**
OL7: A Lyme 1F **105**
SK14: Hyde 5C **120**
SK15: Stal 3F **107**
Richmond Ter. SK6: Mar 4F **161**
Richmond Vw. *OL5: Mos* 2A **94**
(off Bk. Micklehurst Rd.)
Richmond Wlk. M26: Rad 1G **51**
OL9: O'ham 3D **74**
Ricroft Rd. SK6: Comp 6F **137**
Ridd Cotts. OL11: Roch 3G **25**
Riddell Ct. M5: Sal 3C **98**
Riddiough Cl. OL12: Whitw 1E **15**
Riders Ga. BL9: Bury 1D **38**
Ridge, The SK6: Mar 2E **161**
Ridge Av. SK6: Mar 1E **161**
WA15: Haleb 1C **162**
Ridge Cl. SK6: Rom 1C **148**
SK13: Had 3G **123**
Ridge Cres. M45: White 1H **69**
SK6: Mar 2E **161**
Ridgecroft OL7: A Lyme 5H **91**
Ridgedale Cen. SK6: Mar 5D **148**
Ridgedales, The OL1: O'ham 3C **60**
Ridge-End SK6: Mar 3F **161**
Ridge End Fold SK6: Mar 4E **161**
Ridgefield M2: Man 6G **5** (4D **100**)
Ridgefield St. M35: Fail 4F **89**
(not continuous)
Ridgegreen M28: Wors 6E **81**

Ridge Gro. M45: White 1H **69**
RIDGE HILL 2E **107**
Ridge Hill La. SK15: Stal 3D **106**
Ridge La. OL3: Dig 2F **63**
Ridgemont Av. SK4: Stoc 1D **144**
Ridgemont Wlk. M23: Wyth 1F **141**
Ridge Pk. SK7: Bram 1F **167**
Ridge Rd. SK6: Mar 1E **161**
Ridge Wlk. M9: Man 6H **71**
Ridgeway M27: Clif 2B **84**
Ridgeway, The SK12: Dis 6G **161**
Ridgeway Gates BL1: Bolt . . .3F **175** (6D **32**)
Ridgeway Rd. WA15: Tim 6C **140**
Ridgewood Av. M40: Man 6H **87**
OL9: Chad 1G **73**
Ridgmont Dr. M28: Wors 5D **80**
Ridgmont Rd. SK7: Bram 2G **167**
Ridgway, The SK6: Rom 2G **147**
Ridgway St. M40: Man 3G **7** (3H **101**)
Ridgway St. E. M4: Man 4G **7** (3H **101**)
Riding Cl. M29: Ast 4B **80**
M33: Sale 5F **129**
Riding Fold M43: Droy 2D **104**
Ridingfold La. M28: Wors 6C **82**
Riding Ga. BL2: Bolt 5A **20**
Riding Ga. M. BL2: Bolt 5A **20**
Ridings, The SK9: Wilm 5A **172**
Ridings Ct. OL3: Dob 5C **62**
Ridings Rd. SK13: Had 2H **123**
Ridings St. M11: Man 5D **102**
M40: Man 6B **88**
Ridings Way OL9: Chad 3B **74**
Ridley Dr. WA14: Tim 2G **139**
Ridley Gro. M33: Sale 6F **129**
Ridley St. OL4: O'ham 3G **75**
Ridley Wlk. *M15: Man* 2E **115**
(off Wellhead Cl.)
Ridling La. SK14: Hyde 5C **120**
Ridsdale Av. M20: Man 3E **131**
Ridsdale Wlk. *M6: Sal* 6G **85**
(off Langley Rd. Sth.)
Ridyard St. M38: Lit H 4F **65**
Riefield BL1: Bolt 2H **31**
Rifle Rd. M33: Sale 4F **129**
Rifle St. OL1: O'ham 1G **177** (1F **75**)
Riga Rd. M14: Man 6G **115**
Riga St. M4: Man 3B **6** (3E **101**)
Rigby Av. M26: Rad 2C **52**
Rigby Ct. BL3: Bolt 3D **48**
(not continuous)
OL12: Roch 1A **26**
Rigby La. BL2: Bolt 5G **19**
Rigby St. BL3: Bolt 3D **48**
M7: Sal 4B **86**
WA14: Alt 2F **151**
Rigby Wlk. M7: Sal 5C **86**
Rigel Pl. M7: Man 1B **4**
Rigel St. M4: Man 2F **7** (2G **101**)
Righton Gallery 5A **10**
Rigi Mt. OL2: O'ham 1D **58**
Rigton Cl. M12: Man 2C **116**
Riley Cl. M33: Sale 2D **138**
Riley Ct. BL1: Bolt 4D **32**
BL8: Bury 3C **36**
Rileys Snooker Club 2D **116**
Rileywood Cl. SK6: Rom 2F **147**
Rilldene Wlk. OL11: Roch 3H **25**
Rimington Fold M24: Mid 4H **55**
Rimmer Cl. M11: Man 5A **102**
Rimmington Cl. M9: Man 1C **88**
Rimmon Cl. OL3: G'fld 4D **78**
Rimsdale Cl. SK8: Gat 2E **155**
Rimsdale Dr. M40: Man 3E **89**
Rimsdale Wlk. BL3: Bolt 2E **47**
Rimworth Dr. M40: Man 1F **7** (1G **101**)
Ringcroft Gdns. M40: Man 2D **88**
Ringford Wlk. M40: Man 6A **88**
RINGLEY .2F **67**
RINGLEY BROW 1F **67**
Ringley Chase M26: Rad 1D **66**
M45: White 1D **68**
Ringley Cl. M45: White 1D **68**

Ringley Dr.—Robeson Way

Ringley Dr. M45: White 1D **68**
Ringley Gro. BL1: Bolt 6C **18**
Ringley Hey M45: White 1D **68**
Ringley Mdws. M26: Rad 2E **67**
Ringley M. M26: Rad 1B **68**
Ringley Old Brow M26: Rad 2E **67**
Ringley Pk. M45: White 1D **68**
Ringley Rd. M26: Rad 1D **66**
(not continuous)
M45: White 1C **68**
Ringley Rd. W. M26: Rad 1G **67**
Ringley St. M9: Man 3H **87**
Ringlow Av. M27: Swin 4E **83**
Ringlow Pk. Rd. M27: Swin 5E **83**
Ring Lows La. OL12: Roch 5H **15**
Ringmer Dr. M22: Wyth 4A **154**
Ringmere Ct. *OL1: O'ham 1E **75***
(off Godson St.)
Ringmore Rd. SK7: Bram 3A **158**
Ring O' Bells La. SK12: Dis 1H **171**
Rings Cl. M35: Fail 5H **89**
Ringstead Cl. SK9: Wilm 6H **165**
Ringstead Dr. M40: Man 1E **7** (1G **101**)
SK9: Wilm 6H **165**
Ringstone Cl. M25: Pres 6G **69**
RINGWAY .1F 163
Ringway Gro. M33: Sale 1E **141**
Ringway M. M22: Shar 6C **142**
Ringway Rd. M22: Wyth 6C **154**
M90: Man A 6A **154**
Ringway Rd. W. M22: Man A 5A **154**
M90: Man A 5A **154**
Ringway Trad. Est. M22: Wyth 5C **154**
Ringwood Av. BL0: Ram 5A **12**
M12: Man 5D **116**
M26: Rad 6B **52**
M34: Aud 4C **104**
SK7: H Gro 4B **158**
SK14: Hyde 6E **121**
Ringwood Way OL9: Chad 1C **74**
Rink St. M14: Man 2H **131**
Ripley Av. SK2: Stoc 1B **158**
SK8: Chea H 2D **166**
Ripley Cl. M4: Man 1G **11** (5H **101**)
SK7: H Gro 5E **159**
Ripley Cres. M41: Urm 2B **110**
Ripley St. BL2: Bolt 1F **33**
Ripley Way M34: Dent 1F **135**
Ripon Av. BL1: Bolt 4F **31**
M45: White 5F **53**
Ripon Cl. BL3: Lit L 4B **50**
M26: Rad 2D **52**
M45: White 5F **53**
OL9: Chad 3B **74**
SK1: Stoc 5G **179** (3H **145**)
WA15: Hale 4C **152**
Ripon Cres. M32: Stre 4H **111**
Ripon Dr. BL1: Bolt 4F **31**
Ripon Gro. M33: Sale 3H **127**
Ripon Hall Av. BL0: Ram 5B **12**
Ripon Rd. M32: Stre 4H **111**
Ripon St. M15: Man 2E **115**
OL1: O'ham 1D **74**
OL6: A Lyme 2A **106**
Ripon Wlk. SK6: Rom 2G **147**
Rippenden Av. M21: Chor 5G **113**
Rippingham Rd. M20: Man 2F **131**
Rippleton Rd. M22: Wyth 1C **154**
Ripponden Rd. OL1: O'ham 1A **76**
OL3: Dens 3G **45**
OL4: O'ham 1A **76**
Ripponden St. OL1: O'ham 6A **60**
Ripton Wlk. *M9: Man 5F **71***
(off Selston Rd.)
Risbury Wlk. *M40: Man 5E **89***
(off Bridlington Cl.)
Rise, The OL4: Spri 2D **76**
Rises, The SK13: Had 2H **123**
Rishton Av. BL3: Bolt 5D **48**
Rishton La. BL3: Bolt 4D **48**
Rishworth Cl. SK2: Stoc 6D **146**
Rishworth Dr. M40: Man 3G **89**
Rishworth Ri. OL2: Shaw 4F **43**
Rising La. OL8: O'ham 1E **91**
Rising La. Cl. OL8: O'ham 1E **91**
Risley Av. M9: Man 3H **87**
Risley St. OL1: O'ham 1G **177** (1F **75**)
Rissington Av. M23: Wyth 5H **141**
Rita Av. M14: Man 4F **115**
Ritson Cl. M18: Man 1D **116**
Riva Rd. M19: Man 1H **143**
River Bank, The M26: Rad 1C **66**
Riverbank OL3: Dob 6B **62**
Riverbank Dr. BL8: Bury 1A **176** (2D **36**)
Riverbank Garden *BL8: Bury 2D **36***
(off Tottington Rd.)
Riverbank Lawns M3: Sal 1E **5**
Riverbanks BL3: Bolt 2G **49**
Riverbank Twr. M3: Sal 2E **5** (2C **100**)
Riverbank Wlk. M20: Man 6B **130**
Riverbend Technology Cen.
M44: Irl .3E **125**
Riverbrook Rd. WA14: W Tim 2D **138**
Riverdale Rd. M9: Man 6E **71**
River Ho. *M43: Droy 3A **104***
(off Medlock St.)
River La. M31: Part 5D **124**
M34: Dent 4H **119**
Rivermead OL16: Miln 2H **43**
Rivermead Av. WA15: Haleb 6C **152**
Rivermead Cl. M34: Dent 2G **135**
Rivermead Rd. M34: Dent 1G **135**
Rivermead Way M45: White 1G **69**
Riverpark Rd. M40: Man 2C **102**
River Pl. M15: Man 3F **9** (6C **100**)
OL16: Miln 5F **29**
Riversdale Ct. M25: Pres 5G **69**
Riversdale Dr. OL8: O'ham 2G **91**
Riversdale Rd. SK8: Chea 5G **143**
Riversdale Vw. SK6: Wood 4G **135**
Rivers Edge, The OL12: Whitw 4A **14**
Rivershill M33: Sale 3A **128**
Rivershill Dr. OL10: H'ood 4F **39**
Rivershill Gdns. WA15: Haleb 1C **162**
Riverside BL1: Bolt 3E **33**
M7: Sal 2B **4** (2A **100**)
OL1: Chad 6G **57**
SK16: Duk 4A **106**
Riverside, The BL1: Bolt 4E **33**
Riverside Av. M21: Chor 6B **130**
M44: Irl .6F **109**
Riverside Bus. Pk. SK9: Wilm 2F **173**
Riverside Cl. M26: Rad 3D **52**
Riverside Ct. M20: Man 6D **130**
M50: Sal .5G **99**
OL12: Whitw 1B **14**
SK6: Mar B 3E **149**
Riverside Dr. BL9: Sum 1B **22**
M26: Rad 1D **66**
M41: Urm 1D **126**
OL16: Roch 1C **28**
Riverside Ho. OL3: Upp 1D **78**
Riverside M. M15: Man 3F **9**
Riverside Pk. Cvn. Site M22: Nor . . .2C **142**
Riverside Rd. M26: Rad 3D **52**
Rivers La. M41: Urm 2D **110**
Riversleigh Cl. BL1: Bolt 2F **31**
Riversmeade BL7: Bro X 4G **19**
Riverstone Bri. OL15: L'ough 4G **17**
Riverstone Dr. M23: Wyth 4D **140**
River St. BL0: Ram 3C **12**
BL2: Bolt 4H **175** (6E **33**)
M1: Man 3H **9**
M12: Man 2F **11** (5G **101**)
M15: Man 4G **9** (6D **100**)
M26: Rad 4B **52**
OL10: H'ood 2H **39**
OL16: Roch 3C **178** (4H **27**)
SK1: Stoc 6B **134**
SK9: Wilm 1E **173**
Riverton Rd. M20: Man 3F **143**
River Vw. M24: Mid 3E **73**
SK5: Stoc 2A **134**
Riverview SK4: Stoc 3B **144**
River Vw. Cl. M25: Pres 1F **85**
Riverview Ct. M7: Sal 3A **86**
Riverview Wlk. *BL1: Bolt 1B **48***
(off Bridgewater St.)
Riviera Ct. OL12: Roch 1G **25**
Rivington M6: Sal 1C **98**
Rivington Av. M27: Pen 3C **84**
Rivington Ct. M45: White 2C **68**
Rivington Cres. M27: Pen 3C **84**
Rivington Dr. BL8: Bury 4A **36**
OL2: Shaw 6B **44**
Rivington Gro. M34: Aud 5C **104**
M44: Cad 3B **124**
Rivington Hall Cl. BL0: Ram 5C **12**
Rivington Rd. M6: Sal 1C **98**
OL4: Spri 2E **77**
WA15: Hale 3H **151**
Rivington St. OL1: O'ham 6F **59**
OL12: Roch 2H **27**
Rivington Wlk. M12: Man 2B **116**
Rixson St. OL4: O'ham 6B **60**
Rix St. BL1: Bolt 3C **32**
Rixton Ct. *M16: Old T 4H **113***
(off Basford Rd.)
Rixton Dr. M29: Tyld 3A **80**
Rixtonleys Dr. M44: Irl 1F **125**
Roach Bank Ind. Est. BL9: Bury 6H **37**
Roach Bank Rd. BL9: Bury 6H **37**
Roach Ct. *M40: Man 1G **101***
(off Hamerton Rd.)
ROACHES .6A 78
Roaches Ind. Est. OL5: Mos 6A **78**
Roaches M. OL5: Mos 6H **77**
Roaches Way OL5: Mos 6A **78**
Roachill Cl. WA14: Alt 6D **138**
Roach Pl. OL16: Roch 2D **178** (3A **28**)
Roach St. BL9: Bury 3A **38**
(Bury New Rd.)
BL9: Bury 3F **53**
(Manchester Rd.)
Roach Va. OL16: Roch 1C **28**
Roachwood Cl. OL9: Chad 2G **73**
ROAD END .4D 78
Roading Brook Rd. BL2: Bolt 2C **34**
Road Knowl OL2: Shaw 1A **60**
Road La. OL12: Roch 5F **15**
Roads Ford Av. OL16: Miln 4F **29**
Roan Way SK9: A Edg 6H **173**
Roaring Ga. La.
WA15: Hale, Ring 2E **153**
Robert Bolt Theatre, The *4B 128*
(within Waterside Arts Cen.)
Robert Hall St. M5: Sal 2A **8** (5H **99**)
Robert Harrison Av. M20: Man 3D **130**
Robert Lawrence Ct. M41: Urm 6C **110**
Robert Malcolm Cl. M40: Man 6H **87**
Robert Owen Gdns. M22: Nor 3B **142**
Robert Owen St. M43: Droy 3C **104**
Robert Powell Theatre 2H 99
Robert Salt Ct. WA14: Alt 5G **139**
Roberts Av. M14: Man 3F **115**
Robert Saville Ct. *OL11: Roch 5E **27***
(off Half Acre M.)
Robertscroft Cl. M22: Wyth 1A **154**
Robertshaw Av. M21: Chor 3H **129**
Robertson Cl. M18: Man 2E **117**
Robertson St. M26: Rad 3A **52**
Roberts Pas. OL15: L'ough 1B **16**
Roberts Pl. *OL15: L'ough 6F **17***
(off Wordsworth Cres.)
Roberts St. M30: Ecc 4F **97**
Robert St. BL0: Ram 4F **13**
BL2: Bolt 6A **20**
BL8: Bury 2C **36**
M3: Man 1H **5** (2D **100**)
M25: Pres 5A **70**
M26: Rad 3A **52**
M33: Sale 5E **129**
M35: Fail 2A **90**
OL8: O'ham 6B **74**
OL10: H'ood 5A **40**
OL16: Roch 2C **178** (3A **28**)
SK14: Hyde 4A **120**
SK16: Duk 5H **105**
Robeson Way M22: Shar 5C **142**

A-Z Manchester 333

Robe Wlk.—Rooden Ct.

Robe Wlk. *M18: Man* *1F 117*
(off Briercliffe Cl.)
Robin Cl. BL4: Farn 2D **64**
Robin Cft. SK6: Bred 6D **134**
Robin Dr. M44: Irl 4E **109**
Robin Hood St. M8: Man 3D **86**
Robinia Cl. M30: Ecc 5B **96**
Robin La. M45: White 2F **69**
Robin Rd. BL9: Sum 6B **12**
WA14: W Tim 2E **139**
Robinsbay Rd. M22: Wyth 5C **154**
Robins Cl. M43: Droy 2C **104**
SK7: Bram 6G **157**
Robins La. SK7: Bram 6F **157**
Robinson Pk. *SK15: Stal* *4C 106*
(off Robinson St.)
Robinsons Fold OL4: Spri 2F **77**
Robinson's Pl. OL4: Spri 2F **77**
Robinson St. OL6: A Lyme 1H **105**
OL9: Chad 3B **74**
OL16: Roch 3C **178** (4A **28**)
SK3: Stoc 4F **145**
SK14: Hyde 4D **120**
SK15: Stal 5C **106**
Robin St. OL1: O'ham 1E **177** (1E **75**)
Robinsway WA14: Bow 4E **151**
Robinsway Rd. M22: Wyth 3B **154**
Robinwood Lodge *SK13: Gam* *6G 123*
(off Bleaklow La.)
Robson Av. M41: Urm 6G **97**
Robson St. OL1: O'ham 4H **177** (3F **75**)
Roby Rd. M30: Ecc 5E **97**
Roby St. M1: Man 6C **6**
Roch Av. OL10: H'ood 3E **39**
Roch Bank M9: Man 6D **70**
Rochbury Cl. OL11: Roch 5B **26**
Roch Cl. M45: White 6H **53**
Roch Cres. M45: White 5H **53**
ROCHDALE .... **2B 178 (3H 27)**
Rochdale Cen. Retail Cen.
OL11: Roch 5D **178** (5A **28**)
Rochdale Crematorium
OL11: Roch 4D **26**
Rochdale Ent. Generation Cen.
OL12: Roch 4A **178** (4G **27**)
Rochdale Exchange Shop. Cen.
OL16: Roch 3A **178** (3G **27**)
Rochdale FC **3E 27**
Rochdale Ho. M15: Man 2E **9**
Rochdale Ind. Cen. OL11: Roch 5F **27**
Rochdale La. OL2: O'ham 2D **58**
OL10: H'ood 3H **39**
Rochdale Old Rd. BL9: Bury 2A **38**
Rochdale Pioneers Mus. .... **2B 178 (3H 27)**
Rochdale RLFC **3E 27**
Rochdale Rd. BL0: Eden, Ram 2H **13**
BL9: Bury 3C **176** (3G **37**)
M4: Man 3C **6** (2F **101**)
M9: Man 5H **87**
M24: Mid 5C **56**
M40: Man 3C **6** (2F **101**)
OL1: O'ham 1E **177** (6E **59**)
OL2: O'ham 6C **42**
OL2: Shaw 4E **43**
OL3: Dens 2F **45**
OL9: O'ham 1E **177** (6E **59**)
OL10: H'ood 3H **39**
OL16: Miln, Roch 4E **29**
Rochdale Rd. E. OL10: H'ood 3A **40**
Rochdale Station (Rail) .... **6C 178 (5H 27)**
Roche Gdns. SK8: Chea H 1D **166**
Roche Rd. OL3: Del 2A **62**
Rochester Av. BL2: Bolt 4A **34**
M21: Chor 3B **130**
M25: Pres 1A **86**
M28: Wors 2G **81**
Rochester Cl. OL6: A Lyme 4A **92**
SK16: Duk 6E **107**
Rochester Dr. WA14: Tim 2G **139**
Rochester Gro. SK7: H Gro 2E **159**
Rochester Rd. M41: Urm 3F **111**
Rochester Way OL9: Chad 3B **74**
Rochford Av. M45: White 2D **68**
Rochford Cl. M45: White 2D **68**
Rochford Ho. *M34: Aud* *1E 119*
(off Denton Rd.)
Rochford Pl. OL10: H'ood 6B **40**
Rochford Rd. M30: Ecc 5B **96**
Roch Mills Cres. OL11: Roch 6E **27**
Roch Mills Gdns. OL11: Roch 6E **27**
Roch St. OL16: Roch 2B **28**
Roch Va. Cvn. Pk. OL16: Roch 4A **28**
Roch Valley Way OL11: Roch 5E **27**
Roch Wlk. M45: White 6H **53**
Roch Way M45: White 6H **53**
Rock, The BL9: Bury 3B **176** (3E **37**)
Rockall Wlk. *M11: Man* *4B 102*
(off Fairisle Cl.)
Rock Av. BL1: Bolt 3A **32**
Rock Bank M7: Sal 5A **86**
OL5: Mos 2G **93**
Rockdove Av. M15: Man 4G **9** (6D **100**)
Rocket St. M3: Sal 5D **4** (4B **100**)
Rockfield Dr. *M9: Man* *3A 88*
(off Dalbeattie St.)
Rock Fold BL7: Eger 2D **18**
Rock Gdns. SK14: Hyde 2C **136**
Rock Hall Vis. Cen. **5A 50**
Rockhampton St. M18: Man 2F **117**
Rockhouse Cl. M30: Ecc 5E **97**
Rockingham Cl.
M12: Man 6H **11** (1H **115**)
OL2: Shaw 5E **43**
Rockland Wlk. M40: Man 1E **89**
Rockley Gdns. M6: Sal 1H **99**
Rocklyn Av. M40: Man 1E **89**
Rocklynes SK6: Rom 1H **147**
Rockmead Dr. M9: Man 6A **72**
Rock Nook OL15: L'ough 2B **16**
Rock Rd. M41: Urm 5H **111**
Rock St. BL0: Ram 2E **13**
M7: Sal 5B **86**
M11: Man 5G **103**
OL1: O'ham 3G **177** (2F **75**)
(not continuous)
OL7: A Lyme 6G **91**
(not continuous)
OL10: H'ood 4A **40**
SK14: Hyde 2C **136**
Rock Ter. BL7: Eger 2D **18**
OL5: Mos 5G **93**
(Manchester Rd.)
OL5: Mos 6H **77**
(Stockport Rd.)
SK16: Duk 4A **106**
Rocky La. M27: Swin 6F **83**
M30: Ecc 6F **83**
Roda St. M9: Man 4B **88**
Rodborough Gdns. M23: Wyth 2F **153**
Rodborough Rd. M23: Wyth 2F **153**
Rodeheath Cl. SK9: Wilm 2G **173**
Rodenhurst Dr. M40: Man 4C **88**
Rodepool Cl. SK9: Wilm 5H **165**
Rodmell Av. M40: Man 6H **87**
Rodmell Cl. BL7: Bro X 4D **18**
Rodmill Ct. M14: Man 6G **115**
Rodmill Dr. SK8: Gat 1E **155**
Rodney Ct. M4: Man 2E **7**
Rodney Dr. SK6: Bred 4G **135**
Rodney St. M3: Sal 5D **4** (4B **100**)
M4: Man 3F **7** (3G **101**)
OL6: A Lyme 1B **106**
OL11: Roch 3D **40**
Roeacre Bus. Pk. OL10: H'ood 3A **40**
Roeacre Ct. OL10: H'ood 3H **39**
Roeacre St. OL10: H'ood 3A **40**
Roebuck Ct. M33: Sale 5A **128**
Roebuck La. M33: Sale 5A **128**
OL4: O'ham 4E **61**
Roebuck Low OL4: O'ham 4E **61**
Roebuck M. M33: Sale 6B **128**
Roeburn Wlk. M45: White 1A **70**
ROE CROSS **1B 122**
Roe Cross Grn. SK14: Mot 2B **122**
Roe Cross Ind. Pk. SK14: Mot 2C **122**
Roe Cross Rd. SK14: Mot 1B **122**
Roedean Gdns. M41: Urm 5G **109**
Roefield OL12: Roch 3E **27**
Roefield Ter. OL12: Roch 3E **27**
ROE GREEN **3C 82**
Roe Grn. M28: Wors 3B **82**
Roe Grn. Av. M28: Wors 3C **82**
Roe La. OL4: O'ham 4B **76**
Roe St. M4: Man 2E **7** (2G **101**)
OL12: Roch 2E **27**
Rogate Dr. M23: Wyth 6G **141**
Roger Byrne Cl. M40: Man 6D **88**
Roger Cl. SK6: Rom 2F **147**
Roger Hey SK8: Chea H 2D **156**
Rogerson Cl. WA15: Tim 4C **140**
Rogerstead BL3: Bolt 1A **48**
Roger St. M4: Man 1B **6** (2E **101**)
Rokeby Av. M32: Stre 6D **112**
Roker Av. M13: Man 5B **116**
Roker Pk. Av. M34: Aud 6D **104**
Roland Rd. BL3: Bolt 3A **48**
SK5: Stoc 2H **133**
Rolla St. M3: Sal 3F **5** (3C **100**)
Rollesby Cl. BL8: Bury 6D **22**
Rolleston Av. M40: Man 3G **7** (3H **101**)
Rollins La. SK6: Mar B 2E **149**
Rolls Cres. M15: Man 6E **9** (1C **114**)
Rollswood Dr. M40: Man 5C **88**
Romana Sq. WA14: Tim 3G **139**
Roman Ct. M7: Sal 6B **86**
Roman Lakes Leisure Pk. **1F 161**
Roman Rd. M25: Pres 2G **85**
M35: Fail 3A **90**
OL2: O'ham 4D **58**
OL8: O'ham 3A **90**
SK4: Stoc 1F **179** (1G **145**)
(not continuous)
Roman St. M4: Man 4B **6**
M26: Rad 4G **51**
OL5: Mos 6H **77**
Romer Av. M40: Man 2G **89**
Rome Rd. M40: Man 2E **7** (2G **101**)
Romer St. BL2: Bolt 6G **33**
Romford Av. M34: Dent 3G **119**
Romford Cl. OL8: O'ham 4E **75**
Romford Rd. M33: Sale 3G **127**
Romford Wlk. M9: Man 6E **71**
ROMILEY **1A 148**
Romiley Cres. BL2: Bolt 5H **33**
Romiley Dr. BL2: Bolt 5H **33**
Romiley Pools & Target Fitness Cen.
.... **1H 147**
Romiley Pct. SK6: Rom 1A **148**
Romiley Station (Rail) **1A 148**
Romiley St. M6: Sal 6D **84**
SK1: Stoc 1B **146**
Romley Rd. M41: Urm 3F **111**
Romney Av. OL11: Roch 3H **41**
Romney Chase BL1: Bolt 1C **32**
Romney Rd. BL1: Bolt 3E **31**
Romney St. M6: Sal 6H **85**
M40: Man 3C **88**
OL6: A Lyme 4D **174** (2A **106**)
Romney Towers SK5: Stoc 3B **134**
Romney Wlk. OL9: Chad 3B **74**
Romney Way SK5: Stoc 3B **134**
Romsdal Vs. SK6: Rom 1H **147**
Romsey OL12: Roch 2A **178** (3G **27**)
Romsey Av. M24: Mid 4B **56**
Romsey Dr. SK8: Chea H 1E **167**
Romsey Gdns. M23: Wyth 5G **141**
Romsley Cl. M12: Man 1C **116**
Romsley Dr. BL3: Bolt 4A **48**
Ronaldsay Gdns. M5: Sal 4E **99**
Ronald St. M11: Man 4F **103**
OL4: O'ham 2A **76**
OL11: Roch 4E **41**
Rona Wlk. M12: Man 2B **116**
Rondin Rd. M12: Man 5A **102**
Ronnis Mt. OL7: A Lyme 4F **91**
Ronton Wlk. *M8: Man* *3G 87*
(off Mawdsley Dr.)
Roocroft Ct. BL1: Bolt 4B **32**
Rooden Ct. M25: Pres 5A **70**

334 A-Z Manchester

Roods La. OL11: Roch 2G 25
Rookery Av. M18: Man 1H 117
Rookery Cl. SK15: Stal 6H 107
Rookerypool Cl. SK9: Wilm 5H 165
Rooke St. M30: Ecc 5C 96
Rookfield M33: Sale 4C 128
Rookfield Av. M33: Sale 4C 128
Rookley Wlk. M14: Man 4G 115
(off Whitecliffe Cl.)
Rook St. BL0: Ram 3C 12
M15: Man 2C 114
OL4: O'ham 4A 76
Rookswood Dr. OL11: Roch 2D 40
Rookway M24: Mid 2C 72
Rookwood OL1: Chad 6G 57
Rookwood Av. M23: Wyth 4F 141
Rookwood Hill SK7: Bram 4G 157
Rooley Moor Rd.
OL12: Roch 5C 14
(not continuous)
Rooley St. OL12: Roch 2E 27
Rooley Ter. OL12: Roch 2E 27
Roosevelt Rd. BL4: Kea 2B 66
Rooth St. SK4: Stoc 1F 145
Ropefield Way OL12: Roch 6G 15
Rope Race (Indoor Climbing) 1D 160
(within Goyt Mill)
Rope St. OL12: Roch 1B 178 (3H 27)
Ropewalk M3: Sal 2F 5 (2C 100)
Ropley Wlk. M9: Man 2B 88
(off Oak Bank Av.)
Rosa Gro. M7: Sal 5B 86
Rosalind Ct. M5: Sal 2B 8 (5A 100)
Rosamond Dr. M19: Man 4D 4 (3B 100)
Rosamond St. BL3: Bolt 3A 48
M15: Man 5A 10 (1E 115)
Rosamond St. W.
M15: Man 5A 10 (1E 115)
Rosary Cl. OL8: O'ham 2F 91
Rosary Rd. OL8: O'ham 2G 91
Roscoe Rd. M44: Irl 6C 108
Roscoe St. OL1: O'ham 4H 177 (3F 75)
(not continuous)
SK3: Stoc 3F 145
Roscow Av. BL2: Bolt 5A 34
ROSCOW FOLD 5H 33
Roscow Rd. BL4: Kea 2C 66
Rose Acre M28: Wors 4F 81
Roseacre Cl. BL2: Bolt 5G 33
Roseacre Dr. SK8: H Grn 4G 155
Rose Av. BL4: Farn 6G 49
M44: Irl .6D 108
OL11: Roch 1H 25
OL15: L'ough 6F 17
Rosebank BL0: Ram 4G 13
BL6: Los 6C 30
Rose Bank Cl. SK14: Holl 2F 123
Rosebank Cl. BL2: Ain 4E 35
Rose Bank Rd. M40: Man 1D 102
Rosebank Rd. M44: Cad 5A 124
Rosebay Cl. OL2: O'ham 3F 59
Roseberry Av. OL1: O'ham 6H 59
Roseberry Av. BL0: Ram 6C 12
Roseberry St. BL3: Bolt 3A 48
OL8: O'ham 3D 74
SK2: Stoc 1D 158
Rosebery St. M14: Man 4D 114
Rose Cott. Rd. M14: Man 1F 131
Rose Cotts. M14: Man 1H 131
(off Ladybarn La.)
OL3: G'fld 3E 79
Rose Cres. M44: Irl 6D 108
Rosecroft Cl. SK3: Stoc 1G 157
Rosedale Av. BL1: Bolt 6C 18
Rosedale Cl. OL1: O'ham 6H 59
Rosedale Ct. M34: Dent 4E 119
Rosedale Rd. M14: Man 5F 115
SK4: Stoc 4F 133
Rosedale Way SK16: Duk 1A 120
Rosefield SK3: Stoc 6G 145
Rosefield Cres. OL16: Roch 4C 28
Rosefinch Rd. WA14: W Tim 2E 139
Rosegarth Av. M20: Man 5B 130

Rose Gro. BL4: Kea 2B 66
BL8: Bury 3A 36
Rosehay Av. M34: Dent 5F 119
Rose Hey La. M35: Fail 1G 103
ROSE HILL 2E 49
ROSEHILL 3E 151
Rose Hill BL0: Ram 3C 12
BL2: Bolt 2E 49
M34: Dent 4D 118
OL3: Del 4B 62
SK15: Stal 5D 106
Rose Hill Av. M40: Man 1D 102
Rose Hill Cl. BL7: Bro X 4E 19
OL6: A Lyme 6C 92
Rosehill Cl. M6: Sal 3F 99
Rose Hill Cl. M6: Sal 3F 99
OL4: O'ham 1C 76
Rose Hill Cres. OL6: A Lyme 6D 92
Rose Hill Dr. BL7: Bro X 4E 19
Rose Hill Marple Station (Rail) 5B 148
Rosehill M. M27: Clif 3F 83
(off Lit. Moss La.)
Rose Hill Rd. OL6: A Lyme 6D 92
Rosehill Rd. M27: Pen 1H 83
(not continuous)
Rose Hill St. OL10: H'ood 3F 39
Roseland Av. M20: Man 5F 131
Roseland Dr. M25: Pres 3A 70
Roselands Av. M33: Sale 1H 139
Rose La. SK6: Mar 5C 148
Rose Lea BL2: Bolt 1A 34
Rose Leigh M41: Urm 4F 111
(off Crofts Bank Rd.)
Roseleigh Av. M19: Man 2B 132
Rosemary Dr. OL15: L'ough 3F 17
SK14: Hyde 2B 136
Rosemary Gro. M7: Sal 6A 86
Rosemary La. SK1: Stoc . . .3H 179 (2A 146)
Rosemary Rd. OL9: Chad 1G 73
Rosemary Wlk. M31: Part 6D 124
(off Broom Rd.)
Rosemead Ct. SK5: Stoc 3H 133
Rosemount M24: Mid 5B 56
SK14: Hyde 2B 120
Rosemount Cres. SK14: Hyde 2A 120
Roseneath SK7: Bram 4F 157
Roseneath Av. M19: Man 6E 117
Roseneath Gro. BL3: Bolt 5B 48
Roseneath Rd. BL3: Bolt 4B 48
M41: Urm 4E 111
Rosen Sq. OL9: Chad 2B 74
Rose St. BL2: Bolt 6H 175 (2E 49)
M24: Mid 1E 73
OL9: Chad 6A 74
SK5: Stoc 6H 133
Rose Ter. SK15: Stal 4E 107
Rosethorns Cl. M24: Mid 3B 56
Rosette Wlk. M27: Swin 4H 83
Rose Va. SK8: H Grn 4F 155
Rosevale Av. M19: Man 4A 132
Roseville M. M33: Sale 5B 128
Rose Wlk. M31: Part 6C 124
SK6: Mar 5C 148
Roseway SK7: Bram 3H 157
Rosewell Cl. M40: Man 1H 101
Rosewood M34: Dent 4D 118
OL11: Roch 2A 26
SK14: Holl 2F 123
Rosewood Av. BL8: Tot 5A 22
M43: Droy 3B 104
SK4: Stoc 2C 144
Rosewood Cl. SK16: Duk 1B 120
Rosewood Cres. OL9: Chad 6B 58
Rosewood Gdns. M33: Sale 6F 129
(off Hart Av.)
SK8: Gat 5D 142
Rosewood Rd. M9: Man 4H 71
Rosewood Wlk. M23: Wyth 3C 140
Rosford Av. M14: Man 5F 115
Rosgill Cl. SK4: Stoc 1A 144
Rosgill Dr. M24: Mid 6H 55
Rosgill Wlk. M18: Man 2E 117
(off Hampden Cres.)

Rosina St. M11: Man 6H 103
Roslin Gdns. BL1: Bolt 2A 32
Roslin St. M11: Man 3F 103
Roslyn Av. M41: Urm 6A 110
Roslyn Rd. SK3: Stoc 6G 145
Rossall Av. M26: Rad 1C 68
M32: Stre 4C 112
Rossall Cl. BL2: Bolt 5G 33
Rossall Ct. SK7: Bram 1G 167
Rossall Dr. SK7: Bram 1G 167
Rossall Rd. BL2: Bolt 5G 33
(not continuous)
OL12: Roch 1A 28
Rossall St. BL2: Bolt 5G 33
Rossall Way M6: Sal 2G 99
Ross Av. M19: Man 6B 116
M45: White 3F 69
OL9: Chad 6H 73
SK3: Stoc 6G 145
Ross Dr. M27: Clif 5G 67
Rossenclough Cl. SK9: Wilm 6H 165
Rossendale Av. M9: Man 2B 88
Rossendale Cl. OL2: Shaw 6B 44
Rossendale Rd. SK8: H Grn 5G 155
Rossendale Way OL2: Shaw 5H 43
Rossett Av. M22: Wyth 5B 154
WA15: Tim 3A 140
Rossett Dr. M41: Urm 3B 110
Rossetti Wlk. M34: Dent 2G 135
(off Wordsworth Rd.)
Ross Gro. M41: Urm 5E 111
Rosshill Wlk. M15: Man 5D 8
Rossington Pk. SK13: Had 1H 123
Rossington Pl. SK13: Had 2H 123
Rossington St. M40: Man 6F 89
Rossini St. BL1: Bolt 2B 32
Rosslare Rd. M22: Wyth 3C 154
Ross Lave La. M34: Dent 1B 134
SK5: Dent 1B 134
Rosslave Wlk. SK5: Stoc 2C 134
Rosslyn Bldg., The OL11: Roch 3D 40
Rosslyn Gro. WA15: Tim 5A 140
Rosslyn Rd. M16: Old T 5G 113
M40: Man 2C 88
SK8: H Grn 4H 155
Rossmere Av. OL11: Roch 5E 27
Rossmill La. WA15: Haleb 6B 152
Ross St. OL8: O'ham 4D 74
Rostherne M14: Man 6E 115
M16: Old T 4A 114
SK6: H Lan 5C 160
Rostherne Ct. WA14: Alt 2F 151
Rostherne Gdns. BL3: Bolt 3H 47
Rostherne Rd. M33: Sale 6F 129
SK3: Stoc 6G 145
SK9: Wilm 5C 172
Rostherne St. M6: Sal 3E 99
(off White St.)
WA14: Alt 2F 151
Rosthernmere Rd. SK8: Chea H 1B 156
Rosthwaite Cl. M24: Mid 6G 55
Roston Ct. M7: Sal 3C 86
Roston Rd. M7: Sal 3C 86
Rostrevor Rd. SK3: Stoc 6G 145
(not continuous)
Rostron Av. M12: Man 1A 116
Rostron Brow SK1: Stoc 2G 179
Rostron Rd. BL0: Ram 3B 12
Rostron St. M19: Man 6D 116
Rothay Cl. BL2: Bolt 4B 34
M45: White 1A 70
Rothay Dr. M24: Mid 4A 56
SK5: Stoc 1H 133
Rothbury Av. OL7: A Lyme 1E 105
Rothbury Cl. BL8: Bury 3H 35
Rothbury Ct. BL3: Bolt 4H 47
Rotherby Rd. M22: Shar 6C 142
Rotherdale Av. WA15: Tim 6D 140
Rothermere Wlk. M23: Wyth 4E 141
(off Sandy La.)
Rotherwood Av. M32: Stre 4E 113
Rotherwood Rd. SK9: Wilm 3A 172
Rothesay Av. SK16: Duk 6A 106

Rothesay Cres. M33: Sale 1E **139**
Rothesay Rd. BL3: Bolt 4H **47**
  M8: Man .1C **86**
  M27: Pen 4C **84**
  OL1: O'ham 6A **60**
Rothesay Ter. OL16: Roch 1C **42**
Rothiemay Rd. M41: Urm 6A **110**
Rothley Av. M22: Wyth 6B **142**
Rothman Cl. M40: Man 5E **89**
Rothwell Cres. M38: Lit H 4C **64**
Rothwell La. M38: Lit H 4C **64**
Rothwell St. BL0: Ram 3B **12**
  BL3: Bolt 2C **48**
                (not continuous)
  M28: Walk 6B **66**
  M35: Fail 5H **89**
  M40: Man 5E **89**
  OL2: O'ham 4C **58**
  OL12: Roch 2B **28**
Rottingdene Dr. M22: Wyth 4A **154**
ROUGH BANK 1B **44**
Rough Bank OL12: Whitw 4E **15**
Roughey Gdns. M22: Wyth 1B **154**
Rough Hey La. OL3: Dens 2H **45**
Rough Hey Wlk. OL16: Roch 5B **28**
Rough Hill La. BL9: Bury 1B **38**
Roughlee Av. M27: Swin 3F **83**
ROUGHTOWN 1H **93**
Roughtown Ct. OL5: Mos 1H **93**
Roughtown Rd. OL5: Mos 1H **93**
Roundcroft SK6: Rom 6C **136**
Roundham Wlk. M9: Man 3A **88**
                (off Hillier St.)
Round Hey OL5: Mos 3G **93**
Roundhey SK8: H Grn 5F **155**
Round Hill Cl. SK13: Had 4H **123**
Round Hill Way BL1: Bolt . . .1G **175** (4D **32**)
Roundhill Way OL4: O'ham 6C **60**
ROUNDTHORN
  M23 . . . . .5E **141**
  OL4 . . . . .5B **76**
Roundthorn Ind. Est. M23: Wyth . . .5E **141**
                (not continuous)
Roundthorn Rd. M23: Wyth 5F **141**
  M24: Mid 2D **72**
  OL4: O'ham 3H **75**
Roundway SK7: Bram 1F **167**
Roundwood Rd. M22: Nor 4B **142**
Rountree Ho. OL9: O'ham 3D **74**
          (off Manchester St.)
Rousdon Cl. M40: Man 6H **87**
Rouse Cl. M11: Man 4B **102**
Rouse St. OL11: Roch 1E **41**
Routledge Wlk. M9: Man 3A **88**
Roving Bri. Ri. M27: Pen 3D **84**
Rowan Av. M16: W Ran 4B **114**
  M33: Sale 1C **140**
  M41: Urm 4F **111**
Rowan Cl. M35: Fail 5H **89**
  OL12: Roch 6C **14**
Rowan Ct. M14: Man 2H **131**
  SK14: Hyde 6C **120**
          (off Stockport Rd.)
Rowan Cres. SK16: Duk 6D **106**
Rowandale St. M1: Man 2G **9**
Rowan Dr. SK8: Chea H 5E **157**
Rowan Ho. OL6: A Lyme 6C **174**
Rowanlea M25: Pres 5A **70**
Rowan Lodge SK7: Bram 6H **157**
Rowan Pl. M25: Pres 6H **69**
Rowans, The BL1: Bolt 6E **31**
  M28: Wors 4C **80**
  OL5: Mos 2H **93**
Rowans Cl. SK15: Stal 2G **107**
Rowanside Dr. SK9: Wilm 1H **173**
Rowans St. BL8: Bury 1C **36**
Rowan St. SK14: Hyde 6D **120**
Rowanswood Dr. SK14: Hyde 4E **121**
Rowan Tree Dr. M33: Sale 2B **140**
Rowan Tree Rd. OL8: O'ham 2D **90**
Rowan Wlk. M31: Part 6C **124**
  SK13: Had 3G **123**
Rowan Way M7: Sal 4B **86**

Rowanwood OL9: Chad 2G **73**
Rowany Cl. M25: Pres 1G **85**
Rowarth Av. M34: Dent 1G **135**
  SK13: Gam 5F **123**
         (off Grassmoor Cres.)
Rowarth Bank SK13: Gam 5F **123**
         (off Grassmoor Cres.)
Rowarth Cl. SK13: Gam 5F **123**
         (off Grassmoor Cres.)
Rowarth Fold SK13: Gam 5F **123**
         (off Grassmoor Cres.)
Rowarth Rd. M23: Wyth 3F **153**
Rowarth Way SK13: Gam 5F **123**
         (off Grassmoor Cres.)
Rowbotham St. SK14: Hyde 1C **136**
Rowbottom Wlk. OL8: O'ham 4E **75**
Rowcon Cl. M34: Aud 2E **119**
                (not continuous)
Rowdell Wlk. M23: Wyth 1H **141**
Rowden Rd. OL4: O'ham 5C **76**
Rowe Grn. M34: Dent 4F **119**
Rowena St. BL3: Bolt 5G **49**
Rowfield Dr. M23: Wyth 2F **153**
Rowland Av. M41: Urm 4G **111**
Rowland Ct. OL16: Roch 5B **28**
Rowland Ho. OL2: O'ham 3F **59**
ROWLANDS 1D **22**
Rowlands Rd. BL9: Bury, Sum 1C **22**
Rowland St. M5: Sal 5G **99**
  OL16: Roch 5B **28**
Rowlands Way M22: Wyth 3B **154**
Rowland Way OL4: Lees 2C **76**
Rowley Dr. SK7: H Gro 5E **159**
Rowley St. OL6: A Lyme 5B **92**
ROW-OF-TREES 6A **172**
Rowood Av. M8: Man 5F **87**
  SK5: Stoc 5H **117**
Rowrah Cres. M24: Mid 6F **55**
Rowsley Av. BL1: Bolt 4G **31**
  M20: Man 5C **130**
Rowsley Cl. SK13: Gam 5G **123**
Rowsley Grn. SK13: Gam 5G **123**
              (off Edale Cres.)
Rowsley Gro. SK5: Stoc 2G **133**
  SK13: Gam 5G **123**
             (off Rowsley Cl.)
Rowsley M. SK13: Gam 5G **123**
  M32: Stre 4A **112**
Rowsley St. M6: Sal 6H **85**
  M11: Man 3B **102**
Rowsley Wlk. SK13: Gam 5G **123**
             (off Rowsley Cl.)
Rowson Ct. M33: Sale 5D **128**
                (off Oak Rd.)
Rowson Dr. M44: Cad 3B **124**
Rowton St. BL2: Bolt 2F **33**
Roxalina St. BL3: Bolt 3C **48**
Roxburgh St. M18: Man 2F **117**
ROXBURY 4A **76**
Roxbury Av. OL4: O'ham 4B **76**
Roxby Cl. M28: Walk 6F **65**
Roxby Wlk. M40: Man 1F **89**
          (off Blandford Dr.)
Roxholme Wlk. M22: Wyth 5A **154**
Roxton Rd. SK4: Stoc 3E **133**
Roxwell Wlk. M9: Man 3H **87**
           (off Alderside Rd.)
Royal, The M3: Sal 4C **4**
Royal Av. BL9: Bury 6F **23**
  M21: Chor 2G **129**
  M41: Urm 5F **111**
  M43: Droy 3B **104**
  OL10: H'ood 4H **39**
Royal Ct. Dr. BL3: Bolt 5B **32**
Royal Cres. SK8: Chea 3G **155**
Royal Exchange M2: Man 5H **5** (4D **100**)
Royal Exchange Arc. M2: Man 5H **5**
        (within Royal Exchange)
Royal Exchange Theatre 5H **5** (4D **100**)
Royal Gdns. BL0: Ram 6A **12**
  WA14: Bow 3B **150**
ROYAL GEORGE 5A **78**

Royal George Cotts. OL3: G'fld 4A **78**
Royal George St.
  SK3: Stoc 5F **179** (3G **145**)
               (not continuous)
Royal Ho. BL1: Bolt 3B **32**
           (off Tennyson St.)
Royal Oak Ind. Est.
  SK1: Stoc 5H **179**
Royal Oak Rd. M23: Wyth 4F **141**
                (not continuous)
Royal Oak Yd. SK1: Stoc 2G **179**
Royal Pennine Trad. Est.
  OL11: Roch 2F **41**
Royal Rd. SK12: Dis 2H **171**
Royal St. OL16: Roch 1C **28**
Royalthorn Av. M22: Wyth 5B **142**
Royalthorn Dr. M22: Wyth 5B **142**
Royalthorn Rd. M22: Wyth 5A **142**
Royce Av. WA15: Alt 6G **139**
Royce Ct. M15: Man 6D **8**
Royce Rd. M15: Man 5D **8** (1C **114**)
Royce Trad. Est. M17: T Pk 6G **97**
Roydale St. M40: Man 2A **102**
Royden Av. M9: Man 4H **71**
  M44: Irl 1D **124**
Roydes St. M24: Mid 5D **56**
Royds Cl. BL8: Tot 6A **22**
  M13: Man 2A **116**
Royds Pl. OL16: Roch 6A **28**
Royds St. BL8: Tot 4H **21**
  OL16: Miln 6G **29**
  OL16: Roch 6B **28**
Royds St. W. OL16: Roch 6A **28**
Royd St. BL9: Bury 1B **38**
  OL8: O'ham 5C **74**
Roy Grainger Ct. M16: W Ran 4C **114**
Roy Ho. OL2: O'ham 1D **58**
Royland Av. BL3: Bolt 4E **49**
Royland Ct. BL3: Bolt 4D **48**
Royle Barn Rd. OL11: Roch 3E **41**
Royle Cl. OL8: O'ham 6F **75**
  SK2: Stoc 6A **146**
Royle Higginson Ct. M41: Urm 6E **111**
Roylelands Bungs. OL11: Roch 2E **41**
Royle Rd. OL11: Roch 2E **41**
Royles Cotts. M33: Sale 6B **128**
Royles Sq. SK9: A Edg 5G **173**
              (off South St.)
Royle St. M6: Sal 4F **99**
  M14: Man 2H **131**
  M28: Walk 1H **81**
  M34: Dent 2F **119**
  SK1: Stoc 6H **179** (4H **145**)
ROYLEY 5C **58**
Royley OL2: O'ham 4C **58**
Royley Carr Flats SK6: Bred 6F **135**
                (off Field St.)
Royley Clough OL2: O'ham 3C **58**
Royley Cres. OL2: O'ham 4C **58**
Royley Ho. OL2: O'ham 4C **58**
                (off Lea Vw.)
Royley Rd. OL8: O'ham 5E **75**
Royley Way OL2: O'ham 4C **58**
Royon Dr. SK3: Stoc 4D **144**
Royston Av. BL2: Bolt 5F **33**
  M16: W Ran 4B **114**
  M34: Dent 4A **118**
Royston Cl. BL8: G'mount 2H **21**
Royston Ct. M16: W Ran 4B **114**
Royston Rd. M16: Old T 4H **113**
  M41: Urm 4G **111**
Roy St. BL3: Bolt 3H **47**
  OL2: O'ham 3D **58**
ROYTON .3C **58**
Royton Av. M33: Sale 1E **141**
Royton Hall Pk. OL2: O'ham 3E **59**
Royton Hall Wlk. OL2: O'ham 3E **59**
Royton Ho. OL2: Shaw 2H **59**
Royton Sports Cen. 3E **59**
Rozel Sq. M3: Man 1F **9** (5C **100**)
Ruabon Rd. M20: Man 1G **143**
Rubens Cl. SK6: Mar B 3G **149**

Ruby St. BL1: Bolt 2D 32
   BL9: Sum 6C 12
   M15: Man 6A 10 (1E 115)
   M34: Dent 5E 119
Ruby St. Pas. OL11: Roch 6A 178
Rudcroft Cl. M13: Man 5D 10 (1F 115)
Rudding St. OL2: O'ham 5G 59
Ruddpark Rd. M22: Wyth 4B 154
Rudd St. M40: Man 4C 88
Rudford Gdns. BL3: Bolt 3D 48
Rudgwick Dr. BL8: Bury 4C 22
Rudheath Av. M20: Man 2E 131
Rudman Dr. M5: Sal 2A 8 (5A 100)
Rudman St. OL7: A Lyme 4G 105
   OL12: Roch 1G 27
Rudolph St. BL3: Bolt 4D 48
Rudston Av. M40: Man 1D 88
Rudyard Av. M24: Mid 4E 57
Rudyard Dr. M33: Sale 1G 139
   SK4: Stoc 3F 133
Rudyard Rd. M6: Sal 6C 84
Rudyard St. M7: Sal 5B 86
Rufford Av. OL11: Roch 1F 41
   SK14: Hyde 5D 120
Rufford Cl. M45: White 5G 53
   OL2: Shaw 6F 43
   OL6: A Lyme 4A 92
Rufford Dr. BL3: Bolt 5B 48
   M45: White 5F 53
Rufford Gro. BL3: Bolt 5B 48
Rufford Pde. M45: White 5F 53
Rufford Pl. M18: Man 3H 117
Rufford Rd. M16: W Ran 4B 114
Rufus St. M14: Man 2A 132
Rugby Dr. M33: Sale 1A 140
Rugby Pk. SK4: Stoc 2A 144
Rugby Rd. M6: Sal 2A 98
   OL12: Roch 2A 28
Rugby Rd. Ind. Est.
   OL12: Roch 1D 178 (2A 28)
Rugby St. M8: Man 1C 100
Rugeley St. M6: Sal 6H 85
RUINS 1A 34
Ruins La. BL2: Bolt 1A 34
Ruislip Av. M40: Man 6A 88
Ruislip Cl. OL8: O'ham 5H 75
Rumbles La. OL3: Del 3B 62
Rumbold St. M18: Man 1G 117
Rumworth Rd. BL6: Los 1C 46
Rumworth St. BL3: Bolt 3B 48
Runcorn St. M15: Man 4B 8 (6A 100)
Runger La. M90: Man A 6F 153
Runhall Cl. M12: Man 1C 116
Running Hill Ga. OL3: Upp 6F 63
                 (not continuous)
RUNNING HILL HEAD 5G 63
Running Hill La. OL3: Dob 5F 63
Runnymead Ct. OL2: O'ham 3E 59
Runnymeade M6: Sal 5A 84
   M27: Swin 5A 84
Runnymede Ct. SK3: Stoc 4E 145
Runnymede Ct. BL3: Bolt 2B 48
   SK3: Stoc 5E 145
Rupert St. BL3: Bolt 3D 48
   M26: Rad 6B 52
   M40: Man 1G 103
   OL12: Roch 2E 27
   SK5: Stoc 2G 133
Rupert Ter. SK5: Stoc 2G 133
Ruscombe Fold M24: Mid 4H 55
Rush Acre Cl. M26: Rad 4G 51
Rushall Wlk. M23: Wyth 3F 153
Rush Bank OL2: Shaw 5F 43
Rushberry Av. M40: Man 1E 89
Rushbrooke Av. M11: Man 3E 103
Rushbury Dr. OL2: O'ham 3G 59
Rushcroft Cl. M9: Man 1C 88
Rushcroft Rd. OL2: Shaw 5F 43
Rushden Rd. M19: Man 5D 116
Rushen St. M11: Man 4E 103
Rushes, The SK13: Had 3H 123
Rushey Av. M22: Wyth 5A 142

Rushey Cl. WA15: Haleb 6D 152
Rushey Fld. BL7: Bro X 3D 18
Rushey Fold Ct. BL1: Bolt 3B 32
Rushey Fold La. BL1: Bolt 3B 32
Rusheylea Cl. BL1: Bolt 3A 32
Rushey Rd. M22: Wyth 6A 142
Rushfield Dr. M13: Man 4B 116
Rushfield Rd. SK8: Chea H 1C 166
Rushford Av. M19: Man 5C 116
Rushford Ct. M19: Man 5C 116
              (off Rushford Av.)
Rushford Gro. BL1: Bolt 1D 32
RUSHFORD PARK 5C 116
Rushford St. M12: Man 3C 116
Rush Gro. OL3: Upp 2D 78
Rush Hill Rd. OL3: Upp 2D 78
Rush Hill Ter. OL3: Upp 2D 78
Rushlake Dr. BL1: Bolt 4C 32
Rushlake Gdns.
   OL11: Roch 3A 26
Rushley Av. M7: Sal 5H 85
Rushmere OL6: A Lyme 5C 92
Rushmere Av. M19: Man 6D 116
Rushmere Dr. BL8: Bury 6C 22
Rushmere Wlk. M16: Old T 2B 114
Rushmoor Cl. M44: Irl 5E 109
Rush Mt. OL2: Shaw 5F 43
RUSHOLME 4H 115
Rusholme Gdns. M14: Man 5G 115
            (off Wilmslow Rd.)
Rusholme Gro. M14: Man 4G 115
Rusholme Gro. W.
   M14: Man 4G 115
Rusholme Pl. M14: Man 3G 115
Rushside Rd. SK8: Chea H 1B 166
Rush St. SK16: Duk 5D 106
Rushton Cl. SK6: Mar 6E 149
Rushton Dr. SK6: Mar 1D 160
   SK6: Rom 6A 136
   SK7: Bram 3F 157
Rushton Gdns. SK7: Bram 2F 157
Rushton Gro. M11: Man 6G 103
   OL4: O'ham 4C 60
Rushton Rd. BL1: Bolt 4H 31
   SK3: Stoc 4D 144
   SK8: Chea H 1C 166
Rushton St. M20: Man 1F 143
   M28: Walk 1H 81
Rushway Av. M9: Man 1D 88
Rushwick Av. M40: Man 6A 88
Rushworth Ct. SK4: Stoc 4E 133
Rushycroft SK14: Mot 3C 122
Rushyfield Cres. SK6: Rom 6B 136
Rushy Hill Vw. OL12: Roch 2E 27
Ruskin Av. BL4: Kea 2B 66
   M14: Man 3F 115
   M34: Aud 6C 104
   M34: Dent 6D 118
   OL9: Chad 6H 73
Ruskin Cres. M25: Pres 6F 69
Ruskin Dr. M33: Sale 5E 127
Ruskin Gdns. SK6: Bred 6G 135
Ruskin Gro. SK6: Bred 6G 135
Ruskington Dr. M9: Man 4H 87
Ruskin Rd. BL3: Lit L 3D 50
   M16: Old T 4A 114
   M25: Pres 6F 69
   M43: Droy 3A 104
   OL11: Roch 3G 41
   SK5: Stoc 6G 117
Ruskin St. M26: Rad 3C 52
   OL1: O'ham 1D 74
Rusland Ct. M9: Man 6C 72
   M33: Sale 4A 128
   SK2: Stoc 4B 146
            (off Sylvester Av.)
Rusland Dr. BL2: Bolt 3A 34
Rusland Wlk. M22: Wyth 3A 154
Russell Av. M16: W Ran 5B 114
   M33: Sale 4D 128
   SK6: H Lan 6C 160
Russell Ct. BL1: Bolt 5A 32
            (off Russell St.)

Russell Ct. BL4: Farn 1A 66
            (off Russell St.)
   M16: W Ran 4A 114
   M38: Lit H 6G 65
Russell Dr. M44: Irl 5E 109
Russell Fox Ct. SK5: Stoc 2G 133
          (off Broadstone Rd.)
Russell Gdns. SK4: Stoc 2D 144
Russell Pl. M33: Sale 4B 128
Russell Rd. M6: Sal 6B 84
   M16: W Ran 4B 114
   M31: Part 6E 125
Russell St. BL1: Bolt 5A 32
   BL4: Farn 1A 66
   BL9: Bury 1F 37
   M8: Man 1C 100
   M16: W Ran 4D 114
   M25: Pres 5H 69
   M30: Ecc 3H 97
   M38: Lit H 6G 65
   OL6: A Lyme 1B 106
   OL9: Chad 2B 74
   OL10: H'ood 3A 40
   OL11: Roch 6G 27
            (off Grove St.)
   SK2: Stoc 5A 146
   SK6: Comp 6F 137
   SK14: Hyde 4B 120
   SK16: Duk 5A 106
Russet Rd. M9: Man 2H 87
Russet Wlk. BL1: Bolt 1C 32
Russet Way SK9: A Edg 6B 172
Rustons Wlk. M40: Man 2G 89
          (off Glensdale Dr.)
Ruth Av. M40: Man 2G 89
Ruthen La. M16: Old T 3H 113
Rutherford Av. M14: Man 4F 115
Rutherford Cl. SK14: Hyde 5B 120
Rutherford Way
   SK14: Hyde 5A 120
            (Birchfield M.)
   SK14: Hyde 5B 120
             (The Mall)
Rutherglade Cl. M40: Man 5G 87
Rutherglen Dr. BL3: Bolt 1F 47
Rutherglen Wlk.
   M40: Man 6A 88
Ruthin Av. M9: Man 4G 71
   M24: Mid 3C 72
   SK8: Chea H 3A 156
Ruthin Cl. M6: Sal 3G 99
   OL8: O'ham 1B 90
Ruthin Ct. M6: Sal 3G 99
Ruth St. BL0: Eden 3G 13
   BL1: Bolt 5C 32
   BL9: Bury 1F 37
   M18: Man 4F 117
   OL1: O'ham 1H 177 (1F 75)
   OL12: Whitw 4A 14
Rutland OL11: Roch 6A 178 (5G 27)
Rutland Av. M16: Old T 4G 113
   M20: Man 3E 131
   M27: Pen 1H 83
   M34: Dent 5G 119
   M41: Urm 4G 111
Rutland Cl. BL3: Lit L 3D 50
   OL6: A Lyme 3B 106
   SK8: Gat 5F 143
Rutland Ct. M20: Man 4F 131
   SK2: Stoc 6A 146
Rutland Cres. SK5: Stoc 4D 134
Rutland Dr. BL9: Bury 5G 37
   M7: Sal 3A 86
Rutland Gro. BL1: Bolt 4A 32
   BL4: Farn 2G 65
Rutland La. M33: Sale 5F 129
            (not continuous)
Rutland Rd. M28: Walk 2G 81
   M30: Ecc 1H 97
   M43: Droy 3G 103
   M44: Cad 4B 124
   SK7: H Gro 5E 159
   WA14: Alt 5F 139

Rutland St. BL3: Bolt 3B 48
   M18: Man 1G 117
   M27: Swin 2G 83
   M35: Fail 3H 89
   OL6: A Lyme 3B 106
   OL9: O'ham 4C 74
   OL10: H'ood 2H 39
   SK14: Hyde 2B 120
Rutland Way OL2: Shaw 5A 44
Rutter's La. SK7: H Gro 3C 158
Ryall Av. M5: Sal 5H 99
Ryall Av. Sth. M5: Sal 5H 99
Ryan St. M11: Man 6G 103
Ryburn Flats OL10: H'ood 3G 39
             (off Meadow Cl.)
Ryburn Sq. OL11: Roch 5A 26
Rydal Av. M24: Mid 3B 72
   M30: Ecc 1D 96
   M33: Sale 4H 127
   M41: Urm 1C 126
   M43: Droy 4G 103
   OL2: O'ham 5C 42
   OL9: Chad 6G 57
   SK6: H Lan 5C 160
   SK7: H Gro 2C 158
   SK14: Hyde 2A 120
Rydal Cl. BL9: Bury 6E 37
   M34: Dent 5B 118
   SK8: Gat 1F 155
Rydal Ct. BL1: Bolt 4F 31
Rydal Cres. M27: Swin 5H 83
   M28: Walk 2A 82
Rydal Dr. WA15: Haleb 5D 152
Rydal Gro. BL4: Farn 2D 64
   M45: White 1G 69
   OL7: A Lyme 1G 105
   OL10: H'ood 5H 39
Rydal Ho. M28: Walk 1H 81
            (off Sandwich St.)
Rydal Mt. SK5: Stoc 5H 117
   SK9: A Edg 6B 172
Rydal Rd. BL1: Bolt 4G 31
   BL3: Lit L 4C 50
   M32: Stre 4D 112
   OL4: O'ham 2A 76
Rydal Wlk. OL4: O'ham 2B 76
   SK15: Stal 2E 107
Ryde Av. M34: Dent 1H 135
   SK4: Stoc 1D 144
Ryder Av. WA14: Alt 4G 139
RYDER BROW 4F 117
Ryder Brow M18: Man 3F 117
Ryder Brow Rd. M18: Man 3F 117
Ryder Brow Station (Rail) 3F 117
Ryder St. BL1: Bolt 3A 32
   M40: Man 1G 101
   OL10: H'ood 3H 39
Ryde St. BL3: Bolt 3G 47
Rydings La. OL12: W'le . . . .3H 15 & 4A 16
Rydings Rd. OL12: Roch 4A 16
Rydley St. BL2: Bolt 1F 49
Ryebank Gro. OL6: A Lyme 6B 92
Ryebank M. M21: Chor 6F 113
Rye Bank Rd. M16: Old T 5G 113
Ryebank Rd. M21: Chor 6F 113
Ryeburn Av. M22: Wyth 2B 154
Ryeburn Dr. BL2: Bolt 6F 19
Ryeburne St. OL4: O'ham 2A 76
Ryeburn Wlk. M41: Urm 3B 110
Ryecroft M45: White 2C 68
Ryecroft Av. BL8: Tot 5H 21
   M6: Sal .2C 98
   OL10: H'ood 3A 40
Ryecroft Bus. Cen. OL7: A Lyme 4F 105
            (off Ryecroft St.)
Ryecroft Cl. OL9: Chad 6H 73
          (not continuous)
Ryecroft Gro. M23: Wyth 4G 141
Ryecroft Ho. OL7: A Lyme 4G 105
            (off Park St.)
Ryecroft La. M28: Wors 1B 96
   M34: Aud 6E 105
Ryecroft Pk. Sports Club 4B 156

Ryecroft Rd. M32: Stre 6C 112
Ryecroft St. OL7: A Lyme 4F 105
Ryecroft Vw. M34: Aud 5C 104
Ryedale Av. M40: Man 6A 88
Ryedale Cl. SK4: Stoc 6D 132
Ryefield OL7: A Lyme 4F 105
Ryefield Cl. WA15: Tim 6C 140
Ryefield Rd. M33: Sale 1E 139
Ryefields OL12: Roch 5D 16
Ryefields Dr. OL3: Upp 6D 62
Ryefield St. BL1: Bolt 4E 33
Ryelands OL16: Roch 1B 42
Rye St. OL10: H'ood 2A 40
Rye Top La. OL3: Upp 2F 79
Rye Wlk. M13: Man 2G 115
            (off Carmoor Rd.)
   OL9: Chad 3A 74
Rygate Wlk. M8: Man 5D 86
            (off Felthorpe Dr.)
Rylance St. M11: Man 4A 102
Ryland Cl. SK5: Stoc 6H 117
Rylands Ct. M15: Man 6C 8
Rylands St. M18: Man 1G 117
Rylane Wlk. M40: Man 6A 88
Rylatt Ct. M33: Sale 4H 127
            (off Ashton La.)
Ryley Av. BL3: Bolt 2H 47
Ryleys La. SK9: A Edg 5F 173
Ryley St. BL3: Bolt 1A 48
Rylstone Av. M21: Chor 6B 130
Ryther Gro. M9: Man 4F 71
Ryton Av. M18: Man 4E 117

S

Sabden Cl. BL9: Bury 4F 23
   M40: Man 2A 102
   OL10: H'ood 3E 39
Sabden Rd. BL1: Bolt 3E 31
Sabrina St. M8: Man 6C 86
Sack St. SK14: Hyde 2B 120
Sackville Cl. OL2: Shaw 4G 43
Sackville Pl. M1: Man 2B 10
Sackville St. BL2: Bolt 6G 33
   BL9: Bury 2G 37
   M1: Man 1B 10 (5E 101)
   M3: Sal .4E 5
   OL6: A Lyme 4C 174 (2H 105)
   OL11: Roch 3E 41
Saddleback Cl. M28: Wors 5F 81
Saddlecote M28: Wors 1C 96
Saddlecote Cl. M8: Man 3F 87
Saddle Gro. M43: Droy 2D 104
Saddle St. BL2: Bolt 3F 33
Saddlewood Av. M19: Man 1H 143
SADDLEWORTH 1D 78
Saddleworth Bus. Cen. OL3: Del 3B 62
Saddleworth Bus. Pk. OL3: Dig 3E 63
Saddleworth Fold OL3: Upp 6E 63
Saddleworth Mus. & Art Gallery 1D 78
Saddleworth Swimming Pool 2D 78
Saddleworth Youth Cen. 2D 78
Sadie Av. M32: Stre 3A 112
Sadler Ct. M15: Man 6E 9 (2C 114)
Sadler St. BL3: Bolt 3E 49
   M24: Mid 6B 56
Safflower Av. M27: Swin 3F 83
Saffron Dr. OL4: O'ham 5B 60
Saffron Wlk. M22: Wyth 5B 154
   M31: Part 6D 124
            (off Cross La. W.)
Sagars Rd. SK9: Sty 3F 165
Sagar St. M8: Man 1D 100
Sahal Ct. M7: Sal 1B 100
St Agnes Rd. M13: Man 5B 116
St Agnes St. SK5: Stoc 4H 117
St Aidans Cl. M26: Rad 6H 51
   OL11: Roch 6F 27
St Aidan's Gro. M7: Sal 5H 85
St Albans Av. M40: Man 6D 88
   OL6: A Lyme 5H 91
   SK4: Stoc 4E 133

St Albans Cl. OL8: O'ham 5F 75
St Albans Ct. OL11: Roch 5G 27
St Alban's Cres. WA14: W Tim 3E 139
St Albans Cl. SK16: Roch 5A 178 (5G 27)
St Alban's Ter. M8: Man 6C 86
   OL11: Roch 5G 27
St Aldates SK6: Rom 1F 147
St Aldwyn's Rd. M20: Man 4F 131
St Ambrose Ct. OL1: O'ham 6A 60
St Ambrose Gdns. M6: Sal 3F 99
            (off Blodwell St.)
St Ambrose Rd. OL1: O'ham 6A 60
St Andrews Av. M30: Ecc 4G 97
   M43: Droy 4G 103
   WA15: Tim 4G 139
St Andrews Cl. BL0: Ram 4C 12
   M33: Sale 2E 139
   OL15: L'ough 4E 17
   SK4: Stoc 5D 132
   SK6: Rom 2H 147
St Andrews Ct. BL1: Bolt 4G 175
            (off Exchange St.)
   SK1: Stoc 2A 146
   WA15: Hale 2H 151
St Andrew's Dr. OL10: H'ood 4H 39
St Andrews Ho. M38: Walk 6F 65
St Andrews Rd. BL6: Los 6A 30
   M26: Rad 1H 51
   M32: Stre 5B 112
   SK4: Stoc 5D 132
   SK8: H Grn 4G 155
St Andrew's Sq. M1: Man . . .1F 11 (5G 101)
St Andrews St. M1: Man 1E 11 (5G 101)
   M26: Rad 1H 51
St Andrews Vw. M26: Rad 1H 51
St Annes Av. M6: Sal 2E 99
   OL2: O'ham 4D 58
St Annes Ct. M6: Sal 1F 99
            (off Brindle St.)
   M33: Sale 5C 128
   M34: Aud 1E 119
St Anne's Cres. OL4: Gras 4G 77
St Anne's Dr. M34: Dent 3G 119
St Annes Gdns. OL10: H'ood 3B 40
St Annes Mdw. BL8: Tot 4H 21
St Annes M. OL10: H'ood 3A 40
St Annes Rd. M21: Chor 2H 129
   M34: Dent 2F 119
St Annes Sq. OL3: Del 3B 62
St Anne's Rd. M34: Aud 1F 119
St Anne's St. BL9: Bury 1F 37
            (not continuous)
St Ann's All. M2: Man 5G 5
St Ann's Arc. M2: Man 5H 5
St Anns Cl. M25: Pres 6G 69
St Anns Pde. SK9: Wilm 2E 173
St Ann's Pas. M2: Man 5H 5
St Ann's Pl. M2: Man 5G 5
St Anns Rd. M25: Pres 6F 69
   OL16: Roch 3D 28
   SK7: H Gro 3C 158
St Ann's Rd. Nth. SK8: H Grn 4G 155
St Ann's Rd. Sth. SK8: H Grn 4G 155
St Ann's Sq. M2: Man 5H 5 (4D 100)
   SK8: H Grn 5G 155
St Ann's St. M27: Swin 3G 83
   M33: Sale 6F 129
St Ann St. BL1: Bolt 4C 32
   M2: Man 5G 5 (4D 100)
St Anthony's Dr. OL5: Mos 1H 93
St Asaph's Dr. M7: Sal 3D 86
   OL6: A Lyme 5H 91
St Aubin's Rd. BL2: Bolt 1F 49
St Augustine's Ct. BL2: Bolt 4F 33
            (off Thicketford Rd.)
St Augustine's Rd. SK3: Stoc 3D 144
St Augustine St. BL1: Bolt 3B 32
   M40: Man 6H 87
St Austell Av. M29: Ast 3A 80
St Austell Dr. BL8: G'mount 1H 21
   SK8: H Grn 5F 155

St Austell Rd. M16: W Ran 6C 114
St Austells Dr. M25: Pres 4H 69
  M27: Pen 4C 84
St Barnabas Dr. OL15: L'ough 3G 17
St Barnabas Sq. M11: Man 5D 102
St Bartholomew's Dr.
  M5: Sal 1A 8 (5A 100)
St Bartholomew St. BL3: Bolt 3E 49
St Bede's Av. BL3: Bolt 5H 47
St Bees Cl. M14: Man 3E 115
  SK8: Gat 2F 155
St Bees Rd. BL2: Bolt 3G 33
St Bees Wlk. M24: Mid 5A 56
St Benedict's Av. M12: Man 1B 116
St Bernards Av. M6: Sal 6A 86
St Bernards Cl. M6: Sal 6A 86
St Boniface Rd. M7: Sal 1A 100
St Brannocks Rd. M21: Chor 6A 114
  SK8: Chea H 6D 156
St Brelades Dr. M7: Sal 3D 86
St Brendan's Rd. M20: Man 2F 131
St Brendan's Rd. Nth. M20: Man . . .2F 131
St Bride St. M16: Old T 2B 114
St Brides Way M16: Old T 2B 114
St Catherines Dr. BL4: Farn 1D 64
St Catherine's Rd. M20: Man 2F 131
St Chads Av. SK6: Rom 1A 148
St Chad's Cl.
  OL16: Roch 4C 178 (4H 27)
St Chad's Ct. OL16: Roch 4C 178
St Chads Cres. OL3: Upp 1E 79
  OL8: O'ham 2D 90
St Chads Gro. SK6: Rom 1A 148
St Chads Rd. M20: Man 2H 131
St Chad's St. M4: Man 1A 6 (1E 101)
St Charles Cl. SK13: Had 2H 123
St Christopher's Av. OL6: A Lyme 5C 92
St Christophers Cl. M20: Man 3D 130
St Christopher's Dr. SK6: Rom 1G 147
St Christophers Ho. SK1: Stoc 6H 179
St Christopher's Rd. OL6: A Lyme 5B 92
St Clair Rd. BL8: G'mount 1H 21
St Clement Cl. M41: Urm 6F 111
                  (off Manor Av.)
St Clements Ct. M25: Pres 5A 70
  M44: Irl 4F 109
  OL8: O'ham 6G 177
  OL11: Roch 3E 27
St Clements Dr. M5: Sal 4A 8 (6H 99)
St Clements Fold M41: Urm 5G 111
St Clement's Rd. M21: Chor 1G 129
St Cuthbert's Fold OL8: O'ham 2G 91
St Davids Cl. SK6: Rom 1H 147
St Davids Cl. M33: Sale 6A 128
  OL6: A Lyme 4B 92
St Davids Ct. M8: Man 6E 87
St Davids Rd. SK7: H Gro 4C 158
  SK8: Chea 6C 144
St David's Wlk. M32: Stre 5A 112
St Domingo St.
  OL9: O'ham 3E 177 (2E 75)
St Dominic's M. BL3: Bolt 4A 48
St Dominics Way M24: Mid 2C 72
St Dunstan Wlk. M40: Man 5C 88
               (off Craiglands Av.)
St Edmund Hall Cl. BL0: Ram 5C 12
St Edmund's Cl. M40: Man 5A 88
St Edmund St.
  BL1: Bolt 3E 175 (6C 32)
St Edmund's Wlk. M38: Lit H 5F 65
St Elisabeth's Way SK5: Stoc 2G 133
St Elizabeth Pk. M34: Dent 4D 118
St Elmo Av. SK2: Stoc 4D 146
St Elmo Pk. SK12: Poy 3A 170
St Ethelbert's Av. BL3: Bolt 2H 47
St Gabriels Cl. OL11: Roch 4F 41
St Gabriel's Ct. OL11: Roch 3E 41
St Gabriel's Hall M14: Man 3G 115
St Gabriels M. M24: Mid 2E 73
ST GEORGES 4C 8 (1B 114)
St George's Av.
  M15: Man 4C 8 (1B 114)
  WA15: Tim 4A 140

St Georges Ct. BL1: Bolt 5C 32
                  (off Back La.)
  BL1: Bolt 2D 175
                 (All Saints St.)
  BL9: Bury 4A 54
  M15: Man 4D 8
                 (off Angela St.)
  M30: Ecc 4H 97
             (off Bentcliffe Way)
  M32: Stre 6C 112
  SK14: Hyde 5C 120
  WA14: B'ath 4D 138
St George's Cres. M6: Sal 2A 98
  M28: Walk 1H 81
  WA15: Tim 3A 140
St Georges Dr. M40: Man 4D 88
  SK14: Hyde 6B 120
St George's Gdns. M34: Dent 6G 119
St George's Ho. SK15: Stal 3E 107
             (off Cambridge St.)
St Georges Pl. M6: Sal 6G 85
               (off Gerald Rd.)
St Georges Rd. BL1: Bolt . . .3E 175 (5C 32)
  BL9: Bury 3A 54
  M14: Man 2A 132
  M31: C'ton 3H 125
  M32: Stre 5C 112
  M43: Droy 2H 103
  OL11: Roch 3B 26
St Georges Sq.
  BL1: Bolt 2G 175 (5D 32)
  OL9: Chad 6F 73
St George's St.
  BL1: Bolt 2F 175 (5D 32)
  SK15: Stal 2D 106
St Georges Way M6: Sal 1G 99
St Germain St. BL4: Farn 1G 65
St Giles Dr. SK14: Hyde 5D 120
St Gregorys Cl. BL4: Farn 2G 65
St Gregory's Rd.
  M12: Man 3F 11 (6G 101)
St Helena Rd. BL1: Bolt 3E 175 (6C 32)
St Helens Cl. WA3: Rix 6A 124
St Helens Rd. BL3: Bolt 6G 47
  BL5: O Hul 6G 47
St Helier's Dr. M7: Sal 3D 86
St Helier Sq. M19: Man 4B 132
St Helier St. BL3: Bolt 3B 48
St Herberts Ct. OL9: Chad 2B 74
St Hilarys Pk. SK9: A Edg 5G 173
St Hilda's Ct. M22: Nor 2C 142
St Hilda's Dr. OL1: O'ham . . .1E 177 (1D 74)
St Hilda's Rd. M16: Old T 2A 114
  M22: Nor 2B 142
  M34: Aud 1E 119
St Hilda's Vw. M34: Aud 2E 119
St Hugh's Cl. WA14: Tim 3G 139
St Ignatius Wlk. M5: Sal 5H 99
           (off King Edward St.)
St Ives Av. SK8: Chea 5C 144
St Ives Cres. M33: Sale 2A 140
St Ives Rd. M14: Man 5F 115
St Ives Way OL2: O'ham 3G 59
St James Av. BL2: Bolt 5A 34
  BL8: Bury 1B 36
St James Cl. M6: Sal 2B 98
  OL16: Roch 5C 42
St James Ct. BL8: Bury 1B 36
            (off St James Av.)
  M6: Sal .2B 98
  M20: Man 6F 131
            (off Moorland Rd.)
  M20: Man 2F 143
               (Millgate La.)
  OL4: O'ham 1A 76
  SK8: Chea H 1B 166
  SK14: Hat 5H 121
  WA15: Alt 2D 174 (1G 151)
St James Dr. M33: Sale 6A 128
  SK9: Wilm 3D 172
St James Gro. OL10: H'ood 3G 39
           (off W. Church St.)
  WA14: Tim 2H 139

St James Ho. M6: Sal 2F 99
           (off Pendleton Way)
  SK4: Stoc 6F 133
St James Lodge SK3: Stoc 1A 158
            (off The Crescent)
St James Rd. M7: Sal 5C 86
  SK4: Stoc 4D 132
St James's Sq. M2: Man 6H 5
St James St. BL4: Farn 2E 65
  M1: Man 1H 9 (5E 101)
  M30: Ecc 3G 97
  OL1: O'ham 2H 75
  OL2: Shaw 6H 43
  OL6: A Lyme 3B 106
  OL10: H'ood 3G 39
  OL16: Miln 5F 29
St James Ter. OL10: H'ood 3G 39
St James Way OL12: W'le 5C 16
  SK8: Chea H 1B 166
St Johns Av. M43: Droy 3B 104
St Johns Cl. SK6: Rom 1H 147
  SK16: Duk 5C 106
St Johns Ct. BL0: Ram 3C 12
                 (off Cross St.)
  M6: Sal .3F 99
              (off Milford St.)
  M7: Sal .5B 86
          (off Wellington St. W.)
  M26: Rad 5C 52
  OL4: Lees 2D 76
  OL16: Roch 5B 28
            (off St John's Dr.)
  SK14: Hyde 4D 120
  WA14: Bow 2F 151
St Johns Dr. OL16: Roch 5B 28
  SK14: Hyde 4D 120
St John's Gdns. OL5: Mos 1H 93
St John's Ind. Est. OL4: Lees 3C 76
St Johns M. BL8: Tot 4H 21
             (off Kirklees St.)
St John's Pas. M3: Man 1F 9 (5C 100)
St John's Pl. SK4: Stoc 1A 144
St Johns Rd. BL6: Los 4B 46
  M13: Man 3B 116
  M16: Old T 3A 114
  M28: Wors 4D 80
  M34: Dent 2F 119
  SK4: Stoc 1A 144
  SK7: H Gro 4B 158
  SK9: Wilm 6B 172
  WA14: Alt 2E 151
St Johns Sq. M3: Sal 4D 4
St John's St. BL4: Kea 1A 66
  M7: Sal .5B 86
  M26: Rad 5B 52
  OL9: O'ham 4C 74
St John St. M3: Man 1F 9 (5C 100)
  M27: Pen 5D 84
  M28: Walk 5G 65
  M30: Ecc 4F 97
  M44: Irl .5E 109
  OL4: Lees 3C 76
  SK16: Duk 5C 106
            (not continuous)
St Johns Wlk. OL9: O'ham 3C 74
  SK3: Stoc 3D 144
               (off Oak St.)
St Johns Wood BL6: Los 3B 46
St Joseph's Av. M45: White 2H 69
St Josephs Cl. OL2: Shaw 5A 44
St Joseph's Dr. M5: Sal 5H 99
  OL16: Roch 1B 42
St Joseph St. BL1: Bolt 3B 32
              (off Hobart St.)
St Kilda Av. BL4: Kea 3B 66
St Kilda's Av. M43: Droy 2H 103
St Kilda's Dr. M7: Sal 3D 86
St Lawrence Cl. M34: Dent 5F 119
St Lawrence Quay M50: Sal 6F 99
St Lawrence Rd. M34: Dent 4F 119
St Lawrence St.
  M15: Man 6C 8 (1B 114)
St Leonard's Av. BL6: Los 4A 30

St Leonard's Ct. M33: Sale 5H 127
St Leonards Dr. WA15: Tim 5H 139
St Leonards Rd. SK4: Stoc 4F 133
St Leonards Sq. M24: Mid 6C 56
(off Clarke Brow)
St Leonards St. M24: Mid 6C 56
St Lesmo Ct. SK3: Stoc 4E 145
St Lesmo Rd. SK3: Stoc 3D 144
St Lukes Ct. BL1: Bolt 5A 32
OL9: Chad 2A 74
OL11: Roch 6H 27
St Lukes Cres. SK16: Duk 5A 106
St Luke's Rd. M6: Sal 3D 98
St Luke St. OL11: Roch 6H 27
St Lukes Wlk. M40: Man 5C 88
(off Rollswood Dr.)
St Margaret's Av. M19: Man 3B 132
St Margarets Cl. BL1: Bolt 5H 31
M25: Pres 3A 70
WA14: Alt 1E 151
St Margaret's Gdns. OL8: O'ham 6C 74
St Margaret's Rd. BL1: Bolt 5H 31
M25: Pres 3A 70
M40: Man 6F 73
SK8: Chea 5C 144
WA14: Alt 1E 151
St Marks Av. OL2: O'ham 3G 59
WA14: Alt 6C 138
St Marks Cl. OL2: O'ham 3G 59
St Marks Cl. M22: Wyth 3A 154
(off Stoneacre Rd.)
OL9: Chad 1B 74
SK16: Duk 4H 105
St Marks Cres. M28: Walk 2H 81
St Mark's La. M7: Sal 4D 86
M8: Man 4D 86
St Marks Sq. BL9: Bury 1F 37
St Marks St. BL3: Bolt 2D 48
M19: Man 6E 117
SK6: Bred 5G 135
SK16: Duk 4H 105
St Mark's Vw. BL3: Bolt 2D 48
St Mark's Wlk. BL3: Bolt 3C 48
St Martin's Av. SK4: Stoc 1E 145
St Martin's Cl. M43: Droy 2H 103
SK14: Hyde 5E 121
St Martin's Dr. M7: Sal 3D 86
St Martins Rd. M33: Sale 3F 127
OL8: O'ham 1G 91
SK6: Mar 5E 149
St Martins St. OL11: Roch 4F 41
St Mary's Apartments M25: Pres 5G 69
(off The Coppice)
St Mary's Av. BL3: Bolt 2H 47
M34: Dent 1G 135
St Mary's Cl. M25: Pres 5G 69
OL16: Roch 1B 42
St Marys Cl. SK1: Stoc 2H 179 (2A 146)
St Marys Ct. M8: Man 2D 86
(off St Mary's Hall Rd.)
M19: Man 6C 116
(off Elbow St.)
M25: Pres 5G 69
M40: Man 3D 88
OL1: O'ham 2F 177
St Mary's Crest OL3: G'fld 4E 79
St Mary's Dr. OL3: G'fld 4E 79
SK5: Stoc 3H 133
SK8: Chea 5B 144
St Mary's Ga. OL1: O'ham 2G 177
St Marys Ga. M1: Man 4H 5 (3D 100)
OL2: Shaw 6H 43
OL3: Upp 1D 78
OL12: Roch 4A 178 (4G 27)
OL16: Roch 4A 178 (4G 27)
SK1: Stoc 2H 179 (1H 145)
St Mary's Hall Rd. M8: Man 2D 86
St Mary's Ind. Pk. SK14: Hyde 1E 121
St Mary's Parsonage
M3: Man 5F 5 (4C 100)
St Mary's Pl. BL9: Bury 4A 176 (3E 37)
St Marys Rd. M25: Pres 5G 69
M28: Walk 5G 65

St Marys Rd. M30: Ecc 3H 97
M33: Sale 4H 127
M40: Man 4D 88
SK12: Dis 2H 171
SK14: Hyde 2C 120
WA14: Bow 3D 150
(not continuous)
St Mary's St. M3: Man 5G 5 (4D 100)
M15: Man 2C 114
OL1: O'ham 1G 177 (1F 75)
St Mary St. M3: Sal 4D 4
St Mary's Vw. SK14: Hyde 2D 120
(off Bradley Grn. Rd.)
St Marys Way OL1: O'ham . . .2E 177 (2E 75)
SK1: Stoc 1A 146
St Matthews Cl. M32: Stre 6C 112
St Matthews Dr. OL1: Chad 5A 58
St Matthews Grange BL1: Bolt 4C 32
(off Mount St.)
St Matthew's Rd. SK3: Stoc 3F 145
St Matthews Ter. BL1: Bolt 4C 32
(off Barnwood Dr.)
SK3: Stoc 3F 145
St Matthews Wlk. BL1: Bolt 4C 32
(off Rushlake Dr.)
St Mawes Ct. M26: Rad 2E 51
St Michael's & All Angels Church . . .6D 174
St Michael's Av. BL3: Bolt 5F 49
SK7: Bram 6G 157
St Michaels Cl. BL8: Bury 5H 35
St Michaels Ct. M27: Ward 1F 83
M30: Ecc 5C 96
M33: Sale 3G 127
St Michaels Gdns. M45: White 6H 53
St Michael's Pl. M4: Man 1B 6
St Michaels Rd. SK14: Hyde 5E 121
St Michael's Sq. M4: Man 2B 6 (2E 101)
OL6: A Lyme 5D 174 (2A 106)
St Modwen Rd. M32: Stre 2H 111
St Nicholas Rd. M15: Man 4E 9 (6C 100)
St Osmund's Dr. BL2: Bolt 6A 34
St Osmund's Gro. BL2: Bolt 6A 34
St Oswalds Rd. M19: Man 5D 116
St Ouen Cen. M28: Walk 6G 65
St Pauls Cl. M26: Rad 6A 52
St Pauls Ct. BL9: Bury 2G 37
M7: Sal 2A 86
M28: Walk 6H 65
OL8: O'ham 5F 75
St Paul's Gdns. M7: Sal 2A 86
(off St Paul's Rd.)
SK14: Hyde 4C 120
(off St Paul's St.)
St Paul's Hill Rd. SK14: Hyde 5D 120
St Paul's M. SK1: Stoc 6B 134
(off St Paul's St.)
St Paul's Pl. BL1: Bolt 2A 32
St Paul's Ri. M7: Sal 2A 86
(off St Paul's St.)
St Paul's Rd. M7: Sal 2A 86
M20: Man 3G 131
M28: Walk 1A 82
SK4: Stoc 5D 132
St Pauls St. BL0: Ram 3C 12
BL9: Bury 2G 37
SK1: Stoc 6A 134
SK14: Hyde 4C 120
SK15: Stal 3G 107
St Pauls Trad. Est. SK15: Stal 3G 107
St Paul's Vs. BL9: Bury 2G 37
St Peter's Av. BL1: Bolt 3G 31
St Petersburgh Way M22: Wyth 2A 154
St Peters Cl. OL7: A Lyme 3F 105
St Peter's Ct. BL2: Bolt 1E 49
(off Hilden St.)
M32: Stre 4E 113
(off Burleigh Rd.)
St Peter's Dr. SK14: Hyde 5D 120
St Petersgate SK1: Stoc 3F 179 (2G 145)
St Peters Ho. BL2: Bolt 1F 49
St Peter's Rd. BL9: Bury 6F 37
M27: Swin 4G 83

St Peter's Sq. M2: Man 1H 9 (5D 100)
SK1: Stoc 2F 179 (2G 145)
St Peters St.
OL6: A Lyme 6A 174 (3G 105)
OL16: Roch 5B 28
St Peter's Ter. BL4: Farn 2H 65
St Peter's Way BL1: Bolt . . .2G 175 (5D 32)
BL2: Bolt 2G 175 (5D 32)
BL3: Bolt 5D 32
St Philip's Av. BL3: Bolt 3B 48
St Philip's Pl. M3: Sal 4C 4 (3B 100)
St Philip's Rd. M18: Man 3F 117
St Philips Sq. M3: Sal 4C 4
(off Bank St.)
St Phillip's Dr. OL2: O'ham 6E 59
St Saviour's Rd. SK2: Stoc 6C 146
Saintsbridge Rd. M22: Wyth 3A 154
St Simons Cl. SK2: Stoc 3C 146
St Simon St. M3: Sal 1D 4 (2B 100)
St Stephen's Av. M34: Aud 5E 105
St Stephens Cl. BL2: Bolt 2G 49
M13: Man 6H 11 (2H 115)
St Stephens Ct. M9: Man 4H 87
(off Shieldborn Dr.)
St Stephens Gdns. BL4: Kea 3C 66
M24: Mid 5C 56
St Stephens St. BL4: Kea 3C 66
OL1: O'ham 1G 75
St Stephen St. M3: Sal 4D 4 (3B 100)
St Stephens Vw. M43: Droy 3A 104
St Teresa's Rd. M16: Old T 4G 113
St Thomas Circ. OL8: O'ham 4D 74
St Thomas Cl. M26: Rad 4A 52
St Thomas Ct. BL9: Bury 3G 37
St Thomas Pde. OL4: Lees 3C 76
(off High St.)
St Thomas' Pl. M8: Man 1E 101
St Thomas's Pl.
SK1: Stoc 5G 179 (3H 145)
St Thomas St. BL1: Bolt 3B 32
St Thomas St. Nth. OL8: O'ham 4D 74
St Thomas St. Sth. OL8: O'ham 4D 74
St Vincent St. M4: Man 4F 7 (3G 101)
St Werburgh's Rd. M21: Chor 6A 114
St Wilfred's Dr. OL12: Roch 6F 15
St Wilfrid's St. M15: Man 5E 9 (1C 114)
St Williams Av. BL3: Bolt 4C 48
St Winifred's Pl. SK15: Stal 3D 106
(off West St.)
Salcombe Av. BL2: Ain 4F 35
Salcombe Cl. M33: Sale 4G 127
Salcombe Gro. BL2: Bolt 1B 50
Salcombe Rd. M11: Man 5F 103
SK2: Stoc 3C 146
Salco Sq. WA14: Alt 5F 139
Salcot Wlk. M40: Man 1F 7
SALE 3B 128
Sale Circ. M23: Wyth 1H 141
Sale Heys Rd. M33: Sale 6H 127
Sale La. M29: Tyld 3B 80
Sale Leisure Cen. 4C 128
SALEM 4B 76
Salem Gro. OL4: O'ham 3B 76
Sale Rd. M23: Wyth 1F 141
Sale Sharks RUFC 6E 179 (4G 145)
Sales's La. BL9: Bury 2G 23
Sale Station (Metro) 5B 128
Sale St. OL15: L'ough 3H 17
Sale Water Pk. 2D 128
SALFORD 4D 4 (5H 99)
Salford App. M3: Sal 3G 5 (3D 100)
Salford Central Station (Rail)
. . . . .5E 5 (4C 100)
Salford City Reds RLFC 3D 98
Salford Crescent Station (Rail) 3H 99
Salford Ent. Cen. M50: Sal 4C 98
Salford Foyer M6: Sal 2F 99
Salford Mus. & Art Gallery . . .4A 4 (3A 100)
SALFORD QUAYS 6F 99
Salford Quays Station (Metro) 6G 99
Salford Rd. BL5: O Hul 2A 64
Salford Roman Catholic Cathedral 4D 4
Salford Shop. City M6: Sal 2F 99

Salford Sports Village 4G 85
Salford St. BL9: Bury 1G 37
  OL4: O'ham 4A 76
Salford University Bus. Pk.
  M6: Sal 1A 4 (2H 99)
Salford University Climbing Wall . . .2A 4
Salford Watersports Cen. 6F 99
Salik Gdns. OL11: Roch 6H 27
Salisbury Av. OL10: H'ood 5G 39
Salisbury Cotts. SK13: Had 2H 123
  (off Salisbury St.)
Salisbury Cres. OL6: A Lyme 4B 92
Salisbury Dr. M25: Pres 1A 86
  SK16: Duk 5E 107
Salisbury Ho. M1: Man 2B 10
  M3: Sal 3E 5
Salisbury Rd. M21: Chor 6H 113
  M26: Rad 2G 51
  M27: Swin 4G 83
  M30: Ecc 1H 97
  M41: Urm 3F 111
  OL4: O'ham 3H 75
  WA14: B'ath 4F 139
Salisbury St. BL3: Bolt 1B 48
  M14: Man 3E 115
  M24: Mid 6D 56
  M45: White 1F 69
  OL2: Shaw 5F 43
  SK5: Stoc 1H 133
  SK13: Had 2H 123
Salisbury Ter. BL3: Lit L 4E 51
Salisbury Way M29: Ast 3A 80
Salix Ct. M6: Sal 2G 99
Salkeld St. OL11: Roch 6H 27
Salley St. OL15: L'ough 1A 16
Sally's Yd. M1: Man 3A 10
Salmesbury Hall Cl. BL0: Ram 4B 12
Salmon Flds. OL2: O'ham 4E 59
Salmon Flds. Bus. Village
  OL2: O'ham 4F 59
Salmon St. M4: Man 4B 6 (3E 101)
  M6: Sal .1G 99
Salop St. BL2: Bolt 5H 175 (1E 49)
Saltash Cl. M22: Wyth 4B 154
Saltburn Wlk. M9: Man 3A 88
  (off Princedom St.)
Saltdene Rd. M22: Wyth 4A 154
Saltergate Cl. BL3: Bolt 3E 47
Saltergate M. M5: Sal 4G 99
  (off Cavell Way)
Saltersbrook Gro. SK9: Wilm 6H 165
  (off Fairywell Cl.)
Salterton Dr. BL3: Bolt 5F 47
Salterton Wlk. M40: Man 4C 88
  (off Hugo St.)
Salteye Rd. M30: Ecc 4C 96
Saltford Av. M4: Man 4F 7 (3G 101)
Saltford Ct. M4: Man 4G 7 (3H 101)
Salthill Av. OL10: H'ood 6A 40
Salthill Dr. M22: Wyth 3C 154
Salthouse Cl. BL8: Bury 5C 22
Saltire Gdns. M7: Sal 3C 86
Saltney Av. M20: Man 2D 130
Saltram Cl. M26: Rad 2E 51
Saltrush Rd. M22: Wyth 3B 154
Salts Dr. OL15: L'ough 3G 17
Salts St. OL2: Shaw 6G 43
Saltwood Gro. BL1: Bolt 4D 32
  (off Kentford Rd.)
Salutation St. M15: Man 5H 9 (1D 114)
Salvin Wlk. M9: Man 6A 72
  (off Rockmead Dr.)
Sam Cowan Cl. M14: Man 4E 115
Samian Gdns. M7: Sal 6A 86
Samlesbury Cl. M20: Man 6D 130
  OL2: Shaw 6F 43
Sammy Cookson Cl. M14: Man 4E 115
Samouth Cl. M40: Man 2G 7 (2H 101)
Sampson Sq. M14: Man 3E 115
Sam Rd. OL3: Dig 2E 63
Samson St. OL16: Roch 3C 28
Sam Swire St. M15: Man 2D 114
Samuel La. OL2: Shaw 5E 43

Samuel Ogden St.
  M1: Man 2B 10 (5E 101)
Samuel St. BL9: Bury 2G 37
  M19: Man 1D 132
  M24: Mid 5C 56
  M35: Fail 3H 89
  OL11: Roch 3E 41
  SK4: Stoc 6F 133
  SK14: Holl 2E 123
Sanby Av. M18: Man 3E 117
Sanby Rd. M18: Man 3E 117
Sanctuary, The
  M15: Man 6F 9 (1C 114)
Sanctuary Cl. M15: Man 2F 115
Sandacre Rd. M23: Wyth 4H 141
Sandal St. M40: Man 2A 102
Sandbach Av. M14: Man 1D 130
Sandbach Rd. M33: Sale 6F 129
  SK5: Stoc 5G 117
Sandbank Gdns.
  OL12: Whitw 3A 14
Sand Banks BL1: Bolt 5D 18
SANDBED 1F 93
Sandbed La. OL3: Del 2C 62
  OL5: Mos 1G 93
Sand Beds La.
  BL0: Eden, Roch 1H 13
Sandbrook Pk. OL11: Roch 1G 41
Sandbrook Way M34: Dent 2F 119
  OL11: Roch 1G 41
Sandby Dr. SK6: Mar B 3F 149
Sanderling Dr. M8: Man 6C 86
Sanderling Rd. SK2: Stoc 6G 147
Sanderson Cl. M28: Wors 3D 82
Sanderson Ct. M40: Man 4A 88
  (off Redbrook Av.)
Sanderson St. BL9: Bury 2G 37
  M40: Man 6A 88
Sanderstead Dr. M9: Man 6A 72
Sandfield Dr. BL6: Los 1C 46
Sandfield Rd. OL16: Roch 6B 28
Sandfold SK5: Stoc 5G 117
Sandfold La. M19: Man 5E 117
  SK5: Stoc 5G 117
Sandford Av. M18: Man 1F 117
Sandford Cl. BL2: Bolt 1A 34
Sandford Rd. M33: Sale 6F 129
Sandford St. M3: Sal 2E 5 (2C 100)
  M26: Rad 3D 52
Sandgate Av. M11: Man 3F 103
  M26: Rad 2D 66
Sandgate Dr. M41: Urm 3E 111
Sandgate Rd.
  M45: Pres, White 2H 69
  OL9: Chad 3B 74
Sandham St. BL3: Bolt 3D 48
Sandham Wlk. BL3: Bolt 3D 48
  (off Teal St.)
Sandheys M34: Dent 2F 119
Sandheys Gro. M18: Man 3G 117
Sandhill Cl. BL3: Bolt 3D 48
Sandhill La. SK6: Mar B 1H 149
Sandhill St. SK14: Hyde 3D 120
Sandhill Wlk. M22: Wyth 3H 153
Sand Hole La. OL11: Roch 4H 41
Sandhole La. OL11: Roch 6A 26
Sandhole Rd. BL4: Kea 3C 66
Sandhurst Av. M20: Man 3E 131
Sandhurst Cl. BL8: Bury 2B 36
Sandhurst Ct. BL2: Bolt 1A 50
Sandhurst Dr. BL2: Bolt 1A 50
  SK9: Wilm 6G 165
Sandhurst Rd. M20: Man 1F 143
  SK2: Stoc 6B 146
Sandhurst St. OL8: O'ham 5A 76
Sandhutton St. M9: Man 2H 87
Sandilands Rd. M23: Wyth 3D 140
Sandilea Ct. M7: Sal 2G 85
Sandileigh Av. M20: Man 4F 131
  SK5: Stoc 5B 134
  SK8: Chea 5C 144
  WA15: Hale 2H 151

Sandileigh Dr. BL1: Bolt 2E 33
  WA15: Hale 2H 151
Sandimoss Ct. M33: Sale 5H 127
Sandiway M44: Irl 5E 109
  OL10: H'ood 3A 40
  SK6: Bred 6F 135
  SK7: Bram 3G 157
Sandiway Cl. SK6: Mar 3D 148
Sandiway Dr. M20: Man 6E 131
Sandiway Pl. WA14: Alt 6F 139
Sandiway Rd. M33: Sale 5H 127
  SK9: Hand 2H 165
  WA14: Alt 5F 139
Sandmere Wlk. M9: Man 6A 72
  (off Rockmead Dr.)
Sandon St. BL3: Bolt 3B 48
Sandown Av. M6: Sal 3E 99
Sandown Cl. OL1: O'ham 6G 59
  SK9: Wilm 1G 173
Sandown Cres. BL3: Lit L 5C 50
  M18: Man 4F 117
Sandown Dr. M33: Sale 6G 127
  M34: Dent 1H 135
  WA15: Haleb 1D 162
Sandown Gdns. M41: Urm 5C 110
Sandown Rd. BL2: Bolt 2A 34
  BL9: Bury 4G 53
  SK3: Stoc 3D 144
  SK7: H Gro 3F 159
Sandown St. M18: Man 1G 117
Sandpiper Cl. BL4: Farn 2D 64
  OL11: Roch 4B 26
  SK16: Duk 6C 106
Sandpiper Dr. SK3: Stoc 5F 145
Sandpits OL10: H'ood 5B 40
Sandpits Bus. Pk. SK14: Hat 4A 122
Sandray Cl. BL3: Bolt 2F 47
Sandray Gro. M5: Sal 4E 99
Sandridge Cl. BL4: Kea 1A 66
Sandridge Wlk. M12: Man 1A 116
  (off Martindale Cres.)
Sandringham Av. M34: Aud 1D 118
  M34: Dent 4A 118
  SK15: Stal 2E 107
Sandringham Cl. WA14: Bow 4B 150
Sandringham Ct. M9: Man 4E 71
  (off Deanswood Dr.)
  M23: Wyth 3C 140
  SK9: Wilm 3D 172
  (off Cavendish St.)
Sandringham Dr. BL8: G'mount 2A 22
  OL16: Miln 5G 29
  SK4: Stoc 2C 144
  SK12: Poy 4D 168
  SK16: Duk 6D 106
Sandringham Grange M25: Pres 6C 70
Sandringham Ho. SK6: Mar 5B 148
Sandringham Rd. M28: Wors 5E 81
  SK6: Bred 6C 134
  SK7: H Gro 3F 159
  SK8: Chea H 2C 156
  SK14: Hyde 2C 136
Sandringham St. M18: Man 3E 117
Sandringham Way OL2: O'ham 1C 58
  SK9: Wilm 3D 172
Sands Av. OL9: Chad 6F 57
Sands Cl. SK14: Hat 6H 121
Sandsend Cl. M8: Man 1C 100
Sandsend Rd. M41: Urm 4E 111
Sandstone Rd. OL16: Miln 4F 29
Sandstone Way M21: Chor 2B 130
Sand St. M40: Man 1G 101
  SK15: Stal 5D 106
Sands Wlk. SK14: Hat 6H 121
Sandusky Dr. BL1: Bolt 2E 33
Sandwell Dr. M33: Sale 3B 128
Sandwich Rd. M30: Ecc 2H 97
Sandwich St. M28: Walk 1H 81
Sandwick Cres. BL3: Bolt 2B 48
Sandwood Av. BL3: Bolt 2E 47
Sandy Acre OL5: Mos 3G 93
Sandy Bank OL2: Shaw 5F 43
Sandy Bank Av. SK14: Hat 6H 121

Sandybank Cl. SK13: Had 3G **123**
Sandy Bank Rd. M8: Man 3D **86**
Sandybrook Cl. BL8: Tot 5H **21**
Sandybrook Dr. M9: Man 1G **87**
Sandy Brow M9: Man 1H **87**
Sandy Cl. BL9: Bury 3F **53**
Sandycroft Av. M22: Wyth 2B **154**
Sandygate Cl. M27: Swin 4G **83**
Sandy Gro. M6: Sal 2E **99**
  M27: Swin 3H **83**
  SK16: Duk 5B **106**
Sandy Haven Cl. SK14: Hat 6H **121**
Sandy Haven Wlk. SK14: Hat 6H **121**
Sandyhill Cl. M9: Man 6E **71**
Sandyhill Rd. M9: Man 6E **71**
Sandyhills BL3: Bolt 3C **48**
Sandylands Dr. M25: Pres 2G **85**
Sandy La. M6: Sal 2E **99**
  M21: Chor 1H **129**
  M23: Wyth 4E **141**
  M24: Mid 1E **73**
  M25: Pres 6F **69**
  M32: Stre 6B **112**
  M43: Droy 2C **104**
  M44: Irl 4E **109**
  OL2: O'ham 3D **58**
  OL3: Dob 5C **62**
  OL11: Roch 4E **27**
  SK5: Stoc 6G **133**
  SK6: Rom 1A **148**
  SK9: Wilm 1A **172**
  SK16: Duk 5B **106**
Sandy Meade M25: Pres 6G **69**
Sandy Nook SK15: Stal 5E **107**
Sandys Av. OL8: O'ham 6D **74**
Sandyshot Wlk. M22: Wyth 2D **154**
Sandy Va. SK16: Duk 4C **106**
Sandy Wlk. OL2: O'ham 3D **58**
Sandywarps M44: Irl 1E **125**
Sandyway M25: Pres 6G **69**
Sandywell Cl. M11: Man 6F **103**
Sandywell St. M11: Man 5F **103**
Sandywood M6: Sal 2E **99**
Sangster Cl. M5: Sal 5G **99**
Sankey Gro. M9: Man 6F **71**
Sankey St. BL9: Bury 3D **36**
Santiago St. M14: Man 4F **115**
Santley St. M12: Man 4C **116**
Santon Av. M14: Man 1A **132**
Sapling Gro. M33: Sale 1F **139**
Sapling Rd. BL3: Bolt 5H **47**
  M27: Swin 6F **83**
Sarah Butterworth Ct.
  OL16: Roch 5B **28**
      (off Sarah Butterworth St.)
Sarah Butterworth St.
  OL16: Roch 5B **28**
SARAH MOOR 6F **59**
Sarah St. BL0: Eden 2H **13**
  M11: Man 5B **102**
  M24: Mid 1B **72**
  M30: Ecc 4D **96**
  OL2: Shaw 2G **59**
  OL8: O'ham 1D **90**
  OL11: Roch 6D **178** (5A **28**)
Sargent Dr. M16: W Ran 3C **114**
Sargent Rd. SK6: Bred 1D **146**
Sark Rd. M21: Chor 5G **113**
Sarn Av. M22: Wyth 1B **154**
Sarnesfield Cl. M12: Man 3C **116**
Sarnia Ct. M7: Sal 4B **86**
      (off Bk. Hope St.)
Satinwood Wlk. M3: Sal 2E **5**
Saturn Gro. M6: Sal 1A **100**
Saunton Av. BL2: Bolt 2B **34**
Saunton Rd. M11: Man 5F **103**
Sautridge Cl. M24: Mid 6F **41**
Savernake Rd. SK6: Wood 4A **136**
Savick Av. BL2: Bolt 6B **34**
Saville Rd. M26: Rad 6H **35**
  SK8: Gat 5F **143**
Saville St. BL2: Bolt 4H **175** (1E **49**)
  M24: Mid 2F **73**

Saviours Ter. BL3: Bolt 2A **48**
      (off Bankfield St.)
Savio Way M24: Mid 2C **72**
Savoy Cinema
  Stockport 6D **132**
Savoy Ct. M45: White 5E **53**
Savoy Dr. OL2: O'ham 5D **58**
Savoy St. OL4: O'ham 4H **75**
  OL11: Roch 3E **27**
Sawley Av. M45: White 5F **53**
  OL4: O'ham 5B **76**
  OL15: L'ough 2G **17**
Sawley Dr. SK8: Chea H 1D **166**
Sawley Rd. M40: Man 1H **7** (1H **101**)
Sawmill, The BL9: Bury 5D **176** (4F **37**)
Saw Mill Way OL15: L'ough 5G **17**
Sawston Wlk. M40: Man 6E **73**
Saw St. BL1: Bolt 3C **32**
Sawyer Brow SK14: Hyde 3D **120**
Sawyer St. BL8: Bury 1B **36**
  OL12: Roch 2H **27**
Saxbrook Wlk. M22: Wyth 2D **154**
Saxby Av. BL7: Bro X 3D **18**
Saxby St. M6: Sal 6C **84**
Saxelby Dr. M40: Man 5F **87**
Saxfield Dr. M23: Wyth 5A **142**
Saxholme Wlk. M22: Wyth 3A **154**
Saxon Av. M8: Man 2E **87**
  SK16: Duk 5A **106**
Saxon Cl. BL8: Bury 3B **36**
Saxon Ct. M33: Sale 6B **128**
Saxon Dr. M34: Aud 6E **105**
  M43: Droy 3B **104**
  OL9: Chad 1G **73**
Saxonholme Rd. OL11: Roch 6E **41**
Saxon Ho. M16: W Ran 4B **114**
  OL15: L'ough 4H **17**
Saxonside M24: Mid 4A **56**
Saxon St. M24: Mid 1D **72**
  M26: Rad 4H **51**
  M34: Dent 4F **119**
  M40: Man 2A **102**
  M43: Droy 3B **104**
  OL4: O'ham 2A **76**
  OL5: Mos 6H **77**
Saxthorpe Cl. M33: Sale 4F **127**
Saxthorpe Wlk. M12: Man 2A **116**
      (off Britnall Av.)
Saxwood Av. M9: Man 2H **87**
Saxwood Cl. OL12: Roch 2B **26**
Scafell Av. OL7: A Lyme 1F **105**
Scafell Cl. OL1: O'ham 6F **59**
      (not continuous)
  SK6: H Lan 5C **160**
Scalby Wlk. M22: Wyth 4B **154**
Scale St. M5: Sal 4G **99**
      (off Christopher St.)
Scant Row BL6: Hor 2C **30**
Scarborough St. M40: Man 3C **88**
Scarcroft Rd. M12: Man 2C **116**
Scarfield Dr. OL11: Roch 2A **26**
Scargill Cl. M14: Man 1G **131**
Scargill Rd. BL3: Bolt 3G **47**
Scarisbrick Av. M20: Man 6H **131**
Scarisbrick Rd. M19: Man 1B **132**
Scarr Av. M26: Rad 5C **52**
Scarr Dr. OL12: Roch 6H **15**
Scarr La. OL2: Shaw 6A **44**
Scarr Ter. OL12: Whitw 3B **14**
Scarr Wheel M7: Sal 4A **86**
Scarsdale Av. BL1: Bolt 4G **31**
Scarsdale Rd. M14: Man 3A **116**
Scarsdale St. M6: Sal 2H **99**
Scarthwood Cl. BL2: Bolt 6A **20**
Scawfell Av. BL2: Bolt 3F **33**
Scawton Wlk. M9: Man 4F **71**
Schofield Cl. M24: Mid 4C **56**
Schofield Pl. OL15: L'ough 1B **16**
Schofield Rd. M30: Ecc 4C **96**
  M43: Droy 4B **104**
Schofield St. M11: Man 4E **103**
  M26: Rad 3B **52**
  M35: Fail 3H **89**

Schofield St. OL2: O'ham 2D **58**
  OL8: O'ham 6E **75**
  OL10: H'ood 3H **39**
  OL11: Roch 1A **42**
  OL15: L'ough 1B **16**
  OL16: Miln 6G **29**
Scholar Grn. Rd. M32: Stre 2A **112**
Scholars Ct. M27: Clif 6G **67**
Scholars Dr. M20: Man 2E **131**
Scholars Ri. BL7: Bolt 4D **18**
Scholars Way BL9: Bury 1G **37**
      (off Taylor St.)
  M24: Mid 6B **56**
Scholes Cl. M7: Sal 3D **86**
Scholes La. M25: Pres 6H **69**
Scholes St. BL8: Bury 2C **36**
  M27: Swin 3A **84**
  M35: Fail 3A **90**
  OL1: O'ham 3H **177** (2G **75**)
  OL9: Chad 5A **74**
  OL11: Roch 4E **41**
Scholes Wlk. M25: Pres 6H **69**
Scholey St. BL2: Bolt 2E **49**
Scholfield Av. M41: Urm 6H **111**
School Av. M32: Stre 4F **113**
  OL6: A Lyme 5B **92**
School Brow BL9: Bury . . .2B **176** (2E **37**)
      (not continuous)
  M28: Wors 5B **82**
  SK6: Rom 1G **147**
School Cl. SK12: Poy 4F **169**
School Ct. BL0: Ram 4G **13**
  BL7: Eger 1C **18**
  M4: Man 4E **7** (3G **101**)
  SK3: Stoc 5H **145**
School Cres. SK15: Stal 2D **106**
School Dr. SK16: Duk 1C **120**
School Gro. M20: Man 3G **131**
  M25: Pres 1G **85**
School Hill BL1: Bolt 1E **175** (5C **32**)
School Ho. BL7: Bolt 4D **18**
      (off School St.)
School Ho. Flats
  OL8: O'ham 1B **90**
School Ho. Rd. OL4: O'ham 4A **76**
School La. BL9: Bury 3E **23**
  M9: Man 1G **87**
  M19: Man 6F **131**
  M20: Man 6F **131**
  M31: C'ton 3A **126**
  M44: Cad 4B **124**
  M44: Irl 5D **108**
  OL11: Roch 3G **25**
  OL16: Roch 4C **178** (4H **27**)
  SK4: Stoc 4E **133**
  SK6: Comp 5F **137**
  SK8: Chea H 5B **156**
      (not continuous)
  SK12: Poy 3F **169**
  SK14: Hyde 2C **136**
  SK15: C'ook 4A **94**
  WA14: D Mas 4A **138**
School M. SK7: Bram 6G **157**
School Rd. M30: Ecc 5E **97**
  M32: Stre 5C **112**
  M33: Sale 4B **128**
      (not continuous)
  M35: Fail 4H **89**
  OL8: O'ham 1B **90**
  SK9: Hand 3H **165**
  WA15: Hale 2H **151**
      (off Stamford Pk. Rd.)
Schools Hill SK8: Chea 2H **155**
Schoolside Cl. M8: Man 5F **87**
Schoolside La. M24: Mid 2F **71**
Schools Rd. M18: Man 2G **117**
School St. BL0: Ram 4B **12**
  BL3: Lit L 4D **50**
  BL7: Bro X 4D **18**
  BL9: Bury 4H **37**
  M4: Man 2C **6** (2E **101**)
  M7: Sal 1C **100**

School St.—Sesame Gdns.

School St. M26: Rad . . . 4H **51**
M30: Ecc . . . 2D **96**
OL3: Upp . . . 1D **78**
OL4: Spri . . . 3E **77**
OL8: O'ham . . . 4D **74**
OL10: H'ood . . . 3G **39**
OL12: Roch . . . 2B **178** (3H **27**)
OL15: L'ough . . . 4E **17**
SK7: H Gro . . . 3E **159**
School St. Ind. Est. SK7: H Gro . . . 3E **159**
School Ter. *OL12: Whitw . . . 4A* ***14***
(off Lloyd St.)
School Wlk. M16: Old T . . . 2B **114**
School Yd. SK4: Stoc . . . 1A **144**
Schuster Rd. M14: Man . . . 4H **115**
Schwabe St. M24: Mid . . . 1G **71**
Scobell St. BL8: Tot . . . 6H **21**
Scoltock Way OL1: O'ham . . . 2G **177** (2F **75**)
Scope o' th' La. BL2: Bolt . . . 1G **33**
Score St. M11: Man . . . 4C **102**
Scorton Av. BL2: Bolt . . . 6B **34**
Scorton St. *BL1: Bolt . . . 5A* ***32***
(off Wyresdale Rd.)
Scorton Wlk. *M40: Man . . . 1F* ***89***
(off Blandford Dr.)
Scotforth Cl. M15: Man . . . 4E **9** (6C **100**)
Scotland Hall Rd. M40: Man . . . 6D **88**
Scotland La. BL9: Bury . . . 3A **24**
Scotland Pl. BL0: Ram . . . 3C **12**
Scotland Rd. M4: Man . . . 2A **6** (2E **101**)
Scotland St. M40: Man . . . 6E **89**
OL6: A Lyme . . . 5D **174** (2A **106**)
Scotson Fold M26: Rad . . . 5H **51**
Scotta Rd. M30: Ecc . . . 5D **96**
Scott Av. BL9: Bury . . . 1F **53**
M21: Chor . . . 5H **113**
M30: Ecc . . . 2E **97**
Scott Cl. SK5: Stoc . . . 5H **133**
Scott Dr. SK6: Mar B . . . 3G **149**
WA15: Alt . . . 1H **151**
Scottfield OL8: O'ham . . . 6F **177** (4E **75**)
Scottfield Rd. OL8: O'ham . . . 4F **75**
Scott Ga. M34: Aud . . . 6E **105**
Scott Pl. M3: Man . . . 6G **5** (4C **100**)
Scott Rd. M25: Pres . . . 6F **69**
M34: Dent . . . 6E **119**
M43: Droy . . . 4A **104**
Scotts Ind. Pk.
OL16: Roch . . . 5A **28**
Scott St. M26: Rad . . . 2F **67**
M29: Ast . . . 6A **80**
OL8: O'ham . . . 4F **75**
SCOUT . . . 4G 93
Scout Dr. M23: Wyth . . . 1F **153**
Scout Grn. M24: Mid . . . 4C **56**
SCOUTHEAD . . . 1F 77
Scout Vw. BL8: Tot . . . 5A **22**
Scovell St. M7: Sal . . . 5B **86**
Scowcroft La. OL2: Shaw . . . 2G **59**
Scowcroft St. BL2: Bolt . . . 4F **33**
Scroggins La. M31: Part . . . 5D **124**
Scropton St. M40: Man . . . 5H **87**
Seabright Wlk. *M11: Man . . . 4B* ***102***
(off Pilgrim Dr.)
Seabrook Cres. M41: Urm . . . 3E **111**
Seabrook Rd. M40: Man . . . 1E **103**
Seacombe Av. M14: Man . . . 6E **115**
Seacombe Gro. SK3: Stoc . . . 3D **144**
Seaford Rd. BL2: Bolt . . . 5A **20**
M6: Sal . . . 6H **85**
Seaford Wlk. M9: Man . . . 6G **71**
OL9: Chad . . . 3B **74**
Seaforth Rd. BL1: Bolt . . . 6C **18**
Seaham Dr. BL8: Bury . . . 6C **22**
Seaham Wlk. *M14: Man . . . 4F* ***115***
(off Head Pl.)
Sealand Cl. M33: Sale . . . 1E **141**
Sealand Dr. M30: Ecc . . . 5C **96**
Sealand Ho. M25: Pres . . . 4A **70**
Sealand Rd. M23: Wyth . . . 1F **141**
Sealand Way *SK9: Hand . . . 3H* ***165***
(off Henbury Rd.)
Seale Av. M34: Aud . . . 6D **104**
Sealey Wlk. *M40: Man . . . 1A* ***102***
(off Filby Wlk.)
Seal Rd. SK7: Bram . . . 5H **157**
Seamons Dr. WA14: Alt . . . 5D **138**
Seamons Rd. WA14: Alt, D Mas . . . 5C **138**
Seamons Wlk. *WA14: Alt . . . 6D* ***138***
(off Seamons Rd.)
Searby Rd. M18: Man . . . 3D **116**
Searness Rd. M24: Mid . . . 5G **55**
Seascale Av. M11: Man . . . 2D **102**
Seascale Wlk. M24: Mid . . . 5A **56**
Seathwaite Cl. M24: Mid . . . 5H **55**
Seathwaite Rd. BL4: Farn . . . 2D **64**
Seathwaite Wlk. *M18: Man . . . 2E* ***117***
(off Hampden Cres.)
Seatoller Ct. OL2: O'ham . . . 3E **59**
Seatoller Dr. M24: Mid . . . 6G **55**
Seaton Cl. SK7: H Gro . . . 4D **158**
Seaton M. OL7: A Lyme . . . 1E **105**
Seaton Rd. BL1: Bolt . . . 3A **32**
Seaton Way M14: Man . . . 3E **115**
Sebastian Cl. SK6: Mar B . . . 4F **149**
Second Av. BL1: Bolt . . . 6H **31**
BL3: Lit L . . . 3B **50**
BL9: Bury . . . 1B **38**
M11: Man . . . 2F **103**
M17: T Pk . . . 2D **112**
M27: Swin . . . 6F **83**
M29: Ast . . . 6A **80**
OL8: O'ham . . . 1C **90**
SK12: Poy . . . 6D **168**
SK15: C'ook . . . 6A **94**
Second St. BL1: Bolt . . . 1F **31**
Section St. BL3: Bolt . . . 5F **175** (1D **48**)
Sedan Cl. M5: Sal . . . 4G **99**
Sedburgh Cl. M33: Sale . . . 1F **139**
Sedbury Cl. M23: Wyth . . . 2F **141**
Seddon Av. M18: Man . . . 1F **117**
M26: Rad . . . 2D **52**
Seddon Cl. M26: Rad . . . 3A **52**
Seddon Gdns. M26: Rad . . . 1C **66**
Seddon La. M26: Rad . . . 1C **66**
Seddon Rd. WA14: Hale . . . 3F **151**
Seddons Av. BL8: Bury . . . 5A **36**
Seddon St. BL3: Lit L . . . 4D **50**
M12: Man . . . 5D **116**
M26: Rad . . . 4A **52**
M38: Lit H . . . 4D **64**
Sedgeborough Rd. M16: W Ran . . . 3C **114**
Sedge Cl. SK5: Stoc . . . 1A **134**
Sedgefield Cl. M5: Sal . . . 3F **99**
Sedgefield Dr. BL1: Bolt . . . 2H **31**
Sedgefield Pk. OL4: O'ham . . . 3B **76**
Sedgefield Rd. M26: Rad . . . 1H **67**
Sedgefield Wlk. M23: Wyth . . . 1F **141**
Sedgeford Cl. SK9: Wilm . . . 6H **165**
Sedgeford Rd. M40: Man . . . 6H **87**
Sedgemoor Cl. SK8: Chea H . . . 3D **156**
Sedgemoor Va. BL2: Bolt . . . 3B **34**
Sedgemoor Way
OL1: O'ham . . . 2F **177** (2E **75**)
Sedgley Av. M25: Pres . . . 1A **86**
OL16: Roch . . . 1B **42**
Sedgley Bldgs. M43: Droy . . . 5A **104**
Sedgley Cl. M24: Mid . . . 2E **73**
SEDGLEY PARK . . . 1B 86
Sedgley Pk. Rd. M25: Pres . . . 1A **86**
Sedgley Pk. RUFC . . . 3E 69
Sedgley Pk. Trad. Est. M25: Pres . . . 2H **85**
Sedgley Rd. M8: Man . . . 3E **87**
Sedgley St. M24: Mid . . . 2E **73**
Sedley Av. M25: Pres . . . 4F **69**
SEEDFIELD . . . 6E 23
Seedfield Rd. BL9: Bury . . . 6F **23**
SEEDLEY . . . 3E 99
Seedley Av. M38: Lit H . . . 5F **65**
Seedley Pk. Rd. M6: Sal . . . 3E **99**
Seedley Rd. M6: Sal . . . 2E **99**
Seedley St. M14: Man . . . 4F **115**
Seedley Ter. M6: Sal . . . 2E **99**
Seedley Vw. Rd. M6: Sal . . . 2E **99**
Seed St. BL1: Bolt . . . 6A **32**
Seel St. OL5: Mos . . . 2F **93**
Sefton Cl. M13: Man . . . 5D **10** (1F **115**)
M24: Mid . . . 1A **72**
OL1: O'ham . . . 3B **60**
Sefton Ct. BL1: Bolt . . . 1E **175**
BL9: Bury . . . 5F ***23***
(off Sefton St.)
Sefton Cres. M33: Sale . . . 3B **128**
Sefton Dr. BL9: Bury . . . 5G **23**
M27: Swin . . . 5F **83**
M28: Wors . . . 6C **82**
SK9: Wilm . . . 5G **165**
Sefton Rd. BL1: Bolt . . . 3H **31**
M21: Chor . . . 1H **129**
M24: Mid . . . 1A **72**
M27: Pen . . . 2H **83**
M33: Sale . . . 4B **128**
Sefton St. BL9: Bury . . . 5F **23**
M8: Man . . . 3E **87**
M26: Rad . . . 6C **52**
M45: White . . . 2F **69**
OL9: O'ham . . . 1B **90**
OL10: H'ood . . . 4A **40**
OL11: Roch . . . 6H **27**
Segal Cl. M7: Sal . . . 4B **86**
Selborne Rd. M21: Chor . . . 6H **113**
Selbourne Cl. BL5: W'ton . . . 6A **46**
SK5: Stoc . . . 5G **117**
Selbourne St. OL8: O'ham . . . 2G **91**
Selby Av. M45: White . . . 5F **53**
OL9: Chad . . . 6H **57**
Selby Cl. M26: Rad . . . 2D **52**
M32: Stre . . . 4A **112**
OL16: Miln . . . 5E **29**
SK12: Poy . . . 2D **168**
Selby Dr. M6: Sal . . . 2B **98**
M41: Urm . . . 2B **110**
Selby Gdns. SK8: Chea H . . . 1E **167**
Selby Rd. M24: Mid . . . 4B **56**
M32: Stre . . . 4A **112**
Selby St. M11: Man . . . 5D **102**
OL16: Roch . . . 3B **28**
SK4: Stoc . . . 5F **133**
Selby Wlk. BL8: Bury . . . 3H **35**
Selden St. OL8: O'ham . . . 4D **74**
Selham Wlk. M13: Man . . . 4E **11**
Selhurst Av. M11: Man . . . 3E **103**
Selkirk Av. OL8: O'ham . . . 5D **74**
Selkirk Dr. M9: Man . . . 6B **72**
Selkirk Pl. OL10: H'ood . . . 4E **39**
Selkirk Rd. BL1: Bolt . . . 6B **18**
OL9: Chad . . . 5H **73**
Sellars Sq. M43: Droy . . . 5A **104**
Selsby Av. M30: Ecc . . . 3D **96**
Selsey Av. M33: Sale . . . 6H **127**
SK3: Stoc . . . 4B **144**
Selsey Dr. M20: Man . . . 3G **143**
Selside Ct. M26: Rad . . . 1D **66**
Selside Wlk. *M14: Man . . . 1G* ***131***
(off Boland Dr.)
Selstead Rd. M22: Wyth . . . 4A **154**
Selston Rd. M9: Man . . . 5F **71**
Selwood Wlk. *M9: Man . . . 4H* ***87***
(off Carisbrook St.)
Selworth Av. M33: Sale . . . 5E **129**
Selworth Cl. WA15: Tim . . . 5G **139**
Selworthy Rd. M16: W Ran . . . 3C **114**
Selwyn Av. M9: Man . . . 3H **87**
Selwyn Dr. SK8: Chea H . . . 6E **157**
Selwyn St. BL2: Bolt . . . 1E **49**
OL8: O'ham . . . 6E **177** (4E **75**)
Seminar Cen. . . . ***5D 100***
(in Manchester International Convention Cen.)
Senior Av. M14: Man . . . 2A **132**
Senior Rd. M30: Ecc . . . 5B **96**
Senior St. M3: Sal . . . 2F **5** (2C **100**)
Sepal Cl. SK5: Stoc . . . 6A **118**
Sepia Gro. M24: Mid . . . 6B **56**
Sequoia St. M9: Man . . . 3A **88**
Sergeants La. M45: White . . . 2C **68**
Serin Cl. SK2: Stoc . . . 6F **147**
Service St. SK3: Stoc . . . 3D **144**
Sesame Gdns. M44: Irl . . . 4G **109**

A-Z Manchester 343

Setantii Vis. Cen. 5C 174 (2H 105)
Set St. SK15: Stal 4D 106
Settle Cl. BL8: Bury 3H 35
Settle St. BL3: Bolt 4B 48
   BL3: Lit L 4E 51
Settstones La. OL3: Del 2B 62
Seven Acres OL3: Del 2B 62
Seven Acres Country Pk. 4H 33
Seven Acres La.
   OL12: Roch 1A 26
Sevenoaks Av. M41: Urm 3F 111
   SK4: Stoc 4C 132
Sevenoaks Dr. BL3: Bolt 4C 48
   M27: Swin 5A 84
Sevenoaks Rd. SK8: Gat 5F 143
Sevenoaks Wlk. M13: Man 6F 11
Seven Stiles Dr. SK6: Mar 4C 148
Seventh Av. OL8: O'ham 2C 90
Severn Cl. BL9: Bury 4F 23
   WA14: Alt 5E 139
Severn Dr. OL16: Miln 5G 29
   SK7: Bram 1E 167
Severn Rd. OL8: O'ham 2B 90
                (not continuous)
   OL9: Chad 1H 73
   OL10: H'ood 2E 39
Severnside Trad. Est.
   M17: T Pk 2B 112
Severn Way BL4: Kea 3D 66
   SK5: Stoc 4A 134
Sevilles Bldgs. OL5: Mos 6G 77
Sevilles Pl. OL4: Lees 4C 76
               (off Church St.)
Seville St. OL2: O'ham 5E 59
   OL2: Shaw 2G 59
Sewell Way M38: Lit H 6D 64
Sewerby St. M16: W Ran 3D 114
Sexa St. M11: Man 5F 103
Sexton St. OL10: H'ood 3G 39
Seymour Av. M11: Man 3F 103
Seymour Cl. M16: Old T 2A 114
Seymour Ct. M7: Sal 3D 86
   M26: Rad 4B 52
   SK4: Stoc 1A 144
Seymour Dr. BL2: Bolt 5G 19
Seymour Gro. BL4: Farn 6E 49
   M16: Old T 2H 113
   M33: Sale 5B 128
   OL16: Roch 2B 42
   SK6: Mar 5C 148
   WA15: Tim 6A 140
Seymour Pl. M16: Old T 2H 113
Seymour Rd. BL1: Bolt 2D 32
   M8: Man 2D 86
   SK2: Stoc 6B 146
   SK8: Chea H 5C 156
Seymour Rd. Sth. M11: Man 4F 103
Seymour St. BL2: Bolt 5G 19
   M18: Man 1F 117
   M26: Rad 4B 52
              (Church St. W.)
   M26: Rad 4B 52
              (Darbyshire St.)
   M34: Dent 4D 118
   OL10: H'ood 4F 39
              (not continuous)
Seymour Wlk. M26: Rad 4B 52
              (off Haworth Wlk.)
Shackleton Ct. M40: Man 1E 103
Shackleton Gro. BL1: Bolt 3E 31
Shackleton St. M30: Ecc 2E 97
Shackliffe Rd. M40: Man 1D 88
Shaddock Av. OL12: Roch 2B 26
Shade Av. OL4: Spri 4D 76
Shade Ter. SK6: H Lan 6D 160
Shadowbrook Av. M23: Wyth 1G 153
Shadowbrook Cl. OL1: O'ham 6E 59
Shadow Moss Rd. M22: Wyth 6C 154
Shadows La. OL5: Mos 5A 78
Shadows M. OL5: Mos 5A 78
Shadwell St. E. OL10: H'ood 2H 39
Shadwell St. W. OL10: H'ood 2H 39
Shadworth Cl. OL5: Mos 5A 78

Shadworth La. OL3: Mos 5B 78
Shady La. BL7: Bro X 5F 19
   M23: Wyth 4D 140
Shady Oak Rd. SK2: Stoc 5F 147
Shaftesbury Av. M30: Ecc 5E 97
   OL15: L'ough 6F 17
   SK8: Chea H 4E 157
   WA15: Tim 6A 140
Shaftesbury Cl. BL1: Bolt 4C 32
             (off Ashford Wlk.)
Shaftesbury Dr. OL10: H'ood 5G 39
   OL12: W'le 6D 16
Shaftesbury Gdns. M41: Urm 5G 109
Shaftesbury Rd. M8: Man 4E 87
   M27: Swin 4H 83
   SK3: Stoc 5C 144
Shafton Wlk. M40: Man 1F 89
           (off Blandford Dr.)
Shakespeare Av. BL9: Bury 1F 53
   M26: Rad 3G 51
   M34: Dent 1F 135
   SK15: Mill 1H 107
Shakespeare Cl. OL15: L'ough 2A 16
Shakespeare Cres. M30: Ecc 3F 97
   M43: Droy 3A 104
Shakespeare Dr. SK8: Chea 5B 144
             (not continuous)
Shakespeare Rd. M25: Pres 6F 69
   M27: Swin 3F 83
   M43: Droy 3A 104
   OL1: O'ham 5H 59
   SK6: Bred 5F 135
Shakespeare Wlk.
   M13: Man 6F 11 (1G 115)
Shakleton Av. M9: Man 6C 72
Shalbourne Rd. M28: Walk 6G 65
Shaldon Dr. M40: Man 1G 103
Shalfleet Cl. BL2: Bolt 6A 20
Shamrock St. M28: Walk 6F 65
Shandon Av. M22: Nor 2B 142
Shanklin Cl. M21: Chor 6G 113
   M34: Dent 1H 135
Shanklin Ho. M21: Chor 6G 113
Shanklin Wlk. BL3: Bolt 2G 49
Shanklyn Av. M41: Urm 5E 111
Shanley Ct. OL9: Chad 1B 74
Shannon Cl. OL10: H'ood 2E 39
Shannon Rd. M22: Wyth 2C 154
Shap Av. WA15: Tim 6D 140
Shap Cres. M28: Walk 2B 82
Shap Dr. M28: Walk 1B 82
Shapwick Cl. M9: Man 3H 87
           (off Coningsby Dr.)
Sharcott Cl. M16: W Ran 3D 114
Shardlow Cl. M40: Man 1G 7
Shargate Cl. SK9: Wilm 6G 165
Sharman St. BL3: Bolt 2F 49
Sharnbrook Wlk. BL2: Bolt 4F 33
   M8: Man 1C 86
Sharnford Cl. BL2: Bolt 1F 49
Sharnford Sq. M12: Man 1C 116
             (off Bridgend Cl.)
SHARON 4A 78
Sharon Av. OL4: Gras 4H 77
Sharon Cl. OL7: A Lyme 4E 105
SHARPLES .1C 32
Sharples Av. BL1: Bolt 5C 18
Sharples Community Leisure Cen. 6D 18
Sharples Dr. BL8: Bury 1H 35
Sharples Hall Dr. BL1: Bolt 5D 18
Sharples Hall Fold BL1: Bolt 6D 18
Sharples Hall M. BL1: Bolt 5D 18
Sharples Hall St. OL4: O'ham 1B 76
Sharples Pk. BL1: Bolt 1B 32
Sharples St. SK4: Stoc 6G 133
Sharples Va. BL1: Bolt 2C 32
Sharp St. BL8: Bury 1B 36
   M4: Man 2C 6 (2F 101)
   M24: Mid 1C 72
   M25: Pres 5G 69
   M28: Walk 6A 66
Sharrington Dr. M23: Wyth 5E 141

Sharrow Wlk. M9: Man 4H 87
           (off Broadwell Dr.)
SHARSTON .5C 142
Sharston Grn. Bus. Pk.
   M22: Shar 5D 142
Sharston Ind. Area M22: Shar 4B 142
             (not continuous)
Sharston Rd. M22: Shar 4C 142
Shaving La. M28: Walk 2H 81
SHAW 1H 59
Shaw, The SK13: Had 4H 123
Shaw Av. SK14: Hyde 1D 136
Shawbrook Av. M28: Wors 3F 81
Shawbrook Rd. M19: Man 3B 132
Shawbury Gro. M33: Sale 1H 139
Shawbury Rd. M23: Wyth 1H 153
Shawbury St. M24: Mid 2E 73
SHAWCLOUGH 6G 15
Shawclough Cl. OL12: Roch 6F 15
Shawclough Dr. OL12: Roch 6E 15
Shawclough Ri. OL12: Roch 1F 27
           (off Shawclough Rd.)
Shawclough Rd. OL12: Roch 5E 15
Shawclough Trad. Est.
   OL12: Roch 6F 15
Shawclough Way OL12: Roch 6E 15
Shawcroft Cl. OL2: Shaw 2G 59
Shawcroft Vw. BL1: Bolt 2F 33
Shaw & Crompton Station (Rail) 1A 60
Shawcross Fold SK1: Stoc 1G 179
Shawcross La. M22: Nor 3D 142
Shawcross St. M6: Sal 4H 99
   SK1: Stoc 5H 179 (3A 146)
   SK14: Hyde 1D 136
Shawdene Rd. M22: Nor 3A 142
SHAW EDGE 3G 59
Shawe Hall Av. M41: Urm 1C 126
Shawe Hall Cres. M41: Urm 1C 126
Shawe Rd. M41: Urm 5C 110
Shawe Vw. M41: Urm 5C 110
SHAWFIELD .1B 26
Shawfield Cl. M14: Man 1E 131
Shawfield Ct. SK2: Stoc 6D 146
Shawfield Gro. OL12: Roch 1B 26
Shawfield La. OL12: Roch 2A 26
Shawfield Rd. SK13: Had 4H 123
Shawfields SK15: Stal 2H 107
Shawfold OL2: Shaw 6H 43
Shawford Cres. M40: Man 1E 89
Shawford Rd. M40: Man 1E 89
Shaw Ga. OL3: Upp 2F 79
Shawgreen Cl. M15: Man 6D 8 (1B 114)
SHAW HALL .3B 78
SHAWHALL .2E 121
Shaw Hall M14: Man 3H 115
          (off Daisy Bank Hall)
Shaw Hall Av. SK14: Hyde 2F 121
SHAW HALL BANK 4B 78
Shaw Hall Bank Rd. OL3: G'fld 4B 78
Shaw Hall Cl. OL3: G'fld 4B 78
Shaw Head Dr. M35: Fail 5H 89
SHAW HEATH 6E 179 (4F 145)
Shaw Heath SK2: Stoc 6G 179 (4H 145)
   SK3: Stoc 5E 179 (3G 145)
Shawheath Cl. M15: Man 6D 8 (1B 114)
Shawhill Wlk. M40: Man 3A 102
           (off Millhead Av.)
Shaw Ho. BL4: Farn 2H 65
          (off Moorfield Chase)
   OL2: Shaw 2H 59
Shaw La. OL16: Miln 2G 29
   SK13: Had 5G 123
             (not continuous)
Shawlea Av. M19: Man 3A 132
Shaw Lee OL3: Dig 3F 63
Shaw Lodge OL12: W'le 6C 16
            (off Lodge St.)
Shaw Moor Av. SK15: Stal 4G 107
Shaw Rd. OL1: O'ham 6G 59
   OL2: O'ham 4E 59
   OL16: Miln 2H 43
   OL16: Roch 4B 42
   SK4: Stoc 4D 132

Shaw Rd. Sth. SK3: Stoc 5G **145**
(not continuous)
Shaws OL3: Upp 2E **79**
Shaws Fold OL4: Spri 2F **77**
SK9: Sty 4D **164**
SHAW SIDE 2H **59**
Shaws La. OL3: Upp 1E **79**
Shaw's Rd. WA14: Alt 2A **174** (1F **151**)
Shaw St. BL3: Bolt 2C **48**
BL4: Farn 5G **49**
BL9: Bury 2H **37**
M3: Man 2H **5** (2D **100**)
OL1: O'ham 2H **177** (1F **75**)
OL2: O'ham 3E **59**
OL3: G'fld 3C **78**
OL4: Spri 3E **77**
OL6: A Lyme 2B **106**
OL12: Roch 1B **28**
SK14: Mot 3C **122**
Shaw Ter. SK16: Duk 4A **106**
Shay Av. WA15: Haleb 4E **153**
Shayfield Av. M22: Wyth 6B **142**
OL9: Chad 2G **73**
Shayfield Dr. M22: Wyth 5B **142**
Shayfield Rd. M22: Wyth 6B **142**
Shay La. WA15: Haleb 4C **152**
Sheader Dr. M5: Sal 3C **98**
Sheaf Fld. Wlk. M26: Rad 3A **52**
Sheard Av. OL6: A Lyme 5B **92**
Sheardhall Av. SK12: Dis 2H **171**
Shearer Way M27: Pen 3D **84**
Shearing Av. OL12: Roch 2B **26**
Shearsby Cl. M15: Man 6F **9** (2C **114**)
Shearwater Dr. M28: Walk 6G **65**
Shearwater Ho. M19: Man 5H **131**
Shearwater Rd. SK2: Stoc 6F **147**
Sheddings, The BL3: Bolt 3E **49**
Shed St. OL12: Whitw 4B **14**
Sheepfoot La. M25: Pres 6B **70**
OL1: O'ham 6D **58**
Sheep Gap OL12: Roch 2D **26**
Sheep Ga. Dr. BL8: Tot 6G **21**
Sheep Hey BL0: Ram 4G **13**
Sheep La. M28: Wors 3D **80**
Sheerness St. M18: Man 2F **117**
Sheffield Rd. SK14: Hyde 3D **120**
(not continuous)
Sheffield St. M1: Man 1D **10** (5F **101**)
SK4: Stoc 6G **133**
Shefford Cl. M11: Man 5B **102**
Sheiling Ct. WA14: Alt 1E **151**
Shelbourne Av. BL1: Bolt 3H **31**
Shelden Cl. SK13: Gam 6F **123**
(off Brassington Cres.)
Shelden Fold SK13: Gam 6F **123**
(off Brassington Cres.)
Shelden M. SK13: Gam 6F **123**
Shelden Pl. SK13: Gam 6F **123**
(off Brassington Cres.)
SHELDERSLOW 2E **77**
Shelderton Cl. M40: Man 4C **88**
Sheldon Av. M41: Urm 5D **110**
Sheldon Cl. BL4: Farn 5F **49**
M31: Part 6D **124**
Sheldon Ct. OL7: A Lyme 6H **91**
Sheldon Rd. SK7: H Gro 6E **159**
SK12: Poy 5A **170**
Sheldon St. M11: Man 3D **102**
Sheldrake Cl. SK16: Duk 6C **106**
Sheldrake Rd. WA14: B'ath 3D **138**
Shelfield OL11: Roch 2B **26**
Shelfield Cl. OL11: Roch 2B **26**
Shelfield La. OL11: Roch 2A **26**
Shelford Av. M18: Man 3D **116**
Shellbrook Gro. SK9: Wilm 6H **165**
(off Rossenclough Rd.)
Shelley Av. M24: Mid 5D **56**
Shelley Ct. SK8: Chea H 4C **156**
Shelley Gro. M43: Droy 3A **104**
SK14: Hyde 2B **120**
SK15: Mill 1H **107**
Shelley Ri. SK16: Duk 6F **107**

Shelley Rd. M25: Pres 6F **69**
M27: Swin 3F **83**
M38: Lit H 4E **65**
OL1: O'ham 6A **60**
OL9: Chad 6H **73**
SK5: Stoc 6F **117**
Shelley St. M40: Man 3E **89**
Shelley Wlk. BL1: Bolt 4B **32**
(off Darley St.)
Shelley Way M34: Dent 1F **135**
Shelmerdine Cl. SK14: Mot 5B **122**
(off Chain Bar La.)
Shelmerdine Gdns. M6: Sal 1C **98**
Shelton Av. M33: Sale 5F **127**
Shenfield Wlk. M40: Man 1G **7**
Shenhurst Cl. SK9: Wilm 5B **172**
Shentonfield Rd. M22: Shar 5C **142**
Shenton Pk. Av. M33: Sale 1E **139**
Shenton St. SK14: Hyde 3A **120**
Shepherd Ct. OL16: Roch 5B **28**
Shepherd Cross St. BL1: Bolt 4A **32**
Shepherd Cross St. Ind. Est.
BL1: Bolt 3B **32**
(off Shepherd Cross St.)
Shepherds Brow WA14: Bow 2C **150**
Shepherds Cl. BL8: G'mount 2H **21**
Shepherd's Dr. BL6: Hor 2A **30**
Shepherds Grn. OL3: G'fld 4F **79**
Shepherds St. BL8: G'mount 2H **21**
BL9: Bury 5D **176** (4F **37**)
M9: Man 2A **88**
OL2: O'ham 3E **59**
(not continuous)
OL10: H'ood 3G **39**
OL11: Roch 2H **25**
OL12: Roch 1B **178** (3H **27**)
Shepherds Way OL16: Miln 6F **29**
Shepherd Wlk. M34: Dent 1F **135**
Shepley Av. BL3: Bolt 2A **48**
Shepley Cl. SK7: H Gro 5D **158**
SK16: Duk 5B **106**
(off Jeffreys Dr.)
Shepley Dr. SK7: H Gro 4D **158**
Shepley Ho. SK7: H Gro 4E **159**
Shepley Ind. Est. Nth. M34: Aud . . .6G **105**
Shepley Ind. Est. Sth. M34: Aud . . .1G **119**
Shepley La. M34: Aud 2D **160**
Shepley La. Ind. Est. SK6: Mar 2D **160**
Shepley Rd. M34: Aud 1F **119**
Shepley St. M34: Aud 6F **105**
M35: Fail 2A **90**
OL4: Lees 3C **76**
SK13: Had 4G **123**
SK14: Hyde 5C **120**
SK15: Stal 3E **107**
Shepton Cl. BL1: Bolt 4B **18**
Shepton Dr. M23: Wyth 3G **153**
Shepway Ct. M30: Ecc 3D **96**
Sheraton Rd. OL8: O'ham 5E **75**
Sherborne Ct. M26: Rad 2F **51**
Sherborne Ho. M24: Mid 4C **56**
Sherborne Rd. SK3: Stoc 4C **144**
Sherborne St. M3: Man 1G **5** (1D **100**)
M8: Man 1D **100**
Sherborne St. W. M3: Sal . . .1F **5** (2C **100**)
Sherbourne Cl. OL8: O'ham 5A **76**
SK8: Chea H 1D **166**
Sherbourne Ct. M25: Pres 5G **69**
Sherbourne Dr. OL10: H'ood 3H **39**
Sherbourne Rd. BL1: Bolt 4G **31**
M24: Mid 4C **56**
M41: Urm 4G **111**
Sherbrook Av. M25: Pres 5G **69**
Sherbrooke Av. OL3: Upp 6E **63**
Sherbrooke Cl. M33: Sale 6H **127**
Sherbrook Ri. SK9: Wilm 3F **173**
Sherdley Ct. M8: Man 2E **87**
Sherdley Rd. M8: Man 2E **87**
Sherford Cl. SK7: H Gro 3A **158**
Sheridan Ct. M40: Man 6A **88**
(off Ridgewood Av.)

Sheridan Way M34: Dent 1F **135**
OL9: Chad 1G **73**
Sheriffs Dr. M29: Tyld 2B **80**
Sheriff St. BL2: Bolt 4F **33**
OL12: Roch 2A **178** (2G **27**)
(not continuous)
OL16: Miln 6G **29**
Sheringham Dr. BL8: Bury 6D **22**
M27: Swin 5H **83**
SK14: Hyde 4E **121**
Sheringham Pl. BL3: Bolt 2B **48**
Sheringham Rd. M14: Man 2H **131**
Sherlock St. M14: Man 2H **131**
Sherratt St. M4: Man 3D **6** (3F **101**)
Sherrington St. M12: Man 4C **116**
Sherway Dr. WA15: Tim 4C **140**
Sherwell Rd. M9: Man 6F **71**
Sherwin Way OL11: Roch 4F **41**
Sherwood Av. M7: Sal 4H **85**
M14: Man 1G **131**
M26: Rad 5H **35**
M33: Sale 4C **128**
M43: Droy 3C **104**
SK4: Stoc 2C **144**
SK8: Chea H 3B **156**
Sherwood Bus. Pk. OL11: Roch 3F **41**
Sherwood Cl. BL8: Tot 4H **21**
M5: Sal 2D **98**
OL6: A Lyme 4A **92**
SK6: Mar 1D **160**
Sherwood Dr. M27: Pen 4B **84**
Sherwood Ind. Pk. OL11: Roch 3F **41**
Sherwood M. OL6: A Lyme 1B **106**
(off Board St.)
Sherwood Rd. M34: Dent 4B **118**
SK6: Wood 4H **135**
Sherwood St. BL1: Bolt 2D **32**
M14: Man 1G **131**
OL1: O'ham 6D **58**
OL11: Roch 3F **41**
(off Queensway)
Sherwood Way OL2: Shaw 5E **43**
Shetland Circ. M41: Urm 2E **111**
Shetland Rd. M40: Man 1G **7** (2H **101**)
Shetland Way M26: Rad 2A **52**
M41: Urm 2E **111**
Shevington Gdns. M23: Wyth 2H **141**
Shieldborn Dr. M9: Man 4H **87**
Shield Cl. OL8: O'ham 5E **177** (3E **75**)
Shield Dr. M28: Ward 4E **81**
Shiel St. M28: Walk 6H **65**
Shiers Dr. SK8: Chea 1A **156**
Shiffnall St. BL2: Bolt 5G **175** (1E **49**)
Shilford Dr. M4: Man 2E **7** (2G **101**)
Shillingford Rd. BL4: Farn 1F **65**
OL9: Chad 5A **74**
Shillingstone Cl. BL2: Bolt 2B **34**
Shillingten Cl. M28: Walk 6D **64**
Shiloh La. OL4: O'ham 5E **61**
Shilton Gdns. BL3: Bolt 2C **48**
(off Derby St.)
Shilton St. BL0: Ram 4B **12**
Shilton Wlk. M40: Man 1F **89**
(off Blandford Dr.)
Ship Canal Ho. M15: Man 2E **9** (5C **100**)
Shipgate BL1: Bolt 3G **175**
Shipla Cl. OL9: O'ham 2E **177** (2E **75**)
Ship La. OL3: Del 2E **61**
OL4: Del 1E **61**
Shipley Av. M6: Sal 2C **98**
Shipley Vw. M41: Urm 2B **110**
Shipperbottom La. BL0: Ram 4D **12**
(not continuous)
Shippey St. M14: Man 2H **131**
Shipston Cl. BL8: Bury 2B **36**
Shipton St. BL1: Bolt 4H **31**
Shirburn OL11: Roch 6A **178** (5G **27**)
Shirebrook Dr. M26: Rad 3B **52**
Shireburn Av. BL2: Bolt 5G **33**
Shiredale Cl. SK8: Chea H 1D **156**
Shiredale Dr. M9: Man 4H **87**
Shire Gdns. M26: Rad 3H **51**

Shiregreen Av. M40: Man 6G 87
Shirehills M25: Pres 6G 69
Shireoak Rd. M20: Man 2H 131
Shires, The M26: Rad 2A 52
Shires Rd. M43: Droy 2D 104
Shires Vw. OL5: Mos 2G 93
Shirley Av. M7: Sal 4G 85
M27: Pen 4C 84
M30: Ecc 5E 97
M32: Stre 4F 113
M34: Aud 5C 104
M34: Dent 4H 117
OL9: Chad 1G 89
SK6: Mar 5C 148
SK8: H Grn 6G 155
SK14: Hyde 2B 120
Shirley Cl. SK7: H Gro 3C 158
Shirley Ct. M33: Sale 5C 128
Shirley Gro. SK3: Stoc 6G 145
Shirley Rd. M8: Man 4E 87
Shirley St. OL11: Roch 2E 41
Shoecroft Av. M34: Dent 4E 119
SHOLVER 3B 60
Sholver Hey La. OL1: O'ham 3B 60
Sholver Hill Cl. OL1: O'ham 3C 60
Sholver La. OL1: O'ham 3B 60
Shone Av. M22: Wyth 3D 154
SHORE 3F 17
Shore Av. OL2: Shaw 4A 44
Shorecliffe Ri. M26: Rad 5C 52
Shoreditch Cl. SK4: Stoc 4D 132
SHORE EDGE 5C 44
Shorefield Cl. OL16: Miln 4F 29
                        (off Silver Hill)
Shorefield Mt. BL7: Eger 3C 18
Shore Fold OL15: L'ough 3F 17
Shoreham Cl. M16: W Ran 3C 114
Shoreham Wlk. OL9: Chad 3A 74
Shore Lea OL15: L'ough 3F 17
Shore Mt. OL15: L'ough 3F 17
Shore Rd. OL15: L'ough 3F 17
Shore St. OL1: O'ham 2G 75
OL16: Miln 5F 29
Shoreswood BL1: Bolt 6B 18
Shorland St. M27: Swin 4E 83
Shorrocks St. BL8: Bury 2H 35
Short Av. M43: Droy 5H 103
Shortcroft St. M15: Man 3G 9 (6D 100)
Shortland Cres. M19: Man 6H 131
Shortlands Av. BL9: Bury . . .6D 176 (4F 37)
Short St. M4: Man 5B 6 (4E 101)
M7: Sal 1E 5 (2C 100)
OL10: H'ood 4F 39
SK4: Stoc 6F 133
SK7: H Gro 2D 158
Short St. E. SK4: Stoc 6G 133
Shortwood Cl. M40: Man 6C 88
                        (off Harmer Cl.)
Shottery Walks SK6: Bred 6F 135
Shotton Wlk. M14: Man 4F 115
                        (off Ellanby Cl.)
Shottwood Fold OL15: L'ough 3A 16
Showcase Cinema
Belle Vue 2D 116
Shrewsbury Cl. M16: Old T 2B 114
Shrewsbury Gdns. SK8: Chea H 1E 167
Shrewsbury Rd. BL1: Bolt 5H 31
M25: Pres 6G 69
M33: Sale 1A 140
M43: Droy 3A 104
Shrewsbury St. M16: Old T 2A 114
OL4: O'ham 1A 76
Shrewsbury Way M34: Dent 6G 119
                        (off Trowbridge Rd.)
Shrigley Cl. SK9: Wilm 6H 165
Shrigley Rd. SK10: P Shr 5A 170
SK12: Adl, P Shr, Poy 5A 170
SK12: Poy 4A 170
Shrigley Rd. Nth. SK12: Poy 4A 170
Shrivenham Wlk. M23: Wyth 4F 141
                        (off Pitfield Gdns.)
Shropshire Av. SK5: Stoc 3C 134
Shropshire Rd. M35: Fail 5A 90

Shropshire Sq. M12: Man 1B 116
                        (off St Benedict's Av.)
Shrowbridge Wlk. M12: Man 1C 116
                        (off Clowes St.)
Shrubbery, The BL6: Los 6C 30
                        (off Old Hall Clough)
Shrub St. BL3: Bolt 5A 48
Shude Hill M4: Man 4A 6 (3E 101)
Shudehill Rd. M28: Wors 3E 81
Shude Hill Stop (Metro) 3A 6 (3E 101)
Shurmer St. BL3: Bolt 3A 48
Shutt La. OL3: Dob 5B 62
Shuttle Cl. OL5: Mos 2G 93
Shuttle St. M26: Rad 6C 52
M30: Ecc 3H 97
SHUTTLEWORTH 1E 13
Shuttleworth Cl.
M16: W Ran 1C 130
Shutts La. SK15: Stal 5H 107
Siam St. M11: Man 5B 102
Sibley Rd. SK4: Stoc 6D 132
Sibley St. M18: Man 2F 117
Siblies Wlk. M22: Wyth 4H 153
Sibson Ct. M21: Chor 6G 113
Sibson Rd. M21: Chor 6G 113
M33: Sale 5A 128
Sickle St. M2: Man 5A 6 (4E 101)
OL4: O'ham 4G 75
Sidbury Rd. M21: Chor 1A 130
Sidcup Rd. M23: Wyth 6F 141
Siddall St. M12: Man 5C 116
M26: Rad 3A 52
M34: Dent 4F 119
OL1: O'ham 1G 177 (1F 75)
OL2: Shaw 6H 43
OL10: H'ood 5A 40
SIDDAL MOOR 6H 39
Siddington Av. M20: Man 2E 131
SK3: Stoc 5E 145
Siddington Rd. SK9: Hand 2H 165
SK12: Poy 5F 169
Side Av. WA14: Bow 4E 151
Sidebotham St. SK6: Bred 5F 135
Sidebottom St. M43: Droy 4H 103
OL4: O'ham 1C 76
SK15: Stal 3E 107
SIDE OF THE MOOR 5B 20
Side St. M11: Man 3D 102
OL8: O'ham 1C 90
Sidford Cl. BL3: Bolt 2H 49
Sidings, The BL9: Bury 5B 176
M28: Wors 6C 82
Sidlaw Cl. OL8: O'ham 1F 91
Sidley Av. M9: Man 5B 72
Sidley Pl. SK14: Hyde 4D 120
                        (off St John's Dr.)
Sidley St. SK14: Hyde 4D 120
Sidmouth Av. M41: Urm 4A 110
Sidmouth Dr. M9: Man 1H 87
Sidmouth Gro. SK8: Chea H 6B 156
Sidmouth Rd. M33: Sale 4F 127
Sidmouth St. M34: Aud 6D 104
                        (not continuous)
OL9: O'ham 4C 74
Sidney Rd. M9: Man 2H 87
Sidney St. BL3: Bolt 2D 48
M1: Man 4B 10 (6E 101)
M3: Man 6G 5 (4D 100)
M3: Sal 4D 4
OL7: O'ham 6G 59
Sidwell Wlk. M4: Man 5H 7
Siebers Bank OL12: Roch 1F 27
Siemens Rd. M20: Man 4C 130
M44: Cad, Irl 4C 124
Sienna Cl. M44: Irl 3C 124
Sienna Ct. OL9: Chad 1A 74
Sighthill Wlk. M9: Man 3H 87
                        (off Coningsby Dr.)
Signal Cl. M30: Ecc 3D 96
Signal Dr. M40: Man 5H 87
Signet Wlk. M8: Man 6F 87
Silas St. OL6: A Lyme 6B 92
Silburn Way M24: Mid 2G 71

Silbury Wlk. M8: Man 6D 86
                        (off Barrow Hill Rd.)
Silchester Dr. M40: Man 5H 87
Silchester Wlk. OL1: O'ham 2G 177
Silchester Way BL2: Bolt 4A 34
Silfield Cl. M11: Man 4A 102
Silkhey Gro. M28: Walk 2H 81
Silkin Cl. M13: Man 4C 10
Silkin Ct. M13: Man 4C 10
Silk Mill SK12: Poy 3B 168
Silk Mill Way M24: Mid 1B 72
Silk St. M3: Sal 2C 4 (2B 100)
M4: Man 3D 6 (3G 101)
M24: Mid 1B 72
M30: Ecc 4H 97
M40: Man 5E 89
OL11: Roch 1E 41
Silsden Av. M9: Man 4F 71
Silsden Wlk. M7: Sal 3F 85
Silton St. M9: Man 4B 88
Silvamere Cl. M6: Sal 2E 99
Silverbirch Cl. M33: Sale 1F 139
Silver Birches M34: Dent 6H 119
Silver Birch Gro. M27: Pen 5B 84
Silver Birch M. SK16: Duk 6C 106
Silverbirch Way M35: Fail 4H 89
Silver Blades Ice Rink
Altrincham 2C 174 (1G 151)
Silver Cl. SK16: Duk 6H 105
Silver Ct. M45: White 6E 53
Silvercroft St. M15: Man 3E 9 (6C 100)
Silverdale M27: Clif 1A 84
WA14: Alt 1E 151
Silverdale Av. M25: Pres 1C 86
M34: Dent 5G 119
M38: Lit H 4E 65
M44: Irl 3F 109
OL9: Chad 3A 74
Silverdale Cl. BL9: Bury 5G 37
SK6: H Lan 5C 160
Silverdale Dr. OL4: Lees 3D 76
SK9: Wilm 5D 172
Silverdale Rd. BL1: Bolt 6A 32
BL4: Farn 6E 49
M21: Chor 6A 114
SK4: Stoc 5E 133
SK8: Gat 1F 155
Silverdale St. M11: Man 6H 103
Silver Hill OL16: Miln 4F 29
Silver Hill Rd. SK14: Hyde 6C 120
Silver Jubilee Wlk. M4: Man 4C 6
Silverlea Dr. M9: Man 1G 87
Silvermere Ct. BL0: Ram 4B 12
Silver Spring SK14: Hyde 1D 136
Silverstone Dr. M40: Man 1F 103
Silverstone St. BL0: Ram 3C 12
BL9: Bury 4B 176 (3E 37)
M1: Man .1A 10
                        (Abingdon St.)
M1: Man 6B 6 (4E 101)
                        (Chorlton St.)
M44: Irl 3F 109
M45: White 6E 53
OL1: O'ham 4F 177 (3E 75)
Silverthorne Cl. SK15: Stal 4E 107
Silverton Cl. SK14: Hat 5A 122
                        (not continuous)
Silverton Gro. BL1: Bolt 1D 32
M24: Mid 3H 55
Silverton Ho. M6: Sal 2A 98
                        (off Devon Cl.)
Silverwell La. BL1: Bolt 4G 175 (6D 32)
Silverwell St. BL1: Bolt 4G 175 (6D 32)
M40: Man 6F 89
Silverwell Yd. BL1: Bolt 4G 175
Silver Wings Sports Club 1C 152
Silverwood OL9: Chad 2G 73
Silverwood Av. M21: Chor 1H 129
Silvine Wlk. M40: Man 1H 101
Simeon St. M4: Man 2C 6 (2F 101)
OL16: Miln 5F 29
SIMISTER 1C 70

Simister Dr. BL9: Bury 5G **53**
Simister Grn. M25: Pres 1C **70**
Simister La. M24: Mid 6E **55**
  M25: Pres 1B **70**
Simister Rd. M35: Fail 4H **89**
Simister St. M9: Man 3A **88**
Simkin Way OL8: O'ham 2F **91**
SIMMONDLEY 6H **123**
Simmondley La. SK13: Glos 6H **123**
Simmons Ct. M16: W Ran 4C **114**
Simms Cl. BL0: Ram 4A **12**
  M3: Sal 4C **4** (3B **100**)
Simonbury Cl. BL8: Bury 3H **35**
Simon Freeman Cl.
  M19: Man 2E **133**
Simon Ho. SK4: Stoc 3E **133**
Simon La. M24: Mid 5E **55**
Simons Cl. M33: Sale 6A **128**
Simonsway M23: Wyth 2H **153**
Simpson Av. M27: Clif 1C **84**
SIMPSON CLOUGH 6G **25**
Simpson Gro. M28: Wors 5E **81**
Simpson Hill Cl. OL10: H'ood 2B **40**
Simpson Rd. M28: Wors 5E **81**
Simpsons Pl. OL12: Roch 2H **27**
             (off Whitworth Rd.)
Simpson Sq. OL9: Chad 6C **74**
Simpson St. M4: Man 2B **6** (2E **101**)
  M11: Man 4C **102**
  OL9: Chad 5B **74**
  SK9: Wilm 3C **172**
  SK14: Hyde 5B **120**
Sinclair Av. M8: Man 2D **86**
Sinclair St. OL11: Roch 2F **41**
Sinderland La. WA14: D Mas 2A **138**
Sinderland Rd. M31: Part 5G **125**
  WA14: D Mas 2C **138**
Sindsley Ct. M27: Ward 2F **83**
              (off Moss La.)
Sindsley Gro. BL3: Bolt 4C **48**
Sindsley Rd. M27: Ward 1F **83**
Singapore Av. M90: Man A 5G **153**
Singleton Av. BL2: Bolt 6A **34**
Singleton Cl. M7: Sal 2A **86**
Singleton Gro. BL5: W'ton 6B **46**
Singleton Lodge M7: Sal 2B **86**
         (off Cavendish Rd.)
Singleton Rd. M7: Sal 2A **86**
  SK4: Stoc 5D **132**
Singleton St. M26: Rad 3F **51**
Sion St. M26: Rad 5H **51**
Sir Charles Groves Hall M15: Man . . .5A **10**
Sirdar St. M11: Man 5H **103**
Sir Isaac Newton Way OL16: Miln . . .6C **28**
Sirius Pl. M7: Sal 1C **4**
Sir Matt Busby Way M16: Old T 2F **113**
Sir Richard Fairey Rd. SK4: Stoc . . .3C **132**
Sir Robert Thomas Ct. M9: Man 3H **87**
         (off Coningsby Dr.)
Sir Williams Ct. M23: Wyth 5G **141**
Siskin Cl. SK2: Stoc 6F **147**
Sisley Cl. M7: Sal 3H **85**
Sisson St. M35: Fail 4H **89**
Sisters St. M43: Droy 5A **104**
Sixpools Gro. M28: Wors 3G **81**
Sixth Av. BL1: Bolt 6H **31**
  BL3: Lit L 3B **50**
  BL9: Bury 1B **38**
  OL8: O'ham 2C **90**
Sixth St. M17: T Pk 2D **112**
Size St. OL12: Whitw 4B **14**
SK14 Ind. Pk. SK14: Hyde 2A **120**
SKAGEN 1E **175** (4C **32**)
Skagen Ct. BL1: Bolt 1E **175** (4C **32**)
Skaife Rd. M33: Sale 5E **129**
Skarratt Cl. M12: Man 1B **116**
Skegness Cl. BL8: Bury 6D **22**
Skellorn Grn. La. SK10: Adl 6F **169**
Skelton Gro. BL2: Bolt 5B **34**
  M13: Man 5B **116**
Skelton Rd. M32: Stre 4D **112**
  WA14: Tim 4G **139**
Skelwith Av. BL3: Bolt 5D **48**

Skelwith Cl. M41: Urm 3C **110**
Skerry Cl. M13: Man 4D **10** (6F **101**)
Skerton Rd. M16: Old T 2H **113**
Skiddaw Cl. M24: Mid 4H **55**
Skilgate Wlk. M40: Man 5E **89**
         (off Queensferry St.)
Skip Pl. M3: Man 1A **6** (2E **101**)
Skipton Av. M40: Man 2F **89**
  OL9: Chad 6H **57**
Skipton Cl. BL8: Bury 3H **35**
  SK5: Stoc 1G **133**
  SK7: H Gro 5D **158**
Skipton Dr. M41: Urm 2B **110**
Skipton St. BL2: Bolt 5G **33**
  OL8: O'ham 5H **75**
Skipton Wlk. BL2: Bolt 5G **33**
            (off Skipton St.)
Skye Cl. OL10: H'ood 4D **38**
Skye Rd. M41: Urm 2F **111**
Skye Wlk. M23: Wyth 1G **153**
SLACKCOTE 6G **45**
Slackcote La. OL3: Del 6G **45**
Slackey Brow BL4: Kea 3E **67**
Slack Fold La. BL3: Bolt 5A **48**
  BL4: Farn 5A **48**
Slack Ga. OL12: Whitw 1G **15**
  OL12: W'le 1G **15**
Slackgate La. OL3: Dens 4H **45**
Slack Hall OL4: Aus 1D **76**
Slack La. BL2: Bolt 4H **19**
  BL5: W'ton 4A **46**
  BL8: Aff 4C **20**
  M27: Pen 2A **84**
  OL3: Del 6G **45**
Slack Rd. M9: Man 2G **87**
Slack St. OL16: Roch 3C **178** (4H **27**)
  SK14: Hyde 3D **120**
Slade Gro. M13: Man 4B **116**
Slade Hall Rd. M12: Man 5C **116**
Slade La. M13: Man 6B **116**
  M19: Man 1B **132**
Slade Mt. M19: Man 1B **132**
Sladen St. OL12: Roch 2H **27**
Slades La. OL3: Upp 6G **63**
Slade St. BL3: Lit L 4C **50**
Slades Vw. Cl. OL3: Dig 2E **63**
Slaidburn Av. BL2: Bolt 1B **50**
Slaidburn Cl. OL16: Miln 6F **29**
Slaidburn Dr. BL8: Bury 2G **35**
Slaithwaite Rd. M11: Man 3E **103**
Slateacre Rd. SK14: Hyde 2D **136**
Slate La. M34: A Lyme 5E **105**
  M34: Aud 5C **104**
Slaterfield BL3: Bolt 2C **48**
Slater Ho. M5: Sal 3B **8** (6A **100**)
Slater La. BL1: Bolt 1H **175** (4E **33**)
Slater St. BL1: Bolt 1E **175** (5C **32**)
  BL4: Farn 1H **65**
  M30: Ecc 3D **96**
  M35: Fail 2H **89**
  OL8: O'ham 5E **177**
  OL9: O'ham 4E **177**
Slater Way SK14: Mot 5B **122**
Slate Wharf M15: Man 2D **8** (5B **100**)
SLATTOCKS 1F **57**
Slattocks Link Rd. M24: Mid 2F **57**
Slaunt Bank OL12: Roch 1H **25**
Slawson Way OL10: H'ood 2B **40**
Sleaford Cl. BL8: Bury 6D **22**
  M40: Man 1G **7** (2H **101**)
Sleddale Cl. SK2: Stoc 6D **146**
Sledmere Cl. BL1: Bolt 3D **32**
  M11: Man 4C **102**
Sledmoor Rd. M23: Wyth 2F **141**
Slimbridge Cl. BL2: Bolt 4C **34**
Sloane Av. OL4: Lees 1C **76**
Sloane St. BL3: Bolt 4H **47**
  OL6: A Lyme 2A **106**
Slough Ind. Est. M5: Sal 2B **8** (5A **100**)
SMALLBRIDGE 6C **16**
Smallbridge Cl. M28: Wors 3G **81**
Smallbridge Ind. Pk. OL16: Roch . . .1C **28**
Small Brook Rd. OL2: Shaw 3A **44**

Smalldale Av. M16: W Ran 4D **114**
Smalley St. OL11: Roch 3E **41**
Smallfield Dr. M9: Man 3H **87**
Small La. WA16: Mob 6A **162**
Smallridge Cl. M40: Man 2G **7** (2H **101**)
SMALLSHAW 6A **92**
Smallshaw Fold OL6: A Lyme 6H **91**
Smallshaw La. OL6: A Lyme 6A **92**
Smallshaw Rd. OL12: Roch 5C **14**
Smallshaw Sq. OL6: A Lyme 6H **91**
Smallwood St. M40: Man 5E **89**
Smart St. M12: Man 4C **116**
Smeaton Cl. M32: Stre 5E **113**
Smeaton St. M8: Man 5G **87**
SMEDLEY 5F **87**
Smedley Av. BL3: Bolt 4E **49**
  M8: Man 5F **87**
Smedley La. M8: Man 5F **87**
Smedley Rd. M8: Man 5F **87**
Smedley St. M8: Man 5E **87**
Smethurst Ct. BL3: Bolt 5H **47**
         (off Smethurst La.)
Smethurst Hall Rd. BL8: Bury 1C **38**
Smethurst La. BL3: Bolt, Farn 5H **47**
  BL4: Farn 5H **47**
Smethurst St. BL8: Bury 1B **36**
  M9: Man 2H **87**
  M24: Mid 2F **73**
  OL10: H'ood 3F **39**
Smith Farm Cl. OL4: Aus 1D **76**
Smithfield Bldgs. M4: Man 5B **6**
Smithfield Ent. Est. M11: Man 6F **103**
            (off Press St.)
Smithfold La. M28: Walk 6E **65**
Smith Hill OL16: Miln 5F **29**
Smithies Av. M24: Mid 5C **56**
Smithies St. OL10: H'ood 3A **40**
Smithills Cft. Rd. BL1: Bolt 2G **31**
Smithills Dean Rd. BL1: Bolt 1G **31**
Smithills Dr. BL1: Bolt 3F **31**
Smithill's Hall 1H **31**
Smithills Hall Cl. BL0: Ram 4C **12**
Smithills Hall Country Pk. 1H **31**
Smithill's Open Farm 6A **18**
Smith La. BL7: Eger 2D **18**
Smiths Lawn SK9: Wilm 4D **172**
Smith's Rd. BL3: Bolt 4H **49**
Smith St. BL0: Ram 4B **12**
  BL9: Bury 1G **37**
  M16: Old T 5A **8** (1A **114**)
  M28: Walk 6H **65**
  M34: Dent 5F **119**
  OL4: Lees 1C **76**
  OL5: Mos 1F **93**
  OL7: A Lyme 4F **105**
  OL10: H'ood 3H **39**
  OL15: L'ough 4H **17**
         (off Barehill St.)
  OL16: Roch 3C **178** (4H **27**)
  SK8: Chea 5B **144**
  SK14: Hyde 2B **120**
  SK16: Duk 5G **105**
SMITHY BRIDGE 6F **17**
Smithybridge Rd.
  OL15: L'ough 5E **17**
Smithy Bridge Station (Rail) 6F **17**
Smithy Ct. SK6: Mar 5D **148**
Smithy Cft. BL7: Bro X 3D **18**
Smithy Fld. OL15: L'ough 3G **17**
Smithy Fold OL12: Roch 2D **26**
Smithy Fold Rd. SK14: Hyde 6C **120**
SMITHY GREEN 6C **156**
Smithy Grn. OL16: Miln 1C **44**
  SK6: Wood 4H **135**
  SK8: Chea H 5C **156**
Smithy Gro. OL6: A Lyme 1A **106**
Smithy Hill BL3: Bolt 3G **47**
Smithy La. M3: Man 5G **5** (4D **100**)
  M31: Part 6D **124**
  OL3: Upp 1D **78**
  SK14: Hyde 6C **120**
  WA14: D Mas 2A **150**
Smithy Nook OL15: L'ough 2A **16**

Smithy St. BL0: Ram 3C **12**
   SK7: H Gro 2D **158**
Smithy Yd. OL3: Upp 1D **78**
   (off Smithy La.)
Smyrna St. M5: Sal 4E **99**
   M26: Rad 3H **51**
   OL4: O'ham 3A **76**
   OL10: H'ood 4G **39**
Smyrna Wlk. M26: Rad 3H **51**
   (off Smyrna St.)
Snapebrook Gro. SK9: Wilm 6A **166**
   (off Colshaw Dr.)
Snape St. M26: Rad 1H **51**
   (not continuous)
Snell St. M4: Man 6G 7 (4H **101**)
Snipe Av. OL11: Roch 4B **26**
Snipe Cl. SK12: Poy 3A **168**
Snipe Retail Pk. OL7: A Lyme 5D **104**
Snipe Rd. OL8: O'ham 1H **91**
Snipe St. BL3: Bolt 2D **48**
Snipeway OL7: A Lyme 5D **104**
Snowberry Wlk. M31: Part 6C **124**
   (off Wood La.)
Snowden Av. M41: Urm 1D **126**
Snowden St. BL1: Bolt 5C **32**
   OL8: O'ham 5F **75**
   OL10: H'ood 5A **40**
Snowden Wlk. M40: Man 1E **89**
   (off Pleasington Dr.)
Snowdon Rd. M30: Ecc 2A **98**
Snowdon St. OL11: Roch 3A **42**
Snowdrop Wlk. M7: Sal 5B **86**
   (off Bury New Rd.)
Snow Hill Rd. BL3: Bolt 2H **49**
Snydale Cl. BL5: W'ton 5A **46**
Snydale Way BL3: Bolt, W'ton 6C **46**
Soapstone Way M44: Irl 1E **125**
Soap St. M4: Man 4B **6**
Soccer Village 3F **29**
Society St. OL2: Shaw 6H **43**
Sofa St. BL1: Bolt 4H **31**
Soho St. BL3: Bolt 5F **175** (1D **48**)
   OL4: O'ham 2H **75**
Solent Av. M8: Man 1E **87**
Solent Dr. BL3: Bolt 2G **49**
Solness St. BL9: Bury 5F **23**
Soloman Rd. WA14: W Tim 2E **139**
Solway Cl. BL3: Bolt 4B **48**
   M27: Clif 5G **67**
   OL8: O'ham 4E **75**
Solway Rd. M22: Wyth 1C **154**
Somerby Dr. M22: Wyth 4A **154**
Somerdale Av. BL1: Bolt 6G **31**
Somerfield Rd. M9: Man 2H **87**
Somerford Av. M20: Man 1E **131**
Somerford Rd. SK5: Stoc 5H **117**
Somerford Way SK9: Hand 2H **165**
   (off Spath La.)
Somersby Ct. SK7: Bram 4G **157**
Somersby Dr. BL7: Bro X 3D **18**
Somersby Wlk. BL3: Bolt 2D **48**
   (off Hallington Cl.)
Somerset Av. OL2: Shaw 6F **43**
Somerset Cl. M44: Cad 3B **124**
   SK5: Stoc 5C **134**
Somerset Dr. BL9: Bury 5F **37**
Somerset Gro. OL11: Roch 3C **26**
Somerset Pl. M33: Sale 3B **128**
Somerset Rd. BL1: Bolt 5H **31**
   M30: Ecc 1A **98**
   M35: Fail 5G **89**
   M43: Droy 2H **103**
   WA14: Alt 5F **139**
Somerset St. OL4: O'ham 3A **76**
Somers Rd. SK5: Stoc 6H **117**
Somerton Av. M22: Wyth 2A **154**
   M33: Sale 6C **128**
Somerton Ct. M9: Man 6C **72**
Somerton Rd. BL2: Bolt 1B **50**
Somerville Gdns. WA15: Tim 4H **139**
Somerville Sq. BL1: Bolt 2A **32**
Somerville St. BL1: Bolt 2A **32**

Somerwood Wlk. M12: Man 1B **116**
   (off Kelsall St.)
Sommerville Ct. M7: Sal 3B **86**
   (off Park La.)
Sonning Dr. BL3: Bolt 5G **47**
Sonning Wlk. M8: Man 5F **87**
Sopwith Dr. M14: Man 6E **115**
Sorby Rd. M44: Irl 2D **124**
Sorrel Bank M6: Sal 1F **99**
Sorrel Dr. OL15: L'ough 3F **17**
Sorrell Bank SK5: Stoc 6A **118**
Sorrel St. M15: Man 5E 9 (1C **114**)
Sorrel Way OL4: O'ham 5C **60**
Sorton St. M1: Man 3B 10 (6E **101**)
Souchay Ct. M20: Man 5F **131**
   (off Clothorn Rd.)
Soudan Rd. SK2: Stoc 5A **146**
Soudan St. M24: Mid 6E **57**
Sound, The OL3: Del 3B **62**
SOURACRE .1E **107**
Souracre Fold SK15: H'rod 2F **107**
Southacre Dr. SK9: Hand 4H **165**
Southall St. M3: Man 1G **5** (2D **100**)
Southampton Ct. M7: Sal 6B **86**
Southam St. M7: Sal 4D **86**
South Av. BL4: Kea 3B **66**
   M19: Man 2B **132**
   M27: Swin 6F **83**
   M45: White 6E **53**
   OL3: G'fld 3D **78**
   OL10: H'ood 3F **39**
South Bk. Rock BL9: Bury 3B **176**
   (not continuous)
Sth. Bank Cl. SK9: A Edg 4H **173**
Sth. Bank Rd. BL9: Bury 6A **176** (4E **37**)
Southbank Rd. M19: Man 4H **131**
Southbourne Av. M41: Urm 5H **111**
Southbourne St. M6: Sal 3E **99**
Southbrook Av. M8: Man 6D **70**
Southbrook Cl. SK13: Had 3G **123**
Southbrook Gro. BL3: Bolt 4D **48**
Southchurch Pde. M40: Man 1G **101**
   (off Whitley Rd.)
Southcliffe Rd. SK5: Stoc 3H **133**
Sth. Cliffe St. M11: Man 6H **103**
South Cl. BL9: Bury 4G **53**
   SK9: Wilm 3C **172**
   SK13: Tin 1H **123**
Southcombe Wlk. M15: Man 2D **114**
South Ct. OL16: Roch 2D **178** (3A **28**)
South Cres. M11: Man 3F **103**
South Cft. OL8: O'ham 6H **75**
Southcross Rd. M18: Man 4F **117**
Sth. Cross St. BL9: Bury 4D **176** (3F **37**)
   (not continuous)
Sth. Croston St. M16: Old T 3B **114**
Southdene Av. M20: Man 5C **130**
Southdown Cl. OL11: Roch 1E **41**
   SK4: Stoc 1F **145**
Southdown Cres. M9: Man 1C **88**
   SK8: Chea H 5B **156**
Southdown Dr. M28: Wors 5D **80**
Sth. Downs Cl. OL2: Shaw 5F **43**
Sth. Downs Dr. WA14: Hale 5F **151**
Sth. Downs Rd. WA14: Bow 4E **151**
South Dr. BL1: Bolt 1E **175** (4C **32**)
   BL2: Bolt 2A **34**
   M21: Chor 3H **129**
   M41: Urm 2B **110**
   SK8: Gat 1E **155**
   SK9: Wilm 3E **173**
   WA15: Tim 4A **140**
Southend Av. M15: Man 5C **8** (1B **114**)
Southend St. BL3: Bolt 4A **48**
Southerly Cres. M40: Man 6F **73**
Southern App. M27: Clif 1C **84**
Southernby Cl. M13: Man 3B **116**
   (off Holmfirth St.)
Southern Cl. M34: Dent 1F **135**
   SK7: Bram 4H **157**
Southern Cres. SK7: Bram 3H **157**
Southern Ho. BL1: Bolt 4B **32**
   (off Kirkhope Dr.)

Southern Ind. Est. M28: Walk 4H **65**
Southern Rd. M33: Sale 3A **128**
Southern St. M3: Man 2F **9** (5C **100**)
   M6: Sal 3E **99**
   M28: Walk 4H **65**
Southey Cl. OL15: L'ough 1F **29**
Southey Ct. M34: Dent 1G **135**
Southey Wlk. M34: Dent 2G **135**
   (off Burns Rd.)
Southfield Av. BL9: Bury 4F **23**
Southfield Cl. SK9: Hand 4G **165**
   (off Knowle Pk.)
   SK16: Duk 1B **120**
South Fld. Ind. Est.
   M17: T Pk 1C **112**
Southfield Rd. BL0: Ram 1A **22**
Southfields WA14: Bow 3E **151**
Southfields Av. M11: Man 3E **103**
Southfields Dr. WA15: Tim 4B **140**
Southfield St. BL3: Bolt 3F **49**
Southgarth Rd. M6: Sal 2E **99**
Southgate BL2: Bolt 1A **34**
   M3: Man 5G **5** (4D **100**)
   M21: Chor 2H **129**
   M41: Urm 1D **126**
   OL3: Dob 5C **62**
   OL12: Whitw 2E **15**
   SK4: Stoc 4E **133**
Southgate Av. M40: Man 1C **102**
Southgate Dr. M33: Sale 4C **128**
Southgate Ind. Est. OL10: H'ood 4A **40**
Southgate M. SK4: Stoc 4E **133**
Southgate Rd. BL9: Bury 4F **53**
   OL9: Chad 1H **73**
Southgate St. OL1: O'ham . . .4H **177** (3F **75**)
Southgate Way OL7: A Lyme 4G **105**
   (off John St.)
South Gro. M13: Man 2H **115**
   M28: Walk 1G **81**
   M33: Sale 6B **128**
   SK9: A Edg 5G **173**
Southgrove Av. BL1: Bolt 5C **18**
Sth. Hall St. M5: Sal 2B **8** (5A **100**)
South Hill OL4: Spri 4D **76**
Sth. Hill St. OL4: O'ham 3G **75**
Sth. King St. M2: Man 5G **5** (4D **100**)
   M30: Ecc 3D **96**
Southlands BL2: Bolt 5A **34**
   SK3: Stoc 1H **157**
   (off Bramhall La.)
Southlands Av. M30: Ecc 5B **96**
Southlands Ct. SK3: Stoc 5H **145**
Sth. Langworthy M50: Sal 5E **99**
Southlea Rd. M19: Man 4H **131**
   M20: Man 4H **131**
Southleigh Dr. BL2: Bolt 1C **50**
Southlink OL4: O'ham 3G **75**
Southlink Bus. Pk. OL4: O'ham 2H **75**
Southlink Bus. Pk. Workshops
   OL4: O'ham 3G **75**
Southlink Ind. Pk. OL4: O'ham 2H **75**
Sth. Lonsdale St. M32: Stre 4E **113**
South Manchester Gymnastics Cen.
 . . . . .6C **142**
South Mead SK12: Poy 2B **168**
South Meade M21: Chor 2H **129**
   M25: Pres 1B **86**
   M27: Swin 5G **83**
   WA15: Tim 4A **140**
South Meadway SK6: H Lan 6D **160**
Southmere Cl. M40: Man 6E **73**
Sth. Mesnefield Rd. M7: Sal 4G **85**
Southmill St. M2: Man 1G **9** (5D **100**)
Southmoor M23: Wyth 4F **141**
Southmoor Bus. Pk. M23: Wyth 4E **141**
Southmoor Ind. Est.
   M23: Wyth 5F **141**
Southmoor Rd. M23: Wyth 4F **141**
Southmoor Wlk. BL3: Bolt 2C **48**
   (off Parrot St.)
Sth. Oak La. SK9: Wilm 3C **172**
Southolme Gdns.
   M19: Man 5A **132**

South Pde.—Spring Clough

South Pde. OL16: Roch 3B 178 (4H 27)
SK7: Bram 3H 157
South Pk. Dr. SK12: Poy 3E 169
South Pk. Rd. SK8: Gat 5F 143
South Pl. OL16: Roch 3A 28
Southpoint SK4: Stoc 1C 144
Southpool Cl. SK7: Bram 3A 158
Sth. Pump St. M1: Man 1C 10 (5F 101)
Sth. Radford St. M7: Sal 4G 85
SOUTH REDDISH 3H 133
South Ridge M34: Dent 2F 119
South Rd. M20: Man 1F 143
M27: Clif 1D 84
WA14: Bow 3E 151
(not continuous)
WA14: Hale 5F 151
South Row M25: Pres 2F 85
Sth. Royd St. BL8: Tot 4H 21
Southsea St. M11: Man 6F 103
South Side SK14: Hyde 6D 120
Southside SK6: Bred 3E 135
South Stage M50: Sal 5F 99
South St. BL0: Ram 3D 12
(Derby St.)
BL0: Ram 3D 12
(Peel Brow)
BL3: Bolt 4C 48
M11: Man 5D 102
(not continuous)
M12: Man 2A 116
OL7: A Lyme 5E 105
OL8: O'ham 1B 90
OL10: H'ood 3F 39
OL16: Roch 2D 178 (3A 28)
SK9: A Edg 5G 173
South Ter. BL0: Ram 3F 13
BL9: Bury 6D 36
OL12: Roch 2B 26
SK9: A Edg 6G 173
South Ter. Ct. OL16: Roch 6A 28
South Va. Cres. WA15: Tim 6H 139
South Vw. *M14: Man 5G 115*
(off Taylor St.)
OL11: Roch 5A 26
SK5: Stoc 4H 117
SK6: Wood 3A 136
SK15: C'ook 5B 94
SK16: Duk 4A 106
South Vw. Gdns. SK8: Chea 2G 155
South Vw. Rd. OL16: Roch 6E 17
South Vw. St. BL2: Bolt 6G 33
South Vw. Ter. OL16: Roch 5E 17
Southview Wlk. OL4: O'ham 6C 60
South Wlk. SK15: Stal 4E 107
Southwark Dr. SK16: Duk 1B 120
Southway M30: Ecc 3H 97
M40: Man 1H 89
M43: Droy 5A 104
OL7: A Lyme 5H 91
OL8: O'ham 1E 91
WA14: Alt 5G 139
Southwell Cl. BL1: Bolt 5B 32
SK6: Rom 2G 147
Southwell Ct. M32: Stre 6C 112
Southwell Gdns. OL6: A Lyme 4H 91
Southwell St. M9: Man 4A 88
Southwick Rd. M23: Wyth 1G 141
Sth. William St. M3: Sal 5C 4
Southwold Cl. M19: Man 6E 117
Southwood Cl. BL3: Bolt 4D 48
Southwood Dr. M9: Man 4E 71
Sth. Woodley Gdns. M26: Rad 1C 68
Southwood Rd. SK2: Stoc 1B 158
Southworth Ct. M3: Sal 4C 4
Southyard St. M19: Man 1D 132
Sovereign Ent. Pk. M50: Sal 5G 99
Sovereign Hall Cvn. Pk. OL5: Mos 2F 93
Sovereign Ho. SK8: Chea 5B 144
Sovereign Point M50: Sal 6F 99
Sovereign St. M6: Sal 1G 99
Sowerby Cl. BL8: Bury 3H 35
Sowerby Wlk. *M9: Man 5F 71*
(off Chapel La.)
Spa Cl. SK5: Stoc 1G 133
Spa Cres. M38: Lit H 3D 64
Spa Gro. M38: Lit H 3E 65
Spa La. M38: Lit H 3E 65
OL4: Lees 4B 76
Spalding Dr. M23: Wyth 3G 153
Sparkford Av. M23: Wyth 2D 140
Sparkle St. M1: Man 6D 6 (4F 101)
Spark Rd. M23: Wyth 4F 141
Spa Rd. BL1: Bolt 4E 175 (1B 48)
Sparrow Cl. SK5: Stoc 5G 117
Sparrowfield Cl. SK15: C'ook 4A 94
Sparrow Hill OL16: Roch 4A 178 (4G 27)
Sparrow St. M13: Man 6G 11 (2H 115)
OL2: O'ham 5E 59
Sparta Av. M28: Walk 1G 81
Sparta Wlk. *M11: Man 5C 102*
(off Mill St.)
Sparth Bottoms Rd.
OL11: Roch 6A 178 (5F 27)
Sparth Ct. SK4: Stoc 6F 133
Sparthfield Av. OL11: Roch 6G 27
Sparthfield Rd. SK4: Stoc 6F 133
Sparth Hall SK4: Stoc 6F 133
Sparth La. SK4: Stoc 6F 133
Sparth Rd. M40: Man 6F 89
Spa St. M15: Man 2F 115
Spathfield Ct. SK4: Stoc 6F 133
Spath Holme M20: Man 6E 131
Spath La. SK8: Chea H 2B 166
(not continuous)
SK9: Hand 2H 165
Spath La. E. SK8: Chea H 2D 166
Spath Rd. M20: Man 5D 130
Spath Wlk. SK8: Chea H 2D 166
Spaw St. M3: Sal 4E 5 (3C 100)
Spean Wlk. *M11: Man 4E 103*
(off Bill Williams Cl.)
Spear St. M1: Man 5B 6 (4E 101)
Spectator St. M4: Man 4H 7 (4H 101)
Specton Wlk. M12: Man 4D 116
Spectrum Bus. Pk. SK3: Stoc 5D 144
Spectrum Way SK3: Stoc 5E 145
Speedwell SK13: Tin 1H 123
Speedwell Cl. SK13: Tin 1H 123
Speke Wlk. M34: Dent 6E 119
Spencer Av. BL3: Lit L 4E 51
M16: W Ran 5A 114
M45: White 5E 53
SK14: Hyde 2B 120
Spencer La. OL11: Roch 6A 26
Spencer St. BL0: Ram 4B 12
BL8: Bury 2C 36
M26: Rad 3C 52
M30: Ecc 4E 97
OL1: O'ham 2G 75
OL5: Mos 2F 93
OL9: Chad 5B 74
SK5: Stoc 1H 133
SK16: Duk 5A 106
Spencers Wood *BL7: Bro X 4D 18*
(off Hough La.)
Spender Av. M8: Man 5E 87
Spen Fold BL8: Bury 5A 36
OL15: L'ough 5G 17
Spenleach La. BL8: Haw 1F 21
Spenlow Cl. SK12: Poy 6E 169
Spennithorne Rd. M41: Urm 5D 110
Spenser Av. M26: Rad 3G 51
M34: Dent 1G 135
Spenwood Rd. OL15: L'ough 4F 17
Spey Cl. WA14: Alt 5E 139
Spey Ho. SK5: Stoc 5H 117
Speyside Cl. M45: White 1G 69
Spindle Av. SK15: Stal 2G 107
Spindle Ct. *OL2: O'ham 3E 59*
(off High Barn St.)
Spindle Cft. BL4: Farn 1H 65
Spindlepoint Dr. M28: Wors 3G 81
Spindles, The OL5: Mos 3H 93
Spindles Shop. Cen.
OL1: O'ham 4F 177 (3E 75)
Spindlewood Cl. SK15: Stal 3H 107
Spinks St. OL4: O'ham 4H 75
Spinners Gdns. OL12: Roch 5C 16
Spinners Grn. OL12: Roch 1H 27
Spinners Hall BL1: Bolt 2F 175
Spinners La. SK12: Poy 3C 168
Spinners M. BL1: Bolt 1E 175 (5C 32)
Spinners Way OL4: O'ham 3C 60
Spinney, The BL1: Bolt 6H 31
BL7: Tur 1G 19
M28: Wors 6D 82
M41: Urm 5C 110
M45: White 2C 68
OL4: Scout 1E 77
OL12: Roch 6F 15
SK8: Chea 2A 156
SK12: Poy 3C 168
Spinney Cl. SK9: Hand 4G 165
Spinney Dr. BL9: Bury 5E 23
M33: Sale 6F 127
Spinney Gro. M34: Dent 2F 119
Spinney Nook BL2: Bolt 3H 33
Spinney Rd. M23: Wyth 4H 141
Spinningdale M38: Lit H 3B 64
Spinningfields *BL1: Bolt 5B 32*
(off Vermont St.)
Spinningfield Way OL10: H'ood 6H 39
Spinning Mdw. BL1: Bolt 5B 32
Spinnings, The BL9: Sum 6C 12
Spire Wlk. M12: Man 1H 11
Spirewood Gdns. SK6: Rom 2G 147
Spodden Cotts. OL12: Whitw 3B 14
Spodden Fold OL12: Whitw 1E 15
Spodden St. OL12: Roch 3F 27
Spodden Wlk. M45: White 6A 54
Spod Rd. OL12: Roch 2E 27
Spokeshave Way OL16: Roch 1C 28
Spooner Rd. M30: Ecc 4E 97
SPORTCITY 3B 102
Sportlife Fitness Cen. 6H 65
Sportside Av. M28: Walk 6A 66
Sportside Cl. M28: Walk 5H 65
Sportside Gro. M28: Walk 5H 65
Sportsmans Dr. OL8: O'ham 6G 75
SPOTLAND BRIDGE 3F 27
SPOTLAND FOLD 2E 27
Spotland Rd.
OL12: Roch 2A 178 (3F 27)
Spotland Stadium 3E 27
Spotland Tops OL12: Roch 2D 26
Spout Brook Rd. SK15: H'rod 6F 93
Spreadbury St. M40: Man 4C 88
Spring Av. M45: White 5E 53
SK14: Hyde 1D 136
Spring Bank M6: Sal 2E 99
M29: Ast 5A 80
OL3: Upp 1D 78
OL12: Whitw 4B 14
SK15: Stal 4F 107
WA14: Bow 2F 151
Springbank OL9: Chad 2A 74
SK13: Had 2H 123
Spring Bank Av. M34: Aud 6D 104
OL6: A Lyme 6H 91
Springbank Cl. SK6: Wood 3A 136
Springbank Ct. M8: Man 1D 86
SK6: Wood 4H 135
Spring Bank La. OL11: Roch 3A 26
(not continuous)
SK15: H'rod 6G 93
Springbank Pl.
SK1: Stoc 4F 179 (3G 145)
Springbank Rd. SK6: Wood 3A 136
Spring Bank St. OL8: O'ham 5C 74
Spring Bank Ter. M34: Aud 6C 104
Springbridge Ct. M16: W Ran 6D 114
Spring Bri. Rd. M16: W Ran 5D 114
Springburn Cl. M28: Wors 5E 81
Springburn Way OL3: Upp 1D 78
Spring Cl. BL0: Ram 3B 12
BL8: Tot 5G 21
OL4: Lees 4B 76
Spring Clough M28: Wors 6D 82
OL7: A Lyme 5G 91

Spring Clough Av. M28: Walk 1B 82
Spring Clough Dr. M28: Walk 1B 82
Springclough Dr. OL8: O'ham 5H 75
Spring Cotts. OL5: Mos 1G 93
(off Bk. Mill La.)
Spring Ct. OL12: Roch 1C 178 (2H 27)
Spring Ct. M. SK14: Holl 2E 123
Springdale Gdns. M20: Man 6E 131
SPRINGFIELD 6H 175 (1E 49)
Springfield BL2: Bolt 5H 175 (1E 49)
M26: Rad 3E 67
M41: Urm 5E 111
OL4: O'ham 2A 76
(off Moorgate St.)
Springfield Av. M8: Man 3F 87
OL15: L'ough 2G 17
SK5: Stoc 2G 133
SK6: Mar 5D 148
SK7: H Gro 2D 158
Springfield Cl. M35: Fail 3G 89
OL10: H'ood 4A 40
SK13: Had 3G 123
Springfield Dr. SK9: Wilm 4A 172
Springfield Gdns. BL4: Kea 3C 66
Springfield Ind. Est. M35: Fail 3G 89
Springfield La. M3: Sal 2F 5 (2C 100)
M44: Irl 5D 108
OL2: O'ham 6C 42
OL16: Roch 6D 16
Springfield Pk. 6C 26
Springfield Rd. BL0: Ram 1A 22
BL1: Bolt 4C 18
BL4: Farn 6E 49
BL4: Kea 3A 66
M24: Mid 6B 56
M33: Sale 5B 128
M43: Droy 3H 103
SK8: Gat 1F 155
WA14: Alt 1B 174 (6F 139)
Springfield St. BL3: Bolt 3E 49
M34: Aud 1F 119
OL6: A Lyme 6C 92
OL10: H'ood 3E 39
Spring Gdns. BL2: Bolt 1B 34
M2: Man 5A 6 (4E 101)
M6: Sal 2F 99
M24: Mid 5C 56
OL3: Upp 1D 78
(off Moorgate St.)
OL15: L'ough 4H 17
SK1: Stoc 3H 179 (2A 146)
SK7: H Gro 2D 158
SK13: Had 2H 123
SK14: Hyde 3B 120
WA15: Tim 6C 140
Spring Gdn. St. OL2: O'ham 3D 58
Spring Gro. M45: White 5E 53
OL3: G'fld 4D 78
(off Chew Valley Rd.)
Spring Hall Ri. OL4: O'ham 3D 60
SPRINGHEAD 3E 77
Springhead Av. M20: Man 2E 131
OL4: Spri 4E 77
SPRING HILL 6B 60
Springhill OL2: O'ham 3D 58
OL16: Roch 2B 42
Spring Hill Ct. OL4: O'ham 1B 76
Springhill High School Sports Hall
. . . . .6C 28
Spring La. M26: Rad 4A 52
OL4: Lees 4C 76
Springlawns BL1: Bolt 5F 31
Springlees Ct. OL4: Spri 3D 76
Springmeadow La. OL3: Upp 1E 79
Spring Mill Cl. BL3: Bolt 3C 48
(off Aldsworth Dr.)
Spring Mill Dr. OL5: Mos 6A 78
Spring Mill Wlk. OL16: Roch 1C 28
Spring Pl. OL12: Whitw 2B 14
Spring Ri. OL2: Shaw 4G 43
Spring Rd. SK3: Stoc 3E 145
SK12: Poy 5F 169
WA14: Hale 3F 151

Springs, The OL11: Roch 4A 26
WA14: Bow 3D 150
(not continuous)
Spring Side OL12: Whitw 1B 14
Springside SK4: Stoc 2F 133
Springside Av. M28: Walk 6A 66
Springside Cl. M28: Walk 6A 66
Springside Gro. M28: Walk 6A 66
Spring Side La. OL12: W'le 3H 15
Springside Rd. BL9: Bury 3D 22
Springside Vw. BL8: Bury 4B 22
Springside Vw. Cotts. BL8: Bury 4C 22
Springside Wlk. M15: Man 6D 8
Springs La. SK15: Stal 2D 106
Springs Ri. SK15: Stal 2D 106
(not continuous)
Springs Rd. M24: Mid 3G 73
Spring St. BL0: Ram 3B 12
(Bolton St.)
BL0: Ram 2D 12
(Henry St.)
BL3: Bolt 2D 48
BL4: Farn 6H 49
BL8: Bury 1H 35
BL8: Tot 1H 21
BL9: Bury 4D 176 (3F 37)
(not continuous)
M12: Man 5C 116
OL3: Upp 1D 78
OL4: O'ham 1A 76
OL4: Spri 3E 77
OL5: Mos 1G 93
SK9: Wilm 2D 172
SK8: B'tom 6C 122
SK14: Holl 2E 123
SK15: Stal 3E 107
Spring Ter. BL8: Tot 4H 21
(off Spring St.)
OL9: Chad 2A 74
OL11: Roch 3C 26
OL16: Miln 2H 43
Spring Thyme Fold OL15: L'ough 4G 17
Spring Va. M24: Mid 1C 72
M25: Pres 1G 85
SK7: H Gro 3E 159
Springvale Cl. OL7: A Lyme 6F 91
Springvale Ct. M24: Mid 6D 56
Spring Va. Dr. BL8: Tot 4G 21
Spring Va. St. BL8: Tot 5G 21
Spring Va. Ter. OL15: L'ough 4H 17
(off Church St.)
Spring Va. Way OL2: O'ham 2G 59
Springville Av. M9: Man 4B 88
Springwater Av. BL0: Ram 6A 12
Springwater Cl. BL2: Bolt 2A 34
Spring Water Dr. SK13: Had 4G 123
Springway M45: White 5E 53
Springwell Cl. M6: Sal 3E 99
Springwell Gdns. SK14: Hat 6A 122
Springwell Way SK14: Hat 6A 122
Springwood OL3: Del 2A 62
Springwood Av. M27: Pen 5B 84
OL9: Chad 6G 57
Springwood Cres. SK6: Rom 1C 148
Springwood Est. OL3: Del 2A 62
Springwood Hall OL7: A Lyme 4G 91
Springwood Hall Rd. OL8: O'ham . . .1G 91
Springwood La. SK6: Rom 1D 148
Springwood St. BL0: Ram 2B 12
Springwood Way OL7: A Lyme 5G 91
Spruce Av. BL9: Bury 3H 37
Spruce Ct. M6: Sal 3H 99
Spruce Cres. BL9: Bury 4F 23
Spruce Lodge SK8: Chea 5H 143
Spruce St. BL0: Ram 6A 12
M15: Man 6E 9 (1C 114)
OL16: Roch 5B 28
Spruce Wlk. M33: Sale 3E 127
Sprucewood OL9: Chad 1F 73
Spur, The OL8: O'ham 6G 75
Spurn La. OL3: Dig 4D 62

Spurstow M. SK8: Chea H 5D 156
Spur Wlk. M8: Man 4D 86
(off Broomfield Dr.)
Sput Grn. SK14: Mot 2C 122
(off Old Rd.)
Square, The BL3: Bolt 4F 47
BL9: Bury 4C 176 (3F 37)
M27: Swin 6G 83
M45: White 1D 68
OL3: Dob 5C 62
OL3: Upp 1D 78
SK4: Stoc 6E 133
SK14: Hyde 5B 120
SK16: Duk 6D 106
WA15: Haleb 5C 152
Square Fold M43: Droy 3B 104
Square St. BL0: Ram 3C 12
Squire Rd. M8: Man 4D 86
Squire's Ct. M5: Sal 3A 98
Squirrel Dr. WA14: B'ath 3E 139
Squirrel's Jump SK9: A Edg 5H 173
Stable Fold M26: Rad 3A 52
Stablefold M28: Wors 6C 82
OL5: Mos 3G 93
Stableford Av. M30: Ecc 1E 97
Stables, The M25: Pres 6A 70
M43: Droy 2D 104
OL12: Whitw 4A 14
Stables Fitness & Leisure Club 1A 36
Stable St. OL1: O'ham 1H 75
OL9: Chad 1A 90
Stablings, The SK9: Wilm 4D 172
Stafford Ct. OL16: L'ough 5E 17
Stafford Rd. M27: Swin 3H 83
M28: Wors 2G 81
M30: Ecc 2G 97
M35: Fail 6A 90
Stafford St. BL8: Bury 1D 36
OL9: O'ham 5C 74
Stafford Wlk. M34: Dent 6G 119
(off Lancaster Rd.)
Stag Ind. Est. WA14: B'ath 5D 138
Stag Pasture Rd. OL8: O'ham 2D 90
Stainburne Dr. SK2: Stoc 5C 146
Stainburn Rd. M11: Man 5D 102
Staindale OL4: O'ham 3B 76
Stainer St. M12: Man 4C 116
Stainforth Cl. BL8: Bury 2H 35
Stainforth St. M11: Man 5B 102
Stainmoor Ct. SK2: Stoc 5D 146
Stainmore Av. OL6: A Lyme 4B 92
Stainsbury St. BL3: Bolt 3A 48
Stainton Av. M18: Man 3G 117
Stainton Cl. M26: Rad 2H 51
Stainton Dr. M24: Mid 4H 55
Stainton Pk. 3G 51
Stainton Rd. M26: Rad 2G 51
Staircase House (Mus.) 1G 179
Staithes Rd. M22: Wyth 5B 154
Stakeford Dr. M8: Man 3G 87
STAKEHILL 2F 57
Stake Hill Ind. Est.
M24: Mid 3G 57
Stakehill Ind. Est. M24: Mid 2F 57
Stakehill La. M24: Mid 1F 57
Staley Cl. SK15: Stal 3G 107
Staley Hall Cres. SK15: Stal 2G 107
Staley Hall Rd. SK15: Stal 2G 107
Staley Rd. OL5: Mos 3H 93
(not continuous)
Staley St. OL4: O'ham 3H 75
OL4: Spri 2G 77
Stalham Cl. M40: Man 1G 7 (2H 101)
Stalmine Av. SK8: H Grn 5F 155
STALYBRIDGE 4F 107
Stalybridge Celtic FC 5G 107
Stalybridge Country Pk. 4C 94
Stalybridge Rd. SK14: Mot 3C 122
Stalybridge Station (Rail) 3D 106
Stalyhill Dr. SK15: Stal 6H 107
Staly Ind. Est. SK15: Stal 3F 107
Stambourne Dr. BL1: Bolt 1D 32
Stamford Arc. OL6: A Lyme 5D 174

Stamford Av. SK15: Stal 3C 106
  WA14: Alt 6C 138
Stamford Brook Rd.
  WA14: W Tim 3E 139
Stamford Cl. SK15: Stal 3C 106
Stamford Ct. OL6: A Lyme 3B 106
Stamford Dr. M35: Fail 5B 90
  SK15: Stal 3C 106
Stamford Grange
  WA14: Alt 2A 174 (1E 151)
Stamford Gro. SK15: Stal 3D 106
Stamford New Rd.
  WA14: Alt 3B 174 (1F 151)
Stamford Pk. 3C 106
Stamford Pk. Rd. WA15: Alt 2G 151
Stamford Pl. M33: Sale 5C 128
  SK9: Wilm 2E 173
Stamford Rd. M7: Sal 5H 85
  M13: Man 4A 116
  M31: C'ton 3H 125
  M34: Aud 6D 104
  M41: Urm 5D 110
  OL4: Lees 1D 76
  OL5: Mos 1G 93
  SK9: A Edg 5H 173
  SK9: Wilm 6E 165
  WA14: Bow 3D 150
Stamford St SK15: Stal 3C 106
  (not continuous)
Stamford Sq. OL6: A Lyme 3B 106
  WA14: Alt 2B 174
Stamford St. M16: Old T 2A 114
  (not continuous)
  M27: Pen 2A 84
  M33: Sale 3A 128
  OL4: Lees 3C 76
  OL5: Mos 2F 93
  OL6: A Lyme 6B 174 (3H 105)
  OL10: H'ood 4A 40
  OL16: Roch 5B 28
  SK15: Mill 1H 107
  WA14: Alt 1B 174 (6F 139)
Stamford St. Central
  OL6: A Lyme 5D 174 (2A 106)
Stamford St. E. OL6: A Lyme 2A 106
  (not continuous)
Stamford St. W.
  OL6: A Lyme 6A 174 (3G 105)
Stamford Way
  WA14: Alt 1B 174 (6F 139)
Stampstone St. OL1: O'ham 1H 75
Stanage Av. M9: Man 5B 72
Stanbank St. SK4: Stoc 5G 133
Stanbridge Ct. SK4: Stoc . . .1E 179 (1G 145)
Stanbrook St. M19: Man 1E 133
Stanbury Cl. BL9: Bury 4B 38
Stanbury Dr. SK16: Duk 5B 106
Stanbury Wlk. M40: Man 1H 7
Stancliffe Rd. M22: Shar 6C 142
Stancross Rd. M23: Wyth 2C 140
STAND 2C 68
Standall Wlk. *M9: Man* 2A 88
  (off Dalbeattie St.)
Stand Av. M45: White 6E 53
Stand Cl. M45: White 1C 68
Standedge Rd. OL3: Dig, Dob 4D 62
Standedge Wlk. *SK15: C'ook* 5A 94
  (off Crowswood Dr.)
Standfield Cen. M28: Wors 5E 81
Standfield Dr. M28: Wors 4E 81
Standish Rd. M14: Man 1H 131
Standish Wlk. M34: Dent 6E 119
Stand La. M26: Rad 5B 52
  M45: White 1D 68
Stand Lodge *M26: Rad* 6C 52
  (off Stand La.)
Standmoor Ct. M45: White 2D 68
Standmoor Rd. M45: White 2D 68
Standon Wlk. *M40: Man* 1F 89
  (off Blandford Dr.)
Standrick Hill Ri. SK15: C'ook 6A 94
Standring Av. BL8: Bury 5A 36

Stand Ri. M26: Rad 1B 68
Stanford Cl. M26: Rad 2E 67
Stanford Hall Cres. BL0: Ram 5B 12
Stanhope Av. M25: Pres 4G 69
  M34: Aud 1E 119
Stanhope Cl. M34: Dent 2E 119
  SK9: Wilm 1G 173
Stanhope Ct. M25: Pres 3G 69
Stanhope Rd. M6: Sal 6E 85
  WA14: Bow 3C 150
Stanhope St. M19: Man 6D 116
  M34: Aud 2E 119
  OL5: Mos 3G 93
  OL6: A Lyme 1B 106
  OL11: Roch 6H 27
  SK5: Stoc 2G 133
Stanhope Way M35: Fail 3G 89
Stanhorne Av. M8: Man 1E 87
Stanhurst M30: Ecc 2G 97
Stanier Av. M30: Ecc 2F 97
Stanier St. M9: Man 3A 88
Stanion Gro. SK16: Duk 5B 106
Stan Jolly Wlk. M11: Man 5E 103
Stanlaw Ho. M30: Ecc 4G 97
Stanley Av. M14: Man 4G 115
  SK6: Mar 4B 148
  SK7: H Gro 2D 158
  SK14: Hyde 3C 120
Stanley Av. Nth. M25: Pres 3G 69
Stanley Av. Sth. M25: Pres 3G 69
Stanley Casino 2F 175
Stanley Cl. M16: Old T 2A 114
  M45: White 6F 53
Stanley Ct. BL9: Bury 2D 176 (2F 37)
Stanley Dr. M45: White 3F 69
  WA15: Tim 6A 140
STANLEY GREEN 1A 166
Stanley Grn. Bus. Pk.
  SK8: Chea H 2A 166
Stanley Grn. Ind. Est.
  SK8: Chea H 1A 166
  (not continuous)
Stanley Grn. Retail Pk.
  SK8: Chea H 1B 166
Stanley Gro. M12: Man 3B 116
  M18: Man 3B 116
  M21: Chor 1G 129
  (off Crossland Rd.)
  M41: Urm 5F 111
  SK4: Stoc 5D 132
Stanley Hall La. SK12: Dis 6G 161
Stanley M. BL2: Bolt 6H 33
Stanley Mt. M33: Sale 6A 128
Stanley Pk. Grange SK9: Hand 2H 165
Stanley Pk. Wlk. BL2: Bolt 5G 33
Stanley Pl. OL12: Roch 1A 178 (3G 27)
Stanley Rd. BL1: Bolt 4H 31
  BL4: Farn 1C 64
  M7: Sal 3C 86
  M16: Old T 2H 113
  M16: W Ran 5C 114
  M26: Rad 1G 51
  M27: Swin 3A 84
  M28: Walk 1H 81
  M30: Ecc 4E 97
  M34: Dent 4B 118
  M45: White 6F 53
  OL9: Chad 5B 74
  SK4: Stoc 5D 132
  SK8: Chea H 1H 165
  SK9: Hand 1H 165
Stanley Rd. Ind. Est. M45: White 6F 53
Stanley Sq. SK15: Stal 4D 106
Stanley St. BL0: Ram 4B 12
  M3: Sal 6E 5 (4C 100)
  (not continuous)
  M8: Man 1B 6 (1E 101)
  M11: Man 6F 103
  M25: Pres 5A 70
  M40: Man 6B 88
  M45: White 6F 53
  OL4: Lees 4C 76
  OL4: Spri 3E 77

Stanley St. OL9: Chad 2B 74
  OL10: H'ood 4H 39
  OL12: Roch 1A 178 (2G 27)
  SK1: Stoc 1A 146
  SK15: Stal 4D 106
Stanley St. Sth. BL3: Bolt 1C 48
Stanlo Ho. M1: Man 2B 10
Stanmere Ct. BL8: Haw 1D 20
Stanmore Av. M32: Stre 5B 112
Stanmore Dr. BL3: Bolt 2A 48
Stanmore Ho. M34: Aud 5C 104
Stannard Rd. M30: Ecc 4B 96
Stanneybrook Cl. OL16: Roch 3B 28
Stanney Cl. OL16: Miln 6E 29
Stanneylands Cl. SK9: Wilm 5G 165
Stanneylands Dr. SK9: Wilm 5F 165
Stanneylands Rd. SK9: Sty 3F 165
Stanney Rd. OL16: Roch 3B 28
Stannybrook Rd. M35: Fail 4D 90
Stanrose Cl. BL7: Eger 2C 18
Stanrose Vs. BL7: Eger 1C 18
Stansbury Pl. SK2: Stoc 5E 147
Stansby Gdns. M12: Man 6H 11 (1A 116)
Stansfield Cl. BL2: Bolt 5F 33
Stansfield Dr. OL11: Roch 2B 26
Stansfield Hall OL15: L'ough 2A 16
Stansfield Rd. M35: Fail 3A 90
  SK14: Hyde 3C 120
Stansfield St. M11: Man 5F 103
  M40: Man 1F 103
  OL1: O'ham 1E 75
  OL9: Chad 4B 74
Stansted Wlk. M23: Wyth 2D 140
Stanthorne Av. M20: Man 2E 131
Stanton Av. M7: Sal 5H 85
  M20: Man 5C 130
Stanton Ct. M32: Stre 3D 112
Stanton Gdns. M20: Man 5D 130
  SK4: Stoc 2D 144
Stanton St. M11: Man 3E 103
  M32: Stre 3D 112
  OL9: Chad 6B 74
Stanway Av. BL3: Bolt 1B 48
Stanway Cl. BL3: Bolt 1B 48
  M24: Mid 3D 72
Stanway Dr. WA15: Hale 2H 151
Stanway Rd. M45: White 1H 69
Stanway St. M9: Man 3A 88
  M32: Stre 4D 112
Stanwell Rd. M27: Swin 4H 83
  M40: Man 2E 89
Stanwick Av. M9: Man 5E 71
Stanworth Av. BL2: Bolt 6A 34
Stanworth Cl. M16: W Ran 4C 114
Stanyard Ct. M5: Sal 5G 99
STANYCLIFFE 4E 57
Stanycliffe La. M24: Mid 4D 56
Stanyforth St. SK13: Had 3H 123
Stapleford Cl. BL8: Bury 3A 36
  M23: Wyth 1F 153
  M33: Sale 4E 129
Stapleford Wlk. M34: Dent 6E 119
Staplehurst Rd. M40: Man 1C 102
Staplers Wlk. *M14: Man* 4G 115
  (off Stenbury Cl.)
Stapleton Av. BL1: Bolt 4E 31
Stapleton St. M6: Sal 6C 84
Starbeck Cl. BL8: Bury 3H 35
Starcliffe St. BL3: Bolt 5H 49
Star Ct. OL16: Roch 4C 178
Starfield Av. OL15: L'ough 1F 29
Star Gro. M7: Sal 5C 86
Star Ind. Est. OL8: O'ham 6G 177 (4F 75)
Starkey St. OL10: H'ood 2H 39
Starkie Rd. BL2: Bolt 6F 33
  (Bury Rd.)
  BL2: Bolt 4F 33
  (Tonge Moor Rd.)
Starkies BL9: Bury 6E 37
Starkie St. M28: Wors 4C 81
STARLING 3G 35

Starling Cl. M22: Shar 5C 142
  M43: Droy 2D 104
Starling Dr. BL4: Farn 2D 64
Starling Rd. BL8: Bury 5G 35
  M26: Rad 5G 35
Starmoor Dr. M8: Man 5E 87
Starmount Cl. BL2: Bolt 1C 50
Starring Gro. OL15: L'ough 4F 17
                        (off Starring Rd.)
Starring La. OL15: L'ough 4E 17
Starring Rd. OL15: L'ough 3E 17
Starring Way OL15: L'ough 4F 17
Starry Wlk. M7: Sal 1B 4 (1A 100)
Starting Chair OL4: Scout 1G 77
Stash Gro. M23: Wyth 4H 141
Statham Cl. M34: Dent 4G 119
Statham Fold SK14: Hyde 3E 121
Statham Wlk. M13: Man 3D 10
Station App. M1: Man 6C 6 (4F 101)
                            (Ducie St.)
  M1: Man 2A 10 (5E 101)
                       (Whitworth St.)
  OL3: Del 4B 62
  SK8: H Grn 5E 155
  WA15: Alt 1C 174 (6G 139)
Station App. Bus. Est.
  OL11: Roch 6C 178
Station Bri. M41: Urm 5F 111
Station Cl. SK14: Hyde 5A 120
Station Cotts. M31: Part 5E 125
  SK8: Chea H 3D 156
  WA14: W Tim 3F 139
Stationers Entry
  OL16: Roch 3B 178 (4H 27)
Station Ho. WA14: Alt 1B 174
Station Ho's. OL3: Dig 2F 63
Station La. OL3: G'fld 4C 78
  OL4: Grot 4E 77
Station Lofts OL6: A Lyme 6C 174
Station M. M35: Fail 3G 89
Station Rd. BL4: Kea 2B 66
  BL8: G'mount 2H 21
  M8: Man 2E 87
  M27: Swin, Pen 3H 83
  M30: Ecc 4F 97
  M32: Stre 4D 112
  M41: Urm 5F 111
  M44: Irl 2C 124
  OL3: Dig 2F 63
  OL3: Upp 1D 78
  OL4: Grot 4E 77
  OL5: Mos 2H 93
  OL11: Roch 6C 178 (5H 27)
  OL12: Whitw 2B 14
                (Cowm Pk. Way Nth.)
  OL12: Whitw 4D 14
                    (Market St.)
  OL15: L'ough 4H 17
  OL16: Miln 6F 29
  SK1: Stoc 4F 179 (3G 145)
  SK3: Stoc 4E 179 (3G 145)
  SK4: Stoc 2A 144
  SK5: Stoc 5G 117
  SK6: Mar 5D 148
  SK6: Stri 4G 161
  SK6: Wood 4H 135
  SK8: Chea H 3C 156
  SK9: Hand 4H 165
  SK9: Sty 4E 165
  SK9: Wilm 2E 173
  SK13: Had 2H 123
  SK14: Hyde 5F 121
  SK22: N Mil 4G 161
Station Rd. Ind. Est. SK5: Stoc 5G 117
Station Sq. OL5: Mos 2G 93
Station St. BL3: Bolt 6G 175 (1D 48)
  OL4: Spri 3D 76
  SK7: H Gro 3D 158
  SK16: Duk 4H 105
Station Vw. M19: Man 6C 116
  M43: Droy 6A 104
  SK15: Stal 3D 106
                (off Rassbottom St.)

Staton Av. BL2: Bolt 5G 33
Staton St. M11: Man 5E 103
Statter St. BL9: Bury 3G 53
Staveleigh Mall
  OL6: A Lyme 5C 174 (2H 105)
Staveley Av. BL1: Bolt 5C 18
  SK15: Stal 2E 107
Staveley Cl. M24: Mid 5A 56
  OL2: Shaw 1B 60
Staveley Wlk. OL2: O'ham 3E 59
             (off Royton Hall Wlk.)
Staverton Cl. M13: Man 4E 11 (6G 101)
Staveton Cl. SK7: Bram 2H 157
Stavordale OL12: Roch 2A 178
Staycott St. M16: W Ran 3D 114
Stayley Cotts. SK15: C'ook 4A 94
                  (off School La.)
Stayley Dr. SK15: Stal 3G 107
Stead St. BL0: Ram 3C 12
Steadway OL3: G'fld 4E 79
Stedman Cl. M11: Man 4A 102
Steele Ho. M5: Sal 3B 8 (6A 100)
Steeles Av. SK14: Hyde 4C 120
Steeple Cl. M8: Man 6D 86
Steeple Dr. M5: Sal 4G 99
Steeple Vw. OL2: O'ham 3D 58
Stelfox Av. M14: Man 6E 115
  WA15: Tim 4C 140
Stelfox La. M34: Aud 6E 105
Stelfox St. M30: Ecc 5D 96
Stella St. M9: Man 5F 71
Stelling St. M18: Man 2F 117
Stenbury Cl. M14: Man 4G 115
Stenner La. M20: Man 1E 143
Stenson Sq. M11: Man 6F 103
                      (off Ettrick Cl.)
Stephen Cl. BL8: Bury 3C 36
Stephen Lowry Wlk. M40: Man 4C 88
                  (off McConnell Rd.)
Stephen Oake Cl. M8: Man 6D 86
Stephenson Av. M43: Droy 4A 104
Stephenson Ct. SK5: Stoc 5H 117
Stephenson Rd. M32: Stre 5D 112
Stephenson St. M35: Fail 2A 90
  OL4: O'ham 1B 76
Stephens Rd. M20: Man 4G 131
  SK15: Stal 1D 106
Stephens St. BL2: Bolt 6H 33
Stephens Ter. M20: Man 6F 131
                 (off Kings Lynn Cl.)
Stephen St. BL8: Bury 3C 36
  M3: Man 1H 5 (1D 100)
  M41: Urm 5G 111
  SK1: Stoc 3B 146
Stephen St. Sth. BL8: Bury 4C 36
                  (off Stephen St.)
STEPPING HILL 2D 158
Steps Mdw. OL12: Roch 5D 16
Stern Av. M5: Sal 5G 99
Sterndale Rd. M28: Wors 5D 80
  SK3: Stoc 6G 145
  SK6: Rom 2H 147
Sterratt St. BL1: Bolt 6B 32
Stetchworth Dr. M28: Wors 5F 81
Steuber Dr. M44: Irl 4D 124
Steven Ct. M21: Chor 1A 130
Stevenson Ct. BL4: Kea 2A 66
                     (off Bent St.)
Stevenson Dr. OL4: O'ham 3C 60
Stevenson Pl. M1: Man 5C 6
Stevenson Rd. M27: Swin 3G 83
Stevenson Sq. M1: Man 5C 6 (4F 101)
  OL12: Roch 6C 16
Stevenson St. M3: Sal 5C 4 (4B 100)
  M28: Walk 6F 65
Stevens St. SK9: A Edg 5G 173
Stewart Av. BL4: Farn 2F 65
Stewart St. BL1: Bolt 4C 32
  BL8: Bury 2B 36
                 (not continuous)
  OL7: A Lyme 3F 105
  OL16: Miln 2H 43

Steynton Cl. BL1: Bolt 5F 31
Stickens Lock La. M44: Irl 1E 125
Stile Cl. M41: Urm 5G 109
Stiles Av. SK6: Mar 4D 148
Stiles Cl. SK13: Had 2G 123
Stillwater Dr. M11: Man 3C 102
Stilton Dr. M11: Man 5C 102
Stirling M30: Ecc 3G 97
                     (off Monton La.)
Stirling Av. M20: Man 1D 130
  SK6: Mar 6D 148
  SK7: H Gro 4D 158
Stirling Cl. SK3: Stoc 5E 145
Stirling Ct. SK4: Stoc 4E 133
Stirling Dr. SK15: Stal 2E 107
Stirling Gro. M45: White 1G 69
Stirling Pl. OL10: H'ood 4D 38
Stirling Rd. BL1: Bolt 6C 18
  OL9: Chad 5H 73
Stirling St. OL9: O'ham 2C 74
Stirrup Brook Gro.
  M28: Wors 6D 80
Stirrup Ga. M28: Wors 6C 82
Stitch La. SK4: Stoc 6F 133
Stitch Mi La. BL2: Bolt 3A 34
Stiups La. OL16: Roch 1B 42
Stobart Av. M25: Pres 1A 86
STOCK BROOK 2A 74
Stockburn Dr. M35: Fail 4C 90
Stockbury Gro. BL1: Bolt 4D 32
                 (off Halliwell Rd.)
Stock Cl. OL12: Roch 1G 27
Stockdale Av. SK3: Stoc 6H 145
Stockdale Gro. BL2: Bolt 4B 34
Stockdale Rd. M9: Man 5A 72
Stockfield Mt. OL9: Chad 3B 74
Stockfield Rd. OL9: Chad 2B 74
Stock Gro. OL16: Miln 4F 29
Stockholm Rd. SK3: Stoc 5F 145
Stockholm St. M11: Man 3D 102
Stockland Cl. M13: Man 4C 10 (6F 101)
Stock La. OL9: Chad 2B 74
Stockley Av. BL2: Bolt 3A 34
Stockley Wlk. M15: Man 6D 8
Stockmar Grange BL1: Bolt 5E 31
STOCKPORT 3F 179 (2G 145)
Stockport Air Raid Shelters
  . . . . .2G 179
Stockport Art Gallery 4G 179 (3H 145)
Stockport Cemetery & Crematorium
  SK1: Stoc 4A 146
Stockport County FC 6E 179 (4G 145)
Stockport Garrick Theatre
  . . . . .3F 179 (2G 145)
STOCKPORT GREAT MOOR 1C 158
STOCKPORT LITTLE MOOR 3B 146
Stockport Mus. 1B 146
Stockport Rd. M12: Man . . .5F 11 (1G 115)
  M13: Man 1G 115
  M19: Man 4C 116
  M34: Dent 4F 119
  OL4: Lyd 4G 77
  OL5: Mos 1G 93
  OL7: A Lyme 5F 105
  SK3: Stoc 4B 144
  SK6: Mar 5H 147
  SK6: Rom 1H 147
  SK8: Chea 5H 143
  SK14: Hat, Mot 6A 122
  SK14: Hyde 6C 120
  WA15: Alt, Tim 1C 174 (6G 139)
Stockport Rd. E. SK6: Bred 5F 135
Stockport Rd. W. SK6: Bred 6C 134
Stockport Station (Rail) 4E 179 (3G 145)
Stockport Trad. Est. SK4: Stoc 2E 145
Stockport Viaduct 1F 145
Stockport Village SK1: Stoc 2F 179
Stock Rd. OL12: Roch 1A 28
Stocksfield Dr. M9: Man 6A 72
  M38: Lit H 4D 64
Stocks Gdns. SK15: Stal 4G 107
Stocksgate OL12: Roch 1D 26
Stocks Ho. M41: Urm 1B 126

Stocks Ind. Est.—Striding Edge Wlk.

Stocks Ind. Est. M30: Ecc . . . 3E **97**
Stocks La. SK15: Stal . . . 4F **107**
Stocks St. M8: Man . . . 1A **6** (2E **101**)
OL11: Roch . . . 3D **40**
Stocks St. E. M8: Man . . . 1A **6** (2E **101**)
Stock St. BL8: Bury . . . 6E **23**
Stockton Av. SK3: Stoc . . . 3D **144**
Stockton Dr. BL8: Bury . . . 6B **22**
Stockton Pk. OL4: O'ham . . . 3B **76**
Stockton Rd. BL4: Farn . . . 5G **49**
M21: Chor . . . 1G **129**
SK9: Wilm . . . 5C **172**
Stockton St. M16: W Ran . . . 3C **114**
M27: Swin . . . 4G **83**
OL15: L'ough . . . 4G **17**
Stockwood Wlk. M9: Man . . . 4H **87**
Stoke Abbot Cl. SK7: Bram . . . 6G **157**
Stokesay Cl. BL9: Bury . . . 2F **53**
OL2: O'ham . . . 3G **59**
Stokesay Dr. SK7: H Gro . . . 4C **158**
Stokesay Rd. M33: Sale . . . 4G **127**
Stokesby Gdns. BL6: Los . . . 5B **30**
Stokesley Wlk. *BL3: Bolt . . . 4C **48***
(off Belford Dr.)
Stokes Mill *SK15: Stal . . . 3F **107***
(off Higher Tame St.)
Stokes St. M11: Man . . . 3F **103**
Stokoe Av. WA14: Alt . . . 6C **138**
Stonall Av. M15: Man . . . 4D **8** (1B **114**)
Stoneacre BL6: Los . . . 5A **30**
Stoneacre Ct. M27: Swin . . . 4H **83**
Stoneacre Rd. M22: Wyth . . . 4A **154**
Stonebeck Cl. BL5: O Hul . . . 6F **47**
Stonebeck Rd. M23: Wyth . . . 6F **141**
STONE BREAKS . . . 3F **77**
Stonebreaks Rd. OL4: Spri . . . 3E **77**
Stonebridge Cl. BL6: Los . . . 1C **46**
Stonechat Cl. M28: Wors . . . 3F **81**
M43: Droy . . . 2C **104**
Stonechurch BL3: Bolt . . . 2B **48**
Stonecliffe Av. SK15: Stal . . . 3E **107**
Stonecliffe Ter. SK15: Stal . . . 2F **107**
Stone Cl. BL0: Ram . . . 5A **12**
STONECLOUGH . . . 2D **66**
Stoneclough M. OL1: O'ham . . . 6E **59**
Stoneclough Ri. M26: Rad . . . 1D **66**
Stoneclough Rd. BL4: Kea . . . 2B **66**
M26: Rad . . . 2B **66**
Stonecroft OL1: O'ham . . . 2F **177**
Stonedelph Cl. BL2: Ain . . . 4F **35**
Stone Dr. OL2: O'ham . . . 2E **59**
Stonefield M29: Tyld . . . 2A **80**
Stonefield Dr. M8: Man . . . 6C **86**
Stonefield St. OL16: Miln . . . 6F **29**
Stoneflat Ct. OL12: Roch . . . 3F **27**
Stonehaven BL3: Bolt . . . 4F **47**
Stonehead St. M9: Man . . . 4B **88**
Stonehewer St. M26: Rad . . . 5B **52**
Stonehill Cres. OL12: Roch . . . 6C **14**
Stonehill Dr. OL12: Roch . . . 6C **14**
Stone Hill Ind. Est. BL4: Farn . . . 3H **65**
Stone Hill La. OL12: Roch . . . 1C **26**
Stone Hill Rd. BL4: Farn . . . 3H **65**
Stonehill Rd. OL12: Roch . . . 6C **14**
Stonehouse BL7: Bro X . . . 4F **19**
Stonehouse Wlk. *M23: Wyth . . . 4E **141***
(off Sandy La.)
Stonehurst SK6: Mar . . . 1C **160**
Stonehurst Cl. M12: Man . . . 1C **116**
Stonelands Way OL4: Grot . . . 5E **77**
Stoneleigh Av. M33: Sale . . . 4F **127**
Stoneleigh Dr. M26: Rad . . . 2D **66**
Stoneleigh Rd. OL4: Spri . . . 2E **77**
Stoneleigh St. OL1: O'ham . . . 6H **59**
Stonelow Cl. M15: Man . . . 5H **9** (1D **114**)
Stonemead SK6: Rom . . . 6C **136**
Stonemead Av. WA15: Haleb . . . 6C **152**
Stonemead Cl. BL3: Bolt . . . 3D **48**
Stonemead Dr. M9: Man . . . 5H **71**
Stonemere Dr. M26: Rad . . . 6C **52**
Stonemill Ter. SK5: Stoc . . . 6H **133**
Stonepail Cl. SK8: Gat . . . 6D **142**
Stonepail Rd. SK8: Gat . . . 6E **143**
Stone Pale M45: White . . . 2F **69**
Stone Pits BL0: Eden . . . 2H **13**
Stone Pl. M14: Man . . . 4G **115**
Stoneridge SK13: Had . . . 2H **123**
Stone Row SK6: Mar . . . 5E **149**
Stonesby Cl. M16: W Ran . . . 3B **114**
Stonesdale Cl. OL2: O'ham . . . 2E **59**
Stonesteads Dr. BL7: Bro X . . . 3E **19**
Stonesteads Way BL7: Bro X . . . 3E **19**
Stone St. BL2: Bolt . . . 4F **33**
M3: Man . . . 2F **9** (5C **100**)
OL16: Miln . . . 6F **29**
Stoneswood Dr. OL5: Mos . . . 1H **93**
Stoneswood Rd. OL3: Del . . . 4A **62**
Stoney Bank M26: Rad . . . 2E **67**
STONEYFIELD . . . 6H **27**
Stoneyfield SK15: Stal . . . 1E **107**
Stoneyfield Cl. M16: W Ran . . . 5D **114**
Stoneygate Wlk. *M11: Man . . . 6F **103***
(off Botha Cl.)
Stoneyholme Av. M8: Man . . . 4F **87**
Stoney Knoll M7: Sal . . . 5B **86**
Stoney La. OL3: Del . . . 6H **45**
SK9: Wilm . . . 4C **172**
Stoney Royd OL12: Whitw . . . 4B **14**
Stoneyside Av. M28: Walk . . . 5A **66**
Stoneyside Gro. M28: Walk . . . 5A **66**
Stoneyvale Ct. OL11: Roch . . . 1H **41**
Stonie Heyes Av. OL12: Roch . . . 1B **28**
Stony Bri. La. WA15: Tim . . . 4A **140**
Stonyford Rd. M33: Sale . . . 5D **128**
Stony Head *OL15: L'ough . . . 1A **16***
(off Higher Calderbrook Rd.)
Stonyhurst Av. BL1: Bolt . . . 6C **18**
Stopes Rd. BL3: Lit L . . . 4E **51**
M26: Rad . . . 3E **51**
Stopford Av. OL15: L'ough . . . 5E **17**
Stopford St. M11: Man . . . 6G **103**
SK3: Stoc . . . 3F **145**
Stopford Wlk. M34: Dent . . . 4F **119**
Stopley Wlk. *M11: Man . . . 5C **102***
(off Mill St.)
Store Pas. *OL15: L'ough . . . 4G **17***
(off John St.)
Stores Cotts. OL4: Gras . . . 3A **78**
Stores Rd. M90: Man A . . . 1G **163**
Stores St. M25: Pres . . . 5A **70**
Store St. M1: Man . . . 1D **10** (5F **101**)
M11: Man . . . 6D **102**
M26: Rad . . . 3D **52**
OL2: Shaw . . . 5A **44**
OL7: A Lyme . . . 5G **91**
OL11: Roch . . . 2A **26**
SK2: Stoc . . . 1C **158**
Storeton Cl. M22: Wyth . . . 3C **154**
Stormer Hill Fold BL8: Tot . . . 3H **21**
Stortford Dr. M23: Wyth . . . 1H **141**
Stothard Rd. M32: Stre . . . 6B **112**
Stott Dr. M41: Urm . . . 6H **109**
Stottfield OL2: O'ham . . . 4B **58**
Stott Ho. OL8: O'ham . . . 6F **177** (4E **75**)
Stott La. BL2: Bolt . . . 4F **33**
M6: Sal . . . 2B **98**
M24: Mid . . . 2B **56**
Stott Milne St. OL9: Chad . . . 4B **74**
Stott Rd. M27: Swin . . . 5F **83**
OL9: Chad . . . 6G **73**
Stott's La. M40: Man . . . 5F **89**
Stott St. M35: Fail . . . 5F **89**
OL12: Roch . . . 2H **27**
OL16: Miln . . . 1F **43**
OL16: Roch . . . 6D **16**
Stourbridge Av. M38: Lit H . . . 3E **65**
Stour Cl. WA14: Alt . . . 5E **139**
Stourport Cl. SK6: Rom . . . 2G **147**
Stour Rd. M29: Ast . . . 3A **80**
Stovell Av. M12: Man . . . 5C **116**
Stovell Rd. M40: Man . . . 3C **88**
Stow Cl. BL8: Bury . . . 6D **22**
Stowell Ct. BL1: Bolt . . . 4C **32**
Stowell St. BL1: Bolt . . . 4C **32**
*M5: Sal . . . 4E **99***
(off Dolbey St.)
Stowfield Cl. M9: Man . . . 5F **71**
Stow Gdns. M20: Man . . . 3E **131**
St Peter's Square Stop (Metro)
. . . 1H **9** (5D **100**)
Stracey St. M40: Man . . . 2A **102**
(not continuous)
Stradbroke Cl. M18: Man . . . 2E **117**
Strain Av. M9: Man . . . 5H **71**
Straits, The M29: Ast . . . 5A **80**
Strand, The OL11: Roch . . . 3H **41**
Strand Ct. M32: Stre . . . 1C **128**
Strandedge Cl. BL0: Ram . . . 5C **12**
Strand Way OL2: O'ham . . . 5D **58**
STRANGEWAYS . . . 1G **5** (1D **100**)
Strangford St. M26: Rad . . . 3F **51**
Strang St. BL0: Ram . . . 3C **12**
Stranton Dr. M28: Wors . . . 3E **83**
Stratfield Av. M23: Wyth . . . 2D **140**
Stratford Av. BL1: Bolt . . . 4G **31**
BL9: Bury . . . 3E **23**
M20: Man . . . 4D **130**
M30: Ecc . . . 5E **97**
OL8: O'ham . . . 6E **75**
OL11: Roch . . . 6G **27**
Stratford Cl. BL4: Farn . . . 6D **48**
Stratford Gdns. SK6: Bred . . . 6F **135**
Stratford Rd. M24: Mid . . . 4D **72**
Stratford Sq. SK8: H Grn . . . 6G **155**
Strathaven Pl. OL10: H'ood . . . 4D **38**
Strathblane Cl. M20: Man . . . 2F **131**
Strathblane Ho. *SK8: Chea . . . 5H **143***
(off Ashfield Rd.)
Strathfield Dr. M11: Man . . . 3E **103**
Strathmere Av. M32: Stre . . . 4D **112**
Strathmore Av. M16: W Ran . . . 5H **113**
M34: Dent . . . 5H **119**
Strathmore Cl. BL0: Ram . . . 5C **12**
Strathmore Rd. BL2: Bolt . . . 4A **34**
Stratton Rd. M16: W Ran . . . 5H **113**
M27: Pen . . . 2H **83**
SK2: Stoc . . . 3C **146**
Strawberry Bank *M6: Sal . . . 2H **99***
(off Strawberry Rd.)
Strawberry Cl. WA14: B'ath . . . 4D **138**
Strawberry Flds. M43: Droy . . . 3C **104**
Strawberry Hill M6: Sal . . . 2H **99**
Strawberry Hill Rd. BL2: Bolt . . . 2F **49**
Strawberry La. SK9: Wilm . . . 3B **172**
Strawberry Rd. M6: Sal . . . 2G **99**
Stray, The BL1: Bolt . . . 1F **33**
Stray St. M11: Man . . . 5G **103**
Streamside Cl. WA15: Tim . . . 1B **152**
Stream Ter. SK1: Stoc . . . 2B **146**
Street, The OL2: Shaw . . . 6C **44**
STREET BRIDGE . . . 4A **58**
Street Bri. Rd. OL1: Chad . . . 5A **58**
STREET END . . . 3A **90**
Streetgate M38: Lit H . . . 4D **64**
Streethouse La. OL3: Dob . . . 6B **62**
Street La. M26: Rad . . . 5G **35**
SK10: Adl . . . 6C **168**
Street Lodge OL11: Roch . . . 4D **40**
STRETFORD . . . 6D **112**
Stretford Ho. *M32: Stre . . . 6C **112***
(off Chapel La.)
Stretford Leisure Cen. . . . 3F **113**
Stretford Motorway Est.
M32: Stre . . . 2A **112**
Stretford Pl. OL12: Roch . . . 6G **15**
Stretford Rd. M15: Man . . . 2A **114**
M16: Old T . . . 6C **8** (2A **114**)
M41: Urm . . . 6F **111**
Stretford Station (Metro) . . . 6D **112**
Stretton Av. M20: Man . . . 6G **131**
M32: Stre . . . 4A **112**
M33: Sale . . . 5G **127**
Stretton Cl. M40: Man . . . 6H **87**
Stretton Rd. BL0: Ram . . . 1A **22**
BL3: Bolt . . . 3H **47**
BL8: G'mount . . . 1A **22**
Stretton Way *SK9: Hand . . . 2H **165***
(off Sandiway Rd.)
Striding Edge Wlk. OL1: O'ham . . . 6G **59**

Strike Ten Bowl & Laser Quest 1G 41
STRINE DALE 3D 60
STRINES 4G 161
Strines Ct. SK14: Hyde 3C 120
STRINESDALE 4F 61
Strinesdale Cen. 6D 60
Strines Rd. SK6: Mar, Dis ..5E 149
Strines Station (Rai) 4H 161
Stringer Av. SK14: Mot 5B 122
Stringer Cl. SK14: Mot 5B 122
Stringer St. SK1: Stoc 1A 146
Stringer Way SK14: Mot 5B 122
Stroma Gdns. M41: Urm 2E 111
Stromness Gro. OL10: H'ood .4D 38
Strong St. M7: Sal 1C 100
STRONGSTRY 3F 13
Strongstry Rd. BL0: Ram 3F 13
Strontian Wlk. M11: Man 4E 103
  (off Edith Cavell Cl.)
Stroud Av. M30: Ecc 2D 96
Stroud Cl. M24: Mid 4C 72
Struan Ct. WA14: Alt 6E 139
Stuart Av. M44: Irl 5D 108
  SK6: Mar 4A 148
Stuart Ho. M43: Droy 5A 104
Stuart Pl. M43: Droy 2F 103
Stuart Rd. M32: Stre 4D 112
  SK6: Bred 3D 134
  WA14: B'ath 4D 138
Stuart St. M11: Man 3C 102
  M24: Mid 1E 73
  OL8: O'ham 6E 177 (4E 75)
  OL16: Roch 5A 28
  (not continuous)
Stuart St. E. M11: Man 3C 102
Stuart Wlk. M24: Mid 2B 72
STUBBINS 4F 13
Stubbins Cl. M23: Wyth 2E 141
Stubbins La. BL0: Eden, Ram .2C 12
Stubbins Rd. BL0: Ram 4F 13
Stubbins Va. Rd. BL0: Ram ..4F 13
Stubbins Va. Ter. BL0: Ram ..1B 12
Stubbs Cl. M7: Sal 3H 85
STUBLEY 4F 17
Stubley Gdns. OL15: L'ough .4G 17
Stubley La. OL15: L'ough 4F 17
Stubley Mill Rd. OL15: L'ough .5E 17
  (not continuous)
Student Village M1: Man 3H 9
Studforth Wlk. M15: Man 2E 115
  (off Botham Cl.)
Studland Rd. M22: Wyth 2D 154
Studley Cl. OL2: O'ham 3G 59
STYAL 4D 164
Styal Av. M32: Stre 4A 112
  SK5: Stoc 3H 133
Styal Country Pk. 5D 164
Styalgate SK8: Gat 6D 142
Styal Gro. SK8: Gat 2E 155
Styal Rd. M22: Wyth 1D 164
  SK8: Gat, H Grn 4E 155
  SK9: Sty 4E 155
Styal Station (Rail) 3E 165
Styal St. BL1: Bolt 5H 31
Styal Vw. SK9: Wilm 5F 165
Styhead Dr. M24: Mid 4H 55
Style St. M4: Man 2B 6 (2E 101)
Styperson Way SK12: Poy 4E 169
Sudbury Cl. M16: Old T 2A 114
  (off Stanley Rd.)
Sudbury Dr. BL6: Los 1C 46
  SK8: H Grn 5G 155
Sudbury Rd. SK7: H Gro 5E 159
SUDDEN 1E 41
Sudden St. OL11: Roch 1E 41
Sudell St. M4: Man 2D 6 (2F 101)
  (not continuous)
Sudell St. Ind. Est. M4: Man ..2D 6
Sudgen Sports Cen. 4B 10 (6E 101)
Sudley Rd. OL11: Roch 6E 27
Sudlow St. OL16: Roch 1B 28
Sudren St. BL8: Bury 2H 35

Sue Patterson Wlk. M40: Man 6H 87
  (off Aldbourne Cl.)
Suffield Wlk. M22: Wyth 4B 154
Suffolk Av. M43: Droy 2A 104
Suffolk Cl. BL3: Lit L 2D 50
Suffolk Dr. SK5: Stoc 3C 134
  SK9: Wilm 6G 165
Suffolk Rd. WA14: Alt 1D 150
Suffolk St. M6: Sal 6G 85
  OL9: O'ham 6B 74
  OL11: Roch 5B 178 (5H 27)
Sugar La. OL3: Dob 5C 62
Sugar Mill Sq. M5: Sal 3D 98
Sulby Av. M32: Stre 5E 113
Sulby St. M26: Rad 2D 66
  M40: Man 3C 88
Sulgrave Av. SK12: Poy 3F 169
Sullivan St. M12: Man 4C 116
Sultan St. BL9: Bury 5F 37
Sulway Cl. M27: Swin 4A 84
Sumac St. M11: Man 3F 103
Sumbland Ho. M27: Clif 1B 84
Summer Av. M41: Urm 5G 111
Summer Castle
  OL16: Roch 4D 178 (4A 28)
Summer Ct. M33: Sale 1E 139
Summercroft OL9: Chad 6B 74
Summerdale Dr. BL0: Ram ...1B 22
Summerfield Av. M43: Droy ..2G 103
Summerfield Ct. M21: Chor ..6F 113
Summerfield Dr. M24: Mid ...5E 57
  M25: Pres 2G 85
Summerfield Pl. SK9: Wilm ..4D 172
Summerfield Rd. BL3: Bolt ...3F 49
  M22: Wyth 3A 154
  M28: Wors 4C 82
Summerfields Village Cen.
  SK9: Wilm 6H 165
Summerfield Vw. OL8: O'ham .6A 76
Summer Hill OL5: Mos 1H 93
  (off Roughtown Rd.)
Summer Hill Cl. BL1: Bolt ...5B 18
Summerhill Vw. OL3: Dens ...4H 45
Summerlea SK8: Chea H 5D 156
Summer Pl. M14: Man 5G 115
Summers Av. SK15: Stal 3G 107
Summerseat 1C 22
Summerseat Cl. M5: Sal 5G 99
  OL4: Spri 2E 77
Summerseat La. BL0: Ram 6A 12
  (not continuous)
Summerseat Station
  East Lancashire Railway 1C 22
Summersgill Cl. OL10: H'ood 4A 40
Summershades La. OL4: Gras ..3H 77
Summershades Ri. OL4: Gras ..3H 77
Summers St. OL9: Chad 2C 74
Summerton Ho. M5: Sal 4G 99
  (off Buckingham St.)
Summervale Ho. OL9: O'ham ..3D 74
  (off Manchester St.)
Summerville Av. M9: Man 4B 88
Summerville Rd. M6: Sal 6E 85
SUMMIT
  OL2 ....5C 42
  OL10 ....3E 39
  OL15 ....1B 16
Summit Cl. BL9: Bury 1D 38
Summit St. OL10: H'ood 3D 38
Sumner Av. BL2: Ain 4F 35
Sumner Rd. M6: Sal 6D 84
Sumner St. BL3: Bolt 5H 47
  OL2: Shaw 2H 59
Sumner Way M41: Urm 5E 111
Sunadale Cl. BL3: Bolt 2H 47
Sunbank Cl. OL12: Roch 1F 27
Sunbank La. WA15: Ring 2D 162
Sunbeam Wlk. M11: Man 4B 102
  (off Hopedale Cl.)
Sunbury Cl. SK9: Wilm 5A 166
  SK16: Duk 5D 106

Sunbury Dr. M40: Man 1F 103
Sundance Ct. M50: Sal 5E 99
Sunderland Av. OL6: A Lyme ..1A 106
Sundew Pl. M24: Mid 2F 73
Sundial Cl. SK14: Hat 4H 121
Sundial Rd. SK2: Stoc 4D 146
Sundial Wlk. SK14: Hat 4H 121
Sundridge Cl. BL3: Bolt 4G 47
Sunfield SK6: Rom 6H 135
Sunfield Av. OL4: O'ham 4C 60
Sunfield Cres. OL2: O'ham ...4E 59
Sunfield Dr. OL2: O'ham 4F 59
Sunfield Est. OL3: Dig 3E 63
Sunfield La. OL3: Dig 3E 63
Sunfield Rd. OL1: O'ham ...1G 177 (1E 75)
Sunfield Way OL4: Lees 2C 76
Sunflower Gro. OL9: Chad ...1H 73
Sunflower Mdw. M44: Irl 5F 109
Sun Ga. OL15: L'ough 2F 29
SUN HILL 2D 76
Sun Hill OL4: Lees 2D 76
Sunhill Cl. OL16: Roch 3B 42
Sunk La. M24: Mid 1C 72
Sunlight Rd. BL1: Bolt 6A 32
Sunningdale Av. M11: Man ...3D 102
  M26: Rad 2F 51
  M33: Sale 6E 129
  M45: White 2C 68
Sunningdale Cl. BL8: Bury ...5A 36
  SK14: Hyde 2D 120
Sunningdale Ct. BL3: Lit L ..4D 50
  M34: Dent 4B 118
Sunningdale Dr. M6: Sal 6A 84
  M25: Pres 4G 69
  M44: Irl 4D 108
  OL10: H'ood 5H 39
  SK7: Bram 6A 158
Sunningdale Ho. M33: Sale ..6E 129
Sunningdale Rd. M34: Dent ..6G 119
  M41: Urm 6D 110
  SK8: Chea H 6C 156
Sunningdale Wlk. BL3: Bolt ...2B 48
  (off Dinsdale Dr.)
Sunninghey Ct. SK9: A Edg ..4F 173
Sunning Hill St. BL3: Bolt ...3B 48
Sunny Av. BL9: Bury 6F 23
SUNNY BANK 4G 53
Sunny Bank M26: Rad 1C 66
  OL4: Lees 4C 76
Sunnybank SK9: Wilm 3D 172
Sunnybank Av. M30: Ecc 2H 97
  M43: Droy 4H 103
  SK4: Stoc 5B 132
Sunnybank Dr. SK9: Wilm ...5A 172
Sunny Bank Rd. BL9: Bury ..4F 53
  M13: Man 4A 116
  WA14: Bow 4E 151
Sunnybank Rd. BL1: Bolt 3A 32
  M43: Droy 4H 103
Sunny Bower St. BL8: Tot ...5H 21
Sunny Brow Rd. M18: Man ...2E 117
  M24: Mid 1A 72
Sunny Dr. M25: Pres 5F 69
Sunnyfield Rd. M25: Pres 2A 70
  SK4: Stoc 6B 132
Sunnylea Av. M19: Man 4A 132
Sunny Lea M. SK9: Wilm 3D 172
  (off Victoria Rd.)
Sunnymead Av. BL1: Bolt 1D 32
Sunnymede Va. BL0: Ram 6A 12
Sunnyside M43: Droy 2H 103
  OL7: A Lyme 6F 91
Sunnyside Av. M43: Droy 1H 103
Sunny Side Cotts. M32: Stre ..5F 113
  OL12: Roch 1F 25
Sunnyside Ct. M20: Man 6G 131
  M43: Droy 2H 103
Sunnyside Cres. OL6: A Lyme .3B 106
Sunnyside Gro. OL6: A Lyme ..3B 106
Sunnyside Rd. BL1: Bolt 3A 32
  M43: Droy 2H 103
Sunny Top BL8: Haw 1E 21
Sunnywood Cl. BL8: Tot 5H 21

Sunnywood Dr. BL8: Tot 5A 22
Sunnywood La. BL8: Tot 5A 22
Sunrise Vw. OL15: L'ough 2B 16
Sunset Av. M22: Nor 1B 142
Sunset Bus. Pk. BL4: Kea 4E 67
Sun St. BL0: Ram 2B 12
OL5: Mos 2G 93
Sun Vw. OL2: O'ham 4G 59
Sunwell Ter. SK6: Mar 1D 160
Surbiton Rd. M40: Man 1D 160
Surma Cl. OL9: O'ham 2D 74
OL16: Roch 6B 28
Surrey Av. M43: Droy 2H 103
OL2: Shaw 6F 43
Surrey Cl. BL3: Lit L 3D 50
Surrey Dr. BL9: Bury 5F 37
Surrey Pk. Cl. OL2: Shaw 5H 43
Surrey Rd. M9: Man 1H 87
Surrey St. M9: Man 1G 87
OL6: A Lyme 6B 92
OL9: O'ham 4C 74
Surrey Way SK5: Stoc 5C 134
Surtees Rd. M23: Wyth 1G 141
Sussex Av. BL9: Bury 4C 38
M20: Man 5F 131
Sussex Cl. M27: Clif 1A 84
OL9: Chad 3B 74
Sussex Dr. BL9: Bury 5F 37
M43: Droy 2A 104
Sussex Pl. SK14: Hyde 2D 120
Sussex Rd. M31: Part 6C 124
M44: Cad 3A 124
SK3: Stoc 3D 144
Sussex St. M2: Man 5H 5 (4D 100)
M7: Sal 1C 4 (1B 100)
OL11: Roch 5B 178 (5H 27)
Sutcliffe Av. M12: Man 5D 116
Sutcliffe Pl. OL11: Roch 1A 42
(off Wareings Yd.)
Sutcliffe St. BL1: Bolt 3C 32
M24: Mid 1E 73
OL2: O'ham 4G 59
OL7: A Lyme 4F 105
OL8: O'ham 6F 177 (4E 75)
OL15: L'ough 3H 17
Sutherland Cl. OL8: O'ham 2F 91
Sutherland Flats OL10: H'ood 3G 39
(off Meadow Cl.)
Sutherland Gro. BL4: Farn 1G 65
Sutherland Rd. BL1: Bolt 4G 31
M16: Old T 4G 113
OL10: H'ood 4C 38
Sutherland St. BL4: Farn 1G 65
M27: Swin 2G 83
M30: Ecc 2D 96
OL6: A Lyme 2C 106
Suthers St. M26: Rad 6C 52
OL9: O'ham 3C 74
Sutton Cl. BL8: Bury 5B 36
Sutton Dr. M43: Droy 2G 103
Sutton Ho. M6: Sal 2F 99
Sutton Mnr. M21: Chor 6G 113
Sutton Rd. BL3: Bolt 3F 47
M18: Man 4E 117
SK4: Stoc 6E 133
SK9: A Edg 5F 173
SK12: Poy 5G 169
Suttons La. SK6: Mar 6E 149
Sutton Way M6: Sal 2G 99
(off Salford Shop. City)
SK9: Hand 2A 166
(off Sandiway Rd.)
Swailes St. OL4: O'ham 3H 75
Swaine St. SK3: Stoc 3E 179 (2G 145)
Swainsthorpe Dr. M9: Man 3A 88
Swain St. OL12: Roch 2G 27
Swalecliff Av. M23: Wyth 2D 140
Swale Cl. SK9: Wilm 5A 166
Swaledale Cl. OL2: O'ham 2E 59
Swale Dr. WA14: Alt 5E 139
Swallow Bank Dr.
OL11: Roch 2D 40
Swallow Cl. SK15: C'ook 4B 94

Swallow Ct. SK9: Wilm 6F 165
Swallow Dr. BL9: Bury 1H 37
M44: Irl 4E 109
OL11: Roch 4B 26
Swallowfield M44: Irl 5E 109
Swallow Fold SK13: Glos 6H 123
Swallow La. SK15: C'ook 4B 94
Swallow St. M11: Man 4B 102
M12: Man 5C 116
OL8: O'ham 1D 90
SK1: Stoc 6H 179 (4H 145)
Swanage Av. M23: Wyth 2D 140
SK2: Stoc 5D 146
Swanage Cl. BL8: Bury 5C 22
Swanage Rd. M30: Ecc 2D 96
Swanbourne Gdns. SK3: Stoc 5E 145
Swan Cl. SK12: Poy 3B 168
Swan Ct. OL2: Shaw 1H 59
Swanhill Cl. M18: Man 1H 117
Swan La. BL3: Bolt 3B 48
Swanley Av. M40: Man 6A 88
Swann Cl. SK8: Chea H 4D 156
Swann Gro. SK8: Chea H 4D 156
Swann La. SK8: Chea H 4C 156
Swan Rd. BL8: G'mount 1H 21
WA15: Tim 2A 140
Swansea St. OL8: O'ham 5H 75
Swan St. M4: Man 3B 6 (3E 101)
OL6: A Lyme 5D 174 (2A 106)
SK9: Wilm 2E 173
Swan Ter. M30: Ecc 5E 97
Swanton Wlk. M8: Man 5D 86
(off Kilmington Dr.)
Swan Wlk. M22: Wyth 3B 154
Swarbrick Dr. M25: Pres 1F 85
Swayfield Av. M13: Man 4B 116
Swaylands Dr. M33: Sale 2B 140
Sweet Briar Cl. OL12: Roch 1G 27
Sweetbriar Cl. OL2: Shaw 6H 43
Sweetbriar Ho. OL2: Shaw 6H 43
(off Glebe St.)
Sweet Briar La. OL12: Roch 1G 27
Sweetlove's Gro. BL1: Bolt 6C 18
Sweetlove's La. BL1: Bolt 6C 18
Sweetnam Dr. M11: Man 3D 102
Swettenham Rd. SK9: Hand 2H 165
Swift Cl. SK6: Wood 4A 136
Swift Rd. OL1: O'ham 2C 60
OL11: Roch 4B 26
Swift St. OL6: A Lyme 6B 92
Swiftsure Av. M3: Sal 5C 4 (4B 100)
Swift Wlk. M40: Man 6E 89
(off Dakerwood Cl.)
Swinbourne Gro. M20: Man 2G 131
Swinburne Av. M43: Droy 2A 104
Swinburne Grn. SK5: Stoc 6F 117
Swinburne Way M34: Dent 2G 135
Swinburn St. M9: Man 2B 88
Swindells St. M11: Man 6G 103
(off Stanley St.)
SK14: Hyde 2C 120
Swindon Cl. M18: Man 2F 117
Swinfield Av. M21: Chor 1F 129
Swinford Gro. OL2: O'ham 2G 59
Swinford Wlk. M9: Man 6A 72
(off Woodmere Dr.)
Swinley Chase SK9: Wilm 6B 166
Swinside Cl. M24: Mid 5G 55
Swinside Rd. BL2: Bolt 5B 34
Swinstead Av. M40: Man 6A 88
SWINTON 3H 83
Swinton Ct. M27: Swin 4A 84
(off Park St.)
Swinton Cres. BL9: Bury 6G 53
Swinton Gro. M13: Man 2G 115
Swinton Hall Rd. M27: Pen, Swin 3H 83
Swinton Ind. Est. M27: Swin 3A 84
Swinton Leisure Cen. 3H 83
Swinton Library Art Gallery 3H 83
(off Chorley Rd.)
Swinton Lions RLFC 3E 69
SWINTON PARK 4A 84
Swinton Pk. Rd. M6: Sal 6B 84

Swinton Shop. Cen. M27: Swin 3H 83
Swinton Station (Rail) 2H 83
Swinton St. BL2: Bolt 6A 34
OL4: O'ham 4A 76
Swiss Hill SK9: A Edg 5H 173
Swithin Rd. M22: Wyth 5C 154
Swithun Wells Ct. M38: Lit H 4E 65
Swythamley Cl. SK3: Stoc 3C 144
Swythamley Rd. SK3: Stoc 3C 144
Sybil St. OL15: L'ough 3G 17
Sycamore Av. M26: Rad 1H 67
M29: Tyld 2B 80
M34: Dent 5F 119
OL4: O'ham 1B 76
OL9: Chad 6H 73
OL10: H'ood 5A 40
OL16: Miln 2G 43
WA14: Alt 6C 138
Sycamore Cl. M20: Man 2G 131
OL6: A Lyme 2C 106
OL15: L'ough 4F 17
SK9: Wilm 6F 165
SK16: Duk 5D 106
Sycamore Ct. M6: Sal 2G 99
M16: W Ran 4B 114
M33: Sale 3E 127
(off Carrington La.)
M40: Man 2A 102
SK4: Stoc 6D 132
(off Heaton Moor Rd.)
Sycamore Cres. OL6: A Lyme 6A 92
Sycamore Dr. BL9: Bury 5F 23
M26: Rad 2A 52
Sycamore Gro. M35: Fail 4B 90
Sycamore Lodge SK7: Bram 6H 157
Sycamore Pl. M45: White 3F 69
Sycamore Rd. BL8: Tot 6H 21
M30: Ecc 1C 96
M31: Part 6B 124
SK6: Bred 5G 135
Sycamores, The M26: Rad 3D 66
M33: Sale 6C 128
(off Beaufort Av.)
OL4: Lees 1C 76
OL5: Mos 2A 94
SK13: Had 4H 123
SK15: Stal 5F 107
WA14: Alt 1D 150
Sycamore Wlk. SK8: Chea 5A 144
Syddal Cl. SK7: Bram 2F 167
Syddal Cres. SK7: Bram 3F 167
Syddal Grn. SK7: Bram 2F 167
Syddall Av. SK8: H Grn 5H 155
Syddall St. SK14: Hyde 6B 120
Syddall Rd. SK7: Bram 2F 167
Sydenham St. OL1: O'ham 6G 59
(not continuous)
Sydenham Ter. OL12: Roch 6F 15
Sydney Av. M30: Ecc 3F 97
M90: Man A 5G 153
Sydney Barns Cl. OL11: Roch 3D 40
Sydney Gdns. OL15: L'ough 2A 16
Sydney Jones Ct. M40: Man 2E 89
Sydney Rd. SK7: Bram 2H 167
Sydney St. M6: Sal 3E 99
M27: Swin 4F 83
M32: Stre 5D 112
M35: Fail 4G 89
OL5: Mos 3H 93
SK2: Stoc 4C 146
SYKE 5H 15
Syke Cft. SK6: Rom 6B 136
Syke La. OL12: Roch 5H 15
Syke Rd. OL12: Roch 5H 15
OL15: L'ough 1H 29
Sykes Av. BL9: Bury 3H 53
Sykes Cl. OL3: G'fld 4D 78
Sykes Ct. OL16: Roch 5B 28
(off Sykes St.)

Sykes Mdw. SK3: Stoc 5F **145**
Sykes St. OL16: Miln 1G **43**
  OL16: Roch 5B **28**
  SK5: Stoc 1H **133**
  SK14: Hyde 6D **120**
  (off Knight St.)
Sykes Wlk. *SK5: Stoc* 1H **133**
  (off Sykes St.)
Sylvan Av. M16: W Ran 4B **114**
  M33: Sale 6C **128**
  M35: Fail 6G **89**
  M41: Urm 4F **111**
  SK9: Wilm 4C **172**
  WA15: Tim 3H **139**
Sylvan Cl. M24: Mid 5H **55**
Sylvandale Av. M19: Man 6C **116**
Sylvan Gro. WA14: Alt 1A **174** (6F **139**)
Sylvan St. OL9: O'ham 2C **74**
Sylvester Av. SK2: Stoc 5B **146**
Sylvester Cl. SK14: Hat 5A **122**
Sylvester Way M34: Dent 2G **135**
  SK14: Hat 5A **122**
  (off Sylvester Cl.)
Sylvia Gro. SK5: Stoc 2G **133**
Symond Rd. M9: Man 4A **72**
Symons Rd. M33: Sale 4B **128**
Symons St. M7: Sal 4C **86**
Syndall Av. M12: Man 5G **11** (1H **115**)
Syndall St. M12: Man 5G **11** (1H **115**)

T

Tabley Av. M14: Man 5F **115**
Tabley Ct. WA14: Alt 1B **174**
Tabley Gdns. M43: Droy 4B **104**
  SK6: Mar 1E **161**
Tabley Gro. M13: Man 5B **116**
  SK5: Stoc 2G **133**
  WA15: Tim 2H **139**
Tableymere Gdns. SK8: Chea H . . .2B **156**
Tabley M. WA14: Alt 1B **174**
Tabley Rd. BL3: Bolt 3H **47**
  M33: Sale 1E **141**
  SK9: Hand 2H **165**
Tabley St. M6: Sal 6H **85**
  OL5: Mos 3H **93**
  SK16: Duk 5C **106**
Tabor St. M24: Mid 5B **56**
Tackler Cl. M27: Swin 4H **83**
Tadcaster Dr. M40: Man 5H **87**
Tadcaster Wlk. OL1: Man 2G **177**
Taddington Pl. *SK13: Gam* 6G **123**
  (off Castleton Cres.)
Tadman Gro. WA14: Alt 5C **138**
Tadmor Cl. M38: Lit H 5D **64**
Tagge La. M6: Sal 5F **85**
  M27: Pen 5E **85**
Tagg Wood Vw. BL0: Ram 4A **12**
Tagore Cl. M13: Man 3A **116**
Tahir Cl. M8: Man 4F **87**
Tait M. SK4: Stoc 1B **144**
Talavera St. M7: Sal 6B **86**
Talbenny Cl. BL1: Bolt 5F **31**
Talbot Av. BL3: Lit L 3C **50**
Talbot Cl. OL4: O'ham 1A **76**
Talbot Ct. BL1: Bolt 1D **32**
  M32: Stre 4E **113**
Talbot Gro. BL9: Bury 5G **23**
Talbot Pl. M16: Old T 2H **113**
Talbot Rd. M14: Man 2A **132**
  M16: Old T 4E **113**
  M32: Stre 4E **113**
  M33: Sale 5E **129**
  SK9: A Edg 4H **173**
  SK14: Hyde 2C **120**
  WA14: Bow 3D **150**
  (not continuous)
Talbot St. M24: Mid 5C **56**
  M30: Ecc 4G **97**
  OL6: A Lyme 5A **174** (2G **105**)
  OL11: Roch 6B **178** (6H **27**)
  SK1: Stoc 2F **179**

Talbot St. SK7: H Gro 1E **159**
Talford Gro. M20: Man 4E **131**
Talgarth Rd. M40: Man 1G **101**
Talkin Dr. M24: Mid 4A **56**
Talland Wlk. *M13: Man* 2G **131**
  (off Plymouth Gro.)
Tallarn Cl. M20: Man 2G **131**
Tallis St. M12: Man 4C **116**
Tallow Way M44: Irl 1E **125**
Tall Trees M7: Sal 2B **86**
Tall Trees Cl. OL2: O'ham 3C **58**
Tall Trees Pl. SK2: Stoc 5C **146**
Tallyman Way M27: Pen 4E **85**
Talmine Av. M40: Man 6A **88**
Tamar Cl. BL4: Kea 4D **66**
  M45: White 1G **69**
Tamar Cl. M15: Man 6C **8** (1B **114**)
Tamar Dr. M23: Wyth 1G **153**
Tamarin Cl. M27: Ward 2E **83**
Tamar Way OL10: H'ood 2E **39**
Tame Bank Cl. OL5: Mos 6H **77**
Tame Barn Cl. OL16: Miln 5G **29**
Tame Cl. SK15: Stal 2G **107**
Tame Ct. *SK15: Stal* 3F **107**
  (off Portland Pl.)
Tame La. OL3: Del 6G **45**
Tamerton Dr. M8: Man 5E **87**
Tameside Bus. Development Cen.
  M34: Dent 4D **118**
Tameside Ct. SK14: Hat 5A **122**
  SK16: Duk 6H **105**
Tameside Hippodrome 5B **174** (2H **105**)
Tameside Leisure Pool 4H **105**
  (off Queen St.)
Tameside Pk. Ind. Est. SK16: Duk . . .5H **105**
Tameside Stadium 1E **105**
Tameside Work Cen. *OL7: A Lyme* . . .4F **105**
  (off Ryecroft St.)
Tame St. M4: Man 6G **7** (4H **101**)
  M34: Aud 6F **105**
  M34: Dent 3E **119**
  OL3: Upp 1D **78**
  OL5: Mos 6A **78**
  SK15: Stal 4C **106**
TAME VALLEY 4B **106**
Tame Valley Cl. OL5: Mos 6A **78**
Tame Vw. OL5: Mos 1G **93**
Tame Wlk. SK9: Wilm 6H **165**
TAME WATER 6B **62**
Tamewater Vs. OL3: Dob 6B **62**
Tamworth Av. M45: White 2H **69**
Tamworth Cl. M15: Man 2C **114**
  SK7: H Gro 5D **158**
Tamworth Ct. M15: Man 2C **114**
  OL9: O'ham 4C **74**
  (off Tamworth St.)
Tamworth Dr. BL8: Bury 6C **22**
Tamworth Grn. SK1: Stoc 1B **146**
Tamworth St. M15: Man 3C **114**
  OL9: O'ham 4C **74**
  SK1: Stoc 1B **146**
Tandis Ct. M6: Sal 2A **98**
Tandle Hill Country Pk. 1A **58**
Tandle Hill Countryside Cen. 1B **58**
Tandle Hill Rd. OL2: O'ham 1B **58**
Tandle Hill Ter. OL11: Roch 4B **42**
Tandlewood M. M40: Man 6E **89**
Tandlewood Pk. OL2: O'ham 1B **58**
Tanfield Dr. M26: Rad 2D **66**
Tanfield Rd. M20: Man 3F **143**
TANG 2H **147**
Tang, The SK6: Rom 2H **147**
Tangmere Av. OL10: H'ood 6A **40**
Tangmere Cl. M40: Man 6E **73**
Tangmere Ct. M16: W Ran 4B **114**
Tangshutts La. OL3: G'fld 1B **148**
Tanhill Cl. SK2: Stoc 5E **147**
Tanhill La. OL8: O'ham 1G **91**
Tanhouse Av. M29: Ast 4B **80**
Tanhouse Rd. M41: Urm 4H **109**
Tanner Brook Cl. *BL3: Bolt* 3C **48**
  (off John Cross St.)
Tanner Bus. Cen., The OL3: G'fld . . .5E **79**

TANNERS 3B **12**
Tanners Cft. BL0: Ram 3B **12**
Tannersfield Lodge
  M35: Fail 5G **89**
Tanners Fold OL8: O'ham 1G **91**
Tanners Grn. M6: Sal 2F **99**
  (off Nursery St.)
Tanners St. BL0: Ram 3B **12**
  M18: Man 2G **117**
Tanner St. SK14: Hyde 4B **120**
Tannery Way M18: Man 2G **117**
  WA14: Tim 4G **139**
Tannock Ct. SK7: H Gro 4F **159**
Tannock Rd. SK7: H Gro 4F **159**
Tanpit Cotts. OL10: H'ood 1H **39**
Tan Pits Cl. M29: Ast 4A **80**
Tanpits Rd. BL9: Bury 2A **176** (2E **37**)
Tanpit Wlk. M22: Wyth 3A **154**
Tansey Gro. M7: Sal 4D **86**
Tansley Rd. M8: Man 1F **87**
Tanworth Wlk. *BL1: Bolt* 3C **32**
  (off Wolfenden St.)
Tan Yd. Brow M18: Man 3G **117**
Tanyard Dr. WA15: Haleb 1C **162**
Tanyard Grn. SK5: Stoc 4H **133**
Tanyard La. WA15: Alt 2A **162**
Taper St. BL0: Ram 3B **12**
Tapley Av. SK12: Poy 5E **169**
Taplin Dr. M18: Man 2F **117**
Taplow Gro. SK8: Chea H 3B **156**
Taplow Wlk. *M14: Man* 4A **116**
  (off Binstead Cl.)
Tarbet Dr. BL2: Bolt 6B **34**
Tarbet Rd. SK16: Duk 6A **106**
Tarbet Wlk. M8: Man 5D **86**
Tarbolton Cres. WA15: Hale 2C **152**
TARDEN 6H **149**
Tariff St. M1: Man 5C **6** (4F **101**)
Tarland Wlk. *M11: Man* 4E **103**
  (off Kincraig Cl.)
Tarleton Cl. BL8: Bury 4H **35**
Tarleton Ho. *M6: Sal* 1C **98**
  (off Moss Mdw. Rd.)
Tarleton Pl. BL3: Bolt 4G **47**
Tarleton Wlk. M13: Man 6G **11** (1H **115**)
Tarnbrook Cl. M45: White 1A **70**
Tarnbrook Wlk. *M15: Man* 2E **115**
  (off Wellhead Cl.)
Tarn Dr. BL9: Bury 1E **53**
Tarn Gro. M28: Walk 2B **82**
Tarn Ho. M15: Man 4C **8**
Tarns, The SK8: Gat 2F **155**
Tarnside Cl. OL16: Roch 6C **16**
  SK2: Stoc 5F **147**
Tarnside Ho. M8: Man 1D **86**
Tarporley Av. M14: Man 1E **131**
Tarporley Cl. SK3: Stoc 6F **145**
Tarporley Wlk. *SK9: Wilm* 5A **166**
  (off Picton Dr.)
Tarran Gro. M34: Dent 6H **119**
Tarran Pl. WA14: Alt 5G **139**
Tarrington Cl. M12: Man 2C **116**
Tartan St. M11: Man 3D **102**
Tarves Wlk. *M11: Man* 4D **102**
  (off Kincraig Cl.)
Tarvin Av. M20: Man 2E **131**
  SK4: Stoc 2F **133**
Tarvin Dr. SK6: Bred 5E **135**
Tarvington Cl. M40: Man 5G **87**
Tarvin Rd. SK8: Chea 6C **144**
Tarvin Wlk. BL1: Bolt 3C **32**
Tarvin Way SK9: Hand 2H **165**
Tasle All. M2: Man 6H **5** (4D **100**)
Tatchbury Rd. M35: Fail 4A **90**
Tate St. OL8: O'ham 5H **75**
Tatham Cl. M13: Man 4B **116**
Tatham St. OL16: Roch 4A **28**
Tatland Dr. M22: Wyth 2D **154**
Tattenhall Wlk. *M14: Man* 1H **131**
  (off Ravenhead Cl.)
Tattersall Av. BL1: Bolt 3E **31**
Tattersall St. OL9: O'ham 3D **74**
Tatton Bldgs. SK8: Gat 6F **143**

Tatton Cl. SK7: H Gro 1F **159**
   SK8: Chea 1C **156**
Tatton Ct. M14: Man 1H **131**
   SK4: Stoc 5E **133**
Tatton Gdns. SK6: Wood 4B **136**
Tatton Gro. M20: Man 3F **131**
Tatton Ho. BL1: Bolt 6A **32**
Tatton Mere Dr. M43: Droy 4B **104**
Tattonmere Gdns.
   SK8: Chea H 1C **156**
Tatton Pl. M13: Man 3A **116**
   M33: Sale 4B **128**
Tatton Rd. M33: Sale 4B **128**
   M34: Dent 6G **119**
   SK9: Hand 2A **166**
Tatton Rd. Nth. SK4: Stoc 4E **133**
Tatton Rd. Sth. SK4: Stoc 5E **133**
Tatton St. M5: Sal 2A **8** (5H **99**)
   M15: Man 5C **8** (1B **114**)
   SK1: Stoc 2G **179** (2H **145**)
   SK14: Hyde 2C **136**
   SK15: Stal 3F **107**
Tatton Ter. *SK16: Duk* 4H **105**
                     (off Hill St.)
Tatton Vw. M20: Man 3F **131**
TAUNTON .6E **91**
Taunton Av. M30: Ecc 2D **96**
   M41: Urm 1D **126**
   OL7: A Lyme 1G **105**
   OL11: Roch 4D **26**
Taunton Brook La. OL7: A Lyme 6E **91**
Taunton Cl. *BL1: Bolt* 4A **32**
                 (off Valletts La.)
   SK7: H Gro 3G **159**
Taunton Dr. BL4: Farn 6D **48**
Taunton Grn. OL7: A Lyme 6F **91**
Taunton Gro. M45: White 3G **69**
Taunton Hall Cl. OL7: A Lyme 6F **91**
Taunton Lawns OL7: A Lyme 6G **91**
Taunton Pl. OL7: A Lyme 6F **91**
Taunton Platting *OL7: A Lyme* 5F **91**
                   (off Ney St.)
Taunton Rd. M33: Sale 5F **127**
   OL7: A Lyme 1G **105**
   OL9: Chad 5A **58**
Taunton St. M4: Man 5H **7** (4H **101**)
               (off Mancunian Rd.)
Taunton Wlk. *M34: Dent* 6G **119**
               (off Mancunian Rd.)
Taurus St. OL4: O'ham 1A **76**
Tavern Ct. M35: Fail 4A **90**
Tavern Ct. Av. M35: Fail 4A **90**
Tavern Rd. SK13: Had 4G **123**
Tavery Cl. M4: Man 4F **7** (3G **101**)
Tavistock Cl. SK14: Hat 5A **122**
Tavistock Dr. OL9: Chad 6H **57**
Tavistock Rd. BL1: Bolt 1B **48**
   M33: Sale 4F **127**
   OL11: Roch 3H **41**
Tavistock Sq. *M9: Man* 4H **87**
                (off Grangewood Dr.)
Tawton Av. SK14: Hat 4A **122**
Tay Cl. OL8: O'ham 6F **177** (4E **75**)
Tayfield Rd. M22: Wyth 3A **154**
Taylor Av. OL11: Roch 3B **26**
Taylor Bldgs. BL4: Kea 3D **66**
Taylor Grn. Way OL4: Lees 5D **76**
Taylor Ho. BL8: Bury 5C **22**
Taylor Rd. M41: Urm 6G **97**
   WA14: Alt 6C **138**
Taylor's La. BL2: Bolt 6D **34**
   M40: Man 6E **89**
Taylorson St. M5: Sal 6H **99**
Taylorson St. Sth. M5: Sal 1G **113**
Taylors Pl. *OL12: Roch* 2H **27**
                   (off Taylor St.)
Taylor's Rd. M32: Stre 3D **112**
Taylor St. BL3: Bolt 5G **175** (1D **48**)
   BL9: Bury 1F **37**
   M14: Man 5G **115**
   M18: Man 1E **117**
   M24: Mid 1C **72**
                  (not continuous)

Taylor St. M25: Pres 5A **70**
   M26: Rad 4A **52**
   M34: Dent 3F **119**
   M43: Droy 4H **103**
   OL1: O'ham 1A **76**
   OL2: O'ham 2D **58**
   OL4: Lees 3C **76**
   OL9: Chad 2A **74**
   OL10: H'ood 3G **39**
   OL12: Roch 2H **27**
   OL12: Whitw 1F **15**
   SK14: Holl 2F **123**
   SK14: Hyde 4D **120**
   SK15: Stal 4F **107**
Taylor Ter. *OL15: L'ough* 4H **17**
                 (off Beswicke St.)
   SK16: Duk 4H **105**
                    (off Hill St.)
Tayton Cl. M29: Tyld 2A **80**
Taywood Rd. BL3: Bolt 5D **46**
Teak Dr. BL4: Kea 5F **67**
Teak St. BL9: Bury 3H **37**
Teal Av. SK12: Poy 3A **168**
Tealby Av. M16: Old T 3A **114**
Tealby Ct. M21: Chor 6A **114**
Teal Cl. M18: Man 3D **116**
   SK2: Stoc 6F **147**
   WA14: B'ath 3D **138**
Teal Ct. OL11: Roch 4B **26**
Teal St. BL3: Bolt 3D **48**
Teasdale Cl. OL9: Chad 6G **73**
Tebbutt St. M4: Man 2D **6** (2F **101**)
Tedburn Wlk. M40: Man 1F **89**
Tedder Cl. BL9: Bury 5H **53**
Tedder Dr. M22: Wyth 6D **154**
Teddington Rd. M40: Man 2E **89**
Ted Jackson Wlk. *M11: Man* 5B **102**
                 (off Newchurch St.)
Teer St. M40: Man 4H **7**
Teesdale Av. M41: Urm 3C **110**
Teesdale Cl. SK2: Stoc 5E **147**
Teesdale Wlk. *M9: Man* 6A **72**
                 (off Haverfield Rd.)
Tees St. OL16: Roch 5B **28**
Tees Wlk. *OL8: O'ham* 4E **75**
                    (off Lee St.)
Teignmouth Av. M40: Man 1G **101**
Telegraphic Ho. M50: Sal 6G **99**
Telegraph Rd. M17: T Pk 6A **98**
Telfer Av. M13: Man 5A **116**
Telfer Rd. M13: Man 5A **116**
Telford Cl. M34: Aud 6E **105**
Telford M. OL3: Upp 1D **78**
Telford Rd. SK6: Mar 1E **161**
Telford St. M8: Man 6G **87**
Telford Wlk. M16: Old T 3B **114**
Telford Way OL11: Roch 3A **42**
Telham Wlk. M23: Wyth 6G **141**
Tellson Cl. M6: Sal 5D **84**
Tellson Cres. M6: Sal 5D **84**
Tell St. OL12: Roch 4F **27**
Telryn Wlk. *M8: Man* 3G **87**
                   (off Stakeford Dr.)
Temperance Sq. SK14: Mot 3C **122**
Temperance St. BL3: Bolt 2C **48**
   M12: Man 2E **11** (5G **101**)
                  (not continuous)
Temperance Ter. *SK6: Mar* 5D **148**
                 (off Hollins La.)
Tempest Chase BL6: Los 3B **46**
Tempest Ct. BL6: Los 3C **46**
Tempest Rd. BL6: Los 4B **46**
   SK9: A Edg 5H **173**
Tempest St. BL3: Bolt 3H **47**
Temple Cl. OL4: Lees 1C **76**
Templecombe Dr.
   BL1: Bolt 5B **18**
Temple Dr. BL1: Bolt 2A **32**
   M27: Swin 4B **84**
Temple La. OL15: L'ough 2A **16**
Temple Rd. BL1: Bolt 2A **32**
   M33: Sale 5D **128**
Temple Sq. M8: Man 6F **87**

Temple St. M24: Mid 6D **56**
   OL1: O'ham 2H **75**
                    (off Dalton Cl.)
   OL10: H'ood 3H **39**
Templeton Dr. WA14: Alt 5D **138**
Tempus Apartments M3: Man 2G **5**
Temsbury Wlk. M40: Man 6A **88**
Ten Acre Ct. M45: White 2C **68**
Ten Acre Dr. M45: White 2D **68**
Ten Acres Astro Cen. 6C **88**
Ten Acres La. M40: Man 6C **88**
Tenax Circ. M17: T Pk 5B **98**
Tenax Rd. M17: T Pk 6B **98**
Tenbury Cl. M6: Sal 2F **99**
Tenbury Dr. M24: Mid 4C **72**
Tenby Av. BL1: Bolt 4G **31**
   M20: Man 3F **131**
   M32: Stre 3F **113**
Tenby Dr. M6: Sal 6D **84**
   SK8: Chea H 4D **156**
Tenby Gro. OL12: Roch 2E **27**
Tenby Rd. OL8: O'ham 1B **90**
   SK3: Stoc 4D **144**
Tenby St. OL12: Roch 2E **27**
Tenement La.
   SK7: Bram, Chea 2E **157**
                    (not continuous)
Teneriffe St. M7: Sal 6B **86**
Tenham Wlk. *M9: Man* 6A **72**
                 (off Ravenswood Dr.)
Ten Ho's. OL8: O'ham 1A **92**
Tennis St. BL1: Bolt 2B **32**
   M16: Old T 3H **113**
Tennyson Av. BL9: Bury 1F **53**
   M26: Rad 3G **51**
   M34: Dent 2G **135**
   SK16: Duk 6E **107**
Tennyson Cl. SK4: Stoc 1D **144**
Tennyson Gdns. M25: Pres 6F **69**
Tennyson Rd. BL4: Farn 3F **65**
   M24: Mid 5D **56**
   M27: Swin 3F **83**
   M43: Droy 3A **104**
   SK5: Stoc 6F **117**
   SK8: Chea 5B **144**
Tennyson St. BL1: Bolt 4B **32**
   M13: Man 2G **115**
   OL1: O'ham 6A **60**
   OL11: Roch 6A **28**
Tennyson Wlk. *BL1: Bolt* 3C **32**
                   (off Irving St.)
Tenpin 10 Bowling 2H **143**
Tensing Av. OL7: A Lyme 6H **91**
Tensing Fold SK16: Duk 4H **105**
Tensing St. OL8: O'ham 3G **91**
Tenter Brow SK15: Stal 3D **106**
Tentercroft OL1: O'ham 2F **177** (2E **75**)
   OL12: Roch 3A **178** (3G **27**)
                    (not continuous)
Tenterden Wlk. *M22: Wyth* 2A **154**
                 (off Poundswick La.)
Tenterhill La. OL11: Roch 1H **25**
TENTERSFIELD 3D **36**
Tenters St. BL9: Bury 4A **176** (3D **36**)
Tenth St. M17: T Pk 1D **112**
Terence St. M40: Man 6F **89**
Terminal Rd. E. M90: Man A 6H **153**
Terminal Rd. Nth.
   M90: Man A 6H **153**
Tern Av. BL4: Farn 1D **64**
Tern Cl. OL11: Roch 4B **26**
   SK16: Duk 6C **106**
   WA14: B'ath 3D **138**
Tern Dr. SK12: Poy 3B **168**
Ternhill Ct. BL4: Farn 1H **65**
Terrace, The M25: Pres 6H **69**
Terrace St. OL4: O'ham 2H **75**
Terrington Cl. M21: Chor 2C **130**
Tetbury Dr. BL2: Bolt 5B **34**
Tetbury Rd. M22: Wyth 4H **153**
Tetlow Fold SK14: Hyde 4F **121**

Tetlow Gro. M30: Ecc 4E **97**
Tetlow La. M7: Sal 3C **86**
Tetlow St. M24: Mid 1C **72**
  M40: Man 6F **89**
  OL8: O'ham 3D **74**
  SK14: Hyde 2C **120**
Tetlows Yd. OL15: L'ough 1B **16**
Tetsworth Wlk. M40: Man 1F **89**
  (off Blandford Dr.)
Teviot St. M13: Man 3A **116**
Tewkesbury Av. M24: Mid 4B **56**
  M41: Urm 3F **111**
  M43: Droy 2A **104**
  OL6: A Lyme 4A **92**
  OL9: Chad 5A **58**
  WA15: Hale 2C **152**
Tewkesbury Cl.
  SK8: Chea H 1D **166**
  SK12: Poy 2D **168**
Tewkesbury Dr. M25: Pres 1A **86**
Tewkesbury Rd.
  M40: Man 2H **7** (2H **101**)
  SK3: Stoc 5D **144**
Texas St. OL6: A Lyme 3A **106**
Textile Apartments M3: Sal 4G **5**
Textile St. M12: Man 6C **102**
Textilose Ho. SK1: Stoc 3F **179**
Textilose Rd. M17: T Pk 2B **112**
Teynham Wlk. M22: Wyth 4A **154**
  (off Selstead Rd.)
Thackeray Cl. M8: Man 5E **87**
Thackeray Gro. M43: Droy 3A **104**
Thackeray Rd. OL1: O'ham 6A **60**
Thames Cl. BL9: Bury 4F **23**
  M11: Man 5D **102**
Thames Ind. Est.
  M12: Man 3G **11** (6H **101**)
Thames Rd. OL16: Miln 5B **29**
Thames St. OL1: O'ham 1H **177** (1G **75**)
  OL16: Roch 5B **28**
Thames Trad. Cen. M44: Irl 2D **124**
Thanet Cl. M7: Sal 6C **86**
Thankerton Av. M34: Aud 4D **104**
Thatcher Cl. WA14: Bow 5E **151**
Thatcher St. OL8: Stoc 5G **75**
THATCH LEACH 4H **73**
Thatch Leach OL9: Chad 4H **73**
Thatch Leach La.
  M45: White 2G **69**
Thaxmead Dr. M40: Man 1F **103**
Thaxted Dr. SK2: Stoc 6G **147**
Thaxted Pl. BL1: Bolt 5A **32**
Thaxted Wlk. M22: Wyth 5A **154**
The ....
  Names prefixed with 'The' for example
  'The Acorn Cen.' are indexed under the
  main name such as 'Acorn Cen., The'
Theatre Ho. M6: Sal 1E **99**
  (off Langworthy Rd.)
Theatre Royal 5B **120**
Thekla St. OL9: O'ham 1D **74**
Thelma St. BL0: Ram 3B **12**
Thelwall Av. BL2: Bolt 5H **33**
  M14: Man 1D **130**
Thelwall Cl. WA15: Alt 5G **139**
Thelwall Ct. M14: Man 1E **131**
Thelwall Rd. M33: Sale 6E **129**
Theobald Rd. WA14: Bow 4F **151**
Theta Cl. M11: Man 3D **102**
Thetford OL12: Roch 2A **178** (3G **27**)
Thetford Cl. BL8: Bury 6D **22**
Thetford Dr. M8: Man 4F **87**
THICKETFORD BROW 4G **33**
Thicketford Brow BL2: Bolt 4H **33**
Thicketford Cl. BL2: Bolt 3G **33**
Thicketford Rd. BL2: Bolt 4F **33**
Thimble Cl. OL12: Roch 5D **16**
Thimbles, The OL12: Roch 5D **16**
Third Av. BL1: Bolt 6H **31**
  BL3: Lit L 3B **50**
  BL9: Bury 1B **38**

Third Av. M11: Man 2E **103**
  M17: T Pk 2D **112**
    (not continued)
  M27: Swin 6G **83**
  M29: Ast 6A **80**
  OL8: O'ham 1C **90**
  SK12: Poy 6D **168**
  SK15: C'ook 5A **94**
Third St. BL1: Bolt 1F **31**
Thirkhill Pl. M30: Ecc 3H **97**
Thirlby Dr. M22: Wyth 4B **154**
Thirlmere Av. M27: Swin 4A **84**
  M32: Stre 4C **112**
  OL7: A Lyme 1F **105**
Thirlmere Cl. SK9: A Edg 5F **173**
  SK15: Stal 1E **107**
  (off Springs La.)
Thirlmere Dr. BL9: Bury 6E **37**
  M24: Mid 5A **56**
  M38: Lit H 4E **65**
Thirlmere Gro. BL4: Farn 1C **64**
  OL2: O'ham 1D **58**
Thirlmere M. M24: Mid 4A **56**
Thirlmere Rd. M22: Wyth 3H **153**
  M31: Part 5C **124**
  M41: Urm 4A **110**
  OL11: Roch 1D **40**
  SK1: Stoc 4B **146**
Thirlspot Cl. BL1: Bolt 5C **18**
Thirlstone Av. OL4: O'ham 3D **60**
Thirsfield Dr. M11: Man 3E **103**
Thirsk Av. M33: Sale 6E **127**
  OL9: Chad 6H **57**
Thirsk Cl. BL8: Bury 6B **22**
Thirsk M. M7: Sal 5B **86**
  (off Bury New Rd.)
Thirsk Rd. BL3: Lit L 5C **50**
Thirsk St. M12: Man 3E **11** (6G **101**)
Thistle Bank Cl. M9: Man 2G **87**
Thistle Cl. SK15: Stal 6H **107**
Thistle Grn. OL16: Miln 4E **29**
Thistle Ho., The *SK15: Mill* 1H **107**
  (off Bramble Ct.)
Thistle Sq. M31: Part 6C **124**
Thistleton Rd. BL3: Bolt 4F **47**
Thistle Wlk. *M31: Part* 6C **124**
  (off Thistle Sq.)
Thistle Way OL4: O'ham 5B **60**
Thistlewood Dr. SK9: Wilm 2G **173**
Thistleyfield OL16: Miln 4E **29**
Thistley Flds. SK14: Hyde 1A **136**
Thomas Cl. M34: Dent 3G **119**
Thomas Cl. *BL7: Bro X* 4E **19**
  (off Toppings Grn.)
  M15: Man 4D **8**
Thomas Dr. BL3: Bolt 2B **48**
Thomas Garnet Ct. *BL4: Farn* 1G **65**
  (off Glynne St.)
Thomas Gibbon Cl. M32: Stre 6C **112**
  (off Mitford St.)
Thomas Henshaw Ct. OL11: Roch 1E **41**
Thomas Holden St. BL1: Bolt 5B **32**
Thomas Ho. *OL2: O'ham* 3F **58**
  (off Royton Hall Pk.)
Thomas Johnson Cl. M30: Ecc 4E **97**
  (off Green La.)
Thomas More Cl. BL4: Kea 3B **66**
Thomason Sq. OL15: L'ough 4G **17**
Thomas Regan Ct. *M18: Man* 1F **117**
  (off Ansell Cl.)
Thomasson Cl. *BL1: Bolt* 4C **32**
  (off Barnwood Dr.)
Thomasson Ct. BL1: Bolt 6H **31**
Thomas St. BL3: Bolt 2B **48**
  BL4: Farn 1A **66**
  (Bridgewater St.)
  BL4: Farn 2A **66**
  (Old Hall St.)
  M4: Man 4B **6** (3E **101**)
  M7: Sal 3D **86**
  M8: Man 3D **86**
  M26: Rad 4B **52**

Thomas St. M32: Stre 3D **112**
  OL2: O'ham 4F **59**
  OL2: Shaw 1A **60**
  OL4: Lees 4C **76**
  OL12: Whitw 3B **14**
  OL15: L'ough 5F **17**
  OL16: Roch 1D **178** (3A **28**)
  SK1: Stoc 6H **179** (4H **145**)
  SK6: Bred 6G **135**
  SK6: Comp 1F **143**
  WA15: Alt 2C **174** (1G **151**)
Thomas St. W.
  SK1: Stoc 6G **179** (4H **145**)
Thomas Telford Basin
  M1: Man 6E **7** (4G **101**)
Thompson Av. BL2: Ain 4F **35**
  M45: White 2G **69**
Thompson Cl. M34: Dent 4C **118**
Thompson Ct. M34: Dent 4B **118**
  SK15: Stal 3D **106**
  (off Thompson Fold)
Thompson Dr. BL9: Bury 2A **38**
Thompson Fold SK15: Stal 3D **106**
Thompson La. OL9: Chad 5A **74**
Thompson Rd. BL1: Bolt 4H **31**
  M17: T Pk 5G **97**
  M34: Dent 4B **118**
Thompson St. BL3: Bolt 2D **48**
  M3: Man 1G **5**
  M4: Man 2C **6** (3F **101**)
  M40: Man 6B **88**
  OL9: O'ham 2D **74**
  (off Main Rd.)
Thomson Rd. M18: Man 3E **117**
Thomson St. M13: Man 6F **11** (1G **115**)
  SK3: Stoc 5F **179** (3G **145**)
Thoralby Cl. M12: Man 2C **116**
Thorburn Dr. OL12: Whitw 2D **14**
Thoresby Cl. M26: Rad 2E **51**
Thoresway Rd. M13: Man 4A **116**
  SK9: Wilm 4C **172**
Thorgill Wlk. *M40: Man* 4C **88**
  (off Walderton Av.)
Thor Gro. M5: Sal 2B **8** (5A **100**)
Thorley Cl. OL9: Chad 1G **89**
Thorley Dr. M41: Urm 5F **111**
  WA15: Tim 6B **140**
Thorley La. M90: Man A 4F **153**
  WA15: Ring 4E **153**
  WA15: Tim 5B **140**
Thorley M. SK7: Bram 6H **157**
Thorley Rd. WA15: Tim 6C **140**
Thorley St. M35: Fail 3H **89**
Thornaby Wlk. *M9: Man* 5H **87**
  (off Kirklinton Dr.)
Thornage Dr. M40: Man 1F **7** (1G **101**)
Thorn Av. M35: Fail 5G **89**
Thorn Bank SK15: C'ook 4B **94**
Thornbank OL10: H'ood 6A **40**
Thornbank E. BL3: Bolt 1A **48**
Thornbank Est. *BL3: Bolt* 1A **48**
  (off Thornbank E.)
Thorn Bank Lodge SK4: Stoc 5D **132**
Thornbank Nth. BL3: Bolt 1A **48**
Thornbank Sth. BL3: Bolt 1A **48**
Thornbank W. BL3: Bolt 1A **48**
Thornbeck Dr. BL1: Bolt 4F **31**
Thornbeck Rd. BL1: Bolt 4F **31**
Thornbridge Av. M21: Chor 1H **129**
Thornbury OL11: Roch 6A **178** (5G **27**)
Thornbury Av. SK14: Hat 4A **122**
Thornbury Cl. *BL1: Bolt* 5C **32**
  (off Prince St.)
  SK8: Chea H 4E **157**
Thornbury Rd. M32: Stre 3E **113**
Thornbury Way M18: Man 2E **117**
Thornbush Way OL16: Roch 3C **28**
Thornby Wlk. M23: Wyth 6G **141**
Thorncliff Av. OL8: O'ham 6E **75**
THORNCLIFFE 1E **123**
Thorncliffe Av. OL2: O'ham 1C **58**
  SK16: Duk 6A **106**

Thorncliffe Gro. M19: Man 6E 117
Thorncliffe Pk. OL2: O'ham 1C 58
Thorncliffe Rd. BL1: Bolt 6C 18
 SK13: Had 4H 123
Thorncliffe Va. SK14: Holl 1E 123
Thorncliffe Wood SK14: Holl 2E 123
Thorn Cl. OL10: H'ood 2F 39
Thorncombe Rd. M16: W Ran 4C 114
Thorn Ct. M6: Sal 3H 99
 SK15: Stal 3E 107
 (off Waterloo Rd.)
Thorncross Cl. M15: Man 4B 8 (6A 100)
Thorndale Cl. OL2: O'ham 2E 59
Thorndale Ct. M9: Man 1G 87
 (off Marshbrook Dr.)
 WA15: Tim 6A 140
 (off Stockport Rd.)
Thorndale Gro. WA15: Tim 6A 140
Thornden Rd. M40: Man 1H 101
Thorndyke Gdns. M25: Pres 6H 69
 (off Bury New Rd.)
Thorndyke Wlk. M25: Pres 6H 69
Thorne Av. M41: Urm 4C 110
Thornedge WA15: Tim 3H 139
Thorne Ho. M14: Man 5H 115
Thorneside M34: Dent 2F 119
 (not continuous)
Thorne St. BL4: Farn 6G 49
Thorneycroft Av. M21: Chor 4H 129
Thorneycroft Cl. WA15: Tim 6B 140
Thorneycroft Rd. WA15: Tim 6B 140
Thorney Dr. SK8: Chea H 1E 167
Thorney Hill Cl. OL4: O'ham 3G 75
Thorneyholme Cl. BL6: Los 1C 46
Thorneylea OL12: Whitw 4B 14
Thornfield Ct. SK4: Stoc 6C 132
 (off Thornfield Rd.)
Thornfield Cres. M38: Lit H 4D 64
Thornfield Dr. M27: Swin 4G 83
Thornfield Gro. M38: Lit H 4D 64
 OL6: A Lyme 2C 106
 SK8: Chea H 3C 156
Thornfield Hey SK9: Wilm 1H 173
Thornfield Ho. SK8: Chea H 3C 156
Thornfield Rd. BL8: Tot 4F 21
 M19: Man 4A 132
 SK4: Stoc 6C 132
Thornfield St. M5: Sal 4D 98
 (off Foster St.)
Thornfield Ter. OL6: A Lyme 3A 106
Thornford Wlk. M40: Man 1F 89
 (off Blandford Dr.)
Thorngate Rd. M8: Man 6E 87
Thorn Gro. M14: Man 1H 131
 M33: Sale 5B 128
 SK8: Chea H 1C 166
 WA15: Hale 2G 151
Thorngrove Av. M23: Wyth 4D 140
Thorngrove Dr. SK9: Wilm 3F 173
Thorngrove Ho. M23: Wyth 4D 140
Thorngrove Rd. SK9: Wilm 3F 173
Thornham Cl. BL8: Bury 5C 22
Thornham Ct. OL2: Roch 5C 42
Thornham Dr. BL1: Bolt 5D 18
THORNHAM FOLD 6H 41
Thornham La. M24: Mid 1F 57
 OL2: O'ham 5C 42
Thornham New Rd. OL11: Roch 5F 41
Thornham Old Rd. OL2: O'ham 6A 42
Thornham Rd. M33: Sale 1G 139
 OL2: O'ham 6D 42
Thornhill Cl. BL1: Bolt 2A 32
 M34: Dent 5A 118
Thornhill Dr. M28: Walk 2A 82
Thornhill Rd. BL0: Ram 2A 22
 M43: Droy 3B 104
 SK4: Stoc 1B 144
Thornholme Cl. M18: Man 4D 116
Thornholme Rd. SK6: Mar 1D 160
Thorn Ho. SK15: Stal 3E 107
 (off Waterloo Rd.)

Thorniley Brow
 M4: Man 4A 6 (3E 101)
Thorn Lea BL2: Bolt 1H 33
Thornlea M9: Man 1C 88
 M43: Droy 4G 103
 WA15: Alt 1H 151
Thornlea Av. M27: Swin 5F 83
 OL8: O'ham 2C 90
Thorn Lea Cl. BL1: Bolt 6F 31
Thornlea Dr. OL12: Roch 1D 26
Thornlee Ct. OL4: Grot 4F 77
Thornleigh Rd. M14: Man 6E 115
Thornley Av. BL1: Bolt 3A 32
Thornley Cl. OL4: Grot 4E 77
Thornley Cres. OL4: Grot 4E 77
 SK6: Bred 5G 135
Thornley La. OL4: Grot, O'ham 5E 77
Thornley La. Nth. M34: Stoc 4H 117
Thornley La. Sth.
 M34: Dent, Stoc 5H 117
 SK5: Stoc 5H 117
Thornley Pk. Rd. OL4: Grot 4E 77
Thornley Ri. M34: Aud 6D 104
Thornley Rd. M25: Pres 2A 70
Thornleys Rd. M34: Dent 3G 119
Thornley St. M24: Mid 6D 56
 M26: Rad 5B 52
 SK14: Hyde 6C 120
Thornmere Cl. M27: Ward 1E 83
Thorn Rd. M27: Swin 5G 83
 OL8: O'ham 6A 76
 SK7: Bram 2F 167
Thorns, The M21: Chor 2H 129
Thorns Av. BL1: Bolt 2B 32
Thorns Cl. BL1: Bolt 2B 32
Thorns Clough OL3: Dig 2E 63
Thornsett CI. M9: Man 3A 88
THORNS GREEN 2C 162
Thornsgreen Rd. M22: Wyth 5B 154
Thorns Rd. BL1: Bolt 2B 32
Thorn St. BL1: Bolt 3D 32
 BL9: Sum 6C 12
Thorns Villa Gdns. M28: Wors 6E 81
Thornton Av. BL1: Bolt 4F 31
 M34: Aud 5C 104
 M41: Urm 5C 110
Thornton Cl. M33: Lit L 4E 51
 BL4: Farn 2F 65
 M16: Old T 2A 114
 M28: Wors 4C 80
Thornton Cres. M25: Pres 4F 69
Thornton Dr. SK9: Hand 4H 165
Thornton Ga. SK8: Gat 5E 143
Thornton Pl. SK4: Stoc 5D 132
Thornton Rd. M14: Man 5E 115
 M28: Wors 4C 80
 SK8: H Grn 4G 155
Thornton St. BL2: Bolt 3H 175 (6E 33)
 M40: Man 1G 101
 OL4: O'ham 6H 177 (4F 75)
 OL11: Roch 6H 27
Thornton St. Nth. M40: Man 1H 101
Thorntree Cl. M9: Man 4A 88
Thorntree Pl. OL12: Roch 3F 27
Thorn Vw. BL9: Bury 2A 38
Thorn Wlk. M31: Part 6C 124
Thornway M28: Wors 4E 81
 SK6: H Lan 6D 160
 SK7: Bram 5E 167
Thornway Dr. OL7: A Lyme 3F 105
Thornwood Av. M18: Man 3G 117
Thornydyke Av. BL1: Bolt 6C 18
Thorold Gro. M33: Sale 5E 129
THORP 2C 58
Thorp Clough OL2: O'ham 3B 58
Thorpe Av. M26: Rad 2D 52
 M27: Swin 2G 83
Thorpebrook Rd. M40: Man 5C 88
Thorpe Cl. M34: Dent 3F 119
 OL4: Aus 1E 77
 WA15: Tim 4C 140
Thorpe Gro. SK4: Stoc 3F 133
Thorpe Hall Gro. SK14: Hyde 1D 120

Thorpe La. M34: Dent 2F 119
 OL4: Aus, Scout 1D 76
Thorpeness Sq. M18: Man 1F 117
Thorpe St. BL0: Ram 4B 12
 BL1: Bolt 3B 32
 M16: Old T 3A 114
 M24: Mid 2G 71
 M28: Walk 5H 65
Thorp Rd. M40: Man 5C 88
 OL2: O'ham 3D 58
Thorp St. M30: Ecc 5D 96
 M45: White 5E 53
Thorp Vw. OL2: O'ham 1C 58
Thorsby Av. SK14: Hyde 5D 120
Thorsby Cl. BL7: Bro X 3D 18
 M18: Man 2G 117
Thorsby Rd. WA15: Tim 6G 139
Thorsby Way M34: Dent 6G 119
 (off Tatton Rd.)
Thorverton Sq. M40: Man 3E 89
Thrapston Av. M34: Aud 4D 104
Threadfold Way BL7: Bolt 4D 18
Threadmill La. M27: Swin 3F 83
Threaphurst La. SK7: H Gro 5A 160
Threapwood Rd. M22: Wyth 4C 154
Three Acre Av. OL2: O'ham 3G 59
Three Acres Dr. SK5: Stoc 4G 133
Three Acres La. SK8: Chea H 6A 156
Three Counties Rd. OL5: Mos 1H 93
Three La. Ends M34: Dent 5F 119
Three Owls Bird Sanctuary 2G 25
Three Owls Bird Sanctuary Vis. Cen.
 . . . . .2H 25
Three Pits M24: Mid 2E 57
Threlkeld Cl. M24: Mid 6G 55
Threlkeld Ct. M24: Mid 6G 55
Threlkeld Rd. BL1: Bolt 5B 18
 M24: Mid 6G 55
Thresher Cl. M33: Sale 6F 129
 (off Windmill Rd.)
Threshfield Cl. BL9: Bury 4F 23
Threshfield Dr. WA15: Tim 4B 140
Threxton Pl. BL3: Bolt 4F 47
 (off Cressington Rd.)
Throstle Bank St. SK14: Hyde 3A 120
Throstle Ct. OL2: O'ham 4D 58
Throstle Gro. BL8: Bury 6C 22
 SK6: Mar 6B 148
Throstle Hall Ct. M24: Mid 6B 56
Throstles Cl. M43: Droy 2C 104
Throstles Grn. M16: Old T 2G 113
Thrum Fold OL12: Roch 6F 15
Thrum Hall La. OL12: Roch 6F 15
 (not continuous)
Thrush Av. BL4: Farn 1D 64
Thrush Dr. BL9: Bury 1H 37
Thrush St. OL12: Roch 2E 27
Thruxton Cl. M16: W Ran 4C 114
Thurcaston Rd. WA14: W Tim 2E 139
Thurland Rd. OL4: O'ham 3A 76
Thurland St. OL9: Chad 1G 73
Thurlby Av. M9: Man 4A 72
Thurlby St. M13: Man 3H 115
Thurleigh Rd. M20: Man 5F 131
Thurlestone Av. BL2: Ain 4F 35
Thurlestone Dr. M41: Urm 4E 111
 SK7: H Gro 3B 158
Thurlestone Rd. WA14: Alt 5D 138
Thurloe St. M14: Man 4G 115
Thurlow St. M50: Sal 5F 99
 (not continuous)
Thurlston Cres. M8: Man 4E 87
Thurlwood Av. M20: Man 2E 131
Thurnham St. BL3: Bolt 4A 48
Thursby Av. M20: Man 3E 131
Thursby Wlk. M24: Mid 5G 55
Thursfield St. M6: Sal 6H 85
Thurstane St. BL1: Bolt 3A 32
Thurston Cl. BL9: Bury 5G 53
Thurston Clough Rd.
 OL3: Dob, O'ham 6G 61
 OL4: Scout 6G 61
Thurston Grn. SK9: A Edg 5G 173

Thyme Cl. M21: Chor 5B **130**
Thynne St. BL3: Bolt 6G **175** (1D **48**)
  BL4: Farn 6G **49**
Tiber Av. OL8: O'ham 2C **90**
Tib La. M2: Man 6H **5** (4D **100**)
Tib St. BL0: Ram 4B **12**
  M4: Man 5B **6** (4E **101**)
  M34: Dent 5F **119**
Tideswell Av. M40: Man 2G **7** (2H **101**)
Tideswell Bank
  SK13: Gam 6G **123**
    (off Edale Cres.)
Tideswell Cl. SK8: H Grn 5H **155**
Tideswell Rd. M43: Droy 2G **103**
  SK7: H Gro 5E **159**
Tideswell Wlk. *SK13: Gam* 6G **123**
    (off Riber Bank)
Tideswell Way M34: Dent 1G **135**
Tideway Cl. M7: Sal 3F **85**
Tidworth Av. M4: Man 4G **7** (3H **101**)
Tiefield Wlk. *M21: Chor* 2C **130**
    (off Marham Cl.)
Tiflis St. OL12: Roch 1A **178** (3G **27**)
Tig Fold Rd. BL4: Farn 1C **64**
Tilbury St. OL1: O'ham 1E **177** (1E **75**)
Tilbury Rd. M40: Man 1G **7** (1H **101**)
Tilby Cl. M41: Urm 5A **110**
Tildsley St. BL3: Bolt 3C **48**
Tile St. BL9: Bury 1C **176** (2F **37**)
Tilgate Wlk. *M9: Man* 6A **72**
    (off Haverfield Rd.)
Tillard Av. SK3: Stoc 3D **144**
Tillerman Cl. M27: Pen 3D **84**
Tillhey Rd. M22: Wyth 3B **154**
Tillington Cl. *BL1: Bolt* 2C **32**
    (off Eckersley Rd.)
Tilney Av. M32: Stre 6E **113**
Tilshead Wlk. M13: Man 6F **11**
Tilside Gro. BL6: Los 6B **30**
Tilson Rd. M23: Wyth 6E **141**
Tilstock Wlk. M23: Wyth 3E **141**
Tilston Wlk. SK9: Wilm 6A **166**
Tilton St. OL1: O'ham 6A **60**
Timberbottom BL2: Bolt 1G **33**
Timbercliffe OL15: L'ough 2B **16**
Timberhurst BL9: Bury 3B **38**
Timbersbrook Gro. *SK9: Wilm* 5H **165**
    (off Colshaw Dr.)
Timber Wharf M15: Man 3C **8** (6B **100**)
Times Retail Pk. OL10: H'ood 3G **39**
Times St. M24: Mid 1D **72**
Timothy Cl. M6: Sal 2B **98**
TIMPERLEY 4H **139**
Timperley Cl. OL8: O'ham 1G **91**
Timperley Cricket, Hockey,
  Tennis & Lacrosse Club 6H **139**
Timperley Fold OL6: A Lyme 5A **92**
Timperley Rd. OL6: A Lyme 5H **91**
Timperley Station (Metro) 3H **139**
Timperley St. M11: Man 5E **103**
  OL9: O'ham 2E **75**
Timpson Rd. M23: Wyth 4E **141**
Timsbury Cl. BL2: Bolt 2B **50**
Timson St. M35: Fail 4H **89**
Tim's Ter. OL16: Miln 5F **29**
Tindall St. M30: Ecc 5D **96**
  SK5: Stoc 4H **117**
Tindle St. M28: Walk 6B **66**
Tinker's Pas.
  SK14: Hyde 5C **120**
    (off Lumn Rd.)
Tinker St. SK14: Hyde 4B **120**
Tinline St. BL9: Bury 3G **37**
Tinningham Cl. M11: Man 6G **103**
Tinsdale Wlk. M24: Mid 6G **55**
Tinshill Cl. M12: Man 2C **102**
Tinsley Cl. M40: Man 3H **7** (3A **102**)
Tinsley Gro. BL2: Bolt 5F **33**
Tin St. BL3: Bolt 2C **48**
Tintagel Ct. M26: Rad 2E **51**
  SK15: Stal 3D **106**
Tintagel Wlk. SK14: Hat 4A **122**

Tintern Av. BL2: Bolt 3F **33**
  M20: Man 4D **130**
  M29: Ast 4A **80**
  M41: Urm 1C **126**
  M45: White 6F **53**
  OL10: H'ood 1G **39**
  OL12: Roch 6G **15**
  OL15: L'ough 2G **17**
Tintern Cl. SK12: Poy 2D **168**
Tintern Dr. WA15: Hale 3C **152**
Tintern Gro. SK1: Stoc 2B **146**
Tintern Pl. OL10: H'ood 1G **39**
Tintern Rd. M24: Mid 4B **56**
  SK8: Chea H 1D **166**
Tintern St. M14: Man 5F **115**
Tipperary St. SK15: C'ook 6A **94**
Tipping St. WA14: Alt 2F **151**
Tipton Cl. M26: Rad 2F **51**
  SK8: Chea H 1D **156**
Tipton Dr. M23: Wyth 1H **141**
Tiptree Wlk. *M9: Man* 3A **88**
    (off Batley St.)
Tiree Cl. SK7: H Gro 4F **159**
Tirza Av. M19: Man 2B **132**
Tissington Bank *SK13: Gam* 6F **123**
    (off Youlgreave Cres.)
Tissington Grn. *SK13: Gam* 6F **123**
    (off Youlgreave Cres.)
Tissington Ter. *SK13: Gam* 6F **123**
    (off Youlgreave Cres.)
Titchfield Rd. OL8: O'ham 5A **76**
Tithe Barn Cl. OL12: Roch 5D **16**
Tithe Barn Ct. SK4: Stoc 5B **132**
Tithe Barn Cres. BL1: Bolt 1F **33**
Tithe Barn Rd. SK4: Stoc 5B **132**
Tithebarn Rd. WA15: Haleb 5C **152**
Tithebarn St. BL9: Bury ...3C **176** (3F **37**)
  M26: Rad 3D **52**
Titian Ri. OL1: O'ham 2B **60**
Titterington Av. M21: Chor 5H **113**
Tiverton Av. M33: Sale 6H **127**
Tiverton Cl. M26: Rad 2F **51**
  M29: Ast 4A **80**
Tiverton Dr. M33: Sale 6H **127**
  SK9: Wilm 6H **165**
Tiverton Ho. *M6: Sal* 2A **98**
    (off Devon Cl.)
Tiverton Pl. OL7: A Lyme 6G **91**
Tiverton Rd. M41: Urm 3G **111**
Tiverton Wlk. *BL1: Bolt* 4A **32**
    (off Valletts La.)
Tiviot Dale SK1: Stoc 1G **179**
Tiviot Way SK5: Stoc 6H **133**
Tivoli St. *M3: Man* 6G **5**
    (off Stoney St.)
Tixall Wlk. M8: Man 1C **86**
Toad La. OL12: Roch 2B **178** (3H **27**)
  OL16: Roch 2B **178** (3H **27**)
Toad Pond Cl. M27: Swin 5E **83**
Tobermory Cl. M11: Man 4F **103**
Tobermory Rd. SK8: H Grn 4G **155**
Todd's Pl. M8: Man 2G **87**
Todd St. M3: Man 3A **6** (3E **101**)
  M7: Sal 5B **86**
  OL10: H'ood 3E **39**
  OL16: Roch 4D **178** (4A **28**)
Todmorden Rd.
  OL15: L'ough ....1B **16** & 3H **17**
Toft Rd. M18: Man 3E **117**
Toft Way SK9: Hand 3A **166**
Toledo St. M11: Man 4F **103**
Tolland La. WA15: Hale 5H **151**
Tollard Av. M40: Man 6H **87**
Tollard Cl. SK8: Chea H 1D **166**
Tollar Bar St. M12: Man 1A **116**
  SK1: Stoc 4H **179** (1H **145**)
Tollemache Cl. SK14: Mot 2C **122**
Tollemache Rd. SK14: Mot 2C **122**
Tollesbury Cl. M40: Man 1H **101**
Toll Ga. Cl. M13: Man 3A **116**
Tollgate Way OL16: Roch 3C **28**
Toll St. M26: Rad 3F **51**
Tolworth Dr. M8: Man 4F **87**

Tomcroft La. M34: Dent 5D **118**
Tom Husband Leisure Complex
  ....2A **4** (2H **99**)
Tom La. WA14: Rost 6A **150**
Tomlinson Cl. OL8: O'ham 4E **75**
Tomlinson St. M15: Man 6F **9** (1C **114**)
  M40: Man 6E **73**
  OL11: Roch 1E **41**
Tomlin Sq. BL2: Bolt 6G **33**
Tom Lomas Wlk. *M11: Man* 3D **102**
    (off Frankland Cl.)
Tommy Browell Cl. M14: Man 4E **115**
Tommy Johnson Wlk. *M14: Man* ..4E **115**
    (off Up. Lloyd St.)
Tommy La. BL2: Ain 4E **35**
Tommy Taylor Cl. M40: Man 6E **89**
Tom Pendry Sq. *SK15: Stal* 4E **107**
    (off Melbourne St.)
Tom Shepley St. SK14: Hyde 5C **120**
TONACLIFFE 2E **15**
Tonacliffe Rd. OL12: Whitw 4E **15**
Tonacliffe Ter. OL12: Whitw 2E **15**
Tonacliffe Way OL12: Whitw 3E **15**
Tonbridge Cl. BL8: Bury 4C **22**
Tonbridge Pl. BL2: Bolt 4E **33**
Tonbridge Rd. M19: Man 1D **132**
  SK5: Stoc 1H **133**
Tong Clough BL7: Bro X 3D **18**
    (not continuous)
Tonge Bri. Ind. Est. BL2: Bolt 5F **33**
Tonge Bri. Way BL2: Bolt 5F **33**
Tonge Bri. Workshop BL2: Bolt ...5F **33**
Tonge Cl. M45: White 6H **53**
Tonge Ct. M24: Mid 1D **72**
TONGE FOLD 6G **33**
Tonge Fold Rd. BL2: Bolt 6G **33**
Tonge Grn. SK15: Mat 1A **122**
Tonge Hall Cl. M24: Mid 1D **72**
Tonge Mdw. M24: Mid 1D **72**
TONGE MOOR 3F **33**
Tonge Moor Rd. BL2: Bolt 4F **33**
TONG END 3A **14**
Tong End OL12: Whitw 3A **14**
Tonge Old Rd. BL2: Bolt 6G **33**
Tonge Pk. Av. BL2: Bolt 4G **33**
Tonge Roughs M24: Mid 1F **73**
Tonge St. M12: Man 3H **11** (6H **101**)
  M24: Mid 3G **73**
  OL10: H'ood 3H **39**
  OL16: Roch 5D **178** (5A **28**)
Tong Flds. BL7: Eger 3D **18**
Tong Head Av. BL1: Bolt 1F **33**
Tong La. OL12: Whitw 4A **14**
Tongley Wlk. *M40: Man* 1F **89**
    (off Blandford Dr.)
Tong Rd. BL3: Lit L 3C **50**
Tong St. BL4: Kea 2H **65**
Tonman St. M3: Man 1F **9** (5C **100**)
Tontin St. M5: Sal 3H **99**
Tooley Ho. M30: Ecc 5F **97**
Tootal Dr. M5: Sal 2C **98**
  M6: Sal 2C **98**
Tootal Gro. M6: Sal 3C **98**
Tootal Rd. M5: Sal 3C **98**
Topcliffe Rd. M9: Man 6D **72**
Topcroft Cl. M22: Nor 3C **142**
Topfield Rd. M22: Wyth 1A **154**
Topfields Gro. M7: Sal 4B **86**
Topgate Brow M27: Pen 3D **84**
Topham St. BL9: Bury 6D **176** (5G **37**)
    (not continuous)
Topley St. M40: Man 5H **87**
TOP OF HEAP 3D **38**
Top of Heap OL10: H'ood 3D **38**
TOP OF HEBERS 4A **56**
TOP OF LANE 6E **77**
TOP OF MOOR 1B **76**
TOP O'TH' BROW 3H **33**
Top o' th' Brow BL2: Bolt 5A **20**
Top o' th' Flds. M45: White 2F **69**
Top o' th' Gorses BL2: Bolt 2H **49**
Top o' th' Grn. OL9: Chad 5C **74**

Top o' th' La. BL3: Bolt 2H 49
TOP O' TH' MEADOWS 6E 61
Top o' th' Mdws. La. OL4: Wat 6E 61
TOP O' TH' WOOD 6F 25
Topphome Ct. BL4: Farn 2A 66
    (off Longcauseway)
Topping Fold Rd. BL9: Bury 2A 38
TOPPINGS .4E 19
Toppings, The SK6: Bred 6G 135
Toppings Grn. BL7: Bro X 4E 19
Topping St. BL1: Bolt 4C 32
    BL9: Bury 1D 176 (2F 37)
Topp St. BL4: Farn 2A 66
Topp Way BL1: Bolt 2E 175 (5C 32)
Top Schwabe St. M24: Mid 1G 71
Topsham Wlk. M40: Man 6F 89
    (off Silverwell St.)
Top St. M24: Mid 6B 56
    OL4: O'ham 1B 76
Torah St. M8: Man 1E 101
Tor Av. BL8: G'mount 2H 21
Torbay Cl. BL3: Bolt 1A 48
    (off Blackshaw La.)
Torbay Dr. SK2: Stoc 4B 146
Torbay Rd. M21: Chor 1A 130
    M41: Urm 6G 111
Torbrook Gro. SK9: Wilm 5H 165
    (off Bosley Cl.)
Torcross Rd. M9: Man 4F 71
Tor Hey M. BL8: G'mount 1H 21
TORKINGTON 3E 159
Torkington Av. M27: Pen 2H 83
Torkington Ho. SK7: H Gro 3F 159
Torkington La. SK6: H Gro 2B 160
Torkington Mnr. SK7: H Gro 2H 159
Torkington Rd. SK7: H Gro 3E 159
    SK8: Gat 6F 143
    SK9: Wilm 3F 173
Torkington St. SK3: Stoc 4F 145
Torksey Wlk. M9: Man 4F 71
Torness Wlk. M11: Man 4D 102
    (off Emily Beavan Cl.)
Toronto Av. M90: Man A 6H 153
Toronto Rd. SK2: Stoc 5A 146
Toronto St. BL2: Bolt 5A 34
Torpoint Wlk. M40: Man 2E 89
Torquay Cl. M13: Man 6G 11
Torquay Gro. SK2: Stoc 1B 158
Torra Barn Cl. BL7: Eger 1C 18
Torrax Cl. M6: Sal 5B 84
Torre Cl. M24: Mid 4C 56
Torrens St. M6: Sal 6D 84
Torridon Rd. BL2: Bolt 6B 34
Torridon Wlk. M22: Wyth 5A 154
Torrin Cl. SK3: Stoc 6H 145
Torrington Av. BL1: Bolt 3C 32
    M9: Man 1C 88
Torrington Dr. SK14: Hat 5H 121
Torrington Rd. M27: Pen 5B 84
Torrington St. OL10: H'ood 5A 40
Torrisdale Cl. BL3: Bolt 2H 47
Torside M. SK13: Had 1H 123
Torside Way M27: Pen 1H 83
Torver Dr. BL2: Bolt 5B 34
    M24: Mid 5H 55
Torver Wlk. M22: Wyth 4H 153
Torwood Rd. OL9: Chad 6G 57
Total Fitness
    Altrincham 3A 174
    Bolton 4D 32
    Handforth 3B 166
    Walkden .5G 65
    Whitefield 6F 53
Totland Cl. M12: Man 4D 116
Totley Av. SK13: Gam 6F 123
    (off Youlgreave Cres.)
Totley Cl. SK13: Gam 6F 123
    (off Youlgreave Cres.)
Totley Gdns. SK13: Gam 6F 123
    (off Youlgreave Cres.)
Totley Grn. SK13: Gam 6F 123
Totley Lanes SK13: Gam 6F 123
    (off Youlgreave Cres.)

Totley M. SK13: Gam 6F 123
Totley Pl. SK13: Gam 6F 123
    (off Melandra Castle Rd.)
Totnes Av. OL9: Chad 6H 57
    SK7: Bram 3A 158
Totnes Rd. M21: Chor 1A 130
    M33: Sale 4F 127
Totridge Cl. SK2: Stoc 6D 146
Tottenham Dr. M23: Wyth 4D 140
TOTTINGTON 4H 21
Tottington Av. OL4: Spri 2D 76
Tottington Fold BL2: Bolt 6A 20
    (off Tottington Rd.)
Tottington La. M25: Pres 4E 69
Tottington Rd. BL2: Bolt 6A 20
    BL7: Tur 1B 20
    BL8: Bury 6B 22
Tottington St. M11: Man 3E 103
Totton Rd. M35: Fail 4H 89
Touchet Hall Rd. M24: Mid 3F 57
Touch Rd. BL9: Bury 4E 23
Touchstones 4A 178 (4G 27)
Tourist Info. Cen.
    Altrincham 2B 174 (1F 151)
    Ashton-under-Lyne
    . . . . .4C 174 (2H 105)
    Bolton 4F 175 (6D 32)
    Bredbury 6G 135
    Brinnington 4C 134
    Bury 3B 176 (3E 37)
    Heywood 3G 39
    Manchester 1H 9 (4D 100)
    Manchester Airport 5G 153
    Oldham 3G 177 (2F 75)
    Poynton 3E 169
    Ringway 6H 153
    Rochdale 3B 178 (4H 27)
    Saddleworth 1D 78
    Salford Quays 6E 99
    Stockport, Chestergate
    . . . . .2H 179 (2G 145)
    Stockport, Market Pl.
    . . . . .1G 179 (1H 145)
    Wilmslow 3E 173
Tours Av. M23: Wyth 1G 141
Towcester Cl. M4: Man 5H 7 (4H 101)
Tower Av. BL0: Ram 4A 12
Tower Bldgs. BL6: Hor 2A 30
Tower Ct. BL8: G'mount 3H 21
Tower Dr. BL7: Tur 1G 19
Tower Grange M7: Sal 3B 86
Towers Av. BL3: Bolt 3G 47
Towers Bus. Pk. M20: Man 2G 143
Towers Cl. SK12: Poy 2F 169
Tower Sq. M13: Man 5E 11
Towers Rd. SK12: Poy 6F 159
Towers St. OL4: O'ham 6B 60
Tower St. M26: Rad 4D 52
    OL10: H'ood 4F 39
    SK14: Hyde 6B 120
    SK16: Duk 4B 106
Tower Ter. BL8: G'mount 3H 21
Towey Cl. M18: Man 1F 117
Towncliffe Wlk. M15: Man 6D 8
Towncroft M34: Dent 3G 119
Towncroft Av. M24: Mid 5B 56
Towncroft La. BL1: Bolt 5E 31
Townend St. SK14: Hyde 5C 120
TOWNFIELD 2H 75
Townfield M41: Urm 6D 110
Townfield Gdns.
    WA14: Alt 1A 174 (6F 139)
Townfield Rd. WA14: Alt 1A 174 (6F 139)
Townfields Cl. BL9: Bury 5C 176 (4F 37)
Townfield St. OL4: O'ham 2H 75
Townfield Wlk. M15: Man 5D 8
Town Fold SK6: Mar B 4F 149
Towngate Bus. Cen. M38: Lit H 4C 64
Town Ga. Dr. M41: Urm 5G 109
Towngreen Ct. M8: Man 1D 86
Town Hall La. M2: Man 5H 5
Town Hall Sq. OL16: Roch 3B 178
TOWN HEAD 1C 178 (2H 27)

Town Ho. Rd. OL15: L'ough 2H 17
    (not continuous)
Town La. M34: Dent 5D 118
    SK16: Duk 5A 106
Town La. Ct. M34: Dent 5E 119
Townley Fold SK14: Hyde 1F 121
Townley Pk. Ind. Est. M24: Mid 6C 56
Townley Rd. OL16: Miln 5F 29
Townley St. M8: Man 6D 86
    M11: Man 5B 102
    M24: Mid 6C 56
Townley Ter. SK6: Mar 5E 149
    (off Canal St.)
Town Mdws. OL16: Roch 3A 178
Town Mill Brow OL12: Roch 6G 15
    (off Whitworth Rd.)
    OL12: Roch 3A 178
    (College Bank)
Townrow St. OL10: H'ood 1H 39
Townscliffe La. SK6: Mar B 4F 149
Towns Cft. Lodge
    M33: Sale 3G 127
    (off Green La.)
Townsend Rd. M27: Pen 2H 83
TOWNS GATE 5G 109
Townsgate Way M44: Irl 6F 109
Townside Row BL9: Bury . . .5D 176 (4F 37)
Townsley Gro. OL6: A Lyme 6C 92
Town Sq. M33: Sale 5B 128
Town Sq. Shop. Cen.
    OL1: O'ham 4G 177 (3F 75)
Town St. SK6: Mar B 4F 149
Towns Vw. SK15: Stal 4F 107
Towns Yd. OL2: O'ham 3E 59
    (off Park St.)
Towton St. M9: Man 3A 88
Towyn Av. M5: Sal 3G 99
Toxteth St. M11: Man 6G 103
Tracey St. M8: Man 2E 87
Traders Av. M41: Urm 1G 111
Trafalgar Av. M34: Aud 6C 104
    SK12: Poy 4G 169
Trafalgar Bus. Pk. M8: Man 1C 100
Trafalgar Cen., The OL16: Roch 3B 28
Trafalgar Cl. SK12: Poy 4G 169
Trafalgar Ct. BL9: Bury 6A 176
    M16: W Ran 5C 114
Trafalgar Gro. M7: Sal 6B 86
Trafalgar Ho. M34: Aud 6C 104
    (off Audenshaw Rd.)
    WA14: Alt 5F 139
Trafalgar Pl. M20: Man 5E 131
Trafalgar Rd. M6: Sal 3A 98
    M33: Sale 3C 128
Trafalgar Sq. OL5: Mos 2F 93
    OL7: A Lyme 4F 105
    (not continuous)
    OL16: Roch 3A 28
Trafalgar St. M7: Sal 6C 86
    OL1: O'ham 1E 177 (1E 75)
    OL7: A Lyme 5F 105
    OL16: Roch 3A 28
    (not continuous)
Trafalgar Wlk. M11: Man 5C 102
    (off Herne St.)
    M15: Man 2C 114
Trafford Athletics Stadium 6F 113
Trafford Av. M41: Urm 4G 111
Trafford Bank Rd. M16: Old T 2A 114
Trafford Bar Station (Metro) 2H 113
Trafford Boulevard M41: Urm 1E 111
Trafford Cen., The M41: Urm 1F 111
Trafford Ct. M15: Man 6C 8
Trafford Dr. M38: Lit H 4F 65
    WA15: Tim 3B 140
Trafford Ecology Pk. 6C 98
Trafford Gro. BL4: Farn 6A 50
    M32: Stre 6D 112
Trafford Ho. M32: Stre 2F 113
    (off Chester Rd.)
Trafford Mans. M16: Old T 5H 113
TRAFFORD PARK 2C 112
Trafford Pk. Heritage Cen. 1C 112

Trafford Pk. Rd. M17: T Pk 5B 98
    (Moorings Rd.)
  M17: T Pk 2G 113
    (Wharf End)
Trafford Park Station (Rail0 . . . . . . .4C 112
Trafford Pl. M15: Man 6C 8 (1B 114)
  SK9: Wilm 3G 173
Trafford Plaza M16: Old T 3H 113
Trafford Retail Pk. M41: Urm 2E 111
Trafford Rd. M5: Sal 1G 113
  M30: Ecc .5F 97
  M50: Sal .6G 99
  SK9: A Edg 5G 173
  SK9: Wilm 6F 165
Trafford St. BL4: Farn 6H 31
  M1: Man 2F 9 (5C 100)
  OL8: O'ham 6F 177 (4E 75)
  OL11: Roch 6G 27
Trafford Water Sports Cen. 3E 129
Trafford Way M30: Urm 6E 97
Trafford Wharf Rd. M17: T Pk 6D 98
Tragan Cl. SK2: Stoc 5D 146
Tragan Dr. SK2: Stoc 5D 146
Trail St. M6: Sal 3E 99
Trajan Ho. OL1: O'ham 2G 177 (2F 75)
Tramore Wlk. M22: Wyth 3B 154
Tram St. M11: Man 5E 103
Tramway Rd. M44: Irl 2D 124
  OL6: A Lyme 4D 174 (1A 106)
Tranby Cl. M22: Wyth 1D 154
Tranmere Cl. M18: Man 2D 116
Tranmere Dr. SK9: Hand 4H 165
Tranmere Rd. SK3: Stoc 3D 144
Trans Pennine Trad. Est.
  OL11: Roch 2F 41
Transvaal St. M11: Man 4F 103
Travis Brow SK4: Stoc 2F 145
Travis Ct. OL2: O'ham 3E 59
Travis St. M1: Man 2D 10 (5F 101)
  OL2: Shaw 6H 43
  OL16: Miln 1H 43
  SK14: Hyde 5C 120
Trawden Av. BL1: Bolt 3A 32
Trawden Dr. BL9: Bury 3E 23
Trawden Grn. SK2: Stoc 1D 158
Traylen Way OL12: Roch 2C 26
Traynor Cl. M24: Mid 6B 56
Treacle Brow SK14: Hyde 1D 130
    (off Mottram Old Rd.)
Tree Av. M43: Droy 2A 104
Tree Ho. Av. OL7: A Lyme 5F 91
Treelands Wlk. M5: Sal 1H 113
Treen Rd. M29: Ast 3A 80
Tree Tops BL7: Bro X 5G 19
Treetops Av. BL0: Ram 6A 12
Treetops Cl. OL3: Dob 5B 62
  SK6: Mar 4C 148
Tree Wlk. M32: Stre 6C 112
Trefoil Way OL15: L'ough 3F 17
Tregaer Fold M24: Mid 1E 73
Tremain Wlk. M9: Man 4H 87
    (off Stockwood Wlk.)
Trenam Pl. M5: Sal 3H 99
Trenant Rd. M6: Sal 6D 84
Trenchard Dr. M22: Wyth 6D 154
Trencherbone M26: Rad 2G 51
Trengrove St. OL12: Roch 2E 27
Trent Av. OL9: Chad 1G 73
  OL10: H'ood 2E 39
  OL16: Miln 5G 29
Trent Bri. Wlk. M16: Old T 4G 113
Trent Cl. SK5: Stoc 4C 134
  SK7: Bram 1E 167
Trent Ct. M15: Man 6C 8
  SK3: Stoc 4G 145
Trent Dr. BL9: Bury 3F 23
  M28: Walk 1F 81
Trentham Av. BL4: Farn 6G 49
  SK4: Stoc 6B 132
Trentham Cl. BL4: Farn 6G 49
Trentham Gro. M40: Man 2C 88
Trentham Lawns M6: Sal 1G 99
Trentham Rd. M16: Old T 4G 113

Trentham St. BL4: Farn 6G 49
  M15: Man 4B 8 (6A 100)
  M27: Swin 2G 83
Trent Ind. Est. OL2: Shaw 5H 43
Trent Rd. OL2: Shaw 5G 43
Trent St. OL16: Roch 5B 28
Trent Wlk. M43: Droy 5B 104
Trent Way BL4: Kea 4D 66
    (not continuous)
Tresco Av. M32: Stre 6E 113
Trevarrick Ct. OL4: O'ham 1A 76
Trevelyan St. M30: Ecc 3A 98
Trevor Av. BL3: Bolt 4B 48
  M33: Sale 1H 139
Trevor Dr. M40: Man 1G 89
Trevor Gro. SK1: Stoc 3A 146
Trevor Rd. M27: Swin 5F 83
  M30: Ecc .2D 96
  M41: Urm 4B 110
Trevor St. M11: Man 6G 103
  OL11: Roch 2D 40
Triangle, The M4: Man 4H 5 (3D 100)
  WA15: Tim 4B 140
Tribune Av. WA14: B'ath 4D 138
Trident Rd. M30: Ecc 6B 96
Trillo Av. BL2: Bolt 1F 49
Trimdon Cl. M11: Man 3D 102
Trimingham Dr. BL8: Bury 6C 22
Trimley Av. M40: Man 6H 87
Tring Wlk. M9: Man 6F 71
Trinity Av. M33: Sale 5D 128
Trinity Bri. Ho. M3: Sal 4F 5
Trinity Bldgs. OL5: Mos 1H 93
Trinity Cl. SK16: Duk 5C 106
Trinity Ct. M3: Sal 4D 4
  OL6: A Lyme 2G 105
Trinity Cres. M28: Walk 1A 82
Trinity Edge M3: Sal 4E 5
Trinity Gdns. M3: Sal 3D 4 (3B 100)
  SK3: Stoc 2H 157
Trinity Grn. BL0: Ram 1B 22
Trinity Ho. OL1: O'ham 1F 177 (1E 75)
Trinity Retail Pk.
  BL2: Bolt 6H 175 (1E 49)
Trinity Rd. M33: Sale 5C 128
Trinity Sports Cen. 1E 115
Trinity St. BL2: Bolt 6E 175 (1C 48)
  BL3: Bolt 6E 175 (1C 48)
  BL9: Bury 5C 176 (4F 37)
  M24: Mid 1B 72
  OL1: O'ham 1F 177 (1E 75)
  OL12: Roch 1A 26
  SK6: Mar 6D 148
  SK15: Stal 3E 107
  SK3: Stoc 2H 157
    (not continuous)
Trinity Wlk. M14: Man 4F 115
    (off Ellanby Cl.)
Trinity Way M3: Man 2D 100
  M3: Sal 5D 4 (3C 100)
Trippier Rd. M30: Ecc 5B 96
Tripps M. M20: Man 5D 130
Triscombe Way M16: W Ran 4C 114
Tristam Cl. M13: Man 5E 11 (1G 115)
Trojan Gdns. M7: Sal 6A 86
Trongate M9: Man 4A 88
    (off Carisbrook St.)
Troon Cl. BL3: Bolt 4F 47
  SK7: Bram 6A 158
Troon Dr. SK8: H Grn 4G 155
Troon Rd. M23: Wyth 5F 141
Trough Ga. OL8: O'ham 1D 90
Troutbeck Av. M4: Man 4F 7 (3H 101)
Troutbeck Cl. BL8: Haw 1D 20
Troutbeck Dr. BL0: Ram 1C 12
Troutbeck Rd. SK8: Gat 2F 155
  WA15: Tim 6D 140
Troutbeck Wlk. OL2: O'ham 3E 59
    (off Shaw St.)
Troutbeck Way
  OL11: Roch 1D 40
Trowbridge Dr. M40: Man 2E 89
Trowbridge Rd. M34: Dent 6G 119
Trows La. OL11: Roch 4F 41

Trowtree Av. M12: Man 1A 116
Troydale Dr. M40: Man 6C 88
Troy Wlk. M5: Sal 6H 99
TRUB 5F 41
Trumpet St. M1: Man 2G 9 (5D 100)
Truro Av. M32: Stre 5E 113
  OL6: A Lyme 4B 92
  SK5: Stoc 4C 134
Truro Cl. BL8: Bury 2D 36
  SK7: Bram 6H 157
Truro Dr. M33: Sale 5F 127
Truro Rd. M29: Ast 3A 80
  OL9: Chad 6A 58
Truro Wlk. M34: Dent 6F 119
Trust Rd. M18: Man 4E 117
Tucana Av. M7: Sal 1B 4 (2A 100)
Tudbury Way M3: Sal 3D 4 (2B 100)
Tudor Av. BL1: Bolt 6H 31
  BL4: Farn 2F 65
  M9: Man .2A 88
  OL9: Chad 6F 73
  SK15: Stal 2H 107
Tudor Cl. OL5: Mos 2A 94
  SK5: Stoc 2G 133
Tudor Ct. BL1: Bolt 1E 175 (5C 32)
  M16: Old T 2A 114
    (off Stanley Rd.)
  M25: Pres 6A 70
  OL10: H'ood 4G 39
  OL12: Roch 2B 28
Tudor Grn. SK9: Wilm 6A 166
Tudor Gro. M24: Mid 4H 55
Tudor Hall St. OL11: Roch 3E 41
Tudor Ho. M21: Chor 1D 130
    (off Mauldeth Rd.)
Tudor Ind. Est. SK16: Duk 1G 119
Tudor Rd. SK9: Wilm 6A 166
  WA14: B'ath 4D 138
Tudors SK7: Bram 1F 167
Tudor St. BL3: Bolt 3A 48
    (off Venice St.)
  M24: Mid 1D 72
  OL2: Shaw 6H 43
  OL8: O'ham 6E 177 (4D 74)
    (not continuous)
Tuer St. M13: Man 6B 10 (1E 115)
Tuffley Rd. M23: Wyth 2G 153
Tufton Wlk. M9: Man 4H 87
Tugford Cl. M16: W Ran 3C 114
Tuley St. M11: Man 6B 102
Tulip Av. BL4: Farn 6E 49
  BL4: Kea .3B 66
Tulip Cl. M33: Sale 5E 127
  OL9: Chad 2G 73
  SK3: Stoc 6F 145
Tulip Dr. WA15: Tim 5H 139
Tulip Gro. OL12: Roch 6G 15
Tulip Rd. M31: Part 6C 124
Tulip Wlk. M7: Sal 1C 4 (1B 100)
Tulketh St. Ind. Est. M40: Man 3B 88
Tulle Ct. M25: Pres 5G 69
Tully St. M7: Sal 4C 86
Tully St. Sth. M7: Sal 5C 86
Tulpen Sq. OL9: Chad 2B 74
Tulworth Rd. SK12: Poy 3D 168
Tumblewood Dr. SK8: Chea 1A 156
Tumbling Bank M9: Man 6H 71
Tumbling Bank Ter. OL4: Lees 4D 76
Tunbridge Sq. M5: Sal 4G 99
Tunshill Gro. OL16: Miln 5G 29
Tunshill La. OL16: Miln 4H 29
Tunshill Rd. M23: Wyth 2E 141
Tuns Rd. OL8: O'ham 1H 91
Tunstall Cl. BL9: Bury 6G 37
Tunstall Rd. OL4: O'ham 3A 76
Tunstall St. M11: Man 6G 103
  SK4: Stoc 1G 145
TUNSTEAD 3F 79
Tunstead Av. M20: Man 3D 130
Tunstead La. OL3: G'fld 3E 79
Tupelo St. M13: Man 2H 115
Turbary Wlk. OL16: Miln 5D 28
Turf Cl. OL2: O'ham 4E 59

TURF HILL 1B 42
Turf Hill Rd. OL16: Roch 6B 28
Turf Ho. Cl. OL15: L'ough 2F 17
Turfland Av. OL2: O'ham 4E 59
Turf La. OL2: O'ham 4E 59
(not continuous)
OL9: Chad 6H 73
TURF LEA 4F 161
Turf Lea Fold SK6: Mar 4F 161
Turf Lea Rd. SK6: Mar 3E 161
Turfnell Way M28: Wors 6C 82
Turf Pk. Rd. OL2: O'ham 4E 59
Turf Pit La. OL4: O'ham 4C 60
Turf Pits OL4: O'ham 4C 60
Turf St. M26: Rad 4H 51
Turf Ter. OL15: L'ough 3G 17
Turfton Rd. OL2: O'ham 4F 59
Turks Rd. M26: Rad 2F 51
Turk St. BL1: Bolt 5A 32
Turley St. M8: Man 5F 87
Turnberry BL3: Bolt 4F 47
Turnberry Cl. M29: Ast 3A 80
Turnberry Dr. SK9: Wilm 1F 173
Turnberry Rd. SK8: H Grn 4G 155
Turnberry Wlk. M8: Man 3G 87
(off Stakeford Dr.)
Turnbull Av. M25: Pres 2A 70
Turnbull Rd. M13: Man 5B 116
M18: Man 3H 117
WA14: W Tim 3D 138
Turnbury Cl. M33: Sale 3B 128
Turnbury Rd. M22: Shar 6C 142
Turncliff Cres. SK6: Mar 4B 148
Turncroft La. SK1: Stoc 2A 146
Turncroft Way M28: Wors 4D 80
Turner Av. M35: Fail 5G 89
M44: Irl 4E 109
Turner Bri. Rd. BL2: Bolt 5G 33
Turner Dr. M41: Urm 5H 111
Turnerford Cl. BL7: Eger 2C 18
Turner Gdns. SK14: Hyde 3C 120
Turner La.
OL6: A Lyme 4C 174 (1H 105)
SK6: Bred 2F 135
SK14: Hyde 3D 120
Turner Rd. SK6: Mar 5D 148
Turners Pl. OL12: Roch 6G 15
Turner St. BL1: Bolt 1H 175 (5E 33)
M4: Man 4B 6 (3E 101)
M7: Sal 4C 86
M11: Man 4E 103
M16: Old T 5B 8 (1A 114)
M18: Man 2F 117
M34: Dent 2E 119
OL4: Lees 1C 76
OL6: A Lyme 4C 174 (1H 105)
OL12: Roch 2G 27
SK1: Stoc 1G 179 (1H 145)
Turnfield Cl. OL16: Roch 6D 16
Turnfield Rd. SK8: Chea 2G 155
Turnhill Rd. OL16: Roch 2B 42
Turn Moss Rd. M32: Stre 1F 129
Turnough Rd. OL16: Miln 4F 29
Turnpike, The SK6: Mar 4B 148
Turnpike Cl. OL3: Dig 2E 63
Turnpike Grn. M6: Sal 2F 99
(off Nursery St.)
Turnpike Wlk. M11: Man 4B 102
(off Albert St.)
Turn Rd. BL0: Ram 1E 13
Turnstone Rd. BL2: Bolt 6H 175 (1E 49)
SK2: Stoc 6F 147
Turn St. OL6: A Lyme 1A 106
Turton Av. BL3: Lit L 3C 50
Turton Cl. BL8: Bury 5A 36
OL10: H'ood 3E 39
Turton Community Leisure Cen. 4F 19
Turton Ct. BL1: Bolt 1H 175 (5E 33)
Turton Hgts. BL2: Bolt 5F 19
Turton La. M25: Pres 4F 69
Turton Rd. BL2: Bolt 5F 19
BL7: Bro X 5F 19
BL8: Tot 1C 20

Turton St. BL1: Bolt 1G 175 (5D 32)
M11: Man 6F 103
Turves Rd. SK8: Chea H 4A 156
Turville Ho. SK9: Wilm 5H 165
Tuscan Rd. M20: Man 3F 143
Tuscany Vw. M7: Sal 3H 85
Tutbury St. M4: Man 6H 7 (4H 101)
Tuxford Wlk. M40: Man 6H 87
(off Palgrave Av.)
Tweedale Av. M9: Man 4G 71
(not continuous)
Tweedale St.
OL11: Roch 6A 178 (6G 27)
Tweedale Way OL9: Chad 1H 89
Tweed Cl. OL8: O'ham 6F 177 (4E 75)
WA14: Alt 5E 139
Tweedle Hill Rd. M9: Man 5F 71
Tweedsdale Cl. M45: White 6H 53
Tweenbrook Av. M23: Wyth 2G 153
Twelve Yards Rd. M30: Ecc 2D 108
(not continuous)
M44: Irl 3A 108
Twigworth Rd. M22: Wyth 3A 154
Twillbrook Dr. M3: Sal 2F 5 (2C 100)
Twinegate OL12: Roch 6G 15
Twingates Cl. OL2: Shaw 2H 59
Twining Brook Rd. SK8: Chea H 1D 156
Twining Rd. M17: T Pk 5F 97
Twinnies Rd. SK9: Wilm 6F 165
Twin St. OL10: H'ood 4A 40
Twirl Hill Rd. OL6: A Lyme 2C 92
Twisse Rd. BL2: Bolt 6B 34
Twoacre Av. M22: Wyth 6A 142
Two Acre Dr. OL2: Shaw 6F 43
Two Acre La. OL4: O'ham 5E 61
Two Bridges Rd. OL16: Miln 2H 43
Two Brooks La. BL8: Haw 1D 20
Two Mills La. OL5: Mos 2H 93
Two Trees La. M34: Dent 5F 119
Twyford Cl. M20: Man 6D 130
Tybyrne Cl. M28: Wors 4D 80
Tydden St. OL8: O'ham 6F 75
Tydeman Wlk. OL16: Miln 6G 29
Tyersall Cl. M30: Ecc 1G 97
TYLDESLEY 2A 80
Tyldesley St. M14: Man 4E 115
Tyler St. SK9: A Edg 5G 173
Tymm St. M40: Man 3E 89
Tyndall Av. M40: Man 2C 88
Tyndall St. OL4: O'ham 3A 76
Tyne Cl. M28: Walk 6G 65
Tynedale Cl. SK5: Stoc 4G 133
Tynesbank M28: Walk 1G 81
Tynesbank Cotts. M28: Walk 6G 65
(off Tynesbank)
Tyne St. OL4: O'ham 2A 76
Tynwald St. OL4: O'ham 2A 76
Tynwell Wlk. M40: Man 6G 87
(off Glendower Dr.)
Tyrol Wlk. M11: Man 5B 102
Tyrone Cl. M23: Wyth 3D 140
Tyrone Dr. OL11: Roch 6B 26
Tyro St. OL8: O'ham 6F 75
Tyrrell Gro. SK14: Hyde 6E 121
Tyrrell Rd. SK5: Stoc 6H 117
Tysoe Gdns. M3: Sal 3D 4 (3B 100)
Tyson St. M8: Man 3D 86
Tytherington Dr. M19: Man 6F 117
Tywald Mt. OL2: O'ham 4E 59

Ullswater Dr. BL4: Farn 2C 64
BL9: Bury 6E 37
M24: Mid 5B 56
Ullswater Gro. OL10: H'ood 5H 39
Ullswater Rd. M22: Wyth 3H 153
M41: Urm 3A 110
SK1: Stoc 4B 146
SK9: Hand 3G 165
Ullswater Ter. SK15: Stal 1E 107
Ullswater Wlk. M9: Man 4A 72
(off Rockmead Dr.)
Ulster Av. OL11: Roch 6G 27
Ulundi St. M26: Rad 4A 52
Ulverston Av. M20: Man 2E 131
OL9: Chad 3A 74
Uncouth Rd. OL16: Roch 4E 29
Underhill SK6: Rom 1H 147
Underhill Rd. OL1: O'ham 6E 59
Underhill Wlk. M40: Man 1D 102
Under La. OL4: Grot 5F 77
OL9: Chad 6B 74
Underwood OL12: Roch 3A 178 (4G 27)
Underwood Cl. M18: Man 1H 117
Underwood Rd. SK9: A Edg 5H 173
SK14: Hat 5G 121
Underwood St. SK16: Duk 5H 105
Underwood Vs. OL15: L'ough 5E 17
(off Oakley St.)
Underwood Wlk. SK14: Hat 5H 121
Underwood Way OL2: Shaw 5B 44
Undsworths Ct. OL10: H'ood 3H 39
Unicorn St. M30: Ecc 5D 96
Union Arc. BL9: Bury 3C 176 (3F 37)
Union Bldgs. BL2: Bolt . . .5G 175 (1D 48)
Union Ct. BL2: Bolt 3E 33
Union Rd. BL2: Bolt 3E 33
OL6: A Lyme 1A 106
OL12: Roch 5E 17
SK6: Mar 5D 148
Union St. BL0: Ram 3C 12
BL7: Eger 1B 18
BL9: Bury 3C 176 (3F 37)
M4: Man 4B 6 (3E 101)
M6: Sal 1G 99
M12: Man 3F 11 (6G 101)
M14: Man 4F 115
M18: Man 1G 117
M24: Mid 6C 56
M27: Pen 3A 84
M27: Swin 3G 83
OL1: O'ham 4F 177 (3F 75)
OL2: O'ham 3D 58
OL4: Lees 3C 76
OL6: A Lyme 4C 174 (2H 105)
OL9: Chad 5B 74
OL12: Roch 1B 178 (3H 27)
OL12: Whitw 1E 15
OL16: Roch 2C 178 (3H 27)
SK1: Stoc 5G 179 (3H 145)
SK14: Hyde 5C 120
Union St. W. OL8: O'ham 5E 177 (3F 75)
(not continuous)
Union Ter. M7: Sal 3D 86
(off Bury Old Rd.)
Union Yd. OL4: O'ham 3H 75
Unison Bus. Cen. M41: Urm 6G 97
United Rd. M16: Old T 1E 113
United Trad. Est. M16: Old T 2E 113
Unity Cl. OL10: H'ood 4F 39
Unity Cres. OL10: H'ood 4F 39
Unity Dr. M7: Sal 5D 86
Unity St. OL10: H'ood 4F 39
Unity Way SK1: Stoc 5H 179 (3H 145)
UNIVERSITIES 1E 115
University of Bolton
Chadwick Campus 1F 49
Deane Campus 1C 48
University of Manchester
Beyer Building 6B 10
Denmark Road Building 2F 115
Dryden St. 6E 11
Ellen Wilkinson Building 2F 115
Granby Row 2C 10

U

Uganda St. BL3: Bolt 5A 48
Ukraine Rd. M7: Sal 5H 85
Uldale Dr. M24: Mid 6A 56
Ullesthorpe OL12: Roch 2A 178
Ulleswater Cl. BL3: Lit L 4B 50
Ulleswater St. BL1: Bolt 3D 32
Ullock Wlk. M24: Mid 5H 55
Ullswater Av. OL2: O'ham 1D 58
OL7: A Lyme 1G 105
OL12: Roch 2E 27

University of Manchester
Greenheys Bus. Cen. 2E 115
Institute of Science and Technology
. . . . .2C 10 (5F 101)
John Rylands University Library
. . . . .6G 5 (4D 100)
McDougall Sports Cen. 2E 115
Manchester Business School East
. . . . .5B 10 (1E 115)
Manchester Business School West
. . . . .5B 10 (1E 115)
Sackville Street Building
. . . . .2C 10 (5F 101)
Stopford Building 6D 10 (2F 115)
University Place 5C 10
Up. Brook St. 4C 10 (1F 115)
University of Salford
Adelphi Building 3B 100
Adelphi House 3C 4 (3A 100)
Irwell Valley Campus 1H 99
Newton Building 3A 4 (3H 99)
Salford University Bus. Pk. 1H 99
Technology House 2H 99
(off Frederick Rd.)
University Rd. M5: Sal 1A 4 (2H 99)
University Rd. W. M5: Sal 3H 99
UNSWORTH 4A 54
Unsworth Av. M29: Tyld 3A 80
Unsworth St. M26: Rad 3H 51
Unsworth Way OL1: O'ham . . .1F 177 (1E 75)
Unwin Av. M18: Man 3F 117
Unwin Ct. M6: Sal 3F 99
(off Rosehill Cl.)
Upavon Ct. M7: Sal 5D 86
Upavon Rd. M22: Wyth 2D 154
Upcast La. SK9: A Edg 6A 172
SK9: Wilm 6A 172
Upland Dr. M38: Lit H 3D 64
Upland Rd. OL8: O'ham 5E 75
Uplands M24: Mid 2C 72
Uplands, The OL5: Mos 2H 93
Uplands Av. M26: Rad 5C 52
Uplands Rd. M41: Urm 1A 126
SK14: Hyde 3E 137
Up. Brook St. M13: Man . . .4C 10 (6F 101)
SK1: Stoc 3H 179 (2H 145)
Up. Broom Way BL5: W'ton 5A 46
Up. Camp St. M7: Sal 6B 86
Up. Chorlton Rd. M16: W Ran 4A 114
Up. Cliff Hill OL2: Shaw 4A 44
Up. Conran St. M9: Man 3A 88
Up. Cyrus St. M40: Man 3A 102
Upper Downs WA14: Alt 2E 151
Up. George St. OL12: Roch 2H 27
Up. Gloucester St. M6: Sal 2G 99
Up. Hayes Cl. OL16: Roch 3C 28
Up. Helena St. M40: Man . . .3H 7 (3A 102)
Up. Hibbert La. SK6: Mar 1D 160
Up. Kent Rd. M14: Man 4A 116
Up. Kirby St. M4: Man 5F 7 (4G 101)
Up. Lees Dr. BL5: W'ton 6A 46
Up. Lloyd St. M14: Man 4E 115
Upper Mead BL7: Eger 2D 18
Up. Medlock St.
M15: Man 5H 9 (1D 114)
UPPERMILL 6D 62
Uppermill Dr. M19: Man 6A 132
Up. Monsall St. M40: Man 5A 88
Up. Moss La. M15: Man 6E 9 (1C 114)
Up. Park Rd. M7: Sal 2B 86
M14: Man 3G 115
Up. Passmonds Gro. OL11: Roch . . .3D 26
Up. Stone Dr. OL16: Miln 5D 28
Up. West Gro. M13: Man 2H 115
Up. Wharf St. M5: Sal 5B 4 (4A 100)
Up. Wilton St. M25: Pres 5A 70
Uppingham Dr. BL0: Ram 2B 12
Upton OL11: Roch 6A 178 (5G 27)
Upton Av. SK4: Stoc 5A 132
SK8: Chea H 5C 156
Upton Cl. M24: Mid 4C 72
Upton Dr. WA14: Tim 3G 139
Upton La. M29: Tyld 3A 80

Upton Wlk. OL7: A Lyme 4G 105
(off John St. E.)
Upton Way BL8: Bury 6H 21
SK9: Hand 2H 165
(off Beeston Rd.)
Upwood Wlk. M9: Man 6A 72
(off Sanderstead Dr.)
Urban Av. WA15: Alt 3D 174 (1G 151)
Urban Dr. WA15: Alt 3D 174 (1G 151)
Urban Rd. M33: Sale 5A 128
WA15: Alt 3D 174 (1G 151)
Urbis .3H 5 (3E 101)
Urmson St. OL8: O'ham 6F 75
URMSTON 5F 111
Urmston La. M32: Stre 6A 112
Urmston Leisure Cen. 5D 110
Urmston Pk. M41: Urm 5G 111
Urmston Station (Rail) 5F 111
Urwick Rd. SK6: Rom 2H 147
Usk Cl. M45: White 2A 70
Utley Fld. Vw. WA15: Hale 2G 151
Uttley St. BL1: Bolt 3B 32
OL11: Roch 1E 41
Uvedale Ho. M30: Ecc 4F 97
(off Adelaide St.)
Uxbridge Av. M11: Man 3E 103
Uxbridge St. OL6: A Lyme . .5A 174 (2G 105)

V

Vaal St. OL8: O'ham 6C 74
Valance Cl. M12: Man 1C 116
Valdene Cl. BL4: Farn 2H 65
Valdene Dr. BL4: Farn 2H 65
M28: Walk 3H 81
Vale, The OL5: Mos 2F 93
Vale Av. BL9: Bury 6D 36
M26: Rad 2E 67
M27: Pen 2A 84
M33: Sale 4E 129
M41: Urm 6A 110
SK14: Hyde 4E 121
Vale Cl. SK4: Stoc 1B 144
SK6: Rom 1D 148
SK7: H Gro 1E 159
Vale Coppice BL0: Ram 6C 12
Vale Cotts. OL15: 'Lough 4G 17
SK14: Hyde 3A 120
(off Arnside Dr.)
Vale Ct. M24: Mid 1D 72
WA14: Bow 4D 150
Vale Cres. SK8: Chea H 3B 156
Vale Dr. M25: Pres 1G 85
OL9: O'ham 3D 74
Vale Edge M26: Rad 2A 52
Vale Head SK9: Hand 5H 165
Vale Ho. SK4: Stoc 2A 144
Vale La. M35: Fail 1A 104
Vale Mill Cl. BL0: Eden 1G 13
Valemount SK13: Had 2H 123
Valencia Rd. M7: Sal 5H 85
Valentia Rd. M9: Man 5H 71
Valentine St. M35: Fail 4G 89
OL4: O'ham 3A 76
Vale Pk. Way M8: Man 4G 87
Valerie Wlk. M15: Man 4H 9
Vale Rd. M43: Droy 2B 104
OL2: Shaw 1B 60
SK4: Stoc 2B 144
SK6: Rom 2H 147
SK9: Wilm 1B 172
SK15: C'ook 5A 94
WA14: Bow 4D 150
WA15: Tim 6A 140
Vale Side OL5: Mos 3G 93
Vale St. BL2: Bolt 6C 34
M11: Man 3E 103
M24: Mid 1D 72
OL7: A Lyme 5G 91
OL10: H'ood 3A 40
(not continuous)
Vale Top Av. M9: Man 4B 88

Valetta Cl. M14: Man 1F 131
Vale Vw. BL7: Bolt 4D 18
OL5: Mos 6A 78
WA14: Bow 4E 151
(off Vicarage La.)
Valewood Av. SK4: Stoc 2C 144
Valiant Wlk. M40: Man 2G 89
(off Nuthurst Rd.)
Vallea Ct. M4: Man 1A 6 (2E 101)
Valletts La. BL1: Bolt 4A 32
Valletts Sth. Bldgs. BL1: Bolt 4A 32
Valley Av. BL8: Bury 1B 36
Valley Cl. OL5: Mos 1F 93
SK8: Chea 2A 156
Valley Ct. SK4: Stoc 2D 144
Valley Dr. SK9: Hand 4G 165
Valley Gdns. SK14: Hat 6A 122
Valley Gro. M34: Dent 5H 119
Valley M. OL3: G'fld 5E 79
Valley Mill BL7: Bolt 4D 18
Valley Mill La. BL9: Bury 4G 37
Valley New Rd. OL2: O'ham 4E 59
Valley Pk. Rd. M25: Pres 4F 69
Valley Ri. OL2: Shaw 4G 43
Valley Rd. M24: Mid 5D 56
M41: Urm 4H 109
OL2: O'ham 4E 59
SK4: Stoc 2B 144
SK6: Bred 5D 134
SK7: Bram 4H 157
SK8: Chea 2A 156
SK13: Glos 6H 123
SK14: Hat 1H 137
Valley Rd. Sth. M41: Urm 5G 109
Valley Vw. BL7: Bro X 4E 19
OL12: Whitw 1B 14
SK14: Hyde 3E 121
Valley Wlk. M11: Man 4B 102
Valley Way SK15: Stal 4G 107
Valpy Av. BL2: Bolt 2F 33
Vancouver Quay M50: Sal 6F 99
Vandyke Av. M6: Sal 2B 98
Vandyke St. OL12: Roch 2B 26
Vane St. M30: Ecc 3E 97
Vanguard Cl. BL8: Bury 2C 36
M30: Ecc 6B 96
(off Avroe Rd.)
Vantomme St. BL1: Bolt 1C 32
Varden Gro. SK3: Stoc 6F 145
Varden Rd. SK12: Poy 4E 169
Vardon Dr. SK9: Wilm 3G 173
Varey St. M18: Man 2F 117
Varley Rd. BL3: Bolt 3G 47
Varley St. M40: Man 1H 7 (1H 101)
Varna St. M11: Man 6F 103
Vasser Rd. M18: Man 2D 116
Vauban Dr. M6: Sal 2B 98
Vaudrey Dr. SK7: H Gro 3E 159
SK8: Chea H 2C 156
WA15: Tim 3A 140
Vaudrey La. M34: Dent 5G 119
Vaudrey Rd. SK6: Wood 4G 135
Vaudrey St. SK15: Stal 4E 107
Vaughan Av. M40: Man 3C 88
Vaughan Gro. OL4: Lees 3D 76
Vaughan Ho. M13: Man 6C 10
Vaughan Ind. Est. M12: Man 6B 102
Vaughan Rd. M21: Chor 1B 130
SK4: Stoc 6F 133
WA14: W Tim 2E 139
Vaughan St. M12: Man 6B 102
M30: Ecc 2D 96
OL2: O'ham 4E 59
Vauxhall Av. M40: Man 1G 101
(off Hamerton Rd.)
Vauxhall Ind. Est. SK5: Stoc 3G 133
Vauxhall St. M40: Man 1F 101
Vavasour Ct. OL16: Roch 5B 28
Vavasour St. OL16: Roch 5B 28
Vawdrey Dr. M23: Wyth 1F 141
Vaynor OL12: Roch 1A 178 (3G 27)
Vega St. M8: Man 1C 100
Vela Wlk. M7: Sal 2B 4 (2A 100)

Velmere Av.—Victoria St. E.

Velmere Av. M9: Man 4E 71
Velour Cl. M3: Sal 1C 4 (2B 100)
Velvet Ct. M1: Man 2B 10
Vendale Av. M27: Swin 5F 83
Venesta Av. M6: Sal 2B 98
Venetia St. M40: Man 6E 89
Venice Ct. *M1: Man 2B 10*
(off Samuel Ogden St.)
Venice St. BL3: Bolt 3A 48
M1: Man 2B 10 (5E 101)
Venlo Gdns. SK8: Chea H 4D 156
Ventnor Av. BL1: Bolt 2D 32
BL9: Bury 4F 53
M19: Man 1E 133
M33: Sale 3B 128
Ventnor Cl. M34: Dent 1H 135
Ventnor Rd. M20: Man 6G 131
SK4: Stoc 1C 144
Ventnor St. M6: Sal 1H 99
M9: Man 3H 87
OL11: Roch 6H 27
Ventura Cl. M14: Man 6E 115
Venture Scout Way M8: Man 6D 86
Venture Way SK12: Poy 4F 169
Venwood Ct. M25: Pres 1F 85
Venwood Rd. M25: Pres 1F 85
Verbena Av. BL4: Farn 6E 49
Verbena Cl. M31: Part 6D 124
Verdant La. M30: Ecc 5B 96
Verdant Way OL16: Roch 2C 42
Verdun Av. M6: Sal 2B 98
Verdun Cres. OL11: Roch 3E 27
Verdun Rd. M30: Ecc 1D 96
Verdure Av. BL1: Bolt 5E 31
M33: Sale 2C 140
Verdure Cl. M35: Fail 4B 90
Vere St. M50: Sal 4F 99
Verity Cl. M20: Man 3F 131
OL2: O'ham 5D 58
Verity Wlk. M9: Man 6F 71
Vermont Gdns. SK8: Chea H 2D 166
Vermont St. BL1: Bolt 5B 32
Verna St. BL0: Ram 3C 12
Verne Av. M27: Swin 3G 83
Verne Dr. OL1: O'ham 2C 60
Verney Rd. OL2: O'ham 5E 59
Vernham Wlk. BL3: Bolt 3C 48
Vernon Av. M30: Ecc 3H 97
M32: Stre 6D 112
SK1: Stoc 1B 146
Vernon Cl. SK8: Chea H 4A 156
SK12: Poy 5D 168
Vernon Ct. M7: Sal 2A 86
Vernon Dr. M25: Pres 1G 85
SK6: Mar 4A 148
Vernon Gro. M33: Sale 5E 129
Vernon Ho. SK1: Stoc 2B 146
Vernon Lodge *SK12: Poy 5D 168*
(off Copperfield Rd.)
Vernon Mill SK1: Stoc 1A 146
Vernon Pk. WA15: Tim 4A 140
Vernon Rd. BL8: G'mount 2H 21
M7: Sal 2A 86
M43: Droy 3G 103
SK6: Bred 1E 147
SK12: Poy 5D 168
Vernon St. BL1: Bolt 5C 32
BL4: Farn 1A 66
BL9: Bury 1D 176 (1F 37)
M7: Sal 6B 86
M9: Man 4A 88
M16: Old T 2A 114
OL5: Mos 1G 93
OL6: A Lyme 1A 106
SK1: Stoc 1G 179 (1H 145)
SK7: H Gro 2D 158
SK14: Hyde 5C 120
Vernon Vw. *SK6: Bred 6G 135*
(off Thomas St.)
Vernon Wlk. BL1: Bolt 1E 175 (5C 32)
SK1: Stoc 2F 179
Verona Dr. M40: Man 1E 103
Veronica Rd. M20: Man 6G 131
Verrill Av. M23: Wyth 2A 142
Verwood Wlk. *M23: Wyth 6G 141*
(off Beckfield Rd.)
Vesper St. M35: Fail 3A 90
Vesta St. BL0: Ram 3B 12
M4: Man 5F 7 (4G 101)
Vestris Dr. M6: Sal 2B 98
Viaduct Rd. WA14: B'ath 4F 139
Viaduct St. M3: Sal 3F 5 (3C 100)
M12: Man 6H 7 & 2H 11 (4A 102)
SK3: Stoc 3E 179 (2G 145)
Vicarage Av. SK8: Chea H 5D 156
Vicarage Cl. BL9: Bury 3E 23
M6: Sal 2B 98
OL4: Spri 2D 76
SK16: Duk 5C 106
Vicarage Ct. SK14: Hyde 6B 120
Vicarage Cres.
OL6: A Lyme 6B 92
Vicarage Dr. OL16: Roch 6C 16
SK16: Duk 5B 106
Vicarage Gdns. SK3: Stoc 3F 145
SK14: Hyde 5D 120
Vicarage Gro. M30: Ecc 3H 97
Vicarage La. BL1: Bolt 2B 32
M24: Mid 2F 73
SK12: Poy 2E 169
WA14: Bow 4E 151
Vicarage Rd. M27: Swin 3G 83
M28: Walk 5G 65
M41: Urm 3D 110
M44: Irl 5E 109
OL7: A Lyme 6H 91
SK3: Stoc 5G 145
Vicarage Rd. Nth. OL11: Roch 4E 41
Vicarage Rd. Sth. OL11: Roch 4E 41
Vicarage St. BL3: Bolt 2B 48
M26: Rad 4A 52
OL2: Shaw 6H 43
OL8: O'ham 6C 74
Vicarage Vw. OL11: Roch 4F 41
Vicarage Way OL2: Shaw 1G 59
Vicars Dr. OL16: Roch 4B 178 (4H 27)
Vicars Ga. OL16: Roch 4B 178 (4H 27)
Vicars Hall Gdns. M28: Wors 5D 80
Vicars Hall La. M28: Wors 6D 80
Vicars Rd. M21: Chor 1G 129
Vicars St. M30: Ecc 3H 97
Viceroy Ct. M20: Man 1F 143
Vicker Cl. M27: Clif 1H 83
Vicker Gro. M20: Man 4D 130
Vickerman St. BL1: Bolt 3B 32
Vickers Row *BL4: Farn 1F 65*
(off Mossfield Rd.)
Vickers St. BL3: Bolt 2B 48
M40: Man 1H 7 (2A 102)
Victor Av. BL9: Bury 1E 37
Victoria Av. M9: Man 4E 71
M19: Man 1C 132
M20: Man 6E 131
M27: Swin 3A 84
M30: Ecc 2H 97
M45: White 1G 69
SK6: Bred 6F 135
SK7: H Gro 2E 159
SK8: Chea H 3C 156
WA15: Tim 4G 139
Victoria Av. E. M9: Man 5A 72
Victoria Bri. St. M3: Sal 4G 5 (3D 100)
Victoria Bldg., The M50: Sal 6F 99
Victoria Cl. M28: Wors 5E 81
SK3: Stoc 6F 179 (4G 145)
SK7: Bram 1G 167
Victoria Ct. BL4: Farn 5G 49
BL8: Tot 5H 21
M11: Man 5E 103
(off Brigham St.)
M32: Stre 5C 112
M45: White 2F 69
OL7: A Lyme 4G 105
Victoria Cres. M30: Ecc 2H 97
Victoria Dr. M33: Sale 6D 128
Victoria Farm SK16: Duk 6B 106
Victoria Gdns. OL2: Shaw 6H 43
SK14: Hyde 3D 120
Victoria Grange *M20: Man 5E 131*
(off Barlow Moor Rd.)
Victoria Gro. BL1: Bolt 4A 32
M14: Man 1G 131
SK4: Stoc 4E 133
Victoria Hall *M13: Man 3G 115*
(off Up. Brook St.)
M15: Man 5A 10
(not continuous)
Victoria Ho. M11: Man 5E 103
M30: Sal 1A 98
Victoria La. M27: Swin 3F 83
M45: White 2F 69
Victoria Lodge M7: Sal 6A 86
Victoria M. BL9: Bury 5H 53
SK16: Duk 1A 120
Victoria Mill M43: Droy 4A 104
SK5: Stoc 1G 133
Victorian Lanterns BL9: Sum 1C 22
Victoria Pde. M41: Urm 5F 111
Victoria Pk. M14: Man 3A 116
SK1: Stoc 3B 146
Victoria Pl. M17: T Pk 1F 113
M34: Dent 1G 135
Victoria Plaza BL1: Bolt 4F 175
Victoria Rd. BL1: Bolt 6D 30
BL4: Kea 3C 66
M6: Sal 1A 98
M14: Man 1F 131
M16: W Ran 5B 114
M19: Man 6B 116
M22: Nor 3B 142
M30: Ecc 2G 97
M32: Stre 5D 112
M33: Sale 6D 128
M41: Urm 5D 110
M44: Irl 6D 108
SK1: Stoc 2B 146
SK9: Wilm 3D 172
SK16: Duk 1A 120
WA15: Hale 2G 151
WA15: Tim 5A 140
Victoria Sq. BL1: Bolt 4F 175 (6D 32)
M4: Man 3D 6 (3F 101)
M28: Walk 6H 65
(off Ellesmere Shop. Cen.)
M45: White 2F 69
Victoria Station (Rail) 2A 6 (2E 101)
Victoria Sta. App.
M3: Man 3H 5 (3D 100)
Victoria Station Stop (Metro) 2E 101
Victoria St. BL0: Ram 3B 12
BL2: Ain 4E 35
BL4: Farn 5F 49
BL8: Bury 3D 36
(not continuous)
BL8: Tot 4G 21
M3: Man 4H 5 (3D 100)
M11: Man 5E 103
M24: Mid 1C 72
M26: Rad 4A 52
M28: Wors 5E 81
M34: Dent 4E 119
(not continuous)
M35: Fail 5F 89
OL2: Shaw 1H 59
OL4: Lees 3C 76
OL4: O'ham 3G 75
OL7: A Lyme 4G 105
OL8: O'ham 3F 91
OL9: Chad 2B 74
OL10: H'ood 4A 40
OL12: Roch 2H 27
OL12: Whitw 1E 15
OL15: L'ough 4H 17
SK14: Hyde 3C 120
SK15: Mill 1H 107
SK15: Stal 3D 106
SK16: Duk 5B 106
WA14: Alt 1B 174 (6F 139)
Victoria St. E. OL7: A Lyme 3G 105

Victoria Ter. M12: Man 3B **116**
  M13: Man *3G* **115**
    (off Hathersage Rd.)
  OL2: O'ham *2D* **58**
    (off Albert St.)
  OL10: H'ood 1G **39**
  OL16: Miln 6G **29**
Victoria Trad. Est.
  OL9: Chad, O'ham 6B **74**
    (not continuous)
Victoria Wlk. OL9: Chad 6C **58**
Victoria Way OL2: O'ham 1C **58**
  SK7: Bram 1F **167**
Victor Mann St. M11: Man 6A **104**
Victor St. M3: Sal 4D **4** (3B **100**)
  M40: Man 1E **7** (1G **101**)
  OL8: O'ham 2B **90**
  OL10: H'ood 5A **40**
VICTORY 5A **32**
Victory Gro. M34: Aud 6C **104**
Victory Pk. Ind. Est. M35: Fail 4H **89**
Victory Rd. BL3: Lit L 3C **50**
  M44: Cad 5A **124**
Victory St. BL1: Bolt 5A **32**
    (not continuous)
  M14: Man 4G **115**
Victory Trad. Est. BL3: Bolt 2E **49**
Vienna Rd. SK3: Stoc 5F **145**
Vienna Rd. E. SK3: Stoc 5F **145**
Viewfield Wlk. *M9: Man* *4A* **88**
    (off Nethervale Dr.)
Viewlands Dr. SK9: Hand 5H **165**
View St. BL3: Bolt 2B **48**
Vigo Av. BL3: Bolt 4H **47**
Vigo St. OL4: O'ham 4B **76**
  OL10: H'ood 4A **40**
Viking Cl. M11: Man 4B **102**
Viking St. BL3: Bolt 3E **49**
  OL11: Roch 3E **27**
VILLAGE, THE 1B **126**
Village M17: T Pk 2D **112**
Village, The M41: Urm 6B **110**
Village Circ. M17: T Pk 1C **112**
Village Ct. M17: T Pk 1C **112**
  OL12: Whitw 4A **14**
  SK9: Wilm 6H **165**
Village Grn. *OL3: Upp* *1D* **78**
    (off New St.)
Village Leisure Club, The 1A **156**
Village Mnr. OL3: Upp 6D **62**
Village St. M7: Sal 6A **86**
Village Vw. *SK15: Mill* *1H* **107**
    (off Victoria St.)
Village Wlk. *M11: Man* *4E* **103**
    (off Bob Massey Cl.)
Village Way M4: Man 4B **6**
  M17: T Pk 1B **112**
  SK9: Wilm 6H **165**
Villa Rd. OL8: O'ham 5F **75**
Villdale Av. SK2: Stoc 4C **146**
Villemomble Sq. M43: Droy 4A **104**
Villiers Ct. M45: White 2G **69**
Villiers Dr. OL8: O'ham 6E **177** (4E **75**)
Villiers Ind. Est. M6: Sal 1G **99**
Villiers St. BL9: Bury 2G **37**
  M6: Sal 1F **99**
  OL6: A Lyme 3B **106**
  SK14: Hyde 5D **120**
Vinca Gro. *M7: Sal* *5B* **86**
    (off Hilton St. Nth.)
Vincent Av. M21: Chor 6G **113**
  M30: Ecc 1F **97**
  OL4: O'ham 1A **76**
Vincent Ct. BL3: Bolt 4C **48**
Vincent St. BL1: Bolt 1B **48**
  M11: Man 5E **103**
  M24: Mid 5C **56**
  OL15: L'ough 3G **17**
  OL16: Roch 6A **28**
  SK14: Hyde 6D **120**
Vine Av. M27: Pen 3B **84**
Vine Cl. M33: Sale 4E **127**
  OL2: Shaw 6H **43**

Vine Ct. M32: Stre 6D **112**
  OL16: Roch 4B **28**
Vine Fold M40: Man 2H **89**
Vine Gro. SK2: Stoc 5C **146**
Vine Pl. OL11: Roch 6C **178** (6H **27**)
Vinery Gro. M34: Dent 4E **119**
Vine St. BL0: Ram 5A **12**
  M7: Sal 3H **85**
  M11: Man 6G **103**
  M25: Pres 4A **70**
  M30: Ecc 4E **97**
  OL9: Chad 6B **74**
  SK7: H Gro 2E **159**
Vineyard Cl. OL12: W'le 5C **16**
Vineyard Cotts. OL12: W'le 5C **16**
Vineyard Ho. *OL12: W'le*
    (off Knowl Syke St.)
Vineyards, The *M7: Sal* *3A* **86**
    (off Nevile Rd.)
Vineyard St. OL4: O'ham 2H **75**
Viola St. BL1: Bolt 2C **32**
  M11: Man 3F **103**
Violet Av. BL4: Farn 6E **49**
Violet Ct. M22: Wyth 2B **154**
Violet Hill Ct. OL4: O'ham 1C **76**
Violet St. M18: Man 1H **117**
  SK2: Stoc 5H **145**
Violet Way M24: Mid 2F **73**
VIP Cen., The OL1: O'ham 6A **60**
Virgil St. M15: Man 5B **8** (1A **114**)
Virgin Active
  Castlefield 1G **9** (5D **100**)
  East Didsbury 2H **143**
  The Printworks 4A **6**
Virginia Chase SK8: Chea H 5B **156**
Virginia Cl. M23: Wyth 4D **140**
Virginia St. BL3: Bolt 3H **47**
  OL11: Roch 1G **41**
Viscount Dr. M90: Man A 6F **153**
  SK8: H Grn 6H **155**
Viscount St. M14: Man 4G **115**
Vista, The M44: Cad 5A **124**
Vivian Pl. M14: Man 3A **116**
Vivian St. OL11: Roch 6G **27**
Vixen Cl. M21: Chor 2C **130**
Voewood Ho. SK1: Stoc 3B **146**
Voltaire Av. M6: Sal 2B **98**
Vorlich Dr. OL9: Chad 1H **73**
Vue Cinema
  Bury 1H **53**
  Salford Quays 6F **99**
Vulcan St. OL1: O'ham 6H **59**
Vulcan Ter. *OL15: L'ough* *4F* **17**
    (off Spenwood Rd.)
Vulcan Works M4: Man 6G **7** (4H **101**)
Vyner Gro. M33: Sale 3H **127**

W

Wadcroft Wlk. *M9: Man* *3A* **88**
    (off Towton St.)
Waddicor Av. OL6: A Lyme 5C **92**
Waddington Cl. BL8: Bury 3G **35**
Waddington Fold OL16: Roch 3C **42**
Waddington Rd. BL1: Bolt 4G **31**
Waddington St. OL9: O'ham 1C **74**
Wadebridge Av. M23: Wyth 4D **140**
Wadebridge Cl. BL2: Bolt 4E **33**
Wadebridge Dr. BL8: Bury 3H **35**
Wadebrook Gro. *SK9: Wilm* *6H* **165**
    (off Malpas Cl.)
Wade Cl. M30: Ecc 4H **97**
Wadeford Cl. M4: Man 2E **7** (2G **101**)
    (not continuous)
Wade Hill La. OL3: Dob 1A **78**
Wade Ho. *M30: Ecc* *4H* **97**
    (off Wade Cl.)
Wade Row OL3: Upp 1D **78**
Wade Row Top *OL3: Upp* *1D* **78**
    (off Wade Row)
Wadesmill Wlk. M13: Man 4C **10**
Wadeson Rd. M13: Man 3D **10** (6F **101**)

Wade St. BL3: Bolt 4D **48**
  M24: Mid 3F **73**
Wade Wlk. *M11: Man* *5C* **102**
    (off Mill St.)
Wadham Gdns. SK6: Wood 4A **136**
Wadham Way WA15: Hale 4H **151**
Wadhurst Wlk. *M13: Man* *2G* **115**
    (off Lauderdale Cres.)
Wadlow Cl. M3: Sal 2E **5** (2B **100**)
Wadsley St. BL1: Bolt 5C **32**
Wadsworth Cl. SK9: Hand 4A **166**
Wadsworth Ind. Pk. BL3: Bolt 3C **48**
Wadsworth M. M43: Droy 4H **103**
Wagg Fold OL15: L'ough 2F **17**
Waggoners Ct. *M27: Swin* *4H* **83**
    (off Wayfarers Way)
Waggon Rd. BL2: Bolt 4H **33**
  OL5: Mos 3G **93**
Wagner St. BL1: Bolt 2B **32**
Wagstaff Dr. M35: Fail 4H **89**
Wagstaffe St. M24: Mid 6C **56**
Wagstaff St. SK15: Stal 4C **106**
Wagtail Cl. M28: Wors 3H **81**
Waincliffe Av. M21: Chor 5B **130**
Wain Cl. M30: Ecc 3D **96**
Waingap Cres. OL12: Whitw 1F **15**
Waingap Ri. OL12: Roch 5G **15**
Waingap Vw. OL12: Whitw 2F **15**
Wainman St. M6: Sal 6H **85**
Wainscot Cl. M29: Ast 4A **80**
Wainstones Grn. SK2: Stoc 6E **147**
Wainwright Av. M34: Dent 4H **117**
Wainwright Cl. OL4: Spri 2E **77**
  SK2: Stoc 4A **146**
Wainwright Rd. WA14: Alt 6D **138**
Wainwright St.
  OL8: O'ham 6F **177** (4E **75**)
  SK16: Duk 4B **106**
Waithlands Rd. OL16: Roch 5B **28**
Wakefield Cres. SK6: Rom 2G **147**
Wakefield Dr. M27: Clif 5F **67**
  OL1: Chad 6C **58**
Wakefield M. BL7: Bolt 4D **18**
Wakefield Rd. SK15: Stal 3F **107**
  OL1: Chad 6C **58**
Wakefield St. M1: Man 3A **10** (6E **101**)
  OL1: Chad 6C **58**
Wakefield Wlk. *M34: Dent* *6G* **119**
    (off Mancunian Way)
Wakeling Rd. M34: Dent 1E **135**
Walcott Cl. M13: Man 2H **115**
Wald Av. M14: Man 2A **132**
Waldeck St. BL1: Bolt 5A **32**
Waldeck Wlk. *M9: Man* *6A* **72**
    (off Ravenswood Dr.)
Walden Av. OL4: O'ham 5B **60**
Walden Cl. M14: Man 1E **131**
Walden Cres. SK7: H Gro 2C **158**
Walden Flats *OL10: H'ood* *3G* **39**
    (off Brunswick St.)
Walderton Av. M40: Man 4C **88**
Waldon Av. SK8: Chea 6H **143**
Waldon Cl. BL3: Bolt 3A **48**
Wales St. OL1: O'ham 6A **60**
Walford St. M16: W Ran 3C **114**
Walk, The OL16: Roch 3B **178** (4H **27**)
WALKDEN 6G **65**
Walkden Ct. *M28: Walk* *5G* **65**
    (off Mountain St.)
Walkdene Dr. M28: Walk 6F **65**
Walkden Mkt. Pl. *M28: Walk* *6G* **65**
    (off Ellesmere Shop. Cen.)
Walkden Rd. M28: Walk, Wors 1H **81**
Walkden Station (Rail) 1H **81**
Walker Av. BL3: Bolt 4D **48**
  M35: Fail 5B **90**
  M45: White 3G **69**
  SK15: Stal 3G **107**
Walker Cl. BL4: Kea 3C **66**
  SK14: Hyde 5D **120**
Walker Fold SK14: Hyde 5D **120**
Walker Fold Rd. BL1: Bolt 2C **30**
Walker Grn. M30: Ecc 6D **82**

Walker Ho. M5: Sal 1G 113
   M30: Ecc 4F 97
                 (off Barlow La.)
Walker La. SK14: Hyde 5C 120
Walker Rd. M9: Man 5A 72
   M30: Ecc .1C 96
   M44: Irl .6D 108
   OL9: Chad 1H 89
WALKERS .3D 76
Walkers OL4: Spri 3E 77
Walkers Bldgs. M1: Man 6D 6
Walkers Cl. OL3: Upp 1D 78
Walkers Ct. BL4: Farn 1H 65
   OL4: Spri 3E 77
Walker's Cft. M3: Man . . .3H 5 (3D 100)
Walkers Fold *OL5: Mos* 2F 93
               (off Barkwell La.)
Walker's La. OL4: Spri 3E 77
Walker's Rd. OL8: O'ham 1C 90
Walker St. BL1: Bolt 1B 48
   BL9: Bury 5E 37
   M24: Mid .2F 71
              (not continuous)
   M26: Rad 6C 52
   M34: Dent 3E 119
   OL8: O'ham 3D 74
                (off Larch St.)
   OL10: H'ood 4G 39
   OL16: Roch 4A 28
   SK1: Stoc 2F 179 (2G 145)
   SK13: Had 2H 123
Walkers Vw. OL4: Spri 3E 77
Walkerwood Dr. SK15: Stal 2H 107
Walkmill OL3: Dob 6B 62
Walk Mill Cl. OL12: Roch 5D 16
Walkway, The BL3: Bolt 2F 47
Wallace Av. M14: Man 4H 115
Wallace St. OL8: O'ham 5F 75
Wallasey Av. M14: Man 6E 115
WALLBANK 2D 14
Wallbank Dr. OL12: Whitw 2D 14
Wall Bank La. OL12: Whitw 2D 14
Wallbank Rd. SK7: Bram 4A 158
Wallbrook Cres. M38: Lit H 3E 65
Wallbrook Rd. M9: Man 2G 87
Wallbrook Gro. BL4: Farn 5F 49
Walled Garden, The M27: Swin 5F 83
Wallen Gdn., The M16: W Ran 5C 114
Waller Av. M14: Man 1G 131
Walley St. BL1: Bolt 2C 32
Wallhead Rd. OL16: Roch 4D 28
WALL HILL 6A 62
Wall Hill Rd. OL3: Dob 6A 62
Wallingford Rd. M41: Urm 4G 111
   SK9: Hand 2G 165
Wallis St. M40: Man 6E 89
   OL9: Chad 5A 74
WALLNESS 3A 4 (3H 99)
Wallness Bri. M6: Sal 1A 100
Wallness La. M6: Sal 1A 4 (1H 99)
Wallshaw Pl. OL1: O'ham 2G 75
Wallshaw St. OL1: O'ham . . .2H 177 (2G 75)
               (not continuous)
Wall St. OL8: O'ham 6G 177 (4F 75)
WALLSUCHES 2A 30
Wallsuches BL6: Hor 2A 30
Wall Way M18: Man 3G 117
Wallwork Cl. OL11: Roch 2A 26
Wallwork Rd. M29: Ast 5B 80
Wallwork St. M11: Man 5G 103
   M26: Rad 3A 52
   SK5: Stoc 5H 117
Wallworth Av. M18: Man 2F 117
Wallworth Ter. SK9: Wilm 1B 172
Wally Sq. M7: Sal 5C 86
Walmer Dr. SK7: Bram 4A 158
WALMERSLEY 4E 23
Walmersley Ct. SK6: Mar 6D 148
Walmersley Old Rd.
   BL9: Bury, Ram 3F 23
Walmersley Rd.
   BL9: Bury, Ram 1D 176 (1E 23)
   M40: Man 1G 89

Walker St. M14: Man 4F 115
   M18: Man 1G 117
Walmer St. E. M14: Man 4G 115
Walmley Gro. BL3: Bolt 4A 48
Walmsley Av. OL15: L'ough 6F 17
Walmsley Gro. M41: Urm 5F 111
Walmsley St. BL8: Bury 1B 36
   SK5: Stoc 6H 133
   SK15: Stal 5E 107
Walney Rd. M22: Wyth 1B 154
Walnut Av. BL9: Bury 2H 37
   OL4: O'ham 1B 76
Walnut Cl. M27: Clif 5F 67
   SK9: Wilm 1H 173
   SK14: Hyde 5E 121
Walnut Gro. M33: Sale 5A 128
Walnut Rd. M30: Ecc 1C 96
   M31: Part 6B 124
Walnut St. BL1: Bolt 3D 32
   M18: Man 1F 117
Walnut Tree Rd. SK3: Stoc 3C 144
Walnut Wlk. M32: Stre 1C 128
Walpole St. OL16: Roch 4A 28
Walsall St. M6: Sal 6G 85
Walsden St. M11: Man 3E 103
Walsh Av. M9: Man 1G 87
WALSHAW 1H 35
Walshaw Brook Cl. BL8: Bury 1H 35
Walshaw Dr. M27: Swin 4H 83
Walshaw La. BL8: Bury 1H 35
Walshaw Rd. BL8: Bury 1H 35
Walshaw Wlk. BL8: Tot 6H 21
Walshe St. BL9: Bury 4A 176 (3D 36)
Walsh Fold BL7: Tur 1A 20
Walsingham Av. M20: Man 5D 130
   M24: Mid 4C 72
Walter Greenwood Ct. *M6: Sal* 2G 99
              (off Belvedere Rd.)
Walter Scott St. OL1: O'ham 1H 75
Walters Dr. OL8: O'ham 6G 75
Walter St. M9: Man 3H 87
   M16: Old T 3A 114
   M18: Man 1G 117
   M25: Pres 5F 69
   M26: Rad 1H 51
   M28: Walk 1H 81
   OL1: O'ham 4H 177 (3F 75)
Waltham Dr. SK8: Chea H 1D 166
Waltham Gdns. M26: Rad 3G 51
Waltham Rd. M16: W Ran 6C 114
Waltham St. OL4: O'ham 5A 76
Walton Cl. M24: Mid 6G 55
   OL10: H'ood 5H 39
Walton Dr. BL3: Bolt 3D 48
Walton Ho. M35: Fail 3H 89
Walton Hall Dr. M19: Man 6F 117
Walton Pk. Leisure Cen. 1A 140
Walton Pk. Miniature Railway 1A 140
Walton Pl. BL4: Kea 2A 66
Walton Rd. M9: Man 4H 71
   M33: Sale 2H 139
   WA14: Alt 6D 138
Walton St. M24: Mid 5C 56
   OL7: A Lyme 6G 91
   OL10: H'ood 5H 39
   SK1: Stoc 6H 179
Walton Way M34: Dent 6H 119
Walworth Cl. M26: Rad 2E 67
Walworth St. BL3: Bolt 3A 48
Walwyn Cl. M32: Stre 6E 113
Wandsworth Av. M11: Man 3F 103
Wanley Wlk. M9: Man 6B 72
Wansbeck Cl. M32: Stre 6E 113
Wansbeck Lodge M32: Stre 6E 113
Wansfell Wlk. M4: Man 4H 7
Wansford St. M14: Man 4E 115
Wanstead Av. M9: Man 6D 72
Wapping St. BL1: Bolt 3B 32
Warbeck Cl. SK5: Stoc 5A 118
Warbeck Rd. M40: Man 1F 89

Warbreck Cl. BL2: Bolt 6B 34
Warbreck Gro. M33: Sale 6D 128
Warbrick Dr. M41: Urm 6D 110
Warburton Cl. SK6: Rom 2G 147
   WA15: Haleb 1D 162
Warburton Dr. WA15: Haleb 1D 162
WARBURTON GREEN 1D 162
Warburton La. M31: Part 6C 124
Warburton Rd. SK9: Hand 3H 165
Warburton St. BL1: Bolt 3D 32
   M5: Sal .1H 113
   M20: Man 6F 131
   M30: Ecc .5G 97
Warburton Way WA15: Tim 4C 140
Warcock Rd. OL4: O'ham 2A 76
Wardale Cl. M33: Sale 5C 128
Ward Ct. OL3: Dig 3E 63
Wardend Cl. M38: Lit H 3E 65
Warden La. M40: Man 5D 88
Warden St. M40: Man 5D 88
Warde St. M15: Man 6E 9 (1C 114)
Ward La. OL3: Dig 3E 63
WARDLE 6C 16
Wardle Brook Av. SK14: Hat 4G 121
Wardle Brook Wlk. *SK14: Hat* 4H 121
          (off Wardle Brook Av.)
Wardle Cl. M26: Rad 2G 51
   M32: Stre 5E 113
Wardle Edge OL12: Roch 6B 16
WARDLE FOLD 5C 16
Wardle Fold OL12: W'le 5C 16
Wardle Gdns. OL12: Roch 6C 16
Wardle Rd. M33: Sale 6B 128
   OL12: Roch 4C 16
Wardle St. BL2: Bolt 2G 49
   M40: Man 2H 7 (2A 102)
   OL4: O'ham 3H 75
   OL15: L'ough 3G 17
WARDLEY .1F 83
Wardley Av. M16: W Ran 6C 114
   M28: Walk 6F 65
Wardley Gro. BL1: Bolt 6H 31
Wardley Hall Ct. M27: Ward 1E 83
Wardley Hall La. M28: Wors 3C 82
            (not continuous)
Wardley Hall Rd. M28: Wors 2D 82
Wardley Ho. *M6: Sal* 1C 98
           (off Moss Mdw. Rd.)
Wardley Ind. Est.
   M28: Ward 2E 83
            (not continuous)
Wardley Point M28: Ward 2E 83
Wardley Rd. M29: Tyld 3B 80
Wardley Sq. M29: Tyld 3B 80
Wardley St. M27: Swin 3H 83
Wardlow Av. *SK13: Gam* 6F 123
          (off Youlgreave Cres.)
Wardlow Fold *SK13: Gam* 6F 123
          (off Youlgreave Cres.)
Wardlow Gdns. *SK13: Gam* 6F 123
          (off Youlgreave Cres.)
Wardlow Gro. *SK13: Gam* 6F 123
          (off Youlgreave Cres.)
Wardlow M. SK13: Gam 6F 123
Wardlow St. BL3: Bolt 3H 47
Wardlow Wlk. *SK13: Gam* 6F 123
          (off Youlgreave Cres.)
Ward Rd. M43: Droy 4B 104
WARDSEND 6G 169
Wardsend Wlk. M15: Man 6D 8
Ward St. M9: Man 1G 87
   M20: Man 6F 131
   M35: Fail 3G 89
   M40: Man 3B 88
   OL1: O'ham 1E 177 (1D 74)
   OL9: Chad 2C 74
   SK1: Stoc 6H 179 (4A 146)
   SK6: Bred 6F 135
   SK14: Hyde 5C 120
Wareham Gro. M30: Ecc 2E 97
Wareham St. M8: Man 2F 87
   SK9: Wilm 2E 173
Wareing Way BL3: Bolt 1C 48

Warfield Wlk. *M9: Man* 6A *72*
  (off Sanderstead Dr.)
Warford Av. SK12: Poy 5G *169*
Warford St. M4: Man 1C 6 (1F *101*)
WARHILL 4C *122*
Warhurst Fold *SK13: Had* 2H *123*
  (off Old Hall Sq.)
Warke, The M28: Wors 5B *82*
Warley Cl. SK8: Chea 5A *144*
Warley Gro. SK16: Duk 6A *106*
Warley Rd. M16: Old T 4G *113*
Warley St. OL15: L'ough 3H *17*
Warlingham Cl. BL8: Bury 4B *36*
Warlow Crest OL3: G'fld 5C *78*
Warlow Dr. OL3: G'fld 5C *78*
Warmco Ind. Pk.
  OL5: Mos 1H *93*
Warmington Dr.
  M12: Man 6H 11 (1A *116*)
Warmley Rd. M23: Wyth 3D *140*
Warne Av. M43: Droy 3C *104*
Warner Wlk. *M11: Man* 4B *102*
  (off Hopedale Cl.)
Warnford Cl. M40: Man 1F *103*
War Office Rd. OL11: Roch 5A *26*
Warren Av. SK8: Chea 6H *143*
Warren Bank M9: Man 6H *71*
Warren Bruce Rd.
  M17: T Pk 1D *112*
Warren Cl. M24: Mid 6B *56*
  M34: Dent 5D *118*
  SK7: Bram 3F *157*
  SK12: Poy 3B *168*
Warren Dr. M27: Swin 6F *83*
  WA15: Haleb 6D *152*
Warrener St. M33: Sale 5D *128*
Warren Hey SK9: Wilm 1H *193*
Warren La. OL8: O'ham 5H *75*
Warren Lea SK6: Comp 1F *149*
  SK12: Poy 2E *169*
Warren Rd. M17: T Pk 1B *112*
  M28: Walk 6A *66*
  SK3: Stoc 5G *145*
  SK8: Chea H 3D *156*
Warren St. BL8: Bury 4B *36*
  M7: Sal .3D *86*
  M9: Man 1G *87*
  SK1: Stoc 1G 179 (1H *145*)
  (not continuous)
Warre St.
  OL6: A Lyme 4B 174 (2H *105*)
Warrington Rd. M9: Man 5G *71*
Warrington St. OL4: Lees 4C *76*
  OL6: A Lyme 4C 174 (4H *105*)
  SK15: Stal 4F *107*
Warsall Rd. M22: Shar 4C *142*
Warslow Dr. M33: Sale 2E *141*
Warsop Av. M22: Shar 6C *142*
Warth Cotts. OL3: Dig 3E *63*
WARTH FOLD 6D *36*
Warth Fold Rd. M26: Rad 1C *52*
Warth Ind. Pk. BL9: Bury 6D *36*
Warth Rd. BL9: Bury 6D *36*
Warton Cl. BL8: Bury 4H *35*
  SK7: Bram 6A *158*
Warton Dr. M23: Wyth 6G *141*
Warwick Av. M20: Man 5D *130*
  M27: Ward 1F *83*
  M34: Dent 6F *119*
  M45: White 2H *69*
Warwick Cl. BL8: Bury 1B *36*
  BL8: G'mount 2A *22*
  M24: Mid 4C *72*
  M45: White 2G *69*
  OL2: Shaw 6F *43*
  SK4: Stoc 5F *133*
  SK8: Chea H 1C *156*
  SK16: Duk 1A *120*
Warwick Ct. M16: Old T 4G *113*
  M24: Mid 1C *72*
  M34: Dent 1G *135*
  (off Wordsworth Rd.)
  SK4: Stoc 5F *133*

Warwick Dr. M33: Sale 5D *128*
  M41: Urm 3D *110*
  SK7: H Gro 5D *158*
  WA15: Hale 4G *151*
Warwick Gdns. BL3: Bolt 5H *47*
Warwick Gro. M34: Aud 5C *104*
Warwick Ho. *M19: Man* 5C *116*
  (off Central Av.)
  M33: Sale 5D *128*
  (off Temple Rd.)
Warwick Mall SK8: Chea 5H *143*
Warwick Rd. M16: Old T 2F *113*
  M21: Chor 6H *113*
  M24: Mid 3D *72*
  M26: Rad 1H *51*
  M28: Wors 2G *81*
  M35: Fail 6H *89*
  M44: Cad 4B *124*
  OL6: A Lyme 6A *92*
  SK4: Stoc 6E *133*
  SK6: Rom 1G *147*
  WA15: Hale 4G *151*
Warwick Rd. Sth. M16: Old T 4G *113*
Warwick St. BL1: Bolt 1C *32*
  M1: Man 4C 6 (3F *101*)
  M15: Man 6G 9 (2D *114*)
  M25: Pres 5G *69*
  M27: Pen 2H *83*
  OL9: O'ham 5C *74*
  (not continuous)
  OL12: Roch 1B *28*
Warwick Ter. *SK16: Duk* 4H *105*
  (off Hill St.)
Wasdale Av. BL2: Bolt 4B *34*
  M41: Urm 4D *110*
Wasdale Dr. M24: Mid 5A *56*
  SK8: Gat 2F *155*
Wasdale Rd. M23: Wyth 1F *153*
Wasdale Ter. SK15: Stal 1E *107*
Wasdale Wlk.
  OL1: O'ham 1H 177 (1H *75*)
Washbrook OL9: Chad 5B *74*
Washbrook Av. M28: Wors 2F *81*
Washbrook Cl. OL9: Chad 5B *74*
Washbrook Dr. M32: Stre 6B *112*
Wash Brow BL8: Bury 1B *36*
Wash Fold BL8: Bury 6B *22*
Washford Dr. M23: Wyth 3D *140*
Washington Cl. SK8: Chea H 5B *156*
Washington St. BL3: Bolt 1A *48*
  OL9: O'ham 2C *74*
Wash La. BL9: Bury 2G *37*
Wash La. Ter. BL9: Bury 3H *37*
Wash Ter. BL8: Bury 6B *22*
Washway Rd. M33: Sale 2G *139*
Washwood Cl. *M38: Lit H* 3F *65*
  (off Wallbrook Cres.)
Wasnidge Wlk. M15: Man 6H 9
Wasp Av. OL11: Roch 2A *42*
Wasp Mill Dr. OL12: W'le 6C *16*
Wastdale Av. BL9: Bury 4G *53*
Wastdale Rd. M23: Wyth 1F *153*
Waste St. OL1: O'ham 2G *75*
Wast Water St. OL1: O'ham 6G *59*
Watchgate Cl. M24: Mid 4H *55*
Watchgate La. SK7: H Gro 3C *158*
Waterbridge M28: Wors 6B *82*
Watercroft OL11: Roch 2H *25*
Waterdale Cl. M28: Wors 5F *81*
Waterdale Dr. M45: White 1G *69*
Waterfield Cl. BL9: Bury 4F *23*
Waterfield Way M35: Fail 5A *90*
Waterfold Bus. Pk. BL9: Bury 4H *37*
Waterfold La. BL9: Bury 4A *38*
Waterfold Pk. BL9: Bury 4H *37*
Waterfoot Cotts. *SK14: Mot* 3C *122*
  (off Rushycroft)
Waterford Av. M20: Man 6B *130*
  SK6: Rom 1D *148*
Waterford Pl. SK8: H Grn 5F *155*
Waterfront, The M11: Man 3C *102*
Waterfront Ho. M30: Ecc 2E *97*
Waterfront Quay M50: Sal 6F *99*

Water Ga. OL3: Upp 1D *78*
Watergate M34: Aud 5C *104*
Watergate Dr. BL5: O Hul 2A *64*
Watergate La. BL5: O Hul 1A *64*
Watergate Milne Ct.
  OL4: O'ham 1B *76*
Watergrove Reservoir Vis. Cen. 4C *16*
Water Gro. Rd. SK16: Duk 6D *106*
WATERHEAD 6C *60*
Waterhead Av. M40: O'ham 1C *76*
Waterhouse Cl. OL12: W'le 4C *16*
Waterhouse Rd. M18: Man 3G *117*
Waterhouse St.
  OL12: Roch 2B 178 (3H *27*)
Waterhouse Way SK5: Stoc 2G *133*
Water La. BL0: Ram 3G *13*
  BL4: Kea .2A *66*
  M26: Rad 4H *51*
  M43: Droy 4G *103*
  (not continuous)
  OL3: Del .1D *62*
  OL16: Miln 6G *29*
  SK9: Wilm 2D *172*
  SK13: Had 3G *123*
  SK14: Holl 2F *123*
Water La. St. M26: Rad 4H *51*
  (not continuous)
WATERLOO .6G *91*
Waterloo Cotts. SK6: Rom 1C *148*
Waterloo Ct. BL9: Bury 5E *37*
  M20: Man 4E *131*
  (off Lapwing La.)
  SK15: Stal 3D *106*
  (off Hully St.)
Waterloo Gdns. OL6: A Lyme 6C *92*
Waterloo Ind. Est.
  SK1: Stoc 3H 179 (2H *145*)
Waterloo Ind. Pk.
  BL1: Bolt 1H 175 (5E *33*)
Waterloo Pl. SK1: Stoc 3H *179*
Waterloo Rd. M8: Man 6D *86*
  OL6: A Lyme 6H *91*
  SK1: Stoc 3H 179 (2H *145*)
  SK6: Rom 1C *148*
  SK7: Bram 4H *157*
  SK12: Poy 5G *169*
  SK15: Stal 3E *107*
Waterloo St. BL1: Bolt 1H 175 (4D *32*)
  BL8: Bury 3D *36*
  M1: Man 1A 10 (5E *101*)
  M8: Man 3G *87*
  M9: Man 3G *87*
  OL1: O'ham 3H 177 (2F *75*)
  OL4: O'ham 5H 177 (3G *75*)
  OL6: A Lyme 1B *106*
Watermans Cl. M9: Man 3B *88*
Waterman Vw. OL16: Roch 3C *28*
Watermead M33: Sale 2A *140*
Watermead Cl. SK3: Stoc 1G *157*
Water Mead Works BL1: Bolt 4E *33*
Watermeetings La. SK6: Rom 1C *148*
Watermill Cl. OL16: Roch 5D *28*
Water Mill Clough OL2: O'ham 5C *58*
Watermill Ct. OL7: A Lyme 6G *91*
Watermillock Gdns. BL1: Bolt 1D *32*
Waterpark Hall *M7: Sal* 2C *86*
  (off Montpellier M.)
Waterpark Rd. M7: Sal 3C *86*
Water Rd. SK15: Stal 3D *106*
Waters Edge BL4: Farn 5E *49*
  M28: Walk 1B *82*
  OL3: G'fld 4C *78*
  OL5: Mos 5A *78*
  OL6: A Lyme 6C *92*
  SK6: Mar B 2E *149*
Waters Edge Bus. Pk. M5: Sal 1H *113*
Watersedge Cl. SK8: Chea H 2D *156*
Waters Edge Fold OL1: O'ham 3A *60*
Watersfield Cl. SK8: Chea H 5B *156*
WATERSHEDDINGS 6A *60*
Watersheddings St. OL4: O'ham 6B *60*
Watersheddings Way
  OL4: O'ham 6B *60*

Waterside BL3: Bolt	. . . .	.3G 49
M17: T Pk	. . . .	.1F 113
M33: Sale	. . . .	.4C 128
OL3: G'fld	. . . .	.5E 79
SK6: Mar	. . . .	.1D 160
SK13: Had	. . . .	.1H 123
SK14: Hat	. . . .	.6H 121
Waterside Arts Cen.	. . . .	.4B 128
Waterside Av. SK6: Mar	. . . .	.6D 148
Waterside Bus. Pk. SK13: Had	. . . .	.1H 123
Waterside Cl. M21: Chor	. . . .	.5B 130
M26: Rad	. . . .	.3D 52
OL1: O'ham	. . . .	.3A 60
SK14: Hat	. . . .	.5H 121
Waterside Ct. M41: Urm	. . . .	.5H 109
Waterside Ho. M28: Wors	. . . .	.6C 82
Waterside Ind. Pk. BL3: Bolt	. . . . . .	.3H 49
Waterside La. OL16: Roch	. . . .	.3B 28
Waterside Plaza M33: Sale	. . . . . .	.4B 128
		(off Tatton Rd.)
Waterside Rd. BL9: Sum	. . . .	.1B 24
SK12: Dis	. . . .	.6H 161
Waterside Vw. M43: Droy	. . . .	.5G 103
Waterside Wlk. SK14: Hat	. . . .	.5G 121
Waterslea M30: Ecc	. . . .	.3E 97
Waterslea Dr. BL1: Bolt	. . . .	.5F 31
Watersmead Cl. BL1: Bolt	. . . .	.3D 32
Watersmead St. BL1: Bolt	. . . .	.3D 32
Watersmeet M32: Stre	. . . .	.3D 112
Waters Meeting Rd. BL1: Bolt	. . . . .	.2D 32
WATER'S NOOK	. . . .	.6A 46
Water's Nook Rd. BL5: W'ton	. . . . .	.6A 46
Waterson Av. M40: Man	. . . .	.4C 88
Waters Reach M17: T Pk	. . . .	.1F 113
SK6: H Lan	. . . .	.6C 160
SK12: Poy	. . . .	.2F 169
Water St. BL0: Ram	. . . .	.4B 12
BL1: Bolt	. . . .	.3G 175 (6D 32)
BL7: Eger	. . . .	.1B 18
M3: Man	. . . .	.2C 8 (5B 100)
		(not continuous)
M9: Man	. . . .	.3H 87
M12: Man	. . . .	.2F 11
M24: Mid	. . . .	.1B 72
		(not continuous)
M26: Rad	. . . .	.4H 51
M34: Aud	. . . .	.6F 105
M34: Dent	. . . .	.3C 118
OL2: O'ham	. . . .	.3G 59
OL6: A Lyme	. . . .	.5B 174 (2H 105)
OL12: Whitw	. . . .	.1E 15
OL16: Miln	. . . .	.5F 29
OL16: Roch	. . . .	.3C 178 (4H 27)
SK1: Stoc	. . . .	.1H 145
SK14: Hyde	. . . .	.4B 120
SK15: Stal	. . . .	.3E 107
Waterton Av. OL5: Mos	. . . .	.1F 93
Waterton La. OL5: Mos	. . . .	.1F 93
Waterview OL16: Miln	. . . .	.2H 43
Waterway Ent. Pk. M17: T Pk	. . . . .	.1F 113
Waterworks Rd. OL3: Del	. . . .	.1C 62
OL4: O'ham	. . . .	.6C 60
Watfield Wlk. M9: Man	. . . .	.4H 87
		(off Foleshill Av.)
Watford Av. M14: Man	. . . .	.5F 115
Watford Cl. BL1: Bolt	. . . .	.3C 32
		(off Chesham Av.)
Watford Rd. M19: Man	. . . .	.3C 132
Watkin Av. SK13: Had	. . . .	.3G 123
Watkin Cl. M13: Man	. . . . .	.6E 11 (1G 115)
Watkins Dr. M25: Pres	. . . .	.6C 70
Watkin St. M3: Sal	. . . . . .	.1D 4 (2C 100)
OL16: Roch	. . . .	.1A 42
SK14: Hyde	. . . .	.2E 121
Watling Ga. WA14: Tim	. . . .	.2G 139
Watling St. BL8: Aff	. . . .	.1B 20
BL8: Bury	. . . .	.4H 35
Watlington Cl. OL1: O'ham	. . . . . .	.4B 60
Watson Gdns. OL12: Roch	. . . . . .	.1F 27
Watson Rd. BL4: Farn	. . . .	.1D 64
Watsons M. SK9: Wilm	. . . .	.2E 173
Watson Sq.		
SK1: Stoc	. . . .	.3H 179 (2H 145)

Watson St. M3: Man	. . . . . .	.2G 9 (5D 100)
M26: Rad	. . . .	.3A 52
M27: Swin	. . . .	.2H 83
M30: Ecc	. . . .	.3E 97
M34: Dent	. . . .	.4H 119
OL4: O'ham	. . . .	.1A 76
Watton Cl. M27: Pen	. . . .	.1H 83
		(off Hinchley Way)
Watts St. M19: Man	. . . .	.1D 132
OL8: O'ham	. . . .	.1D 90
OL9: Chad	. . . .	.2B 74
OL12: Roch	. . . . . .	.1D 178 (3A 28)
Waugh Av. M35: Fail	. . . .	.5H 89
Wavell Dr. BL9: Bury	. . . .	.6G 53
Wavell Rd. M22: Wyth	. . . .	.3B 154
Waveney Dr. SK9: Wilm	. . . .	.5H 165
WA14: Alt	. . . .	.5E 139
Waveney Flats OL10: H'ood	. . . . . .	.3G 39
		(off Fox St.)
Waveney Rd. M22: Wyth	. . . . . .	.1C 154
OL2: Shaw	. . . .	.5G 43
Waverley Cl. OL12: Roch	. . . . . .	.1A 178
Waverley Av. BL4: Kea	. . . .	.3B 66
M32: Stre	. . . .	.4E 113
Waverley Ct. M9: Man	. . . .	.4E 71
Waverley Cres. M43: Droy	. . . . .	.2A 104
Waverley Dr. SK8: Chea H	. . . . .	.1D 166
Waverley Pl. M26: Rad	. . . .	.4A 52
Waverley Rd. BL1: Bolt	. . . .	.2C 32
M9: Man	. . . .	.4B 88
M24: Mid	. . . .	.4C 56
M27: Pen	. . . .	.4C 84
M28: Wors	. . . .	.2F 81
M33: Sale	. . . .	.3C 128
SK3: Stoc	. . . .	.4E 145
SK14: Hyde	. . . .	.1B 136
Waverley Rd. W. M9: Man	. . . . .	.4B 88
Waverley Sq. BL4: Farn	. . . . . .	.3G 65
Waverley St. OL1: O'ham	. . . . .	.1H 75
OL11: Roch	. . . .	.4E 41
Waverton Av. SK4: Stoc	. . . . .	.2F 133
Waverton Rd. M14: Man	. . . . .	.6E 115
Wavertree Ct. BL1: Bolt	. . . . . .	.1E 175
Wavertree Rd. M9: Man	. . . . . .	.5G 71
Waybridge Ind. Est. M50: Sal	. . . .	.5D 98
Wayfarers Way M27: Swin	. . . . .	.4G 83
Wayfaring BL5: W'ton	. . . .	.5A 46
Wayford Wlk. M9: Man	. . . . . .	.4G 87
		(off Hendham Va.)
Wayland Rd. M18: Man	. . . . . .	.3F 117
Wayland Rd. Sth. M18: Man	. . . .	.4F 117
Wayne Cl. M43: Droy	. . . .	.1C 104
Wayne St. M11: Man	. . . .	.5G 103
Wayside Dr. SK12: Poy	. . . . . .	.3C 168
Wayside Gdns. SK7: H Gro	. . . .	.3G 159
Wayside Gro. M28: Walk	. . . . . .	.5A 66
Weald Cl. M13: Man	. . . . .	.5E 11 (1G 115)
Wealdstone Gro. BL2: Bolt	. . . . .	.3F 33
		(off Scawfell Av.)
Weardale Rd. M9: Man	. . . . . .	.4F 71
Wearhead Row M5: Sal	. . . . . .	.4F 99
WEASTE	. . . .	.3D 98
Weaste Av. M38: Lit H	. . . . . .	.5F 65
Weaste Dr. M5: Sal	. . . .	.2D 98
Weaste La. M5: Sal	. . . .	.3D 98
M6: Sal	. . . .	.2C 98
Weaste Rd. M5: Sal	. . . .	.3D 98
Weaste Station (Metro)	. . . . . .	.4D 98
Weaste Trad. Est. M5: Sal	. . . . .	.3D 98
Weatherall St. Nth. M7: Sal	. . . .	.4D 86
Weatherley Cl. OL8: O'ham	. . . .	.2F 91
Weatherley Dr. SK6: Mar	. . . . .	.5B 148
Weaver Av. M28: Walk	. . . . . .	.1E 81
Weaver Cl. WA14: Bow	. . . . .	.4E 151
Weaver Ct. M15: Man	. . . .	.6C 8
Weaver Dr. BL9: Bury	. . . .	.3F 23
Weaverham Cl. M13: Man	. . . .	.4B 116
Weaverham Wlk. M33: Sale	. . . .	.6E 129
		(off Mottram Rd.)
Weaverham Way		
SK9: Hand	. . . .	.3A 166
Weaver Ho. M7: Sal	. . . .	.6A 86
		(off Victoria Lodge)

Weavers Ct. BL3: Bolt	. . . .	.2C 48
M24: Mid	. . . .	.6B 56
SK14: Mot	. . . .	.3C 122
Weavers Grn. BL4: Farn	. . . . . .	.2H 65
Weavers La. SK7: Bram	. . . . . .	.1F 167
Weavers Rd. M24: Mid	. . . . . .	.6B 56
Weaver Wlk. M11: Man	. . . . . .	.6F 103
		(off Ogden La.)
Webb Gro. SK14: Hat	. . . .	.6A 122
Webb La. SK1: Stoc	. . . .	.3A 146
		(not continuous)
Webb St. BL8: Bury	. . . .	.2D 36
Webbdale Dr. M40: Man	. . . . . .	.4C 88
Weber Dr. BL3: Bolt	. . . .	.2B 48
Webster Gro. M25: Pres	. . . . . .	.1F 85
Webster St. BL3: Bolt	. . . .	.3F 49
OL5: Mos	. . . .	.1G 93
OL8: O'ham	. . . . . .	.6G 177 (4F 75)
Wedgewood St. M40: Man	. . . . .	.1B 102
Wedgwood Rd. M27: Clif	. . . . . .	.1C 84
Wedhurst St. OL4: O'ham	. . . . .	.2A 76
Wedneshough Grn. SK14: Holl	. . .	.2E 123
Weedall Av. M5: Sal	. . . .	.1G 113
Weeder Sq. OL2: Shaw	. . . . . .	.5C 44
Weedon St. OL16: Roch	. . . . . .	.3B 28
Weeton Av. BL2: Bolt	. . . .	.6B 34
Weighbridge Ct. M44: Irl	. . . . .	.4G 109
Weir Rd. OL16: Miln	. . . .	.4E 29
Weir St. M15: Man	. . . .	.2C 114
M35: Fail	. . . .	.4G 89
Welbeck Av. M41: Urm	. . . . . .	.4G 111
OL9: Chad	. . . .	.6F 73
OL15: L'ough	. . . .	.3G 17
Welbeck Cl. M45: White	. . . . . .	.5F 53
OL16: Miln	. . . .	.5E 29
Welbeck Gro. M7: Sal	. . . .	.4C 86
Welbeck Ho.		
OL6: A Lyme	. . . . .	.6A 174 (3G 105)
Welbeck Rd. BL1: Bolt	. . . . . .	.5G 31
M28: Wors	. . . .	.5D 82
M30: Ecc	. . . .	.1G 97
OL6: A Lyme	. . . .	.1B 42
SK5: Stoc	. . . .	.6H 117
SK14: Hyde	. . . .	.5D 120
Welbeck St. M18: Man	. . . . . .	.1G 117
Welbeck St. Nth.		
OL6: A Lyme	. . . . .	.6A 174 (3G 105)
Welbeck St. Sth.		
OL6: A Lyme	. . . . .	.6A 174 (3G 105)
		(not continuous)
OL7: A Lyme	. . . .	.3G 105
Welbeck Ter.		
OL6: A Lyme	. . . . .	.6A 174 (3G 105)
Welburn Av. M22: Wyth	. . . . . .	.2C 154
Welburn St. OL11: Roch	. . . . . .	.6H 27
Welby Rd. M23: Wyth	. . . . . .	.2F 141
Welby St. M13: Man	. . . .	.3H 115
Welch Rd. SK14: Hyde	. . . . . .	.3D 120
Welcomb Cl. SK6: Bred	. . . . . .	.5F 135
Welcomb St. M11: Man	. . . . . .	.6D 102
Welcomb Wlk. M45: White	. . . . .	.2F 69
Welcome Pde. OL8: O'ham	. . . .	.6A 76
Welcroft St. SK1: Stoc	. . .	.4H 179 (3H 145)
Weldon Av. BL3: Bolt	. . . .	.5G 47
Weldon Cres. SK3: Stoc	. . . . . .	.1G 157
Weldon Dr. M9: Man	. . . .	.4H 71
Weldon Rd. WA14: Alt	. . . . . .	.5E 139
Weld Rd. M20: Man	. . . .	.2H 131
Welfold Ho. OL4: O'ham	. . . . .	.4H 75
Welford Cl. SK9: Wilm	. . . . . .	.1H 173
Welford Grn. SK5: Stoc	. . . . .	.4H 133
Welford Rd. M8: Man	. . . .	.6D 70
Welford St. M6: Sal	. . . .	.1H 99
Welkin Rd. SK6: Bred	. . . . . .	.6C 134
Welkin Rd. Ind. Est.		
SK6: Bred	. . . .	.6C 134
Wellacre Av. M41: Urm	. . . . . .	.5H 109
Welland Av. OL10: H'ood	. . . . .	.2E 39
Welland Cl. M15: Man	. . . . .	.6C 8 (1B 114)
Welland Ct. M15: Man	. . . . . .	.6C 8
Welland Rd. OL2: Shaw	. . . . . .	.5G 43
SK9: Chea, Wilm	. . . . . .	.5H 165

Welland St. M11: Man	5F **103**
SK5: Stoc	6H **117**
Wellbank M25: Pres	6F **69**
SK15: Stal	5H **107**
Wellbank Av. OL6: A Lyme	5C **92**
Wellbank Cl. BL3: Lit L	4D **50**
OL8: O'ham	5G **75**
Wellbank St. BL8: Tot	5H **21**
Wellbank Vw. OL12: Roch	2B **26**
Wellbridge Rd. SK16: Duk	1H **119**
Well Brow OL3: Del	3B **62**
(off King St.)
Well Brow Ter. OL12: Roch	2F **27**
Wellbrow Wlk. M9: Man	6A **72**
(off Haverfield Rd.)
Wellburn Pl. BL3: Bolt	5F **47**
Welldale M. M33: Sale	4E **129**
Wellens Way M24: Mid	2G **71**
Weller Av. M21: Chor	2B **130**
SK12: Poy	5D **168**
Weller Cl. SK12: Poy	5D **168**
Weller Gdns. M21: Chor	2B **130**
Wellesbourne Dr. M23: Wyth	4F **141**
Wellesley Av. M18: Man	1F **117**
Wellfield SK6: Rom	5A **136**
Wellfield Cl. BL9: Bury	1E **53**
Wellfield Gdns. WA15: Hale	2C **152**
Wellfield La.
WA15: Hale, Tim	1C **152**
Wellfield Pl. OL11: Roch	6A **28**
Wellfield Rd. BL3: Bolt	2A **48**
M8: Man	3E **87**
M23: Wyth	4G **141**
SK2: Stoc	5C **146**
Wellfield St. OL11: Roch	6A **28**
Wellgate Av. M19: Man	1D **132**
WELL GREEN	2C **152**
Wellgreen Cl. WA15: Hale	2C **152**
Well Green Lodge WA15: Hale	2C **152**
(off Wellfield La.)
Well Gro. M45: White	5E **53**
Wellhead Cl. M15: Man	2D **114**
Wellhouse Dr. M40: Man	6E **73**
Well-i-Hole Rd. OL3: G'fld	3A **78**
Welling Rd. M40: Man	3G **89**
Welling St. BL2: Bolt	4F **33**
Wellington Av. M16: W Ran	5B **114**
Wellington Cen. OL6: A Lyme	3A **106**
Wellington Cl. M33: Sale	3C **128**
Wellington Clough
OL7: A Lyme	5F **91**
BL8: Tot	5H **21**
OL6: A Lyme	2A **106**
(off Adam St.)
OL8: O'ham	5D **74**
(off Frederick St.)
Wellington Cres. M16: Old T	4A **114**
Wellington Dr. M29: Tyld	2C **80**
Wellington Gdns. BL8: Bury	4B **36**
Wellington Gro. M15: Man	6D **8** (1B **114**)
SK2: Stoc	4H **145**
Wellington Ho. BL8: Bury	4B **36**
(off Haig Rd.)
M20: Man	2G **131**
(off Wilmslow Rd.)
M32: Stre	6C **112**
(off Sandy La.)
Wellington Lodge OL15: L'ough	3H **17**
(off Lodge St.)
Wellington Mill SK3: Stoc	3F **179**
Wellington Pde. SK16: Duk	4H **105**
(off Queen St.)
Wellington Pl. M3: Man	1E **9**
OL16: Roch	3A **28**
WA14: Alt	3A **174** (1F **151**)
Wellington Rd. BL9: Bury	6B **176** (5E **37**)
M8: Man	3F **87**
M14: Man	2G **131**
M16: W Ran	5C **114**
M20: Man	2G **131**
M27: Swin	3H **83**
M30: Ecc	3G **97**

Wellington Rd. OL3: G'fld	3C **78**
OL6: A Lyme	4A **174** (2G **105**)
(not continuous)
OL8: O'ham	6E **177** (5C **74**)
SK7: H Gro	5H **159**
WA15: Tim	5G **139**
Wellington Rd. Nth.
SK4: Stoc	1E **179** (2D **132**)
Wellington Rd. Sth.
SK1: Stoc	3F **179** (2G **145**)
SK2: Stoc	3F **179** (2G **145**)
SK3: Stoc	3F **179** (2G **145**)
Wellington Sq. BL8: Bury	4B **36**
Wellington St. BL3: Bolt	1B **48**
BL4: Farn	1H **65**
BL8: Bury	4C **36**
M3: Sal	3D **4** (3B **100**)
M18: Man	2F **117**
M26: Rad	3C **52**
(not continuous)
M32: Stre	6C **112**
M34: Aud	1F **119**
M35: Fail	2A **90**
OL1: O'ham	4H **177** (3F **75**)
OL4: O'ham	5G **177** (3F **75**)
OL6: A Lyme	6B **174** (3H **105**)
OL9: Chad	1B **74**
OL12: Roch	2H **27**
(not continuous)
OL15: L'ough	4H **17**
OL16: Miln	5G **29**
SK1: Stoc	3F **179** (2G **145**)
SK7: H Gro	2F **159**
SK14: Hyde	4A **120**
Wellington St. E. M7: Sal	4B **86**
Wellington St. W. M7: Sal	5B **86**
Wellington Ter. M5: Sal	3D **98**
OL15: L'ough	4H **17**
(off Lodge St.)
SK16: Duk	4H **105**
(off Queen St.)
Wellington Vs. BL8: Bury	4C **36**
Wellington Wlk. BL3: Bolt	1C **48**
Well i' th' La. OL11: Roch	6A **28**
Well La. M45: White	5F **53**
Well Mead SK6: Bred	6E **135**
Wellmead Cl. M8: Man	6D **86**
Well Mdw. SK14: Hyde	3B **120**
Well Mdw. Ct. SK14: Hyde	3B **120**
(off Well Mdw.)
Wellmeadow La. OL3: Upp	1E **79**
Wellpark Wlk. M40: Man	6E **89**
(off Langcroft Dr.)
Wells Av. M25: Pres	1A **86**
OL9: Chad	6A **58**
Wells Cl. M24: Mid	2G **71**
M29: Ast	3A **80**
M43: Droy	5H **103**
SK8: H Grn	6G **155**
Wells Ct. SK16: Duk	1A **120**
Wells Dr. SK4: Stoc	1A **144**
SK16: Duk	1A **120**
Wellside Wlk. M8: Man	5E **87**
(off Dinnington Dr.)
Wells Rd. OL1: O'ham	2C **60**
Wells St. BL9: Bury	6A **176** (4E **37**)
Wellstock La. M38: Lit H	3D **64**
Well St. BL1: Bolt	3H **175** (6E **33**)
BL2: Ain	4E **35**
M4: Man	4A **6**
OL10: H'ood	4A **40**
OL11: Roch	6A **28**
Well St. Nth. BL0: Ram	3F **13**
Well St. W. BL0: Ram	4B **12**
(off Holt St. W.)
Wellwood Dr. M40: Man	4C **88**
Wellyhole St. OL4: O'ham	3B **76**
Welman Way WA15: Alt	3D **174** (1H **151**)
Welney Rd. M16: Old T	4H **113**
Welshpool Cl. M23: Wyth	1H **141**
Welshpool Way M34: Dent	6G **119**
Welton Av. M20: Man	1G **143**
Welton Cl. SK9: Wilm	5C **172**

Welton Dr. SK9: Wilm	5B **172**
Welton Gro. SK9: Wilm	5B **172**
Welwyn Cl. M41: Urm	2D **110**
Welwyn Dr. M6: Sal	6A **84**
Welwyn Wlk. M40: Man	3G **7**
Wembley Cl. SK3: Stoc	6F **145**
Wembley Gro. M14: Man	1G **131**
Wembley Rd. M18: Man	4E **117**
Wembury St. M9: Man	3A **88**
Wembury St. Nth. M9: Man	3A **88**
Wembury Wlk. SK14: Hat	4A **122**
(off Cambourne Rd.)
Wemsley Gro. BL2: Bolt	4F **33**
Wem St. OL9: Chad	5A **74**
Wemyss Av. SK5: Stoc	6H **117**
Wendlebury Grn. OL2: O'ham	2G **59**
Wendon Rd. M23: Wyth	6H **141**
Wendover Dr. BL3: Bolt	2E **47**
Wendover Ho. M5: Sal	4G **99**
Wendover Rd. M23: Wyth	2D **140**
M41: Urm	5E **111**
Wenfield Dr. M9: Man	6D **72**
Wenlock Av. OL6: A Lyme	6H **91**
Wenlock Cl. SK2: Stoc	5G **147**
Wenlock Ct. M12: Man	1B **116**
(off Wenlock Way)
Wenlock Rd. M33: Sale	1A **140**
Wenlock St. M27: Swin	3F **83**
Wenlock Way M12: Man	1B **116**
Wenning Cl. M45: White	6A **54**
Wensley Ct. M7: Sal	2G **85**
(off Wensley Rd.)
Wensleydale Av. SK8: Chea	5G **143**
Wensleydale Cl. BL9: Bury	4G **53**
M23: Wyth	2F **153**
OL2: O'ham	2C **58**
Wensley Dr. M20: Man	4F **131**
SK7: H Gro	6D **158**
Wensley Rd. M7: Sal	3G **85**
SK5: Stoc	5H **133**
SK8: Chea	5G **143**
Wensley Way OL16: Roch	5C **28**
Wentbridge Rd. BL1: Bolt	5B **32**
Wentworth Av. BL4: Farn	2G **65**
BL8: Bury	1B **36**
M6: Sal	2C **98**
M18: Man	1G **117**
M41: Urm	6D **110**
M44: Irl	4E **109**
M45: White	2D **68**
OL10: H'ood	5H **39**
WA15: Tim	5A **140**
Wentworth Cl. M24: Mid	1A **72**
M26: Rad	3F **51**
SK6: Mar	3D **148**
Wentworth Cl. M35: Fail	5H **89**
M45: White	1E **69**
Wentworth Dr. M33: Sale	4H **127**
SK7: Bram	6A **158**
Wentworth Rd. M27: Swin	5F **83**
M30: Ecc	1A **98**
SK5: Stoc	5D **134**
Wentworth Wlk. SK14: Hyde	2D **120**
WERNETH	5C **74**
Werneth Av. M14: Man	5F **115**
SK14: Hyde	1D **136**
Werneth Cl. M34: Dent	5F **119**
SK7: H Gro	1E **159**
Werneth Ct. SK14: Hyde	6C **120**
(off Stockport Rd.)
Werneth Cres. OL8: O'ham	5C **74**
Werneth Hall Rd.
OL8: O'ham	6E **177** (4D **74**)
Werneth Hollow SK6: Wood	3H **135**
Werneth Low Country Pk.	1F **137**
Werneth Low Rd. SK6: Rom	5B **136**
SK14: Hyde	5B **136**
Werneth Recreation Cen.	1F **147**
Werneth Ri. SK14: Hyde	2D **136**
Werneth Rd. SK6: Wood	4H **135**
SK14: Hyde	5D **120**
Werneth St. M34: Aud	2F **119**
SK1: Stoc	1B **146**

Werneth Vw. SK7: H Gro 5H **159**
Werneth Wlk. *M34: Dent* 5F **119**
         (off Werneth Cl.)
Wesley Cl. OL12: Roch 6B **16**
Wesley Ct. BL8: Tot 5G **21**
  M28: Walk 5G **65**
         (off Mountain St.)
  SK4: Stoc 1B **144**
Wesley Dr. M28: Wors 3B **82**
  OL6: A Lyme 5B **92**
Wesley Ho. BL8: Tot 4G **21**
Wesley M. BL2: Bolt 6E **33**
Wesley Mt. *SK4: Stoc* 1G **145**
         (off Dodge Hill)
Wesleys, The BL4: Farn 1D **64**
Wesley Sq. M41: Urm 5C **110**
Wesley St. BL3: Bolt 2C **48**
  BL4: Farn 2A **66**
  BL7: Bro X 3E **19**
  BL8: Tot 4G **21**
  M11: Man 5C **102**
  M27: Swin 3H **83**
  M30: Ecc 3E **97**
  M32: Stre 4E **113**
  M35: Fail 2A **90**
         (not continuous)
  OL2: O'ham 4E **59**
  OL10: H'ood 3G **39**
  OL12: Roch 6B **16**
  OL16: Miln 5E **29**
  SK1: Stoc 3H **179** (2H **145**)
  SK7: H Gro 2E **159**
  SK13: Had 2H **123**
Wessenden Bank E. SK2: Stoc 6D **146**
Wessenden Bank W. SK2: Stoc 6D **146**
Wessex Pk. Cl. OL2: Shaw 5H **43**
Wessington Bank *SK13: Gam* 5G **123**
         (off Hathersage Cres.)
Wessington Fold *SK13: Gam* 5G **123**
         (off Wessington M.)
Wessington Grn. *SK13: Gam* 5G **123**
         (off Wessington M.)
Wessington M. SK13: Gam 5G **123**
Westage Gdns. M23: Wyth 4G **141**
W. Ashton St. M50: Sal 4F **99**
West Av. BL4: Farn 1F **65**
  M18: Man 2G **117**
  M19: Man 2B **132**
  M28: Walk 6G **65**
  M40: Man 3F **89**
  M45: White 5E **53**
  OL12: Roch 6C **16**
  SK8: H Grn 4G **155**
  SK15: Stal 3E **107**
  WA14: Alt 6C **138**
West Bank M11: Man 6A **104**
  SK9: A Edg 6G **173**
Westbank Rd. BL6: Los 1D **46**
  M20: Man 4H **131**
W. Bank St. M5: Sal 1A **8** (5A **100**)
Westbourne Av. BL3: Bolt 4E **49**
  M27: Clif 4F **67**
  M45: White 6D **52**
Westbourne Gro. OL7: A Lyme 1G **105**
  SK9: Wilm 1G **173**
Westbourne Gro. M9: Man 3H **87**
  M20: Man 3E **131**
  M33: Sale 5A **128**
  SK5: Stoc 1H **133**
Westbourne Pk. M41: Urm 4F **111**
Westbourne Range M18: Man 3H **117**
Westbourne Rd. M14: Man 1H **131**
  M30: Ecc 2D **96**
  M34: Dent 5E **119**
  M41: Urm 5F **111**
Westbourne St. OL9: O'ham 2D **74**
Westbrook Cl. OL11: Roch 5F **41**
Westbrook Ct. BL2: Bolt 6H **175** (1E **49**)
  M18: Man 4G **117**
Westbrook Rd. M17: T Pk 6C **98**
  M27: Swin 4G **83**
Westbrook Sq. M12: Man 1C **116**
Westbrook St. BL2: Bolt . . .6H **175** (1E **49**)

Westbrook Trad. Est. M17: T Pk 6D **98**
Westbrook Wlk. M20: Man 1E **131**
Westbury Av. M33: Sale 2E **139**
Westbury Cl. BL5: W'ton 6A **46**
  BL8: Bury 4A **36**
Westbury Dr. SK6: Mar 5C **148**
Westbury Rd. M8: Man 2F **87**
Westbury St. OL6: A Lyme .4D **174** (2A **106**)
  SK14: Hyde 2A **120**
Westbury St. Ind. Est.
  SK14: Hyde 2A **120**
Westbury Way OL2: O'ham 5D **58**
Westby Cl. SK7: Bram 6A **158**
Westby Gro. BL2: Bolt 5G **33**
W. Central Dr. M27: Swin 4B **84**
W. Charles St. M5: Sal 5A **4** (4H **99**)
W. Church St. OL10: H'ood 3G **39**
Westcliffe Ho. OL12: Roch 5D **16**
Westcliffe Rd. BL1: Bolt 5D **18**
Westcombe Building, The
  OL11: Roch 3D **40**
         (off Sydney Barnes Cl.)
Westcombe Dr. BL8: Bury 1C **36**
West Cotts. OL3: G'fld 4B **78**
Westcott Av. M20: Man 3E **131**
Westcott Cl. BL2: Bolt 6A **20**
Westcott Ct. M15: Man 4D **8**
Westcott Gro. OL2: O'ham 2G **59**
Westcourt Rd. BL3: Bolt 5B **48**
  M33: Sale 3H **127**
W. Craig Av. M40: Man 6E **73**
W. Craven St. M5: Sal 6H **99**
West Cres. M24: Mid 2B **72**
W. Croft Ind. Est. M24: Mid 2H **71**
Westcroft Rd. M19: Man 5H **131**
  M20: Man 5H **131**
W. Crown Av. M5: Sal 5H **99**
Westdale Gdns. M19: Man 4C **132**
Westdean Cres. M19: Man 4B **132**
WEST DIDSBURY 4D **130**
Westdown Gdns. OL2: Shaw 5F **43**
W. Downs Rd. SK8: Chea H 2B **156**
West Dr. BL1: Bolt 1E **175** (4C **32**)
  BL9: Bury 6E **23**
  M6: Sal 5E **85**
  M27: Swin 4B **84**
  M43: Droy 4H **103**
  SK8: Gat 1E **155**
  SK13: Tin 1G **123**
W. Duke St. M5: Sal 6C **4**
W. Egerton St. M5: Sal 4H **99**
West End SK14: B'tom 6B **122**
West End Av. SK8: Gat 5E **143**
West End St. OL9: O'ham 2D **74**
West End Trad. Est. M27: Swin 2H **83**
Westerdale OL4: O'ham 3A **76**
         (not continuous)
Westerdale Dr. BL3: Bolt 2G **47**
  OL2: O'ham 2C **58**
Westerham Av. M5: Sal 4G **99**
Westerham Cl. BL8: Bury 4C **22**
Westerhill OL6: A Lyme 3H **91**
Wester Hill Rd. OL8: O'ham 2G **91**
Westerling Way M16: W Ran 4C **114**
Western Av. M27: Clif 1D **84**
Western Circ. M19: Man 3B **132**
Western Pk. M50: Sal 5E **99**
Western Rd. M41: Urm 6A **110**
Western St. M6: Sal 2E **99**
  M18: Man 1G **117**
Westerton Ct. BL3: Bolt 2B **48**
Westfield M6: Sal 1E **99**
  WA14: Alt 2E **151**
Westfield Av. M24: Mid 2C **72**
Westfield Cl. OL11: Roch 2B **26**
Westfield Dr. OL4: Gras 4A **78**
  SK6: Wood 4A **136**
Westfield Gro. M34: Aud 2E **119**
Westfield Rd. BL3: Bolt 5H **47**
  M21: Chor 6H **113**
  M43: Droy 3G **103**
  SK8: Chea H 3B **156**

Westfields WA15: Hale 5H **151**
Westfield St. BL4: Farn 1F **65**
  M7: Sal 2B **86**
  OL9: Chad 1C **74**
Westford Villa SK8: Chea 6G **143**
Westgate M33: Sale 5A **128**
  M41: Urm 6D **110**
  OL12: Whitw 2D **14**
  SK9: Wilm 4D **172**
  WA15: Hale 3G **151**
Westgate Av. BL0: Ram 1A **22**
  BL1: Bolt 4A **32**
  BL9: Bury 6A **176** (4E **37**)
  M9: Man 1G **87**
Westgate Cl. OL12: Whitw 2D **14**
Westgate Dr. M27: Swin 5H **83**
  M29: Ast 5A **80**
Westgate Ho. *OL8: O'ham* 1D **90**
         (off Hollins Rd.)
W. Gate Rd. M90: Man A 1F **163**
Westgate Rd. M6: Sal 6B **84**
Westgate St. OL7: A Lyme 4G **105**
WEST GORTON 1B **116**
West Grn. M24: Mid 2F **71**
West Gro. M13: Man 2H **115**
  M33: Sale 6B **128**
  OL5: Mos 3G **93**
Westgrove Av. BL1: Bolt 5C **18**
West Heaton Bowling & Tennis Club
  . . . . .5C **132**
Westhide Wlk. M9: Man 2B **88**
W. High St. M5: Sal 3G **99**
West Hill OL11: Roch 5G **27**
W. Hill Cl. SK15: Stal 3D **106**
Westholm Av. SK4: Stoc 2D **132**
Westholme Ct. *SK9: A Edg* 4G **173**
         (off Horseshoe La.)
Westholme Rd. M20: Man 4F **131**
  M25: Pres 2A **70**
W. Hope St. M5: Sal 4H **99**
Westhorne Fold *M8: Man* 1C **86**
         (off Counthill Dr.)
Westhoughton Leisure Cen. 6A **46**
WEST HULME 6E **59**
Westhulme Av. OL1: O'ham 6D **58**
Westhulme St. OL1: O'ham 6D **58**
Westhulme Way OL1: O'ham 6C **58**
Westinghouse Rd. M17: T Pk 1A **112**
W. King St. M3: Sal 3E **5** (3C **100**)
Westland Av. BL1: Bolt 4G **31**
  BL4: Farn 3G **65**
  SK1: Stoc 2B **146**
Westland Dr. M9: Man 5H **71**
Westlands M45: White 3F **69**
Westlands, The M27: Pen 5B **84**
West Lea M34: Dent 4G **119**
Westlea Dr. M18: Man 4F **117**
Westleigh SK4: Stoc 5C **132**
Westleigh Dr. M25: Pres 6B **70**
Westleigh St. M9: Man 2A **88**
W. Malling Cl. OL10: H'ood 6B **40**
Westmarsh Cl. *BL1: Bolt* 4C **32**
         (off Kentford Rd.)
W. Marwood St. M7: Sal 5C **86**
Westmead Dr. WA15: Tim 4B **140**
West Meade BL3: Bolt 5B **48**
  M21: Chor 2G **129**
  M25: Pres 1B **86**
  M27: Swin 5G **83**
Westmeade Rd. M28: Walk 4G **65**
West Mdw. SK5: Stoc 6A **118**
Westmere Dr. M9: Man 5G **87**
Westminster Av. BL4: Farn 1G **65**
  M16: W Ran 5A **114**
  M26: Rad 3F **51**
  M45: White 1F **69**
  OL2: O'ham 1C **58**
  OL6: A Lyme 4B **92**
  SK5: Stoc 2G **133**
Westminster Cl.
  M33: Sale 6F **127**
  OL2: Shaw 5H **43**
  SK6: Mar 4B **148**

Westminster Dr. SK8: Chea H 1D 166
   SK9: Wilm 5D 172
Westminster Ho. M3: Sal 3E 5
Westminster Rd. BL1: Bolt 6C 18
   M28: Walk 1H 81
   M30: Ecc 2G 97
   M35: Fail 3B 90
   M41: Urm 3F 111
   WA15: Hale 2A 152
Westminster St. BL4: Farn 1G 65
   BL9: Bury 6B 176 (4E 37)
   M15: Man 4B 8 (6A 100)
   M19: Man 6D 116
   M27: Swin 2F 83
   OL1: O'ham 1H 75
   OL11: Roch 6F 27
Westminster Wlk. BL4: Farn 1G 65
   (off Westminster St.)
Westminster Way SK16: Duk 1A 120
Westmoor Gables SK4: Stoc 5C 132
Westmoreland Cl. WA14: Bow 5D 150
Westmorland Av. OL7: A Lyme 1H 105
   SK16: Duk 5C 106
Westmorland Cl. BL9: Bury 1E 53
   SK5: Stoc 3C 134
Westmorland Dr. OL12: W'le 6D 16
   SK5: Stoc 3B 134
Westmorland Rd. M20: Man 1E 143
   M30: Ecc 6A 84
   M33: Sale 1C 140
   M41: Urm 6E 111
Westmorland Wlk.
   OL2: O'ham 3E 59
   (off Royton Hall Wlk.)
W. Mosley St. M2: Man 6A 6 (4E 101)
West Mt. OL3: G'fld 4B 78
   (off Shaw Hall Bank Rd.)
Westmount Cl. M40: Man 5G 87
W. Oak Pl. SK8: Chea H 4C 156
Weston Av. M27: Clif 5G 67
   M40: Man 2G 89
   M41: Urm 6D 110
   OL16: Roch 1B 42
Weston Ct. M14: Man 5H 115
Weston Dr. M34: Dent 4G 119
   SK8: Chea H 1F 157
W. One Retail Pk. M30: Ecc 3A 98
W. One Way M30: Ecc 4A 98
Weston Gro. M22: Nor 3C 142
   SK4: Stoc 3E 133
Weston Hall M1: Man 2B 10 (5E 101)
Weston Rd. M44: Irl 5E 109
   SK9: Wilm 3G 173
Weston St. BL3: Bolt 3D 48
   OL8: O'ham 5A 76
   OL16: Miln 5E 29
   (not continuous)
   SK5: Stoc 5G 133
West Over SK6: Rom 3G 147
Westover St. M27: Swin 2G 83
West Pde. M33: Sale 6E 127
West Pk. BL1: Bolt 6A 32
   SK14: Hyde 2C 136
West Pk. Av. M34: Dent 5H 119
   SK12: Poy 3A 168
West Pk. Rd. SK1: Stoc 1B 146
   SK7: Bram 3F 157
West Pk. St. M5: Sal 3A 8 (6H 99)
West Pl. M19: Man 2B 132
West Point M16: Old T 2A 114
   (off Chester Rd.)
W. Point Ent. Pk. M17: T Pk 6A 98
W. Point Lodge M19: Man 1B 132
   (off Slade La.)
Westray Cres. M5: Sal 4E 99
Westray Rd. M13: Man 5A 116
Westridge Chase
   OL2: O'ham 2D 58
West Rd. M25: Pres 4F 69
   M41: Urm 6G 97
   WA14: Bow 3E 151
West Row M25: Pres 2F 85

W. Starkey St. OL10: H'ood 2G 39
West St. BL0: Ram 4B 12
   BL1: Bolt 6A 32
   BL4: Farn 6A 50
   M9: Man 6E 71
   M11: Man 3D 102
   M24: Mid 5C 56
   M26: Rad 4A 52
   M35: Fail 4G 89
   OL1: O'ham 3F 177 (2E 75)
   OL4: Lees 4C 76
   OL6: A Lyme 4B 174
   OL9: O'ham 3D 74
   OL10: H'ood 3H 39
   OL15: L'ough 4H 17
   OL16: Roch 1D 178 (3A 28)
   (Ball St.)
   OL16: Roch 4D 28
   (Cross St.)
   SK3: Stoc 2F 145
   SK9: A Edg 5G 173
   SK13: Tin 1H 123
   SK14: Hyde 2B 120
   SK15: Stal 3D 106
   SK16: Duk 4H 105
WEST TIMPERLEY 3E 139
West Twr. M. SK6: Mar 1E 161
W. Towers St. M6: Sal 4F 99
West Va. M26: Rad 2A 52
W. Vale Rd. WA15: Tim 5H 139
West Vw. BL0: Ram 3F 13
   M34: Aud 6E 105
   OL3: Del 1G 61
   OL15: L'ough 4H 17
West Vw. Gro. M45: White 6D 52
West Vw. Rd. M22: Nor 3C 142
Westville Gdns. M19: Man 4A 132
West Wlk. BL7: Eger 1B 18
Westward Ho. OL16: Miln 5F 29
Westward Rd. SK9: Wilm 3C 172
West Way BL1: Bolt 2F 33
   M38: Lit H 4E 65
Westway M9: Man 3F 71
   M43: Droy 6A 104
   OL2: Shaw 1H 59
   OL4: Lees 4C 76
Westwell Gdns. BL1: Bolt 4D 32
   (off Adisham Dr.)
Westwick Ter. BL1: Bolt 3C 32
   (off Boardman St.)
WESTWOOD 2C 74
Westwood WA14: Alt 1D 150
Westwood Av. M7: Sal 3C 86
   M28: Walk 6E 65
   M40: Man 2G 89
   M41: Urm 6H 111
   SK14: Hyde 4F 121
   WA15: Tim 4H 139
Westwood Bus. Cen. OL9: O'ham 3E 74
Westwood Cl. BL4: Farn 1H 65
Westwood Cres. M30: Ecc 2C 96
Westwood Dr. M27: Pen 5C 84
   M33: Sale 1B 140
   OL9: O'ham 2D 74
Westwood Ho. BL4: Farn 1H 65
   (off Hesketh Wlk.)
Westwood Ind. Est. OL9: O'ham 2C 74
WESTWOOD PARK 1E 97
Westwood Rd. BL1: Bolt 5A 32
   M32: Stre 5B 112
   M33: Sale 1B 158
   SK8: H Grn 5F 155
Westwood St. M14: Man 3D 114
Westwood Trad. Est. SK6: Mar 6B 148
W. Works Rd. M17: T Pk 3C 112
Westworth Cl. BL1: Bolt 5B 32
Wet Earth Colliery 4H 67
Wet Earth Grn. M27: Pen 3D 84
Wetheral Dr. BL3: Bolt 3C 48
Wetherall St. M19: Man 6D 116
Wetherby Dr. OL2: O'ham 2C 58
   SK7: H Gro 3G 159
Wetherby St. M11: Man 6G 103

Wexford Wlk. M22: Wyth 3C 154
Weybourne Av. M9: Man 1C 88
Weybourne Dr. SK6: Bred 5F 135
Weybourne Gro. BL2: Bolt 1F 33
Weybridge Cl. BL1: Bolt 1E 175
Weybridge Rd. M4: Man 4F 7 (3G 101)
Weybrook Rd. M19: Man 2D 132
Weycroft Cl. BL2: Bolt 1C 50
Wey Gates Dr. WA15: Haleb 6C 152
Weyhill Rd. M23: Wyth 6G 141
Weylands Gro. M6: Sal 6B 84
Weymouth Rd. M30: Ecc 2D 96
   OL6: A Lyme 5C 92
Weymouth St. BL1: Bolt 3C 32
Weythorne Dr. BL1: Bolt 1D 32
   BL9: Bury 6D 24
Whalley Av. BL1: Bolt 2F 31
   M16: W Ran 4B 114
   M19: Man 5D 116
   M21: Chor 2A 130
   M33: Sale 4C 128
   M41: Urm 4G 111
   OL15: L'ough 3G 17
Whalley Cl. M45: White 6F 53
   OL16: Miln 5E 29
   WA15: Tim 3H 139
Whalley Dr. BL8: Bury 3H 35
Whalley Gdns. OL12: Roch 2D 26
Whalley Gro. M16: W Ran 5B 114
   OL6: A Lyme 4A 92
WHALLEY RANGE 4B 114
Whalley Rd. BL0: Eden, Ram 4H 13
   M16: W Ran 4A 114
   M24: Mid 4B 56
   M45: White 6F 53
   OL10: H'ood 3E 39
   OL12: Roch 2D 26
   SK2: Stoc 4C 146
   WA15: Hale 3A 152
Wham Bar Dr. OL10: H'ood 3F 39
Wham Bottom La. OL12: Roch 5F 15
Wham La. OL3: Dens 4H 45
Whams OL4: Spri 2D 76
Wham St. OL10: H'ood 3F 39
Wharf, The OL3: Dob 5D 62
Wharf Circ. M17: T Pk 6C 98
Wharf Cl. M1: Man 6D 6 (4F 101)
   WA14: Alt 4F 139
   (off Bridgewater Rd.)
Wharf Cotts. OL3: G'fld 3C 78
   OL5: Mos 2H 93
Wharfedale BL5: W'ton 5A 46
Wharfedale Av. M40: Man 2C 88
Wharfedale Rd. SK5: Stoc 1G 133
Wharf End M17: T Pk 1G 113
Wharf Rd. M33: Sale 4C 128
   WA14: Alt 4F 139
Wharfside BL8: Bury 1D 36
Wharfside Av. M30: Ecc 5F 97
Wharfside Bus. Cen. M17: T Pk 1F 113
Wharfside Way M17: T Pk 1E 113
Wharf St. OL9: Chad 6B 74
   SK4: Stoc 6G 133
   SK16: Duk 4H 105
WHARMTON 2C 78
Wharmton Ri. OL4: Gras 3H 77
Wharmton Vw. OL3: G'fld 3C 78
   OL5: Mos 6A 78
Wharncliffe Cl. SK13: Had 3G 123
Wharton Av. M21: Chor 2B 130
Wharton La. M38: Lit H 4B 64
Wharton Lodge M30: Ecc 2G 97
Wheat Cl. M13: Man 2G 115
Wheatcroft SK3: Stoc 6H 145
   SK13: Had 3G 123
Wheater's Cres. M7: Sal 1A 100
Wheater's St. M7: Sal 1B 100
Wheater's Ter. M7: Sal 1B 100
Wheatfield SK15: Stal 6H 107
Wheatfield Cl. BL9: Bury 4F 23
   SK6: Bred 5G 135
Wheatfield Cres. OL2: O'ham 4C 58
Wheatfield St. BL2: Bolt 2F 49

Wheathill St.—Whitethorn Cl.

Wheathill St. OL16: Roch 1A 42
Wheatley Rd. M27: Ward 1F 83
Wheatley Wlk. *M12: Man 1C 116*
(off Woolfall Cl.)
Wheatsheaf Cen., The
OL16: Roch 2C 178 (3H 27)
Wheatsheaf Ind. Est.
M27: Pen 2B 84
Wheeldale OL4: O'ham 3B 76
Wheeldale Cl. BL1: Bolt 3C 32
Wheel Forge Way M17: T Pk 6H 97
Wheelock Cl. SK9: Wilm 6H 165
Wheelton Cl. BL8: Bury 4A 36
Wheelwright Cl. OL11: Roch 1D 40
SK6: Mar 3D 148
Wheelwright Dr. OL16: Roch 6C 16
Whelan Av. BL9: Bury 6E 37
Whelan Cl. BL9: Bury 6E 37
Wheler St. M11: Man 5F 103
Whelmar Est. SK8: Chea H 1D 156
Whernside Av. M40: Man 2C 88
OL6: A Lyme 4A 92
Whernside Cl. SK4: Stoc 6G 133
Whetstone Hill Cl. OL1: O'ham 5H 59
Whetstone Hill La. OL1: O'ham 6A 60
(not continuous)
Whetstone Hill Rd.
OL1: O'ham 5H 59
Whewell Av. M26: Rad 2D 52
Whickham Cl. M14: Man 4F 115
Whiley St. M13: Man 3B 116
Whimberry Cl. M5: Sal 3A 8 (6H 99)
Whimberry Dr. SK15: C'ook 6H 93
Whimberry Way M20: Man 3H 131
Whimbrel Rd. M29: Ast 5A 80
SK2: Stoc 6G 147
Whinberry Rd. WA14: B'ath 4D 138
Whinberry Way OL4: O'ham 3C 60
Whinchat Cl. SK2: Stoc 1G 159
Whinfell Dr. M24: Mid 6G 55
Whingroves Wlk. *M40: Man 5C 88*
(off Halliford Rd.)
Whinmoor Wlk. *M40: Man 4D 88*
(off Bellscroft Av.)
Whins Av. BL4: Farn 1C 64
Whins Crest BL6: Los 6C 30
Whinslee Ct. BL6: Los 6C 30
Whinslee Dr. BL6: Los 6C 30
Whinstone Way OL1: Chad 6G 57
Whipney La. BL8: Haw 1F 21
Whipp St. OL10: H'ood 2F 39
Whirley Cl. SK4: Stoc 4F 133
Whiston Dr. BL2: Bolt 1G 49
Whiston Rd. M8: Man 3F 87
Whitbrook Way M24: Mid 2F 57
Whitburn Av. M13: Man 5A 116
Whitburn Cl. BL3: Bolt 3E 47
Whitburn Dr. BL8: Bury 6C 22
Whitburn Rd. M23: Wyth 1G 153
Whitby Av. M6: Sal 2C 98
M14: Man 1A 132
M16: W Ran 4B 114
M41: Urm 5G 111
OL10: H'ood 2G 39
Whitby Cl. BL8: Bury 3H 35
SK8: Chea 5G 143
SK12: Poy 3C 168
Whitby Rd. M14: Man 1H 131
OL8: O'ham 6A 76
Whitby St. M24: Mid 6E 57
OL11: Roch 6A 28
Whitchurch Dr. M16: Old T 2B 114
Whitchurch Gdns. *BL1: Bolt 3C 32*
(off Gladstone St.)
Whitchurch Rd. M20: Man 2D 130
Whiteacre Rd. OL6: A Lyme 2A 106
Whiteacres M27: Swin 4F 83
Whiteacre Wlk. *M15: Man 2C 114*
(off Shearsby Cl.)
White Ash BL9: Bury 6C 24
White Ash Ter. BL9: Bury 5C 24
Whitebank Av. SK5: Stoc 5C 134
White Bank Rd. OL8: O'ham 2D 90
Whitebarn Rd. SK9: A Edg 6H 173
Whitebeam Cl. M6: Sal 2G 99
OL16: Miln 2G 43
WA15: Tim 6E 141
Whitebeam Ct. M6: Sal 2G 99
Whitebeam Wlk. *M33: Sale 4F 127*
(off Manor Av.)
Whitebeck Ct. M9: Man 5C 72
Whitebirk Cl. BL8: G'mount 1H 21
Whitebrook Ct. M33: Sale 6B 128
White Brook La. OL3: Upp 3F 79
(Old Thorn La.)
OL3: Upp 1E 79
(Springmeadow La.)
Whitebrook Rd. M14: Man 6F 115
WHITE BROW 2F 53
White Brow BL9: Bury 2F 53
Whitecar Av. M40: Man 2G 89
White Carr La. BL9: Bury 2G 23
Whitecarr La. WA15: Hale 2D 152
Whitechapel Cl. BL2: Bolt 6A 34
Whitechapel St. M20: Man 6F 131
White City Circ. M16: Old T 2G 113
White City Retail Pk. M16: Old T 2G 113
White City Way M16: Old T 2G 113
Whitecliff Cl. M14: Man 4G 115
White Ct. M27: Swin 4F 83
White Cft. BL1: Bolt 1E 175 (5C 32)
Whitecroft Av. OL2: Shaw 6B 44
Whitecroft Dr. BL8: Bury 2H 35
Whitecroft Gdns. M19: Man 5A 132
Whitecroft Mdw. M24: Mid 1C 72
Whitecroft Rd. BL1: Bolt 4F 31
SK6: Stri 4G 161
Whitecroft St. OL1: O'ham 6A 60
WHITEFIELD 2F 69
Whitefield SK4: Stoc 6F 133
Whitefield Av. OL11: Roch 3B 26
Whitefield Rd. BL9: Bury 6D 36
(not continuous)
M33: Sale 4H 127
SK6: Bred 5E 135
Whitefield Station (Metro) 6F 53
White Friar Ct. M3: Sal 2E 5
Whitefriars Wlk. M22: Wyth 5B 154
WHITE GATE 6A 74
Whitegate BL3: Bolt 5C 46
OL15: L'ough 5E 17
Whitegate Av. OL9: Chad 5H 73
Whitegate Bus. Cen. OL9: Chad 4H 73
Whitegate Cl. M40: Man 2G 89
Whitegate Dr. BL1: Bolt 6D 18
M5: Sal 2D 98
M27: Clif 1B 84
WHITE GATE END 6G 73
Whitegate La. OL9: Chad 5H 73
(not continuous)
White Gate Mnr. OL10: H'ood 2H 39
Whitegate Pk. M41: Urm 5A 110
Whitegate Rd. OL9: Chad 6F 73
Whitegates *BL7: Eger 2C 18*
(off Turnerford Cl.)
OL4: Scout 5F 61
SK8: Chea 6H 143
SK14: B'tom 6C 122
Whitegates Cl. WA15: Tim 6B 140
Whitegates La. OL4: Scout 5E 61
Whitegates Rd. M24: Mid 3E 57
SK8: Chea 6H 143
Whitehall OL4: O'ham 3D 60
Whitehall Cl. SK9: Wilm 4D 172
Whitehall La. OL4: O'ham 3D 60
Whitehall Rd. M20: Man 6G 131
M33: Sale 1B 140
Whitehall St.
OL1: O'ham 1H 177 (1F 75)
OL12: Roch 1B 178 (2H 27)
OL16: Roch 2C 178 (3H 27)
White Hart Mdw. M24: Mid 5C 56
White Hart St. SK14: Hyde 3B 120
Whitehaven Gdns. M20: Man 1E 143
Whitehaven Pl. SK14: Hyde 2A 120
Whitehaven Rd. SK7: Bram 2E 167
Whitehead Cl. OL3: G'fld 4A 78
Whitehead Cres. BL8: Bury 5C 22
M26: Rad 2E 67
Whitehead Rd. M21: Chor 1F 129
M27: Clif 1B 84
Whiteheads Pl. OL4: Spri 2D 76
Whitehead St. M24: Mid 6E 57
M28: Walk 5H 65
M34: Aud 6E 105
OL2: Shaw 5F 43
OL16: Miln 5E 29
White Hill Cl. OL12: Roch 5F 15
Whitehill Cotts. BL1: Bolt 5B 18
Whitehill Dr. M40: Man 4C 88
Whitehill Ind. Est. SK4: Stoc 3G 133
(not continuous)
Whitehill La. BL1: Bolt 5B 18
Whitehill St. SK4: Stoc 5G 133
SK5: Stoc 5G 133
(not continuous)
Whitehill St. W. SK4: Stoc 5F 133
Whiteholme Av. M21: Chor 5B 130
White Horse Gdns. *M27: Swin 5E 83*
(off Worsley Rd.)
White Horse Gro. BL5: W'ton 5A 46
White Horse Mdws. OL16: Roch 3C 42
White Ho. Av. M8: Man 6C 70
Whitehouse Av. OL4: O'ham 3A 76
Whitehouse Cl. OL10: H'ood 6H 39
Whitehouse Dr. M23: Wyth 6G 141
WA15: Hale 5B 152
Whitehouse La. WA14: D Mas 4A 138
Whitehurst Dr. M11: Man 5C 102
Whitehurst Rd. SK4: Stoc 5B 132
Whitekirk Cl. M13: Man 5D 10 (1F 115)
White Lady Cl. M28: Walk 6D 64
Whitelake Av. M41: Urm 5B 110
Whitelake Vw. M41: Urm 4B 110
Whiteland Av. BL3: Bolt 2H 47
Whitelands OL6: A Lyme 6D 174 (3A 106)
Whitelands Ind. Est. SK15: Stal 3C 106
Whitelands Rd.
OL6: A Lyme 6D 174 (3A 106)
Whitelands Ter. OL6: A Lyme 3A 106
Whitelea Dr. SK3: Stoc 6F 145
Whitelees M. OL15: L'ough 4G 17
Whitelees Rd. OL15: L'ough 4G 17
Whitelegge St. BL8: Bury 1B 36
Whiteley Dr. M24: Mid 2E 73
Whiteley Pl. WA14: Alt 5F 139
Whiteleys Pl. OL12: Roch 2A 178 (3G 27)
Whiteley St. M11: Man 3D 102
OL9: Chad 5B 74
White Lion Brow BL1: Bolt 4E 175 (6C 32)
Whitelow Rd. BL9: Bury 3E 13
M21: Chor 1G 129
SK4: Stoc 6C 132
White Mdws. M27: Swin 4H 83
Whitemoss OL12: Roch 1D 26
White Moss Av. M21: Chor 1A 130
White Moss Gdns. M9: Man 1C 88
White Moss Rd. M9: Man 6A 72
Whiteoak Cl. SK6: Mar 4C 148
Whiteoak Ct. M14: Man 1G 131
Whiteoak Rd. M14: Man 1G 131
Whiteoak Vw. BL3: Bolt 2H 49
Whites Cft. M27: Swin 3H 83
Whiteside Cl. M5: Sal 3D 98
Whiteside Fold OL12: Roch 2C 26
Whitesmead Cl. SK12: Dis 2H 171
Whitestar Ct. *M44: Irl 5E 109*
(off Ferry Rd.)
Whitestone Cl. BL6: Los 1D 46
Whitestone Ho. OL1: O'ham 1E 177
White St. BL8: Bury 4C 36
M6: Sal 4E 99
M15: Man 6C 8 (1B 114)
White Swallows Rd. M27: Swin 5A 84
White Swan Ind. Est. OL1: O'ham 1A 76
White Ter. SK14: Hyde 1A 136
Whitethorn Av. M16: W Ran 4B 114
M19: Man 2B 132
Whitethorn Cl. SK6: Mar 4C 148

Whitewater Dr. M7: Sal 4F 85
Whiteway St. M9: Man 4A 88
Whitewell Cl. BL9: Bury 6D 36
   OL16: Roch 3C 28
Whitewillow Cl. M35: Fail 5A 90
WHITFIELD 3H 43
Whitfield Bottoms OL16: Miln 2H 43
Whitfield Cres. OL16: Miln 2H 43
Whitfield Dr. OL16: Miln 6E 29
Whitfield Ri. OL2: Shaw 4G 43
Whitfield St. M3: Man 1A 6 (1E 101)
Whitford Wlk. M40: Man 1G 7
Whiting Gro. BL3: Bolt 1E 47
Whitland Av. BL1: Bolt 5F 31
Whitland Dr. OL8: O'ham 1B 90
Whit La. M6: Sal 5F 85
   (not continuous)
Whitley Gdns. WA15: Tim 4B 140
Whitley Pl. WA15: Tim 4C 140
Whitley Rd. M40: Man 1G 101
   SK4: Stoc 6D 132
Whitley St. BL3: Bolt 5H 49
Whitlow Av. WA14: B'ath 3D 138
Whitman St. M9: Man 3B 88
Whitmore Rd. M14: Man 6F 115
Whitnall St. M16: W Ran 3C 114
   SK14: Hyde 2B 120
Whitney Ct. OL4: O'ham 3G 75
   (off Hamilton St.)
Whitsand Rd. M22: Shar 6C 142
Whitsbury Av. M18: Man 4F 117
Whitstable Cl. OL9: Chad 3B 74
Whitstable Rd. M40: Man 2E 89
Whitsters Hollow BL1: Bolt 2A 31
Whitswood Cl. M16: W Ran 4C 114
Whittaker Cl. M25: Pres 5A 70
Whittaker Dr. OL15: L'ough 1F 29
Whittaker Ho. M26: Rad 3A 52
Whittaker La. M25: Pres 5A 70
   OL11: Roch 2H 25
Whittaker St. M24: Mid 1B 72
   M26: Rad 3B 52
   M40: Man 3B 88
   OL2: O'ham 2D 58
   OL6: A Lyme 6B 92
   OL11: Roch 2A 26
Whittingham Dr. BL0: Ram 5C 12
Whittingham Gro. OL1: O'ham 1D 74
Whittington Cl. BL3: Lit L 3D 50
Whittington St. OL7: A Lyme 4G 105
WHITTLE BROOK 1B 82
Whittle Brook Cl. BL9: Bury 2A 54
Whittle Brook Gro. OL10: H'ood 6A 40
Whittlebrook Ho. M28: Walk 1A 82
   (off Trinity Cres.)
Whittle Dr. M28: Walk 4G 65
   OL2: Shaw 5B 44
Whittle Gdns. M28: Walk 1A 82
   (off Whittle St.)
Whittle Gro. BL1: Bolt 4H 31
   M28: Walk 6A 66
Whittle Hill BL7: Eger 1C 18
Whittle La. OL10: H'ood 2E 55
Whittles Av. M34: Dent 4G 119
Whittles Cft. M1: Man 6D 6
   (Ducie St.)
   M1: Man 6D 6 (4F 101)
   (Pigeon St.)
Whittles St. OL12: Whitw 1B 14
Whittles Ter. OL16: Miln 1H 43
Whittle St. BL8: Bury 2C 36
   M4: Man 4C 6 (3F 101)
   M27: Swin 4G 83
   M28: Walk 6H 65
   OL15: L'ough 4F 17
Whittles M34: Dent 5G 119
Whitwell Bank SK13: Gam 5F 123
   (off Melandra Castle Rd.)
Whitwell Cl. SK13: Gam 5F 123
Whitwell Fold SK13: Gam 5F 123
   (off Hathersage Cres.)
Whitwell Grn. SK13: Gam 5G 123
   (off Hathersage Cres.)

Whitwell Lea SK13: Gam 5F 123
   (off Calver M.)
Whitwell Wlk. M13: Man 3A 116
Whitwell Way M18: Man 2E 117
WHITWORTH 4A 14
Whitworth Art Gallery, The 3F 115
Whitworth Cl. OL6: A Lyme 1A 106
Whitworth La. M14: Man 6H 115
Whitworth Leisure Cen. 3B 14
Whitworth Mus. 4A 14
Whitworth Pk. Mans.
   M14: Man 3E 115
Whitworth Rake OL12: Whitw 1F 15
Whitworth Rd.
   OL12: Roch 1C 178 (5F 15)
Whitworth Sq.
   OL12: Whitw 1F 15
Whitworth St. M1: Man 2A 10 (5E 101)
   (not continuous)
   M11: Man 6C 102
   OL16: Miln 5F 29
   OL16: Roch 1C 28
Whitworth St. E. M11: Man 6C 102
Whitworth St. W. M1: Man 2F 9 (5C 100)
Whitworth Water Ski Cen. 3A 14
Whixhall Av. M12: Man 1A 116
Whoolden St. BL4: Farn 6G 49
Whowell Fold BL1: Bolt 2A 32
Whowell St. BL3: Bolt 1C 48
Wibbersley Pk. M41: Urm 5B 110
Wichbrook Rd. M28: Walk 6D 64
Wicheaves Cres. M28: Walk 6D 64
Wicheries, The M28: Walk 6D 64
Wicken Bank OL10: H'ood 6A 40
Wickenby Dr. M33: Sale 5A 128
Wicken St. SK2: Stoc 4C 146
Wickentree Holt OL12: Roch 1C 26
Wickentree La. M35: Fail 2H 89
Wicker La. WA15: Haleb 5B 152
Wicket Gro. M27: Clif 5G 67
Wickham Ter. M24: Mid 6C 56
Wickliffe Pl. OL11: Roch 5B 178
Wickliffe St. BL1: Bolt 2E 175 (5C 32)
Wicklow Av. SK3: Stoc 4D 144
Wicklow Dr. M22: Wyth 3C 154
Wicklow Gro. OL8: O'ham 6E 75
Wickmere Wlk. M8: Man 5D 86
   (off Waterloo Rd.)
Widcombe Dr. BL2: Bolt 2B 50
Widdop St. OL9: O'ham 2D 74
Widecombe Cl. M41: Urm 3D 110
Widgeon Cl. M14: Man 1F 131
   SK12: Poy 3B 168
Widgeon Rd. WA14: B'ath 3D 138
Wigan Rd. BL3: Bolt 5D 46
Wiggins Teape Rd. BL9: Bury 1H 53
Wiggins Wlk. M14: Man 4D 115
   (off Bembridge Cl.)
Wighurst Wlk. M22: Wyth 4B 154
Wigley St. M12: Man 6A 102
Wigmore Rd. M8: Man 4F 87
Wigmore St. OL6: A Lyme 1B 106
Wigsby Av. M40: Man 1E 89
Wigwam Cl. SK12: Poy 3C 168
Wike St. BL8: Bury 2D 36
Wilberforce Cl. M15: Man 2C 114
Wilbraham Rd. M14: Man 6G 113
   M16: W Ran 6G 113
   M21: Chor 6G 113
   M28: Walk 6H 65
Wilburn St. M5: Sal 1C 8 (5B 100)
   (not continuous)
Wilby Av. BL3: Lit L 2C 50
Wilby Cl. BL8: Bury 6D 22
Wilby St. M8: Man 5F 87
Wilcockson Ho. BL4: Farn 1H 65
   (off Hesketh Wlk.)
Wilcock St. M16: W Ran 3C 114
Wilcott Dr. M33: Sale 4G 127
   SK9: Wilm 5C 172
Wilcott Rd. SK8: Gat 6E 143
Wildbank Chase SK15: Stal 1A 122
Wildbrook Cl. M38: Lit H 6C 64

Wildbrook Cres. OL8: O'ham 6G 75
   (not continuous)
Wildbrook Gro. M38: Lit H 6C 64
Wildbrook Rd. M38: Lit H 5C 64
Wildbrook Ter. OL8: O'ham 1G 91
Wild Clough SK14: Hyde 6D 120
Wildcroft Av. M40: Man 2C 88
Wilders Moor Cl. M28: Wors 3G 81
Wilderswood Cl. M20: Man 4G 131
Wild Ho. OL8: O'ham 6G 177 (4F 75)
Wildhouse Ct. OL16: Miln 4F 29
Wild Ho. La. OL16: Miln 4F 29
Wildman La. BL4: Farn 1D 64
Wildmoor Av. OL4: O'ham 5C 76
Wildmoor Wood Cl. SK15: C'ook 6H 93
Wilds Bldgs. OL16: Roch 4D 28
Wild's Pas. OL15: L'ough 5E 17
   (New Rd.)
   OL15: L'ough 1B 16
   (Todmorden Rd.)
Wilds Pl. BL0: Ram 4B 12
Wild's Sq. OL5: Mos 1G 93
Wild St. M26: Rad 3D 52
   M34: Dent 4F 119
   OL1: O'ham 2G 75
   OL2: Shaw 1A 60
   OL4: Lees 3C 76
   OL10: H'ood 3A 40
   SK2: Stoc 5A 146
   SK6: Bred 1F 147
   SK7: H Gro 3D 158
   SK16: Duk 5B 106
Wildwood Cl. BL0: Ram 5A 12
   SK2: Stoc 6A 146
Wileman Cl. M5: Sal 3D 98
   (off Sheader Dr.)
Wilford Av. M33: Sale 1A 140
Wilfred Dr. BL9: Bury 1H 37
Wilfred Geere Ho., The
   BL4: Farn 1C 64
Wilfred Rd. M28: Walk 1H 81
   M30: Ecc 5C 96
Wilfred St. BL7: Bro X 4E 19
   M3: Sal 1F 5 (1C 100)
   M40: Man 3C 88
   OL4: O'ham 3H 75
Wilfrid St. M27: Swin 3H 83
Wilham Av. M30: Ecc 4F 97
Wilkes St. OL1: O'ham 3B 60
Wilkin Cft. SK8: Chea H 4A 156
Wilkins La. SK9: Sty 2C 164
Wilkinson Av. BL3: Lit L 3C 50
Wilkinson Rd. BL1: Bolt 6A 18
   SK4: Stoc 1E 179 (1G 145)
   (not continuous)
Wilkinson St. M24: Mid 1B 72
   M33: Sale 5D 128
   OL6: A Lyme 3G 105
Wilks Av. M22: Wyth 3D 154
Willand Cl. BL2: Bolt 1C 50
Willand Dr. BL2: Bolt 1C 50
Willan Ent. Cen. M17: T Pk 1C 112
Willan Ind. Est. M50: Sal 4F 99
Willan Rd. M9: Man 5G 71
   M30: Ecc 3G 97
Willard St. SK7: H Gro 2D 158
Willaston Cl. M21: Chor 2G 129
Willaston Way SK9: Hand 2H 165
   (off Sandiway Rd.)
Willbutts La. OL11: Roch 3E 27
Willdale Cl. M11: Man 3C 102
Willdor Gro. SK3: Stoc 5D 144
Willenhall Rd. M23: Wyth 1A 142
Willerby Rd. M7: Sal 6C 86
Willert St. M40: Man 6H 87
Willesden Av. M13: Man 4A 116
Will Griffith Wlk. M11: Man 5A 102
   (off Rylance St.)
William Chadwick Cl.
   M40: Man 1F 7 (2G 101)
William Cl. M41: Urm 6E 111
William Coates Ct.
   M16: W Ran 4B 114

William Fairburn Way
M4: Man 4B **6** (3E **101**)
William Ford Ho. SK14: Mot 3C **122**
William Greenwood Cl.
OL10: H'ood 3G **39**
William Henry St. OL11: Roch 6A **28**
William Jessop Ct. M1: Man 6E **7**
William Kay Cl. M16: W Ran 3C **114**
William Lister Cl. M40: Man 1F **103**
Williams Ct. *M14: Man* *3H* **115**
(off Hope Rd.)
Williams Cres. OL9: Chad 6H **73**
Williamson Av. M26: Rad 1H **51**
SK6: Bred 5G **135**
Williamson La. M43: Droy 5B **104**
Williamson St. M4: Man 1C **6** (2F **101**)
OL6: A Lyme 5B **174** (2H **105**)
SK5: Stoc 2H **133**
Williamson's Yd. OL1: O'ham 2H **75**
Williams Rd. M18: Man 2E **117**
M40: Man 4D **88**
Williams St. BL3: Lit L 4D **50**
M18: Man 2E **117**
William St. BL0: Ram 4F **13**
M3: Sal 4E **5** (3C **100**)
(not continuous)
M12: Man 2G **11** (5H **101**)
M20: Man 6F **131**
M24: Mid 1D **72**
M26: Rad 3B **52**
M35: Fail 2A **90**
OL7: A Lyme 3F **105**
OL11: Roch 6B **178** (5H **27**)
OL12: Whitw 4A **14**
OL15: L'ough 4G **17**
OL16: Roch 5D **16**
SK14: Hyde 5B **120**
William Wlk. *WA14: Alt* *2F* **151**
(off Yarwood St.)
Willingdon Cl. BL8: Bury 4C **22**
Willingdon Dr. M25: Pres 4H **69**
Willis Rd. SK3: Stoc 5G **145**
Willis St. BL3: Bolt 3A **48**
Williton Wlk. M22: Wyth 2D **154**
Willock St. M7: Sal 5D **86**
Willoughby Av. M20: Man 5G **131**
Willoughby Cl. M33: Sale 4A **128**
Willow Av. M24: Mid 2E **73**
M41: Urm 5G **111**
SK5: Stoc 5H **133**
SK8: Chea H 3B **156**
Willow Bank *M9: Man* *4A* **88**
(off Church La.)
M14: Man 1G **131**
OL3: Upp 1D **78**
SK8: Chea H 1C **166**
WA15: Tim 5A **140**
Willowbank M26: Rad 1H **67**
M27: Clif 1A **84**
OL4: Lees 1C **76**
Willowbank Av. BL2: Bolt 1F **49**
Willow Bank Cl. SK2: Stoc 4D **146**
Willow Bank Ct. M20: Man 3F **143**
Willowbrook Av. M40: Man 4C **88**
Willowbrook Gdns. M22: Wyth 1A **154**
Willow Cl. BL3: Bolt 3H **47**
BL9: Bury 5H **53**
SK12: Poy 4E **169**
SK16: Duk 6D **106**
Willow Ct. M14: Man 1G **131**
M33: Sale 4E **129**
SK6: Mar 6C **148**
SK8: Gat 5E **143**
Willowdale Av. SK8: H Grn 3F **155**
Willowdene Cl. BL7: Eger 3D **18**
M40: Man *6G* **87**
(off Dalbury Dr.)
Willow Dr. BL9: Bury 5H **53**
M33: Sale 1G **139**
SK9: Hand 4H **165**
Willowfield Rd.
OL4: O'ham 5B **60**
Willow Fold M43: Droy 5B **104**

Willow Gro. M18: Man 3G **117**
M34: Dent 4E **119**
OL9: Chad 1B **74**
SK6: Mar 6D **148**
Willow Hey BL7: Bro X 4G **19**
Willow Hill Rd. M8: Man 2E **87**
Willow Lawn *SK8: Chea H* *2C* **156**
(off Vaudrey Dr.)
Willow Mead SK6: Rom 6B **136**
Willowmead Way
OL12: Roch 1C **26**
Willowmoss Cl. M28: Walk 2A **82**
Willow Pk. M14: Man 1G **131**
SK2: Stoc *4E* **146**
(off Wicken St.)
Willow Ri. OL15: L'ough 6F **17**
Willow Rd. M25: Pres 3G **69**
M30: Ecc 1C **96**
M31: Part 6C **124**
OL3: Upp 2E **79**
SK6: H Lan 6D **160**
WILLOWS 3A **48**
Willows, The 3D **98**
Willows, The BL2: Bolt 2C **50**
M21: Chor 2G **129**
M31: Part 6D **124**
M33: Sale 1F **139**
OL4: Lees 4D **76**
OL5: Mos 2A **94**
OL12: Whitw *4E* **15**
(off Tonacliffe Rd.)
SK4: Stoc 6C **132**
Willows Cotts. OL16: Miln 5E **29**
Willows Dr. M35: Fail 1H **103**
Willows End SK15: Stal 2H **107**
Willows La. BL3: Bolt 3H **47**
OL16: Roch 5D **28**
Willows Rd. M5: Sal 3D **98**
Willow St. BL9: Bury 3H **37**
(not continuous)
M8: Man 1C **100**
M11: Man 4C **102**
M27: Swin 6F **83**
M28: Wors 4E **83**
OL1: O'ham 2G **75**
OL10: H'ood 3H **39**
Willow Tree Ct. *M30: Ecc* *4E* **97**
(off Aldred St.)
M33: Sale 6B **128**
Willow Tree M. SK8: H Grn 5F **155**
Willowtree Rd. WA14: Alt 3F **151**
Willow Wlk. M43: Droy 3C **104**
Willow Way M20: Man 6G **131**
SK7: Bram 6E **157**
Willow Wood Cl. OL6: A Lyme 2C **106**
Wilma Av. M9: Man 5G **71**
Wilmcote Cl. M40: Man 1D **46**
Wilmcote Gdns. SK6: Bred 6F **135**
Wilmcote Rd. M40: Man 1H **101**
Wilmers OL15: L'ough 1B **16**
Wilmington Rd. M32: Stre 5B **112**
Wilmot St. BL1: Bolt 2A **32**
Wilmott St. M15: Man 4H **9** (6D **100**)
(Hulme St.)
M15: Man 5A **10** (1E **115**)
(Knowles Pl.)
WILMSLOW 2E **173**
Wilmslow Av. BL1: Bolt 6C **18**
Wilmslow By-Pass
SK9: Wilm . . . . .5D **172** & 3F **173**
Wilmslow Ct. SK9: Hand 4H **165**
Wilmslow Leisure Cen. 2E **173**
Wilmslow Old Rd. WA15: Ring 1F **163**
WILMSLOW PARK 1G **173**
Wilmslow Pk. Nth. SK9: Wilm 2F **173**
Wilmslow Pk. Sth. SK9: Wilm 2F **173**
Wilmslow Rd. M14: Man 3G **115**
M20: Man 5F **131**
SK7: W'ford 6D **166**
SK8: Chea 6H **143**
(not continuous)
SK8: Chea, H Grn 3H **155**
(not continuous)

Wilmslow Rd. SK9: A Edg 4G **173**
SK9: Hand 2H **165**
(not continuous)
SK9: Sty 1F **163**
WA15: Ring 1F **163**
Wilmslow Station (Rail) 2F **173**
Wilmur Av. M7: Sal 5C **86**
M45: White 2G **69**
Wilpshire Av. M12: Man 4D **116**
Wilshaw Gro. OL7: A Lyme 5G **91**
Wilshaw La. OL7: A Lyme 6G **91**
Wilshaw Pl. OL7: A Lyme 6G **91**
Wilson Av. M27: Clif 1B **84**
OL10: H'ood 3E **39**
Wilson Brook Cl. SK14: Hyde 4C **120**
Wilson Cres. OL6: A Lyme 1C **106**
Wilson Fold Av. BL6: Los 5A **30**
Wilson Rd. M9: Man 2H **87**
SK4: Stoc 5D **132**
Wilsons Brow BL4: Kea 6B **50**
Wilsons Pk. M40: Man 6A **88**
Wilson St. BL4: Farn 1A **66**
BL9: Bury 4D **37**
M11: Man 5C **102**
M13: Man 6F **11** (1G **115**)
M26: Rad 3H **51**
M32: Stre 3E **113**
M33: Sale 4B **128**
OL3: G'fld 4C **78**
OL8: O'ham 5E **75**
OL12: Roch 1B **178** (3H **27**)
SK14: Hyde 5C **120**
Wilson Way OL1: O'ham 1G **177** (1F **75**)
Wilsthorpe Cl. M19: Man 3E **133**
Wilton Av. M16: Old T 4G **113**
M25: Pres 1B **86**
M27: Pen 4C **84**
SK8: H Grn 6G **155**
Wilton Ct. M25: Pres 1C **70**
M34: Dent 3A **118**
Wilton Cres. SK9: A Edg 4F **173**
Wilton Dr. BL9: Bury 2G **53**
WA15: Haleb 5C **152**
Wilton Gdns. M26: Rad 2C **52**
Wilton Gro. M34: Dent 3A **118**
OL10: H'ood 4H **39**
Wilton Paddock M34: Dent 3A **118**
Wilton Pl. M3: Sal 4C **4** (3B **100**)
Wilton Polygon M8: Man 2D **86**
Wilton Rd. BL1: Bolt 6C **18**
M6: Sal 1B **98**
M8: Man 1D **86**
M21: Chor 1H **129**
M34: Dent 3A **118**
Wilton St. BL1: Bolt 2D **32**
M13: Man 6C **10** (1F **115**)
M24: Mid 2F **71**
M25: Pres 5A **70**
M34: Dent 3E **119**
M45: White 2F **69**
OL9: Chad 6B **74**
OL10: H'ood 3F **39**
SK5: Stoc 5H **117**
Wilton Ter. OL12: Roch 3G **27**
Wiltshire Av. SK5: Stoc 5C **134**
Wiltshire Cl. BL9: Bury 5G **37**
Wiltshire Rd. M35: Fail 5A **90**
OL9: Chad 4B **74**
Wiltshire St. M7: Sal 4C **86**
Wimberry Cl. OL3: G'fld 4D **78**
Wimbledon Dr. OL11: Roch 6F **27**
SK3: Stoc 4E **145**
Wimbledon Rd. M35: Fail 3B **90**
Wimbledon Ter. M40: Man 1D **102**
Wimborne Av. M41: Urm 3F **111**
OL9: Chad 6A **58**
Wimborne Cl. BL6: Los 4A **30**
SK8: Chea H 1E **157**
Wimpenny Ho. OL8: O'ham 6F **177**
Wimpole St. OL1: O'ham 6G **59**
OL6: A Lyme 4D **174** (2A **106**)
Wimpory St. M11: Man 6F **103**
Winbolt St. SK2: Stoc 1C **158**

Winby St. OL11: Roch 6A **28**
Wincanton Av. M23: Wyth 3D **140**
Wincanton Dr. BL1: Bolt 4B **18**
Wincanton Pk. OL4: O'ham 3B **76**
Wince Brook M24: Mid 1C **72**
Wince Brook Ct. M24: Mid 1D **72**
Wince Cl. M24: Mid 3E **73**
Wincham Cl. M15: Man 6D **8**
Wincham Rd. M33: Sale 1G **139**
Winchester Av. M25: Pres 1A **86**
    M29: Ast .4A **80**
    M34: Dent 6F **119**
    OL6: A Lyme 3B **92**
    OL9: Chad 6H **57**
    OL10: H'ood 5G **39**
Winchester Cl. BL8: Bury 4C **22**
    OL11: Roch 4C **26**
    SK9: Wilm 4B **172**
Winchester Dr. M33: Sale 5F **127**
    SK4: Stoc 1D **144**
Winchester Pk. M20: Man 6D **130**
Winchester Rd. M6: Sal 1C **98**
    M26: Rad 2F **51**
    M30: Ecc 1A **98**
    M32: Stre 4F **111**
    M41: Urm 4F **111**
    SK16: Duk 6E **107**
    WA15: Hale 4C **152**
Winchester Way BL2: Bolt 4H **33**
Wincle Av. SK12: Poy 5G **169**
Wincombe St. M14: Man 5F **115**
Windale M28: Walk 6F **65**
Windcroft Cl. M11: Man 5B **102**
Windermere Av. BL3: Lit L 3C **50**
    M27: Swin 4A **84**
    M33: Sale 1D **140**
    M34: Dent 5A **118**
Windermere Cl. M11: Man 5C **102**
    M25: Pres 4F **69**
    M32: Stre 4C **112**
Windermere Cres. OL7: A Lyme . . .1F **105**
Windermere Dr. BL0: Ram 2C **12**
    BL9: Bury 6E **37**
    SK9: A Edg 5F **173**
Windermere Ho. *M28: Walk 1H **81**
    (off Sandwich St.)
Windermere M. M24: Mid 4A **56**
Windermere Rd. BL4: Farn 1C **64**
    M24: Mid 5G **55**
    M41: Urm 6E **111**
    OL2: O'ham 6D **42**
    SK1: Stoc 5B **146**
    SK6: H Lan 5C **160**
    SK9: Hand 3G **165**
    SK14: Hyde 2A **120**
    SK15: Stal 2E **107**
    SK16: Duk 5A **106**
Windermere St. BL1: Bolt 3D **32**
    OL12: Roch 1H **27**
Windermere Wlk. OL4: O'ham 1B **76**
    (not continuous)
Winder St. BL1: Bolt 1F **175** (5D **32**)
Winders Way M6: Sal 1H **99**
Windfields Cl. SK8: Chea H 2D **156**
Windgate Ri. SK15: C'ook 6H **93**
Windham St. OL16: Roch 6C **16**
Windle Av. M8: Man 6D **70**
Windle Ct. SK2: Stoc 6E **147**
WINDLEHURST 5B **160**
Windlehurst Ct. SK6: H Lan 6B **160**
Windlehurst Dr. M28: Wors 4F **81**
Windlehurst Hall SK6: H Lan 4D **160**
Windlehurst Old Rd. SK6: Mar 3D **160**
Windlehurst Rd. SK6: H Lan 5B **160**
Windley St. BL2: Bolt 5E **33**
Windmill Av. M5: Sal 3A **8** (6H **99**)
Windmill Cl. M28: Walk 4G **65**
    M34: Dent 5B **118**
    OL2: O'ham 5D **58**
Windmill Cl. OL16: Roch 5B **28**
Windmill La. M34: Dent 5A **118**
    SK5: Stoc 6H **117**
Windmill La. Ind. Est. M34: Dent . . .4C **118**

Windmill Rd. M28: Walk 4G **65**
    M33: Sale 6F **129**
Windmill St. M2: Man 1G **9** (5D **100**)
    OL16: Roch 5B **28**
Windmill Trad. M34: Dent 4D **118**
Windover St. BL3: Bolt 3G **47**
Windrush, The OL12: Roch 5E **15**
Windrush Av. BL0: Ram 1A **22**
Windrush Dr. M9: Man 4H **87**
Windsor Av. BL3: Lit L 4C **50**
    M27: Clif 1A **84**
    M33: Sale 3B **128**
    M35: Fail 3B **90**
    M38: Lit H 4F **65**
    M41: Urm 5B **110**
    M44: Irl 4F **109**
    M45: White 2G **69**
    OL9: Chad 5A **74**
    OL10: H'ood 3F **39**
    SK4: Stoc 6C **132**
    SK8: Gat 6D **142**
    SK9: Wilm 2C **172**
Windsor Bri. M5: Sal 3H **99**
Windsor Cl. BL8: G'mount 2A **22**
    SK12: Poy 3D **168**
Windsor Ct. BL3: Bolt 5B **48**
    M9: Man 4E **71**
    M26: Rad 3B **52**
    *M33: Sale 4H **127**
    (off Wentworth Dr.)*
    *M34: Dent 1G **135**
    (off Wordsworth Rd.)*
    OL2: Shaw 5H **43**
Windsor Cres. M25: Pres 6C **70**
Windsor Dr. BL8: Bury 5B **36**
    M34: Aud 4D **104**
    OL7: A Lyme 1F **105**
    SK6: Bred 6C **134**
    SK6: Mar 6C **148**
    SK15: Stal 2E **107**
    SK16: Duk 6D **106**
    WA14: Bow 4B **150**
    WA14: Tim 3H **139**
Windsor Gdns. SK7: Bram 1G **167**
Windsor Gro. BL1: Bolt 4A **32**
    M26: Rad 2D **66**
    OL6: A Lyme 4A **92**
    SK6: Rom 1C **148**
    SK8: Chea H 5B **156**
Windsor Ho. *M21: Chor 1D **130**
    (off Mauldeth Rd.)*
    M34: Dent 4A **118**
Windsor Rd. BL7: Bro X 4E **19**
    M9: Man 4A **88**
    M19: Man 6C **116**
    M25: Pres 1C **86**
    M34: Dent 4A **118**
    M40: Man 1G **103**
    M43: Droy 3F **103**
    OL8: O'ham 4D **74**
    (not continuous)
    SK7: H Gro 3F **159**
    SK14: Hyde 2B **136**
Windsor St. M5: Sal 4H **99**
    M18: Man 3E **117**
    M35: Fail 3A **90**
    M40: Man 1G **103**
    OL1: O'ham 6G **59**
    OL11: Roch 6A **28**
    SK2: Stoc 5A **146**
Windsor Ter. *OL16: Miln 5E **29**
    (off Moorhouse Farm)*
    OL16: Roch 4C **28**
    *SK2: Stoc 5A **146**
    (off Russell St.)*
Windsor Wlk. SK2: Stoc 5H **145**
Windybank M9: Man 4G **71**
Windy Harbour La. BL7: Bro X 3F **19**
    (not continuous)
Windyhill Dr. BL3: Bolt 4G **47**
Winfell Dr. M40: Man 2H **7** (2H **101**)
Winfield Av. M20: Man 3H **131**
Winfield Dr. M18: Man 1F **117**

Winfield Gro. SK6: Mar B 2F **149**
Winfield St. SK14: Hyde 5D **120**
Winford Rd. M24: Mid 3E **73**
Winford St. M9: Man 3A **88**
Wingate Av. BL8: Bury 3B **36**
Wingate Dr. M20: Man 1G **143**
    M45: White 6E **53**
    WA15: Tim 6A **140**
Wingate Rd. M38: Lit H 5F **65**
    SK4: Stoc 5E **133**
Wingate St. OL11: Roch 2A **26**
Wingfield Av. SK9: Wilm 3B **172**
Wingfield Dr. M27: Swin 5A **84**
    SK9: Wilm 3B **172**
Wingfield St. M32: Stre 3D **112**
Wingrave Ho. M5: Sal 3G **99**
Wings Gro. OL10: H'ood 6H **39**
Winifred Av. BL9: Bury 1D **38**
Winifred Rd. BL4: Farn 6E **49**
    M20: Man 6F **131**
    M40: Man 4D **88**
    M41: Urm 5E **111**
    SK2: Stoc 6A **146**
Winifred St. BL0: Ram 4B **12**
    M30: Ecc 4D **96**
    OL12: Roch 2D **26**
    SK14: Hyde 2C **136**
Winmarith Dr. WA15: Haleb 6D **152**
Winmarleigh Cl. BL8: Bury 4H **35**
Winnall Wlk. *M40: Man 5E **89**
    (off Rothman Cl.)*
Winnie St. M40: Man 3C **88**
Winning Hill Cl. M18: Man 3F **117**
Winnington Grn. SK2: Stoc 5D **146**
Winnington Rd. SK6: Mar 3D **148**
Winnipeg Quay M50: Sal 6F **99**
Winnows, The M34: Dent 4D **118**
Winscombe Dr. M40: Man 1G **101**
Winser St. M1: Man 2A **10** (5E **101**)
Winsfield Rd. SK7: H Gro 5D **158**
Winsford Dr. OL11: Roch 6B **26**
Winsford Gro. BL3: Bolt 2F **47**
Winsford Rd. M14: Man 6E **115**
Winsford Wlk. *M33: Sale 6E **129**
    (off Mottram Rd.)*
Winskill Rd. M44: Irl 1E **125**
Winslade Cl. OL4: O'ham 6B **60**
    SK7: H Gro 3A **158**
Winslade M. BL4: Farn 6H **49**
Winsley Rd. M23: Wyth 1F **141**
Winslow Av. SK14: Mot 5B **122**
Winslow Pl. M19: Man 3B **132**
Winslow Rd. BL3: Bolt 4C **46**
Winslow St. M11: Man 5C **102**
Winson Cl. BL3: Bolt 3C **48**
Winstanley Cl. M6: Sal 6D **84**
Winstanley Rd. M33: Sale 4C **127**
    M40: Man 1G **7** (2H **101**)
Winster Av. M7: Sal 5H **85**
    M20: Man 5C **130**
    M32: Stre 4A **112**
Winster Cl. BL2: Bolt 4B **34**
    M45: White 1H **69**
Winster Dr. BL2: Bolt 4A **34**
    M24: Mid 5A **56**
Winster Grn. M30: Ecc 5D **96**
Winster Gro. SK2: Stoc 5A **146**
Winster Ho. M41: Urm 4B **110**
Winster M. *SK13: Gam 5G **123**
    (off Melandra Castle Rd.)*
Winster Rd. M30: Ecc 5D **96**
Winston Av. BL3: Lit L 4E **51**
    OL11: Roch 5A **26**
Winston Cl. M26: Rad 2G **51**
    M33: Sale 4H **127**
    SK6: Mar 4B **148**
Winston Rd. M9: Man 3B **88**
    (not continuous)
Winswell Cl. M11: Man 3D **102**
Winterbottom Gro. SK14: Mot 5B **122**
Winterbottom St. OL9: O'ham 3D **74**
Winterbottom Wlk. *SK14: Mot 5B **122**
    (off Winterbottom Gro.)*

Winterburn Av. BL2: Bolt 5F **19**
  M21: Chor 5A **130**
Winterburn Grn. SK2: Stoc 6E **147**
Winterdyne St. M9: Man 4A **88**
Winterfield Dr. BL3: Bolt 4G **47**
Winterford Av. M13: Man . . .6H **11** (2H **115**)
Winterford La. OL5: Mos 1H **93**
Winterford Rd. M7: Sal 4D **86**
  M8: Man 4D **86**
  OL5: Mos 1H **93**
Winter Gdn. M4: Man 4A **6**
Wintergreen Wlk. M31: Part 6D **124**
  (off Wychelm Rd.)
Wintermans Rd. M21: Chor 2C **130**
Winterslow Av. M23: Wyth 2D **140**
Winter St. BL1: Bolt 2B **32**
Winterton Cl. BL5: W'ton 6A **46**
Winterton Rd. SK5: Stoc 6A **118**
Winthrop Av. M40: Man 6H **87**
WINTON 3D **96**
Winton Av. M34: Aud 6D **104**
  M40: Man 2F **89**
Winton Cl. SK7: Bram 4F **157**
Winton Ct. WA14: Bow 3E **151**
Winton Grn. BL6: Los 5A **30**
Winton Gro. BL3: Bolt 3E **47**
Winton Rd. M6: Sal 5D **84**
  WA14: Bow 3E **151**
Winton St. OL6: A Lyme 4B **174** (2H **105**)
  OL15: L'ough 4H **17**
  SK15: Stal 4F **107**
Winward St. BL3: Bolt 3G **47**
Winwood Dr. M24: Mid 5D **56**
Winwood Fold M24: Mid 3B **56**
Winwood Rd. M20: Man 3G **143**
Wirral Cl. M27: Clif 1A **84**
Wirral Cres. SK3: Stoc 3C **144**
Wisbech Dr. M23: Wyth 2F **141**
Wisbeck Rd. BL2: Bolt 5G **33**
Wiseman Ter. M25: Pres 5A **70**
Wishaw Sq. M21: Chor 2C **130**
Wisley Cl. SK5: Stoc 1A **134**
Wistaria Rd. M18: Man 2F **117**
Witham Av. M22: Shar 6C **142**
Witham Cl. OL10: H'ood 5B **26**
Witham St. OL6: A Lyme 1C **106**
Withenfield Rd. M23: Wyth 3F **141**
Withens Av. SK2: Stoc 5E **147**
Withern Flats OL10: H'ood *3G **39***
  (off Hill St.)
Withies, The M30: Ecc *3D **96***
  (off Worsley Rd.)
WITHINGTON 3E **131**
Withington Dr. M29: Ast 4A **80**
Withington Grn. M24: Mid 3C **56**
Withington Leisure Cen. 3F **131**
Withington Rd. M16: W Ran 3B **114**
  M21: Chor 1B **130**
Withington St. OL10: H'ood 5A **40**
Withinlea Cl. BL5: W'ton 5A **46**
Withins Av. M26: Rad 2C **52**
Withins Cl. BL2: Bolt 5A **34**
Withins Community Leisure Cen. . . .3A **34**
Withins Dr. BL2: Bolt 5A **34**
Withins Gro. BL2: Bolt 5A **34**
Withins Hall Rd. M35: Fail 5B **90**
Withins La. BL2: Bolt 5A **34**
  M26: Rad 2C **52**
Withins Rd. OL8: O'ham 1B **90**
Withins St. M26: Rad 3C **52**
Withnell Dr. BL8: Bury 4A **36**
Withnell Rd. M19: Man 6H **131**
Withycombe Pl. M6: Sal 6G **85**
Withy Gro. M4: Man 4A **6** (3E **101**)
Withypool Dr. SK2: Stoc 6B **146**
Withy Tree Gro. M34: Dent 5G **119**
Witley Dr. M33: Sale 3F **127**
Witley Rd. OL16: Roch 4B **28**
Witney Cl. BL1: Bolt *3C **32***
  (off Draycott St.)
Wittenbury Rd. SK4: Stoc 1D **144**
Wittenham Ho. SK9: Wilm 5H **165**
Witterage Cl. M12: Man 1B **116**

Witton Wlk. M8: Man *5D **86***
  (off Cranlington Dr.)
Woburn Abbey OL3: Upp 6C **62**
Woburn Av. BL2: Bolt 2G **33**
Woburn Cl. OL16: Miln 5E **29**
Woburn Ct. SK12: Poy 3F **169**
Woburn Dr. BL9: Bury 2F **53**
  WA15: Hale 3B **152**
Woburn Grn. M24: Mid 5C **56**
Woburn Rd. M16: Old T 5G **113**
Woburn St. M16: W Ran 4D **114**
Woden's Av. M5: Sal 3A **8** (6A **100**)
Woden St. M5: Sal 3B **8** (6A **100**)
Woking Rd. SK8: Chea H 1B **166**
Woking Ter. BL1: Bolt *4C **32***
  (off Woking Gdns.)
Wolfenden Cres. BL4: Farn 6C **48**
Wolfenden St. BL1: Bolt 3C **32**
Wolfenden Ter. BL1: Bolt *3C **32***
  (off Wolfenden St.)
Wolf Grange WA15: Hale 4G **151**
Wolford Dr. M29: Tyld 2A **80**
Wolfreton Cres. M27: Clif 6A **68**
Wollaton Wlk. M34: Dent 6E **119**
Wolseley Ho. M33: Sale *3C **128***
  (off Dargle Rd.)
Wolseley Pl. M20: Man 4F **131**
Wolseley Rd. M33: Sale 3B **128**
Wolseley St. BL8: Bury 4B **36**
  OL16: Miln 1H **43**
Wolsey Cl. M26: Rad 4A **52**
Wolsey Dr. WA14: Bow 4C **150**
Wolsey St. M26: Rad 4A **52**
  OL10: H'ood 4G **39**
Wolstenholme Av. BL9: Bury 5F **23**
Wolstenholme Coalpit La.
  OL11: Roch 1F **25**
WOLSTENHOLME FOLD 1G **25**
Wolstenholme La. OL12: Roch 1G **25**
Wolstenvale Cl. M24: Mid 6D **56**
Wolver Cl. M38: Lit H 3F **65**
Wolverhampton Ho. SK9: A Edg . . .5G **173**
  (off George St.)
Wolverton Av. OL8: O'ham 6D **74**
Wolverton Dr. SK9: Wilm 6G **165**
Wolverton St. M11: Man 6B **102**
Wolvesey OL11: Roch 6A **178**
Woodacre M16: W Ran 6C **114**
Woodacre Cl. M33: Sale 1A **140**
Woodacres Ct. SK9: Wilm 3C **172**
Woodall Cl. M33: Sale 5D **128**
Woodark Cl. OL4: Spri 4D **76**
Woodbank BL2: Bolt 3H **33**
  SK9: A Edg 4G **173**
Woodbank Av. SK1: Stoc 3C **146**
  SK6: Bred 6E **135**
Woodbank Ct. M41: Urm 4D **110**
Woodbank Dr. BL8: Bury 1C **36**
Woodbank Pk. SK1: Stoc 2B **146**
Woodbank Pk. Athletic Track 2C **146**
Woodbank Rd. OL15: L'ough 6G **17**
Wood Bank Ter. OL5: Mos 1H **93**
Woodbank Works Ind. Est.
  SK1: Stoc 1B **146**
Woodbine Av. M44: Cad 5B **124**
Woodbine Cres. SK2: Stoc 4H **145**
Woodbine Pas. OL15: L'ough *4G **17***
  (off William St.)
Woodbine Rd. BL3: Bolt 4A **48**
  (not continuous)
Woodbine St. M14: Man 3E **115**
  OL16: Roch 6A **28**
Woodbine St. E. OL16: Roch 6B **28**
Woodbine Ter. M44: Irl 5F **109**
Woodbourne Ct. M33: Sale 1B **140**
Woodbourne Rd. M33: Sale 1A **140**
  SK4: Stoc 3E **133**
Woodbray Av. M19: Man 4A **132**
Woodbridge Av. M34: Aud 6D **104**
Woodbridge Dr. BL2: Bolt 4F **33**
Woodbridge Gdns. OL12: Roch 1E **27**
Woodbridge Gro. M23: Wyth 2G **141**
Woodbridge Rd. M41: Urm 4H **109**

Woodbrook Av. OL4: Spri 2F **77**
Woodbrooke Av. SK14: Hyde 5D **120**
Wood Brook La. OL4: Lyd, Spri 2F **77**
Wood Brook Rd. OL4: Spri 2E **77**
Woodbrook Rd. SK9: A Edg 5H **173**
Woodburn Dr. BL1: Bolt 2H **31**
Woodburn Rd. M22: Nor 3B **142**
Woodbury Cres. SK16: Duk 6H **105**
Woodbury Pk. SK7: H Gro 2G **159**
Woodbury Rd. SK3: Stoc 3D **144**
Woodchurch Cl. BL1: Bolt *4C **32***
  (off Kentford Rd.)
Woodchurch Wlk. M33: Sale *6F **129***
  (off Mottram Rd.)
  OL9: Chad 3B **74**
Woodcliffe Lodge M25: Pres 1H **85**
Woodcock Cl. M43: Droy 2C **104**
  OL11: Roch 4B **26**
Woodcote Av. SK7: Bram 3E **157**
Woodcote Rd. M31: C'ton 1C **138**
  WA14: D Mas 2C **138**
  WA14: W Tim 2F **139**
Woodcote Vw. SK9: Wilm 6B **166**
Woodcote Wlk. M8: Man *3G **87***
  (off Nunthorpe Dr.)
Wood Cott. Cl. M28: Walk 6D **64**
Wood Cotts. SK6: Wood 3G **135**
Woodcott Bank BL1: Bolt 1C **32**
Woodcott Gro. SK9: Wilm *6A **166***
  (off Picton Dr.)
Wood Cres. OL4: O'ham 6C **76**
Woodcroft SK2: Stoc 5D **146**
Woodcroft Av. M19: Man 5A **132**
Woodeaton Cl. OL2: O'ham 3G **59**
Wooded Cl. BL9: Bury 6F **23**
Wood Edge Cl. BL3: Bolt 5G **49**
WOOD END .5H **43**
WOODEND
  OL5 . . . . .1H **93**
  SK6 . . . . .5H **161**
  SK9 . . . . .3F **165**
Woodend OL2: Shaw 5A **44**
  SK7: Bram 3F **157**
Woodend Cen. Ind. Pk. OL5: Mos . . .1H **93**
Woodend Cl. SK14: Hyde 6B **120**
Woodend Dr. SK15: Stal 1H **121**
Woodend La. OL12: W'le 6D **16**
  SK14: Hyde 6A **120**
  SK15: Stal 1H **121**
  WA16: Mob 6E **163**
Woodend Mill OL5: Mos 1H **93**
Woodend Mills Ind. Est.
  OL4: Spri 4D **76**
Woodend Rd. M22: Wyth 1B **154**
  SK3: Stoc 1H **157**
Woodend St. OL1: O'ham 6E **59**
  OL4: Spri 4D **76**
Woodend Vw. OL5: Mos 1H **93**
Woodfield M22: Wyth 2B **154**
Woodfield Av. OL12: Roch 1G **27**
  SK6: Bred 5G **135**
  SK14: Hyde 1B **136**
Woodfield Cl. OL8: O'ham 5C **74**
  SK13: Had 2H **123**
Woodfield Ct. SK2: Stoc 1A **158**
Woodfield Cres. SK6: Rom 1F **147**
Woodfield Dr. M28: Wors 5F **81**
Woodfield Gro. BL4: Farn 3G **65**
  M30: Ecc 4E **97**
  M33: Sale 3A **128**
Woodfield M. SK14: Hyde 1B **136**
Woodfield Rd. M6: Sal 1D **98**
  M8: Man 2E **87**
  M24: Mid 3A **72**
  SK8: Chea H 6D **156**
  WA14: Alt 5E **139**
WOOD FIELDS 1B **176** (2E **37**)
Woodfields Retail Pk.
  BL9: Bury 2B **176** (2E **37**)
Woodfields Ter.
  BL9: Bury 1B **176** (2E **37**)
Woodfield St. BL3: Bolt 4E **49**
Woodfield Ter. OL10: H'ood 2A **40**

Wood Fold BL7: Bro X 5G **19**
Woodfold Av. M19: Man 5C **116**
WOODFORD 5G **167**
Woodford Av. M30: Ecc 3D **96**
  M34: Dent 3G **119**
  OL2: Shaw 6B **44**
Woodford Ct. M43: Droy 5B **104**
Woodford Dr. M27: Swin 1G **83**
Woodford Gdns. M20: Man 1E **143**
Woodford Gro. BL3: Bolt 3A **48**
Woodford Rd. M35: Fail 3A **90**
  SK7: Bram, W'ford 2G **167**
  SK12: Poy 3A **168**
Wood Gdns. SK9: A Edg 4H **173**
Woodgarth Av. M40: Man 6F **89**
Woodgarth Dr. M27: Swin 5G **83**
Woodgarth La. M28: Wors 6B **82**
Woodgate Av. BL9: Bury 1B **38**
  OL11: Roch 5C **26**
Woodgate Cl. SK6: Bred 6F **135**
Woodgate Dr. M25: Pres 3A **70**
WOODGATE HILL 1B **38**
Woodgate Hill Rd. BL9: Bury 2A **38**
(not continuous)
Woodgate Rd. M16: W Ran 6C **114**
Woodgate St. BL3: Bolt 4E **49**
Woodgrange Cl. M6: Sal 3E **99**
Woodgreen Dr. M26: Rad 1A **68**
Wood Gro. M34: Dent 3F **119**
  M45: White 4E **53**
  SK6: Wood 4G **135**
Woodhall Av. M20: Man 2E **131**
  M45: White 3D **68**
Woodhall Cl. BL2: Bolt 3G **33**
  BL8: Bury 6D **22**
  SK7: W'ford 4G **167**
Woodhall Cres. SK5: Stoc 5A **134**
Woodhall Rd. SK5: Stoc 5H **133**
Woodhall St. M35: Fail 3H **89**
Woodhalt Rd. M8: Man 3E **87**
Woodham Rd. M23: Wyth 2F **141**
Woodham Wlk. BL3: Bolt 2B **48**
Woodhead Cl. BL0: Ram 5C **12**
  OL4: Lees 2C **76**
Woodhead Dr. WA15: Hale 4H **151**
Woodhead Rd. WA15: Hale 4H **151**
Woodhead St. M16: W Ran 3C **114**
WOODHEY 6B **12**
Wood Hey Cl. M26: Rad 4F **51**
Woodhey Ct. M33: Sale 2G **139**
Wood Hey Gro. M34: Dent 5G **119**
  OL12: Roch 5H **15**
Woodhey Rd. BL0: Ram 6A **12**
Woodheys SK4: Stoc 6B **132**
Woodheys Cotts. SK6: Mar B 5H **137**
Woodheys Dr. M33: Sale 2F **139**
Woodheys Rd. OL15: L'ough 1G **29**
Woodheys St. M6: Sal 3F **99**
(off Derg St.)
WOODHILL 2D **36**
Woodhill M24: Mid 5B **56**
Wood Hill Cl. M12: Man 3D **116**
Woodhill Cl. M24: Mid 5B **56**
Woodhill Dr. M25: Pres 1H **85**
WOODHILL FOLD 2D **36**
Woodhill Fold BL8: Bury 2D **36**
Woodhill Gro. M25: Pres 6H **69**
Woodhill Rd. BL8: Bury 2D **36**
Woodhill St. BL8: Bury 1D **36**
Woodhill Va. BL8: Bury 2D **36**
Woodhouse Ct. M41: Urm 3C **110**
(off Davyhulme Rd.)
Woodhouse Farm Cotts.
  OL12: Roch 1H **25**
WOODHOUSE GREEN 4C **90**
Woodhouse Knowl OL3: Del 3A **62**
Woodhouse La. M22: Wyth 1B **154**
  M33: Sale 2D **138**
(not continuous)
  M90: Man A 6B **154**
  OL12: Roch 1H **25**
  WA14: D Mas 2A **150**
(not continuous)

Woodhouse La. E. WA15: Tim 2A **140**
Woodhouse La. Nth. M22: Wyth . . .5B **154**
WOODHOUSE PARK 4H **153**
Woodhouse Pk. Lifestyle Cen. 4H **153**
Woodhouse Rd. M22: Wyth 5B **154**
  M41: Urm 3B **110**
  OL2: Shaw 4A **44**
  WA14: D Mas 1A **150**
WOODHOUSES 1E **139**
  M33 . . . . .1E **139**
  M35 . . . . .5C **90**
Woodhouse St. M18: Man 2G **117**
  M40: Man 6B **88**
Wooding Cl. M31: Part 5E **125**
Woodlake Av. M21: Chor 5A **130**
Woodland Av. BL3: Bolt 5F **49**
  M18: Man 3G **117**
  SK7: H Gro 4E **159**
Woodland Cres. M25: Pres 1H **85**
Woodland Gro. BL7: Eger 1B **18**
Woodland Pk. OL2: O'ham 1B **58**
Woodland Rd. M18: Man 3G **117**
  M19: Man 1C **132**
  OL10: H'ood 2A **40**
WOODLANDS . . . .
  M41 . . . . .6G **109**
  SK15 .6H **107**
Woodlands M35: Fail 1G **103**
  M41: Urm 4E **111**
  SK14: Hyde 5D **120**
  SK15: Stal 6G **107**
Woodlands, The BL6: Los 5C **30**
  BL8: Bury 6D **22**
  M25: Pres 2F **85**
  M27: Swin 4B **84**
  M43: Droy 2G **103**
  OL10: H'ood 5A **40**
Woodlands Av. M27: Swin 5E **83**
  M30: Ecc 5C **96**
  M32: Stre 5D **112**
  M41: Urm 5G **109**
  M44: Irl 4E **109**
  M45: White 6E **53**
  OL11: Roch 5C **26**
  SK6: Wood 4G **135**
  SK8: Chea H 3C **156**
Woodlands Cl. M28: Wors 4A **82**
  SK8: Chea H 5C **156**
  SK13: Tin 1H **123**
  SK14: B'tom 6B **122**
  SK15: Stal 6H **107**
Woodlands Ct. SK2: Stoc 3E **147**
  SK9: A Edg 6G **173**
  WA15: Tim 6G **139**
(off Woodlands Parkway)
Woodlands Dr. M33: Sale 2C **140**
  SK2: Stoc 3C **146**
  SK6: Wood 4G **135**
Woodlands Gro. BL8: Bury 2B **36**
  SK14: B'tom 6B **122**
Woodlands La. WA15: Tim 6G **139**
Woodlands on Stamford, The
  OL6: A Lyme 3B **106**
(off Stamford St. E.)
Woodlands Pk. SK14: Hyde 5E **121**
Woodlands Pk. Rd. SK2: Stoc 3D **146**
Woodlands Parkway WA15: Tim . . .5G **139**
Woodlands Rd. BL0: Ram 3G **13**
  M8: Man 3E **87**
  M16: W Ran 6C **114**
  M28: Wors 4A **82**
  M33: Sale 4C **128**
  OL6: A Lyme 5C **92**
  OL16: Miln 6E **29**
  SK4: Stoc 1H **143**
  SK9: Hand 4A **166**
  SK9: Wilm 6D **164**
  SK12: Dis 1E **171**
  SK15: Stal 6H **107**
  WA14: Alt 1B **174** (6F **139**)
  WA15: Alt 1B **174** (6F **139**)
Woodlands Road Stop (Metro) 4F **87**
Woodlands St. M8: Man 3E **87**

Woodland St. M12: Man 2D **116**
  OL10: H'ood 3H **39**
  OL12: Roch 1A **28**
Woodlands Vw. OL16: Roch 3C **28**
Woodlands Way M24: Mid 3B **72**
Woodland Ter. M7: Sal 6B **86**
  M31: Part 6C **124**
Woodland Vw. BL7: Bro X 3F **19**
  SK14: Hyde 4D **120**
Wood La. BL0: Ram 3G **13**
  M24: Mid 2D **72**
  M31: Part 6B **124**
  OL6: A Lyme 6H **91**
  SK6: Mar 6B **148**
  WA15: Tim 6A **140**
  WA16: Mob 6A **162**
WOOD LANE END 6H **169**
Wood La. Nth. SK10: Adl 6H **169**
Wood La. W. SK10: Adl 6F **169**
Woodlark Cl. M3: Sal 5D **4**
Woodlawn Ct. M16: W Ran 4A **114**
Woodlea M28: Wors 3A **82**
  M30: Ecc 1E **97**
  OL9: Chad 2F **73**
  WA15: Alt 1H **151**
Woodlea Av. M19: Man 3A **132**
Woodlea Chase M27: Clif 4F **67**
Woodleigh WA14: Alt 6C **138**
Woodleigh Ct. SK9: A Edg 4G **173**
Woodleigh Dr. M43: Droy 1C **104**
Woodleigh Rd. OL4: Spri 2E **77**
Woodleigh St. M9: Man 2B **88**
WOODLEY 4G **135**
Woodley Av. M26: Rad 6B **52**
Woodley Bank SK14: Hyde 3A **136**
Woodley Cl. SK2: Stoc 4D **146**
Woodley Pct. SK6: Wood 4G **135**
Woodley Station (Rail) 4H **135**
Woodley St. BL9: Bury 5F **37**
Woodliffe St. M16: Old T 2A **114**
Woodlinn Wlk. M9: Man 4H **87**
(off Ravelston Dr.)
Woodman Dr. BL9: Bury 5E **23**
Woodman St. SK1: Stoc . . .1F **179** (1G **145**)
Woodmeadow Ct. OL5: Mos 1G **93**
Woodmere Dr. M9: Man 6A **72**
Wood Mt. WA15: Tim 6B **140**
Woodmount Cl. SK6: Rom 1C **148**
Woodnewton Cl. M18: Man 3E **117**
WOOD PARK 3D **90**
Woodpark Cl. OL8: O'ham 6G **75**
Woodpecker Pl. M28: Wors 3H **81**
Woodridings WA14: Bow 2D **150**
WOOD ROAD 2C **22**
Wood Rd. M16: W Ran 4A **114**
  M33: Sale 2B **140**
  WA15: Tim 2B **140**
(not continuous)
Wood Rd. La. BL8: Bury 3B **22**
  BL9: Bury 3B **22**
Wood Rd. Nth. M16: Old T 4A **114**
Woodrow Wlk. M12: Man 1B **116**
(off Clowes St.)
Woodrow Way M44: Irl 2D **124**
Woodroyd Cl. SK7: Bram 4F **157**
Woodroyd Dr. BL9: Bury 2A **38**
Woodruffe Gdns. SK6: Rom 3G **147**
Woodruff Wlk. M31: Part 6D **124**
Woods, The OL4: Grot 3F **77**
  OL11: Roch 1E **41**
  WA14: Alt 5G **139**
Woods Ct. BL1: Bolt 3G **175** (6D **32**)
  M24: Mid 1G **71**
Woodseaves Cl. M44: Irl 6F **109**
WOODS END 4A **110**
Woodsend Circ. M41: Urm 4H **109**
Woodsend Cres. Rd. M41: Urm 5H **109**
Woodsend Grn. M41: Urm 4H **109**
Woodsend Rd. M41: Urm 3H **109**
Woodsend Rd. Sth. M41: Urm 5A **110**
(not continuous)
Woods Gro. SK8: Chea H 6D **156**

Woodshaw Gro. M28: Wors 3G 81
Woodside OL2: Shaw 5B 44
 OL16: Miln 1A 44
 SK4: Stoc 2B 144
 SK12: Poy 3F 169
Woodside Av. M19: Man 4B 132
 M28: Walk 1B 82
Woodside Cl. OL4: Lees 3C 76
Woodside Dr. BLO: Ram 4A 12
 (off Hillside Rd.)
 M6: Sal 2C 98
 SK6: H Lan 6C 160
 SK14: Hyde 6C 120
Woodside Gdns. M31: Part 5D 124
 (off Lock La.)
Woodside La. SK12: Poy 3E 169
Woodside M. SK7: Bram 3E 157
Woodside Pl. BL2: Bolt 2G 49
Woodside Rd. M16: W Ran 5H 113
Woodside Sq. BL2: Bolt 2G 49
Woodside St. SK15: C'ook 5A 94
Woodside Tennis Club 1C 170
Woods La. OL3: Dob 6C 62
 SK8: Chea H 6D 156
Woods Lea BL1: Bolt 6F 31
Woodsleigh Coppice
 BL1: Bolt 6F 31
Woodsley Rd. BL1: Bolt 3F 31
WOODS MOOR 1B 158
Woodsmoor La. SK2: Stoc 1A 158
 SK3: Stoc 1A 158
Woodsmoor Rd. M27: Swin 4F 83
Woodsmoor Station (Rail) 1B 158
Woods Pas. OL15: L'ough 4F 17
Wood Sq. M43: Droy 5A 104
 OL3: G'fld 3D 78
Woods Rd. M44: Irl 1D 124
Woodstock Av. SK5: Stoc 4H 133
 SK8: Chea H 6C 156
Woodstock Bus. Pk. OL2: O'ham . . .4G 59
Woodstock Cl. OL10: H'ood 3A 40
Woodstock Ct. SK9: Hand 2A 166
Woodstock Cres. SK6: Wood 4G 135
Woodstock Dr. BL1: Bolt 4G 31
 BL8: Tot 4F 21
 M27: Swin 5A 84
 M28: Wors 6C 82
Woodstock Grn. OL8: O'ham 6G 75
Woodstock Rd. M16: Old T 4H 113
 M40: Man 2E 89
 SK6: Wood 4G 135
 WA14: B'ath 3E 139
Woodstock St.
 OL4: O'ham 6H 177 (4F 75)
 OL12: Roch 2E 27
Wood St. BLO: Ram 4B 12
 BL1: Bolt 4G 175 (6D 32)
 BL8: Bury 2C 36
 M3: Man 6F 5 (4C 100)
 M11: Man 5D 102
 M24: Mid 5H 55
 M26: Rad 1G 67
 M30: Ecc 4H 97
 M34: Dent 3F 119
 OL1: O'ham 1H 75
 OL2: Shaw 5E 43
 OL6: A Lyme 6B 174 (3H 105)
 OL10: H'ood 3H 39
 OL15: L'ough 4H 17
 OL16: Miln 1A 44
 OL16: Roch 5D 178 (5A 28)
 SK3: Stoc 3E 179 (3F 145)
 SK8: Chea 5H 143
 SK14: Holl 2F 123
 SK14: Hyde 5C 120
 SK15: Stal 3E 107
 SK16: Duk 1A 120
 WA14: Alt 2B 174 (1F 151)
Wood Ter. BL2: Ain 4F 35
Woodthorpe Ct. M25: Pres 1B 86
Woodthorpe Dr. SK8: Chea H 3C 156
Woodthorpe Grange M25: Pres 1B 86

Wood Top BLO: Ram 2B 12
 (off Glen St.)
Wood Top Av.
 OL11: Roch 6B 26
Wood Top Cl. SK2: Stoc 4E 147
Woodvale M24: Mid 3C 56
 WA14: Bow 3E 151
Woodvale Av. BL3: Bolt 5B 48
Woodvale Dr. BL3: Bolt 5B 48
Woodvale Gdns. BL3: Bolt 5B 48
Woodvale Gro. BL3: Bolt 5B 48
Woodvale Rd. M26: Rad 6B 52
Woodvale Wlk. M11: Man 4B 102
 (off Redfield Cl.)
Wood Vw. M22: Nor 2B 142
 OL10: H'ood 1G 39
Woodview Av. M19: Man 4B 132
Woodville Dr. M33: Sale 4A 128
 SK6: Mar 6B 148
 SK15: Stal 2H 107
Woodville Gro. SK5: Stoc 3H 133
Woodville Rd. M33: Sale 4A 128
 WA14: Alt 1E 151
Woodville Ter. M40: Man 2B 88
Woodward Cl. BL9: Bury 6F 23
Woodward Ct. M4: Man 3G 7 (3H 101)
Woodward Pl. M4: Man 4F 7 (3G 101)
Woodward Rd.
 M25: Pres 1F 85
Woodward St. M4: Man 4F 7 (3G 101)
Woodwise La. M23: Wyth 2E 141
Wood Yd. OL16: Roch 4D 42
Woolden Rd. M44: Cad 1A 124
Woolden St. M30: Ecc 2D 96
Woolfall Cl. M12: Man 1C 116
WOOLFOLD 1B 36
Woolfold Trad. Est. BL8: Bury 1B 36
Woollacot St.
 OL1: O'ham 3H 177 (2F 75)
Woollam Pl. M3: Man 1D 8 (5B 100)
Woolley Av. SK12: Poy 5D 168
WOOLLEY BRIDGE 3F 123
Woolley Bri. SK13: Had 3G 123
Woolley Bri. Rd.
 SK13: Had 3G 123
Woolley Cl. SK14: Holl 3F 123
Woolley La. SK14: Holl 3E 123
 (Market Pl.)
 SK14: Holl 1F 123
 (Woolley Mill La.)
Woolley Mill La. SK13: Tin 1F 123
Woolley St. M8: Man 1D 100
 OL6: A Lyme 5C 92
Woolley Ter. SK16: Duk 4H 105
 (off Queen St.)
Woolmore Av. OL1: O'ham 6E 59
Woolpack Grn. M6: Sal 2F 97
 (off Arbour Cl.)
Wool Rd. OL3: Dob 6D 62
Woolston Dr. M29: Tyld 3A 80
Woolston Ho. M6: Sal 1C 98
 (off Moss Mdw. Rd.)
Woolton Cl. M40: Man 1E 89
 (off Pleasington Dr.)
Woolton Hall M14: Man 6H 115
Wootton St. SK14: Hyde 3B 120
Worcester Av. M23: Wyth 3F 141
 M34: Dent 6G 119
 SK5: Stoc 4C 134
Worcester Cl. BL9: Bury 5G 37
 M6: Sal 1C 98
 OL6: A Lyme 3B 92
 SK6: Rom 2G 147
Worcester Rd. BL3: Lit L 4B 50
 M6: Sal 1C 98
 M24: Mid 4B 72
 M27: Ward 1F 83
 M33: Sale 6F 127
 SK8: Chea H 1C 156
Worcester St. BL1: Bolt 4C 32
 BL8: Bury 1D 36
 OL9: O'ham 4B 74
 OL11: Roch 1G 41

Wordsworth Av. BL4: Farn 2F 65
 BL9: Bury 1F 53
 M8: Man 5E 87
 M26: Rad 4G 51
 M43: Droy 3A 104
Wordsworth Cl. SK16: Duk 6E 107
Wordsworth Cres. OL7: A Lyme . . .6E 91
 OL15: L'ough 1F 29
Wordsworth Gdns. M25: Pres 6F 69
Wordsworth Ind. Est. BL1: Bolt . . .3B 32
 (off Wordsworth St.)
Wordsworth Rd. M16: Old T 4H 113
 M24: Mid 5D 56
 M27: Swin 2F 83
 M34: Dent 2G 135
 M38: Lit H 4F 65
 OL1: O'ham 6H 59
 SK5: Stoc 6F 117
Wordsworth St. BL1: Bolt 4B 32
Wordsworth Way OL11: Roch 5A 26
Workesleigh St. M40: Man 6E 89
World Trade Cen. M5: Sal 1G 113
World Way M90: Man A 5H 153
Worrall St. M5: Sal 3A 8 (6A 100)
 M40: Man 5C 88
 OL12: Roch 1F 27
 SK3: Stoc 6E 179 (4G 145)
 (not continuous)
Worrell Cl. M26: Rad 3H 51
Worsbrough Av. M28: Walk 1G 81
Worsefold St. M40: Man 3C 88
Worsel St. BL3: Bolt 3A 48
WORSLEY 4A 82
Worsley Av. M28: Walk 6E 65
 M40: Man 2B 88
Worsley Brow M28: Wors 5B 82
Worsley Bus. Pk. M28: Wors 3D 80
Worsley Ct. M14: Man 5G 115
 M28: Walk 6H 65
Worsley Cres. SK2: Stoc 4C 146
Worsley Gdns. M28: Walk 5G 65
 (off Mountain St.)
Worsley Gro. M19: Man 6C 116
 M28: Walk 1E 81
Worsley Mill M3: Man 3D 8 (5B 100)
Worsley Pl. OL2: Shaw 1G 59
 OL16: Roch 4B 28
Worsley Point M27: Swin 5G 83
Worsley Rd. BL3: Bolt 3G 47
 BL4: Farn 3H 65
 M27: Swin 6B 82
 M28: Wors 6B 82
 M30: Ecc 1C 96
Worsley Rd. Ind. Est. BL4: Farn . . .3H 65
Worsley Rd. Nth. M28: Walk 4H 65
Worsley St. BL3: Bolt 2C 48
 BL8: Tot 4G 21
 M3: Sal 4F 5 (3C 100)
 M15: Man 3C 8 (6B 100)
 M27: Pen 1H 83
 M27: Swin 4A 84
 OL8: O'ham 4H 75
 OL16: Roch 4B 28
Worsley Trad. Est. M38: Lit H 4C 64
Worsley Vw. M29: Ast 6A 80
Worston Av. BL1: Bolt 2F 31
Worth Ct. SK12: Poy 5D 168
Worthenbury Wlk. M13: Man 4A 116
Worthing Cl. SK2: Stoc 5D 146
Worthing St. M14: Man 5F 115
Worthington Av. M31: Part 6D 124
 OL10: H'ood 6A 40
Worthington Cl. OL7: A Lyme 6G 91
 SK14: Hat 5A 122
Worthington Ct. M33: Sale 5E 129
Worthington Dr. M7: Sal 2B 86
Worthington Rd. M33: Sale 5E 129
 M34: Dent 6H 119
Worthington St. BL3: Bolt 4A 48
 M16: Old T 3A 114
 M40: Man 3E 89
 OL7: A Lyme 6G 91
 SK15: Stal 4D 106

Worthington Way
  M34: Dent 3E **119**
Worth's La. M34: Dent 2G **135**
Wortley Av. M6: Sal 2C **98**
Wortley Gro. M40: Man 1D **88**
Wragby Cl. BL8: Bury 6D **22**
Wrath Cl. BL2: Bolt 6F **19**
Wray Cl. M22: Wyth 1B **154**
Wray Gdns. M19: Man 1E **133**
Wray Pl. OL16: Roch 5C **28**
Wraysbury Wlk. M40: Man 4C **88**
              (off Hugo St.)
Wrayton Lodge M33: Sale 6B **128**
Wrekin Av. M23: Wyth 2G **153**
Wren Av. M27: Clif 6B **68**
Wrenbury Av. M20: Man 2D **130**
Wrenbury Cres. SK3: Stoc 5E **145**
Wrenbury Dr. BL1: Bolt 5D **18**
  OL16: Roch 2C **42**
  SK8: Chea 5A **144**
Wrenbury Wlk. M33: Sale 6E **129**
          (off Mottram Rd.)
Wren Cl. BL4: Farn 1D **64**
  M34: Aud 4C **104**
  SK2: Stoc 6F **147**
Wren Dr. BL9: Bury 1H **37**
  M44: Irl 3E **109**
Wren Gdns. M24: Mid 3F **71**
Wrengate Ho. M20: Man 6D **130**
Wren Grn. OL16: Roch 5C **28**
Wrens Nest Av. OL2: Shaw 5A **44**
Wren St. OL4: O'ham 3A **76**
Wrenswood Dr. M28: Wors 3G **81**
Wren Way M11: Man 5A **102**
Wrexham Cl. OL8: O'ham 1B **90**
Wrigglesworth Cl. BL8: Bury 2H **35**
Wright Robinson Cl. M11: Man 5A **102**
Wright Robinson Hall
  M1: Man 2C **10**
Wrights Bank Nth. SK2: Stoc 6E **147**
Wright St. M16: Old T 6A **8** (1A **114**)
  M26: Rad 4H **51**
  M34: Aud 5E **105**
  M35: Fail 3H **89**
  OL1: O'ham 3H **177** (2G **75**)
  OL6: A Lyme 1B **106**
  OL9: Chad 4B **74**
  WA14: B'ath 4E **139**
Wright Tree Vs. M44: Cad 4B **124**
Wrigley Cres. M35: Fail 4H **89**
Wrigley Fold M24: Mid 4G **55**
Wrigley Head M35: Fail 3H **89**
Wrigley Head Cres.
  M35: Fail 3H **89**
Wrigley Pl. OL15: L'ough 6F **17**
Wrigley's Pl. OL8: O'ham 6E **75**
Wrigley Sq. OL4: Lees 3D **76**
  SK14: Hyde 2C **136**
        (off Rowbotham St.)
Wrigley St. OL4: Lees 3C **76**
  OL4: O'ham 2H **75**
  OL4: Scout 1F **77**
  OL6: A Lyme 1H **105**
Wroe St. M3: Sal 5C **4**
  M27: Pen 6H **67**
  OL4: Spri 3D **76**
Wroe Ter. M27: Clif 6H **67**
Wrotham Cl. M5: Sal 4G **99**
Wroxeter Wlk. M12: Man 1B **116**
        (off Witterage Cl.)
Wroxham Av. M34: Dent 4A **118**
  M41: Urm 4D **110**
Wroxham Cl. BL8: Bury 6D **22**
Wroxham Rd. M9: Man 6F **71**
WUERDLE 5E **17**
Wuerdle Cl. OL16: Roch 6E **17**
Wuerdle Farm Way
  OL16: Roch 5E **17**
Wuerdle Pl. OL16: Roch 5E **17**
Wuerdle St. OL16: Roch 5E **17**
Wyatt Av. M5: Sal 3A **8** (6H **99**)
Wyatt St. SK4: Stoc 1E **179** (1G **145**)
  SK16: Duk 5A **106**

Wybersley Rd.
  SK6: H Lan 5E **161**
Wychbury St. M6: Sal 3E **99**
Wychelm Rd. M31: Part 6D **124**
Wycherley Rd.
  OL12: Roch 1D **26**
          (not continuous)
Wych Fold SK14: Hyde 2C **136**
          (not continuous)
Wych St. OL6: A Lyme 6B **174** (3H **105**)
Wychwood WA14: Bow 4D **150**
Wychwood Cl. M24: Mid 2D **72**
Wycliffe Av. SK9: Wilm 2D **172**
Wycliffe Ct. M41: Urm 5E **111**
          (off Flixton Rd.)
Wycliffe Rd. M41: Urm 5E **111**
Wycliffe St. M30: Ecc 3E **97**
          (off Watson St.)
  SK4: Stoc 1F **145**
Wycombe Av. M18: Man 1G **117**
Wycombe Cl. M41: Urm 2E **111**
Wycombe Dr. M29: Ast 4A **80**
Wye Av. M35: Fail 4H **89**
Wyecroft Cl. SK6: Wood 4H **135**
Wye St. OL8: O'ham 4D **74**
Wyke St. BL8: Bury 5A **22**
Wykeham Gro.
  OL12: Roch 2D **26**
Wykeham M. BL1: Bolt 6G **31**
Wykeham St. M14: Man 4E **115**
Wyke Pk. OL4: O'ham 3B **76**
Wylam Wlk. M12: Man 4D **116**
Wylde, The
  BL9: Bury 3B **176** (3E **37**)
Wynchgate Rd.
  SK7: H Gro 2G **159**
Wyndale Dr. M35: Fail 6H **89**
Wyndale Rd. OL8: O'ham 6F **75**
Wyndcliffe Dr. M41: Urm 6A **110**
          (not continuous)
Wyndham Av. BL3: Bolt 5G **47**
  M27: Clif 1H **83**
Wyndham Cl. SK7: Bram 6G **157**
Wyne Cl. SK7: H Gro 2G **159**
Wynfield Av. M22: Wyth 6D **154**
Wynford Sq. M50: Sal 4F **99**
Wynford St. SK8: Chea H 4B **156**
  WA15: Hale 5H **151**
Wynne Av. M27: Clif 6H **67**
Wynne Cl. M11: Man 5B **102**
  M34: Dent 6F **119**
Wynne Gro. M34: Dent 6F **119**
Wynne St. BL1: Bolt 3C **32**
  M6: Sal 1A **4** (2H **99**)
  M38: Lit H 5E **65**
Wynnstay Gro. M14: Man 1G **131**
Wynnstay Rd. M33: Sale 4B **128**
Wynn St. M40: Man 2G **89**
Wynyard Cl. M33: Sale 1D **140**
Wynyard Rd. M22: Wyth 2A **154**
Wyre Cl. M45: White 6H **53**
Wyre Dr. M28: Wors 4F **81**
Wyresdale Rd. BL1: Bolt 5A **32**
Wyre St. M1: Man 2D **10** (5F **101**)
  OL5: Mos 2G **93**
Wythall Av. M38: Lit H 3F **65**
Wythburn Av. BL1: Bolt 4G **31**
  M8: Man 5G **87**
  M41: Urm 4D **110**
Wythburn Rd. M24: Mid 4A **56**
  SK1: Stoc 4B **146**
Wythburn St. M6: Sal 3E **99**
WYTHENSHAWE 2A **154**
Wythenshawe Community Farm
. . . . .3H **141**
Wythenshawe Hall
  (Art Gallery & Mus.) 3H **141**
Wythenshawe Pk. 3G **141**
Wythenshawe Rd.
  M23: Wyth 3E **141**
  M33: Sale 5E **129**
Wythens Rd. SK8: H Grn 5F **155**
Wythop Gdns. M5: Sal 4G **99**
Wyvern Av. SK5: Stoc 4G **133**

Wyverne Rd. M21: Chor 6B **114**
Wyville Cl. SK7: H Gro 2G **159**
Wyville Dr. M6: Sal 2F **99**
  M9: Man 3F **71**
  M27: Swin 5G **83**
Wyvis Cl. OL9: Chad 6A **58**

X

XQ7 Building M5: Sal 1G **113**
XS Superbowl 3E **83**

Y

Yale Rd. M18: Man 2D **116**
Yarburgh St. M16: W Ran 4C **114**
Yardley Av. M32: Stre 5A **112**
Yardley Cl. M32: Stre 5A **112**
Yarmouth Dr. M23: Wyth 2H **141**
Yarn Cft. M29: Ast 3A **80**
Yarnton Cl. OL2: O'ham 2G **59**
Yarrow Cl. OL11: Roch 6H **27**
Yarrow Pl. BL1: Bolt 4C **32**
Yarrow Wlk. M45: White 6A **54**
Yarwell OL12: Roch 1A **178**
Yarwood Av. M23: Wyth 4F **141**
Yarwood Cl. OL10: H'ood 2A **40**
Yarwoodheath La.
  WA14: Rost 5A **150**
Yarwood St. BL9: Bury 3G **37**
  WA14: Alt 2F **151**
Yasmin Gdns. OL1: O'ham 6D **58**
Yates Dr. M28: Walk 6E **65**
Yates St. BL2: Bolt 4E **33**
  M24: Mid 2G **71**
  OL1: O'ham 1G **75**
  SK1: Stoc 6B **134**
Yattendon Av. M23: Wyth 3D **140**
Y Club, The 1E **9** (5C **100**)
Yeadon Rd. M18: Man 4F **117**
Yea Fold OL15: L'ough 6E **17**
Yeoman Av. SK4: Stoc 5F **133**
Yealand Cl. OL11: Roch 5D **26**
Yeardsley Cl. SK7: Bram 2G **157**
Yeargate Ind. Est. BL9: Bury 3B **38**
Yellow Lodge Dr.
  BL5: W'ton 6B **46**
Yeoford Dr. WA14: Alt 5D **138**
Yeoman Cl. SK7: H Gro 2D **158**
Yeomanry Ct. M16: W Ran 4B **114**
Yeoman's Cl. OL16: Miln 4F **29**
Yeoman Wlk. M11: Man 4B **102**
Yeovil St. M16: W Ran 4D **114**
Yew Cl. BL3: Bolt 3A **48**
Yew Ct. OL12: Roch 1B **28**
Yew Cres. OL4: O'ham 1B **76**
Yewdale M27: Clif 1B **84**
Yewdale Av. BL2: Bolt 3B **34**
Yewdale Dr. M24: Mid 6A **56**
  M35: Fail 3C **90**
Yew Dale Gdns.
  OL11: Roch 1D **40**
Yewdale Gdns. BL2: Bolt 3B **34**
Yewdale Rd. SK1: Stoc 5B **146**
Yewlands Av. M9: Man 4H **71**
Yew St. BL9: Bury 2A **38**
  M7: Sal 5A **86**
  M15: Man 6E **9** (2C **114**)
  M34: Aud 2F **119**
  OL10: H'ood 3F **39**
  SK4: Stoc 3D **144**
YEW TREE 6D **106**
Yew Tree Av. M14: Man 5E **115**
  M19: Man 6C **116**
  M22: Nor 2B **142**
  SK7: H Gro 4F **159**
Yew Tree Cl. OL7: A Lyme 5G **91**
  OL11: Roch 4B **42**
  SK6: Mar 6C **148**
  SK9: Wilm 2G **173**

Yew Tree Cotts. OL3: Dig 1E **63**
  SK6: Comp 6F **137**
Yew Tree Cres. M14: Man 6F **115**
Yew Tree Dr. BL6: Los 1B **46**
  M22: Nor 2B **142**
  M25: Pres 5H **69**
  M33: Sale 5E **129**
  M41: Urm 3B **110**
  OL9: Chad 2F **73**
  SK6: Bred 6D **134**
Yew Tree Gro. SK8: H Grn 2E **155**
Yew Tree La. BL1: Bolt 6E **19**
  M23: Wyth 1H **141**
                    (not continuous)
  SK16: Duk 6C **106**
Yewtree La. SK12: Poy 5E **169**
Yew Tree Pk. Rd.
  SK8: Chea H 1D **166**
Yew Tree Rd. M14: Man 4F **115**
  M20: Man 1F **131**
  M34: Dent 6E **119**
  SK3: Stoc 2H **157**
  SK10: Adl 6H **169**
Yew Wlk. M31: Part 6C **124**
York Arc. M1: Man 6B **6**
                    (off Parker St.)
York Av. BL3: Lit L 4C **50**
  M16: W Ran 5A **114**
  M25: Pres 1B **86**
  M27: Swin 1F **83**
  M33: Sale 4B **128**
  M41: Urm 4G **111**
  OL8: O'ham 5D **74**
  OL11: Roch 5C **26**
York Cl. M34: Dent 3F **119**
  SK8: Chea 6C **144**
York Cres. SK9: Wilm 2F **173**
Yorkdale OL4: O'ham 2B **76**
York Dr. BL0: Ram 5A **12**
  M90: Man A 6F **153**

York Dr. SK7: H Gro 3G **159**
  WA14: Bow 4F **151**
York Ho. M33: Sale 4B **128**
York Pl. OL6: A Lyme 3G **105**
York Rd. M21: Chor 1H **129**
  M33: Sale 4A **128**
  M34: Dent 3E **119**
  M43: Droy 2H **103**
  M44: Cad 4B **124**
  OL9: Chad 1H **73**
  SK4: Stoc 4D **132**
  SK14: Hyde 1C **136**
  WA14: Bow 4E **151**
York Rd. E. M24: Mid 4E **73**
York Rd. W. M24: Mid 4E **73**
Yorkshire St. M3: Sal 4F **5** (3C **100**)
  OL1: O'ham 3G **177** (2F **75**)
  OL6: A Lyme 4B **174** (1H **105**)
                    (not continuous)
  OL12: Roch 1D **178** (3A **28**)
  OL16: Roch 3B **178** (4H **27**)
                    (not continuous)
Yorkshire Ter. OL5: Mos 2G **93**
                    (off Mill St.)
York St. BL4: Farn 1A **66**
  BL9: Bury 3G **37**
  M1: Man 2A **10** (5E **101**)
  M2: Man 5A **6** (4E **101**)
  M9: Man 3A **88**
                    (not continuous)
  M13: Man 4B **10** (6E **101**)
  M19: Man 1C **132**
  M20: Man 6F **131**
  M26: Rad 2D **52**
  M34: Aud 5E **105**
  M45: White 1F **69**
  OL9: O'ham 4E **177** (3E **75**)
  OL10: H'ood 3H **39**
  OL16: Roch 5B **28**
  SK3: Stoc 4E **179** (3G **145**)

York St. WA15: Alt 2G **151**
York Ter. BL1: Bolt 3C **32**
                    (off Boardman St.)
  M33: Sale 3A **128**
Youlgreave Cres.
  SK13: Gam 6F **123**
Young St. BL0: Ram 3B **12**
  BL4: Farn 2A **66**
  M3: Man 6F **5** (4C **100**)
  M26: Rad 2H **51**
Yulan Dr. M33: Sale 5E **127**
Yule St. SK3: Stoc 3F **145**

Z

Zama St. BL0: Ram 5A **12**
Zandra Ho. M16: W Ran 4B **114**
                    (off Dudley Rd.)
Zealand St. OL4: O'ham 1A **76**
Zedburgh OL12: Roch 1A **178** (3G **27**)
Zeta St. M9: Man 4B **88**
Zetland Av. BL3: Bolt 5H **47**
  BL3: Bolt 5H **47**
Zetland Pl. OL16: Roch 3B **28**
Zetland Rd. M21: Chor 1H **129**
Zetland St. SK16: Duk 4A **106**
Zinc Ct. M25: Pres 4G **69**
                    (off Longfield Cen.)
Zinnia Dr. M44: Irl 1C **124**
Zion Arts Cen. 6F **9** (1C **114**)
Zion Cres. M15: Man 6F **9**
Zion Ter. OL12: Roch 1A **26**
Zorbit M. SK14: Hyde 3B **120**
Zulu St. BL2: Bolt 6F **33**
Zurich Gdns. SK7: Bram 2G **157**
Zyburn Ct. M6: Sal 2A **98**

HOSPITALS and HOSPICES
covered by this atlas

with their map square reference

N.B. Where Hospitals and Hospices are not named on the map,
the reference given is for the road in which they are situated.

ALEXANDRA (BMI) HOSPITAL, THE 5H **143**
Mill Lane
CHEADLE
SK8 2PX
Tel: 0161 4283656

ALPHA HOSPITAL, BURY 4C **36**
Buller Street
BURY
BL8 2BS
Tel: 0161 762 7200

ALTRINCHAM GENERAL HOSPITAL 2A **174** (1F **151**)
Market Street
ALTRINCHAM
WA14 1PE
Tel: 0161 9286111

ALTRINCHAM PRIORY HOSPITAL 5A **152**
Rappax Road
Hale
ALTRINCHAM
WA15 0NX
Tel: 0161 9040050

BEALEY COMMUNITY HOSPITAL 3D **52**
Dumers Lane
Radcliffe
MANCHESTER
M26 2QD
Tel: 0161 7232371

BEAUMONT BMI HOSPITAL, THE 5C **30**
Old Hall Clough
Chorley New Road
Lostock
BOLTON
BL6 4LA
Tel: 01204 404404

BEECHWOOD CANCER CARE CENTRE 6F **145**
Chelford Grove
STOCKPORT
SK3 8LS
Tel: 0161 4760384

BIRCH HILL HOSPITAL 4E **17**
Union Road
ROCHDALE
OL12 9QB
Tel: 01706 377777

BOLTON HOSPICE 6B **32**
Queens Park Street
BOLTON
BL1 4QT
Tel: 01204 663066

BOLTON, SALFORD & TRAFFORD MENTAL HEALTH NHS TRUST
(PRESTWICH SITE) 4F **69**
Bury New Road
Prestwich
MANCHESTER
M25 3BL
Tel: 0161 773 9121

BOOTH HALL CHILDREN'S HOSPITAL 6B **72**
Charlestown Road
MANCHESTER
M9 7AA
Tel: 0161 795 7000

BURY HOSPICE 3D **52**
Dumers Lane
Radcliffe
MANCHESTER
M26 2QD
Tel: 0161 7259800

CASUALTY PLUS WALK-IN CENTRE (CHEADLE) 5H **143**
The Alexandra Hospital
Mill Lane
CHEADLE
SK8 2PX
Tel: 0161 4282161

CHARLES HOUSE 1F **99**
1 Charles Street
SALFORD
M6 7DU
Tel: 0161 745 7900

CHEADLE ROYAL HOSPITAL 3G **155**
100 Wilmslow Road
CHEADLE
SK8 3DG
Tel: 0161 4289511

CHERRY TREE HOSPITAL 6C **146**
Cherry Tree Lane
STOCKPORT
SK2 7PZ
Tel: 0161 4831010

CHRISTIE HOSPITAL 3F **131**
550 Wilmslow Road
MANCHESTER
M20 4BX
Tel: 0845 226 3000

DR. KERSHAW'S HOSPICE 4F **59**
Turf Lane
Royton
OLDHAM
OL2 6EU
Tel: 0161 6242727

FAIRFIELD GENERAL HOSPITAL 1C **38**
Rochdale Old Road
BURY
BL9 7TD
Tel: 0161 7646081

FALL BIRCH HOSPITAL 4A **30**
Fall Birch Road
Lostock
BOLTON
BL6 4LQ
Tel: 01204 695714

FRANCIS HOUSE CHILDREN'S HOSPICE 1G **143**
390 Parrswood Road
MANCHESTER
M20 5NA
Tel: 0161 4344118

HIGHBANK PRIORY REHABILITATION CENTRE 1E **23**
Walmersley House
Walmersley Road
BURY
BL9 5LX
Tel: 01706 829540

HIGHBANK PRIORY REHABILITATION CENTRE (ELTON UNIT)
....1H **35**
Walshaw Road
Elton
BURY
BL8 3AL
Tel: 01706 829540

HIGHFIELD BMI HOSPITAL, THE 6F **27**
Manchester Road
ROCHDALE
OL11 4LZ
Tel: 01706 655121

HOPE HOSPITAL 2B **98**
Stott Lane
SALFORD
M6 8HD
Tel: 0161 7897373

HYDE DAY HOSPITAL 6D **120**
Grange Road South
HYDE
SK14 5NY
Tel: 0161 6043445

MANCHESTER LIFESTYLE BMI HOSPITAL, THE 3H **115**
108-112 Daisy Bank Road
MANCHESTER
M14 5QH
Tel: 0161 249 3000

MANCHESTER ROYAL EYE HOSPITAL 2F **115**
Nelson Street
MANCHESTER
M13 9WH
Tel: 0161 276 1234

MANCHESTER ROYAL INFIRMARY 2G **115**
Oxford Road
MANCHESTER
M13 9WL
Tel: 0161 276 1234

MANCHESTER SPIRE HOSPITAL 4B **114**
Russell Road
Whalley Range
MANCHESTER
M16 8AJ
Tel: 0845 6050112

MEADOWS HOSPITAL, THE 4E **147**
Owens Farm Drive
STOCKPORT
SK2 5EQ
Tel: 0161 419 6000

NEIL CLIFFE CANCER CARE CENTRE 1F **153**
Wythenshaw Hospital
Southmoor Road
MANCHESTER
M23 9LT
Tel: 0161 2912912

NHS WALK-IN-CENTRE (BOLTON) 4F **175** (6D **32**)
Lever Chambers
27 Ashburner Street
BOLTON
BL1 1SQ
Tel: 01204 872725

NHS WALK-IN CENTRE (BURNAGE) 3B **132**
Burnage Health Care Centre
347 Burnage Lane
MANCHESTER
M19 1EW
Tel: 0161 443 0600

NHS WALK-IN CENTRE (BURY) 3C **176** (3F **37**)
18 Parsons Lane
BURY
BL9 0JZ

NHS WALK-IN CENTRE (CENTRAL MANCHESTER PCT) 2G **115**
Manchester Royal Infirmary
Oxford Road
MANCHESTER
M13 9WL

NHS WALK-IN CENTRE (MANCHESTER PICCADILLY) ...6C **6** (4F **101**)
1st Floor Gateway House
Station Approach
Piccadilly South
MANCHESTER
M1 2GH
Tel: 0161 233 2525

NHS WALK-IN CENTRE (OLDHAM) 4E **177** (3E **75**)
Lindley House
1 John Street
OLDHAM
OL8 1DF

NHS WALK-IN CENTRE (PRESTWICH) 4G **69**
Fairfax Road
Prestwich
MANCHESTER
M25 1BT

NHS WALK-IN CENTRE (ROCHDALE) 2H **27**
90 Whitehall Street
ROCHDALE
OL12 0ND

NHS WALK-IN CENTRE (WITHINGTON) 4D **130**
Withington Community Hospital
Nell Lane
MANCHESTER
M20 2LR
Tel: 0161 217 3015

NHS WALK-IN CENTRE (WYTHENSHAWE FORUM) 3A **154**
Health Care Centre
Forum Square
Civic Centre
Simonsway
Wythenshawe
MANCHESTER
M22 5RX
Tel: 0161 490 8082

NORTH MANCHESTER GENERAL HOSPITAL 2F **87**
Delaunays Road
MANCHESTER
M8 5RB
Tel: 0161 795 4567

OAKLANDS HOSPITAL 2B **98**
19 Lancaster Road
SALFORD
M6 8AQ
Tel: 0161 7877700

ORCHARD HOUSE DAY HOSPITAL 3E **59**
Milton Street
Royton
OLDHAM
OL2 6QX
Tel: 0161 6336219

RAMSBOTTOM COTTAGE HOSPITAL 4B **12**
Nuttall Lane
Ramsbottom
BURY
BL0 9JZ
Tel: 01706 823123

ROCHDALE INFIRMARY 2G **27**
Whitehall Street
ROCHDALE
OL12 0NB
Tel: 01706 377777

ROYAL BOLTON HOSPITAL 6D **48**
Minerva Road
Farnworth
BOLTON
BL4 0JR
Tel: 01204 390390

ROYAL MANCHESTER CHILDRENS HOSPITAL 4C **84**
  Hospital Road
  Pendlebury
  Swinton
  MANCHESTER
  M27 4HA
  Tel: 0161 7944696

ROYAL OLDHAM HOSPITAL, THE 6D **58**
  Rochdale Road
  OLDHAM
  OL1 2JH
  Tel: 0161 624 0420

ST ANN'S HOSPICE 5E **65**
  Peel Lane
  Little Hulton
  MANCHESTER
  M28 0FE
  Tel: 0161 702 8181

ST ANN'S HOSPICE 3G **155**
  St Ann's Road North
  Heald Green
  CHEADLE
  SK8 3SZ
  Tel: 0161 4378136

ST MARY'S HOSPITAL FOR WOMEN & CHILDREN 3G **115**
  Oxford Road
  MANCHESTER
  M13 0JH
  Tel: 0161 276 1234

SPRINGHILL HOSPICE 2B **42**
  Broad Lane
  ROCHDALE
  OL16 4PZ
  Tel: 01706 649920

STEPPING HILL HOSPITAL 1C **158**
  Poplar Grove
  STOCKPORT
  SK2 7JE
  Tel: 0161 4831010

STRETFORD MEMORIAL HOSPITAL 4H **113**
  226 Seymour Grove
  MANCHESTER
  M16 0DU
  Tel: 0161 8815353

TAMESIDE GENERAL HOSPITAL 1C **106**
  Fountain Street
  ASHTON-UNDER-LYNE
  OL6 9RW
  Tel: 0161 3316000

TRAFFORD GENERAL HOSPITAL 4C **110**
  Moorside Road
  Urmston
  MANCHESTER
  M41 5SL
  Tel: 0161 7484022

UNIVERSITY DENTAL HOSPITAL OF MANCHESTER
  ....6B **10** (1E **115**)
  Higher Cambridge Street
  MANCHESTER
  M15 6FH
  Tel: 0161 275 6666

WILLOW WOOD HOSPICE 2C **106**
  Willow Wood Close
  ASHTON-UNDER-LYNE
  OL6 6SL
  Tel: 0161 3301100

WITHINGTON COMMUNITY HOSPITAL 4D **130**
  Nell Lane
  MANCHESTER
  M20 2LR
  Tel: 0161 434 5555

WOODLANDS HOSPITAL 5D **64**
  Peel Lane
  Worsley
  MANCHESTER
  M28 0FE
  Tel: 0161 7031040

WYTHENSHAWE HOSPITAL 1F **153**
  Southmoor Road
  Wythenshawe
  MANCHESTER
  M23 9LT
  Tel: 0161 998 7070

The representation on the maps of a road, track or footpath is no evidence of the existence of a right of way.
The Grid on this map is the National Grid taken from Ordnance Survey® mapping with the permission of the Controller
of Her Majesty's Stationery Office.
No reproduction by any method whatsoever of any part of this publication is permitted without the prior consent of
the copyright owners.

Copyright of Geographers' A-Z Map Company Ltd.

Printed and bound in the United Kingdom by Polestar Wheatons Ltd., Exeter.